D1604979

WORLD ERAS

VOLUME 2

RISE AND SPREAD OF ISLAM
622 - 1500

Detroit • New York • San Diego • San Francisco • Cleveland • New Haven, Conn. • Waterville, Maine • London • Munich

World Eras Vol 2
Rise and Spread of Islam
622–1500

Editorial Directors
Matthew J. Bruccoli and Richard Layman

Series Editor
Anthony J. Scotti Jr.

LIBRARY OF CONGRESS CATALOGING-IN-PUBLICATION DATA

World Eras vol. 2: Rise and Spread of Islam, 622-1500 /
    edited by Susan L. Douglass.
      p. cm.—(World eras; v.2)
    "A Manly, Inc. book."
    Includes bibliographical references and indexes.
    ISBN 0-7876-4503-6 (alk. paper)
    1. Civilization, Islamic. 2. Islamic Empire—History.
      I. Douglass, Susan L. (Susan Lynn), 1950–

DS36.85 .W67 2001
909.07—dc21

00-050380

Printed in the United States of America
10 9 8 7 6 5 4 3 2 1

ADVISORY BOARD

For Our Families

بسم الله الرحمن الرحيم

يَا أَيُّهَا النَّاسُ إِنَّا خَلَقْنَاكُم مِّن

ذَكَرٍ وَأُنثَىٰ وَجَعَلْنَاكُمْ شُعُوبًا

وَقَبَائِلَ لِتَعَارَفُوا إِنَّ أَكْرَمَكُمْ عِندَ

اللَّهِ أَتْقَاكُمْ إِنَّ اللَّهَ عَلِيمٌ خَبِيرٌ

*O mankind! We created you from a single soul,
male and female, and made you into nations and
tribes, so that you may come to know one another.
Truly, the most honored of you in God's sight is
the greatest of you in piety. God is All-Knowing,
All-Aware.* (Qur'an 49: 13)

CONTENTS

ABOUT THE SERIES xv

TIMELINE xvii

INTRODUCTION xxv

ACKNOWLEDGMENTS xxxi

CHAPTER 1: WORLD EVENTS

Chronology. 1

CHAPTER 2: GEOGRAPHY

Chronology. 66

Overview 69

Topics in Geography

The Geography of Muslim Lands. 70
The Legacy of Near Eastern Science. 71
Muslim Geographical Studies 72
The Technology of Geography 76
Topography and Climate. 78

Significant People

Abu Rayhan al-Biruni 79
Abu Abdullah al-Idrisi 79

Documentary Sources. 80

CHAPTER 3: THE ARTS

Chronology. 82

Overview 85

Topics in the Arts

Arabic Poetry. 86
Arabic Prose Literature 90
Calligraphy 99
Decorative Arts 101
Domestic and Secular Architecture. 105
Early Religious Architecture and City Planning 107
Later Masjid Architecture in the Arab World and Africa. 114
Later Masjid Architecture in the Turco-Iranian World and India 118
Music. 120
Oral Poetry, Storytelling, and Folklore 123
Persian Poetry 124
Persian Prose Literature. 125
The Prohibition of Images 127

Significant People

Hafiz 131

Al-Hariri 131

Abu Uthman al-Jahiz 132

Abd al-Qahir al-Jurjani 132

Al-Khansa' 133

Al-Mas'udi 133

Al-Mutanabbi 134

Sibawayh 135

Al-Walid ibn Abd al-Malik 135

Documentary Sources 136

CHAPTER 4: COMMUNICATION, TRANSPORTATION, AND EXPLORATION

Chronology 138

Overview 139

Topics in Communication, Transportation, and Exploration

Communication 141

Land Transportation 146

Sea and River Transport 151

Scientific Exploration 155

Significant People

Ibn Battuta 158

Ibn Fadlan 158

Ibn Jubayr 159

Abu Dulaf al-Khazraji 159

Shams al-Din Abu 'Abd Allah Muhammad al-Muqaddasi 159

Documentary Sources 160

CHAPTER 5: SOCIAL CLASS SYSTEM AND THE ECONOMY

Chronology 162

Overview 166

Topics in Social Class System and the Economy

Agriculture and Pastoralism 168

Artisans, Manufacturing, and Commerce 171

The Class System and Social Change 176

Converts and Social Integration 182

The Decentralization of Society 184

Significant People

Al-Zahir Baybars 190

Abu al-Fadl Ja'far ibn 'Ali al-Dimashqi 191

Harun al-Rashid 191

Salah al-Din al-Ayyubi 192

'Umar ibn 'Abd al-'Aziz 192

'Umar ibn al-Khattab 193

Documentary Sources 194

CHAPTER 6: POLITICS, LAW, AND THE MILITARY

Chronology. 196

Overview 201

Topics in Politics, Law, and the Military

The Authority of the Khilafah. 203
The Judicial System. 206
Jurisprudence and Law 209
Laws on Commerce. 211
Laws on Crime 212
Laws on Family Life 213
Laws on Foreign Relations and War 215
Legal Developments 217
Military Developments 221
Mongol Invasions 228
The Spread of Islam 230
Sultanates 232

Significant People

Abu Hanifah 233
'Ali ibn Abi Talib 234
Ahmad Ibn Hanbal 235
'Abd al-Rahman Ibn Khaldun. 235
Ja'far al-Sadiq. 236
Malik ibn Anas 237
Nizam al-Mulk 238
Muhammad ibn Idris al-Shafi'i 238
Shajarat al-Durr 239

Documentary Sources. 240

CHAPTER 7: LEISURE, RECREATION, AND DAILY LIFE

Chronology. 242

Overview 245

Topics in Leisure, Recreation, and Daily Life

Adapting to Climates and Landscapes 247
Characteristics of Islamic Daily Life 248
Clothing and Textiles 250
Dwelling Spaces 261
Food. 268
Games and Leisure Activities 276
Holidays and Religious Observances. 280

Significant People

Abu Hurayrah 288
Muhammad ibn Ismail al-Bukhari 288
Ahmad Badi al-Zaman al-Hamadhani 289
Ibn Khallikan. 289
Anas Ibn Malik 290

    Juha 290

    Nasr al-Din Khoja 290

    Muslim Abu al-Husayn Muslim 291

Documentary Sources 291

CHAPTER 8: THE FAMILY AND SOCIAL TRENDS

Chronology 294

Overview 296

Topics in the Family and Social Trends

    Child-Rearing Methods 297

    Education 302

    Marriage 307

    Sexuality 312

    Social Roles and Responsibilities 315

Significant People

    'A'isha bint Abi Bakr 319

    Ahmad ibn 'Abd al-Rahim 319

    'Aish'a bint Muhammad ibn 'Abd al-Hadi 320

Documentary Sources 321

CHAPTER 9: RELIGION AND PHILOSOPHY

Chronology 324

Overview 332

Topics in Religion and Philosophy

    Din and Theology in Qur'an and Sunnah 335

    Free Will and the Rise of Islamic Sectarianism 343

    Origins and Development of Systematic Theology 354

    The Rise of Falsafah: The Philosophical Tradition 366

    The Sunni Critique of Kalam and Falsafah 381

Significant People

    Abu Hamid Muhammad al-Tusi al-Ghazali 393

    Muhyi al-Din Ibn al-'Arabi 393

    Muhammad 394

    Rabi'ah al-Adawiyyah 395

    Jalal al-Din Rumi 396

Documentary Sources 397

CHAPTER 10: SCIENCE, TECHNOLOGY, AND HEALTH

Chronology 400

Overview 403

Topics in Science, Technology, and Health

    The 'Alim and Muslim Science 405

    Astronomy 407

    Botany 409

Cartography and Navigation 411

Chemistry 413

Mathematics 415

Mechanics 418

Medicine and Health. 419

Military Advances 424

Mineralogy and Geology. 426

The Muslim Agricultural Revolution 426

Optics and Ophthalmology. 428

Technology 429

Zoology. 432

Significant People

Jabir ibn Hayyan 434

Abu Bakr Muhammad ibn Zakariya al-Razi. 435

Nasir al-Din al-Tusi. 435

Documentary Sources. 436

GLOSSARY 439

GENERAL REFERENCE 447

CONTRIBUTORS 457

INDEX OF PHOTOGRAPHS 459

INDEX 467

ABOUT THE SERIES

PROJECT DESCRIPTION

Patterned after the well-received *American Decades* and *American Eras* series, *World Eras* is a cross-disciplinary reference series. It comprises volumes examining major civilizations that have flourished from antiquity to modern times, with a global perspective and a strong emphasis on daily life and social history. Each volume provides in-depth coverage of one era, focusing on a specific cultural group and its interaction with other peoples of the world. The *World Eras* series is geared toward the needs of high-school students studying subjects in the humanities. Its purpose is to provide students—and general reference users as well—a reliable, engaging reference resource that stimulates their interest, encourages research, and prompts comparison of the lives people led in different parts of the world, in different cultures, and at different times.

The goal of *World Eras* volumes is to enrich the traditional historical study of "kings and battles" with a resource that promotes understanding of daily life and the cultural institutions that affect people's beliefs and behavior.

What kind of work did people in a certain culture perform?

What did they eat?

How did they fight their battles?

What laws did they have and how did they punish criminals?

What were their religious practices?

What did they know of science and medicine?

What kind of art, music, and literature did they enjoy?

These are the types of questions *World Eras* volumes seek to answer.

VOLUME DESIGN

World Eras is designed to facilitate comparative study. Thus volumes employ a consistent ten-chapter structure so that teachers and students can readily access standard topics in various volumes. The chapters in each *World Eras* volume are:

1. World Events
2. Geography
3. The Arts
4. Communication, Transportation, and Exploration
5. Social Class System and the Economy
6. Politics, Law, and the Military
7. Leisure, Recreation, and Daily Life
8. The Family and Social Trends
9. Religion and Philosophy
10. Science, Technology, and Health

World Eras volumes begin with two chapters designed to provide a broad view of the world against which a specific culture can be measured. Chapter 1 provides students today with a means to understand where a certain people stood within our concept of world history. Chapter 2 describes the world from the perspective of the people being studied—what did they know of geography and how did geography and climate affect their lives? The following eight chapters address major aspects of people's lives to provide a sense of what defined their culture. The ten chapters in *World Eras* will remain constant in each volume. Teachers and students seeking to compare religious beliefs in Roman and Greek cultures, for example, can easily locate the information they require by consulting chapter 9 in the appropriate volumes, tapping a rich source for class assignments and research topics. Volume-specific glossaries and a checklist of general references provide students assistance in studying unfamiliar cultures.

CHAPTER CONTENTS

Each chapter in *World Eras* volumes also follows a uniform structure designed to provide users quick access to the information they need. Chapters are arranged into five types of material:

- **Chronology** provides an historical outline of significant events in the subject of the chapter in timeline form.

- **Overview** provides a narrative overview of the chapter topic during the period and discusses the material of the chapter in a global context.

- **Topical Entries** provide focused information in easy-to-read articles about people, places, events, institutions, and matters of general concern to the people of the time. A references rubric includes sources for further study.

- **Biographical Entries** profiles people of enduring significance regarding the subject of the chapter.
- **Documentary Sources** is an annotated checklist of documentary sources from the historical period that are the basis for the information presented in the chapter.

Chapters are supplemented throughout with primary-text sidebars that include interesting short documentary excerpts or anecdotes chosen to illuminate the subject of the chapter: recipes, letters, daily-life accounts, and excerpts from important documents. Each *World Eras* volume includes about 150 illustrations, maps, diagrams, and line drawings linked directly to material discussed in the text. Illustrations are chosen with particular emphasis on daily life.

INDEXING

A general two-level subject index for each volume includes significant terms, subjects, theories, practices, people, organizations, publications, and so forth, mentioned in the text. Index citations with many page references are broken down by subtopic. Illustrations are indicated both in the general index, by use of italicized page numbers, and in a separate illustrations index, which provides a description of each item.

EDITORS AND CONTRIBUTORS

An advisory board of history teachers and librarians has provided valuable advice about the rationale for this series. They have reviewed both series plans and individual volume plans. Each *World Eras* volume is edited by a distinguished specialist in the subject of his or her volume. The editor is responsible for enlisting other scholar-specialists to write each of the chapters in the volume and of assuring the quality of their work. The editorial staff at Manly, Inc., rigorously checks factual information, line edits the manuscript, works with the editor to select illustrations, and produces the books in the series, in cooperation with Gale Group editors.

The *World Eras* series is for students of all ages who seek to enrich their study of world history by examining the many aspects of people's lives in different places during different eras. This series continues Gale's tradition of publishing comprehensive, accurate, and stimulating historical reference works that promote the study of history and culture.

The following timeline, included in every volume of *World Eras*, is provided as a convenience to users seeking a ready chronological context.

TIMELINE

This timeline, compiled by editors at Manly, Inc., is provided as a convenience for students seeking a broad global and historical context for the materials in this volume of World Eras. *It is not intended as a self-contained resource. Students who require a comprehensive chronology of world history should consult a source such as Peter N. Stearns, ed.,* The Encyclopedia of World History, *sixth revised edition (Boston & New York: Houghton Mifflin, 2001).*

CIRCA 4 MILLION TO 1 MILLION B.C.E.
Era of *Australopithecus,* the first hominid

CIRCA 1.5 MILLION TO 200,000 B.C.E.
Era of *Homo erectus,* "upright-walking human"

CIRCA 1,000,000-10,000 B.C.E.
Paleothic Age: hunters and gatherers make use of stone tools in Eurasia

CIRCA 250,000 B.C.E.
Early evolution of *Homo sapiens,* "consciously thinking humans"

CIRCA 40,000 B.C.E.
Migrations from Siberia to Alaska lead to the first human inhabitation of North and South America

CIRCA 8000 B.C.E.
Neolithic Age: settled agrarian culture begins to develop in Eurasia

5000 B.C.E.
The world population is between 5 million and 20 million

CIRCA 4000-3500 B.C.E.
Earliest Sumerian cities: artificial irrigation leads to increased food supplies and populations in Mesopotamia

CIRCA 3000 B.C.E.
Bronze Age begins in Mesopotamia and Egypt, where bronze is primarily used for making weapons; invention of writing

CIRCA 2900-1150 B.C.E.
Minoan society on Crete: lavish palaces and commercial activity

CIRCA 2700-2200 B.C.E.
Egypt: Old Kingdom and the building of the pyramids

CIRCA 2080-1640 B.C.E.
Egypt: Middle Kingdom plagued by internal strife and invasion by the Hyksos

CIRCA 2000-1200 B.C.E.
Hittites build a powerful empire based in Anatolia (present-day Turkey) by using horse-drawn war chariots

CIRCA 1792-1760 B.C.E.
Old Babylonian Kingdom; one of the oldest extant legal codes is compiled

CIRCA 1766-1122 B.C.E.
Shang Dynasty in China: military expansion, large cities, written language, and introduction of bronze metallurgy

CIRCA 1570-1075 B.C.E.
Egypt: New Kingdom and territorial expansion into Palestine, Lebanon, and Syria

CIRCA 1500 B.C.E.
The Aryans, an Indo-European people from the steppes of present-day Ukraine and southern Russia, expand into northern India

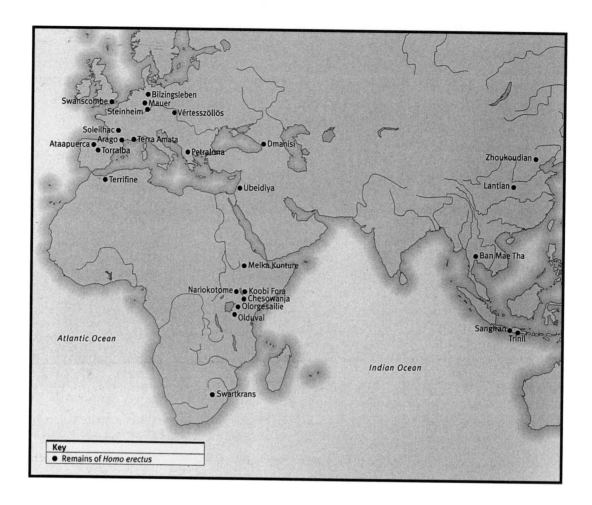

Key
● Remains of *Homo erectus*

CIRCA 1500 B.C.E.
Phoenicians create the first alphabet

CIRCA 1400-1200 B.C.E.
Hittites develop the technology of iron-smelting, improving weaponry and agricultural implements, as well as stimulating trade

CIRCA 1200-800 B.C.E.
Phoenicians establish colonies throughout the Mediterranean

CIRCA 1122- 221 B.C.E.
Zhou Dynasty in China: military conquests, nomadic invasions, and introduction of iron metallurgy

CIRCA 1100-750 B.C.E.
Greek Dark Ages: foreign invasions, civil disturbances, decrease in agricultural production, and population decline

1020-587 B.C.E.
Israelite monarchies consolidate their power in Palestine

CIRCA 1000-612 B.C.E.
Assyrians create an empire encompassing Mesopotamia, Syria, Palestine, and most of Anatolia

and Egypt; they deport populations to various regions of the realm

1000 B.C.E.
The world population is approximately 50 million

CIRCA 814-146 B.C.E.
The city-state of Carthage is a powerful commercial and military power in the western Mediterranean

753 B.C.E.
Traditional date of the founding of Rome

CIRCA 750-700 B.C.E.
Rise of the polis, or city-state, in Greece

558-330 B.C.E.
Achaemenid Dynasty establishes the Persian Empire (present-day Iran, Turkey, Afghanistan, and Iraq); satraps rule the various provinces

509 B.C.E.
Roman Republic is established

500 B.C.E.
The world population is approximately 100 million

The ROMAN EMPIRE
before the Barbarian Invasions

CIRCA 400 B.C.E.
Spread of Buddhism in India

338-323 B.C.E.
Macedon, a kingdom in the central Balkan peninsula, conquers the Persian Empire

323-301 B.C.E.
Ptolemaic Kingdom (Egypt), Seleucid Kingdom (Syria), and Antigonid Dynasty (Macedon) are founded

247 B.C.E.-224 C.E.
Parthian Empire (Parthia, Persia, and Babylonia): clan leaders build independent power bases in their satrapies, or provinces

215-168 B.C.E.
Rome establishes hegemony over the Hellenistic world

206 B.C.E. TO 220 C.E.
Han Dynasty in China: imperial expansion into central Asia, centralized government, economic prosperity, and population growth

CIRCA 100 B.C.E.
Tribesmen on the Asian steppes develop the stirrup, which eventually revolutionizes warfare

1 C.E.
The world population is approximately 200 million

CIRCA 100 C.E.
Invention of paper in China

224-651 C.E.
Sasanid Empire (Parthia, Persia, and Babylonia): improved government system, founding of new cities, increased trade, and the introduction of rice and cotton cultivation

340 C.E.
Constantinople becomes the capital of the Eastern Roman, or Byzantine, Empire

CIRCA 320-550 C.E.
Gupta Dynasty in India: Golden Age of Hindu civilization marked by stability and prosperity throughout the subcontinent

395 C.E.
Christianity becomes the official religion of the Roman Empire

CIRCA 400 C.E.
The first unified Japanese state arises and is centered at Yamato on the island of Honshu; Buddhism arrives in Japan by way of Korea

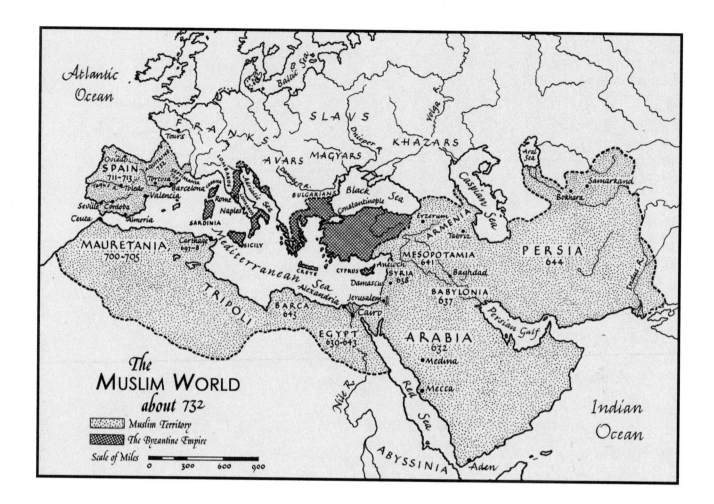

The MUSLIM WORLD about 732

Muslim Territory
The Byzantine Empire

Scale of Miles
0   300   600   900

CIRCA 400 C.E.
The nomadic Huns begin a westward migration from central Asia, causing disruption in the Roman Empire

CIRCA 400 C.E.
The Mayan Empire in Mesoamerica evolves into city-states

476 C.E.
Rome falls to barbarian hordes and the Western Roman Empire collapses

CIRCA 500-1500 C.E.
Middle Ages, or medieval period, in Europe: gradual recovery from political disruption and increase in agricultural productivity and population

618-907 C.E.
Tang Dynasty in China: territorial expansion, government bureaucracy, agricultural improvements, and transportation and communication networks

632-733 C.E.
Muslim expansion and conquests in Arabia, Syria, Palestine, Mesopotamia, Egypt, North Africa, Persia, northwestern India, and Iberia

CIRCA 700 C.E.
Origins of feudalism, a political and social organization that dominates Europe until the fifteenth century; based on the relationship between lords and vassals

CIRCA 900 C.E.
Introduction of the horseshoe in Europe and black powder in China

960-1279 C.E.
Song Dynasty in China: civil administration, industry, education, and the arts

962-1806 C.E.
Holy Roman Empire of western and central Europe, created in an attempt to revive the old Roman Empire

1000 C.E.
The world population is approximately 300 million

1096-1291 C.E.
Western Christians undertake the Crusades, a series of religiously inspired military campaigns, to recapture the Holy Land from the Muslims

1200 to 1400 C.E.
The Mali empire in Africa dominates the trans-Saharan trade network of camel caravans

1220-1335 C.E.
The Mongols, nomadic horsemen from the high steppes of eastern central Asia, build an empire that includes China, Persia, and Russia

Circa 1250 C.E.
Inca Empire develops in Peru: Civil administration, road networks, and sun worshipping

1299-1919 C.E.
Ottoman Empire, created by nomadic Turks and Christian converts to Islam, encompasses Asia Minor, the Balkans, Greece, Egypt, North Africa, and the Middle East

1300 C.E.
The world population is approximately 396 million

1337-1453 C.E.
Hundred Years' War, a series of intermittent military campaigns between England and France over control of continental lands claimed by both countries

1347-1350 C.E.
Black Death, or the bubonic plague, kills one-quarter of the European population

1368-1644 C.E.
Ming Dynasty in China: political, economic, and cultural revival; the Great Wall is built

1375-1527 C.E.
The Renaissance in Western Europe, a revival in the arts and learning

1428-1519 C.E.
The Aztecs expand in central Mexico, developing trade routes and a system of tribute payments

1450 C.E.
Invention of the printing press

1453 C.E.
Constantinople falls to the Ottoman Turks, ending the Byzantine Empire

1464-1591 C.E.
Songhay Empire in Africa: military expansion, prosperous cities, control of the trans-Saharan trade

1492 C.E.
Discovery of America; European exploration and colonization of the Western Hemisphere begins

Circa 1500-1867 C.E.
Transatlantic slave trade results in the forced migration of between 12 million and 16 million Africans to the Western Hemisphere

1500 C.E.
The world population is approximately 480 million

1517 C.E.
Beginning of the Protestant Reformation, a religious movement that ends the spiritual unity of western Christendom

1523-1763 C.E.
Mughal Empire in India: military conquests, productive agricultural economy, and population growth

1600-1867 C.E.
Tokugawa Shogunate in Japan: shoguns (military governors) turn Edo, or Tokyo, into the political, economic, and cultural center of the nation

1618-1648 C.E.
Thirty Years' War in Europe between Catholic and Protestant states

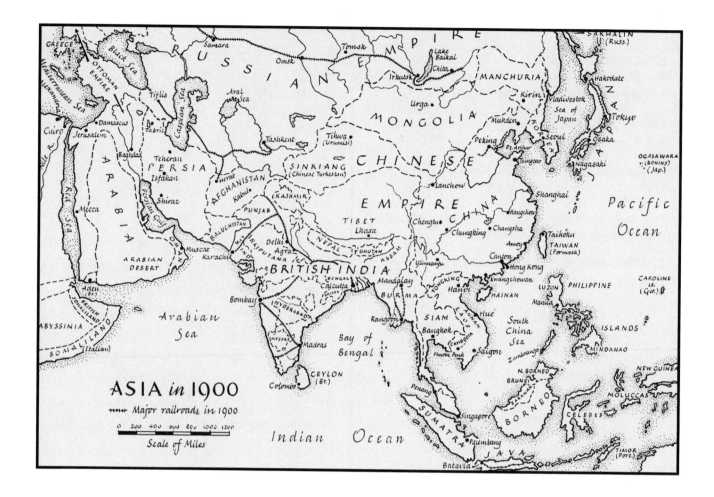

ASIA in 1900
⊬⊬⊬⊬ Major railroads in 1900

0 200 400 600 800 1000 1200
Scale of Miles

1644-1911 C.E.
Qing Dynasty in China: military expansion and scholar-bureaucrats

1700 C.E.
The world population is approximately 640 million

CIRCA 1750 C.E.
Beginning of the Enlightenment, a philosophical movement marked by an emphasis on rationalism and scientific inquiry

1756-1763 C.E.
Seven Years' War: England and Prussia versus Austria, France, Russia, Saxony, Spain, and Sweden

CIRCA 1760-1850 C.E.
Industrial Revolution in Britain is marked by mass production through the division of labor, mechanization, a great increase in the supply of iron, and the use of the steam engine

1775-1783 C.E.
American War of Independence; the United States becomes an independent republic

1789 C.E.
French Revolution topples the monarchy and leads to a period of political unrest followed by a dictatorship

1793-1815 C.E.
Napoleonic Wars: Austria, England, Prussia, and Russia versus France and its satellite states

1794-1824 C.E.
Latin American states conduct wars of independence against Spain

1900 C.E.
The world population is approximately 1.65 billion

1914-1918 C.E.
World War I, or the Great War: the Allies (England, France, Russia, and the United States) versus Central Powers (Austria-Hungary, Germany, and the Ottoman Empire)

1917-1921 C.E.
Russian Revolution: a group of Communists known as the Bolsheviks seize control of the country following a civil war

1939-1945 C.E.
World War II: the Allies (China, England, France, the Soviet Union, and the United States) versus the Axis (Germany, Italy, and Japan)

1945 C.E.
Successful test of the first atomic weapon; beginning of the Cold War, a period of rivalry, mistrust, and, occasionally, open hostility between the capitalist West and communist East

1947-1975 C.E.
Decolonization occurs in Africa and Asia as European powers relinquish control of colonies in those regions

1948
Israel becomes the first independent Jewish state in nearly two thousand years

1949
Communists seize control of China

1950-1951
Korean War: the United States attempts to stop Communist expansion in the Korean peninsula

1957 C.E.
The Soviet Union launches *Sputnik* ("fellow traveler of earth"), the first man-made satellite; the Space Age begins

1965-1973
Vietnam War: the United States attempts to thwart the spread of Communism in Vietnam

1989 C.E.
East European Communist regimes begin to falter and multiparty elections are held

1991 C.E.
Soviet Union is dissolved and replaced by the Commonwealth of Independent States

2000 C.E.
The world population is 6 billion

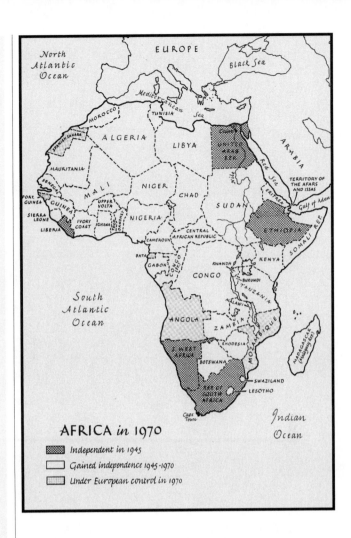

AFRICA *in* 1970

- Independent in 1945
- Gained independence 1945-1970
- Under European control in 1970

INTRODUCTION

The Origins of Islam. Islam is a world religion that represents a continuation and—according to Muslims—the culmination of the monotheistic tradition. Although its beginning is traditionally dated to the seventh century of the Common Era, its origins actually lie much farther back in time, with Adam, who is considered the first prophet of Islam. The teachings of Islam embrace all of the major events in the relationship between God and humankind described in the Hebrew Bible and the New Testament. While the historical religion of Islam was first established in Arabia, all the Fertile Crescent and the Holy Land are included in Islam's narrative of revelation and its unfolding in history.

Religion and Civilization. Islam is the only world civilization named for its religion. Scholars seldom speak of "Hindu civilization" or "Buddhist civilization." Instead, they name the civilizations that include the Hindu and Buddhist religions in geographic or cultural terms, such as "Indian civilization" or "Chinese civilization." Similarly, "Western civilization" has become common shorthand for the culture and history that originated in a relatively limited part of western Eurasia, which also happens to be part of Christendom. Western civilization is no longer called "Christendom," because it is well known that Western civilization includes Jews and even some Muslims and that Christendom includes non-European Christians.

An "Islamic" Civilization? The problem with the concept of *Islamic civilization* is that it tends to hide many cultural differences under a single "Islamic" cloak. While cultural history seeks to highlight the differences among peoples, periods, and regions, cultural artifacts from Mughal India or medieval Anatolia, Persia, North Africa, Yemen, and Syria are all too often classified as "Islamic" rather than as "Indian," "Anatolian," or "Persian." Premodern literary or scientific works written in the Arabic language may also be classified as "Islamic" even if Christians or Jews wrote them. Sacred and secular forms of architecture alike are also called "Islamic," and one even finds references to "Islamic trade routes" and "Islamic technology," although the teachings of the Islamic religion make no reference to the "Islamization" of such phenomena.

Defining Terms. Because the misuse of the term *Islamic* is so pervasive in academic and general literature, it is often difficult for the student to distinguish between what is truly Islamic in origin and what persists from pre-Islamic times or belongs to secular realms. This problem even extends to identifying as "Islamic" certain beliefs and practices that go against Islamic teachings. Some scholars have attempted to solve this "adjective problem" by coining more accurate terms, but they have come at the cost of elegance and simplicity. One such coinage is the adjective *Islamicate*, which Marshall G. S. Hodgson defines in *The Venture of Islam* (1974) as referring "not directly to the religion, Islam, itself, but to the social and cultural complex historically associated with Islam and the Muslims, both among Muslims themselves and even when found among non-Muslims." This term includes cultural and social phenomena influenced by Islamic beliefs and practices, along with the material, artistic, and literary creations of people who were not Muslim but who were influenced by Islamic cultural forms. Other scholars have simply juggled the terms *Muslim* and *Islamic* in various ways but have never solved the problem because they use the same terms to refer to different things at different times and in different contexts. The test of applying similar terms to other non-Islamic cultures makes these problems apparent. For example, if Urdu and Persian are called "Islamic" languages, why are Swedish and French not called "Christian" languages? In this volume the word *Islamic* is used specifically to designate the religion of Islam and its teachings, while *Muslim* is used to designate the civilization developed by adherents of the Islamic faith.

Regional Diversity and Change. During the nearly nine hundred years from 622 to 1500, Islam and Muslim civilization spread over a vast area that includes Asia, Africa, Europe, and regions bordering the Indian Ocean. It became the faith of the majority, or a significant minority, of people in regions with differing climates and terrains, from the driest deserts to the monsoon tropics, from snow-capped mountains to grasslands and temperate forests. Geographically, the lands in which Islam became the dominant religion were at the center of the known world, where continents are joined together by land bridges and navigable bodies of water. Historically, the heartland of Muslim civilization, the Arabian Peninsula, which lies at the intersection of three continents and several major bodies of water, has been a pathway for repeated migrations and is crisscrossed by trade routes that link Europe, Africa, and Asia and eventually reach into the Western Hemisphere. The ethnic groups, cultures, religions, and languages of the Arabian Peninsula had already mingled before the rise of Islam, but they maintained much of their diversity even after the disparate cultural groups were united by the common threads of belief, language, and practice.

Spread of Islam. It is important to understand that the vast territory that some call the "Muslim World" did not become "Islamic" all at once. The territory under Muslim rule did expand rapidly during the first century after 622, but the spread of the Islamic religion was a separate process that took centuries. The conversion of local populations to Islam occurred over many generations, even in the lands that came under Muslim rule as early as the seventh and eighth centuries. The spread of Islam beyond these regions was still more gradual, occurring mainly through the effects of trade and migration. The configuration of Muslim civilization also underwent great changes over the period 622–1500, beginning from relatively homogeneous Arab roots, becoming more complex and heterogeneous during the early development of Muslim civilization, and then changing again under the influence of new ruling groups, circumstances, and cultural influences. Students must avoid the tendency to think of Muslim societies as monolithic and unchanging. Previous approaches to world history have tended to concentrate on the history of Muslim civilization during its first centuries and have often neglected later changes in thought, institutions, and economy, as though Muslim civilization was a cart full of goods that was pushed forward at some point in time and continued to roll on the same path with the same cargo. Writing the chapters for this volume was a daunting challenge for each contributor not only because of the wealth and variety of available materials on each topic but also because of the broad regional span and the long period of time that he or she was required to cover.

Study of Islam and Muslim History. In research, there is a constant interaction between the researcher and his or her subject. This subjectivity has long been recognized in the humanities, but now even physicists acknowledge that the process of research can affect the results of an experiment. Over many centuries, the study of Muslim civilization by Western scholars was adversely affected by the uneasy relationship between the two cultures and their religions. Although the differences between western European "Christendom" and North African and southwest Asian "Islamdom" have often seemed unsurpassable, these two civilizations have in fact had much in common. During the early centuries of Islam, Christianity was also beginning to spread in Europe, and the Roman Church was becoming established as an institution. The formation of states that later colonized Muslim regions had barely begun. In contrast, by the early 700s an expanding Muslim empire had reached the Iberian Peninsula, Sicily, and Crete, chal-

lenged the Byzantine Empire in Anatolia, and penetrated as far east as Central Asia. It is hard to say whether the military threat to European states or the religious challenge of Islam to the Christian Church weighed heavier in the European tendency to regard Muslims as opponents, enemies, or unfamiliar "others." The rarity of northern European travel to the Muslim world and the frequency of Muslim travel to nearly everywhere but Europe kept the two sides physically and conceptually separated. Conversions to Islam by Spanish and Italian Christians bred fear among Church officials, creating a situation in which they did not study Islam objectively but instead perceived a contest between the claims of each faith. Because Islam venerated Jesus but denied that he was the Son of God, the relationship between the Islamic and Christian religions became especially complicated. When the soldiers of the Reconquista and the Crusades took Muslim territory in Spain and the Holy Land, the two sides engaged in many cultural exchanges and even major transfers of knowledge, but at the same time religious hostility increased. Medieval scholarship about Islam from within Christendom was hostile and propagandistic as well as ill informed, sometimes making the absurd claim that Islam was a religion of idol worship. Transfers of Greek and Arabic philosophy through the translation of Muslim texts in the twelfth and thirteenth centuries engendered much respect for Muslim scholarship and thought among European scholars. This awareness, however, did not extend much beyond a small group of intellectuals and was soon counterbalanced by a fear of Ottoman military prowess—especially after the fall of Constantinople in 1453. The subsequent Ottoman expansion into Europe fanned the flames of hostility even though information exchange and trade continued. The words used to describe Muslims in the medieval and Renaissance periods reveal Europeans' profound ignorance of Islam and Muslims in the West, ranging from misguided names such as "Mahometan" and "Mohammedan," which implied that Muslims worshiped Muhammad, to overgeneralized ethnic terms such as "Saracen," "Turk," and "Arab."

Orientalism. By the nineteenth century the balance of military, technological, and economic superiority had tipped decisively toward Europe, and Muslim regions fell under European colonial domination. Although the physical distance between Muslim and European regions had dwindled because of advances in transportation and communication, much residual hostility and ignorance remained. Europeans were becoming aware of themselves as a civilization with distinct secular values. European study of Islam and Muslims became colored by a strong missionary impulse, along with a tendency to feel suspicious toward religion and its "superstitions," while regarding the secular as safe and "rational." During this time the study of Islam and Muslim culture became a major discipline in European universities. European scholars produced many valuable studies, made important archaeological finds, and obtained art objects, manuscripts, and documents. These discoveries occurred, however, under conditions that were intimately linked to the political and economic domination of Muslim regions. The overwhelming technological and economic superiority of the West was accompanied by a sense that Western civilization was superior to all others, and Europeans assumed that modernization in other places would have to follow the same pattern. The West, they believed, would play a leading role in bringing about the modernization of Muslim regions without giving up its economic, political, or military dominance. Part of this mind-set was the "glory that was Islam" approach to studying Muslim culture. This prescriptive attitude asserted that Islam, while glorious in the past, had become the repository of outdated traditions that hindered social and scientific progress. Islam, like other "traditional" religions, they asserted, would have to be reformed so that it would no longer intrude on the modernization process. The contradictions inherent in this Western approach to the study of Islam and Muslim societies is an important part of what Edward Said and many of his contemporaries have called "Orientalism" and described as a flawed approach to culture history that affected the Western study of other world cultures as well.

Challenges to Orientalism. By the late twentieth century, Orientalism had been thoroughly critiqued, and research into the study of Islam by Western scholars had become a subdiscipline by itself. Over the past fifty years an ever-increasing group of scholars within and outside the Muslim world have changed attitudes and approaches to the study of Islam and Muslims and created a more balanced perspective on the relative virtues and vices of both Western and Muslim civilizations. The legacy of Orientalism, however, has not vanished, and present scholarship still builds on the achievements of earlier Western writers. In the twenty-first century, scholars strive for a more authentic and less prejudiced reading of the past, but no one imagines that subjectivity in historical writing will ever disappear. The contributors to this volume are well aware of these issues and seek to bring to students the best that recent scholarship can offer toward understanding and appreciating the richness and complexity of Islam and Muslim civilization.

Why This Volume? The study of world history is in the process of dramatic and fruitful change. When advanced civilizations have attempted to write histories of the world, they have usually placed their own cultural assumptions and geographic locations at the center of the story. Western versions of world history, such as those taught in European and American classrooms for decades, have been no different. Since the nineteenth century, the center of the Western world-history narrative has been an investigation of the biblical, classical, and medieval heritage of Western civilization and the rise of Western nations to dominance since the 1500s. Information about non-Western regions and civilizations was added later to surveys of world history, but they have typically appeared on the margins of the main narrative. Some of the achievements and contribu-

tions of these civilizations have been noted, but the story of their interactions with one another and with Europe has remained largely untold. Furthermore, geographic regions of great importance to world history have often been left out at crucial points of the story, such as the Indian Ocean and its trade before the arrival of European explorers, and the Central Asian steppes and the role of nomadic groups in migration and trade. The history of science and technology has also been viewed in isolation, giving little emphasis to contributions from non-Western civilizations before the Scientific Revolution in Europe, which in fact owed much to the work of earlier Muslim scientists.

New Approaches. Over the past fifty years or so, proponents of "new historiography" have begun to explore the defects of this narrow view of world history and have experimented with new ways of understanding and teaching about world history. By the 1990s this approach had begun to appear in high-school and collegiate world-history surveys. As the title of this World Eras series suggests, world-history courses are now being built around a framework of eras instead of a series of discrete and isolated civilizations. During their study of each era, students learn how human societies and civilizations developed, changed, interacted with, and influenced each other in time and geographic space. The contrast between the old and the new approach is like the difference between viewing a portrait gallery and examining a series of panoramic landscapes. One cannot see much beyond the subject in a portrait, but many things—mountains, sky, plants, animals, and even people—may inhabit a landscape. Furthermore, one can zoom in on various subjects in a landscape for closer study and analyze how their activities or position relate to each other. As one approaches each new landscape in a series, one may see both familiar faces and new ones, and the scene gradually becomes more complex. Sometimes the viewer might recognize that the scene is becoming familiar. The chapters in this volume are like such a series of landscapes. They depict a world civilization whose development and influence extends across a wide geographic area and continues through many eras. Like other works in this series, this volume is designed to aid in-depth study of a major world civilization during each of its relevant eras, adding necessary detail to the reader's personal stock of images, ideas, and impressions about the human experience.

How to Use This Book. The main goal of this series is to produce for students and for teachers of new world-history survey courses a reference tool that is readable, accurate, and thorough in covering civilizations through historical eras. In order to make it easy for introductory students to gather detailed information about different periods and groups—and to compare and contrast various aspects of history and cultural developments—all the volumes in the series are organized in the same way. Each volume has the same basic table of contents, and each of the chapters covers a general set of topics that most major civilizations have in common. These topics include the environment of each civilization, the economy that sustains its people, the way in which society is organized, behaviors that prevailed and changed over time, how the states in each civilization were ruled and how they defended or expanded their territory, what languages they used to communicate, and what patterns of thought, invention, and creativity appeared in their cultural productions. This design is intended to facilitate comparison among civilizations and across eras, but its topical arrangement should also be used to draw comparisons within each volume and to make connections among historical realms covered in the chapters. Each discipline—art history, economic and social history, and political, military, and intellectual history—views the civilization from a different perspective. By reading and comparing, the connections between language and culture, economy and communication, politics and social organization, technology and environment, and science and art become clear. The authors of the chapters have tried to avoid repetition, but some overlap cannot and should not be avoided, because many aspects of a civilization intersect and affect others in a complex society.

The Arabic Language. The universal language of Islamic worship and premodern Islamic scholarship is Arabic, and Arabic-Islamic terms have entered all the languages spoken by Muslims across the globe. There are several reasons for this widespread importation of Arabic vocabulary. Chief among them is the requirement that all Muslims must perform the daily prayer and read the Qur'an, the Islamic holy book, in the original Arabic. Thus, they must begin memorizing Arabic liturgy and scripture at an early age. Memorizing the entire Qur'an or large parts of it is the goal of Muslims everywhere. Because of this emphasis on learning the language of Islam, Arabic devotional expressions, greetings, and supplications to God are interspersed in the speech of Muslims around the world, no matter what vernacular language they speak. The universal greeting *assalaamu alaikum* (peace be unto you) and the ubiquitous expression praising God, *alhamdulillah,* are the most commonly used expressions, but there are many others as well. Arabic was for many centuries the universal language of learning through which knowledge of Islam was transmitted, and many of its terms cannot be fully understood except in the original language. Because many of these terms come from the Qur'an or were introduced by the Prophet Muhammad, it has been a simple matter to assimilate them into the vernacular from the language already used by Muslims for worship and reading scripture. Among literate, educated Muslims, whether or not they are fluent Arabic speakers, the language of the Qur'an and the Prophet is acknowledged as the language in which religious knowledge, with its extensive terminology, is conveyed. The framework provided by this knowledge in turn guides the behavior of Muslim individuals and their societies. The most common terms include the five pillars of Islamic practice—*shahadah* (the affirmation that "there is no god but God and Muhammad is the Messenger of God"), *salat* (the five required daily prayers), *zakat* (the required poor

tax), *siyam* (fasting during the month of Ramadan), and *hajj* (pilgrimage to Makkah)—as well as terms designating the parts of the Qur'an, the movements and phrases used in daily prayers, and the names of annual celebrations. Words describing aspects of Islamic law and practice, such as *haram* (forbidden) and *halal* (permitted), are also widely known in areas where other languages are spoken.

The Spread of Arabic. During the early centuries of Islamic history, Arabic became the most widespread language in most of southwest Asia and North Africa, and it had a profound effect on the many other languages spoken by Muslim peoples, including Persian, Turkish, Urdu, Malay, and African languages of the Sahara, the Niger, and the Swahili coast. Arabic script was adopted for transcribing these languages. It remains dominant in Persian and Urdu, but it was replaced in Turkey by the Latin alphabet when the Kemalists came to power after World War I; in Central Asia by the Cyrillic alphabet when the region came under the control of the Russian-dominated Soviet government; and in other Muslim regions as a result of colonization and globalization.

The Qur'an and the Writing System. The standard for Arabic is the language of the Qur'an. Because of its constant use and the literary and intellectual production it stimulated, this language has been preserved in its seventh-century Arabian classical form, but it has also remained a living language that grows along with the introduction of new ideas and material objects. There are also many regional dialects of spoken Arabic. Because Qur'anic recitation has played a central role in Islam as an authentic oral tradition, the original pronunciations of Arabic words have been passed down from the time of the Prophet to successive generations. Refinements in the script during the early Islamic centuries were adopted to distinguish among similarly written words, thus preserving and transmitting correct reading and pronunciation. As a result, trained and educated modern readers can accurately reproduce the original pronunciation of classical Arabic, despite the variety of local dialects that have emerged during the fourteen centuries of Islam. Arabic is written in an alphabet of twenty-five symbols, in addition to several diacritical marks that aid in the correct vocalization of words. Like the other Semitic languages, such as Aramaic and Hebrew, Arabic is inflected: nouns change endings depending on their case or position in the sentence, and verbs change endings with tense and subject. Prepositions and pronouns are not inflected. The majority of words in classical Arabic start with three-letter consonant roots. By changing vowel sounds, doubling consonants, and adding prefixes, suffixes, or internal syllables, words with a wide variety of related meanings and modes are formed. These various forms give structure to the language and allow close analysis of meaning. For example, the root *k-t-b* relates to writing. The verb *kataba* means "he wrote," a book is *kitab,* an office or place for writing is *maktab,* a library is *maktaba,* a grammar school for children is *kuttab,* and the passive "it was written" is *kutiba.* The same or similar patterns can be found with thousands of words. In addition, the Arabic language includes an enormous variety of words—exasperating for the foreign student of the language and useful for the poet. For example, there are 350 words for *lion*, 50 words for *clouds*, 88 words for *water wells*, and 21 words for *light*, and a seemingly infinite number of adjectives for human qualities and characteristics.

Alphabet. The twenty-eight Arabic consonant sounds represented by letter symbols are *a, b, t, th, j, h, kh, d, zh, r, z, s, sh, ss, dd, tt, zz, 'ain, ghain, f, q, k, l, m, n, h, w, y.* The Arabic alphabet uses a few basic letter forms differentiated by one, two, or three dots placed above or below the symbol. (A chart of the Arabic alphabet is included in Chapter 4: Communication, Transportation, and Exploration.) To guide pronunciation of written words, a few additional vocalization marks placed above or below the letter indicate that a consonant is doubled, followed by a short *a, u,* or *i,* or without a vowel sound. There is also a symbol called *hamza,* which indicates a glottal stop in the middle or at the end of a word, as in the middle of the phrase *"Me?! Angry?"* Pronunciation rules also indicate that, when words are joined together—most commonly when the definite article *al* (the) is joined to its noun— the *l* sometimes assimilates to the first letter of the word. This change is similar to the English practice of saying *an apple,* which is easier to say than *a apple.* In Arabic the words for *the light* assimilate to *an-noor* in a sentence, not *al-noor;* but *al-kitab,* "the book," does not assimilate. The highest standards for the pronunciation of the Arabic language are found in the tradition of *tajwid* (pronounced "tahj-WEED"), complex rules for the rhythmic recitation of the Qur'an, which were passed down in unbroken oral transmission from the Prophet to generations of Qur'an reciters. The Qur'an cannot be recited properly without applying these rules, but few people are masters of all its intricacies.

Spelling and Pronunciation. The spellings of Arabic, Persian, and Turkish words that appear in this volume are the result of considerable improvement among academics, publishers, and journalists over the past few decades in transliterating Islamic terminology and Muslim cultural vocabulary. These changes parallel improvements in transliteration of many other languages, including Chinese and Japanese, that have resulted from direct contact between Western and indigenous scholars and better knowledge of the languages in the West. The goal of the spellings used in this book is to reproduce the original sound of the Arabic language as accurately and simply as possible. Gone are the days when adherents of Islam were called "Saracens," "Musulmans," "Mohammedans," or even "Moslems." The simple spelling *Muslim* (pronounced MUSS-lim) has replaced earlier forms almost everywhere. The Prophet's name is now spelled *Muhammad* (pronounced moo-HAHM-mad) rather than Mohammed. The name of God in Arabic, *Allah,* a word that Arabic-speaking Christians also use for God, is pronounced with the stress on the second, not the first, syllable (al-LAH). Though the trans-

literation has not changed, most Western readers now clearly understand that Allah refers not to an exclusive, tribal god of the Arabs, but to the universal Creator, the God of the monotheistic tradition. The traditional spellings of the two most important Islamic place-names, *Mecca* and *Medina,* have given way to *Makkah* and *Madinah,* which more accurately indicate the proper pronunciation. A Muslim leader or tribal elder is no longer called a "shiek" (which rhymed with *shriek*), but properly, a *shaykh.* An extremely important word encountered in the study of Islam and Muslim civilization is the one designating a house of worship, which has long been called a *mosque* in English and *mosquée* in French. The proper word, used in this volume, is *masjid* (MAS-jid), which literally means "place of kneeling down," referring to the posture of kneeling with the forehead touching the ground in Islamic prayer. The older term *mosque* emerged in Europe during the medieval period as a double corruption of the original Arabic. In Spanish *masjid* became *mezquita,* which the French adapted to *mosquée,* losing touch with its meaning in the process. The correct plural for masjid is *masajid* (mass-AH-jid), but for the sake of simplicity, the Anglicized plural (*masjids*) has been used in this volume.

Transliteration. Some difficulties remain because there are a few Arabic letters that represent sounds not found in English. This volume avoids the diacritical points routinely used among specialists in the past for hard and soft consonants, long and short vowels, as well as the tortured letter combinations such as "dj" or "dsch" for *j* and unfamiliar marks representing sounds not used in English, such as *'ain, ghain,* and the emphatic *dd, ss, tt,* and *zh* sounds. Apart from these unavoidable difficulties, Arabic spelling is straightforward. The transliterations used in this book consciously err on the side of simplicity for the sake of the general reader.

Acknowledgments. All praise is due to the Creator, in gratitude for health and capacity to work. May our humble efforts be accepted. The sacrifice of time and energy for a project like this one cuts sharply into what belongs to our families. As the book is dedicated to the families of all the contributors, I leave it to each to make amends for what was lost so that the reader of this volume might gain. I must especially acknowledge the sacrifice and generous assistance of my husband and fellow educator Usama Amer, and remember my children, Anas, Ayman, Maryam, and Sarah, who encouraged me to make these efforts. We must acknowledge also Shabbir Mansuri, Founding Director of the Council on Islamic Education in Fountain Valley, California, who has earned recognition for his dedication to the cause of learning and teaching, and whose efforts brought most of the contributors together during the past decade. The greatest pleasure in compiling this volume has been to learn from and interact with the contributors, who are noted scholars in their fields. They have taken time from busy schedules as directors and heads of departments, professors, teachers, and researchers to write these introductory chapters for nonspecialists. Their willingness to do so is part of a healthy trend toward collaboration among precollegiate educators and scholars at the upper reaches of academia and also shows the eagerness of scholars in the Islamic disciplines to convey recent dramatic advancements in the field to a wider audience of educated people. I thank them for their fine chapters, and I am sure that the difficulties of this enterprise will fade in comparison with the fine result they have achieved. Among the scholars and other colleagues who provided suggestions on the content of the volume and its contributors were Professor Ross E. Dunn of San Diego State University, Professor John O. Voll of Georgetown University, Elizabeth Barlow, retired Outreach Coordinator at the Center for Middle East and North African Studies at the University of Mich-

igan, Ann Arbor, and Zeina Seikaly, Outreach Coordinator at the Center for Contemporary Arab Studies, Georgetown University. I owe all of them thanks, as well as the admiration, affection, and respect they have always earned. Gratitude is due to Dr. Karen Rood, senior editor, whose cheerful, patient, and scholarly efforts brought this volume to completion. Finally, this book was inspired by my students and the teachers, textbook editors, and writers with whom I have worked over the years, whose desire to understand and appreciate history—and whose occasional resistance to enjoying history—have motivated preparation of this book.

Susan L. Douglass

ACKNOWLEDGMENTS

This book was produced by Manly, Inc. Karen L. Rood, senior editor, was the in-house editor and Anthony J. Scotti Jr. is series editor.

Production manager is Philip B. Dematteis.

Administrative support was provided by Ann M. Cheschi, Amber L. Coker, and Angi Pleasant.

Accountant is Ann-Marie Holland.

Copyediting supervisor is Sally R. Evans. The copyediting staff includes Phyllis A. Avant, Brenda Carol Blanton, Melissa D. Hinton, Charles Loughlin, Rebecca Mayo, Nancy E. Smith, and Elizabeth Jo Ann Sumner.

Editorial associates are Michael S. Allen, Michael S. Martin, and Pamela A. Warren.

Database manager is José A. Juarez.

Layout and graphics supervisor is Janet E. Hill. The graphics staff includes Karla Corley Brown and Zoe R. Cook.

Office manager is Kathy Lawler Merlette.

Photography supervisor is Paul Talbot. Photography editor is Scott Nemzek.

Permissions editors are Ann-Marie Holland and Kathy Lawler Merlette.

Digital photographic copy work was performed by Joseph M. Bruccoli.

The SGML staff includes Linda Dalton Mullinax and Jason Paddock.

Systems manager is Marie L. Parker.

Typesetting supervisor is Kathleen M. Flanagan. The typesetting staff includes Patricia Marie Flanagan, Mark J. McEwan, and Pamela D. Norton.

Walter W. Ross supervised library research. He was assisted by Pamela A. Warren and the following librarians at the Thomas Cooper Library of the University of South Carolina: circulation department head Tucker Taylor; reference department head Virginia W. Weathers; Brette Barclay, Marilee Birchfield, Paul Cammarata, Gary Geer, Michael Macan, Tom Marcil, Rose Marshall, and Sharon Verba; interlibrary loan department head John Brunswick; and interlibrary loan staff Robert Arndt, Hayden Battle, Barry Bull, Jo Cottingham, Marna Hostetler, Marieum McClary, Erika Peake, and Nelson Rivera.

WORLD ERAS

VOLUME 2

RISE AND SPREAD OF ISLAM
622 - 1500

WORLD EVENTS:
SELECTED OCCURRENCES OUTSIDE THE MUSLIM WORLD

by MUNIR A. SHAIKH

622

- Byzantine emperor Heraclius I attempts to safeguard his possessions in Asia Minor from the Sasanid (Persian) empire by granting his generals civil as well as military authority over the regions they occupy.

- Over the next nine years, Swithila, king of the Visigoths, extends Visigoth authority throughout Spain.

- The eastern plain of China is ruled by Emperor Kao-tsu (reigned 618–626), founder of the T'ang dynasty (618–907), who brings northern and southern China under his control by 624. He claims to be a descendant of Lao-tzu, the first philosopher of Chinese Taoism. Though they are officially Taoists, the T'ang emperors also accord royal support to Buddhism.

- Prince Shotoku of Japan dies, having served as regent for his aunt Empress Suiko (ruled 592–628) since the beginning of her reign. During his regency he established relations with China, sending scholars there to study Buddhism and Chinese culture.

- Over roughly the next five centuries northwestern and central India are ruled by four dynasties of Rajputs (Sons of Kings).

626

- The Avars, a nomadic people from eastern Europe, attack Constantinople and nearly succeed in occupying this capital of the Byzantine Empire.

626-628

- The Celtic Christian Church of southern Ireland adopts the Roman Christian form of worship. Northern Irish churches make the change in 692.

627

- Bishop Paulinus of Kent, the first of the seven Anglo-Saxon kingdoms of England to have been converted to Christianity (597), goes on a mission to Northumbria, where he converts King Edwin and many of his subjects.

*DENOTES CIRCA DATE

627
(CONT'D)

- Chinese emperor Kao-tsu's son Li-Shih-min forces his father to abdicate and takes the throne as Emperor T'ai-tsung. Ruling until 649, he becomes known for tolerance, patronage of the arts, and establishing contacts with the Sasanid and Byzantine empires, as well as India and Central Asia.

628

- Having achieved a decisive victory against the Sasanids at the Battle of Ninevah in December 627, Byzantine emperor Heraclius I is able to end a war that has continued off and on for decades. The Byzantines recover all conquered territory, which includes Jerusalem and Alexandria in Egypt. This victory is mentioned in the Qur'an.

629

- Dagobert, king of Austrasia (the part of Frankish territory from the Meuse River to the Bohemian forests), becomes king of the entire Frankish realm, with territory corresponding roughly to modern France with parts of the Low Countries and western Germany. He is the last strong ruler of the Merovingian dynasty, founded in 481 by Clovis I, who converted to Roman Christianity in about 498.

630*

- The Anglo-Saxon kingdoms of East Anglia and Wessex are converted to Christianity.

630

- Chinese troops conquer the eastern Turks (centered in Mongolia), who have earlier attacked the eastern Chinese capital at Ch'ang-an in 624 and 626.

- Mahendravarman I dies. Under his reign, which began circa 600, the Pallava dynasty of southern India reaches the height of its power.

633

- Because of a revival of paganism in Northumbria after the death of King Edwin in 632, his successor, Oswald, invites the monk Aidan of Iona to spread Christianity throughout northern England. The mission begins the temporary ascendancy in England of Celtic Christianity over that of the Roman Church.

634

- Byzantine Empire troops are defeated by a Muslim army between Gaza and Jerusalem, beginning centuries of ultimately unsuccessful struggle against a succession of Muslim Empires.

635

- Byzantine emperor Heraclius I forms an alliance against the Avars with Kubrat, King of the Bulgars, a nomadic people of Turkic origin.

- A Nestorian missionary arrives in the Chinese capital of Ch'ang-an, where he is allowed to preach and is given a church (638). The Nestorians are a Christian sect centered in Persia that believes the divine and human natures of Jesus Christ are independent, two persons only loosely united.

*DENOTES CIRCA DATE

638

- In an attempt to strengthen political support against Muslim incursions in Syria and Egypt, Heraclius I tries to placate Monophysites (members of a heretical Christian sect who believed that Jesus Christ had only one, divine nature)—and perhaps respond to the strict monotheism of Islam—by promulgating the doctrine of Monothelitism, the belief that Christ had two natures (divine and human) but only one will. The compromise is ineffective. Muslim troops conquer Syria later this year and complete their conquest of Egypt in 642.

639

- Dagobert I dies, having given Austrasia to his son Sigibert in 632, and leaving Neustria (roughly the northwestern part of modern France bounded by the Meuse, the Loire, and the Atlantic) and Burgundy to his son Clovis II. Though members of the Merovingian dynasty continue to rule in name until 751, power passes to nobles known as mayors of the palaces: Ebroïn in Neustria and in Austrasia, Pepin I of Landen, founder of what becomes known as the Carolingian dynasty.

641

- Heraclius I dies, having ruled the Byzantine Empire since 610, the year in which Muhammad began receiving divine revelation. By the end of the year the throne has passed through two sons to Heraclius's grandson Constans II, who is unable to check either the advance of the Muslim Empire or internal dynastic strife.

- After the Byzantine city of Oderzo in Italy falls to the Lombards, a Germanic people who conquered much of Italy in the sixth century, the seat of the Byzantine exarchate of Ravenna moves to Venice.

642*

- Kubrat, King of the Bulgars, dies and his five sons divide their people into five hordes, three of which are absorbed into other peoples over the next few decades. Bezmer, or Bat-Bayan, leads his horde north, where it eventually settles around the confluence of the Volga and Kama Rivers. Asparukh leads his horde westward, eventually crossing the Danube River.

642-643

- The Chinese make the khanate of the western Turks (in part of present-day Turkestan) a tributary state.

643

- King Rothari codifies the laws of the Lombards.

- The powerful Soga family of Japan kills Prince Shotoku's son Yamashiro Oe and all his family.

645

- China forms alliances with the Khitans of Manchuria and the Korean states of Paekche and Silla to invade the Korean state of Koguryo. Forced to withdraw after heavy losses, China makes another unsuccessful invasion attempt in 647.

*Denotes Circa Date

645
(CONT'D)

• Chinese Buddhist monk Hsüan-tsang returns home after a fifteen-year pilgrimage in India and heads a commission that translates seventy-five Sanskrit books into Chinese.

• Prince Nakano Oe and Nakatomi Kamatari stage a coup in Japan, killing the Soga family and re-establishing the power of the royal family.

646

• The Japanese royal family institutes the Taikwa reforms, re-establishing a central Japanese state and limiting the power of the nobility.

649

• At the Lateran Synod in Rome, Pope Martin I condemns the doctrine of Monothelitism as heretical.

650*

• Two Slavic tribes, the Croats and the Serbs, settle in Bosnia.

• The Bulgars of the Volga region are conquered by Turkic tribes known as Khazars, who have established an empire in southern Russia.

651*

• Indian philosopher-poet Bhatrihari dies.

651

• Yazdigard III, the last Sasanid ruler of Persia, dies as the Muslim conquest of his empire becomes complete.

653

• The exarch (military ruler) of Ravenna, one of the Byzantine enclaves on the Italian peninsula that was not conquered by the Lombards, arrests Pope Martin I for his condemnation of Monothelitism and sends him to Constantinople, where he dies in exile in 655.

655

• Wu Hou, a junior concubine of Chinese emperor T'ai-tsung and later the favorite concubine of his heir Kao-tsung (reigned 649–683), triumphs over all her rivals, including the emperor's wife, to marry Kao-tsung and become Empress Wu Hou. By 660 she, not her husband, is the real ruler of China.

656

• The son of Pepin I of Landen, Mayor of the Palace Grimoald, attempts to make his son Childebert king of Austrasia, sparking a surge of support for the Merovingians in which father and son are killed.

657

• Wulfhere, King of Mercia, begins efforts to convert his Anglo-Saxon kingdom to Christianity.

*DENOTES CIRCA DATE

657-659
- The western Turks disperse, some traveling across southern Russia and eventually reaching Hungary, others going to India.

660
- The Korean kingdom of Paekche is invaded by China and calls on Japan for help.

662
- Prince Nakano Oe becomes emperor of Japan.

663
- Intending to regain Italian territory conquered by the Lombards and to prevent Muslim troops from conquering Sicily and Italy, Byzantine emperor Constans II transfers his capital to Italy, dreaming of restoring imperial Rome.
- The Japanese army in Korea is defeated by the Chinese and withdraws from the peninsula.

664
- Though at first Roman and Celtic Christian missionaries worked together in Britain, differences have developed, especially over how to calculate the date of Easter. The Synod of Whitby firmly establishes Roman Christianity as the dominant religion of England.

668
- Constans II is killed during a mutiny of his troops in Syracuse and is succeeded by his son Constantine IV, who reigns until 685 during a period in which the Byzantine Empire is under constant attack not only from the Muslim Empire but also from Bulgar and Slavic peoples of the Balkans.
- China forces Korea to become a vassal state.
- The *Hua Hu Ching*, a fourth-century apocryphal text claiming that Lao-tzu is a prior avatar of Buddha, is banned in China.

669
- Pope Vitalian appoints Theodore of Tarsus the first archbishop of Canterbury, in Kent, giving him authority over all English churches.

672
- The death of Emperor Tenji, who has ruled Japan since 668, sparks warfare over the succession. Tenji's younger brother is victorious and rules as Emperor Temmu. During his reign he codifies the Taika reforms as the Asuka Kiyomihara Code, establishing criminal and civil codes as well as governmental structure and dividing the people into freemen and slaves (about 10 percent). All land is the property of the state, which distributes it for the use of the people.

674-678
- Constantinople is besieged by Arab naval forces. The conflict ends with a truce that lasts thirty years.

*DENOTES CIRCA DATE

675
- China completes its conquest of the Korean peninsula.

679
- The Chinese check the advances of Tibetans who have been raiding northern China since the 630s.

680*
- Ebroïn, mayor of the palace of Neustria, attempts to unify the mayoralties of Neustria and Austrasia under one house and is murdered.

680–711
- Visigoth authorities intensify their persecution of Spanish Jews and try to compel them to convert to Christianity.

681
- The Byzantine Empire recognizes by treaty that the land between the Balkans and the Danube is under the control of Asparukh's horde of Bulgars, delimiting the territory in which the modern state of Bulgaria was later created and weakening the hold of the Avars in the region.

681–687
- The Anglo-Saxon kingdom of Sussex is converted to Christianity.

681–737
- The Khazars become embroiled in a series of wars with the Muslim Empire and eventually withdraw north of the Caucasus Mountains, where they provide a buffer between the Muslims and eastern Europe.

683
- On the death of Emperor Kao-tsung his son Wu Chao becomes Emperor Chung-tsung. A month later, after his wife attempts to exercise the same sort of power wielded by her mother-in-law, however, Empress Wu deposes this son and places another, Jui-tsung, on the throne. He rules in name only while his mother governs China. In 690 she usurps the throne.

685
- Justinian II succeeds his father, Constantine IV, to the throne of the Byzantine Empire.

687
- Pepin II of Heristal, grandson of Pepin I of Landen, defeats the Neustrians at the Battle of Tetry, becoming mayor of the palaces of Austrasia and Neustria and unifying the northern Frankish kingdom over the next decade.

692
- Byzantine forces are badly beaten by a Muslim army at the Battle of Sevastopol.

*DENOTES CIRCA DATE

692
(CONT'D)

- Byzantine emperor Justinian II convenes the Quinisext Council at Constantinople. Not recognized by Rome, the council settles the biblical canon and other doctrinal matters that set eastern Christianity apart from the Church in the West.

694

- A Manichaean missionary arrives at the Chinese court from Persia and is permitted to preach his religion. A dualist faith that holds all matter to be unalterably evil and the spirit (God) to be perfectly good, Manichaeanism was founded in the third century by Mani, who considered himself the successor to a long line of prophets, including Buddha, Zoroaster, and Jesus.

695

- Leontius leads a successful rebellion against Justinian II and becomes Byzantine emperor, beginning two decades of anarchy in the empire.

696

- The Khitans of Manchuria rebel against their Chinese governor and invade part of the Hopeh province of northeast China.

- The *Hua Hu Ching,* a fourth-century apocryphal text linking Taoism and Buddhism, is accorded official toleration in China.

697

- With the help of the Turks, Chinese troops drive the Khitans out of Hopeh.

- According to historical tradition, Paolo Lucio Anafesto becomes the first doge (leader) of Venice, a major Italian seaport that is part of the Byzantine Empire.

698

- The Byzantine army deposes Leontius and places Tiberius II on the throne.

- Carthage, the last major Byzantine stronghold in North Africa, falls to the Muslims.

- China's one-time allies, the Turks, invade Hopeh but are driven out by Chinese forces.

700*

- By this date the Lombards of Italy have converted from Arian Christianity (the belief that Christ was human, not divine; that is, a creation of God the Father) to orthodox Roman Christianity.

- Tapestry weaving is well established in Peru.

- Porcelain is produced in China.

- The West African kingdom of Ghana arises on the Niger River bend.

701

- In Japan the Taiho Code refines laws set forth in the Asuka Kiyomihara Code.

*DENOTES CIRCA DATE

703
- The Venerable Bede, a monk at the monastery of Jarrow in the Anglo-Saxon kingdom of Northumbria, writes *On Times,* in which he introduces the counting of dates backward (B.C.) and forward (A.D.) from the birth of Christ.

705
- Aided by the Bulgars, Justinian II reclaims the throne of the Byzantine Empire.
- Leading Chinese officials seize the palace of Empress Wu and force her to abdicate in favor of her son Emperor Chung-tsung, whose wife, Empress Wei, attempts to wield power by openly selling offices and influence at court.

710
- After the death of Witiza, Roderick, Duke of Baetica, claims the throne of Spain.
- Emperor Chung-tsung of China dies, probably poisoned by his wife, Empress Wei, who tries to claim the throne for herself; but Wu's daughter T'ai-p'ing helps Prince Li Lung-chi, a son of former emperor Jui-tsung, Chung-tsung's brother, to restore Jui-tsung to the throne.
- The Japanese court establishes its first permanent capital at Nara.

711
- Supporters of Witiza's son call on the Muslims of North Africa for aid. Berber general Tariq ibn Ziyad invades Spain, defeating Roderick and the Visigoths at the Battle of Guadalete River on 19 July. The Visigoth kingdom collapses, and by 719 the Muslims have reached the Pyrenees.
- The Turkish khan Mo-ch'o has gained control of the Central Asian steppes from the Chinese frontier to Transoxiana and is a threat to China itself. When he is murdered in 716, his empire collapses.

711-717
- Insurgent troops led by Philippicus defeat and kill Justinian II. Philippicus becomes emperor only to be overthrown by another military uprising in 713 that places Anastasius II on the throne; he is overthrown in 715 and replaced by Theodosius III. None of these weak emperors is able to check the advances of Muslim forces.

712
- Liutprand becomes king of Lombard Italy. During his reign, which lasts until 744, he steadily reduces Byzantine territory in Italy.
- In China, T'ai-p'ing's attempts to control her weak brother Jui-tsung result in the emperor's abdication in favor of his son Li Lung-chi, who becomes Emperor Hsüng-tsung. His reign, which lasts until 756, is marked by the height of the T'ang dynasty's power and influence and the high renaissance of Chinese art, literature, and music. China is in a period of prosperity and population growth.

714
- The death of Pepin II of Heristal begins a period of upheaval in Austrasia and Neustria.
- The Tibetans begin yearly raids into northwest China that continue for decades.

*DENOTES CIRCA DATE

716–719
- Charles Martel (the Hammer), illegitimate son of Pepin II of Heristal, defeats Neustrian forces, establishing himself as mayor of Austrasia and Neustria, and sets out to reassert Frankish authority in southern Gaul. He supports the efforts of English missionary Wynfrid (St. Boniface) to convert the pagans of Germany to Christianity, recognizing its value in the consolidation of political power.

717
- Leo III, an excellent general and administrator, forces the abdication of Theodosius III and is proclaimed ruler of the Byzantine Empire. The founder of the Isaurian (Syrian) dynasty, he remains on the throne until his death in 741.

717–718
- Constantinople is under siege by Muslim forces, which are eventually defeated by Leo III.

718–721
- Visigoth noble Pelayo establishes the Christian kingdom of Asturias.
- Spurning an offer of alliance from Turkish khan Bilge, successor to Mo-ch'o, Emperor Hsüng-tsung of China goes to war against him and is forced to sue for peace.

720
- By this date the Byzantine Empire—which once nearly ringed the Mediterranean from Italy to much of the coast of North Africa and southernmost Spain—has lost much of the eastern rim of the Mediterranean and all its North African territory to the Muslim empire, which also controls Arabia, Persia, and the Iberian peninsula.

726
- Byzantine emperor Leo III promulgates the Ecloga, a revision according to Christian principles of the Roman law by which his empire has been governed, and issues his first ban on religious images (icons) in churches.

727
- Leo III's Iconoclastic pronouncements spark an unsuccessful Greek revolt.
- Orso Ipato becomes the first elected doge of Venice.

727–729
- China engages in a full-scale war with Tibet.

729–749
- During his reign, the devout Emperor Shomu of Japan establishes Buddhist temples and monasteries in every province and calls for the casting of the Great Buddha, a fifty-three-foot bronze statue dedicated at Todai Temple in Nara in 752.

730s
- Though a settlement is reached in 730, fighting between China and Tibet flares up again within a decade and continues well into the 750s.

*DENOTES CIRCA DATE

730
- Leo III proclaims Iconoclasm the official policy of the Byzantine Empire. Pope Gregory II (reigned 715–731) and his successor, Gregory III (reigned 731–741), object to the imposition of Iconoclasm on churches in Byzantine areas of Italy, leading to further estrangement of the eastern and western Christian Churches. Ravenna revolts against Iconoclasm and makes an alliance with the Lombards, while Venice helps the Byzantines to retain some of their Italian territory.

731
- A Byzantine fleet fails to restore Ravenna to the empire.
- Pope Gregory III excommunicates all Iconoclasts.

732
- Charles Martel is victorious at the Battle of Tours, near Poitiers in southern France, ending the Muslim advance.

735-736
- Charles Martel drives the Muslims from Aquitaine in southern France.

740*
- As aristocrats and generals gain power in China, Emperor Hsüng-tsung exercises less and less authority. The aristocratic minister Li Lin-fu becomes virtual dictator.

741
- Charles Martel dies, and his lands and powers are divided between his sons; Carloman becomes mayor of Austrasia, and Pepin III (the Short) gets Neustria.
- On the death of Leo III his son Constantine V becomes Byzantine emperor, suppressing a revolt led by his brother-in-law Artavasdos.

744
- On the northern border of China, the Uighur Turks establish an empire that remains a powerful force in the region until 840.

745
- Constantine V achieves important victories against the Muslims in northern Syria.

747
- Carloman enters a monastery, and Pepin III (the Short) has himself crowned king of all Carolingian holdings, with the support of Pope Zacharias.

749
- Not long before his death the Buddhist monk Gyogi promotes the belief that Shinto, the native belief system of Japan, and Buddhism are two aspects of the same religion, leading to the gradual amalgamation of the two faiths.
- Greek theologian John of Damascus, an eloquent defender of the value of icons in Christian worship, dies on 4 December.

*Denotes Circa Date

751
- Supported by Pope Zacharias, Pepin III (the Short) deposes Childeric III, the last Merovingian king.
- The Lombards invade Ravenna, ending the Byzantine exarchate there. Though Venice is still nominally a Byzantine possession, it becomes increasingly independent of empire control.

752
- Pope Stephen makes Pepin III (the Short) patrician of the Romans and consecrates his sons, establishing the legitimacy of the dynasty.
- After the death of Li Lin-fu, Yang Kuo-chung—a relative of Emperor Hsüng-tsung's favorite concubine, Yang Kuei-fei—begins to dominate the Chinese court.

753
- The Chinese monk Ganjin arrives at the Japanese court in Nara, where he establishes the Ritsu sect of Buddhism.

754-755
- Pepin III (the Short) goes to the aid of the Pope in his disputes with the Lombards.

755-756
- An Lu-shan, the powerful military governor of three provinces on the northwest frontier of China, marches his troops toward the capital city Ch'ang-an and proclaims himself emperor. As Emperor Hsüng-tsung flees, his guard mutinies, kills Yang Kuo-chung, and demands that the emperor execute Yang Kuei-fei.

755-775
- The Byzantines engage in repeated campaigns against the Bulgars, eventually weakening, but not crushing, them.

756
- Pepin III (the Short) returns to Italy, defeating the Lombards and making the Donation of Pepin, which establishes the basis for a papal state (and the temporal power of the papacy). The donation also sets up the Franks as the protectors of the papacy.

757
- An Lu-shan is assassinated by some of his own men, but his rebellion against the dynasty in China continues until 763. From this time until its fall in 907, the T'ang dynasty is too weak to assert any real authority, and China is ruled by warlords and plagued by raids from the north.

757-796
- During the reign of Offa II, Mercia becomes the dominant kingdom in England.

*DENOTES CIRCA DATE

759
- Frankish troops force the final withdrawal of Muslim troops from southern France, as Pepin III (the Short) conquers Septimania and reasserts Frankish authority in Aquitaine, extending his kingdom south to the Pyrenees.
- Not long after this date the *Man'yoshu*, an anthology of some 4,500 ancient and contemporary poems written in Japanese, is compiled. The poems are by writers from all classes of Japanese society.

762
- The great Chinese poet Li Po dies in Tang-t'u, China.
- At about this time the Japanese begin making pictorial books of wood-block prints.

762-763
- Uighur Turks attack Chinese rebel forces and sack the eastern capital at Loyang. One of the Uighur leaders is converted to Manichaeism, which becomes the state religion of the Uighur empire.

764
- Civil war erupts in Japan after the powerful Buddhist priest Dokyo, backed by former empress Koken, eliminates his main political rival, Oshikatsu, minister to Emperor Junnin and a member of the influential Fujiwara family. Junnin is deposed and Koken takes the throne as Empress Shotoku. During her reign, which lasts until 770, Dokyo is prime minister and high priest of state.

768
- Pepin III (the Short) dies, and his kingdom is divided between his two sons, Charles (Charlemagne) and Carloman.

770
- On the death of Empress Shotoku of Japan, the powerful Fujiwara family banishes from the capital her favorite, Donyo, who has attempted to have himself proclaimed emperor. The Fujiwaras place Emperor Konnin on the throne, considerably lessening the influence of the wealthy and powerful Buddhist establishment on the politics of Japan. The Fujiwaras remain a major force in Japanese government until the mid twelfth century.

771
- Carloman dies, and the kingdom of the Franks is reunited under Charlemagne, who establishes his capital at Aachen (Aix-la-Chapelle).

772-804
- Charlemagne's troops engage in a difficult but ultimately successful campaign to conquer Saxony.

774
- Charlemagne conquers Lombard Italy, incorporating it into his empire and fulfilling his father's promise of establishing a papal state.

*DENOTES CIRCA DATE

775
- After the death of Constantine V, the Byzantine throne goes to his son Leo IV, who dies prematurely in 780.

775*
- Monks on the Scottish island of Iona begin what is now known as the Book of Kells, an illuminated manuscript of the four Gospels in the ornate Celtic style. After Vikings (Norsemen) raid the island in 802, it is taken to the Abbey of Kells in Ireland, where it is probably completed.

778-824
- Borobudur Temple in Java is built as a microcosm of the universe according to the ideas of Mahayana Buddhism.

778
- Charlemagne's forces are attacked by Basques at Roncesvalles in the Pyrenees as they return from an unsuccessful foray into Spain. The battle later becomes the inspiration for the early-twelfth-century French epic *La Chanson de Roland* (The Song of Roland).

780
- Ten-year-old Constantine VI inherits the Byzantine throne. His mother, Empress Irene, becomes his regent.

781
- Charlemagne gives the throne of Italy to his son Pepin and makes his son Louis I (the Pious) king of Aquitaine.
- Byzantine forces suffer a major loss to Muslim troops in Asia Minor.

784
- Hoping to lessen the influence of the powerful monasteries of Nara, Emperor Kammu, who ascended the Japanese throne in 781, moves his capital to Nagaoka.

787
- The first recorded incursion of Danes takes place in England, beginning a long series of European raids by Danes, Norsemen, and Swedes, known collectively as Vikings.
- Under the instigation of Empress Irene, the Council of Nicaea allows icons to be returned to Byzantine churches, decreeing that they should be revered and venerated but not worshiped.

788
- Charlemagne conquers Bavaria.

790
- The Byzantine army forces Empress Irene into retirement, but Constantine VI recalls his mother two years later and makes her coruler.

*DENOTES CIRCA DATE

792
- The Bulgars rise again and win a major victory against the Byzantines.

794
- Emperor Kammu moves his court to Heian-kyo, later known as Kyoto, which remains the capital of Japan until 1868.

797
- Empress Irene orders her son Constantine VI deposed and blinded, claiming the Byzantine throne for herself.

800*
- Chinese alchemists discover how to make gunpowder.
- At his court in Aachen, Charlemagne establishes a palace school headed by the English monk Alcuin of York, beginning a revival of learning in western Europe that becomes known as the Carolingian Renaissance.
- Charlemagne defeats the Avars.
- The rulers of the Khmer (Cambodian) empire found the city of Angkor, which remains their capital until the fifteenth century.

800
- On Christmas Day, Pope Leo III crowns Charlemagne "Emperor of the Romans," a conscious attempt to signal the birth of a Christian Empire (the precursor of the Holy Roman Empire) to rival the expanding Muslim Empire and to equal ancient Rome in its power and glory. At about this time Charlemagne sends an ambassador to the court of Abbasid khalifah (caliph) Harun al-Rashid. The Byzantine Empire refuses to recognize the new western empire.

801
- Charlemagne's forces take Barcelona, creating a Spanish March (buffer zone) between the Frankish Empire and Muslim Spain.

802
- High-ranking Byzantine officials depose Empress Irene and place Nicephorus I on the throne.

804-806
- The Byzantine territories of Anatolia, Cyprus, and Rhodes suffer repeated Muslim raids.

805
- The Chinese Buddhist monk Saicho founds the Tendai Sect in Japan.

806
- The Chinese Buddhist monk Kukai goes to Japan, where he founds the Shingon Sect. A devout Buddhist, Emperor Kammu encourages the growth of the Tendai and Shingon sects to counter the influence of the powerful Buddhist sects centered at Nara.

*Denotes Circa Date

809
- King Krum of the Bulgars begins a war with the Byzantines.

811
- Emperor Nicephorus I is defeated and killed in a costly battle with the Bulgars. Emperor Michael I Rhangabe is equally unsuccessful in stopping the Bulgar advance on Constantinople.

812
- The Byzantines sign a treaty with Charlemagne that allows them to keep their territory in southern Italy, Venice, and Dalmatia.

813
- The Byzantine army deposes Emperor Michael I Rhangabe and places Leo V (the Armenian) on the throne.
- On 11 September, Charlemagne has his last surviving son, Louis I (the Pious), crowned coruler of his Empire.

814
- Charlemagne dies on 28 January and is succeeded by Louis I (the Pious).

815
- Under Emperor Leo V (the Armenian) the Council of St. Sophia revives Iconoclasm in the Byzantine Church.

817
- Louis I (the Pious) announces that on his death his empire will be divided among three sons: Lothar I (Italy), Pepin I (Aquitaine and Burgundy), and Louis II (the German) (Bavaria).
- Byzantine Emperor Leo V (the Armenian) wins a major victory over the Bulgars at the Battle of Mesembria and forces them to sign a thirty-year peace treaty.

820
- Emperor Leo V (the Armenian) is assassinated, and Michael II, the first emperor of the Phrygian dynasty, is placed on the Byzantine throne.

825
- Egbert, King of Wessex, defeats Beorhtric, King of Mercia, at the Battle of Ellendune, destroying the dominance of Mercia over the other Anglo-Saxon kingdoms. Kent, Sussex, Surrey, and Essex accept Egbert as their king.

826*
- Muslims from North Africa capture the island of Crete from the Byzantines and use it as a base for pirate ships until 961, when it is reconquered by the Byzantines.

*DENOTES CIRCA DATE

826
- At the request of King Harald of Denmark, the Benedictine monk Ansgar begins his mission to convert Scandinavia to Christianity.

829
- Egbert becomes king of Mercia.
- Byzantine emperor Michael II is succeeded by his son Theophilus.

830
- Lothar I, Pepin I, and Louis II try unsuccessfully to overthrow their father; another attempt in 833 also fails.
- The Magyars, an ethnic blend of Ugric and Turkish peoples, have migrated southwest through the Khazar empire from western Siberia and have reached the west bank of the Don River.

831
- Abbot Paschasius Radbertus of Corbey writes *De corpore et sanguine Christi* (Concerning Christ's Body and Blood), clearly setting forth the doctrine of transubstantiation, which later becomes the dominant interpretation of the Eucharist in the Western Christian Church.

834
- The use of a crank to turn a rotary grindstone is documented in western Europe for the first time.

838
- Louis I (the Pious) gives Neustria (modern northwestern France) to his son Charles II (the Bald), who is also given Aquitaine after his brother Pepin's death in this year.
- Egbert achieves a major victory over invading Vikings (Danes) and their Cornish Briton allies at the Battle of Hingston Down.
- Emperor Theophilus is defeated by Muslim forces, who capture the important Byzantine frontier fortress at Armoria.

840*
- Vikings (Norsemen) found the towns of Dublin and Limerick on the Irish coast as bases for trade with their homeland.

840
- Louis I (the Pious) dies. His son Lothar I begins efforts to gain control of all Carolingian lands.

840-841
- Though Venice is still nominally a part of the Byzantine Empire, by this time the great trading city is making international agreements in its own name and is essentially self-ruling.

*Denotes Circa Date

841

- Lothar I is defeated by his brothers, Louis II (the German) and Charles II (the Bald), at the Battle of Fontenoy.

- France is invaded by Vikings (Norsemen), who settle in the region that becomes known as Normandy. By 843 they have made it all the way to the shores of the Mediterranean Sea.

842

- Louis II (the German) and Charles II (the Bald) renew their alliance against Lothar I in the Strasbourg Oaths. Charles makes his declaration in *lingua romana* (Old French) and Louis makes his in *lingua teudisca* (Old German), creating a manuscript that documents an early stage in the evolution of modern German and French.

- Michael III ascends the Byzantine throne with his mother, Theodora, as regent.

843

- The Treaty of Verdun gives Lothar I control of northern Italy and Lorraine; Louis II (the German) receives the lands east of the Rhine River; Charles II (the Bald) becomes the king of the West Franks (modern-day France).

- Genoa becomes a republic.

- Icons are restored to Byzantine churches.

- Kenneth I MacAlpin becomes the first king to rule both the Scots and the Picts.

843-845

- T'ang emperor Wu-tsung, a Taoist, persecutes Buddhists, Manichaeans, Nestorians, and Maddens (members of a Persian sect), ending a long period of general religious tolerance in China. Only Buddhism survives.

845

- Vikings (Norsemen) sack Paris.

850*

- Groups of Jews settle in Germany. The Yiddish language begins to develop from Hebrew, Aramaic, and German roots.

- Under Vijayawada, who reigns until 870, the prosperous Hindu Cola (or Cholla) dynasty of Tamil kings begins its territorial expansion in southern India.

850-900*

- Salerno University is founded in Italy and rapidly becomes well known for its medical faculty.

851

- Egbert's successor, Aethelwulf, defeats a Viking (Danish) army that has attacked Canterbury and London, but is having difficulty defending the long, unfortified English coastline from repeated raids.

*DENOTES CIRCA DATE

855
- Lothar I dies. His lands are divided among his three sons: Louis II is given Italy; Charles gets Provence; and Lothar II obtains Lotharingia (modern-day Lorraine).

856
- Theodora is forced to retire as regent for Michael III. Her brother Bardas takes advantage of his nephew's weakness to become de facto ruler of the Byzantine Empire.

858
- Fujiwara Yoshifusa, father-in-law of the emperor of Japan, becomes the first commoner to serve as regent when his nine-year-old grandson, Seiwa, takes the throne.
- Photius is named patriarch of Constantinople, replacing Ignatius, who has fallen into disfavor with Bardas. Pope Nicholas I challenges Photius's elevation, sparking the Photian Controversy between the eastern and western Christian Churches.

860*
- Viking (Norse) explorers discover Iceland.

860
- Sailing down the Dnieper from Kiev to the Black Sea, the Russians launch an unsuccessful naval attack on Constantinople.

862
- Charles II (the Bald) grants Flanders to his son-in-law, Baldwin I (Iron Arm).

862-885
- Byzantine missionaries Cyril and Methodius preach Christianity among the Slavs of Moravia and Bohemia. Cyril adapts the Greek alphabet to the Slavic tongue, and it becomes known as the Cyrillic alphabet.

865
- Boris I of Bulgaria is converted to Christianity, eventually affiliating with the Eastern Church.
- Louis II (the German) divides his kingdom among his three sons: Carloman (Bavaria and Carinthia), Charles the Fat (Swabia); and Louis the Younger (Franconia, Thuringia, and Saxony).

866
- Emperor Seiwa of Japan achieves his majority, but his grandfather continues to serve as regent, inaugurating nearly two centuries of clan dominance known as the Fujiwara period (866–1160).
- A Viking (Danish) army of nearly three thousand men attacks England and captures Northumbria.
- Bardas is murdered by Basil, a favorite of Byzantine emperor Michael III.

*Denotes Circa Date

867

- In the midst of the continuing Photian Controversy, Photius condemns and excommunicates Pope Nicholas I for refusing to recognize him as patriarch of Constantinople.

- Basil orders Emperor Michael III deposed and murdered, replacing him on the throne as Emperor Basil I, the founder of the Macedonian dynasty. He deposes Photius, who has protested the murder of Michael III, and restores Ignatius to the office of patriarch.

868

- Empress Shotoku of China orders the printing of the first known book, the *Diamond Sutra*, a collection of Buddhist incantations.

869

- Lothar II dies and his lands are divided between his uncles Louis II (the German) and Charles II (the Bald).

869–870

- The Council of Constantinople excommunicates Photius and attempts to smooth over differences with the Roman Church, but friction remains.

871

- Having already captured York and East Anglia, Vikings (Danes) raid London and meet fierce resistance in Wessex. Late in the year Alfred (the Great) becomes king of Wessex and negotiates a temporary peace.

871–879

- Taking advantage of internal dissent within the Muslim Empire, the Byzantines engage in sporadic border warfare with the Muslims and make some inroads.

874

- Ingólfr Arnarson becomes the first permanent Norse settler of Iceland.

875

- Louis II dies; Charles II (the Bald) invades Italy and is crowned the Holy Roman Emperor.

- Byzantine forces capture Bari in southern Italy. They later take Tarentum (880) and Calabria (885), re-establishing a large foothold on the peninsula.

876

- Charles II (the Bald) attempts, but fails, to take the territory of Louis II (the German), who dies in August. His son Louis III (the Younger) defeats his uncle at the Battle of Andernach on 8 October. Louis's son Charles III (the Fat) becomes king of Swabia.

877

- The death of Charles II (the Bald) leaves the Empire in a state of anarchy. His son Louis II (the Stammerer) becomes king of the West Franks but refuses to become emperor.

*DENOTES CIRCA DATE

877
(CONT'D)

• On the death of Ignatius, Photius is restored as patriarch of Constantinople, causing a renewal of friction with Rome.

878

• The Vikings, led by the Danish king Guthrum, are defeated by King Alfred the Great at the Battle of Edington in Wiltshire. Alfred establishes the Peace of Wedmore, in which Guthrum accepts Christianity and agrees to withdraw to the "Danelaw," England north of Watling Street from Chester to London and the Thames from London to the sea.

879

• Seeking Byzantine support against the Muslims of Spain, who are conducting naval raids along the Italian coastline, Pope John VIII recognizes Photius as patriarch of Constantinople and sends legates to a new Church council held in Constantinople.

880

• Fujiwara Mototsune becomes the first *kampaku* (civil dictator), the de facto ruler of Japan. With one exception, until 1160 a member of the Fujiwara clan serves as *kampaku* during the reign of adult emperor or as regent when a minor is on the throne.

• After the death of Louis II (the Stammerer) in April 879, his sons Carloman and Louis III divide the kingdom of the West Franks.

880-881

• The Byzantines achieve several naval victories over Muslims in the eastern Mediterranean.

881

• Charles III (the Fat) becomes Holy Roman Emperor.

882

• Louis III dies, and his brother Carloman becomes sole ruler of the West Franks.

• Louis III (the Younger) dies, and his brother Charles III (the Fat) gains Saxony.

884

• On the death of Carloman, King of the West Franks, Charles III (the Fat) gains control of West Frankish lands, uniting under his rule all the territory controlled by Charlemagne except Provence.

885-886

• Vikings (Norsemen) lay siege to Paris, but the city is defended by Count Eudes (Odo). Charles III (the Fat) fails in his attempt to aid Eudes.

886

• After repelling a Danish invasion of Kent in 885, Alfred the Great captures London and is acknowledged as king of all England south of the Danelaw.

*DENOTES CIRCA DATE

886
(CONT'D)

- Basil I dies and is succeeded as Byzantine emperor by his son Leo IV (the Wise), who has been co-emperor since 870 and completes the codification of Byzantine law begun by his father.

887

- Charles III (the Fat) is deposed by the German magnates, marking the final dissolution of Charlemagne's empire. Charles's nephew Arnulf, the illegitimate son of Carloman, becomes king of Germany.

888

- Eudes, Count of Paris, is elected king of the West Franks. Another faction backs Charles III (the Simple), younger brother of West Frankish kings Louis III and Carloman, and a five-year civil war ensues.

889

- The Pechenegs, a Turkic people, enter the area between the Don and lower Danube Rivers, driving the Magyars to the eastern edges of their territory.

- Boris I retires to a monastery and is succeeded as ruler of the Bulgars by his son Vladimir.

891

- Fujiwara Mototsune dies, and Emperor Uda, whose mother is not a Fujiwara, refuses to appoint a new *kampaku*. Having ascended the Japanese throne in 887, Uda rules independently of the Fujiwaras until his death in 897. He is supported in his efforts by the powerful scholar-poet-politician Sugawara Michizane (later deified as Tenjin).

- The Vikings (Norsemen) are defeated at the Battle of the Dyle (in present-day Belgium) by Arnulf of Germany.

- With the help of the Magyars, Arnulf attacks the Moravians, who are making incursions into Germany.

- After a vacancy on the throne since 887, Guido of Spoleto is crowned Holy Roman Emperor.

893

- Charles III (the Simple) becomes king of France and rules from Laon. He is the last Carolingian king to exert any true authority in France.

- Boris I comes out of retirement, puts down a revolt against his son Vladimir, deposes and blinds him, and makes his son Simeon I (the Great) king of the Bulgars.

894

- Emperor Uda appoints Sugawara Michizane Japanese envoy to the T'ang dynasty of China, but Michizane convinces the emperor that contact with the Chinese is undesirable because of growing influence from the Near East and that China no longer has anything to teach Japan. Although unofficial contact between the two countries continues, this break in diplomatic relations marks the end of some three centuries of Chinese influence on Japanese culture.

*DENOTES CIRCA DATE

894-924
- Simeon I (the Great) of Bulgaria engages in a series of wars with the Byzantine Empire, hoping to place himself on the imperial throne. Despite repeated attempts, he is never able to take Constantinople.

896
- Led by Arpad, the Magyars settle in Hungary, subjugating the resident Slavs and Huns.
- Arnulf of Germany invades Italy, capturing Rome. With his victory he is crowned Holy Roman Emperor by Pope Formosus.

899
- Arnulf of Germany dies and is succeeded by his six-year-old son, Louis IV (the Child), the last Carolingian ruler of Germany.
- Alfred I of England dies and is succeeded by his son Edward (the Elder).

899-955
- The Magyars conduct raids in Central Europe.

900*
- The Chimú kingdom arises in the Moche Valley of Peru, beginning to fill a vacuum left by the collapse of the Huaris.
- Bantu-speaking people establish city-states on the east coast of Africa.
- The classic period of Mayan civilization in present-day Guatemala, Honduras, southern Mexico, Belize, and El Salvador comes to an end. At its height the Mayan Empire consisted of some forty cities and had a total population of about two million people. While the lowland cities are abandoned after 900, the cites in the highlands of the Yucatán peninsula continue to flourish for several more centuries.
- By this time the last inhabitants of Teotihuacán, near present-day Mexico City, have abandoned what is left of their once-great city, devastated by fire some 150 years earlier. They have been driven away by the arrival of warlike peoples such as the Toltecs.
- The Mataram dynasty is established in Java, Indonesia.

900s
- Many works of vernacular European literatures—Celtic, Old French, Old High German, and Old Norse—are written down for the first time.

902
- The Byzantine island of Sicily falls to the Muslims after a long series of raids that began in 827.
- Work begins on the Campanile of St. Mark's in Venice.

905
- Edward the Elder of England defeats an internal struggle for his throne initiated by his cousin Aethelwald, who had Danish support.

*Denotes Circa Date

907
- A Russian delegation led by Prince Oleg arrives in Constantinople to discuss a trade agreement, signed in 911.
- The T'ang dynasty, which has ruled China since 618, falls because of internal rebellions and Turkish invasions, ending a golden age of Chinese culture and beginning the break-up of China into separate kingdoms.
- Khitan Mongol leader A-pao-chi proclaims himself ruler of the Khitan nation, and by 916 he has created a Chinese-style dynasty to rule a nation that includes Mongolia and much of Manchuria.

910
- Duke William I of Aquitaine donates land to found the Benedictine Abbey of Cluny in France.

911
- Charles III (the Simple) cedes to the Norseman Rollo the Duchy of Northmen (Normans), which becomes known as Normandy. Rollo converts to Christianity, is baptized Robert, and becomes Charles's vassal. Charles gains control of Lorraine.
- On the death of Louis III (the Child), the last Carolingian king of the East Franks, Germany splinters into many smaller principalities. Their rulers elect Conrad I, Duke of Franconia, king of Germany, but he has to fight challenges from Swabia and Bavaria.

912
- Danes in East Anglia are forced to submit to the authority of Edward the Elder.

913
- Leo VI's seven-year-old son, Constantine VII (Porphyrogenitus), becomes Byzantine emperor and reigns until 959. A scholarly, artistic man, Constantine leaves the work of government to the strongmen associated with him.

914
- Bulgar ruler Simeon I (the Great) extends his power in the Balkans through raids in Macedonia, Albania, and Serbia.

919
- Henry I (the Fowler), Duke of Saxony and the strongest opponent of Conrad I, is elected king of Germany. The Swabian and Bavarian dukes are brought to heel, and Henry forms an alliance with Charles III (the Simple) of France.

920
- Romanus I (Lecapenus) is made co-emperor of the Byzantine Empire with his son-in-law Constantine VII (Porphyrogenitus) and becomes de facto ruler of the empire.

922*
- The Volga Bulgars convert to Islam.
- Robert, Duke of Paris, seizes the crown of France from Charles III (the Simple).

*DENOTES CIRCA DATE

923
- Charles III (the Simple) kills Robert in a battle at Soissons, only to be captured by Hebert, Count of Vermandois, in whose custody he dies in 929. Robert's son-in-law Rudolf, Duke of Burgundy, becomes king.

924
- Edward the Elder dies and is succeeded by his son, Aethelstan, who annexes Northumbria in 926 on his way to controlling most of England.

925
- Simeon I (the Great) proclaims himself tsar of all the Bulgars, presiding over the first Bulgarian empire. Having proclaimed the independence of the Bulgarian Church from Constantinople, he is recognized by the Pope but not by the Byzantines.

926
- In return for helping the Juchens of Manchuria to conquer northern China, Khitan ruler A-pao-chi is given the northeast corner of China, which includes the city of Beijing.

927
- German king Henry I (the Fowler) launches an attack on, and defeats, the Heveller, a Slavic tribe that has a strong fortress on the Havel River that was thought to be invincible.

932
- Chinese minister Fong Tao orders the printing of a collection of Chinese classics in 130 volumes.

933
- German king Henry I (the Fowler) defeats the Magyars at Riade on the Unstrut River. The Magyars, who have invaded with a force of nearly one hundred thousand men, are crushed by two German armies.

935-941
- The provincial military class in Japan revolts unsuccessfully against imperial rule.

936
- Henry I (the Fowler) dies and is succeeded as king of Germany by his son, Otto I (the Great).
- On the death of King Rudolf, Louis IV, son of Charles III (the Simple), becomes king of France, but the kingdom is actually ruled by Hugh the Great, son of King Robert.

937
- Aethelstan's English forces defeat Scottish and Danish armies at the Battle of Brunanburh, helping to unify the Anglo-Saxon kingdom.

939
- Vietnam gains its independence from China.

*Denotes Circa Date

941
- Igor, Duke of Kiev, launches a naval attack on Constantinople, but his fleet is defeated by the Greeks. His second attempt, in 944, fails as well.

942
- Kettledrums and trumpets arrive in western Europe from Muslim regions.

944
- Romanus I (Lecapenus) is deposed by his sons Stephen and Constantine, who force him to become a monk. After exiling Romanus's sons in 945, Constantine VII (Porphyrogenitus) becomes sole ruler again, but the Byzantine Empire is largely governed by the powerful general Bardas Phocas, who is under the influence of Constantine's wife, Empress Helena, and her favorite, Basil.

947
- The Khitans of northeastern China proclaim the Liao dynasty, which rules that portion of their empire until 1125.
- Quetzalcoatl, revered by the Toltecs as a god, is born in Mexico.

950*
- The war-like Toltecs build their capital city, Tula, about fifty miles north of present-day Mexico City.

951
- Otto I (the Great) invades Italy, largely to open the passages through the mountains.

954
- On the death of Louis IV of France his eldest son, Lothaire, becomes king. The kingdom is controlled by Hugh the Great until 956 and then by Hugh's uncle, Archbishop Bruno of Cologne, brother of King Otto I (the Great) of Germany.

955
- The Magyars attempt another invasion of Germany, but they are defeated at the Battle of the Lechfeld by Otto I (the Great) and driven back into Hungary, where they establish a permanent kingdom.
- A treaty between Ordoño III and 'Abd al-Rahman-al-Nasir secures the independence of Leon and Navarre.

957
- Olga, widow of Prince Igor of Kiev and regent for their son Svyatoslav, is baptized in Constantinople and begins efforts to convert Russians to Christianity. She is later canonized as the first saint of the Russian Orthodox Church.

959
- Byzantine emperor Constantine VII (Porphyrogenitus) dies and is succeeded by his son Romanus II, who allows the eunuch Joseph Bringas to run affairs of state and leaves military affairs to Nicephorus Phocas, son of Bardas Phocas.

*DENOTES CIRCA DATE

960* • Monasticism undergoes a revival in England.

960 • Chao K'uang-yin stages a coup in China and proclaims himself Emperor T'ai-tsu, establishing the Sung dynasty which remains in power until 1279. In the Sung period China undergoes a revival of Confucianism; Chinese trade goods such as porcelain and steel become world famous; and artists, particularly watercolor landscape painters, flourish. During his reign, which lasts until 976, T'ai-tsu begins the reunification of the Chinese empire.

961 • Byzantine general Nicephorus Phocas recaptures Crete from the Muslims.

962 • After invading Italy for the second time, Otto I (the Great) is crowned Holy Roman Emperor by the Pope. During his reign he sends an ambassador to the Umayyad capital in Cordoba, Spain, to learn about Muslim society and military capacities.

• The Germans are working silver and copper mines in the Hartz Mountains.

963 • Byzantine emperor Romanus II dies on 15 March, leaving Joseph Bringas in charge of the affairs of state and naming his twenty-year-old empress, Theophano, regent for his two sons, Basil (age six) and Constantine (age three). After the people of Constantinople revolt against Bringas, the imperial army places Nicephorus Phocas on the throne (16 August) as Nicephorus II, and he marries Theophano (20 September).

966-969 • With the aid of Prince Svyatoslav of Kiev, the Byzantines defeat the Bulgars. Svyatoslav refuses to cede his conquest to the Byzantines and announces plans to establish a Russo-Bulgarian empire.

967 • Otto I (the Great) forces Pope John XIII to crown his son, Otto II, as joint Holy Roman Emperor.

969 • Byzantine emperor Nicephorus II (Phocas) is murdered in a plot devised by his wife, Empress Theophano, and his relative and trusted lieutenant John Tzimisces, who has been having an affair with Theophano. When Patriarch Polyeuctus of Constantinople insists that he do penance in order to become Emperor John I, Tzimisces banishes Theophano to a convent and punishes the murderers.

971 • Prince Svyatoslav of Kiev invades the Byzantine Empire, where he is defeated by John I (Tzimisces) and forced to evacuate Bulgaria. John annexes eastern Bulgaria to the Byzantine Empire.

*DENOTES CIRCA DATE

972

- The Chinese begin printing with movable type.

973

- On the death of his father, Otto I (the Great), Otto II becomes king of Germany and Emperor of the Romans.

- Commercial relations are established between Italy and Fatimid Egypt.

974-976

- In campaigns against the Fatimid Muslims in Syria, John I (Tzimisces) takes Antioch, Damascus, and other cities but dies—probably of typhoid—before he can take Jerusalem.

975-1025*

- *Beowulf,* an Old English epic that has evolved over several centuries, is written down for the first time.

976

- On the death of John I (Tzimisces), Basil II and Constantine VIII, sons of Romanos II and Theophano, become the rulers of the Byzantine Empire. They are under the influence of their granduncle Basil the Chamberlain (also known as Basil the Eunuch), illegitimate son of Romanus I (Lecapenus).

- During his reign, which lasts until 997, T'ai-tsung, brother and successor of T'ai-tsu, completes the reunification of the Chinese empire.

978

- Otto II of Germany puts down a revolt by Henry II of Bavaria.

- Aethelred II (the Unready) becomes king of England and is soon facing new Danish raids.

979

- Bardas Phocas defeats Bardas Skleros, who has led a military uprising against Byzantine emperor Basil II.

980

- Samuel becomes tsar of Bulgaria, establishing his capital in Macedonia and extending his empire into the northern part of present-day Albania and northern Greece.

982

- Banished from Iceland for manslaughter, Norseman Erik the Red settles on the island he later calls Greenland.

- German king Otto II's troops are defeated by Muslim forces near Stilo in southern Italy.

983

- On the death of Otto II, his three-year-old son Otto III becomes king of Germany and Emperor of the Romans. His mother and grandmother rule as regents.

***Denotes Circa Date**

985
- Returning to Iceland, Erik the Red recruits settlers for Greenland, choosing the name to make the island seem more attractive than Iceland.
- Byzantine emperor Basil II exiles Basil the Chamberlain to end his influence on imperial policy.
- On the death of King Lothaire, his weak son Louis V becomes king of France.

986
- Icelanders led by Erik the Red establish two main settlements in Greenland.
- Blown off course during a storm, Icelander Bjarni Herjulfsson and his crew make the first recorded European sighting of the North American continent.

987
- The last Carolingian king of the West Franks, Louis V, dies and is succeeded by Hugh Capet, the first Capetian king of France.

989
- With the help of Prince Vladimir of Kiev, Byzantine emperor Basil II puts down a revolt led by his generals Bardas Phocas and Bardas Skleros. Basil rewards Vladimir with the hand of his sister Anna, on the condition that he and his subjects convert to Christianity. A mass conversion of Russians to Eastern Christianity follows.

994
- The Danes, led by Sweyn I Forkbeard, invade England and impose tribute.

995
- Fujiwara Michinaga becomes head of his clan and de facto ruler of Japan, fostering a Japanese literary renaissance while struggling to suppress rebellions by warrior families who resent the Fujiwaras' centralized control of the nation.
- Military victories at Aleppo and Homs strengthen the Byzantines' position in Syria.

996
- Emperor Basil II recovers Byzantine holdings in Greece by defeating Tsar Samuel of Bulgaria at the Battle of Spercheios River.
- Hugh Capet of France dies and is succeeded by his son Robert II (the Pious).

998
- The Feast of All Saints is celebrated for the first time at Cluny.

999*
- Influenced by the success of Christian missionaries sent by Olaf I Tryggvason, king of Norway, the Althing, or Icelandic assembly, decides that all Icelanders must abandon the old Norse religion in favor of Christianity.

*DENOTES CIRCA DATE

1000*

- Over the past three thousand years, people speaking the Bantu family of languages have spread out from western Africa and now dominate the cultures of most of sub-Saharan Africa, diffusing their knowledge of iron work and agriculture.

- The West African city-state of Benin emerges in what is now Nigeria, becoming renowned for its metalwork. By the late fifteenth century, when Portuguese explorers visit it for the first time, it has become a large, powerful, and prosperous walled city.

- The Incan civilization begins to develop in South America.

- Struggles between rival religious groups begin to weaken the Toltec state of central Mexico.

- Among the Eastern Woodlands peoples in the northwestern part of present-day New York State the introduction of corn sparks the development of the Owasco culture, the foundation of the groups Europeans later call the Five Iroquois Nations: the Mohawks, Senecas, Onondagas, Oneidas, and Cayugas. Once they begin practicing horticulture, their population grows and competition for land increases, leading eventually to the construction of fortified hilltop towns.

- The Navajo and Apache peoples from the far north in Canada arrive in the American Southwest, where they encounter Pueblo Indians, including the Zuni and Hopi, who have been in the region for thousands of years. The Navajo learn agriculture, weaving, and artistic styles from the Pueblo tribes, but the Apache remain mostly hunter-gatherers. Only a few groups of their people supplement their diet by growing maize and other vegetables.

- At Cahokia, near present-day East St. Louis, Illinois, members of the group archaeologists call Mississippians begin building the largest earthen structures in pre-Columbian North America. Following a tradition begun around 2300 B.C. these mound builders place structures such as the council house, chiefs' houses, and their temple on their mounds. Situated on land well suited for agriculture and strategically located for trade, Cahokia becomes a prosperous and influential city, with a population that eventually reaches about twelve thousand people. Its political and religious rituals, symbols, and costumes spread throughout the Southeast.

- Maori people settle New Zealand following long voyages across the Pacific Ocean.

1000

- Leif Eriksson, son of Erik the Red, converts to Christianity during a visit to Norway.

- The Danes, led by Sweyn I, defeat the forces of Olaf Tryggvason of Norway.

1001

- Leif Eriksson and his crew sail to places they call Vinland, Helluland, and Markland, possibly Nova Scotia, Labrador, and Newfoundland.

1002*

- Leif Eriksson and his party return to Greenland, where he proselytizes for the Christian religion, first converting his mother, who builds the first Christian church on the island.

***Denotes Circa Date**

1002

- Otto III dies and his cousin Henry II becomes king of Germany. He is crowned Emperor of the Romans in 1014.

- Danish settlers are massacred in England, prompting the Danish king to send regular raiding parties to the island for the next twelve years.

- Byzantine emperor Basil II takes Macedonia from the Bulgars.

1003

- Tsar Samuel of Bulgaria recovers Macedonia from the Byzantines.

1004

- Thorfinn Karlsefni and his wife, Gudrid, lead an expedition of about 130 people from Greenland to the North American continent, landing possibly at Baffin Island, traveling south, and settling along what was probably the Gulf of St. Lawrence. After three years they abandon the settlement they call Vinland and return to Greenland. Thorfinn and Gudrid's son, Snorri (born circa 1005), may be the first European born in mainland North America.

1005

- Malcolm II Mackenneth becomes king of Scotland and rules until 1034.

1007

- Byzantine emperor Basil II subdues Macedonia, but conflict with the Bulgars continues.

1013–1014

- Danish king Sweyn I invades England and is acknowledged as king, but after his death in Gainsborough, Aethelred the Unready regains the throne.

1014

- Rajendra becomes king of a Cola empire that includes southern India, the Laccadive and Maldive Islands, and northern Ceylon (Sri Lanka). During his thirty-year reign, he extends the northern boundaries of his kingdom, completes the invasion of Ceylon, and conquers portions of the Malay Peninsula and Archipelago.

- King Brian of Ireland defeats the Vikings (Norsemen) at Clontarf, ending Viking control of Ireland. Many Norse settlers remain in Ireland.

- Byzantine emperor Basil II annihilates the Bulgarian army at the Battle of Balathista, earning the byname "Bulgaroctonus" (Slayer of Bulgars). He blinds several thousand Bulgar soldiers and sends them to Tsar Samuel, who—according to tradition—dies from the shock of seeing them.

1016*

- The victory of Malcolm II Mackenneth at the Battle of Carham makes him the first Scottish king to rule over a country with roughly the same boundaries as modern Scotland.

*DENOTES CIRCA DATE

1016

- On the death of Aethelred the Unready of England in April, his son Edmund II Ironside is proclaimed king in London, but nobles in Southampton offer the throne to Canute I (the Great), son of Sweyn I of Denmark. The dispute is finally resolved by Edmund's death in November. Canute rules England until his death in 1035.

1018

- Lombard and Norman forces led by the nobleman Melus invade Italy and are defeated at Cannae by a Byzantine army, which secures Byzantine holdings in southern Italy.

- On the death of his father, Sweyn I, Canute I (the Great) of England becomes Canute II of Denmark.

1022

- The Byzantines, who have been annexing portions of Armenia since 968, gain possession of the Armenian kingdom of Vaspurakan, and the ruler of the Armenian kingdom of Ani is compelled to make Emperor Basil II heir to his estates.

1024

- On the death of Henry II, his cousin Conrad II becomes king of Germany; in 1027 he is crowned Emperor of the Romans. He is regularly challenged by revolts in Italy and Germany, but he manages to suppress them and rules until 1039.

1025-1028

- After the death of Basil II, his brother, Constantine VIII, rules the Byzantine Empire until his death three years later.

1026

- The Danes defeat an attempt by the Swedes and Norwegians to conquer their country.

1028

- The death of Fujiwara Michinaga begins the decline of Fujiwara control in Japan, as other clans begin to usurp power in the countryside.

- Canute the Great of England and Denmark becomes king of Norway.

- After the death of Constantine VIII, his daughters Zoë and Theodora are named co-empresses of the Byzantine Empire. Theodora lives in retirement until Zoë exiles her to a monastery, and Zoë rules the empire until 1050 with a succession of three husbands, the first of which is her father's handpicked successor, Romanus III (Argyropolus). During the early part of their reign, Zoë and Romanus allow the patriarch of Constantinople to persecute the Monophysties of Syria, engendering hatred for the Byzantines in the region and causing thousands of Syrians to flee to Muslim territory.

1030-1031

- Conrad II of Germany leads an unsuccessful expedition against the Hungarians but follows it by defeating the Poles and forcing them to pay homage.

- Romanus III is severely defeated in 1030 by Muslims who have attacked Syria, but the following year General Georgios Maniakes preserves the Byzantine hold on the territory.

*Denotes Circa Date

1031
- Robert II (the Pious) dies and is succeeded by his son Henry I in France.

1034
- Malcolm II of Scotland dies and is succeeded by his daughter's son, Duncan I.
- Byzantine emperor Romanus III (Argyropolus) dies, reputedly poisoned by his wife, Empress Zoë, who marries Romanus's young chamberlain and makes him Emperor Michael IV (the Paphlagonian).

1034-1040
- The Byzantine fleet achieves several significant naval victories over the Muslims in the eastern Mediterranean.

1035
- Harold I (Harefoot), the illegitimate son of Canute I (the Great), becomes regent in England and seizes the throne outright in 1037.
- William II becomes the duke of Normandy.

1039
- Conrad II dies and is replaced as king of Germany and Emperor of the Romans by his son Henry III (the Black). During his reign, which lasts until 1056, Henry controls Poland, Bohemia, and Saxony.

1040
- Danish king Hardecanute, the legitimate son of Canute I (the Great), invades England and unseats his half brother, Harold, from the throne.
- Byzantine troops crush a Bulgar uprising. Bulgaria is incorporated into the Byzantine Empire, and its autonomous church comes under the jurisdiction of the patriarch of Constantinople.
- Macbeth rises up against his young cousin Duncan I, kills him in a battle near Elgin on 14 August, and is crowned king of Scotland.

1041-1042
- On the death of Michael IV (the Paphlagonian) Empress Zoë elevates her favorite Michael V (Kalaphates), who attempts to make himself sole emperor by exiling Zoë to a convent. Members of the nobility depose Michael, blind him, and imprison him, placing Zoë and her sister Theodora on the throne as co-empresses.

1042
- Edward the Confessor, son of Aethelred the Unready, takes the throne of England on the death of his half brother Hardecanute; Edward rules England until 1066.
- Byzantine empress Zoë marries Constantine IX (Monomachus), elevating him to emperor and relegating Theodora to the background.
- General Georgios Maniakes fends off a Norman invasion of Byzantine holdings in southern Italy. In 1043 he leads disaffected troops against Constantinople, but the rebellion falls apart after he is accidentally killed en route.

*DENOTES CIRCA DATE

1044
- Englishman Robert of Chester prepares a treatise on chemistry based on Arabic learning.

1045
- Byzantine emperor Constantine IX (Monomachus) occupies Ani and takes over the government of all Armenia.

1048
- Byzantine forces defeat an army of Saljuk Turks, who have been moving westward from Central Asia and threatening the Byzantine and Muslim Empires.

1050*
- The astrolabe and other Arab astrological tools come into use in Europe.
- Over the next 250 years the Pueblo peoples of the American Southwest build their cliff houses at Mesa Verde and apartment-like housing at Chaco Canyon and other sites.
- The Pechenegs, who have been raiding Byzantine territory since the defeat of the Bulgars, are now a constant threat in Byzantine Thrace and Macedonia.

1050
- After the death of Empress Zoë, her third husband, Constantine IX (Monomachus), rules the Byzantine Empire alone until 1055.

1051
- William II of Normandy defeats Geoffrey Martel and captures Anjou.

1054
- Angry at Pope Leo IX's support for Norman conquests in Byzantine southern Italy, Patriarch Michael Kerularios of Constantinople anathematizes the Roman Church, an act widely regarded as the beginning of the schism between the Western and Eastern Christian Churches.

1055
- On the death of Constantine IX (Monomachus), Empress Theodora reasserts her claim to rule the Byzantine Empire.

1056
- A bishop's seat is established in Iceland.
- Henry III dies and is succeeded as king of Germany and Emperor of the Romans by six-year-old Henry IV, who reigns until 1106.
- On the death of Empress Theodora in August, Michael VI (Stratioticus) becomes the Byzantine emperor. He is deposed the following August by members of the military aristocracy, who put Isaac I Comnenus on the throne.

1057
- Macbeth of Scotland is killed in battle on 15 August by Malcolm III Canmore, the son of Duncan I. Malcolm rules Scotland until his death in 1093.

*DENOTES CIRCA DATE

1059
- Byzantine emperor Isaac I Comnenus abdicates in favor of Constantine X (Ducas).

- Pope Nicholas II decrees that the cardinal clergy of Rome are responsible for electing a new Pope, thus eliminating secular rulers from the election process. Though he is unable to enforce the decree against opposition from the Emperor of the Romans, he establishes the important precedent of reserving power within the Church to the ecclesiastical hierarchy.

1060
- Henry I of France dies and is succeeded by his son Philip I.

1061
- Norman brothers Robert and Roger Guiscard begin a long campaign to capture Sicily from the Muslims. The invasion is not entirely complete until the fall of Muslim forces at Messina in 1091. In 1072 Roger becomes Roger II, Count of Sicily.

1064
- Ani, in Armenia, falls to the Saljuk Turks.

1066
- On the death of Edward the Confessor, Harold Godwinsson becomes king of England and defeats an invading army led by King Harald Hardrada of Norway at the Battle of Stamford Bridge (25 September) in Yorkshire.

- Norman troops under William the Conqueror land on the southern coast of England and defeat Harold Godwinsson's weary army at the Battle of Hastings (14 October). Harold Godwinsson is killed, ending Saxon rule of England. William the Conqueror becomes William I of England on Christmas Day and rules until 1087, imposing systematic feudal land tenure.

- During the Norman Conquest a celestial body later named Halley's Comet is seen in the skies.

1068
- On the death of Byzantine emperor Constantine X (Ducas), Romanus IV Diogenes marries the widowed Empress Eudoxia and becomes co-emperor with Constantine's minor son, Michael VII (Ducas).

1070*
- Italian merchants found the Order of St. John (later Order of Knights Hospitalers of St. John) to protect Christian pilgrims to the Holy Lands in Jerusalem. The order eventually becomes known as the Knights of Malta.

1071
- After a three-year siege, a Norman fleet commanded by Robert Guiscard conquers Bari, the last important Byzantine stronghold in southern Italy.

- Byzantine emperor Romanus IV Diogenes is defeated and taken captive by Saljuk Turks at the Battle of Malazgirt (Manzikert). The power of the Byzantine state is broken.

*DENOTES CIRCA DATE

- Michael VII (Ducas) becomes sole ruler of the Byzantine Empire.

1072
- The Scots are forced to pay homage to William I (the Conqueror), who takes hostage Duncan, son and heir of Malcolm III of Scotland.

1074
- Michael VII (Ducas) calls on the Saljuks for help against Roussel de Bailleul, a Norman mercenary who tries to establish his own kingdom in Asia Minor, thus paving the way for the Saljuks' conquest of most of Anatolia.

1076–1122
- Pope Gregory VII and Emperor Henry IV and their successors engage in the long dispute known as the Investiture Controversy, a power struggle over whether secular rulers have the right to select and install bishops.

1077*
- Work begins on the 230-foot-long, 20-inch-wide Bayeux Tapestry, depicting events leading up to and including the conquest of England by William I (the Conqueror) in 1066.

1078
- After riots over grain policy break out in Constantinople, rival generals, Nicephorus Bryennius in Albania and Nicephorus Botaneiates in Anatolia, march on the city to claim the throne. Michael VII (Ducas) abdicates, and Botaneiates becomes Emperor Nicephorus III. His ascent is greeted by military insurrections, which are put down by General Alexius Comnenus.

1081
- Alexius Comnenus seizes the Byzantine throne, ruling as Alexius I Comnenus until 1118.

1081–1085
- Led by Robert Guiscard and his sons, Bohemond and Roger Borsa, Normans from southern Italy invade Byzantine territories in western Greece (1081), Macedonia (1083), and Corfu (1083). Alexius I Comnenus wins the support of Venice by granting it extensive trading privileges (1082), and in 1085 the Byzantine and Venetian fleets defeat the Normans near Corfu, a loss that, with the death of Robert, convinces the Normans to abandon their invasion.

1085
- Alfonso VI of Castile captures the Muslim city of Toledo in Spain, which becomes a major center for the translation into Latin of Arabic scientific, medical, and philosophical manuscripts, including ancient Greek and Roman writings.

1085–1086
- William I (the Conqueror) of England has the *Domesday Book* compiled to determine the taxable capacity of his kingdom.

*DENOTES CIRCA DATE

1087
- William I (the Conqueror) is fatally wounded in a fall from a horse during warfare with Philip I of France. He is replaced on the English throne by his son, William II (Rufus), who rules until 1100.

1088
- The University of Bologna is founded.
- Arabic medicine is taught at Salerno.

1091
- Alexius I Comnenus defeats the Pechenegs.

1094
- Spanish mercenary soldier Rodrigo Diaz de Vivar captures Valencia from the Muslims in Spain.

1095
- Responding to a call from Alexius I Comnenus for help against the Saljuks, Pope Urban II calls for a Crusade to claim the Holy Land for Christianity.

1096-1099
- Crusader victories during the First Crusade enable Alexius I Comnenus to recover the western coast of Anatolia for the Byzantines, but rather than turning over all conquered territories the Crusaders establish the Latin Christian kingdoms of Jerusalem, Edessa, Antioch, and Tripoli—which only grudgingly acknowledge the Byzantine emperor as their overlord.

1100*
- Inuits, a people of North America, settle in northern Greenland.
- Troubadour poetry emerges in southern France under the patronage of Duke William IX of Aquitaine and his descendants Eleanor of Aquitaine and Marie of France.
- The French epic poem *La Chanson de Roland* (The Song of Roland) tells the tale of a French warrior killed while defending the rearguard of Charlemagne's troops at Roncesvalles in 778.
- In western Europe, Gothic architecture begins to supplant the earlier Romanesque style.

1100
- William II (Rufus) of England is killed while hunting. His brother Henry I (Beauclerc) becomes king and rules until 1135.

1100-1300
- Tahitian chiefs make a series of voyages to the Hawaiian Islands.

*DENOTES CIRCA DATE

1104
- Alfonso I (the Battler) becomes king of Aragon and Navarre, ruling until 1134.

1106
- A second bishopric is established in Iceland.
- An army led by Henry I of England defeats the troops of his brother, Robert II (Curthose), Duke of Normandy, on 28 September at the Battle of Tinchebrai in northwest France. Robert is imprisoned.
- On the death of Henry IV, his son Henry V becomes king of Germany and Emperor of the Romans.

1108
- Philip I of France dies and is succeeded by his son Louis VI (the Fat).

1113
- Pope Paschal II issues a bull naming and formally recognizing the Order of Knights Hospitalers of St. John (Knights of Malta).

1113-1150*
- During his reign Khmer king Suryavarman II builds Angkor Wat, a huge temple complex in his capital city.

1115
- The religious and military order of the Knights Templar is founded to protect Christian pilgrims in the Holy Land. These knights become bankers and money brokers who handle transactions between different provinces and states.

1117
- Alexius II Comnenus defeats the Saljuks at Philomelion and recovers a large portion of Anatolia.

1117-1128*
- Peter Abelard's *Sic et Non* (Yes and No) helps to establish Scholasticism as the dominant teaching method in the universities of western Europe.

1118
- Alfonso the Battler captures the province of Saragossa in northeast Spain, which Muslims have held for nearly four hundred years.
- On the death of Alexius II Comnenus, his son John II Comnenus becomes Byzantine emperor.

1119
- A loose grouping of schools is established at Paris. By 1215 it has become the University of Paris.
- The use of a compass for sea navigation is documented for the first time in China.

*DENOTES CIRCA DATE

1120
- Construction begins on Chartres Cathedral in France, one of the greatest examples of Gothic architecture. It is essentially completed by 1220.

1120–1121
- John II Comnenus continues his father's campaign against the Saljuks and recovers still more of Anatolia for the Byzantines.

1122
- John II Comnenus defeats the Pechenegs, alleviating their threat to the Byzantine Empire.

1122–1126
- After John II Comnenus refuses to renew the generous trade agreements granted by his father, a Venetian fleet ravages Byzantine islands in the Aegean until John complies with their demands.

1123
- The Juchens conquer the Liao dynasty lands in northern China and proclaim the Chin dynasty, which rules until 1234.

1125*
- Latin translations of Arabic writings and Arabic manuscripts of classical works discovered in Muslim lands begin to flood western Europe.

1125
- Henry V dies without an heir. Lothar II is elected the king of Germany.

1126
- The Juchens of Manchuria conquer the northern portion of the Sung empire in China.
- A bishop's seat is established in Greenland.
- Deriving his knowledge from Arabic manuscripts, Adelard of Bath introduces Euclidean geometry into Europe.

1127
- Sung prince Kao-tsung escapes from Juchen invaders and rules the portion of the empire that lies south of the Yangtze River.

1130
- Roger II becomes ruler of the newly formed kingdom of Sicily. He patronizes many scientific projects, including the creation of sophisticated maps, such as those completed by al-Idrisi in 1154, the year of Roger's death.

*Denotes Circa Date

1135
- On the death of Henry I of England, his nephew Stephen, a grandson of William the Conqueror, claims the English throne, having earlier been forced by Henry to recognize his daughter, Empress Matilda of Germany, as the rightful heir. A civil war breaks out between Stephen and Matilda.

1137
- Byzantine troops complete a three-year campaign to conquer Cilician (Little) Armenian, which has been under the control of the Latin Christian state of Antioch. Raymond of Antioch is forced to do homage to the Byzantine Empire.
- Louis VI (the Fat) of France dies and is succeeded by his son Louis VII (the Young).

1138
- Following the death of Lothar II in 1137, Conrad III is elected king of Germany. He loses Saxony to Bavaria but expands German control in the Scandinavian areas.

1143
- On the death of John II Comnenus, his son Manuel I Comnenus becomes Byzantine emperor.

1147
- European troops led by Louis VI of France and Conrad III of Germany arrive in the East for the Second Crusade, which ends in 1149, after their poorly coordinated offensive accomplishes little of importance. Relations between the Crusaders and the Byzantines worsen.
- Prince Yury Vladimirovich Dolgoruky, prince of Suzdal, founds the Russian city of Moscow.

1150*
- Imported Muslim musical instruments begin to influence western European music.
- The Spanish epic *Cantar del mio Cid* (Poem of the Cid), recounts the deeds of a hero based on Castilian warrior Rodrigo Díaz de Vivar during warfare to recapture Valencia from the Muslims.

1152
- On the death of his uncle Conrad III, Frederick I (Barbarossa) is elected king of Germany and becomes Emperor of the Romans. During his thirty-eight-year reign, he leads six expeditions into Italy.

1152-1154
- The Byzantines defeat the Hungarians, who have attempted to take Serbia and Bosnia.

1153
- King Stephen of England recognizes Henry of Anjou (Henry II), the son of his rival, Empress Matilda, as his heir.

*Denotes Circa Date

1154
- On the death of King Stephen, Henry II assumes the English throne.

1156
- Civil war breaks out in Japan as retired emperor Sutoku attempts unsuccessfully to regain power from his brother, reigning emperor Go-Shirakawa. The emperor is backed by samurai warriors led by Taira Kiyomori and by the Fujiwaras, who—despite their support of the winning side—continue to lose influence as the Taira family begins its ascent.
- Austria is formed from the duchy of Bavaria.

1157
- Valdemar I (the Great) becomes king of Denmark. During his reign, which lasts until 1182, he greatly improves Danish military capabilities.
- In Moscow, Prince Yury Vladimirovich Dolgoruky begins building the fortifications that become the Kremlin.

1158-1159
- The Byzantines send a military expedition against the Latin Christian kingdom of Antioch and force its ruler, Raymond, to renew his homage to the Byzantine Empire.

1159
- The Spanish Jew Benjamin of Tudela begins a journey across the Mediterranean, through Constantinople to India and back to Spain via Egypt.

1160
- Minamoto Yoshitomo and Fujiwara Nobuyori, who were allied with Taira forces in 1156, are defeated in a coup attempt against the Taira family, ending the Fujiwara period in Japan and leaving Taira Kiyomori in control of the entire country.

1165-1168
- The Byzantine Empire engages in a successful war against Hungary and incorporates Dalmatia, Bosnia, and part of Croatia into the empire.

1169-1170
- Hoping to break the trade monopoly of Venice, Byzantine emperor Manuel I Comnenus signs treaties with Genoa and Pisa, arousing animosity among Venetians.

1170*
- A large number of scholars have come together in the English town of Oxford, forming the basis for the University of Oxford.

1170
- Chrétien de Troyes writes Arthurian legends such as *Lancelot*.
- Archbishop Thomas Becket is murdered at Canterbury Cathedral in England because of his resistance to King Henry II's demands for greater royal control over the clergy.

*DENOTES CIRCA DATE

1171
- The severing of relations between Venice and the Byzantine Empire is followed by naval warfare.

1173
- Construction begins on the bell tower for the cathedral of Pisa, which is completed in 1174 and becomes known as the Leaning Tower of Pisa.

1174
- The Toltec Empire of central Mexico falls after internal chaos and invasions by less-civilized nomads.

1175-1176
- The Venetians and Normans form an alliance against the Byzantines, forcing them to pay a heavy indemnity.

1176
- Byzantine emperor Manuel I Comnenus attacks the Saljuks and suffers a severe defeat at the Battle of Myriocephalon. Though the Byzantines achieve some military success in 1176, the Battle of Myriocephalon is often identified as a harbinger of the fall of the Byzantine Empire.

1179
- The Mayan city of Chichén Itzá is burned and destroyed.

1180*
- Glass mirrors with lead backing come into use in Europe.
- Windmills with vertical sails begin to appear in Europe.

1180
- Taira Kyomori places his two-year-old grandson on the throne of Japan as Emperor Antoku, provoking a rebellion led by Minamoto Yoritomo, whose father Kyomori had executed after his coup attempt in 1160.
- Manuel I Comnenus dies and is succeeded as Byzantine emperor by his eleven-year-old son, Alexius II Comnenus, whose mother, Mary, daughter of Raymond of Antioch, serves as regent. She entrusts the government to Manuel's unpopular nephew Alexius.
- Louis VII (the Young) dies without issue and is succeeded on the French throne by his brother Philip II Augustus.

1182
- Canute VI becomes king of Denmark upon the death of his father, Valdemar the Great. During his reign, which lasts until 1202, Canute expands Danish influence to Pomerania, Holstein, and Mecklenburg.
- Philip II Augustus of France expels the Jews from all the territory he controls.

*DENOTES CIRCA DATE

1183
- After growing resentment and rioting over the influence of Latins (western Europeans) in the Byzantine government, Andronicus I Comnenus, a cousin of Manuel I Comnenus, seizes the throne from Alexius II Comnenus, has him strangled, and marries his thirteen-year-old widow.

1185
- The Minamoto clan defeats the Tairas and establishes the Kamakura shogunate. During this period of feudalism, which lasts until 1333, emperors are ceremonial figureheads, and powerful military governors known as shoguns are the real rulers of Japan.
- Isaac Comnenus, Byzantine governor of Cyprus, declares himself the independent ruler of the island.
- King William II (the Good) leads his Norman Sicilian troops across Greece and occupies Thessalonica, the second most important city of the Byzantine Empire. News of the defeat sparks a revolt in Constantinople. Andronicus I Comnenus is killed by a street mob. Isaac II Angelus seizes the throne.

1185-1191
- The Byzantines drive the Normans from Greece and the Balkans.

1186-1188
- The Byzantines are unable to put down a revolt in Bulgaria that leads to the establishment of a new Bulgarian state north of the Balkans.

1187
- The Latin state of Jerusalem falls to the forces of Salah al-Din (known in the West as Saladin) and comes under Muslim control.

1189
- Richard I (the Lionhearted), eldest son of Henry II, becomes king of England. With Frederick I (Barbarossa) of Germany and Philip II Augustus of France, he leads the Third Crusade, which lasts until 1192.

1190
- Frederick I (Barbarossa) drowns in Cilicia; Henry VI becomes king of Germany and is crowned Emperor of the Romans in 1191.

1190-1194
- The Byzantines suffer major defeats in a war with Bulgaria.

1191
- Crusaders led by Richard I (the Lionhearted) and Philip II Augustus take Acre, in the kingdom of Jerusalem, and slaughter the inhabitants. Richard seizes Cyprus from Isaac Comnenus.

*DENOTES CIRCA DATE

1192

- After Latin Christian forces fail to retake Jerusalem, the Third Crusade ends. Richard I (the Lionhearted) sells Cyprus to Guy of Lusignan, the deposed ruler of the Latin kingdom of Jerusalem.

- Defeated by Indian troups at Taraori in 1191, Muslim Ghurid leader Mu'izz al-Din returns to win a great victory that opens the way for his subordinates to establish Ghurid control over northern India.

1194

- While returning from the Third Crusade, Richard I (the Lionhearted) is captured in Austria by King Leopold and is ransomed to England. After his release he begins a war against Philip II Augustus, who has prepared to attack Henry's French lands.

1195

- Isaac II Angelus is deposed and blinded by his brother Alexius III, who seizes the Byzantine throne. During his reign, which lasts until 1203, the already-decaying government and military bureaucracy of the empire collapses completely.

1196

- Emperor Henry VI, heir to Norman domains, demands Durazzo (in present-day Albania) and Thessalonica (in Greece) from the Byzantines, but Henry's death in 1197 removes any immediate threat from the West, as civil war breaks out between rivals for the German crown: Henry's brother Philip of Swabia, supported by France, and Otto of Brunswick, who is backed by England and is recognized by Pope Innocent III as Otto IV of Germany in 1201.

1198

- Innocent III becomes Pope and recognizes the sovereignty of Serbia, Hungary, and Bulgaria—all of which have been refused recognition by the Byzantines. Innocent calls for another crusade but finds little enthusiasm for the endeavor. During his pontificate, which lasts until 1216, the exercise of papal authority over secular rulers reaches its height.

1199

- Richard I (the Lionhearted) of England is mortally wounded while making war against Philip II Augustus in France. His successor is his brother John I (Lackland), who continues the war against France.

1200*

- Kabbalism, a Jewish mystic philosophy, develops in southern Europe.

- The Chimú kingdom builds an impressive capital at Chan Chan in the Moche Valley of Peru. Basing their wealth on llamas and agricultural products, the kingdom begins a period of expansion around 1370, becoming the most powerful civilization in Peru before the rise of the Incas.

- The major city-state of Great Zimbabwe dominates southern Africa, founded by the Shona, one of the Bantu-speaking peoples who have come to the region. Its rulers largely control the trade in gold, slaves, and ivory between the inland regions and the Indian Ocean coast.

*DENOTES CIRCA DATE

1200*
(CONT'D)

- Khmer king Jayavarman VII builds the temple complex Angkor Thom in his capital city.

- Specialized agriculture has been established in various regions throughout Europe. Burgundy and Bordeaux specialize in wine, while the area around Toulouse in southern France focuses on cloth dye. Northern England is known for its sheep and wool, while northern Germany is known for its cattle.

- Known to the Muslims since the mid eighth century and in the West since the tenth century, when it arrived via Spain and Sicily, the Chinese invention of paper is coming into widespread use in Europe.

- Amsterdam, Holland, is founded as a small fishing village.

1200-1250*

- French poet Guillaume de Loris writes the first part of *Roman de la Rose* (Romance of the Rose).

1202-1241

- Much of the Baltic region comes under the control of the Danes during the reign of Valdemar II.

1202-1204

- The Fourth Crusade is led by Boniface of Montferrat and Venetian doge Enrico Dandolo.

1203

- Sumanguru, ruler of the Susu kingdom of Kaniaga (in the southwestern part of present-day Mali), plunders the Ghanian capital of Kumbi.

- Motivated by the wish of Pope Innocent III to reunite the Byzantine and Roman Churches and by the long-standing trade disputes between the Venetians and the Byzantines, Latin Christian knights attack Constantinople. Responding to an earlier request for help from Alexius, son of Isaac II Angelus, the Crusaders depose Alexius III and place Isaac and his son on the throne. Alexius IV governs as a puppet of the Crusaders.

1204

- Popular discontent in Constantinople leads to the deposition and murder of Alexius IV. Alexius V (Ducas) seizes the throne, and the Crusaders respond by sacking the city with such brutality that the Pope and the crusade movement are discredited. The Crusaders place Baldwin I (of Flanders) on the throne of the Latin kingdom that controls Constantinople until 1261. Boniface of Montferrat is made king of Thessalonica, and the Venetians gain control of important harbors and islands on their trade routes. Members of Byzantine royal families establish enclaves at Trebizond on the Black Sea, Epirus in northwest Greece, Nicaea in Anatolia, and elsewhere, but the Byzantine Empire never recovers from the sack of its capital.

1206

- Temujin, great-grandson of Mongol leader Kabul Khan, is proclaimed Genghis Khan (Emperor within the Seas), uniting the Mongol tribes into a single nation and forging them into a powerful fighting force.

*DENOTES CIRCA DATE

1206 (CONT'D)

- Muslim conquerors establish the Sultanate of Delhi in northwestern India, establishing a dynasty that rules until 1266. It depends on Hindu soldiers, civil servants, to maintain the kingdom.

1208-1209

- After the assassination in 1208 of Philip of Swabia, one of the claimants to the German throne, Pope Innocent crowns Otto IV Emperor of the Romans in 1209.

1209

- The Latin Christian Church launches an internal European Crusade in southern France against the Cathars, a Christian dualist sect.

- Francis of Assisi founds the brotherhood of friars that becomes known as the Franciscan order, which Pope Innocent III approves in 1210.

- In England some scholars migrate from Oxford to Cambridge, forming the basis for the University of Cambridge.

1211

- Led by Genghis Khan, the Mongols begin their invasion of the Chin state in northern China.

1212

- Frederick II, who has gained the support of Pope Innocent III, becomes king of Germany.

- At the Battle of Las Navas de Tolosa, the Christian kingdoms of Leon, Castile, Aragon, Navarre, and Portugal severely defeat the Almohad army, opening the way for the Christian conquest of southern Iberia.

1214

- Philip II Augustus of France and Frederick II of Germany defeat John of England and Emperor Otto IV at the Battle of Bouvines. Frederick becomes Emperor of the Romans (crowned 1220).

1215

- English barons meet with King John at Runnymede and force him to sign the Magna Carta (15 June), a feudal charter that limits the powers of the king and protects individual liberties.

- Pope Innocent III calls the Fourth Lateran Council, which sets out fundamental rules of Christian practice and belief.

1216

- The Cola empire of southern India begins to break up.

- On the death of John of England his nine-year-old son, Henry III, becomes king.

- Pope Innocent III approves the founding of the Dominican Order.

*DENOTES CIRCA DATE

1218
- The Fifth Crusade begins, with efforts concentrated on Egypt. It ends in 1221 after Crusaders fail to take Cairo.
- The University of Salamanca is founded.

1219
- Control of the Kamakura shogunate in Japan passes from the Minamoto family to the Hojo family.

1220
- Genghis Khan completes his conquest of Persia.

1221
- King Lalibela, of Ethiopia, who sponsored the building of eleven rock-hewn churches in Aksum, dies.

1223
- The Mongols defeat the Russian and Cuman forces at the Battle of the Kalka River in Southern Russia but then return to Asia rather than continuing the invasion.
- Philip II Augustus of France dies and is succeeded by his son Louis VIII.

1224
- Sumanguru conquers the Mandingo (or Mande) peoples of Kangaba (near the modern border of Mali and Guinea) and makes their kingdom part of his West African empire.

1226
- On the death of his father, Louis VIII, Louis IX (the Pious) becomes king of France and rules for forty-four years.

1227
- Genghis Khan dies. His kingdom is divided among his sons, with Ogodei, the eldest, as Great Khan, or overlord.

1228-1229
- Against the wishes of the pope, Emperor Frederick II launches the Sixth Crusade. Capturing Jerusalem, Bethlehem, and Nazareth, he is proclaimed king of Jerusalem.

1230
- The Mongols continue their conquest of Iran and Central Asia.
- Sundiata begins the expansion of the Malian Empire.

1231
- Mongol troops occupy Korea.

*DENOTES CIRCA DATE

1231
(CONT'D)

- Emperor Frederick II captures Sicily.

- Pope Gregory IX founds the papal Inquisition to deal with the continuing existence of heretical Christian sects, such as the Cathars and Waldenses, especially in southern France and northern Italy.

1234

- The Mongols annex the Chin empire of northern China.

1235

- Sundiata, Mandingo king of Kangaba, defeats Sumanguru at the Battle of Kirina (near the modern city of Koulikoro in Mali), re-establishing the independence of his kingdom and beginning the expansion of the powerful empire of Mali.

1237

- Mongol armies under Batu, grandson of Genghis Khan, renew their invasion of Russia, conquering the Volga Bulgars.

1240*

- The Mongols capture Moscow and force its princes to accept them as overlords.

- The Great Council of England begins to be called "Parliament."

1240

- Mongol troops take Kiev, ending their conquest of southern and central Russia. The western part of the Mongol Empire becomes known as the Golden Horde.

- Sundiata destroys Kumbi, former capital of Ghana, annexing Ghana and taking control of its gold-trade routes.

1241

- Mongol armies menace Eastern Europe, successfully invading Poland and Hungary and reaching the Adriatic Sea. Great Khan Ogodei dies, and his wife becomes regent for his son Guyuk.

1242

- The Mongol threat to Europe ends when Batu withdraws his troops to conquered Russian territory and establishes the capital of the western part of the empire at Sarai on the lower Volga.

1244

- Jerusalem is recaptured by the Saljuk Turks.

1245

- Pope Innocent IV sends Giovanni di Plano Carpini and Lawrence of Portugal on a mission to the Mongol court.

***DENOTES CIRCA DATE**

1248
- Louis IX (the Pious) of France leads the Seventh Crusade, which ends in 1250.
- Great Khan Guyuk dies. He is succeeded by his nephew Mongke.

1250*
- The city of Cahokia is in a decline that may have been triggered by factors such as climate changes, a breakdown of its economy, or internal and external strife. Though its society disappears, the political and religious influence continues.
- Christian laypeople and clergy in Italy begin the religious practice of flagellation. The practice spreads into Germany and the Low Countries, and flagellant brotherhoods are formed.

1250-1300*
- French poet Jean de Meun completes *Roman de la Rose* (Romance of the Rose).

1250
- On the death of Frederick II, Conrad IV becomes king of Germany.

1253
- The Venetians and the Genoese engage in ongoing naval warfare over trade rights in the eastern Mediterranean.

1254-1273
- The death of Conrad IV is followed by a long interregnum, during which many German princes struggle for power.

1255
- Sundiata dies after having extended borders of the Malian empire north to the Sahara, west to the Senegal River, south to the gold fields of Wangara, and east into present-day Sudan.

1258
- Mongol armies led by Hulegu, brother of Great Khan Mongke, take Baghdad. Hulegu founds the Ilkhanid dynasty to rule Persia as part of the vast Mongol empire.
- An English committee draws up the Provisions of Oxford, establishing a baronial veto over decisions made by the king. In 1261 Henry III reneges on his oath to support the provisions, leading to the outbreak of a civil war known as the Barons' War.

1259
- Great Khan Mongke dies while leading his army in China and is succeeded by his brother Kublai.

*DENOTES CIRCA DATE

1261

- The Latin kingdom of Constantinople is conquered by Michael VIII Palaeologus of Nicaea, a Byzantine aristocrat. The Byzantine rulers of Epirus and Thessaly refuse to acknowledge Michael as emperor, and separate Byzantine states continue to exist in Greece and Anatolia. Because Michael blinds and banishes John IV Lascaris, his coruler of Nicaea, Arsenius, the new patriarch of Constantinople, excommunicates the emperor.

- Having previously been self-governing, the people of Greenland and Iceland swear allegiance to the king of Norway, who has sought to unite all Norwegian Viking settlements under his reign.

1264

- Henry III is captured by his brother-in-law, Simon de Montfort, Earl of Leicester, at the Battle of Lewes (14 May). Simon forces Henry to renew his pledge to the reforms of 1258.

1265

- With the help of troops from the Welsh borderlands, Prince Edward (later Edward I) comes to the aid of his father, Henry III, defeating and killing Montfort at the Battle of Evesham (4 August).

- Byzantine emperor Michael VIII Palaeologus exiles Patriarch Arsenius of Constantinople, replacing him with Joseph. The empire splits into Arsenites (opponents of Michael and his pro-Latin policies) and Josephites (supporters of Michael).

1266

- Charles of Anjou, brother of Louis IX of France, defeats Manfred of Sicily at the Battle of Benevento and establishes himself as Charles I of Sicily.

1266-1273

- Thomas Aquinas writes his *Summae theologae* (Comprehensive Theology), a cornerstone of all subsequent Roman Catholic theology.

1267

- Roger Bacon describes gunpowder, marking its introduction to Europe, probably via Arabic sources.

1268

- Charles I of Sicily captures Conradin, his rival claimant to Sicily, and has him beheaded in Naples.

1269

- Peter of Maricourt (Peter the Pilgrim) describes magnetic polarity and other experiments with a "lodestone."

1270

- Louis IX of France and Edward I of England launch the Eighth—and final—Crusade. Louis dies in Tunis and is succeeded by his son Philip III (the Bold).

*Denotes Circa Date

1271
- The Eighth Crusade ends, having accomplished nothing.

- The Roman Christian Church canonizes Louis IX.

- Kublai Khan proclaims the Yuan dynasty in China, establishing his capital at Ta-Tu (present-day Beijing). He rules until 1294, promoting cultural life and religious tolerance while oppressing all opponents of Mongol rule.

- Marco Polo leaves Venice to travel to China.

1272
- Henry III dies. Called back from crusade, Edward I assumes the throne in 1274 and rules until 1307.

1273
- Rudolf of Habsburg becomes Rudolf I, king of Germany and Holy Roman Emperor, establishing the Habsburg dynasty.

1274
- Kublai Khan's fleet is virtually destroyed in an attempt to invade Japan.

- A delegation sent by Byzantine emperor Michael VIII Palaeologus to the Council of Lyon submits the Eastern Christian Church to the authority of the Pope, a diplomatic ploy to gain papal protection and avoid a repetition of the events of the Fourth Crusade. Because of violent opposition, leading to persecution and imprisonment of many Eastern Christians, the union of the two Churches never comes about.

1275*
- Moses of Leon writes his *Sefer ha-zohar* (Book of Splendor), the fundamental work of Jewish mysticism.

1275
- Marco Polo arrives at the court of Kublai Khan and lives in his domains for the next seventeen years.

1279
- Kublai Khan completes his conquest of the Sung kingdom in southern China, reunifying all of China under Mongol rule.

- The last king of the Indian Cola dynasty dies.

1281
- Mongol hopes of conquering Japan are dashed when a typhoon ("kamikaze") destroys Kublai Khan's great invasion fleet.

1281-1282
- Charles I of Sicily makes two attempts to wrest Albania from the Byzantines. His second invasion fails after a rebellion at home removes him from power. Defending his empire in the West prevents Emperor Michael VIII from protecting his eastern provinces from the Turks, and by Michael's death in 1282 they have advanced well into western Anatolia.

*DENOTES CIRCA DATE

1282
- Edward I of England leads an army into Wales to put down a second revolt led by Welsh prince Llywelyn ap Gruffudd. Llywelyn is killed, and his brother David is hanged, drawn, and quartered in 1283.

- Erik V (Glipping), the king of Denmark from 1259 to 1286, is forced to grant the nobles a constitution, which recognizes a national assembly and puts the king under its authority.

- Andronicus II becomes Byzantine emperor. Ruling until 1328, he repudiates the union between Eastern and Western Churches.

1285
- Philip IV (the Fair) succeeds his father, Philip III (the Bold), as king of France.

1289
- Pope Boniface VIII sends John of Monte Corvino on a mission to China.

1290
- Edward I expels the Jews from England.

1291
- The Crusader state of Acre is conquered by Mamluks, ending the presence of Latin military states in the eastern Mediterranean.

1292
- Supported by Edward I of England, John de Balliol becomes the successor to Alexander III (died 1286) after a long dispute over the Scottish throne.

- Marco Polo leaves China and reaches Venice three years later. Soon thereafter he is taken prisoner during a sea battle and is imprisoned in Genoa, where he begins dictating the story of his travels to a fellow prisoner.

1293
- Perhaps because of prolonged drought in the thirteenth century and conflicts with Navajo and Apache peoples, the Pueblo peoples abandon their cliff dwellings, moving southward and eastward and establishing new, large villages. Designs on the pottery of this so-called Regressive Pueblo period are naturalistic representations of animals and people rather than the geometric patterns of earlier periods.

- Turkish leader Othman (for whom the Ottoman Empire is named) emerges as the prince of a border principality in northeastern Anatolia and begins to seize Byzantine territory.

1294
- King John Balliol of Scotland is angered by Edward I's demand for help in a projected war against Germany and signs a treaty with France.

1295
- Edward I of England calls the Model Parliament, with the broadest representation to date, including clergy, knights, burgesses, and aristocrats as well as commoners representing shires, towns, and parishes.

*DENOTES CIRCA DATE

1296

- Edward I of England invades Scotland with around thirty thousand infantrymen and five thousand cavalry, destroying Berwick and massacring the inhabitants before defeating Scottish forces at the Battle of Dunbar and removing Balliol from the throne. The Scots are forced to acknowledge Edward as their king.

- The Serbs conquer western Macedonia and northern Albania, and in 1298 they force Byzantine emperor Andronicus II to acknowledge their sovereignty there.

1297

- Scottish nobleman William Wallace gathers an army and defeats the English at Stirling Bridge.

1298

- Edward I sends another army against the Scots, who are defeated at the Battle of Falkirk.

1300-1350*

- The Salado Indians build Casa Grande (Big House), a four-story unreinforced-clay fortress topped by an adobe watchtower in the Gila Valley of present-day Arizona. It is near the site of a village and irrigation system built by Hohokam Indians circa 300 B.C.E.–500 C.E.

1302

- Flemish burghers defeat an army of French knights at the Battle of Courtrai (Battle of the Golden Spurs).

- Philip IV (the Fair) of France calls the first Estates-General, which has members from the clergy, nobility, and common people.

1303

- Pope Boniface VIII founds the University of Rome.

- Pope Boniface VIII enters into a dispute with Philip IV (the Fair) of France, who has his agents kidnap the Pope. Boniface dies later this year.

1303-1307

- Byzantine emperor Andronicus I hires an army of Catalan mercenaries to fight the Turks, but after one successful engagement against them, the Catalans attack Constantinople.

1305*

- Florentine painter Giotto paints the frescoes for the Arena Chapel in Padua.

1305

- The English capture Wallace, who is found guilty of treason, hanged, drawn, and quartered.

1306

- Robert I the Bruce murders John Comyn, his rival for the Scottish throne (10 February), and is crowned king at Scone (25 March).

*DENOTES CIRCA DATE

1307
- Mansa Musa, the grandson or grandnephew of Sundiata, becomes the emperor of the Malian empire. He is renowned worldwide for his wealth, his devotion to Islam, and his patronage of the arts.
- John of Monte Corvino becomes the first archbishop of Beijing.
- Edward I of England dies and is succeeded by his son, Edward II.

1309
- Amid political factionalism in Italy, Pope Clement V moves the seat of the papacy from Rome to Avignon, France, where it remains until 1377.

1310
- English nobles force Edward II to accept the Lords Ordinances, reforms that require parliamentary consent to royal appointments, declarations of war, and the king's departure from the realm.

1311
- After failing to take Constantinople, the Catalans advance through Greece, conquer Athens, and create the Catalan Duchy of Athens and Thebes.

1314
- Robert I the Bruce defeats an English army at the Battle of Bannockburn.
- Philip IV (the Fair) of France dies and is succeeded by his son Louis X (the Stubborn).

1315
- A group of barons led by Thomas of Lancaster, a cousin of King Edward II, takes virtual control of the English government.

1316
- Louis X (the Stubborn) of France dies and is succeeded by an infant son, John I, who lives only a few days. The crown goes to Louis's brother Philip V (the Tall).

1317
- Mongol rule in Persia begins to collapse because of factional struggles among the Mongol ruling class, economic troubles, and the decline of the ruling family.

1320–1328
- Byzantine emperor Andronicus II disinherits his grandson Andronicus, who responds by starting a civil war that devastates much of the empire. Andronicus II is finally forced to yield the throne to Andronicus III, who rules until 1341.

1321
- Dante completes his *Commedia* (Divine Comedy).

*DENOTES CIRCA DATE

1322
- Forces loyal to Edward II defeat Thomas of Lancaster at Boroughbridge, Yorkshire. Edward has Lancaster beheaded and revokes the Lords Ordinances.
- Philip V (the Tall) of France dies and is succeeded by his brother Charles IV (the Fair).

1324
- Mansa Musa makes a pilgrimage to Mecca, stopping in Cairo with a retinue that is said to include one hundred camels, each carrying three hundred pounds of gold.

1325*
- Ibn Battutah leaves Tangiers for some thirty years of travels that provide the basis for his writings about Asia and Africa, major sources of information about those continents for Westerners.
- The Mexica (Aztecs) build their great capital city of Tenochtitlán on the site of present-day Mexico City.

1325
- Mansa Musa annexes the Songhai kingdom of Gao (in the western part of modern Mali), making it part of the empire of Mali.

1325-1327
- Queen Isabella of England, wife of Edward II and daughter of Philip IV of France, goes to France, where she conspires with her lover, the exiled English baron Roger Mortimer. In September 1326 they lead an invasion of England, depose Edward II, and have Isabella and Edward's fifteen-year-old son, Edward III, crowned king. Edward II dies in prison (September 1327), probably murdered. The reign of Edward III is marked by constant conflict with France.

1326
- Gunpowder cannons are mentioned for the first time in European records.

1327
- Exiled from Florence, Petrarch (Francesco Petrarca) goes to Avignon, France, where he meets the woman he addresses as "Laura" in his sonnets.

1328*
- After an unsuccessful military campaign in 1327, Edward III of England signs the Treaty of Northampton, recognizing Scottish independence. Edward's seven-year-old sister, Joanna, is married to Robert I the Bruce's four-year-old son, David.

1328
- Charles IV (the Fair) of France dies without issue and is succeeded by Philip VI, son of Charles of Valois and a nephew of Philip IV.

*Denotes Circa Date

1329
- Scottish king Robert I the Bruce dies and is succeeded by his son David II.

1330*
- The bubonic plague, or Black Death, begins to kill huge numbers of people in northeastern China. The epidemic is carried westward by traders, travelers, and nomadic peoples.

1330
- After a three-year regency during which England has been ruled by Roger Mortimer and Queen Isabella, Edward III overthrows their rule and has Mortimer executed.

1332*
- Mansa Musa, emperor of Mali, dies, having made the cities of Niano, Tombocktu, and Gao into important religious and cultural centers with mosques, libraries, and Muslim schools. He leaves his empire strong and prosperous, but by the end of the century quarrels over royal succession divide Mali and leave it vulnerable to invasion. Around this time Mali is the source of about two-thirds of the gold circulating in the Eastern Hemisphere.

1332
- Edward de Balliol, son of John de Balliol, invades Scotland. He is crowned king in September but is driven out of the country in December.

1333
- The English defeat a Scottish army at Halidon Hill and restore Edward de Balliol to the Scottish throne. David II flees to France.
- Richard of Wallingford describes his astronomical clock at the monastery of St. Albans. It shows the movement of stars, the sun, and planets, as well as striking hours on a bell.
- Emperor Go-Daigo of Japan successfully overthrows the Kamakura shogunate, but his subsequent actions provoke civil war.
- Togon-temür becomes the last Yuan (Mongol) emperor of China. During his reign his anti-Chinese policies result in frequent rebellions, and in 1368 he is forced to flee to the steppes of inner Asia, clearing the way for Ming dynasty rule of China (1368–1644).

1335
- The Sultanate of Delhi now dominates most of the Indian subcontinent.
- After the death of Il-Khan Abu Sa'id, the Mongol empire in Persia breaks into separate kingdoms ruled by Ilkhanid princes until 1353.

1336
- Ashikaga Takauji, who has proclaimed himself shogun, drives Emperor Go-Daigo of Japan from the capital and places Kogon on the throne, establishing the Ashikaga shogunate, under which Japanese feudalism enters its golden age. During the Ashikaga period, which lasts until 1568, aristocrats depend on armed retainers (samurai), who followed a strict code of conduct (bushido).

1337

• After losing all northwestern Anatolia to the Ottoman Turks, the Byzantines come to terms with the Ottomans and other Turkish emirs, a move that enables the Byzantines to hire Turkish soldiers to help them against European enemies such as the Italians, Serbs, and Bulgars.

• The French and the English start an intermittent struggle known as the "Hundred Years' War," which begins when Edward III of England, grandson of Philip IV, claims the French throne, which has gone to Philip IV's nephew Philip VI. Edward lands an army in Flanders.

1340

• The Christian forces of Alfonso XI of Castile and Alfonso IV of Portugal defeat Granadan Muslim forces at the Battle of Río Salado, retaining Castilian control over the Strait of Gibraltar and thwarting Muslim efforts to reclaim lost territory bordering the kingdom of Granada.

1341

• Petrarch (Francesco Petrarca) is named poet laureate of Rome.

• On the death of Andronicus III Palaeologus his minor son John V Palaeologus becomes Byzantine emperor, and civil war breaks out in the empire.

• In the wake of widespread resentment of English control over King Edward Balliol, David II returns from France and regains the Scottish throne.

1345

• The Ottoman Turks extend their conquest of Byzantine territory into Europe.

1346

• Bubonic plague reaches the Golden Horde, beginning the disintegration of Mongol rule in Russia.

• Stefan Dusan, king of Serbia since 1331, has himself crowned emperor of the Serbs and Greeks. He has already conquered much of coastal Albania and part of Greece, and by 1348 his empire includes all of northern Greece.

• In a major victory at the Battle of Crécy (26 August), English longbowmen and foot soldiers prove their superiority to French troops.

1347

• Bubonic plague reaches Constantinople and other parts of the Byzantine Empire.

• John Cantacuzenus, who has opposed the forces of John V Palaeologus in the Byzantine civil war, takes Constantinople and seizes the throne, reigning as John VI until 1354.

• After a long siege the English take Calais in France.

1348

• Bubonic plague reaches North Africa, mainland Italy, Spain, England, and France.

*DENOTES CIRCA DATE

1349
- Pope Clement VI condemns the religious practice of flagellation.
- Bubonic plague reaches Austria, Hungary, Switzerland, Germany, and the Low Countries.

1349-1351*
- Italian poet Giovanni Boccaccio writes *The Decameron*, set during the plague that ravaged Florence in 1348.

1350
- Bubonic plague reaches Scandinavia and the Baltic lands.
- Philip VI of France dies and is succeeded by his son John II (the Good).

1351
- Serbs led by Stefan Dusan lay siege to Thessalonica.

1354
- John V Palaeologus retakes Constantinople and forces the abdication of John VI Cantacuzenus as the Turks advance steadily on Byzantine territory.

1355
- Stefan Dusan is advancing on Constantinople when his sudden death puts an end to his efforts to expand the Serbian empire.

1356
- At the Battle of Poitiers (19 September) Edward the Black Prince, son of Edward III of England, defeats and captures King John II (the Good) of France.

1360
- The Treaties of Bretigny and Calais give Edward III full sovereignty over French lands he previously held as vassal to the king of France. In return, Edward renounces his claim to the French throne. John II of France is ransomed but remains in England, where he dies in 1364.

1364
- Charles V (the Wise) of France inherits the throne from his father, John II. Refusing to accept the provisions of peace agreements with England, he re-opens hostilities.

1369
- Chu Yuan-chang overthrows the Mongol Yuan dynasty of China and proclaims himself emperor Hung-wu, establishing his capital at Nanking and founding the Ming dynasty, which rules China until 1644.

1370
- On the orders of Charles V, the French begin building the fortress known as the Bastille in Paris.

*Denotes Circa Date

1371
- David II of Scotland dies and is succeeded by his cousin Robert II, the first Stuart king of Scotland.

1373
- The Turks force John V Palaeologus, who has unsuccessfully sought help in the West, to become their vassal.

1374
- John of Gaunt, Duke of Lancaster, strikes a bargain with Alice Perrers, influential mistress of the aging Edward III, and becomes virtual ruler of England. He and his supporters are opposed by a faction led by Edward the Black Prince, heir to his father's throne.

1375-1400*
- Englishman Geoffrey Chaucer writes his *Canterbury Tales*.

1376
- In the midst of revolutions backed by the Turks, the Genoese, and the Venetians, Byzantine emperor John V Palaeologus is deposed and succeeded by his son Andronicus IV.
- At the Good Parliament of 1376, supporters of Edward the Black Prince impeach some of John of Gaunt's supporters, the first parliamentary impeachment of government officials in English history. The death of Prince Edward on 8 June, however, robs Parliament of the ability to deal with John of Gaunt.

1378
- After Pope Gregory XI moves the papacy back to Rome in 1377, there begins a period known as the Great Western Schism (1378–1417), during which cardinals in Rome and Avignon each elect their own pope.
- Edward III of England dies and is succeeded by his grandson, ten-year-old Richard II, son of Edward the Black Prince. Until Richard comes of age in 1389, England is ruled by a council headed by John of Gaunt.
- After some twenty years of disputes between England and the papacy, John Wycliffe of Oxford begins a systematic attack on the doctrines of the Latin Christian Church. Though his actions do not lead to schism in the Church, he is considered a precursor of the Protestant Reformation.

1379
- Byzantine emperor John V Palaeologus regains his throne.

1380
- The death of Charles V of France halts the gradual reduction of English territory in France. He is succeeded by his eleven-year-old son, Charles VI, who reigns until 1422, largely a figurehead. France is controlled by prominent members of the nobility.
- John Wycliffe plans the first English translation of the Bible, which he carries out with the help of John Purvey and Nicholas of Hereford.
- Prince Dmitry of Moscow defeats the Mongols at the Battle of Kulikovo.

***Denotes Circa Date**

1381

- Protesting (among other things) the attempt of some landowners to return English peasants to the feudal system of servitude, which has been considerably weakened by the labor shortage that followed the plague, Wat Tyler starts the Peasants' Revolt, the first popular uprising in English history, leading a large group of Kentish laborers who capture the city of Canterbury and then go on to London. Richard II offers concessions but Tyler counters with more-radical demands, which included the confiscation of all Church lands. Tyler is wounded in fighting that breaks out during negotiations and then is captured and beheaded on the orders of the lord mayor of London. After Tyler's death the rebellion ends quickly.

1382

- Mongol troops recapture and plunder Moscow.

1390

- Robert II of Scotland dies and is succeeded by his son John, who rules as Robert III.

1391

- Manuel II, second son of John V Palaeologus, ascends the throne of a Byzantine Empire that for much of his reign is reduced to the cities of Thessalonica and Constantinople and Morea.

1392

- The Yi dynasty is established in Korea, where it rules until 1910.

1399

- Henry Bolingbroke—son of the late John of Gaunt, Duke of Lancaster, and, like Richard, a grandson of Edward III—deposes Richard II and rules England as Henry IV, first king of the House of Lancaster. During his reign, which lasts until 1413, Henry faces a series of internal rebellions, as well as Scottish and French invasion attempts.

1400*

- The Incan civilization begins a period of expansion that leads to its domination of the Andean region.

1405-1433

- Cheng Ho (Zheng He) leads a fleet of Chinese treasure ships to lands in and around the Indian Ocean, reaching Indonesia, India, East Africa, and many islands.

1413

- On the death of Henry IV, his son Henry V becomes king of England.

1413-1414

- At the Disputation of Tortosa between Spanish Jews and Christians, Joseph Albo defends Judaism.

*Denotes Circa Date

1415
- Taking advantage of civil war over the succession to the French throne, Henry V renews English claims to the crown of France and wins a major victory at the Battle of Agincourt on 25 October, greatly enhancing the standing of England as a major European power.

1417-1420
- After his success at Agincourt, Henry V of England forms an alliance with the Burgundian faction and conquers all of northern France. The Treaty of Troyes (1420) recognizes Henry as the regent and heir apparent to the mad king Charles VI (deposing the dauphin, later Charles VII) and arranges Henry's marriage to Charles VI's daughter Catherine.

1420
- The Ming dynasty of China moves its capital from Nanking to Beijing, where it has constructed the enormous palace and temple complex known as the Forbidden City.

1422
- Sultan Murad II of the Ottoman Empire lays siege to Constantinople and invades Greece.
- Henry V of England dies suddenly and is soon followed by Charles VI of France. The English acclaim Henry's nine-month-old son, Henry VI, king of England and France, while Charles's son Charles VII asserts his claim to the French throne, and fighting in France continues.

1423
- The Byzantines hand over Thessalonica to the Venetians.

1424
- On the death of the king of Siam, his two sons compete for the throne by fighting to the death on elephants.

1425
- The Portuguese begin a series of voyages to explore the west coast of Africa.
- Spanish Jew Joseph Albo completes his *Sefer ha-'iqqarim* (Book of Principles), in which he set out the dogmas and beliefs that are valid for both Judaism and other religions. The book is published in 1485.
- Byzantine emperor Manuel II Palaeologus dies and is succeeded by his son John VIII.

1429
- Joan of Arc leads French troops to end the English siege of Orléans and make possible the coronation of Charles VII at Reims.

1430
- Ottoman sultan Murad II captures Thessalonica.

*DENOTES CIRCA DATE

1431
- Having captured Joan of Arc, the English try her for witchcraft and burn her at the stake in Rouen. They then crown Henry VI king of France at Paris.

1434
- The Medici family rises to power in Italy, ruling Florence for most of the period from 1434 to 1737 (except for intervals in 1494–1512 and 1527–1530).

1434–1471
- Under Pachacuti the Incas greatly expand their territory.

1436
- The forces of French king Charles VII retake Paris from the English.

1439
- To gain much-needed support from the West, Byzantine emperor John VIII Palaeologus accepts a union of the Eastern and Western Christian Churches, creating opposition at home that serves to negate the value of Western help.

1444
- A Christian army sent to aid the Byzantines is decisively defeated by the Turks at the Battle of Varna.

1445–1456
- Johannes Gutenberg invents a method of printing with movable type. The books from his press include the *Constance Mass Book* (1450) and the first printed Bible (1456).
- The Incas build the great city of Machu Picchu in Peru. It is inhabited for about a century and then abandoned.
- Europeans begin trading in African slaves.

1448
- Constantine XI Palaeologus inherits the throne from his brother. He is the last Byzantine emperor.
- The Hungarians are defeated by Ottoman sultan Murad II at the Battle of Kosovo.

1448–1453
- The forces of Charles VII gradually conquer all English holdings in France except Calais, bringing an end to the Hundred Years' War. (Calais is ceded to the French in 1558.)

1450*
- The East African kingdoms of Kilwa and Zimbabwe are in decline.

1453
- Muhammad II (the Conqueror) captures Constantinople for the Ottoman Empire, bringing to an end the one-thousand-year-old Byzantine Empire.

*DENOTES CIRCA DATE

1455
- The thirty-year Wars of the Roses begin in England between supporters of two rival claimants to the throne. The Lancastrians, who wear red roses, support King Henry VI. The Yorkists, who wear white roses, back Richard, Duke of York, who—as a descendent of Edward III's third son, Lionel, Duke of Clarence—has a better claim, according to the rules of primogeniture, than Henry, who is descended from John of Gaunt, Duke of Lancaster, Edward's fourth son.

1460
- Yorkist forces led by Richard Neville, Duke of Warwick, defeat the Lancastrians at the Battle of Northampton (10 July) and capture Henry VI, who comes to a compromise with Richard, Duke of York, by which Richard will succeed to the English throne on Henry's death. Angry that her son, Prince Edward, is thus disinherited, Henry's queen, Margaret of Anjou, gathers her own forces, who kill York at Wakefield in December.

1461
- York's son and heir, Edward, Duke of York, takes London on 26 February and is proclaimed King Edward IV of England on 4 March. Henry, Margaret, and their son flee to Scotland.
- Charles VI of France dies and is succeeded by his son Louis XI.

1462
- Ivan III (the Great) of Moscow becomes the first sovereign to rule a unified Russian nation. He reigns until 1505.

1469
- The Wars of the Roses resume in England. Edward IV's brother George, Duke of Clarence, and Edward's former ally Richard Neville, Duke of Warwick, rise up against the king, defeating his supporters at Edgecote and taking the king prisoner.

1470
- After Edward IV regains control of England, Warwick and Clarence flee to France, where they ally themselves with Louis XI and Henry VI's wife, Margaret of Anjou. Returning to England in September, they depose Edward IV and return Henry VI to the throne.

1471
- Having fled to the Netherlands and gained the support of the Burgundians, Edward IV returns to England and defeats the Lancastrians. On 4 May Margaret of Anjou is captured and Henry VI's son Edward is killed. Henry VI is murdered in the Tower of London on 21 May, and Edward IV resumes the English throne.

1476
- Under the patronage of Edward IV, William Caxton sets up the first English printing press at Westminister. Among the roughly one hundred books he prints over the next fifteen years are Geoffrey Chaucer's *Canterbury Tales* (1477) and Sir Thomas Malory's *Morte Darthur* (1485).

*DENOTES CIRCA DATE

1478

- Pope Sixtus IV authorizes the Spanish Inquisition to discover, and reform or punish, Christians who hold heretical or unorthodox beliefs, including converts to Christianity from Judaism or Islam who are suspected of retaining their prior beliefs and practicing those religions in secret.

1479

- Queen Isabella, wife of King Ferdinand of Aragon, inherits the throne of Castile, leading to the union of the two Spanish kingdoms under their joint monarchy.

1480

- Ivan III (the Great) repels the last Mongol advance on Moscow, ending Mongol power in Russia.

1483

- Tomás de Torquemada becomes Grand Inquisitor for the Spanish kingdoms of Castile, León, Aragon, Catalonia, Valencia, and Majorca. By 1498 he has had some two thousand "heretics" burned at the stake.

- On the death of Edward IV of England on 9 April, his twelve-year-old son, Edward V, becomes king, with his father's brother Richard, Duke of Gloucester, serving as lord protector. In June, Richard usurps the throne and is proclaimed Richard III.

- Louis XI of France dies and is succeeded by his son, Charles VIII.

- Martin Luther, the founder of the Protestant Reformation, is born in the German state of Saxony.

1485

- In England, the Wars of the Roses begin anew as Yorkists angry with Richard III turn to the Lancastrian claimant, Henry Tudor, Earl of Richmond, whose forces defeat and kill Richard III at the Battle of Bosworth Field on 22 August. The victor ascends the throne as Henry VII.

1486

- Henry VII of England unites the Houses of York and Lancaster by marrying Edward IV's daughter Elizabeth of York.

1491-1492

- Michelangelo sculpts two of his earliest works, *Madonna of the Stairs* and *Battle of the Centaurs*.

1492

- The Muslim kingdom of Granada falls to Spanish Christian forces, ending Muslim political rule in the Iberian peninsula and setting the stage for the Christianization of premodern Spain and Portugal.

- Seeking a westward route to Asia for the Spanish rulers Ferdinand and Isabella, Christopher Columbus discovers the Americas, reaching the Bahamas and Cuba.

*DENOTES CIRCA DATE

1493
- Muhammad I Askia seizes the throne of the Songhai empire of West Africa, greatly expanding its territory during his twenty-five-year reign.

1494-1496
- Charles VIII of France conquers Naples, claiming he has inherited it through his father, but the Holy League (Emperor Maximilian I, Pope Alexander VI, Spain, Venice, Milan, and England) force him to withdraw.

1495
- At the Imperial Diet at Worms, Emperor Maximilian I proclaims "perpetual peace."

1495-1497
- Leonardo da Vinci paints *The Last Supper*.

1497-1499
- Looking for a sea route to India, Portuguese explorer Vasco da Gama commands an expedition around the Cape of Africa into the Indian Ocean. He reaches the southwestern coast of India in May 1498 before starting back to Portugal.

1498
- Charles VIII of France dies while planning another expedition to Italy and is succeeded by his cousin Louis XII, son of Charles, Duke of Orléans.

1500
- Portuguese mariner Gaspar de Corte Real explores the east coast of Greenland and the Labrador peninsula.

*Denotes Circa Date

CHAPTER TWO

GEOGRAPHY

by MUNIR A. SHAIKH

CONTENTS

CHRONOLOGY
66

OVERVIEW
69

TOPICS IN GEOGRAPHY

The Geography of
Muslim Lands. 70

The Legacy of
Near Eastern Science 71

*Why Muslims
Study Geography* 72

**Muslim Geographical
Studies**. 72

Defining Geography 74

**The Technology
of Geography** 76

*Sources of Geographical
Information* 76

**Topography
and Climate**. 78

**SIGNIFICANT
PEOPLE**

Abu Rayhan al-Biruni 79

Abu Abdullah al-Idrisi 79

**DOCUMENTARY
SOURCES**

80

Sidebars and tables are listed in italics.

632

- The death of the Prophet Muhammad signals the completion of his mission and the end of the revelation of the Qur'an. Many verses of this divine scripture convey geographical, astronomical, and cosmological ideas on which the Islamic geographical tradition is partly established.

637

- Under the leadership of the second khalifah (caliph) Umar ibn al-Khattab, Muslims defeat the Sasanid Persians in battle.

638

- Muslims gain control of Jerusalem and conquer Syria from the Byzantines, expanding their rule.

661

- The founding of the Umayyad dynasty marks the creation of a centralized empire based in Damascus. Muslim scholarship in Qur'anic studies, *hadith* (traditions and sayings of the Prophet Muhammad), Arabic grammar and linguistics, and law is initiated. The Umayyads foster translations of some Greek and Syriac texts.

- Muslims have continued to conquer and settle in the Fertile Crescent, central Asia, and North Africa during the late seventh and early eighth centuries under the Umayyad khalifahs, intermingling with local inhabitants. By 711 Muslim armies have reached Spain in the West and the Sind in the East, expanding the empire and encompassing many cultural groups.

750

- The Abbasids lead a revolt against the Umayyads and acquire the khilafah (caliphate).

763

- After moving their capital to the newly founded city of Baghdad, the Abbasids patronize literary and scientific endeavors in keeping with imperial court culture.

786-809

- During his reign the famous Abbasid khalifah Harun al-Rashid promotes learning, poetry, and high culture, making Baghdad an important meeting place for scholars, merchants, and emissaries from throughout the Eastern Hemisphere.

830

- Abbasid khalifah al-Ma'mun establishes the Bayt al-Hikmah (House of Wisdom) in Baghdad, which functions as a scientific academy and translation center, where Greek, Persian, and Indian works are rendered into Arabic. Ptolemy's geographical works are among the sources translated.

848

- Abbasid postmaster Ibn Khurdadhbih writes *Kitab al-Masalik wa al-Mamalik* (Book of the Routes and Kingdoms), describing the main trade routes in different parts of the empire, as well as China, Japan, and Korea.

* DENOTES CIRCA DATE

860*
- Al-Farghani, a noted astronomer and civil engineer working in the Abbasid administration, writes *Ikhtiyar al-Majisti* (selections from the *Almagest*), a translation and commentary on Ptolemy's well-known astronomical and mathematical work. Al-Farghani also produces a book on the construction of sundials, and other works.

873
- Abu al-Husayn Muslim dies three years after Muhammad Ibn Ismail al-Bukhari. Both men gathered authentic hadith of the Prophet, including those encouraging travel for the sake of knowledge. Their collections are central to the Muslim scholarly tradition.

929
- Al-Battani dies. Perhaps the greatest astronomer of the medieval era, he revised and updated many of Ptolemy's calculations and theories about the earth and its relationship to heavenly bodies.

969
- The Fatimids establish control in North Africa, found Cairo as an independent khalifal capital, and promote regional astronomical and geographical study.

985
- Abu Abdullah al-Muqaddasi writes *Ahsan al-Taqasim fi Ma'rifat al-Aqalim* (The Best Divisions for the Knowledge of the Climes), which includes maps of fourteen regions within the Islamic empire.

998
- Mahmud of Ghazna becomes a major local ruler in Afghanistan and begins to extend Muslim rule to parts of India, paving the way for Muslim geographers and travelers such as al-Biruni to study eastern lands.

1030*
- Al-Biruni writes *Tahqiq al-Hind* (Facts about India), an important work of regional geography and ethnology based on his travels in India.

1055
- The Saljuk Turk Tughrul Beg seizes control of Baghdad and is given the title of sultan by the khalifah. In exchange for support from the ulama' (religious leaders), the Saljuks subsequently establish the madrasah, a college for religious studies, and patronize scientific learning.

1085
- The city of Toledo, a major scientific center in Muslim Spain, falls into the hands of the Christian king Alfonso VI of Castile. Beginning in the twelfth century, scientists from England, Germany, Italy, France, and other parts of Europe flock to Toledo to participate in the translation of many Arabic scientific works into Latin.

* DENOTES CIRCA DATE

1095

- The First Crusade is launched, bringing Christian knights, merchants, officials, and travelers from western Europe in greater contact with Muslim civilization and scientific activities for several centuries.

1138

- King Roger II of Sicily employs the Muslim geographer al-Idrisi to develop various maps and representations of the known world.

1147

- The Berber Almoravid dynasty is displaced by that of the Almohads. Both dynasties provide some unity and stability for Muslim civilization in North Africa and Spain in the face of increasing pressure from Christian states in northern Spain.

1258

- The Mongols of central Asia sweep through Iran and Iraq, sacking the Abbasid capital at Baghdad. The Mongols subsequently assimilate to Persian Islamic culture and patronize learning and science in the eastern Islamic lands.

1274

- Nasir al-Din al-Tusi dies. A prolific writer, he prepared critical commentaries on Greek works and wrote new works in Persian, such as the *Zij-i Ilkhani* (The Ilkhanid Tables) for computing the positions of the planets. He developed a new theory of linear motion based on the sum of two circular motions, known as the Tusi Couple, a major breakthrough in explaining elliptical orbits.

1293

- Othman emerges as the ruler of a border principality in northeastern Anatolia and begins to seize Byzantine territory. After his death in 1326, his successors, the Ottoman Turks, expand Turkish rule in Anatolia, the Middle East, and the Balkans.

1369-1405

- During his rule, Timur (Tamerlane), a fierce warrior who devastated central and western Asia, brought scholars to his court in Samarkand and patronized scientific endeavors.

1420*

- Timur's grandson Ulugh Beg builds a famous observatory in Samarkand.

1453

- The Ottoman Turks capture Constantinople, which they call Istanbul. The city becomes a prosperous, advanced center for commerce and learning. Turkish geographical scholarship and cartography begins.

1487

- Bartolomeo Diaz rounds the Cape of Good Hope. He is followed in 1497–1498 by Vasco da Gama, with the help of Arab seafarer Ibn Majid. Da Gama's sea route to India gives Europeans easier access to Asia than the old overland trade routes, increasing their wealth and power.

* DENOTES CIRCA DATE

OVERVIEW

Study of the Earth and Its Inhabitants. Geography is the study of the earth as the home of humankind. The discipline encompasses the realms of nature and culture and the relationship between the two. Consequently, the understanding of ecological, biophysical, socioeconomic, and political processes may all be considered components of geographical analysis. The Muslim geographical tradition, which spans fourteen centuries, embraces these same concerns and views the study of geography as an integral part of human life and activity on earth.

Impetus for Learning. Following the Muslim conquests in the Near East during the late seventh and early eighth centuries, the scientific knowledge of the ancient world passed into the nascent Islamic civilization. Muslim and non-Muslim scientists living in the lands of Islam inherited a significant body of scientific literature from the Greeks, Persians, Indians, and Chinese. Taking seriously the encouragement in the Qur'an that they practice inquiry, critical thinking, and reflection on the natural and man-made world, Muslim investigators took the materials at hand as a starting point for further development. Their aims were to advance knowledge for its own sake and to gain a better understanding of the Muslims' place in the world, as a community of believers and as members of the larger human family.

Pre-Renaissance Men. Unlike modern scholars, who often assign distinct boundaries to academic disciplines, premodern science and inquiry spanned a range of disciplines. From Aristotle to Galen to Ibn Rushd, many a scholar of politics or religion was equally skilled as a physician, a mathematician, and a philosopher. Inherently aware that human, cultural, and physical geographies were an interrelated totality rather than separate subdisciplines, medieval Muslim geographers were able to explore the full range of geographical inquiry. This approach has its roots in a holistic view of the world in which human existence is tied to the natural environment and to spiritual and metaphysical concepts.

Advances in Science. The scientists who helped create a new Islamic civilization in the Near East and beyond worked diligently to produce new knowledge and develop new instruments and techniques to advance understanding. More than mere transmitters of ancient knowledge (as respected as it was), these scientists engaged in previously unperformed empirical studies and traveled widely within the expanded boundaries of a large empire that shared a common Islamic culture, debating among each other and writing for a literate audience that included rulers, administrators, educated elites, and merchants. Scholars constantly invented new devices—such as astrolabes, compasses, and observatories—and devised new concepts in sophisticated theoretical treatises.

The Modern World. The bulk of medieval and premodern learning in the sciences was produced by scholars in Muslim lands, and the steady incorporation of this knowledge in European learned circles, beginning in the late Middle Ages, helped western European nations become prominent and powerful participants in Eastern Hemisphere trade and politics. The discovery of the "New World" was a direct result of European exposure to Muslim theories about the sphericity and circumference of the Earth. The subsequent expansion of European rule in the East and the West set the stage for the rise of modern nation-states following the Age of Imperialism.

TOPICS IN GEOGRAPHY

THE GEOGRAPHY OF MUSLIM LANDS

Dar al-Islam. From the earliest period the Dar al-Islam (abode of Islam) has encompassed a diverse territory. From the rocky valley of Makkah (Mecca) and the oases of the Arabian Hijaz and the lava fields of Madinah (Medina), where the first Muslim communities arose, to the steppes of Uzbekistan and the tropics of Singapore and the jungles of Africa, where Islam spread in the course of centuries, it is impossible to associate a single climate, terrain, or mode of life with Islam. Contrary to the popular image of nomads on camels sailing across a yellow, endless desert, Islam has primarily been an urban phenomenon, though even that general view has varied depending on location. Furthermore, local weather patterns, land forms, and available building materials have shaped Muslim life. For example, the mud-brick masjids (mosques) found in Djenne, Mali, are quite different from those built on stilts in Burma and other monsoon areas.

Origins. While Islam does not have a single geographic milieu, it does have a single geographic origin. Islam springs from the same region as its sister faiths, Judaism and Christianity. Islam has had a long-standing association with the Near East, both as a faith tradition that believers identify with Adam and most of the biblical prophets and as a religious community established under the leadership of the Prophet Muhammad from the year 610 onward.

Successors. Following the death of the Prophet in 632, after a twenty-three-year mission during which the majority of the inhabitants of the Arabian peninsula embraced Islam, the khalifahs (caliphs) who succeeded him presided over the expansion of Muslim territory. Muslim armies defeated Byzantine and Persian forces and settled in newly conquered territories to the north, intermingling with local inhabitants. The Umayyad dynasty brought Iberia, North Africa, the Middle East, Transoxiana, and the western edge of the Indian subcontinent into the fold of Dar al-Islam. The Abbasids displaced the Umayyads in 750 and inherited the empire. During the early part of their reign, they directed their energies to preserving existing borders with Europe, Central Asia, southern Africa, China, and India, and turned inward to develop a high culture and rich Islamic civilization that could sustain itself. In the tenth century, the Abbasids lost centralized control of the empire, and the Saljuk Turks from Central Asia began ruling on their behalf in Persia, Iraq, Syria, and Arabia, and wrested the lands of Anatolia from the Byzantines. In the west the Fatimids and Almoravids ruled North Africa, while in the east, the Ghaznavids of Afghanistan began expanding the empire into India. Beginning in the late eleventh century, the Muslims began facing serious challenges on their frontiers, resulting in some contraction of Muslim lands. Crusaders attempted to capture the Holy Land in a series of Holy Wars between 1096 and 1270. Muslim rulers in Iberia were gradually defeated by their Christian rivals to the north and left with only the kingdom of Granada in the south after 1248, and during the same century the Mongols, who eventually adopted Islam, devastated much of the eastern Muslim lands, bringing an end to the Abbasid khilafah (caliphate) in 1258. In the sixteenth century the lands of Islam expanded once again. The Ottomans extended their rule into the Balkans, Greece, and parts of eastern Europe. At the same time, the Mughals extended Islamic rule southward in India.

Expansion through Trade. From the thirteenth century onward, Islam was introduced in southeast Asia (Malaysia, Indonesia) by Muslim merchants from Yemen, the Persian Gulf, and India, who were involved in long-distance trade in the Indian Ocean. Small colonies of Muslim merchants gave rise to regional Muslim populations comprising immigrants and indigenous Muslims, with a significant Muslim presence developing by the early 1500s. In northwestern and southwestern China, the Mongols encouraged Muslim settlers, who assimilated to Chinese culture and formed a nucleus around which a Chinese Muslim community grew. Likewise in sub-Saharan Africa, Islam was spread by the migration of Muslim merchants, scholars, and immigrants. Local rulers sometimes adopted Islam and provided momentum for the Islamization of African culture. Ghana in the eleventh century and Mali in the thirteenth through sixteenth centuries were strong Muslim states. Subsequent empires, with their trade networks and scholarly connections to Arab Muslim lands, expanded the practice of Islam in west and central Africa.

Muslims in Europe and America. The spread of Islam did not stop after 1500. Increasing trade and diplomatic relations between Muslims and Europeans, especially following

Ibn Hawqal's tenth-century map of western Asia and the eastern Mediterranean (Suleymaniye Library, Istanbul)

Napoleon's expedition in Egypt (1798–1801), led to the establishment of small Muslim student and professional communities in European countries. In the nineteenth century Muslim refugees and immigrants formed communities in the United States, France, England, and other European states. Following the world wars and the decolonization of Muslim lands in the early twentieth century, Muslim communities in western countries increased through further immigration and the birth of Muslim citizens in these countries. Conversion to Islam by westerners has also contributed to the growth and participation of Muslim communities in the West. Advances in transportation, increased communications, and global economic opportunities have stimulated Muslim settlement in countries as diverse as Japan, the Netherlands, and Argentina. Islam is practiced in virtually every country of the world.

Sources:
Marshall Hodgson, *The Venture of Islam*, 3 volumes (Chicago: University of Chicago Press, 1977).

Ira Lapidus, *A History of Islamic Societies* (Cambridge & New York: Cambridge University Press, 1988).

Francis Robinson, *Atlas of the Islamic World since 1500* (New York: Facts On File, 1982).

Roelof Roolvink, with Saleh A. el Ali, Hussain Mones, and Mohd Salim, *Historical Atlas of the Muslim Peoples* (Amsterdam: Djambatan, 1957).

THE LEGACY OF NEAR EASTERN SCIENCE

Legacy. The Muslim conquest of the Near East, North Africa, Iberia, and parts of South Asia in the late seventh and early eighth centuries established a new political and spiritual universe within a single century after the death of the prophet Muhammad. Early Muslims from Arabia and converts to Islam living in the newly conquered territories existed in close proximity to long-standing Christian, Jewish, and Zoroastrian communities. These groups maintained the traditions, culture, and scientific knowledge cultivated in the Near East over the preceding centuries under the aegis of Greek, Roman, Byzantine, Arab, and Persian rule. Early Muslim scholars and scientists—and their counterparts within the other religious communities—were heirs to the wisdom of the ancients. Natural curiosity, a lack of restrictive parochialism, and religious inducements toward the acquisition of knowledge—such as the famous hadith "Seek knowledge even unto China"—propelled Muslim scholars who were interested in the sciences.

Disciplines of Knowledge. Having emerged as a distinct religious group within the rich matrix of Near Eastern civilization, the Muslims diversified their interests, some elab-

WHY MUSLIMS STUDY GEOGRAPHY

For Muslims, living a righteous and productive life in this world is a means to achieving reward and happiness in the afterlife. A variety of impulses spurred Muslims to study geography and make sense of the world, including:

Qur'anic Injunctions: Verses such as "And He [God] has set up on the earth mountains standing firm lest it should shake with you; and rivers and roads; that you may guide yourselves, and marks and signposts; and by the stars men guide themselves" (16:14–16) encouraged Muslims to expand their horizons.

Daily Worship: Muslims pray at five different times during the course of the day and night. Determining times for prayer in different parts of the empire required accurate astronomical observations and measurements of distances between locations.

The Hajj (Pilgrimage): Each year during Dhu al-Hijja (month of the pilgramage) in the Islamic lunar calendar, Muslims from all over the world perform a pilgrimage to Makkah. In medieval times, the journey took months or years, and routes to Makkah from distant places had to be determined, provisioned, and protected.

The Search for Knowledge: Muslim scholars and scientists had a natural inquisitiveness and empirical minds. They emphasized direct observation and believed that knowledge was a treasure that could be found anywhere.

Commerce: Engaging in a productive livelihood and interaction with fellow human beings was an important part of an Islamic lifestyle. Merchants traveled far, seeking new opportunities, and consulted each other for useful geographical and maritime information.

The Ummah (community of the Prophet): Regardless of their own origins, Muslims view themselves as part of a global community of believers. A desire to meet fellow Muslims in other parts of the world has existed from the earliest times, in order to strengthen their sense of brotherhood.

orating religious doctrine, others fleshing out a legal framework for adjudicating personal and communal matters, and still others investigating the natural world and its phenomena. Of course, individual scholars often expressed interest in and excelled in several of these fields simultaneously. In almost all cases, the starting point for each endeavor was an assessment of existing knowledge and a desire to contribute to its advancement. The Muslims, especially after the establishment of the Abbasid khilafah in 750, accelerated their efforts, with royal support, to bring to light Greek, Persian, and Indian scholarship through translations of texts into Arabic. The Persian influence is mainly identified with pre-Islamic activity at Jundi-Shapur, a great center of learning and research. Several works were translated into Arabic, such as *A'in-nama*

(Book of Customs), which combined astronomical information with geographical information and were related to the limits and divisions of the Sasanian empire of Persia. The Persian influence on Arab thought is mainly evidenced in maritime literature and cartography. The Indian influence came through translations of the Sanskrit astronomical treatise *Surya-siddhanta* during al-Mansur's reign (754–775). Other Indian works that were translated include the *Aryabhatiya* (with astronomical calculations) and the *Khandakhadyaka* (on lunar and solar eclipses and planetary alignments), both of which belong to the Gupta period (fourth-seventh centuries). Indian astronomy had a greater impact than Indian geography on Arab thought. Most important, many Greek/Syriac works in various fields were translated into Arabic and other languages used within Muslim civilization, serving as the baseline for subsequent scholarship. Works by Greek thinkers such as Aristotle in philosophy, Diascorides in botany, Galen in medicine, and Ptolemy in astronomy and geography became available to early Muslim thinkers and scientists. Early Muslim geographical writing was particularly indebted to the second century Alexandrian Ptolemy, whose *Geography* was translated several times in the Abbasid period alone. Ptolemy's *Almagest* and *Apparitions of Fixed Stars* were also influential. The well-known Arab scholar al-Kindi (died 873) is credited with translating such works; his geography was titled *Rasm al-Rub al-Ma'mur* (Description of the Habitable Quarter). Ptolemy developed Hipparchus's idea that a map should be based on points of which the latitude and longitude are known. His geography includes sections on the latitudes and longitudes of roughly eight thousand places, the distance measured in terms of walking/marching time.

Sources:
Nafis Ahmad, *Muslim Contribution to Geography* (Lahore: Sh. Muhammad Ashraf, 1972).

S. Maqbul Ahmad, "Djughrafiya," in *Encyclopedia of Islam*, new edition, CD-ROM (Leiden: Brill, 1999).

MUSLIM GEOGRAPHICAL STUDIES

Early Writings. Early Arabic/Muslim writings, like those of the predecessor civilizations, tended to include many geographical myths and fantastic narratives or notions. One interesting conception, perhaps purely didactic in intent, was the idea that the known inhabited land mass resembled a great bird. The head was China, the right wing India, the left wing al-Khazar, the chest Syria, Iraq, and Arabia, and the tail North Africa. With vast lands stretched before them, Muslims wanted to learn about the unknown, a desire that led to the production of *aja'ib* literature, which recounted the wonders and strange creatures and plants of far-away lands. One such work is *Kitab al-Ajnas ala Mithal al-Ghareeb* (Book of Species Which Show Peculiar Characteristics) by Nadar ibn Shima'il (born 740). The great literateur al-Jahiz (died 868) wrote *Kitab al-Amsar wa Aja'ib al-Buldan* (Book of Cities and Marvels of Countries).

Practical Motives. At the same time, pragmatic considerations and a penchant for accuracy set in. Muslims

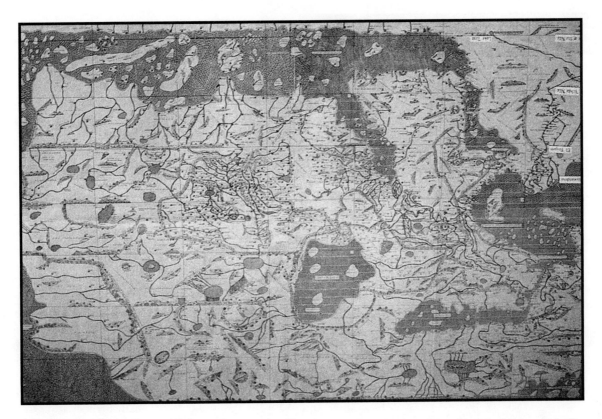

Al-Idrisi's twelfth-century map of the Mediterranean, northern Africa, and southwestern Asia (Bodleian Library, Oxford)

needed to determine the direction of Makkah from various locations for the performance of prayers and to fix the times for the five daily prayers, which varied according to latitude. They also needed an understanding of terrain, routes, and locales for provisioning of animals in order to plan for the annual pilgrimage to Makkah, as well as to execute the day-to-day business of the empire. The knowledge of geography, distance, and the characteristics of different climes also helped them to anticipate conditions for fasting during Ramadan.

Foundations. The well-known mathematician Muhammad ibn Musa al-Khawarizmi is said to have laid the foundations for Arabic geographical science in the ninth century. Working at the Bayt al-Hikmah (House of Wisdom) established in 830 by Khalifah al-Ma'mun in Baghdad, al-Khawarizmi prepared a book titled *Kitab Surat al-Ard* (Book of the Image of the World). He was followed closely by al-Kindi (died 873) and Ahmad al-Sarakhsi (died 899) who wrote what may be the first Arabic work titled *Kitab al-Masalik wa al-Mamalik* (Book of Routes and Kingdoms). Another mid-ninth-century author of this kind of book was Ibn Khurdadhbih, an Abbasid postmaster well known for his thorough work, written in 848, which includes not only information on the Muslim world but also descriptions of China, Japan, and Korea. Around this time, Ahmad al-Ya'qubi (died 897), sometimes called the "father of Muslim geography," wrote a compendium titled *Kitab al-Buldan* (Book of Countries), which provided sig-

nificant details of various countries or regions and their inhabitants. During this early period there were three main strands of geographical writing: human geography, administrative geography, and the geography of individual countries. These studies were bolstered by astronomical and mathematical data as astronomical and mathematical works, like those of geography, gained their own space in the body of scientific knowledge. The *surat al-ard* works include the Greek notion of climes or zones, in addition to Islamic cosmological diagrams and maps, and they locate the position of the earth in the heavens, a process related to *ilm al-hay'a* (knowledge of the structure of the universe), involving the hierarchical order of the spheres and the divisions of the Zodiac. The *masalik wa al-mamalik* literature, on the other hand, was mainly concerned with fixing the geographical positions of places relative to each other, rather than the larger, more schematic approach.

Journeys. Travel accounts also contributed to geographical knowledge. The famous Ibn Battuta, who traveled more than seventy-five thousand miles over a period of more than thirty years, described pearl fisheries in the Persian Gulf, the markets along the Nile, the coral islands of the Maldives, the intense cold of the Ukraine, and many other facets of terrain and human life. Other travelers, such as Ibn Jubayr of Valencia and Hafiz Abru of Persia, provided similar details in their accounts.

New Developments. During the tenth century, Muslim geographic works became increasingly sophisticated. The

DEFINING GEOGRAPHY

The Muslim geographer and traveler Abu Abdullah al-Muqaddasi was a keen observer of human activity and its relationship to the physical environment. In 985 he outlined his broad view of the scope of geography, stating that it "is an account of a region—comprising a description of its deserts and seas, the lakes and rivers that it contains, its famous cities and noted towns, the resting places on its roads and its highways of commerce, the places of growth and production, its exports, and staple commodities, an account of the inhabitants of the different countries, of the diversity of language and manner of speech; of their dialects and complexion, and their religious tenets; of their measures and weights, their coins, with information about their food and drink, a description of their hills, plains and mountains, thick and thin soils, their fertile or infertile lands, unirrigated lands and forests, and an account of their industries and literary achievements."

Source: Abu Abdullah al-Muqaddasi, *Ahsan al-Taqasim*, translated by G. S. A. Ranking and R. F. Azoo in Bibliotheca Indica, no. 137, new series 899, 952, 1001, and 1258 (Calcutta: Asiatic Society, 1897-1910), p. 304; quoted in S. M. Ali, *Arab Geography* (Aligarh: Muslim University, 1960), p. 5.

seventh volume of the encyclopedia the Persian Abu Ali Ibn Rustah wrote in Isfahan in 903 deals with geography. It discusses the extent of the earth, the founding of Makkah and Madinah, seas and rivers, climate, and the geography of Iran and surrounding lands. Ahmad Ibn Fadlan's account of his journey as ambassador to the court of the Volga Bulgars in 921 provides a thorough description of the regions around the Caspian Sea and to the northeast of the Black Sea, areas about which Ptolemy and the first century Greek geographer Strabo knew little. In 945 Coptic Christian scholar Ibn Serapion compiled a work in which he described Mesopotamia and its rivers and extensive canal system. Another Christian, Abu al-Faraj, an accountant working in the revenue department at Baghdad, wrote *Kitab al-Kharaj* (Land Tax Book, 928), in which he summarizes the taxable lands and commodities in various areas of the empire.

Cartography. Muslim mapmaking became more prevalent around the tenth century. Abu Zaid al-Balkhi (died 934), a student of al-Kindi, was one of the early Muslim mapmakers. He valued a statistical approach to information, and his works focus on explanations of charts. Abu Ishaq al-Istakhri, who lived in the mid tenth century, wrote a "routes and kingdoms" book in which he included colored maps for each country. The well-known traveler and geographer Shams al-Din 'Abd Allah Muhammad al-Muqaddasi (circa 945 – circa 990) wrote *Ahsan al-Taqasim fi Ma'rifat al-Aqalim* (The Best Divisions for the Knowledge of the Climes). Always seeking to improve geographical knowledge, Al-Muqaddasi studied his predecessors' works, dis-

cussing their merits and drawbacks and stating that geography had received insufficient attention from earlier scientific writers. He therefore set about collecting from all parts of the Islamic world data based on personal travel and direct observation. He divided the Muslim lands into fourteen regions and prepared separate maps for each one, using various cartographic symbols and representing relief. Routes were colored red; deserts, yellow; salt seas, green; rivers, blue; and mountains, brown. Unlike many of his ancient predecessors, he considered the earth to be nearly spherical (an idea rooted in the Qur'an), dividing it into two equal parts by the equator, the southern being mostly water and the northern mainly land. Abu al-Qasim Ibn Hawqal (born circa 925) traveled extensively for thirty years before preparing his *surat al-ard* book. Such travel was essential for the creation of increasingly sophisticated maps. Abu al-Hasan al-Mas'udi (died 956), born in Baghdad, traveled far and wide on the Indian Ocean, in Palestine, Syria, and elsewhere. His *Muruj al-Dhahab wa Ma'adin al-Jawahir* (Meadows of Gold and Mines of Precious Stones, 947) is an historical-geographical encyclopedia, discussing earthquakes, geological formations, the nature of the Dead Sea, and windmills in Sijistan. Prefiguring Charles Darwin's theory, al-Mas'udi's last book deals with the notion of evolution. In the eleventh century the great geographer al-Biruni wrote that the earth is round and charted latitudes and longitudes for many places. In the twelfth century al-Idrisi made accurate, detailed maps of the Mediterranean region.

Bronze astrolabe from Iraq, circa 927–928 (Kuwait National Museum)

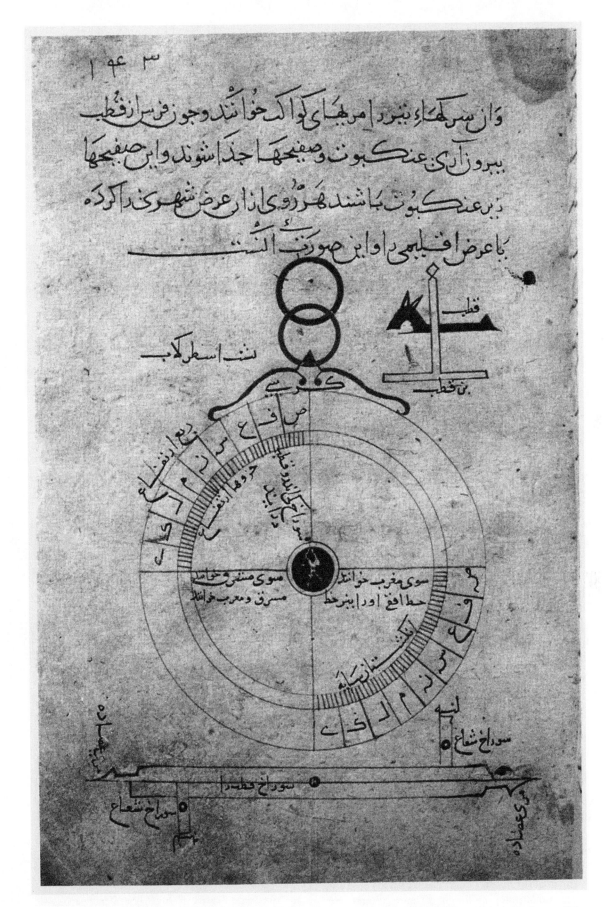

Description of the astrolabe in a twelfth-century manuscript for al-Biruni's *Kitab al-Tafhim* (Book of Astrology), one of the works in which he discussed the calculation of longitudes and latitudes (Majles Library, Tehran)

Sources:

Nafis Ahmad, *Muslim Contribution to Geography* (Lahore: Sh. Muhammad Ashraf, 1972).

S. Maqbul Ahmad, "Djughrafiya," in *Encyclopedia of Islam*, new edition, CD-ROM (Leiden: Brill, 1999).

Seyyed H. Nasr, *Science and Civilization in Islam* (London: Islamic Texts Society, 1987).

Ahmad Nazmi, "Some Aspects of the Image of the World in Muslim Tradition, Legends, and Geographical Literature," *Studia Arabistyczne i Islamistyczne*, 6 (1998): 87–102.

THE TECHNOLOGY OF GEOGRAPHY

Methods. Personal observation was the first and foremost means by which Islamic geographers gathered information about the earth and its flora and fauna, land forms, bodies of water, and resources. Looking down at the ground, however, provided only part of the picture; geography could not exist without the use of external bodies—the sun, moon, planets, and stars—as reference points. The complex orbits and rotations of the various spheres, including the Earth, necessitated astronomical and mathematical studies. Advances in these fields served geographers' need to explain climate, tides, atmospheric conditions, and to fix precisely the location of cities and places relative to each other. Observatories made such advances possible. Muslims maintained the observatory at Jundi-Shapur and built new ones at Baghdad, Palmyra, and Cairo, as well as in the hills outside Damascus. In Muslim Spain observatories were built in Toledo and Cordoba. In the thirteenth century Nasir al-Din al-Tusi directed studies at an observatory built by the Mongol Hulagu Khan at Maragha in Persia. The observatory had a variety of instruments and a library of about four hundred thousand books. The ruler Ulugh Beg built an observatory at Samarkand, at which he himself studied the stars.

Devices. Instruments of various kinds were vital for geographical study. The Muslim scientists inherited tools such as the annulus (a circular device for charting the heavens), the quadrant (a quarter-circle-shaped instrument for measuring angles from a vertical reference), and the clepsydra (water clock). The astrolabe existed in primitive form during Greek times and was essentially reinvented by the Muslims. Al-Zarqali (died 1087) of Toledo invented a new version called a *safiha*. Another new instrument was the *dhat al-awtar*, an advanced sundial comprising four square posts arranged so as to ascertain the time at different latitudes. There is an ongoing debate about the origins of the magnetic compass. Whether it originated in China or the Muslim lands, it was widely used in the Indian Ocean by Arab and Persian seafarers, and helped sailors venture far from the coasts. Navigators such as Ibn Majid, who wrote *Al-Fawa'id fi Usul al-Bahr wa al Qawa'id* (Principles of Navigation, circa 1490), used such devices along the coast of Africa, preparing the way for a sea route from Europe to India around the tip of Africa. The increasingly accurate astronomical and latitude and longitude data gathered over the centuries by Muslim scientists were compiled in a variety of charts known as *zij* that became vital research tools. Al-Zarqali, for example, corrected Ptolemy's estimate of the length of the Mediterranean sea from 62 degrees to the nearly correct 42 degrees. His *zij* was translated into Latin in the twelfth century. Muslim navigation charts also gave impetus to the rise of *portolani* (charts listing sailing directions from one point to another) such as the *Catalan Atlas* (1375) among European ship captains.

Mapmakers. Maps drawn by Muslim scientists were also important resources. Al-Idrisi's maps were known to European scholars. An official Chinese map of 1331 was drawn by Muslim geographers or by geographers using Muslim sources. Perhaps the most interesting example of the advanced state of Muslim mapmaking is the map prepared around 1513 by

SOURCES OF GEOGRAPHICAL INFORMATION

In the medieval era geography was often viewed as one of several interrelated sciences rather than a distinct field, and much nonscientific literature also included geographical information. Modern scholars of Muslim history study a wide range of sources to ascertain the nature of Muslim geographic study and the way in which Muslims have viewed their place in the world, including:

Geographical Works: Muslim geographers wrote specialized treatises dealing with the shape of the earth, the extent and features of the inhabited land mass, trade and navigation routes, and ethnography.

Astronomical Works: Astronomers devised ways to determine the direction of Makkah and the daily times for Muslim worship, which in turn helped geographers to develop methods for creating accurate maps for travelers and pilgrims and for determining distances between places.

Conquest Accounts: The astounding speed with which the Muslims expanded their empire necessitated the constant flow of updated information to administrators, including accounts of the resources they encountered, the settlement patterns of tribes in various locales, and other geographic and ethnographic details.

Biographical Dictionaries: Islamic religious and legal studies placed great emphasis on the reputation of scholars and teachers. Specialized dictionaries provide valuable details about their lives and their places of origin.

Routes: As dynasties took stock of their territories, they commissioned studies of the best routes for military and commercial uses.

Travel Accounts: Merchants and scholars often kept journals, reporting on the strange new peoples, customs, and sites they encountered.

Popular Tales and Stories: Fictional works such as *Alf Layla wa Layla* (The Thousand and One Nights) and the *Maqamat* stories, picaresque morality tales often featuring a rogue, reveal much information about far-off places, agriculture, and trade goods produced in different environments.

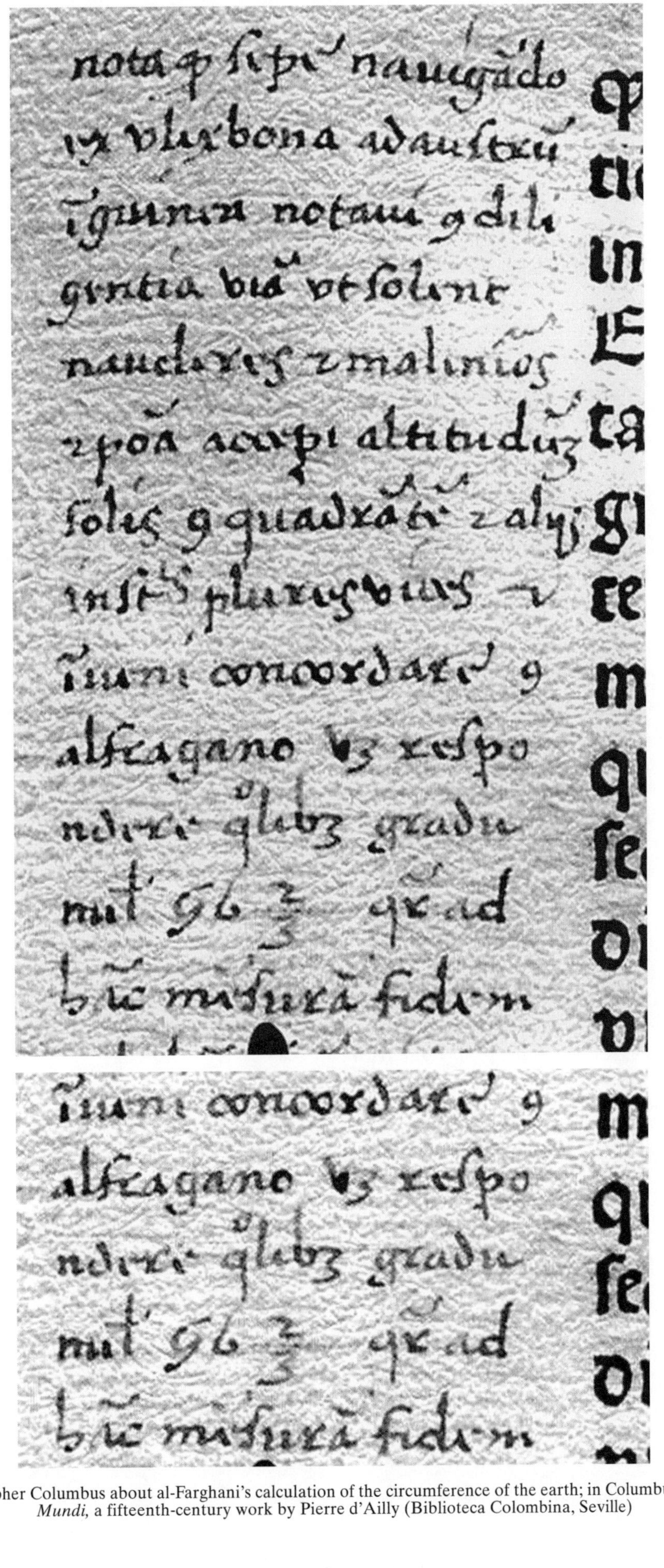

nota q̃ sepe nauegãdo
iz̃ vlixbona adaustꝝ
iguinm notaui q dili
gꝛntia bm̄ vt solent
nauclerez z malinios
z pꝛon̄ acupi altituduz
folez g quadrãtẽ z alij
inst̃s plurꝫbuiaſ z
Iuum concordate q
alfagano vz̃ reſpo
ndꝛct̃ qlibꝫ gradn
mit̃ g6 ⅔ grad
bn̄c mnſuṝã fidem

Iuum concordate q
alfagano vz̃ reſpo
ndꝛct̃ qlibꝫ gradn
mit̃ g6 ⅔ grad
bn̄c mnſuṝã fidem

Notes by Christopher Columbus about al-Farghani's calculation of the circumference of the earth; in Columbus's copy of *Imago Mundi*, a fifteenth-century work by Pierre d'Ailly (Biblioteca Colombina, Seville)

Ottoman admiral Piri Reis. He used about twenty source maps, some ancient and some more recent, including one said to have been drawn by Christopher Columbus. He reduced his sources to a single scale, a difficult task at the time, and included the Antarctic landmass (under the ice), which went "undiscovered" until modern sonar determined its shape.

Sources:

Nafis Ahmad, *Muslim Contribution to Geography* (Lahore: Sh. Muhammad Ashraf, 1972).

S. M. Ali, *Arab Geography* (Aligarh: Muslim University, 1960).

Seyyed H. Nasr, *Science and Civilization in Islam* (London: Islamic Texts Society, 1987).

TOPOGRAPHY AND CLIMATE

Varied Landscapes. Muslim rulers presided over an increasingly vast region of diverse land forms, climates, soils, wildlife, and vegetation, extending from North Africa and Spain to the borders of India. Geography affected concentrations of populations and helped define the borders of successive ruling groups. From Madinah, the early Muslims expanded into the Fertile Crescent, an agricultural zone arching from Egypt north into Syria, across Iraq and Iran and down toward the Persian Gulf, incorporating several key river systems such as the Nile, Orontes, Tigris, and Euphrates. The Umayyads and Abbasids inherited this prosperous irrigable region where grains, vegetables, and fruits could be grown and goods from across the hemisphere could be traded.

Breakdown of Centralization. However, the centralized empire was short-lived, as various rulers vied with each other for regional control. In 756 a lone Umayyad prince, Abd al-Rahman, claimed *al-Andalus* (Andalusia, a portion of Iberia) for his own. By the ninth century, the Idrisids in Morocco, the Aghlabids in Tunisia, and the Tulunids in Egypt ruled independently. Shi'i and Khariji states emerged in North Africa at this time as well, such as the Ibadis at Tahert, followed in the tenth century by the Fatimids, an Isma'ili dynasty that founded Cairo. Zaydi Shi'is ruled in Yemen. In order to prop up their dominions, the Abbasids increasingly relied on Turkic soldiers and horsemen from the Central Asian steppes, a flat, arid region where life revolved around pastoralism. After 1055, the Saljuk Turks ruled on behalf of the Abbasids in Iraq, Iran, and Syria. The famous Salah al-Din, who led a successful resistance against the Crusaders, defeated the Fatimids in 1171 and established the Ayyubid dynasty in Egypt. In 1250 the Mamluks, Turkish and Circassian soldiers, overthrew the Ayyubids and took control, ruling Egypt until the coming of the Ottomans in 1517.

Late Medieval Dynasties. In the thirteenth century Mongol armies from Central Asia devastated Iran, Iraq, and surrounding areas. The Ilkhanids, a Mongol-Persian regime, ruled much of Iran and Inner Asia. In the fourteenth century, Timur absorbed these territories into a new empire based around his capital at Samarqand, which lasted until the advent of the Safavids around 1500. In the west, the Almoravids, Almohads, Marinids, and Hafsids successively ruled portions of Morocco, Algeria, and Spain between the eleventh and sixteenth centuries, while the Nasrids ruled the kingdom of Granada in Spain until 1492. In the east the Ghaznavids ruled in Afghanistan from the tenth to the twelfth century, while Muslim sultanates based in Delhi ruled portions of India from the thirteenth century until the arrival of Mughals in the sixteenth. During the same time period, sub-Saharan states in Ghana and Mali prospered as well, and port cities such as Mogadishu in East Africa bustled with activity.

Natural Boundaries. High mountain ranges such as the Atlas in Morocco and the Hindu Kush in Afghanistan and great deserts such as the Sahara in Africa provided natural boundaries between political rivals. Large open spaces, such as the dry Spanish meseta and the arid Central Asian steppes, provided a buffer between Muslim and non-Muslim lands. River valleys such as the Guadalquivir in Spain, the Orontes in Syria, and the Indus in Pakistan invited agricultural expansion and cultivation, stimulating the growth of new communities of Muslims with local customs and identities. The Mediterranean Sea provided both a buffer and a zone of trade and interaction between Italian city-states, France, Spanish Christian states, and Byzantium and the Muslim states of North Africa and the Levant. Another major commercial zone was the Indian Ocean. Relying on the annual monsoon winds, Muslim merchants traversed the vast ocean and brought goods, fabrics, and luxury items to the Malay archipelago in southeast Asia, leading to the establishment of Muslim colonies there that were nuclei for the growth of Islam among local inhabitants from the thirteenth century onward.

Sources:

Nafis Ahmad, *Muslim Contribution to Geography* (Lahore: Sh. Muhammad Ashraf, 1972).

J. H. Kramers, "Geography and Commerce," in *The Legacy of Islam*, edited by Thomas Arnold and Alfred Guillaume (Oxford: Clarendon Press, 1931).

SIGNIFICANT PEOPLE

ABU RAYHAN AL-BIRUNI

973-1048
GEOGRAPHER

The Importance of Geography. One of the greatest Muslim geographers was al-Biruni, who once said, "This subject is an all-important one for travellers and merchants. It is desired by princes and noble personages, sought for by judges and doctors of law, the delight of commoners and men of rank."

Intellectual Achievements. Born in Khalwarizm, Khorasan (in present-day Turkmenistan), al-Biruni was considered one of the foremost Persian scholars and scientists of his age. Writing in Arabic, he could also speak Turkish, Persian, Sanskrit, Hebrew, and Syriac, and in addition to his geographical works, he wrote on astrology, mathematics, physics, medicine, and history.

Royal Geographer. In 1017 al-Biruni was captured during a war with the sultanate of Ghazna (in Afghanistan) and was made royal geographer to Sultan Mahmud. While traveling with the sultan on military expeditions he became an expert on the peoples, cultures, and physical geography of India, writing *Tahqiq al-Hind* (Facts About India, circa 1030).

Geographical Writings. In his works on geography al-Biruni discussed the roundness of the Earth and gave latitudes and longitudes of many places. Despite political divisions, Muslim lands represented a vast territory of common culture in which travel and research could take place. As al-Biruni said, "To obtain information concerning places of the earth has now become incomparably easier and safer. Now we find a host of places which in the Ptolemaic Geography are indicated as lying to the east of other places, actually situated to the west of the others named, and vice versa." Al-Biruni and other Muslim geographers were able to use advances in mathematics such as algebra and trigonometry to determine more accurately the exact locations of places on the Earth and thus revise the latitude and longitude information in their charts.

Sources:
D. J. Boilot, "al-Biruni," in *Encyclopedia of Islam*, CD-ROM version (Leiden: Brill, 1999).

Ainslie Embree, *Alberuni's India* (New York: Norton, 1971).

Seyyed Hossein Nasr, *Science & Civilization in Islam*, second edition (Cambridge, U.K.: Islamic Texts Society, 1987).

ABU ABDULLAH AL-IDRISI

1099-1165 OR 1166
GEOGRAPHER

Mapmaking. Known as one of the greatest medieval geographers, Abu Abdullah al-Idrisi is best known for his *Kitab Nuzhat al-Mashtaq fi Ikhtiraq al-Afaq* (Amusement for One Who Desires to Travel Around the World, 1154), which includes detailed maps of the Mediterranean region.

Early Life and Career. Born in Ceuta, North Africa, al-Idrisi was educated at Cordoba. He visited Asia Minor when he was only sixteen, and continued his extensive travels around the Mediterranean, observing the flora and fauna of Muslim lands.

Court Geographer. In about 1145 al-Idrisi was invited to work at the court of the Norman king Roger II in Palermo, Sicily, where Roger formed the Academy of Geographers and invited other scholars to help al-Idrisi create the most scientifically accurate map in the world and to gather together all available geographical information. The result was *Kitab Nuzhat al-Mashtaq fi Ikhtiraq al-Afaq*, also known as *Kitab al-Rujari* (The Book of Roger), a major contribution to the geographical knowledge of his time. Al-Idrisi also made a celestial sphere on which the constellations were inscribed on a three-hundred-pound silver disk bearing a map of the known world. Shortly after Roger's death in 1154, his court was attacked by Byzantine invaders, who melted down the silver disk to make weapons. Al-Idrisi escaped with the Arabic version of his *Book of Roger*, but the Latin version was destroyed and the work was not translated into Latin again until the seventeenth century.

Sources:
J. H. Kramers, "Geography and Commerce," in *The Legacy of Islam*, edited by Thomas Arnold and Alfred Guillaume (Oxford: Clarendon Press, 1931).

G. Oman, "al-Idrisi," in *Encyclopedia of Islam*, CD-ROM version (Leiden: Brill, 1999).

DOCUMENTARY SOURCES

Abu Rayhan al-Biruni, *Tahqiq al-Hind* (Facts About India, circa 1030)—An important contribution to the field of regional geography and ethnography.

Shihab al-Din Hafiz Abru, *Zubdat al-Tawarikh* (1415)—A Persian geographical compendium based on a combination of older Arabic works and new observations.

Abu al-Qasim Ibn Hawqal, *Kitab Surat al-Ard* (A Book on the Shape of the Earth, late tenth century)—An important source describing the major territories and cities of the Muslim east and west.

Muhammad Ibn Jubayr, *Rihlat Ibn Jubayr* (Ibn Jubayr's Travels, circa 1200)—An excellent example of the genre of travel literature that was common among Muslims, written by a Spanish Muslim.

Abu al-Qasim Ibn Khurdadhbih, *Kitab al-Masalik wa al-Mamalik* (Book of the Routes and Kingdoms, 848)—A postmaster's summary of the main trade routes through the various kingdoms of the Muslim lands and a description of other regions such as China and Japan, this work was a model for similar later works.

Abu al-Hasan al-Mas'udi, *Muruj al-Dhahab wa Ma'adin al-Jawahir* (Meadows of Gold and Mines of Precious Stones, 947)—A compendium of accounts about Abbasid high culture, examples of poetry and literature, and descriptions of natural, agricultural, and mineral resources that propelled trade and commerce in diverse Muslim lands.

Shams al-Din 'Abd Allah Muhammad al-Muqaddasi, *Ahsan al-Taqasim fi Ma'rifat al-Aqalim* (The Best Divisions for the Knowledge of the Climes, 985)—Based on earlier Greek notions about the division of the world into climes, this work breaks new ground by incorporating prior Muslim geographical learning into a new synthesis, with maps of fourteen regions within the Muslim empire.

THE ARTS

by MANAR DARWISH and KHALID YAHYA BLANKINSHIP

CONTENTS

CHRONOLOGY
82

OVERVIEW
85

TOPICS IN THE ARTS

Arabic Poetry 86
Pre-Islamic Poetry 87
Arabic Prose Literature 90
Language and Rhetoric 94
The Verse of Light 97
Calligraphy 99
Decorative Arts 101
Poet of Pessimism 102
Domestic and
   Secular Architecture 105

Early Religious Architecture
   and City Planning 107
The Maqama of the Yellow One . . 110
Later Masjid Architecture
   in the Arab World
   and Africa 114
The Maqama of the Spindle 115
Later Masjid Architecture
   in the Turco-Iranian World
   and India 118
Music 120
Oral Poetry, Storytelling,
   and Folklore 123
Hafiz 123
Persian Poetry 124
Persian Prose Literature 125
The Prohibition of Images 127
Alive, The Son of Awake 128

SIGNIFICANT PEOPLE

Hafiz 131
Al-Hariri 131
Abu Uthman al-Jahiz 132
Abd al-Qahir al-Jurjani 132
Al-Khansa' 133
Al-Mas'udi 133
Al-Mutanabbi 134
Sibawayh 135
Al-Walid ibn Abd al-Malik . . .135

DOCUMENTARY SOURCES
136

Sidebars and tables are listed in italics.

622
- The Prophet Muhammad migrates from Makkah (Mecca) to Madinah (Medina), where he founds a house of worship (masjid or mosque) in the courtyard of his house. This building becomes the prototype for all later masjids.

632*
- Over a period of about twenty-three years the Muslim scripture, the Qur'an, has been revealed to the Prophet Muhammad in installments. The Qur'an is the first book known to have been written down in Arabic, and it has a major influence on all subsequent Muslim literature, whether in Arabic or in other languages.

691
- In Jerusalem, Umayyad khalifah Abd al-Malik ibn Marwan (ruled 685–705) constructs the Dome of the Rock, the oldest standing Muslim building that still retains its original form. Bearing the earliest dated inscription attesting to verses from the Qur'an, the Dome is the first building of a huge construction program undertaken by Abd al-Malik and his son and successor, al-Walid I (ruled 705–715).

692
- The Ka'bah in Makkah, God's Inviolable House toward which Muslims bow in worship, is rebuilt in its present form after having been damaged in a civil war.

696
- The Byzantine gold coins that have been in circulation in the khilafah (caliphate) are replaced with epigraphic coins bearing Qur'anic verses and other Islamic inscriptions. The silver coinage is similarly reformed in 698, when the Sasanian coins that have been in use are replaced by epigraphic Muslim ones similar in design to the new gold coins.

721
- Khalifah (Caliph) Yazid II issues an iconoclastic proclamation ordering the elimination of public images of humans and animals throughout the khilafah.

762
- Abbasid khalifah al-Mansur constructs the royal city of Baghdad in Iraq as the new capital of the khilafah. The city soon replaces Kufah as the central metropolis of Islam.

767*
- Muqatil ibn Sulayman al-Balkhi and Muhammad ibn Ishaq die. They are the authors of the first two surviving full-length books in Arabic after the Qur'an: Muqatil's commentary on the Qur'an and ibn Ishaq's biography of the Prophet Muhammad.
- Malik completes *al-Muwatta'* (The Trodden Way), the first substantial Muslim law book and goes on to teach law for thirty years in Madinah. Other law books soon follow.

836
- Khalifah al-Mu'tasim moves his capital from Baghdad farther up the Tigris in Iraq to Samarra', which becomes a large city by 892, when the capital reverts to Baghdad.

* Denotes Circa Date

849-851	• Khalifah al-Mutawakkil builds the Great Masjid of Samarra' with its spiral minaret.
915	• In Baghdad, al-Tabari completes his history of the first three centuries of Islam.
963	• Modern Persian prose literature begins when the Samanid ruler Mansur I commissions Bal'ami to translate al-Tabari's history in Islam into Persian.
1010	• Persian literature becomes well established with the completion of Firdawsi's *Shahnamah* (Book of Kings), an epic poem about the pre-Islamic Iranian kingdoms.
1033*	• Syrian poet Abu al-'Ala' al-Ma'arri writes his *Risalat al-ghufran* (Treatise of Forgiveness), a poetic description of a journey through heaven and hell that predates Dante's *Divine Comedy* (1321).
1108	• Al-Hariri publishes his satirical *al-Maqamat* (assemblies, or occasional discourses), describing the adventures of an impoverished but eloquent scoundrel in various Muslim cities.
1183-1184	• The Citadel of Salah al-Din (Saladin) is constructed in Cairo. One of the most extensive medieval fortresses ever built, it is the usual residence of the sultans of Egypt throughout the medieval period.
1261-1273	• Rumi composes his six-volume poetic masterpiece, *Mathnawi-i ma'nawi*, in Persian at Konya, Turkey.
1333-1392	• Yusuf I (ruled 1333–1354) and Muhammad V (ruled 1354–1359, 1362–1391), Nasrid rulers of Granada, Spain, build most of the Alhambra Palace.
1356-1361	• The masjid of Sultan Hasan is built in Cairo.
1375*	• The Khirki Masjid is built in Delhi, India.

* DENOTES CIRCA DATE

THE ARTS

1423	• The Jami' Masjid is built in Ahmadabad, India.
1472-1474	• The Mausoleum of Sultan Qa'itbay is built in the Northern Cemetery of Cairo.

* DENOTES CIRCA DATE

Tile made in Egypt or Syria during the first half of the fifteenth century (British Museum, London)

OVERVIEW

Ancient Background. Art has been part of everyday life from the time of the earliest civilizations in the ancient Near East, which form the background for the civilizations of Islam and the modern West. Art seems to have developed from ordinary necessities. People needed shelter, and the art of domestic architecture developed, with the rich and powerful living in larger, more-decorated dwellings than the poor. People needed places to worship and carry out the rituals of their organized religions, and beautiful temples survive from as far back as the time of the ancient Egyptians and Iraqis (known in the West as Mesopotamians). Ancient people adorned themselves with fine jewelry made from precious metals and gemstones as well as from more ordinary materials such as bone, ivory, tusks, and ebony. Even ordinary utensils were often beautifully decorated. As for the linguistic arts, people have expressed themselves through poetry and prose for thousands of years; Sumerian and Akkadian tablets reveal the literary prowess of the ancient Iraqis, and papyri and wall inscriptions on temples and tombs demonstrate similar abilities in the ancient Egyptians. Musical instruments, as well as statues and pictures of musicians, have been discovered in the excavations of tombs of these two ancient civilizations, pointing to ancient humans' interest in music.

Graeco-Roman Culture. Much later, when the ancient Greeks had become the dominant power in the Mediterranean, their art forms, including their dramas and theatrical productions, were widely cultivated. The Romans continued the trend, and many examples of art and literary works have survived from the time of the Roman Empire. Beginning in the fourth century when Emperor Constantine accepted Christianity and made it the official religion of the Roman Empire, artistic production was channeled toward producing works of arts that served the new faith.

Near Eastern Predecessors. Often ancient Graeco-Roman culture has been viewed as the major influence on Islamic culture, but recent research has shown that the continuity of Near Eastern civilization was more important than any outside influence. The predecessors of the Muslim khilafah (caliphate) included the long-lasting Achaemenid, Parthian, and Sasanian empires of Iran, which together spanned the years 550 B.C.E.–651 C.E., with a break only from 330 to 248 B.C.E. when no Iranian empire

existed. When the khilafah expanded, it absorbed the entire Iranian cultural world and its heritage. While the Zoroastrian religion of the Iranian rulers seems to have had little direct influence on Islam, the Iranian, or Persian, cultural contribution was enormous, and important Indian influences also came through Iran. Aside from the Iranian and Indian cultures, the Aramaic-Syrian Semitic culture of the inner lands of the Fertile Crescent also had a clear influence, especially perhaps in linguistic and literary matters, as the prevalent Aramaic, or Syriac, language of that region is closely related to Arabic. Also, the Coptic culture of Egypt may have had some influence on decorative motifs, especially on Egyptian woodwork produced under Muslim patronage.

Muslim Civilization. The Muslim civilization that arose and flourished in the period 622–1500 was directly influenced by the earlier civilizations and cultures of the Near East, including the Graeco-Roman. First-generation Muslims wedded these influences to Arabian motifs to create a general Muslim artistic synthesis. After the establishment of Islam as a religion in the seventh century, a body of artistic production with unified basic themes and shared aesthetic standards gradually developed in all the lands where Islam spread. The religious ideology of Islam managed to unify people in many lands far distant from each other and helped them develop a rich and impressive civilization.

Coherence of the Concept of Muslim Art. From Morocco to China, one may find many examples of magnificent masjids (mosques) with domes and soaring minarets, as well as nonreligious buildings with similar architecture. The majority of such masjids and other structures have gilded inscriptions and decorative floral arabesques adorning their exteriors and interiors. Islamic art collections in major museums the world over include examples of illuminated manuscripts with vividly decorated pages, enameled-glass lamps with delicate designs, bronze ewers inlaid with silver and gold, wooden chests and doors meticulously inlaid with mother-of-pearl, ceramic bowls and tiles glazed in brilliant colors, as well as samples of textiles and rugs. Such objects were made as early as the ninth century in countries ranging from Iran in the east to Spain in the west. What immediately becomes clear is that all these objects share something in common: similarities in their use of decorative themes and color. What unifies all these objects is the fact that they were produced in lands where Islam spread under the patronage of rulers who believed in the religion of Islam and thus adhered to certain standards when commissioning works of art.

Regional Variations. Of course, it is also true that there are considerable regional variations in Muslim art, as well as new trends, styles, and developments over time. When the spread of Islam started in the early part of the seventh century, from the cities of Makkah and Madinah in western Arabia, it rapidly led to the formation of the vast empire called the khilafah. Within its first century, Islam had already extended as far as India in the southeast and Spain in the northwest. This huge territory encompassed peoples with many different languages, cultures, aesthetics, and ancient heritages. Thus, it is unsurprising that local themes and trends existed, mixed with general Muslim themes on the arrival of Islam, and then produced new local styles and genres. By 1500 these local cultures included the Arabo-Berber, the West African, the East African or Swahili, the Anatolian Turkish, the Iranian, the Central Asian, the South Asian, the Southeast Asian, and the Chinese. Early on, each region continued to produce art according to its localized tradition, but increasingly there was a universal artistic idiom used by artisans and craftsmen in all Muslim regions. While variations from one region to another remained, one can easily recognize works of art produced under the patronage of the Muslims and see the common motifs that make them Muslim.

Genres of Islamic Art and Architecture. Every civilization or cultural zone establishes some forms of artistic endeavor and lacks others. In fact, most artistic products are culturally bound. This chapter examines all the known genres of Muslim artistic effort. Although these artistic expressions were produced for Muslims and are sometimes referred to as examples of "Islamic art," they are by no means limited to religious works. The words "Muslim" and "Islamic" should be understood here as general cultural terms, under whose umbrella secular as well as religious works were created by or for Muslims. Also, it should be recognized that the concepts of *religious* and *secular* are essentially modern ones that have little to do with the way Muslims have looked at their culture or its products. Thus, the boundary between the two often cannot be clearly drawn.

TOPICS IN THE ARTS

ARABIC POETRY

Pre-Islamic Poetry. At the time of the revelation of Islam, a highly developed oral poetry already existed in Arabic. Although all languages produce poetry, especially in their primal phase before the introduction of writing, the Arabic language is exceptionally poetic because of its morphological structure, in which words are built up from three-letter roots according to a limited number of fixed patterns, and there is relatively little elaboration of words through prefixes and suffixes. These linguistic facts have made the Arabic language a particularly effective vehicle for poetry and other literature, especially after the civilizational development it has gone through over the course of its existence. Even in the pre-Islamic era, poetry was an important and ubiquitous vehicle of public expression. Poets exercised great influence through their ability to praise or to condemn eloquently. Some have likened their effect on their people to that of the press in a modern society. Their poems were probably even more effective when they were set to music. As popular songs, poems were widely circulated, memorized, and sung. Rulers had to take the power of poetry into account and were thus always careful to cultivate the great poets of their time, often bestowing gifts and prizes on them in the hope of getting favorable comments from them in their poems. By the time Islam appeared, Arabic poetry was principally cultivated in the form of the *qasidah* (ode), which goes on for at least several dozen verses—frequently more than a hundred—and includes several stock themes, which had to be included for the poem to be acceptable. In all classical Arabic poetry, rhythm is carefully observed and limited to sixteen classical meters. Each line consists of two hemistichs (half lines divided by a caesura, or pause) and each line ends in a consonant and vowel that are repeated without variation throughout the poem. This repetition is possible in Arabic because of its rhythmic nature, but it cannot be done in English and many other languages. This rhyme scheme is used in fifteen of the classical meters. The only exception is the popular *rajaz* meter, considered the easiest, in which hemistichs end in the same consonant and vowel, but the lines do not, producing in effect a poem of rhyming couplets, with no continuous rhyme throughout the poem. This meter is closer than the others to some English poetry,

In the Ka'bah, the "cubic" central shrine of Islam, poems were hung on the walls because of their recognized excellence among the Arabs. These poems—about the exploits of tribal heroes, nature, and pastoral life in the Arabian desert—represent the highest literary achievement in Arabic language before Islam. The following excerpt is from "The Poem of Antar," one of the best-known examples:

Have the poets left in the garment a place for a patch to be patched by me; and did you know the abode of your beloved after reflection?

The vestige of the house, which did not speak, confounded thee, until it spoke by means of signs, like one deaf and dumb.

Verily, I kept my she-camel there long grumbling, with a yearning at the blackened stones, keeping and standing firm in their own places.

It is the abode of a friend, languishing in her glance, submissive in the embrace, pleasant of smile.

Oh house of 'Ablah situated at Jiwaa, talk with me about those who resided in you. Good morning to you, O house of 'Ablah, and be safe from ruin.

I halted my she-camel in that place; and it was as though she were a high palace; in order that I might perform the wont of the lingerer.

And 'Ablah takes up her abode at Jiwaa; while our people went to Eazan, then to Mutathallam.

She took up her abode in the land of my enemies; so it became difficult for me to seek you, O daughter of Mahzam.

. . .

She passes her evenings and her mornings on the surfaceof a well-stuffed couch, while I pass my nights on the back of a bridled black horse.

And my couch is a saddle upon a horse big-boned in the leg, big in his flanks, great of girth.

Would a Shadanian she-camel cause me to arrive at her abode, who is cursed with an udder scanty of milk and cut off?

After traveling all night, she is lashing her sides with her tail, and is strutting proudly, and she breaks up the mounds of earth she passes over with her foot with its sole, treading hard.

As if I in the evening am breaking the mounds of earth by means of an ostrich, very small as to the distance between its two feet, and earless.

The young ostriches flock toward him, as the herds of Yemenian camels flock to a barbarous, unintelligible speaker.

They follow the crest of his head, as though it was a howdah on a large litter, tented for them.

. . .

When my people) defended themselves with me against the spears of the enemy, I did not refrain from the spears through cowardice, but the place of my advance had become too strait.

When I heard the cry of Murrah rise, and saw the two sons of Rabi'ah in the thick dust,

While the tribe of Muhallam were struggling under their banners, and death was under the banners of the tribe of Mulhallam,

I made sure that at the time of their encounter there would be a blow, which would make the heads fly from the bodies, as the bird flies from off her young ones sitting close.

When I saw the people, while their mass advanced, excite one another to fight, I turned against them without being reproached for any want of bravery.

They were calling 'Antarah, while the spears were as though they were well-ropes in the breast of Adham.

They were calling 'Antarah, while the swords were as though they were the flash of lightning in a dark cloud.

They were calling 'Antarah, while the arrows were flying, as though they were a flight of locusts, hovering above watering places.

They were calling "O 'Antarah," while the coats of mail shone with close rings, shining as though they were the eyeballs of frogs floating in a wavy pond.

I did not cease charging the enemy, with the prominent part of his throat and breast, until he became covered with a shirt of blood.

Then he turned on account of the falling of the spears on his breast, and complained to me with tears and whining.

If he had known what conversation was, he would have complained with words, and verily he would have, had he known speech, talked with me.

And verily the speech of the horsemen, "Woe to you, 'Antarah, advance, and attack the enemy," cured my soul and removed its sickness. . . .

Source: Charles F. Horne, ed., *The Sacred Books and Early Literature of the East*, volume 5: *Ancient Arabia* (New York: Parke, Austin, & Lipscomb, 1917), pp. 19–40.

such as the heroic couplets of John Dryden or even sonnets. The *rajaz* meter was used for shorter poems as well as odes and was originally less formal than the others.

Continuation. Although not Muslim in origin, the Arabic oral poetic tradition was—alongside the Qur'an—the second foundational element of the Muslim literary tradition. Apparently, the early poetry continued to be transmitted mainly in oral form for a considerable period after Islam had become established, at least until the time when it was collected by Hammad al-Rawiyah (circa 694 – circa 772). Even after poetry began to be collected and written down, oral recitation and memorization continued. Indeed, oral poetry is still an important cultural feature in Arab and most other Muslim societies. Arabic poetry from before the revelation of the Qur'an is known as pre-Islamic, or Jahili, poetry and continues to be held in the highest regard among all Arabic verse. This poetry is characterized by brilliant imagery and a varied, rare, and now-archaic vocabulary that is both a guarantee of its authenticity and an obstacle to its being easily understood without a commentary. The oldest surviving Arabic poetry dates from after 500. From about 600, works by many poets have survived. The most important early poems are generally held to be the seven odes known as *al-Mu'allaqat* (The Suspended Ones), which are said to have been woven in gold thread and displayed in the Ka'bah before Islam. These are odes attributed to Imru' al-Qays (died circa 540), Tarafah ibn al-Abd (died circa 569), Zuhayr ibn Abi Salma (died circa 627), Labid ibn Rabi'ah (died circa 661), 'Amr ibn Kulthum (died circa 600), al-Harith ibn Hillizah (late sixth century), and 'Antarah ibn Shaddad (died circa 615). Some of these poets overlapped the start of the Muslim era, and none flourished more than a century before the appearance of Islam. What helped gain acceptance for poetry as a Muslim literary form was that several poets praised the Prophet Muhammad, celebrated his victories, defended Islam, and attacked the opponents of the newly founded faith. The best known of these poets was Hassan ibn Thabit (died circa 660). Another was Ka'b ibn Zuhayr ibn Abi Salma, one of several Makkan poets who at first had attacked the Prophet in their poetry, a tradition commonly known as *hija'*. After the surrender of Makkah to the Muslims in 630, however, Ka'b asked for forgiveness, which the Prophet granted. To show his gratitude, Ka'b recited a friendly poem for him, and in return the Prophet gave his cloak, known in Arabic as a *burdah*, to Ka'b as a present—an incident signaling the Prophet's approval of poetry. A whole new genre of poetry based on this story developed later, taking its name from the Prophet's *burdah*. The best-known poem in this genre is *Burdah* by al-Busiri (1213 – circa 1296), which became the most favored and commented on of all Arabic poems. Another poet from the earliest era of Islam is a woman, al-Khansa' (circa 575 – circa 644), who used vivid language for mourning poems and other verse and became a Muslim for about the last fifteen years of her life—demonstrating that women as well as men could be poets in Islam.

The Early Khilafah. Under the early khilafah (632–661) and especially under the Umayyads (661–750), the khalifahs (caliphs) and by their provincial governors continued to cultivate the classical forms of Arabic poetry and were served by many poets who extolled their patrons' virtues and generosity. Being traditional, both the Umayyad rulers and their poets continued to cultivate the early poetic ideal, recalling Bedouin campsites and desert journeys, even though these motifs did not reflect the lives of most Arabian Muslims, let alone those who inhabited the bustling new urban centers of Islam, such as Damascus, Kufah, and Basrah. Despite rulers' attempts to evoke the simplicity of the past in their isolated castles on the fringes of cultivated areas, new factors inevitably introduced change, which is already apparent in the poems of the best-known Umayyad poets, the Christian al-Akhtal (circa 640 – 710), as well as Jarir (circa 653 – circa 728) and al-Farazdaq (circa 641 – circa 728). These poets had links to both the unlettered oral poetic tradition of pre-Islamic times and to the new age of far flung empire, mixing of peoples, khalifal politics, and writing. Some poets expressed political opposition, such as the sophisticated Kufan Shi'i, al-Kumayt al-Asadi (680–743). Even more a sign of the times was the well-known poet of courtly love 'Umar ibn Abi Rabi'ah (644 – circa 711), who—while basing himself in part on earlier Arabic models—virtually founded a new tradition of pure love poetry, along with his lesser-known contemporaries Kuthayyir 'Azzah (circa 650 – 723) and Jamil Buthaynah (circa 660 – 701). Their poems concentrate on the suffering caused by unfulfilled passion, which became the great theme of most subsequent love poetry. There were also several women poets in this period, including Umm Hakim, the noble-born wife of Khalifah Hisham, who ruled 724–743.

Abbasid poetry. Under the early Abbasid khilafah (750–945), poetry, and literature in general, really began to move in new, unprecedented directions. While continuing to employ the same sixteen meters, poets began to abandon traditional modes of poetry. Among the most innovative of these poets was Abu Nuwas (circa 762 – 813), who held the classical conventions of poetry up to ridicule by parodying them. Other well-known poets of Abbasid times include the sarcastic blind Iranian poet Bashshar ibn Burd (circa 714 – circa 784), who became the first non-Arab to reach the first rank of Arabic poets; the ascetic and world-rejecting Abu al-'Atahiyah (748–826), whose poems were set to music as popular songs; the traditionalist Abu Tammam (804–845); and the urbane al-Buhturi (821–897). Often these poets are said to have reached a new peak of excellence in variety and quality of expression. Though many students of poetry have stated a preference for the Jahili poets, works by the Abbasid poets are popular because they use Arabic vocabulary and constructions that are closer to modern standard Arabic, making them easier to understand. Indeed, the Arabic of the early Abbasid writers and that of the present day do not differ much either in vocabulary or grammar, so it may be said that the standard Arabic language

A literary group in a Baghdad garden, circa 1237; illumination from a manuscript
for the *Maqamat* (Assemblies) of al-Hariri (Bibliothèque Nationale, Paris)

became more or less fixed by the literary activity of those early writers.

Later Poets. Other poets followed, associated with the time of Abbasid political decline (945–1258). A versatile poet best known for his beautiful descriptions of nature was al-Sanawbari (circa 888 – 945), whose patrons were the provincial Hamdanid dynasty in Aleppo. The works of the well-known al-Mutanabbi (915–965), whom the Hamdanids also supported, are often said to represent the acme of technical perfection in Arabic poetry, and he may possibly be the best poet. The sarcastic poet of asceticism, Abu al-'Ala' al-Ma'arri (973–1058) was not above criticizing the religious leaders of Islam along with everyone else. His well-known *Risalat al-ghufran* (The Epistle of Forgiveness, circa 1033) is a mixture of poetry and prose describing a soul's journey through the reaches of heaven and hell. After this period, Arabic poetry is sometimes said to have declined, but such assertions are based on the tendency to value the distant past over more-recent times. In fact, good poetry continued to be cultivated and written. Not merely recirculating worn-out themes, poets remained creative while also taking into consideration the growing number of poetic pre-

cedents left by their forebears. Poetry tended to become more self-consciously intellectual than before, a feature that also characterizes much modern Western poetry. One particularly fertile genre was mystical poetry, especially by the renowned Egyptian Ibn al-Farid (1180–1235) and the great Andalusian Sufi Muhyi al-Din Ibn al-'Arabi (1165–1240). Yet, overall the poets of the later Middle Ages are not as well known as their predecessors.

Spain and North Africa. One area where the greatest cultural flourishing took place somewhat later was the Muslim West, North Africa, and Spain, where new genres such as *muwashshah* and *zajal* poetry appeared in the eleventh and twelfth centuries respectively. These poems are distinguished from the old odes by more-complex rhyming structures, including stanzas, and by the use of a less formal and more colloquial language. These forms subsequently spread to the Arabic-speaking East. While they were not usually highly regarded by scholars, they eventually found their place in popular expression and as songs. Spanish Muslim poetry is especially known for its themes of love and descriptions of nature. One Spanish Muslim poet is 'A'ishah bint Ahmad al–Qurtubiyyah (died 1009), who was born into a literary family of Qurtuba (Cordoba), the capital of Muslim Spain and lived at the height of Umayyad rule there, when the city was perhaps the largest in Europe (with the possible exception of Byzantine Constantinople). 'A'ishah was considered a wonder of her age, excelling in learning, including religious learning, literary ability, and poetry. In fact, her poetic talent surpassed that of her uncle, who was also a poet, and she was known for the purity of her style. She was also a well-known calligrapher and made many copies of the Qur'an. Her independence is illustrated by the lines of poetry in which she which she responded to an unwelcome marriage proposal from a poet she did not like:

> I am a lioness, and will never consent to let
> My body be the stopping place for anyone.
> But if I should choose that, I would not hearken
> To a dog,—and how many a lion I have turned down!

Ibn Zaydun (1003–1070), a court official who specialized in love poetry, has often been considered the most important poet of Muslim Spain. His poetry celebrates his long and tortuous affair with the haughty Umayyad princess Walladah (circa 1008 – 1091), who was also a poet. Indeed, the theme of ill-fated lovers is a common one in Arabic poetry, especially its Andalusian branch. Another well-known pair is al-Mu'tamid al-'Abbadi (1040–1095), the ruler of Seville and the best-known poet of his generation, and his beloved wife al-Rumaykiyyah (died 1091), also a poet. Their kingdom suffered a sudden downfall, and they died in exile. A third unfortunate pair was Abu Ja'far Ahmad ibn Sa'id (died 1164) and Hafsah al-Rakuniyyah (died 1184 or 1190). Always set to music, such Spanish Arabic poetry set the standard for courtly love in Western Europe during the later Middle Ages, and its influence on the French troubadours should not be underestimated. Writing in a different vein, Ibn Khafajah (1058–1117) was so well known for his celebration of nature that he was later called "the Sanawbari of al-Andalus," comparing him to the early Syrian nature poet but connecting him to Muslim Spain. The later court poets Ibn al-Khatib (1313–1374) and Ibn Zamrak (1333–1393) served as ministers to the ruler of Granada, the last Muslim outpost in Spain, and continued the Andalusian poetic tradition with undiminished brilliance.

Sources:

Julia Ashtiany and others, *Abbasid Belles Lettres* (Cambridge, U.K. & New York: Cambridge University Press, 1990).

H.A.R. Gibb, *Arabic Literature: An Introduction*, second revised edition (Oxford: Clarendon Press, 1963).

James Kritzeck, *Anthology of Islamic Literature, from the Rise of Islam to Modern Times* (New York: Holt, Rinehart & Winston, 1964).

Ilse Lichtenstadter, *Introduction to Classical Arabic Literature* (New York: Twayne, 1974).

Mustansir Mir and Jarl E. Fossum, eds., *Literary Heritage of Classical Islam* (Princeton: Darwin, 1993).

John Alden Williams, *The Word of Islam* (Austin: University of Texas Press, 1994).

ARABIC PROSE LITERATURE

Foundations. From early on Islam produced a broad prose literature of enduring significance. By 1500 the Muslim literary tradition—by then nearly nine hundred years old—was one of the leading traditions of the world and probably the largest in size at that time. Although Muslim literature later came to be written down in a considerable number of languages, until 1500 it was almost entirely written in just two, Arabic and Persian. Though the Muslim canon in either language was enormous by 1500, the Arabic was somewhat larger, in part because it was older, having begun in the seventh century, while Persian Muslim literature began in the tenth. Arabic is the foundational language of Muslim civilization, occupying a role similar to Greek in the classical Graeco-Roman tradition or Sanskrit in the ancient Indian civilization. Under Islam, Persian was an Arabicized form of the pre-Islamic language of Iran and written in the Arabic script. Arabic written literature begins with the foundational sacred book of Islam, the Qur'an, which came down in a series of separate revelations to the Prophet Muhammad from about 609 to 632. No other significant written literature in Arabic appears to have preceded the Qur'an; indeed, there are scarcely any examples of Arabic writing prior to it apart from a few inscriptions. Thus, the seminal role of the Qur'an in Arabic literature—a place it shares with pre-Islamic Arabic oral poetry—can hardly be underestimated. Because there is no earlier written literature, the Qur'an has informed and influenced all subsequent developments in written Arabic, much as Homer's two epics did for Greek. It is no proof against its influence to say that the Qur'an is in a category by itself and was not subsequently imitated or reproduced. The same could be said of the Homeric poems; yet—despite their peculiar language, form, and subject matter—they exerted a pervasive influence in the classical civilizations of Greece and Rome. In fact, the language of the Qur'an has always been celebrated by Muslims as the best, most effective, and most moving of any speech.

The Rise of Prose Literature. The central role of Arabic poetry decreased after the thirteenth century and had perhaps begun to lose its dominance considerably earlier. Arabic prose in the meantime arose and flourished throughout the period 750–1500. For about the first 150 years of Islam, the Qur'an prevailed alongside poetry and oral narratives; before 750, little prose literature was written, apart from a handful of treatises, epistles, and speeches, mostly connected with the government, such as those attributed to the Umayyad khalifal secretary Abd al-Hamid ibn Yahya (died 750). An Abbasid prime minister of Persian origin, Ibn al-Muqaffa' (circa 720 – circa 756), also wrote some prose treatises. Most of them are translations from Middle Persian, or Pahlavi literature, but a few of them are original or have original passages. His longest and best-known surviving work is the tale of talking animals, *Kalilah wa-Dimnah*, an example of a "mirror for princes" (advice book for rulers), translated from Sanskrit through Pahlavi and into Arabic, with some reworking by Ibn al-Muqaffa' to make it accept-

Page from a manuscript for *Kalilah wa-Dimmah* by Ibn al-Muqatta', an eighth-century collection of animal fables narrated by two jackals, Kalilah and Dimmah, who are counselors to a lion king (Bodleian Library, Oxford)

able to Muslim sensibilities. After these beginnings, a never-ending stream of Arabic prose composition in various genres of literature has been unbroken to the present day. The establishment of paper mills in Turkestan shortly after 750 and in Iraq before 800 made available an inexpensive writing material and facilitated an outpouring of prose composition and compilation. Unlike the compositions of Ibn al-Muqaffa', however, later Arabic prose literature was increasingly inspired by the religion of Islam. The Arabic reading public in that age of calligraphy and handwritten manuscripts consisted almost entirely of Muslims, and most of these readers and writers worked in the religious field. Therefore, it is hardly surprising that most of the Arabic literature of the period 750–1500 is religious or ancillary to the religious writings. The two earliest surviving long prose works are the Qur'an commentary (*tafsir*) by Muqatil ibn Sulayman al-Balkhi (died 767) and the biography (*sirah*) of the Prophet Muhammad by Muhammad ibn Ishaq (circa 704–circa 767). Several other almost as early Qur'an commentaries also exist, and many others have been written down to the present, forming a major category of Arabic literature. The earliest commentaries were followed a short time later by the first significant treatise on Muslim law, *al-Muwatta'* by Malik ibn Anas (circa 712–795), which includes many traditions attributed to the Prophet Muhammad as well as Malik's own legal opinions. Subsequently, two major themes of Malik's work became separate genres of Muslim religious literature, the first being *fiqh* (legal prescriptions, discussions, and opinions) and the second, hadiths (traditions attributed to the Prophet). Each of these earliest surviving works is a sophisticated piece of writing that is obviously not the beginning of a new genre but rather at an already advanced stage in the development of its tradition. The massive catalogue of Arabic literature by Ibn al-Nadim (circa 936–995), *al-Fihrist*, lists thousands of early works that were subsequently lost.

Preserving Islamic Knowledge. The motivation for writing in the genres of *tafsir, sirah, fiqh,* and *hadith* was a desire of the early Muslims in the diverse and changing Muslim khilafah to cultivate and preserve knowledge about Islam. From the beginning, Madinah, the Prophet's city in Arabia, held pride of place as the unquestioned center of religious knowledge, and a few of the earliest Muslim writings can be traced to that city, including those by Malik and Ibn Ishaq. Yet, the real development of early Muslim scholarship and its methodologies centered in Iraq, in the large Muslim cities of Kufah and Basrah, and, after 762, in the new Abbasid capital of Baghdad. Soon the new Arabic written scholarship spread all over the khilafah, to Damascus, al-Fustat (later Cairo), al-Qayrawan, Cordoba, Marw, Balkh, Nishapur, Bukhara, and Samarqand. After Iraq, Transoxiana, or Turkestan, became the second center where much early Arabic literature was composed. Although this new Arabic literature was cultivated by Muslims of all kinds of different ethnic backgrounds, the Iranian element was dominant among authors, and Arabs were in a minority. The scholarly methodology that characterizes the influential early works of Ibn Ishaq and Malik, among others, subsequently became a signature feature of most Muslim literature, both religious and secular. In this methodology of tradition, all statements are attributed with great care and in precise detail to a chain of sources said to have transmitted that particular piece of information. In Arabic, this chain is called the *isnad*. An *isnad* might say, "A got it from B, who got it from C . . ." all the way back to the Prophet. Although comparable systems of tracing statements to sources occur in embryonic form in ancient Greek, Roman, and Jewish literature, such systems do not have the meticulous completeness found in the Muslim sources. As such, the Muslim scholastic method points the way to later developments of scholarly method in Europe, as has been established by the American scholar George Makdisi. In the ninth century, the genres of Qur'an commentary, law, and Prophetic tradition became voluminous. Many multivolume sets were produced that surpassed in length the largest literary monuments of the ancient world. This development has continued into the present, and these religious works with their commentaries and supercommentaries constitute the largest body of Muslim religious literature.

Creativity. Sometimes critics have stated that these early compositions and compilations lack creativity because they consist largely of statements taken from earlier works. Such disparagement of medieval Muslim literature is the result of imposing modern ideas of "originality" and "creativity" on a body of work created according to different criteria. Indeed, a Muslim religious scholar's excellence was measured precisely by the care with which he copied the statements of his predecessors, especially in the area of hadiths. A similar respect for tradition—and lack of regard for what modern writers consider creativity—was also common in medieval Western Europe, as well as other ancient and medieval societies. The overall creativity of Muslim scholarship is unquestionable; a huge body of scholarly knowledge was brought into existence where none had existed before. Furthermore, the concept of valuing individual authorship did not exist at the beginning and arose only gradually. Abu 'Ubaydah (728–824), a Basran philologist, and al-Jahiz (circa 776–869), a Basran essayist and satirist, are among the early writers to whom original works may be attributed. Finally, many of the early works do exhibit creativity and original authorship, and even compilations of quotations from various sources require the selection and arrangement of the material, which can be important and creative contributions to knowledge in their own right. Still, literary historians are interested in what part of a particular writer's work is his original creation. In the case of much medieval Muslim literature, that assessment has yet to be undertaken, much less completed and agreed on, and finding out the exact sources of many ideas and contributions may prove impossible. In this respect, early Muslim literature resembles ancient classical literature, where, for example, it is impossible to ascertain how

ملاحشاتك مشقضا أوشّا أويس من الهبالة

الأوس الاعطاء وأويس هو الذّب وقال الهذلي

ما فعل اليوم وأويس الغنم

وقال اُمّية بن أبى الصّلت

وأبو الثامى كان يحسن أوسهم ويحوّطهم في كلّ عام جاحد

وتقولون اجمق من نعامة قالوا ذلك لأنّها تدع الحضن على بيضها شاعة الحاجة الى الطّعم

فإن في وخر وجما ذلك زان بيض لعامة قد خرجت للطعم حضنت بيضها ولشيت بنّض

نفتها ولعل نلك ان نصاد فلا ترجع الى بضها حتى نملك قالوا ولذلك قال ابن

هرمة

Illumination of an ostrich sitting on its eggs in a manuscript for *Kitab al-hayawan* (The Book of Animals), an eight-volume compendium of information by the ninth-century writer al-Jahiz (Ambrosiana Library, Milan)

LANGUAGE AND RHETORIC

Several prose genres arose to serve the needs of scholars studying the enormous body of Islamic religious literature. Among them were lexicography, grammar, and rhetoric—initially motivated by a desire to understand as fully as possible the language of the Qur'an. These investigations were initiated by Abu 'Amr ibn al-'Ala' (circa 689 – circa 770) of Basrah, one of the seven canonical "readers" of the Qur'an. These linguists studied the most ancient sources of Arabic, pre-Islamic poetry, alongside the Qur'an. They also investigated the speech of the Bedouin Arabs, which was considered the purest Arabic. The pioneer theorist and scholar of language in this effort was one of Abu 'Amr's students, Khalil ibn Ahmad (died between 776 and 791), who produced the first Arabic dictionary. The earliest Arabic surviving grammatical work is by Khalil's student Sibawayh (died circa 796). The extensive linguistic studies that followed made Arabic the most completely described and best analyzed language until modern times. Grammatical and rhetorical studies have been a basic part of the Muslim school curriculum since the earliest times. Medieval Arabic grammatical and linguistic works often show great insight. For example, the linguistic writings of Ibn Jinni (913–1002), who lived in Iraq, Syria, and Iran, anticipated many modern developments in that field. Ibn Jinni also wrote on rhetoric, as did Abd al-Qahir al-Jurjani (died circa 1078), whose analyses of how metaphor and figurative language work prefigure modern academic thought on such subjects. Muslim linguists also devised the principles (usul) of methodology for various Islamic sciences. Often these writings dealt with questions about the nature and basis of knowledge, thus entering into the realm of philosophy as well.

Sources: C. Rabin, "Arabiyya," *Encyclopedia of Islam*, CD-ROM version (Leiden: Brill, 1999).

A. Hadj Salah, "Lugha," *Encyclopedia of Islam*, CD-ROM version (Leiden: Brill, 1999).

much of the corpus of writings attributed to Aristotle was actually written by him.

Religious Disciplines. In Arabic literature, Qur'an commentaries and the less-plentiful *sirah* literature seem to be the earliest genres to appear separately. Qur'an commentaries range from large encyclopedia-sized works to small single volumes and marginal notes in copies of the Qur'an. Many are comprehensive, but others cover only a part of the Qur'an, sometimes a single chapter. Although such commentaries might appear derivative and therefore not in the realm of what is usually considered to be literature, from the Muslim viewpoint they are at the center of literature and not marginal to it. The commentaries include various sorts of material, including linguistic analyses, explanations attributed to the Prophet and other early authorities, opinions of the authors, narrative details of the Qur'anic stories of the Prophets, and philosophical and theological arguments. Among the largest, most widely distributed, and best known are those of al-Tabari (839–923), exhaustively collecting early exegetical traditions; al-Zamakhshari (1075–1144), providing brilliant linguistic insights; al-Razi (1149–1209), emphasizing philosophy; al-Qurtubi (died 1273), specializing in law; and Ibn Kathir (circa 1300–1374), criticizing many traditions and establishing a kind of norm for conservative interpretation. Each of these works is a multivolume set ranging from four to thirty volumes. Among the Shi'is, the *tafsir* of al-Tabarsi (1075–1153) is the most famous. More than one thousand Arabic commentaries on the Qur'an have been written, most of them before 1500.

Legal Writings. The next genre of early literature to be widely cultivated was, following Malik, the *fiqh* works, or the compendia of Muslim practice according to the Shari'ah legal schools. These works became exceedingly long and numerous in the ninth century and have continued in like manner ever since. Among the earliest products in this area are the multivolume sets attributed to Abu Yusuf (732–798), Abd al-Razzaq al-San'ani (744–827), Muhammad ibn Hasan al-Shaybani (750–805), al-Shafi'i (767–820), and Sahnun (777–854), the last compiled from Malik's teachings. These writings—which include legal material, Prophetic hadiths, and other traditions—are the longest works composed in Arabic up to their time. Later, even longer juristic encyclopedias, focusing more on the law than the traditions, were written by al-Sarakhsi (died 1090), Ibn Rushd (1063–1126), al-Nawawi (1133–1177), and Ibn Qudamah (1147–1223) and dozens of others. Hundreds of shorter works were compiled and circulated, often having more influence than the longer ones, because the smaller ones were more often studied and memorized. An example of one of these short works is *al-Risalah* (The Treatise) by Ibn Abi Zayd al-Qayrawani (922–996), which was taken to America much later by enslaved African Muslims who had memorized it, some of whom left partial manuscripts of its contents in Arabic. The large law books are reference works that had a huge impact on Muslim society by setting its standards in detail, and they remain perhaps the best known embodiment of Islam, a form of literature that has contributed to the unity of Muslim beliefs and practice across space and time.

Hadith Collections. To support the pronouncements of the law books, it was necessary to quote not only the Qur'an but also hadiths, authoritative traditions reporting what the Prophet Muhammad said, did, or approved. Each hadith consists of a discrete text, often only a few words but sometimes extending to several pages in length. Each text is accompanied by its own chain of guarantors or transmitters describing who got the text from whom, extending back to the Prophet. The grading of the traditions according to their authenticity, mostly on the basis

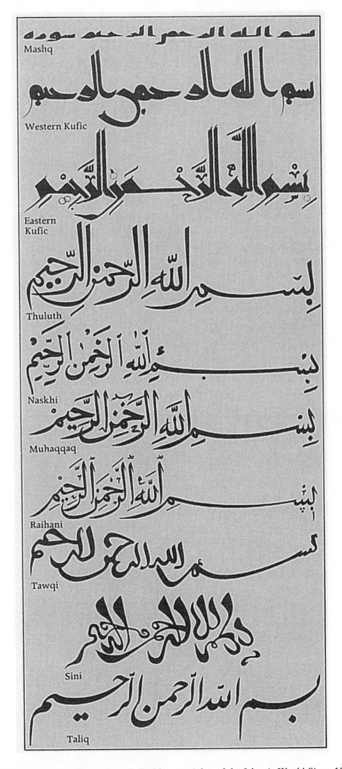

| Mashq |
| Western Kufic |
| Eastern Kufic |
| Thuluth |
| Naskhi |
| Muhaqqaq |
| Raihani |
| Tawqi |
| Sini |
| Taliq |

Arabic calligraphy styles (from Francis Robinson, *Atlas of the Islamic World Since 1500*, 1982)

of the reliability of their chains of transmitters, became an exacting science because hadiths are the second primary source of legal and behavioral norms for Muslims after the Qur'an, Muslims wanted to be especially careful about the authenticity of these traditions. Therefore, a movement arose to compile books including only traditions of the Prophet Muhammad. Between roughly 775 and 1075, Muslims produced about two hundred extant original collections of hadiths, in addition to others that have not survived. These works range in size from small booklets to huge multivolume sets. Nearly all the large collections have survived. With a few exceptions this literature was compiled in Turkestan and northern Iran, or it was compiled by writers from those two regions who lived elsewhere, usually in Iraq. Also with few exceptions, the redactors of hadiths in Arabic were from Iranian ethnic groups. The most important and reliable of such works are the *Sahihs* (Sound Traditions) by Muhammad ibn Ismail al-Bukhari (810–870) and Abu al-Husayn Muslim (821–875), which may be viewed as entirely normative for Sunnis, who accept all the traditions collected in these two works. Thus, they are among the mostly widely read books of all Muslim literature. Four other collections considered highly reliable, in order of rank, are those of Abu Dawud (817–889), al-Tirmidhi (824–892), al-Nasa'i (830–915), and Ibn Majah (824–887). Together with al-Bukhari and Muslim, these works make up the "Six Books" of the Sunnah. All six books are organized according to subject matter and follow the same order as the books of law or *fiqh*.

Hadith Commentaries. Many long commentaries were subsequently written on most hadith collections. Some of these commentaries became well-known works of Muslim literature in their own right, especially that of Ibn Hajar al-'Asqalani (1372–1449) on al-Bukhari and that of al-Nawawi on Muslim. Also, many secondary compilations of the hadith were taken from the original collections, and several of these works became quite influential. In response to "the Six Books" of the Sunnis, the Shi'is created a traditional corpus of four collections that they recognize as authoritative: those of al-Kulayni (died circa 940) and Ibn Babwayh (circa 918 – 991) and two by al-Tusi (995–1067).

Devotional Prose. In addition to works in the categories of *tafsir, fiqh,* and *hadith,* a great body of devotional and argumentative religious literature arose. Some of this literature was written in the form of esoteric *tafsir* and ascetic hadith compilations. But eventually this writing became a separate genre that can be broadly described as esoteric or Sufi literature, which became as vast as other religious genres. In its early phases this writing is associated with al-Muhasibi (died 857), al-Junayd (died 910), and al-Qushayri (986–1072). Later, the teachings of Abd al-Qadir al-Jilani (1078–1166) became prominent and popular. Abd al-Qadir was a strict Hanbali legalist who emphasized the moral teachings of Islam as well as the practice of the law. Ibn 'Ata' Allah (died 1309) is admired for the pietistic aphorisms in his *Hikam* (Wise Sayings). The more philosophical trend in Sufism is represented by the controversial Andalusian Muhyi al-Din Ibn 'Arabi (1165–1240), whose many writings include his esoteric encyclopedia of Sufi piety, *al-Futuhat al-Makkiyyah* (The Makkan Openings).

Philosophical Prose. Devotional and esoteric literature often dealt with philosophical issues as well, and there are also many separate philosophical writings. The best-known Muslim philosophers include al-Kindi (circa 801 – circa 866), who first systematized a Muslim philosophy that borrows from the Greeks but is also depended on the Qur'an; al-Razi (circa 854 – 925 or 935), a well-known physician; al-Farabi (circa 870– 950), who wrote about a kind of utopia; Ibn Sina' (980–1037, known in the West as Avicenna), a great physician and Neoplatonist; al-

Ghazali (1059–1111, known in the West as Algazel), the synthesizer of the Sunni tradition, and Ibn Rushd (1126–1198, known in the West as Averroës), a great defender of Aristotelianism.

Historiography. Muslims also cultivated historical writing to help explain religious texts and, perhaps, to instruct the rulers. The first writing of this kind was the Prophet's biography, which was followed by hundreds of narrative historical works, many in multivolume sets of encyclopedic length, a body of work whose size dwarfs that of historical writings in any other language before 1500. The best-known Arabic narrative histories include those of the Qur'an commentator al-Tabari, covering the first three hundred years of Islam; al-Mas'udi (circa 890–956), who wrote extensively on non-Muslim peoples outside the khilafah; Ibn Khaldun (1332–1406), a social analyst and philosopher of history; and al-Maqrizi (1364–1442), a great political, economic, and social historian of Egypt. Indeed, with regard to al-Maqrizi and his contemporaries, the fifteenth century has often been considered the high point of Muslim historiography in Egypt and Syria. Muslim historical narratives often concern rulers and capital cities, as do other medieval chronicles. Thus, in general, they are political histories and do not concern themselves with peaceful religious developments, even when they are written by ulama' (religious leaders) such as Ibn Kathir. Their purpose was mainly to provide the literate classes with historical information about the general course of Islam. Although the historical narratives were sometimes read to the rulers, they were often unfavorable to them, especially in describing the intrigues, scandals, and failures of past rulers with great frankness and detail. Muslim narrative histories also include much economic, social, and religious information. While medieval Muslim histories do not follow modern historical methodologies, they scrupulously document their sources, in many cases achieving a greater degree of such documentation than previous historians elsewhere. Another useful kind of Muslim history writing is local history centered on one city or province.

Biographical Works. There are also many Muslim biographical dictionaries. In fact the number of such biographies produced by medieval Muslims exceeds that of all other ancient and medieval civilizations combined. Muslim religious scholars used these works to verify the reliability of hadith transmitters and other sorts of scholars. Some of these works include only information about hadith transmitters of the first three centuries of Islam. The earliest work of this sort is by Ibn Sa'd (circa 784–845). In Ibn Hajar al-'Asqalani's biographical dictionaries of transmitters, the biographies usually consist of short notices giving the names, dates, places of birth and death, teachers, students, and estimates of the trustworthiness of the person in question. Other biographical dictionaries have much fuller information, especially the seventy-volume work of Ibn 'Asakir (1105–1176), detailing the lives of everyone who had anything to do with Damascus and including

much of the early Syrian historical tradition. Al-Dha-habi's (1274–1348) longer works, such as *Siyar a'lam al-nubala'* (The Biographies of Outstanding Nobles) and *Ta'rikh al-Islam* (The History of Islam), also include a great deal of detail. A large number of other biographical dictionaries cover only specific fields of endeavor, including those on poets, prose writers, or Sufis.

Geography and Travel Writing. Another sort of literature useful to religious scholars and historians is geographical writing. Muslim geographers definitely surpassed all other ancient and medieval geographers in both the quantity and quality of their output. Geographical writings helped rulers, merchants, and religious scholars to understand their world. The central location of the Muslims in proximity to Europe, Africa, South Asia, Southeast Asia, China, and Turkestan probably enhanced the value of their work. Two of the most important Muslim geographers were al-Muqaddasi (born 947), who based his innovative description of the world on firsthand observations, and al-Biruni (973–at least 1050), a geographer and ethnographer, especially of India, which he visited. A related genre is the travel narrative, of which there are several medieval Muslim examples. The best known is the account of the Moroccan Ibn Battuta (1304-1369), who dictated it in 1357. Ibn Battuta traveled longer and more widely than anyone before him, visiting China, India, Central Asia, East Africa, and West Africa, as well as most of the central Muslim lands.

Adab. Less strictly religious than other prose genres, *adab,* or cultured prose writing, tended to serve a somewhat different public than *tafsir, sirah, fiqh,* or *hadith.* While it often included poetic quotations as well, *adab* is basically less-religious prose writing as contrasted with poetry. The audience for *adab* literature included rulers and government officials, as well as religious scholars, who greatly enjoyed relief from reading serious religious books. Also, most rulers, princes, and government officials received some religious training and read religious works and commentaries as a foundation of their education. Some, such as al-Mahdi Ibn Tumart (circa 1080–1130), the founder of the messianic al-Muwahhid movement, which established a dynasty in Morocco, had extensive religious training, qualifying them as scholars in their own right. Conversely, *adab* literature was usually written by religious scholars. Like most Muslim poets but unlike writers of strictly religious works, *adab* writers tended to have rulers as patrons. The first great Muslim writer of *adab,* or cultured, literature is usually considered to be al-Jahiz (circa 776–869) of Basrah. Although al-Jahiz wrote treatises on many subjects, including religious and political topics, he is best known for his amusing essays and treatises, such as *Kitab al-bukhala'* (The Book of Misers). Some of his writing seems to be drawn from the works of Ibn al-Muqaffa'. Al-Jahiz had a considerable influence on the standards for courtly literature. Although his elaborate style is often deemed most appropriate for the cultivated elite, he has remained popular among vari-

---

THE VERSE OF LIGHT

Muslims do not view the Qur'an as literature because they believed it to be the direct Word of God, and therefore it is not subject to literary evaluation. The language of the Qur'an is considered to be inimitable, reaching the pinnacle of eloquence in Arabic. Thus, the Qur'an sets the standard for Arabic literary expression. It even includes the challenge to produce verses like it—a challenge that has never been met. Among the most-beautiful and best-known passages are "The Verse of Light, and the verses (or *ayat*), that follow it.

Allah is the Light of the heavens and the earth. The parable of His Light is as if there were a Niche and within it a lamp: the Lamp enclosed in Glass: the glass as it were a brilliant star: lit from a blessed Tree an Olive neither of the East nor of the West whose Oil is well-nigh luminous though fire scarce touched it: Light upon Light! Allah doth guide whom He will to His Light. Allah doth set forth Parables for men: and Allah doth know all things.

[Lit is such a light] in houses which Allah hath permitted to be raised to honor; for the celebration in them of His name: in them is He glorified in the mornings and in the evenings [again and again]

By men whom neither traffic nor merchandise can divert from the Remembrance of Allah nor from regular Prayer nor from the practice of regular Charity: their [only] fear is for the Day when hearts and eyes will be transformed [in a world wholly new]

That Allah may reward them according to the best of their deeds and add even more for them out of His Grace: for Allah doth provide for those whom He will without measure.

But the Unbelievers their deeds are like a mirage in sandy deserts which the man parched with thirst mistakes for water; until when he comes up to it he finds it to be nothing: but he finds Allah [ever] with him and Allah will pay him his account: and Allah is swift in taking account.

Or [the Unbelievers' state] is like the depths of darkness in a vast deep ocean overwhelmed with billow topped by billow topped by [dark] clouds: depths of darkness one above another: if a man stretches out his hand he can hardly see it! for any to whom Allah giveth not light there is no light!

Source: Qur'an, Surah 24, ayat 35–40, Yusuf Ali translation; from *The Alim for Windows* Multimedia Edition 4.5 (Baltimore: ISL Software Corporation, 1996).

---

ous classes of Muslims. His successor Ibn Qutaybah (828–889) was an Iraqi religious scholar who produced strictly religious writings but is better known for his cultured literature, which includes encyclopedic compendia of curious and amusing information and stories as well as substantial books on poetry. Ibn Qutaybah brought a simpler, more popular style to bear, as Abu al-'Atahiyah had done for poetry a couple of generations earlier. Ibn Abd

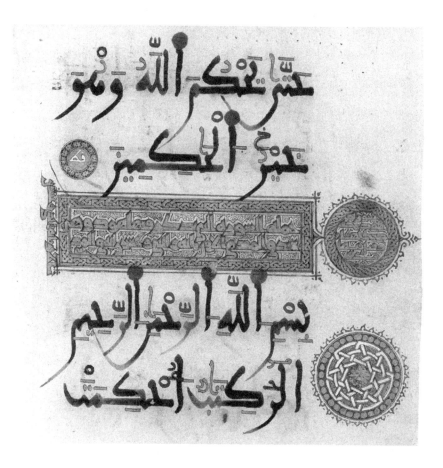

Pages from manuscripts for the Qur'an: (top) in Kufic script from ninth-century Iraq (British Library, London) and (bottom) in Maghribi script from tenth-century Andalusia (from *Aramco World*, September-October 1989)

Rabbih (860–940) was an Andalusian who wrote a great and popular encyclopedia of information and lore about the Muslims in the East. Abu Faraj al-Isfahani (897–967) compiled *Kitab al-aghani* (The Book of Songs), an enormous encyclopedia on early Muslim poets, with many quotations of poetry and stories about the poets. Similar encyclopedias of cultured literature and information continued to be produced throughout the Middle Ages. Al-Qalqashandi (1355–1418) compiled a specialized encyclopedia of everything a governmental correspondence secretary was expected to know, and there were several other encyclopedias later in the medieval period.

Maqamat. A significant genre of rhymed prose (*saj'*) is that of the *maqamat* (assemblies, or occasional discourses; singular: *maqamah*), fictional stories told in the first person by an author as if he were narrating them from their source, who is usually an eloquent vagabond—and sometimes a scoundrel and swindler as well. Contrasting a highly classical Arabic language with plotlines about disreputable members of society and their tricks, *maqamat* are highly amusing and must have appealed to both the elite and the merchant class. The concept of the polished vagabond is a commonplace in literature that extends back to the story called "The Eloquent Peasant" in ancient Egypt circa 2000 B.C.E. *Maqamat* writers often wove into their stories much subtle but sharp social commentary and criticism. This genre was originally established by the Iranian Ahmad Badi al-Zaman al-Hamadhani (968–1008) as a story related by a narrator about a disreputable but eloquent person. The well-known writer al-Tanukhi (939–994) employed this theme slightly earlier. Al-Hamadhani adopted rhymed prose as its vehicle, producing a humorous and bouncy effect, endowing the writing with a special verve. Al-Hamadhani was said to have produced four hundred *maqamat,* but only fifty-two are known. The form was further popularized by al-Hariri (1054–1122) of Basrah, who heightened the effect of his stories by using a loftier vocabulary than al-Hariri. Al-Hariri's *maqamat* enjoyed great popularity in his own lifetime and are still read, studied, and celebrated. Writers still employ the *maqamat* genre, especially when they want to engage in sly or sarcastic social criticism. In fact, no century after al-Hariri has lacked authors working in this genre.

A Muslim Robinson Crusoe. In his well-known book *Hayy ibn Yaqzan* (Alive, the son of Awake) the Spanish Muslim philosopher Abu Bakr Muhammad ibn Tufayl (died 1185) imagines a pious Muslim, Asal, who seeks a solitary spiritual retreat on a lush island he believes to be uninhabited. To his astonishment, he discovers there a feral human man who was raised by a gazelle and knows no human language, but nonetheless has arrived through reflection at a complete philosophical system, including faith in the Creator. Asal names the man Hayy ibn Yaqzan and teaches him language and the religion of Islam. The message in the story is that faith in God is natural, and that given completely uninfluenced natural conditions, the human being will arrive at it. An English translation of Ibn Tufayl's work was published eleven years before Daniel Defoe's *Robinson Crusoe* (1719) and—along with the true story of the 1704–1709 adventures of Scottish sailor Alexander Selkirk—may have influenced Defoe's novel.

Sources:

Julia Ashtiany and others, *Abbasid Belles Lettres* (Cambridge, U.K. & New York: Cambridge University Press, 1990).

Muhammad ibn Ismail al-Bukhari, *The Translation of the Meanings of Sahih Al-Bukhari: Arabic-English*, 9 volumes, edited and translated by Muhammad Muhsin Khan (Beirut: Dar al-Fikr, 1981).

H. A. R. Gibb, *Arabic Literature: An Introduction,* second revised edition (Oxford: Clarendon Press, 1963).

James Kritzeck, *Anthology of Islamic Literature, from the Rise of Islam to Modern Times* (New York: Holt, Rinehart & Winston, 1964).

Ilse Lichtenstadter, *Introduction to Classical Arabic Literature* (New York: Twayne, 1974).

Mustansir Mir and Jarl E. Fossum, eds., *Literary Heritage of Classical Islam* (Princeton: Darwin, 1993).

Abu al-Husayn Muslim, *Sahih Muslim*, 4 volumes, translated by Abdul Hamid Siddiqi (Lahore: Shaikh Muhammad Ashraf, 1971–1975).

Ibn al-Nadim, *The Fihrist of al-Nadim: A Tenth-Century Survey of Muslim Culture,* edited and translated by Bayard Dodge, 2 volumes (New York: Columbia University Press, 1970).

John Alden Williams, *The Word of Islam* (Austin: University of Texas Press, 1994).

CALLIGRAPHY

Highest Art Form. Because Muslim art generally follows the prohibition of figural representations of people or animals, calligraphy, writing in decorative scripts, became a highly developed Muslim art form. Such writing ranges from attractive handwriting to monumental calligraphic decorations on buildings that involve carved stone or wood as well as painted letters on colored tiles or writing in colored mosaic. Indeed, most genres of Muslim art, including common crafts, use calligraphy for decoration. Calligraphic writing appears on cloth—especially that meant for public display, such as woven borders, brocades, banners and tapestries—as well as on metal ewers and trays and ceramic ware such as dishes and cups. Such writing can be either religious or secular, according to what is deemed appropriate for its location. Thus, masjid decoration almost always include religious phrases, usually from the Qur'an, while ordinary household objects might bear verses from the Qur'an or nonreligious poetry. In the masjids, the most common locations for calligraphy are in, around, or above the mihrab (prayer niche) and around the walls in a continuous band just below the ceiling. Masjids often display calligraphy on their outside walls as well, frequently in a continuous band running around the top of the wall and paralleling the band on the inside. Humble masjids may display no calligraphy, and because of the religious nature of most calligraphy, it was not used in places or on objects that might demean its religious message. Indeed, religious scholars formulated rules regulating its use, including a ban on putting it in public or private bathrooms, lest God's word or name or the name of the Prophet, should be dishonored. Similarly, calligraphy was not written on anything that would be trodden underfoot, such as carpets or

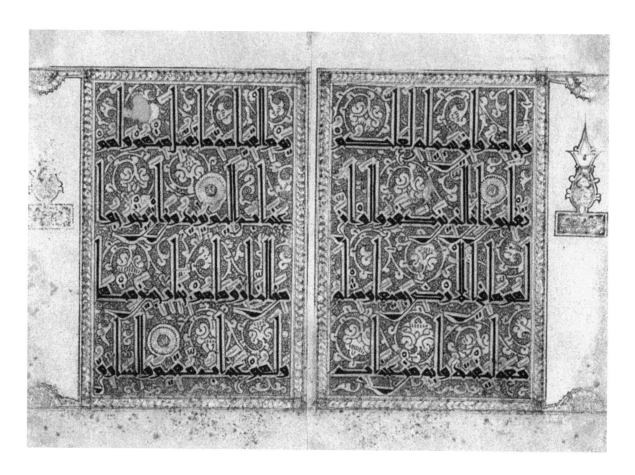

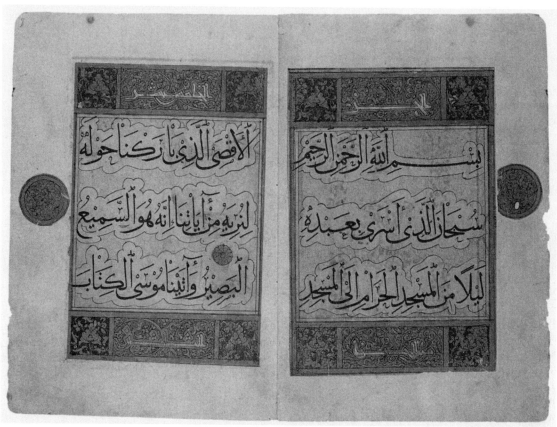

Pages from manuscripts for the Qur'an: (top) illumination in Kufic script, eleventh century (Vever Collection, Arthur M. Sackler Gallery, The National Museum of Asian Art, Smithsonian Institution, Washington, D.C.) and (bottom) illumination in Muhaqqaq script by Yaqut al-Musta'simi of Baghdad, 1282–1283 (Khalili Collection, Isfahan)

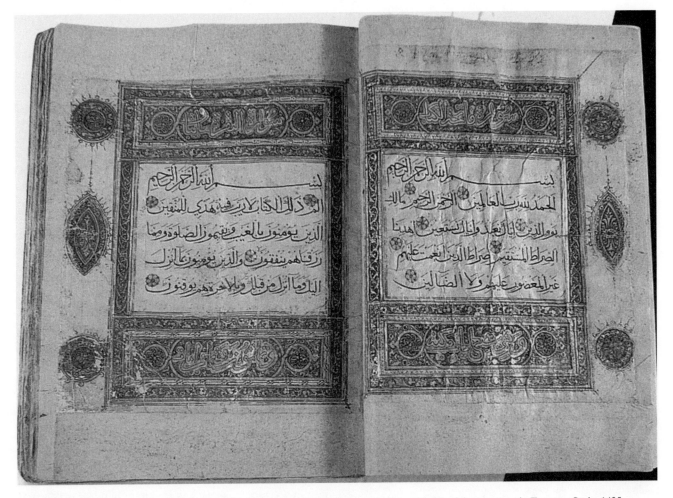

Pages from a copy of the Qur'an written and illuminated in Muhaqqaq script under Mamluk patronage in Egypt or Syria, 1425
(Bayt al-Qur'an, Bahrain)

paving stones. In other cases the attempt of the religious scholars to regulate the public use of calligraphy did not succeed. While they tried to discourage any display of writing on masjid buildings, inside or outside, this ruling was generally ignored. Scarcely any large masjid in the Muslim world lacks Qur'anic calligraphy.

Styles. Arabic calligraphy has been created in a wide variety of styles. As the Arabic alphabet was derived from the Syriac, the earliest Arabic script is close to the form of its source, in which thick letters mostly curve upward from a line that connects the letters of a word. From this source, the earliest Arabic calligraphers developed a fancy script called Kufic (after Kufah in Iraq, the first Muslim metropolis). Kufic script tends to emphasize sharp angles and square or rectangular shapes for the letters and was particularly suitable for carving on stone or wood. After about 800, as paper replaced expensive parchment and papyrus, rounder, more-cursive scripts were developed and generally replaced Kufic script in Qur'an copies by the tenth century and in monumental inscriptions by the twelfth century—except where Kufic script was used for an archaic effect. Muslims in North and West Africa, however, continued to use a form of the more angular Kufic script, which is still represented in Qur'an copies from these regions. The rounder scripts that became dominant farther east included

naskh, ruq'ah, and *thuluth.* Persian calligraphers developed another style, called *nasta'liq,* which emphasizes the thinness of the letters and makes them lean more, and this form eventually became the script of choice for Persian and Turkish languages, and—after 1500—for Indian Muslim languages as well.

Sources:
Basil Gray, ed., *The Arts of the Book in Central Asia, 14th-16th Centuries* (Boulder, Colo.: Shambhala, 1980).

Gabriel Mandel Khan, *Arabic Script: Styles, Variants, and Calligraphic Adaptations* (New York: Abbeville Press, 2001).

B. W. Robinson and others, eds., *Islamic Painting and the Arts of the Book* (London: Faber & Faber, 1976).

DECORATIVE ARTS

Motifs. Although the decorative arts of Islam are sometimes referred to as the "minor arts," they in fact express much of the genius of Muslim art. The artist working for a Muslim patron had to conform to the Muslim standards for religious art if his production was to be displayed in a religious institution. Because of the prohibition on portraying people and animals, Islamic decoration consists basically of three major motifs: the geometrical, the vegetal, and the calligraphic. Of these, the geometric is by far the most common, with plant decorations or calligraphy usually serving as embellishments.

Born in Ma'arah, Syria (near Alepp), Abu al-'Ala' Ma'arri (973–1058) became blind as a youth and relied in his writing on memory and sound. As the following examples demonstrate, his poetry and prose are known for his pessimistic and ascetic style, beliefs that were controversial from an Islamic standpoint.

III
Vain are your dreams of marvelous empire,
Vainly you sail among uncharted spaces,
Vainly seek harbor in this world of faces
If it has been determined otherwise.
V
You that must travel with a weary load
Along this darkling, labyrinthine street—
Have men with torches at your head and feet
If you would pass the dangers of the road.
XI
Myself did linger by the ragged beach,
Whereat wave after wave did rise and curl;
And as they fell, they fell—I saw them hurl
A message far more eloquent than speech:
XII
We that with song our pilgrimage beguile,
With purple islands which a sunset bore,
We, sunk upon the desecrating shore,
May parley with oblivion awhile.
L
Alas! I took me servants: I was proud
Of prose and the neat, the cunning rhyme,
But all their inclination was the crime
Of scattering my treasure to the crowd.
LVIIII
There is a palace, and the ruined wall
Divides the sand, a very home of tears,
And where love whispered of a thousand years
The silken-footed caterpillars crawl.
LXIX
And where the Prince commanded, now the shriek
Of wind is flying through the court of state:
"Here," it proclaims, "there dwelt a potentate
Who could not hear the sobbing of the weak."
CII
How strange that we, perambulating dust,
Should be the vessels of eternal fire,
That such unfading passion of desire
Should be within our fading bodies thrust.

Source: *The Diwan of Abu'-Ala,* translated by Henry Baerlein (New York: Dutton, 1914), pp. 34, 35, 36, 44, 45, 48, 54.

Rounded lines are used especially with vegetal or calligraphic motifs.

Woodworking. Muslim artists developed woodworking as an art in itself and as a subsidiary to architectural decoration, in both cases producing masterpieces. The large number of carved ceilings, doors, windows, and screens that have survived for centuries in all Muslim countries attest to the dexterity of the Muslim woodcarvers. Boxes inlaid with mother-of-pearl as well as highly ornate pieces of inlaid furniture have survived in Iran, Syria, Egypt, North Africa, and India. Masjids, madrasahs (colleges for religious studies), and other religious buildings were provided with ceilings, doors, and windows of carved wood. In addition, a masjid usually had a *minbar* (pulpit), a *kursi* (a raised seat for the Qur'an reader to sit on while reciting), and a chest to hold the Qur'an—all carved from wood. The woodworker usually carved his wood in different depths to create different impressions through light and shadow. The Muslim artists particularly excelled at making *mashrabiyyahs*, screens made of turned wood fitted together in geometric patterns. Several museums around the world, including the Museum of Islamic Art in Cairo, have excellent examples of woodwork from the earliest periods.

Metalworking and Jewelry. Museums worldwide also have examples of Muslim metalworking—including utilitarian ware such as ewers, basins, jugs, incense burners, lamps, and handwarmers. Metalworkers also made finials for the tops of masjid domes and minarets, which usually end in a crescent, as well as elaborate window grilles and locks. Weapons were often elaborately and expensively decorated with bronze and brass metalware inlaid with silver. Rulers could afford to have their swords embellished not only with silver but also with gold. Entry doors for various religious institutions, as well as some houses and palaces, consisted of a solid wooden core entirely covered with worked metal. There is a story that when the Sultan Hasan Masjid in Cairo was first built, the windows and the doors separating the large prayer hall from the mausoleum were covered with gold, and the day after they were installed they disappeared forever without a trace. One thing that seems to unite all human cultures from the dawn of history is a fascination with and production of jewelry for personal adornment. Since the medieval period, gold and silver bracelets, rings, earrings, and clasps for scarves and belts have survived throughout the Muslim world.

Glass. One of the crafts at which Muslim artists excelled was glassmaking. Islamic collections in museums nearly always feature fine examples of vases, cups, and especially lamps from medieval times. Endowment deeds for the masjids and other religious institutions that were built during the Mamluk period (1250–1517) attest to the large number of glass lamps made to light the new buildings. The decorations on glass products resemble those used on metalware and ceramics and in book illumination. Inscriptions as well as figural and geometric motifs

Yet, occasionally plant decoration has been quite important, and calligraphy is usually present in some measure. Muslim geometric decoration tends to consist of complex webs of interlocking lines, which are more often straight than curved, producing an angular effect in the designs.

Inlaid brass bowl and handwarmer typical of vessels Muslim craftsmen made for the European
market during the fifteenth century (British Museum, London)

decorate the Mamluk lamps. Colored enamel was used, and most of these lamps were also gilded. Surviving examples also bear the coats of arms of the Mamluks who commissioned them.

Ceramics. Under Muslim patronage, potters produced a wide array of ceramic products, including plates, bowls, cups, jugs, and lidded jars. They produced colored tiles to decorate the walls and floors of palaces, residences, and masjids. The quality of surviving ceramic products ranges from crude to refined. Centers of ceramic production were spread all over the Muslim world, with some places being most prominent at various times. Kashan in central Iran was so important that the Arabic word for ceramic tiles is *kashani*. Surviving ceramics were created with molds and hand building as well as on potters' wheels. Muslim potters decorated their wares with slip, underglaze, overglaze, and luster painting. Slip, also referred to as *engobe*, is diluted clay used to decorate a clay pot when it is leather hard, or "green," before the first firing. Underglaze, slip, or diluted clay to which colored pigment has been added can be applied to a pot or tile when it is leather hard or after it has been fired. After a piece is fired, it is covered with a transparent glaze and refired, making it shiny and sealing it so that no water can seep through. Overglaze is applied after the first firing. Luster painting, decoration with metallic colors such as gold, is a demanding process. Decorative themes on Muslim ceramics include geometric patterns and floral motifs as well as figural compositions. Inscriptions were also used, sometimes incised into the pot, a technique known as sgraffito, or in other cases painted on. There is no doubt that the techniques and colors of Chinese ceramics had a profound influence on early Islamic pottery. The blue-and-white Chinese pottery seems to have been favored by Muslim potters, but they did not blindly copy Chinese pottery; rather, they combined Chinese indigenous motifs.

Textiles. Medieval sources document that Muslim rulers commissioned luxurious textiles from early on. Textiles were ordered not just for clothing but also for curtains, rugs, and furniture coverings used in the domestic and religious spheres. They were also used as gifts from the ruler, or sultan, to his amirs and other rulers and were given to visitors to the court whom the ruler wished to distinguish with robes of honor. Textiles were important because they identified the various classes within each society—through the quality and decoration of individuals' garments and of their horse and camel saddles. Also, banners identifying various court officials were displayed at ceremonies. Surviving materials include cotton, linen, wool, and silk, all of which were originally brightly colored and highly decorated. Colors used included but were not confined to shades of blue, green, and gold. The decorative motifs of textiles surviving in museums vary and include bands of inscription, floral and geometric motifs, and animal and bird figures. The inscriptional band, known as a *tiraz*, usually mentions a sultan's titles and wishes him glory, honor, or long life. The animals and birds include real animals and imaginary ones, such as griffins. Some stand peacefully in rows, and some are engaged in fights. Luxurious textiles were hand embroidered, while those for everyday use had block-printed designs. By the fourteenth century, Muslim textiles were being exported to Europe, as is documented in several

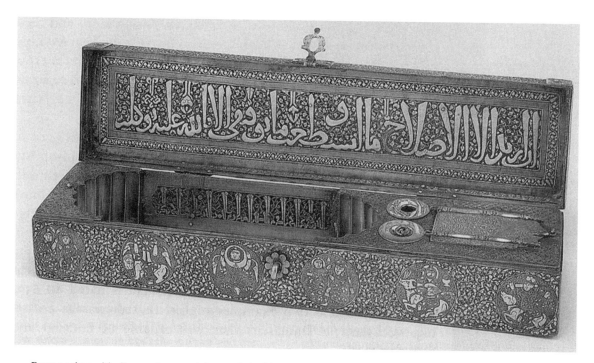

Brass penbox with silver and copper inlay, made in thirteenth-century Iraq; the inscription is a verse from the Qur'an:
"I desire only to set things right as far as I am able. My succor is only in God, in Him I put my trust"
(Victoria and Albert Museum, London).

paintings by well-known artists. Production of textiles was spread all over the Muslim world, and the surviving examples point to the fact that there was an exchange of ideas and techniques with other countries, such as China and India. Because textiles are more fragile than wood, metal, glass, or ceramic, examples surviving from before 1500 are very rare.

Rugs. Rugs were produced all over the Muslim world with some centers, such as Tabriz and Shiraz in Iran, gaining prominence. Handwoven Persian carpets are among the best known in the world, and have been for centuries. They are renowned for their intricate designs and high-quality fibers, usually wool, and much care and work goes into making each one. Rug designs include many of the same motifs found in other decorative arts, such as illuminated manuscripts and woodworking. Since they would be placed on floors and walked on, however, carpets were to a great extent devoid of inscriptions. For the same reason, animal representation is more common on rugs than on other decorative items. Rug sizes varied from super large for the audience halls in palaces, to narrow and long prayer rugs for the rows of worshipers in masjids. Unlike rugs from other parts of the Muslim world, Mamluk rugs from Egypt, which are among the most beautiful, seem to have suddenly appeared fully developed toward the end of the fifteenth century. In almost all cases they were woven from wool dyed red, blue, and green. Their central pattern uses interlacing geometric motifs, similar to decorative motifs in illuminated manuscripts and woodworking, and their borders consist of medallions alternating with oval cartouches. Some scholars have explained the sudden development of Egyptian rug making as a result of political unrest in Iran.

Egyptian rulers may have given refuge to Iranian artisans, who established a rug-weaving industry there.

Kiswah. Annually the Egyptian sultans provided the kiswah, the outer covering made especially for the Ka'bah, the cubical stone building at the heart of the Great Mosque in Makkah. This black cloth covering, large enough to cover the Ka'bah in its entirety, was carefully handwoven and embroidered with a large border of Qur'anic verses in gold thread near the top. When it was completed, a pilgrim caravan delivered it to Makkah. It was the duty of the amir of the pilgrimage to deliver the material. This practice was first documented in 1272, at the time of Sultan Baybars I, and continued well into the twentieth century. After the new kiswah arrived the old was then cut into pieces that were distributed to the pilgrims.

Qur'an Illumination. One area in which Muslim artists excelled was the illumination of sacred and secular books. The religious motivation that drove the artists to excellence in illuminating copies of the Qur'an spilled over into the secular domain. The Qur'an was revealed to the Prophet Muhammad over a period of twenty-three years. Every time the Prophet received a new revelation, he taught it to his followers, who memorized it, and he also had it recorded in a written form. That tradition has continued to the present day; Muslims memorize the Qur'an and pass it on orally from teacher to student, from generation to generation. At the same time, there is a standard Qur'an in Arabic that continues to be copied to the present. Early copies of the Qur'an were written on kidskin and parchment, materials too thick and bulky to accommodate the whole book in one volume. Therefore, the Qur'an was traditionally made in thirty volumes, one volume for each of its parts. When a ruler ordered the construction of a new religious foundation, he always provided at least one lavishly illuminated copy of the Qur'an, which was typically embellished with gold leaf and pigments made from powdered semiprecious stones. Because of the prohibition on figural representation, no people or animals are depicted in copies of the Qur'an. The most elaborate illumination in medieval Qur'ans usually appear on the opening two pages, which usually have colorful floral borders encircling them entirely. The rest of the pages of a volume of the Qur'an may be similarly, but less elaborately, illuminated, or they may be left undecorated. Other decorative elements in copies of the Qur'an include medallions that mark the division of each part of the Qur'an into halves and quarters, to make it easy for the reader to measure out passages for recitation and reading.

Secular Book Illumination. While illuminators of religious books other than the Qur'an observed the ban on figural representation, illuminations in works of science and literature sometimes include humans and animals, especially when such illustration was needed. For example, books on anatomy and veterinary and human medicine include elaborate figural representations, as do other works, even on astronomy, zoology, or literatures. Probably illuminators were permitted to break the rule because their illuminations were two-dimensional and in private copies of books that were not on public display.

Persian Miniatures. From illustrations in private copies of secular books developed the genre called "Persian miniatures," which especially flourished in the eastern Muslim world. Whereas painters in medieval Europe were becoming increasingly concerned with techniques for the naturalistic presentation of figures, surroundings, landscapes, and especially perspective, in the Persian world the emphasis was more on hierarchy, complex design, and brilliance of color. Muslim artists did not pay attention to one-point perspective with the figures diminishing in size to produce the illusion of distance. Rather, the most important person in a painting is the largest, no matter where he or she is placed. Rugs are painted as if floating in space, allowing the viewer to admire their entire designs, instead of being presented in visually correct perspective, which would allow the viewer to see only a portion of the design. Figures are larger than their architectural surroundings, and buildings tend to appear stacked up, instead of diminishing in size to create the illusion of space. Rock formations and other features show the influence of Chinese painting.

Sources:
Esin Atil, W. T. Chase, and Paul Jett, *Islamic Metalwork* (Washington, D.C.: Freer Gallery of Art, Smithsonian Institution, 1985).

John R. Hayes, ed., *The Genius of Arab Civilization: Source of Renaissance* (Cambridge: MIT Press, 1983).

Seyyed Hossein Nasr, *Islamic Art and Spirituality* (New York: State University of New York Press, 1987).

Venetia Porter, *Islamic Tiles* (New York: Interlink, 1995).

Rachel Ward, *Islamic Metalwork* (New York: Thames & Hudson, 1993).

DOMESTIC AND SECULAR ARCHITECTURE

Family Privacy. Muslim domestic architecture has historically been dominated by concepts different from those of modern western architecture. Whereas modern western homes are designed for nuclear families, Muslim homes have, whenever possible, provided an enclosure for an extended family, often consisting of dozens of people. While modern western housing is open to the outside via large picture windows and gardens that can be seen from the street, classical Muslim houses are built to ensure maximum privacy, closing off the outside world as completely as possible with solid walls on the property line, few or no windows at street level, and carved wooden screens on all windows, which are usually in the upper stories only. Through such screens, those inside can see out, but outsiders cannot see the interior of the house. Inside this enclosed space, rooms often open onto an interior courtyard, which sometimes contains a garden, a fountain, or both. The structure of Muslim houses was motivated principally by the social system of Islam, which discouraged contacts between outsider males and the women of the house. Another feature of traditional Muslim interior design is the separation of the semipublic space, where male guests can be entertained, from the private family space, which outside guests are not allowed to enter. This private space of the family consists of most of the house, and the guest room is usually a single room near the main entrance. This room is known by different names in Arabic, including *qa'ah, mandharah, midyafah,* and *majlis.* In grand houses the guest room might be quite elaborate, with carved decorations and a fountain in the center. In some cases it is located outside the family house entirely, even separated from it by a street, although such a situation is inconvenient for providing hospitality to the guests.

Ancient Roots. Although Muslim home-design concepts differ from modern western ones, they resemble premodern domestic designs from most areas of the world. Ancient Greek, Roman, Indian, and Chinese domestic architecture all favored houses built around courtyards, with maximum family privacy, and were designed to discourage male outsiders from mixing with the women of the household, unless a marriage was being negotiated. Examples of Muslim domestic architecture from before 1500 have survived less well than public religious and secular structures, so few medieval houses exist in anything like their original form. Those that remain are generally palaces that were inhabited by rulers or governors rather than ordinary people. While showing great diversity in design and decoration, such palaces generally follow the principles of Muslim house design, with interior courtyards and surrounding rooms as a principle architectural feature, but they are also not typical because of their grander scale and their semipublic functions. This difference in scale is especially apparent in the magnificent palace of the Alhambra (*al-Hamra'* in Arabic) of

Fountains in the Court of Lions and a double-arched window with muqarnas (stalactite) decoration and Arabic
calligraphy at the thirteenth-century Alhambra palace in Granada, Spain

Granada in Spain, built by the Nasrid dynasty (1232–1492), mostly in the thirteenth century.

Public Lodgings. The other main kind of secular architecture surviving from the medieval period is that of caravanserais, the hotels of the Middle Ages. They were known by several names that indicate their various functions: *khan, funduq, wakalah,* and *ribat.* Quite a few of these buildings, all of which are built around central courtyards, still exist in Morocco, Tunisia, Egypt, Turkey, and Iran. Because animals were the means of transportation and carrying of goods from place to place, these buildings were generally built with stables on the lower floor, as well as storerooms to hold trade goods. The upstairs, consisting of one or more floors, provided lodging for the traveling merchants and their employees. Such merchants would usually travel in caravans, sometimes quite large ones, for safety, journeying about thirty miles per day. Other surviving secular structures include fortresses and towers, city walls and gates, markets, *bimaristans* (hospitals), and baths. There are only a handful of examples of these secular structures, however, whereas the medieval masjids even in a single city can number in the hundreds. Medieval books and documents record many examples of domestic architecture that are no longer extant, including pictures and plans.

Sources:
Jonathan Bloom and Sheila Blair, *Islamic Arts* (London: Phaidon, 1997).

David Talbot Rice, *Islamic Art,* revised edition (London: Thames & Hudson, 1975).

The Dome of the Rock in Jerusalem, completed in 691

EARLY RELIGIOUS ARCHITECTURE AND CITY PLANNING

Preservation. Most surviving medieval Muslim buildings are masjids (mosques). As with churches and cathedrals in Europe and the temples of ancient civilizations, Muslim religious buildings have survived in better condition and in far greater numbers than Muslim secular structures. The much higher survival rate for masjids than secular buildings may be attributed to several factors. It is suggested in the Qur'an (22: 40 and 72: 18) and established in Muslim law that once a masjid has been used for worship, it should never be alienated, sold, or turned to any other purpose. Furthermore, because of the respect people have for houses of worship in general, they tend to invest more money in them and build them with better materials and better engineering than secular structures. As a result, people feel obliged to spend more effort maintaining them as significant investments and cultural artifacts. Masjids were clearly the most important public spaces in medieval Islam. Since Islam was often the religion and ideology of the state, Muslim rulers financed much masjid construction, established charitable trusts for their maintenance, and also sought to preserve the buildings of their predeces-

sors. The rulers were no doubt motivated by a Prophetic hadith stating that a Muslim's charities continue to intercede with God even for him or her after that Muslim has died. Rewards for those who build masjids are also suggested in the Qur'an (9: 18) and specified in the hadiths. Other religious structures that have survived are madrasahs (religious schools), which in the majority of cases are part of a masjid, khanqahs (buildings for Sufi meditational retreats and congregational chants), and tekkes (tombs).

Masjids (Mosques). The motivation for having a specific place assigned for worship in Islam grew directly from the requirement that all Muslims offer five fixed prayers, or salats, each day to worship God. It is preferable that, if possible, these prayers be performed in congregation. The prayers consist of standing, bowing, and prostrating oneself (*sujud*) with the forehead touching the ground a prescribed number of times, while reciting certain phrases in Arabic, including passages from the Qur'an. In order to be able to perform the prayers, a worshiper has to be in a state of purity, which may require either major ablution (*ghusl*), a shower or bath, or the minor one (*wudu'*), washing the hands, face, arms, and feet and wiping the head. To be ready to pray, the worshiper must also be properly dressed.

Ruins of Qasr Mushatta, the desert palace built by Umayyad khalifah al-Walid II, circa 743–744

One then must face in the direction of the Ka'bah, God's Holy House in Makkah. All Muslim prayers are done toward the Ka'bah, whether one is standing, sitting, bowing, or kneeling with face on the ground. This direction is known as the *qiblah,* and the tradition of facing Makkah is based on the Qur'an (2: 144, 149–150). Whenever the Muslims settled in a new land, they determined the correct direction to Makkah, and it then became established for the inhabitants of that place to face that way when praying. In Egypt, for example, people generally pray toward the southeast, since Egypt is northwest of Makkah.

Locations for Prayer. As for the place for prayer, any location that is clean and dry is considered fit. No particular building or house of worship is required, nor are any furniture or ritual implements. Early tradition urged worshipers to prostrate themselves on earth, gravel, or straw mats, which probably reveals the simple conditions of earliest Madinah. Later, however, masjids generally became equipped with carpets. In its original essence, the Arabic word *masjid* refers to a place of prostration, or *sujud.* Indeed—as implied in the Qur'an (2:115) and clearly stated in the hadiths—the whole earth is a masjid suitable for the performance of prayers. Beginning in the time of the Prophet Muhammad, however, Muslims have always felt the need of a space specifically for worship and religious teachings. There is no evidence that there was a space dedicated solely for Muslim prayers during the period of the Prophet's public preaching at Makkah (612–622), but one of his first acts on his arrival at Madinah after his *hijrah*

(migration) from Makkah in 622 was to establish a masjid, a place dedicated to Muslim worship, in the courtyard of his house. The tradition of facing Makkah during prayer was established in 624. Before that time, worshipers faced Jerusalem. The space was used first for the five daily prayers, second for the important Friday congregational prayer, which included a sermon (Qur'an 62: 9–11), and third as an center for religious lessons, which may be alluded to in Qur'an 9: 122. The first masjid seems to have served other purposes as well. It was a meeting place for the community, where problems and concerns were discussed; the place where the Prophet received delegations, which came to Madinah with increasing frequency toward the end of his life; the place where the troops were mustered and from which military campaigns were launched; and also, perhaps, a place for visitors to stay and a shelter for the poor. The original masjid built by the Prophet at Madinah was a building of great simplicity. It consisted mostly of an open courtyard a little more than fifty meters square. This space was large enough to accommodate several thousand worshipers packed closely together at one time, thus setting the trend for early masjids to have large, unobstructed open areas. The whole building was surrounded by a wall of mud brick a little over a meter high and with a base of stone. A colonnade made of palm trunks lined the north side and supported a roof of thatched palm leaves, for shading worshipers and guests from the midday sun. When the *qiblah* was changed from Jerusalem to Makkah in 624, the front of the masjid was moved from the north wall to the south wall, and a second shaded colonnade was constructed on the south side of the courtyard. At first, the Prophet used to give the Friday sermon beside one of the palm-trunk columns, but in 628 he had *minbar* (a pulpit), consisting of three steps, built for delivering his sermons. Despite its simplicity and the humble conditions from which it arose, the Prophet's masjid in Madinah became a model for all later Muslim houses of worship, especially the great courtyard masjids that have remained one of the major styles of masjid buildings.

Masjid Plans. In the subsequent development of the masjid, there came to be two main designs that, with some secondary variations, have been employed through history: the arcaded plan and the *iwan* (arched hall) plan. Regardless of which plan is used, all masjids have the following features in common: a main sanctuary that houses the *mihrab* (prayer niche), which marks the *qiblah* and is normally built into the *qiblah* wall. A *minbar* from which an imam delivers the Friday sermon is placed on the right side of the *mihrab*. Traditionally, the roofed "sanctuary" area by the *qiblah* wall has been larger and more impressively decorated than the rest of a masjid.

Arcaded Masjids. Deriving from the masjid the Prophet built in Madinah, the arcaded plan (also known as the hypostyle plan) is the earlier of the two masjid designs. In the arcaded plan the masjid has a large *sahn* (courtyard) in its center, and columns or pillars form arcades or colonnades that are covered by a wood-beamed roof. The side facing Makkah usually has more rows of columns and is thus deeper. The arcade plan was used for all the large early masjids and has continued in use because of its simplicity and versatility. It allows a building to be constructed from expensive materials or just palm trunks, depending on the availability of raw materials and the builder's financial means. Because it requires only repetitions of post-and-lintel structures, the execution of an arcaded masjid is cheaper and requires less engineering skill than other possible plans. Because it is supported by a forest of columns, it does not require the spanning of wide spaces to hold up the roof, and the many columns produce a dignified and pleasing appearance. Also, an arcaded building can easily be enlarged by demolishing one wall and adding more rows of columns. The Prophet's masjid and most of the other great early masjids have been enlarged by this method several times each. Eventually domes were added to the original arcaded-masjid plan. It became common to have a small dome above the center aisle of the roofed sanctuary area, at the place where it meets the courtyard, to create a central axis leading to the *mihrab*. Also—or instead—in many instances a dome was erected on top of the *mihrab* itself. In other cases, three small domes were placed at the *qiblah* wall, one on top of the *mihrab*, and two on either side at the lateral corners of the sanctuary. These domes project up from the otherwise flat roof, looking from above like large bubbles on a flat surface. Eventually, large dome chambers, usually housing mausoleums, were attached to one side of the masjid structure, in defiance of Islamic rules prohibiting tombs in masjids. Adding a dome gives more structural variety and beauty to the outside and inside of a building and windows in the drum of the dome admit more light to the interior.

Iwan Masjids. When roofs covered large areas of masjids, lighting became a problem. One solution was the second major masjid design, the iwan plan, which has two to four iwans, or large arched halls, open on the side facing a courtyard. This kind of structure thus shares the courtyard feature of arcaded masjids but has higher, soaring halls with pointed or "cathedral" ceilings. The iwan plan was introduced and developed in Iran by Muslim builders who were following the example of pre-Islamic Sassanian architecture, and it was likely transferred via Muslim Spain to Europe, where it influenced Romanesque architecture. Building a vaulted iwan requires more architectural knowledge and technical skill than constructing an arcaded masjid. As time passed, domes were also added to iwan masjids. In some countries, such as Egypt, arcaded and iwan masjids eventually came to exist side by side. In other places one plan was employed to the exclusion of the other. For example, iwan-style masjids were rarely built in North Africa and Spain, while in Iran they predominate.

Models for Islamic Architecture and Design. The Muslim state expanded rapidly during last few years of the Prophet Muhammad's life. By the time he died in 632, he had gained control over most of western Arabia and Yemen and had been extending his influence into eastern Arabia as well. Islam not only survived the crisis of the Prophet's death but immediately began a long political expansion under his successors, the khalifahs. Right after his death, Muslim armies were sent to the various neighboring lands to the north to claim them for the rule of God's religion (Qur'an 2: 193, 9: 33, 48: 28, and 61: 9). Everywhere the Muslims settled they erected a central arcaded masjid. Generally, these earliest arcaded masjids fit into two subtypes. In the new cities founded by Muslims, such as Kufah and Basrah in Iraq, huge new masjids were erected on the model of the Prophet's Masjid in Madinah and performed the same functions. The main difference was that the new masjids of Kufah and Basrah were one hundred meters square or ten thousand square meters, more than four times the size of the masjid in Madinah. Islam had grown, but Muslims still believed that all the male population of a place should attend the Friday congregation together at the same time. This concept has left its trace in Muslim law. Both Sunnis and Shi'is acknowledge the preferability of having only one Friday congregation in a given city. Despite the difficulty of gathering everyone in one place once a week, as late as the time of Salah al-Din (ruled 1171–1193) and the Ayyubids in Egypt, for example, the ruler was still trying to hold the Friday congregation in only one place. Later, numbers and practicality forced the Sunnis to allow multiple congregations in a city if the largest masjid could not hold all the worshipers, but the Shi'is still follow the old way. Obviously, requiring only one congregation in a city had a profound effect on

Interior of the Great Masjid of Córdoba, Spain, begun in 785

and square form of the minaret prevailed for centuries in much of North Africa and Spain as well as Syria. Another feature adopted from earlier Syrian architecture was the use of mosaic for decoration. Besides the major types of masjids, there are also smaller, humbler local masjids that do not necessarily follow either of the major plans. Such minor masjids were first built in Madinah, which is a large oasis where it quickly proved impossible for all Muslims to go to the central masjid five times a day to pray. Thus, smaller, local masjids were established near the dwellings of the various clans. The existence of such masjids even in the Prophet's lifetime is indicated in the Qur'an, in which masjids are mentioned in the plural (2: 187, 22: 40, 72: 18). Eventually, and probably quite early, these smaller masjids were used for Friday prayers as well. Smaller masjids to serve local districts or quarters in a city were soon built elsewhere as well. The survival of these humble structures has been rare, so little is known about their design. Some may have been only open places marked off by on the ground a mere semicircle of stones, with an indentation indicating the *qiblah*. Others were buildings with small rooms. Some may have been originally built for other purposes and then later turned into masjids.

The Harams of Makkah, Madinah, and Jerusalem. Like all other great religions, Islam has holy sites that func-

architecture. The digging of trenches around the new masjids suggests that they were also built to double as military bastions of last resort, and indeed that need has arisen occasionally in Muslim history. When a masjid was established in a city that already existed, Muslim builders usually borrowed from the local population and their indigenous traditions. For example, when the Muslims settled in Syria, they were influenced by the great architecture they saw around them, which attested to the prowess of the Roman and Byzantine builders and artisans. Yet, even when they adopted ideas from the earlier structures and adapted them to their own use, Muslims created a formula for building and decoration that is distinctively Islamic in its spirit and expressiveness. The structures that the Muslim patrons commissioned, even when they bear resemblance to existing, pre-Islamic edifices, were meant from the beginning to serve a different function, which necessitated some adaptations from the start, particularly in public religious buildings. Thus, early masjids in Syria have the usual masjid features, but the form and arrangement of the arcades of columns, the roof, the windows, and the walls were all influenced by existing structures. One particular addition that appears to have come from Syrian church structures is the minaret, the tower from which the muezzin calls the worshipers to prayer five times a day. The origin of this structure appears to be Syrian church towers, and the wide

THE MAQAMA OF THE YELLOW ONE

Ahmad Badi al-Zaman al-Hamadhani (968–1008) was the originator of the literary form known as *maqamat* (assemblies; singular: *maqama*) for literary gatherings in which eloquence and wit in Arabic was prized. Maqamat anecdotes consist of prose passages often combined with poetry and feature a rogue hero whose exploits reveal much about Muslim life of the time. "The Maqama of the Yellow One" is a riddle whose solution is "a pair of gold coins"; their child is "a reputation for generosity":

'Isa ibn Hisham tells the following story. When I was about to start for home after the Pilgrimage, a man came to me saying, "I have with me a lad of yellow paternity, who'd tempt me to join the ungodly fraternity; he dances on the fingertips, and much travel has polished him up. Charity impels me to come to you, to present his plea unto you; he seeks from you a yellow bride, admired beyond measure, to all eyes a pleasure. If you consent, there will be born of them a child that will reach all lands and all ears, and when you're bent upon return and have wound up your concern, he'll be before you in your homeland, so will you please display what's in your hand?" This speech I relished, and the wit of his demand, so I did what he wished. In reply he declaimed: "The begging hand puts paid to pride, but generosity has all on its side."

Source: *Maqamat al-Hamadhani*, quoted in *Abbasid Belles Lettres*, edited by Julia Ashhtiany, T. M. Johnstone, J. D. Latham, R. B. Sargeant, and G. Rex Smith (Cambridge: Cambridge University Press, 1990), pp. 131–132.

tion as focal points for worship. There are three places of special significance to Muslims: the cities of Makkah, Madinah, and Jerusalem. As primary centers of worship and pilgrimage from the inception of Islam to the present, each of these cities has an important sacred enclosure set aside for worship. Although they share certain common features with arcaded masjids, they encompass larger areas than other masjids and have some special features. These sacred enclosures are known as "inviolable sanctuaries," or *harams*. The word *haram* is an Arabic term for a holy place. In Islam a *haram* is a sanctuary holy to God, and special rules guarantee and honor its sanctity. While Makkah and Madinah are associated specifically with the mission of the Prophet Muhammad, the third Muslim holy city, Jerusalem, is also sacred to Judaism and Christianity, the other two main monotheistic religions. Occasionally, the main masjid of al-Khalil (Hebron) in the West Bank, said to have been established by the Prophet Ibrahim (Abraham), is also considered a *haram*, but it is not designated as such in either in the Qur'an or the hadiths.

Makkah as a Muslim city. The Prophet of Islam, Muhammad, was born in Makkah around 569, and when he was about forty he received his first revelation of the Qur'an there. Makkah is mentioned or alluded to in many Qur'anic verses, and its exalted rank is further emphasized in hadiths. Moreover, Makkah houses the Ka'bah, the House of God. According to the Qur'an, the Ka'bah was built by the Prophet Ibrahim and his son Isma'il (2: 127). It has been restored several times both in pre-Islamic times and after the advent of Islam. By 624, when Muslims began prostrating themselves toward it for prayers, the Ka'bah had become the focal point of worship. The Ka'bah is also the primary destination of both the *hajj* (greater pilgrimage) and the *'umrah* (or lesser pilgrimage). Many of the pilgrims' rituals are performed near the Ka'bah, especially the *tawaf* (circumambulation) around the Ka'bah. These pilgrimages became standard Muslim practices soon after 628, when the Prophet Muhammad attempted to lead Muslim pilgrims from Madinah to Makkah on the first lesser pilgrimage. Although turned back that time, the Prophet did successfully lead a lesser pilgrimage in 629. Then, after the surrender of Makkah to him, he made a lesser pilgrimage again in 630 and sent others to lead greater pilgrimages in 630 and 631, leading a greater pilgrimage himself only once, in 632, the year of his death. That pilgrimage became the exemplar for all future Muslim pilgrimages. The Ka'bah had been a venerable sanctuary for years before the advent of Islam, and pilgrims from all over the Arabian peninsula traveled to it. By the time the Prophet was born, pilgrims were coming annually to pay homage to the many pagan deities worshiped by the various tribes, and statues in their honor had been placed all around the Ka'bah. According to Islam, this practice was a corruption in the original monotheistic religion of Ibrahim. When the residents of the city of Makkah finally surrendered to the Prophet and accepted Islam as their religion, the idols were demolished, and the Ka'bah and its sanctu-

ary were purified and dedicated to the worship of Allah alone. The present Ka'bah dates to 692, when it was completely rebuilt; it underwent a further, partial reconstruction in 1627. The existing building is believed to follow closely the plan of the Ka'bah at the time of the Prophet Muhammad. The whole building, a cube-shaped structure built of huge, rough-hewn stones, measures about eleven by thirteen meters at its base and is sixteen meters high. It has a door but no windows, and the inside contains only pillars, lamps, and inscriptions. The interior is not used for worship. Thus, the Ka'bah itself is not a masjid. It is draped with a huge, gold-embroidered black cloth, the *kiswah*, which is changed annually. Because the Ka'bah is the focal point of Muslim worship, its surrounding enclosure, the Inviolable Sanctuary (al-Masjid al-Haram) has many distinctive features, but its architecture in general is similar to that of other arcaded masjids. All around the Ka'bah is a giant courtyard large enough to accommodate several hundreds of thousands of people. This courtyard is enclosed by a colonnade built originally by the Abbasid khalifah al-Mahdi (ruled 775–785). In this courtyard, because the Ka'bah itself is the focal point of Muslim worship, the worshipers perform their prayers facing it in concentric circles rather than in straight rows. Thus, the Inviolable Sanctuary lacks a *qiblah* wall and *mihrab*.

Madinah. Madinah, short for Madinat al-Nabi, or the City of the Prophet, was known in pre-Islamic times as Yathrib. Its inhabitants welcomed the Prophet and his companions in 622, when they fled persecution by unbelievers in Makkah. The site of the first masjid built by the Prophet after the founding of Islam, Madinah was the place where he resided during the last ten years of his life, teaching and establishing the norms of Islamic practice. When he died in 632, he was buried in his first masjid, and the first two khalifahs were subsequently buried beside him. Visiting the Prophet's tomb is a meritorious act that a devout Muslim usually performs before or after a pilgrimage to Makkah.

Jerusalem. Jerusalem was the first *qiblah* until 624, when God ordered the believers to face Makkah instead during prayers. This change is alluded to in the Qur'an (2: 144). In addition, Jerusalem has a degree of sanctity for Muslims because it was the focus of worship for the Israelite prophets, who are also recognized as prophets of Islam. Also, the Prophet Muhammad allowed pilgrimages to three masjids: the *harams* of Makkah, Madinah, and Jerusalem although only the pilgrimage to Makkah is required. Early Muslim texts identify the entire area within the walls of the *haram* area in Jerusalem as al-Masjid al-Aqsa (the Farthest Place of Worship). Muslims believe that verse 17: 1 of the Qur'an, which refers to the Prophet's miraculous night journey, is about the sanctuary in Jerusalem. They hold that the Prophet was transported to this site in Jerusalem, where he led all of the previous prophets in prayer. Then, accompanied by the archangel Gabriel, he ascended into heaven, where he spoke to various prophets and the angels, and finally he was returned to Makkah—all in the same night. When the Muslims took Jerusalem from its Byzantine rulers in 638, they considered al-Masjid al-Aqsa sacred both on account of the Prophet's ascension from that spot to heaven and because of his leading a communal prayer in the same vicinity. When the Muslims took Jerusalem, they found the *haram* site in ruins and completely abandoned, without any functioning buildings or habitations. They cleaned and restored the site as a place for the worship of God.

The Noble Sanctuary of Jerusalem. Known as al-Haram al-Sharif, or the Noble Sanctuary, the haram of Jerusalem consists of a quadrilateral area almost five hundred meters long and three hundred meters wide. Located atop a long hill running north to south, the area is enclosed by high stone walls on all sides and consists of a large platform paved with giant stones. The al-Aqsa Masjid, located at the south end of the platform on the *qiblah* wall, is constructed with rows of columns and a flat roof with a small silver dome, according to the arcaded-masjid design, with the rest of the platform acting as its courtyard. In the middle of the *haram* area stands the oldest building commissioned by the early Muslim rulers that is still substantially intact: the Dome of the Rock, which is also one of the most beautiful and fascinating buildings in the world. Completed in 691, fewer than sixty years after the death of the Prophet Muhammad, the Dome of the Rock is believed to retain much of its original decoration and overall appearance, having undergone far fewer reconstructions than the older, adjacent al-Aqsa Masjid, which was originally constructed under Khalifah 'Umar (634–644) in about 643–644 and was later rebuilt and enlarged several times. Both buildings have been in continuous use as masjids since their construction, except when they were converted into Christian churches during the first Crusader occupation of Jerusalem (1099–1187). The Dome of the Rock stands on a stone platform built above the level of the rest of the haram and is built over and around an irregular rock outcropping that protrudes above the foundation. This rock takes up space that otherwise would be devoted to prayers and worship, making the Dome of the Rock unique among Muslim buildings. The reason for including the rock as a vital part of the building is a puzzle that has not been solved, though it has aroused much speculation. Octagonal in shape, the building is surmounted by a large golden dome, which is supported by columns arranged in a circle around the rock outcropping, outside of which is an unobstructed ambulatory, which is also used for prayers. The interior walls are richly decorated with mosaics in geometric and vegetational patterns. Outside, the building is adorned with glazed blue tiles decorated with Qur'anic verses in decorative calligraphy. The design and color scheme of the outside dates to early Ottoman restorations of the sixteenth century. Medieval sources give much information about the reasons behind the erection of the Dome of the Rock, including the exact dates for the initiation and completion of its construction. One of the earliest descriptions was written in 903 by Ibn al-Faqih, who wrote: "In the Dome

every night they light 300 lamps. It has four gates roofed over, and at each gate are four doors, and over each gate is a portico of marble. The building is covered with white marble, and its roof with red gold. In its walls, and high in (the drum of its dome), are fifty-six windows, glazed with glass of various hues. The Dome, which was built by the Umayyad Khalifah Abd al-Malik ibn Marwan (ruled 685–705), is supported on twelve piers and thirty pillars." This description closely accords with the present appearance of the Dome. One of the most noticeable features of the building is the long Arabic inscription in mosaic on the inside, which was placed there by the Khalifah Abd al-Malik. Except for the date and founder's name, it consists entirely of Qur'anic verses and, in fact, is the earliest dated Qur'an text. The verses are an integral part of the building and help to establish the legitimacy of Islam in relation to other religions in the holy city of Jerusalem, especially Byzantine Christianity.

Development of Architecture. Like the original masjid of the Prophet in Madinah, the earliest masjids are described in literary sources as having been plain and unadorned. Indeed, the Prophet is said to have warned about placing any decoration in masjids because it might detract from the concentration of the worshipers. Nevertheless, it did not take long for the Muslim rulers to commission elaborate and costly structures. The third khalifah, 'Uthman (ruled 644–656), is said to have begun enlarging the Prophet's masjid and was criticized for it. The Umayyad dynasty (ruled 661–750) began a great program of masjid expansion and adornment, and several examples of their work survive, setting a precedent for later rulers, whatever popular or religious opinion might have been. Defending his decision to build the opulent Dome of the Rock in Jerusalem, the Khalifah Abd al-Malik said that the Christians had impressive churches and that he was afraid that some Muslims would be distracted by the beauty of those churches. Thus, he said that Muslims needed equally impressive structures of their own. Muslim rulers spared no expense when commissioning masjids and other structures. Generally, from the first century of Islam, rulers in all the lands where Muslims settled initiated huge building campaigns, ordering the construction of masjids, schools, palaces, public baths, markets, hospitals, hotels, walls, fortifications, and even in a few cases whole cities with streets, roads, and all the necessary infrastructure to support them. The production and development of great works of art and architecture coincided with the establishment of new dynasties of rulers, who took control of vast amounts of territory. From the eighth century onward, as the khilafah fell apart, regional states were established, leading to greater variety and production of art. The capital of each new regional state became a center of artistic production—among them Samarra' in Iraq, Fez in Morocco, and Cairo in Egypt. Cairo was the center of power for several successive dynasties of rulers, and it still has hundreds of monuments built before 1500 in a relatively good state of preservation. Examples of Egyptian woodwork, metalwork,

Scholars in a public library at Hulwan, near Baghdad; illumination from a 1237 manuscript
for al-Hariri's *Maqamat* (Bibliothèque Nationale, Paris)

glass, ceramics, and jewelry from before 1500 may be found in many museums. Syria was the domain of the first Muslim dynasty, the Umayyads, who were avid builders. In addition to their masjids, they left palaces and fortifications, several of which are located in the desert area of present-day Jordan, including Mushatta, Khirbat al-Mafjar, Qusayr 'Amrah, Qasr al-Hayr al-Gharbi, and Qasr al-Hayr al-Sharqi. The best known of these secular remains is the bath that is thought to have belonged to the palace of Qusayr 'Amrah. The bath is a small domed structure, whose architectural style is indebted to Byzantine construction techniques. On the interior are fresco paintings and mosaic decorations. The themes of the frescoes are not typical of other Islamic wall painting because they depict naturalistically painted human beings—providing a glimpse of the private domain, away from the scrutiny of the religious establishment and the general populace. A scene on one of the walls repre-

sents the Muslim ruler enthroned, with the rulers of the other major empires standing around him submissively.

Great Masjids. Perhaps the best-known Umayyad monument is the Great Masjid of Damascus, which was the chief masjid of the whole khilafah. This magnificent building was part of the construction program of the Khalifah al-Walid I (ruled 705–715), who governed at the zenith of Umayyad power. He also undertook the reconstruction and expansion of the masjids of Makkah, Madinah, al-Ta'if, Jerusalem, and San'a'—and probably others of which all traces have been lost. Al-Walid's masjid in Damascus, which is still nearly intact, is known especially for its beautiful Byzantine-style mosaics, which show their Muslim character by portraying only buildings, vegetation, and landscapes. Another feature it has—which probably appeared for the first time in an earlier masjid of Damascus—is the *maqsurah,* a part of the masjid designated for the khalifah and his entourage and partitioned off from the rest of the sanctuary by a wooden screen. This innovation has been attributed to either Mu'awiyah (ruled 661–680) or Marwan I (ruled 684–685).

Abbasid Architecture. When the Abbasids succeeded the Umayyads as the ruling dynasty in 750, the seat of power was moved from Syria to Iraq. Baghdad was built as the new capital in 762 and quickly acquired a reputation as an important cultural center. Located on the west bank of the Tigris River, the new city was founded mainly as a royal residence for the khalifah, his family, and his legions of troops, supporters, and servants. The city plan is in the form of a large circle with the ruler's palace and a great masjid at the center. Inspired by earlier Sassanian constructions, this round city was surrounded by high walls, which the builders thought would be easier to defend because they lacked corners. Within fewer than fifty years other quarters grew up in the vicinity of the original round city, and most of Baghdad moved to the east bank of the Tigris. Eventually, the khalifahs followed, building new palaces farther east and abandoning the round city, which vanished without a trace. In 1258 Baghdad was severely sacked by the Mongols, and it was sacked again by Timur (Tamerlane) in 1393. In addition to the loss of the khalifal library, which had been catalogued in detail by Ibn al-Nadim (circa 936–995), most architectural monuments in Baghdad did not survive. Another early Abbasid city, Samarra', was founded in 836 by the Abbasid khalifah al-Mu'tasim (833–842) to house his army. The city contained a great masjid (built 849–851), one of the largest ever built, measuring 240 by 156 meters, more than 37,000 square meters in area, enough to accommodate 60,000 worshipers. Unlike the round city of Baghdad, much of this masjid has survived, including its outer walls, foundations and an outline of its interior, and its minaret. It was built on the arcaded plan, with rows and rows of pillars surrounding a large courtyard on four sides. The walls were made of mud brick, a building material readily available in Iraq—thanks to the Tigris and the Euphrates Rivers—and commonly used for most construction since the days of Sumer and Akkad in the fourth millennium B.C.E. The minaret, also built of baked bricks and located just outside the walls, had a particularly unusual spiral design created by a wide ramp wrapped around it and leading to the top. The design of that minaret was copied only twice, once in Iraq and once in Egypt. Sometimes this design is viewed as a throwback to the "stairways to heaven" built by the ancient Sumerians and Babylonians on their ziggurats. Actually, it seems to bear little resemblance to any known previous structure and may be seen as an example of creativity in engineering and design. Another important structure in Samarra' was the palace of the ruler, which had intricate decorative designs of molded plaster and carved wood. Although many grand palaces were built, few have survived. The most notable example may be the desert fortress-palace of Ukhaydir, built for an Abbasid prince circa 778. A ruin in a fair state of preservation, it reveals a continuity with Sassanian build-ing techniques and the architectural design of the earlier Umayyad desert palaces.

Sources:

K. A. C. Creswell, *A Short Account of Early Muslim Architecture*, revised by James W. Allan (Cairo: American University in Cairo Press, 1989).

Creswell, *Early Muslim Architecture* (New York: Hacker Art Books, 1979).

Martin Frishman and Hasan-Uddin Khan, ed., *The Mosque: History, Architectural Development and Regional Diversity* (New York: Thames & Hudson, 1994).

Aptullah Kuran, *The Mosque in Early Ottoman Architecture* (Chicago: University of Chicago Press, 1968).

LATER MASJID ARCHITECTURE IN THE ARAB WORLD AND AFRICA

The Development of Regional Styles. The disintegration of the khilafah, which began with the independence of western North Africa (modern Morocco and Algeria) as early as 740, continued thereafter at an increasing pace and led to the development of regional architectures, even though Islam remained unified in religion, law, and expressions of spirituality under the banner of Sunnism, reflecting the popular understanding and will. By 900 the political unity of the khilafah was largely broken. From 945 until 1152 the khalifahs did not even rule in Baghdad, and their brief temporal restoration from 1152 to 1258 was purely local and lasted only until the Mongols destroyed the khilafah with the sack of Baghdad. Different styles of architecture developed under the patronage of regional rulers who claimed various degrees of independence from the khalifahs and wanted to show their independence by stamping their monuments with a signature style. Because these regional styles underwent gradual development over a long period, it is impossible to point to a specific date when any of them began. But generally they began to appear after 900. The regional styles that emerged before 1500 include what can be broadly called the Iranian, Egyptian (or Syro-Egyptian), North African–Andalusian, and Indian. Mostly subsequent to 1500, far more divergent styles appeared on the edges of the Islamic cultural regions, including the Turkish, West African, and Malay-Indonesian styles. Many other substyles were either derived from one of these regional styles or existed between two or more of them.

Egypt, Syria, the Hijaz, and Yemen. After the early phase of khalifal unity, Syria remained politically subordinate to Egypt through most of the medieval period. Independent Egypt was successively ruled by the Tulunids (868–905), the Ikhshidids (935–969), the Fatimids (969–1171), the Ayyubids (1171–1250), and the Mamluks (1250–1517), and Syria was usually subject to these same rulers. Each of these dynasties contributed to the development of an independent architectural tradition. The Hijaz—the birthplace of Islam in the western part of the Arabian peninsula—was also politically and architecturally dominated by Egypt at this time, and Egyptian architecture seems to have been the main influence in Yemen as well, although local traditions also persisted there. Islamic architecture and decoration in

THE MAQAMA OF THE SPINDLE

The answer to the riddle in the following maqama by al-Hamadhani is explained at the end:

'Isa ibn Hisham related to us and said: I entered Basra when I was wide of fame and abundant of reputation, and there came to me two young men. One of them said: "May God strengthen the Shaikh! this youth entered our house and seized a kitten with vertigo in its head, with the sacred cord and a whirling sphere around its middle. Gentle of voice, if it cries; quick to return, if it flees; long of skirt, if it pulls; slender of waist, weak of chest. of the size of a plump sheep. Staying in the town, yet not abandoning travel. If it be given a thing, it returns it. If it be tasked with a journey, it goes energetically, and if it is made to draw the rope, it lengthens it. There it is, bone and wood. It contains property, immoveable and moveable, a past and a future." Said the young man: "Yes, may God strengthen the Shaikh! for he forcibly took from me:—

"Pointed is his spearhead, sharp are his teeth,
His progeny are his helpers, dissolving union is his business.
He assails his master, clinging to his moustache;
Inserting his fangs into old and young.
Agreeable, of goodly shape, slim, and abstemious.
A shooter, with shafts abundant, around the beard and the moustache."
So I said to the first: "Give him back the comb in order that he may return to thee the spindle."

Source: *Maqamat of Badi al-Zaman al-Hamadhani*, translated by W. J. Prendergast (London: Curzon, 1973), pp. 16–17.

Egypt were influenced by the origin and background of its rulers, with tastes in architecture changing along with the rise of new ruling dynasties, each with its own political affiliations and ethnic background. At first the Iraqi influence of the Abbasid khilafah (750–945) prevailed. There are no remains from this period in Egypt, apart from a few windows in the Masjid of 'Amr ibn al-'As. The Iraqi influence can still clearly be seen in the early masjid of Ahmad Ibn Tulun, founder of the Tulunid dynasty, who seceded from Abbasid control in 868. Later, the North African influence became prevalent with the advent of the Fatimid rulers from Tunisia in 969. Ruling Egypt for two hundred years, they exerted a strong North African influence on the architectural style and its decoration. From the thirteenth to the beginning of the sixteenth century, Anatolian/Syrian influences were predominant. The rulers of that period, the Mamluks, had been brought in from the Turkic world of Central Asia and Anatolian Turkey as military leaders and took over the rule of Egypt in 1250. They also established themselves in Syria.

Abbasid Architecture. During the Iraqi phase of Egyptian architecture, the building material of choice was mud brick, in conformity with what was available in Iraq. Later, almost all major examples of public architecture were constructed of stone, a material readily available in Egypt. The Masjid of Ibn Tulun, built in 876–879, is a huge arcaded structure with an enormous courtyard, much like the Great Masjid at Samarra' in Iraq. The Masjid of Ibn Tulun has the same layout, with outer walls measuring 162 by 162 meters and inner walls 140 by 122 meters—about 17,000 square meters, enough for nearly 30,000 worshipers. It was built with the same materials as the masjid in Samarra' and has similar decorative elements, stylized floral patterns and intricately interlacing circles and other geometric shapes. The minaret was an exact copy of the minaret in Samarra' until it was partially rebuilt in the twelfth century after suffering damage in an earthquake.

Fatimid Architecture. When Egypt came under the rule of the Fatimids in 969, the new dynasty launched an impressive building campaign. In effect, the city of Cairo was founded by the Fatimids. Originally it was the royal headquarters, with two lavishly decorated and furnished palaces that faced one another and that gave to the main thoroughfare the name Bayn al-Qasrayn (Between the Two Palaces). This road still exists as the main north-south street in the heart of medieval Cairo, but all traces of the palaces have disappeared. The royal quarter was incorporated into the still growing city.

Fatimid Masjids. The Fatimids built many masjids, which vary in size from quite large to quaint and small. All Fatimid masjids follow an arcaded plan. The best known of the structures they commissioned, which is still in use, is the Masjid of al-Azhar, first constructed in 970–972 and often rebuilt and expanded. From the start, it was meant as both a congregational masjid and a teaching institution, perhaps modeled on the earlier Nizamiyyah madrasahs of Iraq. With its traditional plan of columned sanctuary and large courtyard, the al-Azhar Masjid was easily suited for use as a school. Each of the notable scholars was assigned a specific column at which he sat during teaching hours and around which his students sat in a circle. Thus, al-Azhar Masjid became the original site of al-Azhar University, said to be the oldest surviving university in the world. As is the case with all public religious structures, the decoration of al-Azhar Masjid is based on geometric and stylized floral patterns. At first al-Azhar Masjid had an arcade on only one side of its courtyard, but under the Fatimid Khalifah al-Hafiz (1129–1149), arcades were added to the other three sides, and a dome was constructed over the entrance to the sanctuary area. On its interior, the dome is beautifully decorated with designs carved in the stucco. Originally, the stucco was painted and gilded. The inspiration for this dome came from the design and decoration of the Fatimid masjid at al-Mahdiyyah, in Tunisia, from which the dynasty had originally come. The other surviving Fatimid masjids in Cairo include those of al-Hakim (built 990–1003), al-Juyushi (1085), al-Aqmar (1125), and al-Salih Tala'i' (1160). The Masjid of al-Salih Tala'i' has wonderful

An artist's reconstruction of the plastered-mudbrick masjid built in Djenné, Mali, as early as the thirteenth century
(drawing by Pierre Maas; from *Aramco World*, November-December 1990)

screens made of turned wood on the front porch of the main facade. Moreover, this masjid has room beneath it for shops, and the revenue generated from renting them was used for the upkeep of the masjid. This use of space is one of the earliest examples of a common practice found in the Muslim world, that of the *waqf*, or endowment. A patron usually designated a plot of land or the revenue from trade to the upkeep of a masjid. The many surviving *waqfiyyah* documents attest to the care patrons took to ensure the maintenance of masjids for years to come. Such a document specified in great detail the amounts of money that were to be spent and how, the jobs that had to be filled at all times, and the wages for the muezzin, the imam, and others. Later, in the cases of madrasahs, *waqfiyyahs* specified the number of teachers, their wages, and the stipend for students. Care was also taken to provide meals for students and water for passersby to drink or for ablutions before prayers. The practice of endowment continued into modern times, when it was largely replaced by government appropriations.

Fatimid City Walls. In addition to masjids, the Fatimids built a great stone wall around the city of Cairo (1087–1092). Like other medieval cities, Cairo needed a wall with gates for protection against invaders and against robbers at night. Three gates from the Fatimid wall have survived in good condition, two on the north end of the Fatimid city and one on the south. It is fascinating to visit the surviving portions of the wall and gates and marvel at the beauty of the stone architecture. A narrow spiral staircase in the north wall is particularly amazing because each stone had to be cut precisely to fit.

Fatimid Tombs. Though memorial funerary architecture eventually became prominent, construction of elaborate memorials began late in Egypt and the rest of the

Muslim world. The earliest domed tombs commemorate past religious figures, and once that practice became accepted rulers sought similar commemoration. The earliest surviving domed tomb in Egypt, that of Yahya al-Shabih (circa 1150), dates from the Fatimid period. Earlier domed tombs in Egypt have not survived, and there are a few commemorative domed memorial structures that apparently do not contain graves. One such structure, the Masjid of al-Juyushi, dates from 1085, earlier than the earliest domed tomb in Egypt.

Ayyubid Architecture. The Ayyubid dynasty, which followed the Fatimids in 1169, also left some magnificent buildings in Cairo, including the citadel of Salah al-Din (known in the West as Saladin), built 1183–1184, as well as masjids and mausoleums. The best-known Ayyubid mausoleum was that of Imam Shafi'i (built in 1211), honoring the early jurist and founder of one of the four main Sunni schools of thought (762–820).

Mamluk Architecture. The most glorious period of Egyptian Muslim architecture is undoubtedly that of the alien Mamluks, who ruled Egypt for almost three hundred years (1250–1517), although this impression may be partly owing to the fact that so many structures have survived from the Mamluk period. These buildings are predominantly masjids, largely because of the stipulation against tearing them down. The Mamluks also built homes, palaces, baths, hospitals, madrasahs, mausoleums, and caravanserais (known in Egypt as *wakalahs*). The earliest Mamluk monuments were commissioned by the ruler al-Zahir Baybars (1260–1277), the founder of the Mamluk state in Cairo. What has survived of the masjid he constructed reveals that it was a large arcaded masjid (built 1266–1269), almost a copy of the Fatimid masjid of al-Mahdiyyah in Tunisia. Baybars's masjid is the last of the great arcaded masjids constructed around a large courtyard to be built in Egypt. After this time, Egyptian masjids were generally constructed as roofed buildings without open-air courtyards. This change represents a retreat from the effort to get worshipers to attend Friday congregational prayer in a few large masjids rather than in many smaller neighborhood ones. It is probably connected to the growth and increased crowding of cities, as illustrated by the fact that Baybars had to build his large masjid outside the city walls. The next major building effort from which structures have survived was that of Sultan Qala'un (1279–1290), who left an impressive complex of buildings, including a masjid, a mausoleum, and a hospital. Few traces of the hospital have survived, but the masjid and the mausoleum are still in existence. The mausoleum, in particular, is in a good state of preservation. Like the Dome of the Rock, it has large columns supporting a central dome, and its stucco, mosaic, and marble decorations also attest to influences from earlier buildings. Both the square shape of the lower part of the minaret of the Masjid of Qala'un and its stucco decoration attest to the persistence of some North African influence, even after the downfall of the Fatimids. Since the time of the Fatimids, mausoleums had been erected both as independent structures and as attachments to a religious complex. After Qala'un, they became almost a required accoutrement of power; not only the sultans but also nobles built them. Indeed, only a few Mamluk religious structures were built without attached mausoleums. Although prophetic teachings (hadiths) disapproved of the proximity of masjid to mausoleum, such structures expressed the hope of a patron that worshipers would also visit his tomb and pray for him. In addition to the development of the royal tomb as an elaborate architectural form, there were other interesting trends in masjid construction during the reign of Qala'un. One of the most significant developments of this time was the shift from the arcaded masjid of the past to the iwan-style masjid developed in Iran. While the iwan style had been known before, it came into general use in Egypt only from the period of Qala'un. Most of the later Mamluk masjids in Egypt were built with four vaulted halls opening onto a courtyard. Yet, the form of architecture remained distinct from the Iranian style because it did not adopt most other details of Iranian architecture but represents instead a distinct local style. Two iwan-style masjids of the Mamluk period are especially notable. One is the Masjid of Sultan Hasan (built 1356–1361), which was constructed as a school as well as a tomb for the sultan, who was never buried in it, and of course as a masjid for worship. The other is the Mausoleum of Sultan Qa'itbay (built 1472–1474) in the Northern Cemetery, with its exquisite, delicate proportions and ornate decoration. Dozens of other beautiful Mamluk foundations survive as well.

Mamluk Architectural Trends. Enough Mamluk architecture has survived to allow scholars to trace the evolution of design from one epoch to another. At first,

Mihrab (prayer niche) in the Mamluk masjid at the Sultan Hassan madrasah, built in Cairo in 1356

brick was the primary building material, as in Ibn Tulun's Masjid. Shortly thereafter, stone replaced brick for most parts of buildings except domes. Gradually, domes were also built of stone. The first stone domes were simple ribbed domes, similar to and probably influenced by the brick domes of Iran. Then intricate patterns were introduced. By the fifteenth century, complex arabesques carved in varying depth had become prominent features of domes. Many domes, such as that crowning the Mausoleum of Qa'itbay, are breathtaking in their beauty. That dome—large, elongated, and elegant—attests to the prowess of the medieval architects and artisans. The dome is completely formed of large interlocking stones, the surface of which was artfully transformed into a carpet-like design of intertwining geometric forms and naturalistic floral forms. The tall, slender, elegant minaret is also well proportioned. The whole building is decorated inside and out with delicate designs carved in the marble and the wood used as surface materials. The building is considered a model for much modern masjid construction in Egypt. Qa'itbay was an avid builder. During his reign as many as eighty separate structures were erected, including the citadel he ordered built in Alexandria on the site where the famous Pharos lighthouse, since fallen into ruin, had once stood.

Sources:
Nurhan Atasoy and others, *The Art of Islam* (Paris: Unesco, 1990).

Sheila S. Blair and Jonathan M. Bloom, *The Art and Architecture of Islam 1250–1800* (New Haven: Yale University Press, 1994).

Abbas Daneshvari, ed., *Essays in Islamic Art and Architecture: In Honor of Katharina Otto-Dorn* (Malibu, Cal: Undena, 1981).

Martin Frishman and Hasan-Uddin Khan, ed., *The Mosque: History, Architectural Development and Regional Diversity* (New York: Thames & Hudson, 1994).

George Michell, ed., *Architecture of the Islamic World: Its History and Social Meaning* (New York: Morrow, 1978).

Henri and Anne Stierlin, *Splendours of an Islamic World: Mamluk Art in Cairo 1250–1517* (London & New York : Tauris Parke, 1997).

LATER MASJID ARCHITECTURE IN THE TURCO-IRANIAN WORLD AND INDIA

Iranian Architecture. Even after the breakdown of the khilafah that started around 740 and the development of regional styles that began after 900, Iran, as one of the largest cultural regions under Islam, took the lead in establishing an important regional style, even though local dynasties frequently changed, and none ruled the whole of Iran. Eventually, the Iranian area of influence embraced most of the Turco-Iranian world, not only the modern country of Iran, but also Afghanistan and Central Asia to the east and Turkey to the west. Iranian themes also strongly influenced the Muslim architecture of India, which soon, however, took off in its own direction. Likewise, on the west in Anatolia, the rivalry between Ottoman Turkey and Safavid Iran after 1500 helped push the Turks more quickly along the road to their own influential regional tradition. The architecture of the Arabic-speaking country of Iraq, the seat of the khilafah until 1258, also followed the Iranian pattern. The most important Iranian contribution to Muslim architecture was perhaps the vaulted halls called iwans. Such high vaulting was an established feature of Iranian architecture even before the rise of Islam, as shown by the Sassanian palace at Salman-pak near Baghdad, Iraq. It took some time, however, before it was adopted by Muslims even in Iran, for the early masjids there were all of the arcaded type. The oldest example of an iwan-style masjid—with only one iwan—is the one built in Nayriz around 975. After this time, the design spread rapidly, developing into masjids with two and with four iwans during the Saljuk dynasty (1037–1194), especially in the period circa 1080–1160. The oldest surviving masjid originally designed and built according to a four-iwan plan is the Jami' Masjid of Zavara in Iran, constructed in 1135. Masjids of this style began to be built with regularity in Egypt from the thirteenth century onward, and the iwan design influenced Turkish architecture profoundly. The notable examples of Iranian architecture that have survived the test of time are mostly masjids, madrasahs, and tombs. The preferred building material was brick. Early buildings had intricate brick designs for decoration. Gradually some bricks were covered in colored tiles, and eventually entire walls were covered in tiles with patterned designs painted on them. Even the ribbed domes that crowned the buildings soon were covered with tiles—no doubt a time-consuming, labor-intensive, and hazardous feat. This trend led to the establishment of the signature style of Iranian decoration: glazed blue tiles covered in Arabic calligraphy, usually in white. The beauty of Iranian masjids and other public buildings owes much to the ingenious use of colored tiles as part of their decorative scheme. The best-known Iranian-style masjids are perhaps the large complexes of Isfahan and Mashad in Iran and Bukhara and Samarqand in Uzbekistan. Each of these was constructed and reconstructed over a period of some centuries. Representing the culmination of iwan-type architecture, these complexes are characterized by enormous courtyards capable of holding more than one hundred thousand worshipers; lofty, elongated, vaulted iwan halls frequently topped by domes; beautiful tilework, usually in blue and embellished with Qur'anic verses and other Arabic inscriptions; and large, high, round minarets that usually tapered to a narrower top. High iwan halls were also adapted for use as entrance portals, appearing as extremely lofty, pretentious gateways on the outside. This style was already being copied outside Iran under the last Abbasids, as, for example, in 1223 at al-Mustansiriyyah Madrasah in Baghdad. Construction of religious buildings according to this design has continued to the present.

Domes. The dome, which had already been a feature of Sassanian architecture, rose to greater and greater heights between 900 and 1500. It seems to have originated in the "kiosk-type" masjid, which consisted of a small, square chamber with doors on three sides and the *qiblah* wall on the fourth, topped by a dome nearly as large as the building. This structure provided a small but unobstructed worship space. An example of this type of masjid is the Jami' Masjid of Gulpayagan in Iran, built in 1104–1118. The dome then became wedded to the iwan structure, creating loftier interior spaces. In contrast, the traditional arcaded masjid design, with its relatively low ceiling and forest of columns may have seemed limiting, clumsy, and repetitious as the buildings grew in size. The domed tomb may also have derived from the kiosk masjid. According to the hadiths, tombs raised above the ground or otherwise permanently marked are not allowed in Islam, but—as with other restrictions on habits of conspicuous consumption by the wealthy—such prohibitions were often subverted or disobeyed by the rulers. Such violations of tradition frequently began in Iran and Iranian-influenced areas, with their heritage from ancient civilizations. The oldest partially extant domed tomb is Qubbat al-Sulaybiyyah at Samarra' in Iraq, dating from the ninth century. This structure was followed by the earliest mausoleum ever built for a ruler, a no-longer-extant tomb for the mother of the Abbasid ruler al-Muqtadir (ruled 908–932) at al-Rusafah in Syria. Almost as old, the earliest surviving example of such a tomb is one built for a member of the Samanid dynasty in Bukhara, dating from before 943 and tastefully executed with brick decoration. After this time, domed tombs for the rulers spread everywhere in the Muslim world, despite frequent opposition from religious scholars. In Iranian architecture double-

Decorative brickwork on a tomb built in Bukhara for a member of the Samanid dynasty during the first half of the tenth century

domed structures were built quite often. Constructing two shells, one on top of the other, made the outer dome large enough to be viewed from a distance while the inner dome was proportionate to the interior of the building and low enough for the viewer to see its decoration.

South Asian Architecture. Muslim architecture in South Asia drew its inspiration from Iranian examples. The most splendid Muslim architecture of the region dates from after 1500, but impressive structures from the period 1200–1500 have survived. Some of them are still in use, while others survive only partially or in ruins. Most are religious buildings erected for royal patrons, particularly masjids and tombs. In India tombs have had the highest survival rate. The buildings are widely scattered geographically, but many are clustered around the capital city of Delhi and around the old provincial capitals, especially Ahmadabad in Gujarat, which has many masjids dating from before 1500, notably the exquisite Jami' Masjid, built in 1423. After the first Muslim rulers of India migrated there from the Iranian world just before 1200, the Persian influences they brought with them were quickly subordinated to a new local style that was strongly affected by Indian traditions of ornate decoration. Most Indian masjids are built on raised platforms. The early masjids of South Asia follow the arcaded form of masjid architecture, which is quite similar to the local model of Hindu temples with their "thousand-pillared halls." Several variations on this style exist. The Khirki Masjid at Delhi (circa 1375) and others are built on a

Ruins of Aq Suray, a Timurid palace built at
Shahr-I Sabz, Uzbekistan, during the
early fifteenth century

cruciform plan with four small arcaded courtyards
arranged in a square pattern around the central cross,
which is also arcaded. This style bears some affinity
with the Anatolian masjid design of the same date. It
did not become the dominant pattern in India, where
masjids eventually came to consist of rather small halls
with pillars supporting domes on one side of an enormous, open-air courtyard.

Sources:
Nurhan Atasoy and others, *The Art of Islam* (Paris: Unesco, 1990).

Sheila S. Blair and Jonathan M. Bloom, *The Art and Architecture of Islam
1250–1800* (New Haven: Yale University Press, 1994).

K. A. C. Creswell, *Early Muslim Architecture* (New York: Hacker Art
Books, 1979).

Abbas Daneshvari, ed., *Essays in Islamic Art and Architecture: In Honor of
Katharina Otto-Dorn* (Malibu, Cal. : Undena, 1981).

Martin Frishman and Hasan-Uddin Khan, ed., *The Mosque: History,
Architectural Development and Regional Diversity* (New York: Thames
& Hudson, 1994).

Aptullah Kuran, *The Mosque in Early Ottoman Architecture* (Chicago:
University of Chicago Press, 1968).

George Michell, ed., *Architecture of the Islamic World: Its History and Social
Meaning* (New York: Morrow, 1978).

Arthur Upham Pope, *An Introduction to Persian Art Since the Seventh Century A.D.* (Westport, Conn.: Greenwood Press, 1977).

Henri Stierlin, *Turkey: From the Selcuks to the Ottomans* (Köln, Germany &
New York: Taschen, 1998).

Henri and Anne Stierlin, *Splendours of an Islamic World: Mamluk Art in
Cairo 1250-1517* (London & New York: Tauris Parke, 1997).

MUSIC

Islam and Musical Expression. Music produced by
Muslims varies greatly from one country to another, and
even more from region to region. The music of each
Muslim cultural zone probably takes some of its traditional inspiration from the music that prevailed in that
geographical area before Islam was introduced there.
Since Islam began in the Arabic and Persian-speaking

Middle East and has flourished there the longest, however, it is likely that the music of the early Middle Eastern Muslims, Arabs and Iranians especially, has tended to influence all subsequent Muslim musical development even outside of its own cultural area. Because Islam does not, on the whole, use music in any of its forms of worship, and especially not in the obligatory prayers, this transfer of central Muslim cultural influence to other Muslim cultures has been less pronounced in music than in other areas of cultural influence. This important factor helps to account for the great diversity of music among various Muslim culture groups. Indeed, music is a controversial topic in Islamic law. Muslims appreciate and are amazed by the music of nature, which is all around in birds' songs and the splashing of waves and waterfalls. While the Qur'an never mentions music, it describes the languages of birds and other creatures and emphasizes that they are praising God by their sounds (17: 44, 21: 79, 24: 41, 27: 16). Even the thunder praises God (13: 13), and the mountains do likewise (38: 18). Natural music aside, however, Muslims have been wary of music and of the playing of musical instruments because they are condemned in some of the accepted hadiths. This reservation about music has been found among some conservative Christians as well. The hadiths that condemn music disapprove of it because some music has traditionally been associated with activities such as the consumption of drugs and alcohol, flirtation, and casual sex—things that are not been conducive to the piety or self-discipline of devout Muslims. Because the only music available was live music, and paying musicians to play could be expensive, the discouragement of music was also a device to limit the social-class difference between rich and poor. On the other hand, some hadiths, while not actually declaring all music allowable, describe various instances when the Prophet heard some kind of music, permitted it, or approved of it. When the Prophet Muhammad first arrived in Madinah, he was welcomed by inhabitants who had been eagerly awaiting his arrival and had composed a song in his honor. The words of the song are still sung in all the Muslim countries, and children learn it at an early age. Drums would probably have accompanied the first performance of this song, and the use of drums and tambourines is mentioned in other hadiths. Celebrations accompanied by singing and music, or at least percussion instruments, were also specifically approved for weddings and feast days. Generally, even the strictest Muslims allow certain kinds of music if it encourages the following of Islam and its rules and reminds the Muslims of God. There is, for example, the *musahhirati*, the man who during the month of Ramadan goes from door to door before first light chanting and beating his drum to wake up Muslims to have their *suhur* (early morning meal) so that they can get ready to fast during daylight.

Musicians in a tavern playing a tambourine, short-necked lute, and harp; illumination from a circa 1256 manuscript for al-Hariri's *Maqamat* (British Library, London)

Muslim trumpeters; illumination from a 1468–1469 manuscript for a Persian glossary of rare words (British Library, London)

Sufi Music. The Sufis' use of music in their ecstatic ceremonies was controversial and often met with disapproval from the ulama'. The purpose of Sufi music was to bring the worshiper nearer to God. Such music was played on the same instruments that produced secular music, and, if words were sung as well, their poetry about love of God often paralleled secular love poetry. These musical performances were sometimes accompanied by dancing as well, as in the Mawlawis order of Turkey, which can be traced back to the great Persian poet Jalal al-Din Rumi (1207–1273). These performances were not mixed social dancing; they were divided by gender. Some deeply religious people were devoted to such practices, while other devout Muslims firmly felt that such music and dancing was undignified and not sanctioned by the Prophet's tradition for religious purposes, and the controversy still continues among Muslims.

Secular Music. Although restrictions on music may have been supported by some religious leaders, however, music has flourished everywhere and among most social classes throughout Muslim history. The popularity of music is demonstrated, for example, by the *Kitab al-aghani* (Book of Songs) compiled by Abu al-Faraj al-Isfahani (897–967). This enormous collection of poets' lives from before the Muslim era down through the first three centuries of Islam includes quotations from their poetry with written notes indicating how to play the music to which the poems should be sung. These musical notations

are insufficient for modern performers to reproduce the music today, however, and early Muslim music—like that of ancient Greece and Rome—has been lost. Nevertheless, *Kitab al-aghani* demonstrates that Arabic poetry was often—probably even usually—sung and that there were many different styles in a musical tradition that appears to have been rich and complex. Theoretical discussions of music had already begun under the Umayyads (ruled 661–750). Under the early Abbasids (750–945), classicists and modernists existed, the former represented by the well-known composer- singers Ibrahim al-Mawsili (742–804) and his son Ishaq (767–850), the latter by the Abbasid prince Ibrahim ibn al-Mahdi (779–839). During this period there were eight modes of classical music, which were expanded later through Persian influence to eighteen. *Kitab al-aghani* was followed by a large body of musical literature in both Arabic and Persian, which preserves many songs and describes the complicated structures of formal concerts given before the rulers. Several Muslim philosophers—including al-Kindi (circa 801 – circa 866), al-Farabi (circa 870 – 950), and Ibn Sina (980–1037)—wrote extensively on musical theory. The first musical notation that can be interpreted by modern musicians was created by Safi al-Din al-Urmawi (died 1294), and the earliest presently reproducible song was written down by Qutb al-Din al-Shirazi (1236–1311).

Instruments. Muslim music of the Middle East used many different instruments, including the *'ud* (lute), *tanbur* (a large long-necked lute), *ribab* (rebec), *qanun* (zither), *duff* (tambourine), *mizmar* (reeded pipe) and various kinds of *nay* (flute) and *tabl* (drum). As Middle Eastern Muslim music spread to other regions local instruments were added. The lute was regarded as the most fundamental of these instruments, for musical theory was built on a description of its frets (the finger positions on its neck that produce the different notes). Certain European instruments are descended from Muslim instruments. The guitar, for example goes back to the lute.

Source:
Isma'il R. and Lois L. al-Faruqi, *The Cultural Atlas of Islam* (London: Collier Macmillan, 1986).

ORAL POETRY, STORYTELLING, AND FOLKLORE

Oral Epics. An abiding, popular form of colloquial poetry is the epic form produced spontaneously along particular story lines by illiterate poets. Arabic epics bear comparison with the Greek *Iliad* and *Odyssey* of Homer in length, form, and content; indeed, the Arabic epics are longer than Homer's. All such epics have three principal characteristics: they are heroic, poetic, and narrative. While they have well-known story lines like folktales, these oral epics do not have fixed texts. Rather, they are told differently every time they are narrated, even by the same poet on different occasions. In his recitation the oral poet makes use of various stock phrases called "formulaic language." The classical Arabic oral epics include *Sirat 'Antar* (Romance of Antar), which dates as early as the twelfth century; *Sirat Abi Zayd al-Hilali* (Romance of Abi Zayd al-Hilali), including a fictional elaboration of certain events of the eleventh century; and *Sirat al-Zahir Baybars* (Romance of al-Zahir Baybars), on the heroic Mamluk sultan Baybars (ruled 1260–1277). Poets tended to specialize in singing only one such cycle, and each had its own rules. Although all these epics survived into the nineteenth century and have been recorded in written versions, it is mainly *Sirat Abi Zayd* that continues to be sung today, with a complete version consisting of as many as two hundred thousand lines of rhymed quatrains. When performing an oral epic, the poet usually sings the verses of only a single episode to the accompaniment of a musical instrument, often a *ribab* (rebec), a small two-stringed instrument that looks somewhat like a violin. It is played with a bow and held vertically like the cello.

The Thousand and One Nights. The stories called *Alf laylah wa-laylah* (The Thousand and One Nights) were collected gradually in the Middle Ages. Originating in a Persian storybook that was in turn based largely on stories from India, an Arabic work with this name was documented by tenth-century writers and by a ninth-century papyrus fragment. The stories seem to have existed in Arabic in the eighth century, but the collection was later greatly expanded, in Iraq and in Egypt from about the twelfth to the fourteenth century, by which time it was nearly complete in its present form. Although Westerners often think of *Alf laylah wa-laylah* as representative Arabic

HAFIZ

Persian poet Shams al-Din Muhammad Shirazi (circa 1325 –circa 1390), known as Hafiz wrote mainly in the *ghazal* form, creating mystical works whose meanings were both secular and religious. In Ghazal 38 he wrote:

I cease not from desire till my desire
Is satisfied; or let my mouth attain
My love's red mouth, or let my soul expire,
Sighed from those lips that sought her lips in vain.
Others may find another love as fair;
Upon her threshold I have laid my head,
The dust shall cover me, still lying there,
When from my body life and love have fled.
My soul is on my lips ready to fly,
But grief beats in my heart and will not cease,
Because not once, not once before I die,
Will her sweet lips give all my longing peace.
My breath is narrowed down to one long sigh
For a red mouth that burns my thoughts like fire;
When will that mouth draw near and make reply
To one whose life is straitened with desire?
When I am dead, open my grave and see
The cloud of smoke that rises round thy feet:
In my dead heart the fire still burns for thee;
Yea, the smoke rises from my winding-sheet!
Ah, come, Beloved! for the meadows wait
Thy coming, and the thorn bears flowers instead
Of thorns, the cypress fruit, and desolate
Bare winter from before thy steps has fled.
Hoping within some garden ground to find
A red rose soft and sweet as thy soft cheek,
Through every meadow blows the western wind,
Through every garden he is fain to seek.
Reveal thy face! that the whole world may be
Bewildered by thy radiant loveliness;
The cry of man and woman comes to thee,
Open thy lips and comfort their distress!
Each curling lock of thy luxuriant hair
Breaks into barbed hooks to catch my heart,
My broken heart is wounded everywhere
With countless wounds from which the red drops start.
Yet when sad lovers meet and tell their sighs,

Not without praise shall Hafiz' name be said,
Not without tears, in those pale companies
Where joy has been forgot and hope has fled.

Source: Gertrude Bell, *The Teachings of Hafiz* (London: Octagon Press, 1985), n. pag.

and Muslim literature, it is really more comparable to *Grimms' Fairy Tales* than to other kinds of Arabic and Muslim literature, and it does not have an especially high reputation in the Muslim world. The stories come from a great variety of sources, including ancient Sumer, Assyria, and Egypt, as well as India, Iran, and Arabia, and have delighted many over the ages. Although some of its stories filtered individually into medieval Europe, the first western appearance of *The Thousand and One Nights* as a large collection came in 1704 with a French translation that seems to have have augmented the original Arabic collection with stories from other sources.

Source:

Michael Zwettler, *The Oral Tradition of Classical Arabic Poetry: Its Character and Implications* (Columbus: Ohio State University Press, 1978).

PERSIAN POETRY

Language. Middle Persian, or Avestan, was a written language during the entire twelve centuries of the ancient Persian empires (550 B.C.E. – 651 C.E.), and some of the ancient literature in that language is still read by followers of the Zoroastrian religion. But after the Muslims established control of most of Iran (638–651), the Avestan language lost the state patronage that was important for its survival. The decline of Avestan was accelerated by the Arabicization of public records that began during 700–742 in different areas of the khilafah. As Iranians began to adopt Islam, especially in northeastern Iran, Arabic became the primary language for all kinds of writing while Persian remained the spoken tongue of the people, including Muslims. Indeed, even the descendants of the original Arab immigrants to Iran and the rest of the Muslim East came to speak Persian as their mother tongue. As the unity of the khilafah waned and certain marginal regions became independent, they began to cultivate forms of Persian written in the Arabic script, perhaps to underline their cultural independence within the Muslim world. These areas included especially Sistan—the remote region where the modern borders of Iran, Afghanistan, and Pakistan meet—where the Saffarid dynasty (861–1003) cultivated Persian poetry and probably other writing in Persian. The term *Modern Persian* is used to describe the Persian language since the introduction of Islam, and especially since Arabic script was first used to write Persian. Beginning in the mid tenth century, the use of Persian as a literary language expanded both suddenly and widely. This development was probably connected with the continuing decline of the central authority of the Abbasid khilafah in Baghdad and the concomitant growth of Persian-speaking local dynasties, the most prominent of which were the Samanid (873–1005), Buyid (945–1055), and Ghaznawid (977–1187) ruling groups. After this time Persian spread widely in the eastern part of the Muslim world and tended to displace Arabic except in religious literature. It not only became the lingua franca of the Iranians, many of whom spoke Iranian languages other than Persian, but was also generally used by Muslim speakers of Turkish and Indian languages. When Islam became securely established in India after 1200, the local Muslims used the Persian language as their main vehicle of written expression, thus greatly enriching Persian literature. The same can be said to a lesser extent for the Anatolian and Central Asian Turks, who also used Persian as their literary vehicle.

Models. Poetry has always been the most highly respected form of Persian literature. Poetry written in Modern Persian, an exceptionally rich and extensive liter-

ary form equal to any other world literature, came into existence in the earliest Muslim period. Its existence is documented by a few fragments from the eighth and ninth centuries. The earliest extensive surviving Modern Persian poetry, however, starts in the tenth century with the poets Rudaki (died circa 940 – 950) and Daqiqi (circa 935 – circa 980). The earliest surviving poetic works date from the beginning of the eleventh century, with Firdawsi (circa 941 – 1020), Farrukhi (died 1038), 'Unsuri (died 1040), and Manuchihri (died circa 1041). Early Modern Persian poetry was primarily influenced by Arabic models, including meter and rhyme—which might be compared to English poetry using Latin meter and rhyme schemes for much of its history. Such borrowing is understandable in the case of Persian poetry, as Arabic poetry represented the highest level of literary achievement for the Muslim elite, whether of Arab, Iranian, or another origin. Until the thirteenth century most Persian poems, like their Arabic models, were in the form of the *qasidah* (ode) and consisted of a prologue, a panegyric, and an appeal to the patron. In the eleventh century the *ghazal* (love poem), based on a common prologue theme for the *qasidah*, appeared, and it was the dominant poetic form from the thirteenth to the eighteenth century. Also based on earlier Arabic models, the *ghazal* form was specifically used for love poetry, but all other forms of Persian poetry also celebrate love, whether earthly or divine. Indeed, Persian love poetry may perhaps be considered the most extensive and refined expression of romantic emotion in all human literature. As a great gulf exists between the structures of the Arabic and Persian languages, Persian poets began to establish their own forms. One Persian invention was *ruba'i*, two lines of two rhymed hemistichs each: in effect, four rhymed lines. The greatest creation of classical Persian literature was the *mathnawi*, an epic poem written in rhymed couplets (with each couplet written as a single line of verse). Although one meter of Arabic poetry, the *rajaz*, is also written in rhymed couplets, there is no form in Arabic poetry that compares to the development of the Persian *mathnawi*, especially in its ability to sustain poems of thousands of lines. Except for colloquial oral epics, such lengthy poems are lacking in Arabic. Already in existence by the tenth century, the *mathnawi* consists of three types: the heroic epic based on ancient, pre-Islamic Persian traditions, the romantic epic celebrating a famous pair of lovers, and the didactic *mathnawi*, which is only epic in its use of narrative to illustrate the moral, spiritual, or philosophical truths that it tries to inculcate. Some Persian poems follow other forms, or mix them, but the forms mentioned here are the dominant ones.

Important Persian Poets. Rudaki is in many respects the founder of Modern Persian verse and the inventor of some of its forms. Only one hundred lines of his poetry have survived: one complete poem and fragments quoted by later anthologists. Firdawsi created the foundational epic of Persian poetry, which is also the national epic of Iran, the massive *Shahnameh* (Book of Kings) of more than forty-eight thousand *mathnawi* verses (up to sixty thousand in some versions), one of the longest poems in any language and the earliest long poem surviving in Persian. Written between about 980 and 1010, Firdawsi's monumental epic tells the story of the ancient Iranian kingdoms through the Sasanids (224–651), whose history occupies the last third of the work. The work uses fewer Arabic words than later Persian poems. Firdawsi may be considered the Persian Homer, and his work has had a major influence on all subsequent Persian literature. Abd Allah-i Ansari (1005–1089), who wrote in both Persian and Arabic, became the founder of Persian mystical poetry with his *Munajat*, a mixture of prose and poetry. 'Umar Khayyam (1048–1131), though widely known as a poet, has always been better known among Muslims as a scholar, scientist, and mathematician. 'Umar's poems are quatrains, and only perhaps 250 of them survive, a small output compared to the quantity of work produced by writers who are primarily poets. He has become known as a great poet in the West chiefly because of the famous, creative, and loose translation of his *Ruba'iyyat* by Edward FitzGerald (1809–1883), which has strongly influenced subsequent Western views of Persian poetry and Muslim philosophy. Although it represents 'Umar's poetry to some extent, FitzGerald's work also promotes his own materialistic and antireligious beliefs in a manner that many late-nineteenth-century British readers found attractive. That 'Umar questioned God's actions in his poetry was not especially remarkable; Sufis, even the great mystic Abd Allah-i Ansari did the same. Likewise, the wine drinking and hedonism implied by some of the 'Umar's poems may be found in the hedonistic Arabic poetry of Abu Nuwas, and 'Umar's poetry also exhibits a struggle to repent that matches that of Abu Nuwas. 'Umar and Abu Nuwas, like other poets, lived their lives as Muslims within the framework of Islam, even while they struggled with the prevailing interpretations of it.

The Beloved. As it developed, Persian poetry began to put a heavy emphasis on love as the means of reaching union with God, the Beloved. Often written in the *ghazal* form, Persian Sufi love poetry was derived from the earlier ode celebrating the poet's patron, who was replaced by God or by the shaykh (spiritual leader) as a representative of God. At the same time the undying devotion and absolute obedience of the lover to the beloved becomes a symbol for complete surrender, devotion, and obedience to God. While perhaps not a practitioner of Sufism like most other Muslim mystic poets, Sana'i (died 1131) wrote the first large body of Muslim pietistic poetry, in particular the first large group of *ghazals*. He also wrote the first religious *mathnawi*. Continuing the religious *mathnawi* form, Nizami of Ganjah (1141 – circa 1209) wrote the romantic epic *Layla wa-Majnun* (Layla and the Crazy One) about the chaste devotion and unrealized love of a Bedouin Arab couple. The story had circulated for centuries before Nizami wrote his poem, but his version in Persian is often considered the best and has become the quasi-official version. *Layla wa-Majnun* has the mystical overtones that characterize most Persian love poetry, especially because the love described is that of devo-

tion and obedience to the beloved without expectation of reward. Nizami's near contemporary Farid al-Din al-'Attar (circa 1143 – circa 1220) wrote poetic epics with mystical content, generally teaching that God is within each individual and that one has only to realize his presence to achieve salvation. This theme is present in his *Mantiq al-tayr,* widely available in English as *The Conference of the Birds.* Jalal al-Din Rumi (1207–1273) wrote during an important period for Persian verse, when several prolific major poets were living at the same time. Rumi is the most famous of all Persian poets and indeed the best known and most widely read Muslim author in English. His surviving *ghazals* are included in his *Diwan-i Shams-i Tabrizi* (The Collected Poems of Shams-i Tabrizi) of more than forty thousand verses. He also wrote a *Mathnawi* of more than twenty-six thousand verses. Although he is primarily considered a Sufi poet, he was also a poet of passionate love. These two aspects are brought together by the idea that the beloved is really God, even though the expressions of love may seem earthly. In the view of Rumi and his followers such passion is the most ideal state to which humans may aspire and is thus a suitable way in which to express one's love of God. Such ideas have helped to endear Rumi to a large segment of the western public. Another important Sufi poet was the daring and well-traveled Fakhr al-Din 'Iraqi (1213–1289), also known chiefly for his mystical love poetry. Sa'di (circa 1216 – 1292) is considered to have brought the *ghazal* to its peak. In his *Gulistan* (Rose Garden) he developed a mixture of prose and poetry that has remained a popular form. Sa'di's poetry is shrewd, entertaining, and full of practical worldly advice. Amir-i Khusraw (1253–1325), who wrote both *ghazals* and panegyric "historical" poems, became the premier Muslim poet of medieval India. Hafiz (circa 1325 – 1390), whose complete works consist of only a few hundred short *ghazals,* is often held to represent the pinnacle of Persian literature. Jami (1414–1492) brought Sufi love poetry to its highest perfection, writing a large number of poems characterized by ornate, elaborate expression and filled with complicated references and metaphors. He may also have expressed a more conservative or orthodox religious sentiment than most of his predecessors who wrote Persian love poetry, and his poems tend to inculcate lessons, offer advice, and voice admonishment.

Sources:

Franklin D. Lewis, *Rumi: Past and Present, East and West: The Life, Teaching and Poetry of Jalal al-Din Rumi* (Oxford & Boston: Oneworld, 2000).

George Morrison, ed., *History of Persian Literature: From the Beginning of the Islamic Period to the Present Day* (Leiden: Brill, 1981).

PERSIAN PROSE LITERATURE

Courtly and Popular Literature. While the classical Arabic literature was largely produced by a class of religious scholars for themselves and only secondarily for the class of political rulers and their employees, classical Persian literature seems to have been directed mainly at a secular elite. This difference can be explained by the fact that religious scholars were conversant with the Arabic language because—except for mystical Sufi works—Muslim religious writings were exclusively in Arabic regardless of an author's mother tongue. (Indeed, until the twentieth century nearly all Muslim religious writing continued to be written in Arabic.) Princes, although they were often tutored in Arabic and religious subjects, frequently did not feel as comfortable with the Arabic language and preferred literature in Persian, which was either their mother tongue—as in the case of dynasties such as the Saffarids (861–1003), Samanids (873–1005), and Buyids (945–1055)—or was a preferred lingua franca for them—as with the later Turkish dynasties such as the Ghaznawids (977–1187) and Saljuks (1037–1194).

Persian Histories. The earliest surviving long prose work in Persian is Samanid minister Bal'ami's translation, abridgment, and revision of al-Tabari's Arabic history. Bal'ami, who died in 974, began his work in 963. Prose history written originally in Persian began with the work of Gardizi (flourished circa 1050). His *Zayn al-akhbar* (The Book of Reports) briefly covers the history of the eastern Muslims until 1041. The slightly later and more important history by Abu al-Fazl Bayhaqi (995–1077) was originally in thirty volumes, but only the volume covering the years 1030–1040 has survived. Somewhat like a memoir, this substantial book is written in chatty, colloquial language. Bayhaqi's work marks the beginning of year-by-year annals in Persian, a methodology already long established in Arabic. This arrangement is the preferred organizing principle of most later Persian chronicles. 'Ali Kufi (flourished circa 1216) translated and possibly amplified an Arabic work on the eighth-century Muslim entry into Sind (now a province of Pakistan) into *Fathnamah-i Sind* (Book of the Opening of Sind), a foundational historical record for Muslims in South Asia. An early local history is Ibn Isfandiyar's *Tarikh-i Tabaristan* (The History of Tabaristan, written circa 1210 – 1217), covering the area south of the Caspian Sea. This book started as a translation of an earlier Arabic history but became an independent work.

State-Sponsored Histories. The unbroken chain of major Persian state-sponsored chronicles begins with *Tabaqat-i Nasiri* (The Nasiri Book of Generations) by Minhaj-i Siraj Juzjani (1193 – after 1265), a long work detailing and exaggerating the depredations of the Mongols until the year 1259. Having migrated to India about 1226, Juzjani wrote his great history by about 1259–1260. It is not only the first of a regular series of Persian chronicles but also the first Persian history of India. The anonymous *Tarikh-i Sistan* (The History of Sistan), written between 1277 and 1281, is a local history of the remote province of Sistan, which draws on early sources and includes much information about the Saffarid dynasty (861–1003) and the early development of Persian poetry. 'Ata-Malik Juwayni (1226–1283), who served as a governor for the Mongols during the years 1259–1281, recorded the history of the Mongols and their early rule in Iran down to 1258 in his massive *Tarikh-i jahangushay* (The History of the Siezer of the World). Rashid al-Din (circa 1247 –

1318), minister for the Mongol Ilkhan dynasty during the years 1298–1318, wrote an enormous encyclopedia of history and ethnography called *Jami' al-tawarikh*, which in some respects represents the high point of medieval Persian historiography. The Ilkhans were served by two other authors of compendious Persian histories: Wassaf (1264–1334) and Hamd Allah Mustawfi Qazwini (circa 1281 – after 1339), the author of *Tarikh-i guzidah* (Selected History), Ziya' al-Din Barani (before 1285 – after 1357) was the first Muslim historian born in India. His *Tarikh-i Firuz Shahi* (The History of Firus Shah) is a valuable chronicle of the early period of the Delhi sultanate in 1266–1357. Like the other classical Persian historians, Barani was connected with the government. Hafiz-i Abru (died 1430) and Mirkhwand (1433–1498) covered the Timurid dynasty in particular. Like Rashid al-Din's *Jami' al-tawarikh* (Collected Histories), Abru's *Majma' al-tawarikh* (Collected History), and Mirkhwand's *Rawzat al-safa'* (Garden of the Pure) are universal accounts starting from the creation of the world and ending with the authors' own lifetimes. Most of these histories are reliable and indispensable for events close to the time when they were written, but to corroborate earlier events one must go back to earlier sources.

Mirrors for Princes. Another important genre, first developed in Arabic but greatly elaborated in Persian, is the advice book for rulers. Sometimes called "mirrors for princes," these works usually comprise a great deal of miscellaneous information, including stories and anecdotes, that is deemed suitable to inculcate cultural refinement in the children of rulers, who probably were not usually proficient in Arabic. Such books were also available and of use to other readers as well. Kayka'us ibn Iskandar (1021 – at least 1083), the ruler of a small Persian principality in northern Iran, wrote the oldest of these works in Persian, the lively *Qabusnamah*. Nizam al-Mulk (died 1092), who served as prime minister to a Saljuk sultan for more than twenty years, wrote a more practical manual, *Siyasatnamah* (Book of Politics) in 1091–1092. Nizami 'Arudi Samarqandi (flourished 1110–1156) wrote *Chahar maqalah* (Four Discourses), which offers advice about secretaries, poets, astrologers, and physicians—all people with whom a prince would have dealings. Other "mirrors for princes" followed these early examples.

Geography and Travel Literature. An extremely early Persian geography book is the anonymous *Hudud al-'alam* (Limits of the World), written in 982 in Guzgan, northern Afghanistan. This work, which is not a translation of an Arabic geography book, may have been written for a Persian-reading prince who did not know Arabic. Much later, geography became an established genre of Persian literature. A related genre, the traveler's narrative, is exemplified by the *Safarnamah* (Travel Book), of Nasir-i Khusraw (1004 – at least 1072), describing the Iranian writer's pilgrimages to Makkah and his long sojourn in Egypt.

Other Prose Genres. *Al-Mu'jam fi ma'ayir shi'r al-'ajam* (Compendium of Standard Persian History) by Shams-i Qays (flourished 1204–1230s) is the oldest Persian work on poetics, and only the first of a considerable body of Persian literature on language and rhetoric. Much theoretical literature about music was also written in Persian, starting with works by Qutb al-Din Shirazi (1236–1311) and Abd al-Qadir Maraghi (died 1435). In the genre of biography, Hujwiri of Ghazna (died 1071) wrote *Kashf al-mahjub* (Revelations of the Hidden), the oldest Persian prose work on Sufism, which includes Sufi biographies and anecdotes. Such biographical works also became a major genre of Persian literature.

Sources:

A. J. Arberry, *Classical Persian Literature* (New York: Macmillan, 1958).

Reuben Levy, *An Introduction to Persian Literature* (New York: Columbia University Press, 1969).

George Morrison, ed., *History of Persian Literature: From the Beginning of the Islamic Period to the Present Day* (Leiden: Brill, 1981).

THE PROHIBITION OF IMAGES

Ethos. Muslim art was influenced by preceding civilizations, but the overall ethos it derives from the Qur'an and from the teachings and the acts of the Prophet Muhammad is a unifying thread in the midst of Muslim diversity. In particular, the doctrine against figural representations of humans and animals has shaped the whole direction of Muslim art. Although this prohibition might seem restrictive to Westerners, from the viewpoint of Muslim artists, it has actually been liberating. Because of humans' fascination with representations of their own species, images of humans tend to dominate the art of cultures in which they are allowed, as evidenced by most ancient Near Eastern, Greek, Roman, Byzantine, Indian, and Western art. The exclusion of figures opens up other possibilities, which have been thoroughly elaborated in Muslim art. In Islam, the word of God replaces the human figure as the center of attention. In general, God's word is represented in two ways: in calligraphy, which adorns the first dated Muslim building still standing, and in decoration with geometric, floral, and vegetational designs.

Religious Images. Even though the Qur'an includes no direct prohibition on the manufacture or veneration of images—as is frequently reiterated in the Bible (Exodus 20:4–5, 23 and 34:17; Leviticus 19:4 and 26:1; Deuteronomy 4:15–18, 23 and 5:8–9; Ezekiel 20:7, 18; 1 Corinthians 10:7, 14; and 1 John 5:21)—it nevertheless disparages them. In fact, it describes such idols, whether carved images or mere stones (*ansab*), as the filth of Satan (Qur'an 5: 90). As in the parallel biblical text, the Qur'an includes an account of how, after the Prophet Musa (Moses) prohibited idol worship, his people in his absence made a golden calf and suffered punishment for their transgression (Qur'an 7: 138–140, 148–152 and 20: 88–91, 97). The Qur'an also relates how the Prophet Ibrahim (Abraham) denounced the veneration of idols (*asnam, tamathil*) by his father and his people as "manifest error" (6: 74 and 21: 52–54), ridiculed idols as powerless and as representing nonexistent gods (21: 63 and 37: 91–92, 95), expressed disgust at their worship (21: 67), and smashed them to pieces (21: 58; 37: 93). At Makkah, Ibrahim prayed to God that his descendants might never worship idols (*asnam*) (14: 35). Although the Prophet Sulayman (Solomon) had power over jinn who make statues (*tamathil*) for him, their connection with their malevolent makers is clear (34: 13). The Qur'an also denies that the idols of the pagan Arabs have any substance whatever (53: 19–23). These and other verses against polytheism—along with certain hadiths—are the basis for the prohibition of religious images.

Figural Representation. Furthermore, the Qur'an insists that God created human beings and then fashioned them in their particular forms (7: 11) with the best of appearances (40: 64 and 64: 3). Thus, the fashioning of forms—as well as the creation of matter and the elements—are manifestations of God's creative power. God permitted the Prophet 'Isa (Jesus) to make clay birds and then breathe life into them to demonstrate God's vivifying and resurrectionary power, but the miracle happened specifically and only by God's permission (3: 49 and 5: 110). Perhaps commenting on these texts, in the extra-Qur'anic tradition of the hadith, the Prophet states that on the Day of Judgment, God will ask people who have made images of humans and animals to blow life into their representations, and when they cannot do so, they will be thrown into hellfire. This statement reserves the fashioning of forms as one of God's exclusive creative prerogatives, disallowing the making of human and animal images by Muslims. The prohibition against human and animal representation in Islam is further reinforced by the history of the Prophet Muhammad and other statements attributed to him. Before Islam, the pagan Arabs who frequented the Inviolable Sanctuary containing the Ka'bah at Makkah, had filled the building and its enclosure with more than three hundred statues and sacred stones representing various deities. In the year 630, after the Prophet Muhammad obtained the surrender of Makkah from the nonbelievers, his first act was to cleanse the sanctuary of all idols. As each of the idols was dumped on its face and hewn to pieces, he recited the Qur'anic verse "Truth has come and falsehood has perished, and falsehood was ever perishing" (17: 81). Down through the centuries this famous action has turned Muslims away from figural representation. The stipulation against figural imagery is still respected by the majority of Muslims, who fear that having images might also drive the angels away; as the Prophet also said in a hadith: "Angels do not enter a house in which there is an image." Such a stipulation has always discouraged Muslim artists and craftsmen from incorporating naturalistic human or animal imagery into their works of art.

Islamic Law and Muslim Practice. Aside from the relevant scriptural texts on the subject of images, one needs also to consider traditional Muslim law that scholars have studied and interpreted for fourteen centuries. In this law the making or owning of images is in general forbidden. Exceptions are sometimes made for carpets and cushions that one might walk on, sit on, or otherwise treat disrespectfully. While some less-strict religious scholars have

The title character of *Hayy ibn Yaqzan* (Alive, the Son of Awake), by Abu Bakr Muhammad ibn Tufayl (died 1185), is a man who grew up on an island far from human contact and without social or religious influences. He achieves enlightenment through reflection, experiment, and intensive study of his surroundings:

Our forefathers, of blessed memory, tell of a certain equatorial island, lying off the coast of India, where human beings come into being without father or mother. This is possible, they say, because of all places on earth, that island has the most tempered climate. And because a supernatural light streams down on it, it is the most perfectly adapted to accept the human form. . . .

. . . the newborn infant got hungrier and hungrier and began to cry, whereupon the doe with the lost fawn responded. . . . the doe that cared for him was richly pastured so she was fat and had plenty of milk, to give the baby the best possible nourishment. . . . So the child grew, nourished by his mother's doe-milk, until he was two years old. By then he'd learned to walk, and, having his teeth, he took to following the doe on her foraging expeditions. . . .

She was inseparable from him and he from her. When she grew old and weak he would lead her to rich pastures and gather sweet fruits to feed her. Even so, weakness and emaciation gradually tightened their hold, and finally death overtook her. All her movements and bodily functions came to a standstill. When the boy saw her in such a state, he was beside himself with grief. . . .

. . . What made him think there was something he could "take away" was his own past experience. He knew that when he shut his eyes or covered them, he saw nothing until the obstruction was removed; if he stopped his ears with his fingers he could not hear until the obstacle was gone. . . . These observations led him to believe that not only his senses, but every one of his other bodily functions was liable to obstructions that might block its work. . . . Hayy hoped that if he could find that organ and remove whatever lodged in it, it would revert to normal, its benefits would once more flow to the rest of the body and all the bodily functions would resume. . . . But there remained some hope of her recovery if he could find the critical organ and take away the hurt. So he decided to cut open her breast and find out what was inside. . . .

. . . Realizing the whatever had lived in that chamber [the heart] had left while its house was intact, before it had been ruined, Hayy saw that it was hardly likely to return. . . . The body now seemed something low and worthless compared to the being he was convinced had lived in it for a time and was now departed. Hayy turned the focus of his thoughts on that being. What was it? What was the manner of its existence? What had bound it to this body? Where had it gone, and how had it gotten out? . . . His mind was filled with these questions. He soon dropped the body and thought no more of it, knowing that the mother who had nursed him and showed him so much kindness could only be that being which had departed. From that— and not from this lifeless body—all those actions had issued. The whole body was simply a tool of his being, like the stick with which he fought the animals. His affection was transferred now from the body to the being that was its master and mover. All his love was directed toward that. . .

Source: *Ibn Tufayl's Hayy ibn Yaqzan*, translated by Lenn Evan Goodman (New York: Twayne, 1972), pp. 103, 105, 109, 111–115.

---

stated that flat or photographic images might be allowed, all agree on prohibiting figures that cast any shadow, including, specifically, pictures of humans or animals on coins. The almost complete absence of representational art from public spaces in Muslim countries until the twentieth century demonstrates the general effectiveness of this law. Yet, it seems that the prohibition against figural representation was not as thoroughly upheld during the early years of Islam. The first coins used by the Muslims were the Persian and Byzantine money that had already been circulating in the area. They not only had pictures of monarchs on one side of each coin but also carried the religious symbol of each state on the other, a cross on the Byzantine coins and a sacred fire tended by two Zoroastrian priests on the Persian money. These coins were the only ones in circulation in the khilafah until the reign of Abd al-Malik ibn Marwan (685–705), who replaced the cross with a pole and who put his own full-length picture on the new khalifal gold coins in 693. Starting in 696, however, the khilafah began replacing these "khalifah-standing" coins with completely epigraphic gold coins (coins bearing only writing and decorative motifs and no figural representations at all). In 698 the old silver coins depicting a Persian king were replaced with epigraphic silver coins. That the khalifah should be forced to remove his picture and his name from the coinage is an indication of the force of the ideological movement during the early years of Islam to ban figural representation. By 700 it was clear that the Islamic ban on figural art was quite complete, as was also the case in Judaism. With a few marginal exceptions, epigraphic designs remained standard for all Muslim coinage until well into the twentieth century.

Defining Style. The move to define a separate Muslim style of art arose partly from the desire for a clear Muslim cultural self-definition, in contradistinction to the Christianity of the Byzantine Empire. With its capital at Constantinople, this empire withstood repeated Muslim attempts to conquer it and continued to hold out, even though greatly diminished, until 1453, when

Calligraphy and geometric designs in the carved
plaster and tilework of the façade of the
Attarine madrasah in medieval Fez

Constantinople fell to the Ottomans. Furthermore, during the period 678–685, the Byzantines successfully took the offensive and threatened the khalifahs in their home province of Syria, extracting a humiliating treaty from the khalifah in 685. In 692 the Byzantines began an ideological offensive as well, changing their coins to show the bust of Christ as well as the emperor, and a few years later the Muslims responded with their epigraphic coins. The opposition to images reached a peak in 721 when Khalifah Yazid II issued his iconoclastic decree commanding that all images of humans and animals, whether religious or secular, be effaced throughout the khilafah. This Muslim image smashing was also picked up by the Byzantines, albeit in a more moderate form. Though he had no objection to secular images, in 726 Byzantine emperor Leo III issued a ban on the use of religious images in churches. More than a century later, in 843—after periods in which images were allowed and again disallowed—religious images were definitively restored to Byzantine churches, again underlining the difference between Muslims and Eastern Christians. Art in any society is inevitably influenced by that society's ideology. In the case of early Islam, the figural art of the pagans, Zoroastrians, and Christians required an alternative, if the new religion and ideology of Islam was to become securely established.

Public Art. Public works of Islamic art and architecture, which have survived in abundance from the medieval period—during which Muslim civilization was one of the greatest cultural forces in the world—are devoid of representational images of humans and animals. Every masjid or other religious institution built under Muslim sponsorship from the time of early Islam to the present has no figural imagery in its decoration. From a quite early period—whether in Iraq, Iran, Syria, Turkey, India, Egypt, North Africa, or Spain—masjids were decorated in a highly ornate manner with floral and geometric motifs and Qur'anic inscriptions. Artists competed to invent beautiful scripts.

Private Art. Most Muslims still try to avoid having representational images in their private domains as well. Even in the medieval period, however, Muslims have sometimes produced works of art including human and animal images for use in private settings, but they have never been incorporated in religious settings. In such works the images are usually schematic, rather than naturalistic or detailed, so that the interest is still on the design more than on the figures.

Ideology and Practice. No doubt a major reason for Muslim preferences in art over the centuries has been the habit of liking what is familiar, but ideological consciousness has always been an important factor as well. For example, the historian Ibn Khaldun (1332–1406) criticized the Spanish Muslims of his time because they "are found to assimilate themselves to the Galician nations [that is, Spanish Christians] in their dress, their emblems, and most of their customs and conditions. This goes so far that they even draw pictures on the walls and have them in buildings and houses. The intelligent observer will draw from this the conclusion that it is a sign of being dominated by others." For Ibn Khaldun, at a time when the Muslims were gradually losing their Spanish territory to Christian forces, the fact that Spanish Muslims had pictures in their houses was a clear indication of their submission and humiliation at the hands of the conquering Spanish Christians. Some western scholars have objected to the claim that the special character of Muslim art

derives from the religious prohibition on images. They point out that Muslim religious texts ban them less directly and strictly than the Bible; yet Christianity, with some few exceptions, has generally cultivated figural art, especially figural representation in religious art. They also point to the many extant exceptions to the prohibition in art produced by Muslims. Yet, however one reads Muslim religious sources, the prohibition is clearly there, and the Muslim reception of these texts, as expressed in Muslim law and practice over the centuries, is more important than the words themselves. There have been some exceptions, such as book illustrations (especially for scientific works), Persian and Indian court miniatures (many from after 1500), and decoration on household objects such as pottery and metalwork. Indeed, there are even European-style portraits of the Ottoman Sultan Muhammad II (ruled 1444–1448, 1451–1481), an early indication of European cultural influence, but the use of such pictures was purely private and limited. These exceptions, however, have almost always been limited to the private sphere and do not change the basic fact that Muslim art includes little figural representation, despite the strong human attraction to such representation that is demonstrated in most other artistic traditions.

Sources:

Isma'il R. and Lois L. al-Faruqi, *The Cultural Atlas of Islam* (London: Collier Macmillan, 1986).

'Abd al-Rahman Ibn Khaldun, *The Muqaddimah: An Introduction to History*, translated by Franz Rosenthal, edited and abridged by N. J. Dawood (Princeton: Princeton University Press, 1967).

SIGNIFICANT PEOPLE

HAFIZ

CIRCA 1325 - 1390
POET

Early Life. Hafiz is the nickname of Shams al–Din Muhammad Shirazi, a major Persian poet who was born and died in Shiraz in southern Iran. His nickname means "Qur'an memorizer" and is given to people who have learned the entire Muslim holy book by heart. Hafiz had humble beginnings and is said to have worked as a baker's apprentice and a manuscript copyist, the latter an occupation through which he may have obtained his broad education. In addition to having memorized the entire Qur'an, he knew Arabic well and was widely read in Persian literature. By the time he was in his twenties, Hafiz had begun serving as a poet who sang the praises of the local rulers of Shiraz. It is uncertain how close he was to the court, and since he seems to have sometimes lectured on the interpretation of the Qur'an at an Islamic college, he may have still been earning his living from sources other than royal largess. His fame spread throughout Persia after about 1360, but he suffered royal disfavor for a period of about ten years (1366–1376), during which he spent a couple of years away from Shiraz in the Iranian cities of Isfahan and Yazd. Although distant rulers invited him to their capitals, he turned down such offers and returned to Shiraz. His lack of travel was rather unusual among well-known Muslim scholars and literary figures.

Poetic Works. Hafiz's poetry is entirely contained in his *Diwan* (Collected Poems), a collection said to have been finalized by Hafiz in 1368 but quite possibly arranged by one of his followers shortly after his death. His great popularity has contributed to a massive accretion of poems falsely attributed to him over the centuries; his authentic poems seem to number about five hundred, which is not a large body of work in comparison with those of other Persian poets. Almost all his poems are short *ghazals*. Though the *ghazal* is the form employed for love poetry, Hafiz often drew the vocabulary for his *ghazals* from the idiom of such love-and-wine poetry but used the convention for another purpose, such as praise of his patron, and some

have suggested that he was a Sufi mystic. His subtleness of expression, use of conventional vehicles to suggest other meanings, technical perfection, and linguistic virtuosity have led many readers to call him the best of all Persian poets. Over the centuries he was especially well known among non-Iranian users of Persian as a literary language in Turkey and India, and enthusiasm for him in Iran revived only in the twentieth century.

Sources:
Elizabeth T. Gray, trans., *The Green Sea of Heaven: Fifty Ghazals from the Díwán of Háfiz* (Ashland, Ore.: White Cloud, 1995).

Michael C. Hillmann, *Unity in the Ghazals of Hafez* (Minneapolis: Bibliotheca Islamica, 1976).

G. M. Wickens, "Hafiz," *Encyclopedia of Islam*, CD-ROM version (Leiden: Brill, 1999).

AL-HARIRI

1054-1122
MAQAMAT WRITER

Life. Al-Hariri was the chief developer and popularizer of a form of Arabic rhymed prose called *maqamat* (assemblies), speeches for particular occasion, often combat or another sort of contest, which are still written and widely read. He was born into the rural gentry near the southern Iraqi city of Basrah and soon migrated to that city, where he was employed as chief of intelligence, a post that enabled him to meet many people—including con men, scoundrels, and crooks—and to ponder the psychology that moved people to behave in various ways. Al-Hariri's literary work, *al-Maqamat*, is based closely on an earlier work of the same name by Ahmad Badi al-Zaman al-Hamadhani (968–1008), who began his work about 990 and continued to add to it over most of the rest of his life. Al-Hariri began to compose his work in 1101, a century after al-Hamadhani, and may have completed it by 1108. Al-Hariri is considered a master of Arabic style, far surpassing al-Hamadhani in excellence of expression, and his work is also highly entertaining, signaling the popularization of a rather highbrow literary form. Al-Hariri is also a skilled satirist, who laughed at his society and the odd characters who inhabited it. The stories of al-Harari's various *maqamat* exhibit great variety and include valuable information about the manners of Muslim society in his time. By the time al-Hariri died in 1122, he had produced more than seven hundred copies of his work, which has never lost its popularity.

Source:
Thomas Chenery, trans., *The Assemblies of al Hariri*, 2 volumes (London: Williams & Norgate, 1867, 1898).

ABU UTHMAN AL-JAHIZ

CIRCA 776 - 869
ADAB WRITER

Career. A native of Basrah in Iraq, al-Jahiz was one of the non-Arabs who made up most of the intellectual and scholarly class in that country. He was apparently of African ancestry, as he is described as black and as he wrote *Risalat mufakharat al-sudan 'ala al-bidan* (Treatise on the Superiority of Blacks over Whites). Educated in the cosmopolitan milieu of Basrah, the chief Indian Ocean port of the khilafah, al-Jahiz belonged to the literary and intellectual circles of the city, which had strong economic and political ties with Turkestan, India, and the Indian Ocean area in general. From about 815, he rose to become one of the literary figures around the Abbasid khalifah al-Ma'mun (ruled 813–833), who greatly valued scholarship. As a result, al-Jahiz moved to the capital, Baghdad, and later to Samarra' after it became the capital from 836. He retained his ties with Basrah as well, perhaps in order to keep his distance from the rulers. Although he held no official posts, he received largess from several Abbasid prime ministers, while also working as a scribe and a teacher. Perhaps after a military revolt that killed his friend and patron in 861, he returned permanently to Basrah, where he died.

Writings. Al-Jahiz composed during his long life at least two hundred works, which qualify him as virtually the founder of cultured prose literature in Arabic (*adab*). Of these works, about thirty survive complete, along with another fifty more or less extensive fragments. Some of these works are short treatises; others are multivolume sets, including his long, incomplete, *Kitab al-hayawan* (The Book of Animals) in eight volumes. This anthology of interesting and entertaining information also includes embryonic ideas of animal psychology and even the evolution of species. Other works include diverse information about language, eloquence, oratory, poetry, and literary skill. Al-Jahiz's work is so foundational that it is somewhat difficult to characterize by genre because the various Arabic prose genres had not yet taken specific forms. Sometimes he is called an essayist, but—while many of his treatises are indeed essays—the term does not do justice to the breadth and complexity of his work. Many of his works, such as *Kitab al-bukhala'* (The Book of Misers), are highly satirical, calling attention to the serious social criticism at the heart of many of al-Jahiz's writings. He also devoted some effort to polemical writings defending the right of the Abbasids to rule and asserting his own somewhat Mu'tazilite views, those of a philosophical school patronized by the Abbasids that emphasized justice and reason. Al-Jahiz became so well-known in his lifetime that he was able to maintain some control over the copying and publishing of his books, a milestone on the road to the recognition and attribution of individual authorship.

Sources:
William M. Hutchins, trans., *Nine Essays of al-Jahiz* (New York: Peter Lang, 1989).

Charles Pellat, "Al-Jahiz," in *Encyclopedia of Islam*, CD-ROM version (Leiden: Brill, 1999).

Pellat, *The Life and Works of Jahiz*, translated by D. M. Hawke (London: Routledge & Kegan Paul, 1969).

ABD AL-QAHIR AL-JURJANI

DIED 1078
LINGUIST

Early Life. Little is known of the life of Abd al-Qahir al-Jurjani, who appears to have spent his entire life in his native city of Gurgan in Iran at the southeastern corner of the Caspian Sea. His only known teacher was Abu al-Husayn Muhammad ibn Hasan al-Farisi, whose uncle Abu 'Ali al-Farisi (900–987) was a well-known grammarian who was from Iran and lived in Baghdad.

Major Works. Al-Jurjani wrote a large number of scholarly works, including popular manuals and detailed commentaries on Arabic grammar, as well as monographs on etymology, prosody, and the inimitability of the Qur'an. He also compiled an anthology of poetry. His main works are *Dala'il al–i'jaz* (The Proofs of the Inimitability [of the Qur'an]) and *Asrar al–balaghah* (The Secrets of Eloquence), which earned him renown as one of the most important thinkers of the Muslim world. In these works he developed a complete linguistic theory which goes far beyond anything achieved in earlier classical times by Greeks, Indians, or Muslims and anticipates many modern discourses in linguistics. In striving to prove that God's word in the Qur'an cannot be imitated, al-Jurjani went beyond classical ideas of meaning and vocabulary, in which eloquence is usually explained as a function of word choice. Rather, he asserted, eloquence is vested in the construction of the linguistic elements into coherent patterns governed by rhetorical rules that are extensions of the rules of grammar. He also explored and compared the construction of language and the formulation of thought. Like modern linguists, he emphasized that language is a system of relations governed by the two facts that linguistic signs are arbitrary and that language is conventional. Thus, individual words can have importance only when they are embedded in syntactic structures. That is, only sentences—not single words—truly generate meaning. Any change in the surface structure of a sentence inevitably changes its meaning as well. Thus, exact translation is impossible. Similarly, each image, or figurative language, is not just an ornament but is a separate act of linguistic creation whose expression of meaning is unique. This conclusion was not widely held until the late twentieth century. Elaborating further, al-Jurjani shows that metaphor is not transference of a word into another meaning, but rather an intermediate usage that retains its original meaning as well and thus exists in a tension of double meaning. This idea anticipated the work of I. A. Richards on metaphor in the twentieth century. Thus al-Jurjani established a more sophisticated and nuanced way of analyzing language and rhetorical phenomena than anyone who preceded him.

Source:
Hellmut Ritter, ed., *Asrar al-balagha, The Mysteries of Eloquence, of 'Abdalqahir al-Jurjani* (Istanbul: Govt. Press, 1954).

AL-KHANSA'

CIRCA 575 – CIRCA 644 OR LATER
POET

Early Life. Tumadir bint 'Amr of the tribe of Sulaym, a pastoral tribe in Najd in central Arabia, was a well-known pre-Islamic poet whose poetry continued to be celebrated in the Muslim era. Her nickname was al-Khansa', possibly meaning "gazelle" or "pug-nosed," the latter being the better-known explanation. A strong-willed woman, she rejected the marriage proposal of a renowned tribal chief, Durayd ibn al-Simmah al-Jushami, because she considered him too old. Perhaps the most traumatic events in her life, perhaps, were the deaths of her brothers Mu'awiyah and Sakhr in tribal battles in 612 and 615. Much of her poetry consists of sorrowful eulogies for them, through which she encouraged her tribe to avenge itself on their killers. Al-Khansa' is also said to have appeared at the festive market of 'Ukaz in Makkah for the poetry contests.

Conversion to Islam. In about 630, late in the Prophet Muhammad's career, al-Khansa is said to have gone to Madinah and embraced Islam, and Muslim tradition states that four of her six sons were slain in 637 while fighting for Islam against the Persians at al-Qadisiyyah, a battle at which she is also said to have been present. Afterward, she returned to her Arabian homeland, where she died.

Poetry. Although she lived into the Muslim era and became a Muslim, al-Khansa's poetry remained rooted strongly in pre-Islamic times and themes. Of her poetic output, nearly a thousand lines remain. Most of her poems are elegies (*marathi*), particularly for her brothers. Al-Khansa' became recognized as a true master of this ancient genre. She greatly added to its breadth of expression, and her innovations became standard in later elegiac tradition. The intensity and force of her expression, coupled with her tenderness and her concentration on the necessity and centrality of grief, make her poetry particu-

larly striking and impressive. A poem commemorating her brother Sakhr includes these lines:

> The rising of the sun reminds me of Sakhr,
> and I remember him with every setting of the sun.
> If not for the numerousness of those bewailing
> their brothers, I would have killed myself!
> But I do not cease seeing one bereft of her child
> and one weeping over the dead on an unlucky day.
> I see her distracted by grief, weeping for her brother
> the evening of his loss or on the day after.
> They do not bewail the like of my brother, but
> I console myself over him through their sorrow.

Al-Khansa's elegies were eventually collected in a *Diwan* (Collected Poems) by Ibn al-Sikkit (802–858), a literary scholar of the early Abbasid era.

Source:
F. Gabrieli, "Al-Khansa'," in *Encyclopedia of Islam,* CD-ROM version (Leiden: Brill, 1999).

AL-MAS'UDI

BEFORE 896 – 956
HISTORIAN

Education and Travels. Abu al-Husayn 'Ali al-Mas'udi was an unconventional Shi'i writer who is accounted one of the most important Muslim historians. Born in Baghdad of Arab origin, he heard and possibly studied with eminent teachers such as Waki' (died 918), al-Nawbakhti, and the well-known Mu'tazili al-Jubba'i (died 915), as well as perhaps al-Tabari (died 923), Ibn Durayd (died 934), and al-Ash'ari (died 935). Al-Mas'udi was also an associate of the well-known Abbasid historian and minister Abu Bakr al-Suli (died 946). These teachers gave him a solid background in the Muslim knowledge and intellectual currents available in the capital. Al-Mas'udi's great scholarly curiosity and drive propelled him to study foreign books and languages, converse with non-Muslims, including Jews, Christians, and Zoroastrians, cultivate an interest in faraway places beyond the Muslim world in both space and time, and undertake extensive travels to research his interests. He was still in Baghdad in 912; by 915 he had reached Persia and then India. (He probably did not voyage to Sri Lanka or China.) In 917, he returned to Iraq via 'Uman. From 918 to 926, he traveled around Syria and may have visited Arabia. From about 932, he visited Armenia and the Caspian Sea region. In 941 or 942, he moved to Egypt, where he apparently spent the rest of his life, apart from another visit to Syria, including Damascus and Antioch, in 943. It is not known how he supported himself during his life, but he seems never to have held any government posts.

Works. During his lifetime al-Mas'udi wrote at least thirty-six works, of which only two survive. The larger of the two is his eclectic history, *Muruj al-dhahab* (Meadows of Gold), a universal history down to the time of its writing in 943 and revision in 947. The first part of this work goes into the history of the surrounding civilizations—including the Frankish, Byzantine, Indian, Chinese, and African—as well as the Muslim, in greater detail than is the case with other Muslim "universal" histories. Al-Mas'udi dwelt greatly on geography, the importance and effects of which he appears to have been well aware. His history includes frequent digressions with amusing stories and is characterized by an easy rather than a florid Arabic style. Although a Shi'i, al-Mas'udi carefully recorded the history of all the khalifahs down to his own time. His second work, *Kitab al-tanbih wa-al-ishraf* (Book of Information and Overview), written at the end of his life in 955–956, includes some of the same information in a summarized form. Despite the relative obscurity of his life, al-Mas'udi's surviving works have had a great influence on history ever since and foreshadowed the broad and ecumenical interests of the much later historian Ibn Khaldun (1332–1406).

Sources:

Al-Mas'udi, *The Meadows of Gold: The Abbasids,* translated and edited by Paul Lunde and Caroline Stone (London: Kegan Paul International, 1989).

Charles Pellat, "Al-Masudi," in *Encyclopedia of Islam,* CD-ROM version (Leiden: Brill, 1999).

Ahmad M. H. Shboul, *Al-Masudi and His World: A Muslim Humanist and His Interest in Non-Muslims* (London: Ithaca Press, 1979).

AL-MUTANABBI

915-965

POET

Early Life. Abu al-Tayyib Ahmad ibn al-Husayn al-Ju'fi, known by the nickname al-Mutanabbi (The One Who Claimed Prophethood), is often considered to be the single most important Arabic poet, and certainly he stands above the other writers of his time in historical stature. The classical age of Arabic poetry had passed by the time he began his colorful career. Born of Arab parents in the Iraqi city of Kufah, al-Mutanabbi fled with his family to escape the Qarmati Ismaili schismatics who captured his home city in 924, leading him to spend more than two years with the pastoral Arabs of the Kalb tribe in the Syrian desert to the west. After returning to Kufah in 927, al-Mutanabbi devoted himself exclusively to poetry, thus showing great precociousness from an early age. At first his models were the two great poets of the preceding century, Abu Tammam (804–845) and al-Buhturi (821–897). When Kufah was sacked by the Qarmatis again, he left the city in 928, heading first to Baghdad and adopting the life of a wanderer.

Revolutionary. During the revolutionary upheavals of his time, which ruined Kufah, al-Mutanabbi became a Shi'i in religion and developed a strongly philosophical and pessimistic character. His philosophical attitude led him to an outward denigration and rejection of worldly things, and the constant insecurity in which he lived only confirmed his ideas. After wandering around in northern Syria for a couple of years, he proclaimed himself a prophet, a completely heretical action, and led a revolt in the Syrian desert among the Kalb, his earlier hosts. He was defeated and captured by the Ikhshidid dynasty in 933 and imprisoned for two years until he recanted and was released. From that time on, the name al-Mutanabbi—indicating a false prophet or one who arrogated to himself prophethood—stuck to him. His poems of this period began to take on a personal tone, which elevated their quality, because of the directness his expression.

Patrons. Soon al-Mutanabbi had to seek sustenance again, and beginning in 937 he returned to praising paying patrons for a living. At first, these patrons were lowly officials who did not reward his efforts well, but eventually al-Mutanabbi's renown spread. During 939–940, he became poet to Badr ibn 'Ammar, the governor of Damascus, but soon, as often happened, al-Mutanabbi had a falling out with his patron and had to flee for his life to the desert again. After working again for a series of minor patrons, al-Mutanabbi stayed with the redoubtable Hamdanid ruler of Aleppo Sayf al-Dawlah (916–967) from 948 to 957. During his career with this patron al-Mutanabbi wrote his best-known poetry and enjoyed the most munificent patronage, as he celebrated Sayf's many campaigns against the Byzantines.

Rivals. Yet, al-Mutanabbi also clashed with a rival poet who was as egotistical as himself, Abu Firas (932–968), was a Hamdanid prince and thus a member of the dynasty. When a military plot arose against Sayf al-Dawlah, al-Mutanabbi felt he had to flee again, passing through Damascus on his way to Egypt, where the ruler Kafur al-Ikhshidi became his patron. Scarcely able to conceal his contempt for Kafur, al-Mutanabbi fled again, this time across Arabia to Iraq, where he visited his hometown of Kufah after an absence of thirty-four years and then stopped again in Baghdad. Here too, he faced the jealousy of other poets and writers, including Abu al-Faraj al-Isfahani, the author of *Kitab al-aghani* (Book of Songs), so he set out once more in 965, this time to Iran to the east. He did not stay there for long. While trying to return to Iraq, he and his son were killed by bandits.

Reputation. After his death, al-Mutanabbi fame continued to grow, especially because of the praise of the well-known linguist Ibn Jinni (died 1002), who had met al-Mutanabbi in Aleppo. Although he was frequently criticized as well, his poetry became a standard for later poets, who tried to emulate or surpass it, and his lines continue to be memorized to this day.

Source:

Charles Pellat, "Al-Mutanabbi," in *Encyclopedia of Islam,* CD-ROM version (Leiden: Brill, 1999).

SIBAWAYH

DIED CIRCA 796
GRAMMARIAN

Career. Little is known about the life of Sibawayh, who, more than any other individual, was the foundational grammarian of Arabic. It is likely that he was born between about 755 and 766 and died around 793–796. Like many well-known grammarians, the language he became expert in was not his mother tongue. He was of Persian origin and migrated at an early age to Basrah, where he studied hadith, law, and grammar with many well-known teachers, including the famous Khalil ibn Ahmad (died between 776 and 791), who had a considerable influence on Sibawayh.

Writings. Sibawayh's only work is called *Kitab Sibawayh* ("The Book of Sibawayh"), which was edited after his early death by his student al-Akhfash al-Awsat (died between 825 and 835). A huge book for its time, this comprehensive treatment of Arabic grammar spans nine hundred pages. Sibawayh started with seven introductory chapters and then dealt with syntax, morphology, and phonology, in that order. He based his findings on three sources: the Qur'an, early Arabic poetry, and the speech of the Bedouins. Finding the most reliable indication in his third source, Sibawayh collected firsthand evidence from the Bedouins, as well as citing secondhand information. He also had the critical acumen to reject some Bedouin evidence as incorrect. Furthermore, he judged speech on the basis of its effectiveness rather than as a set of logical propositions. He also frequently gave psychological or contextual explanations. Sibawayh's grammar book is an original work of great genius that broke new ground. There are no precedents for it in Syriac, Greek, or Latin. Formerly, Greek and Sanskrit had perhaps been the best-described languages. After Sibawayh, Arabic was for centuries the most thoroughly analyzed and elucidated of languages from a grammatical point of view—a claim that may still hold true today.

Source:

M.G. Carter, "Sibawayh," in *Encyclopedia of Islam*, CD-ROM version (Leiden: Brill, 1999).

AL-WALID IBN ABD AL-MALIK

CIRCA 671 - 715

UMAYYAD KHALIFAH

Muslim Expansion. Son of the Umayyad khalifah Abd al-Malik ibn Marwan (circa 647 – 705), al-Walid had a brief but remarkable ten-year reign (705–715). In some sense it represents the high point of the Umayyad khilafah, for it never again attained the level of success that it had under al-Walid. He ruled during the second wave of Muslim expansion. Under him Muslims achieved the final elimination of the Byzantines from North Africa and the pacification of the Berbers there, as well as the conquest of the Visigoth kingdom of Spain, many small Iranian states between the Oxus and the Jaxartes, and the substantial Brahmin kingdom of Sind in present-day Pakistan.

Patron of the Arts. These territorial acquisitions brought a huge new tax income into the coffers of the Muslim state, enabling al-Walid to engage in public works and other projects on a lavish scale. Among these projects were the reconstructions of the great masjids in all the principal cities, including Makkah, Madinah, Jerusalem, Damascus, San'a', and probably other towns. Al-Walid is now principally remembered as the patron of these building projects. The only one of his constructions that is still standing in its original form is the great Umayyad Masjid in Damascus. Its beautiful original mosaics resemble Byzantine art but scrupulously avoid representations of humans and animals, although they do include scenes of houses, public buildings, trees, and shrubs, in addition to geometrical patterns. (As with most other Muslim art, the names of the artists are unknown.)

Source:

Khalid Yahya Blankinship, *The End of the Jihad State: The Reign of Hisham ibn 'Abd al-Malik and the Collapse of the Umayyads* (Albany: State University of New York Press, 1994).

DOCUMENTARY SOURCES

Abu al-Faraj al-Isfahani, *Kitab al-Aghani* (The Book of Songs, circa 917–967) — Vital information about early Muslim music, as well as detailed biographies of the poets of the first three centuries of Islam, with samples of their poetry and indications that they often sang their poems to musical accompaniment.

Ibn al-Nadim, *al-Fihrist* (The Index, 987)—A bibliography of all Arabic writers during the first four centuries of Islam; based on Ibn al-Nadim's knowledge as a bookseller and on extensive research, including perhaps at the khalifal library in Baghdad, *al-Fihrist* demonstrates how much of the medieval Muslim literary output has been lost.

Al-Jahiz (circa 776–869), *Kitab al-Bukhala'* (The Book of Misers, circa 845–850?)—The most popular of al-Jahiz's works, perhaps because of its manageable size and amusing anecdotes; the subject of well-known misers and their stories gave al-Jahiz full scope to display his powers of observation, his skepticism, his humor, and especially his satire.

Al-Maqrizi (1364–1442), *al-Khitat al-Misriyyah* (Egyptian City Descriptions) — A detailed description of Egypt in the time of al-Maqrizi with especially detailed notes on hundreds of important buildings, an indispensable source for architectural historians.

Rumi (1207–1273), *Mathnawi-i ma'nawi* (Conceptual Couplets, 1261–1273)—A twenty-six-thousand-line narrative poem expounding Rumi's religious understanding, commenting on the Qur'an, and providing illustrations through entertaining stories.

COMMUNICATION, TRANSPORTATION, AND EXPLORATION

by RICHARD W. BULLIET

CONTENTS

CHRONOLOGY

138

OVERVIEW

139

TOPICS IN COMMUNICATION, TRANSPORTATION, AND EXPLORATION

Communication 141
Why Scholars Traveled 142

Land Transportation 146
Ibn Battuta Visits the Turks 147
Sea and River Transport 151
The Harbor at Tyre 153
Scientific Exploration 155
The Known World 157

SIGNIFICANT PEOPLE

Ibn Battuta 158
Ibn Fadlan 158
Ibn Jubayr 159

Abu Dulaf al-Khazraji 159
Shams al-Din Abu
‘Abd Allah Muhammad
al-Muqaddasi 159

DOCUMENTARY SOURCES

160

Sidebars and tables are listed in italics.

632-800*
- Muhammad's death in 632 is followed by a period in which the Islamic religion is consolidated, Arab conquests result in the formation of an Islamic empire, and a unified governing structure for that empire is developed.

711
- Muslim troops invade Spain in the West and conquer the Indus Valley in the East.

800-1000*
- As Islamic imperial unity dissolves, many regional Muslim states emerge, and there is an extensive elaboration of social structures and institutions based on the Islamic religion.

921-923
- Ibn Fadlan travels with an embassy from Baghdad to the king of the Volga Bulgars and writes an account of the journey that includes descriptions of the various peoples he encounters along the way.

1000-1500*
- During this period there is a significant resumption of territorial expansion on three frontiers: India, Anatolia and the Balkans, and sub-Saharan Africa, both in West Africa and along the Nile Valley.

1183-1185
- Ibn Jubayr goes on a pilgrimage from Granada, Spain—via Sardinia, Sicily, Crete, and Alexandria—to Makkah and then on to Baghdad. Then he journeys homeward on the caravan route across Syria from Mosul to Aleppo, eventually reaching the Mediterranean coast at Acre and enduring a shipwreck off Sicily before returning home to Spain.

1334
- Ibn Battuta, a native of Tangier, arrives in the northern India city of Delhi, where he spends the next eight years.

1342
- Ibn Battuta sets out on a journey from Delhi to China, traveling through India to Sumatra and then through China from the south coast to Beijing.

1347
- Ibn Battuta begins his return home, arriving in Tangier in 1350.

* DENOTES CIRCA DATE

OVERVIEW

Unity. The world of Islam is often regarded as one of great unity, which is attributed to a common faith. To the degree that Muslims quite consciously think of themselves as belonging to a single worldwide community and look back on the career of the Prophet Muhammad and the text of the divine revelations he received between 610 and 632 as a common heritage, the idea of unity has substance. Yet, there are also many differences among Muslim peoples and the regions they inhabit. This chapter covers aspects of unity and disunity that are not directly related to religious belief. Since it is not uncommon for Muslims and non-Muslims alike to feel that there is something distinctive about living or traveling in the Islamic world, this chapter explores possible historical roots for that feeling in the areas of communication and transportation and the degree to which that feeling was expressed by Muslim travelers, geographers, and cartographers.

Dominant Regions. From the standpoint of world history, this investigation of communication, transportation, and exploration corresponds to a perception that the world seems to have become divided into a handful of broad geographical areas during the half millennium preceding modern times. The Islamic world, European Christendom, and China and nearby Chinese-oriented lands made up the three dominant regions with the Eastern Hemisphere, sub-Saharan Africa, South Asia, and Southeast Asia becoming the three zones of imperialist contestation. The three dominant regions were broadly dissimilar with respect to communication and transportation and had different outlooks on exploration, travel, and cartography.

Regional Differences. Chinese, Islamic, and European writing systems differed in character and appearance; and the three regions had distinctively different language characteristics. In transportation, Christian Europe was a zone of river and sea transport with a dedication to wheeled transport on land. China was bound together by a monumental network of rivers and canals. The Islamic world relied overwhelmingly on pack animals with a comparatively minor interest in seafaring. As for exploration, the European fixation of the early modern period—termed the "era of discovery" in histo-ries of the Western civilization—had few counterparts in the other two zones, even though both of them were more congenial to travel on an everyday basis than Europe. This chapter, therefore, investigates just one part of a broader question of what went into the division of the world, or the perception of the division of the world, into broad zones of similarity in the centuries preceding modern times.

Expansion. Between the Prophet Muhammad's death in 632 and the year 800, Arab warriors carried the banner of Islam to the Atlantic Ocean and Spain in the west and to the Indus River in the east. The territory they conquered constituted the greatest empire known up to that time in world history. They brought with them their faith in Islam, their language, and a clear sense of Arab identity. Between 800 and 1000 great changes beset this empire. Politically, its unity under a monarch known as a khalifah (caliph), residing in Syria (661–750) or Iraq (750–1258), eroded. North Africa, Spain, Egypt, Iran, and Central Asia became more or less independent, and the khalifahs lost temporal power when their capital city, Baghdad, was occupied by Iranian hill tribes in 945. This decline of central power and authority led to the flourishing of many provincial cities.

Islamization of Population. Religiously, the percentage of Muslims among descendants of those people living within the territories conquered two centuries earlier rose from approximately 10 percent to 80 percent, except in Spain, where the conversion process was delayed by the relatively late date (711) of its conquest. An empire in which a ruling minority of mostly Arab Muslims governed a vastly larger population of non-Muslim non-Arabs—mostly Christians, Jews, and Zoroastrians—thus gave way to a heavily Muslim society fractured into independent principalities. Ethnically, the conversion process inevitably diminished the dominance and importance of the Arabs and provided opportunities for Iranians, Turks, Berbers, and others to play important roles in society. Counterbalancing this tendency, intermarriage and the widespread adoption of the Arabic language by the Egyptians, Syrians, and Iraqis (a phenomenon manifested some two centuries later in Algeria and Morocco), led to growing ambiguity regarding Arab identity. When the boundaries of the

Islamic world began to expand significantly from 1000 on, therefore, political, religious, and ethnic circumstances had changed so dramatically that the Islamic societies that developed between 1000 and 1500 in northern India, Anatolia (modern Turkey), sub-Saharan Africa, and here and there in the Balkans bore only scant resemblance to each other or to the society of the early khilafah (caliphate). The history of communication, transportation, and exploration must be seen against this background. Islam, as a belief system, has no intrinsic relationship to these various aspects of human social and spatial relations. Insofar as Islam is relevant to their evolution, therefore, it is as a social system that undergoes substantial change, both generally and locally, during the period in question.

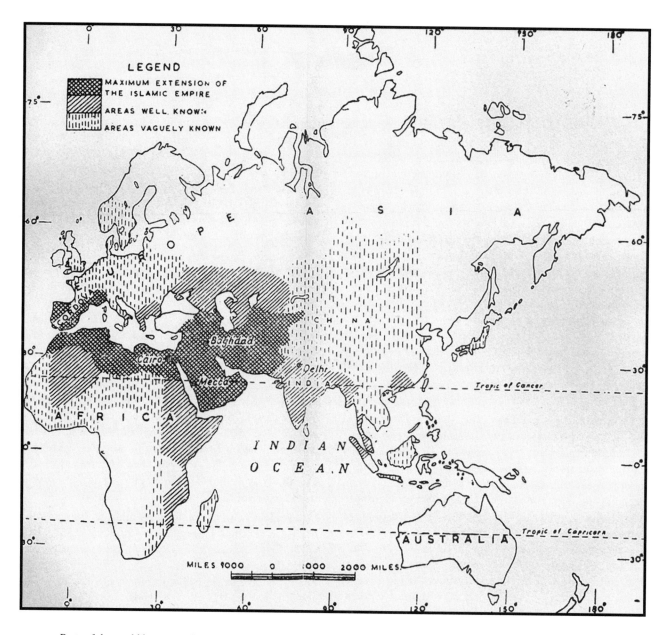

Parts of the world known to the Muslims, circa 700–1500 (from Nafis Ahmad, *Muslim Contributions to Geography*, 1945)

TOPICS IN COMMUNICATION, TRANSPORTATION, AND EXPLORATION

COMMUNICATION

Arabic. Since God's original revelations to Muhammad between circa 610 and 632 first took the form of oral recitation and were later collected in the Qur'an, the Arabic language may rightly be considered intrinsic to the Islamic faith. The function of Arabic as a vehicle for communication within the Muslim community varied greatly over time and space. Initially, most if not all Muslims spoke Arabic and understood the Qur'an when they heard it recited. Though dialectical differences distinguished the Arabic of some parts of the Arabian peninsula from that of other parts, a pre-Islamic tradition of poetry used to extol the virtues or achievements of a tribe had produced a substantial degree of mutual comprehension of poetic diction, which is quite similar to the diction of the Qur'an.

Expansion. From 634 onward, when the first khalifahs rallied the far-flung Arab tribes to carry the Islamic conquests outside the Arabian peninsula, however, it was inevitable that different versions of Arabic would be employed in different conquest areas, depending on the geographic origins of the specific tribal contingents conquering, and subsequently being stationed in, each area. The spread of these different versions eventually contributed to the emergence of the regional dialects of Arabic that still separate the spoken language of one Arab country from that of another. Initially, however, Arabic provided a bond of unity and exclusivity among the new ruling elite and served as a barrier to communication with the conquered peoples. Moreover, the insistence on Arabic as the sole language of sacred writing served as a barrier to the spread of Islam because few non-Arabs—indeed, few Arabs—were literate in Arabic. With bilingual individuals comparatively scarce among both the Muslim and non-Muslim communities, Islam inevitably spread quite slowly. Intermarriage, concubinage, and the enslavement of prisoners of war provided the most obvious social contexts for the development of bilingualism

and thereby the propagation of knowledge about Islam among the conquered population. The geography of Arab settlement was also important. Military frontiers such as Khurasan in northeast Iran, and garrison centers such as Basrah and Kufah in Iraq, Fustat in Egypt, and Qairawan in Tunisia acquired concentrated Arab populations and thus afforded non-Arabs living nearby greater opportunities for exposure to Arabic than non-Arabs had in regions where few Arabs settled. Arab settlements thus became geographical centers from which knowledge of Arabic and of Islam spread.

Migration. A third factor influencing the spread of Arabic was the movement of Arab tribes from the Arabian peninsula and the conversion to Islam of tribes already living in the regions north of the Arabian peninsula. The fact that Egypt, Syria, and Iraq all became Arabic-speaking lands, while Iran did not and North Africa became Arabic-speaking at a substantially later date, is probably related more to the spread of Arab tribes in Egypt, Syria, and Iraq than to the policies of the khalifahs. Since some important Arab tribes in Iraq and Syria remained largely Christian for a century or two after the conquests, the identification between the Arabic language and the Islamic religion was undoubtedly less firm there than in, say, Iran, where most Arabs were Muslims attached to military units. Their lack of military ties to the khilafah probably made it easier for non-Muslim Syrians and Iraqis than for non-Muslim Iranians to accept Arabic as an everyday spoken tongue without at the same time adopting the Islamic faith.

Conversion. While Arabic constituted a barrier to communication in the period 634–800, however, the situation changed dramatically between 800 and 1000. Mass conversion to Islam in the ninth century was accompanied by accelerated urbanization, partly a result of converts desiring to live in the Muslim communities established by the Arabs during the conquest period and partly a result of religious ostracism leading converts

In his account of his 1183–1185 pilgrimage to Mak-kah, Ibn Jubayr explained the motivation of scholars to travel:

The conveniences in this city [Damascus] are beyond computation, more especially for those who commit to memory the Book of Great and Glorious God [the Qur'an] and those devoted to study, to whom the attitude of this town is most extraordinary. All these eastern cities are of this fashion, but this city is more populous and wealthy. Whoever of the young men of the Maghrib [western Muslim lands] seeks prosperity, let him move to these lands and leave his country in the pursuit of knowl-edge and he will find many forms of help. The first of these is the release of the mind from consideration of live-lihood, and this is the greatest and most important. For when zeal is present the student will find the way clear to exert his utmost endeavor, and there will be no excuse for lagging behind, save in the case of those addicted to idle-ness and procrastination, and to them this exhortation is not addressed. We speak only to the zealous, who in their own land find that the search for the means of living comes between them and their aim of seeking knowledge. Well then the door of this East is open, so enter it in peace industrious youth and seize the chance of undistracted [study] and seclusion before wife and children cling to you and you gnash your teeth in regret at the time you have lost. God is the Helper and the Guide. There is no God but He. . . . If in all these eastern lands there were nothing but the readiness of its people to show bounty to strangers and generosity to the poor, especially in the case of the inhabitants of the countryside [it would be enough]. . . . Any stranger in these parts whom God has rendered fit for solitude may, if he wishes, attach himself to a farm and live there the pleasantest life with the most contented mind. Bread in plenty will be given to him by the people of the farm, and he may engage himself in the duties of an imam or in teaching, or what he will, and when he is wea-ried of the place, he may remove to another farm. . . .

Source: Ibn Jubayr, *The Travels of Ibn Jubayr*, translated by R. J. C. Broad-hurst (London: Cape, 1952), pp. 298–300.

from Christianity, Judaism, and Zoroastrianism to leave their home communities and join the Muslim communi-ties. For converts, knowledge of Arabic gave access to the Qur'an and to the increasingly important body of hadiths, traditions of the Prophet—stories of Muham-mad's words and deeds orally transmitted from genera-tion to generation in Arabic. Learning Arabic became a pious obligation, and myriad grammar books and lexi-cons were produced to facilitate such learning.

Ulama'. Pressure to learn Arabic was particularly high in cities and among people who sought, or sought for their children, a clear-cut identity as Muslims, irrespec-tive of ethnic background. During the ninth and tenth centuries there emerged a distinct class of religious scholars, called ulama', or "possessors of knowledge."

Though some ulama' were born in villages, the Arabic learning that they needed to read the Qur'an and master the traditions of the Prophet was mostly available in cit-ies. Thus, the ulama' arose as a distinctly urban class. Intermarried with merchants and landowners, the ulama' became, by the eleventh century, the social core of urban Muslim society. Since they all spoke, read, and wrote Arabic—even if they preferred their mother tongue for everyday use—the culture of the growing cities was expressed predominantly in Arabic. Indeed, it became possible for a religious scholar from Spain to travel all the way to Central Asia and find a community of like-minded Arabic-speaking scholars in every town where he stopped.

Scholarly Travel. Travel in the interest of gathering religious knowledge was commonplace, and it became a dynamic force in Muslim societies. Scholarly travel was initially stimulated by the desire to gather and authenti-cate knowledge of hadiths. Though the traditions of the Prophet were all regarded as originating in Makkah and Madinah during his lifetime, they were considered to have come into general circulation in a variety of loca-tions. A person who witnessed one of the Prophet's deeds, for example, might have related the incident on a trip to Syria or Iran during the period of the conquests, and it might have spread elsewhere from that telling. Given these assumptions, it was plausible to believe that new traditions might be gathered almost anywhere within the range of the early conquests. Hence, ambi-tious ulama' took to the road in substantial numbers to search out places where new traditions might be heard.

Itineraries. Though some non-Muslim scholars of today vehemently reject the notion of geographically dis-persed prophetic traditions that motivated the traveling ulama', a study of ulama' itineraries and attitudes toward the collection of traditions shows clearly that they believed these assumptions about the nature of Muham-mad's traditions. Scholars in northeast Iran, for example, did not travel just to Makkah, Madinah, or Baghdad in search of traditions. Many of them went eastward to the major cities of Central Asia. Study of itineraries also shows, however, that routes of scholarly research fre-quently overlapped trade and pilgrimage routes. Indeed, it is apparent that many traveling scholars engaged in trade to support themselves during journeys that might last for several years. Not all Muslim merchants were scholars, of course, but an appreciable number of schol-ars engaged in one form or another of business. Since Islam did not have clerical or monastic institutions to provide a livelihood for scholars, as medieval Europe did, the need to earn a living and the generally favorable Muslim attitude toward business activities produced a social climate that favored the coming together of reli-gious scholarship, travel, and trade. The rise of the ulama' thus enhanced the role of Arabic as a transre-gional Muslim lingua franca. Far from being a barrier to communication as it had been originally, Arabic became

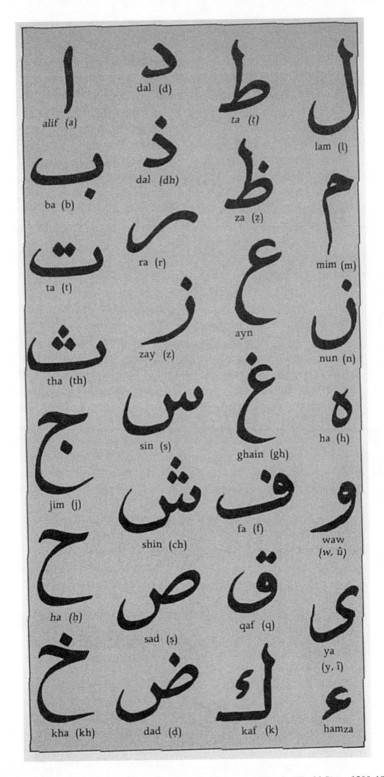

The Arabic alphabet (from Francis Robinson, *Atlas of the Islamic World Since 1500*, 1982)

the foundation for a distinctively Muslim sort of international communication and understanding. However, even though Arabic continues to this day to function in this manner to some degree, inasmuch as Muslim scholars from anywhere in the Islamic world continue to use Arabic as a common language, the next wave of Islamic expansion that began after the year 1000 did little to solidify or enhance a pattern of Arabic dominance.

Persian and Turkish. In Central Asia, northern India, and Anatolia (modern Turkey), Persian became a more important vehicle for Islamic culture than Arabic; and within this same zone, and spreading into the Balkans by 1500, Turkish gradually established itself as a competing literary tongue. Among the new regions brought into the world of Islam after 1000, only in sub-Saharan Africa—specifically Sudan, Chad, Niger, Mauritania, and Mali—

Muslim secretaries of the Abassid period; illumination
from an 1195 Sicilian Christian manuscript by Peter
of Eboli (Burgerbibliothek, Bern)

bordered non-Muslim lands seem to have had better luck than those further removed from the frontier in attracting religiously zealous warriors.

Non-Arab Muslims. Few Arabs took part in the new wave of expansion. In the east, Turks and Afghans predominated in the armies that invaded India. In West Africa, Berbers spearheaded the new wave of expansion. Arabia, Egypt, Syria, and Iraq, which had become the Arabic-speaking core of the old khilafah, bordered on non-Muslim areas only in the north—Anatolia—and in the south—Sudan. In Sudan, Arabs and Arabic did, indeed, play a major role in Muslim expansion from the late twelfth century onward, but Anatolia fell not to Arabs but to Turks invading from northwest Iran. Lest one think that the Arabs were not as zealous for their faith as other Muslim peoples, however, one should remember that the Crusaders who fell upon the Holy Land in 1097 provided a vigorous non-Muslim enemy for close to two centuries.

Language Diversity. The communication gap caused by invading armies speaking languages unknown to the peoples they conquered was not quite the same as it had been in the days of the first conquests. While the Arabs of the generation after Muhammad identified Islam strongly with being Arab, by 1000 it was assumed throughout the Muslim community that Islamic faith was independent of ethnic identity, inasmuch as anyone could become a Muslim through conversion and be accepted as an equal by other Muslims. When people brought under Muslim rule during the second great wave of Islamic conquest entered into relations with their conquerors, therefore, they were under no illusion that learning the conquerors' language was tantamount to conversion to Islam. Some of those living under the new rulers had to learn Persian or Turkish to get along, but Arabic was needed only by converts seeking a religious education. Hence, Arabic had little impact in northern India, or even in Anatolia, which bordered Arabic-speaking Syria and Iraq.

The Rise of New Persian. New Persian, a language written in Arabic script by Muslim Iranians, was gaining widespread acceptance as an alternative religious language to Arabic by the year 1000. The Qur'an and the traditions of the Prophet were studied in Arabic, as they always had been, but increasing amounts of poetry, history, spiritual exhortation, and religious commentary were being written in New Persian. Minimally, the effect of this change was to open the way for Persian speakers to communicate religious sentiments to other Persians in their mother tongue, something that facilitated the deepening of Islamic observance in purely Persian-speaking settings, such as Iranian farming villages; but historical circumstance dictated broader consequences.

The Decline of Iran. For a complex set of reasons, including over-urbanization and the migration into Iran of Turkish pastoral tribes, Iran suffered serious economic decline from approximately 1075 until the devastating invasion of Ghengis Khan's Mongol troops a century and a half later. These two blows to the economy, which seem

did the Arabic of the ulama' become the standard of high literary culture. Several factors contributed to these different outcomes.

Fragmentation. The growing fragmentation of Muslim political unity after 800 ensured that the new wave of expansion was carried out by political and military leaders on the geographical periphery of the khilafah rather than in the center. When Mahmud of Ghazna and his descendants led raids from Afghanistan into India in the decades after the year 1000, they had no idea that Muslim religious activists were agitating among Berber tribes in the western Sahara and stimulating a movement that eventually greatly increased Muslim presence on the southern fringe of the great desert. Nor would Mahmud have cared if he had known. His concern was for his own faith and fortune and that of his family. Perhaps the one common element binding together the new expansion areas was that it was religiously more palatable for a local Muslim warlord to raid non-Muslims across a frontier than to go to war with other Muslim warlords. Their common religion, however, certainly did not prevent Muslims from warring against each other, but warlords whose frontiers

The earliest known fragment of *Alf Laylah wa Laylah* (The Thousand and One Nights), written on paper in 879 by legal scholar Ahmad Ibn Mahfouz (Robert C. Williams American Museum of Papermaking, Atlanta)

to have been felt most severely in the cities, prompted an extensive migration from Iran of the scholarly elite. India, Central Asia, Anatolia, Iraq, and Syria all received and welcomed a significant influx of Iranian scholars. The Iranian exodus affected most strongly India and Anatolia, both ruled by generally Turkish-speaking Muslim warlords. As Muslim communities developed around the court and in the towns of these newly conquered lands, Iranian scholars readily assumed positions of religious leadership. Arab scholars, by contrast, were comparatively few. As a consequence, Persian became firmly implanted in India and Anatolia as the language of culture and religion, although Arabic was still respected as the language of the Qur'an.

International Languages. By 1400 the Islamic world had acquired two international languages: Arabic and Persian. With the adoption of Arabic in the urban areas of North Africa, the Arabic zone stretched from Iraq westward across Africa and into the Sudan and the north-

ern edge of sub-Saharan Africa. The Persian zone stretched from the Aegean Sea eastward across Anatolia through Iran to India and Central Asia. Turkish was a language of the military in parts of both zones; after 1500 it also became a sophisticated literary and religious language in Anatolia and the Balkans. Indeed, by 1500 it had become commonplace for well-educated Muslims in the central lands to learn all three languages, despite the difficulty caused by each tongue belonging to a different language family—Arabic to Semitic, Persian to Indo-European, and Turkish to Ural-Altaic.

Arabic Scripts. Though the ebb and flow of language dominance over nine centuries of Islamic history may seem complicated, three important factors greatly enhanced communication across the vast expanse of the Islamic lands. The first was the adoption of a common writing system, the Arabic script. Though the Arabic alphabet can be written in many styles, they are all more or less readable to someone brought up in the tradition of Arabic script. Since

Arabic, Persian, and Turkish all look similar and share many words, the culture of medieval Islam had a strong element of visual cohesion. Calligraphic architectural decoration, inscriptions, personal names, and the basic appearance of books conveyed a sense of familiarity to travelers wherever they ventured. By contrast, Christian Europe still remains divided by zones of Latin, Greek, and Cyrillic script, making it difficult for the average traveler to read street signs in Greece, Russia, and London.

The Qur'an. The second uniting factor was the shared text of the Qur'an. Every aspect of written culture and many aspects of oral culture were permeated by Qur'anic phraseology and vocabulary. Even non-Muslims became accustomed to the standard religious expressions of their Muslim neighbors—such as *inshallah* meaning "God willing"—sometimes adopting parallel expressions of their own to contribute to an overall impression of a geographically vast territory culturally oriented toward the religion of Islam.

Paper. The third factor was the use of paper, a Chinese invention that spread rapidly after its introduction into the Islamic world sometime in the early eighth century. (The story of the craft being taught by Chinese taken prisoner after a battle on the Talas River in Central Asia in 751 is a picturesque legend.) Because paper can be made virtually anywhere and was much cheaper than parchment, medieval Islamic society took books, libraries, and bookstores for granted long before an equivalent generalizing of literate culture occurred in Europe. One consequence was that Arabic handwriting became standardized earlier and with fewer regional variants than did Latin handwriting in Europe.

Diversity. Observed at the broadest cultural level, these aspects of communication combined to create the impression—both within the Islamic world and from outside—that a great stretch of the globe was united in a single zone of communication. The reality, of course, was much more complex. Spoken languages and dialects, for example, varied widely from place to place. The Arabic of uneducated villagers in Morocco was scarcely recognizable by uneducated villagers in Iraq. Moreover, the differences between Arabic, Turkish, and Persian were by no means negligible. Nevertheless, the impression of unity of communication was an important influence on people's lives. To live in the world of Islam seemed to offer a promise of communication, even with visitors from far away, that was missing when one moved even a short distance to a land using a different script and practicing a different faith.

Sources:

Jonathan Bloom, *Paper Before Print: The History and Impact of Paper in the Islamic World* (New Haven: Yale University Press, 2001).

Dale F. Eickelman and James Piscatori, eds., *Muslim Travellers: Pilgrimage, Migration, and the Religious Imagination* (London: Routledge, 1990).

Johannes Pedersen, *The Arabic Book*, translated by Geoffrey French (Princeton: Princeton University Press, 1984).

Kees Versteegh, *The Arabic Language* (New York: Columbia University Press, 1997).

LAND TRANSPORTATION

Wheeled vehicles. The zone defined by the first great wave of Islamic conquest was so strikingly homogeneous in transportation characteristics as to raise the suspicion that transportation played some role in defining the limits of expansion. The factors that dictated this homogeneity substantially antedated the life of Muhammad. Though some of the earliest evidence for the use of wheeled vehicles anywhere in the world goes back to Mesopotamia circa 3000 B.C.E., there were few wheeled vehicles in use in the regions the Arab armies invaded in the seventh century C.E. Evidence for this statement comes largely from the near absence of references to wheeled transport in medieval Islamic sources. Not only are they rarely mentioned, but Arabic and Persian are deficient in words relating to vehicles, and the infrequent miniature paintings depicting wheeled vehicles are usually so fantastic as to make it clear the artist had never seen the device he was trying to draw. The disappearance of wheeled vehicles seems to have occurred between circa 300 and circa 600, that is, over the three centuries immediately preceding the life of Muhammad (born circa 570). The cause of the disappearance was the progressive replacement of wheeled transport by pack animals, most notably the camel. Documents from the Roman period indicate that, by the year 300, transport by pack camel had become 20 percent cheaper than transport by oxcart. Other documents indicate that Arab camel breeders deliberately used this economic advantage to force carters and wheelwrights out of the transportation business.

Animal Transport. To place these economic issues in perspective, one must look at the role of animal husbandry throughout the zone conquered by the Arabs and contrast it with animal husbandry in Europe to the north, sub-Saharan Africa to the south, and India and Central Asia to the east. The boundaries of early Islamic expansion mirror those most conducive to the use of cheap animal transport. Animal power generally comes from horses, oxen, camels, donkeys, or mules. Each of these species has characteristics that define its utility for transport. Horses are fast, oxen slow, camels in between. Camels are strong, mules less strong, donkeys comparatively weak. More important than these specific characteristics, however, is the cost of the working animal in terms of food, shelter, and care. One-humped camels and donkeys are desert animals, the former adapted to the torrid interior of Arabia and the latter to the similarly punishing climate of northeast Africa. Horses are native to the grasslands of Central Asia and well adapted to extremes of heat and cold. Wild cattle once roamed forests and mountains throughout the Middle East and North Africa, but they are accustomed to moister climates than camels or donkeys. Wild two-humped camels were found in desolate areas of the Middle East, including mountains, but they were more numerous in northern or high altitude areas because they are adapted more to withstand great cold than great heat.

Arid Landscape. The climate of the Middle East and North Africa ranges from dry to extremely dry. Few areas receive enough rainfall to support farming without irrigation, and those that do often find the rainfall unreliable from year to year. Consequently, human settlement has been determined largely by access to water. River valleys such as the Nile and the Tigris-Euphrates offer plentiful water for irrigation. Terracing has been used to turn the seaward slopes of mountains into good farming areas in Lebanon and Israel and a few other places. Oases and wells dot the broad areas of desert, and subterranean canals bring water to Iranian villages suitably situated with respect to nearby mountains that receive rain or snow during the winter. No part of the zone the Arabs conquered in the seventh century is more than fifty miles from land that is either too dry or too mountainous for farming. Human settlement therefore is spotted discontinuously across an arid zone that provides ample pasturage for animals that can live on meager supplies of food and water.

Camels. In the case of camels, it is possible to raise large herds of animals on the abundant wasteland that has no other economic use. Not only does raising a young camel entail no monetary cost, but its omnivorous constitution thrives on low-grade pasturage that would be inadequate to nourish a horse or an ox. A camel also needs no shelter. The costs associated with camel use, therefore, are primarily those of the nomads who raise them and rent or sell them to people requiring camel labor. Oxen, by contrast, require better fodder. Horses require grasslands. In premodern Europe, where grassy steppeland was rare and the climate cold, cattle needed shelter during the winter and had to be fed with stored food. Horses also required shelter and had to be fed rations of grain—grain that might otherwise be eaten by humans—in order to do heavy work. Oxen were cheaper to keep than horses but more expensive than camels. A comparison between Central Asian and European horse breeding is instructive. Horses were abundant in the grasslands of Central Asia where the Turkish and Mongol nomads allowed them to graze but did not feed them grain. As a result, the horses were not particularly strong. A Mongol soldier in the days of Genghis Khan would ride a horse for five or six hours, then had to switch to another and could not remount the first until it had had several days of rest. Hence, Mongol armies had some seven times as many horses as men and required vast pasture lands. A European warhorse, carthorse, or plowhorse was larger and stronger than the typical Mongol horse but had to be fed expensive grain every working day. From these comparisons it should be evident that the superior economy of pack camels in late Roman times was not a temporary phenomenon, but a natural consequence of having abundant desert land where nomads could raise the animals at minimal cost. Why then did camels not replace oxcarts at a much earlier time? The answer to this question lies not in animal husbandry but in the relations between desert nomads and farmers. When camel-riding nomads first appear in the historical record, in biblical passages of the mid second millennium B.C.E. and in Assyrian wall carvings half a millennium later, they are portrayed as desert

IBN BATTUTA VISITS THE TURKS

The best-known Muslim traveler of the medieval era was Ibn Battuta, who traveled to India during the first half of the fourteenth century. In the following passage he described the transportation methods of the Turks living in southeastern Crimea:

The place was in the Qipchaq desert [steppe] which is green and verdant, but flat and treeless. . . . The only method of traveling in this desert is in waggons; it extends for six months' journey, of which three are in the territories of Sultan Muhammad Uzbeg. The day after our arrival one of the merchants in our company hired some waggons from the Qipchaqs who inhabit this desert, and who are Christians and we came to Kafa, a large town extending along the sea-coast, inhabited by Christians, mostly Genoese, whose governor is called Damdir [Demetrio]. . . .

We hired a waggon and traveled to the town of Qiram, which forms part of the territories of Sultan Uzbeg Khan and has a governor called Tuluktumur. . . . He was on the point of setting out for the town of Sara, the capital of the Khan, so I prepared to travel along with him and hired waggons for this purpose. These waggons have four large wheels and . . . . on the waggon is put a light tent made of wooden laths . . . . and it has grilled windows so that the person inside can see without being seen. One can do anything one likes inside, sleep, eat, read or write during the march. . . . At every halt the Turks loose their horses, oxen and camels and drive them out to pasture at liberty, night or day, without shepherds or guardians. This is due to the severity of their laws against theft. Any person found in possession of a stolen horse is obliged to restore in with nine others; if he cannot do this, his sons are taken instead, and if he has no sons he is slaughtered like a sheep.

Source: Ibn Battuta, *Travels in Asia and Africa, 1325–1354*, 3 volumes, translated by H. A. R. Gibb (London: Routledge, 1929), II: 132.

marauders, barbarians capable of raiding farmland but militarily weak. They did not begin to acquire military strength until approximately 200 B.C.E., when a new saddle design made it possible to fight effectively from camelback with sword and spear.

Caravan Cities. As the Arab camel breeders gained military capacity, they applied it to taking control of and reaping the profits from the caravan routes through the desert. These profits, in turn, enabled them to build caravan cities of great magnificence, such as Petra in Jordan and Palmyra in Syria. Though Roman power cut short the period of independent Arab power based on caravan cities by the third century C.E., the Arabs by then no longer needed them. They had become sufficiently aware of the trade and transportation system of the region to carry on and prosper as merchants, caravaneers, and suppliers of pack animals within the Roman provinces of the eastern Mediterranean and North Africa, and they seem to have penetrated the caravan trade of the Sasanid Empire of Iraq and Iran as

A Mongol camel train depicted on a ceramic plate made in fourteenth-century Iran (Landesbildstelle Rheinland, Düsseldorf)

well. The upshot of this complicated transportation history before the coming of Islam was that by means of their acquired dominance in the transportation economy, the pastoral Arabs went from being desert barbarians regarded as enemies by settled farmers to being an integral part of the economy: selling their animals to operate wells, mills, and irrigation devices; providing seasonal transportation for farmers who needed to get crops to market; and dominating the caravan trade across the deserts and increasingly into the surrounding territories.

Islamic Expansion. It would be an exaggeration to say that the transformation of the Arab role in the transportation economy made possible the Islamic conquests, because many other factors contributed as much or more to that historical watershed; but it is a factor that cannot be overlooked, especially in view of the geography of the conquests. Makkah was a caravan city—though it came into being long after the Romans destroyed Petra and Palmyra

and never enjoyed a comparable prosperity. Muhammad and many of his supporters are said to have been merchants or at least quite familiar with caravan trading. Furthermore, the limits of Arab expansion in the first period of conquest make more sense from an economic than from a religious or political perspective.

Frontiers. Unlike the Romans and Greeks before them, the Arabs of the conquest period were little interested in sea transport as an instrument of conquest. They never raided across the Red Sea into Ethiopia or Sudan, for example, and they gave up maritime attacks on the Byzantines in the north after a couple of failures. The Muslim-Byzantine frontier stabilized, in fact, at the line of the Taurus Mountains in southern Anatolia. Though less rugged than the Zagros Mountains of western Iran or the Elburz Mountains of northern Iran, the Taurus represented a transportation frontier. To the south, warm deserts were well suited to camel herding. To the north, the high Anatolian plateau was much less suitable for the Arabs' warm-weather camels. Indeed, oxcarts did not die out there in the pre-Islamic period as they did to the south but remained in use down to the twentieth century. In the west, the Arabs made their way across North Africa to the Atlantic Ocean, but they made a truce with the tribes to the south of Egypt in the Sudan.

Barriers to Trade. The khalifahs' decision to send a military expedition to Morocco but not up the Nile makes sense when looked at from the point of view of camel herding and caravan trading. Trade on the Nile River was primarily by boat, but the first cataract of the Nile, located roughly at the Egyptian-Sudanese frontier, interrupted the trade. To go further south one had to unload, portage around the rapids, and reload above the cataract. If a population of Arab camel pastoralists had been established in the vicinity of the first cataract at the time of the conquest of Egypt, such a detour might have proven a lucrative source of profit; but no Arab tribes ventured anywhere close to the cataract in the conquest period. Hence, there was little reason to push south into a land where trade would be so difficult and so dependent on others.

Mediterranean Trade. By contrast, the Mediterranean coastal plain and desert fringe of North Africa provided good country in which Arabs could raise their animals and establish an east-west caravan trade. Though trade by ship along the coast continued, the land route across Libya to Tunisia attained a prominence in early Islamic times that it had never had before.

The Silk Road. Turning to the eastern edge of the conquest area, the earliest penetration of the Arabs into eastern Iran was across the desert to the south, a route that was more hospitable to their livestock than the colder north. But they soon found that the richest trading route was the Silk Road that went across northern Iran and into Central Asia on its way to China. By the mid eighth century this road, known as the Khurasan Highway, had become the most-famous and most-prosperous trade route in the khilafah. It is not surprising, therefore, that the khalifahs devoted massive military resources to protecting and extending their frontier in Central Asia while they ignored the Sudan and settled for a frontier-raiding relationship with Byzantine Anatolia.

Eastern Limits. Central Asia and India, however, represented a limit to Arab trading enterprise. The Arabs' hot weather camels could not be used in Central Asia because of the frigid winters, and the cheapness of grass-fed horse power in the steppe lands lessened the need for camel power. The Arabs knew little about the two-humped camels bred by the nomads of Central Asia, which were the mainstay of Silk Road traffic north of the fortieth parallel. The Central Asian frontier stabilized, therefore, at approximately the point where caravans shifted from one-humped to two-humped livestock. As for India, despite their seizure of the lower Indus Valley in 711, the Arabs soon settled for a stabilized frontier. Over the course of several centuries, camel herding and camel transport became a major enter-

prise in the Indus region and beyond, but the India the Arabs encountered in the eighth century was basically a land of oxcarts in which Arab merchants with their strings of camels had little place.

The Second Expansion. While considerations of animal husbandry and land transport seem to have played a role in determining that the Islamic khilafah would spread extensively east and west but stabilize its frontiers effectively at the southern and northern limits of Arab nomadism of the pre-Islamic period, these frontiers were not fixed permanently. The second wave of Muslim expansion, after the year 1000, carried the faith into India, Anatolia, and sub-Saharan Africa. Historians usually associate raiding on the Indian frontier with desire for booty or religious zealotry. Be that as it may, the post–1000 time frame seems, from rather scanty evidence, to coincide with the extension of one-humped camel pastoralism into the northwestern portions of India where the raids concentrated.

Spread of One-Humped Camels. The only breed of camel known in ancient India, as in ancient Iran, was the two-humped Bactrian variety, seemingly a rather uncommon animal that was not the focus of a herding culture. The first specification of a camel as "two-humped" occurs in a Sanskrit dictionary compiled in the twelfth century, implying that the one-humped variety had become known in India by that time. This date is in accord with the estimate by scholars that the Baluchi-speaking people, the most-important camel-herding people east of the Arabian peninsula, moved into their current territory in western Pakistan, southern Afghanistan, and southeastern Iran between 1000 and 1200. Subsequently, one-humped camels came into use east of the Indus River, but they were still fairly scarce in the fourteenth century. Though considerations of transport probably had nothing to do with the onset of Muslim raids into India, the expanding area of Muslim control seems to have fostered an expansion eastward of the transport pattern of the Middle East. Camel pastoralism became established in desert regions, and one-humped camels became an inexpensive mode of transport. Since camels had been scarce prior to that time, the competition between camels and wheeled vehicles only then began in India. Unlike the lands further west, however, wheeled transport of a quite efficient nature was well established in India, and camel pastoralists such as the Baluch remained on the fringe of settled society. As a result, Pakistan and India saw the widespread development of one-humped-camel carts, using harnesses that betray their technological lineage by incorporating Arabian saddle designs. (Two-humped-camel carts exist in China and eastern Central Asia.) Thus, the Muslim-dominated areas of north India acquired a distinctive mode of transportation of such low cost that it continues to compete effectively with motorized transport in certain situations down to the present day.

Turkic Migrations. In Anatolia, the crucial transport consideration is that the Turks who defeated the Byzantine army at the Battle of Manzikert in 1071 and then

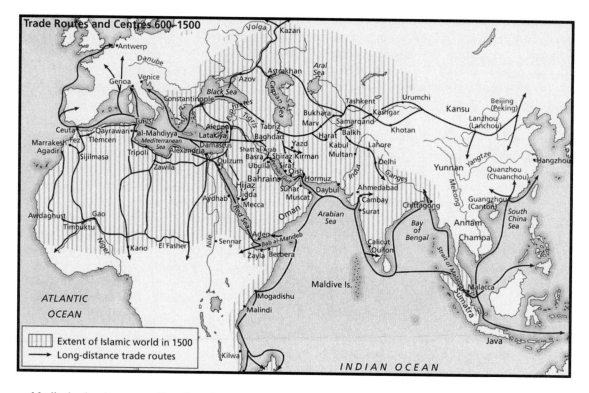

Trade Routes and Centres 600–1500

Extent of Islamic world in 1500
Long-distance trade routes

Muslim land and sea routes (from Francis Robinson, ed., *The Cambridge Illustrated History of the Islamic World*, 1996)

spread westward to the Mediterranean coast were primarily horse breeders. Anatolia offered a cooler climate than other parts of the Middle East, and the grassy mountain valleys surrounding the arid central plateau provided excellent horse pasture. Arab camel pastoralists living to the south of Anatolia in Iraq and Syria did not move northward into the territories newly opened to Muslim settlement because the winter climate was ill-suited to their animals. Thus, Anatolian peasants—and, north of them, peasants in the Balkan regions into which the Turks began to expand in the fourteenth century—continued to use inefficient ox carts down to the twentieth century because cheap camel transportation never materialized.

Saharan Transport. On the Saharan frontier, camel pastoralism was well established among Berber-speaking tribes on the northern and southern fringes of the desert before the Arab conquests of the seventh century. The southern pattern of pastoralism seems to date to the early centuries B.C.E. while pastoralism in the north seems to have developed with the decline of Roman agriculture in the third to sixth century C.E. Breeding conditions kept these two camel cultures largely apart, however. The mating season for camels typically coincides with the best pasture season. Since the gestation period is twelve months, the season of births is more or less the same as the mating season. In the northern Sahara, the best pasture time is in winter, when occasional rains trigger the brief flowering of desert plants. In the south, rains and good pasture come in the summer. Hence, there is little cross-breeding of animals from the north with animals from the south, which helps explain the fact that the two camel cultures also differ in the types of saddles they use, the role camels play in

the society, and even how the camels look. (The south has many camels with splotchy black-and-white or brown-and-white coloring).

The Arab-Berber Alliance. During the first wave of Arab conquests, the invaders undoubtedly came to know about the camel culture of the south, but they made no significant connection with it. By contrast, they saw the camel pastoralists of the north as natural allies pursuing a familiar style of life. This alliance helps explain why the army that invaded Spain in 711 consisted mostly of Berber tribesmen from the north with only a small contingent of Arabs, a rare example of Arab alliance with local forces. The caravan routes of the Middle East were easily extended along the northern frontier of the Sahara from Egypt all the way to Morocco, and North Africa was subsequently considered a part of the Islamic world despite early political separation. Since the Muslims of the north knew of the southern camel herders and the Berbers among them spoke a dialect of the same language, it is not surprising, once North Africa had become integrated into the Middle Eastern caravan network, that trade across the Sahara became a serious venture.

Sub-Saharan Trade. From the late eighth century onward, camel caravans laden with manufactured goods made their way southward, trading for salt at salt mines in the southern Sahara and then trading the salt for sub-Saharan commodities, particularly gold, in the savanna region below the desert. Though prosperous, however, Saharan trade did little to spread Islam south of the Sahara. Arab merchants were received with favor and perhaps converted a few local people to their faith, but sub-Saharan Africa was not a major area of religious expansion. This situation did not begin to change until the eleventh century, when for the first time Berber-speaking Mauritanian tribes (from near the Atlantic coast) imbued with the southern pattern of camel pastoralism adopted Islam and used it as an instrument for political organization and expansion. From that time onward, Islam spread rapidly in the southern Sahara and in the adjoining savanna lands. Northern control of the trans-Saharan caravan routes lapsed, and the Muslim peoples of the south became the new masters.

Urban Life. The expansion of Islam seems closely tied up with the spread of specific forms of land transportation. Yet, Islam had nothing to do with the origin of those forms, which derived mostly from pre-Islamic developments. In the first wave of conquest, Arab camel pastoralism and the network of caravan routes seems to have dictated minimal expansion north and south and phenomenal expansion east and west, the eastern frontiers stabilizing in regions where the mode of transportation along caravan routes normally changed. The second wave of expansion after 1000 was geographically discontinuous and politically uncoordinated, and also involved transport issues. In India it opened the door to significant changes. In Anatolia it made less difference because the animals of the conquerors were used for riding rather than baggage transport, and in sub-Saharan Africa the adoption of Islam by camel pastoralists changed their role in the region and their faith.

Pedestrian Roads. The Islamic world prior to the post-1000 period of expansion was a pedestrian zone. In the absence of wheeled vehicles, every aspect of society and the economy was predicated on movement by foot. Dirt being kinder than stone on human and animal feet, roads and streets were seldom paved, nor did pedestrians have to take into account the length of axles or the turning radius of vehicles. Roads could meander, take sharp turns, incorporate stairs, and vary in width without causing inconvenience. Governments interested in fostering interurban trade concentrated on bridges and rural rest areas—caravanserais—rather than the roads themselves. Within cities, the desirability of living at easy walking distance from congregational mosques, markets, and other centralized amenities raised the value of land near the city center. Space devoted to streets and open areas was therefore scarce, giving the city a high population density. Shops catering to everyday needs—such as baths, bakeries, and butcher shops—were distributed throughout the residential neighborhoods while craftsmen and shops less frequently visited—such as cobblers, coppersmiths, jewelers, and perfumers—were concentrated in one place. A person wanting to buy cotton cloth could walk to the appropriate section of the market and stroll easily from shop to shop. As a result, market areas typically featured close clusters of shops selling the same type of wares.

Limitations of Animal Transportation. Finally, the need to divide loads of freight into units small enough to be carried on animal back militated against monumental construction based on large stones. Brick and wood, commodities that were easily divided, were the building methods of choice. Though transportation was not the sole factor shaping the fabric of urban life, it contributed materially to the way in which travelers from beyond the Islamic world perceived Islamic life. They often reported on cities with narrow, irregular streets; little public space; crowding; and clustering of crafts and stores according to the commodities being sold. Impressions such as these contributed to the image of an Islamic world that was comparatively homogeneous across a broad geographical area, and different from the neighboring regions of Europe, Anatolia, India, and sub-Saharan Africa.

Sources:
Richard W. Bulliet, *The Camel and the Wheel* (Cambridge, Mass.: Harvard University Press, 1975).

Jibrail S. Jabbur, *The Bedouins of the Desert: Aspects of Nomadic Life in the Arab East* (Albany: State University of New York Press, 1995).

Owen Lattimore, *The Desert Road to Turkestan* (New York: Kodansha International, 1995).

SEA AND RIVER TRANSPORT

Access to the Sea. In the area of water transport, the medieval Islamic world presents a double face. The Mediterranean Sea and the Indian Ocean formed water frontiers to which Muslims reacted quite differently. The empire conquered by the Arabs between 632 and 711 incorporated an enormous extent of coastline: the Mediterranean coast of Iberia (Spain), the Atlantic coast of Morocco, the southern and eastern coasts of the Mediterranean Sea, all the east and half of the west coast of the Red Sea, the southern coast of the Caspian Sea, and the entire Indian Ocean coast from Yemen to the mouth of the Indus including the Persian Gulf. No empire had comparable access to the sea until the Portuguese and Spanish explorations of the fifteenth century. These coastlines do not all have the same importance, however, in political and economic calculations. Geographically speaking, most of the Muslims' coastal lands were of restricted value, at least from a transport perspective.

Limits to Navigation. The arid zone that proved so favorable to the pastoralism of its conquerors dictated that there were few navigable rivers and hence few port cities at river mouths. The Nile and the Shatt al-Arab (the river at the head of the Persian Gulf formed by the confluence of the Tigris and Euphrates), provided the only significant river access to the lands behind the coast; but the shifting delta of the Nile prevented the development of a large port city like Basrah in Iraq. In other places steep mountains shadowing narrow coastal plains produced seasonal torrents rather than perennial rivers, as was the case in the Algerian, Lebanese, and Caspian coastlands. Small ports provided stopovers for coastal traders, but they did not connect to major inland trade routes. In still other places, lack of fresh water put a strict limit on human settlement, as on both sides of the Red Sea and Persian Gulf and along the southern coast of Iran and Sind (the lower

Indus valley). Only in southern Arabia, from Mocha in Yemen to Musqat in Oman, did occasional small seaports connect with rich hinterlands, but even there geography was destiny, inasmuch as the great sand sea of the Rub' al-Khali (the Empty Quarter) cut off most of southern Arabia from the lands to the north.

Trade Winds. Since sailing ships were the primary means of water transport, the prevailing winds must also be taken into account. Winter storms over the Mediterranean dictated a more or less complete cessation of sea travel for several months of the year. In the Red Sea, the only point of potential maritime contact between the worlds of the Mediterranean and the Indian Ocean, northerly winds prevailed above the latitude of Makkah, making it comparatively inconvenient to sail northward. In the Indian Ocean, seasonal winds—from west to east in summer and from east to west in winter—strongly influenced trading calendars and itineraries. The wind-determined difficulty in navigating the northern portion of the Red Sea manifested itself in technological discontinuity. Mediterranean ships were built and rigged differently from those in the Indian Ocean and Persian Gulf.

Shipbuilding. Roman ship-building practice favored joining the planks on the ship's hull with mortise-and-tenon joints—that is, put tab A in slot B—held in place by wooden pegs. Ribs were then attached to the inside of the hull for strengthening. This technique changed in the medieval period to that of laying down a keel, attaching a framework of ribs, and nailing the hull planks to the ribs.

An Arab dhow (illustration by Susan L. Douglass)

In both periods, the finished ship was rigged with a square sail and fitted with oars and oarlocks if military operations were anticipated. In the Indian Ocean and Persian Gulf, shipbuilders bored holes in the hull planks, tied them together with palm-fiber cords, and caulked the seams with bitumen, which was plentifully available from the tar seeps that signaled the immense underground oil reserves of the Gulf. For rigging, Indian Ocean shipmasters used a lateen sail. This large, irregular, four-sided sail presented such a narrow edge to the wind that it is often described as triangular. Compared to the Mediterranean square sail, the lateen design permitted ships to sail more directly into the wind and probably made them more stable since the force of the wind was greater on the wide lower portion of the sail than on its pointed peak. A reason for this difference that was more important than technical advantage or disadvantage, however, was the fact that shipwrights and shipmasters from the southern seas seem to have had little contact with those in the Mediterranean world.

Maritime Zones. The differences between the two zones carried over into politics and trade. Despite the principle legendarily ascribed to the early khalifahs that Muslim lands should never be separated by water, Muslim sea raiders did hold—for varying lengths of time—the Belearic Islands, Malta, Sicily, and Crete. And of course the army that conquered Spain had to be ferried across the strait of Gibraltar. Nevertheless, the idea of linking these maritime holdings commercially or politically, after the manner of the ancient Athenians and Carthaginians or the late medieval Venetians, seems never to have been considered. Naval conquests seem to have been less the product of a centralized strategy of Islamic expansion than of the decay of power in the khilafal center and the corresponding rise of independent local states. Sicily, for example, was conquered from, and remained tied to, the quasi-independent government of Tunisia, and the Balearic Islands were an outpost of the totally independent Muslim state in Spain.

Sea Trade. With respect to trade, the maritime route from Spain to Tunisia and Egypt was the most active. Commercial relations with Christian Europe were few in the early Islamic centuries, with most cargoes being shipped by Jewish traders, who were marginally more welcome in Christian lands, where there were communities of co-religionists, than were Muslim traders. The historian Henri Pirenne's well-known dictum that the Muslim conquests permanently severed maritime ties between the northern and southern sides of the Mediterranean has been disproved by archaeological and textual evidence. Southern products did continue to reach Europe in early medieval times, but trade unquestionably declined. Christian and Muslim sea raiders made routes that approached enemy territory too closely unsafe.

Maritime Powers. Not until the conquest of Anatolia in the second wave of Muslim expansion did sea power again become a major concern. Turkish Muslim principalities established along the shores of the Aegean Sea in western Anatolia inherited the seafaring expertise and enterprise of their mostly Greek-speaking populations. At the same time, however, the eleventh-twelfth century revival of urban prosperity in Italy stimulated the Venetians, Genoese, and Pisans to establish themselves as a trading presence on the southern and eastern shores of the Mediterranean from Tunisia to Egypt and Syria, with special emphasis on the Crusader States established after 1097. Trade and warfare eventually culminated in a long struggle between the Ottoman Empire and Venice for Mediterranean domination, a struggle that extended well beyond 1500. Based in shoreline fortresses or castle-protected seaports increasingly equipped with large cannon after 1400, oared galleys rowed out to prey on passing enemy shipping. Yet, even then the Muslim states never developed a clear-cut naval strategy based on their control of the southern Mediterranean shoreline from the strait of Gibraltar to Greece, an expanse of territory that had been completely absorbed into the Ottoman empire by 1520.

Political Disunity. Given the extent of the Muslim lands, and their substantial political disunity between 800 and 1500, it is pointless to search for a deep ideological meaning behind the lack of dedication to seaborne trade and maritime political power. It is easier, perhaps, to explain the relative success of the Christian states in this area by looking at the limited possibilities Venice, Pisa, and Genoa had for expansion by land and the consequent push to the sea as the outlet for their ambitions.

Indian Ocean Trade. In the southern seas, Muslim aggression was even less in evidence, despite the isolated undertaking to send part of an invasion force from Basrah to the Indus valley by sea in 711. Trade flourished from east Africa to China, but no country seems to have sought to dominate it. Africans, Arabs, Iranians, Indians, Malays, Indonesians, and Chinese all participated. Mangrove poles, ivory, and gold from Africa; cotton cloth and spices from India; spices from Southeast Asia; and pottery and other manufactured goods from China became well known in the Muslim cities of the Middle East, but no one conceived of the idea of following the trade to its sources and asserting political control over it by force of arms as the Portuguese and other Europeans did later. Seaport societies were typically multilingual and cosmopolitan, but no Muslim city became politically important as a seaport between 600 and 1500. Basrah, the intermediary trade center at the head of the Persian Gulf, is only an apparent exception. Its undeniable political importance in the seventh and eighth centuries derived not from maritime activities but from the migration of Arab tribes from the deserts of the peninsula to take part in the conquests.

Rivers. Finally, there is the matter of river transport. As in the case of maritime trade, no sources survive that would permit an estimate of the boatloads of grain or

THE HARBOR AT TYRE

The twelfth-century traveler Ibn Jubayr described the harbor at Tyre in Lebanon and explained how seasonal winds affected travel on the Mediterranean:

the strength and impregnability of Tyre is more marvelous than is told of. It has only two gates, one landwards, and the other on the sea, which encompasses the city save on one side. The landward gate is reached only after passing through three or four posterns in the strongly fortified outer walls that enclose it. The seaward gate is flanked by two strong towers and leads into a harbor whose remarkable formation is unique among maritime cities. The walls of the city enclose it on three sides, and the fourth is confined by a mole bound with cement. Ships enter below the walls and there anchor. Between the two towers stretches a great chain which, when raised, prevents any coming in or going forth, and no ships may pass save when it is lowered. At the gate stand guards and trusted watchers, and none can enter or go forth save under their eyes. The beauty of the site of this port is truly wonderful. Acre resembles it in situation and description, but cannot take the larger ships, which must anchor outside, small ships only being able to enter. The port of Tyre is more complete, more beautiful and more animated. . . . The blowing of the winds in these parts has a singular secret. It is that the east wind does not blow except in spring and autumn, and, save at those seasons, no voyages can be made and merchants will not bring their goods to Acre. The spring voyages begin in the middle of April, when the east wind blows until the end of May. It may last longer or less according to what God on High decrees. The autumn voyages are from the middle of October, when the east wind (again) sets in motion. It lasts a shorter time than in the spring, and is for them a fleeting opportunity, for it blows for (only) fifteen days, more or less. There is no other suitable time, for the winds then vary, that from the west prevailing. Voyagers to the Maghrib, to Sicily, or to the lands of the Rum, await this east wind in these two seasons as they would await the fulfillment of a pledge. Glory to God, creating in His wisdom, and miraculous in His power. There is no God but He.

Source: Ibn Jubayr, *The Travels of Ibn Jubayr*, translated by R. J. C. Broadhurst (London: Cape, 1952), pp. 319–320, 326.

other goods carried per year on the Nile or the Tigris-Euphrates system. Yet, the largest cities in the Muslim world, Baghdad and Cairo, were supplied primarily by river. Baghdad received myriad shipments by sailing craft coming up the Tigris from the south and from rafts floated down the Euphrates from the north. River traffic northward from Baghdad was impractical, however, because of the swiftness of the current and general absence of favorable winds. The Nile was more congenial to transportation. Prevailing northerly winds made it comparatively easy to sail southward upstream from the Mediterranean to the region of the first cataract around Aswan. To go in the other direction, one simply floated downstream with the current. Located at

القرآن ثم وبعد اساطير بلاها ورخارف جلاها وقال اركبوا فيها بسم الله مجراها

ومرساها ثمّ نفس نفس المغبرين او عباد الله للكرمين وقل لك اما انا

A ship sailing in the Persian Gulf to the port of Basrah; illumination from a thirteenth-century manuscript
for the *Maqamat al-Hariri* (Bibliothèque Nationale, Paris)

the juncture of the Nile and its delta, Cairo derived maximum benefit from this system. The only other river transport of note involves the rivers of Central Asia and Russia. The Syr Darya (ancient Jaxartes) flows from the Pamir Mountains of Tajikistan and Kyrgyzstan to the Aral Sea in Uzbekistan; the Amu Darya (ancient Oxus) drains the Hindu Kush in Afghanistan and similarly terminates in the Aral Sea. The Aral Sea, however, is landlocked. Though river trade on these substantial rivers was feasible, there is little to indicate that the volume of traffic was large. Trade on the Volga, Don, and Dnieper further to the west is another story. Scandinavian merchants sent furs, amber, and slaves southward by boat for exchange in Byzantine and Muslim territories. Byzantium garnered the lion's share of this trade since the Don and the Dnieper emptied into the Black Sea, but tens of thousands of Islamic coins found in hoards in the Baltic Sea region attest to the vigor of trade with Muslim regions by way of the Volga and the Caspian Sea.

Sources:

George Hourani, *Arab Seafaring in the Indian Ocean in Ancient and Early Medieval Times,* revised and expanded by John Carswell (Princeton: Princeton University Press, 1995).

Patricia Risso, *Merchants and Faith: Muslim Commerce and Culture in the Indian Ocean* (Boulder: Westview Press, 1995).

Aziz Suryal Atiya, *Crusade, Commerce, and Culture* (Bloomington: Indiana University Press, 1962).

G. R. Tibbetts, *Arab Navigation in the Indian Ocean Before the Coming of the Portuguese: Being a Translation of Kitab al-Fawaid fi Usul al-Bahr Wal-Qawaid* (London, 1971).

Auguste Toussaint, *History of the Indian Ocean* (Chicago: University of Chicago Press, 1966).

Alan Villiers, *Sons of Sinbad: An Account of Sailing with the Arabs in Their Dhows, in the Red Sea, around the Coasts of Arabia, and to Zanzibar and Tanganyika: Pearling in the Persian Gulf: and The Life of the Shipmasters, the Mariners and Merchants of Kuwait* (New York: Scribners, 1940).

SCIENTIFIC EXPLORATION

Land Beyond. The concept of exploration does not transfer easily from one culture to another. European history counts exploration as one of its great themes, but only from the fifteenth century onward. While, for example, ancient Greeks and Romans traveled from Morocco to India, they are rarely referred to as explorers. Exploration has implications of first discovery and often of territorial acquisition. European explorers of the fifteenth century and later were much given to claiming the territories they reached for their monarchs and for Christianity, blithely ignoring the interests of the indigenous inhabitants and the fact that traders or travelers from non-European regions might have already been well acquainted with the place. In short, the word *exploration,* when applied to journeys to places previously unknown to the journeys' sponsors, is difficult to use outside the context of European imperialism. It has no exact translation in the languages of the Muslim world. It is often noted, however, that the terms *dar al-Islam* (abode of Islam) and *dar al-harb* (abode of war) played key roles in medieval Islamic thought. Legal texts, in particular, make distinctions between the status of individuals living under the rule of a Muslim government (that is, in the "abode of Islam") and those living under non-Muslim rule (in the "abode of war"). These distinctions have led some scholars to attribute a sort of garrison mentality to medieval Islamic society, a view of the world that started from a principle of conquest and rested on a zealous commitment to bring the entire world into the Muslim fold by force of arms. If this supposition were true, one might expect to find a clear distinction in Muslim geographical texts between the "abode of Islam" and the "abode of war." In fact, geographers made almost no reference to this legalistic division of the world, nor did cartographers inscribe a boundary between the two abodes on their maps. While from a legal point of view—for example, in determining the obligation of individual Muslims to the government of the territory in which they live—the distinction is important, in reality it seems to have been less substantial than the medieval European conception of Christendom as opposed to the land of the infidel.

Pilgrims. More important than legalistic territorial boundaries was the actual experience of travel. Certain elements of medieval Muslim society were much more given to long-distance travel than were most Europeans. Scholars and traders—often one and the same person—sometimes spent years on the road, as did pilgrims to Makkah. Moreover, the accounts of their travels became popular reading, and from the thirteenth century onward narrations of individual pilgrimages to Makkah became an established genre from Morocco to India. These travel writings were not chronicles of exploration, of course. To some degree, they were the opposite. A pilgrim might start from a little known place, possibly outside the orbit of Muslim political dominion, and make his way to the best known of places, the holy cities of Makkah and Madinah. Yet, some travel accounts presumed a reading audience interested in exotic and faraway places and therefore come closer to being accounts of exploration. Ahmad Ibn Fadlan, for example, traveled among and described the Turks of Central Asia as part of an embassy for the Abbasid Khalifah al-Muqtadir (ruled 908–932) to the king of the Volga Bulgars, a Turkic people living north of the Caspian Sea. Four centuries later, the best-known Muslim traveler of all, Ibn Battuta, spent years wandering from his native North Africa to Muslim and non-Muslim lands as far afield as China, India, and sub-Saharan Africa. Needless to say, travelers such as these had no royal commission to claim new territory or plant the flag of Islam. Whether afflicted with wanderlust or following the orders of monarchs, they were private individuals who were also aware of an audience for their narratives. Their actions were as much extensions of the established practice of traveling in pursuit of religious knowledge (*rihla fi talab al-'ilm*), whether through pilgrimage or sitting at the feet of a scholar in a distant city, as they were

Fragment of a pilgrimage certificate issued at Makkah and Madinah in the twelfth century (Museum of Islamic Art, Istanbul)

self-conscious efforts at exploration for the benefit of a royal sponsor.

Geography. In one respect, however, some travelers did overlap in purpose with the later European explorers: they consciously contributed to cartography and the literature of geography. Geography was an important literary genre in the Islamic world from the ninth century onward. Some works are nothing but schematic descriptions of trade routes, listing the nightly stopping points between city A and city B. Others describe cities and towns in greater or lesser detail. Still others focus on the wonders or marvels (*al-'aja'ib*) that might be seen in dif-

ferent places, or on the sites of saintly tombs where a pious traveler might wish to pray. By the eleventh century it had become common to couch parts of such works in rhyming Arabic prose, a style that clearly signaled the writer's desire to be considered a litterateur and not just a compiler of lore. Geographical works of these various types almost always concern broad regions, if not the entire Islamic world. Some include brief descriptions of non-Muslim lands as well. Works of more local interest, such as urban or provincial geographies, were also composed, many of them appearing as sections of local history books rather than as independent works.

In his *Tahqiq al-Hind* (The Precise Description of India), the eleventh-century geographer al-Biruni described the location of India in the known world, beginning with the Indian Ocean:

This southern ocean does not form the utmost southern limit of the inhabitable world. On the contrary, the latter stretches still more southward in the shape of large and small islands which fill the ocean. In this southern region land and water dispute with each other their position, so that in one place the continent protrudes into the sea, whilst in another the sea penetrates deeply into the continent. The continent protrudes far into the sea in the western half of the earth, and extends its shores far into the south. . . . On its coast, and the islands before the coast, live the various tribes of the Zanj.

There are several bays or gulfs which penetrate into the continent on this western half of the earth, the bay of Berbera, that of Klysma (the Red Sea), and that of Persia (the Persian Gulf); and between these gulfs the western continent protrudes more or less into the ocean. In the eastern half of the earth the sea penetrates as deeply into the northern continent as the continent in the western half protrudes into the southern sea, and in many places it has formed bays and estuaries which run far into the continent—bays being parts of the sea, estuaries being the outlets of rivers towards the sea. This sea is mostly called from some island in it or from the coast which borders it. Here, however, we are concerned only with that part of the sea which is bordered by the continent of India, and therefore is called the Indian Ocean.

As to the orographic configuration of the inhabitable world, imagine a range of towering mountains like the vertebrae of a pine stretching through the middle latitude of the earth, and in longitude from east to west, passing through China, Tibet, the country of the Turks, Kabul, Badhakhshan, Tokharistan, Bamiyan, Elghor, Khurasan, Media, Adharbaijan, Armenia, the Roman Empire, the country of the Franks and of the Jalalika (Galicians). Long as this range is, it has also a considerable breadth, and besides, many windings which enclose inhabited plains watered by streams which descend from the mountains both towards north and south. One of these plains is India, limited in the south by the above-mentioned Indian Ocean, and on all three other sides by the lofty mountains, the waters of which flow down to it. But if you have seen the soil of India with your own eyes and meditate on its nature—if you consider the rounded stones found in the earth however deep you dig, stones that are huge near the mountains and where the rivers have a violent current; stones that are of smaller size at greater distance from the mountains, and where the streams flow more slowly; stones that appear pulverized in the shape of sand where the streams begin to stagnate near their mouths and near the sea—if you consider all this, you could scarcely help thinking that India has once been a sea which by degrees has been filled up by the alluvium of the streams.

Source: *Alberuni's India*, translated by Edward C. Sachau, edited by Ainslie T. Embree (New York: Norton, 1971), pp. 196–198.

Maps. Though written descriptions of non-Muslim lands are usually sketchy, world maps are not uncommon in Islamic cartography. In fact, Muslim world maps are the earliest extant attempts from any culture at depicting the entire world. They are usually circular in format with south at the top and north at the bottom. They depict the various continents surrounded by a single great ocean. The geometric center of the encircling sea varies somewhat, but is usually in the vicinity of Iran, perhaps indicating a pre-Islamic cartographic tradition. Almost all the maps made prior to the fifteenth century are highly geometric and schematic and demonstrate a general lack of interest in physical accuracy. They—or more often the provincial maps usually accompanying them—supplement the geographical texts in which they are typically inserted by listing many cities and places and indicating which are connected to which by overland routes. Taken altogether, the particular characteristics of medieval Muslim travel literature, geography, and cartography bespeak a society that, despite changing and often severe political divisions, was conscious of the great territorial expanse of Islam. The divisive politics that accompanied the decline of central khilafal power from the tenth century onward did not erode the cosmopolitan outlook of literate Muslims. On the other hand, this viewpoint diminished sharply when pushed beyond the boundaries of the Islamic world. As with communications and transportation, travel writing, geography, and cartography contributed substantially to the prevailing sense that the Islamic world had a material as well as a doctrinal unity.

Sources:
Ross E. Dunn, *Adventures of Ibn Battuta, A Muslim Traveler of the Fourteenth Century* (Berkeley: University of California Press, 1986).

Dale F. Eickelman and James Piscatori, eds. *Muslim Travellers: Pilgrimage, Migration, and the Religious Imagination* (London: Routledge, 1990).

Ibn Battuta, *Travels in Asia and Africa, 1325–1354*, 3 volumes, translated by H. A. R. Gibb (London: Routledge, 1929).

G. Le Strange, *The Lands of the Eastern Caliphate: Mesopotamia, Persia, and Central Asia from the Moslem Conquest to the Time of Timur* (Cambridge: Cambridge University Press, 1905).

G. R. Tibbetts, *A Study of the Arabic Texts Containing Material on South-East Asia* (Leiden: Brill, 1979).

Andre Wink, *Al-Hind, The Making of the Indi-Islamic World* (Leiden: Brill, 1990).

SIGNIFICANT PEOPLE

IBN BATTUTA

1304 - CIRCA 1378
TRAVELER

Journeys to New Places. Ibn Battuta was born in Tangier in 1304. Following a vow he made during his first pilgrimage to Makkah "never, so far as possible, to cover a second time any road," he accumulated a wealth of travel experience never duplicated in Islamic history. After spending two or three years in Makkah on his third pilgrimage, he decided that henceforth he would travel for the sake of seeing new peoples and places rather than solely for the sake of piety. After familiarizing himself with all parts of the Islamic Middle East, he set out in 1325 to Constantinople, the capital of the Christian Byzantine Empire, and traveled from there across Central Asia to India, by way of Samarqand. He resided in Delhi at the court of the Muslim ruler Muhammad ibn Tughlaq of northern India for eight years.

Embassy to China. In 1342 Ibn Battuta's host sent him on an embassy to China. This trip took him through all parts of India to Sumatra, and then through China from the south coast to Beijing. In 1347 he turned west, again traveling by way of Sumatra and India, and finally reached Tangier in 1350.

Travel Accounts. On subsequent journeys Ibn Battuta visited Spain and traveled across the Sahara to Niger (1352–1353). Before his death around 1378, Ibn Battuta dictated his account of his travels on order of Abu Inan, the ruler of Fez, to Ibn Juzayy, a legal scholar from Spain. In the process, some shaping of the text in terms of itineraries and literary form took place, but by and large Ibn Battuta's work is considered accurate; and his name has become a byword in Muslim cultures for adventurous travel.

Sources:

Ross E. Dunn, *Adventures of Ibn Battuta, A Muslim Traveler of the Fourteenth Century* (Berkeley: University of California Press, 1986).

Ibn Battuta, *Travels in Asia and Africa, 1325–1354*, 3 volumes, translated by H. A. R. Gibb (London: Routledge, 1929).

IBN FADLAN

FLOURISHED 921-923
TRAVELER

Journey to Russia. Little is known about the life of Ibn Fadlan. He was probably of non-Arab ancestry, and he seems to have been in the service of a high-ranking official of the Abbasid court in Baghdad. In June 921 he left Baghdad with a party of jurists and teachers on an embassy to the king of the Volga Bulgars, who had invited Khalifah al-Muqtadir to send instruction on Islam to his people. The journey took approximately two years, and the only surviving account of it is a narrative by Ibn Fadlan. His observations of the various Turkic peoples across whose territory the embassy traveled are an invaluable source for the history and ethnography of Central Asia, as are his descriptions of the Rus, the Scandinavian warrior-traders who traversed the rivers of Russia, in whose name their historical role survives. At one point in his narrative he commented on their appearance and dress:

> I had never seen people of such tall stature—they are as tall as palm trees, blond, and ruddy of complexion. They do not wear shirts or caftans [robes]. Their custom is to wear a length of coarse cloth that they wrap around their sides and throw over the shoulder so that one arm remains bare. Each of them carries with him an ax, a dagger and a sword. They are never seen without these weapons. Their swords are broad with wavy stripes on the blade, and of Frankish [European] manufacture. On one side, from the point to the handle, it is covered with figures and trees and other decorations. The women fasten to their bodice a locket of iron, copper, silver or gold, according to the wealth and position of her husband. On the locket is a ring, and on that is a knife, also fastened to the front of their bodice. They wear silver and gold chains around their necks. If the man possesses ten thousand dirhams [silver coins], he has a chain made for his wife; and if he has twenty thousand, she gets two necklaces; and so she receives one more each time he becomes ten thousand richer. In this way the Rus woman acquires a great number of necklaces. Their most valued jewelry consists of green glass beads like the kind found on the ships.

Source:

C. M. Fraehn, *Ibn Fozlan's und anderer Araber Berichte über die Russen älterer Zeit: Nachdruck der Ausgabe von 1823* (Habsburg: Helmut Buske, 1976). [English translation by Susan Douglass]

IBN JUBAYR

1145-1217

PILGRIM

Journey to Makkah. Ibn Jubayr produced one of the earliest and most influential accounts of a pilgrimage to Makkah. He left Granada in his native Spain in February 1183, embarking at Ceuta on a Genoese ship that over a month-long period took him to Alexandria via Sardinia, Sicily, and Crete, all non-Muslim lands. After making the pilgrimage, he went to Baghdad, the then-declining metropolis of the Abbasid khilafah, and then took the caravan route across Syria from Mosul to Aleppo eventually reaching the Mediterranean coast at Acre. Once again boarding a Genoese ship, he endured a harrowing shipwreck off Sicily before finally returning to Spain in yet another ship in April 1185. He made further voyages in later years, dying during a sojourn in Alexandria in 1217. His description of his first journey, *Rihla Ibn Jubayr* (Travel Account of Ibn Jubayr), is the only one to survive. It became so influential a model for later travelers that extensive portions of it were sometimes quoted without acknowledgement. Though he employed a reportorial day-to-day format, he also included passages in rhymed prose that seem more colorful than accurate.

Source:

Ibn Jubayr, *The Travels of Ibn Jubayr*, translated by R. J. C. Broadhurst (London: Cape, 1952).

ABU DULAF AL-KHAZRAJI

FLOURISHED 943-952

TRAVEL WRITER

Abu Dulaf al-Khazraji exploited the popular interest in travel to enhance his reputation as a litterateur. An Iranian frequenting the court of a local ruler in western Iran during the mid tenth century, he wrote two travel accounts. The first purports to report on a delegation sent by the Samanid ruler Nasr ibn Ahmad (ruled 914–943) of eastern Iran to negotiate a royal marriage with the ruler of China. Abu Dulaf's short, and at times fanciful, descriptions of the peoples he encountered are in seemingly illogical order, and the few words he devoted to an alleged return to Iran by way of China, Malaya, and India have led scholars to doubt that he ever made the journey. More likely, he collected information from travelers in the Samanid capital of Bukhara and fabricated a narrative to please the reading public. Scholars have been more generous in their appraisal of his second account, which is devoted solely to travels within Iran. Even here, however, the information from western Iran is distinctly more plausible and geographically coherent than the lore pertaining to more eastern provinces. In a third work, a long poem with extensive explanatory notes, Abu Dulaf described the activities of another class of travelers in medieval Islamic society, the "guild" of beggars, street performers, and confidence tricksters. This colorful group, known as the Banu Sasan, excited the same sort of interest among Abu Dulaf's audience of educated courtiers that a modern account of underworld or circus life might excite today. Abu Dulaf's work testifies to the popularity of stories about exotic peoples and locales even as it casts doubt on his personal honesty.

Source:

Richard W. Bulliet, "Abu Dolaf al-Yanbu'i, Mes'ar b. Mohalhel al-Kazraji," in *Encyclopaedia Iranica* (London: Routledge & Kegan Paul, 1985), I: 271–272.

SHAMS AL-DIN ABU 'ABD ALLAH MUHAMMAD AL-MUQADDASI

CIRCA 945 - CIRCA 990

TRAVELER-GEOGRAPHER

Describing Islamic Lands. The geography of Abu 'Abd Allah Muhammad al-Muqaddasi is considered the finest achievement in this field of medieval Islamic literature. Born in Palestine and bearing a family name derived from a name for city of Jerusalem (then called al-Bait al-Muqaddas, "the sacred house"), al-Muqaddasi later said that he decided to write his book during a sojourn in Shiraz in southwestern Iran in 985, by which time he had passed the age of forty and had made two pilgrimages to Makkah along with other journeys. Like some previous geographers, he included a wealth of lore about individual cities and regions: climate, products, resources, sacred sites, customs, political and religious factions, and trade routes. His most distinctive contribution, however, is a broad conception of the land of Islam as an integral geographical zone. He thus named his book *Ahsan al-Taqasim fi Ma'rifat al-Aqalim* (The Best Division for Knowledge of the Provinces). Dividing the totality of the Islamic lands into a western, Arab half and an eastern, non-Arab half, he systematically analyzed the structure of each province and subprovince starting with the largest cities and working down through a hierarchy of subordinate towns and locales. His information on routes and products strongly suggests that he saw his work as being of value to merchants, but he also included long descriptive passages composed in rhyming prose to appeal to the taste of the educated reader.

Source:

Basil Anthony Collins, *Al-Muqaddasi: The Man and His Work, with Selected Passages Translated from the Arabic* (Ann Arbor: Department of Geography, University of Michigan, 1974).

DOCUMENTARY SOURCES

Abu Rayhan al-Biruni (died 1048), Tahqiq al-Hind (The Precise Description of India) — An important work written just after the invasions of India by Mahmud of Ghazna; al-Biruni's wide-ranging book explores the physical, economic, mathematical, and cultural geography of the subcontinent, as well as investigating Indian science, history, religion, technology, and thought, making the book an original cultural study with great depth.

The Geniza Collection, Cambridge University—A collection of documents and fragments found in the Geniza, or document depository, of the thousand-year-old Ben Ezra Synagogue in Fustat, the medieval core of the city of Cairo; collected in 1896 these papers comprise 140,000 documents and texts written in Hebrew, Arabic, and several other languages by Jewish clerics, scholars, merchants, scribes, and ordinary people; these texts are an important source of information about, legal, social and economic relations; everyday life; and the development of Jewish thought and religious life under Muslim rule from the seventh to the thirteenth centuries; they include information whose geographic range extends from Spain to the Southeast Asia.

Abu Abd Allah Muhammad Ibn Battuta (1304 – circa 1378), *Rihlah* (Travels) — The best-known travel account of any era in Muslim history, by the widest-ranging Muslim traveler; In addition to describing travels from Morocco to China and from Kilwa to the Volga River during the years 1325–1354, Ibn Battuta's *Rihlah* provides descriptions of religious life and expressions, social customs, everyday life, political and economic relations, and topography.

Ibn Jubayr (1145–1217), *Rihlah* (Travels) — An account of a pilgrimage to Makkah, during the course of which the writer left his native city of Granada, Spain, in 1183 and visited Sardinia, Sicily, Egypt, Iraq, Syria, and Palestine; his account provides glimpses of Baghdad in decline, conditions for Muslims in Norman Sicily, Cairo during the reign of Salah al-Din (Saladin), and the Holy Land during the Crusades, as well as extensive descriptions of the Hejaz and the pilgrimage rites; Ibn Jubayr's *Rihlah* was well known among later Muslim writers, and served as an often unacknowledged source for later Rihlah authors.

Yaqut Hamawi (1179–1229), *Mu'jam al-Buldan* (Dictionary of Countries) — A work describing in alphabetical order all the towns, countries and notable places on which information was available to the well-traveled Yaqut, this dictionary provides the physical description, mathematical geography, historical information, and ethnography of each place and gives detailed descriptions of Muslim lands from Spain to Central Asia and India during the thirteenth century; its major significance lies in its description of Muslim culture and prosperity just before the destruction wrought by the Mongol invasions.

CHAPTER FIVE

SOCIAL CLASS SYSTEM AND THE ECONOMY

by MAHMOOD IBRAHIM

CONTENTS

CHRONOLOGY
162

OVERVIEW
166

TOPICS IN SOCIAL CLASS SYSTEM AND THE ECONOMY

Agriculture
and Pastoralism 168

Crops and Regional
Character 169

Financing a Khilafah 170

Artisans, Manufacturing,
and Commerce 171

Guidebook for the Muhtasib 175

The Class System
and Social Change 176

Peace Treaty 176

Converts and Social
Integration 182

Ethnic Diversity 183

The Decentralization
of Society 184

Urban Occupations 185

SIGNIFICANT PEOPLE

Al-Zahir Baybars 190

Abu al-Fadl Ja'far ibn 'Ali
al-Dimashqi 191

Harun al-Rashid. 191

Salah al-Din al-Ayyubi 192

'Umar ibn 'Abd al-'Aziz. 192

'Umar ibn al-Khattab 193

DOCUMENTARY SOURCES
194

Sidebars and tables are listed in italics.

622
- The Prophet Muhammad leaves Makkah (Mecca) and settles in the northern oasis town of Yathrib, later known as Madinah. Later Khalifah 'Umar ibn al-Khattab (ruled 634–644) designates 622 as the first in the Islamic calendar.

630
- After Makkah surrenders to the forces of Muhammad, most Makkans embrace Islam, marking the beginning of the Prophet's establishment of authority over western Arabia.

632
- The Prophet Muhammad dies after a brief illness, and his longtime companion Abu Bakr becomes his successor, later known as khalifah (caliph).

632-656
- A period of Arab-Islamic expansion is inaugurated under Abu Bakr and continues under the "Four Rightly Guided Khalifahs."

634-644
- During the reign of Khalifah 'Umar ibn al-Khattab, Muslims found the military garrison cities of Basrah and Kufah in Iraq and Fustat (later Cairo) in Egypt, which later become provincial capitals and important Muslim cultural centers.

656-661
- The First Civil War results in a division in Muslim society that leads to the formation of two Islamic sects, the Shi'a (Shi'ites) and the Kharijites, each of which later splits again. (The most important division among the Shi'ites occurred in the eighth century with the formation of two major subsects, the Imamis and the Ismai'lis. The majority of modern Muslims are Sunnis, a sect that develops by the ninth century.

661-750
- The Umayyad Dynasty extends Muslim rule from Central Asia to Spain. During their rule believers in Islamic universalism (the brotherhood of all Muslims) challenged the Umayyads' policies, particularly those according lower social status to non-Arab converts to Islam. The resulting social tension and opposition to the Umayyads' expansionist policies eventually lead to the outbreak of revolts.

685-705
- Umayyad khalifah Abd al-Malik introduces far-reaching administrative and financial reforms that lead to the emergence of Arabic as the language of administration and culture and the unification and standardization of coinage, which gives merchants greater freedom of movement with the growing khilafah (caliphate).

717-720
- During his short reign Umayyad khalifah 'Umar ibn Abd al-Aziz introduces social and fiscal reforms intended to remove social distinctions among Muslims. These reforms are short lived, but the principles he advocates become the slogans of an underground movement that builds secret coalitions to topple the increasingly unpopular Umayyads.

* Denotes Circa Date

747–750
- Led by Abu Muslim, the Abbasid revolution is proclaimed in the eastern province of Khurasan. With Umayyad armies unable to contain the revolt, Abbasid troops march westward toward Damascus, defeating the Umayyads and putting an end to their dynasty.

750–1258
- The Abbasid dynasty rules the Muslim world. During this period Muslim society grows as more converts embraced Islam, and Muslims make major achievements in the sciences, the arts, and literature.

754–775
- The second Abbasid khalifah, al-Mansur, establishes the capital city Baghdad as the center of the khilafah.

785–809
- During the reign of Harun al-Rashid, known as the golden age of Islam, the Abbasid dynasty reaches its high point. Harun corresponds with Charlemagne, ruler of the Holy Roman Empire in western Europe, and an exchange of gifts and ambassadors takes place.

813–833
- During his twenty-year reign, al-Ma'mun, a learned scholar who often participates in the debates he hosts at his palace, attempts to introduce state-sponsored dogma by supporting the rationalist-philosophical doctrines of the Mu'tazila.

830
- Khalifah al-Ma'mun establishes the Bayt al-Hikmah, a school, library, and museum where scholars devote themselves to translating Greek and Indian works on science and philosophy.

847–861
- During his reign, al-Mutawakkil reverses al-Ma'mun's policies favoring the rationalist interpretation of Islam in favor of traditional and literal interpretations. He also introduces the practice of *iqta'*—granting military commanders and their soldiers the tax revenues from certain lands instead of paying them state salaries—a method of taxation that eventually leads to the decentralization of the Abbasid khilafah and the rise of provincial dynasties of governors.

861
- After the death of al-Mutawakkil, a military takeover ushers in nearly a century of military rule.

945
- The Buyids, an Iranian military dynasty and followers of Shi'ism, take over Baghdad but keep the Abbasid khalifahs (caliphs) as figureheads. The decline of agriculture during their rule, which lasts until 1055, may be traced to their abuse of the system of *iqta'* and constant fighting among rival factions, which also disrupts trade.

* Denotes Circa Date

SOCIAL CLASS SYSTEM AND THE ECONOMY

1055
- Recruited initially as military men by the various governors, the Saljuk Turks take Baghdad from the Buyids and rule until 1118.

1071
- The Saljuk Turks defeat the Byzantines at the battle of Malazgirt (Manzikert) in eastern Anatolia, opening up Anatolia to Turkish tribes that started the process of Turkification and Islamization of the territory.

1072-1092
- Wazir Nizam al-Mulk, head of the civilian administration of the Saljuks, regularizes the practice of *iqta'* and establishes colleges in the large cities under their control. The best known is the Nizamiyya of Baghdad.

1096
- The first wave of Crusaders from western Europe arrive in the Holy Land. The Crusader period lasts nearly two hundred years.

1099
- Jerusalem falls to the Crusaders, who establish a Latin Christian kingdom there.

1128
- The Zengid rulers of northern Iraq begin an offensive against the Crusaders. Themselves Turks, the Zengids employ a large number of Kurdish military men in their army, the best known of whom is Salah al-Din (Saladin).

1171-1252
- The Ayyubid dynasty, founded by Salah al-Din, unifies Syria and Egypt and successfully contains the Crusaders to a sliver of territory in the Levant.

1187
- At the Battle of Hattin in northern Palestine, Salah al-Din defeats army Crusaders and retakes Jerusalem. His victory sparks the Third Crusade, led by Richard the Lionhearted.

1258
- The army of the Mongol ruler Hulagu, grandson of Genghis Khan, sacks and loots Baghdad for three days, causing great death and destruction.

1260
- The Mongols advance against Syria and push southward toward Egypt. A hastily convened army of the Mamluks, who have just taken power in Egypt, blocks the advance of the Mongols and hands them their first defeat near 'Ayn Jalut (Goliath's Well). The Mamluks go on to defeat the Mongols again in 1277 and 1281 and to force them to retreat toward Persia, where they establish the Il-Khanid, which lasts until 1349.

* DENOTES CIRCA DATE

1262-1517

• The Mamluks rule Egypt, Syria, and much of western Asia, contributing to the consolidation of Arabic and Arabic culture in the Middle East, at the same time as Turkish becomes the dominant language in Anatolia (present-day Turkey), Persian becomes the language of the land east of the Zagros mountains (Iran and eastward).

1291

• Al-Ashraf Khalil defeats the Crusaders, who evacuate their last stronghold, Acre in northern Palestine, ending the Crusader presence in the eastern Mediterranean.

1453

• Ottoman Turks take Constantinople, causing the fall of the Byzantine Empire.

1497-1499

• Portuguese explorer Vasco da Gama commands an expedition around the Cape of Good Hope into the Indian Ocean, reaching the southwestern coast of India in May 1498 before starting back to Portugal. In efforts to block the Portuguese who appear in the Persian Gulf and the Red Sea after da Gama's successful voyage, the Ottomans move into eastern Anatolia and Syria. By 1517 the Ottomans have defeated the Mamluks and incorporated much of the Middle East and North Africa into their huge empire, which lasts until 1922.

* **DENOTES CIRCA DATE**

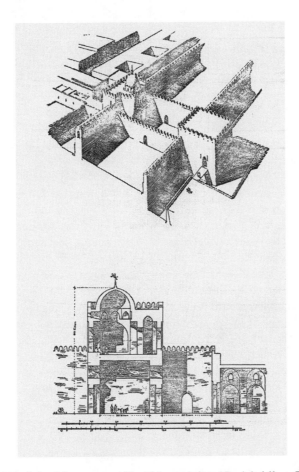

Artist's reconstructions of the gates to Abbasids' round city of Baghdad (from Friedrich Sarre and Ernst Herzfeld, *Archäologische Reise im Euphrat- und Tigris-Gebiet,* volume 2, 1920)

OVERVIEW

Pre-Islamic Arabia. On the eve of the rise of Islam, the society of Makkah was becoming increasingly diversified as more and more nomadic tribes settled in and around the city. Makkan mercantile activities flourished in the Near East, giving rise to the development of a social-class system. As the nomadic and Makkan societies lost their homogeneity, social values based on kinship bonds began to give way to those based on the ownership of capital. In the period of transition during the second half of the sixth century, social disequilibrium began to weaken the effectiveness of many of the institutions that helped Makkah prosper, including the *haram*, sacred center of the Ka'bah, an already important place of worship. If such trends had continued, they would have threatened the social stability and commercial importance of Makkah.

The Rise of Islam. The future prophet of Islam, Muhammad, was born and reared in such conditions. Muhammad began his prophetic career when he reached forty, around the year 610. Having preached with limited success and having faced the deaths of his wife and first believer, Khadijah, and his uncle and protector, Abu Talib, in 618, Muhammad was offered the opportunity to relocate to the city of Yathrib (later Madinah). This event, called the *hijrah*, took place in 622 and was later the event chosen to mark the beginning of the Islamic calendar. In Madinah the Prophet began to lay the foundation of Islamic society and expounded the details of the faith as in the Madinan *surahs* (chapters of the Qur'an, the holy text of the Muslims). Other than the religious dogma called *shahada* and prayer, fasting, pilgrimage, and charitable contributions (collectively known as the pillars of the faith), the Prophet provided three basic institutions that became the basis of Islamic society and civilization. These were divine and prophetic authority, the institution of the *ummah* (the community), and a means of distributing wealth that guaranteed social and economic mobility. Having succeeded in establishing his authority and proving the efficacy of his message through the increasing number of his followers, the Prophet was finally able in 630 to win Makkah, with its sacred center, for Islam. He also succeeded in converting influential Makkan merchant leaders.

Expansion and Integration. In 632, soon after his victory at Makkah, the Prophet died, and the nascent Islamic community elected Abu Bakr, Muhammad's longtime companion, to succeed him in political authority. Given the title of "Successor of the Prophet," later known as khalifah (caliph), Abu Bakr (ruled 632–634) had the enormous tasks of keeping the community together and of directing the initial efforts to expand Muslim control outside of the Arabian peninsula. The second khalifah, 'Umar ibn al-Khattab (ruled 634–644), laid the foundation of the Islamic state, especially after the successes of the Muslims against the Byzantine and Sasanid armies in 636–637.

New Cities. One of 'Umar's most significant acts was the building of the cities of Kufah, Basrah, and Fustat. Founded primarily to house Arab troops and their families, these garrison cities immediately became the cosmopolitan urban centers in which Islamic civilization was developed. They were multicultural cities where Muslims came into contact with diverse ethnic and religious populations. As conversions to Islam began to accelerate, to be a Muslim was no longer virtually synonymous with being Arab. (Even earlier, Greeks, Persians, and Egyptians had converted to Islam). The entry of non-Arabs into Islam, in fact, became a major issue and a significant source of social tension during the first century of Islamic history, especially during the Umayyad khilafah (caliphate, 661–750). Most Umayyad rulers encouraged Arabism through their various policies. During this period, society became divided into various social classes: Arabs as the elite rulers, the dhimmis, or People of the Book (Christians, Jews, and, later, Zoroastrians), the mawali (non-Arab converts to Islam), and at the bottom slaves who were captured during the military campaigns. Many considered such a structure—especially the status of the Mawali—to be contradictory to Islamic teachings. This class system and other policies of the Umayyads led to the rise of opposition groups. Revolution broke out in 747, and three years later the Abbasid khilafah (750–1258) laid the foundation for the transformation of Islamic society. Once social and other restrictions on non-Arab Muslims were removed, more and more ethnic groups became Muslims. Within a fifty-year period fully 45 percent of Persians became Muslims. Berbers in North Africa, Spaniards in Andalusia, Turks in Central Asia, and blacks in West and East Africa also embraced Islam and became part of the thriving multi-ethnic, multicultural world of Islam.

Decentralization. Profound changes in Islamic society took place during the more than five-hundred-year rule of the Abbasids. Arabs no longer dominated the ruling elite. As Persians and others became Muslims, they also shared in the governing structure, some becoming nearly as powerful as the khalifahs who employed them. The military also began to reflect the diverse ethnicity of the khilafah. After the ninth century, Turks began to form the dominant element in the military. The gradual erosion of the khalifahs' authority and the rise of the power of military commanders who assumed the title of sultan began during the tenth century. Khalifahs were increasingly relegated to the status of figureheads while the sultans became the true rulers of the realm. As this development became entrenched, the government of the khilafah was no longer centralized. Provinces began to assume greater autonomy, and petty provincial dynasties emerged. This political fragmentation led to weakness, exposing the land of the khilafah to outside attacks, such as the Reconquista in Spain and the Crusades, which brought invaders to eastern Mediterranean lands in 1096 and continued until 1271, with the last Crusader stronghold falling twenty years later.

Social Classes. Another significant social change that started after the Abbasids took power was the gradual transformation of the status of farmers and the rural population. As the value of land increased and agriculture became the main source of revenue, agricultural producers were required to stay on the land and became more like the serfs of feudal Europe. Because of this requirement the military had to recruit more Turks as soldiers. Distinctions between various ethnic and religious communities began to break down, as is demonstrated by the peasant revolt in the Egyptian delta (832), where for the first time Muslims and Christians revolted together against the taxation policies of the khilafah. The situation for farmers became even more difficult after 860 with the introduction of *iqta'* (land assignments) allowing a member of the military to collect tax revenues on a piece of land as a means of paying his wages, and more rural revolts followed.

Social Divisions. The gradual effect of these social changes is the larger division of the society into the *khassa* (the elite) and the *'amma* (commoners or subjects). Such a division became strict as the khilafah continued to decline and became dominated by Persian concepts of rule and by the Turkish military. There were also divisions based on geographic location as society became divided into urban, rural, and nomadic sectors. Urban populations, especially in Baghdad and other major cities, were divided into neighborhoods, and tensions between the rich and the poor threatened the stability of the cities. Urban gangs and urban unrest were not uncommon.

The Scholarly Class. Despite the rigid social structure, one avenue for social mobility remained open: to become a member of the learned class, the *ulama'*. This class grew more influential, especially those who studied the religious sciences and became lawyers, judges, and formulators of Islamic dogma. The population of physicians, philosophers, mathematicians, geographers, and other scholars increased as the production of paper began in Baghdad and as translations from Greek and other languages increased the availability of books on various sciences. The state encouraged translations, and rulers and prominent officials built libraries and schools for translations, including Dar al-Hikma, founded by Khalifah al-Ma'mun (ruled 812–832). Later, especially after the Saljuk Turks took over Baghdad in 1055, advanced schools or colleges called *madrasahs* were founded in various cities, including the Nizamiyya in Baghdad. The patrons of these schools lavished them with *waqf* (endowments) for their upkeep and provided salaries for teachers and students alike.

TOPICS IN SOCIAL CLASS SYSTEM AND THE ECONOMY

AGRICULTURE AND PASTORALISM

Before Islam. Ancient peoples knew the Arabian peninsula as Arabia Felix, or happy Arabia. Such a description originates from the heavy presence of Arabian merchants in Mediterranean ports. These merchants traded rare and exotic products imported from places like East Africa, India, and China. The southern part of the Arabian peninsula (present-day Yemen and Oman) is home to the frankincense plant, an aromatic shrub whose resin was burned in official and religious ceremonies. Ancient trade in this product was widespread, including China and Greece. It would be misleading to describe the whole of the peninsula as "Happy Arabia" or to imagine that most of its inhabitants were merchants. Arabian society was as complex and varied as the environment in which it evolved. These social and geographic variations eventually influenced later Islamic societies throughout western Asia and North Africa. Indeed, wherever Islam reached, the society that emerged embodied some of the influences from pre-Islamic Arabs.

Agriculture. The Arabian peninsula is a vast area, nearly one-fifth the size of the United States. Most of the peninsula receives little rainfall. Only in the mountainous area of Yemen was there enough rainfall to allow for the development of agriculture. In this region settled, rural communities tilled the land and tended frankincense trees. Towns and cities gradually developed and led eventually to the rise of small states ruled by kings and other officials.

Pastoralism. While the Yemenis were fortunate enough to have enough rainfall for farming, the majority of the Arabian peninsula remained parched for most of the year. When rain came, it was sparse, except for rare, often devastating flash floods. In some scattered areas, water was available from springs, around which oases developed. These

A nomadic encampment; illumination from a fifteenth-century manuscript for
Album of the Conqueror (Topkapi Library, Istanbul)

limited resources fostered the development of a tribal society largely dependent on its animals (sheep, goats, horses, and camels). Because they could not find enough pasture in one place to support them year-round, these tribes were forced to move about in search of fresh pastures for their animals; that is, they became nomadic. Living in temporary encampments in the proximity of oases or near connecting trade routes, they traded among each other at fairs and festivals held during certain months of the year. Each tribe developed a pattern of migration within a somewhat recognizable zone and became fiercely protective of its area and resources, especially watering places.

Agriculture. Since the population of western Asia had always been predominantly rural and agricultural, it was natural that this crucial activity was sustained and encouraged under Muslim rule. From the beginning, the khilafah encouraged agriculture by granting uncultivated land to be reclaimed for farming. The state invested in building canals, dams, and dikes to secure a water supply and extend the area available for cultivation. One of the earliest and most effective ways in which the khilafah increased the amount of land available for cultivation was building new cities—such as Basrah and Kufah during the reign of 'Umar ibn al-Khattab (ruled 634–644)—away from established agricultural areas and near the edge of the desert. This practice required the digging of canals from the Euphrates River to bring water to those cities and thus increased arable land. Generally a person who received such land, called *mawat* (dead land), was exempted from taxation for several years as an incentive to undertake reclamation efforts. To encourage their production, certain agricultural products—such as dyestuffs like indigo and other commercially desirable crops—were also exempted from taxation. The state generally graduated produce taxes according to the investment that went into growing a crop. For example, the tax on rain-fed crops was higher than that for crops that had to be artificially irrigated. Products that had to be transported long distances to a market were taxed at a lower rate than crops produced nearby. An important development in medieval Islamic agriculture was the introduction of new crops and plants that were disseminated all over the Muslim world, including citrus fruits, cotton, rice, and sugarcane. As the khilafah expanded, Arabs in newly conquered areas did not engage in agriculture at first because they were serving in the military, but they gradually settled on the land and became farmers or resided in cities and became urbanized. From 750 onward, ethnic or religious distinctions in the rural population gradually diminished, disappearing altogether in subsequent centuries.

Land and Revenue. After the Abbasids ended the wars of expansion in 750, the state and its army could no longer generate revenue from sources such as spoils of war, booty, or new territories to tax. Rather, all revenue had to be generated internally. Land values immediately increased, and it became necessary to keep people at work cultivating such a resource for state revenue. Eventually, as the decline of the

CROPS AND REGIONAL CHARACTER

In *al-Muqaddimah* (1375–1378, revised 1378–1406) the renowned Muslim historian Ibn Khaldun (1332–1406), who has often been called the Father of Sociology, suggested a connection between the diet of a region and its inhabitants' physical and mental characteristics:

Differences with regard to abundance and scarcity of food in the various inhabited regions and how they affect the human body and character: It should be known that not all the temperate zones have an abundance of food, nor do all their inhabitants lead a comfortable life. In some parts, the inhabitants enjoy an abundance of grain, seasonings, wheat, and fruits, because the soil is well balanced and favourable to plants and there is an abundant civilization. And then, in other parts, the land is strewn with rocks, and no seeds or herbs grow at all. There, the inhabitants have a very hard time. Instances of such people are the inhabitants of the Hijaz and the Yemen, or the Veiled Sinhajah who live in the desert of the Maghrib on the fringes of the sandy wastes which lie between the Berbers and the Sudanese Negroes [West Africans]. All of them lack grain and seasonings. Their nourishment and food consist of milk and meat. Another such people are the Arabs who roam the waste regions. They may get grain and seasonings from the hills, but this is the case only at certain times and is possible only under the eyes of the militia which protects (those parts). Whatever they get is little, because they have little money. They obtain no more than the bare necessity, and sometimes less, and in no case enough for a comfortable or abundant life. They are mostly found restricted to milk, which is for them a very good substitute for wheat. In spite of this, the desert people who lack grain and seasonings are found to be healthier in body and better in character than the hill people who have plenty of everything. Their complexions are clearer, their bodies cleaner, their figures more perfect, their character less intemperate, and their minds keener as far as knowledge and perception are concerned. There is a great difference in this respect between the Arabs and Berbers (on the one hand), and the Veiled (Berbers) and the inhabitants of the hills (on the other). This fact is known to those who have investigated the matter.

Source: 'Abd al-Rahman Ibn Khaldun, *The Muqaddimah: An Introduction to History*, translated by Franz Rosenthal, edited and abridged by N. J. Dawood (Princeton: Princeton University Press, 1967), p. 65.

khilafah began after the tenth century, the rural population and the peasantry were gradually reduced to a status similar to that of serfdom; that is, although legally free, they were bound to the land and became like sharecroppers working largely for the benefit of powerful landlords. While previously Muslim society had been dynamic, providing a great deal of mobility with plenty of opportunities for the individual to gain wealth and status, society became static, and upward mobility became much more difficult.

Policy Shifts. The increase in the importance of land and landlords caused a gradual shift in the orientation and emphasis of the government and of its bureaucracy. Intellectuals and members of the *ulama'* class, who formulated legal opinion and interpreted religious dogma, began to express a viewpoint in line with the interest of the landlords. While maintaining their economic power, merchants and artisans gradually lost their ability to influence government policies or legal and religious interpretation. This trend is most clear in the gradual diminution of rationalist philosophy and in the increase in traditional and literal interpretation of the Qur'an and Islamic dogma. The often-heated debate between the two sides is partially reflected in the efforts of the Khalifah al-Ma'mun (ruled 813–833) when in 832 he declared his support for the rationalist-philosophical doctrines of the Mu'tazila and insisted that an examination be instituted to determine whether employees of the state and public figures adhered to those concepts. This examination, known as the *Mihna*, was given for nearly thirty years before it was abandoned in 853 by al-Mutawakkil, who introduced a radical shift in policy, favoring those who advocated a fixed, literal interpretation of the Qur'an and Islamic dogma. At the same time, al-Mutawakkil removed members of the previous administration and brought in officials who were either landlords or connected to the landed class.

Iqta'. Al-Mutawakkil also introduced the practice of *iqta'*—granting to military commanders and their soldiers the tax revenues from certain farmers' lands in lieu of state salaries. This system evolved and lasted under one name or another until the nineteenth century. The Mongols called it *suyurghal*, and later the Ottomans called it *timar*. In all of these cases the commanders and their troops did not receive the land to own as private property; rather, they were given the right to collect the taxes on that property in lieu of salary, in a system that historians have called "tax farming." While initially this system may have been efficient, abuses such as overtaxation, repetitive taxation, and neglect of the agricultural infrastructure soon appeared to plague the society and the state.

Ilja'. As *iqta'* became widespread, small farmers felt insecure about the exactions of these tax collectors and began joining their lands to those of more powerful neighbors in exchange for protection. Eventually this arrangement, called *ilja'*, resulted in small farmers' losing ownership of their plot of land, after which they either abandoned rural life to move to a city or became landless peasants who worked the land but did not own it, in arrangements similar to sharecropping.

The Plantation Economy. Rural landlords were so well connected during the Abbasid period, especially after al-Mutawakkil's khilafah (847–861), that they eventually amassed huge estates, and a plantation economy began to appear in the mid tenth century. Many of these large plantations produced cash crops such as rice, cotton, and sugarcane. While this system benefited large landowners, however, it was instituted at the expense of small farmers,

---

FINANCING A KHILAFAH

During the Umayyad khilafah (661–750) state revenues came from several sources. The state treasury received one-fifth of the spoils of war, mostly in the form of movable booty, which was called *fai'*. In addition, when a city surrendered to Muslim troops and negotiated a treaty with them, it often agreed to pay an annual tribute. The khilafah also levied taxes. Non-Muslims paid *jizya* (poll tax) and *kharaj* (agricultural produce tax). Levied on able-bodied males, usually between eighteen and forty-five years old, *jizya* was regarded as payment for military protection, in lieu of military service, and the amount varied according to the wealth of the individual. The *kharaj* varied according to the type of crop, the distance from the market, and the type of irrigation used to cultivate it. Some crops were exempted from taxation. Arab Muslims paid the *'ushr* (tithe) and obligatory alms called *zakat* (one of the pillars of Islam). The state revenue was redistributed in stipends to those who participated in fighting, who were paid in kind and in cash. During the first decades in which this system prevailed, almost all Arabs received a stipend in the amount established by Khalifah 'Umar ibn al-Khattab (ruled 634–644), based generally on the individual's participation in the service of Islam.

Source: D. C. Dennets, *Conversion and Poll-Tax in Early Islam* (Cambridge, Mass.: Harvard University Press, 1950).

---

and slaves, especially from East Africa, were imported to clear marshes and prepare the land for agriculture.

Peasant Revolts. It is important to remember that income from land was always nearly 70 percent of the revenue of the state. Such moneys were not always extracted willingly from the rural populations, and after 750, when the exploitation of internal revenue sources increased, rural-based peasant revolts broke out frequently, first in the provinces and then in Iraq, the heartland of the Abbasid khilafah. Four revolts stand out as particularly significant. The revolt of Babak in Azerbaijan lasted for nearly thirty years as Abbasid khalifahs sent one army after another to Azerbaijan, the rugged mountainous region of northwest Iran, until Babak was finally defeated in 838. In 869 the Zanj—mostly slaves from East Africa who were brought to Iraq to clear the salt marshes north of Basrah to create large cash-crop plantations—established a state around the port of Basrah on the Persian Gulf. This state lasted until 883, when it was finally defeated by Abbasid troops. The third revolt was that of Hamdan Qarmat and his followers in Syria and Iraq during the early tenth century. His successors went on to establish a state in eastern Arabia that lasted more than a century. The Bashmuric revolt in the Egyptian delta in 832 is significant because it was made up of Christian and

Muslim peasants who rebelled jointly against the taxation policies of the Abbasids. The frequency and intensity of peasant revolts exposed the weakness of the central government and its institutions.

Agricultural Decline. By the tenth century, with peasant rebellions against *iqta'* becoming more frequent and urban insecurity increasing, the state began to recruit central Asian Turkic pastoral groups to serve in the military and act as an arm of the state in putting down the rebels. This practice ultimately had a major impact on the political and economic structure of the Muslim world. The Turks, led by a powerful family known as the Saljuks, relied primarily on *iqta'* to pay their troops. Politically, the growth of a Turkic military eventually led to loss of political influence for the khalifah (caliph) and his civilian administration, while the military gained strength and gradually assumed autonomy in the provinces. By 1055 the Turks had become the dominant element in the military and politics. The rise of the military led to the political fragmentation of the Islamic world. The agriculture of western Asia suffered tremendously during the centuries of military rule. Having introduced and disseminated new plants and cash crops and reached unprecedented levels of agricultural productivity and wealth, farmers and landlords witnessed the decline, or at least the stagnation, of agricultural production from the eleventh century onward. Several factors led to this situation. Since the army was primarily preoccupied with military matters and viewed the land only as a source of income, they neglected the upkeep of the agricultural infrastructure—including dams, dikes, and canals—which eventually led to smaller crops and, thus, lower *iqta'* revenues. Instead of repairing the infrastructure, army commanders demanded more land for taxation. Increasingly large areas of land lost productivity, forcing the owners either to sell the land or abandon it altogether. Diminished revenue resulting from neglect and corruption prompted commanders to demand either additional tracts or the replacement of their initial grant. The double burden of spiraling demand for revenue and the disregarded needs of the agricultural infrastructure impoverished the countryside, and the rural population reduced the revenue of the central government in favor of Turkish army commanders. The system of *iqta'* made the central government far weaker, especially as most of the revenue remained in the hands of military commanders. In time the practice of land assignment was applied to whole provinces, depending on the rank and importance of the recipient. While these assignments were not given as private property, soon they were passed on as inheritance, encouraging the formation of petty dynasties in the provinces. These conditions were exacerbated by the constant conflicts among the Turkish lords who had taken over southwest Asia by the middle of the eleventh century. An alarming aspect of this conflict was the deliberate destruction of agricultural infrastructure as a military strategy—such as the breaking of a dam in order to flood out enemy soldiers downstream. The decline of agriculture continued

for centuries, reaching its peak during the Mamluk period (1250–1517). When the Black Death struck around 1350, it devastated huge areas of southwest Asia and North Africa, wiping out entire villages. Large sectors of the rural population returned to nomadic, pastoral ways of life, with the consequent decline of cities and their rural hinterlands and a breakdown of civil order.

Sources:

Daniel G. Bates and Amal Rassam, *Peoples and Cultures of the Middle East,* second edition (Saddle River, N.J.: Prentice Hall, 2001).

Michael Dols, *The Black Death in the Middle East* (Princeton: Princeton University Press, 1977).

Philip Khuri Hitti, *History of the Arabs,* tenth edition (New York: St. Martin's Press, 1974).

Peter M. Holt, *The Age of the Crusades: The Near East from the Eleventh Century to 1517* (London & New York: Longman, 1985).

Albert H. Hourani, *A History of the Arab People* (Cambridge & New York: Cambridge University Press, 1991).

Andrew M. Watson, *Agricultural Innovation in the Early Islamic World: The Diffusion of Crops and Farming Techniques, 700–1100* (Cambridge: Cambridge University Press, 1983).

ARTISANS, MANUFACTURING, AND COMMERCE

Pre-Islamic Trade. Before the advent of Islam, a significant commercial culture developed on the basis of agricultural production and trade in the surplus, especially frankincense and other aromatic products such as myrrh and balsam. Other important commodities for local and regional trade included wine, grains, leather goods, and textiles. Writing sometime during the first century C.E., a Greek sailor named Hippalus described the ports of call along the Red Sea and listed these commodities among products a merchant could buy and sell at a profit.

Economic Development under the Khilafahs. After the death of the Prophet Muhammad in 632 and the establishment of the Islamic khilafah, the economy of the growing empire came to depend on three factors. The basic pillar was agricultural production. In fact, most of the areas that the khilafah controlled were rural and agricultural. The second factor was artisanal production and manufacturing, and the third was commerce. Several factors helped artisans and manufacturers in the Muslim world to thrive and to produce high-quality commodities, including clothing and textiles, leather goods, carpets, glass, metalwares, pottery, and paper. These products and others were sought after everywhere Muslim merchants attended markets. One factor was the presence of an ancient and well-established tradition of manufacturing in cities that came under Muslim control, such as Alexandria, Damascus, and Antioch. These cities had already-established glassmaking, metalworking, and textile traditions of long duration. Cottage industries and courtly workshops for the production of textiles and leather goods had also existed in pre-Islamic Arabia. Skilled workers received a major boost from Muslim expansion, which was accompanied by an enormous circulation of wealth in the form of stipends and land grants. With so much money in circulation, the buying power of each individual was enhanced. People could afford not only basic commodities and foodstuffs but also luxury products

Farm laborers cultivating medicinal plants; illumination from *Kitab ad-Diryad* (Book of Antidotes), a late twelfth-century Muslim medical manuscript (Bibliothèque Nationale, Paris)

imported from China, India, and East Africa at substantially increased rates. The port of Basrah quickly became the most important in the Muslim world and remained so for centuries to come.

Marketplaces. Not everything, however, was imported. Demand for manufactured goods increased substantially with the foundation and growth of cities under Muslim rule. This demand spurred local production, especially because the Muslims took over well-established economic centers such as Damascus, Alexandria, and Antioch. Artisans had a ready market for their products, which were sold in centralized and specialized markets in each city. Neighborhood markets are also known to have existed, and markets—especially for livestock—were set up outside towns on weekly, monthly, or seasonal bases. And with the production of leather goods and textiles already widespread in Yemen, interregional trade became very lucrative for merchants and producers alike. One of the largest markets was associated with the annual pilgrimage, or hajj, not only in and around Makkah but also in the major staging areas for pilgrimage caravans, such as Baghdad, Damascus, and Cairo. Along pilgrimage routes, markets were set up to provision the caravans. Pilgrims brought wares and goods to exchange for provisions and foodstuffs such as dried fruits, dates, raisins, and olive oil. Thus, several months ahead of the pilgrimage season, merchants descended on important cities to buy rugs, carpets, woven textiles, brocades, other furnishings, knives, swords, pottery, glass, and ceramic wares. Local and regional products—as well as those from dis-

tant areas of the Muslim world such as eastern Asia, Africa, and Europe—were traded in these markets.

Decline. It is important to recognize that artisanal activity and manufacturing were closely tied to agriculture and depended on political stability. The decline of cotton production, for example, greatly impacted the production of textiles in a given area. Furthermore, political instability and regional conflict hindered the movement of products and decreased the demand for goods. Such conditions existed during the fourteenth and fifteenth centuries, when products that Muslims had exported to Europe—such as glass, pottery, and textiles—began to be imported into the region from budding European manufacturing centers through the activity of Italian merchants. European textiles began to compete with local products and imitate their design and production techniques. Some of the early European centers were in former Muslim territories such as Sicily. Eventually low import duties imposed on European merchants made European textiles competitive with local goods and led to the decline of local textile production.

Commerce. Commercial activity reached unprecedented heights before 1500. Muslim merchants linked much of the Eastern Hemisphere in a network of sea and overland trade routes, facilitating the movement of goods to meet the demands of a growing urban population with a rising standard of living. Muslim merchants were involved in long-distance trade as well as local or regional exchange of luxury products or staples and ordinary foodstuffs. The greatest wealth seems to have been accumulated by merchants engaged in long-distance trade because prices increased with the distance a merchant traveled and the risks he encountered along the journey, such as storms, shipwrecks, and pirates at sea, and bandits, marauders, and political instability on land. Several factors allowed mercantile activities to thrive. First and foremost was a favorable social attitude to merchants and their activity. Contrary to most ancient and medieval civilizations, the Islamic world respected merchants. This positive attitude stems partly from the fact that pre-Islamic Arabian wealth was not based on agriculture, as was the case with the Romans and the Persians, where the landed nobility held power and social influence. Islam was founded in a mercantile environment, and the Prophet Muhammad himself was a merchant. Unlike the medieval Christian Church, Islam did not frown on trade. The Qur'an includes many references to the permissibility of trade as an economic activity, such as: "Allah hath permitted trade and forbidden usury . . . " (2: 275); "Behold! In the creation of the heavens and the earth; in the alternation of the night and the day; in the sailing of ships through the ocean for the profit of mankind . . ." (2: 164); "And the cattle hath He created. . . . they bear your loads for you unto a land you could not reach save with great difficulty to yourselves. Lo! Your Lord is full of pity, merciful" (16: 5–7). The khilafah established after Islamic expansion was founded and largely administered by people with experience as merchants. Therefore, from the beginning of Muslim society, the ideology and the state favored merchants, placing no obstacles to their material or social advancement. Having established mercantile expertise, Arabs, and later other Muslim merchants, took advantage of favorable conditions to increase their activities, wealth, and influence.

Trade Routes. Another factor that helped commerce was the location of southwest Asia as a link among the three continents of the Eastern Hemisphere. With the expansion of the khilafah, the most important trade routes of antiquity came under Muslim control, as well as regional trade networks—such as Mediterranean shipping lanes, the Red Sea, and the Persian Gulf routes that connected Europe, Africa, and Asia—and many ports, such as Basrah and Alexandria, which thrived on the international trade. Muslims also controlled overland routes, such as the silk roads that originated near Beijing and terminated in Antioch, Syria. Finally, North African Muslim merchants traversed the Sahara to reach the gold-producing regions of West Africa and to trade with states such as Ghana and Mali, especially after the eleventh century. The Muslims' extensive trade network combined with their religious and cultural motives to travel—such as the hajj and the search for knowledge and the bounty of Allah—to give merchants and their fellow travelers a primary role in the spread of Islam to areas that Muslim armies never reached, such as Southeast Asia and East and West Africa. Merchants were also largely responsible for the introduction and dissemination of many new plant species and crops. Mercantile activity was given a further boost when Sufis established their centers (zawiya) along trade routes to provide lodging and hospitality to merchants and their caravans. Rulers, governors, and other high officials built khans (hostels) in cities, and caravanserais (caravan staging and provisioning centers) on the outskirts of cities to facilitate commerce.

Trade Policies. From the beginning of the Islamic expansion, merchants were permitted to accompany Muslim armies, supplying soldiers with provisions or purchasing movable booty after battles ended. Encouraged to travel freely even during military campaigns, merchants were given protection and security as well as aman (safe conduct) to leave and enter Muslim domains. The Arab/Muslim expansion helped the merchants in two other ways: an enormous distribution of wealth and the resulting prosperity increased the buying power of the population and the rise of new Muslim cities, and an unprecedented growth of urbanization created ready markets to be supplied by merchants with locally produced goods or imported commodities. Merchants also benefited from state policies such as the standardization of coinage and the stabilization of the exchange rate between gold and silver. Such reforms, introduced by Umayyad khalifah Abd al-Malik (ruled 685–705), unified the markets stretching from Central Asia to Spain, making Muslim coinage one of the most widely accepted currencies during the period and allowing merchants to travel freely with the confidence that their merchandise would not lose value when transported from one region to another. Muslim merchants developed and disseminated many advanced mercantile practices, such as the use of a variety of partnerships, especially what came to be known in medieval Europe as the commenda, and the letter of credit, which acquired the name sakk, the root of the English word check. Many commercial practices based in Shari'ah, or Islamic law, were spread along the trade routes by Muslim merchants and influenced non-Muslim mercantile practices in Asia, Africa, and Europe. The commercial practice of double-entry bookkeeping using Arabic (Hindi) numerals led to their eclipse of Roman numerals in Europe.

Baghdad. The fact that the early centuries of the Abbasid khilafah are known as the golden age of Muslim civilization is largely because of the successful Muslim commercial activities that occurred after the revolution that brought the Abbasid rulers to power in 750. The building and layout of Baghdad, on which construction was completed in 762, is indicative of the enormous advantages provided to merchants. Tens of thousands of skilled workers and artisans were assembled for the enormous undertaking of building the government complex, the Round City, or Madinat al-Salaam, which was planned with the palace at the center surrounded by concentric rings of residences and streets lined with market arcades. During construction, forges were set up on the spot to mint coins with which the workers were paid on a daily basis. While bricks and mortar might be provided locally, much of the material that went into the construction was imported. Baghdad quickly became the most

Travelers Abu Zyd and al-Harith arriving in a Muslim village; illumination from a manuscript
for the *Maqamat* (Assemblies) of al-Hariri (Bibliothèque Nationale, Paris)

important commercial center of the Abbasid khilafah. Its markets were constantly enlarged, and new ones were added to keep up with the consumer demands of the growing population. To safeguard the market, the Abbasids introduced the institution of the *muhtasib*, a market-regulation officer who was usually a respected individual from the *ulama'* class and whose responsibilities included ensuring that proper weights and measures were used in transactions, that fair prices were charged by shopkeepers and merchants, and that the high quality of merchandise was maintained. Those who were found in violation were turned over to the police. During the heyday of Abbasid rule, merchants were not only influential in

the economy but also played important roles in the interpretation of Islam. Many merchants became part of the *ulama'* class, especially during the ninth century. Such power was especially evident during al-Ma'mun's khilafah (813–833), since he supported Mu'tazila doctrines, which seemed to favor merchants and artisans. The influence of the Mu'tazila remained strong during the khilafahs of al-Mu'tasim (833–842) and al-Wathiq (842–847). Their near monopoly of state offices was broken only by al-Mutawakkil (847–861).

Foreign Competition. In the following centuries, commercial activities continued to flourish despite merchants' loss of political influence. Muslims maintained uncontested

GUIDEBOOK FOR THE MUHTASIB

In the twelfth century al-Shayzari (died circa 1193) wrote a guidebook for *muhtasibs* (market inspectors) that included advice on ethical weighing practices:

The most accurate scale is that in which the two sides are equal, the pans are balanced and the hole for the attachment on either side of the center of the beam is one third of the thickness of the attachments. This hole should be one third of the way under the peg of the attachment, and two-thirds above it. This allows for the inclination of the scales by taking the tongue of the balance out of the beam of the attachment, and the pan will descend with the slightest weight. As for the scales from Damascus, the position of the hole for the attachment is different from what we have mentioned. Their inclination is allowed by putting the tongue into the beam of the attachment without the scale going down. The peg might be square, triangular or round. The best is the triangular one because it inclines with more sensitivity than the others.

The muhtasib must order those who use scales to wipe and clean them hourly of any oil or dirt, as a drop of oil may congeal on them and affect the weight.

The merchant must settle the scales before he begins to weigh and should place the merchandise on them gently, not dropping it into the pan from his raised hand, nor moving the edge of the pan with his thumb, as all of this is fraudulent.

Among the hidden swindles used with scales for weighing gold is for the merchant to put his hand in front of his face and to blow gently onto the pan containing the merchandise thus making it descend. The buyer will have his eyes on the scales and not on the mouth of their owner. The merchants also have ruses by which they give short weight when they hold the attachment for the scales. They also sometimes stick a piece of wax on the bottom of the pans and put the silver on it, then they put the weights on the other pan. In this way they take one or two habbas out of every dirham. . . .

The muhtasib must continually inspect the measures and see that the merchants do not make them smaller, for some of them pour gypsum on the bottom, which so adheres to it that it can hardly be noticed. There are others who smear the dregs of oil extracted from grains on the sides and bottom. Yet others take some sap of the fig tree and knead it with oil until it becomes like a cream, then they stick this on the inside of the measures and it cannot be noticed. Some merchants have a ruse they employ when they hold the measure which makes it give less. The muhtasib must therefore never cease to keep an eye on them. But God knows best.

Source: R. P. Buckley, trans., *The Book of the Islamic Market Inspector: Nihayat al-Rutba fi Talab al-Hisba (The Utmost Authority in the Pursuit of Hisba) by Abd al-Rahman b. Nasr al-Shayzari* (Oxford: Oxford University Press, 1999), pp. 43–45.

mastery of the commerce of western Asia and the Indian Ocean. This situation began to change in the eleventh century, in tandem with the decline of agriculture, artisanal activity, and manufacturing. Political instability and fragmentation and regional conflicts (especially those involving fleets of ships) gradually took their toll, and Muslim merchants began to lose their earlier advantages. Competitors, especially merchants from prominent Italian city-states, began to challenge the Muslims in the eastern Mediterranean and North Africa, most notably during the Crusader era (1095–1191). This decline was countered, however, by the efforts of rulers such as Salah al-Din (ruled 1169–1193) and al-Zahir Baybars I (ruled 1260–1277) to revive trade. The Karimi merchants of Egypt, the first multinational, multireligious merchant association, attained a high degree of wealth and influence, often lending money to rulers and acting as emissaries on their behalf. Nonetheless, as competition increased—especially in the fourteenth and fifteenth centuries, when the Mongol successor states (tribal groups known as Aq Quyunlu and Qara Quyunlu) took over most of western Asia—trade routes had shifted northward (north of the Caspian and Black Seas), away from the traditional southern routes along the Persian Gulf and the Red Sea. To make this situation worse, the Mamluk rulers, hard-pressed for revenue, began to monopolize trade and fixed prices to their advantage, a practice that came to be known as *tarh*. During the fourteenth and fifteenth centuries, Muslim merchants suffered greatly from foreign competition and the shortsighted policies of the Mamluks. With agriculture in decline and with Muslim manufactured goods declining in quality, merchants lost much of their previously undisputed power. This situation was exacerbated when the Portuguese mariner Vasco da Gama's 1497–1499 exploration of the route around Africa to India was soon followed by voyages by other Europeans, who began to take control of the trade in the Indian Ocean and gained military control of access to the Red Sea and the Persian Gulf. During the following centuries Muslim merchants were able to regain some influence, but they were unable to halt the advance of European commercial success at their expense.

Sources:
Muhammad M. Ahsan, *Social Life Under the Abbasids, 786–902 A.D.* (London & New York: Longman, 1979).

Eliyahu Ashtor, *A Social and Economic History of the Near East in the Middle Ages* (Berkeley: University of California Press, 1976).

Michael A. Cook, ed., *Studies in the Economic History of the Middle East: From the Rise of Islam to the Present Day* (Oxford: Oxford University Press, 1970).

Michael Dols, *The Black Death in the Middle East* (Princeton: Princeton University Press, 1977).

Ross E. Dunn, *Adventures of Ibn Battuta, A Muslim Traveler of the Fourteenth Century* (Berkeley: University of California Press, 1986).

Philip Khuri Hitti, *History of the Arabs*, tenth edition (New York: St. Martin's Press, 1974)

Mahmood Ibrahim, *Merchant Capital and Islam* (Austin: University of Texas Press, 1990).

David Morgan, *Medieval Persia: 1040–1797* (London & New York: Longman, 1988).

Patricia Risso, *Merchants and Faith: Muslim Commerce and Culture in the Indian Ocean* (Boulder, Colo.: Westview Press, 1995).

Maxime Rodinson, *Islam and Capitalism* (New York: Pantheon, 1973).

Abraham L. Udavitch, *Partnership and Profit in Medieval Islam* (Princeton: Princeton University Press, 1970).

THE CLASS SYSTEM AND SOCIAL CHANGE

Pre-Islamic Society. Because resources were scarce and the food supply was not always guaranteed, and because they were always on the move Arab nomads (*Bedu*, or Bedouins) developed into tightly knit family units whose allegiance was to protect and defend each other against outsiders. The survival of the group depended on each individual, and the survival of the individual depended on the collective group. Living in a seemingly changeless landscape and having meager resources on which to subsist, tribesmen became socially conservative, valuing and following the traditions of their ancestors, which were passed down from generation to generation through folktales and poetry recitals around the campfire or at festivals. The most important of these ideals and values, collectively known as *muruwwa*, were hospitality and courage. Hospitality was necessary because of their environment, where life sometimes depended on the kindness of others. Courage was greatly valued because clansmen were expected to defend, at any time, their fellow tribesmen. Each tribe, large or small (and some could reach several thousands), became a state unto itself, following its own traditions and customs. Each was governed by an elected chief, called a *sayyid*, whose authority was limited by a tribal council, called a *majlis*, made up of the clan heads and patriarchs. Decisions were reached collectively. When it was decided to move, the tribe moved as a whole. Despite the nomadic tendency to be egalitarian and to value each other's individuality, pre-Islamic society, whether nomadic or settled, came to be stratified. Tribal chiefs, clan heads, and patriarchs—the *sayyids*—were the leaders and could form alliances with their equals in other tribes. They become known as *halif* (allies), and thus, larger groups and tribal confederations were formed. When an alliance was made it was usually sealed by marriage, creating kinship or new blood ties. Generally the rank-and-file members of the tribe were freemen cooperating with each other for the collective good of the tribe. They constituted the fighters who went out on raids and were expected to defend the tribe against all attackers. As in many ancient societies, slaves formed the lowest rung of society. People usually became enslaved by being captured in battle and then sold (war slavery), or by losing one's freedom because of inability to pay one's debts (debt bondage). In much of the ancient world debt bondage was the most common form of slavery. In Arab society, unlike many others, however, these slaves were allowed to purchase their freedom. Usually a contract was drawn up between the master and his slave. When the provisions of the contract had been satisfied, the slave became a freedman and acquired a new social status, that of a *mawla* (plural: *mawali*). Though free and able to move up the social ladder, a *mawla* remained part of his master's household. As in most patriarchal, male-dominated societies, women in pre-Islamic

PEACE TREATY

In his history of the early years of the Muslim state, al-Baladhuri quoted from a 636 treaty between the inhabitants of the Byzantine city of Ba'labakk (in present-day Lebanon) and their Muslim conquerors, documenting the khilafah's taxation policies for non-Muslims:

In the name of Allah, the Compassionate, the Merciful. This is a statement of security to so and so, son of so and so, to the inhabitants of Ba'labakk—Greeks, Persians and Arabs—for their lives, possessions, churches and houses, inside and outside the city and also for their mills. The Greeks are entitled to give pasture to their cattle within a space of 15 miles, yet are not to abide in any inhabited town. After [the months of] Rabi' and Jumada I shall have passed, they are at liberty to go where they will. Whosoever of them adopts Islam, shall have the same rights as we and be bound by the same obligations; and their merchants are entitled to go through capitulation [special rights of passage given to merchants]. Those of them who do not adopt Islam are bound to pay jizya [poll tax] and kharaj [produce tax].

Source: Al-Baladhuri, *The Origins of the Islamic State: Being a Translation from the Arabic, Accompanied with Annotations, Geographic and Historic Notes of the Kitab Fituh al-Buldan of al-Imam Abu-l Abbas Ahmad Ibn-Jabir al-Baladhuri*, 2 volumes, translated by Philip Khuri Hitti (Beirut: Khayats, 1966).

Arabia did not enjoy the same rights as men. Although women were legally free, they were considered subservient to men. A husband could repudiate or divorce his wife, but this right was not available to women. Most often they were denied a share of the family's inheritance. Because of poverty, concern for family honor, and perhaps some ancient practice, some families went to the extreme measure of female infanticide, known as *wa'd*. On the whole, women were treated as property, but there were exceptions. Some women chose their own husbands and could stipulate certain conditions in their marriage contracts. Some were wealthy, owning and managing businesses and property, and even employing men.

Formation of New Tribes. When a tribe became too large for its food supply, a section split off and moved away, establishing itself as a new tribe or joining another. This process help to create alliances between tribes in far-flung parts of the Arabian peninsula, which were crucial in the absence of a central government that could enforce laws and ensure peace and security. In a few instances, tribesmen were able to settle down in one place and begin changing to a sedentary lifestyle. Such was the case with the tribe of Quraysh who settled in and around Makkah sometime around the middle of the fourth century C.E.

The Sacred City. By the fourth century, Makkah was already recognized as the foremost holy center in the western region of Arabia. The area of Makkah was considered sacred, or *haram*. Belief in sacred space and sacred time was

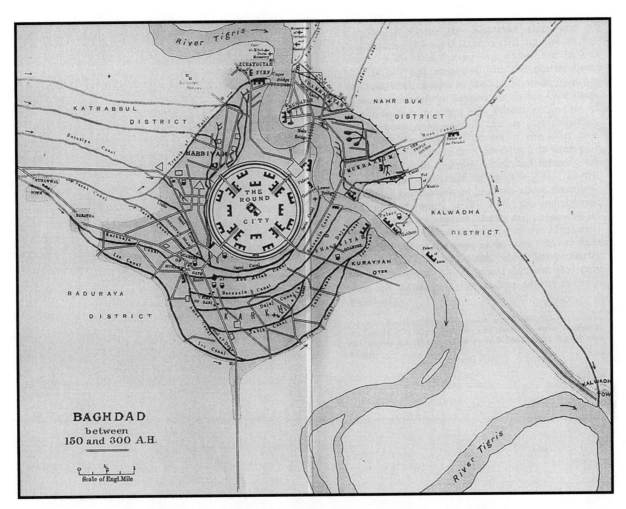

Plan of the Abbasid city of Baghdad as it was in the years 772–992 (from Guy Le Strange, *Baghdad During the Abbasid Caliphate*, 1924)

central to the religious beliefs of the nomads, and it was also important to some settled communities, including those in Yemen. Because everyone who visited them was assured of safety, sacred centers became places where trade was conducted. Travel from one sacred center to another could take place during the four months of the year designated as sacred. While nomads did not build temples in which to worship their gods, relying instead on more temporary or portable shrines, settled communities built great temples in cities across southern Arabia. Among other deities reminiscent of Mesopotamian, Egyptian, and Greek gods, the southern Arabs worshiped the moon god al-Maqah. Temples to al-Maqah were endowed with rich land and other gifts, and temple officials became a powerful influence in society. Settled and nomad groups alike believed in a higher deity, Dahr (loosely translated as Time). In addition, there were Zoroastrians, Jews, and Christians in many parts of the Arabian peninsula, including Makkah, which was located on the trade route between Yemen and Syria, not far from the Red Sea coast. It was also near the juncture of another trade route that connected with Iraq. In Makkah a water well, known as Zamzam, had attracted settlers since the distant past. The site was considered holy and protected, or *haram*. The Arabs believed

that Abraham had built a house dedicated to the worship of God on the site, where he had come with his wife Hagar and son Ismail (Ishmael). This structure became known as the Ka'bah and eventually became the object of pilgrimage during the holy months—Muharram, Rajab, Dhu al-Qi'da, and Du al-Hijjah, the first, sixth, eleventh, and twelfth months, respectively—during which life and property became inviolable and strict taboos were enforced assuring the safety and security of pilgrims. Trade fairs and festivals, including horse racing and poetry recitals, were held during the pilgrimage months (especially at the nearby market fair of 'Ukaz), and the Makkans traded with passing caravans as well as with surrounding communities. Makkan merchants grew in wealth and influence.

The Arrival of Islam. Few changes had taken place by the time the Prophet Muhammad appeared on the scene some two centuries after the Quraysh settled in Makkah, but these changes were significant. The states in southern Arabia were weaker than ever and their authority was limited. The Byzantines and the Sasanids, the two established imperial powers to the north, had been engaged in intermittent conflict with one another for nearly a century. This warfare not only weakened their armies and defenses but also disrupted their lines of communication with the Arabian peninsula so that their merchants were unable to reach the markets in the south. Their absence created room for merchants from various parts of Arabia, especially Makkah, to engage in commerce with merchants in the surrounding regions. Makkah merchants began to grow wealthier and more powerful than others, impacting the social structure in Makkah, hastening its breakdown. Tribal ideals and values became difficult to follow and enforce in a settled, urban environment. Kinship ties, though they never disappeared, became weaker as new identities, loyalties, and affiliations based on profession and wealth began to form. Thus, values based on kinship ties, such as hospitality and taking care of orphans and the poor, were not followed as before. The social structure in Makkah began to show cracks, and the whole population and the reputation of the city were bound to suffer if this state of affairs continued. When Muhammad began to preach Islam around 610, no central government with any meaningful strength existed in the whole of Arabia. Tribal fragmentation and conflict was the order of the day, and *muruwwa* ideals had been largely replaced by social relations oriented toward wealth and its accumulation through trade.

Prophethood. When the Prophet Muhammad began to preach Islam in the Makkan community, he singled out the social ills that had become common in Makkah, advising his townsmen to fear God almighty in their dealings with other members of society. To remind them of their social responsibility, Muhammad pointed out that orphans, widows, the poor, and the homeless were to be treated fairly and kindly. Makkans were asked to purify their souls before Judgment Day by giving alms to the needy. This social component was included in a religious message that preached the worship of one God, Allah, who is ever present, all powerful and eternal. One particular incident in Muhammad's life illustrates the breakdown of the social structure in Makkah. According to tribal tradition, a clan leader had to offer protection to his clansmen and defend them whether he agreed with them or not. Sometime around 618, a change in the leadership of Muhammad's clan brought to power an uncle who was opposed to Muhammad's teachings. This new clan leader, instead of extending the customary familial protection, denounced his nephew and aligned himself with other merchants in opposition to the Prophet. Kinship ties were superseded by the business interests of the clan leader. The willingness of the Makkan leadership to boycott, ostracize, and even torture their own relatives signaled a serious breakdown of traditional kinship relations. The position of Muhammad and his followers in Makkah became precarious, so he looked elsewhere to continue his preaching. By 622 he was able to settle in Madinah, about 215 miles to the north of Makkah, at the invitation of its inhabitants, who pledged to protect him. This event is called the *hijrah*, and it marks the beginning of the Muslim calendar (622 C.E. = 1 A.H.). Those Makkans who followed the prophet (about four hundred to five hundred from various clans) came to be known as the *Muhajirun* (Immigrants). The people in Madinah who welcomed the Prophet and his followers and became Muslims were known as the *Ansar* (Helpers).

Qur'anic Social Principles. In Madinah, Muhammad was able to put into practice the Qur'anic principles, and there the Qur'anic message was expressed in its political and social dimensions. Apart from establishing Islam with its five pillars of the faith in Madinah, Muhammad carried out far-reaching social reforms. Realizing that the tribe was losing effectiveness as a social and political unit and was less responsive to the rapid changes taking place around it, the Prophet introduced the concept of the *ummah*, a community where belief in Allah and the Prophet was the basis of identification and solidarity. Replacing the tribe, the *ummah* became a social and political unit that could be easily expanded since the basis of inclusion was belief in God, not kinship relations. To cement the idea that belief in God was the basis of inclusion, the Prophet introduced the practice of fraternization, pairing as brothers each person of the *Muhajirun* with one from the *Ansar*. During the last years of his life, the Prophet proclaimed that all Muslims are brethren, that they should protect and not wrong each other. Repeatedly during confrontations between the Muslims and their enemies, the *ummah* proved to be an enduring institution. Indeed, the Muslim *ummah* will continue to exist as long as there are Muslims and keep expanding as long as there are more people accepting Islam.

The Status of Women. Another important area of social reform under Islam was in rules pertaining to the position of women, marriage, and divorce. On the whole, through teachings of the Prophet that were reinforced by Qur'anic verse, Islam raised the status of women and introduced legal guarantees for their improved conditions. Men and women were placed on equal footing before Allah spiritually and in their duties and obligations as Muslims. A woman had to be consulted before she could be married and given a dowry that was hers alone, to dispose of as she chose. A woman was given the right to a specific share of the family inheritance, which was regarded as her God-given portion. Among other advances that elevated her position in society, she had the right to own, buy, and sell property and to manage her own business. As revealed in the Qur'an, the Prophet emphasized that the powerful must protect the weak, that widows and orphans must be provided for, and that honesty, justice, and equity should prevail in order to cure the ills of society: "And the believers, men and women, are protecting friends one of another; they enjoin the right and forbid the wrong, and they establish worship and they pay the poor-due, and they obey Allah and His messenger. As for these, Allah will have mercy on them. Lo! Allah is Mighty, Wise" (Surah al-Tauba, v. 72).

Slavery. Islam considered that the natural state of individuals was one of being born in a state of freedom. Yet, Islam did not abolish slavery outright; it mitigated its conditions and created many situations in which a slave could earn freedom. If a war captive converted to Islam, for example, he or she should be immediately set free. If a

A merchant and his porter; illumination from an early thirteenth-century Baghdad manuscript for the *Maqamat* of al-Hariri (Bibliothèque Nationale, Paris)

slave owner missed a prayer or broke his fast during the holy month of Ramadan, then he was to expiate the sin by setting slaves free. Those who owned slaves were admonished to free them as an act of *sadaqa* (charity), and obligatory alms could be spent for the liberation of slaves. A slave woman who gave birth was to be freed and married. Charitable acts were different from *zakat* (alms giving), which became one of the five pillars of Islam. While *sadaqa* was voluntary, *zakat* was a divine requirement incumbent on every Muslim. In earlier periods the amount was set at nearly 2.5 percent of the individual's wealth and came to constitute the genesis of the central treasury of the Islamic state, called *Bayt al Mal*. The Qur'an stipulated that the recipients of the proceeds of the *zakat* should be the homeless, wayfarers, the widows, orphans, and the poor. The rest of the money was to be spent in "God's way." As Muslim society grew, especially after its expansion beyond the Arabian peninsula, the state no longer engaged in the collection and distribution of the *zakat*. Charity once again became an individual responsibility, and it became traditional practice that a wealthy family distributed alms discretely to needy households in its neighborhood just before major Islamic holidays, such as the feast days at the end of Ramadan.

Expansion of the Muslim State. This ideal, egalitarian Islamic society changed soon after the death of the Prophet and the commencement of Muslim expansion outside the Arabian peninsula in 632. Arab Muslim troops quickly defeated Byzantine and Sasanid armies and overran Syria, Iran, and Egypt—the area that, along the Arabian peninsula, came to constitute the core of Islamic lands. After taking over all the land that had been under the control of the defunct Sasanid Empire in Iran, Muslim armies continued to expand eastward, taking cities such as Samarqand and Bukhara. They also moved westward, taking over northern Africa and most of the Iberian peninsula and then crossing the Pyrenees in southern France. When in 732 Charles Martel (Charlemagne's grandfather) stopped the Muslim advance at Tours, the Muslims had already established—after only a century of expansion—the largest land-based empire humanity had known. The success of the Muslim military campaigns was not without several social consequences. Significant and profound changes led to the emergence of a new society.

The People of the Book. First, inhabitants of the conquered territories were adherents of various Jewish and Christian sects. These followers of monotheistic religions were considered "the People of the Book," followers of divinely revealed books (the Torah and the Evangelium). According to treaties and other agreements reached between the Muslims and the inhabitants of various areas, Jews and Christians (regardless of sect) were given the status of *dhimmis* and came to be known as the Protected People. Although *dhimmis* did not necessarily constitute a social class at first, they soon developed into one as the new society continued to take shape. *Dhimmis,* whether Christians or Jews, were economically diversified, as demonstrated by the graduated taxation they were required to pay; it ranged from four gold dinars for the wealthy to one dinar for the less-well-to-do. (The word *dinar* derives from the Greek word *dinarius*). Women, children, the infirm, the old, priests, and monks were exempted from taxation. The economically diverse People of the Book lived either in rural areas as peasants, farmers, or landlords or urban communities, where they were artisans, craftsmen, and merchants, as well as professionals such as physicians and government bureaucrats. In Persia, Zoroastrians, followers of Zoroaster (or Zarathustra), were also given the status of People of the Book.

Urbanization. The expansion of territory under Arab/Muslim rule resulted in an unprecedented level of urbanization in the Near East, as one city after another was built in newly won territories. Garrison cities, built to house the fighters and their families and to make the conquests more permanent and secure, were strategically located close to water supplies and trade routes. Some garrison cities became provincial capitals and later played significant roles in the formation of Islamic civilization. Some, such as Basrah, Cairo, Baghdad, and Fez, continue to flourish today. The first garrison cities to be established were Kufah and Basrah in Iraq and Fustat (later Cairo) in Egypt. After a large area was designated as a public square and the main thoroughfares were marked, the land was distributed to Muslim fighters according to tribal affiliations and alliances. In the initial phases of settlement, the houses were makeshift and temporary, but eventually clay and bricks were used to build permanent structures. Tribal divisions were also transformed into the administratively convenient quarters of the city, or districts for various resident groups.

Since these cities quickly became the most important in the provinces, they also became seats of administration. A governor, who was usually the army commander, was appointed by the khalifah (whether in Madinah or later in Damascus or Baghdad). The governor was usually assisted by a growing number of officials, including a treasurer and various heads of *diwans* (bureaus), who kept track of taxation and other sources of revenue as well as payments to the military and other officials. At first officials were drawn from the local population, and records were kept in the local language or that of the former imperial government, Persian or Greek. Later, as the spread of Arabic literacy increased, records were kept in Arabic as a matter of policy. As the populations of these towns continued to increase, open areas of land were built up. Although cities were initially laid out in a grid pattern, as time passed the pattern of streets and alleyways grew in complexity, becoming more like a maze. This unprecedented urbanization was the basis of Islamic civilization. Even though the population was made up of fighters (*jund*) they were usually mobilized only about four or five months of each year. When these fighters were at home, they engaged in professions or artisanal activity. Merchants benefited the most from the growth of the cities. With growing opportunities for trade and employment, cities also became magnets for newly converted Muslims and for local Christians, Jews, and Zoroastrians (the predominant religious group in Persia). Gradually, Muslim cities became cosmopolitan centers in which various cultural and religious traditions interacted and influenced each other.

Growth of an Intellectual Class. A notable consequence of this interaction was the beginning of an elaboration of Islamic theology. Faced with established religious traditions, Muslims began to ask theological questions that had been asked in other monotheistic religions, such as those pertaining to free will and predestination, the position of man in relation to God, and the nature of Heaven and Hell. Challenged by the traumatic events of the First Civil War (656–661), Muslims sought answers to questions regarding the nature of authority, the community, and human responsibility. When Muslims debated Christians and Jews, who contemplated those very issues, they found that they needed "intellectual tools" to help them respond to such vexing problems. Muslims began to resort to Greek philosophy, and many of the works of Aristotle and Plato, among others, were translated into Arabic. The foremost translator was Hunain ibn Ishaq, who set the standards for accuracy and thoroughness. Eventually, a special educated class of Muslims began to appear. Known collectively as *ulama'* (learned scholars), they studied a variety of subjects, including grammar, the Qur'an, hadith (the Prophet's sayings), biography, history, and geography. Later, hard sciences such as medicine, mathematics, alchemy, optics, and mechanics were added to the list of scholarly disciplines, especially after Greek, Pahlavi, and Sanskrit books on these subjects were translated into Arabic. Astronomy was a particularly relevant science for Muslims, and they excelled in

Covered berths for ships at Alanya, Turkey, built by the Saljuks in 1228

it. Many observatories were built throughout the Islamic world. Astronomy was used to locate the direction of Makkah (so that Muslims could face it during prayer), to predict the occurrence of the new moon for accurately determining the beginnings of the lunar months in the Muslim calendar (especially for pinpointing the start and end of fasting in the holy month of Ramadan), and to determine the times of prayer. Members of the *ulama'* class were also engaged in the study of Islamic law. At first scholars met in the corners or by the pillars of a masjid (mosque), forming a circle around a teacher. These groups began to create what might be called schools of thought.

Charitable Foundations. In time, caliphs, government officials, and wealthy Muslims began to endow special places for the education of the *ulama'*. These endowments—called *waqf*—were established not only for the building and upkeep of schools (called *madrasahs*) but also to provide salaries for the teachers and to cover books and other expenses for students. Some wealthy Muslims established *waqfs* for schools in several cities. Some of these *madrasahs* began to teach specific subjects or a particular approach to Islamic law. The best-known school was the Madrasah Nizamiyya, established by the Saljuk wazir Nizam-i-Mulk in Baghdad. *Waqfs* allowed for the building of several *madrasahs* in each of the major cities, and education became a well-respected endeavor among Muslims, leading to a whole new activity and a new genre of literature: traveling in search of knowledge and writing an account of one's journey. Several travelers—including Nasri-Khusro, Ibn Jubayr, and the noteworthy Ibn Battuta—left accounts of their travel throughout the Islamic world.

Social Status. As the pursuit of knowledge became a respected endeavor in Muslim society, the *ulama'* became a socially respected class whose members were generally assured of upward mobility. As a socially desirable group, they could form alliances, either through marriage or business partnerships, with wealthy families, whether merchants or landowners. Having gained wealth and influence, these *ulama'* were often artisans, merchants, and urban and rural landlords as well.

Sources:
Leila Ahmad, *Women and Gender in Islam: Historical Roots of a Modern Debate* (New Haven: Yale University Press, 1992).

Julia Ashtiyani and others, eds., *The Cambridge History of Arabic Literature: Abbasid Belles Lettres* (Cambridge & New York: Cambridge University Press, 1983).

Daniel G. Bates and Amal Rassam, *Peoples and Cultures of the Middle East,* second edition (Saddle River, N.J.: Prentice Hall, 2001).

George W. Braswell Jr., *Islam: Its Prophet, Peoples, Politics, and Power* (Nashville: Broadman & Holman, 1996).

Elizabeth Warnock Fernea, ed., *Children in the Muslim Middle East* (Austin: University of Texas Press, 1995).

Fernea, ed., *Women and the Family in the Middle East: New Voices of Change* (Austin: University of Texas Press, 1985).

Suzanne Haneef, *What Everyone Should Know about Islam and Muslims* (Chicago: Kazi, 1979).

G. R. Hawting, *The First Dynasty of Islam: The Umayyad Caliphate A.D. 661–750* (Carbondale: Southern Illinois University Press, 1987).

Philip Khuri Hitti, *History of the Arabs,* tenth edition (New York: St. Martin's Press, 1974).

Peter M. Holt, *The Age of the Crusades: The Near East from the Eleventh Century to 1517* (London & New York: Longman, 1985).

Albert H. Hourani, *A History of the Arab People* (Cambridge & New York: Cambridge University Press, 1991).

Mahmood Ibrahim, *Merchant Capital and Islam* (Austin: University of Texas Press, 1990).

Hugh Kennedy, *The Prophet and the Age of the Caliphates: The Islamic Near East from the Sixth to the Eleventh Century* (London & New York: Longman, 1986).

Ira M. Lapidus, *A History of Islamic Societies* (Cambridge & New York: Cambridge University Press, 1988).

Fazlur Rahman, *Major Themes of the Qur'an* (Minneapolis: Bibliotheca Islamica, 1988).

D. A. Spellberg, *Politics, Gender, and the Islamic Past: The Legacy of Aisha bint Abi Bakr* (New York: Columbia University Press, 1994).

Abdullah al-Udhari, *Classical Poems by Arab Women: A Bilingual Anthology* (London: Saqi Books, 2000).

W. Montgomery Watt, *The Formative Period of Islamic Thought* (Edinburgh: Edinburgh University Press, 1973).

Watt, *Muhammad: Prophet and Statesman* (London: Oxford University Press, 1961).

CONVERTS AND SOCIAL INTEGRATION

Non-Arab Muslims. After the Muslim conquest of non-Arab lands in the eighth century, non-Arabs in these regions gradually but steadily converted to Islam, creating a demographic transformation of Muslim society. Arabs were no longer the only Muslims. Modern scholars explain the conversion of non-Arabs in many ways, the most common being economic. Non-Muslims paid two kinds of taxes; *jizya* and *kharaj*, both of which were higher than a Muslim's *zakat* and the *'ushr* taxes. The *jizya* was paid by the People of the Book in lieu of military service and for protection by the state (thus, the designation "Protected People"). Theoretically, if one converted to Islam, such a tax no longer applied. There are several flaws in this widespread theory. First, the number of people who converted to Islam was much greater than those who achieved economic advantage by doing so. The state saw a disadvantage in granting fiscal equality to new Muslims, and some government officials, especially during the Umayyad period (651–750), demanded that converts continue to pay the *jizya* tax. Because Islam regarded all Muslims as equal brethren within the *ummah*, these officials contradicted the teachings of Islam by following such a policy.

Mawali. Umayyad officials also established an inflammatory social policy regarding new converts. Non-Arab Muslims became known as *mawali*, similar to the status accorded freed slaves in pre-Islamic society, creating a hierarchical social structure in which the *mawali* were considered inferior in social status. Pious Muslims of Arab origin objected to this policy and began to argue for a change. A social movement of Arabs and non-Arabs favoring integration formed the nucleus of a growing opposition to the Umayyads. At some point the state policy of distinguishing between non-Arab Muslims and Arab Muslims became useless. Converts assumed Islamic (Arabic) names, increasingly spoke Arabic, and intermarried with Arabs. The ethnic divide became less and less sharply delineated. Family ties and mutual business interests emerged between Arab and non-Arab Muslims, and a growing, vocal segment of the society began to call for integration and equality for the *mawali*. Such demands became so widespread that the reformist Umayyad khalifah 'Umar ibn Abd al-Aziz (ruled 717–720) attempted to introduce social and tax reforms to address the brewing tension. His reforms proved only temporary, however, and when later khalifahs reversed his policies, rebellions flared up even more frequently than before 'Umar's reforms. The Umayyads' failure to make needed social reforms spelled the end of their dynasty. An underground revolutionary movement succeeded in defeating their armies by 750.

The Abbasid Revolution. The Umayyads were followed by the Abbasid dynasty, which ruled from 750 to 1258. During this long period, so many social, political, and economic changes took place that the social structures and organization toward the end of these five centuries little resembled those at the beginning. The most profound change was in the nature of the new society. To integrate the *mawali* into the power structure of the state—and thus uphold the principle of equality for all Muslims—the Abbasids abolished the status of *mawla*, meaning that it no longer defined a social class. Government bureaucrats were increasingly people of mixed origins. The scribes employed by the Abbasid khilafah were largely Persians or Persianized Aramaeans. This group was so large that it constituted a social class, the *kuttab* (scribal class), and they wielded considerable political and social influence. Books were published on Persian ideas, values, and, most important, political practices. Soon books and treatises began to praise the heritage of other ethnic groups. Al-Jahiz (circa 776 – 869), one of the most brilliant literary figures of his time and of partial African descent, wrote a tract in praise of blacks. Arabs responded by writing tracts in praise of their culture. A lively literary debate was carried out in this manner for nearly a century. This literary movement came to be known as the Shuubiyya movement (loosely translated as "people's pride" movement). It may be seen as an indication of the vibrancy of Islamic society at the time and as an indication of that society's multi-ethnic and multicultural makeup.

Persians. The successes of the Abbasids in integrating the Persians may be measured not only by the preponderance of the Persians in the scribal class but also by the powerful new governmental positions that were staffed largely by Persians, particularly the office of the wazir. Holders of this office were at the head of the bureaucracy and became the second most powerful figures in the realm. Depending on the energy and the inclinations of the khalifah, the wazir was sometimes delegated the authority to make all appointments and to lead the army of the khilafah. Indeed, under the Abbassids the *mawali*—especially the Persians—came a long way from their position of inferiority under the Umayyads. In studying patterns of conversion to Islam, Richard Bulliet has found that by 750 (that is, during

In the ninth century, as Muslim society grew increasingly diverse, writers began to describe the merits of their various racial or ethnic groups. In his *Kitab al-Imta'wa al Mu'anasah* (Book of Enjoyment and Good Company) the tenth-century Arabic philosopher and man of letters Abu Hayyan al-Tawhidi commented on this tendency:

It is not in the Persian's nature nor his custom nor his origin to acknowledge the merit of the Arab, and neither is it in the nature of the Arab nor in his habit that he be delighted at the merit of the Persian. And the same applies to the Indian, the Greek, the Turk, the Dailamite, and others, for the consideration of merit and nobility rests upon two things. The first is that by which one people became distinguished from another, at the time of the creation, by the choice of good and bad, by correct and erroneous opinion, and by the contemplation of the beginning and the end. The matter depends upon this, but secondly, every nation has virtues and vices and every people has good and bad qualities, and every group of people is both complete and deficient in its industry and its wielding of influence. And it is decreed that bounties and merits and faults be poured forth over all mankind, scattered among them all.

Thus the Persians have politics, manners of government, restraints, and ceremonies; the Greeks have science and wisdom; the Indians have thought, deliberation, agility, beguilement, and perseverence; the Turks have courage and boldness; the Negroes have patience, the ability for hard labor, and joy; and the Arabs have bravery, hospitable reception, fidelity, gallantry, generosity, responsibility to obligation, oratory, and a gift for explanation.

Moreover, the merits mentioned above, in these famous nations, are not possessed by everyone of their individuals but rather are wide-spread among them. But there are some in their group who are devoid of all of them and are characterized by their opposite; that is, the Persians do not lack a man ignorant of politics and lacking in manners, found among the riffraff and the rabble. Similarly, the Arabs do not lack a cowardly or an ignorant or a foolish or a miserly or an inarticulate man. And the same holds true for the Indians, the Greeks, and others. Accordingly, when the people of merit and perfection from the Greeks are compared with the people of merit and perfection from the Persians, they come together on an even path. There is no difference between them except in the degrees of merit and the extents of perfection, and those are general rather than specific. In a like manner, when the people of shortcoming and vileness of one nation are compared with those of shortcoming and vileness of another nation, they come together on a single path. There is no difference between them except in degrees and extents. And no attention is paid to that nor any blame put upon it. Thus it has become clear from this list that all the nations have divided among themselves merits and shortcomings by the necessity of natural endowment and the choice of thought. Beyond that, people only compete among themselves regarding inheritance, native custom, overwhelming passion of irrascible souls, and the angry impulse of emotional force.

Here is another thing, an important principle which it is not possible to avoid pointing out in our discussion. Every nation has a period of domination over its opponents. . . . And for this reason, Abu Muslim, when asked which people he found most courageous, said, "All people are courageous when their fortune is rising." He had spoken truly. And accordingly, every nation at the beginning of its prosperity is virtuous, courageous, brave, worthy of glory, generous, outstanding, eloquent, perceptive, and reliable. This point of view is extrapolated from a phenomenon common to all nations, to one universal to each nation at a time, to a thing embracing each group, to one prevalent to each tribe, to something customary in each family, to one special to each person and each man. And this change from nation to nation illustrates the abundance of the generosity of God to all His creation and creatures in proportion to their fulfillment of His demand and their readiness to exert themselves at length in attaining it.

Source: "Enjoyment and Good Company," translated by John Damis, in *Introduction to Arabic Literature*, edited by Ilse Lichtenstadter (New York: Schocken, 1976), pp. 353–357.

the Umayyad period) only 7 percent of Persians had converted to Islam, but within fifty years of the advent of the Abbasids and their social programs (that is, between 750 and 800) nearly 45 percent were converted. It took another one hundred years for the majority of the Persians to convert to Islam and for Zoroastrians to dwindle to a small minority.

Sources:

Nabia Abbot, *Two Queens of Baghdad: Mother and Wife of Harun al-Rashid* (Chicago: University of Chicago Press, 1946).

Leila Ahmad, *Women and Gender in Islam: Historical Roots of a Modern Debate* (New Haven: Yale University Press, 1992).

Muhammad M. Ahsan, *Social Life Under the Abbasids, 786–902 A.D.* (London & New York: Longman, 1979).

Julia Ashtiyani and others, eds., *The Cambridge History of Arabic Literature: Abbasid Belles Lettres* (Cambridge & New York: Cambridge University Press, 1983).

Eliyahu Ashtor, *A Social and Economic History of the Near East in the Middle Ages* (Berkeley: University of California Press, 1976).

Daniel G. Bates and Amal Rassam, *Peoples and Cultures of the Middle East*, second edition (Saddle River, N.J.: Prentice Hall, 2001).

Donna Lee Bowen and Evelyn A. Early, eds., *Everyday Life in the Muslim Middle East* (Bloomington: Indiana University Press, 1993).

George W. Braswell Jr., *Islam: Its Prophet, Peoples, Politics, and Power* (Nashville: Broadman & Holman, 1996).

Elizabeth Warnock Fernea, ed., *Women and the Family in the Middle East: New Voices of Change* (Austin: University of Texas Press, 1985).

Dimitri Gutas, *Greek Thought, Arabic Culture: The Greco-Arabic Translation Movement in Baghdad and Early 'Abbasid Society* (London & New York: Rutledge, 1988).

A qadi (judge or magistrate) settling a dispute between a young woman and her father; illumination from an early thirteenth-century Baghdad manuscript for the *Maqamat* of al-Hariri (Bibliothèque Nationale, Paris)

Shirley Guthrie, *Arab Women in the Middle Ages: Private Lives and Public Roles* (London: Saqi Books, 2000).

Albert H. Hourani and S. M. Stern, eds., *The Islamic City: A Colloquium* (Philadelphia: University of Pennsylvania Press, 1970).

Nikki R. Keddie and Beth Baron, eds., *Women in Middle Eastern History: Shifting Boundaries in Sex and Gender* (New Haven: Yale University Press, 1991).

Tarif Khalidi, *Arabic Historical Thought in the Classical Period* (Cambridge: Cambridge University Press, 1994).

George Makdisi, *The Rise of Colleges: Institutions of Higher learning in Islam and the West* (Edinburgh: Edinburgh University Press, 1981).

Louise Marlow, *Hierarchy and Egalitarianism in Islamic Thought* (Cambridge: Cambridge University Press, 1997).

M. A. Shaban, *The 'Abbasid Revolution* (London: Cambridge University Press, 1970).

W. Montgomery Watt, *The Majesty That Was Islam: The Islamic World, 611–1100* (London: Sidgwick & Jackson, 1974).

THE DECENTRALIZATION OF SOCIETY

New Groups. When the Abbasid khilafah was founded in 750, it governed a strong, centralized state with the khalifah as an effective ruler, soon installed in the newly built capital of Baghdad. Gradually the centralized khilafah began to lose its effectiveness, and regional powers began to appear, leading to the decentralization of the khilafah and, in later years, to its fragmentation into autonomous units. By the middle of the tenth century the Arabs, who had been the dominant, ruling elite, began to recede in importance. Iranians, as well as Kurdish and Turkish military groups who had converted to Islam, began to wield more

power. The khalifahs lost their authority and effectiveness and became symbolic figureheads who lent the *ummah* a semblance of unity even as the centralized government continued to break up. The real rulers, military commanders who were recruited largely from Turkish tribes, assumed the title *sultan*. While these sultans carried out military campaigns, they left the civil administration to wazirs.

Civil Order. When the state was strong and its authority recognized, peace and security were the responsibility of officials appointed for this purpose. Each city had its own police force (*shurta*), which was recruited locally. Transgressors were thrown in jail for a term usually specified by a *qadi* (judge) or a governor. In addition to the police, each quarter of a town was administered by a trusted member of the notables (*a'yan*), who worked as a liaison or intermediary between the ruler and his subjects, and a *muhtasib* (market inspector) was appointed to make sure that the marketplace functioned smoothly and that business there was conducted honestly. To assist the *muhtasib*, organizations that are similar to guilds were encouraged. These organizations, came to be known as *sinf*, and their chiefs functioned like government officials, making sure that guild members produced quality goods, charged fair prices, and paid their taxes to the government.

Urban Violence. After Baghdad was founded in 750, it soon surpassed other cities in the Muslim world. Its expan-

In his *Muslim Cities in the Later Middle Ages*, Ira M. Lapidus described the occupations of the middle and lower classes of Damascus during the fourteenth and fifteenth centuries:

Al-'amma proper, sometimes called al-'ammat al nas (common members of the nas [people]), as if to emphasize a degree of respectability, were the trading and working people of the cities. They were the shopkeepers, retailers and artisans, taxpayers, men known and accessible, the honest toilers. Some were of recognized social importance. Middle-class retailers were made responsible for fiscal and monetary measures taken by the regime. Skilled craftsmen such as carpenters, masons, and marble workers were awarded the prized Sultan's robes of honor on the completion of important projects. Other commoners variously called ba'a, suqa, mutaayyishun, or mutasabbibun, who were food dealers, artisans, workers and peddlers, made up the remainder of this working population.

Yet included in the meaning of the word al-'amma was a still lower class of the population, in the eyes of the middle classes a morally and socially despised mass, possessing little or none of the Muslim attributes in family life, occupation, or religious behavior, and often holding heretical religious beliefs. Though the boundaries between the respectable and the disreputable masses were not clearly set, a virtual caste apart from the rest of the common people was an important element in urban social life.

Muslim literary sources from various periods describe a theoretical distinction between the respectable and disreputable on religious grounds. First among the disreputable were the usurers, or all those who profited from chicanery or transactions forbidden by Muslim law—brokers, criers, money changers, slave dealers, and people who sold forbidden objects. In a second category fell people of questionable morality—male or female prostitutes, wine sellers, cock fighters, professional mourners, dancers and other entertainers. Thirdly, people defiled by dead beasts or animal wastes were included among the impure. Barbers and surgeons were valued on other grounds, but butchers, tanners, donkey and dog handlers, hunters, and waste scavengers were despised.

. . . the usurious trades of silver, gold, and silks were not highly regarded, and of course dealing in wine and pork and selling weapons to the enemy was strictly forbidden. The various cooking trades could be either good or evil. In general, bakers, furriers, carpenters, tailors and perfumers were among the finer tradesmen, while silk weavers, wooden clog makers, goldsmiths, porters, wood gatherers, and water pourers belonged to subordinate occupations. The socially rejected tradesmen were weighers, camel and donkey drivers, changers, falconers, cuppers, leather workers and tanners, geomancers, jugglers, and barbers. . . .

The menials shaded over into a second category of despised persons, thieves and common criminals, prostitutes, and gamblers. The menial and the criminal seem to have been closely related. For example, *al-masha'iliyya*, the nightwatchmen and torch bearers who cleaned the latrines, removed refuse from the streets, and carried off the bodies of dead animals served as police, guards, executioners, and public criers, and paraded people condemned to public disgrace whose shame may have consisted in part in being handled by such men. At the same time, al-masha'iliyya made use of their intimacy with nightlife to become involved in gambling, theft and dealing in hashish and wine. . . .

The slaves and servants of the Sultan and the emirs formed another group which did not share in the producing and trading activities of the city or in its normal family and district life. Standing outside the social structure of artisan, quarter and religious life was an undisciplined and turbulent mass of kitchen helpers, stable hands, dog handlers, falconers, and huntsmen. They, too, were often associated with criminals and with traders in wine and hashish. . . . Apart from the menials, criminals, and slaves there were the homeless and poverty stricken. The large towns attracted a floating population of immigrants. Many were wealthy, learned, or had come to make their fortune and soon found a place in society, but the towns also harbored rootless foreigners. These included transient merchants, pilgrims or traveling scholars, and sheikhs who had accommodations, friends and contacts, but poor peasants and Bedouins fleeing rural hardship fell into the nameless and faceless mass.

Source: Ira M. Lapidus, *Muslim Cities in the Later Middle Ages* (Cambridge & New York: Cambridge University Press, 1984), pp. 82–84.

sion in size and population continued for centuries after, spreading into suburbs on both sides of the Tigris River. Within a hundred years, Baghdad was one of the largest cities in the world, perhaps second only to Xian, China. Some scholars have said that Baghdad in the ninth century was larger than Paris in the nineteenth. Urban Muslim society began to experience some of the same problems exhibited in modern, large urban cities, especially urban violence. During the ninth and tenth centuries, many members of the rural population gave up agriculture and moved to the cities, either to escape the taxes and the exactions of the landlords or to find employment in the various manufacturing concerns found in the city. Most often they became day laborers, swelling the ranks of the working class. Only occasionally employed and filled with resentment and frustration, they became fertile ground for recruitment into private militias and for membership in gangs that preyed on neighborhood shops and merchants. These gangs were known by names such as *Zu'aar* (young thugs), *Shuttar* (delinquent youths), and *Ayyarun* (rascals).

The medieval city of Aleppo; from the itinerary of Nasuh al-Matraki, Istanbul, circa 1536 (Istanbul University Library)

Abbasid coins found in a tenth-century grave near Oslo, Norway (from *Aramco World*, November–December 1999)

These groups caused violence and insecurity in the streets, but at other times they restored peace and tranquility, especially when their cooperation was bought by the wealthy of the neighborhood or the city government. In later years, some of these groups gained a measure of respectability, especially those who dedicated themselves to uphold honorable ideals and defend common interests and values. Some of these groups did charitable work. Members of such groups wore distinctive uniforms and associated with the elite and the powerful. These organizations, known as *futuwwa* (to distinguish them from the earlier criminal elements), were in fact cultivated and encouraged by some khalifahs, especially Khalifah al-Nasir (ruled 1180–1225), who had hoped to regain influence and authority through the *futuwwa* organization that he headed.

Sufism. Another consequence of the urban sprawl of Baghdad and other Muslim cities was the rise of mysticism, or Sufism. Pious Muslims found that city life interfered with the performance of their religious duty. Some of them sought a more peaceful existence in which they could contemplate God's creation and reflect on their place in the world. Other Muslims seemed to believe that religious scholars, especially those who dealt with Islamic law, were interpreting Islam too rigidly and formalistically. Eventually, these groups came to believe that the best religious life was an ascetic life that rejected luxury and material things. They began to wear coarse woolen garments (*suf*) and

therefore came to be known as Sufis. People of this inclination began to congregate together in a corner of a masjid and took to repeating certain religious formulas over and over again. This practice of recitation became known as *dhikr*. Since the masjid was intended for prayer (which, aside from the Friday sermon, is performed in silence) and religious instruction, the practice of *dhikr* was noisy and distracting, and the Sufis were forced out of masjids, indeed out of town. After Sufism became accepted by mainstream Islam, and it became advantageous for rulers to bestow upon them, Sufis began to build retreats (called *zawiya* in Arabic, *tekkah* in Turkish and *khanqah* in Persian), where a Sufi master (called *shaykh*) and his devotees (*murids*) would reside and chant their *dhikr* undisturbed and without disrupting prayer or other masjid activities. Because *zawiyas* were erected along trade routes such as the ancient silk route toward China or Saharan routes to western Africa, they became convenient stopping points for caravans. Over the years the Sufis and merchants were largely responsible for spreading Islam to eastern and western Africa, and central, southern, and southeastern Asia. Indeed, Islam spread further and faster after the twelfth century through Sufism than during previous centuries through Muslim territorial expansion. Sufi groups often traveled from town to town to perform their *dhikr* for the public, especially during festivals. In some areas of the Islamic world, a guild might become associated with one

Sufi master or another, reinforcing the "corporate" structure of Islamic society, especially during times when it was faced with external threats.

The Turks. By 1055 the Turks were dominating the military and politics, effectively ruling vast territories while the khalifahs in Baghdad were subservient to them. What had begun as a trickle had become a full-fledged downpour, as hundreds of thousands of Turkomen had migrated first into Iran, then Iraq and the rest of southwest Asia. Their greatest impact was in Anatolia. Following their victory over the Byzantine army in 1071 at the Battle of Malazgirt (Manzikert), the Turks continued to migrate westward and brought about the gradual Turkification and Islamization of the area. By 1290 they had brought into being the Ottoman Empire, which went on to become a major force in regional and world affairs, finally coming to an end in 1922.

Landholding and the Military. Led by a powerful family known as the Saljuks, the Turkish military relied for its primary income on *iqta'*, the system by which they were assigned the rights to collected taxes on a particular piece of property in lieu of salary. As the Turks in the military grew more and more numerous and powerful and gained effective control over larger and larger land areas, the power and the revenue of the central government decreased accordingly. In some cases a whole province might be assigned to a particularly important commander, and though these so-called tax farms were not granted as private property, they began to be passed on as inheritance, creating petty dynasties in the provinces. From the tenth century onward political fragmentation was rife.

Fragmentation. Another alarming concept introduced by the Turks was the idea that the state and its resources were the collective property of the ruling house. Thus, whenever a sultan died, members of his household competed for his office and engaged in armed conflict to replace him. Alliances and counteralliances were forged or broken depending on circumstances and perceived advantages. Agricultural resources were depleted as troops destroyed the irrigation infrastructure for military advantage and trampled fields of crops. Competing armies also disrupted trade routes and sporadically threatened the security of pilgrimage routes to Palestine, providing the pretext for Pope Urban II to call for the First Crusade in 1095. As commerce diminished, urban craft production declined. Such tragic consequences did not diminish the appetite of the military for additional taxes. With the land producing less and less, nomadism increased, and there was a noticeable decline in the population of cities and towns throughout the Near East. The decline in urban population was highlighted by the transformation of Baghdad from a cosmopolitan metropolis and the administrative center of an empire to an insignificant provincial capital.

External Threats. As the once united and powerful khilafah began to fragment into competing regional and autonomous states, its weakness invited outside invasion. By 1091 the Normans had completed their conquest of Sicily (where Muslim culture and Islamic religion continued to flourish for some time). A few years later Muslim society experienced its first serious external threat from the First Crusade.

The Crusades. Largely because Muslim rulers were unable to mount a unified opposition to this European invasion, the Crusaders established the Latin Kingdom of Jerusalem in 1099, as well as other Crusader strongholds in the Levant (the eastern Mediterranean). Hoping to gain ground against their rivals, some petty Muslim rulers cooperated with the Crusaders. The success of the Crusades, however, was not long lasting, nor was the disorganization of the Muslims. By the second decade of the twelfth century, another group of Turks, the Zengids of northern Iraq, took the initiative to unify the realm. The Zengid ruler Mahmud employed a general of Kurdish origin who went on to defeat the Crusaders. In 1169 that leader, the well-known Salah al-Din (Saladin), established the Ayyubid dynasty, unifying Egypt and Syria in 1175 and retaking Jerusalem from the Crusaders in 1187. Salah al-Din went on to further success in the Third Crusade (1189–1192), led by Richard the Lionhearted.

The Reconquista. Another threat to Muslim unity occurred in the extreme western part of the Islamic lands, the Iberian peninsula, during the eleventh century: the Reconquista. Over the next few centuries Spanish Christian forces gradually won back territory from Muslim rulers, including Toledo, which fell in 1085. Despite intermittent setbacks, the Reconquista eventually overran all Muslim territory in Spain, finally conquering the last Muslim foothold, Granada, in 1492.

The Mongols. At the other geographic extreme, in Central Asia, the Muslims found themselves under attack by the Mongols. Grandsons of Genghis Khan extended their rule from China all the way to the Black Sea. Hulagu put an end to the Abbasid dynasty in 1258 when his huge army occupied and sacked Baghdad after laying waste to many other Muslim cities. The devastation of Baghdad put a final end to the Abbasid khilafah.

The Mamluks. The need to fight on many fronts required the Ayyubids to recruit more soldiers than were available in the Middle East. Once more they sought recruits in central Asia. Around 1240 they brought Qipchaq Turks to Egypt to be educated in Islam and trained in the art of warfare. Eventually, these troops became known as the Mamluks. In 1259 Mamluk commanders took power in Egypt. Muslim society was faced with a double threat: the Crusaders from the West and the Mongols from the East, who had taken Baghdad the previous year. The quick action of the Mamluks saved the day. Not only were they able to force the Crusaders to retreat from Cairo and then to evacuate Egypt altogether but they also gathered an army that hurriedly marched out to block the Mongol advance. The two armies met near 'Ayn Jalut (Goliath's Well) in northern Palestine, and the Mongols were defeated in 1262. The Mamluks remained a constant feature of the political

Gates of Sultan Khan, a travelers' inn built by Saljuk ruler 'Ala' al-Din Kayqubad
outside Konya, Turkey, during the thirteenth century

and military life in the region for several centuries, coming to constitute the military governing elite of society. They defeated the Mongols two more times near Hims in central Syria, and in 1291 they reconquered the last Crusader kingdom in Syria.

Social Responses. The various external threats to the Muslim empire endangered not only the physical well-being of Muslims but also their culture. The Crusades and the Reconquista were fought in the name of Christianity, and the Mongols were also fighting in the name of their ideals and way of life. Faced with such a threat and with essentially no central government to offer them protection, Muslim society adopted, as a defensive strategy, a mode of organization that is often described as *corporate society*, a society organized into small groups that share a common interest, such as a profession, a sectarian affiliation, or—as was increasingly the case among Muslims—their membership in mystical brotherhoods.

Cultural Divisions. After the Mamluks stopped their westward advance, the Mongols settled in Persia, where they established their own dynastic state, becoming known as Il-Khanids. Eventually the Middle East became divided into three large cultural zones: Persian in Iran, Turkish in Anatolia, and Arab in what remained of southwest Asia. In northern Africa, Arabo-Berber society continued to evolve separately, with occasional influences from the East. Thus, from the thirteenth century onward, there was no longer a unified Islamic land or a single Islamic society. Other than common beliefs and rituals related to Islam—and the fact they were ruled by various military groups—not much remained to unite the Islamic world. The military rulers were either nomads inexperienced in the art of government or foreigners. Thus, they relied on local expertise to run the affairs of government, and Arabic, Persian, and Turkish became firmly established as languages of administration and culture in their respective regions. Local notables took the role of mediators between the military elite (*khassa*) and the subject population (*'amma*). These notables were drawn from merchants, landlords, and the learned classes (*ulama'*). Added to the *ulama'* class at this time were the Sufi *shaykhs,* who gained influence through Mamluk patronage and encouragement. Islamic society continued to be split along urban, rural, and nomadic lines, and the social classes remained divided according to their function. Peasants continued to make up the bulk of Muslim society.

Diversity. By the fourteenth century, Muslim society had become a vast multiethnic and multiracial composite linked by Islamic faith and practice and by commercial activity. Sufism and commerce helped Islam become truly universal. Islam claimed adherents in regions of the Eastern Hemisphere as far apart as West Africa and coastal China. Muslim merchants from India and Arabia spread the faith into Southeast Asia. In the twenty-first century, Indonesia is the largest Muslim country in the world, and there are large populations of Muslims in Malaysia and the Philippines as well. Between the seventh and fifteenth centuries, southwest Asia, the birthplace of Islam, became a Muslim melting pot, as Arabs were joined by Egyptians, Persians, Indians, Greeks, Visigoths, Berbers, Turks, and finally Mongols. Because Islam was spread by diverse groups and at different times, Islamic practices and beliefs, other than the core beliefs and dogma, became as complex as the ethnic makeup of the Islamic *ummah.*

Sources:

Eliyahu Ashtor, *A Social and Economic History of the Near East in the Middle Ages* (Berkeley: University of California Press, 1976).

Daniel G. Bates and Amal Rassam, *Peoples and Cultures of the Middle East,* second edition (Saddle River, N.J.: Prentice Hall, 2001).

Donna Lee Bowen and Evelyn A. Early, eds., *Everyday Life in the Muslim Middle East* (Bloomington: Indiana University Press, 1993).

Michael Dols, *The Black Death in the Middle East* (Princeton: Princeton University Press, 1977).

Ross E. Dunn, *Adventures of Ibn Battuta, A Muslim Traveler of the Fourteenth Century* (Berkeley: University of California Press, 1986).

Peter M. Holt, *The Age of the Crusades: The Near East from the Eleventh Century to 1517* (London & New York: Longman, 1985).

Albert H. Hourani and S. M. Stern, eds., *The Islamic City: A Colloquium* (Philadelphia: University of Pennsylvania Press, 1970).

R. Stephen Humphreys, *From Saladin to the Mongols: The Ayyubids of Damascus 1193–1260* (Albany: State University of New York Press, 1977).

Alice C. Hunsberger and Nasir Khusraw, *The Ruby of Badakhshan: A Portrait of the Persian Poet, Traveller and Philosopher* (London & New York: I. B. Tauris, 2000).

Robert Irwin, *The Middle East in the Middle Ages: The Early Mamluk Sultanate, 1250–1382* (Carbondale: Southern Illinois University Press, 1986).

Ira M. Lapidus, *A History of Islamic Societies* (Cambridge & New York: Cambridge University Press, 1988).

Amin Maalouf, *The Crusades Through Arab Eyes,* translated by Jon Rothschild (London: al-Saqi, 1983).

David Morgan, *Medieval Persia: 1040–1797* (London & New York: Longman, 1988).

Carl F. Petry, ed., *The Cambridge History of Egypt,* volume 1: *The Islamic Period, 640–1517* (Cambridge: Cambridge University Press, 1999).

W. Montgomery Watt, *A History of Islamic Spain* (Edinburgh: Edinburgh University Press, 1965).

SIGNIFICANT PEOPLE

AL-ZAHIR BAYBARS

1223-1277

MAMLUK SULTAN

Mongol Menace. Al-Zahir Baybars, or Baybars I, (reigned 1260–1277) was the most prominent of Mamluk Sultans and the real founder of the Mamluk state. He was born in 1223 when the Mongols were attacking central Asia in their westward drive. Baybars was sold as a slave (some say he joined the Mamluks on his own) and arrived in Egypt around 1240 to begin his career in the service of one of the last Ayyubid Sultans. He began to distinguish himself as early as 1250 when he fought in the battle of al-Mansura against the armies of Louis IX. In 1260, he commanded the vanguard against the Mongol army at the battle of Ain Jalut in northern Palestine. A brilliant military strategist and untiring military campaigner, he was able to consolidate Mamluk control over Egypt and Syria where he rebuilt the fortresses and citadels that had been destroyed or damaged. A most outstanding legacy of this activity is the citadel of Aleppo, in which the Throne Room still exhibits the fine artistic ability of the era. He also spent considerable effort in building canals, harbors, and *Madrasas* in Cairo and Damascus where the economy, especially trade and industry, began to show improvement after decades of insecurity and decline. Baybars gave the Mamluk regime even greater legitimacy by inviting one of the surviving Abbasids to Cairo to serve as

Khalifah after Baghdad had been demolished by the Mongol army of Hulagu.

Constant Campaigns. His military brilliance is exhibited in his success against the simultaneous threat of the Crusaders and Mongols. From 1265 to 1271, Baybars carried out annual campaigns against the Crusades and took over most of their territories, especially Antioch in 1268. He fought against the Mongols incessantly, carrying out at least nine campaigns against them. Toward the end of his reign he had forced them to retreat behind the Zagros Mountains and succeeded in reducing their control even in Anatolia. His success in the military field is matched by his diplomatic initiatives. He was in contact with the rulers around him, and he may have managed to thwart an impending alliance between the Crusaders and the Mongols. It is said that Baybars was a master of disguises and that he accompanied diplomatic missions incognito so as to assess firsthand the capabilities of his adversaries.

Hunter. Other than being a patron of the arts and of learning, Baybars loved to hunt. He died in July 1277, in Damascus where he is buried in the Zahiriyya Madrasa, built by him near the Umayyad mosque.

Sources:
Syedah Fatima Sadeque, ed., *Baybars I of Egypt* (Dacca: Oxford University Press, 1956).

Peter Thorau, *The Lion of Egypt: Sultan Baybars I and the Near East in the Thirteenth Century*, translated by P. M. Holt (London & New York: Longman, 1992).

ABU AL-FADL JA'FAR IBN 'ALI AL-DIMASHQI

ELEVENTH CENTURY
MERCHANT

Obscure Origins. Abu al-Fadl Ja'far ibn 'Ali al-Dimashqi is the author of *Kitab al-Isharah ila Mahasin at-Tijarah wa Ma'rifat Jayyid al-A'rad wa Radi'iha wa Ghush-ush al-Mudallisin fiha* (A Guide to the Merits of Commerce and to Recognition of Both Fine and Defective Merchandise and the Swindles of Those Who Deal Dishonestly). Little is known about al-Dimashqi's life. Historians generally agree that he was a prosperous merchant who lived in either Egypt or Syria. His life is dated to the eleventh century because in his only book, he mentions a specific Indian coin that circulated in eastern Mediterranean ports during that time period.

Middleman. It is evident from his book that al-Dimashqi engaged as a middleman in the import-export business. He dealt primarily with raw or partly finished goods, such as expensive fabrics and precious stones, as opposed to finished products, such as clothing and jewelry. (Apparently, the former offered a better return on his investments.) Scholars believe that, as a young man, he traveled extensively. His book makes frequent references to sea voyages and major port cities. They also assume that he

composed his work at the end of his career, when he was more sedentary and likely investing in real estate, which he recommended highly.

Practical Advice. Al-Dimashqi's *Guide* is a valuable tool to understanding tenth-century and eleventh-century commercial activity. It is filled with practical advice and warns the reader to use his wealth wisely and not to squander it. Moreover, the *Guide* provides shrewd commentary on a variety of topics, including the evaluation of commodities, proper pricing and record keeping, methods for identifying fraud, and correct sales techniques.

Source:
George N. Atiyeh and others, *The Genius of Arab Civilization: Source of Renaissance*, third edition (New York & London: New York University Press, 1992).

HARUN AL-RASHID

766-809
FIFTH ABBASID KHALIFAH

Zenith of Power. Harun al-Rashid was the fifth Abbasid khalifah (reigned 786–809) during whose rule the khilafah reached its zenith of wealth and power and also began to experience the symptoms and stirrings of provincial autonomy. The khilafah reached "the golden age" as Baghdad had become the wealthiest city in the world. Born in February 766, he was tutored in the arts of politics and culture by Yahya al-Barmaki. The khilafah was in good hands when Harun came to power (with al-Rashid as his title) and appointed Yahya the Barmakid as his Vizir (chief minister). Even though the territories were well administered and Baghdad was well respected, the far western provinces began to disengage from the center, especially Andalusia under the rule of the so-called Umayyads of Spain. This development invited correspondence and exchanges of gifts and ambassadors between Harun and Charlemagne to forge a strategy against their common enemies, the Umayyads and the Byzantines.

Cultural Achievements. During his reign Baghdad became a major cosmopolitan center attracting poets, literati, musicians, singers and other entertainers, physicians, and translators. Harun's court attracted various cultural figures, such as the poet Abu Nuwwas and the musician Ziryab. It is said that Ziryab perfected the Oud, the pear-shaped wooden instrument with six double strings, at the court of Harun. (The Oud was later adapted to western music to become the lute.) The stories found in the *Arabian Nights* or *The 1001 Nights*, although composed and recorded centuries later, were loosely based on this vibrant period of Abbasid history.

Female Influence. Women seemed to have had a great deal of influence on Harun's court as well as the culture of the day. Harun's mother al-Khayzuran was instrumental in ensuring his succession to power. Harun's wife Zubayda became well known for her own public activities and public-works projects, such as the construction of a fresh water aqueduct to supply Makkah from twenty-five miles away. Also, she had rest stops constructed along the pilgrimage route from Basrah to Makkah. This road became known as Darb Zubayda (Zubayda's road) in the Middle Ages.

Protocol of Makkah. In the first years of the ninth century trouble began to appear between the provinces and Baghdad. The major issues in this conflict were the amount of provincial taxation to be forwarded to the capital city and the role of local elite in the administration of the provinces. It seems that Harun was the first khalifah to grant a hereditary governorship in the provinces when he allowed Ibrahim ibn al-Aghlab and his descendants to rule the province of Ifriqiya (Tunis). To remedy the rapidly deteriorating situation, Harun proposed to divide the far-flung territories of the khilafah among his sons (similar to the solution reached among Charlemagne's grandsons). The division, largely between al-Amin and al-Ma'mun, was recorded and solemnized by oaths in the shadow of the Ka'bah. The document, known as the Protocol of Makkah, was entrusted to the inner sanctum of the Ka'bah. Yet, this division eventually led to civil war between the two brothers and ushered in a period of instability that would lead to continued provincial autonomy. Harun al-Rashid died on 24 March 809 in eastern Iran while on his way to Merv, the provincial capital of the eastern-most province of Khurasan.

Sources:

André Clot, *Harun al-Rashid and The World of the Thousand and One Nights,* translated by John Howe (London: Saqi, 1989).

Tayeb El-Hibri, *Reinterpreting Islamic Historiography: Harun al-Rashid and the Narrative of the `Abbasid Caliphate* (Cambridge & New York: Cambridge University Press, 1999).

Al-Tabari, *The Early `Abbasid Empire,* 2 volumes, translated by John Alden Williams (Cambridge & New York: Cambridge University Press, 1988, 1989).

SALAH AL-DIN AL-AYYUBI

1138-1193

AYYUBID SULTAN

Reflective Youth. Salah al-Din al-Ayyubi (Saladin) was of Kurdish origin, being born in 1138 in the town of Takrit in northern Iraq. He went on to found the Ayyubid Dynasty, which ruled Syria, Egypt, and Yemen from 1174 to 1258. He seemed to have been a quiet boy who was more prone to study than to war when he accompanied his father after the latter was appointed governor of Ba'albakk in the Biqa' valley in present-day Lebanon.

Military Experience. Salah al-Din eventually became a commander in the army of Nur al-Din Muhmud Zengi, the principal initiator of the countercrusade. Salah al-Din's fame began to rise after he had accompanied his uncle Shirkuh to Cairo when the Fatimid khalifah requested military aid to shore up his defenses against an impending

Crusader attack. Shirkuh died shortly after arriving and Salah al-Din assumed command and became the Vizir of the Fatimids. Two years later he abolished the Isma'ili Fatimid khilafah and restored Egypt to the Sunni world (it had been under Shi'i control since 969) under the nominal leadership of the Abbasids in Baghdad.

Assassins. His true calling came in 1174 after the death of his mentor and suzerain Nur al-Din and the inability of the latter's children to rule effectively and to end factionalism. Salah al-Din marched toward Damascus, which he took in his own name in the same year. He proceeded to consolidate his control over the rest of Syria and he seized Aleppo in 1183 and Mosul in 1186. One of his urgent tasks during these campaigns was to reduce the power of the Order of the Assassins, who had made two attempts on his life. The Assassins were a dangerous sect who claimed as their victims such figures as Malik Shah, one of the great Saljuk Sultans, his vizir Nizam al-Mulk, Conrad of Montferrat, king of Jerusalem, and Raymond II of Tripoli.

Hattin. Having unified Syria and Egypt and having reformed the economy and administration of the realm, he was prepared to carry out his campaign against the Crusaders who controlled a few coastal strongholds. His most outstanding success came on 3–4 July 1187 at Hattin, near Tiberias in northern Palestine, where he defeated a combined Crusader force. This decisive victory opened the road to Jerusalem against whose walls he appeared a few months later; he easily captured that city in October.

Third Crusade. Salah al-Din's success alarmed Western European rulers who called for fresh crusader reinforcements. King Richard the Lionhearted became the major adversary in the Third Crusade. Between 1189 and 1191 negotiations, exchange of presents, and other contacts were made to produce a treaty between the two sides known as the Peace Treaty of Ramlah (1192). Salah al-Din died shortly thereafter on 19 February 1192.

Sources:

Beha ed-Din, *The Life of Saladin.* (London: Committee of the Palestine Exploration Fund, 1897).

Geoffrey Regan, *Lionhearts: Saladin, Richard I, and the Era of the Third Crusade* (New York: Walker, 1999).

'UMAR IBN 'ABD AL-'AZIZ

CIRCA 680 - 720

UMAYYAD KHALIFAH

Reformer. Although the Umayyad dynasty (661–750) is generally known among Muslim historical writers for repression rather than reform, Khalifah 'Umar ibn 'Abd al-'Aziz (also known as 'Umar II), who reigned for only two and a half years (717–720), is an exception to that characterization. Known for his piety and frugality, he reformed the tax system, putting the *mawali* (non-Arab Muslims) on a equal basis with Arab Muslims.

Career. Born in Madinah, 'Umar was the son of a governor of Egypt and a descendant of Khalifah 'Umar ibn al-Khattab ('Umar I, ruled 634–644). After a traditional education in Madinah, he was made governor of the Hijaz region of Arabia, which includes Makkah and Madinah, in 706. During his tenure as governor, he formed a council of pious Muslims to advise him on his rule. He was elevated to khalifah in 717.

The Role of the State. Having come to power at the high noon of Muslim expansion, but facing a potential Muslim defeat at the siege of the Roman capital of Constantinople in 717–718, 'Umar embarked on an extensive and well thought-out reassessment of the purpose of the Muslim state. He lifted the disastrous siege, ending the third period of Umayyad military conquest, and embarked on a campaign of reform at home, attempting to address the instability caused by discontent over taxation among the *mawali* and by the belief of many Muslims that the Umayyads placed greater priority on their own political interests than on religious principles. He replaced unpopular governors and reformed the system of taxation so that all Muslims, regardless of ethnic origins, had the same fiscal rights. He also began efforts to separate the treasury from the khalifah's own funds. The only khalifah to send missionaries to convert the pagans of North Africa and other areas of the khilafah to Islam, he was also known for his tolerance of Christianity, Judaism, and Zoroastrianism. Despite his popularity among a broad segment of the population, his Umayyad successors reversed 'Umar's reforms, leading to the successful Abbasid revolution of 749–750.

Sources:

M. A. Shaban, *Islamic History: A New Interpretation, Vol. I, A.D. 600–750 (A. H. 132)* (Cambridge: Cambridge University Press, 1971).

Julius Wellhausen, *The Arab Kingdom and Its Fall,* translated by Margaret Graham Weir (Calcutta: University of Calcutta, 1927).

'UMAR IBN AL-KHATTAB

CIRCA 586-644

SECOND KHALIFAH

Charisma. 'Umar ibn al-Khattab or 'Umar I was the second khalifah (reigned 634–644) of the nascent Islamic state and the real founder of the khilafah. During his reign the Muslims achieved major victories against the Byzantines and the Sasanids and consolidated their control of Western Asia. 'Umar had a towering figure and a powerful charismatic personality that had had a considerable influence on Islam and the emerging Islamic polity. Traditional accounts state that while Muhammad preached secretly in his early career, he had prayed to Allah to strengthen his cause by the conversion of 'Umar. Indeed, no sooner than 'Umar became Muslim (perhaps the fiftieth person to do so), he demanded that the Prophet should no longer be deterred by security considerations and that he should begin preaching in public. A *hadith* (prophetic tradition) is said to have stated that no controversy among the Muslims that had been solved by the Qur'an did not take 'Umar's opinion into account.

Devotion. Devoted to the Prophet, 'Umar initially refused to believe that Muhammad the Prophet had died and vowed to punish anyone who said so. However, the shock soon wore off and because of 'Umar's organizational genius and decisive action the Muslim community averted a disaster by nominating Abu Bakr as the successor of the Prophet. Abu Bakr ruled briefly, and he nominated 'Umar to follow him as the most qualified for the position. No one objected.

Successor. Thus, in 634 'Umar became "Successor to the Successor of the Prophet." He correctly realized the cumbersome nature of this title and in its place he introduced the generic title of *Amir al-Mu'minin* (Commander of the Faithful). He also decreed that the year of the *Hijra* be the start of the Muslim calendar (622 or 1 A.H.). Furthermore, he regularized taxation, the collection of revenue, and the distribution of wealth among the *Umma*. He ordered a cadastral survey to be conducted to determine the taxable land and the amount of taxation and established the first bureaus of the government, *Diwan al-Jund* (army register) and *Diwan al-Kharaj* (register of the revenue). For the distribution of wealth, he created what is known as *Diwan 'Umar*, a register of the Muslims according to their precedence in the service of Islam: the earlier one converted, the more exalted the rank and the higher the annual stipend he received. Women and children also received a fixed stipend.

Consolidation. To consolidate the state further, he decreed that all officials, including the khalifah, should receive a salary from the central treasury. He also ordered the establishment of three new cities (Kufah, Basrah, and Fustat) and appointed various officials to administer the conquered provinces.

Confiscations. Powerful and austere, he maintained a tight grip on the activities of prominent Makkans, lest they take advantage of their status. The finances of the khilafah were jealously guarded. He maintained a practice of confiscating half of the wealth of dismissed officials after he realized that they enriched themselves during their tenure.

Consultation. Before he died, 'Umar appointed a council of electors (*Shura*) to select a successor. The concept of *shura* (consultation), whether narrowly or broadly defined, became an important feature of Islamic politics.

Sources:

G. Levi della Vida, "Umar ibn al-Khattab," *Encyclopedia of Islam,* CD-ROM version (Leiden: Brill, 1999).

Muhammad Shibli Nu'mani, *'Umar the Great: The Second Caliph of Islam,* 2 volumes, translated by Zafar Ali Khan [and Muhammad Saleem] (Lahore: Sh. Muhammad Ashraf, 1956–1957).

Documentary Sources

Al-Baladhuri, *Futuh al-Buldan* (History of the Muslim Conquest)—A chronicle of the early Islamic period, considered one of the best primary sources about this time of Islamic history; al-Baladhuri's book includes information about military conquests, land reclamation, and the founding of cities.

Muhammad ibn Ishaq (circa 704–circa 767), *Sirat Rasul Allah* (The Life of Muhammad)—The earliest biography of the Prophet Muhammad, including nearly every detail of his life and activities and information about the foundation and consolidation of Islam; it is not extant in its original form but has been preserved in two later recensions, the best known by Ibn Hisham (died 833), on which many later biographies and histories of the period relied for information.

Ibn Khaldun (1332–1406), *al-Muqaddimah* (The Prolegomena, 1375–1378, revised 1378–1406)—An important philosophy of history that, according to many modern scholars, lays the foundations of the science of sociology.

Usama ibn Munqidh (1095–1188), *Kitab al I'tibar* (Book of Reflections and Considerations)—A memoir of the Crusades period by a high official in Damascus, whose influential family was involved in the political, diplomatic, and military relations between the Muslims and the Crusaders in Syria; his various observations on the "Franks" (as the Muslims called the Crusaders) have helped scholars to understand how the Crusaders and the Muslims viewed one another and to appreciate the adjustments that societies go through during periods of conflict.

Ibn al-Nadim, *al-Fihrist* (The Catalogue, or Survey, of Culture, circa 987)—A bibliography of all the books published in Arabic by the late tenth century, which allows modern scholars to gauge the extent of learning in the Abbasid period.

Al-Jahiz (circa 776–869), *Kitab al-Bukhala'* (The Book of Misers)—A book of anecdotes and a social commentary against materialism by a writer who lived during the great debates of the Mu'tazila.

Al-Maqrizi, *History of the Ayyubid Sultans of Egypt*—The best chronicle of medieval Egyptian history, this work describes Salah al-Din's countercrusade and his dealings with Richard the Lionhearted and describes Egyptian society under the Mamluks in great detail.

Al-Tabari (838–923), *Tarikh al-Rusul wa al-Muluk* (History of Prophets and Kings)—The most detailed account of early Islamic history.

CHAPTER SIX

POLITICS, LAW, AND THE MILITARY

by KHALID YAHYA BLANKINSHIP

CONTENTS

CHRONOLOGY
196

OVERVIEW
201

TOPICS IN POLITICS, LAW, AND THE MILITARY

The Authority
of the Khilafah 203

Let It Be Known 204

The Judicial System 206

*Major Ruling Groups,
622–1500* 207

Jurisprudence
and Law 209

*Madhhabs
(Schools Of Law)* 210

Laws on Commerce 211

Laws on Crime 212

Laws on Family Life 213

Laws on Foreign Relations
and War 215

Legal Developments. 217

Mirrors of Princes 217

Military
Developments 221

Mongol Invasions 228

Religious Expansion 229

The Spread of
Islam 230

Sultanates 232

SIGNIFICANT PEOPLE

Abu Hanifah 233

'Ali ibn Abi Talib 234

Ahmad Ibn Hanbal 235

'Abd al-Rahman
Ibn Khaldun 235

Ja'far al-Sadiq 236

Malik ibn Anas. 237

Nizam al-Mulk. 238

Muhammad ibn
Idris al-Shafi'i 238

Shajarat al-Durr 239

DOCUMENTARY SOURCES
240

Sidebars and tables are listed in italics.

622
- After the Muslims are driven out of Makkah, the Prophet Muhammad settles in Madinah, where he establishes the earliest Muslim polity, beginning the Muslim era.

623
- The first Muslim military expeditions are sent out from Madinah.

624
- At the Battle of Badr the Muslims defeat a force of Quraysh from Makkah of more than twice their number.

627
- After the Battle of the Trench, at which Muslims end a siege of Madinah by forces from Makkah, the Prophet's authority becomes unquestioned at Madinah.

629
- With the taking of the oasis of Khaybar, the Prophet's rule extends beyond Madinah for the first time.

630
- After the surrender of Makkah to a Muslim force, the Prophet appoints his first resident governor away from Madinah, thus making the Muslim polity a territorial state.

631
- During the "Year of Deputations," the Prophet accepts the submission of all West Arabia and of various groups in the Arabian peninsula.

632
- After the death of the Prophet Muhammad, his companion Abu Bakr is saluted as amir by an assembly of resident Muslims.

634
- Abu Bakr sends Muslim military expeditions to Syria in the Byzantine Empire and to the Sasanid Empire in Iraq.
- Abu Bakr dies and is succeeded by 'Umar ibn al-Khattab (ruled 634–644), who assumes the title Amir al-Mu'minin (Commander of the Believers), expressing his superior authority in the state; he is also known as khalifah (caliph), or deputy, and the state is called the khilafah (caliphate).

636-637
- Syria and Iraq are added to the khilafah after the decisive battles of al-Yarmuk (636) and al-Qadisiyyah (637).

638
- New Muslim military-camp cities are founded in Iraq at Basrah and Kufah, which in time become great metropolises.

* DENOTES CIRCA DATE

638
(CONT'D)
- The Byzantines surrender Jerusalem, an honored place in the Islamic religion, to the Muslims.

639-642
- Egypt comes under Muslim rule.

643
- Most of Iran falls to the khilafah.

644
- 'Umar is assassinated. His successor, 'Uthman, a member of the Umayyad family, is elected by a *shura* (consulting committee) appointed by 'Umar on his deathbed, establishing a precedent for consultation and electoral procedures among later Muslims.

655
- Muslim naval forces shatter the Byzantine fleet off the coast of Anatolia.

656
- Khalifah 'Uthman is killed in a revolt, sparking the First Civil War. 'Ali is elected the fourth khalifah and fights the pro-Quraysh party at the Battle of the Camel, where opposition leaders Talhah and al-Zubayr are killed.
- Mu'awiyah, the governor of Syria, refuses allegiance to 'Ali and prepares for war.
- External Muslim military expeditions are suspended.

656-661
- During the First Civil War, the khilafah concludes a defensive truce with the Byzantine Empire.

660
- Mu'awiyah is proclaimed khalifah in Jerusalem.

661
- After the assassination of 'Ali, his followers name his son al-Hasan as his successor, but Hasan reaches an agreement with his rival by which Mu'awiyah becomes khalifah.

680
- Mu'awiyah dies and is succeeded by his son Yazid I.

681-692
- The Second Civil War ends with a continuation of the Umayyad khilafah.

* DENOTES CIRCA DATE

685	• The khilafah signs a defensive truce with the Byzantine Empire, which lasts until 692.
711–715	• Muslims acquire Spain, Turkistan, and the Sind in a series of quick campaigns with only a few battles.
717–718	• A major campaign to take Constantinople fails, and Muslims lose control of the eastern Mediterranean.
740	• In Morocco a great Berber revolt breaks out against the Umayyad khilafah. The rebels set up a rival khalifah, ending the political unity of Muslims, and Umayyad attempts to expand the boundaries of its khilafah.
749	• The Abbasid khilafah is proclaimed at Kufah in Iraq in the midst of the Third Civil War (746–752).
750	• The Umayyad khilafah ends with the death of the last Umayyad khalifah, Marwan II, in Egypt.
762–763	• The unsuccessful revolt of the 'Alid Muhammad al-Nafs al-Zakiyyah against the Abbasid khalifah al-Mansur results in the arrest of legal scholars Abu Hanifah and Malik for lending support to the rebels.
763	• Al-Mansur founds Baghdad in Iraq as his royal capital. The city quickly becomes the central metropolis and main cultural center of the Muslim world, leading to the precipitous decline of nearby al-Kufah.
786*	• In an attempt to establish a hierarchy of judicial authority, Abu Yusuf is appointed the supreme judge of the Abbasid khilafah, depriving the khalifah of all authority in the law and creating a separate status for the judiciary.
811–827	• The Fourth Civil War greatly weakens the khilafah.
861	• A military coup by Turkish troops at Samarra' restricts the temporal authority of the Abbasid khalifahs, who never recover power completely.

* DENOTES CIRCA DATE

909
- Claiming that their leader is divinely guided, the Isma'ili Shi'i Fatimids establish a khilafah in Tunisia in opposition to the Abbasids.

928
- The Umayyad ruler of Spain takes the title of khalifah in opposition to the Fatimids and the Abbasids.

945
- The Shi'i Buyids, an Iranian dynasty, capture Baghdad and place the Abbasid khalifahs under virtual house arrest.

969
- Egypt is captured by the Fatimids of North Africa, who found Cairo, which gradually replaces Baghdad as the central and most important Muslim metropolis.

1055
- Saljuk Turks take Baghdad from its Shi'i Buyid rulers, ending the Buyid amirate and founding a Saljuk sultanate for a "dyarchy" of sultanate and khilafah. The Saljuk sultans favor the Shafi'i school of law, while the Abbasid khalifahs favor the Hanbali school, connecting both to the state for the first time.

1071
- The defeat and capture of Byzantine emperor Romanus IV Diogenes at Malazgirt (Manzikert) cause the Byzantines to lose control over most of Anatolia. Turks then settle widely there and assimilate much of the Greek-speaking population over the next centuries. This victory begins a major expansion of the area influenced by Islam.

1095
- Pope Urban II calls for a Crusade against Islam.

1099
- Western European Crusaders seize Jerusalem from the Fatimids and establish a Latin Christian kingdom there.

1171
- Sultan Salah al-Din al-Ayyubi (1171–1193), known to Western Europeans as Saladin, makes himself sultan, restoring Sunni rule in Egypt and ending the Shi'i Fatimid khilafah.

1187
- Salah al-Din completely defeats the Crusaders at Hittin in Palestine and retakes Jerusalem from them.

1211
- Iltutmish (1211–1236) founds the Sultanate of Delhi in northern India, the first Indian Muslim state.

* DENOTES CIRCA DATE

POLITICS, LAW, AND THE MILITARY

1218-1221
- The first Mongol invasions devastate Muslim Central Asia, Afghanistan, and northern Iran. The eastern half of the Muslim world is severely injured by these invasions.

1258
- Baghdad falls to the Mongols, ending the Abbasid khilafah.

1260
- Mongols sack Aleppo and Damascus, but the Mamluks of Egypt stop their advance at 'Ayn Jalut in Palestine.

1291
- Muslims capture Acre, the last Crusader outpost in Syria, ending the presence of western Crusaders in the Middle East, except on Cyprus.

1295*
- Ghazan Khan, the Mongol ruler of Iran, converts to Islam.

1299*
- The Ottoman sultanate—later the largest, longest-lasting, and most institutional of pre-modern Muslim states—is established as a small principality in northwest Anatolia.

1361
- The Ottoman Turks take Andrianople from the Byzantines and make it their new capital.

1369
- Timur (Tamerlane), a Muslim Turkic leader, rises to power in Transoxania.

1383-1385
- Timur conquers eastern Persia.

1398
- Timur sacks Delhi, India.

1405
- After the death of Timur, his successors are unable to maintain his empire.

1453
- Constantinople is taken by Ottoman Turks led by Sultan Muhammad II al-Fatih, ending the Byzantine Empire.

1492
- The surrender of Granada to Spanish Christian forces ends the last Muslim state in Spain.

* DENOTES CIRCA DATE

OVERVIEW

Revealed Law. At first, political and legal organization in Islam was simple. From the time he began preaching publicly, about 612, the Prophet Muhammad guided a small community of followers at Makkah, all of whom were connected with the local tribe known as the Quraysh. Because they knew each other personally, no institutionalized organization was needed. However, when visitors from the oasis of Yathrib, 450 kilometers to the north, decided to become Muslims in 620, they took an oath of allegiance to the Prophet and renewed it the following year. In 622, when the Prophet and a few dozen of his Makkan companions, called the Muhajirun (Emigrants), settled Yathrib, which was then renamed Madinah (the community governed by divine law), they were joined by large numbers of people from that oasis, called the Ansar (Helpers), and the community required more political organization. The earliest expression of this institutionalization of government is found in a document known as the Constitution of Madinah, which shortly after Muhammad's arrival set down some general guidelines for internal affairs within the Muslim community and its relations with the non-Muslims in the oasis. It also established the Prophet's position as arbitrator and judge. For the Muslims, the new state that gradually emerged was based on obedience to God and His Prophet as emphasized in the Qur'an. Earlier occasional oaths of allegiance became institutionalized as the basis for a new oath of adherence to the Muslim community (Qur'an 9: 111; 48: 10, 18; 60: 12) in which Muslims swore to uphold certain religious duties and moral principles in addition to supporting the Prophet. Such an oath appears to have become regularly administered to new Muslims in the last few years of Muhammad's life.

Sovereignty. As the number of Muslims in Madinah and elsewhere in western Arabia grew, the Prophet's power and sovereignty increased. As early as 627, the Muslims seem to have become a majority of the population of Madinah. By 629, Muslim sovereignty reached the oasis of Khaybar to the north, thus extending beyond the city-state of Madinah for the first time. The important towns of Makkah and al-Ta'if surrendered and accepted Islam in 630 and 631 respectively and received resident governors. Despite this growing political organization, however, the lack of earlier examples of states in Arabia made it difficult for the Prophet to enforce obedience. The Qur'an includes long passages exhorting Muslims to join military expeditions, even in some of the latest parts (Qur'an 9: 38–57, 81–106)—evidence that there was still no mandatory military conscription as late as 631, almost at the end of the Prophet's life. Similarly, there were no bureaucratic institutions. Although the Prophet was the ruler of a nascent state, he apparently had no personal staff or officials to keep a distance between himself and the people (Qur'an 33: 53; 49: 1–5). Also, there were no officials residing outside of Madinah until a governor was appointed for Makkah in 630. This rudimentary level of political organization still existed when the Prophet died in 632. This lack of organization during the Prophet's lifetime, lovingly handed down as precedents in the Sunnah (prophetic tradition) by subsequent generations of Muslims, had enormous consequences. Because tradition did not specify any political system in detail, later Muslim political systems could establish only meager religious justification.

Legitimacy. As the Muslim civilization unfolded after the death of the Prophet, however, it remained true to the positive elements in the teachings laid down by the Prophet. The Qur'an and the Sunnah remained the two underlying bases that informed the development of subsequent Muslim culture through all succeeding ages. The Qur'an was the Book of God revealed to the Prophet as divine guidance. The Prophet's additional teachings and practices constituted his Sunnah, or path to follow. The Sunnah was eventually recorded extensively in written form as the independent reports called the hadiths. (Although Sunnah and hadiths are not quite identical, the two words are often used interchangeably.) Because there is little strictly political matter in the Qur'an and the Sunnah as represented by the hadiths, the state in Islam remained on the whole an ad hoc affair. This tendency to deal with the situation at hand without considering long-term consequences contributed to its loss of legitimacy, until the Ottoman empire (1299–1922) somewhat restored the balance in favor of the state. Meanwhile, however, law formulated by independent scholars, who were usually not under the control or even the influence of the state, drew strength and legitimacy from the same sources that were denied to the state. Hence, the law was always religious in its inspiration. Most of the time, when the law was strong, the state was weak. On the other hand, on the rare occasions when the state was strong, legal scholars tended to become more dependent on and subservient to the state, although there were always those who did not conform.

Sources of Law. The branch of Muslim religious knowledge that provides the principles by which the law may be known, derived, and elaborated is called *usul al-fiqh* (sources of law). Because this area of study defines the principles on which Muslim law is based, it can be viewed as the centerpiece of Muslim legal thinking. Muslim scholars have produced hundreds of books on this subject. The classical schools of law (*madhhabs*) differ first and foremost in their approaches to handling the sources of law. As the religion of Islam and its law are based on divine revelation, which alone can provide infallible knowledge, the first source of the law is the direct revelation of God to the Prophet Muhammad, the Qur'an, and the amplification found in the established practices of the Prophet, the Sunnah.

The Sunnah. At first the Sunnah consisted of all the oral traditions handed down by the early Muslims. Later, these traditions were classified according to who reported them, and those that could be traced back to the Prophet Muhammad were accorded the highest authority. Traditions that could not be traced back to the Prophet but only to his Companions or even to authorities of later generations were not necessarily discarded but had a lesser status. After a considerable time, the oral tradition began to be written down, perhaps at first in small notebooks or booklets that were later incorporated in larger works. The earliest editions of Malik's *al-Muwatta'* (The Trodden Path), the earliest complete law book, which includes various kinds of traditions, may date to circa 765–770. A study of this book reveals that it could not have been the first such book; rather it caps a sophisticated development of thought that must have taken place over a considerable period. After Malik, the Sunnah came increasingly to be written down in compendia that burgeoned in size to multivolume sets. After al-Tayalisi (died 819), books that included only traditions traceable to the Prophet himself began to circulate. These traditions, called hadiths, recorded what the Prophet said, did, or approved. After al-Shafi'i (died 820), the tendency grew to call only the traditions of the Prophet Sunnah, thus equating the Sunnah with the hadiths. This limitation was desirable not only because of the overriding authority of the Prophet but also because only what could be established as coming from the Prophet was held to come from God, even if indirectly, as suggested by such Qur'an verses as 2: 129, 151; 3: 164; and 4:113.

Consensus. In any legal system many issues that are not treated by existing texts may arise, and other principles are needed to extend the law. The first of these principles in Muslim law was the concept of consensus. If a consensus could be shown to exist on an issue not treated clearly in texts, or if there were a consensus on how a rele-

vant text should be interpreted, that consensus itself became a legal argument. Scholars disagreed, however, on who might be a party to such a consensus and whether a consensus had to be unanimous. According to the broadest interpretation a consensus meant agreement of the living scholars of the religion and did not have to achieve absolute unanimity. Eventually, though, consensuses largely became limited to those formed by earlier scholars. With the appearance of schools of law, which interpreted the sources of the law in various different ways, there also arose the idea that a consensus among the scholars of one school was sufficient to establish the rulings of that school. The most restrictive conception was that only a consensus formed by the Companions of the Prophet carried any weight, and that no subsequent consensuses were of any significance. (This opinion was held only by the Zahiris, a literalist Sunni school.)

Analogy. Although establishing consensuses helped to define much of the law, many instances arose in which religious scholars had to give a religious opinion on an issue that had not been clearly covered before or on an issue on which a serious difference of opinion existed. In such cases, the principle of reasoning by analogy was introduced. By drawing analogies only from texts of the Qur'an and the Sunnah, it was possible to maintain a connection with divine revelation while at the same time allowing for reasoning. Some textual literalists dissented from this view and discouraged or disallowed analogy.

Standards. Despite a widespread agreement among the Sunni schools (except for the Zahiris) over these four basic sources of the law—the Qur'an, the Sunnah, consensus, and analogy—great disagreements arose among the schools of law regarding the precise meaning and method of application of each source. Mostly, these disputes were about the nature and role of the Sunnah. The principles for interpretation of the Qur'an, a single text, were largely fixed quite early. The Sunnah, however, consisted of a great mass of statements relating to the practice of the first Muslims and were usually orally transmitted in the early period. If any of the righteous Muslims of the first two or three generations could be shown to have followed a certain practice, that proof could be taken as evidence that the Prophet had also followed the same practice or had at least approved of it. Yet, many differences were obvious, especially from city to city but also among different groups of Muslims in the same city. These discrepancies seemed to require a tightening of the standards for what constituted sufficient proof of the Sunnah. For Malik and the school of Madinah, the received practice of the Madinans was the best evidence of the Prophet's Sunnah, because Madinah had been the scene of his last ten years and had continued his tradition unbroken since that time. Other schools, however, began to demand that a Sunnah, to be valid, had to be traceable to an individual report going back to the Prophet through an unbroken chain of named transmitters. Such reports constituted the hadiths, which were collected in writing in roughly two hundred separate collections from about 770 to 1070, a period of three centuries. To determine their validity, the many reports making up each collection had to be assessed individually by the fairly complex criteria of a form of historical criticism, and the assessment of a particular tradition often differed among the schools. Eventually, however, a consensus emerged on most hadiths. In particular, all those contained in the two sound collections of Muhammad ibn Ismail al-Bukhari (810–870) and Abu al-Husayn Muslim (821–875) were held to be valid for law, and four other books of Sunnah were also identified as generally good sources, making a total of six books. Traditions found in other works continued also to be used as well.

TOPICS IN POLITICS, LAW, AND THE MILITARY

THE AUTHORITY OF THE KHILAFAH

Death and Succession. The Prophet Muhammad's death immediately cut off the Muslim community from its direct, personal divine source of inspiration, revelation, and guidance. The Prophet had not acknowledged anyone else as a prophet or potential prophet, and the Qur'an seems to foreclose that possibility for eternity (33:40). The community met and elected one of the older Companions, Abu Bakr (ruled 632–634), to hold sovereignty in Madinah. At first, perhaps, Abu Bakr bore the title of *amir* (commander), but under the rule of his successor, 'Umar ibn al-Khattab (ruled 634–644), the title became *amir al-mu'minin* (commander of the believers), a more exalted label meant to clarify the superiority of the ruler's authority

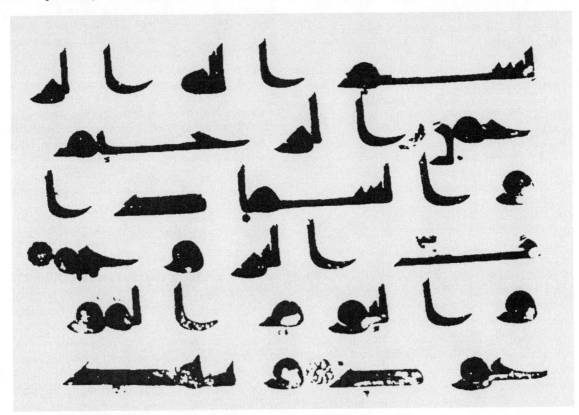

Calligraphy attributed to Khalifah 'Ali ibn Abi Talib, who reigned 656–661 (from Isma'il R. al-Faruqi, and Lois Lamya', *The Cultural Atlas of Islam*, 1986)

The murder of Uthman, the third Khalifah, in 656, resulted from unrest in the province of Egypt, where Uthman's appointed governor was accused of tyranny. When Ali ibn Abi Talib acceded to the Khilafah, he appointed Malik al-Ashtar as governor of Egypt. Because the appointment was so critical to restoring good government and civil order, Ali put in writing a lengthy exposition on just rule in the form of the letter excerpted here. The letter was among the writings and sayings of Ali compiled by al-Sayyid al-Radi (970-1015), an influential Shi'i scholar, based on earlier works.

Let it be known to you, Malik, that I am sending you as a governor to a country which has seen many regimes before this. Some of them were benign, sympathetic and good, while others were tyrannical, oppressive and cruel. People will judge your regime as critically as you have studied the activities of other regimes and they will criticize you in the same way as you have censured or approved other rulers. You must know that a good and virtuous man is known and recognized by the good that is said about him and the praise which Allah has destined him to receive from others. Therefore, make your mind the source and fountain-head of good thoughts, good intentions and good deeds. This can only be attained by keeping a strict control on your desires and yearnings, however much they may try to incite and coerce you. Remember that the best way to do justice to your inner self and to keep it out of harm is to restrain it from vice and from things which the "self" inordinately and irrationally desires.

Malik! You must create in your mind kindness, compassion and love for your subjects. Do not behave towards them as if you are a voracious and ravenous beast and as if your success lies in devouring them. Remember, Malik, that amongst your subjects there are two kinds of people: those who have the same religion as you have; they are brothers to you, and those who have religions other than that of yours, they are human beings like you. Men of either category suffer from the same weaknesses and disabilities that human beings are inclined to, they commit sins, indulge in vices either intentionally or foolishly and unintentionally without realizing the enormity of their deeds. Let your mercy and compassion come to their rescue and help in the same way and to the same extent that you expect Allah to show mercy and forgiveness to you.

Malik! You must never forget that if you are a ruler over them then the caliph is the ruler over you and Allah is the Supreme Lord over the caliph. And the reality is that He has appointed you as the governor and tested you through the responsibility of this governance over them. Never think of raising yourself to such a false prestige that you can declare war against Allah because you cannot ward off His Wrath and you can never be free from the need of His Mercy and Compassion. Do not feel ashamed to forgive and forget. Do not hurry over punishments and do not be pleased and do not be proud of your power to punish. Do not get angry and lose your temper quickly over the mistakes and failures of those over whom you rule. On the contrary, be patient and sympathetic with them. Anger and desire of vengeance are not going to be of much help to you in your administration.

Never say to yourself, "I am their Lord, their ruler and all in all over them and that I must be obeyed submissively and humbly" because such a thought will unbalance your mind, will make you vain and arrogant, will weaken your faith in religion and will make you seek support of any power other than that of Allah. If you ever feel any pride or vanity on account of your influence and rule over your subjects then think of the supreme authority and rule of the Lord over the Universe, the extent of His creations, the supremacy of His Might and Glory, His Power to do things which you cannot even dream of doing and His control over you which is more dominating than that which you can ever achieve over anything around you. Such thoughts will cure your mental weakness, will keep you away from vanity and rebellion (against Allah), will reduce your arrogance and haughtiness and will take you back to the sanity which you had foolishly deserted.

Source: Sayed M. A. Jafery, trans., *Nahjul Balagha: Sermons, Letters and Sayings of Hazrat Ali* (Karachi: Khorasan Islamic Centre, 1971), pp. 491–493.

over that of any other. More generally, the title *khalifah* (caliph), or deputy, also came into use for the ruler, probably because the Prophet had always appointed a deputy to take charge when he was absent from Madinah. This title is usually anglicized as "caliph." Possibly by the reign of the third khalifah, the Umayyad 'Uthman (ruled 644–656), this title was expanded to *khalifat Allah* (God's deputy). Probably this interpretation of the title was elaborated from a single Qur'anic verse (38: 26) referring to the Prophet David's appointment by God as a khalifah on earth. The title *khalifat Allah* became as important under the Umayyad dynasty (661–750) as that of amir al-mu'minin, with which it was used interchangeably.

Authority. From the beginning, Muslims held that—just as they had had to obey the Prophet—they must obey the khalifah, because he too possessed sovereignty over Muslims. This general power was theoretically unfettered, but certain limitations were nonetheless present from the outset. Unlike the Prophet, the khalifahs never claimed to receive special revelations from God, even though they insisted, at least from the time of 'Uthman and probably from that of Abu Bakr, that God had authorized their rule.

Mosaic floor from the bath at the Umayyad desert palace of Khirbat al-Mafjah (Palestine Archaeological Museum)

Their lack of power of prophetic revelation limited their ability to legislate. As the Muslim law was eventually elaborated by independent jurists, the khalifahs saw their freedom of action gradually curtailed. Also, the state ruled by the khalifahs was not in any sense a modern, institutionalized nation-state, but rather the rudimentary state that they had inherited from the Prophet. As it expanded, coming to rule over large populations of non-Muslims by the reign of 'Umar ibn al-Khattab, its main, immediate function was collecting taxes so that it could pay the army, in order to uphold the rule of Islam. Other institutions of government developed slowly, and non-Muslims were left to regulate their own affairs in many areas. During the reign of 'Umar ibn 'Abd al-'Aziz (ruled 717–720) it began to seem necessary to separate the public treasury from the khalifah's private purse, but that reform took a long time to come into effect. Under Hisham (ruled 724–743) the khalifah still had only a single secretary for correspondence and sometimes even wrote his own letters to his governors. This situation continued under later Umayyads, who often resided in isolated private castles at the edge of the desert, remote from the cities and other population centers.

Abbasid Rule. To strengthen their power the Abbasid dynasty (749–1258) tried to elaborate the institutions of the state. Thus, in 763 they established a new capital, Baghdad, that quickly became the main metropolis of the Muslim world and thereby ended the khalifah's isolation. They appointed a wazir (prime minister) to share in the administrative duties of running the state, and after 786 they also tried to impose their superior power over all the provinces by appointing a supreme judge in Baghdad with judicial authority over the whole khilafah (caliphate). Furthermore, they strove to improve the efficiency of their tax-gathering machinery. Nevertheless, the Abbasids encountered several insurmountable obstacles that led to the gradual disintegration of their authority. First, they lacked legitimacy because they had come to power through a revolution against the Umayyads, and they disappointed their Shi'i supporters, who had wanted a descendant of the Prophet's son-in-law 'Ali to rule rather than the descendants of the Prophet's uncle al-'Abbas. Lacking legitimacy, they did not have the moral authority to compel the provinces to submit to a more central organization and taxation system. Instead, the provinces fell away one by one. Indeed, the Abbasids never ruled in Spain, Morocco, and Algeria, so they had to face a multiplicity of Muslim states from the beginning, a fact that seriously undermined their claim to universal dominion. In order to maintain themselves, they had to make deals that involved giving up more and more of their power. Thus, Tunisia and Tripolitania were sold to the Aghlabid family in 800 in exchange for a regular payment, and those countries were henceforth politically independent from the khilafah.

Military Rule. The Abbasids also had to rely on paid professional soldiers to keep them in power. After the Khalifah al-Mu'tasim (833–842) began importing Turkish slave soldiers for this purpose, it was only a matter of time before the generals took over and pushed the khalifahs aside. The first military coup, which overthrew the Khalifah al-Mutawakkil in 861, was the beginning of this trend. Beginning in 934, by which time most of the outer provinces had already been lost, the military dictator's title was formalized as *amir al-umara'* (commander of commanders), and the khalifah's power was at an end. Under the hostile Shi'i Buyids (945–1055), the Abbasid khalifahs were reduced to prisoners in their own palace. Under the Sunni Saljuks (1055–1152), the khalifahs were once again honored but given no access to power, while the Saljuks controlled the state both in fact and in name with the new title of *sultan* (authority). After the decline of the Saljuks, the khalifahs were able to restore their own independent sovereignty once more (1152–1258), but only inside their home province of southern Iraq, an area much smaller than the present-day country of Iraq. Having lost their general authority, except in theoretical legal prescriptions, the Abbasid khilafah in this period functioned merely as one local state in a constellation of local states, until the non-Muslim Mongols put an end to it with their bloody conquest of Baghdad in 1258.

Rival Khalifahs. Meanwhile, a plethora of rival claimants challenged the Abbasids even for their titles of khalifah and amir al-mu'minin. This tendency first arose in North Africa and Spain but eventually was found in many places, devaluing the concept of the khalifah's universal rule. The first to free their lands permanently from the central khilafah's control were the Berbers, whose new states began to emerge in North Africa in 740, even before the end of Umayyad rule. Never again was all Islam in any way associated with a particular state. These new Berber states were at first deemed kharijite (rebel) by the main Muslim tradition, but from their own viewpoint each represented the true khilafah. Later, the Shi'i Fatimids (909–1171), who established themselves in Tunisia and eventually Egypt, seriously challenged the Abbasids' monopoly on the khalifal title in the East as well. When the Umayyad dynasty in Spain (756–1031) revived its claim to the khalifal title in 928 and continued to do so until its end more than a century later, there came to be three major khilafahs simultaneously. Also, many local dynasties in Spain and North and West Africa adopted titles such as *amir al-mu'minin* that were normally accorded in the East only to khalifahs. Later, the full title of the khilafah was claimed by the al-Muwahhids (circa 1132–1269), the Marinids (1269–1465), the Hafsids (1253–1574), and all the later rulers of Morocco to this day. Thus, the various western dynasties did not recognize the eastern khilafah after 909.

End of the Khilafah. In the East the existence of the khilafah was called into question after the taking of Baghdad and the killing of the Abbasid khalifah by the pagan Mongols in 1258. In many respects, this event spelled the end of the khilafah and showed how unimportant and unnecessary the office had become. Although the Mamluk sultans set up an alleged branch of the Abbasids in Egypt (1261–1543), the sultans accorded this branch scant respect or attention, and it was not recognized outside the Egyp-

tian sultanate except by the distant sultanate of Delhi in India (1211–1556). When the Ottoman Turks conquered Egypt in 1517, they temporarily carried off the khalifah, al-Mutawakkil III, to Istanbul, but he had so little importance that later he was allowed to return to Egypt, where he died. The Egyptian Abbasid khilafah did not continue after his death. Thus, by 1500, the khilafah barely existed in the Muslim world, having lost almost all importance and relevance, and it scarcely entered the consciousness of the Muslims any longer, except for the memory of it as an early ideal, especially in the books of the law. Much later, beginning in 1774, the Ottoman sultans made use of the title occasionally until its definitive abolition in 1924. Although the khilafah eventually served no governmental function, it played an early role in providing the somewhat stable political framework within which Islam was preached for more than two centuries (632–861). The khilafah helped to establish Islam on a firm and lasting basis, and then the religion was able to survive and flourish without such a political expression.

Sources:

Antony Black, *The History of Islamic Political Thought: From the Prophet to the Present* (New York: Routledge, 2001).

Marshall G. S. Hodgson, *The Venture of Islam: Conscience and History in a World Civilization*, 2 volumes (Chicago: University of Chicago Press, 1974).

Hugh Kennedy, *The Prophet and the Age of the Caliphates: The Islamic Near East from the Sixth to the Eleventh Century* (London: Longman, 1986).

D. Sourdel and A. K. S. Lambton, "Khalifa," in *Encyclopedia of Islam*, CD-ROM version (Leiden: Brill, 1999).

THE JUDICIAL SYSTEM

Judges. The exercise of legal and judicial decision making was at first in the hands of Muslim political rulers representing the khalifah, who in turn represented the authority of the Prophet. The Prophet had exercised the judicial function in his own community exclusively by himself; his initial role on arriving in Madinah had been as judge for the disparate communities of that oasis (Qur'an 4: 58; 5: 42–43, 48–49). Under the khalifahs, judges were originally legal advisers to the governors. When the governors became too busy with other affairs to handle legal cases themselves and when caseloads increased in proportion to the growing number of Muslims and the multiplication of legal problems in a society that was becoming more complex, the governors transferred jurisdiction over legal cases to the legal advisers completely. The legal advisers who became judges were people who were learned in the Shari'ah (sacred law) and carefully considered it in their rulings. Thus, they served as somewhat of a bridge between the state and the religious community during the early period.

Independent Judiciary. The chronology of the inauguration of the independent judicial system (*qada'*) is obscure. The Prophet is said to have sent Mu'adh ibn Jabal to serve as judge to part of Yemen, but other traditions make it clear that the office of Mu'adh, if historical, was a political governorship that included authority over

Al-Khulafa' al-Rashidun (The Rightly Guided Khalifahs)	632–661	Arabia, Syria, Iraq, Iran, and Egypt
Umayyads	661–750	Arabia, Syria, Iraq, Iran, Egypt, North Africa, and central Asia
Abbasids	749–1258	Arabia, Syria, Iraq, Iran, Egypt, North Africa, and central Asia
Umayyads of Spain	756–1031	Spain
Rustamids	779–909	western Algeria
Idrisids	789–926	Morocco
Aghlabids	800–909	Tunisia, eastern Algeria, and Sicily
Samanids	819–1005	northeastern Iran and central Asia
Rassids	circa 860–1281	Yemen
Saffarids	867–1003	eastern Iran
Tulunids	868–905	Egypt and Syria
Fatimids	909–1171	North Africa, Egypt, and Syria
Buyids	934–1062	Iran and Iraq
Ikhshidids	935–969	Egypt and Syria
Ghaznawids	977–1186	northeastern Iran, Afghanistan, and northern India
Ghurids	end of 10th c.–1215	northeastern Iran, Afghanistan, and northern India
Muluk al-tawa'if (party kings)	11th c.	Spain
Great Saljuks	1037–1194	Iran and Iraq
Saljuks of Kirman	1041–1186	southeastern Iran
Almoravids	circa 1050–1147	North Africa and Spain
Danishmendids	1071–1178	central Turkey
Saljuks of Rum	1077–1307	central and eastern Turkey
Saljuks of Syria	1078–1117	Syria
Almohads	1130–1269	North Africa and Spain
Fahkr al-Din dynasty	12th c.– 16th c.	Somalia
Ayyubids	1171–1260	Egypt, Syria, and part of western Arabia
Marinids	1196–1464	Morocco
Delhi Sultanate	1206–1555	northern India
Chaghatayids	1227–1363	central Asia
Hafsids	1228–1574	Tunisia and eastern Algeria
Rasulids	1229–1454	Yemen
Nasrids	1230–1492	southern Spain
Mamluks	1250–1517	Egypt and Syria
Ilkhanids	1256–1353	Iran and Iraq
Qaramanids	circa 1256–1483	central Turkey
Ottomans	1299–1922	Turkey, Syria, Iraq, Egypt, Cyprus, Tunisia, Algeria, and western Arabia
Timurids	1369–1506	central Asia, Iran, Iraq
Aq Qoyunlu	1378–1508	eastern Turkey and northwestern Iran
Qara Qoyunlu	1380–1468	northwestern Iran and Iraq

Sources: Albert Hourani, *A History of the Arab Peoples* (Cambridge, Mass.: Harvard University Press, 1991), pp. 489–490.

Francis Robinson, ed., *The Cambridge Illustrated History of the Islamic World* (Cambridge: Cambridge University Press, 1996), pp. 308–311.

Discussion on a point of law at the court of a qadi; illumination by Bihzad in a 1488–1489 manuscript for the *Bustan* (Garden) by al-Sa'di (General Egyptian Book Organization, Cairo)

judicial matters, not a pure judgeship. Certain traditions attribute the foundation of the judiciary to the Khalifah 'Umar ibn al-Khattab (634–644), but others state that he was his own judge, which is undoubtedly correct. Probably the first appearance of a separate judiciary may be located in the reign of an early Umayyad, perhaps Mu'awiyah I (661–680). Judges served at the pleasure of the ruler, but this limit did not necessarily compromise their integrity, for juristic knowledge was respected, and judges sometimes held office for long terms. Quite often a judge was continued in office in spite of a change of government. On the other hand, the idea eventually became widespread that a scholar ought to avoid judicial office because of the taint of the state. Many of the first-ranking scholars of Islam never held such office, but a substantial number did accept judgeships, often reluctantly, probably because of the belief that someone had to do it. Among the well-known scholars who held judgeships were Abu Yusuf (732–798), al-Shaybani (750–805), al-Baqillani (died 1013), 'Abd al-Wahhab al-Baghdadi (973–1031), 'Iyad ibn Musa (1083–1149), Abu Bakr Ibn al-'Arabi

(1076–1148), al-Baydawi (died 1286), Ibn Khaldun (1332–1406), and Ibn Hajar al-'Asqalani (1372–1449).

Legal Texts. Although the position of judge in a Muslim court is somewhat analogous to that of a modern judge in a Western court, there are several distinct differences. The law by which the Muslim judge ruled was not built up by cases and precedents, but rather consisted of a body of legal texts elaborated by many different independent scholars over the centuries. While these texts were prescriptive in nature, laying down specific laws to be followed, they also included a huge variety of differing legal opinions on many issues. Over the centuries the body of the law was constantly being renewed by new compositions and compilations. Thus, the judge had a considerable body of texts on which to build his decisions. To some extent, these books of jurisprudence took the place of case precedents and functioned in the same way, as authorities to be cited. The production of such books, once started, has continued throughout Muslim history to the present day. They eventually came to be supplemented by books of religious opinions responding to particular questions, often inquiries by ordinary people. Such opinions are called *fatwas* and their issuer is a *mufti* (jurisconsult). A *fatwa* was never viewed as setting a precedent; rather, it was only a response of a single authority on a single question. It remained for the state to decide whether to put a *fatwa* into force, and such actions were rare, except where the state itself was the inquirer. Nevertheless, *fatwas* also became commonly cited in judges' legal opinions, when their sources were disclosed (and often they were not).

Courts. Once a Shari'ah judge had ruled on a matter, the decision was final in theory. In practice, however, recourse was sometimes had to parallel courts called *mazalim* courts, which functioned more directly under the supervision of the government. They also enforced the Shari'ah but frequently ignored the standards of judicial procedure and evidence set by the Shari'ah in order to be more immediately effective. Another difference from the modern practice of law, which was also the case in other premodern systems, was that everyone, both plaintiffs and defendants, had to answer for themselves in person; attorneys were not to represent anyone. This provision was made because the purchase of eloquence for representation would not be egalitarian since only the rich would then be well represented (a complaint often made today). A person in a Shari'ah court could seek legal advice outside the court, but inside it everyone had to represent himself or herself.

Sources:

Abu'l-Hasan al-Mawardi, *al-Ahkam al-Sultaniyyah: The Laws of Islamic Government,* translated by Asadullah Yate (London: Ta-Ha Publishers, 1996); also translated by Wafaa H. Wahba as *The Ordinances of Government* (Reading, U.K.: Garnet Press, 1996).

J. S. Nielsen, "Mazalim," in *Encyclopedia of Islam,* CD-ROM version (Leiden: Brill, 1999).

Émil Tyan, and Kaldy Nagy Gy, "Kadi" *Encyclopedia of Islam,* CD-ROM version (Leiden: Brill, 1999).

Tyan, *Histoire de l'organisation judiciaire en pays d'Islam,* second edition (Leiden: Brill, 1960).

JURISPRUDENCE AND LAW

Comprehensive Law. Muslim law, based on the divinely revealed and guided sources of the Qur'an and hadiths, forms the centerpiece and backbone of the religion of Islam. Unlike western systems of law, Muslim law covers and prescribes behavior in all areas of life, including both individual actions that are private to the self and relationships involving two or more parties. Thus, Muslim law is more comprehensive than most other legal systems. Indeed, the Qur'an makes clear that there can be no legitimate legal rulings that are not according to what God has revealed (5: 44–45, 47). Muslim law is also different from Western law in its source. It traces the origin of its principles and prescriptions back to texts of divine origin interpreted by scholars not usually in the employ of the state, thus establishing for a whole society a general legal system that is not directly administered by the state. Nevertheless, the rulers usually intervened in those areas of law that had public impact, often adding laws decreed and enforced by themselves. Thus, the Shari'ah (sacred law) became more developed and remained more applied in the private realms

Early fourteenth-century tile gravestone of Qadi Jalal al-Din 'Ali, with an inscription calling him "King of the Learned Men" and including a genealogy going back through seven generations of qadis, as well as a verse from the Qur'an (British Museum, London)

than in the public. In fact, one can place different categories of law on a continuum from more private to more public in order to show in a descending order the extent of the application of the Shari'ah. These categories would be: forms of worship, necessarily the most private and the most ruled by religion, family law, commercial law, criminal law, judicial procedure, foreign relations and war, and lastly the administration of the state. In classical times, both religion and family law were thoroughly governed by the Shari'ah.

Because Muslim scholars differed on some of the secondary sources of the law and the principles for interpreting those sources, different schools of law arose in Islam. At first fairly numerous, these schools began to arise before 700 under the Umayyads and continued to proliferate until about 950. After that time some schools began to die out. There are now four Sunni schools: Hanafi, Maliki, Shafi'i, and Hanbali; three Shi'i schools: Ja'fari or Imami, Zaydi, and Isma'ili (the last of which is considered heterodox by most other Muslims); and one Kharijite school (Ibadi). Over the centuries there have been sporadic efforts to re-establish a fifth Sunni school, the literalist Zahiri school.

Historically, the various schools differ according to their principles for the use and interpretation of the four sources of law (the Qur'an, the Sunnah (traditions), consensus, and analogy). Some schools tend to predominate in one or another geographical region and hence become a part of the religious and cultural expressions of those regions. Thus, the Hanafi school is dominant in most of Muslim Asia, including in Turkey, the Balkans, Central Asia, the Sunni part of Iraq, and South Asia except for the extreme south of India. The countries in these regions include nearly half of all Muslims in the world. The Maliki school has prevailed in Muslim Africa, including North and West Africa, the Sudan, Upper Egypt, and part of the Persian Gulf area in what is now the United Arab Emirates. It was also the main school of the Muslims in Spain. Although the Maliki school is far from the largest, a majority of Arabic speakers have traditionally followed it. The Shafi'i school prevailed among many of the *ulama'* (scholars), and also in Syria, Lower Egypt (including Cairo), southern Yemen, southern Saudi Arabia, the Red Sea coast of Africa, East Africa, Sri Lanka, the state of Kerala in India, and Southeast Asia. The school of the Abbasid khalifahs for around two centuries (circa 1055–1258), the Hanbali school did not prevail anywhere until after 1500; today it is the official school in Saudi Arabia and Qatar. The Zahiri school survived mostly in Spain. Ja'fari Shi'ism is the majority school in Iran, Azerbaijan, Bahrain, and Iraq, and also is the largest school in Lebanon; this distribution had already been largely established by 1500. The Zaydi school, after having existed in northern Iran, ended up only in northern Yemen. The Isma'ilis, usually regarded as heretical by all the other schools, survived as a minority school in India. The Ibadis remain the official school in Oman, where they have had their center for centuries, and they also are found in small numbers in Libya and Algeria.

The various schools sometimes differed over the validity of a particular tradition, but in general they agreed. Wide differences, however, arose over how they should be ranked. For the Hanafis, a tradition needed to have three individual chains of transmission to be binding, and a hadith could not restrict a general prescription of the Qur'an. For the Malikis, the practice of the people of Madinah, which was recorded in books other than the hadith collections, took precedence over isolated individual hadiths, unless these were supported by multiple chains of transmission. For the Shafi'is, on the other hand, individual reports traceable to the Prophet took precedence, even if these produced only probability rather than certainty. For the Hanbalis, even weakly attested hadiths were deemed better than the resort to individual reasoning, and sound hadiths, even if they were attested only by an isolated chain of transmitters, were held to produce certainty. All of these varying evaluations of the Sunnah led to many legal differences between the schools.

Sometimes scholars have characterized some schools as easier and others as stricter than others in their legal rulings. The Hanafi school has sometimes been called the easiest or most liberal and the Hanbali the narrowest and strictest. It is difficult, however, to make such generalizations because the various schools differ not so much in the broad outlines of their principles as in the details of their rulings. Therefore, while one school may be restrictive on one point, it may be liberal on another. Generally, the Hanafi school has allowed a wider scope for the exercise of reason by jurists, while the others, especially the Hanbali school, have placed more emphasis on the tradition. The Maliki school has preferred strictness in the rules of worship but has been more flexible in other areas of the law. The Zahiris never accepted the principle of analogy as a basis for law, and the Hanbalis also expressed a considerable reluctance on this point. The Shafi'is required that the analogy be clearly related to other texts and recognized legal processes. The Malikis, however, stressed the overriding nature of the public interest, while the Hanafis gave their jurists considerable latitude to exercise their reason. These latter two schools were in theory less bound to the texts, but the differences were to a considerable extent only in words, for all the schools had mechanisms for allowing reinterpretations of previous texts. The Hanbali and Zahiri schools, although supposedly the most scrupulously text-bound, never excluded the free exercise of intellectual effort on the part of the religious scholar, as the other schools tended to do. In theory, because the two schools had a literalist understanding of language, they professed that any honest intellectual effort would always lead to the same conclusion, in conformity with the texts. In actual practice, however, no such thing happened, and as a result these schools, like the others, allowed some flexibility of interpretation.

Sources: Muhammad Abu Zahra, *The Four Imams: Their Lives, Works, and Schools of Thought.* (London: Dar al-Taqua, 2001).

Christopher Melchert, *The Formation of the Sunni Schools of Law, 9th–10th Centuries C.E.* (Leiden: Brill, 1997).

The commercial law of the Shari'ah was extensive and detailed, but it could not always be enforced in practice, and the degree of its application varied. The criminal law was not as developed and was not thoroughly applied because the governments felt that the laws of evidence were too exacting to control crime effectively. Therefore, criminal cases were often handled by state *mazalim* courts rather than by Shari'ah courts. Shari'ah rules of judicial procedure were partly, but not completely, applied. Foreign relations, war, and governmental administration were under the total control of the state, which was only rarely swayed by religious arguments away from doing what was expedient.

Sources:

Ahmad Hasan, *Analogical Reasoning in Islamic Jurisprudence: A Study of the Juridical Principle of Qiyas* (Islamabad: Islamic Research Institute, 1986).

Ahmad Ibn Naqib al-Misri, *The Reliance of the Traveller: The Classic Manual of Islamic Sacred Law 'Umdat al-Salik*, 2 volumes, edited and translated by Nuh Ha Mim Keller (Evanston, Ill.: Sunna Books, 1994).

Muhammad ibn Ahmad Ibn Rushd, *The Distinguished Jurist's Primer: A Translation of Bidayat al-Mujtahid*, translated by Imran Khan Nyazee (Reading, U.K.: Garnet Publishing, 1994).

Mohammad Hashim Kamali, *Principles of Islamic Jurisprudence*, revised edition (Cambridge: Islamic Texts Society, 1991).

Chibli Mallat, ed., *Islam and Public Law: Classical and Contemporary Studies* (London: Graham & Trotman, 1993).

Burhan al-Din al-Marghinani, *The Hedaya, or Guide: A Commentary on the Mussulman Laws*, translated by Charles Hamilton (London: Bensley, 1791).

LAWS ON COMMERCE

A Mercantile Economy. Since business is as old as civilization, the early Muslims inherited existing economic systems instead of creating a new system. Indeed, the revelation of the Qur'an may be seen on the economic front as mainly concerned with fairness in dealing within the existing system(Qur'an 6:152; 7:85; 11:35, 84–85; 17:35; 26:181–182; 55:7–9; 83:1–3). Thus, in many respects, the medieval Muslim economy resembled the other economic systems of its time. Other systems were also interested in fair business practices. Even in the relatively arid Middle East, wealth was principally derived from land, so most laws dealing with commerce were based on the central and well-understood background assumption that wealth was vested in land. Like several other premodern systems, the medieval Muslim economy was based on a bimetallic currency standard of gold and silver coins, a situation that extended back to the time of the ancient Greeks, more than a thousand years before Muhammad. There was also a copper-token coinage. The main underlying difference between the medieval Muslim economy and that of other regions was, perhaps, that commerce and trade were more important in the Middle East than elsewhere—partly owing to the aridity of the region but also because the occupation of merchant was not despised, as it often was elsewhere, for example, in western Europe, China, and Japan. Indeed, Muslims could hardly despise buying and selling for a living when the Prophet himself had been a merchant. For this reason, in fact, the Muslims of the Middle East developed more-advanced business practices than existed elsewhere during medieval times. Modern capitalism eventually grew from these practices as trade took the Middle Eastern Muslim experience across the Mediterranean to Europe.

Profit and Risk. Although Muslim commercial law resembled other civilized Old World legal systems in its stress on fair dealing, its effect was somewhat different from that of European law. The limits Muslim law set on business were not always thoroughly enforced, of course, but they were constantly present and thus had a considerable influence. Overall, commercial law was based on respect for private property and preservation of real value, as well as on an aversion to exploitation and dishonesty. In particular, earning money from interest—which is solidly and fiercely condemned in the Qur'an (2:275–278; 3:130; 4:161; 30:39) and some hadiths—was strictly prohibited by the religious leaders. Demanding the payment of interest—which in medieval times was often extracted at usurious rates because there was high risk attached to making loans—was discouraged and prohibited elsewhere too, including medieval Christian Europe. In Islam the prohibition was firmly ensconced in the sacred law (Shari'ah), which was the law of the land, and therefore usury was not permissible at all. For this reason pious Muslims have thus always been cautious about any business activities that include the payment of interest. Likewise, Muslims have always striven to avoid debt, which is commonly related to interest payments.

Ownership and Fairness. Another major feature of Muslim commercial law was the prohibition of uncertainty (*gharar*) in the law of sale. That is, when a sale took place, the parties had to know exactly what was being bought and sold, and the item being sold had to be in the possession of the seller. Thus, fruit not yet grown could not be sold in advance because such transactions had in them an element of speculation. In modern terms, Muslim law forbids not only the sale of products not yet in hand but also trade in futures or the sale of insurance, which is also seen as a species of uncertain speculation. Because the prohibition on interest eliminated the possibility of leveraging (using credit to enhance one's buying capacity) and because of premodern technology, the medieval Muslim economy was relatively stable and—barring unforeseen political upheavals—one could count on life going according to accustomed patterns. In general, Muslim law viewed ownership as restricted to real property and actual objects in the possession of an owner. Because rentals and leases were permitted, rights of use could be rented, but sale of rights of use was not possible because such a transaction would violate the law that the property being sold must be in the possession of the owner. This prohibition appears to militate against such modern concepts as copyright and "intellectual property." However, modern Muslim jurists have overwhelmingly favored extending property rights to these concepts as well.

Financial Instruments. The medieval Muslim economy is well known for its elaboration of advanced financial instruments, such as an early form of bank draft or check (derived from the Arabic word *sakk*). This word

A mechanical beverage dispenser depicted in a thirteenth-century Iranian manuscript for al-Jazari's *Fi ma 'rifat al-hiyal al-handasiyah* (Book of Knowledge of Ingenious Mechanical Devices); the horseman is a copy of a weathervane atop the khalifah's palace in Baghdad, whose lance was said always to point toward rebellion in some part of the empire (Topkapi Museum, Istanbul)

does not occur in the Qur'an, which does describe the document that Muslims should write between one another when one incurs a debt (Qur'an 2:282), and thus the *sakk* has a Qur'anic basis. Because Muslim law approves of the transference of debts, the use of the *sakk* as a system of payment over long distances was established and greatly facilitated interregional and international trade. Indeed, Muslim trade continued to flourish and grow during the medieval period even though it suffered from occasional local setbacks.

Sources:

Ibn Taymiya, *Public Duties in Islam: The Institution of the Hisba*, translated by Muhtar Holland (Leicester: Islamic Foundation, 1982).

M.Y. Izzi Dien, "Shira'," in *Encyclopedia of Islam*, CD-ROM version (Leiden: Brill, 1999).

Izzi Dien, "Suftadja," in *Encyclopedia of Islam*, CD-ROM version (Leiden: Brill, 1999).

J. Schacht, "Bay," in *Encyclopedia of Islam*, CD-ROM version (Leiden: Brill, 1999).

Schacht, "Riba," in *Encyclopedia of Islam*, CD-ROM version (Leiden: Brill, 1999).

LAWS ON CRIME

Penalties. Like the other facets of Muslim law, Muslim criminal law is derived from the Qur'an and the Sunnah. While the Qur'an includes few specific legal prescriptions (far fewer than the Torah), it does prescribe several specific punishments for crimes: capital punishment for murder (2:178 and 17:33) and armed robbery (5:34; compare 29:29); retribution for injuries, specifically the loss of eye, nose, ear, or tooth (5:45, which actually refers to the Torah, Exodus 21:23–25); amputation of the hand for theft (5:38); one hundred lashes for adultery and fornication (24:2); and eighty lashes for making a false accusation of adultery, along with the permanent loss of one's credibility as a witness (24:4). These are called *hadd* (literally "limit") penalties because they are prescribed for the transgression of the bounds set by God. In hadiths, they are considerably elaborated and modified. Thus, the penalty for adultery by married persons becomes death by stoning, as in the Torah (Leviticus 20:10 and Deuteronomy 22:22–24). Also, hadiths prescribe the death penalty for apostasy (renouncing one's religious faith) and desertion from the army in wartime, neither of which has a particular punishment specified in the Qur'an, which reproves both acts and threatens one who commits them with punishment in the afterlife. Finally, hadiths also prescribe forty or eighty lashes for the consumption of alcohol, which the Qur'an also forbids (5:90–91) but without specifying any punishment. Beyond these fixed penalties, the law also ordained that a judge could inflict other punishments, including no more than ten lashes, banishment, imprisonment for certain offenses, and monetary penalties.

Application. Although the law apparently set down stern punishments for a variety of offenses, the application of these penalties was severely limited in several ways. The early Muslim state had little institutional apparatus, and consequently was not at all like a modern state. On the whole, the rulers cared most about political threats to themselves, so they tried to apply capital punishment for apostasy against political rebels. This interpretation was rejected by most jurists, unless a rebellion was accompanied by a severe deviation in matters of belief. Other criminal cases did not often come to court; they were dealt with informally by extended family groups or clans. In big cities, where recourse to the courts was convenient, cases were tried there more often than in rural areas. In these courts jurists applied exacting standards of evidence derived from hadiths, which made it extremely difficult to obtain a conviction. Any crime required the testimony of two witnesses who had seen the crime happen and whose statements concurred. If their statements did not tally, they risked the penalty for bearing false witness. In cases of adultery and fornication, four eyewitnesses were required. Because the Prophet advised that Muslims should not inflict punishments if doubts existed, religious courts generally exacted penalties only if the accused confessed, and it was specifically forbidden to use coercion or torture to obtain a confession. Thus, the religious courts became viewed as too lenient, and the government established another kind of court (*mazalim*) that meted out sundry punishments. The new courts were not necessarily Qur'anic, and did not follow the standards of evidence set by the Shari'ah (sacred law). It has been said that in the entire history of the Ottoman empire only once was a man's hand cut off as a penalty for robbery. Like other ancient and medieval legal systems, Muslim criminal law rarely punished crimes with imprisonment, although it was occasionally used. No doubt the maintenance of an institutionalized prison system was generally beyond the financial means of premodern states, and ancient and medieval law was economical in this regard. Muslim law sought instead to exact justice swiftly and immediately.

Sources:

Mohamed S. El-Awa, *Punishment in Islamic Law* (Indianapolis: American Trust Publications, 1982).

M. Cherif Bassiouni, ed., *The Islamic Criminal Justice System* (London: Oceana Publications, 1982).

Irene Schneider, "Sidjn," in *Encyclopedia of Islam*, CD-ROM version (Leiden: Brill, 1999).

LAWS ON FAMILY LIFE

Prevalence. Family and commercial law are the most developed branches of Muslim law. Even today Muslim family or "personal status" law tends to prevail in most Muslim countries, with the exception of Turkey, Central Asia, and to some extent Tunisia. Family law can be divided into several categories, the most important of which are laws governing marriage, divorce, guardianship and child custody, and inheritance.

Wedlock. Marriage in Islam is more a civil contract between the two parties than a religious rite. Except in the Hanafi school of law, the approval of the bride's guardian is required. The bride must also give her consent. A mutually acceptable dowry is paid by the groom to the bride (Qur'an 4: 4, 19–21, 24–25). In order to facilitate marriage, the law has often emphasized that a dowry need not be large, but in practice it has often been substantial. Part of the dowry may be delayed; that is, if a husband divorces his wife, he must in effect pay a penalty to exit from the marriage; and if the marriage continues until the husband dies, the widow is then entitled to take the delayed amount off the top of his estate. Two witnesses are required for a marriage to be valid, and the marriage must be publicly proclaimed. A man may marry as many as four wives (Qur'an 4: 3), but he must treat them all equally (4: 129). This provision has been interpreted as meaning that he should give them separate and equal dwellings, clothing, food, and gifts, and must divide his time equally among them. In practice, polygamous households have been uncommon throughout Muslim history. The practice of polygamy is meant specifically to ensure the legitimacy of all children, and to prevent recourse to illicit sex outside marriage. A man must treat his wife well (Qur'an 2: 228; 4: 19, 129; 30: 21), which includes giving her sexual satisfaction. In return the wife must give her husband sexual access. She is not required to perform other services; whatever cooking or housework she does is her voluntary contribution. The husband is financially responsible for the household (Qur'an 4: 34), and any money the wife may contribute is a voluntary charity (4: 4). The husband must keep the wife in the manner to which she was accustomed while growing up, providing suitable food, clothing, and accommodations. This responsibility extends to providing for the children as well (Qur'an 2: 233). If one's wife grew up having a servant, the husband should see to it that this level of service continues.

Divorce. Although the Prophet is reported in hadiths to have said that divorce is the permissible action God dislikes most, several kinds of divorce are allowed. However, Muslim divorce is by no means as easy as non-Muslims sometimes imagine. The husband pronounces the divorce by making a clear statement. When he pronounces divorce once, which should be done when the wife is not having her monthly period, the wife remains married to him until she has completed her waiting time ('iddah), which is until the beginning of her third monthly course after the divorce (Qur'an 2: 228; 65: 1). If a woman has no monthly courses, the waiting period is three months (Qur'an 65: 4). Although the woman stays in the household (Qur'an 65: 1), and her husband remains financially responsible for her during this time (65: 6), they are not to have conjugal relations, and if they do, the divorce is canceled. During the wife's waiting time, the husband may cancel the divorce and resume the marriage. After the waiting time elapses, the divorce is final. If the couple then decides they do not want to be divorced, they must remarry with a new marriage contract and dowry (Qur'an 65: 2). If the husband pronounces divorce three times, however, the marriage is ended immediately, and the couple may not remarry one another until the divorced wife has married another man, consummated the marriage with him, and been divorced from him in turn (Qur'an 2: 229–230). The triply divorced wife must still wait until the appearance of her third monthly course to remarry, however. This restriction was made to leave no doubt about the paternity of any child that may be conceived near the time of the divorce and remarriage.

Repudiation. Several other kinds of divorce also exist. If a man says to his wife that she is like his mother's back, they are immediately and definitely divorced, but they can remarry under a new contract and dowry. In addition, because this means of divorce is regarded as sinful, the husband must free a Muslim slave, or fast sixty days, or feed sixty poor people in expiation before he can resume the marriage (Qur'an 33: 4; 58: 1–4), though he need not do so if he marries another. Furthermore, if a man swears that he will not have sexual relations with his wife for four or more months and then carries out the promise, he and his wife are considered divorced at the end of the four months (Qur'an 2: 226–227). If a husband accuses his wife of adultery or denies his paternity of a child she has borne, the marriage is immediately dissolved, and the couple can never remarry at all under any circumstances (Qur'an 24: 6–9) because of the gravity of the accusation. All these forms of divorce are meant to protect the woman from being kept in marriage by a husband who does not want her as a wife but will not divorce her (Qur'an 2: 231; 4: 129). A man is also not entitled to take any of the dowry or his wife's other property by force (2: 229; 4: 19–21).

A Wife's Right to Divorce. There are also several forms of divorce that can be initiated by the wife. If the wife agrees to pay her husband a certain amount of money to divorce her, and he agrees, then they are immediately and definitely divorced and can remarry only under a new contract and dowry (Qur'an 2: 229). If the wife sues the husband for divorce in court, and he is shown to be at fault, the judge dissolves the marriage, and the wife pays the husband nothing. The grounds for such a complaint by the wife vary among the schools of law. All schools consider the husband's impotence a ground for divorce. Others include desertion and lack of maintenance of one's wife and children (Qur'an 2: 233). In the Maliki school, the wife may also sue for divorce on the grounds of cruelty. A husband may also grant the wife the right to pronounce divorce, and that right may be written into the marriage contract. The Hanbali school also allows a woman to insert in the marriage contract a condition stating that she will be automatically divorced should her husband marry a second wife.

Children. Regulations on child guardianship (*wilayah*) and custody (*hadanah*) in Islam vary considerably among the different schools. Usually, guardianship, which includes the responsibility for the education of and provision for the child, belongs to the father, and in default to the nearest relative on the father's side. If no one at all on the father's side is suitable or willing to take guardianship, however, a Muslim judge can grant guardianship to the mother or someone in her family. However, the custody of the child, caring for the child in one's home, belongs to the mother or, in default, to the closest female relative on the mother's side, the first being the mother's mother. If the closest female relative does not take custody, it may revert to the father's side. A father cannot be denied access to his child but also cannot take him or her away from the mother until the child reaches a certain age, which differs greatly among the schools. According to the Hanafi school, when a son is between the ages of seven and nine he should go to live with his father, and a daughter should reside with her father after the age of nine to eleven. For Malikis, the son should go to the father at puberty, but the daughter should stay with her mother until marriage. The Shafi'is hold that the child should start out with its mother and at the age of seven be allowed to chose the parent with whom it would like to live. The Hanbalis accord the right to choose to sons and say all daughters should go to their fathers at the age of seven. The Ja'fari Shi'is transfer custody to the father when a son is two and a daughter is seven. In all the schools the mother may lose custody earlier if she remarries, but in this case custody does not immediately revert to the father but rather to relatives on the mother's side. The priority according to which these relatives are listed varies among the schools, but the first person on any list is the mother's mother. Thus, a grandparent's rights are acknowledged by Muslim law.

Heirs. Inheritance in Islam is regulated by the Qur'an (2: 180–182; 4: 7–9, 11–12, 19, 33, 176). All debts are paid first. Then, if there is a will, bequests made by the testator are paid. No more than one-third of an estate may be disposed of by will, and bequests can be made only to persons or organizations that are not heirs to the remainder of the estate. After these bequests are made, fixed shares are given to relatives entitled to them according to the Qur'an (4: 11–12, 176). Generally, a male gets twice the share of a female because males are required to maintain female family members, while women bear no such financial burdens in the intact Muslim family. A son shares the inheritance with his surviving parent, other siblings, and his grandparents, and all more-distant relatives

Mahmud of Ghazna (998–1030), in eastern Afghanistan, putting on the robe of honor sent to him by the Abbasid khalifah al-Qahir; from a 1306–1307 Tabriz manuscript for *Jami' al-tawarikh* (Universal History) by Rashid al-Din (Edinburgh University Library)

are excluded from inheritance. If the deceased leaves only daughters, they may inherit no more than two-thirds of the estate, or one-half if there is only one daughter, and some of the inheritance goes to more-distant relatives, such as uncles and aunts. Husbands and wives also inherit fixed shares.

Sources:

K. N. Ahmad, *Muslim Law of Divorce* (New Delhi: Kitab Bhavan, 1978).

Asaf A. A. Fyzee, *Outlines of Muhammadan Law,* fourth edition (Oxford: Oxford University Press, 1974).

Chibli Mallat and Jane Connors, eds., *Islamic Family Law* (London: Graham & Trotman, 1989).

LAWS ON FOREIGN RELATIONS AND WAR

Ideals versus Reality. As Muslim law is theoretically a complete scheme for governing all areas of human life, the actions of the state fall under its view. In practice, however, the rules of government have tended to be bent or changed for purposes of expediency. Therefore, the laws for foreign relations and war (*siyar*) have tended to be ideals that are not applicable in changing conditions. Part of the reason for this lack of continuous application is that the early khilafah provided the primary political model on which the laws were based. Prominent in this model was the doctrine that the Muslim polity should be one and united. After all, the Madinan state founded by the Prophet was a single, unified polity under God speaking through Muhammad. The definitive breakdown of the unity of the khilafah that began in 740 and the growth of a multiplicity of Muslim states thereafter eventually gave rise to an acknowledgment, even in the law, of the possibility of multiple Muslim rulers. This concept was

not at first well received, as in the dictum reported in a hadith: "If there are two khalifahs, kill one." Eventually it was acknowledged because of the force of reality. Nevertheless, Muslims were still not supposed to fight each other (Qur'an 49: 9). Like a similar dictum in Christianity, this stricture proved impossible to uphold once Islam had spread over a large territory. Muslim religious scholars, however, still refused to sanction wars against other Muslims as just wars.

International Law. In theory, relations with non-Muslim states were also governed by Muslim law. The early khilafah did not acknowledge equal relations with other states; rather, the khalifah was the supreme representative of God on earth. Apart from accepting Islam and submitting to the khalifah as a Muslim, only two other options were conceivable: to fight or to send tokens of submission without adopting Islam. In the first case the Muslims would mobilize in the cause of just war (*jihad*) to extend the scope of God's rule in the earth. In the latter case the khalifah would decide if the tokens of submission were sufficient or acceptable. Cities that surrendered on terms were usually given a Muslim governor and treaties guaranteeing the protection of the religious freedom, lives, and property rights of the inhabitants in exchange for the payment of a regular tax. This solution is mentioned in the Qur'an (9: 29) and is detailed in hadiths. However, a considerable variety of such treaties existed. Peoples on the fringes of the khilafah were sometimes able to avoid the residence of Muslims among them if they provided their own troops to the Muslim armies, in which case the tribute that they paid was only nominal. Such was the case with the Armenians under the early khilafah. Alter-

A Muslim embassy to the court of an Abyssinian ruler; illumination from a 1306–1307 Tabriz manuscript for *Jami' al-tawarikh* by Rashid al-Din (Edinburgh University Library)

natively, when some regions proved impossible to hold for military reasons, the Muslim commander was satisfied with a single payment and went away.

Legitimate Warfare. Once Muslims embarked on a just war, the idea was that it should be fought to victory (a widely held belief shared by Christian nations as well). To be just, a war also had to be fought under many restrictions, including the strictures that noncombatants were not to be killed or injured and that real property was not to be damaged even as a tactic to obtain the surrender of the enemy. Thus, cattle could not be killed wantonly, but they could be captured, and fruit trees were not to be uprooted. However, one's commander also had to be obeyed, and there was naturally a reluctance in combat situations to examine the orders of the commander for their ethical content before acting. Rather, the troops simply obeyed. As a result, although the legal restrictions on warfare may have had some effect on the way the Muslims fought, they were not always applied.

Treaties. Quite early, situations arose where the Muslims were unable to carry on just wars, even against a resistant opponent such as the Byzantine Empire. Thus, while the Muslims were engaged in civil wars during the years 656–661 and 685–692, the khilafah made humiliating treaties with that empire, paying a substantial tribute to the emperor in exchange for peace. There was a sort of precedent for such agreements in the life of the Prophet. He had made the Peace of al-Hudaybiyyah with the Makkan pagans and their allies in 628 (mentioned in Qur'an 48: 1, 18–26 and 60: 10–11). This treaty required no payment of tribute but included provisions that some Muslims viewed as unfavorable. Still, the Muslims upheld it for two years, until they deemed that the other side had broken it. As the khilafah developed, this treaty and certain verses of the Qur'an (3: 64; 8: 61; 60: 7–9) became precedents for the concept of a temporary truce. That is, the khilafah should not establish any permanent peace with a non-Muslim state that was not submitting to the Muslims, but a truce could be made on that basis. As the khilafah proved unable

to carry on any more significant military campaigns after 740 and failed to acquire any further territory, temporary truces gradually changed into truces for longer and longer periods. During these times of peace, it was sometimes necessary to consult the opposing side. Thus, the exchange of envoys began to take place more and more frequently. Muslim envoys did not, however, reside in non-Muslim territories permanently; rather, they were only sent out as needed. Even so, this practice eventually led to a growing cultural and economic exchange. A masjid (mosque) built for the Muslim prisoners in the prison at Constantinople where prisoners of war were held eventually gave way to a regular masjid for the use of visiting Muslims who were not prisoners. Likewise, a special church for Byzantine use was established at Baghdad (and there were many other churches functioning inside the khilafah).

Aliens and Travelers. Such conditions led to a considerable body of officially recognized laws about protected aliens from states not under Muslim rule. Such a person was described as a *musta'min* (a non-Muslim who has been given safe conduct by a Muslim ruler). For such a person to be received, he also needed a letter or document from his own ruler. This paper became like a passport, while the letter or document of safe conduct from the Muslim side was the equivalent of a visa. Muslims visiting non-Muslim states received similar documents and safe-conduct guarantees. Although these passes may have at first been viewed as temporary expediencies, as medieval times wore on they became regular features and are often mentioned in the travelogues of medieval travelers, both Muslim and non-Muslim. There remained some suspicion of Muslims traveling to non-Muslim lands, because until after 1200 few Muslims lived under non-Muslim control except in Spain and Sicily. The reverse was less true, because great numbers of Christians and Jews lived as protected communities (*ahl al-dhimmah*) in lands under Muslim rule and law. These communities, which were free to practice their religions and govern themselves under their own personal-status laws in exchange for the payment of a tax, often pro-

Nizam al-Mulk (died 1116) served as chief minister under two successive Saljuk rulers, Alp Arslan and Malikshah. As the Saljuks were warrior chiefs unused to administering an empire, Nizam al-Mulk compiled a manual of advice, experience and administrative plans to aid him in constructing stable government and a civil service. Apart from administrative theories and advice, the author often instructs the reader through examples of famous rulers in times past, in the tradition of the "mirrors of princes" literature.

Concerning tax collectors and constant enquiry into the affairs of wazirs:

1.) Tax-collectors, when they are given a fiscal district, must be instructed to deal honorably with their fellow creatures, and to take only the due amount of revenue, and to claim that too with civility and courtesy, and not to demand. any taxes from them until the time comes for them, to pay; because when they demand payment before the time, trouble comes upon the peasants, and to pay the tax they are obliged to sell their crops for half [of what they would be worth when they ripen], whereby they are driven to extremities and have to emigrate. If any peasant is in distress and in need of oxen or seed, let him be given a loan to ease his burden and keep him viable, lest . . . he be cast out from his home into exile.

2.) I heard that in the time of King Qubad there was famine in the world for seven years, and blessings [rain] ceased to come down from heaven. He ordered the tax-collectors to sell all the grain which they had, and even to give some of it away as charity. All over the kingdom the poor were assisted by gifts from the central treasury and [local] treasuries, with the result that not one person died of hunger in those seven years-all because the king chid his officers.

3.) One must enquire constantly into the affairs of the tax-collector. . . . If he comports himself in the manner just described, the fiscal district can be kept in his hands, but if not. he must be changed for someone suitable. If he has taken more than is due from the peasants, it must be recovered from him and given back to them; after that if he has any property left, it must be seized and brought into the treasury. The officer should be dismissed, and never employed again. Others will then take warning and give up practicing extortion.

On obtaining information about the conduct of tax collectors, judges, prefects of police and mayors, and keeping them in check:

1.) Let observation be kept in every city to see who there is in it who shows interest in religious matters, fears God (be He exalted) and is not self-seeking. Let such a person be addressed thus, "We have now made you responsible for the security of this city and its district. All that God asks of us, we shall require of you. We desire that you make constant enquiries and be always well-informed in matters small and great concerning the conduct of the tax . . . collector, the judge, the prefect of police and the inspector (of weights and measures) towards the people. Make us acquainted with the truth whether your findings are kept secret or made public, so that we may give our orders as appropriate." If persons who are of the right quality refuse to accept this trust, they must be coerced and however reluctantly commanded to do it.

Source: Hubert Drake, trans., *The Book of Government or Rules for Kings: The Siyasat nama or Siyar al-Muluk of Nizam al-Mulk* (New Haven: Yale University Press, 1960), pp. 23, 49.

---

vided Muslims with traders and envoys to non-Muslim lands. This role especially fell to the Jews, who as neutrals between the religions of Islam and Christianity could serve as uncommitted intermediaries.

Sources:

Muhammad Hamidullah, *Muslim Conduct of State,* seventh edition (Lahore: Sh. Muhammad Ashraf, 1977).

John Kelsay and James Turner Johnson, eds., *Just War and Jihad: Historical and Theoretical Perspectives on War and Peace in Western and Islamic Traditions* (New York: Greenwood Press, 1991).

Majid Khadduri, *War and Peace in the Law of Islam* (Baltimore: Johns Hopkins Press, 1955).

Muhammad ibn Hasan al-Shaybani, *The Islamic Law of Nations: Shaybani's Siyar, translated by Majid Khadduri* (Baltimore: Johns Hopkins Press, 1966).

LEGAL DEVELOPMENTS

Historical Context. Islam was originally revealed to the Prophet Muhammad in an environment of customary tribal law, not revealed law. But the Qur'an makes clear that, even in the earliest stages of the Muslim community, the Prophet had the power to command. Eventually this power was enhanced by revelation and institutionalized, especially at Madinah after 622. There, the continuing revelation of the Qur'an began to bring an increasing number of legal prescriptions or recommendations, in line with the Constitution of Madinah (622), which made the Prophet Muhammad the arbiter and judge of the whole oasis. Described as having divine origin, these laws were not challenged, and they superseded the previous customary law wherever they differed from it. Indeed, the Qur'an admonished Jews and Christians as well as Muslims to judge only according to the laws God had sent down to them (5: 44-45, 47). The Qur'anic legislation ceased with the death of the Prophet Muhammad in 632, which cut off the introduction of further divine laws into the community. Though legal verses in the Qur'an were revealed over a period of ten years at Madinah, the Qur'an included relatively little legal material overall, most of it concentrated in the latter half of Surah 2 and in Surahs 4, 5, 8, 9, 17, 22, 24, 33, 49, 58, 60, and 65. Also, many of the verses deemed to have legal implications or content provide only general guidelines and exhort to justice rather than prescribe.

The Effect of Expansion. The cessation of direct divine revelation with Muhammad's death, coupled with the astonishing expansion of the relatively small territory ruled by the Prophet into a great empire under the early khalifahs, led to profound new legal developments. The early khalifahs and their Arabian Muslim cohorts showed great care in upholding the rulings of the Qur'an, which they looked on as sufficient for a written legal text, for they and their Arabian Muslim brethren were not well versed in the ways of the urbanized empires that had just come under their rule. They preferred simplicity and informality, ruling according to the customs that had come down to them from the Prophet's time, including those decisions of the Prophet that were remembered and became known as the Sunnah, or the path of the Prophet. During this period most Muslims were still Arabs, and they were far less numerous than the sundry other peoples in the khilafah, who were left to continue governing and policing themselves in their own accustomed ways according to their previously enacted legal systems, including the Roman and the Persian systems, as well as others. Although the early Muslim rulers had to make many legal decisions, most of their time was taken up with various affairs of state, so they did not think of elaborating a written legal system and conducted most of government business in the old languages of those they ruled. Occasionally, they would consult the Companions of the Prophet who were still alive to help them in making a legal decision. But most of the time the khalifahs who ruled until 680, all of whom were Companions of the Prophet themselves, ruled according to their own knowledge and understanding of Islam, and their decisions held binding force in such cases as were brought before them.

The Mawali. Under the reign of the first important khalifah from a generation that had no living memory of the Prophet, 'Abd al-Malik ibn Marwan (ruled 685–705), the state, reeling from a Byzantine counterattack, began to engage in an ideological campaign to define Islam, which inevitably had an impact on the law. The results of this campaign included the building of new, lavishly decorated masjids, of which surviving examples include the Umayyad Masjid in Damascus and the Dome of the Rock in Jerusalem, the minting of Islamic-Arabic coins (to replace Byzantine and Persian coins that had been used in the khilafah), the institution of Arabic as the official language of government business, correspondence, and offices, and the prohibition of human and animal images throughout the khilafah. The khalifah also engaged in ideological correspondence with recognized scholars such as al-Hasan al-Basri (circa 646–728) of Basrah in Iraq. Interacting with the increasing numbers of non-Arab Muslims (*mawali*) as well as non-Muslims of diverse nationalities and cultural

backgrounds across the khilafah, Arab Muslims were challenged to reflect on the meaning of Islam. Furthermore, the *mawali* began to play increasingly important roles in the definition and elaboration of Muslim belief and practice. Such a deepening of Muslim thought resulted from the increasing numbers of noncombatant Muslims in the khilafah. From the beginning of Muslim history, of course, there had been some male noncombatants, as is indicated by Qur'anic verse 9: 122, which shows that as early as the Prophet's time, some people had been designated to stay behind to instruct others in the faith. Nevertheless, the paradigmatic Muslim from a khalifah's point of view was a fighter for the faith under the khalifah's command, and that remained the view for most of the Umayyad khilafah, as the struggle to expand the area under God's rule continued. But, as more people became Muslim, it was not possible to maintain all of the males in the army, and some of the new Muslims were not inclined to such service anyway. These noncombatants, who were most often *mawali*, began to provide instruction in the masjids. This trend continued at an increasing pace after 702, when the Umayyads, responding to a revolt, demobilized most of the Iraqi Muslims, both Arabs and non-Arabs, from the military. At the same time, the Umayyads put the province of Iraq under Syrian military occupation, centered in the new city of Wasit, which was built between Kufah and Basrah to control both military outposts. These oppressive steps led the Iraqis to agitate for the downfall of the Umayyads and a more egalitarian vision of Islam.

Administration. Meanwhile, because of the growing urbanization of Kufah, Basrah, and other cities, most of which had started out as military camps, the government had to take a greater role in administration than had been the case earlier, including settling disputes and enforcing the law in general. Because Muslims wanted to be governed by God's law alone, it was not suitable for new Muslims outside Arabia to continue being governed by the non-Muslim laws of their previous rulers. Because of the need constantly to expand and elaborate the Muslim law, it became impossible for the khalifah and his governors to hear all legal cases as they had done at first, because they did not have the time, nor often the expertise, nor the interest. Thus, they began to seek out local Muslim legal experts, who were the very same group that had already been cultivating a greater knowledge of Islam in the masjids. Some of these experts became first legal advisers, then later actual judges, before the end of the first century. The judges continued to be in touch with the scholars of the masjid circles, however, and they would undoubtedly consult these others on occasion. Reliance on the Qur'an as the first source of law and the remembered Sunnah as the second continued to form the basis of legal practice, but often cases arose where neither of these sources was sufficient. For this reason and because the social and economic situations of the different cities of the khilafah differed enormously, the local schools of law began to diverge somewhat in their inter-

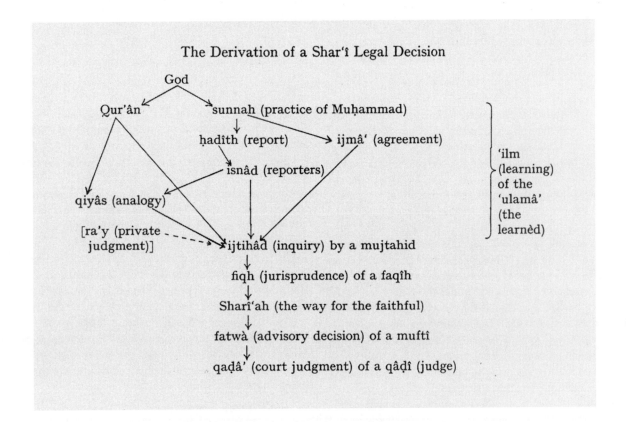

The Derivation of a Shar'î Legal Decision

God

Qur'ân → sunnah (practice of Muḥammad)

ḥadîth (report) → ijmâ' (agreement)

isnâd (reporters)

qiyâs (analogy)

[ra'y (private judgment)] ⤑ ijtihâd (inquiry) by a mujtahid

'ilm (learning) of the 'ulamâ' (the learnèd)

fiqh (jurisprudence) of a faqîh

Sharî'ah (the way for the faithful)

fatwà (advisory decision) of a muftî

qaḍâ' (court judgment) of a qâḍî (judge)

Chart showing how a Muslim judge arrives at a decision on the validity of an Islamic law
(from Marshall G. S. Hodgson, *The Venture of Islam,* 1977)

pretations. In Iraq at Kufah in particular, rational elaboration of the law through the considered opinion of the jurist was considered a legitimate means of extending the scope and detail of the law. This situation existed at the end of the Umayyad khilafah in 750.

Jurists and the Abbasids. While the new Abbasid dynasty was no less autocratic in its expectations and aspirations than its Umayyad predecessor, the political situation did not allow the Abbasids to rule freely or securely. The Abbasids lacked legitimacy in the eyes of many because they had seized power. Their claim to represent the Prophet's family was severely undercut when they were revealed to be descendants of the Prophet's uncle rather than the Prophet himself. While they tried to compensate for their lack of legitimacy by adopting grandiose titles implying messianic links, the falseness of such claims was readily apparent, for they were unable to come up to messianic expectations and rule perfectly. Thus, to gain support, they had to make concessions to parties who were not their backers, including the nascent body of jurists. The second Abbasid khalifah, al-Mansur (ruled 754–775), despite the urging of his Persian prime minister, declined to promulgate a khalifal legal code and left the setting down of the law to private jurists. The importance of this decision for Muslim law can scarcely be overemphasized. Juristic scholars who were also religious leaders and largely outside of the control of the state were able to establish their primacy over the government, contrary to the usual legal model in empires, such as the Byzantine, where the Emperor Justinian I (ruled 527–565) had instituted a set of legal codes that

he had personally approved and which has remained the main and final expression of Roman law.

Schools of Law. In the eighth century, as Islam spread along with literacy and book publishing, the Abbasid khalifahs were less able to exercise the same degree of censorship over the teaching of Islam that the Umayyads had. Thus, the regional schools of law (*fiqh*) that had been developing came out into the open, especially in Iraq, which had become the metropolitan province of the khilafah after the Abbasids moved their capital to Baghdad in 763. The Iraqi school of law tended to be favored by the Abbasid khalifahs because it was the school prevalent in their capital. Most of the inhabitants of Kufah eventually moved to Baghdad, and the Kufan school of law continued in Baghdad, becoming the school of the khalifal center. The Abbasid khalifahs hoped to be able to exert some influence on this school and through it over the schools of the other provinces as well. Thus, while Abu Hanifah (699–767), the founding father of the Kufan school, spent the last four and a half years of his life in the khalifah's prison for political opposition, his students and successors Abu Yusuf (732–798) and Muhammad ibn Hasan al-Shaybani (750–805) accepted judgeships from the khalifah. Indeed, it appears that around 786 the Abbasid khalifah Harun al-Rashid appointed Abu Yusuf as the supreme judge of the khilafah, implying that Abu Yusuf had authority over all the judiciary in all the provinces, which had hitherto been independent. This appointment appears to have been an attempt at judicial centralization, but it did not work, and the khilafah continued to disintegrate politically over the next century and a half. The appointment was also a significant devolution of the khalifah's powers, for before this time the khalifahs themselves had held the supreme judicial authority.

Madinah. Some other locales resisted the nascent dominance of Baghdad. First among them was Madinah, the city of the Prophet, where Muhammad had spent his last ten years molding his community. From the beginning, Islam had been primarily molded and practiced in Madinah. Although the Prophet was from Makkah and the Ka'bah was there, Makkah played little role in the subsequent development of Islam, because the Prophet and his followers had migrated to Madinah when the early community was still quite small, possibly not exceeding a couple of hundred people. It was in Madinah that the Muslim community first became established on a firm basis, and Madinah remained the capital under the first three khalifahs. Even when the capital moved elsewhere after 656, Madinah remained the place where the overwhelming majority of the Companions and their descendants continued to reside. In such an atmosphere, and deprived of all political and military role in the khilafah, the inhabitants of Madinah naturally assumed that their practice of Islam was the norm with which all others should agree. As the residents of the authentic center of Islam, the Madinans did not accept that anyone coming from another place could have a knowledge of Islam superior to their own. Such thinking was reinforced by the awe felt by pious pilgrims going to Makkah on the hajj, almost all of whom stopped in Madinah on the way to and from Makkah. Pilgrims with scholarly intentions would often linger at Madinah to hear the authentic early tradition from the descendants of the Companions. Thus, it came as quite a shock when, after the fall of the Umayyads, the nascent Iraqi school began disagreeing with the Madinans on various points of practice and asserting its own superiority.

Logical Argumentation. Finding their legal positions unwelcome in Madinah, the Iraqis—who were more sophisticated and urbane than the Madinans and better practiced in polemic from a century of opposition to Umayyad oppression in Kufah—resorted to various kinds of argument to best their opponents. One method was to demonstrate the intellectual superiority of their position through logic, but the Madinans, in defiance of rationalizing arguments, relied on the Sunnah of the Prophet as represented in the living practice of their city, inherited in an unbroken chain from the Prophet. In this atmosphere, the Iraqis referred to their own traditions going back to the Prophet and documented every step of the way. The Iraqi scholar Muhammad ibn Hasan al-Shaybani even came to Madinah to study with Malik (circa 712-795), the chief exponent of the Madinan school. On returning to Iraq, al-Shaybani then produced a version of Malik's teaching, called *al-Muwatta'* (The Trodden Path), which replied to the positions taken by Malik on various issues. In another work, *Kitab al-hujjah 'ala ahl al-Madinah* (The Book of Proof against the People of Madinah), al-Shaybani further elaborated his objections to the Madinan version of the law.

Al-Shafi'i. Attempting to resolve the growing dispute between the legal schools of Iraq and Madinah, the Madinan scholar al-Shafi'i (767–820), who had also been a student of Malik, undertook to propose a solution that he hoped all parties would accept. He organized the sources of the law under a few headings and then arranged these in a hierarchical order, so that there should be no dispute about what the correct view on any point should be. First came the Qur'an, then the Sunnah of the Prophet as expressed in hadiths, then the consensus of the scholars, then analogical reasoning from known laws in order to apply their principles to new situations. Al-Shafi'i's organization of the principles for deriving the law and of its sources eventually found wide acceptance and became a central part of Sunni Islam. But the establishment of a set of principles for deriving the law did not eliminate or even reduce the legal disputes between the schools; instead it led to a new framing of arguments by the parties. The followers of al-Shafi'i, unable to cooperate with any of the major existing schools, formed their own school, further contributing to the multiplicity of schools of the law.

Ibn Hanbal. The opposition of traditionalists to the somewhat rationalist methodologies of the *fiqh* schools led to the formation of a traditionalist movement whose most important member was Ahmad Ibn Hanbal (780–855). This movement, which also wanted to preserve Muslim unity, long denied that it was a legal school as such, preferring to say that it was only keeping to the tradition of the Prophet. Thus, the traditionalist school exhibited a degree of literalism in its interpretations and often showed concern with correct creedal beliefs. But even Ibn Hanbal, who had also been influenced by the proto-Hanafi Abu Yusuf, admitted that reason had a role in law. This position led to the rise of a more radically literalist school of tradition, the Zahiri school of Dawud ibn 'Ali ibn Khalaf (circa 817 – 884), which laid emphasis on only following the clear, obvious primary meaning of a text, using no rational interpretation or reasoning by analogy. The teachings of this school were too strict for it to gain anything but a limited and temporary success, primarily in Iraq and in Spain.

Fiqh. During the period 800–1000, the formal schools of *fiqh* gradually crystallized. While this formalization was taking place, many scholars seemed to have held independent positions and did not follow any particular school, and several schools flourished that eventually became extinct, including those of the Syrian al-Awza'i (706–774), the Kufan Sufyan al-Thawri (716–778), the Egyptian Layth ibn Sa'd (713–791), and the Baghdadi Ibn Jarir al-Tabari (839–923). By around 1000, the predominant Iraqi school of *fiqh* had become the Hanafi; the Maliki school was pre-eminent in Madinah, and the Shafi'i school was the most influential in Egypt. Each of these had gradually absorbed its opponents and later become prevalent in particular geographical areas. The coalescence of the Hanafi school was considerably facilitated by the

Muslim cavalrymen jousting; illumination from *Kitab al-Baytarah* (Book of Veterinary Medicine),
a fourteenth-century Egyptian manuscript (Museum of Islamic Art, Cairo)

association of Abu Yusuf and later Hanafi jurists with the Abbasid state; however, after the Abbasids had succumbed to the rule of the Shi'i Buyids in 945, that connection was severed. Later in the thirteenth century, however, the Hanafi school was often the official school in much of the Muslim East, especially under governments of Turkish origin, such as the Ottomans and the Sultanate of Delhi in India. An early association of the Maliki school with the much smaller Umayyad emirate of Spain began in the early 800s and extended to North Africa after the expulsion of the Shi'i Fatimids by 1048. Farther east, the Saljuks favored the Shafi'i school from the beginning of their sultanate in 1037. Finally, in response to the Saljuk conquest of Baghdad in 1055, the Abbasid khalifahs, in order to maintain some independence, adopted the Hanbali school and even produced writings supporting it. Thus, in a long series of steps, the schools of law gained official recognition, began to recognize each other after heated rivalries, and were limited to just four Sunni schools.

Shi'i Schools. The development of the Shi'i and other non-Sunni schools tended to follow developments among the Sunni majority. The Shi'a, on the whole, was mainly a political movement in the earliest period. After the killing of Zayd ibn 'Ali (699–740) and his son Yahya (died 743) in revolts against the Umayyads, Zayd's followers adopted a quietist stance, emphasizing their master's legal teachings, which eventually were formalized as a school of law. Meanwhile, the Ja'fari, or Imami (Twelver), Shi'is continued their political claims, coupled with rather radical departures in belief, and formed their own school, which was traced back to Ja'far al-Sadiq (died 765), the sixth imam.

Sources:
Jonathan E. Brockop, *Early Maliki Law: Ibn 'Abd al-Hakam and His Major Compendium of Jurisprudence* (Leiden: Brill, 2000).

N. J. Coulson, *A History of Islamic Law* (Edinburgh: Edinburgh University Press, 1964).

Yasin Dutton, *The Origins of Islamic Law: The Qur'an, the Muwatta' and Madinan 'Amal* (Richmond, U.K.: Curzon, 1999).

Wael B. Hallaq, *A History of Islamic Legal Theories: An Introduction to Sunni Usul al-Fiqh* (Cambridge: Cambridge University Press, 1997).

Ahmad Hasan, *The Early Development of Islamic Jurisprudence* (Islamabad: Islamic Research Institute, 1970).

Mansour Hasan Mansour, *The Maliki School of Law: Spread and Domination in North and West Africa 8th to 14th Centuries C. E.* (San Francisco: Austin & Winfield, 1995).

Joseph Schacht, *An Introduction to Islamic Law* (Oxford: Clarendon Press, 1964).

MILITARY DEVELOPMENTS

Expansion. The territory of the earliest Muslim state, which modern historians call the khilafah for the period beginning in 632, expanded with startling rapidity. The ideological justification and proximate reason for this expansion was what the early Muslims understood as a divine imperative to claim the entire earth for God's rule (Qur'an 9: 33; 48: 28; 61: 9). This military action continued with several interruptions for more than one hundred years until the beginning of the great Berber revolt against the Umayyads in 740, and it represents one of the greatest sustained military expansions in the history of the world, comparable in duration and extent with the territorial expansions of the Romans, the Mongols, the Spanish, the British, and the Americans. After 740, when the khilafah's sovereignty reached from Morocco to the borders of modern China, this expansion almost completely stopped, to be resumed only partially and intermittently by local states on particular frontiers. Because more than one Muslim state existed after 740, Islam ceased to be associated in any sense with any one particular state, which led to the increasing dissociation of religion from the state throughout the rest of the medieval period.

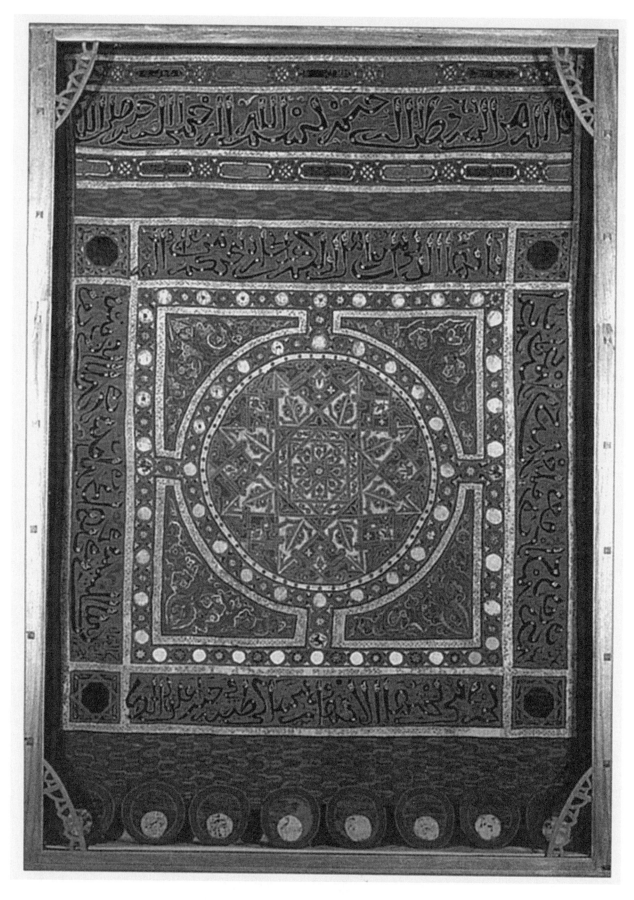

Banner thought to have been the ensign of an Almohad general at the Battle of Las Navas de Tolosa
against Christian Spanish forces in 1212 (Patrimonio Nacional, Madrid)

Chronology. The era of early expansion may be divided into several periods (623–656, 661–683, 692–718, 720–740) broken by hiatuses having various causes. After its foundation by the Prophet Muhammad at Madinah in 622, the Muslim polity gained domination of that oasis by 627, acquired Khaybar to the north in 629, and established hegemony over western Arabia by 632. Under the first khalifah, Abu Bakr (ruled 632–634), the Muslims established firm control over all of Arabia, and no further opposition to Islam arose there. Under 'Umar ibn al-Khattab (634–644), the Muslim state took control of Syria, Egypt, Iraq, and western Iran, annexing most of the Persian empire and depriving the Byzantine Empire of its most populous provinces. During the reign of 'Uthman (644–656) came the final overthrow of the Persian empire, Muslim expeditions to North Africa, and the defeat of the Byzantine fleet, establishing Muslim control of the Mediterranean Sea from 655 to 678. Thus, what had developed under the Prophet from a small religious community to a city-state to a local territorial state in western Arabia with only a few institutions had by the end of 'Uthman's reign became a vast empire ruling over millions of mostly non-Muslim subjects, all within the lifetimes of many of the Companions of the Prophet, who could no doubt recall the early days in Arabia when Muslims had no state. Indeed, the Muslim state by 656 was the largest and strongest in the world apart from T'ang-dynasty China, dwarfing the Byzantine Empire and completely outclassing the insignificant tribal kingdoms of Europe.

Continuing Expansion. The next major advance of the khilafah took place in the period of 692–718. During this period, Muslim armies subdued North Africa (698–710), Spain (called al-Andalus in Arabic, 711–718), Central Asia (or Transoxiana, 709–715), and Sind (part of modern Pakistan, 712–715). This expansion involved the elimination of the Byzantines from North Africa and the overthrow of the Visigoth kingdom of Spain, various Iranian and Turkish principalities in Central Asia, and the Brahmin kingdom of Sind. All these campaigns climaxed under the Umayyad khalifah al-Walid I (ruled 705–715). They were followed by an all-out drive in 717–718 to capture Constantinople, the Byzantine capital, which would have eliminated the main surviving rival. This attempt failed completely, however, and the Muslims lost control of the sea to the Byzantines again. This campaign represents the high noon of Umayyad expansion, for although campaigning was resumed in 720 and continued until 740, it was not successful in making any lasting additions to the khilafah, which thereafter gradually shrank geographically.

Losses and Gains. The Umayyads' successors, the Abbasids, were confronted with the loss of Muslim unity caused by the successful Berber revolt that began in Morocco and Algeria in 740 and the re-establishment in 756 of Umayyad rule in the distant refuge of Spain, where the dynasty ruled until 1031. The Abbasids were scarcely able to secure their rule in the rest of the khilafah and could not renew campaigns outside their borders for a long

time. By 763, they had finally resumed offensive campaigns against the Byzantines in Anatolia, but without any lasting success. Indeed, by the tenth century the Muslims were on the defensive on their frontier with the Byzantines, and the khalifahs lost all their former power to direct campaigns there. The Byzantines even recaptured Antioch in 969 and threatened Aleppo and Damascus. Most further Muslim military efforts occurred on specific fronts under the direction of particular local rulers. The best known of these include the campaigns of the Ghaznawids (977–1187) and the Ghurids (1152–1215) to extend the rule of Islam into Punjab and from there to the rest of northern India. The Ghaznawids conducted their campaigns especially under Mahmud of Ghazna (ruled 997–1030), who acquired a considerable empire in Afghanistan and Punjab and conducted deep raids into India. It was not until the time of the Ghurids that such military expeditions led to a long-lasting extension of Muslim rule east of Lahore. The Ghurid sultan defeated the Hindu princes in 1192; Delhi, Kanauj, and Bihar were taken in 1193; Ajmer in Rajasthan was occupied in 1197; and Bengal was subdued in 1199–1202. This startlingly rapid expansion resulted in the capture of the entire densely populated Ganges River valley in only about ten years. This area remained under Muslim rule until its annexation by the British in 1757–1803. The Ghurids' efforts were followed by the establishment of the independent Muslim Sultanate of Delhi (1211–1556) in India, which continued to extend the area ruled by the Muslims, particularly under the sultans Iltutmish (1211–1236), 'Ala' al-Din Khalji (1296–1316), and Muhammad ibn Tughluq (1325–1351). After the mid fourteenth century, the Sultanate of Delhi tended to disintegrate, but smaller sultanates that broke off from it continued to extend Muslim control in southern India. Unlike the territories of the Umayyad khilafah, all of which eventually became predominantly Muslim except Spain, the areas of India taken after 1192 have all remained mostly Hindu, except for eastern Bengal, now Bangladesh. However, a substantial number of Indians did embrace Islam over the centuries, such that 30 percent of the population in South Asia, including Pakistan, India, and Bangladesh, is now Muslim.

Asia Minor. Another front on which a later Muslim expansion took place was in Anatolia against the Byzantines. The khilafah had taken Egypt and Syria from the Byzantines during the first expansion of 634–642; the Taurus Mountains remained the frontier between the Byzantines and the Muslims for more than three centuries, until 962, when the Byzantines began seriously to advance south of the mountains once more. But in 1071, the Saljuk sultan Alp Arslan (1063–1072) defeated and captured the Byzantine emperor at Malazgirt (Manzikert), and within ten years almost all of Anatolia was under Muslim control. The Muslims tried to consolidate their gains by organizing them under the Saljuk Sultanate of Rum (1077–1308), which was completely independent of the main Saljuk sultanate farther east. In 1097–1099 the First Crusade helped

Laborers building the fort at Khawarnaq, on the Euphrates River in present-day Iraq; from a manuscript for Nizami's
Khamsah (Five), circa 1494, illuminated by Bihzad (British Library, London)

to restore Byzantine rule to part of Anatolia but also led to long disorders and wars. Eventually much of the population became Muslim. The Ottoman sultanate, founded about 1299 as a small principality in northwest Anatolia near Brusa, took up the struggle against the Byzantine Empire, driving the Byzantines from their last major base in Anatolia at Nicomedia in 1337. Since that time, Anatolia has constituted the main region of the country of Turkey. The Ottomans continued their campaigning nonstop into Europe, crossing at Gallipoli in 1355. In 1389, they defeated a coalition of Serbs and others at Kosovo, capping their control of the Balkans. Constantinople, now called Istanbul, was taken in 1453, putting an end to the Byzantine Empire, and the last small Greek states fell in 1460 and 1461. By 1500, the Ottoman Empire was one of the strongest Muslim states. Although Anatolia and part of Thrace became predominantly Muslim—as did Albania, Kosovo, and part of Bosnia—most of the Balkans remained Orthodox Christian under Ottoman rule. Other than these advances in India, Anatolia, and the Balkans, Muslim states and empires after the khilafah period largely did not occupy other areas by military force. On the contrary, in the West Muslims suffered a great reverse when the Spanish Christians drove them from Spain in a long series of campaigns starting with the Christian capture of Toledo in the center of the Iberian peninsula in 1085. Although the Moroccan dynasties of the al-Murabitun, or Almoravids, and the al-Muwahhidun, or Almohads, managed to counter the Christian onslaught for a while, the decisive defeat of the latter by the Christians in 1212 led to the eventual loss of the Muslim metropolises of Cordoba in 1236 and Seville in 1248. After that time, Muslim rule in Spain was confined to a small area around Granada, which finally fell in 1492. Muslims continued to live in Spain a while longer, but all those remaining were eventually either forced to convert to Christianity or expelled in 1609–1614. The Muslims also lost the island of Sicily, which they partly controlled from 827 to 1090, and there as well no Muslims were permitted to remain after the reign of Frederick II (1212–1250). Elsewhere before 1500, Islam often spread as the religion of the state when the local rulers embraced it, especially in West and East Africa and Southeast Asia, in all of which Islam was well established by 1500. Islam was also preached in areas where some of the population, but not the rulers, became Muslims, as in China, for example.

The Crusades. One other series of campaigns that left its mark on Muslim military history was the invasion of Asia Minor and greater Syria by Western European Crusaders, starting in 1097. These campaigns enabled the Byzantines to maintain their hold on part of Anatolia and established colonies, known as Crusader kingdoms (or Latin kingdoms), all along the Syrian coast that lasted for nearly two centuries. Although the Crusaders had some early successes, they were unable to conquer the pivotal country of Egypt (failing in 1167–1169, 1218–1221, and 1248–1250) and in the end they lost all their territory in Syria, including the city of Jerusalem, their ostensible goal, which the Europeans held only in 1099–1187 and 1229–1244. When the Europeans made one last futile attempt to launch a crusade in 1396, the Ottoman Turks completely defeated them at the Battle of Nicopolis. Although it is sometimes said that the Crusades helped to introduce Muslim sciences into Western Europe, little such exchange

Soldiers using a catapult; illumination for a 1306 manuscript for Rashid al-Din's
Jami' al-tawarikh (Edinburgh University Library)

took place in the East. Rather, the great conduits of that cultural flow were through Spain and Sicily. The Crusades did, however, make the Muslims aware of the danger posed by European aggression.

Organization and Technology. Similar to that of other medieval peoples, Muslim military organization and technology evolved over the centuries. From the time the Visigoths defeated and killed the Roman emperor Valens at Adrianople in 378, long before the life of the Prophet Muhammad, cavalry had been the dominant branch of any army and remained so throughout the medieval period as far as the Muslims were concerned. The earliest Muslim armies enjoyed spectacular and unparalleled successes for more than a century during expansion of the khilafah (624–740). Though information about military organization and technology for this early period is scanty, the Muslim armies represented a revolution in military tactics, organization, and perhaps weaponry. The Qur'an (3: 146, 152–159, 173, 186; 61: 4) commands Muslims to fight patiently without flinching, to maintain a solid battle line, and not to be tempted to break ranks to grab spoils, a serious temptation for medieval armies that caused the near defeat of Uhud in 625. Such verses show that the Muslims, even that early in their history, were already far beyond the individualized raiding tactics of the tribes. How this new organization and discipline arose is obscure although it may be supposed that some help came from contacts with the Byzantines or the Persians—as is suggested by the story that a Persian client suggested digging

a trench that confounded the Muslims' opponents at the Battle of the Trench in 627. Muslim army divisions and regiments were organized purely according to tribal affiliations. While there seems to have been no compulsory conscription in the Prophet's time, judging by the many exhortations to volunteer in the Qur'an, the armies of the early khilafah nevertheless consisted of a mass mobilization of free Muslim citizens. Motivation to join came as much from ideological enthusiasm as from hope for material gain. Troops were raised about equally from all regions of Arabia, as there are records of tribal regiments from all areas. The heavily populated region of Yemen, whose inhabitants were farmers, probably contributed half the troops. Elsewhere in Arabia, too, most of the inhabitants were farmers, not nomads. While it is possible that Muslims rode camels as well as horses in some early battles, there is no doubt that the horse quickly asserted itself as the main vehicle of cavalry. Infantry was used as well, but cavalry was dominant, and by law the cavalryman received the greater share of the spoils. When members of the defeated Persian elite cavalry agreed to become Muslims, they were welcomed into the Muslim army, an indication of how highly the Persian cavalry was respected.

Professional Soldiers. The biggest transformation in Muslim military organization to occur during the medieval period was the replacement of the volunteer citizen army with professional soldiers. To some extent, this evolution echoed the change that took place in the Roman army, which was an army of temporarily conscripted citi-

The Mongol sack of Baghdad (1258); illumination from a fourteenth-century manuscript for
Jami' al-tawarikh by Rashid al-Din (Bibliothèque Nationale, Paris)

zens under the republic but became more fully professional under the empire. Professionalization of the Muslim military started when certain princes used the armies of private retainers at the end of the Umayyad khilafah. The transformation did not become complete, however, until al-Mu'tasim turned to Turkish soldiers in 833. From this time onward, professional soldiers began to predominate in the military across the Muslim world. Furthermore, these soldiers were increasingly non-Muslims who were bought from beyond the frontiers of Islam as boys, brought up in Islam, trained to be professional warriors, and freed along the way. As early as 861, these professional military men began to interfere in the government. Often of Turkish origin, they eventually formed the political elite of various states, especially the Mamluk sultanate of Egypt and Syria (1250–1517) and the Sultanate of Delhi (1211–1556). The progress of these professional soldiers was accompanied by technological developments as well. Cavalrymen gradually became more heavily armed and armored. The crossbow, which had vastly more force than the traditional bow, was a heavier yet less maneuverable weapon. Siege techniques improved, but so did defensive walls of stone, so castles were often able to hold out against an enemy even when the surrounding countryside had fallen. Catapults, which had been developed much earlier by the Greeks and Romans, also became heavier.

Naval Forces. On the sea, the Muslims gradually established considerable control over the western part of the Indian Ocean, but in the Mediterranean Sea they only

Funeral procession of Ghazan (ruled 1295–1304), the first Ilkhanid (Mongol) ruler to embrace Islam; illumination from a fourteenth-century manuscript for Rashid al-Din's *Jami' al-tawarikh* (Bibliothèque Nationale, Paris)

occasionally triumphed over the Christians to the north. For the most part the Byzantines maintained their naval dominance for some centuries. Their naval dominance was partly achieved through the invention of "Greek Fire," a naphtha compound that was shot from tubes mounted on Byzantine ships and burst into flames as it hit the enemy ships. Greek Fire was also used against armies besieging Byzantine cities. Only after 1000 were the Byzantines gradually overtaken on the sea by the Italian city-states of Venice, Genoa, and Pisa.

Sources:

Khalid Yahya Blankinship, *The End of the Jihad State: The Reign of Hisham ibn 'Abd al-Malik and the Collapse of the Umayyads* (Albany : State University of New York Press, 1994).

Marshall G. S. Hodgson, *The Venture of Islam: Conscience and History in a World Civilization*, 3 volumes (Chicago: University of Chicago Press, 1974).

P. M. Holt, *The Age of the Crusades: The Near East from the Eleventh Century to 1517* (London: Longman, 1986).

Walter Emil Kaegi, *Byzantium and the Early Islamic Conquests* (Cambridge: Cambridge University Press, 1992).

Hugh Kennedy, *The Prophet and the Age of the Caliphates: The Islamic Near East from the Sixth to the Eleventh Century* (London: Longman, 1986).

MONGOL INVASIONS

Destruction. The Mongol invasions of the Muslim world began in 1219 and lasted until the Mongols eventually embraced Islam as their religion, in 1295 in the Ilkhanid empire of Persia and in 1313 in the Khanate of the Golden Horde in Russia. Even after this time, Muslim Mongol rulers such as Timur (1369–1405) repeated the pattern and some of the destructiveness of the earlier pagan Mongol invasions. Based on the testimony of all the sources and even allowing for exaggeration, it is clear that the Mongol invasions were quantitatively the most destructive episode Muslim Asia ever experienced, and they had deep and widespread repercussions. Cities were totally destroyed and their inhabitants massacred, sometimes almost to the last person. For the purpose of controlling conquered lands, the Mongols deliberately wrecked agricultural systems and irrigation channels and tunnels, reducing the size of the population that the land could support. Even after the immediate destructiveness of the invasions had passed, Muslim society continued in a downward spiral for a considerable time because early Mongol governments tended to be inefficient and rapacious, leading to further neglect of agriculture. When a recovery from these bouts of destruction finally got under way, lands such as Iran and Central Asia found themselves greatly surpassed in population and urbanization by Europe, India, China, and even other parts of the Muslim world.

Turkic Invaders and Migrants. Many migrations into and invasions of southwest Asia by pastoral peoples had taken place over long periods. By Muslim times, these migrants and invaders were Altaic peoples who spoke either Turkic or Mongol languages. In 1037 the Oghuz Turks, led by the Saljuk family, took Nishapur in northeastern Iran. Although the Saljuks' spread was accompanied by some destruction, which may have helped to pave the way for the later ultimate catastrophe of the Mongols, the Saljuks were already Muslims, which tempered their actions toward fellow Muslims somewhat. Thus, when the Saljuks took Baghdad in 1055, they were interested in ruling, not plundering. Later, in 1141, the pagan Kara Khitay conquered Turkestan, including the great Muslim cities of Samarqand and Bukhara, helping to set in motion new invasions of Oghuz Turks, this time from tribes not yet Muslim. By 1153, these Oghuz had managed to capture the Saljuk Sultan Sanjar, opening inroads into northeast Iran, where they visited great destruction and thus paved the way for the Mongols.

Mongol Strategy. The Mongols erupted from their aboriginal homeland in Mongolia and Siberia. Their power was so great that they were able to carry on campaigns against China and the Middle East at the same time and to launch invasions of Russia, Europe, India, Southeast Asia, and Japan. They possessed excellent military organization and augmented their power by enlisting defeated enemies of Turkish stock and exploiting existing political splits and hatreds. Often, the Mongols used their subject allies to perpetrate the worst massacres carried out under their auspices. The terror they inflicted was often enough alone to convince enemies to surrender, and when the Mongols were faced with a determined opposition, they relentlessly pursued the resisters until they were completely wiped out. Probably the first Mongol invasion, led by Genghis Khan (ruled 1206–1227), was the worst. Genghis had already spent years subduing North China, where he visited a destruction as severe as in any Muslim land. During the Mongol invasions, the population of China decreased from about 100 million to 65 million. Of course, most of the 35 million excess deaths probably came about not from direct killing, but because of the destruction of the means of production, especially agricultural, that gave people their livelihoods. In some regions the downward spiral of population continued for some time. In Muslim Central Asia, Genghis advanced from 1219 to 1221, conquering all of Central Asia and most of Afghanistan before returning to Mongolia in 1222. Generals sent by him devastated northern Iran, the Caucasus region, and southern Russia, returning to Mongolia in 1224. This invasion was the first visitation. Although the Mongols did not immediately incorporate all their conquests into their empire, they did keep control over Central Asia and waged campaigns from there, extending their rule over much of Iran (1231) and Anatolia (1242–1243), where they made the Saljuks of Rum their vassals. During the next big campaign, led by Genghis's grandson Hulagu from 1254 to 1260, the Mongols destroyed the Isma'ili castles in Iran and then conquered Baghdad in 1258. From there, they went to Syria but had to withdraw partially in 1260 to face civil war in the Mongol empire. Indeed, the year 1260 was a decisive watershed in Mongol history, after which the Mongol empire split into several mutually hostile areas that soon coalesced into separate states. Hulagu's withdrawal from Syria quickly led to the defeat and expulsion of the rest of his occupying force there by the Mamluks of Egypt. This victory was the first time the Mongols had been stopped. The state founded by Hulagu, the Ilkhan empire, continued in Iran and Iraq. Gradually the

Students of Muslim history often tend to conflate the Arab conquests with the spread of Islam when, in fact, the two events are distinct historical processes separated by centuries. During the first century after the Hijrah, rapid expansion of Muslim territory occurred under the impetus of military campaigns. However, these lands did not at that time suddenly become "Islamic." The spread of Islam among the population of these lands was a gradual process that continued for centuries, even in the regions conquered in the seventh century.

The chronology below traces major milestones in the expansion of Islam. It marks both dates when various regions became exposed to Islam, and also gives a range of dates within which Muslims likely became a majority of the population in those areas.

750s: Muslim soldiers settle in Chang'an (Xian) while Muslim merchants regularly visit and reside in Chinese ports.

Circa 800-850: The majority of the population in present-day Iran is Islamic.

819: The Samanids form the first independent Muslim state in northeastern Iran and Central Asia; by the end of the ninth century, Islam has become the predominant religion in the region.

Circa 850-900: Islam achieves majority status in present-day Iraq, Egypt, and Tunisia.

Circa 940-1000: The Muslim-ruled populations of the Iberian Peninsula become Islamic.

1000s: Muslim traders help to spread Islam in West Africa; Muslims reside in Champa (present-day Vietnam).

1000s-1200s: Some rulers and resident merchant traders of the Sudanic kingdoms are Muslims. The rulers occasionally go on pilgrimages. Trading contacts increase.

1040s: The Almoravids, a Berber group, are established in Mauritania, spreading Islam in the western Sudan. They undertake campaigns against the Soninke kings of Ghana.

1060s: The Almoravids subjugate the Maghrib and al-Andalus; the empire of Ghana, center of western Sudanic trade, grows weaker.

Circa 1200: The majority of the population in Syria is Muslim.

1200s: The Ghana empire collapses while the Mali empire rises. The rulers of Kanem, near Lake Chad, are Muslims by this point.

Late 1200s: Muslims reside in the northern ports of Sumatra, and they maintain close trade and cultural contacts with East Indian coastal cities such as Gujarat.

1295: Ghazan "the Reformer" becomes the first Ilkhan to break with Mongol tradition and embrace Islam, along with most of his Mongol generals.

Circa 1300: The majority of the population in Anatolia is Muslim.

1300s: Mali, Gao, and Timbuktu on the Niger River become important centers of Muslim trade and scholarship.

1324-1325: Mansa Musa, king of Mali, makes his pilgrimage journey to Makkah, strengthening the region's ties with Islam.

1400s: A ruler of Malacca converts to Islam as the port city becomes important to trade in the East Indies. From Malacca Islam spreads to the southern Malay Peninsula and to neighboring islands.

Sources: Richard W. Bulliet, *Conversion to Islam in the Medieval Period: An Essay in Quantitative History* (Cambridge, Mass.: Harvard University Press, 1979).

Marshall G. S. Hodgson, *The Venture of Islam: Conscience and History in a World Civilization*, 3 volumes (Chicago: University of Chicago Press, 1974).

Ilkhanids Mongols accepted the Muslim religion of their subjects, the ruler becoming a Muslim in 1282–1284 and again from 1295.

Successor States. The Mongols who had conquered Russia in 1237–1241 had also established a state, which is known as the Khanate of the Golden Horde. This state waged war mostly against Russian Christians rather than other Muslims, and its ruler of 1258–1266, Berke, became the first important Mongol Muslim. Indeed, he allied with the Mamluks of Egypt against his own relatives, the Ilkhanids, whom he attacked from the north. This attack contributed greatly to curtailing Hulagu's plans for further expansion of the Ilkhanid state. After its Muslim khan had died, however, the Golden Horde went back to paganism until about

1313, when Islam was re-established there on a firmer basis. Although the conversion of the Mongols to Islam usually limited the ferocity of their military campaigns, occasional repeats of their earlier destructiveness continued to occur, mostly in Turkestan, which as a result suffered a considerable fall from its once high estate in Islam. Furthermore, the Turkish or Mongol ruler Timur the Lame (Tamerlane, ruled 1369–1405) severely damaged Delhi in 1398–1399; Iran, Iraq, and Syria in 1400–1401; and Turkey in 1402 during a series of attacks designed to build up the core of his empire in Turkestan. Not only did Mongols in all previously Muslim areas eventually convert to Islam, but Islam also later expanded in some steppe areas where it had not previously prevailed, as in Kazakhstan. Though Islam survived and prevailed, however, the vast destruction caused by the Mongol invasions, especially in the period 1219–1260, was a great setback for the Muslim world.

Sources:

'Ala'al-Din 'Ata-Malik Juwayni, *The History of the World-Conqueror*, translated by J. A. Boyle (Manchester: Manchester University Press, 1958).

David O. Morgan, *The Mongols* (Oxford: Blackwell, 1986).

Morgan, "Mongols," in *Encyclopedia of Islam*, CD-ROM version (Leiden: Brill, 1999).

THE SPREAD OF ISLAM

A Gradual Process. It is often wrongly imagined that as soon as any country came under the political rule of Muslims or a Muslim state, a majority, or even all, of its population started professing Islam as their personal religion, whether from choice or compulsion. In actuality, the spread of Islam as a religion in a particular country has always been a gradual, slow process that has taken decades or, most often, centuries. In fact, this process is still ongoing in most Muslim-majority countries, where there exist religious minorities whose numbers have slowly dwindled over the centuries, often from a point at which their faith was the majority religion.

No Compulsion in Religion. The Qur'an specifies, "There is no compulsion in religion" (2: 256), a statement recognizing that no one can ever be forced to believe anything and commanding Muslims never to try to compel belief. Muslims felt that anyone embracing Islam under duress would be only feigning belief and therefore not be sincere in his or her profession of faith. Even when Muslim rule came to places through conquest, the new rulers rarely required the native populations to embrace Islam. In those rare cases when, contrary to the Qur'anic verse, Islam was required of a non-Muslim, such a conversion could only at best be a verbal assent to something not properly understood and thus not an immediate and complete adherence to a new personal religion. Unlike Christianity, Islam was usually not preached by missionaries to non-Muslims. Rather, throughout history, adherence to Islam has generally been voluntary, and the diverse peoples who have become Muslims have sought out the religion for themselves.

Assimilation. Even after an individual has embraced Islam, he or she may take a long time to learn and apply its rituals and rules, going through many different stages or levels of understanding and practice over time. When such individual

processes of religious assimilation are multiplied across a whole population, different people or even whole social classes have different understandings of Islam at the same time. Thus, it is usually not possible to single out a particular historical period as representing the essence of normative Islam. Also, many local nuances and differences remain even after a society has been Islamized for a long time, further guaranteeing the continued existence of diversity within Islam.

The Process of Conversion. The Prophet Mohammad preached Islam at Makkah and Madinah in Arabia for about twenty-three years. Early on, from about 612 to 622, he preached in public at Makkah, but after the migration to Madinah he appears to have preached only in his own house, which became the first masjid, and only to those people who chose to come to him. Preaching in one's house or in the masjid became the pattern in Islam. Under the first two khalifahs, Islam was required of most of the inhabitants of Arabia who had been pagans, but Christian and Jewish communities were allowed to exist there, particularly in Yemen, where there are still Jews. Outside Arabia, however, the khilafah did not compel non-Arab inhabitants to become Muslims; indeed, it did not even encourage them to do so, fearing a decrease in the state's revenues from its taxes on non-Muslims, a major source of income. Only Khalifah 'Umar ibn 'Abd al-'Aziz (ruled 717–720) made an effort to encourage adherence to Islam, sending out missionaries to North Africa and other areas. Despite this brief attempt during the early khilafah (632–750), non-Arabs became Muslims mainly of their own volition, sometimes migrating to Muslim military-camp cities, where they were normally not supposed to reside, in order to embrace Islam. Such converts may often have been seeking economic or social advantages rather than individual spiritual fulfillment, but their actions nevertheless spread and eventually deepened popular adherence to Islam. Non-Arab Muslims, called *mawali*, were sometimes mistreated by their patrons and rulers, and many threw themselves into learning about their new religion as a means of self-defense and resistance against oppression—themes that appear frequently in the Qur'an and hadiths. More literate than the early rulers, these *mawali*, along with a few of the Arabs, began to produce the enormous body of scholarship on Islamic law and creed. Each group of *mawali* also sought to spread Islam among their relatives and other members of their ethnic group. Thus, Islam spread in spite of political rulers, not because of them. Nevertheless, it is important to remember that during the years 661–750, apart from the Arabs, the overwhelming majority of the inhabitants of the Umayyad khilafah—which stretched from Morocco to China—were not Muslims. Only toward the end of that period, in about 710, did the first major spread of Islam to non-Arabs take place, among the Berber (or Amazigh) population of North Africa. The Berbers embraced Islam rapidly, but their process of Islamization, which is not well documented, took a long time. Within a few centuries, however, the process was well along, and Christianity disappeared completely from North Africa—as it did from no other place in the Muslim world—while Juda-

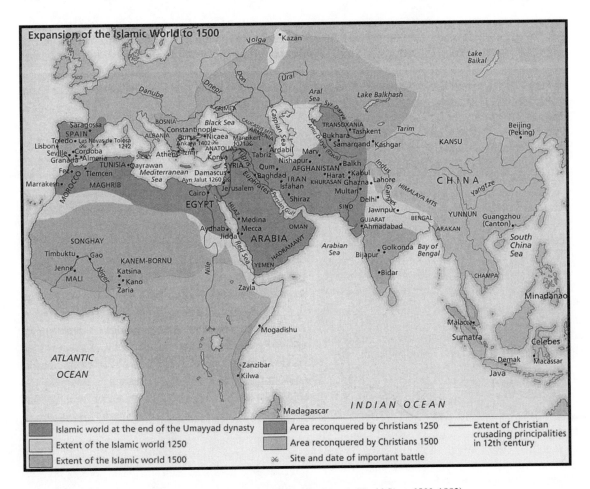

Expansion of the Islamic World to 1500

Legend:
- Islamic world at the end of the Umayyad dynasty
- Extent of the Islamic world 1250
- Extent of the Islamic world 1500
- Area reconquered by Christians 1250
- Area reconquered by Christians 1500
- Site and date of important battle
- Extent of Christian crusading principalities in 12th century

(from Francis Robinson, *Atlas of the Islamic World Since 1500*, 1982)

ism persisted there as a small minority. The second major spread of Islam to non-Arabs also began under the Umayyads, to the Iranians of Central Asia, beginning in about 720. It is interesting that each of these centers of conversion is far from Arabia and produced immediate political problems for the Umayyad rulers. In North Africa, a Berber movement set up a counter khilafah, breaking the political unity of Islam, while in Central Asia, a revolutionary movement arose that replaced the Umayyads with the Abbasids. Islam was no longer the religion of a single ethnic group or ruling elite.

Islamization. In the central lands of Islam, its gradual spread cannot be precisely documented. Nevertheless, some scholars such as Richard Bulliet have proposed that in Egypt only few Egyptians had become Muslims before the year 700 and that the 50-percent mark was only reached in the 900s, three hundred years after the introduction of Islam. By about 1200, Muslims were more than 90 percent of the population, and religious Islamization was moving apace, as expressed by the proliferation of Muslim religious writing in Egypt that began around that time. In geographical Syria, the process was even slower. The 50-percent mark was not reached until 1200, nearly six hundred years after the arrival of Islam. Iraq and Iran probably were closer to the pattern of Egypt than that of Syria, but Islamization was gradual there too. In large parts of Spain and Portugal, Islam was established between

711 and about 1250 and continued to exist until after 1600; it is not clear that a majority of the population there was ever Muslim, and the Spanish Christian reconquest eventually eliminated Islam completely from the Iberian peninsula. (Spain, Portugal, and the island of Sicily are the only places from which Islam has ever been driven out.) In the East, Muslim law treated Zoroastrians, Buddhists, and Hindus just as it treated Jews and Christians, offering them protection of life, property, and freedom of religious practice in exchange for the payment of a tax. In Sind, the largely Buddhist population appears to have embraced Islam rather rapidly, over about two centuries (712–900), a period during which Buddhism disappeared entirely from that region and for the most part from Afghanistan and Central Asia. Hinduism in Sind, however, declined much more slowly than Buddhism. All the lands discussed to this point were part of the khilafah, but after the decline of the khilafah Islam spread to lands outside its boundaries. Anatolia (or Asia Minor), which makes up most of modern Turkey, came under the rule of rather superficially Islamized Turkish tribesmen after 1071, and its population embraced Islam gradually for centuries thereafter. In Anatolia, the spread of Islam was probably facilitated by the alienation of the population from the Byzantine Empire that had ruled oppressively there in its last period. After the Ottoman Turks reached southeastern Europe in the mid four-

teenth century, most Albanians and Bosnians and some Bulgarians became Muslims. Beginning in the fifteenth century, however, the spread of Islam in this area seems to have been impeded by the aversion of the populace to the centralized bureaucracy of the Ottoman Empire, a factor that had not had the same effect in Anatolia because most of the people there had already become Muslims.

Continuing Spread. Beginning in 1192 other Turkish tribesmen took Muslim rule to India, including the area of present-day Bangladesh, and the number of Muslims there gradually increased from that time. The people of Bangladesh were Buddhists, and, beginning about 1300, they—like the Buddhists of Sind—rapidly embraced Islam, leading to a Muslim majority in that region. Elsewhere in India, apart from most of Punjab and Kashmir in the northwest, Hinduism remained the religious system of the majority. In South India and Sri Lanka, Islam was spread by traders and charismatic Sufis, who also extended it to Southeast Asia by 1290, starting in Sumatra and going eastward from there to reach the Moluccas in eastern Indonesia after nearly two more centuries. Although Islam was present throughout the Malay archipelago after that time, it took centuries more for the Islamization process to establish a form of Islam similar to that of the Middle East, and this process is still ongoing. Northeast of the khilafah, Islam gradually extended into the original homelands of the Turks and Mongols, eventually becoming at least the nominal religion of nearly all Turkic-speaking peoples. Beyond those regions, Islam spread into China, where it was to some extent tolerated by the Chinese empire.

Africa. Before 1500, Islam spread widely in sub-Saharan Africa. The first place south of the Sahara documented as having embraced Islam is Gao on the Niger River in Mali, which was Muslim, at least in name, before 990, by a voluntary act of its ruler. By 1040 the Tucolor or Takarir of Senegal became Muslims, and from them Islam spread to the region of present-day Senegal, west Mali, and Guinea in the same century. After the Soninke of the Kingdom of Ghana became Muslims about 1076, Islam began to spread more widely along the Niger, and Muslims established the well-known kingdoms of Mali (thirteenth to fifteenth century) and Songhai (1465 – after 1600). Farther east, Kanem-Bornu around Lake Chad also became Muslim shortly after 1100. As in Turkestan, India, and Indonesia, traders usually introduced Islam at first, were followed a considerable time later by charismatic Sufis, and still later by scholars teaching a more text-oriented form of Islam with an emphasis on the law. This process led eventually to greater Islamization of practice. In Mali, the spread of classical Muslim scholarship seems to date from the early fourteenth century. By 1500, Islam was well established in West Africa throughout the Sahil belt and along the Niger River into modern Nigeria. In East Africa, traders had spread Islam down the coast by the tenth century, and it gradually developed further in the subsequent centuries. In the Sudan, south of Egypt, the population of Nubia gradually became Muslim during the fourteenth century, owing to some immigration of Muslim Arab tribesmen and the preaching of Islam, as well as to the

weakening of the Christian kingdom there. Muslim control and presence, however, did not extend south of the confluence of the Blue and White Niles before 1500.

The State and Islamization. Islam has tended to spread best and fastest when the population of a region is not ruled as a powerful, centralized Muslim state. In such cases—as with the Ottoman Empire in the Balkans during the fifteenth century, or the Sultanate of Delhi and the Mogul empire in northern India—non-Muslim populations seem to have viewed their powerful Muslim rulers as an alien force, and thus resisted conversion to Islam. Whoever did embrace Islam in such circumstances, if not for material gain, usually did so because of the efforts of itinerant Sufi preachers, who were not under the control of the state. On the other hand, when Muslim political regimes were weak, decentralized, disunited, or completely absent, Islam as a religion flourished and often spread to non-Muslims.

Sources:

Richard W. Bulliet, *Conversion to Islam in the Medieval Period: An Essay in Quantitative History* (Cambridge, Mass: Harvard University Press, 1979).

Bulliet, *Islam: The View from the Edge* (New York: Columbia University Press, 1994).

SULTANATES

Dyarchy. The word *sultan* appears in the Qur'an, but only in the meaning "authority" or "proof," never as the title of a person. During the early centuries of Muslim rule, the ruler—because he possessed "authority" and sovereignty—was occasionally called the sultan, but the conversion of the word into a title of office for a supreme ruler dates to its use by the Saljuk Turkish sultans, who in the period 1055–1152 dominated the Muslim East, including Baghdad, which was then still the Muslim metropolis. By using the title *sultan* the Saljuks recognized the theoretically superior authority of the khalifah but exercised all the real power for themselves. Therefore, the Saljuk period introduced to Muslim politics the concept of dyarchy (a government with two rulers): the khalifah was the higher, spiritual head of the Muslims with control over creed, while the sultan was the lesser, political ruler, with the actual power and executive authority. Although it might seem that this state of affairs somewhat parallels the rivalry between Pope and Holy Roman Emperor that was going on at the same time in western Europe, the two situations were actually completely different, for the khalifahs not only lacked any true executive authority except right around Baghdad but also had little spiritual authority outside the capital because, unlike the popes, they were not heads of an ecclesiastical hierarchy. From 1152 to 1258, the Abbasid khalifahs briefly restored their temporal authority in southern Iraq, but they failed to rise above the level of local princes.

Sultanates. Meanwhile, use of the title *sultan* for the effective sovereign head of a Muslim state spread widely. In Egypt and Syria the Ayyubid (1171–1250) and Mamluk (1250–1517) rulers were called sultans throughout their history. Likewise, the rulers of the large Muslim kingdom in India were called the sultans of Delhi (1211–1556). Beginning in the thirteenth century, the Muslim rulers in Southeast Asia were usually known as sultans as well, and during the same century the best known of all sultanates, that of the Ottoman Turks (circa 1299–1922), was founded in Turkey. After the fall of Baghdad to the Mongols in 1258, only the Mamluks and the sultans of Delhi continued to pay lip service to the shadow Abbasid khilafah in Cairo (1261–1543), which seems to have become increasingly irrelevant. Thus, there was no real balance of power between khilafah and sultanate; rather, sultans simply supplanted khalifahs as the real rulers. Nevertheless, ever since the time of the Saljuk "dyarchy," some Muslims have imagined political arrangements in which spiritual and political powers have been separated according to the model of sultanate and khilafah.

Regional Powers. The various sultanates before 1500 differed from the early khilafah in several significant ways. Until 740 the early khalifahs enjoyed dominion over all Muslims and even after that continued to aspire to such a universal rule. None of the sultans ever had enough power or territory even to imagine such a universal rule. Because Islam was constantly expanding, such a rule would have had a wider geographical spread than territories controlled by the early khalifahs. Also,

the early Muslims were only a minority of the subjects of the khilafah, but after 1000 most Muslim sultanates ruled over Muslim majority populations. Muslims expected their sultans to rule justly. The articulate, educated class of *ulama'* (religious scholars) was fully in place by the year 1000, and as the *ulama'* came to have power over education and as the law that the *ulama'* studied and interpreted tended to become more fixed, the freedom and power of the ruler was limited. The weakness and instability of the sultanates and their inability to create governmental institutions undermined their attempts to establish hereditary rule as well. Although some ruling families lasted more than two centuries, most did not. In some cases, such as in the Mamluk sultanate of Egypt and Syria, few sultans were succeeded by their sons; instead unrelated military leaders came to power.

Sources:

Antony Black, *The History of Islamic Political Thought: From the Prophet to the Present* (New York: Routledge, 2001).

J. H. Kramers, O. Schumann, and Ousmane Kane, "Sultan," revised by C. E. Bosworth, in *Encyclopedia of Islam,* CD-ROM version (Leiden: Brill, 1999).

Emil Tyan, *Sultanate et califat* (Paris: Recueil Sirey, 1956).

SIGNIFICANT PEOPLE

ABU HANIFAH

CIRCA 699-767
LEGAL SCHOLAR

The Hanafi School. Though Abu Yusuf (732–798) and Muhammad ibn Hasan al-Shaybani (750–804) also played major roles, Abu Hanifah is considered the founder of the Hanafi school of law. Born in Kufah, Iraq, of non-Arabs who originated in Afghanistan, Abu Hanifah spent most of his life in his native city, traveling only to make a pilgrimage to Makkah in Arabia. Toward the end of his life, when the Abbasid dynasty came to power, he supported a revolt against the khalifah, was arrested, and sent in 763 to the brand-new capital, Baghdad, where he died after four and a half years in prison. Never holding a government office or a judgeship, Abu Hanifah represented the private cultivation of the law in the center of the khilafah, Iraq, and specifically the tradition of the most urbane and sophisticated Iraqi city, Kufah, which had not yet been supplanted by Baghdad. Still concerned with the political issues that had concerned Muslims under the discredited Umayyad

government, Abu Hanifah held a point of view that was at once rationalist, determinist, and politically quietist, while not favorable to the new Abbasid khilafah. Abu Hanifah's quietism was expressed in ideological terms in the assertion that ordinary Muslims ought not to judge the faith of other Muslims, for God will judge all on the last day. Because it suggested that one should suspend one's judgment with the regard to the belief or disbelief of the rulers, this position ultimately fit with the Abbasids' desire to quiet the opposition they were facing, but in Abu Hanifah's lifetime, it did not lead to any cooperation with them.

Followers. Abu Hanifah's student Abu Yusuf continued to develop his teacher's stances, but—unlike Abu Hanifah, who maintained his independence from the state—Abu Yusuf accepted the position of supreme judge in the khilafah from Khalifah Harun al-Rashid (reigned 786–809). This appointment constituted a major change of direction because it associated the Iraqi legal school, the proto-Hanafis, with the state, a link that on the whole continued in many places in later history. The other main founder of the Hanafi school, al-Shaybani (750–805), a student of both Abu Hanifah and Abu Yusuf, also accepted a judgeship from Khalifah al-Rashid, but none of the main

Hanafi legal scholars after them ever held the position of supreme judge, and few were judges at all.

Legacy. Abu Hanifah wrote down little if anything, and only a few works attributed to Abu Yusuf survive. Al-Shaybani produced most of the earliest extant texts of the Hanafi school. Indeed, writings attributed to al-Shaybani constitute the first comprehensive, systematic expression of Muslim law, already in a highly sophisticated form. Without abandoning the rationalist tradition of Abu Hanifah and Abu Yusuf, al-Shaybani relied more than they on the traditions of the Prophet and thus helped to win acceptance for the Iraqi school from its more traditionist rivals. Positions attributed to all three scholars were handed down and together formed the raw material from which the Hanafi legal system was built. This school prevailed in most of Muslim Asia, especially among Turkish populations, and later was the official school of the Muslim empires in Turkey and India.

Legacy. Although Abu Hanifah's role in founding the school that is named after him is thus somewhat indirect, he nevertheless held pride of place as the founder, as he was much better known to the masses than either Abu Yusuf or al-Shaybani. As the teacher of both men, Abu Hanifah provided a blanket of unity that covered all the Hanafi school and its considerable inner diversity. Also, certain principles that he established are still basic to the school. The most notable of these, perhaps, was his use of reasoning to elaborate the law from its basic sources, the Qur'an and the Sunnah. Although Abu Yusuf tended to cite the Sunnah a little more than Abu Hanifah, and al-Shaybani made vastly more use of it (especially in the form of hadith reports) than either of his predecessors, the principle of the use of reason laid down by Abu Hanifah was never shaken.

Sources:

Shibli Nu'mani, *Imam Abu Hanifah: Life and Work: English Translation of Allamah Shibli Nu'mani's "Sirat-i-Nu'man,"* translated by M. Hadi Hussain (Lahore: Institute of Islamic Culture, 1977).

Joseph Schacht, "Abu Hanifa al-Nu'man," in *Encyclopedia of Islam*, CD-ROM version (Leiden: Brill, 1999).

'ALI IBN ABI TALIB

CIRCA 599-661
FOURTH KHALIFAH

Early Years. 'Ali ibn Abi Talib is possibly the second most famous Muslim after Muhammad because of his close family relationship with the Prophet and his famous early political role in establishing Islam. 'Ali's father was the Prophet's benefactor and uncle, Abu Talib (circa 564-619), who sent 'Ali to live in the Prophet's household; although 'Ali was thus the Prophet's first cousin, he was treated as a son. Tradition avers that 'Ali was about ten when Islam was first revealed to Muhammad around 609 and was among the first who accepted it after the Prophet and Khadijah. Thus, 'Ali grew up in the teachings of Islam from a young age, and deeply imbibed its universalizing aspect, as he became freer of the old tribal loyalties than many of the other Companions.

Strong Bonds. At first, perhaps, 'Ali was necessarily subordinate to his much older brother Ja'far (circa 589-629), who was also an early Muslim but spent many years as the head of the Muslim exiles in Abyssinia (circa 615-627). However 'Ali gradually assumed a greater importance, being especially renowned as a warrior in the battles of the Madinan period. In 624, he married the Prophet's youngest daughter, Fatimah (circa 604-632). They had four children who survived to adulthood, two sons, al-Hasan (625-669) and al-Husayn (626-680), and two daughters, Zaynab and Umm Kulthum, and it is only through these that all the Prophet's later descendants are traced (as the line from Fatimah's sister Zaynab through her daughter Umaymah soon became extinct). The young family of 'Ali and Fatimah further endeared 'Ali to the Prophet, who loved children and enjoyed playing with his young grandsons. These circumstances gave 'Ali easy access to the Prophet, which may have also fueled a rivalry with Fatimah's young stepmother 'a'ishah, the daughter of Abu Bakr, who was perhaps slightly younger than Fatimah. This split had important political consequences later.

Succession. Nevertheless, when the Prophet died in 632, 'Ali put aside his own potential legitimist political claims for the sake of internal Muslim harmony. The Shi'ah assert that the Prophet had indeed predesignated him as his successor as imam or leader of the Muslim community, though not as Prophet (Qur'an 33:40). The Sunnis assert that, although the Prophet gave some indirect indications that he preferred Abu Bakr to succeed him, the community had to elect a successor, and chose Abu Bakr as amir or commander, and that he also took the title of *Khalifah* (caliph or deputy). At the time, however, this difference did not cause a final political break, and 'Ali eventually acknowledged Abu Bakr as ruler and paid allegiance to him when Fatimah died about six months after the Prophet. On Abu Bakr's own death in 634, 'Ali likewise paid allegiance to 'Umar, who sometimes consulted him on matters of state. 'Ali also married his youngest daughter by Fatimah, Umm Kulthum, to 'Umar, although possibly with some reluctance. When 'Umar was assassinated in 644, with his last breathe he appointed a council of six high-ranking Quraysh tribe members including 'Ali to elect a successor, and from that time the political split became worse, because 'Ali always had a more universalist view of Islam than the Quraysh nobles, who expected to be the privileged group.

Rebels. 'Ali's broader view may have derived from his close friendship with the Ansar, the native people of Madinah, who had provided most of the troops for the military campaigns in the Prophet's lifetime but found themselves increasingly shunted aside by the Quraysh. When the Umayyad 'Uthman (circa 574-656) was elected as the third Khalifah in succession to 'Umar, tempers flared immediately. 'Uthman's attempted to prevent separatist fiefs from developing in the newly-acquired outer provinces by appointing his close relatives as governors. Such a policy only alienated even his Quraysh supporters, however, so that a revolutionary situation developed which led to his assassination in his house by rebels from the outer provinces. The rebels, in collaboration with the Ansar in Madinah, immediately elected 'Ali to be Khalifah and imam.

Civil War. This revolution broke the fragile legitimacy of the Madinan khilafah that had been dominated by the Quraysh. The Muslims thereupon split into several factions, each of which 'Ali fought in succession in the First Civil War (656-661). He initially defeated the old Quraysh nobles led by 'A'ishah, Talhah, and al-Zubayr, preventing their comeback (656). Then he fought the well-established governor of Syria, Mu'awiyah (circa 600-680) to a stalemate (657). Because he accepted arbitration to save further bloodshed among the Muslims, 'Ali was now denounced by his own true-blue faction, who became the Kharijites. He tried to suppress this group as well (658). Another faction of Muslims held back from fighting altogether and refused to take sides. Thus, the war remained unsettled, much blood had been shed, and 'Ali's title to rule had been severely tested. The fighting ended when 'Ali was himself assassinated in 661, and his son al-Hasan, after gaining promise of an amnesty, surrendered to Mu'awiyah.

Legacy. 'Ali left behind him the memory of a sincere commitment to Islam and to justice, however, and a loyal cadre of followers who commemorated him, who in time became the Shi'ah. The Sunnis likewise claim him as a just ruler, and thus his fame and influence continue to reverberate after fourteen centuries.

Sources:
Wilferd Madelung, *The Succession to Muhammad: A Study of the Early Caliphate* (Cambridge: Cambridge University Press, 1997).

L. Veccia Vaglieri, "'Ali b. Abi Talib," in *Encyclopedia of Islam,* CD-ROM version (Leiden: Brill, 1999).

AHMAD IBN HANBAL

780-855

LEGAL SCHOLAR

Defining Islam. The period in which 'Ahmad Ibn Hanbal lived was filled with ideological controversies about the precise definition of Islam, a discussion that the declining khilafah was unable to dominate. Ibn Hanbal contributed greatly to the emergent Sunni orthodoxy by helping to define the religion, fighting what he saw as heresy, and supporting the hadiths (traditions of the Prophet) as a central source of doctrine and practice alongside the Qur'an. Like the other founding figures of Sunni Islam, he was concerned with establishing firm Sunni conformity to agreed-upon principles.

Life and Works. Born in Baghdad, where his father was one of the Khurasani soldiers who were the chief support of the Abbasid khilafah, Ibn Hanbal spent most of his life in his native city, and does not appear to have traveled much. Thus, he did not meet most of the imams who were later considered founders of legal schools. The only exception was al-Shafi'i, whom Ibn Hanbal seems to have met only once. Nevertheless, he studied under the most important hadith scholars of his time, including Sufyan ibn 'Uyaynah (died 813), and later had many well-known students himself, including the compilers of several important hadith collections: al-Bukhari, Muslim, and in particular Abu Dawud, to whom Ibn Hanbal was closely associated.

Hadith Transmitter. Ibn Hanbal is perhaps best remembered for his complete devotion to the hadiths, which were first handed down in oral form. By Ibn Hanbal's time they had begun to be recorded in writing, and he transmitted a vast collection of more than twenty thousand individual reports of the Prophet's words and deeds. After his death, this collection was edited and expanded by Ibn Hanbal's son. It became the best-known, standard collection of its time and greatly helped to establish the currency of the hadiths as the second source of Islam after the Qur'an. Ibn Hanbal's viewpoint thus came to be regarded as the paradigmatic early expression of the traditionist approach to Islam and its law.

Persecution. Several importatnt consequences emerged from ibn Hanbal's complete devotion to the hadiths. Because the hadiths were increasingly becoming recorded in written form, Sunni Islam was becoming more and more textually oriented, and Ibn Hanbal's work reinforced this trend, which included the tendency to observe the letter of the text (that is, a considerable literalism). On these grounds Ibn Hanbal argued from the Qur'an, and especially the hadiths, that the Qur'an is God's uncreated speech. This view clashed with the rationalist Mu'tazili ideology then patronized by the Abbasid khalifahs as official doctrine, leading to Ibn Hanbal's persecution under the Khalifah al-Mu'tasim after 833, including imprisonment and corporal punishment. This treatment, however, only enhanced Ibn Hanbal's reputation, and beginning in 847 he had the satisfaction of seeing the Khalifah al-Mutakkil abandon Mu'tazilism for standard Sunnism.

Source:
H. Laoust, "Ahmad b. Hanbal," in *Encyclopedia of Islam,* CD-ROM version (Leiden: Brill, 1999).

'ABD AL-RAHMAN IBN KHALDUN

1332-1406

HISTORIAN, LEGAL SCHOLAR

Early Life. The colorful life of historian 'Abd al-Rahman Ibn Khaldun is in some ways typical of the career of a Muslim scholar, as he flourished in many different lands and pursued a diversity of occupations. Ibn Khaldun was born in Tunis, the capital of Tunisia, to a family of Spanish Muslims who had been part of the scholarly gentry for several generations. In 1349, at the age of seventeen, his parents died of the Black Death, the same epidemic that devastated the population of Europe.

Career. In 1350, at only eighteen, Ibn Khaldun took a post as a clerk in a government office in Tunis but aspired to leave his birthplace. After spending a few years in the service of various local governors in Algeria, he reached the court of the Marinid sultan of Morocco at Fas in 1354. He benefited from the opportunity to hear many great scholars of Islam lecture at the Qarawiyyin University in Fas, the greatest center of Muslim learning in North Africa, but he also fell foul of the political intrigues that surrounded the sultan and spent most of 1357 and 1358 in prison. After the sultan died, Ibn Khaldun was freed and worked at minor administrative posts, including a judgeship. From 1362 to 1365, Ibn Khaldun lived in Granada, Spain, where he was a friend of the prime minister, Ibn al-Khatib (1313–1375), who, like Ibn Khaldun, was a scholar as well as a government official. In 1364 Ibn Khaldun was sent on an embassy to the Christian king, Pedro the Cruel, of Castile and Léon, which enabled him to gather more information about a society different from his own. After Ibn al-Khatib became jealous of Ibn Khaldun's talents, he moved on, serving at government posts in eastern Algeria (1365–1372) and Fas (1372–1375), before returning briefly to Granada (1375), and then going on to Tilimsan (1375). Then, fearing for his life after all the often-fatal political intrigues he had witnessed, and particularly the execution of his friend Ibn al-Khatib in Fas, Ibn Khaldun took refuge with his family in a desert castle (1375–1378). During this period he planned and wrote the earliest draft of his great *al-Muqaddimah* (The Introduction to History). In 1378 he returned to his native Tunis, where intrigues and jealousy of his abilities again placed him in danger. Therefore, in 1382 he accepted the invitation of Sultan Barquq of Egypt to move there. Ibn Khaldun obtained permission from the government of Tunis for his wife and daughters to follow him, and in 1384 they all died in a shipwreck near Alexandria. In Egypt, where—except for a brief diplomatic sojourn in Syria (1400–1401)—he spent the rest of his life, Ibn Khaldun avoided politics and concentrated on scholarship and teaching, holding the judgeship of the Maliki school of law six times during the years 1384–1385, 1399–1400, and 1401–1406.

Writings. Like many great Muslim scholars, Ibn Khaldun wrote a large number of books, but few of them are still read or studied apart from his autobiography and his great history, *Kitab al-'ibar* (The Book of Historical Lessons), a seven-volume universal encyclopedia of world history down to his own time. Because his sources are largely those of the Muslim civilization, this work suffers from many of the same limitations as other Muslim "universal histories," but Ibn Khaldun did consult some other sources, translated for him from Latin, which gave him an awareness of the ancient Roman republic that is not found in works by other Muslim historians of the period. Also, he recognized that different civilizations represented distinct and separate ways of thinking. His major accomplishment is the first volume of his *Kitab al-'ibar*, his renowned *al-Muqaddimah,* which constitutes the foundation of history as a social science. Relying on empirical observation to describe society, Ibn Khaldun went on from this grounding to elaborate a complex theory of the rise and fall of states and peoples, basing his theory on the concept of 'asabiyyah (group feeling). He used his theory to explain the rise and fall of various kingdoms in North Africa, Spain, and elsewhere. Much of his analysis is sociological, as he considers the people in general, not merely the ruling elites, using a method that is development oriented, rather than event oriented. Because his work anticipates many recent developments in the academic study of societies, he has frequently been called the "Father of Sociology." Also his emphasis on economic activity, particularly production, prefigures the concerns of Karl Marx almost five centuries later. Widely read in Egypt during Ibn Khaldan's lifetime, *al-Muqaddimah* later became influential in Ottoman Turkey and in Europe beginning in the nineteenth century.

Source:
'Abd al-Rahman Ibn Khaldun, *The Muqaddimah: An Introduction to History,* translated by Franz Rosenthal, edited and abridged by N. J. Dawood (Princeton: Princeton University Press, 1967).

Khaldun, *The Muqaddimah: An Introduction to History,* 3 volumes, translated by Franz Rosenthal (London: Routledge & Kegan Paul, 1958); abridged by N. J. Dawood (Princeton: Princeton University Press, 1967).

M. Talbi, "Ibn Khaldun, Wali al-Din 'Abd al-Rahman b. Muhammad," in *Encyclopedia of Islam,* CD-ROM version (Leiden: Brill, 1999).

JA'FAR AL-SADIQ

CIRCA 702-765

IMAM

Religion and Law. Ja'far ibn Muhammad ibn 'Ali ibn al-Husayn ibn 'Ali ibn Abi Talib (Ja'far al-Sadiq), a lineal descendant of the Prophet Muhammad, is the sixth imam for the Twelver Shi'is, who today are the majority religious group in Iran, Azerbaijan, Bahrain, and Iraq. The Twelvers regarded Ja'far as the founder of their school of jurisprudence, which is called Ja'fari in his honor. Traditions traced back to him, of which there are many, have legal authority for followers of the Ja'fari school.

Patience. Ja'far appears to have lived all of his life in Madinah, the early religious center of Islam. Forewarned by the fate of his great-grandfather, al-Husayn ibn 'Ali, who, while trying to lead a revolt, had been slain with many of his family at Karbala' in Iraq by an Umayyad army in 680, Ja'far preferred a quietist policy. Thereby he was able to avoid confrontation with the Umayyad rulers while nonetheless cultivating his own loyal group of followers, who held him to be the one true imam and proper leader for the Muslim community. Thus, Ja'far was able to expand his following while avoiding entanglement in the failed Shi'i revolts of Zayd ibn 'Ali (740) and Muhammad al-Nafs al-Zakiyyah

(762), which he did not support. On the other hand, at the time of the downfall of the Umayyads (749), Ja'far seems to have been considered by the revolutionary forces in Kufah in Iraq as a possible candidate to be the ruler, but he laid down conditions for his own freedom of action that the revolutionaries felt were too stringent. Also, unlike his great-grandfather, he did not leap at the chance to go to Iraq to establish his claim, but believed instead that when the time was ripe, he would be called to office.

Influence. Although he did not leave behind a law-book in his name as did Malik and al-Shafi'i, he was nevertheless influential in establishing Shi'i law, which bears the stamp of its Madinan origin, as does the Maliki and the Shafi'i. Many of the traditions in later Shi'i legal compilations are traced back to Ja'far. He gathered around him a coterie of supporters who included many philosophically-minded scholars and sectaries. This situation helped contribute to the Ja'fari Shi'is acceptance of several features of Mu'tazili thought, which was influenced by Greek philosophical concepts, including, in particular, the importance of justice as an absolute value.

Sources:
Marshall G. S. Hodgson,, "Dja'far al-Sadik," in *Encyclopedia of Islam*, CD-ROM edition (Leiden: Brill, 1999).

Syed Husain M. Jafri, *The Origins and Early Development of Shi'a Islam* (London & New York: Longman, 1979).

Moojan Momen, *An Introduction to Shi'i Islam: The History and Doctrines of Twelver Shi`ism* (New Haven: Yale University Press, 1985).

MALIK IBN ANAS

CIRCA 712-795

THEOLOGIAN AND SCHOLAR

Madinah. Malik ibn Anas, the founding figure of the Maliki school of jurisprudence, also known as "the school of the people of Madinah," was born at Madinah at the height of the Umayyad khilafah. Although Madinah had by his time long lost the political importance it had once had, the town remained the chief center of transmitted information about Islam in all the lands of the khilafah, because it was the original setting of the Prophet's mission in the crucial last ten years of his life, because the overwhelming majority of Muhammad's Companions had continued to reside there after his death, and because their descendants were still living there in Malik's time. As Muslims elsewhere were often busy with political and military affairs in early Islam, Madinah became the paradigm of sound Muslim practice, an image that was reinforced when Muslims from the Iraq, Iran, Syria, Egypt, North Africa, and Spain necessarily passed through Madinah on their way to Makkah to perform the pilgrimage.

Public Beating. Although Malik's ancestors had come from Yemen, his family had long been settled in Madinah, where they were clients of the Qurashi clan of Taym ibn Murrah. The family also had cultivated Muslim religious studies from an early date, as Malik's great-grandfather, grandfather, father, and uncles all transmitted traditions. Thus, it was quite natural for Malik to pursue such studies as well, which he did from an early age. He was able to study under respected teachers, including Ibn Hurmuz, Rabi'ah ibn Farrukh, Nafi',and Ibn Shihab al-Zuhri. Steeped in the learning of Madinah, he became the chief scholar and exponent of its tradition. Although he held no political offices, he occasionally became entangled in the politics of his time, especially when he supported the hopeless rebellion of Muhammad al-Nafs al-Zakiyyah in 762 against the Abbasids, a stance for which he was publicly beaten by the Abbasid governor. Nevertheless, he was still held in esteem and occasionally consulted by later Abbasid khalifahs, who would sometimes visit him on their way to Makkah for the pilgrimage. He was also visited by scholars from the outer provinces who had heard of his fame. Many of these individuals devoted themselves to his teaching, but a rivalry with the nascent legal school of Iraq began to intensify, especially when the Iraqi Muhammad ibn Hasan al-Shaybani (750-805) began to challenge the teachings of Malik on various points.

Book. The main monument left by Malik to posterity is his book *al-Muwatta'* (The Trodden Path), perhaps composed about 765-770. It is the earliest Muslim law book of any size and Malik used this collection in his teaching and sometimes added to it later. It contains an arrangement of the chapters of the law which became the basis for most subsequent law books. Mostly, it is a collection of traditions, about half of which are traced to the Prophet Muhammad himself and the remainder are traced to his Companions and the generation following them. Thus, it is the earliest major source for the practice of the Prophet and was heavily used by later compilers of Hadith collections. It also includes the statements of Malik himself, including his descriptions of the living practice of the Madinans of his time. This practice was treated by the Maliki *madhhab* (school of law) as one of the most reliable sources of law, because it reflected the living tradition handed down from the time of the Prophet by the inhabitants of the Prophet's city, Madinah. The greater authenticity of its tradition based on Madinah became one of the main arguments for preferring the Maliki legal school.

Legacy. Malik remains one of the most famous of all the scholars Islam has ever produced, and his earliness guaranteed him an influence on later developments, and not only in the Maliki school, for the Shafi'i founder al-Shafi'i (767-820) and Muhammad ibn Hasan al-Shaybani, who was one of the major founders of the Hanafi school, were his students. He was also respected by Ahmad ibn Hanbal (780-855) and other later jurists and transmitters of tradition. He represented the final summation of the influence of Madinah on Muslim jurisprudence. Up to Malik's time, the religious authority of Madinah was easily superior to that of all other Muslim cities, but after him it greatly lost influence, even in the Maliki school, which thereafter was cultivated mainly in North Africa, Iraq and the Persian Gulf, and much later in West Africa.

Sources:
Yasin Dutton, *The Origins of Islamic Law: The Qur'an, the Muwatta' and Madinan 'Amal* (Richmond, U.K.: Curzon, 1999).

Malik ibn Anas, *al-Muwatta'*, translated by 'A'isha 'Abdarahman al-Tarjumana and Ya'qub Johnson (Norwich: Diwan Press, 1982); also translated as *Al-Muwatta' of Imam Malik ibn Anas: The First Formulation of Islamic Law*, translated by 'A'isha 'Abdurrahman Bewley (London: Kegan Paul International, 1989).

Joseph Schacht, "Malik b. Anas," in *Encyclopedia of Islam*, CD-ROM version (Leiden: Brill, 1999).

NIZAM AL-MULK

CIRCA 1019-1092
WAZIR

Prime Minister. Nizam al-Mulk was the Persian prime minister (wazir) of the well-known Saljuk rulers Alp Arslan (ruled 1063–1072) and Malikdhah (ruled 1072–1092). Throughout this period, Nizam al-Milk witnessed a series of wars, as the Saljuk realm expanded. The Saljuks captured their first significant city, Nishapur, in 1037, and only eighteen years later, in 1055, took Baghdad, the capital of the khilafah in 1055, only eighteen years later. When Nizam al-Mulk became prime minister, the Saljuk sultanate was already the single most powerful Muslim kingdom of its day. During his term in office, it attained even greater size, especially after the defeat of the Byzantines at Malazgirt (Manzikert) in 1071 and the capture of Syria in 1072. Probably his role in these conquests was minimal, his position being administrative rather than military; yet, the extend of Saljuk territory put at his command large financial resources to spend on useful projects with lasting effects.

Founder of Colleges. The best-known, longest-lasting, and most influential of Nizam al-Mulk's projects was the founding of Nizamiyyah madrasahs (colleges) in several cities of the Saljuk realm, which at that time covered most of the eastern Muslim world. The first of these colleges was opened at Baghdad in 1067. The madrasah movement contributed to the establishment of a regular system of Muslim higher education, which later provided a model for European universities. Although madrasahs had already been established as separate institutions independent from masjids, his Nizamiyyah madrasahs gave a strong impetus to the madrasah movement, establishing professorships supported by regular stipends from endowments belonging to each school. Part of the motivation for establishing these colleges was ideological. The state the Saljuks overthrew had been Shi'i, and the Nizamiyyah emphasized the teachings of the Sunni Shafi'i school, which the Saljuks supported, thus demonstrating their Sunni legitimacy. Whatever the political motives, however, the colleges raised educational standards throughout the Muslim world.

Literary Legacy. Although Nizam al-Mulk was clearly part of the class of literati, unlike most members of that class he was a politician, not a scholar of religion, and he wrote in Persian, not Arabic. His major work, the *Siyasat-namah* (Political Treatise), is a major medieval Muslim work advising rulers and their assistants about the conduct of state and one of the earliest important works of Persian literature. Throughout this work Nizm al-Mulk helped the trend to raise the status of Persian language for nonreligious uses. The book harks back to earlier Persian models of statecraft but also includes many useful examples from Nizam al-Mulk's own long career. It was meant to instruct the young ruler Malikshah, who ascended the throne at age seventeen. Malikshah eventually tired of the interference of the old prime minister, dismissing him from office in 1092. Shortly thereafter, Nizam al-Mulk was assassinated by a follower of an extreme branch of Shi'ism that the prime minister had worked to suppress.

Sources:
H. Bowen, "Nizam al-Mulk, Abu 'Ali al-Hasan b. 'Ali," revised by C. E. Bosworth, *Encyclopedia of Islam*, CD-ROM version (Leiden: Brill, 1999).

Michael Brett, *Ibn Khaldun and the Medieval Maghrib* (Aldershot, U.K.: Ashgate Variorum, 1999)

Bruce B. Lawrence, ed., *Ibn Khaldun and Islamic Ideology* (Leiden: Brill, 1984).

Nizam al-Mulk, *The Book of Government or, Rules for Kings: The Siyar al-Muluk or Siyasatnama*, translated by Hubert Darke, revised edition (London: Routledge & Kegan Paul, 1978).

S.A.A. Rizvi, *Nizam al-Mulk Tusi, His Contribution to Statecraft, Political-Theory and the Art of Government* (Lahore, 1978).

MUHAMMAD IBN IDRIS AL-SHAFI'I

767-820
THEOLOGIAN AND JURIST

Trial. Muhammad ibn Idris al-Shafi'i was a Qurashi Arab of fairly noble lineage born in Gaza, Palestine in the early Abbasid era. After studying with the great authority of the Madinan school of law, Malik ibn Anas, al-Shafi'i obtained employment in a government office in Yemen, where he was arrested by the khalifal police, accused of belonging to an illegal organization, and sent to Iraq for trial before the Khalifah Harun al-Rashid himself. In Iraq, he was able to defend himself against the charges and win his liberty. Knowing of the serious differences between the legal schools of Iraq and Madinah, the latter being his own school, al-Shafi'i sought out Muhammad ibn Hasan al-Shaybani (750-805), the main living exponent of the Iraqi school, for an exchange of views. Later, al-Shafi'i traveled back and forth between Madinah and Iraq many times, promoting certain principles for the derivation of Muslim law on which he hoped all could agree. These views became the basis for al-Shafi'i's legal theory, the first organized theory of the law that is known in Islam. However al-Shafi'i was disappointed in his expectation that all would respect his principles. During his last visit to Baghdad about 814, he also became somewhat disgusted with the Abbasid rulers, who were engaged in a ruinous civil war. As a result, he withdrew to Egypt, which had drifted out of direct Abbasid control, and there wrote down both his final formulations of the law and his legal theory.

Principles. Al-Shafi'i's legal theory stressed four sources of the law. First, there was the Qur'an, which all were completely agreed upon. Second, there was the Sunnah, which al-Shafi'i equated with the Hadith of the Prophet that had been transmitted and verified by a chain of reliable transmitters. In adopting this point, he favored the school of Iraq over that of Madinah. The equation of the Sunnah with the prophetic Hadith led to an increasing tendency to disregard traditions that could not be traced back all the way to the Prophet. Third, he acknowledged the principle of the consensus of the legal opinion of the community. Fourth, al-Shafi'i allowed the law to be further elaborated from the original texts by the use of analogy. Although these sources, laid down in his *al-Risalah* (The Treatise, 815–820), were accepted by all Sunnis eventually, the various schools made their own interpretations of them, so that they did not lead to unity in the legal system as al-Shafi'i probably hoped. Yet at least they played a major role in framing the legal discourses of Islam. Al-Shafi'i's much-admired principles also led to the establishment of a school of law in his name that was distinct from the other existing schools. At first popular in Lower Egypt, where he taught for the last five or so years of his life, this school eventually became popular with the Sunni religious scholars because of the orderliness of its principles, which had been laid down by the founder from the first and not extracted later from practice, as was the case with the Hanafi and Maliki schools. Thus, al-Shafi'i had a tremendous impact on the formulation of Muslim law.

Sources:

E. Chaumont, "al-Shafi'i," in *Encyclopedia of Islam*, CD-ROM version (Leiden: Brill, 1999).

Muhammad ibn Idris al-Shafi'i, *al-Shafi'i's Risala: Treatise on the Foundations of Islamic Jurisprudence*, translated by Majid Khadduri (Baltimore: Johns Hopkins Press, 1961).

SHAJARAT AL-DURR

CIRCA 1223-1257
SULTANAH OF EGYPT AND SYRIA

Seventh Crusade. Shajarat al-Durr, queen of Egypt and Syria, was a Turkish slave who was the concubine of the Ayyubid sultan al-Malik al-Salih Najm al-Din Ayyub (ruled 1240-1249). Freed by her husband before his accession, she became one of his closest advisers. In late 1249, she went forth with her husband to fight French king Louis IX in the Seventh Crusade (1248–1254). Louis IX had occupied the Egyptian port of Damietta and was trying to seize all of Egypt, and although Sultan al-Salih was ill at the time with tuberculosis, the invasion of the kingdom required his presence. The sultan died in November 1249, and from that time until the arrival of her stepson Turan Shah in February, Shajarat al-Durr ruled the state as a member of a council of three. She kept Sultan al-Salih's death a secret, despite the advance of the Frankish Crusaders, who were decisively defeated in February 1250, shortly before Turan Shah's arrival.

Court Intrigue. Turan Shah proved to be an unworthy ruler, however, and Shajarat al-Durr arranged his assassination in May, whereupon she was acclaimed as sultanah in her own name, a position she held for three months. The refusal of Syria to submit caused the army to enthrone Aybak (reigned 1250-1257) as ruler in her place, and at some point Aybak also married her.

Marriage of Convenience. Although deprived of her title, Shajarat al-Durr retained ruling authority alongside her husband, still issuing royal decrees by herself as late as 1255. While Aybak tended to confine himself to military matters, Shajarat al-Durr ran the state administration. This political marriage eventually turned into a kind of rivalry, ending in Shajarat al-Durr arranging her second husband's assassination in 1257; in turn Aybak's loyal troops murdered Shajarat al-Durr a few days later.

Impact. The historian Ibn al-'Ibri or Bar Hebraeus (1226-1286) called her "the amazing phenomenon of the time who was rivalled by no woman in beauty and no man in determination." Like her contemporary, Sultanah Radiyyah of Delhi (ruled 1236-1240), Shajarat al-Durr demonstrated that women could have significant political roles in classical Islam although such careers were exceptional during that era.

Source:

L. Ammann, "Shadjar al-Durr," in *Encyclopedia of Islam*, CD-ROM version (Leiden: Brill, 1999).

DOCUMENTARY SOURCES

'Abd al-Rahman Ibn Khaldun (1332–1406), *al-Muqaddimah* (The Muqaddimah, 1375–1378, revised 1378–1406) — An important theory of history that prefigures modern theoretical discussions; because he does not focus only on elites but considers the people and their culture as a whole, his work has a lasting relevance and he has sometimes been called "the Father of Sociology."

Ibn Rushd (1126–1198), *Bidayat al-Mujtahid* (The Distinguished Jurist's Primer, circa 1167 and 1188) — An important work of classical Muslim jurisprudence by a well-known Maliki scholar of Córdoba, perhaps the best-known books dealing with differences among the rulings of the various schools of law; most of it was written around 1167, but the chapters on the pilgrimage were added in 1188; Ibn Rushd covers all the major differences of law and practice among the schools; though he concentrates most on his own Maliki school, his treatment is extremely comprehensive, dealing with the four classical schools—Hanafi, Maliki, Shafi'i, and Hanbali—as well as extinct schools such as the Zahiri and early independent jurists; Ibn Rushd was also a major Muslim philosopher whose works were translated into Latin during the Middle Ages and influenced the development of philosophy throughout western Europe, where he was known as Averröes.

Malik ibn Anas (circa 712 – 795), *al-Muwatta'* (The Trodden Path, circa 765–770) — The earliest collection of hadiths and law according to the tradition of Madinah, said to comprise 1,720 traditions.

Al-Mawardi (974–1058), *Al-Ahkam al-Sultaniyyah* (The Ordinances of Government) — The best-known book of a well-known Shafi'i scholar and judge in Baghdad who lived mostly during the decline of the Shi'i Buyid dynasty in Iraq (945–1055), this influential early Muslim treatise on government includes sections on governance, crime, and punishment from a viewpoint of a writer thoroughly grounded in Muslim jurisprudence; though the institutions he described did exist, al-Mawardi's book presents an ideal picture of the functions of the Muslim state that is not altogether consonant with the actualities of his time.

Muhammad ibn Hasan al-Shaybani (750–805), Siyar (Law of Nations — A section on international relations—especially war regulations and truces—from *Kitab al-asl* (Book of Origin), a law book by the most important founder of the Hanafi school of law, who served as the judge of al-Raqqah, the Syrian city where Khalifah Harun al-Rashid (ruled 786–809) sometimes resided.

Al-Tabari (839–923), *Tarikh al-Rusul wa al-Muluk* (History of Prophets and Kings) — The largest and most important of the early Muslim histories, covering the period from creation to the year 915, but giving more coverage to the early periods of Islam than to the years closer to the author's own time and centering on Iraq, the land in which he lived; his biography of the Prophet Muhammad is one of the most important sources on that subject; Al-Tabari—who was born in northern Iran, traveled widely in the Muslim world, and spent most of his career in Baghdad—was a great religious scholar as well as an historian and is best known for his Qur'an commentary, often considered the greatest of all; he also founded his own school of law, which has since disappeared.

LEISURE, RECREATION, AND DAILY LIFE

by SUSAN L. DOUGLASS

CONTENTS

CHRONOLOGY
242

OVERVIEW
245

TOPICS IN LEISURE, RECREATION, AND DAILY LIFE

Adapting to Climates
and Landscapes 247

Characteristics of Islamic
Daily Life 248

Clothing and Textiles 250

Dwelling Spaces 261

The Spread of Muslim Textiles . . 263

Food 268

Juha. 269

Breads 272

Regional Cookery 275

Games and
Leisure Activities. 276

Holidays and Religious
Observances 280

A Merchant of Baghdad. 285

SIGNIFICANT PEOPLE

Abu Hurayrah 288

Muhammad ibn Ismail
al-Bukhari. 288

Ahmad Badi al-Zaman al-
Hamadhani 289

Ibn Khallikan 289

Anas Ibn Malik 290

Juha 290

Nasr al-Din Khoja. 290

Muslim Abu al-Husayn
Muslim 291

DOCUMENTARY SOURCES
291

Sidebars and tables are listed in italics.

622
- Muhammad and his followers make their *Hijrah* (migration) from Makkah to Madinah, where a Muslim society is established under his leadership; the Constitution of Madinah sets down in writing conditions and rights under which Muslims and non-Muslims will live together.

624
- The direction of the *qiblah*, the prayer orientation of Muslims, changes from Jerusalem to Makkah.

630
- Under Muhammad's leadership, victorious Muslims re-enter the city of Makkah, offering a general amnesty to the inhabitants; Muhammad removes all idols from the Ka'bah and rededicates it to worship of the One God.

632
- Muhammad dies, and shortly thereafter Abu Bakr becomes the first "Rightly Guided" Khalifah (caliph), or successor to Muhammad.

634-642
- Muslim troops are successful in battles against the Byzantine and Sasanid Empires, extending Muslim rule into Syria, Palestine (including Jerusalem), Iraq, and Iran.

650-652
- The Qur'an is compiled in definitive written form for the first time, and the text is checked against all available written and oral sources.

661
- The murder of Ali ibn Abi Talib, who had ruled since 656, ends the period of Rightly Guided Khalifahs. The Umayyad dynasty is established in Damascus.

691
- Muslims construct the Dome of the Rock and al-Aqsa Masjid (mosque) in Jerusalem, the third holiest city in Islam.

696
- Arabic is declared as the official language of Muslim administration, replacing Greek and Pahlavi.
- Arabic coins are introduced.

711
- Tariq ibn Ziyad establishes Muslim rule on the Iberian peninsula. Muslim rule also expands into Sind, in northern India.

* DENOTES CIRCA DATE

750-763	• The Umayyads are overthrown, and the Abbasid dynasty comes to power; a new capital, Baghdad, is established on the Tigris River in Iraq.
760-855	• The four major Sunni schools of Islamic law, or *Shari'ah*, are founded: Hanafi, Maliki, Shafi'i, and Hanbali. These schools continue to influence the behavior of ordinary Muslims to the present day.
791	• A papermaking industry is established in Baghdad, making books more widely available and less expensive and simplifying government administration.
800-909	• The Aglabid dynasty completes the transformation of North Africa into Muslim Ifriqiya and captures Sicily.
870	• Muhammad ibn Ismail al-Bukhari dies. He was the best-known compiler of hadiths (words and deeds of Prophet Muhammad), which make up the Sunnah, the source of law second only to the Qur'an.
969	• After establishing their rule in North Africa, the Fatimids found Cairo, promoting architecture and patronizing textile production.
1055	• Saljuk Turk Tughril Beg is recognized as sultan by the khalifah in Baghdad, and the Turkic influence in fashions, food, and elite culture grows.
1071	• The Saljuk Turks defeat the Byzantines in eastern Anatolia, opening the region to Turkic migration, Islamization, and Turkic cultural influences.
1085	• Toledo falls to Spanish Christian forces, resulting in the opening of its libraries to western Europeans and the translation of Arabic texts into Latin; by the end of the twelfth century much of the corpus of Islamic learning has been introduced to Europe.
1096-1291	• The Crusades bring western Europeans to the Holy Land, initiating a period of cultural, military, and commercial exchange.

* DENOTES CIRCA DATE

1236	• Córdoba falls to the Christians; the Masjid of Córdoba is late converted to a cathedral.
1258	• Mongols led by Hulegu sack Baghdad, climaxing a destructive invasion that leaves behind ruined cities, decimated public works, and reduced standards of living.
1262-1517	• Mamluk rule of Egypt and much of southwest Asia influences the architecture and cultural institutions of the region, including masjids, schools, hospitals, and elegant homes.
1453	• The Byzantine capital of Constantinople falls to the Ottoman Turks.
1492	• Granada falls to Spanish Christian monarchs Ferdinand and Isabella, ending Muslim rule in Spain.

* DENOTES CIRCA DATE

Pierced brass and silver-inlaid globe made in Syria for Badr al-Din Baysari, circa 1270 (British Museum)

OVERVIEW

Cultural Interactions. The period from 622 to 1500 belongs to an era of intensifying interactions in the Eastern Hemisphere, and Muslim civilization was a major part of the cultural, technological, economic, and social exchanges taking place. During the first two centuries of the period, the rise and spread of Islam brought an infusion of Islamic beliefs and practices into regional and local cultures, significantly influencing daily life in many areas. In the following centuries a recognizable, but diverse, Muslim culture emerged and continued to spread. By the end of the period, political changes had reconfigured the region many times, and it had undergone extensive urbanization despite periods of warfare and other disasters that caused decline in cities. The backdrop of agricultural, pastoral, and urban life remained fairly constant in its basic outlines, but it had been influenced by the spread of urbanization and changes in makeup of the population caused by significant migrations in several areas. The regions into which Islam had spread were increasingly linked to trading systems in the Eastern Hemisphere and experienced the influences of advancement in agriculture, technology, science, modes of living, and cultural expressions that grew out of a cosmopolitan culture identified closely with Islam.

The Muslim Lifestyle. Islam is commonly described as a way of life, and seemingly minute details of everyday life may be involved in Muslim religious practice. The sources for such prescriptions are found either in the verses of the Qur'an or among the transmitted hadiths (words and deeds) of Prophet Muhammad, whose life was a model of Qur'anic precepts for Muslims. The Sahabah (companions) of the Prophet, especially those closest to him, collectively transmitted the Qur'an by memorizing it and reciting it in the Prophet's presence. They also transmitted to each other, and to subsequent generations of Muslims, details of his daily habits, personal appearance, and likes and dislikes. This second source of Islam, the Sunnah, consists in what Muhammad said, did, and approved of by word or gesture. Some among the Sahabah used to take turns each day spending as much time as they could in his presence, with a careful respect for his privacy. Anas ibn Malik and others who served in his household related information about his personal habits, what and how he ate, what he wore, and the furnishings of his home. His daughter Fatima and his wives reported on his daily habits, and were often asked how Muslims should conduct private matters between husband and wife. The Prophet instructed his companions—men, women, and children—about matters of daily life such as personal grooming, dress, eating, hygiene, and maintaining ritual purity for purposes of worship.

Hadith Collections. After the Prophet's death, the knowledge and transmission of hadiths, which encompassed all areas of knowledge and practice from the most personal level to complex affairs of state, were prized forms of learning. Just as news of the Prophet's doings and pronouncements was spread among members of the community during his life, it continued to be shared, discussed, evaluated, and interpreted after his death. This process culminated in the authentication and compilation of hadith collections during the eighth through tenth centuries, resulting in the hadith collections that are considered standard by legal scholars. As hadiths were related to transmitters in the following generations, this body of knowledge spread to regions that had come under Muslim rule and became a formal and informal guide for Muslim daily living that was elaborated and unified by the writings of jurists. From the earliest years of Muslim cultural development, the hadiths formed a collective fund of wisdom, guidance, expectations, and common understanding among Muslims that was certainly not uniform from place to place—or unadulterated by faulty transmission, local custom, and pre-Islamic survivals—but nonetheless informed the development of Muslim culture from the household to the institutions of state. On a personal level, the body of hadiths established criteria for behavior that was deemed appropriate before and after acceptance of Islam. It included guidelines for the education and socialization of children, and its refinement and interpretation have remained important topics for scholars of *fiqh*, a branch of Islamic Shari'ah that emphasizes practice. Many books dealing with the Sunnah of personal habits, daily life, and family life have been written and copied by succeeding generations. The best evidence for the pervasiveness of this common fund of understanding and custom is its survival among diverse Muslim peoples and its influence on the details of their everyday lives.

Daily Life. The hadiths shed much light on what daily life was like during the time of the Prophet in Arabia. Anecdotes include descriptions of clothing, hairstyles, jewelry, cosmetics, grooming implements, food and its preparation, and articles such as bags, cushions, tools, and decorations. The hadiths also document pagan practices and the Islamic customs of daily life and worship that were substituted for them. Comparable information for later periods and other regions in Muslim history is revealed by archaeological discoveries, artifacts, literature, and, less often, pictorial sources. It is important to note that the exemplar of the Prophet's life cannot be taken as a stencil for the way all Muslims lived their daily lives thereafter. Emulation of his life required quite an effort, even assuming that an individual set the conscious goal of doing so. The hadiths that were recorded by the eighth century were not accessible to every Muslim in the way that they are readily available in books and even searchable CD-ROM disks today. The Muslims who had the most access to hadiths were the people who lived at Madinah in the generations after the Prophet, or who associated with knowledgeable Sahabah who migrated into other lands, or their students. A mass of fabricated hadith material circulated at the time as well, which made the culling out of unsound hadiths from among the mass seem necessary to compilers such as Muhammad Ibn Isma'il al-Bukhari (810–870) and Muslim Abu al-Husayn Muslim (circa 821–875). Ahmad ibn Hanbal (died 855), and Abu Abd al-Rahman ibn Shu'ayb al-Nasa'i (died 915). Pre-Islamic customs persisted as well, perhaps most among those who remained in their ancestral homes, unlike the early converts who left their homes to live in the growing cities with Arab migrants.

Preserving Knowledge of the Prophet. Steps were taken to preserve the record of Muhammad's words and deeds and to ensure that the Qur'an—the revealed word of God, according to Islamic teachings—did not become diluted by variant texts and disputes over its authenticity. Islamic disciplines related to the systematic interpretation of the Qur'an and the hadiths—and the development of Shari'ah law, Arabic grammar and philology, as well as historical writing—all emerged within the century following Prophet Muhammad's death, and expanded with the spread of Islam among the population over the centuries. Institutions such as the masjid (mosque) with its weekly communal prayer and sermon, as well as the law courts, centers of learning, and travel for the sake of knowledge contributed to disseminating information about the Prophet and his way of life.

Islamic Customs and Practices. It is unclear how rapidly Islamic customs and ways of life penetrated the regions to which Islam was spreading. Archaeologists have identified the emergence of specifically Islamic practices in urban and rural sites. Material evidence of daily life across the social spectrum is usually scarce in comparison to the recorded deeds of prominent figures, but there is evidence in the plentiful literature, government records, and artistic productions from Muslim regions. Literature is one of the hallmarks of Muslim societies, and in such poetry and prose, readers can obtain glimpses of daily life among various classes of people. Architecture, art, literature, music, official records, documents, and everyday objects, as well as surviving customs, have enabled historians to assemble a detailed picture of daily life in Muslim regions from Prophet Muhammad's death to the present. Relatively little domestic architecture has survived, and relatively few less-durable items such as clothing and everyday implements have survived, particularly in view of the absence of grave goods. The prohibition against representing the human figure in Muslim art has discouraged detailed depictions of everyday scenes, portraits, or landscapes. Book illustrations, often related to specific purposes such as medical or other scientific works, practical manuals or histories, but also some literary works, fill this gap somewhat. Miniature painting, mostly developed for the Iranian, Turkish, and Indian courts toward the end of the medieval time period, is mostly quite formal in nature, depicting idealized historical material or the daily life of courtly society. Nevertheless, the abundance and quality of literary sources make up for the relative paucity of visual sources. Thus, it is possible to know how people dressed, what they cooked and ate, what sort of houses the various classes occupied, how they socialized, what they played, what crafts they engaged in, and how they moved about their local area or traveled across the known world.

TOPICS IN LEISURE, RECREATION, AND DAILY LIFE

ADAPTING TO CLIMATES AND LANDSCAPES

Muslim Territory. The most obvious challenge to gaining an overview of daily life among Muslims during the almost nine centuries between 622 and 1500 is the size and diversity of the territory where Muslims lived. During this period Islam expanded northward and eastward into the vast Asian steppe and began to spread to tropical islands in the Indian Ocean and Southeast Asia. Islam extended as far west as Spain, as far east as Southeast Asia, as far north as the Caucasus, and as far south as sub-Saharan West Africa and equatorial east Africa. Landscapes in this vast region range from arid desert and steppe to rain-fed cultivated areas in the North African Sahara, Southwest Asia, and Central Asia. It includes the Mediterranean climates and coastal lands in North Africa, Spain, Turkey, and the Levant, as well as mountainous regions of North Africa, Southwest Asia, and the Hindu Kush. The great river valleys of the Niger, the Nile, the Tigris-Euphrates, the Syr and Amu Darya, and the Indus are fertile agricultural regions that contributed to the development of Muslim culture and economy.

Environments and Cultural Forms. Within this range of geographic regions, various pre-Islamic cultures contributed to the diversity of daily life patterns. Muslim regions were predominantly arid landscapes requiring irrigated farming, while rain-fed agriculture was only possible in a few areas. Pastoral (nomadic or seminomadic) communities inhabited the most arid regions and marginal agricultural areas, depending for their livelihoods on herds of sheep and goats, camels, or horses. Pastoral groups supplied animals for transport, guides for travel, and military support, usually maintaining relationships of mutual benefit with settled folk, thus supplementing their diets of meat and milk with grains, fruits, and vegetables. Invasion of settled areas and warfare were sporadic and most often were sparked by drought or regional unrest. Coastal and island communities on the Mediterranean coast, the inland seas of Asia, the Persian Gulf, and the Indian Ocean relied on trading, fishing, and harvesting pearls and coral. From ancient times, cities flourished in the lands that came under Muslim rule. Islam arose in the towns of Makkah and Madinah, and the

growth of cities reached spectacular heights under Muslim rule. The growth of cities was important for the spread of Islam and the development of Muslim civilization. As economic, political, and cultural centers, cities grew with migration and became prominent destinations for various sorts of travelers. Important aspects of daily life changed with the spread of Islam to a given area, but the range of geographic environments and cultural influences during the period 622 to 1500 resulted in enormous diversity in the customs and habits of daily life.

Change. Natural hazards such as drought or catastrophic flooding caused abrupt change in rural communities. Political stability and periods of peace and prosperity led to improved maintenance of irrigation systems and expansion of land under cultivation, while loss of state control and warfare caused contraction. For pastoral communities, drought spurred migration or invasion of other settled lands, but political stability often meant less autonomy for pastoral groups. For urban communities, prosperity in the hinterlands meant adequate food supplies, and regional stability improved trade, allowing positive economic conditions to expand the cities. Invasion, warfare, floods, fires, and political instability caused the shrinkage or even abandonment of urban areas. Pastoral, rural, and urban ways of life intermeshed, waxed, and waned with economic, climatic, and political fortunes, but the three groups generally benefited from the many forms of exchange in various Muslim regions.

Social Class. Daily life varied considerably depending on class and occupation. Between the palaces of the ruling elites and the humble dwellings of workers, porters, laborers, and the poor, there was of course great disparity in ways of meeting basic needs. The urban upper and middle classes included merchants, skilled artisans, the *ulama'* (learned class), landowners, shopkeepers, and petty merchants, all of whom enjoyed some of the amenities of the wealthy in prosperous times but suffered in hard times. Slaves' lifestyles were determined by the class of those whom they served. Those integrated into common households might serve for only a few years and then be freed, marry, and form their own households. Islamic law regulated the practice of slavery and in fact encouraged its demise as an institution, but custom and economic power maintained the practice. It was not, however, based on race, nor did it result in segregation based on race. Slaves or unfree persons constituted part of the ruling classes—as Mamluk rulers, for example—in some Muslim societies, through marriage, military, or civil service to the state.

Sources:
Isma'il R. al-Faruqi and Lois Lamya', *The Cultural Atlas of Islam* (New York: Macmillan / London: Collier-Macmillan, 1986).

Francis Robinson, "The First Nine Centuries, from 622–1500," in his *Atlas of the Islamic World Since 1500* (New York: Facts on File, 1982).

CHARACTERISTICS OF ISLAMIC DAILY LIFE

The Pillars of Islam. The act of accepting Islam was simple. In the presence of two witnesses, the person, male or female, recited the *shahadah*, a testimony of faith in the One God and His Messengers (Muhammad being the seal of the prophethood), with the Arabic formula *la ilaha illa Allah wa Muhammadun rasulullah* (There is no god but God, and Muhammad is the messenger of God). Having fulfilled the first pillar of Islam, an act repeated daily throughout life, one committed oneself to the other four obligatory acts of worship, or pillars. They were the five daily prayers (salat), purification of wealth through charity (zakat), observing the fast during Ramadan if one was healthy and residing at home (siyam), and performing the *hajj*, or pilgrimage to Makkah, once in a lifetime if means and health permitted. Acceptance of Islam thus brought immediate changes in the daily life of an individual, and the spread of Islam within a village or town soon introduced institutions that made these changes a permanent part of community life.

Prayer. The first obligation after speaking the *shahadah* was to perform the five daily prayers. The times for prayer were stated in the Qur'an and exactly fixed by the Prophet Muhammad on the basis of direct instruction by the angel Gabriel (Jibril in Arabic). The first was the dawn prayer, or *fajr*, performed at the first light of dawn or up to the beginning of sunrise. The noon prayer, or *zuhr*, was called just after noon and could be performed up to midafternoon. The afternoon prayer, or *asr*, was called at that time, and could be performed any time before the beginning of sunset, though Muslims were instructed not to delay it. The *maghrib* prayer took place immediately after sunset, with *isha'*, the last obligatory prayer, called between the end of twilight and the passing of the first third of the night. In the Sunan of Abu Dawud, Hadith 393, Abdullah ibn Abbas says:

> The Apostle of Allah (peace be upon him) said: Gabriel (peace be upon him) led me in prayer at the House (i.e. the Ka'bah). He prayed the noon prayer with me when the sun had passed the meridian to the extent of the thong of a sandal; he prayed the afternoon prayer with me when the shadow of everything was as long as itself; he prayed the sunset prayer with me when one who is fasting breaks the fast; he prayed the night prayer with me when the twilight

had ended; and he prayed the dawn prayer with me when food and drink become forbidden to one who is keeping the fast. On the following day he prayed the noon prayer with me when his shadow was as long as himself; he prayed the afternoon prayer with me when his shadow was twice as long as himself; he prayed the sunset prayer at the time when one who is fasting breaks the fast; he prayed the night prayer with me when about the third of the night had passed; and he prayed the dawn prayer with me when there was a fair amount of light. Then turning to me he said: Muhammad, this is the time observed by the prophets before you, and the time is anywhere between two times.

In addition to the obligatory prayers, additional voluntary prayers could be performed, as established by the Prophet Muhammad. Among these was voluntary prayer during the small hours of the night.

Mind and Body. Prayer was a simple act that engaged body and mind. It consisted of movement and recitation called a *rak'a*, performed identically by men, women, and children. All recitation was in Arabic, no matter what language people spoke in their daily lives. Standing, and after beginning the prayer with a recitation similar to the call for prayer, a Muslim recited *al-fatihah* (the opening chapter) of the Qur'an, followed by at least three other Qur'an verses. Next he or she bowed from the waist, called *ruku*, and recited praises to God, standing again, then kneeling with forehead, hands, knees, and toes touching the ground, called *sujud*. Sujud has often been incorrectly translated as "prostration," literally, lying face down rather than kneeling. The word *sujud* was the origin for the term *masjid* (mosque), meaning "place of kneeling in prayer." Each pair of *rak'a* was followed by the *tashahhud* (testimony), words of praise recited in a sitting position. The number of *rak'a* in various prayers ranged from two to four.

Telling Time. In any Muslim community the *adhan*, or call to prayer, could be heard at established times. The *adhan* was called in any place where Muslims gathered for prayer, by an elder such as the head of household, or a boy of sufficient knowledge, or a woman or girl among women. From the Prophet's time, a man with a strong, sonorous voice was chosen to make the call. Later, the office of *muezzin* or *mu'athin* became an honorable occupation in every masjid. The five prayers measured out life in the family and the community into universally understood, exact increments by which one paced daily activities. Appointments between Muslims are still set according to the completion of the noon, afternoon, or *maghrib* prayer. The times for calling the *adhan* may be determined by simple observation of the sun and shadows or calculated with sophisticated mathematical and astronomical precision. Each local muezzin might calculate time on his own, but large cities had access to well-calibrated sundials or water clocks, for which persons of means bore collective responsibility. So life in homes, villages, and cities followed the rhythm of the prayers.

The Masjid. As a place for communal performance of the five daily prayers, the masjid was the first Islamic insti-

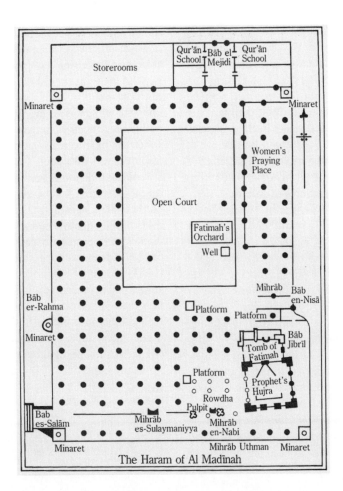

The Haram of Al Madīnah

Plan of the Prophet Muhammad's masjid in Madinah (from Isma'il R. al-Faruqi and Lois Lamya',
The Cultural Atlas of Islam, 1986)

tution to appear in a community. A masjid might be a low earthen wall or line of stones marking out the *musalla* (place of prayer) or an elaborate architectural creation. *Adhan* was called from the roof or a wall of the masjid or from a tower called a minaret. Villages might have a single masjid, while towns and cities had lesser masjids in their various quarters but a central masjid for the obligatory Friday prayer. Performing the prayer in the company of others was preferred, and men were encouraged to perform it at the masjid. Men and older boys were obligated to attend jum'ah, Friday communal prayer. Women and girls were permitted but not required to attend. Pre-Islamic custom in some places discouraged or excluded females from entering the masjid. It is difficult to determine just where and when such practical prohibition was in force, but at the time of the Prophet and for some time after, women could and did attend communal prayer in masjids—a fact that is documented in oral, written, and later pictorial evidence. It is backed up by several hadiths, including: "Ibn 'Umar reports that the Prophet (peace and blessings be upon him) said: 'Do not prevent the women from going to the mosques, of Allah'" (*Hadith Al-Muwatta*, 14:12). Women gathered in the masjid for instruction by the Prophet, spoke during public gatherings in the masjid after the Prophet's death, and served as teachers in the masjid. Indoors or out, women prayed separately from men, arranged in rows behind the men or occasionally alongside

them but separate. This separation was later reinforced in masjids by the erection of physical barriers such as curtains, partitions, or special sections.

Gathering Places. The masjid was a central part of Muslim life. As with the cathedrals in Europe, patronage and donations, as well as the work of local or imported artisans, made certain that a masjid was a showpiece for an area. Privately funded smaller masjids were adorned according to the wealth of the donors. Maintenance of an earthen masjid was a communal effort carried out after the annual rainy seasons, earthquakes, or floods. The masjid was a place of education for adults through weekly sermons and recitation, and for children, who learned to recite the Qur'an in the *kuttab* (primary school). Each year the entire Qur'an was recited at the masjid during the nearly thirty nights of Ramadan. The masjid was a classroom, a place where the homeless or travelers could sleep and expect to receive charity, and a sanctuary. Along with congregational prayer, educational, social, business, and political affairs were conducted in and around the masjid. Judges sometimes heard cases in a masjid.

Purification for Prayer. Purifying the body, clothing, and surroundings was a part of Islamic belief, and seeking forgiveness from God for sins was equated with cleansing. Islam prescribed guidelines for bodily cleanliness that begin with purification for prayer, called *wudu'*, done with water collected from a pure source. A Muslim first washed the hands three times, then cleansed the face, rinsing the mouth and nostrils three times, then washed the forearms thrice (right first), then wiped the head and ears, and finally washed the right foot and the left foot to the ankle. If no water could be found, a Muslim could strike his or her hands on pure earth, sand, or dust, shake it off, and symbolically cleanse the hands and face. The symbolic act of washing for prayer was a metaphor for the benefits of prayer in this hadith: "When a servant of Allah—a Muslim or a believer—washes his face (in course of ablution), every sin he contemplated with his eyes will be washed away from his face along with water, or with the last drop of water; when he washes his hands, every sin they wrought will be effaced from his hands with the water, or with the last drop of water; and when he washes his feet, every sin towards which his feet have walked will be washed away with the water, or with the last drop of water, with the result that he comes out pure from all sins" (*Sahih Muslim*, hadith 475). The place for prayer had to be free of any filth, and it occupied an established location in many homes. Away from home, prayer was to be performed in any clean place, at a distance from latrines or graves. The masjid was to be kept clean and pure, either informally or by hired custodians. According to the *Sunan of Abu-Dawood*, "The Apostle of Allah (peace be upon him) commanded us to build mosques in different localities (that is, in the locality of each tribe separately) and that they should be kept clean and be perfumed" (Hadith 455).

Hygiene and Cleanliness. Keeping the home and the streets clean of filth was required of Muslims. Removing a dangerous object or obstacle from the road was considered an act of charity. A part of the belief in emulating the Prophet, personal cleanliness, or *taharah*, included frequent bathing, combing one's hair, using perfume, and wearing clean clothing free of impure substances. The Prophet taught prayers and supplications to accompany these and many other daily acts. Weekly baths before Friday prayer, bathing after sexual relations and menstrual periods, and washing private parts with water after using the toilet were universally recognized Islamic requirements for personal hygiene. The Prophet Muhammad practiced frequent cleaning of his teeth, using a fibrous twig called a *siwak* that was chewed to make a brush-like ending. Such natural toothbrushes are still widely used among Muslims. According to *Sahih al-Bukhari*, "Allah's Apostle said, 'If I had not found it hard for my followers or the people, I would have ordered them to clean their teeth with siwak for every prayer'" (Hadith 2.12). Other matters of personal grooming were also attributed to the Prophet's recommendations, such as keeping nails clipped and removing some body hair. In a widely recorded hadith, the Prophet's wife Hafsah reported, "The Messenger of Allah, upon whom be peace, reserved his right hand for eating, drinking, putting on his clothes, taking and giving. He used his left hand for other actions" (Sunan of Alan Dawood, hadith 321). Dressing and washing began on the right. One stepped into a masjid with the right foot and out with the left. Even left-handed Muslims followed this pattern based on the Sunnah, such as entering a latrine with the left foot and exiting with the right. A Muslim should not show himself or herself to others, talk, stand up, or face in the direction of prayer or its opposite while answering the call of nature. For the sake of public hygiene, urination in elevated places, into a source of water, or in any place that would defile public space or resources was forbidden. Such teachings established a lowest common denominator in terms of standards of living in seventh-century Arabia, and these customs were far ahead of their time considering that nothing was known about disease microorganisms and that cholera and dysentery epidemics were frequently caused by sewage entering sources of public drinking water. These basic principles of hygiene could be applied in undeveloped surroundings or more advanced circumstances. In later periods, the need to maintain these practices encouraged development of hydraulic technologies and public-health measures that led to urban plumbing systems, influenced the design of houses and public latrines, and guided their placement in the urban or rural landscape.

Sources:
Richard W. Bulliet, *Islam: The View from the Edge* (New York: Columbia University Press, 1994).

Timothy Insoll, *The Archaeology of Islam* (Oxford: Blackwell, 1999).

Martin Lings, *Muhammad: His Life Based on the Earliest Sources*, revised edition (London: Islamic Texts Society, 1991).

Francis Robinson, "Religious Life," in his *Atlas of the Islamic World Since 1500* (New York: Facts on File, 1982).

CLOTHING AND TEXTILES

Early Muslim Dress. Because textiles are extremely perishable, and figurative representation was a sparsely practiced art form in Muslim societies, detailed knowledge of dress for the earliest period is limited. Depictions of clothed figures before the 1500s are largely limited to book illustrations, ceramics, and metalwork, and an artist often gave only a mere suggestion of the style and construction of garments. Literary descriptions in prose and poetry, however, make up for the lack of pictorial evidence. Basic garments worn in Arabia during the time of Prophet Muhammad were adapted to suit the local environment and made use of products from societies with whom Arabs traded. Arabia produced only leather goods and homespun fabrics made from the hair of goats, sheep, and camels, ranging from coarse to fine in quality. Cotton, linen, silk, and woolen garments were imported through Yemen, Syria, and Africa, forming a staple of trade. Such garments were frequently mentioned in the hadith literature by place of origin or type. The Prophet often received garments as gifts and distributed many of them to others, both men and women, before or after wearing them.

Early Garments. Secondary sources describe the basic items of clothing worn in Arabia as identical or similar for men and women. An undergarment, a long shirt, a long gown or tunic, and an overgarment such as a mantle, coat, or wrap were worn with shoes or sandals and head cover-

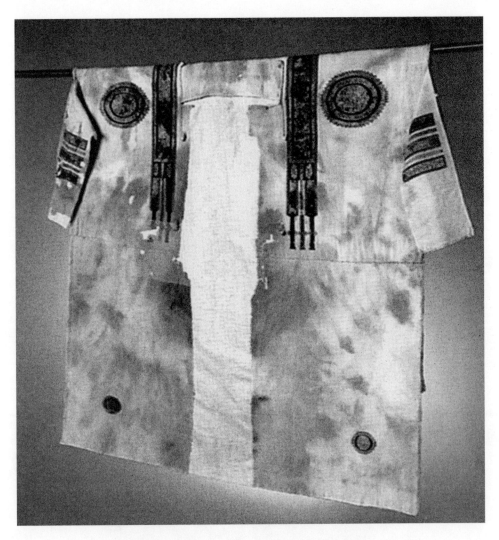

A sixth- or seventh-century Egyptian man's wool tunic with tapestry ornamentation
(Whitworth Art Gallery, University of Manchester)

ings. Garments were layered depending on weather, wealth, and occasion. The *izar* was a basic garment, essentially a length of cloth that could be wrapped or draped over parts of the body or worn around the waist. It was most commonly worn as a long or short wrapped loincloth, meeting the Islamic requirement for men to cover the body between waist and knees. During hard work or hot weather, men wore it alone. *Sirwal* (pants) were common cotton or linen undergarments that were probably Persian in origin. In early Islamic times, according to the Prophet's example, both men and women wore *sirwal* to preserve modesty while seated. Pants were long or short, close-fitting or wide. In later Islamic periods, an enormous variety of *sirwal* appeared, from ankle-length pantaloons to short, close-fitting briefs. The body shirt, or *kamis* (from the Latin word *camisia*), was made from fine or heavy fabrics and was worn by Muslim men and women in their homes. Children typically wore a short version. The *kamis* was often belted and worn under an outer garment. The simplest was an unsewn wrap thrown over the shoulders or draped over one shoulder. A woolen tunic called a *jubba* had narrow sleeves. Another common garment was the *aba'a*, or *abaya*, a wide, sleeveless outer robe. Often made of

fine fabrics, the *hulla* was a long, flowing coat of Persian origin slit in back or front and fastened with buttons. Two common outer garments often mentioned in the hadith were the *rida*, a man's mantle that was also ceremonial, and a *burda*, a woven, striped wrap of Yemeni origin that often had a border. Examples of both were worn by the Prophet. Outer garments were often named according to the fabric or place of origin. Footwear for men and women was either sandals made of leather or woven palm fiber or soft leather boots, called *khuff*, that came to the ankle or calf.

Headdresses. In the Prophet's time, head coverings were worn by both men and women. Wrapped cloaks were often pulled over the head and held with a band or a separate piece of cloth. The typical Arab head wrap for men was called an *imama*, a turban made from a long strip of cloth wound around the head. The Prophet Muhammad used to extend one end of the turban down his back between his shoulders, a habit faithfully imitated by many Muslims since. The head cover was also pulled over the face while traveling to keep out the dust or strangers' gazes. The turban later became a distinctive mark of the Muslim, worn as a simple wrap or as an elaborate headdress over a variety of caps and made from costly gold-worked materials

Fragment of tiraz brocaded silk woven during the twelfth century in Muslim Spain (Musée de Cluny)

or studded with jewels. In the early period, women covered their heads with a shawl draped around the head and across the chest, abandoning the pagan custom of exposing the breasts, and sometimes pulling the same wrap across part of the face. A full veil was made of sheer, dark material that permitted the wearer to see out but hid facial features from others. Such veils were loosely draped over the head, extending down to chest or waist level. A large outer garment called a *jilbab* was pulled up to cover the head and draped over the body to the ground, leaving part of the face exposed. Long, wide overgarments for Muslim women are still called *jilbabs* in Arabic. A common head veil was the *mandil* (from which the Spanish word *mantilla* derives),

which was secured by a comb or pins. A smaller rectangle called a *niqab* might cover all or part of the face. Arab men sometimes covered their faces when riding or traveling, as the Tuareg men of the Sahara still do. The feared Umayyad governor al-Hajjaj first appeared before the rebellious people of Kufah with his face covered in 694.

Occasions. Special styles of clothing included mourning dress, an undyed garment worn by a woman from the death of her husband until the completion of the *iddah* (waiting period) of more than four months. The *ihram*, worn by men during the hajj, consisted of two white, unsewn sheets, one wrapped around the waist, the other draped over the shoulder. Women did not cover their faces during the *hajj* and wore ordinary modest garments. Customs modeled on the Sunnah included asking a blessing on wearing new clothes for the first time and not purposely dragging men's clothes on the ground out of arrogance. Men were allowed the silk garments only if they had a skin condition irritated by other fabrics, but women were allowed to wear silk. Gold jewelry was allowed only to women, but men were permitted to wear other metals.

Umayyad-Era Clothing. The expansion of territory brought great wealth to the Arab ruling classes and exposed them to new styles and articles of dress. Because of their attachment to the example of Prophet Muhammad, Muslims continued to wear the basic articles of clothing used by the early Arabs throughout the Umayyad period (661–750). Embroidered, brocaded, and patterned fabrics in stripes and other designs became increasingly common, refining the appearance of the *thawb* (a long one-piece garment with sleeves), the *kamis,* and especially outer garments and headgear. Despite the Prophet's injunction, silk became more common for elite men's clothing. Special, plain white robes of state for the khalifah (caliph) can be traced to the reign of the Umayyad al-Walid I (ruled 705–715).

Embellishments. The Umayyad court used embroidered and woven designs called *tiraz* for the khalifah's robes and those given to others as a sign of official favor. Muslim historian Ibn Khaldun (1332–1406) described the role of *tiraz* fabrics in Islamic history:

> It is part of royal and government pomp and dynastic custom to have the names of rulers or their peculiar marks embroidered on the silk, or brocade, or pure silk garments that are prepared for their wearing. The writing is brought out by weaving a gold thread or some other colored thread of a color different from that of the fabric itself into it. . . . Royal garments are embroidered with such a tiraz in order to increase the prestige of the ruler or the person of lower rank who wears such a garment, or in order to increase the prestige of those whom the ruler distinguishes by bestowing upon him his own garment when he wants to honor them or appoint them to one of the offices of the dynasty. . . . In the Umayyad and Abbasid dynasties the greatest importance was attached to the tiraz.

The practice of court manufacture probably originated with diplomatic gifts from the Byzantines to the Muslim rulers, whose state textile factories had earlier adopted sophisticated Persian techniques and styles. Arab rulers took over weaving establishments in Syria and former Sasanian Persia. Hisham ibn 'Abd al-Malik (ruled 724–743) was the first Umayyad whose *tiraz* factories are mentioned in extant sources. They flourished under the Abbasids (749–1258) and their successors. By the thirteenth century, the state was less involved in the production of fine fabrics, and *tiraz* fabrics had become so commercially popular in the Mediterranean trade that they were devalued as political statements. The inscriptions became less associated with any ruler, the letters less intelligible and merely symbolic. *Tiraz* symbols worked into brocade fabrics with geometric, plant, and animal motifs were widely imitated in Italy and beyond, where the lettering gradually became more assimilated into the design.

A Textile Society. Woven cloth and garments were a store of household wealth and a form of currency, as well as a commodity needed by everyone. Chests of clothing and household textiles were a pillar of the family's worth and inheritance. A daughter's trousseau was assembled during her childhood, demonstrating the skill she acquired in sewing, weaving, or embroidery. It spared the family the expense of purchasing such goods and might become a source of income in time of need. Because of long-standing pre-Islamic local traditions and because they were marks of one's social class, garments and fabrics to be given by the groom to the bride and her family were an important part of marriage negotiations. Clothing and the fabrics used to make it were an expression of social class, a mark of respectability, and a way of conferring privilege and prestige. They were used as payment for services or as a means of reward. As such, they were a ubiquitous item of trade, and entire sections of urban marketplaces were assigned to the textile trades.

Textiles as Currency. When fabrics became more varied, luxurious, and finely made, their usefulness as a store of value and a form of liquid currency increased. Because producing such fabrics required many artisan hours and considerable resources marshaled from various regions, textiles were accumulated for a time when they would be needed. The list of fabulous fabrics stored in the warehouses of the fabled khalifah Harun al-Rashid (ruled 786–809) is not an indication of mindless extravagance and resources sunk in conspicuous consumption. Fabrics and ready-made garments were a form of wealth that the state treasury purchased or received as tax or tribute. Khalifal purchases were a form of economic stimulus that might bring a city, province, or foreign state into the commercial sphere of the khilafah (caliphate). The government extracted profit from the trade and regulation of fabrics imported, exported, and traded within the empire. The inventory of the wardrobe stores left by Harun al-Rashid lists: "Four thousand jubba of variegated silk said by Ghazuli . . . woven with gold; Four thousand jubba of khazz silk lined with the fur of the sable, the marten and other animals; ten thousand qamis and ghilala (shirts & chemises); ten thousand kaftan (a kind of robe resembling the qa'ba); two thousand sirwal (trousers) of different materials; four thousand 'imama (turbans); one thousand rida' (wrappers) of different stuffs; one thousand taylasan (robes furnished with a hood); five thousand mandil (handkerchiefs) of different materials; one thousand mintaq (girdles) which Ghazuli described as studded with gold; four thousand pairs of khuff (boots), most of them lined with the fur of the marten, sable and other animals; four thousand pairs of jawrab (stockings)." *Tiraz* factories under state control ensured a supply of fine fabrics for the court, and they attracted scarce, highly skilled artisans, creating employment for a host of secondary and tertiary craftsmen, merchants, and laborers. As *tiraz* fabrics spread to the commercial sector the khalifal

Traditional Turkestani man's coat (*chalat*) of ikat velvet with brocade lining and embroidered cuffs and bindings
(Whitworth Art Gallery, University of Manchester)

name and insignia added value to them. A robe of honor with the khalifal insignia woven in became—like signed home-run baseballs or presidential pens—an instant collectible that could be turned into money if necessary. State textile assets were quite liquid, being distributed as a part of the salaries (fringe benefits) of courtly officials and servants. They were spent in the form of gifts to supporters and foreign powers in exchange for loyalty, backing, and achievement of foreign-policy goals. The textiles were carefully inventoried and kept in special buildings under the administration of a high official. While the language of taste varied among cultures of the Eastern Hemisphere, fabrics were universally prized and knowledgeably scrutinized across regional boundaries.

Regional Styles. Costume in the regions newly under Muslim rule must have been vastly diverse. Locally available fibers and dyes were used for fabrics and garments that were suited to the climate and continued little changed for centuries in rural regions. Trade, prosperity, and cultural influences spread to Muslims from Byzantines, Persians, Indians, and Chinese. After the Arab conquest, regional styles changed gradually and influenced Muslim dress perhaps as much as they were influenced by Muslim costume. At the start, Arab dress was inherently dissimilar to that of the other groups, but in time—probably by the reign of the Umayyad reformer Khalifah Umar ibn 'Abd al-'Aziz (ruled 717–720)—aspects of Muslim dress had been copied by non-Muslims, and Muslims had adopted styles from wealthy non-Muslims. The *ghiyar* (sumptuary policies) followed on and off by Muslim rulers decreed that non-Muslims had to distinguish themselves in dress from Muslims. The inherent contradiction lay in the problem of who was to differentiate themselves from whom. The sense of a hadith attributed to Prophet Muhammad was that the Muslims should separate themselves in appearance from those who had not accepted Islam. It is more likely, however, that Muslims adopted the dress of wealthy classes in the regions where they ruled and lived than that non-Muslims were indistinguishable because they imitated Muslim dress. Use of the coercive power of the state to force non-Muslims not to imitate Muslims was somewhat contradictory, and such laws were both hated and ineffective. Nonetheless, various khalifahs decreed that *dhimmis* (non-Muslims) had to wear differentiating garments and distinguish themselves from Muslims in other ways. It is doubtful that such decrees were ever widely enforced, and, though they periodically reappeared under various Muslim regimes, sumptuary laws were often withdrawn or circumvented, or they fell into disuse. Secretarial and merchant classes in the eastern Mediterranean and Persia influenced adoption of certain garments and use of more luxurious fabrics, but styles were generally subdued because of the Prophet's opposition to ostentation, especially his prohibition against men wearing silk and gold. This prohibition never extended to women, however, allowing them to wear fine fabrics and ornaments in the regions where Islam spread. In Abbasid times, as earlier, the cities were home to a wide variety of styles in dress based on ethnic group, class, and occupation, and became more so with in-migration. Arab, Turkish, Persian, Slavic, and Greek costumes could be seen in the streets and markets of growing Muslim cities during the eighth through the twelfth centuries.

Production and Diversification. The importance of clothing, the widespread production of fabrics, innovations in technology, and developments in artistic style in Muslim regions led historian André Clot to refer to Islam as a "textile civilization." Textiles became the most developed product of Muslim regions of the Eastern Hemisphere during the Abbasid period and continuing well beyond 1500, though production centers shifted. Spinning and weaving were part of the domestic village economy nearly everywhere, producing textiles ranging from the coarse fabrics worn by the poor and laborers to local specialties. In areas where wool, cotton, linen, and silk were cash crops, spinning and weaving were carried out on a commercial scale to produce goods for urban and export markets. Woolen goods were made in Syria, Iraq, North Africa, Spain, and various areas in Central Asia, such as Bukhara, Armenia, and Azerbaijan. These goods included mohair (from the Arabic word *mukhayyar*), softest camel hair, thick highland woolen goods, and durable woolen yarns for carpets. Linen, a well-known export from Egypt, spread to other Muslim centers, such as Fars and Khuzestan, whose linens rivaled theirs. Cotton cultivation, which had not spread much beyond India before the seventh century, spread widely under the influence of Islam. Cotton textiles quickly became popular not only for their washability, absorbency, and variable weight, but especially for their ability—unlike their nearest competitor, flax—to absorb brightly colored dyes. During the T'ang period (618–907), cotton became a popular fabric in China under the influence of Muslim textile exports, and the Chinese began to cultivate it. By the tenth century,

cotton production had spread to Iraq, the eastern Mediterranean, Egypt, and Spain. Cotton was introduced as an import to Europe, where it could not be grown in the colder climate. Mosul, Iraq, gave its name to the basic cotton fabric called *muslin*, whose weight could vary from the finest gauze to thick, sturdy stuff. Merv, Nishapur, Aleppo, Hama, and Egypt produced specialty cottons ranging from voile to tent canvas. Textile-producing centers on the western Indian coast and inland perfected cotton production for export. Gujurati wraps used tie-dyed or starch-resist methods to make an indigo-blue-and-white or red-and-white bordered pattern called *bandhana* related to the red-and-white or blue-and-white bandannas worn today. Calicut produced wood-block printed muslins with flowers, borders, and paisley designs that were already being exported to Fustat, Egypt, by the eighth century. Their bright red, black, brown, and violet shades were fast colors from vegetable dyes to which mordants, or fixatives, such as alum and iron oxides, were added. Though imported, these cotton textiles were priced within the reach of ordinary people. Brought from India by Muslim merchants, these friendly prints traveled around the world in the period after 1500 to become the ubiquitous *calico* prints seen in quilts, American pioneer dresses, and even wallpaper designs. Painted fabrics made use of larger designs, borders, and scenes, including the twill-woven cottons called chintz that were a fad during the seventeenth century. From the finest gauzes to richly embroidered shawls and silks encrusted with jewels, Indian textile centers on the coast answered to the rising demand for luxury and ordinary fabrics. Arab textile trade with India was of long standing, having begun long before Islam, facilitated by the annual monsoon winds that bore ships between India and Yemen.

Silk. Silkworm cultivation and manufacture had been successfully adopted from China by the Sassanid Persians and probably spread from there to Byzantine workshops (notwithstanding the story of silkworms carried in a Christian missionary's walking stick). Muslim silk production replaced Byzantine and Persian production in the region and, despite Italian connections to the Byzantines, overtook Byzantine silk exports to Europe. By the Abbasid period, the Islamic prohibition against silk for men was circumvented or ignored except by ascetics or those who could not afford it. Well-known export centers included Sicily, Spain, Egypt, Syria (especially damask brocades), Iraq, and Khorasan, and *tiraz* production spread to virtually all court centers after the breakup of the Abbasid state. Silk velvets; fringes and tassels; carpets; striped, printed, embroidered, and brocaded silks—with gold and silver threads picked out with pearls and jewels—were produced for local sale and export to those who could afford even a single piece of finery. The Chinese draw loom either was reinvented or underwent considerable refinement in western Asia, and by the Abbasid period, its ability to raise individual threads allowed weavers of *tiraz* and other textiles to form complex designs of animals, plants, geometric patterns, and lettering

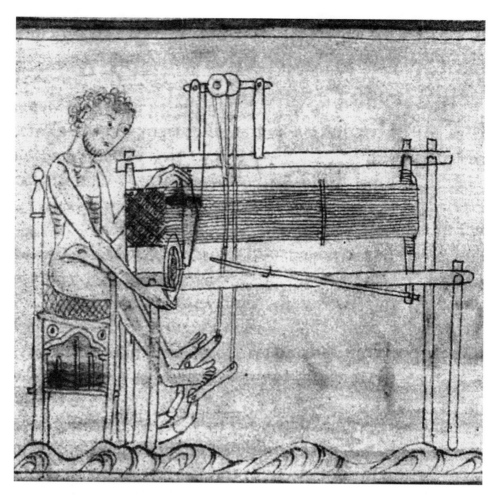

A medieval horizontal loom; illumination from a mid-twelfth-century manuscript (Trinity College, Cambridge)

in brocaded fabrics. During the tenth through twelfth centuries, Fatimid Egypt and Sicily were particularly important brocade manufacturing centers for exports to Europe, and from the latter, the complex treadle looms and their fabric designs spread to Europe. People wearing vestments and garments bearing Islamic designs are depicted in European paintings. Islamic textiles appeared commonly as altar cloths and vestments in European churches, and they have been exhumed from the graves of church officials and royalty in Europe. More than one bishop was buried in grave clothes bearing Arabic inscriptions, including one example with the Islamic creed *La ilaha illa Allah* (There is no god but God) now preserved in the textile collection at the Cleveland Museum of Art. By the thirteenth century, silk brocade weaving in Norman Sicily was being produced for export to Europe and was copied in Italian and French centers as well. Beginning in the same century, complex weaving and dyeing techniques spread from Sicily, North Africa, and Spain to various European textile centers.

Leather and Fur. Leather goods were widely produced and used, stimulating the importation of plants and minerals used in tanning and dyeing. Bookbinding in leather was an associated art for which gold stamping and tooling were developed as decorative techniques. A related industry made saddles and trappings for riding animals such as don-

keys, horses, camels, and elephants. The finest examples were made for court ceremonies. Furs, mainly imported from Asian forests, including Rus trade routes along the Volga, were used to edge and line winter garments such as shoes and mantles. Sable, ermine, and less luxurious pelts were used as the wearer's budget allowed, and courtly dress often featured the finest furs.

Abbasid Era Clothing. The Sunnah influenced the styles of garments that persisted over the long term, especially with the gradual spread of Islam among the population. Because modesty was required in private and in public among men and women, loose-fitting, dignified overgarments, undergarments, and head coverings became standard characteristics of men's and women's dress in Muslim regions, but such garments had a wide variety of shapes and appearances. By the Abbasid era, the shapeless, rustic garments of the early Muslims had faded into disuse. The rough, woolen robe of the Arabian peninsula known as the *khirka* came to mean a "rag" or "dishcloth" in Abbasid-era vernacular. The rustic tunic called the *midra'a* came to be associated only with the extremely poor. The poor also wore a *shamla*, a woolen robe that doubled as a blanket. Workingmen in hot weather wore the *tubban*, or short trousers that came to the knee, and sandals made of coarse fiber. Hunters, fish sellers, builders, and other laborers wore similar garments. Bedouins wore the *aba'a* in wool. Some garments were common to all classes but varied in the quality of material. The *izar* continued in use as a common wrap in fabrics of varying weights. It might be used as a head covering, waist wrap, or apron. Under Indian influence, the longer version of the *izar* became known as a *futa* (sheet), which when made of fine fabric resembles an Indian sari. As a waist wrap, the *izar* was a mandatory minimum garment in public baths and was worn by both men and women, who were separated by gender. Almost everyone wore a *ghilala* (light chemise) and *sirwal* (loose, long or short pants with a drawstring) as undergarments and by themselves in private. Women considered it inelegant to wear white garments, so their underclothes were often grayish or pastel in tone. The *kamis* had wide sleeves often with an inside pocket big enough to hold a book, coins, or writing supplies. At the palace, one had to wear the *durra'*, a fancy, sleeved outer garment that was often highly decorated with embroidery or even precious stones. Women wore wide-sleeved dresses with drawstrings to pull the neckline together for a high bodice. They wore an enveloping wrap for public outings, as well as a *futa*. Women wore a black headdress similar to a turban together with a fine face veil. Fashionable footwear consisted of sandals, leather slippers, or leather ankle boots, which were also used to carry things. The materials used in women's footwear ranged from fur-lined and jeweled to rough leather or bast. Men as well as women covered their heads. A man most often wore a turban, which was given a lot of importance during Abbasid times as an emblem of Islam and a requirement for a man's dignified appearance. Some wore felt caps under their turbans. A sort of Persian hat called a tall *kalansuwa*, or *danniyya*, came into fashion for a while; one of its names is derived from the word *dann* (an amphora-shaped storage jug). The Persian secretarial class employed by the Abbasid state influenced Muslim manners (*adab*), literary tastes, and clothing. Socks and colorful shoes became common under Persian influence, though clashing colors were considered in poor taste. A well-known garment that entered courtly and urban fashions from Persia during the Abbasid period was the *khaftan*, a robe made from fine material with buttons down the front. (It was named after a *cuirass*, or armored breastplate). Under the Turkish influence that began in the twelfth century, this garment became a typical Turkish coat and acquired its common name of *caftan*.

Courtly Dress. The khalifah's robes, banded with embroidered inscriptions in Arabic, came to be viewed as robes of office, and black was the official Abbasid color. The *burda* (going back to a mantle worn by the Prophet), the staff, and sword were further insignia of office. The *kalansuwa* (cap) worn with a turban was the equivalent of a crown. Servants of the Abbasid state wore black as a sign of duty and loyalty. Jurists wore sober versions of prevailing formal garments, including the *danniyya*, and wore the *taylasan*, a long piece of cloth draped across the shoulders. This garment of office evolved into the doctoral hood that

is worn by western scholars with Ph.D.s, one of the many results of the medieval academic connections between Europe and Muslim scholarship. State ministers and secretaries wore the *durra'* overcoat, and a *khatib*, or preacher, wore a turban and carried a staff. For the Friday sermon he might also wear a long *izar* wrapped around him instead of wide pants. Poets favored bright colors, gold-worked clothing, and silken robes. Fantastic descriptions of courtly robes for men and women are found in *adab* literature. Harun al-Rashid and his wife Zubaidah are said to have possessed jewel-encrusted shoes and belts, a fantastic number of brocaded robes (a Byzantine emperor once sent him three hundred), jeweled tiaras, rings, necklaces, and other jewelry. Diaphanous silks, gold-worked velvet, fur-trimmed jackets and coats, and the finest undergarments and shirts are mentioned in the lore of khalifal wardrobe excess. When the state was at the height of its wealth and power and Baghdad was a trade hub for the Eastern Hemisphere, such accounts may not have been much exaggerated. A well-known court fabric was a gold-worked silk called *washi*, produced in centers such as Yemen and Syria. The Abbasids' extravagance extended to their courtiers and other lucky people. Abbasid khalifahs bestowed robes of honor (*khila'*) on scholars, scientists, poets, singers, military leaders, visiting dignitaries, and diplomats. An entire outfit rather than just a robe, the *khila'* included a lined coat or cloak (*mubattana*), a sleeved robe (*durra'*), a body shirt (*qamis*), pants or drawers (*sarwal*), and a turban (*'imama*). All these garments were made of fine cloth and court workmanship, though khalifal stores included suits of varying degrees of luxury. On occasion special honor was conferred by giving a robe worn by the khalifah himself, instead of a "standard issue" suit from the khalifal storehouses. Twice-yearly gifts of a suit of clothes were given after the fast of Ramadan as an obligation of the court to its officials. This tradition, which probably pre-dates Islam, percolated down through the social classes of society to include households with servants, and gifts from the head of the household to wives and children. Clothing was the most expensive of the basic necessities, so it was carefully stored and worn and patched and mended until it could no longer be worn. Then it was cut up for cushions, coverlets, and other uses.

Fatimid-Era Clothing. When the Fatimid dynasty came to power in Egypt in 973, Egyptians had produced textiles for millennia, and linen remained an important fiber crop. Fatimid Egyptian artisans exported techniques and luxury textiles to other Muslim lands and to Europe. A well-known example is the gold-embroidered red-silk robe with an Arabic inscription at the hem that the Norman ruler Roger II wore for his coronation as king of Sicily in 1130. Tiraz fabrics of linen, silk, and wool set the style in the Mediterranean and influenced the developing Italian textile industry so profoundly that Italian silk-brocade designs are indistinguishable from their Islamic models. The name *Dar al-Kiswa* given to Fatimid *tiraz* manufacture refers to the black brocaded *kiswa*, heavily

Syrian dress and home furnishings during the Mamluk period; illumination from a 1237 manuscript
for the *Maqamat* (Assemblies) of al-Hariri (British Library, London)

embroidered with gold and silver Qur'an verses, made as a covering for the Ka'bah and taken on the annual pilgrimage to Makkah in an ornate camel litter. A government ministry oversaw production and storage of costumes and fabrics. The Fatimid khalifah, who wore splendid white clothing embroidered in gold and silver on ceremonial occasions, topped his costume with an enormous turban of fine fabric wound over a cap and decorated with jewels and silk bands. Twice a year in season, every government official from the highest minister to the lowliest clerk or servant in livery received a *badla,* or outfit that consisted of a dozen garments. The quality, color, and cut of the costume differed according to the recipient's rank. Fabulous textiles produced in Egypt included *khusrawani* (royal brocade, named after the Persian shah Khusraw Parwiz, who ruled the Sasanid empire in 591–628), *siglaton* (gold brocade), and linens from transparent gossamers to heavy fabrics. Goods were usually named after the place of production, such as *dumyati* (Damietta) and *rashidi* (Rosetta), and garments were embellished with the ruler's name, attributes, and a blessing woven or embroidered onto tiraz bands. The basic garments differed little from those of the Umayyad and Abbasid periods, an assortment of wraps, tunics, mantles, dresses, and typical undergarments accompanied by shawls, veils, scarves, belts, and turbans. These articles became common parts of Islamic costume in cosmopolitan Muslim cities almost everywhere. As the well-known traveler Ibn Battuta (1304 – circa 1378) moved from place to place receiving gifts of garments, he was able to identify them by place of export, accepting and wearing them as customary clothing, without any sense that they were strange or ill suited.

Common Egyptian Dress in the Fatimid Period. Ordinary people in Egypt during the Fatimid period (973–1171) wore similar garments whether they were Muslim, Christian, or Jewish and followed courtly styles as closely as their means allowed. The custom of giving complete outfits and the use of *tiraz*-like decorative elements was practiced on a smaller but proportionately ostentatious scale in the households of wealthy and middle-class Egyptians. A valuable source of information about Fatimid-era costumes worn by the bourgeoisie are the Geniza documents, some of which list bridal trousseaus in detail. Written by Jewish residents of Cairo, these documents also provide evidence that sumptuary laws were not enforced. The urban poor wore clothing similar in coverage to that of other Egyptians but consisting of fewer garments and coarser fabrics. Beyond the cities, regional styles remained distinctive long after the spread of Islam into the countryside. Traditional dress included shirred black sari-style wraps for women, basic cotton print wide dresses over pants, and the *tarhah*, a fine black veil worn over a *mandil*, or scarf. The people of the Sinai and the Libyan desert also continued to wear their traditional costumes. Variations among towns and religious groups were noticeable, but Egyptian men's dress was probably more like the basic universal Muslim costume of the cities, with local variations and stylistic panache.

Turkish Influence under the Saljuks, Ayyubids, and Mamluks. During the tenth century, Abbasid rulers began to rely heavily on Turkish soldiers, who brought new influences on costume from their exuberant pastoral tradition. Their stylistic influence spread gradually with their growing military power and the increasing in-migration of Turkic groups. The Turks, who accepted Islam and established dynasties in various parts of the Muslim lands from the eleventh to the sixteenth centuries, were influenced by Muslim dress but also introduced new garments and a distinctive sense of style, shape, and color. The central Asian styles they introduced included ceremonial court dress and military outfits suited for fighting from horseback. Turkish women also rode horses, necessitating clothing that was less voluminous and sparer, though not less colorful or elaborately decorated. Long or short coats were worn over the usual undergarments, and the body shirt was cut longer to show under the coat. The front of a new style of "Turkish coat," modeled perhaps on a Chinese style, crossed the chest diagonally to the waist and was preferred by Saljuk and Ayyubid rulers from the eleventh through the thirteenth centuries and on through the period of Turkic ascendancy. The Mamluks wrapped their coats left side over right, as typical men's shirts in the West button today. Wide belts or cummerbunds were worn over the coat. Mamluk princes wore belts of decorated metal plaques linked together. The Turks introduced the custom of ranking a person by the width of his sleeves, which reached below the hands in length. A turban was worn over a red or yellow *kalawta* cap. Turkish soldiers wore native headgear called the *sharbush*, a stiff cap with a triangular front often trimmed with fur. A short-sleeved coat called a *bughlutak*, made of fine fabrics and sometimes trimmed with fur, was sometimes worn with an outer coat. As Turkish influence grew, many urbanites adopted the full-length caftan, and women wore a closer-fitting coat called a *yelek*. Most other articles of clothing remained the same but acquired Turkish names.

Maghrib and Andalusia. Since the Arab conquest in the seventh century, the Muslim lands in northwestern Africa and the Iberian peninsula were known for their special styles of dress, built on traditions of the Berbers and combining Punic, late Roman, and Christian influences. Major eastern Muslim influences, such as Persian and Turkic,

reached the West only gradually and indirectly, and even then only in coastal cities and the Iberian Peninsula. One type of pre-Islamic Berber man's dress was a short, wide tunic worn without a belt. Another group wore the burnous, a long mantle with straight panels, sleeves, and a peaked hood that was edged with wool or silk-braided cord and embroidery, later worn with a *kamis* under it. In the Altas Mountains, woolen mantles or capes of rough Berber weave were wrapped or draped over the shoulders. The capes sometimes carried a design in the shape of a large eye on the bottom. Women's native dress was similar to eastern Arab desert dress, often an *izar* cloth wrapped around the body and over the head. Fancy woven belts of wool and much silver jewelry were used to decorate the simple pieces. During the Islamic period, Egyptian influences spread westward. Syrian ruling classes brought Eastern tastes in clothing, furnishings, and fabrics to the Iberian peninsula. The well-known Iraqi singer Ziryab, a trendsetter in the Umayyad court at Córdoba during the mid ninth century, successfully transplanted influences in dress and manners from the eastern cities to Andalusia. Ziryab wore different clothes in each season, introducing the *djubba* (a wide, long outer garment with an open front and sleeves cut into the garment) for both men and women, and defining the cut and color of robes. The Persian tall cap called the *kalansuwa* and the *taylasan* were worn more widely in Andalusia after Ziryab arrived. Women's dress was fashionable. Covering the head was not taken as seriously in Andalusia as in other parts of the Muslim world until after the Almohad period (1130–1269), though the same forms of veils appeared there as in other Muslim regions. Peasant dress remained similar to pre-Islamic styles, and influence from the Christian north continued. Instead of the turbans, which were seldom seen, men wore a soft felt hat similar to a pillbox that was usually red or green. Styles and colors of dress changed as Andalusia became an important silk-weaving center and known especially for a gilded silk called *washy* that was made in Almeria, Murcia, and Malaga.

West Africa. Between the twelfth and the fifteenth centuries, when Islamic influence became marked in the region and the wealth of the Niger bend region increased through trade, garments worn by Muslim rulers and dignitaries of West African cities took on new form and meaning. The indigenous weaving used native cotton on narrow looms with strips sewn together edge to edge to form larger widths. The caftan-like, one-piece garment for men that evolved from this fabric was long and extremely wide, with sleeves reaching nearly to the hem. The neck was slit open vertically, creating a v-neck front and back that added to the drape of the garment. On one side of this style of clothing was a large elaborately embroidered pocket. Wider looms, silk weaving, and embroidery were introduced by Muslim traders and West African Muslims who made the hajj. In the growing cities of the Niger bend, ruling families sponsored scholarship and commerce. There emerged a class of scholar-tailors who supported their Qur'anic studies by weaving and

Fourteenth-century Spanish silk fabric with a
geometric pattern similar in style to designs
at the Alhambra Palace in Granada
(Musée Historique des Tissus, Lyon)

silk using treadle looms to create weft-and-warp striped patterns. (The lengthwise threads on a loom are called the *warp*, and the crosswise threads are the *weft*.) The name for raffia fiber—from which plush, tufted cushions and fine mats were woven—came from a word in their language (*rofia*).

Central Asia. The region from the Caspian Sea to the borders of China included settled oasis cities such as Bukhara, Samarqand, and Tashkent, as well as the arid steppe and grasslands to the north. Across this huge area, pastoral people possessed a long history of tribal textiles made from the wool of their herds, and an exuberant sense of design and color. Felt and leather work were highly developed decorative arts, in addition to carpet and tapestry weaving in geometric, animal, and vegetal designs. Influences from Iran and China moved back and forth along the Silk Roads, bringing refined, courtly styles and elegant modes of dress. Among the most typical fabrics for coats was *ikat*, warp-dyed silk woven on cotton. These brightly colored fabrics with bold designs were made into gowns and sleeved coats that might be worn in layers to display the owner's wealth. *Ikat* fabrics had as many as seven colors—red, blue, yellow, green, and purple, as well as black and white. Warp dyeing gave the design a vibrant quality because the edges of the motif were not sharply defined. The ikat technique was also used in some *tiraz* inscriptions, particularly in the Yemen. Other distinctive garments were the embroidered caps worn by men and boys, as well as unmarried girls, who wore them with a veil. In the western lands of Central Asia, specific types of embroidery were attached to tribal and regional groupings.

Mongol Influences. Central Asian styles that influenced Muslim fashions include mandarin short-sleeved robes with decorations on front and back and with a long-sleeved tunic worn underneath, a fur-trimmed, peaked felt cap, and fur-trimmed robes. Silk and jeweled hats built on a light frame were the fashion for Mongol princesses, who wore sheer veils and feathers atop such hats. In the Timurid period of the fifteenth century, closer-fitting garments came in, including a long, open coat with braided-frog closures, and a *kumar* band (cummerbund sash) worn around the waist. This elegant sword belt, originally for military use, is still worn with European-style men's formal and semiformal dress. The coats—with long or short sleeves or sleeveless—were made of elegant fabrics such as velvet, brocade, and fine wool and often worn in layers over the kamis.

Sources:

Muhammad M. Ahsan, *Social Life Under the Abbasids, 786–902 A.D.* (London & New York: Longman, 1979).

Andre Clot, *Harun al-Rashid and the World of the Thousand and One Nights*, translated by John Howe (New York: New Amsterdam Press, 1989).

Jennifer Harris, ed., *Textiles, 5000 Years: An International History and Illustrated Survey* (New York: Abrams, 1993).

T. Majda, "Libas," in *Encyclopedia of Islam*, CD-ROM version (Leiden: Brill, 1999).

Clive Rogers, ed. *Early Islamic Textiles* (Brighton, U.K.: Rogers & Podmore, 1983).

embroidering dignified garments. Though Ibn Battuta in the fourteenth century complained that West African women were too scantily clad, they became more observant of Islamic requirements for coverage. Women wore head wraps and wide, long dresses made of colorful resist-dyed cotton fabrics, as well as imported fabrics that came across the Sahara. Gradually, with Portuguese explorations along the West African coast during the late 1400s, the first European-influenced fabrics, not yet mainly of European manufacture, began to arrive. There was also a tradition of unraveling and reweaving imported fabrics to create brilliant plaid and striped designs, perhaps because of the desire to work in colors for which indigenous dyes were not available.

East Africa. Because this region was in contact with Yemen, Egypt, and the lands around the northern rim of the Indian Ocean, it was exposed to a wide range of styles, fabrics, and goods from as far away as China. Ibn Battuta mentioned, for example, receiving from the sultan of Mogadishu a traditional robe of honor made from Jerusalem fabric. As in many trading centers of the Muslim world, cloth and finished garments were virtually a form of currency. The ceremonial dress the sultan and his retinue wore for Friday prayer featured voluminous robes, embroidery, and rich colors. Madagascar, whose island population included people of African, Malay, and Arab descent, knew how to weave shawls from a native type of

Typical Houses. Like other aspects of Muslim daily life, housing varied enormously across the many geographic regions to which Islam spread. Within regions, dwellings varied according to ethnicity, religion, class, way of life (rural or urban, agricultural or pastoral), and historical periods. Archaeologists and social historians have dealt with diversity in domestic spaces by identifying common features and creating an idealized schema for the Muslim home. The scheme is based on attributes of Islamic family life: gender separation, private and public life, and the sanctity of the *haram*, or sacred, protected space. The prototype for this sort of house is the one built by the Prophet Muhammad in Madinah. It is a courtyard house of a basic type found in western Arabia during the seventh century, but it was consciously constructed to fulfill the requirements of the Prophet's extended family and public responsibilities. It was both a dwelling and a meeting place with a rectangular, walled courtyard. On one or more sides of the courtyard it had rooms for sleeping and storage, and each wife and her children had their own chamber. Words for house in Arabic include *bayt* or *manzil*, and a compound was called *dar*, usually designated with a family name, such as *Dar al-Khatib*. The typical layout of the Muslim courtyard house was rectangular with a street entrance opening into a room for receiving male guests that let onto a main, semiprivate courtyard, with entrances to the kitchen and men's quarters. Entrances to private quarters also opened onto the main courtyard and then onto a second, private courtyard around which the women's and children's quarters were arranged. In rural areas there might be an enclosure for domestic animals. Commentators on Muslim societies have often erred in describing public and private spaces, maintaining often that the men enjoyed the public space, while women were confined to private spaces. In fact, Muslim women entertained female visitors and received tradeswomen and messengers, just as men entertained male visitors, so it is more appropriate to speak of male communal areas and female communal areas rather than public and private space as gender-exclusive realms. Nor is it true that women did not share at all in the public life of the city. Literary and pictorial evidence shows that they were present in public. The basic plan of a Muslim house has often been described as inward-turning, with a relatively unadorned exterior of adobe or stucco with high, narrow windows and a door that opens on an entryway angled to discourage looking into the house. (On the other hand, medieval books also include illustrations of houses with ornamented exteriors, both in rural and urban areas.) The typically bland exterior has been contrasted with the richly ornamented interior decor, replete with mosaics, carpets, textile hangings, cushions, and furnishings, and a courtyard garden with flowers and fountains. Some aspects of this house type predate Islam and bear a relationship to previous cultures and religious groups that, like Muslims, valued privacy. For example, the desire for family privacy was also common in pre-Islamic Byzantine society, where women were

Woman wearing tiraz fabrics; detail from a fifteenth-century *Adoration of the Magi*, by Gentile da Fabriano (Uffizi Gallery, Florence)

not prominent in public. The features of the archetypical Muslim house are also related to the hot, arid climate in much of the Muslim world, and the need to keep dust out of the house and to shade the interior from direct sunlight as much as possible. Although the courtyard house was typical for many North African and Southwest Asian regions during the period, there were many variations on the theme of divided private and communal spaces for family members: one-floor houses, multistory dwellings, domestic compounds consisting of a walled or fenced space with multiple buildings, and elaborate palaces and palatial complexes.

Urban Context. The urban setting in which houses were placed was as important a part of daily life as the houses themselves. Much has been written over the twentieth century about the structural patterns of the stereotypical "Islamic" city, and much has been reconsidered by recent scholars. New evidence has called into question the supposedly typical patterns identified by earlier scholars, who have been criticized because the concepts they used to discuss cities in Muslim regions were derived from European urban models to which Muslim cities were often unfavorably compared. For example, these early scholars often expressed the notion that the grid pattern of classical cities deteriorated under Muslim rule, so that cities took on a random "rabbit warren" or "labyrinth" pattern. Orientalist scholars used to attribute this change to a tendency toward fragmentation and disorder inherent in Islam. Recent scholarship shows that Muslim cities arose from a variety of historical contexts and developed along many planning patterns. Garrison cities, for example, were often organized on a grid modeled on a military encampment, with separate sections to house the tribal groups who made up the Arab armies. The grid was later modified by non-military migration to the towns and the expansion of commercial and cultural institutions and activities in and around the older core. In contrast, capital cities such as Fustat (Cairo) and Baghdad started out as expressions of a single ruler or group but expanded beyond the complex of palaces, dwellings for officials, places of worship, and administrative offices, often spreading beyond city walls and forming suburbs as the population grew. Just as modern cities have ethnic neighborhoods, migrants to centers of Islam settled in close-knit, relatively homogenous neighborhoods. Over the centuries, neighborhoods became quarters with district governments and leadership structures such as guilds, and they were designated, but not necessarily segregated, according to religion and ethnicity. Ultimately, both capital and garrison cities became much larger than the original complexes, and the cities became important for reasons that overshadowed their original function. Older cities such as Damascus, Jerusalem, and Córdoba grew along functional lines, under the influence of prestige-enhancing construction projects such as monuments, palaces, and religious institutions. Present-day historical study focuses less on the identification of archetypes and more on the layout and development of actual cities—both those newly developed by Muslims and those that overlaid existing cities—and the social forces that brought about change in urban patterns.

The Masjid. The concept of a uniform Muslim urban layout may be highly questionable, but the existence of many common features in cities, as in individual dwellings, sheds light on the daily life of the people who lived there. Among the most important common features, the masjid is the most universal. Large cities had a jami' (main, or Friday) masjid at a central, open site, often near the residence of the governor or ruler, with dwelling quarters in blocks around it. Surrounding quarters often had internal squares and smaller neighborhood masjids, or in the case of non-Muslim quarters, other houses of worship. The rationale for the central jami' masjid was that jum'ah prayer on Friday was a time for people of different groups to mingle, learn to know and care about each other, and reinforce the unity of the ummah (community of the Prophet) as a whole. The khutbah, or sermon, was a powerful tool for mobilizing public opinion, and it was carefully watched by the rulers.

Markets. Places of worship were often associated with weekly or permanent markets. They might be as simple as a mat laid out in an open space or wide street, or a series of tent-shaded market stalls set up near the masjid or along a major thoroughfare. A public project in major cities was the construction of the bazaar (from Persian) or covered market arcades, the original shopping malls. As early as the eighth century in Damascus, each category of goods had a permanent market (suq), and these markets collectively evolved into a network of covered bazaars or urban commercial areas. In some cities, markets were furnished with amenities such as arcades that drew in the cooling breezes. One form of natural air conditioning in bazaars was a series of small domes over the arcades, with openings to the sky. Warm air rose up and out through the openings in the domes, which also provided a source of light for the covered area of the shops. Earthen, paved, or tiled floors protected the goods from dust and mud. Animal traffic and loading took place in side streets parallel to the pedestrian walkways. Other shops, stalls, and occasional markets were set up in quarters to meet the needs of neighborhoods, and fresh produce markets were placed near the gardens and hinterlands that provided for the city. Major markets for craft production, exports, and imports were set up in special areas close to transportation routes such as ports, waterways, and entry points for overland routes, often close to the city gates. The craft markets were planned and regulated by the institution of the muhtasib (market inspector). The various crafts were regulated for integrity of production and honesty in commerce, and their workplaces were situated in such a way as to meet their requirements for water, fuel, or access to roads, to reduce hazards from noxious odors, runoff, and danger of fire. Tanneries, for example, had to be downwind and on the outskirts of the cities, while businesses such as perfumers, booksellers, and fabric markets could be placed anywhere, especially near a masjid.

Such zoning regulations determined where people lived and worked and where and at what times they moved about the city, while limiting the bustle, noise, and smells of urban commerce and manufacture in most parts of the city.

Baths. Another important feature of everyday city life was the public bath, called *hammam*. Literary accounts mention thousands of public baths in some cities. These either public or commercial establishments were regulated by market or health inspectors. Except for the inhabitants of palaces and extravagant residences, which had their own baths, everyone used public baths, which varied in the degree of luxury according to location. Many public baths served both men and women, designating different sections or different days for each sex; some baths were exclusively male or female. Modeled on the baths of Rome, the *hammams* in Muslim cities and towns were made from stone or brick, with the floors and lower walls paved with mosaics or marble. In Iraq earthen brick was plastered with bitumen to make it waterproof and shiny like polished marble. Designs were formed in the bitumen for decoration. This inexpensive but effective construction was also used for latrines in middle-class homes.

Rooms in the Bath. Bathers visited a series of rooms in sequence. In the first room, which had a counter from which attendants handed out bath supplies, bathers undressed and hung their outer clothing on pegs. This room was cool and along its walls it had stone or wooden benches covered with carpets and cushions where clients could rest and chat. To enter the second room, which was warmed and humidified, bathers put on the *mizar*, or waist wrap, and remained there until they were accustomed to the heat. The third room was the tepidarium, which was warmed by a heat source in its thick walls or under the floor. The domed ceiling of the tepidarium had round, thick glass inserts to let in light, but there were no openings to allow the escape of steam. Next to this steam room was a furnace room where water was boiled, then piped into the tepidarium. Used water flowed into runnels outside the building and was not allowed to flow directly into rivers or canals. Water was often carried to the baths via aqueducts or a diverted stream, or draft animals or waterwheels supplied fresh water. The tepidarium was tiled, faced with marble, or plastered with bitumen; it was fitted with stone basins, benches, and alcoves with earthenware pipes bringing hot and cold water. Drinking hot water and sitting in the warm room, the bathers sweated and then entered cubicles where they or an attendant scrubbed and lathered the skin, removed body hair, and gave a massage. The last step was taking a dip in a large swimming pool at the center of the tepidarium. After the bath, the bather went to a relaxation room—which often had a pool, fountains, and wooden benches with cushions and carpets—where refreshments were served. Needless to say, the baths were as much a gathering place as a means of staying healthy and meeting religious requirements for cleanliness. Market inspectors established strict instructions for keeping baths sanitary, including regular fumigation, daily laundering of

THE SPREAD OF MUSLIM TEXTILES

When Ibn Battuta visited Mogadishu in East Africa around 1330 local officials gave him gifts of clothing from various parts of the Muslim empire:

On the fourth day, which was a Friday, the qadi and . . . one of the Shaikh's viziers came to me, bringing a set of robes; these robes consist of a silk wrapper which one ties around his waist in place of sarwal (for they have no acquaintance with these), a tunic of Egyptian linen with an embroidered border, a furred mantle of Jerusalem stuff, and an Egyptian turban with an embroidered edge. . . . They also brought robes for my companions suitable to their position. . . .

Source: Ross E. Dunn, *Adventures of Ibn Battuta: A Muslim Traveler of the Fourteenth Century* (Berkeley: University of California Press, 1986).

towels and wraps, preventing wastewater from polluting fresh, and cleaning the basins and tanks.

Construction and Materials. Geography determined building materials. In the arid, sparsely treed belt that stretched across much of the Muslim world from West Africa to Central Asia, unbaked mud bricks were used for ordinary homes, and baked bricks were employed in more-expensive public structures. The majority of rural housing in the Muslim world was unbaked brick, or adobe, usually one story in height but widely varying in size. The word *adobe* came to English through Spanish from the Arabic word for an earthen brick, *al-tuba*. The climatic forces that limited tree growth made such houses practical and durable, with annual upkeep limited to replastering in regions where there were appreciable seasonal rains. Wood was used only for roof beams, doors, and basic furnishings in these areas. In West Africa, where Islam had begun to dominate by 1500, public buildings such as masjids were typically constructed with porcupine-like wooden beams protruding from towers and high elevations and serving as built-in scaffolding for plastering after the rains. West African houses included rectangular mud-brick styles with wood and stucco decorative elements, round mud-brick houses with thatch roofs, and round dwellings constructed entirely of matting. In the marshy area of southern Iraq and lake areas of Chad and Western Africa, houses were built of reeds and grasses. Among the best-known unbaked-brick structures are the multistory mud-tower houses of the Yemen, some of which have stood for more than a thousand years. On the seacoasts and in Egypt, houses were built with wind towers: large, rectangular shafts with wooden vents on the sides or an opening at the top to catch the prevailing winds and channel them into the rooms of the house. Regions such as the eastern Mediterranean coast, the Atlas Mountains of the Maghrib, and parts of Spain and East Africa had plentiful supplies of stone, which was used for foundations in combination with wood or adobe. Dwellings for the wealthier classes might be built

Interior of a *suq* (bazaar); from an early-thirteenth-century manuscript for the
love story of Warqa and Gulsah (Topkapi Museum, Istanbul)

entirely of finely dressed stone, as were public buildings and fortifications for towns, which formed a backdrop and security zone for individual dwellings in their quarters. The use of Jerusalem stone in Palestine was typical of such construction. In Asia Minor, which by 1500 had experienced the major migration of Turkish tribes that began in the eleventh century, houses in rural areas were constructed of stone and wood, which were much more plentiful there than in many other Muslim regions and could be more readily imported for urban construction.

Urban Construction. Palaces were built on large estates surrounded by gardens and fortifications, but the homes in most urban quarters were spaced close together on narrow alleyways. The city was divided into sections linked by wider roads, but streets in the quarters usually were only wide enough to allow riding animals to pass one another. The narrow streets were shaded by walls, keeping the city cooler, and some streets were covered or bridged so that upper stories or rooftops could form another layer of movement in the city, allowing women to move from house to house without going outdoors. Narrow streets were the focus of regulations forbidding protrusions, such as bay windows, from blocking the streets. Residents were responsible for sweeping and watering the alley in front of their houses to keep the dust down.

Mobile Homes. Among pastoral peoples of the Arabian and Saharan deserts, the rectilinear, divided, or undivided tent made of goat or camel's hair had already been developed centuries before Islam and has persisted to the present day. Many Turkic peoples of Central Asia used less-rectilinear and more pavilion-like tents, which were sometimes mounted on wagons, such as the one Ibn Battuta described when he was crossing the Asian steppe. The elaborate framework of tent poles and rigging was most like that of circus tents used in western Europe and North America, with a high, peaked dome from which the sides were suspended. Such a tent could be made rectangular, square, or round on the same model. An interesting form of such "mobile homes" was the yurt, which became familiar in the Muslim world after the Mongol invasions of the thirteenth century and the subsequent conversion of many Mongol tribes to Islam within about a century. Originating many centuries before Islam, the yurt was a round, igloo-shaped

home large enough for a single family to sleep, cook, and live in during severe weather. It was constructed of thick wool felt laid over a collapsible wooden latticework frame. The felt provided a warm and waterproof covering to keep out strong winds and snow. Inside, a yurt was comfortable and roomy without wasting space; pile carpets, hangings, and woven and embroidered cushions were arranged around the sides for sleeping and sitting. Intricate, boldly colored designs were worked into the felt of the interior. Like a typical Turkic peaked tent, the design of the yurt also influenced regional architecture in permanent materials, especially mausoleums in tent-like forms. Both the pavilion and the yurt could be elaborately decorated and enormous in size when used to house a prominent ruler or military commander. Fine materials such as silk, embroidered and appliqued panels, linings, and furnishings made royal tents like mobile palaces.

Decoration. Among the most common decorative materials were surface embellishment or perforations of the building material around the roof, walls, windows, or balconies. Raised designs made of plasterwork and stucco could be plain, carved, or inlaid with tiles as simply or elaborately as the budget allowed. One could gauge the wealth of a home by the elaborately carved panels and friezes in the rooms. Facing the building in full or in part with stone, tile, or textured brickwork was common. In regions where it was too scarce to use as a construction material, wood might be used as a decorative element. Among the best were tropical woods from East Africa and imported Indian teak, which was weatherproof, well suited to carving, and durable. In most places windows were shuttered rather than glazed, and in hot, arid lands, latticework on windows and upper door panels let in breezes and allowed people to look out without being seen. Curtains or wooden louvers preserved privacy when inner rooms were lighted at night. Among the best-known elements of multistory buildings in southwest Asian cities was the *mashrabiyyah,* a multifunctional set of decorative window lattices made from small pieces of turned wood. Its combination of shutters, grilles, and frames gave maximum cooling, shade, and privacy during the day and evening. The name *mashrabiyyah* comes from the root word *sharaba* (to drink) and the related word *mashraba* means "a place or niche where earthenware water jugs were kept to cool the water by evaporation." The *mashrabiyyah* originated in Cairo but was influenced by Indian perforated windows done in marble and earlier in iron or bronze. Carved wood moldings on rooms and the use of inlays in painted and unpainted doors were common. In Yemen, Iraq, and Syria, colored glass and thin, translucent slices of stone were shaped into designs and embedded in stuccoed frames, creating an effect similar to a leaded stained-glass window. Muslims also worked in stained glass, and their designs, along with their recipes and the minerals they used to make colored glass, probably influenced European glasscraft, which employed geometric designs reminiscent of Islamic art.

Interior Spaces. Many city and village residents lived in humble one-room huts or houses, with perhaps a walled enclosure for animals attached. In rural areas, animals were kept in the house, and fowl such as chickens, pigeons, and ducks were often kept on the rooftop, where the family also slept in summer. Rural and poor families used their dwelling spaces in flexible ways dictated by local traditions and economic activities such as weaving and crafts. Men socialized in communal public spaces rather than at home, and women visited each other's homes but also socialized at communal work areas such as wells, riverbanks, and fields.

Multiroom Houses. The reception room in Muslim regions—such as the parlor, salon, or living room in many cultures—displayed the owners' wealth in its furnishings. The reception room was typically decorated with tiled or paneled dados and niches to hold decorative items on the walls, as well as moldings on the ceilings. It was furnished with mats or carpets, curtains, cushions, tables, or trays for presentation of refreshments and was ventilated by openings onto the main courtyard. Braziers were brought in to warm it in winter, while sprinkled sand and earthen water jugs cooled it in summer. To the sides of the reception rooms, adjoining the main courtyard, were men's private quarters and a kitchen, with private quarters and a private courtyard for the family beyond. Archaeologists have excavated single-story houses of fifty rooms and more, and two-to-eight-story buildings were found in cities such as Fustat, with the upper apartments used variously for guest reception or private apartments. Near the back of the house, and often detached from it, were privies that emptied into a pit that might be closed off when filled or was emptied by paid workmen. The refuse was dried for fuel or fertilizer. Only the houses of the wealthy had private baths, and most people used water from pitchers and large vessels for washing themselves and their clothing at home. Water came from wells, rivers, and canals or was bought from water carriers. Digging private wells in cities was not usually practical because of the congestion and danger of contamination, but the wealthy piped in water through cement, earthen, and wooden piping systems. Public water systems were the pride of public works, featuring norias (water wheels with buckets attached to their rims), cisterns, and aqueducts, some of which pre-dated Islam. In some places the groundwater level was low and the water

brackish. Runoffs for used household water led into the streets and, in places where urban order was well administered, the disposal of wastewater was regulated so that it did not create a health problem. Palaces had elaborate, self-contained facilities for water supply and drainage. Among the rooms that were sometimes added to the basic public and private spaces in a house were additional reception rooms, apartments, and guest quarters. Under the influence of the positive attitude toward learning, the wealthy acquired books and built personal libraries to house them. In Baghdad and parts of Persia and Central Asia, underground or sunken rooms were dug for cooling, with running water channeled through them. Another social space was the raised porch, or *dukkan*, at the doorway of a house, a raised platform where the owner could sit and watch the street or receive guests informally. Students sometimes took lessons from masters on the *dukkan*. Such platforms might be small front stoops in narrow alleyways of the city, but in areas where homes were less densely clustered, the *dukkan* approached the dimensions of a veranda and might be canopied or roofed over with wood, while its floor was covered with carpets or mats for sitting. The informal evening round of visitations in villages and towns still makes use of this architectural element for much of its social vitality. A passerby can offer a greeting without stopping, stop for a few moments, or sit for an extended period with refreshments.

Gardens. Surrounding the homes of the wealthy and the palaces of the ruling classes were elaborately laid-out gardens for relaxation and entertainment and for growing fruits, vegetables, and herbs for the kitchen. Courtyards in humble urban homes might have a few plants and trees, and even a simple fountain or water basin. Hydraulic technologies developed in Muslim regions combined ideas from China, Persia, India and Central Asia, and Rome. Waterwheels and windmills, pumps, gears, and siphons made fountains spout water. Engineering books from the medieval period depict elaborate waterworks built to entertain princes and their courts. Palaces such as the Alhambra in Granada show the imaginative use of light, shade, water, and vegetation in decorating the interior and exterior spaces of a living complex. The art of gardening was well developed in India and Persia, where many of the common garden flowers and fruits known around the world were first domesticated. Orange, lemon, and fig trees, palms, shrubs, and scented flowers such as the rose and jasmine spread across the Eastern Hemisphere with the growing urbanization of Muslim regions. Quite a few domesticated fruits, medicinal plants, flowers, and herbs were first brought to the palace gardens and were then grown in other areas of a city. Musical and literary gatherings were held in the gardens of humble homes and royal palaces alike.

Furnishings. Furnishings in Muslim homes were on a horizontal plane. During the medieval period, none but the wealthiest people used framed, raised furniture such as *diwans* (raised sofas), chairs, and benches, and even those

A khalifah in the bath house; illumination by Bihzad in a 1494–1495 manuscript
for the *Khamsah* (Five) of Nizami (British Library, London)

seats were quite low. Most people sat on mats, carpets, cushions, mattresses, or low platforms. The custom of low seating was encouraged by the precedent of Prophet Muhammad, who sat on the floor, slept on a coarse mat, and had no throne despite the high esteem in which he was held. In addition, the horizontal aspect of Islamic prayer reinforced this custom, as did the value placed on gathering knowledge while sitting at the feet of a learned person in the *halaqa,* or circle, in the masjid or *madrasah* (school). These forms of furniture created a demand for domestic textiles, which were produced in increasing variety and traded among Muslim cities and regions. Just as clothing was an important form of wealth in households great and small, domestic textiles—such as mats, cushions, and curtains—were traded, displayed, and inherited. Eating also took place at floor level, with the food spread out on skins, mats, cloths, trays, or low tables. Storage chests were the most prominent vertical furniture in homes. Chests were fitted with metal hinges, plates, and locks, and elaborate chests were carved, inscribed, or inlaid with designs in ivory, metal, mosaics, and exotic woods. Embossed leather boxes and basketry were alternatives to wooden chests. Articles could also be stored in niches in the thick earthen and stucco walls, with doors or curtains to conceal the contents. Open niches displayed trinkets and held lamps. Lamps were made of metal, stone, glass, or ceramic and burned olive oil, scented oils, and other flammable, slow-burning substances. Engineers such as al-Jazari and the Banu Musa produced designs for perpetual lamps and self-trimming wicks, curiosities for the wealthy or public spaces. Knotted and woven carpets, whose Asian and African origins date to prehistoric times, became a highly refined Muslim textile product that was widely traded and exported. Muslim carpets came to be prized in European homes and palaces, where the custom of walking on interior floors with boots and shoes differed from the practice further south and east. The stunning array of colors and designs used in Muslim carpets represent local tastes and traditions, and carpets were the most valuable, durable, and useful domestic items of everyday use.

Everyday Implements. Domestic articles from Muslim society are well represented in museums, and their shapes and decoration may be traced to cultural influences across the Eastern Hemisphere. Literary accounts and miniature illustrations show the high standard of living attained by some Muslims, who had a dazzling variety of objects for everyday use. At one end of the economic spectrum were carpets woven of silk and wool; velvet cushions and mattresses stuffed with feathers; chests inlaid with ivory and gold; vessels of brass, glass, gold, pewter, silver, or jade; trinkets encrusted with jewels; and other objects of fine workmanship from the most renowned centers of production. Less affluent households possessed less opulent objects that might nonetheless be beautifully made. The most basic household items were woven mats for sleeping and sitting, clay vessels for cooking and holding water, some wooden or metal cooking utensils, and a few personal

items such as combs, leather bags, and coarse fabrics for various purposes. Made of rushes, reeds, palm fiber, and grasses, mats lasted for years even with hard use. In Egypt smooth mats were made from papyrus reeds woven on a base of hemp or palm-fiber twine. Inexpensive cushions and mattresses were also made from these durable natural fibers, as were sandals, baskets, and other household items, including cradles. Among the basic items in common households was a tall pitcher called a ewer. It was used to pour water for washing hands before and after meals and for ritual washing before prayer. Drinking vessels included earthenware jars that were left unglazed to cool the water by evaporation. Some water jars had a pouring spigot near the bottom. Earthenware also served as storage for foodstuffs in the kitchen, but some substances—such as oils, perfumes, and spices—required glazed containers. Cooking pots, trays, and other vessels of spun, beaten, or cast metal were commonly used for cooking and serving. Some metals, such as copper, were known to have toxic properties, so, for example, acidic foods were not cooked in copper pots unless they were lined with tin. Engraving, chasing (pressing raised designs into the metal), and inlaying decorations in metal were renowned crafts among Muslims. Museums possess excellent examples of brass buckets, ewers, pen boxes, mirrors, bowls, plates, and candlesticks inlaid with silver and gilt designs depicting scenes, arabesques, inscriptions, and vegetal patterns. Ceramic and glass household objects—and sometimes porcelain imported from China—included candlesticks, cups, and jars, and their decorations show a range of design influences and glazing techniques. Muslim advances in ceramics included attempts to duplicate porcelain by developing white glazes for dark clays on which designs could be overglazed. They also devised a recipe for stoneware that used pulverized quartz and high-temperature firing to make an extremely white and durable ceramic that is thicker than porcelain and still used today. Household items used to entertain guests or beautify the house included incense burners of wood, brass, silver, ceramic, and stone, shaped according to local tradition. A particularly well-known style is the perforated incense ball that contained a gimbel, or small pan, that rocked on two pins to keep the burning coals upright when the burner moved or hung from the ceiling. This innovation was later adapted for use as a cradle to keep magnetic compasses level onboard ships.

Personal Objects. For personal use, a comb and a mirror and a case to hold kohl eyeliner made from antimony were essentials and might be finely crafted from precious materials. As literacy spread, writing implements and writing tables became common, especially in homes of scholars or literary figures. Paper arrived in Muslim society early in its development and greatly aided the spread of literacy and the proliferation of books, libraries, literary gatherings, and institutions, affecting the layout of cities and homes and the mobility of people devoted to learning. Paper did not remain a luxury item, becoming available in many different forms and qualities. The first use for Arabic-language

Brass candlestick inlaid with copper and silver, made in Iran, circa 1220–1250 (Victoria and Albert Museum, London)

printing (circa 800–1400) was the mass production of amulets containing Qur'anic verses and recommended supplications to God. Printed or handwritten inscriptions were worn in lockets, placed in beds and homes, and worn by children. Among pastoral and rural families, saddles, trappings, saddlebags, and the implements for transporting family goods were important everyday items.

Sources:

Muhammad M. Ahsan, *Social Life Under the Abbasids, 786–902 A.D.* (London & New York: Longman, 1979).

Khatib al-Baghdadi, *The Topography of Baghdad in the Early Middle Ages*, translated by Jacob Lassner (Detroit: Wayne State University Press, 1970).

Timothy Insoll, *The Archaeology of Islam* (Oxford: Blackwell, 1999).

Ira M. Lapidus, *Muslim Cities in the Later Middle Ages* (Cambridge & New York: Cambridge University Press, 1984).

Lapidus, ed., *Middle Eastern Cities: A Symposium on Ancient, Islamic, and Contemporary Middle Eastern Urbanism* (Berkeley: University of California Press, 1969).

Bassam Musallam, "The Ordering of Muslim Societies," in *Cambridge Illustrated History of the Islamic World*, edited by Francis Robinson (Cambridge: Cambridge University Press, 1996).

Nezar al-Sayyad, *Cities and Caliphs: On the Genesis of Arab Muslim Urbanism* (New York & London: Greenwood Press, 1991).

FOOD

Lawful and Prohibited Foods. Despite their vast geographic, social, and chronological diversity, Muslims share the concepts of *halal* (permitted) and *haram* (forbidden) foods. The verse of the Qur'an outlining these prohibitions says, "He has only forbidden you dead meat and blood and the flesh of swine and any (food) over which the name of other than Allah has been invoked. But if one is forced by necessity without willful disobedience nor transgressing due limits then Allah is Oft-Forgiving Most Merciful." (16: 115). The verse thus forbids four categories of flesh but allows for their consumption in cases of desperate hunger. The Qur'an also requires special rites for slaughtering animals: "To every people did We appoint rites (of sacrifice) that they might celebrate the name of Allah over the sustenance He gave them from animals (fit for food) but your Allah is one Allah: submit then your wills to Him (in Islam) and give thou the Good News to those who humble themselves" (22: 34). The ritual sacrifice that marks various Islamic celebrations always involves distribution of the meat among family, friends, and the needy. As the Qur'an says, "It is not their meat nor their blood that reaches Allah: it is your piety that reaches Him. . . ." (22: 37). Beyond the few forbidden foods, Muslims are encouraged to "Eat of the things which Allah hath provided for you lawful and good: but fear Allah in Whom ye believe" (5: 88).

Tayyibat. The word used for good and lawful food is *tayyibat*, or beneficial provisions of God. Many such permissible and beneficial foods are mentioned in the Qur'an, including various fruits, vegetables, herbs, grains, milk, and honey. All kinds of seafood are permitted in Islam and do not require ritual slaughter. The prohibition against pork and its derivatives virtually eliminated the raising of pigs in Southwest Asia, North Africa, and parts of Central Asia, but the hot weather and the earlier prohibition against pork among Jews made pork rare in these regions even before Islam, in contrast to East Asia and Europe. In other regions where Islam spread, archaeologists use the lack of pork remains as evidence for identifying Muslim settlements within non-Muslim areas. Other meat prohibitions included animals that had been killed by a predator, by goring, or by falling, unless the animal could be slaughtered before it died. It was significant, however, that Muslims were specifically permitted to eat meat slaughtered by Jews and Christians. This provision fostered social mingling because Muslims could break bread with the People of the Book, and it made family life in mixed marriages much easier than it would otherwise have been. A society that required dietary isolation among the people who worship the same God would have effectively prohibited sharing among neighbors and visits among all sorts of associates, creating great difficulties among people who converted to Islam as they tried to follow the Islamic requirement to keep good relations with the families of their birth. The ability to share food prevented isolationism. Among religiously heterogeneous neighbors in Muslim regions, sharing of food among neighbors of different faiths was common, and it is frequently mentioned in literature.

Alcoholic Beverages. The well-known Islamic prohibition against wine extended to all fermented, alcoholic beverages that might be made from dates or grains (such as beer and distilled spirits). Addressing the Prophet and the questions raised by his followers, the Qur'an states, "They ask you concerning wine and gambling. Say: 'In them is great sin and some profit for people; but the sin is greater than the profit.' They ask thee how much they are to spend; say: 'What is beyond your needs.' Thus does Allah make clear to you His Signs: in order that ye may consider" (2: 219). Muslim legal scholars unanimously interpreted the prohibition as meaning any intoxicating substance, including drugs that clouded the mind. During Muhammad's prophethood, the prohibition was introduced gradually, beginning with the injunction not to come to prayer beclouded with drink, which sharply limited when a person might drink and still make the five daily prayers. Hadith transmitter Anas Ibn Malik reported that when the final prohibition was revealed at Madinah, whoever was serving wine at the time dumped out their vessels immediately. As the news spread through the city, it was reported, wine ran in the streets. For later Islamic periods, it is difficult to gauge the degree to which this prohibition was honored as the Muslim presence expanded into areas where wine was produced and used by people of other religions.

Pre-Islamic and Early Islamic Arabia. Settled Arab farmers lived in oases and highland areas with rainfall, growing dates, barley, and, less often, wheat. In addition to these staples they grew vegetables such as onions, gourds, cucumbers, palm hearts, various greens, herbs, and fruits such as grapes and pomegranates. The diet of the pastoral people consisted mainly of milk and occasionally meat from a slaughtered sheep or goat, but only rarely a camel. They supplemented their diet with wild fruits, vegetables, herbs, game, and small desert animals such as lizards. From the oases they acquired dates and grain for bread, illustrating the relationship between pastoral and settled groups at its most basic level. Through their interaction, both groups gained variety and additional nutrients in their diets. Dates are a highly nutritious, healthful staple, providing many vitamins, minerals, and carbohydrates. The date palm had many other uses as a source of wood, fiber, and thatching material. Bread was something of a luxury among pastoral tribes. Dates, raisins, and thin strips of roasted meat were sun-dried to preserve them. Honey was a rare but appreciated sweetener mentioned in the Qur'an as a healing and blessed substance, and milk was also celebrated in prophetic lore. Milk was drunk fresh and preserved as clarified butter or cheese. Foods were cooked by roasting, boiling, or baking on hot stones. Cuisine was simple, as in *hays*, a mixture of dates, butter, and milk, or *tharid*, a broth made of meat and vegetables with crumbled bread. Broths and porridges were made. Since eating dry bread was not considered a meal, bread was dipped into a condiment such as oil, vinegar, or salt if nothing else. While spices such as cinnamon and saffron and aromatics such as mastic were known and traded through the region, their use was probably sparse because they were expensive. Expeditions and caravans carried the components for *sawik*—dried barley meal to which water and clarified butter or fat from the tails of sheep was added. The irrigated agriculture of southern

JUHA

A legendary Muslim who is said to have lived in the eighth century, Juha (who is sometimes called Goha and Abu Nuwas) has been the subject of jokes and comic stories throughout the Muslim world for centuries. The following anecdote demonstrates how this comic figure often exposes the foibles of others:

Goha went to the public baths in the town. As usual, he was poorly dressed and so the attendants did not treat him with any respect. He was given only the smallest piece of soap and a little towel that didn't look very clean. During his time in the baths he was not served tea and cakes like the other customers. In fact, the attendants made it obvious they would not mind if they never saw him there again. But when he left the baths Goha gave the two attendants a gold coin each. They were amazed at how this poorly dressed man, whom they had treated roughly, should suddenly be so generous to them. Perhaps the next time, they told themselves, he would be even more generous. The following week Goha again went to the public baths. This time, despite the fact that he was dressed in the same clothes, he was treated like a king. When he left he handed to each of the attendants the smallest copper coin instead of the gold one he had given them after his first visit. "This copper coin," explained Goha to the surprised men, "is for the previous visit when I was treated like a beggar. The gold coins I gave you were for this time."

Source: Denys Johnson-Davis, trans., *Goha* (Cairo: British Council, 1993), p. 30.

Arabia allowed more variety in fruits, vegetables, and grains, producing wheat, sesame, beans, and capers. Date groves, orchards, and vineyards were common.

Cuisines. With the expansion of Islam into the Fertile Crescent, North Africa, and Central Asia, the rich agriculture and culinary heritages of Rome, Persia, India, and Egypt were added to the simple Arab fare. The tendency for migrating people to import their native food habits over all else may have led the Arabs to introduce their simple fare into new lands, but this diet was counterbalanced by the newly available variety of foods in the rich agricultural regions of the Fertile Crescent. The many new ingredients and methods of preparation in the Fertile Crescent and elsewhere soon overcame the simple diet of the Arab migrants, though it continued with little change in the Arabian peninsula. Among converts in the new territories, the Islamic prohibitions against *haram* foods modified existing dietary practices and influenced the further development of cuisines in those areas.

Crop Transfers. Another factor that altered the diet in Muslim regions after the seventh century was the introduction of new crops fostered by expansion, migration, travel, and trade. Literary sources from the medieval Muslim world show that a great deal of travel, migration, and trade took place. For humble pilgrims, scholars, merchants, and diplomatic envoys, traveling within the Dar al-Islam (Abode of Islam) meant the possibility of traversing much of inland Asia, the coasts of the Indian Ocean from China to East Africa, North and West Africa, and the lands around the Mediterranean, including Spain. Travelers took with them knowledge of the farming techniques, plant life, and cuisine of their native regions, and they were exposed to the knowledge and products of the lands they visited. The result was an important period of exchange in crops, agricultural methods, and foods. Botanical exchanges that took place between the seventh and the fifteenth centuries in the Muslim world include many important food crops, such as sorghum, rice, hard wheat, sugar cane, citrus, and nutritious vegetables.

Supplying Cities. The degree of urbanization in Muslim society points to an efficient and well-developed system of agriculture and food distribution, as well as crafts related to the processing of staples such as oil, cheeses, and other dairy products and preserving meat, fish, fruits, and flour for city populations. Major towns and cities had commercial establishments for storing and selling ice even in summer. In the central Muslim lands, ice was usually gathered from snow-capped mountains, where it was compacted, packed, and transported in straw or sawdust, canvas, and lead-lined boxes. At the point of sale, ice was stored in lined pits underground. Occasional hail or snow was made into slabs and preserved, and winter river-ice from north of the Caspian Sea was imported. While ice was a luxury enjoyed profusely in the palaces of the wealthy, it was common in lesser quantities in prosperous homes, and as an occasional treat for others. One of its best-known appearances in Islamic history was the iced sherbet offered by the legendary Salah al-Din (Saladin) to Richard the Lionhearted when the English king fell ill.

Fats. Olive oil had been a Mediterranean staple since ancient times, produced for local use and export using several types of oil presses whose gradual development was one of the earliest forms of mechanical engineering. Beam presses, screw presses, and vertical and horizontal grindstones were all used to extract the oil from the olive or seed cake. Many Muslim regions—including Syria, Palestine, and Tunis—were well known for exporting olive oil. Where it was plentiful, olive oil was also used for lighting in homes and masjids, a use mentioned in the well-known "Verse of Light" in the Qur'an (Qur'an, Ayat al-Nur). Olive oil was eaten as a condiment with bread, mixed with herbs such as oregano and mint, combined with other fresh ingredients, and added to cooking. Other prized vegetable oils were sesame from fresh and roasted seeds, cottonseed, and poppy-seed oil. Almond, pistachio, and other nut oils were used in baking sweets. Linseed and castor oil were pressed for industrial uses. Animal fat was clarified for preservation and used in cooking, mostly by the lower classes. Butter was used fresh or clarified by removing the protein, leaving pure butter fat, called *saman*, which kept well. It was mixed into foods or used for frying.

Salt. Salt was traded on a large scale as a health essential and important preservative. Books for the *muhtasib* (market inspector) include guidance that this officer should make sure that the leftover fish each day be salted to preserve it and to prevent its being sold as fresh the next day. Meats were preserved with salt, fats, and spices as sausages, and the *muhtasib* was also responsible for overseeing its manufacture. The gold-for-salt trade in West Africa was carried on to provide inland people in salt-poor areas with an essential dietary supplement. Another stimulus to the gold-salt trade in West Africa may have been the need to preserve the plentiful catch of fish during the season of flooding in the inland delta of the Niger River, which became a series of lakes and wetlands during the wet season, and was near the cities of Djenne, Gao, and later Timbuktu—all regional centers for grain, cotton, and animal products that developed and sustained long-distance trade.

Cheese and Curds. Milk could be preserved by curdling, or souring, and salting. Medieval sources mention soft and hard cheeses made from goat, sheep, and camel milk. Curds of milk were dried and used in cooking sauces. Yogurt was introduced by the pastoral Turks and became known to Europeans through visitors to the Ottoman Empire near or after 1500. Fresh and curdled milk were featured in recipes for vegetables, meat, and sweet dishes.

Beverages. Milk was mentioned as a favored drink in the Qur'an and hadiths. Milk from goats, camels, sheep, and buffalo was drunk fresh; soured, salted, and diluted with water; and sometimes traditionally fermented. The Turks in their native Asian steppe drank mare's milk and fermented it for use in a strong, ceremonial beverage called *koumiss*. Water was the basic drink of rich and poor, a welcome refreshment in warm, arid lands. Drinking water after a meal was a practice of the Prophet, who warned believers to fill their stomachs one-third full with food and one-third full with water and to leave one-third empty. Construction of wells and public fountains was a common charitable activity, and shopkeepers kept pottery jars of air-cooled water at their doorsteps. In pastoral regions, water skins continued in use after the time of the Prophet, and they are frequently mentioned in hadiths. Watersellers were ubiquitous in public places, and with their tanks, belts, and shining cups they can still be seen in Muslim cities today. Literary sources mention containers and methods for drawing water from rivers and wells, filtering it, and allowing it to settle until it was crystal clear. The wealthy mixed water with snow. Drinks prepared from pressed or soaked fruits were common, but the jurists warned people not to allow them to ferment. The propriety of using drinks that fermented quickly was debated, since they were used as a base for all sorts of alcoholic drinks before Islam. Sugar, honey, and treacle were used to preserve fruit juices. Fruit juices and fragrant syrups were even bottled for export to the cities, and they were frequently mixed with water and iced for drinking after dinner and on other occasions. Prepared drinks were also made with ginger, tamarind, jujubes, licorice, and flowers. *Laymun* was a sherbet (sweet-

Metalwork banquet dishes with blessings and the owner's name engraved
around the borders, circa 1000 (drawing by Ann Searwright)

ened "drink") that resembles lemonade. Such drinks were prescribed in medical works. Pharmacies and perfumers sold dried substances from which infusions could be made.

Alcohol. Beer-like drinks prepared from almost any fruits or grains were common in all pre-Islamic societies. Despite the Islamic prohibition on alcoholic beverages, neither wine drinking nor the cultivation of grapes for wine was eliminated from lands chiefly populated by Muslims. Wine was specifically allowed to *dhimmis* (non-Muslim People of the Book) since it was used in religious practices such as communion. There are many historical and literary references to the persistence of wine drinking despite Islamic law. Contemporary historians reported that some prominent rulers regularly drank, not at courtly dinners but in more intimate gatherings of like-minded courtiers. Celebration of wine also appears in literature that depicts the life of scoundrels and thieves. Incongruously, in some Arabic and Persian poetry wine became a metaphor for both worldly love and love of the divine in a purely spiritual sense.

Social Practice. It is difficult to tell, however, how widely wine was drunk in actual social practice. While alcoholic beverages certainly did not disappear from Mus-

lim societies altogether, it is nonetheless probable that the prohibition against drinking, selling, manufacturing, and transporting alcohol by Muslims (though not by non-Muslims) exercised a dampening effect, and that common folk generally obeyed this ban, since it is still widely observed in Muslim countries. However, use of wine and other forms of intoxicating drink certainly took place among some ordinary medieval Muslims, at least in secret, and it was drunk fairly openly in privileged circles. Nonetheless, criminal punishments were designated and carried out for those who broke the taboo, and a brisk production or trade in wine among Muslims does not seem to have arisen.

Rice. Except for some wild varieties, rice was originally domesticated from grasses in the Far East as early as 3000 B.C.E. It is the only grain that can be cooked and eaten whole. Most others need to be pounded or ground into flour. Rice has a high yield and nutrition value per acre, but growing it requires a lot of hand labor and water. Its cultivation spread to Persia and possibly parts of the Mediterranean before Islam, but its diffusion as a major crop outside East and South Asia took place with the spread of Islam, during which it became a staple crop in Iraq and Persia, and it appeared in North Africa and as far west as Spain by

Leavened and unleavened breads were the most typical daily food in most of the region from North Africa to Central Asia. (In India and Southeast Asia, where Islam spread toward 1500, breads were less of a staple.) Baked in loaves—round or other shapes—breads varied widely from region to region—even from city to city, village to village, and household to household. Regional variations may be explained in part because different climates are best suited to growing different grains. Regional techniques of milling grain, leavening the dough, baking bread, and serving it usually predated Islam. Dissemination of these practices into new areas accelerated with migration, trade, and the spread of Islam. The basic steps for making bread were universal, but the details differed, producing a huge variety of breads.

Grinding the Flour: Bread was made from grains such as wheat, barley, oats, rice, millet, and sorghum, or beans such as chickpea and lentil. The first step was to make them digestible by grinding or pounding. The simplest implements used in the early Islamic period go back to the beginnings of human settled life and persisted in isolated Muslim regions throughout the medieval period (and even to the present). A mortar and pestle made of stone or wood or a stone quern—either a rectangular trough with a smaller upper stone or a circular trough with two stones rotating on an axis—were the most common ways to grind in rural areas. Urban and even village populations used communal mills run by animal power, and by the tenth century, water- and wind-powered flour mills were common nearly everywhere. Some grains, such as rice, required pounding rather than grinding, and water-powered trip-hammers were used. Fine, white wheat flour was the most prized for making bread, barley was the coarsest and poorest grain, and combinations of grains varied according to the kind of bread and the locale. Sufis were sometimes known to subsist on rice bread. With the spread of hard-wheat (durum) cultivation, breads that had to be made with highly glutinous flour increasingly entered the daily diet in Muslim regions.

Making and Shaping the Dough: The simplest bread dough consisted of grain and water mixed or kneaded on a board or in a wooden bowl. Leavened bread dough began with a yeast sponge or sourdough starter; then sieved flour was added and the dough was kneaded. Other additions might include salt, milk, and oil. Because the freshness and purity of bread was highly valued, making dough was a daily task for the women or servants in every household. Even urban households did not purchase bread from outside, and only the poor, travelers, and the homeless usually bought from bakers. The simplest breads were formed into a thin pancake by hand. *Raqiq* wheaten breads could be rolled out on a board with a rolling pin into wide, thin sheets. A poet attending a wedding dinner in Aleppo once mistook the bread for cloth and wanted to ask his host to give him a piece to make a shirt, until he saw the guests begin to eat it. Thick, leavened bread was shaped into round, long, oval, rectangular, or ringed loaves of varying size and thickness. Bread borax was sometimes brushed on with a feather to glaze the loaf before baking. For decoration, knife cuts or rope-like designs made some loaves distinctive. In Central Asia many varieties of round, leavened breads were stamped with designs in the center, forming a soft outer part and a chewier, thinner center. Poppy, sesame, and white or black cumin seeds added decoration, flavor, and nutrition to some local specialty breads. Sweet breads mentioned in Abbasid-era cookbooks included almond, pistachio, or sesame paste folded into the dough or spread on bread in layers; loaves could also be stuffed with honey, sugar, or mastic, and prepared with rose

water. Among Chinese Muslims a traditional holiday bread was made by the poor people living in masjid courtyards, with more-affluent families supplying the ingredients and receiving a share of the bread. This custom commemorated a tradition according to which an old woman made a simple gift of bread to the Prophet because she had nothing else at home. In West Africa and the Sudan, millet and sorghum breads were commonly eaten, in addition to some breads made with indigenous grains.

Baking: The simplest arrangements for baking in rural areas involved a campfire or an earthen fire pit. Nomadic bakers sometimes buried their loaves in sand under hot coals, or put them on a hot stone or a bed of hot pebbles. Pancake-style breads were baked on a flat or curved iron plate. A metal pot or portable hearth served the same purpose as more permanent earthen or brick ovens. A *tannur* (or *tandoor*) oven was also simple to make, either as a free-standing, domed, cylindrical oven a few feet high and less than a meter across, or as a clay-lined pit in the ground. Either way, the hot coals gave heat from below, and the leavened bread was wetted and slapped onto the side, where it stuck until the stamped or textured loaf was done to a golden brown. Fuels included dried dung, bundled rice, wheat straw, and dry brushwood, such as cotton, cane, or thorns. In some areas, wood and coal were available for use as fuel. In larger villages, towns, and cities, bread was baked in communal ovens. People took their dough to the baker, or it was collected from the neighborhood homes and marked for each customer. The guidebooks for *muhtasib* provide rules for bakers: "The bakers must raise the ceilings of their shops, open the doors and make wide holes in the roofs of their ovens for the smoke to come out. . . . When the baker has finished lighting the tannur he should first wipe inside it with a clean rag before baking the bread. . . . The bakers should not take the bread out of the oven until it is well baked without burning. It is for the common good that the muhtasib stipulates that each shop must bake a certain amount of bread every day. . . . The muhtasib should dispense them [oven keepers] among the roads, quarters and outskirts of the town because of their utility and great importance for the people. He should order them to maintain the chimneys and to clean every hour the tiles of the oven of burnt seeds, cinders and scattered sand so that none of it sticks to the bottom of the bread. The oven keeper must have some water in a clean container with him, so that when he has finished baking the bread he can use it to swill out any debris left in the oven. . . . On the following day he must wash the oven. . . . [and] the board he uses to stack the dough on. . . . If the people bring him many bowls of dough, whenever he finishes baking one of them he should separate it from the others by marking it so they do not become confused and indistinguishable. . . . The oven keeper's servants and hirelings should be immature boys because they enter the people's houses and meet their womenfolk. But God knows best."

Eating: Out of respect for the substance of life and provision of Allah, not even a crumb of bread was wasted. Bread was broken with the hands, not cut. Pieces of thin breads (*raqiq*) and flatbreads were torn off into the right hand and used to pick up food from a platter shared with other diners. Bread was also crumbled into broth or sauce to make a meal.

Sources: Muhammad M. Ahsan, *Social Life Under the Abbasids, 786–902 A.D.* (London & New York: Longman, 1979).

Jeffrey Alford and Naomi Duguid, "On the Flatbread Trail," *Aramco World,* 46 (September–October 1995): 16–25.

C. Pellat, "Khubz," in *Encyclopedia of Islam,* CD-ROM version (Leiden: Brill, 1999).

the tenth century. Beginning as a luxury dish that remained popular among the Muslim upper classes, rice bread also became a staple for the lower classes in Abbasid cities. In Muslim cookery, rice was boiled by itself and flavored with salt and spices, or it was added to meat and vegetable stews. Nutritious chickpeas, lentils, or pistachio nuts were added to rice—with or without spiced meat—as versions of a dish called *aruzz mufalfal*, which appeared in medieval Muslim cookbooks. (This dish is somewhat like the later Turkish rice pilaf.) Rice was the main ingredient in a sweet pudding called *muhallabiya*, which is still popular in the region; for this dish washed rice is cooked in fresh milk and seasoned with mastic (aromatic Arabic gum), camphor, and cinnamon; sugar or honey could be added and sometimes meat or chicken. Rice was also made into vinegar, and it had other uses, such as a thickening agent, a powder for washing hands and scenting clothes, and probably a glue and sizing agent for paper and cloth.

Hard Wheat. Another important food crop for nutritional value and versatility in cooking was durum wheat, which may have originated in the eastern Mediterranean or East Africa. Its cultivation spread widely under Muslim influence, reaching North Africa, Spain, and Central Asia, as well as southern and eventually northern Europe (where the predominant medieval grain was rye). Hard wheat is drought resistant and can be stored for a long time without spoiling. It is high in gluten, which makes dough made from its flour rise well and stretch easily into thin sheets. Thus, hard wheat is the only kind of grain suitable for making pasta such as noodles, macaroni, and North African couscous, and fine pastry dough for use in layered, nut-filled, honeyed sweets such as baklava. Macaroni was invented by travelers who made dough into balls or tubes with holes, which were light and easy to carry when strung together. Then they could be cooked quickly in salted water for a substantial, nutritious meal. Sauces, legumes, vegetables, and meat could be added, and pasta was also sweetened. Hard wheat flour was also an important component of the many kinds of flatbreads enjoyed in cities and countrysides across the central, grain-producing Muslim regions.

Citrus Fruits. Some citrus fruits may have arrived in the Mediterranean region in pre-Islamic times. Cultivation of varieties such as kumquats, sweet and sour oranges, lemons, and limes began in China, Malaysia, and India. Fruits often spread through gifts to royal gardens, such as the well-known Patio de los Naranjos in Córdoba. From there, citrus trees moved to ordinary backyard gardens, family courtyards, and village orchards.

Bananas. The versatile banana, raw or cooked, ripe or green, was introduced from tropical Southeast Asia. It was first cultivated on a larger scale in India and disseminated along the monsoon routes before Islam. By the eighth century, banana cultivation—which requires cuttings rather than seeds—had spread to many Muslim regions. By the fifteenth century it had reached around the Mediterranean to Spain, and bananas were grown in much of Africa.

Bananas—an important source of minerals, vitamins, and starches—are one of the natural "perfect foods." The word *banana*, meaning "fingers of the hand," is found in the Qur'an, but *mauz* is the Arabic word used for the fruit.

Other Fruits and Nuts. Specific varieties of grapes used for juice and raisins, cherries, quinces, apricots, peaches, and pomegranates also spread across Muslim lands during the medieval time. Apricots, certain nuts, and melons such as the watermelon disseminated along the Silk Road in pre-Islamic times, and they were widely cultivated and traded in fresh and dried form for the use of urban populations. For the wealthiest clientele in Baghdad or Damascus, melons from Bukhara or Samarqand were shipped in lead cases filled with ice and were a commonly stocked item in khalifal kitchens. In Central Asia particularly, melons were a delicacy enjoyed by all classes for quenching thirst in the heat and for good digestive health, as they were valued everywhere they grew. Fruit markets were called melon houses in some places. The arid belt from North Africa to Arabia and Central Asia was well known for dried fruits such as dates, raisins, figs, and apricots, as well as for nuts, including almonds, pistachios, walnuts, and hazelnuts. These nutritional staples were important as a source of carbohydrates, protein, vitamins, and minerals. Dried fruits of high quality were important items of local, regional trade, and the best quality fruits were prized long-distance trade items such as Smyrna figs. When trade traffic was brisk, even bulky fresh fruits were transported if underground cold storage was available locally to hold over apples, pomegranates, and grapes. Some regions sent fresh or dried fruit such as apples to the khalifahs' storehouses in payment of the *kharaj* land tax. For the wealthiest customers, shipping in lead ice boxes insulated with straw was sufficient to transport valuable specialties over considerable distances.

Vegetables. Of the many vegetables that were used in Muslim kitchens during the period, spinach, originally grown in Nepal, was known as the "queen of vegetables," and made its way westward, along with its Arabic name, *isbanakh*. Asparagus was highly prized in Abbasid times, and root vegetables such as carrots, turnips, beets, and onions, as well as gourds and squashes; legumes such as lentils, peas, and beans; and greens such as lettuce, parsley, mint, and watercress were widely eaten in Baghdad during the Abbasid period and in other cities. Many variations of recipes for these ingredients have been passed down. Pickling vegetables with brine and vinegar was a common, inexpensive method of preservation. Olives, cucumbers, turnips, carrots, and eggplants were some of the most common daily food items preserved by pickling, and they were ubiquitous items on the tables of rich and poor alike. Poor families might have pickles as the only relish for their meal of bread.

Sugar. Of all the crops that moved across Muslim regions during the medieval period, sugar cane has the most interesting history. It began as a domesticated grass in Southeast Asia, was cultivated on a large scale in ancient India, and was introduced to China and Persia, where it

A lustre-glazed ceramic dish made in Valencia, Spain, during the early fifteenth century (Victoria and Albert Museum, London)

was a rare delicacy. Small quantities may have reached the royal courts of other lands to the west before Islam, but sugar did not begin to spread rapidly until the development of Muslim cities with their prosperity and sophisticated urban lifestyle. Growing sugar cane produces more human food per acre than any other crop, and what is left after the extraction of its juice makes excellent animal fodder. Sugar-cane juice was drunk as a nonalcoholic beverage and made into cane sugar, molasses, or other syrups. Cultivation and processing of sugar cane required sophisticated agricultural, irrigation, and processing techniques. Wind and waterpower were used to crush the cane and extract the juice. Workers were highly organized to perform the steps of its production. Sugar was traded regionally and exported, and Muslim techniques for processing sugar were transferred to China.

Uses of Sweeteners. There were many grades of sugar and molasses, from the darkest syrup to the purest white powder, which people purchased according to their means. Sugar was purchased in solid molds or cones from which the cook broke or shaved the amount needed. (Sugar was still sold in this form in colonial America.) Treacle, or sugar syrups of various kinds, was made by boiling fruits to a concentrated juice, with or without additional sweetener. A sweet paste made of carob pulp or dates was also a sweetener of less refinement. Like many newly introduced plants, sugar was thought to have medicinal value, but its important contribution to Islamic medicine was the innovation of mixing medicines with syrups to make them more palatable. Syrups were also believed to speed medicine to the organs, an idea supported by modern knowledge of the rapid rate at which sugar is metabolized. Evidence indi-

cates that sugar cane was grown in Egypt by the mid eighth century and spread across North Africa, reaching Spain and Sicily by the tenth or eleventh century. The Crusaders were introduced to sugar in the eastern Mediterranean and Cyprus, areas that exported the luxury sweetener to Christian Europe. European visitors, especially the scholars who flocked to Spain during the twelfth century to translate Arabic philosophical and scientific works, were certainly exposed to delights such as marzipan, the tasty sweet made from ground almonds and sugar, a Toledo specialty as well known as its libraries. Sugar was used in fruit preserves such as apricot jams and candied or crystallized oranges and lemons and in the preparation of fruit and flower syrups—such as violet, rose, jasmine and orange blossom—for sherbet. It was used alongside honey for sweetening cooked dishes, and in urban medieval cooking, where novelty was a virtue, sugar was even added to meat dishes.

Flavorings and Spices. Locally grown flavorings such as mint, parsley, coriander, fennel, scallions, dill, garlic, onions, sumac, sage, and exotic herbs figured in the cuisines of various Muslim regions. Some were mentioned in the Qur'an and earlier scriptures and had figured in pre-Islamic folk literature and medicine for ages. They were used fresh, pounded into paste, and dried for storage. Herbs played a part in traditional medicine. They were mentioned in botanical encyclopedias and pharmacological treatises of the ancient Greeks and Persians and passed into Muslim pharmacological works. Foods were eaten for their medicinal properties. According to ancient and medieval theories of bodily "humors," which were accepted in western Europe as well as the Muslim world, foods and their flavorings were considered humid, dry, cold, or hot according to the "humors" they produced, and were combined to enhance or counter these effects. A variety of rhubarb that was imported along the Silk Road from China cured dysentery in children and adults. Many spices—such as pepper, cinnamon, cardamom, saffron, frankincense, vanilla, clove, and mastic—were available only through regional or long-distance trade, but cumin and coriander were grown in local gardens. Aromatic substances such as attar of roses and jasmine were used for perfuming the body, the home, and the *masjid* in addition to flavoring foods. Having inherited the Indian art of gardening, Persia was a source for the most fragrant flowers. Use of spices by the wealthy and middle classes of Muslims brought these flavorings to the attention of European traders and visitors to Muslim courts, helping to stimulate European maritime exploration for trade routes to the spice-producing regions of Asia and Africa.

Sources:

Muhammad M. Ahsan, *Social Life Under the Abbasids, 786–902 A.D.* (London & New York: Longman, 1979).

Jeffrey Alford and Naomi Duguid, "On the Flatbread Trail," *Aramco World,* 46 (September–October 1995): 16–25.

Andre Clot, *Harun al-Rashid and the World of the Thousand and One Nights,* translated by John Howe (New York: New Amsterdam Press, 1989).

The similarity in cooking and diet across the lands of Islam can be attributed to trade, migration, Islamic food prohibitions and preferences, and the dissemination of important crops; the differences that emerged among regions may be explained by local conditions and tastes. Nearness to mountains, sea, river, desert, grassland, or forest might determine what could be caught, grown, and raised. Proximity to cosmopolitan trade and invasion routes brought enormous variety to the cooking of the eastern Mediterranean and the Central Asian Silk Road, while lands where tropical fruits, vegetables, and spices grow had a different kind of variety in their diet. Remote or less-fertile regions had a more limited range of ingredients to work with, and in most places families with lesser means had to be content with simple fare. The following is a sampling of dishes from various regions taken from literary sources and cookery books.

North Africa and the Maghrib. Kuskusu, or couscous, is an ancient dish of ground grain that was soaked, salted, sieved, and steamed to be eaten alone or with stews. This fine pasta probably originated with the Berbers and was served from western Egypt to the Maghrib. When hard durum wheat reached North Africa in about the year 1000, it became the most common grain used in couscous pellets. A typical recipe included the following instructions: Place semolina in a trough and sprinkle with salted water. Roll the semolina with the hands to form small pellets. Pour the pellets into a coarse sieve and roll them around with the palm until they fall through the screen. Sieve again, using a finer screen. Repeat until all the couscous grains are evenly sized. Place the sieved grains in a woven basket and steam twice over plain water. Cool. Spread the grains on a large sheet to dry in the sun, raking and turning until completely dry. Store in jars away from humidity.

Al-Andalus. A thirteenth-century Valencian manuscript included the following recipe for a royal feast dish made in the Muslim kingdom of Andalusia in Spain: Take a fat, young sheep, skinned and cleaned. Open it and remove what is in the stomach. In the stomach place a stuffed goose, and in the goose's belly a stuffed hen, and in the hen's belly a stuffed young pigeon, and in the pigeon's belly a stuffed thrush, and in the thrush's belly another stuffed or fried bird. Sprinkle with the sauces customary for stuffed dishes. The opening of the sheep is sewn together and the sheep is baked in a hot clay oven until done and crisp

on the outside. It is sprinkled with more sauce, and then put in the cavity of a young calf that has already been cleaned. The calf is stitched together and put in the hot oven until it is done and crisp on the outside. Take out of the oven and present to the guests.

Iraq and Persia. *Sikbadj*, a well-known sweet-and-sour stew, was eaten year round, but the ingredients might differ with the season. Fat meat was boiled in water, with fresh coriander, cinnamon bark, and salt. The froth was skimmed off, and dry coriander, onions, leeks, carrots, and stewed and peeled eggplant were added. When the stew was almost cooked, a mixture of date juice and vinegar was added, and the stew was boiled a little longer. Then some broth was taken out, mixed with saffron, and returned to the stew. Peeled sweet almonds, currants, raisins, and dried figs were added, and the stew was cooked a little more. Finally, just before the stew was served, it was sprinkled with rose water.

Central Asia. Pilaf is a traditional lamb and rice dish that arose from the relationship between the pastoral peoples of the steppe (shepherds) and the settled folk of the river valleys (rice farmers), who came together in caravan cities where they exchanged the products of their labors. In pilaf, lamb is cooked in broth, and the meat and bones are removed. Rice is heated with fat or butter, then cooked slowly in the broth with salt and some dried spices. Soaked lentils, other legumes, and raisins can be cooked with rice. Toasted almonds are sprinkled on top of the pilaf, which was typically served with yoghurt.

East Africa. When Ibn Battuta visited Mogadishu in about 1330, he described a meal provided by a local dignitary: "Their food is rice cooked with ghee (clarified butter), which they put into a large, wooden platter, and on top of this they set platters of kushan (pottery). This is the seasoning made of chickens, meat, fish and vegetables. They cook unripe bananas in fresh milk and put this in one dish, and in another dish they put curdled milk, on which they place pieces of pickled lemon, bunches of pickled pepper steeped in vinegar and salted, green ginger, and mangos. . . . When they take a mouthful of rice, they eat some of these salted and vinegar conserves after it."

Sources: Tor Eiglund, "The Cuisine of Al-Andalus," *Aramco World*, 40 (September–October 1989): 29.

Ibn Battuta, *Travels in Asia and Africa, 1325–1354*, 3 volumes, translated by H. A. R. Gibb (London: Routledge, 1929).

Greg Noakes and Laidin C. Noakes, "Couscous: The Measure of the Magrib," *Aramco World*, 49 (November/December 1998): 16–25.

Ahmad Y. al-Hassan and Donald R. Hill, *Islamic Technology: An Illustrated History* (Cambridge & New York: Cambridge University Press / Paris: Unesco, 1986).

Timothy Insoll, *The Archaeology of Islam* (Oxford: Blackwell, 1999).

C. Pellat, "Khubz," in *Encyclopedia of Islam*, CD-ROM version (Leiden: Brill, 1999).

M. Rodinson, "Ghidha," in *Encyclopedia of Islam*.

J. Sadan, "Mashrubat," in *Encyclopedia of Islam*.

'Abd al-Rahman ibn Nasr al-Shayzari, *The Book of the Islamic Market Inspector: Nihayat al-Rutba fi Talab al-Hisba (the Utmost Authority in the Pursuit of Hisba),* translated by R. P. Buckley (Oxford: Oxford University Press on behalf of the University of Manchester, 1999).

Andrew M. Watson, *Agricultural Innovation in the Early Islamic World: The Diffusion of Crops and Farming Techniques, 700–1100* (Cambridge: Cambridge University Press, 1983).

GAMES AND LEISURE ACTIVITIES

Recitation. The tradition of reciting oral literature was among the most widespread and common leisure activities among Muslims of the medieval period. As a restorative or "recreational" activity in the literal sense of the word, reading or reciting the Qur'an aloud in rhythmic cadences, or listening to a skilled *qari'* (Qur'an reciter), was probably the most universal Muslim activity apart from daily work. On the occasion of Friday prayers, at any commemorative service, and as a daily activity for many, the remembrance of Allah through reciting scripture, performing *dhikr* (formulaic, often rhythmic, repetitions of words in remembrance of God) were regular activities among the pious. The practice of *dhikr* became a sophisticated art among Sufi orders, whose music and rhythmic movement led to ecstasy and whose practices at their most extreme met with jurists' disapproval. From children's earliest introduction to Qur'an recital in the *kuttab* (primary school) school at age three to five, to the time a Muslim lay on the deathbed, recitation of the Qur'an and other oral religious expressions was a ubiquitous aspect of daily life.

Oral Poetry. Among the early Arabs, whose literary tradition was almost entirely oral, the pleasure of reciting poetry in Arabic was of enormous significance, as was the ability to compose it extemporaneously and to recall its great masters. Poetry contests were held at market fairs, the best-known being the market of Ukaz, and the most-renowned poems were those posted in the environs of the Ka'bah. Muhammad did not forbid the composition and recital of poetry, but the Qur'an denies the accusation that Muhammad was merely a poet and affirms the divine source of the revelation. Poets whose skills were not in the service of truth were reviled in the Qur'an. Poetry was a part of the psychology and culture of the Arabs, accompanying work, encouraging armies during battle, and commemorating great events. Pre-Islamic traditions of Arabic poetry influenced Muslim literature and social life for centuries to come. Styles changed and were influenced by other sources, but the practice of reciting and listening to poetry has continued unbroken to the present. Whether the setting was a circle of people around a campfire, a courtly gathering in a palace, or neighbors meeting in a public place or a private garden, recited poetry or prose was

enjoyed by all classes. During a period of political unrest under Harun al-Rashid (ruled 786–809), even a camel driver was heard to recite verses passing judgment on the actions of the khalifah. Poetry could be recited alone or with musical accompaniment using drums, which were expressly permitted according to the hadiths, or using stringed instruments or flutes, which were questionable according to Islamic law.

Oral Histories. Pre-Islamic oral histories of tribes, which included their genealogies and great struggles, occupied leisure time and served as a repository of tribal history that was held and passed on by elders. During the early Islamic centuries, the oral narration of hadiths was woven into two related traditions. The transmission of knowledge about the precedents set by Prophet Muhammad and his companions, which developed into the legal sciences, was both a popular pursuit among the pious and a serious scholarly activity. The other tradition was the oral transmission of *ayyam* (battle days), which built on the tribal-history tradition and included both the history of the nascent Muslim community under Prophet Muhammad's leadership and later narratives of the *futuhat* (openings), military struggles to open new territories to Muslim rule. Tribal history and military history merged in the composition of poems celebrating victories or lamenting defeats. After the Crusaders massacred the inhabitants of Jerusalem in 1099, the few survivors made their way to the Abbasid court and horrified their listeners with a poetic account of the event. As a courtly institution, poets were commissioned to write poems or rewarded for reciting them on great occasions, a tradition that continued at Persian, Turkish, and Indian Muslim courts and public ceremonies.

Pre-Islamic Ties. Several examples of the storytelling tradition in Muslim culture demonstrate how widespread and enmeshed with pre-Islamic cultures it was. The best-known literary example of this interconnectedness is *Alf Laylah wa-Laylah* (The Thousand and One Nights), a frame tale that includes stories from Indian, Persian, and other traditions and illustrates the continuity of the tradition in Islam and its many roots. Other works, such as animal fables from Greek, Indian, and Persian sources, found their way into both high culture and popular culture. Examples of linkage between Muslim and pre-Islamic traditions in other places include the oral history transmitters called griot in West Africa and the performers of heroic tales from Hindu and indigenous sources in Southeast Asia, who used shadow puppets with elaborate percussion accompaniment.

Storytellers. The *hakawati* (storytellers) plied a trade that was passed down from father to son at public or private social gatherings. Female storytellers, whose material might be secular or religious, were also cherished. Sheherezad, the narrator of *Alf Layla wa-Laylah,* is the best-known example. At urban gatherings, storytellers commemorated famous people and events, such as the Crusades, or transmitted stories of local history and local heroes. Their stories could also be a form of political com-

Bayad singing and playing the 'ud; illumination from a thirteenth-century Spanish or Moroccan manuscript for *Bayad wa Riyad* (Bayad and Riyad), a rare example of Muslim figurative painting in Spain (Vatican Library, Rome)

mentary or satire on the current leadership. Some of these popular entertainments included dramatic enactments involving props, puppets, actors, or mimes.

Religious Stories. Stories in the pious vein included the stories of the prophets (*Qassas al-Anbiya'*) and stories from the Prophet Muhammad's life (Sirah), which were passed on through family and social gatherings as well as in sermons and scholarly circles. Many stories of the prophets were versions based on Jewish and Christian scriptures and oral traditions and were viewed as valid only where corroborated by the Qur'an and hadiths. Nonetheless, the telling of these embellished stories persisted because of their emotive impact and ability to invoke a sense of piety in the hearers, especially the young and those without formal education. Another strand of the storytelling tradition was picked up by Sufi teachers who instructed their followers by means of symbolic, didactic stories, tapping into an age-old tradition of spiritual teaching and collective wisdom. One of the best-known literary works in this tradi-

tion is the *Mathnawi* of Jalal al-Din Rumi (1207–1273), which includes allegorical tales and poems to enhance spiritual growth and moral uplift.

Musical Entertainment. Public performance of music, except vocal or percussive, and the use of rhythmic movements to accompany it are both activities considered forbidden by many Muslim jurists and frowned upon by the pious. Yet, music and dance survived from pre-Islamic cultures in both popular and courtly cultures, but these arts underwent modification with the spread of Islam and its consolidation. After the rise of Islam, folk dances tended to be performed in gender-separate groups, became more subdued in their movements, and were purged of pagan symbolism and sexual suggestiveness. The tradition of formal dance cultivated at courts was distant from Islamic practice but continued to be widespread within that narrow sphere of Muslim society. Courtly dance was based on refined and sophisticated musical traditions from Greek, Persian, Indian, and other ancient origins. The use of highly trained female slave singers at the courts is celebrated in literary works and historical accounts. *Abu al-Faraj al-Isfahani's Kitab al-Aghani* (Book of Songs, circa 917–967) is evidence of the breadth and sophistication of musical performance traditions in Muslim society during the tenth century. The courtly tradition filtered down to the upper and middle classes, and the popular tradition took on greater sophistication in urban settings, incorporating elements that demonstrate the heterogeneous, mobile nature of Muslim culture. Musical instruments, especially the large variety of stringed instruments that spread across the lands of Islam, had their origins in the folk traditions of the Mediterranean, Africa, and Central and South Asia. Among these instruments are the kettledrum, the tambourine, the rebec (forerunner of the violin and related instruments), the lute and its derivatives (such as the mandolin, guitar, and banjo), and the qanun (similar to a zither, autoharp, or sitar). Military or processional music was a part of public spectacles, providing entertainment and galvanizing public support for the ruling groups. Horns and drums accompanied processions to announce a celebration, attracting attention over a wide area. With the rising influence of Turkic groups in the Abbasid state and successor governments and their migration into Southwest Asia, the Turkic tradition of martial music added to these influences a rousing forerunner of the military marching band. Turkish, and later Ottoman, military engagements with European armies influenced the development of the orchestra and the marching band in European musical history.

Games of Strategy and Chance. The two most popular and enduring Muslim table games are chess and backgammon. The game of chess (*shatranj*) was widely praised for its value in developing the intellect and military-strategy skills and was widely played in courtly or polite society. The game originated in India before Islam, and after passing into Persia, it became an integral part of Muslim culture. Harun al-Rashid is said to have given a chess set as a diplomatic gift to Charlemagne. Poems were written about chess; children were taught chess as part of their education; and theoretical works were written about the game. The Abbasid khalifahs held competitions and played matches. Backgammon (*nard*) is another game of great renown in Muslim society. It was played on a board divided into twelve color-contrasting diamond-shaped points to represent the months in a year. Thirty pieces represented the number of days in the month, and two dice—the determining variable in the game—were considered symbols of human submission and divine will. The game is said to have originated in Persia with a King Ardashir, though it may have antecedents in India as well. Another strategy game, called *mancala,* is an indigenous African game that dates back to ancient Egypt and was widely played in Muslim West Africa. There are many variations of mancala all over Africa, and it may have spread to Southeast Asia and elsewhere around the Indian Ocean during the medieval period. It was played on a board with rows (two, three, four, or more) of depressions into which seeds or other

counters were placed, the object being to move the counters in complete laps around the board, keeping all of them in competition. The game requires skill and sophisticated strategy. Medieval Muslims played it on a beautifully carved game board in an elegant setting or in depressions on the ground with seeds or pebbles as counters. In addition to these three intellectual games, a variety of games of chance continued from their pre-Islamic origins, many involving dice or sheep's knuckles. Gambling—whether with cards, dice, or arrows—or any other game of chance or skill was strictly forbidden, but the wealthy and powerful and the lower elements of urban Muslim society both gambled to some extent. Some members of the courtly classes are said to have squandered fortunes, some personal and some the property of the state. To the horror of Muslim jurists, people also gambled on fights between animals such as cocks, dogs, and large and small beasts of prey—as a throwback to pagan times. Some dissolute members of the royalty had arenas constructed for this purpose.

Child's Play. Medieval Muslim literature describes many games for children. Nearly all girls, and many boys, played with dolls, which might be as simple as a figure made of twisted straw or as sophisticated as a carved-wood, fabric-dressed figure sold in the toy market. For the holidays, some dolls were made of molded sugar or bread dough filled with sweets. Little animal-shaped figures made of scented substances were tossed out at festivals. Playing with dolls even received the sanction of a hadith, which records how Muhammad's youngest wife, Aisha, played with a likeness of Solomon's winged horse, with the approval of the Prophet. In the many cultures of the Muslim world, children played a wide variety of guessing games, hide-and-seek, and games of rivalry and competition. Other games imitated adult activities, such as weddings and work, and included play with model animals.

Military Sports. Pastimes and popular sports related to military exercises had pre-Islamic roots and grew in variety and sophistication under the mingling of cultures and the prosperity in Muslim civilization. Wrestling and weight-lifting remained popular, incorporating regional customs from Indo-Iranian and Greek traditions and—in the eastern part of the Muslim world—partaking of the Asian martial-arts legacy. Celebrated by Prophet Muhammad, archery increased greatly in popularity with the rise of the Turks, who brought the remarkable skills and technology of Central Asian horse archers. This tradition continued through the Ottoman period.

Equestrian Sports. Horse breeding and equestrian arts were a vital part of military and elite society. Treatises on horse breeding, training, and riding, as well as genealogies of horses and collections of the veterinary knowledge needed to maintain them, were passed to other cultures, where they continue to influence world equestrian circles. Equestrian skills were shown in official processions and demonstrations, and horse racing was an important activity, which was approved by Islamic law so long as it was not coupled with gambling. Horse racing over long and

A hunter attacking a lion; illumination by Bihzad in a manuscript for the *Shahnameh* (Book of Kings) of Firdawsi, circa 1400 (Topkapi Museum, Istanbul)

short distances reached sophisticated levels. Unable to afford the expensive sport of horse racing, people outside elite social circles raced dogs, camels, donkeys, and homing pigeons. Rulers built hippodromes for racing horses and playing polo, a sport whose roots also lie in the broad grasslands of Central Asia among horse-breeding pastoral groups. Among such peoples, where most learned to ride before they could walk, racing was a popular sport that played an important role in the culture. A polo-like game that is still played at festivals on the Asian steppe involves a swinging goat carcass, which one team tries to grab from the other for the victory. Polo itself evolved into a sophisticated game, which the khalifah and his guests watched from lavishly appointed seating. Another version, called *tabtab*, was also played from horseback but with a sort of wooden racquet. Elite women sometimes participated in racing and equestrian sports, as they did in Central Asian pastoral society.

Hunting. Another sport that crossed rural and urban, elite and common, lines was hunting. Pastoral Arabs preferred hunting to farming. For the nonelite, hunting was a source of food as well as enjoyment. Ordinary people hunted and fished with whatever means were available, including hounds, falcons, traps, nets, and decoys. The Arab, Persian, Indian, and Turkish ruling classes inherited hunting from pre-Islamic royal traditions and shared its passion for the sport with the royalty of European, Asian, and African cultures—creating an intermingling of influ-

ences that can no longer be traced with any certainty. Royal hunting was a valiant, luxurious, and often massively wasteful pastime. It was considered a measure of virility and readiness to do battle, a source of vigorous exercise that was beneficial to health—even though kings and princes were killed while engaging in it. Large hunting parties included soldiers who practiced military skills and developed new ones. The popularity of hunting also stimulated the sciences of zoology, veterinary medicine, animal behavior, and military technology. The use of trained hunting birds and other animals was among the hallmarks of Muslim hunting. Falconry reached a high degree of sophistication. Many treatises were written about falconry, and its skills were also passed down orally. Other animals such as dogs, horses, wolves, panthers, tigers, lynx-caracal weasels, and ferrets were used in the hunt, but the most prized of the royal hunting animals was the cheetah. Cheetahs were trained to ride on a pillion, or platform, attached to a horse. The animal stalked the prey, or the hunting party would run down and tire a herd of gazelle and then allow the cheetah to take one gazelle as a finale. Other animals trailed the quarry using their keen sense of smell or eyesight, flushed the quarry from thickets, or dug them out of holes. These tracking animals were trained to sharpen their instincts and taught to give up their prey to the human hunter in return for a token piece of meat. Hunting animals were sold for large sums of money and presented as diplomatic gifts of high esteem. Lion hunting was a royal pas-

LEISURE, RECREATION, AND DAILY LIFE

279

time of great prestige and danger, and many royals enjoyed the far less-dangerous pastime of hunting water fowl as well. Whatever the quarry, elite hunting parties ranged over large stretches of territory, not only royal reserves but also open countryside that was under cultivation or in use by pastoralists. Hunting could cause considerable damage to crops and flocks, and adequate, or generous, compensation was expected and generally given by the official hunting party. Royal hunting parties were known to stop at rustic homes for refreshment, an honor that might also be richly compensated. Abuses were surely not unknown, but the jurists in whom ruling groups sought legitimacy were firm on the matter of compensation for losses incurred by lesser folk from the pastimes of the powerful.

Sources:

Muhammad M. Ahsan, *Social Life Under the Abbasids* (London & New York: Longman, 1979).

Andre Clot, *Harun al-Rashid and the World of the Thousand and One Nights,* translated by John Howe (New York: New Amsterdam Press, 1989).

Mounah A. Khouri, "Literature," in *The Genius of Arab Civilization: Source of Renaissance,* edited by J. R. Hayes (New York: New York University Press, 1975).

HOLIDAYS AND RELIGIOUS OBSERVANCES

'Id. The term *'id,* meaning "day of celebration," was introduced by the Prophet Muhammad to designate the two annual Islamic celebrations prescribed in the Qur'an verse 2: 67: "Unto each nation have We given sacred rites which they are to perform; so let them not dispute with thee of the matter, but summon thou unto thy Lord. Lo! thou indeed followest right guidance." The greater of the two celebrations is 'Id al-Adha, the feast of the sacrifice, and the lesser is 'Id al-Fitr, the feast of breaking the fast. The dates of these two celebrations are determined by the lunar calendar, so they shift in the solar calendar by about eleven days each year. Thus, over several decades, they rotate through the seasons.

Jum'ah. Friday is the day of jum'ah, or congregational prayer. This day is not, as in the Jewish or Christian traditions, a day of rest, but the day on which obligatory public worship takes place. From the early days of Islam, following the practice of the Prophet, jum'ah prayer was held in a single masjid in each city. Thus, people from disparate quarters of a city gathered at one large jami' masjid—a tradition that some jurists considered a condition for proper performance of the jum'ah prayer. All adult men who were not ill or traveling were expected to attend. Women were exempted, but men were enjoined by the Prophet not to forbid women's participation in the masjid. At jum'ah, readings from the Qur'an were followed by the *adhan* (call to prayer), and the sermon was delivered from *minbar* (raised pulpit), in two parts, with the *khatib* (preacher) sitting briefly between the two parts. The service ended with a prayer of two *rak'a.* By the Abbasid period at the latest, Friday had become a day off for officials and students, but businesses reopened after prayer. The presence of Jews and Christians in Muslim society tended to influence the weekly rhythms of life, and Saturday or Sunday was sometimes a local day of enjoyment for all, though some rulers took action against this habit among Muslims, requiring the market stewards to ensure that Muslims' shops were not closed in observation of the *dhimmi* Sabbath.

Ramadan. 'Id al-Fitr follows the fast during the ninth lunar month of Ramadan, the time when all adult Muslims of sound mind and body are obliged to abstain from food, drink, and sexual intercourse from dawn until sunset, for a period of twenty-nine or thirty days. A traveler or sick person may fast a like number of days at another time. People who are ill or in any condition that would make fasting a health risk, including pregnancy or nursing, may compensate by preparing the *iftar,* or fast-breaking meal for fasting people or the needy. Children often participate in the fast occasionally or for part of a day but are not required to do so until reaching puberty. During Ramadan the day began when drummers walked through villages and quarters beating drums or calling to wake people for the predawn meal, or *suhur,* which might be as little as a few dates and some water to a communal household meal including meat, rice, sweets, fruit, salads, and beverages. After performance of the dawn prayer, some people slept for a few more hours. During the day, many Muslims in rural areas went about their usual tasks, but in the cities schedules underwent a shift. Much of the afternoon was devoted to preparation of the *iftar,* served at sunset. The Ramadan fast was a time of increased fellowship among family members, neighbors, and friends, who shared *iftar* on many nights. Masjids and homes of prominent members of society were open for charity during Ramadan, and it was considered meritorious to provide food for fasting people. People hurried through the streets of cities and villages to arrive on time for the meal served at sunset, which many began by eating a few dates and water, just as the Prophet Muhammad had done. This fast-breaking meal was followed by the sunset (*maghrib*) prayer, and in many places the major meal of the evening took place some time later. The streets came to life after *iftar,* as people went to masjids to take part in extended prayers. Ramadan was a time of increased concentration on worship; reading the Qur'an and remembering Allah accompanied the physical rigor of fasting. Over the course of the month of Ramadan, the whole Qur'an was recited in conjunction with supererogatory prayers called tarawih. According to a tradition of the Prophet, the Lailat ul-Qadr (Night of Power) takes place on a late, odd-numbered night of Ramadan. Lailat ul-Qadr commemorates the night in the cave of Hira' when the Angel Jibril first transmitted the revelation of the Qur'an to Muhammad. It was traditional to celebrate the occasion with all-night prayers in the masjid, following the tarawih. During the last ten nights of Ramadan, males could take part in the *i'tikaf,* or withdrawal into the masjid for worship.

'Id al Fitr. The end of Ramadan and the beginning of Shawwal was called 'Id al Fitr (Feast of the Fast Breaking). Its arrival was marked by the appearance of the new crescent moon. Watching for it from the rooftops and high

اما الحج مبارك تأوبنا واذلج ا ولا اعيامل اجمالا واخدلجا

Pilgrims on the road to Makkah, accompanied by drummers and trumpeters playing festive music; illumination by al-Wasiti from a 1237 manuscript for the *Maqamat* of al-Hariri (Bibliothèque Nationale, Paris)

places was a celebration in itself. The night of its appearance was filled with preparations and excited children. After the dawn prayer, Muslims made their way to public prayer, which was traditionally held in a large open space to accommodate the large number of worshipers, who wore festive, new, or holiday-best clothes. The public prayer consisted of two *rak'a* with many recitations of the glorification of Allah, followed by a sermon, during which worshipers were supposed to keep silent. Following this prayer, Muslims in city and village exchanged greetings and congratulations, visited each other, gave presents and gifts of money to children, and visited the graves of loved ones. 'Id al-Fitr, though formally considered the lesser of the two festivals, often took on greater prominence because of the communal hardship of the Ramadan fast and the mood of celebration that accompanied its successful completion.

'Id al-Adha. The second, greater festival of the Islamic calendar was 'Id al-Adha, the Feast of the Sacrifice. It was celebrated on the tenth of Dju al-Hijja, the month in which the hajj (pilgrimage) rites take place, approximately two months after Ramadan. 'Id al-Adha was celebrated by Muslims everywhere to commemorate Abraham's obedience to and faith in God, which he demonstrated by preparing to sacrifice his first-born son, Isma'il (Ishmael), who willingly submitted to the test of faith. Isma'il was ransomed by God through the miraculous appearance of a ram. For Muslims who did not take part in the hajj, 'Id al-Adha was a festival of public prayer and exchange of visits for the whole community. The prayer service, held in the open air and performed between sunset and the moment when the sun has reached its zenith on the tenth of Dhu al-Hijjah, consisted only of two *rak'a* with more glorification of Allah than ordinary prayers. Resembling the oldest forms of communal prayer, this 'Id prayer was followed by a sermon, or *khutbah*, after which people rose and greeted each other. A major event of the day was the sacrifice of a sheep, cow, or camel, whose meat was divided among family, friends, neighbors, and the poor.

Festivities. At both 'Id celebrations, each of which in practice lasted three or four days, Muslims wore their best clothes; people visited, congratulated, and gave gifts to each other, especially to children, who often received gifts of money from relatives, friends, and neighbors. People also visited cemeteries, often staying there for many hours, or even spending the whole night there in tents. The annual festivals offered rulers a legitimate way to impress their subjects with their generosity and wealth. Rulers vied with each other to put on lavish displays. The great Muslim geographers compared the virtues of celebrations of various cities and peoples. Ibn Jubayr (1145–1217) and al-Muqaddasi (circa 945–circa 990) described the Ramadan celebrations in Makkah, and others described them in Sicily and Baghdad. Decoration of the city was a common element, with illumination playing a starring role. Ceremonial gates were put up in different quarters, and processions passed through the city gates on the way to the ruler's palace. These parades featured the ruler dressed in carefully selected, beautiful clothing and included other officials, including the military commanders and wazirs (governors or ministers), dressed in livery and costumes according to their rank, station, and position. Bright banners, riding animals wearing ornamental trappings, and spectacles—such as burning-naphtha throwers, acrobats, and other entertainers—accompanied the parade of notables. Medieval reports of the 'Id al-Fitr festival in Baghdad have described that city as decorated like a bride with miles of colored fabric, paper, carpets, and lamps everywhere from the humblest houses or shops to the most splendid palaces. The Tigris was filled with decorated and torch-lit boats, from the ceremonial barges and floats of the khalifah, which might be shaped like animals or mechanized with moving parts, to the less spectacular imitations put afloat by persons of means. People feasted in homes, shops, gardens, and palaces. It was a time of generosity when the wealthy hosted common folk and provided them with food and entertainment, as well as gifts of coins and clothing. Similar spectacles took place on 'Id al-Adha, but the main feature of this celebration was the sacrifice of animals and the distribution of their meat among members of the family and the community.

Pilgrims. Medieval Muslim literature is full of accounts of hajj journeys made by well-known and ordinary individuals, including the pilgrimages of Ibn Battuta and Ibn Jubayr. The arrival of pilgrims at the major caravan departure cities was greeted with processions, food, and merriment, as was the return of the caravans, and the return of pilgrims to their hometowns. Pilgrim camps on the outskirts of the cities had the atmosphere of a long-running celebration. Like moving cities, the great caravans departed with much fanfare, and preparations for them must have provided an enormous annual economic stimulus to local economies. Whenever a khalifah or sultan went on the hajj (pilgrimage), his retinue displayed the wealth of the ruler and the state. A full retinue of servants, aides, and other hangers-on made up a caravan the size of a town. The khalifahs of Baghdad made gifts of money, fresh vegetables, iced drinks in desert towns, and tens or hundreds of thousands of dirhams in cash in and on the way to Makkah. One of the best-known pilgrimages in history was the 1324 journey of the West African Mansa Musa, king of Mali, whose generosity in distributing gold is said to have depressed the price of gold for some time after he left a place.

Hajj Rituals. A series of rituals were performed in and around Makkah during the hajj season. Rituals during vis-

its to Makkah at other times of the year were called 'umrah and made up only part of the hajj rituals. These rites commemorated events in the life of Abraham and his family, were established on the basis of the Qur'an, and were performed according to the precedent set by Prophet Muhammad. The rites began at predetermined points distant from Makkah with men putting on the *ihram*, a white, unsewn two-piece wrap worn with sandals. Women wore ordinary clothing that concealed the body, but their faces and hands had to be left uncovered. The *muhrim*, a person wearing *ihram*, was not allowed to hunt or kill any animal, cut his or her hair or nails, wear perfume, propose or enter a contract of marriage, or have sexual intercourse. Upon arriving in Makkah, the hajji (pilgrim) went directly to the Masjid al-Haram and circumambulated the Ka'bah seven times (a ritual known as *tawaf*), prayed at the station of Abraham, and drank water from the well of Zamzam, which was associated with miraculously slaking the thirst of Hajar and Abraham's son Isma'il. The hajji then performed the sa'yy, walking seven times back and forth between Safa and Marwa, the two hills where Hajar ran desperately searching for water. The hajj continued on the eighth of Dhu al-Hijjah at Mina, a camp five or six kilometers outside Makkah, where the hajji spent the day and night in prayer. After dawn the hajji left for Arafat, an area about twenty kilometers southeast of Makkah, and remained there until sunset on the ninth of Dhu al-Hijja. Called the standing of Arafat, this stop was one of the most important rites of the hajj. Muslims who were not on the hajj traditionally fasted on this day and, like the hajji, spent the day praising Allah, repenting, and asking for forgiveness and guidance. After sunset the hajji left for Muzdalifah, eight or nine kilometers north of Arafat, where he or she stayed the night. After the dawn prayer on the tenth of Dhu al-Hijja, the day of 'Id al-Adha, the hajji left for Mina, stopping at the Jamarat al 'Aqabah, three stone pillars symbolizing Satan. There the hajji threw small pebbles at the pillars to symbolize overcoming evil. At Mina, any time after sunrise, the hajji completed the hajj rites by sacrificing a sheep—or a cow or camel, either of which may be shared among seven people—and distributing its meat in thirds. After cutting his or her hair, the hajji is released from the state of *ihram*. The last act of the pilgrimage was the performance of a farewell *tawaf* around the Ka'bah. It was considered meritorious to repeat the hajj, and some Muslims made the journey to Makkah more than once.

The Significance of the Hajj. As a central ritual of Islam, the hajj played a major role in unifying Muslim society. At a time when most people in the world were oriented toward, and scarcely looked beyond, their home village or city and its environs, acceptance of Islam brought a new and wider orientation. The fifth pillar of Islam, the intention to fulfill the obligation of performing the hajj, is also embodied in the second pillar and in the five daily prayers, which are oriented geographically toward Makkah and the Ka'bah. The concept of all believers facing a single central point on earth was a spiritual departure from the tradition-

وقال لي هل نرى اليوم فني لا نقمر الفوم فني ما ادسنه نم نبصر ودع السوم

A Muslim burial scene; illumination by al-Wasiti from a 1237 manuscript for the *Maqamat*
of al-Hariri (Bibliothèque Nationale, Paris)

ally powerful pull of local orientation and involvement. Through this orientation, even the humblest Muslim, whose possibilities for travel were limited, might dream of performing the hajj and vicariously participate, and find fulfillment in others' pilgrimages to Makkah. In a worldly sense, the obligation of local officials and knowledgeable persons to determine the direction of Makkah for orientation of the masjid involved a significant re-orientation of the community toward the larger world. Village, province, or state officials had the responsibility of ensuring that pilgrims could complete the annual hajj and faced shame should the ways be blocked. A simple peasant might yearn his entire life to make the hajj journey to a destination that was unimaginably far away but palpably and spiritually near. A neighbor, kinsman, or traveler might return from such a pilgrimage to tell about it, returning with a heightened sense of the scope of the Muslim ummah (community) and its diversity. Different foods, manners of dress,

languages, crafts, and technologies spread with this regular traffic of pilgrims. Since the hajj was traditionally combined with scholarly pursuits, returning pilgrims were considered authorities on Islamic practice, reinforcing its unity over the centuries by drawing their knowledge from a single, central source. The annual hajj has never been suspended for more than the briefest of periods because of war or other disruptions.

Social Benefits of the Hajj. Muslim science, technology, trade, arts, and literature all benefited from the mobility of Muslim society set in motion by the institution of the hajj. The hajj created an enduring need to construct roads, to ensure facility of transport, and to perfect navigation from all points of the Muslim state that went beyond the usual establishment of imperial communication and fiscal-collection systems. One of the first uses to which Muslim scientists put their knowledge of geography and astronomy was determining the direction of Makkah and determining the times for prayer and dates for celebrations. This enterprise resulted in advancements in mathematical geography, such as determining the coordinates of cities. Road systems have historically been constructed to meet the need of secular governments and have fallen into disrepair and disuse with the weakening of centralized power. The hajj, however, created an enduring need that required the continued upkeep of roads and ongoing communication among Muslim officials, even as the khilafah broke down into smaller states, maintaining the links among the several centers from which the hajj caravans departed and the lands from which pilgrims originated. Furthermore, after one's first hajj journey, one was allowed to conduct business on one's pilgrimage, thus, the practice of going on hajj contributed to the growth of trade among the various regions of the Muslim world. Because the hajji was on a holy pilgrimage, travel became an activity associated with honor, and travelers were not accorded outsider status, as was the case with travelers in many cultures. Hosting a traveler, especially one on the hajj, was an act of charity that enabled the host to share in the blessings of the traveler's journey. Charitable foundations and donations established drinking places, caravanserais, hostels, and places where travelers were fed. Sponsorship of pilgrims by the wealthy and the powerful was viewed as a way of purifying one's wealth as well as displaying it. Zubaydah, the wife of Khalifah Harun al-Rashid (ruled 786–809), was well known for sponsoring drinking places along the hajj routes.

Weddings. Among the most common Muslim family observances during the Middle Ages, the ones most closely associated with the Sunnah were weddings and celebrating the birth of a child. Weddings in Islam celebrate the conclusion of an agreement between the man and the woman and the joining of their respective families. In pre-Islamic times the search for a partner and marriage process differed widely according to ethnic and regional customs, but within an Islamic context the center of the event was the marriage contract, which required the full, though possibly silent, consent of the bride and gave the couple the right to cohabit and produce legitimate offspring. Preparing the bride and groom for the wedding night included dressing them in traditional finery and regaling them with entertainment and honors. The details of these customs differed widely across the Muslim world between 622 and 1500. Some typical aspects included bringing the bride to her new home; a procession to deliver the household furnishings; various ceremonies to confer fertility, health, and blessings; and even customs that played on the challenges of marital life.

Celebrating a Birth. During the celebration of a birth, which might occur after seven days or multiples thereof, a child's locks were cut, charity was given in its name, and one sheep was slaughtered for a female child or two for a male child. The meat was distributed as part of the parents' obligation, according to their means.

Royal Celebrations. The birth of a child to a ruler's household was celebrated on a grand scale, with processions, gifts, congratulatory audiences, and donations of robes, coins, and sometimes precious scents such as musk and ambergris. During the Abbasids' heyday coins and semiprecious stones were tossed into the crowds. Similarly, the circumcision of a ruler's child might be celebrated grandly. Sometimes orphans and poor boys were circumcised with the son of the ruler, and the lucky children received charitable donations. Rulers' weddings were on a scale corresponding to their means and the tenor of the times, and they also staged elaborate celebrations for events such as a new ruler's inauguration, naming of an heir, or learning the Qur'an. Chroniclers recorded the moneys allocated, perhaps inflating the sums to show the munificence of the ruler, and perhaps to comment subtly on such extravagance. A victorious return from battle sparked an official celebration. Ceremonial arches and gates were constructed; pavilions and bunting were put up; and carpets were spread for the procession. In this sort of celebration, money and other gifts were thrown to people along the route of the procession.

Mawlid un-Nabi. Among regional celebrations, the most important and widespread was Mawlid un-Nabi, which commemorated the birthday of the Prophet Muhammad. It has been said that Muhammad, though he is neither worshiped nor depicted in images (with a few exceptions in courtly illuminated manuscripts not viewed by common people), is nevertheless the most thoroughly imitated human being in history. The Prophet's Sunnah became the definitive model to follow in remembering God in word, deed, and prayer. Second only to the Qur'an, the hadiths were the standard by which a Muslim's behavior and religious knowledge were judged. Many details are known about his life, and many of its major events are well known and dated. Commemoration of his birth spread even though there is no evidence that Muhammad himself celebrated this occasion, which was recorded as having been on a Monday, the twelfth day of the month of Rabi' II. Some evidence suggests that the Prophet's birth may have been commemorated as early as the time of Khayzuran, the mother of Harun al-Rashid, who transformed the humble house in Makkah where Muhammad was born into a place that was frequently visited by pilgrims. Yet, the practice of celebrating the day of his birth at Makkah may not have begun until much later, when it was mentioned by the twelfth-century Andalusian pilgrim Ibn Jubayr. Commemorative processions, special sermons, and recitation of poems in praise of the Prophet developed in Fatimid Cairo, during the eleventh century, especially at the court, and in thirteenth-century Iran. From about that time onward, the practice spread widely among common people, often in connection with the growth of the Sufi orders and the increase in number of common followers. The Ottoman Sultan Murad III introduced the celebration of the Mawlid un-Nabi at his court in 1588. Because celebration of the Mawlid un-Nabi was not sanctioned in the Sunnah, it was controversial. The Egyptian scholar al-Suyuti (1445–1505) wrote a piece discussing its pros and cons from a legal point

The following satirical anecdote about a bragging host and his unfortunate guest offers a good look at the daily life of a merchant in tenth-century Baghdad, including details about the merchant's neighborhood, his house, his relations with his wife and servant, his diet, his furnishings, and even his lavatory. The story is from *Maqamat al-Hamadhani* (The Assemblies of al-Hamadani).

'Isa Ibn Hisham related to us and said: "I was in Basra and with me was Abu'l-Fath al-Iskanderi . . . . We were present with him at a merchant's entertainment and there was placed before us Madirah [meat stew] . . . . When it took its place upon the table and its home in the hearts, Abu'l-Fath al-Iskanderi arose cursing it. . . . We thought he was joking, but. . . . He withdrew from the table and abandoned cooperation with his brethren. So we ordered it to be removed . . . eyes traveled behind it, mouths watered for it, lips were licked for it . . . and hearts followed in its trail. . . . we enquired of him the fact concerning it."

He answered: ". . . While I was in Baghdad a merchant invited me to partake of Madirah and he clung to me with the clinging of a pressing creditor . . . till I accepted his invitation to it, so we started. Now the whole way he was praising his wife . . . saying, 'Sir, if you were to see her with the apron tied round her waist, going about the rooms, from the oven to the cooking-pots, . . . blowing the fire with her mouth, pounding the spices with her hands; and if you were to see the smoke discoloring that beautiful face and affecting that smooth cheek, thou wouldst behold a spectacle at which eyes would be dazed. I love her because she loves me, and it is a mark of a man's good fortune. . . . He bored me with his wife's virtues till we reached his quarter, whereupon he said: 'Sir, do you see this quarter? It is the best quarter in Baghdad. . . . none but merchants live in it. . . . My house is in the middle of its belt of buildings. . . . How much do you think, Sir, was spent upon each house in it? . . . This is my house, how much dost thou reckon I spent on this window? . . . How dost thou find its workmanship and shape? I adjure thee by God. . . . Observe the fine finish of it. Ponder its curves which seem to have been drawn with a compass. Regard the skill of the carpenter in the make of this door. Of how many planks did he make it? Say, How do I know? It is made of teakwood from one piece which was neither worm-eaten nor rotten. When it is moved it creaks, and, when it is struck with the finger, it rings. . . . Now this knocker; dost thou observe it? I bought it in the fancy bazaar from 'Imran, the curiosity dealer, for three Muizzi dinars. How much brass does it contain, Sir? There are in it six pounds. It revolves on a pin in the door. I adjure thee by God, turn it, then sound it and observe it. . . .'

"Then he knocked at the door, we entered the vestibule and he said: 'May God prosper thee, O house! and not destroy thee, O wall! How strong are thy walls . . . and how firm thy foundations! By heavens! observe its staircase, the entrance and the exit, . . . I bought this mat in an auction. . . . If thou hast heard of Abu 'Imran, the mat-weaver. . . . By my life! do not buy mats except at his shop. . . .'

"Let us return to the story of the Madirah for noontide has approached. 'Boy! the basin and the water!' I said 'Great God! perhaps deliverance is nigh, and escape has become easy.' . . . 'Put down the basin and bring the ewer.' The slave put it down and the merchant picked it up, . . . sounded it and said: 'Look at this brass, it seems like a burning brand, or a piece of gold. Its

brass is Syrian and it is of Iraq workmanship. It is not a worn-out curio. It has known and made the round of the palaces of kings; consider its beauty . . . Boy, the ewer!' And he brought it. And the merchant took it up, turned it over and said: 'The spout is of one piece with it. This ewer is fit only for this basin, and this basin is only suitable for this company. . . . Boy! pour the water, for food time is nigh. I adjure thee by God, dost thou see this water? How pure it is! Blue as the eye of the cat, clear as a crystal wand, drawn from the Euphrates, and it is used after standing for the night when it has become like the flame of a torch and translucent as a tear. . . . Nothing proves the purity of the vessel more correctly than the purity of the liquid. Now this napkin . . . is a fabric of Jurjan. . . . I made some of it into a napkin . . . gave it to the embroiderer . . . and preserved it for refined guests . . . .'

"'Boy! The table! . . .' The slave brought the table. The merchant then turned it over sounded it with his fingers, and bit it with his teeth and said: 'May God prosper Baghdad, how excellent are her goods and skilful her artisans! By Heavens! observe this table. . . .'

"Said I: 'This is the make but when is the meal?' . . . Said Abu'l-Fath, 'My spirit boiled,' and I said: 'There remains the baking and its implements, the bread and its properties, the wheat and where the grain was first bought . . . in which mill it was ground and the vessel in which it was kneaded, which oven was heated . . . and there remains the wood and how it was dried . . . Then there are left the baker and his description . . . the flour and its praise, the leaven and its tale, the salt and its savor; and then . . . the dishes and . . . who made them. Then the vinegar, how its grapes were picked . . . how its press was plastered, how the essence was extracted . . . and how much its vat is worth. Then there remain the vegetables and . . . the garden . . . the Madirah and how its meat was bought and its extra fat was got, how its cooking pot was set up, how its fire was kindled, how its spices were pounded, till, finally, it was well-cooked and its gravy became consistent. But this is a mighty matter and a never-ending affair?'

"So I arose. He asked: 'Where do you intend to go?' I replied, 'I intend to go to discharge a need.' He enquired: 'Sir, dost thou want a privy [toilet] that makes the spring quarters of the prince, and the autumn residence of the wazir appear contemptible? Its top has been plastered with gypsum and its bottom with mortar, its roof has been made flat and its floor paved with marble. The ant slips down from its wall and cannot cling, and the fly tries to walk upon its floor but slides. It has a door whose [ventilation slats] are made alternately of teak and ivory and joined together with an excellent joining so that the guest desires to eat in it.' Said I: 'Eat thou from this bag, the privy was not in the reckoning.' And I went out towards the door . . . and began to run. . . . 'Abu'l-Fath! the Madirah! 'And the boys thought Madirah was a title of mine, and took up his cry. So out of excessive vexation I threw a stone at one of them, but a man received it on his turban and it sank into his skull. Therefore I was attacked with sandals . . . then I was placed in prison and remained . . . for two years. So I vowed not to eat Madirah as long as I lived. Now ye men of Hamadhan am I unjust in this?" Said 'Isa ibn Hisham: "So we accepted his excuse, we vowed the same vow and said: 'Long since did Madirah sin against the noble and prefer the base to the good.'"

Source: Badi al-Zaman al-Hamadhani, *The Maqamat of Badi al-Zaman al-Hamadhani*, translated by W. J. Prendergast (London: Curzon Press, 1973), pp. 88–92.

of view and declaring it not necessarily harmful as long as it was celebrated in a restrained manner, without excessive adulation or inappropriate expression.

Ghadir Khumm. The festival known as Ghadir Khumm was celebrated by Shi'i Muslims in commemoration of the eighteenth day of Dhu al-Hijja in 632, which followed the Prophet's farewell pilgrimage to Makkah. The name refers to a pool of water at which Prophet Muhammad gave a speech in praise of his cousin and son-in-law 'Ali ibn Abi Talib (circa 596–661), who had just returned from Yemen. This speech was considered by 'Ali's followers to form the basis of his claim to be the rightful successor of Muhammad and to rule over the Muslim state. According to hadiths that are also related by Sunni Muslims (who interpreted the speech as only a general statement in support of 'Ali's character), the Prophet took 'Ali by the hand and asked his followers whether he, Muhammad, was not closer to the believers than they were to themselves; the crowd is reported to have replied: "It is so, O Apostle of God!" He then stated, "He of whom I am the mawla (patron), of him 'Ali is also the mawla (*man kuntu mawlahu fa 'Ali mawlahu*)." The fact of the speech is not in dispute, but there is more than one version of exactly what the Prophet said and the occasion on which he said it, the ending of the revelation of the Qur'an. After the political and religious split between Sunni and Shi'i Muslims occurred during the late seventh century, writers in those regions where Sunni rulers held sway seemed to avoid reporting the association of the speech with this event, probably because they feared it would lend legitimacy to 'Ali's claim. Shi'is have considered 18 Dhul al-Hijja a day of solemn celebration because of the importance in their eyes of Muhammad's discourse at Ghadir Khum. Its celebration seems to date from the mid-to-late tenth century, when it became one of the most important religious commemorations.

Persian Festivals. Among pre-Islamic celebrations that persisted in the lands that became Islamized between the seventh and sixteenth centuries, Persian festivals were among the most prominent, both because of the influence Persian culture has had in Islam since the Abbasid period and because of Iranian cultural influences over a wide area before Islam. The most important of several pre-Islamic Persian festivals was Nawruz (New Year's Day), the beginning of the Persian solar calendar in the spring. Although it has no foundation in Islam, it was a popular six-day festival that was widely celebrated by people of various faiths, including Muslims, and it is still celebrated in Persian-speaking regions. At the Nawruz festival people poured, splashed, or sprinkled fresh water on themselves and each other for good luck gesture and to purify their homes and wash away the soot of indoor fires. People exchanged gifts, burned illuminations and incense, dyed eggs in various colors, and served fresh foods, including fruits. Another Persian festival celebrated during Abbasid times and later was Mihrjan (meaning "love of the spirit"), which marked the beginning of winter. It had been a traditional time under the Sasanids for collecting land taxes, nominating governors, transfer-

ring posts, minting coins, and performing other acts that required auspicious conditions. The Abbasid governors and khalifahs allowed its celebration and waited in their palaces to receive gifts. People also changed over to winter clothing on this day, a practice said to have been popularized by the courtier Ziryab in Andalusia but quite possibly originating with the Persians. Courtiers and officials who paid their respects to their ruler also received gifts of clothing. Official audiences were held at this time, and the festivities included songs, sporting exhibitions, illuminations, and beating of drums. Mihrjan was also associated with perfumes and certain foods as guarantees against illness. The practice of celebrating Mihrjan spread with the breakup of the Abbasid state, but declined with the dominance of Turkic and Mongol rulers. Earlier these Persian-influenced celebrations had encountered official disapproval from time to time, and survived as festivals without their original religious content. Another old Persian festival was Sadaq (Night of Fires), which took place during the winter. It is reminiscent of yuletide celebrations in Christian Europe (and pre-Christian, Indo-European regions). At Sadaq bonfires were lit, houses fumigated to ward off misfortune, music played, and boats were set afloat with fires and illuminations on board, while people enjoyed themselves through the night.

Cross-Cultural Influences. As in many multicultural societies characterized by a high degree of peaceful co-existence, holiday celebrations in Muslim lands tended to cross religious lines. In Egypt, Sham un-Nasim, which is associated both with the coming of the spring season and with the Christian Easter celebration, also included elements that seem to have been traditional in pre-Islamic Egypt. Similarly, a practice that may be from pharaonic times was absorbed into Ramadan as a lantern procession of children singing about the coming of the holy month of Ramadan. Among the common people eager for a diversion, and sometimes among the courtly classes, who seldom missed an opportunity for celebration and display, any festive occasion was reason enough for festive food, entertainment, and outdoor spectacles. Such practices were discouraged by many rulers, jurists, and other religious leaders, but sometimes with little effect.

Funerals. Rituals surrounding the death of a Muslim were most often carried out according to Islamic precedent, displaying considerable unity of practice across time and space. The Sunnah encouraged the dying person to recite the testimony of faith and to turn his or her face toward Makkah. As it was not acceptable in Islam to postpone the burial unless it was night, preparation of the body was simple and prompt. Except for martyrs who fell in battle, a corpse was in most cases washed by a person of the same sex, who poured on water in a specific order similar to the ritual washing for prayer. Camphor, or other herbs, was added to the water. The eyes and mouth were closed, and a woman's hair was plaited in three braids. The grave clothes, or winding sheet, put on the corpse were usually white in color and of simple construction and material. For rulers and the wealthy, richer and more elaborate materials were sometimes used. Some Muslims reserved their hajj garments for use as shrouds, underlining the significance of the hajj as an analogy for the believers' appearance before God on the Last Day. The body was carried on an open bier covered by a cloth and taken quickly to the place of burial. To avoid lamentation that would add to the suffering of the dead person, in early Islam women did not customarily accompany the corpse to the grave site. It was customary to stand as a funeral passed, to walk in the procession, and to help carry the bier, which was brought to a masjid and placed in front of the first row of worshipers. They stood during the funeral prayer, as the imam stood by the head of a man or by the side of a woman. Prayers were also said at the grave site. Graves were dug so that the corpse could be oriented on its right side, facing Makkah, and only one body was placed in each grave. The grave was dug as a narrow trench with a niche or roof of stones to allow the body to sit up when questioned by the angels. Relatives went into the grave to loosen the shroud and position the body with its face toward Makkah. No grave goods were supposed to be placed with the body, but in some outlying regions people followed pre-Islamic customs and placed simple possessions of the dead person in the grave. The grave was covered with earth, sometimes with a slight mound. The earliest Muslim graves were unmarked, but grave markers were gradually introduced, and marked and inscribed headstones became widespread after the first few centuries of Islam. Coffins, mausoleums, and tombs with raised burial chambers became more common after the twelfth or thirteenth century, and about the same time women began to take more prominent roles in funerals, including as professional mourners. After the burial, family members received condolences and held Qur'an readings for the deceased. With the help of neighbors and relatives, the family hosted a funeral meal and in some areas made gifts of food to the poor. It was the custom in some places, especially in Persian-influenced regions, to commemorate the death forty days after the funeral. Other customs varied from place to place. If they were modified by Islamic norms, they changed gradually. After the deaths of parents or children, Muslims remembered and honored them often, making regular supplications on their behalf. It was

permissible for the heirs to fast on days when the deceased had intended to do so, and as an act of piety, if the person had been unable to perform the hajj in his or her lifetime, to use funds from the inheritance to make the pilgrimage on the deceased's behalf. The Sunnah outlined limits on mourners, prescribing that the period of mourning and withdrawal from normal life should not exceed three days for anyone except a wife, whose mourning period, or 'iddat, should last four months and ten days. During that time, a widow should abstain from wearing dyed clothing, kohl, or perfume, and not entertain proposals of marriage. According to a hadith collected by al-Bukhari:

> We were forbidden to mourn for more than three days for a dead person, except for a husband, for whom a wife should mourn for four months and ten days. [While in the mourning period] we were not allowed to put kohl in our eyes, nor perfume ourselves, nor wear dyed clothes, except a garment of 'Asb [special clothes made in Yemen]. But it was permissible for us that when one of us became clean from her menses and took a bath, she could use a piece of a certain kind of incense. And it was forbidden for us to follow funeral processions" (7: 254).

The color of mourning clothes was black in some regions and white in others. In practice, local and pre-Islamic traditions and customs made the mourning period and its outward expressions differ from place to place. An eleventh-century Andalusian poem by al-Kalif al-Husri Kairouan (died 1095) provides an eloquent comment on the color of mourning worn there: "If white is the color of mourning in Andalusia, that is only just. Don't you see that I have put on the white of old age out of mourning for my youth?"

Sources:
Muhammad M. Ahsan, *Social Life Under the Abbasids* (London & New York: Longman, 1979).

James Bellamy and Patricia Owen Steiner, trans., *The Banners of the Champions: An Anthology of Medieval Arabic Poetry from Andalusia and Beyond* (Madison: Hispanic Seminary of Medieval Studies, 1989).

Timothy Insoll, *The Archaeology of Islam* (Oxford: Blackwell, 1999).

J. Knappert, "Mawlid," in *Encyclopedia of Islam*, CD-ROM version (Leiden: Brill, 1999).

Ian Richard Netton, *Seek Knowledge: Thought and Travel in the House of Islam* (Surrey, U.K.: Curzon Press, 1996).

F. E. Peters, *The Hajj: The Muslim Pilgrimage to Mecca and the Holy Places* (Princeton: Princeton University Press, 1994).

SIGNIFICANT PEOPLE

ABU HURAYRAH

DIED 678
COMPANION OF THE PROPHET

Father of the Kitten. Abu Hurayrah al-Dawsi al-Yamani was one of the best known Companions of the Prophet Muhammad and a narrator of hadiths. It is said that he was given the name Abu Hurayrah (Father of the Kitten) because he had a kitten and used to play with it while herding people's goats for a living.

Late Convert. Abu Hurayrah was among the converts to Islam who arrived in Madinah around 629, the seventh year after the migration, and after that he associated closely with Muhammad. He was one of the poor people known as the Ahl al-Suffa, who inhabited the platform in the Prophet's masjid and depended on charity.

Hadith Narrator. Although he arrived at Madinah only about four years before the Prophet's death, he is best known as a narrator of hadiths about the Prophet's daily life and other affairs. More than 3,500 of these traditions are attributed to him, and eight hundred different hadith collectors received traditions from him. According to Ibn Saad (784–845), the well-known biographer of the Sahabah (Companions of the Prophet) and the Tabiun (the second generation after the original Companions), Abu Hurayrah passed on more traditions than other Companions—including Aisha, the Prophet's young wife—because he occupied himself only with remembering the words and deeds of the Prophet, while others had different priorities and pursued other activities. The story is also told that Abu Hurayrah's memory was blessed by the Prophet. Some of the hadiths attributed to Abu Hurayrah were not transmitted by him and are thus not authentic; because of his reputation for reliability, others sought to lend credence to nongenuine traditions by attaching them to his. The careful process of winnowing his traditions by analyzing their content and chain of transmission still resulted in many authentic ones appearing in the authoritative collections of al-Bukhari and Muslim. The traditions passed on by Abu Hurayrah are an important source of information about the daily life of the Prophet and his Arab contemporaries.

Source:
"Abu Hurayrah," in *The Alim for Windows, Multimedia Edition,* Release 4.5 (Baltimore: ISL Software, 1996).

Schottenius, "De underjordiska källorna," in *På jorden: 1960–1990,* volume 4 of *Nordisk kvinnolitteraturhistoria,* edited by Unni Langås (Höganäs: Wiken, 1997), pp. 412–419.

MUHAMMAD IBN ISMAIL AL-BUKHARI

810-870
HADITH COLLECTOR

Traveling Scholar. Muhammad ibn Ismail al-Bukhari is one of the best-known compilers of hadiths, or traditions, of the words and deeds of the Prophet Muhammad. He began to memorize hadiths at the age of ten. He had an excellent memory and traveled widely—from Central Asia to Egypt—in search of people from whom he could learn traditions. This extensive research made him able to correct the oral and written hadith collections of his contemporaries by winnowing out less-reliable and unreliable traditions by checking the veracity of the *isnad,* or links, of the transmitters back to the Prophet himself.

Collecting Hadiths. Al-Bukhari went on to compile one of the most authoritative collections, applying the same standards and categorizing hadiths according to their reliability. For his best-known work, *Sahih al-Bukhari,* he selected 7,397 hadiths that he judged to have complete and reliable isnad, from a body of some 600,000 purported hadiths then in circulation. He stated that before he added each hadith to his collection, he first performed the wudu' (ritual Islamic washing) and prayed. *Sahih al-Bukhari* is divided into 97 books with 3,450 chapters classified according to subject matter. While al-Bukhari was a well-respected scholar during his lifetime, it was not until a century or so after his death that the *Sahih al-Bukhari* took its place at the head of hadith collections in the Sunni tradition. Along with the *Sahih Muslim,* it continues to enjoy that respect. Al-Bukhari also wrote biographies of the hadith transmitters.

Sources:

Muhammad Asad, *Sahih al-Bukhari: The Early Years of Islam* (Gibraltar: Dar al-Andalus, 1981).

J. Robson, "al-Bukhari" and "Hadith," in *Encyclopedia of Islam,* CD-ROM version (Leiden: Brill, 1999).

AHMAD BADI AL-ZAMAN AL-HAMADHANI

968-1008

MAQAMAT WRITER

Prodigy. Ahmad Badi al-Zaman al-Hamadhani, whose middle name (Badi al-Zaman) means the Prodigy of the Age, was an Arabo-Persian writer born at Hamadan in 968. He began his early studies in Hamadan and soon showed an exceptional talent in Arabic and Persian language, as well as an excellent memory. At about twenty-two years of age, he settled at Rayy, where the atmosphere was suited to an ambitious writer, and received the patronage of the Buyid wazir. As was fashionable at the time, he may also have mingled with the local association of beggars and with the poet Abu Dulaf, who also enjoyed "slumming" with the local low life. While still in his early twenties al-Hamadhani lived in Nishapur and Jurjan, both famous Iranian intellectual centers, and made some important connections. As al-Hamadhani gained renown as a writer, he began traveling in intellectual court circles, reaching the status of favorite panegyrist, or poet of praise, at the court of Amir Salaf, and he also joined the court of Mahmud of Ghazna in that role. In 1008, at the age of just forty, al-Hamadhani died at Herat.

Maqamat. Al-Hamadhani gained a reputation as a poet and letter writer, but he is most often remembered as the creator of a distinctive genre in Arabic language, the *Maqamat* (Assemblies). Maqamat are short anecdotes or sketches composed in prose and poetry to show off the writer's style. Beginning about 990, and continuing for many years, he wrote more than four hundred maqamat, from which fifty-two have survived. Maqamat are a rich source of social history, describing middle-class and common people, as well as intellectuals. They are often satirical and feature the exploits of picaresque figures, including low-life types, but some were also written in praise of patrons. Al-Hamadhani laid the groundwork for this genre, to which subsequent Arabic writers have contributed for nearly a thousand years.

Source:

R. Blanchere, "al-Hamadhani," in *Encyclopedia of Islam,* CD-ROM version (Leiden: Brill, 1999).

IBN KHALLIKAN

1211-1284

JURIST AND WRITER

Biographer. Ibn Khallikan was the author of one of the best-known Arabic biographical dictionaries, an important source of information on notable Muslims who are not mentioned in other collections. The book also includes much interesting information about Muslim life during the medieval period.

Early Life. Ibn Khallikan was born in 1211 to a prominent family in Irbil, Iraq. His father was a teacher at the local college, where Ibn Khallikan's studies began, and he traveled during the course of his education to Mosul, Aleppo, and Damascus. He made the acquaintance of several important Muslim historians, including Ibn al-Athir, and served for several years as deputy to the head judge of Egypt.

Career. In 1261 the Mamluk sultan Baybars appointed Ibn Khallikan the head judge of Damascus, where he administered justice over the whole of Syria. He lost this post in 1266 during a reorganization of the office but was called back by Baybars's successor and received with great honor, only to be dismissed again during a revolt, recalled again, and dismissed for a third time. Despite his political ups and downs, Ibn Khallikan gained a reputation as a just man who was knowledgeable about the law. In his writings, he displayed a sharp mind and acute observation of character. As a sociable and witty personality, he was well suited to collecting information on well-known people in Islamic history. His biographical dictionary, *Waf ayat al-a'yan wa anba' abna' al-zaman*, is arranged alphabetically. It omits the Sahabah (Companions of the Prophet), the hadith transmitters, and the khalifahs—all of whom were covered elsewhere—and included scientists, philosophers, and other figures of the past, as well as some of his own contemporaries. His information is considered invaluable, because he relied on sources that have been lost or not published and included people who are not mentioned elsewhere in other biographical dictionaries. He began his book in 1256 at Cairo and completed there in 1274, after much editing and re-arranging. He died at Damascus in 1284.

Sources:

J. W. Fuch, "Ibn Khallikan," in *Encyclopedia of Islam,* CD-ROM version (Leiden: Brill, 1999).

Ibn Khallikan, *Biographical Dictionary,* 4 volumes, translated by Bn Mac Guckin de Slane (Paris: Oriental Translation Fund of Great Britain and Ireland, 1843–1871).

ANAS IBN MALIK

DIED CIRCA 700
COMPANION OF THE PROPHET

Servant to the Prophet. With Aisha and Abu Huraira, Anas Ibn Malik was one of the most prolific transmitters of hadiths. When Anas was ten, his mother placed him in the care of the Prophet Muhammad as a servant. At Madinah he lived in close proximity to the Prophet and later passed on to historians much information about daily life in Muhammad's household, including details such as the household implements and furnishings he had, the clothing he wore, and the food he ate. Anas was present at the Battle of Badr in 624, but, because of his young age, he took no part in the combat. He remained in Muhammad's service until the Prophet's death in 632.

Later Life. Anas Ibn Malik later served in the military during the expansion of Islam. He became imam at Basrah, Iraq, a center of hadith transmission, and was involved to some extent in the First Fitna, or civil war (656–661). He died at Basrah around the year of 700, when he was perhaps more than one hundred years old. Since he was close to the Prophet Muhammad and then lived for many years in Basrah, where scholars were actively recording and collecting hadiths, it is natural that many of the traditions Anas related were preserved and passed on. It is also understandable that false traditions were attributed to one so respected as an authority. Hadiths passed on by Anas appear in many hadith collections. Al-Bukhari and Muslim recorded 278 traditions attributed to Anas, and 128 of them appear in both collections; 80 other were recorded only by al-Bukhari, and 70 more only by Muslim.

Source:
"Anas Ibn Malik," in *The Alim for Windows, Multimedia Edition*, Release 4.5 (Baltimore: ISL Software, 1996).

JUHA

EIGHTH CENTURY
COMIC FIGURE

Biographical Data. Juha is a popular comic hero, found under various names—including Goha and Abu Nuwas—in the jokes of North Africa, Southwest Asia, East Africa, and Iran. Over the centuries, well-known scholars have debated whether he really lived and when. Several early works mention him as a member of the tribe of Banu Fazara and a resident of al-Kufah in Iraq. He is said to have lived a hundred years, to have been connected with some well-known people of the eighth century, and to have died during the reign of Khalifah al-Mansur (754–775). The earliest reference to him is from the early ninth century in

the essays of al-Jahiz, who mentioned him among other people known for their follies.

Comic Character. Juha appeared as the central figure in a collection of anecdotes called *Kitab Nawadir Djuha*, which is mentioned in the tenth-century literary encyclopedia of Ibn Nadim. By that time, Juha had come to represent a Charlie Chaplin–like figure who constantly blunders and gets involved in futile schemes but comes up with witty retorts that expose other people's vanity, gullibility, and stupidity. His proverbial silliness often includes nuggets of wisdom and compassion for the human condition. Later authors, including the well-known historian al-Suyuti (1445–1505), thought Juha was an invented personage, and he lovingly said, "No one should laugh at him on hearing of the amusing stories told against him; on the contrary it is fitting that everyone should ask God to give him profit from the blessings of Juha." In fact, Juha's self-sacrifice for the sake of laughter is considered laudable. Modern authors have concentrated on cataloguing the several hundred anecdotes about him and believe they can trace back a core group of more than one hundred original stories to the spread of the Arabic language and Islam in the period 632–656. Local lore was added to the original body of stories over the centuries, and in modern times books, television, and motion pictures have spread Juha's fame throughout the Muslim world.

Source:
C. Pellat, "Djuha," in *Encyclopedia of Islam*, CD-ROM version (Leiden: Brill, 1999).

NASR AL-DIN KHOJA

THIRTEENTH-FOURTEENTH CENTURY
COMIC FIGURE

Biographical Data. Nasr al-Din Khoja (Nasreddin Hoca in modern Turkish) is the best-known humorous character in Turkish-Islamic culture from the Balkans to Central Asia. Like the Arabic jester Juha, Nasr al-Din Khoja was a legendary figure whose historical existence is unprovable. He is supposed to have been active around the thirteenth and fourteenth centuries, perhaps in Persia.

Comic Figure. Early manuscripts of the adventures of Nasr al-Din Khoja include more than one hundred anecdotes, and by modern times around four hundred had been collected from oral and written sources. Like Juha, whom Egyptians melded with Nasr al-Din into one jokester hero, Nasr al-Din Khoja has various names, including Mulla Nasr al-Din (in Persian), Ependi or Apandi, Efendi (giving rise to the Chinese word A-fan-t'i for trickster), and Nastradin (in Greek, Albanian, Serbian, and Croatian). Modern scholarship has shown that tales attributed to Nasr al-Din in the later Islamic tradition may be traced back to the fund of Juha tales that can be reconstructed from early Arabic literature. As this base of tales was augmented, a distinctive character evolved, taking on the dialects, dress, and social contexts of a changing society and its ethnic and linguistic makeup. Juha/Nasr al-Din is a donkey-riding, good-natured member of the vaguely learned class, who mingles Islamic values and folk wisdom. Sometimes rural and sometimes urban, he has attributes of both the poor and the middle classes. Pious humor and sharply off-color jokes have been attached to him. He is a kind of flexible Everyman, underdog, and hero, both learned and stupid, who provides a mirror of everyday life and the concerns of ordinary people.

Source:
U. Marzolph, "Nasr al-Din Khoja," *Encyclopedia of Islam*, CD-ROM version (Leiden: Brill, 1999).

MUSLIM ABU AL-HUSAYN MUSLIM

CIRCA 821 – 875

HADITH COLLECTOR

Traveling Scholar. Muslim Abu al-Husayn Muslim was one of the most important early traditionists, or compilers of hadiths. His best known work is *al-Jami al-Sahih*, which stands with the *Sahih al-Bukhari* as one of the two most authoritative collections. In fact, some scholars consider Muslim's work the most reliable collection. Like al-Bukhari, Muslim began gathering hadiths at an early age and traveled widely in Iraq, Syria, the Hijaz, and Egypt in order to hear traditions from the masters. In compiling and carefully sifting a body of 300,000 alleged hadiths, he followed the meticulous method of checking the veracity of the *isnad*, or links reaching back to the Prophet Muhammad. Muslim's collection comprises approximately 3,000 hadiths, not counting variant versions. Modern historians find his collection to be the most useful of the six authoritative collections because texts concerning aspects of Islamic legal concepts are clustered together and not repeated in various chapters and because his method of organization allows historians to trace and analyze traditions.

Sources:
J. Robson, "Hadith," in *Encyclopedia of Islam*, CD-ROM version (Leiden: Brill, 1999).

Abdul Hamid Siddiqi, trans., *Sahih Muslim*, 4 volumes (Lahore: Sh. Muhammad Ashraf, 1980).

DOCUMENTARY SOURCES

Muhammad Ibn Sa'd al-Basri (born circa 790), *Kitab al-Tabaqat al-Kabir* (Great Book of the Generations)— A collection of biographical notices on the narrators of hadiths (traditions of the Prophet Muhammad) written by a native of Basrah, an early center of scholarship on hadith transmission, history, and Arabic language; Ibn Sa'd's biographical entries on the first and second generations of hadith transmitters provide valuable information on daily life and the peoples of the time.

Abu Abd Allah Muhammad Ibn Battuta (1304–circa 1378), *Rihlah* (Travels)—A travel account by a native of Tangier, who between 1325 and 1356 traversed nearly all the major Muslim trade and pilgrimage routes in Asia and Africa, visiting towns and cities, using many different modes of transportation, and seeing ordinary people, heads of state, jurists, and merchants from many of the Muslim cultures and ethnic groups; a valuable source for social historians, his account includes details about foods, dress, housing, transport, governance, customs, and geography.

Ibn Jubayr (1145–1217), *Rihlah* (Travels)—An account of an extended pilgrimage journey to Makkah, Egypt, the eastern Mediterranean, and Iraq during the time of the well-known Muslim leader Salah al-Din (Saladin, ruled 1169–1193) and the European Crusades; Ibn Jubayr was an excellent observer who recorded many significant details of daily life, and his descriptions of Baghdad and the Hijaz (the sacred environs of Makkah and Madinah) are rich in detail.

Abu Uthman al-Jahiz (circa 776–869), *Kitab al-Bayan wal-Tabyin* (Elegance of Expression and Clarity of Exposition)—A work that describes costume and habits of dress during the Abbasid period.

Al-Jahiz (circa 776–869), *Kitab al-Bukhala'* (Book of Misers)—A work filled with details about cooking, clothing, and household goods among various classes during the Abbasid period.

Al-Jahiz (circa 776–869), *Kitab al-Hayawan* (Book of Animals)—A work describing hunting and the various animals Muslims kept for pleasure, work, and sport during the Abbasid period.

Al-Khatib al-Baghdadi (died 1091), *Tarikh Baghdad* (History of Baghdad)—One of the most important descriptions of the construction and development of Baghdad, written as an introduction to a biographical dictionary of prominent residents of the city; because little or no archaeological work has been done on the medieval city, which was destroyed by the Mongols in 1258, historians consider *Tarikh Baghdad* an important source, which is especially valuable because the chains of authority cited by the author can be verified in other sources.

Abd al-Rahman ibn Nasr ibn Abdullah al-Shayzari (died circa 1193), *Nihayat al-Rutba fi Talab al-Hisba* (The Utmost Authority in Pursuit of the Duty to Promote Good and Forbid Evil)—One of several medieval guidebooks for the Muslim *muhtasib* (market inspector), which include details about crafts, professions, buying and selling everything from bread and water to metal and leather goods and medical services; the author of *Nihayat al-Rutba fi Talab al-Hisba* was probably of Syrian origin but active in Egypt.

Brass and silver-inlaid canteen made in Syria by a Muslim craftsman for sale to a Christian visitor to the Holy Land during the thirteenth century (Freer Gallery of Art, The National Museum of Islamic Art, Smithsonian Institution, Washington, D.C.)

C H A P T E R   E I G H T

THE FAMILY AND SOCIAL TRENDS

by JUDITH TUCKER

CONTENTS

CHRONOLOGY
294

OVERVIEW
296

TOPICS IN THE FAMILY AND SOCIAL TRENDS

Child-Rearing Methods. 297
The Story of Moses. 299
Education 302

*Elegy for a Scholarly
    Daughter*. 303
Marriage. 307
Divorce Records 308
Sexuality 312
Social Roles and
    Responsibilities 315

SIGNIFICANT PEOPLE

'A'isha bint Abi Bakr. 319
Ahmad ibn
    'Abd al-Rahim 319

'Aish'a bint Muhammad ibn
    'Abd al-Hadi 320

DOCUMENTARY SOURCES
321

Sidebars and tables are listed in italics.

622
- After a period of persecution in Makkah, the Prophet Muhammad and his followers make their *Hijrah* (migration) to the city of Madinah, marking the birth of the new religion of Islam and the starting point of the official Muslim calendar.

622-950
- During the expansion and consolidation of the Muslim empire, the Qur'an (God's revelations to Muhammad) and the hadiths (accounts of Muhammad's own words and deeds) are recorded in written form.
- Muslim scholars focus on Islamic theology and law, which have major implications for family and social life in the Muslim community. The many religious texts authenticated during this period later serve as a touchstone for thinkers and interpreters of the meaning of Islam for social life.

632
- By the death of Muhammad, the Arabian peninsula has been won to the cause of Islam.

632-661
- The Muslim community is under the rule of the Four "Rightly Guided" Khalifahs (caliphs), all of whom have been Companions of the Prophet.
- During this period, Muslim military conquest is rapid and far-reaching, as Arab armies had integrated most of the Middle East and North Africa into the Muslim khilafah (caliphate) in fewer than thirty years.

661
- The center of power shifts from Madinah to Damascus under the Umayyad dynasty, which continues territorial expansion, consolidating an empire that reaches from the Iberian peninsula (Spain) in the West to the Indus Valley of India in the East.

750
- The Umayyad dynasty is replaced by the Abbasids, who established their capital at Baghdad in present-day Iraq.

750-950
- During the Abbasid period the majority of the population of the Middle East converts to Islam, and a flourishing court culture emerges.

950-1258
- The beginning of Turkish tribal incursions into the Middle East inaugurates a period of political change during which the Abbasid khilafah becomes fragmented and Turkic states are established in India (the Ghaznavids) and in Persia and Anatolia (the Saljuks).

* DENOTES CIRCA DATE

950-1258
(CONT'D)

- The new Turkish political elite pays particular attention to the demands of rule, and many intellectuals examine issues of statecraft. The result is a rapid institutionalization of administration in areas including tax collection and education. Under the patronage of the Turkish dynasties, the arts and sciences flower as rulers commission monuments, poems, and histories that celebrate and help to legitimize their reigns.

1211

- The Sultanate of Delhi, the first Indian Muslim state, is founded in northern India.

1250

- The Mamluks, Turco-Circassians brought to Egypt as slaves to serve in the military, found a dynasty in Egypt.

1258

- As Mongol invasions sweep the region, Baghdad falls to the Mongols, signaling the official end of the long-ailing Abbasid dynasty.

1258-1300*

- After an initial period of rapid military successes, the Mongols consolidate their power primarily in Persia, ruling as the Ilkhanid dynasty, which gradually adopts Persian culture and by 1295 officially converts to Islam.

- In other parts of the former Muslim khilafah, states come under the rule of Turkish elites. Family and social life under Islam develop differently in various areas of the region as Arab, Turkish, and Mongol cultural traditions interacted with the ongoing high culture of the Islamic learned elite (ulama').

1299*

- The Ottoman dynasty is founded in Anatolia.

1370*

- Timur (Tamerlane), a Muslim Turkic leader, rises to power in Transoxania.

1453

- Constantinople is captured by Ottoman Turks, marking the fall of the Byzantine Empire.

1500*

- Muslim regions stand on the threshold of renewed political centralization as the Ottomans are vigorously expanding their territory in the West, and the Safawids emerge as the uncontested rulers of Persia. These two empires come to dominate much of the Muslim world.

* DENOTES CIRCA DATE

OVERVIEW

Diversity. During the long period between 622 and 1500, over a territory that extended from Spain to India, Muslim family and social life—including marriage, sexual customs, child rearing, education, and social roles and responsibilities—developed in many ways. There were a large number of changes not only in political structures but also in the ways of life of people in urban areas, the countryside, and the desert regions. Townsfolk, peasants, and nomads had different sources of livelihood, and their access to legal, educational, and social institutions varied enormously. Much of the information about this period comes from the records and observations of urbanites, and scholars do not presume that rural and nomadic peoples necessarily lived the same way. In addition, the various classes had different lifestyles. The world of the official and intellectual elites stood in stark contrast to that of the urban poor or the rural peasantry. Variations produced by geography and class were further heightened by diverse cultural influences. As Arabs, Persians, Turks, and Mongols—among others—left their imprints on social mores, people's values and ideals changed.

Unity. At the core of understanding Muslim social life in this period stand the precepts of Islam. With the Qur'an as the bedrock of Islamic scripture, Muslim intellectuals labored over the years to interpret Islamic texts in order to guide Muslims in their daily lives. Any study of Muslim social life between 622 and 1500 must focus in large measure on how the principles and precepts of Islam were understood and put into practice over time. In part, this process was an interaction of Islamic practices with preexisting cultural traditions such as those of the Byzantines and the Sasanids, as well as with later influences from the Turks and the Mongols. Many individuals shaped the social history of Muslim communities as well. It was not only the ulama' (Muslim intellectuals) who decided what constituted an "Islamic" way of life but also ruling elites, whose edicts and examples influenced others' lifestyles. The common people as well helped to shape Islamic history by adapting the precepts of Islam to their immediate and varied conditions.

The Family. In discussing Muslim family and social life, the question of gender often emerges as a central concern. Family life and social trends were dramatically affected by the society's view of the male and the female: the characteristics, rights, and responsibilities of people were all highly "gendered" in the sense that being male or female determined one's identity and social roles more than any other single factor. Islamic doctrine and law emphasized the complementarity rather than the similarity of the male and female, and men and women were assigned quite different rights and duties. Distinctions between males and females were sustained and elaborated in marriage, sexual mores, methods of child rearing, the educational system, and the organization of public life. Over the many years between 622 and 1500, however, these distinctions were modified in many ways, and in some cases the boundaries between male and female even disappeared.

TOPICS IN THE FAMILY AND SOCIAL TRENDS

CHILD-REARING METHODS

Procreation. Although sexual activity was not necessarily linked to procreation—as it was in the medieval Christian tradition—children were often an outcome. The Qur'an says that children come by God's will: "The kingdom of the heavens and the earth belongs to God. He creates what He pleases, for some He grants females, for some He grants males, for some He grants males and females, and some He makes childless. He is Wise and Capable" (49: 50). It also says that all children should be welcomed, explicitly condemning the pre-Islamic practice of female infanticide and asking for what crime the infant girl should be killed. Despite such Qur'anic positions, Muslim religious thinkers in the medieval period had to remind people that male and female children should be equally valued. In a critique of what was no doubt customary behavior, al-Ghazali (1058–1111) called on men not to make a great show of joy at the birth of a son or to express sadness at the birth of a daughter, for "there is no way of knowing who will prove to be good." Both religious and medical scholars of the period understood that, through sexual intercourse, mother and father contributed equally to the making of a child. These scholars believed that the developing fetus was bestowed with a soul at the end of the fourth month of gestation, at which point it became a human person. After 120 days of gestation, they concluded, abortion was no longer permitted, and a miscarried fetus should be properly buried. A fetus acquired full rights as a person (such as inheritance rights), however, only after birth. A baby who died at birth must have breathed or moved in order to qualify for its inheritance (which in the case of its death belonged to its heirs).

Infancy. The infant lived in a perilous world. Although there is no data on infant mortality for this period, historians assume that it was extremely high by modern standards, probably peaking in the fourteenth century when the region was swept by epidemics of plague, which took their highest toll among children. Medical and religious authorities devoted considerable thought to the care of infants, and both medical and legal treatises emphasized the special needs and vulnerabilities of infants and children. Care of the infant focused on the basic issue of nutrition.

Breast Feeding. The importance of breast feeding to the health and survival of a baby was clearly understood and discussed as a right of the child. Medical literature of the time preferred that the mother nurse her own child for a period of approximately two years if she were able to do so. Both medical and legal thinkers encouraged couples to avoid the risk of pregnancy during this period so that the baby could enjoy a full and uninterrupted period of nursing. Islamic legal scholars held, however, that a mother could not be coerced into breast feeding her baby: she must have some choice in the matter. But if the baby's mother was not breast feeding—whether through inability or choice—then the baby's father was responsible for securing the services of a wet nurse; animal milk and other foods were not recommended for an infant. If the father could not find or afford a suitable wet nurse, however, the mother did have an absolute responsibility to nurse her child. There was much discussion, both medical and legal, about the qualifications for a wet nurse, suggesting that wet nursing was part of the culture, at least in more-affluent urban circles. It seems to have been a common practice in the towns of the Arabian peninsula at the time of the rise of Islam, when town dwellers thought that putting an infant out to nurse with the desert tribes was a healthy practice. Early biographers of the Prophet Muhammad say that he was sent to a wet nurse named Halima. 'Abd al-Malik Ibn Hisham included her account of how she acquired Muhammad as a nursling:

> So I went and took him for the sole reason that I could not find anyone else. I took him back to my baggage, and as soon as I put him in my bosom, my breasts overflowed with milk which he drank until he was satisfied, as also did his foster-brother. Then both of them slept, whereas before this we could not sleep with him. My husband got up and went to the old she-camel and lo, her udders were full; he milked it and I drank of her milk until we were completely satisfied, and we passed a happy night. In the morning my husband said: "Do you know Halima, you have taken a blessed creature?" I said, "By God, I hope so." . . . We ceased not to recognize this bounty as coming from God for a period of two years when I weaned him.

Muhammad maintained a close relationship with Halima throughout the rest of his life, referring to her as his mother

A man hurrying home for the birth of his son; illumination by al-Wasiti from a 1237 Baghdad manuscript for the *Maqamat* (Assemblies) of al-Hariri (Bibliothèque Nationale, Paris)

and weeping at the news of her death. The ties established by wet nursing were the equivalent of a blood relationship—milk brothers and sisters, for example, were considered siblings and therefore not eligible to be marriage partners. The well-being of the infant was paramount in the discussion of breast feeding. The Qur'an 2: 233 states:

> Mothers shall suckle their children for two whole years; (that is) for those who wish to complete the suckling. The duty of feeding and clothing nursing mothers in a seemly manner is upon the father of the child. No one should be charged beyond his capacity. A mother should not be made to suffer because of her child, nor should he to whom the child is born (be made to suffer) because of his child. And on the (father's) heir is incumbent the like of that (which was incumbent on the father). If they desire to wean the child by mutual consent and (after) consultation, it is no sin for them; and if ye wish to give your children out to nurse, it is no sin for you, provided that ye pay what is due from you in kindness. Observe your duty to Allah, and know that Allah is Seer of what ye do.

Parents were advised to give an infant only breast milk until the first teeth appeared at about seven months. Then the infant could be gradually introduced to supplemental solid food. Full weaning should not occur until the age of two or so, and then it should be done slowly and cautiously to preserve the health of the child, preferably in the fall when the cooler weather would stimulate the child's appetite. Many mothers probably nursed their children longer than the recommended two years, for there is ample evidence of children who were nursed at least partially until they were four or five.

Nurturing. Pediatric medical treatises also included other information on the care of the young child. Parents were instructed on bathing and swaddling a baby, on the best kinds of beds, on comforting a crying baby, on the importance of association with other children, and even on the benefits of introducing infants to music and dancing. Throughout this literature there is a clear sense that infants and children have bodies and minds that are different from those of adults. The authors were interested in the stages of infancy and discussed such issues as the use of baby walkers for the child who is ready to take steps and the encouragement of first attempts at speech. They were also aware of the pathology of childhood: one such text had fifteen chapters on childhood diseases and their treatments. Mothers were presumed to be not only the safest feeders but also the best caretakers for their own infants. If a man died or divorced his wife, she retained the right to keep her infant, in accordance with a hadith reporting the ruling of the Prophet in such a case:

> If a separation takes place between a husband and a wife who are possessed of an infant child, the right of nursing and keeping it rests with the mother, because it is recorded that a woman once applied to the Prophet; saying "O Prophet of God! this is my son, the fruit of my womb, cherished in my breast, and his father is desirous of taking him away from me into his own care" to which the Prophet replied, "thou hast a right in the child prior to that of thy husband as long as thou dost not marry with a stranger."

A divorced or widowed woman thus had the right to keep her infant with her unless she subsequently married a man who was a "stranger," that is, someone not related to the child. In that case, she could lose custody of the infant.

Weaning and Childhood. After infants were weaned (and presumably toilet trained) at approximately the age of two, they would usually remain with their parents during childhood. The common practice in medieval Europe of sending a child out to be fostered in another family as part of a period of training or apprenticeship does not seem to have been prevalent among Muslims. On the contrary, religious and legal thought assumed that children would be raised within their families of birth. In the patrilineal society of this period, children ultimately "belonged" to their father's family: their father's name formed part of their name. That is, everyone was known by a given name plus the name of his or her father, as in "Muhammad son of Ahmad" or "Fatima daughter of Ahmad." The child's father was his or her natural guardian, who was fully responsible for the child, the child's property, and decisions about the child's upbringing until he or she reached legal majority. If the father were absent or deceased, guardianship was supposed to devolve on another member of the paternal line, such as the paternal grandfather or uncle. But, as in the case of infants, divorced or widowed mothers also had some rights to their children who were past infancy. Generally speaking, children were presumed to be better off with their mothers at least until they reached an age when they could look after their own basic needs. A mother, should she be divorced or widowed, had the right to custody of young children, usually defined as boys up to the age of seven and girls until age nine or even puberty (depending on the school of law). In the standard legal texts of the period, such as that written by al-Marghinani, a prominent jurist of the twelfth century, the mother was held to be more capable of providing for the basic needs of the child, but a father should be entrusted with the education of his son after the age of seven or so and with the protection of his daughter after puberty:

> The right of *hidanah* (custody), with respect to a male child, belongs to the mother, grandmother, or so forth, until he becomes independent of it himself, that is to say, becomes capable of moving, eating, drinking, and performing the other natural functions without assistance; after which the charge devolves upon the father, or next paternal relation entitled to the office of guardian, because, when thus far advanced, it then becomes necessary to attend to his education in all branches of useful and ornamental science, and to initiate him into a knowledge of men and manners, to effect which the father or paternal relations are best qualified. . . . But the right of *hidanah* with respect to a girl belongs to the mother, grandmother, and so forth, until the first appearance of the menstrual discharge (that is to say, until she attains the age of puberty) because a girl has occasion to learn such manners and accomplishments as are proper to women, for the teaching of which the female relations are most competent; but after that period the charge of her properly belongs to the father, because a girl, after maturity, requires some person to superintend her conduct, and for this the father is most completely qualified.

Such a division treated boys and girls quite differently. The tasks of coddling and meeting the physical needs of boys was assigned to the mother, but the father was viewed as essential to a boy's socialization process. For a girl, however, a mother was capable of meeting basic needs and providing the required socialization and training, underlining the diverse roles males and females would be playing in society, where the definitions of "manners" and "accomplishments" differed for men and women. A well-known hadith reported by al-Bukhari emphasizes the lifelong importance of the maternal link over the paternal one, which has bearing on the emotional attachment, the duties it entails, and its enduring cultivation throughout the sons' or daughters' lives: "A man came to Allah's Apostle and said, 'O Allah's Apostle! Who is more entitled to be treated with the best companionship by me?' The Prophet said, 'Your mother.' The man said, 'Who is next?' The Prophet said, 'Your mother.' The man further said, 'Who is next?' The Prophet said, 'Your mother.' The man asked for the

---

THE STORY OF MOSES

The Qur'anic version of the story of Moses, whose mother abandoned him so he would not be executed by the pharaoh as a male child born to Hebrews, highlights a mother's attachment to, and anxiety for, her child. God understands her grief and intervenes to make sure there is no other available wet nurse so that Moses is returned to his mother for nursing:

So we suggested to Moses' mother: Suckle him and when thou fearest for him, cast him into the sea, neither fearing nor grieving; for We are going to restore him to thee, and to make him one of the envoys. . . . On the morrow the heart of Moses' mother was empty . . . She said to her sister: "Follow him"; so she watched him from afar, without their being aware. Now before this We had put a ban upon the breasts (nurses) for him, so she (Moses' sister) said (to Pharaoh's daughter): "Shall I direct you to a household who will take charge of him for you and be to him good counselor? So we restored him to his mother, that she might be comforted and not grieve.

Source: *The Qur'an,* 2 volumes, translated by Richard Bell (Edinburgh: Clark, 1937, 1939), 28: 7–12.

fourth time, 'Who is next?' The Prophet said, 'Your father.' " (Sahih al-Bukhari, 8: 2)

Islamic Instruction. The inculcation of belief and religious training began immediately after birth. The Islamic call to prayer and the initiatory words of prayer were recited in the ears of the newborn. On the seventh day after birth, the father named the child and slaughtered an animal to express gratitude and joy for his or her arrival and survival. Boys were also circumcised in a religious ceremony, although this operation could be performed at any point from infancy up to the beginning of adolescence. As soon as the child began to talk, he or she was supposed to be taught the basic principles of faith.

Celebration of a child's birth; illumination by a student of Bihzad from a 1485 manuscript for *Layla wa-Majnun* (Layla and Majnun) by 'Amir Khosrow Dihlavi (Chester Beatty Library, Dublin)

Systematic religious training began at the age of seven, when a child reached the age of "discernment." At this point, boys were sent to the primary school, or *kuttab*, for instruction in the Qur'an and basic literacy skills. Most boys completed their educations around the age of puberty, after which their fathers were responsible for helping them choose and train for a vocation. Although there are no statistics on child labor during this period, the presence of many primary schools and the high value placed on at least some form of elementary religious education probably limited the use of child labor, at least in urban areas. The children of the ruling and intellectual elites enjoyed a longer period of education. Those from ruling families were often tutored at home, and their education included training in the martial arts as well as the religious sciences, history, and poetry. Children of the intellectual elite often undertook long years of study as they trained for scholarly careers. Information on the training and education of girls is less reliable than that on the schooling of boys. Many were educated at home, where their parents might teach them a combination of basic literacy and household-management skills. There is some evidence that girls could attend kuttabs, where they studied alongside boys, and at least a few kuttabs for girls did exist in the medieval period. In general, girls were supposed to be educated to their religious duties just as boys were. Girls should be taught to pray and fast so that they could be ready as adults to participate fully in religious life. Daughters of the elite had other educational opportunities, usually through the employment of home tutors or the attention of literate family members.

Legal Ties. Marriage was presumed to be an important part of almost any child's future. The father played a special role in arranging marriages for his children. As long as children were still in their legal minority (before puberty), a father as natural guardian had the right to arrange a marriage for his son or daughter. While it is unlikely that many marriages contracted for children were consummated before the children reached puberty (at the earliest), the father's arrangements were binding on his children. If children reached the age of puberty without having a marriage contract signed for them, they then acquired some rights to choose a spouse or at least refuse a marriage (depending on the legal school). It may be, however, that the weight of local custom prevented many young people from exercising these rights. The idea that boys and girls should be subject to the authority of their fathers or other paternal relatives was not always realized in practice, however. The higher mortality rates of premodern society meant that many parents died while their children were still relatively young. In the case of the death of a father, mothers were often able to retain custody of their children beyond the statutory limits and play an active role in managing their affairs. Court records from fourteenth-century Jerusalem, for example, include cases of widows who were retaining custody of their children, both boys and girls, while collecting income for them and managing their property. Divorced women were apparently not likely to be able to keep their children with them, especially if they remarried, but there are many cases of widows who became their children's legal guardians.

Orphans. Orphans (children who had lost their fathers, not necessarily both parents) were of particular concern to medieval Muslim society. The Qur'an and subsequent legal discussion accorded orphans special protections. The Qur'an calls on all Muslims to deal justly with orphans, and Islamic law put safeguards on their property and affairs. For example, the process of dividing up an individual's estate, the procedures for which are carefully prescribed in Islamic law, did not have to be done in a court of law unless the rights of a minor orphan were involved; in that case it was the responsibility of the Islamic judge to make sure the orphan received his or her due. There were also many religious endowments (*waqfs*) set up to benefit needy orphans in various ways. For example, a property could be endowed so that the income provided trousseaus for orphaned girls or educational fees for orphaned boys. Although some *waqfs* were established to support institutions for orphans, there is little evidence that these places were orphanages in the usual sense of the term but rather schools or other training facilities. The prevailing view was that children belonged in families, and an orphan typically found a home with relatives or neighbors, even though formal adoption, including the taking of another family's name, was forbidden under Islamic law.

Legal Majority. Once any child reached puberty, he or she entered legal majority and was no longer considered a child, at least under law. Both boys and girls at this age were adults in the sense that they could enter into contracts and generally manage their own affairs. But since unmarried adolescents continued to live with their parents or other relatives, it seems unlikely that they enjoyed much individual freedom at this stage. There is also evidence that boys tended to work with their fathers and follow them into their professions, an arrangement that would preclude much independence. Even marriage did not necessarily entail separation from parents: many young men brought their wives to live in the paternal household. Girls, on the other hand, usually stayed with their parents only until they married, often in their teens, and then moved to their husbands' parents' houses.

Emotional Ties. Many other ties continued to bind parents and children beyond the formal termination of childhood. A young woman who experienced difficulties in her marriage often returned to her parents' house for a period. If she could not be reconciled with her husband, and a divorce ensued, she would ordinarily remain with her parents until she contracted another marriage. Parents were expected to help their children if they needed financial assistance, and grown children were considered both legally and socially responsible for their parents. The Islamic laws of inheritance, which specified which relatives must inherit and in what proportions, made parents and children reciprocal heirs: all children shared in their mother's or father's estate, although boys inherited double the share of girls based on the greater share of financial responsibility they shouldered within the extended-family system. Should a child predecease his or her parents, both the mother and father inherited from him or her. It is more difficult to understand from such a distance in time what kinds of emotional ties bound parents and children. Not only did the law recognize the special love of mothers for their children, but the Qur'an also includes a moving testimony to maternal love in the story of the infant Moses. The biblical version of this story does not go into the emotions of Moses' mother when she bears a male child who is under the threat of the pharaoh's decree that all such children born to the Hebrews must die, nor does it describe her feelings when she takes the dire step of placing him in the river. The Qur'an, by contrast, tells the story with particular attention to the mother's emotional turmoil. A hadith recorded by al-Bukhari tells about the Prophet's tears of grief on the death of his infant son Ibrahim, providing an example of fatherly bonds to infants; according to Anas ibn Malik: "We went with Allah's Apostle to the blacksmith Abu Saif, and he was the husband of the wet nurse of Ibrahim (the son of the Prophet). Allah's Apostle took Ibrahim and kissed him and smelled him and later we entered Abu Saif's house and at that time Ibrahim was in his last breaths, and the eyes of Allah's Apostle started shedding tears. 'Abdur Rahman bin 'Auf said, 'O Allah's Apostle, even you are weeping!' He said, 'O Ibn 'Auf, this is mercy.' Then he wept more and said, 'The eyes are shedding tears and the heart is grieved, and we will not say except what pleases our Lord, O Ibrahim! Indeed we are grieved by your separation' " (Sahih al-Bukhari, 2: 390).

Consolation Treatises. Another source of evidence for the strong emotional attachment between parents and their children, including infants, is the popularity of the consolation treatise from the thirteenth century to the sixteenth. Consolation treatises, written for parents whose children had died, offered solace through several themes. For example, parents were told that the unweaned infant would continue to nurse in paradise, where he would be loved and cared for; and bereaved parents were promised that their child's death gained them entrance to paradise, where they would be reunited with their child and be automatically saved from hellfire. Most of these treatises wavered between comforting the parent by dwelling on the child's happiness in the hereafter and exhorting the mourning parent to remember that these children were given to God, so excessive displays of grief were unwarranted, if not sacrilegious. Even the existence of these treatises suggests that despite high rates of infant mortality, parents did allow themselves to develop strong bonds with their infants and young children and deeply mourned their loss.

Sources:

Avner Giladi, *Children of Islam: Concepts of Childhood in Muslim Society* (New York: St. Martin's Press, 1992).

Giladi, *Infants, Parents and Wet Nurses* (Leiden: Brill, 1999).

Alfred Guillaume, *The Life of Muhammad: A Translation of Ishaq's Sirat Rasul with Introduction and Notes* (London: Oxford University Press, 1955).

Muhammad M. Khan, *The Translation of the Meanings of the Sahih al-Bukhari*, 9 volumes (Madinah: Dar al-Fikr, 1981).

'Ali ibn Abi Bakr al-Marghinani, *The Hedaya*, translated by Charles Hamilton (Lahore: Premier Book House, 1957).

B. F. Musallam, *Sex and Society in Islam* (Cambridge: Cambridge University Press, 1983).

Barbara Stowasser, *Women in the Qur'an, Traditions, and Interpretations* (New York & Oxford: Oxford University Press, 1984).

EDUCATION

Seeking Knowledge. As it developed in the medieval period, Islamic culture placed major emphasis on education and learning. "Seek knowledge, even as far as China," said the Prophet, according to a well-known hadith. The intellectual elite, the ulama' who spent years acquiring knowledge in the religious sciences and then served as teachers, jurists, and bureaucrats in their communities, commanded great respect. Clad in distinctive robes and turbans, they derived their authority and prestige from their years of studying theology and law, along with other supporting subjects. Education was not the province of a small elite, however. All Muslims were encouraged to study in order to gain a basic familiarity with the Qur'an and the hadiths. In addition, every Muslim should seek and receive the education necessary for his or her station in life, in order to know what God required as well as what practices to avoid. Because learning was key to living a good life as a Muslim, the ulama' had a special responsibility to educate all members of their communities. In a fourteenth-century treatise, Ibn al-Hajj urged the scholar to "be humble and approachable to any student or any other who attends him," and to teach common people who approach him as well,

> because if religious knowledge is forbidden to the common people, the elite [ulama'] will not benefit from it either, as has been explained. To lock the door of a madrasah is to shut out the masses and prevent them from hearing the [recitation] of knowledge and being blessed by it and by its people [the ulama'].

Schools. Institutions evolved to provide settings for the important business of education. Primary education took place in a kuttab, a school usually attached to a masjid (mosque) or an institution of higher learning. Children came to the kuttab for basic instruction in Arabic and the Qur'an: the focus at this level was on learning enough Arabic to read and memorize the Qur'an. At about the age of puberty, those children who were continuing their education (probably a minority) left the kuttab for more advanced instruction elsewhere. Originally, most teaching of the Islamic religious and legal sciences took place in masjids, where "teaching circles" formed around learned individuals who offered lessons to whomever assembled. Beginning in the tenth century, khans, or hostelries, came to be established next to masjids so that students could live and study in the same complex. Finally, by the eleventh century the madrasah had emerged. This separate building dedicated to teaching and learning rapidly spread throughout Muslim lands. By the late twelfth century, for example, the city of Damascus boasted thirty operating madrasahs. The madrasah did not entirely replace other venues for learning: students continued to study in masjid circles or in khanqahs, the equivalent of Sufi monasteries.

Charitable Foundations. Madrasahs and the other educational institutions were almost entirely funded by religious endowment, the *waqf*. A prominent member of the ruling elite or even a middle-class person could choose to convert a piece of private property into a *waqf*, the income from which would be assigned to a religious or charitable purpose. Typically, *waqf* proceeds would pay for the upkeep of the building

A *nasib* (elegy) written by the Egyptian father Abu Hayyan (born 1256) for his daughter Nudar (born 1301) praises the talent and knowledge of his scholar-poet daughter and is one example of how literature provides evidence that women of the elite classes were educated:

My soul turned
away from this world
after Nudar settled
in the moist earth,

So my ear is deaf
when someone speaks;
my eye stares
far away.

How can I mind
whom I'm with
when I can't see
Nudar's shining face?

No. And I can't hear
her voice
whose finest words
were pearls.

If strung in verse
they'd be the blazing stars;
if scattered in prose,
they'd be the brightest blossoms.

Though she may be veiled
from my eye,
still her figure
is etched in my heart;

I've stayed by the grave
where she settled,
where fragrant musk
lingers.

There with her dwell
knowledge and virtue;
she was renowned for them
among the leading men.

In excellence,
no other woman could compare—
can a rock ever match
a jewel?

She recited the Qur'an
freshly, clearly,
without an error,
without distortion,

And adorned in ink
her page—an
embroidered tapestry
of revealing lines—

With tales of the Chosen Prophet,
with grammar and jurisprudence,
and with poetry,
always well-composed.

Source: "An Elegy (Nasib) for Nudar," translated by Th. Emil Homerin, in *The Literary Heritage of Classical Islam: Arabic and Islamic Studies in Honor of James Bellamy*, edited by Mustansir Mir (Princeton: Darwin Press, 1993), pp. 107–117.

and provide stipends for teachers and students. A student stipend might include the costs of a dormitory room and meals in the complex, usually available to the student as long as he pursued his studies and remained unmarried. Not all higher education was fully funded, however. Some of the instruction that took place in the varied locales such as masjids, khanqahs, or private houses was given on a fee-for-service basis. Although many of these schools were well established and lavishly endowed, they did not have the corporate identity of modern colleges and universities. Schools did not grant degrees, nor did they have any other method of formally recognizing a student's progress.

Teachers. Higher education was a personal relationship between a student and teacher. A student came to a madrasah, a masjid, a khanqah, or a teacher's home to study with a certain individual. A teacher was chosen because of his general reputation and his specialties, which, in turn, hinged on the reputations and specialties of his teachers. Students read and mastered particular texts with an individual teacher, texts the teacher had mastered before them through a process of transmission from teacher to student. The full meaning of the text was secured through a process of reading the text aloud and hearing the teacher's commentary. When a student had "learned" the text, he received a certificate (*ijazah*) from his teacher specifying his mastery of a particular text, and a student's collection of such certificates was the equivalent of his "degree." This personal relationship made teachers powerful authority figures for their students. Beginning at the elementary level, students were expected to be respectful and obedient, and corporal punishment was condoned for any lapses in behavior. At the higher levels students were cautioned always to behave in a deferential and considerate fashion toward their teacher. A student was taught to have clean clothes, hair, and nails in the presence of his teacher; to take care of his teacher's children and their descendants; and to continue to honor his teacher after his death by visiting his grave.

Children in a masjid school; illumination by al-Wasiti from a 1237 Baghdad manuscript for the *Maqamat* of al-Hariri (Bibliothèque Nationale, Paris)

Teaching Methods. The core subject, covered by many of the texts that students studied, was the foundations and development of Islamic law. The interpretation of the Qur'an, the study of the hadiths, Arabic grammar, and medicine were additional subjects essential to the study of the law. These areas of study, which constituted the "religious sciences" and their auxiliary subjects, formed the core of an Islamic higher education. Other fields of study—such as the "rational sciences" of philosophy, logic, and mathematics—were more marginal to the standard curriculum, but a student might seek instruction in them insofar as they contributed to his progress in the study of the religious sciences. Several fields in which there was abundant material and considerable intellectual activity at the time—such as literature, history, and astronomy—were not usually studied in an institutional setting. Students probably pursued these subjects on their own by gaining access to privately or publicly held collections of books, or perhaps through private instruction that was not institutionally based. The literary figure al-Jahiz (circa 776–869) mentioned the practice of renting a bookseller's shop for a period of time in order to read from works in its contents. Ibn Khallikan (1211–1284) mentioned an accusation against Abu 'Ali Ibn Sina (980–1037)—the Muslim philosopher-scientist known

in the West as Avicenna—who secured exclusive permission to study in the library of a prince of Khorasan:

> Abu Ali was then received into the favor of that prince, and he frequented his library, which was of incomparable richness, as it contained not only all the celebrated works which are found in the hand of the public, but others not to be met with anywhere else, and of which not only the titles but the contents were unknown. Here Abu Ali discovered treatises on the sciences of the ancients and other subjects, the essence of which he extracted, and with the greater part of which sciences he became acquainted. It happened, some time afterwards, that this library was consumed by fire, and Abu Ali remained the sole depository of the knowledge which it contained. Some persons even said that it was he who set fire to the library, being induced to do so for the reason that he alone was acquainted with its contents, and that he wished to pass off as his own the information which he had there acquired.

Oral Transmission. Teaching methods were geared to the demands of personal instruction and the emphasis placed on the value of oral transmission. Children began their education by memorizing the Qur'an: to truly know the text was to commit it to memory. Various treatises on education stressed the importance of such memorization and recommended memo-

"Layla and Majnun at School"; illumination attributed to Qasim Ali from a 1494 manuscript for *Khamsah* (Five) by Nizami
(British Library, London)

rization tools such as using tooth picks or eating honey, raisins, coriander, eggplant, and bitter apples to stimulate their memories. Older students committed other texts to memory as well, and some educational texts were set in verse to ease this task. Oral recitation of the text was also essential, for it was only through correct phrasing and pronunciation that the true meaning of the text was secured. At a time when hand-copied versions of a work were the only texts available, there was ample room for error: a careless copyist or a slip of the pen could alter the meaning of a word, line, or idea. Oral transmis-

sion—reading the text aloud with a competent teacher—helped to guard against such distortions and errors. Students also typically studied aloud even when working on their own. Masjids and madrasahs must have been constantly abuzz with the noise of teachers reciting text and students studying aloud.

Traveling Scholars. Students in higher education often journeyed in search of instruction. Most prominent scholars had traveled extensively in their youth in order to study with renowned teachers in several of the main centers of learning. The educational travels of the student Ahmad ibn 'Abd al-

Rahim (died 1423) from Cairo, for example, took him to Makkah, Madinah, Damascus, and Jerusalem in order to study with the leading scholars of the day. During such journeys students acquired both knowledge and credentials. There are many instances of fathers making these trips with children far too young to absorb sophisticated lessons. Still, their contact with a famous teacher and their physical presence at his lesson conferred prestige and even perhaps an *ijazah* that would be useful later in life. Many prominent ulama' continued to make such journeys throughout their careers, so the learned elite of the Muslim world developed many intellectual and social ties among themselves. A learned man could find familiar ideas and a similarly educated elite in any city in the vast territory that stretched from Spain in the west to India in the east.

Women. The Prophet had taught that seeking knowledge is the duty of every Muslim. Social attitudes toward the education of women, however, were marked by ambivalence. The women of the early Islamic community were praised for their learning, and all Muslim women had a responsibility to learn at least to read the Qur'an if possible. Yet, it was the opinion of some males that to educate a woman was to invite trouble; if she had full literacy skills, she might put them to bad use. As institutions of higher learning took shape during the medieval period, women were by and large excluded as students and teachers. Although some wealthy women endowed schools and, as founders, might even participate in the ongoing administration of the institution, they were not teachers or stipend-holding students in the madrasahs, masjid schools, or khanqahs of the period. Furthermore, the career paths available to these students in the religious, legal, and bureaucratic professions were all closed to women. Yet, the absence of women from the rolls of these schools does not necessarily mean that women were entirely barred from education. The informal and personal nature of much education made women's learning possible in several settings. Many young girls did attend neighborhood kuttabs in order to receive a basic education in the Qur'an, and others studied privately. Educated families often took an interest in their girls' education, and females commonly studied at home with their fathers, grandfathers, uncles, or even their mothers. Once married, young women sometimes continued to study with their husbands. Girls from the milieu of the educated elite were taken as young children to hear lectures and hadith transmissions, as were their brothers, and some girls frequented teaching circles held in private homes, masjids, and madrasahs even if they were not formally enrolled.

Female Scholars. Although some girls might study texts in the fields of law, theology, or grammar, beyond the elementary stages most females focused on the hadiths. The vast majority of women who acquired reputations as scholars and teachers did so in the transmission of these traditions. The role that Muhammad's wife 'A'isha played as the source of much hadith material certainly helped to validate female abilities. In addition, several women took part in the early collection of the Qur'an, a process that entailed recalling from memory orally transmitted revelations. Finally, women

shared with certain men the advantages that early exposure to reputable hadith transmitters could confer, especially if they lived long enough. A girl who was taken as a child to hear an elderly transmitter, and then lived to a ripe old age herself, might acquire major stature as a teacher of hadiths with a special link to previous generations. 'A'isha bint Muhammad 'Abd al-Hadi, a fourteenth-century Damascus woman, found herself in such a prominent position.

Accomplished Women. Muslim courtly society placed a high value on the abilities and talents of women in poetry, the arts, and general refinements—all of which required education and training, and measures were taken to ensure that women received such education. Shahrazad, the legendary protagonist of *Alf Laylah wa-Laylah* (The Thousand and One Nights), is one example. Other literary evidence points to the presence of such women among the elite during many periods of Muslim history. Muslim literature mentions the refinements of the women of the courts in music, dance, poetry, and other educated arts. Other families of sufficient means also placed value on the education of women, so that they could participate in cultured society and marry well. The degree to which a woman was educated probably increased along with social class and with the general level of education available in a given family, though her education was not equal to that of men in similar circumstances. Individual talent, proclivity, and opportunity probably accounted for additional exceptions. Literary evidence shows that, after promising beginnings, Muslim women's roles in formal and professional educated society declined over time, with some exceptions, but women of the courts and educated classes could probably expect to receive an education that enabled them to hold their own among their social peers, and some achieved exceptionally above this level.

Common Folk. The informal nature of many of the classes held in madrasahs and masjids, which enabled some women who were not enrolled in the schools to attend, also made educational opportunities available to a general public. Many madrasahs and masjids were located in the heart of the city, so people who were not preparing for scholarly careers could take advantage of classes offered for the layperson. Some of these institutions employed men whose primary task was to provide basic instruction in the Qur'an and writing. For the more advanced layperson, many madrasahs and masjids employed a "reader" who read books of hadith and Qur'an interpretation for the benefit of the urban masses. Some scholars also took their lessons to the streets. Most urban centers had "narrators" who established themselves on busy streets and "taught" passersby: they might recite verses of the Qur'an, hadiths, or stories of the early Muslim community. Their educational mission was broad in scope, ranging from helping the uneducated understand their religious duties to sheer entertainment through the narration of exciting stories. At least in the urban centers, the informal and fluid organization of education gave a broad spectrum of the population access to educational services and dispelled tensions between the educated elite and the ordinary people. Indeed, the urban centers of this period were remarkably free of the town-gown conflicts that pitted scholars against their uneducated neighbors in medieval Europe.

Sources:

Jonathan Berkey, *The Transmission of Knowledge in Medieval Cairo* (Princeton: Princeton University Press, 1992).

Gavin Hambly, ed., *Women in the Medieval Muslim World* (New York: St. Martin's Press, 1998).

Ibn Khallikan, *Ibn Khallikan's Biographical Dictionary*, 4 volumes, Bn Mac Guckin de Slane (Paris: Printed for the Oriental Translation Fund of Great Britain and Ireland, 1842–1871).

Nikki R. Keddie and Beth Baron, eds., *Women in Middle Eastern History: Shifting Boundaries in Sex and Gender* (New Haven: Yale University Press, 1991).

Guity Nashat and Judith Tucker, *Women in the Middle East and North Africa: Restoring Women to History* (Bloomington: Indiana University Press, 1998).

MARRIAGE

Islamic Marriage. Scholars who study the evolution of Muslim marriage practices between 622 and 1500 are still debating if the rise of Islam signaled new practices in the institution of marriage; to what extent the message brought by the Prophet Muhammad introduced new ideas that shaped Muslim marital life over the following centuries; and whether Islamic marriage gave women more rights and power than they had in the pre-Islamic period. The Qur'an, which records the word of God as revealed to Muhammad, praises the institution of marriage as natural and desirable for all Muslims, saying that God "created for you mates from yourselves that you might find rest in them, and ordained between you love and mercy" (30: 21). Men are enjoined to treat their wives with kindness and to provide them with support and protection. In return, women are expected to obey their husbands. Although these Qur'anic verses call for marriage to be a loving and supportive relationship, it is a relationship of complementarity rather than complete equality between husband and wife. The husband also has more leeway than his wife when it comes to divorce. He can divorce his wife at will, although the Qur'an does expect him to fulfill certain obligations to her and his children.

Pre-Islamic Marriage. Scholars have taken three distinct positions on whether the stipulations made in the Qur'an represent a departure from pre-Islamic practice and whether the Muslim marriage described by the Qur'an was more or less favorable to women than unions in pre-Islamic Arab society. First, some scholars argue that pre-Islamic marriage in the Arabian peninsula accorded women considerable power. They point to evidence that some women freely chose their marriage partners and brought their husbands to live with them and their families (a matrilocal marriage arrangement). In addition, the offspring of these women were considered part of the woman's family or clan, not her husband's, and the line of descent was reckoned through the mother, or matrilineally. Finally, a woman could divorce her husband at will, simply by turning her tent around so that the entrance was no longer where her husband expected it to be when he returned home. According to this view the patrilocal and patrilineal Muslim marriage represented a real reversal for women. Other scholars, however, assert that Islam ushered in a set of positive

changes and even revolutionary progress for women in marriage. They stress that in pre-Islamic Arabia, divorce was easy and casual for men as well. They could enter and leave a marriage at will without incurring any obligations. In this view the Qur'an—by outlining the obligations of the husband for the support of his wife and children and by detailing the responsibilities of the husband to his wife in the wake of divorce—introduced regulation of the marital relationship in ways that brought new security to women. Furthermore, although the Qur'an accepted the practice of polygyny, the right of a man to be married to more than one woman at a time, it was strictly regulated. The Qur'an limited the number of legal wives to four and exhorted a man to marry only one if he could not treat multiple wives with fairness (4: 2–3). Thus, in this second view, Islam brought order and security to an institution that had been plagued by arbitrary practices. A third view tends to focus on the extent to which Islamic marriage exhibits continuity with prior practices in the Middle East. These scholars point out that Islamic marriage as discussed in the Qur'an represents a blend of pre-existing social practices. The diverse marriage practices of the pre-Islamic nomadic peoples of the Arabian peninsula, which included the possibility of polygamy for both men and women as well as several forms of marriage and divorce, was one set of traditions that contributed to the Islamic tradition. But the settled pre-existing urban cultures of the region (such as the Sasanians and the Byzantines), which tended to subordinate the wife to the husband and severely restricted her ability to choose her own husband or leave a marriage, also contributed to the cultural mix. The Qur'an drew on both traditions and tempered the blend with a stress on ethical and compassionate behavior.

The Prophet's Marriages. The Qur'an was not the only source of guidance on marriage for early Muslims. They also looked to the example set by the Prophet Muhammad, whose life was studied carefully and deemed worthy of emulation. Muhammad married several women during his lifetime, but two of his marriages have received the most attention. His first marriage, to Khadijah, on which he entered when he was still a young man, proved central to his spiritual mission. Khadijah was a wealthy widow and businesswoman who had considerable trading interests. Fifteen years Muhammad's senior, she had first hired him to work for her and later proposed marriage to him. By all accounts, their relationship was close and supportive. Her wealth allowed him to pursue his spiritual path, and she not only provided material support but was the first to believe in the authenticity of the revelations he received from God. Therefore, she was the first convert to Islam. As long as she lived, Muhammad took no other wife, and after her death he mourned and revered her throughout the rest of his life. Once Khadijah was gone, however, Muhammad married several women. The most prominent and beloved of these wives was 'A'isha. The daughter of Abu Bakr, one of Muhammad's closest supporters, 'A'isha was married to the Prophet when she was nine years old and was his companion and confidante until he died nine years later. Islamic texts highlight the level of intimacy between them: Muhammad washed from the same vessel as 'A'isha; he

DIVORCE RECORDS

Though a man was permitted to divorce a wife without bringing the case before a judge, divorced couples sometimes appeared in court to make a formal declaration of the end of their marriage and the fulfillment of all related obligations. The following declaration was made in a Jerusalem court in 1304:

In the name of God, the Compassionate, the Merciful. She acknowledged—Fatima daughter of 'Abd-Allah son of Muhammad, the Hebronite, who is present in Jerusalem—in conformity with the shari'a, while she was in a sound body and mind and legally capable of conducting her affairs, that she has no claim on her divorcer, the Shakyh, the Imam, the Unique and Perfect Scholar, Burhan al-Din Ibrahim son of the late Zayn al-Din Allah, al-Nasiri, one of the Sufis of the khanqah of al-Salahiyya in Jerusalem, may God the Most High strengthen him; [she claims] no right or any remainder of a right, nor a bride price or any remainder of a bride price, no [expense of] clothing or maintenance, and no alimony, and absolutely nothing from the matrimonial rights in the past and up to its [the document's] date. [She acknowledged] that she received from him her fixed share allotted to her child by him for a period of three months and a half, in conformity with the legal payment. In regard to this she was born witness to, on the fourth of Shawwal al-Mubarak of the year seven hundred and eighty two. Praise be to God, Lord of the two worlds. . . .

Source: Huda Lutfi, "A Study of Six Fourteenth Century Iqrars from al-Quds Relating to Muslim Women," *Journal of the Social and Economic History of the Orient*, 26 (October 1983): 259.

prayed and received revelations in her presence; and when he realized he was mortally ill, he chose to die in her arms. Her close relationship with Muhammad made her a special source of information on his life. She had witnessed his actions and heard his opinions on many topics, and thus she became an authoritative voice in the transmission of hadiths, the accounts of what the Prophet said and did during his lifetime that came to serve as guides for the actions and beliefs of later communities of Muslims. It is thanks to 'A'isha, for example, that Muslims know the Prophet helped with the housework and even shared a toothbrush with her. These accounts of Muhammad as a loving husband with a gift for intimacy do not seem to accord well with the historical fact that Muhammad married several different women and, after the death of Khadijah, routinely practiced polygyny. Admittedly, many of his marriages were made to cement political alliances and in some cases to provide support and protection for widows. Furthermore, he always stressed the need to treat all wives equally and with fairness, and—later commentators added—not all his marital practices were necessarily meant to be followed by Muslims in general. That is, the Prophet and his wives were special people whose example was not to be followed exactly in every matter.

Islamic Marriage Law. The task of melding Qur'anic material and the example of the Prophet to develop and interpret Islamic rules applicable to all Muslim marriages took place largely in a legal context. Medieval Muslim jurists, who came from the ranks of the ulama', spent considerable time and energy on the project of defining Islamic marriage as they elaborated the shari'ah (the corpus of Islamic law). Working with the Qur'an and the hadiths, they shaped the laws regulating Islamic marriage. Distinct legal schools, with differing rules for marriages and divorce, emerged in the ninth and tenth centuries and then continued to undergo a process of development and refinement. All these schools viewed Islamic marriage as a contract between the bride and groom entailing specific rights and obligations that differed for the man and the woman. Both parties had to agree to the contract, and the groom paid the bride a specified dower (*mahr*), which became her personal property. Once the marriage was consummated, the husband was responsible for the material support of his wife, and in return she was expected to give him her obedience. He could restrict her freedom of movement by forbidding her to leave his house, for example, but he was expected to treat her fairly and kindly. A husband did not have any rights to the control of his wife's property, however. Everything she brought to the marriage and any property she earned or was given were hers to enjoy and dispose of as she wished. While Islamic law permitted a man to have as many as four wives (as well as an unlimited number of slave concubines), women were required to practice monogamy.

Divorce Law. A man could divorce his wife without citing grounds, although he did incur a number of legal obligations in the wake of divorce: he was required to pay any balance of the dower and any other debts he owed his wife; he was required to support her during a "waiting period" of three months or, should she be pregnant, until she delivered the child; and he was completely responsible for the material support of all children born of the marriage. The ulama' ruled that a wife, however, could obtain a divorce from an Islamic judge only if she could demonstrate that the marriage was defective in some way. The legal schools differed in what they considered valid reasons for a woman to demand a divorce, but they were generally quite restrictive, ranging from a husband's impotence or fatal communicable disease to his desertion or nonsupport. If she could not prove such a defect in the marriage, a woman could try to obtain a *khul'* divorce, a female-initiated action in which the woman obtained a divorce from her husband in return for forgoing the balance of her dower, giving up her rights to support during her waiting period, and perhaps taking on responsibility for child support as well.

Interpretation and Practice. The legal rules for marriage evolved as a process of juristic interpretation of Islamic texts in connection with actual legal practice. Islamic courts were established at a local level, and individuals brought their claims and questions about marriage to the Islamic judge for rulings. Islamic jurists with reputations for great learning and wisdom became *muftis*, people who were qualified to give legal opinions outside the court to anyone who asked. Although there are few surviving Islamic court records from before the sixteenth century, there are many extant collections of legal opinions issued by prominent muftis. These opinions reveal the extent to which individual Muslims participated in the process of fashioning the law by bringing their questions about marriage to the attention of jurists. For example, the basic concept that a husband owes his wife material support during their marriage called for clarification and elaboration. Over the years, in response to questions brought to the muftis and the courts, the jurists came to define such support in great detail: a man must support his wife in the manner to which she is accustomed and in keeping with the lifestyle of her social class in her specific environment. That is, a woman from a comfortable family could insist on a house servant or perhaps daily servings of meat. It was laymen and -women, seeking detailed guidance, who pressed the jurists to continue elaborating and interpreting the law in the context of changing societies. Yet, because of the lack of extensive records for the medieval period, it is difficult to ascertain to what extent the legal rules for marriage were actually observed. Still, there are some indications that the laws on marriage were taken seriously. In fourteenth-century Jerusalem, for example, a husband and wife might come to court after a divorce to register their divorce settlement. The former wife would testify that she had received her rights: the balance of her dower, the costs of her waiting period, any debts her husband owed her, and child support. The registration of such a settlement (not required under law) suggests that the couple, and in particular the former husband, were trying to avoid future legal action over divorce obligations and were establishing an official record to prove that all such obligations had been discharged. Clearly they expected the Islamic rules of divorce to be enforced in their community. Although there are no statistics on overall divorce rates during this period, the ease of divorce—and the absence of any discernable stigma attached to the practice—probably resulted in a perception of marriage as an impermanent institution and high rates of divorce. Women as well as men were likely to have serial marriages: women of the Mamluk elite in thirteenth-, fourteenth-, and fifteenth-century Egypt often made several marriages over their lifetimes. For example, Khadijah, the daughter of the Mamluk prince Hajji ibn al-Baisari, married six different men in the course of her marital career.

Courtly Marriages. Islamic religious texts and the laws derived from them were not the only forces that shaped the institution of marriage in the medieval period. Particularly in elite circles, other cultural influences came into play. Historians have noted that the respect enjoyed by the wives of Muhammad and his contemporaries in the early Islamic period seem to have persisted into the days of the Umayyad dynasty (661–750). 'Attika, the wife of the Umayyad ruler 'Abd al-Malik (ruled 685–705), was well known for her wealth and beneficence, and many sought her intercession with her husband. Umm al-Banin, the wife of al-Walid I (ruled 705–715), was known to summon and scold officials on her own.

Concubines. By the time of the late Umayyad and early Abbasid periods, however, it had become common practice for rulers to keep large harems of secluded women, in which legal wives of free origin were vastly outnumbered by slave concubines. Slave concubinage predated Islam and came to be regulated by Islamic law. According to the law, men were permitted to have sexual access to any female slave they owned. As the Arab empire expanded under the Umayyads and early Abbasids, newly conquered territories were the source of large numbers of slaves, many of whom became the personal property of the ruler and his top officials. After the initial conquest of a region, the conquerors continued to procure slaves through trade with neighboring lands. Slave women, many of whom were educated and trained in various social graces, became a standard feature of elite harems, where they often displaced legal wives. As concubines, they did not enjoy the legal privileges of free wives. They could be bought and sold at will, and they had no rights to marital support. Only in the event that a concubine bore a child to her master did she acquire some limited rights: she could not be sold; she would be freed on the death of her master (according to some, she became free on the birth of the child); and her child was the free and legitimate heir of his father. A few concubines were able to function more or less as legal wives if they gained their master's support and affection. Khayzuran, the concubine of the Abbasid ruler al-Mahdi (ruled 775–785), managed to become his legal wife and the mother of two of his successors as khalifah, playing an active role in the making of state policy. In general, the rise of slave concubinage as a common practice tended to depress the status of wives. All the women of the elite came to be confined to the quarters of the harem, and the boundaries between free wife and concubine were blurred.

Powerful Women. With the arrival and eventual takeover of power by Turks and Mongols in the thirteenth century, the marriage practices of the elite underwent some modification. The power and influence of wives in the states established by Turks and Mongols suggest that the nomadic cultural traditions of these groups accorded women considerable power within a marriage. In the Ilkhanid state, established by the Mongols after the capture of Baghdad and downfall of the Abbasids in 1258, royal wives participated in the highest Mongol council, the Kuriltay, and were thus part of the power structure. In the Ayyubid dynasty in Egypt, the power and involvement of the wife of the ruler came to a climax in the reign of al-Malik al-Salih, Najm al-Din, who died in 1249 while fighting against the Crusaders. His wife, Shajarat al-Durr, concealed his death for three months and then had herself proclaimed sultana and ruled first in the name of a child-prince and then in consort with the leader of the Mamluk soldiers, who founded a new dynasty. In the context of these elites, marriage was a political project, one of the most important bonds that undergirded elite loyalties and power struggles. Although historians know quite a bit about elite

People pouring gold coins over a groom as he leaves his bride's room on the day after their wedding; illumination from a 1396 Baghdad manuscript for the *Diwan* (Collected Poems) of Khwaju Kirmani (British Library, London)

A Muslim qadi (magistrate) hearing a dispute between a husband and wife; illumination by al-Wasiti from a 1237 manuscript for the *Maqamat* of al-Hariri (Bibliothèque Nationale, Paris)

marriage thanks to the availability of chronicles and biographies of the period, they know far less about marriage for ordinary people. Elaborate harem quarters housing multiple wives and slave concubines were far too expensive for most of the population.

Common Folk. No doubt the majority of the urban poor and the peasantry in the countryside could not afford to imitate the marriage practices of the wealthy and powerful. Scholars lack the historical materials, however, to ascertain the extent to which the bulk of the population adhered to Islamic regulations on marriage and divorce. An occasional glimpse of life at the more mundane level may be found in fragmentary records from Islamic courts. In fourteenth-century Jerusalem, for example, a widow of average means acknowledged to the court that she had received her due from her late husband's estate. The debts the estate owed her included the remainder of her bridal gift and a sum of money for her clothing, as well as her share as one of the heirs in his estate. Even the presence of such a document suggests that the local community took these marital claims seriously. In the wake of a husband's death, his widow's rights to her dower and other marital debts took precedence over all other claims on the estate.

Love in Marriage. Emotional ties are difficult to document. Even among the literate intellectual Muslim elite, there was a certain reticence when it came to dis-

playing feelings about one's wife or husband. One striking exception was Sultan Sulayman (born 1494), who ruled the Ottoman Empire in 1520–1566 and who wrote passionate love poetry to his concubine turned wife, Hurrem Sultan. An example of a middle-class merchant's devotion to his wife is revealed in an anecdote from tenth-century Baghdad recorded by al-Hamadhani in his *Maqamat*. The passage also describes the common practice of cousin marriage:

> While I was in Baghdad a merchant invited me to partake of madirah [a meat dish] and he clung to me with the clinging of a pressing creditor . . . till I accepted his invitation to it, so we started. Now the whole way he was praising his wife and ready to sacrifice his heart's blood for her, eulogizing her cleverness in her art, and her excellent taste in cooking, saying, "Sir, if you were to see her with the apron tied round her waist, going about the rooms, from the oven to the cooking pots, and from the cooking pots to the oven, blowing the fire with her mouth, pounding the spices with her hands; and if you were to see the smoke discoloring that beautiful face and affecting that smooth cheek, thou wouldst behold a spectacle at which eyes would be dazed. I love her because she loves me, and it is a mark of a man's good fortune that he should be given a lawful helpmeet and that he should be aided by his spouse, and especially when she is of his own clay. In near relationship she is my paternal uncle's daughter, her clay is my clay, her town is my town, her paternal uncles are my paternal

uncles and her origin is my origin. But in disposition she is more generous than I am, and in form more beautiful."

Ibn Khaldun, the great fourteenth-century historian whose theories on the rise and decline of civilization still seem relevant, experienced the loss of his wife and daughters in a shipwreck as they were en route to join him in Cairo. Observers noted that this tragedy transformed him, and he was irascible and distant to the end of his days some twenty-two years later. The meaning and practice of marriage varied greatly across class and community. Although it is possible to discern an Islamic vision of marriage, it was a vision with variations, and it had the flexibility to accommodate practices ranging from vast royal harems to monogamous relationships with precisely defined rights and obligations.

Sources:

Leila Ahmed, *Women and Gender in Islam: Historical Roots of a Modern Debate* (New Haven: Yale University Press, 1992).

Maulana Muhammad Ali, trans., *A Manual of Hadith* (Guilford, U.K.: Curzon Press, 1983).

Abu Hamid al-Ghazali, *Ghazali's Book of Council for Kings*, translated by F. R. C. Bagley (London & New York: Oxford University Press, 1964).

Husain Haddawy, trans., *The Arabian Nights*, edited by Muhsin Mahdi (New York & London: Norton, 1990).

Ahmad Badi al-Zaman al-Hamadhani, *The Maqamat of Badi al-Zaman al-Hamadhani*, translated by W. J. Prendergast (London: Curzon Press, 1973).

Gavin Hambly, ed., *Women in the Medieval Muslim World* (New York: St. Martin's Press, 1998).

Nikki R. Keddie and Beth Baron, eds., *Women in Middle Eastern History: Shifting Boundaries in Sex and Gender* (New Haven: Yale University Press, 1991).

'Ali ibn Abi Bakr al-Marghinini, *The Hedaya*, translated Charles Hamilton (London: W. H. Allen, 1870).

Guity Nashat and Judith Tucker, *Women in the Middle East and North Africa: Restoring Women to History* (Bloomington: Indiana University Press, 1998).

Leslie Peirce, *The Imperial Harem: Women and Sovereignty in the Ottoman Empire* (New York: Oxford University Press, 1993).

Ruth Roded, *Women in Islamic Biographical Collections: From Ibn Sa'd to Who's Who* (Boulder: Lynne Rienner, 1994).

Roded, ed., *Women in Islam and the Middle East, A Reader* (London: Tauris, 1999).

Denise Spellburg, *Politics, Gender, and the Islamic Past: The Legacy of 'A'isha bint Abi Bakr* (New York: Columbia University Press, 1994).

Barbara Stowasser, *Women in the Qur'an, Traditions, and Interpretations* (New York & Oxford: Oxford University Press, 1984).

SEXUALITY

Mutuality. A central aspect of all marriages was the sexual component, which attracted considerable attention and discussion during the years 622–1500. The Qur'an places a positive value on the sexual dimension of the marital relationship. In an explicit reference to sexual companionship, men are told that their wives "are an apparel for you and you for them," and the Qur'an further specifies that couples can have sexual relations even on most of the nights of Ramadan, the holy month of fasting—abstaining only for the last ten days of the month (2: 187), during which a man might choose to participate in a state of self-seclusion called *ihtikhaf*. Islamic jurists in the following centuries

elaborated on the role of sex in marriage and wrote marriage manuals aimed primarily at instructing men how to treat their wives. They stressed a woman's right to sexual satisfaction within a marriage, and called on men to provide their wives with a good sexual experience. Their explicit validation of female sexuality drew on the Qur'an and the words and deeds of the Prophet, as illustrated by the instructions for intimate relations given in the eleventh century by al-Ghazali, who advised the husband to

proceed with gentle words and kisses. The Prophet said, "Let none of you come upon his wife like an animal, and let there be an emissary between them." He was asked, "What is this emissary, O Messenger of God?" He said, "The kiss and [sweet] words." He also said, "There are three qualities which are considered deficiencies in a man: one, that he should meet someone whose acquaintance he wishes to make but parts from him before learning his name and lineage; second, that he should be treated kindly and reject the kindnesses done unto him; and third, that he should approach his concubine or wife and have sexual contact with her before exchanging tender words and caresses, consequently, he sleeps with her and fulfills his needs before she fulfills hers."

Birth Control. The attitude of Islamic jurists toward birth-control practices also stressed the positive nature of sex within marriage. In general, jurists in this period thought that Islam permitted the practice of birth control, most commonly withdrawal, or coitus interruptus, as long as the couple had acceptable reasons to avoid pregnancy. Such reasons could include the safeguarding of the health and beauty of the woman and the hardship that the support of an additional child might bring. On the other hand, the desire to avoid more female children or a woman's personal distaste for childbirth and nursing did not justify the planned prevention of births. In the case of sexual relations with a concubine, the preservation of property was also a legitimate concern: because a concubine who became pregnant by her master would be automatically freed, birth control could legitimately be used to prevent her pregnancy and eventual manumission. Whether practicing birth control with a wife or concubine, however, a man was instructed to be careful that his actions not deprive his partner of sexual satisfaction. The female's right to sexual pleasure overrode all other considerations. For this reason, some jurists thought that withdrawal should only be practiced with the explicit permission of the wife. It is impossible to tell with any certainty if medieval Muslims practiced birth control in any systematic fashion or if the prescriptive literature of the jurists had any impact on the decisions people made about the size of their families. Yet, there is indirect evidence that birth control was being widely practiced. From the eleventh century onward, Islamic jurists felt the need to discuss the issue in detail, suggesting that they thought it was of interest and relevance to the members of their communities. In addition, there were other forms of literature circulating among the literate elite that included information on birth control. Pharmacopoeias, the standard lists of drugs and their uses

An Afghan princess and her attendants; illumination from a 1335–1340 manuscript for the *Shahnameh* (Book of Kings) by Firdawsi (Vever Collection, Arthur M. Sackler Gallery, The National Museum of Asian Art, Smithsonian Institution, Washington, D.C.)

that were available to medical and laypeople, included many abortifacients and instructions for their employment. The erotica of the period also discussed birth-control practices in some depth as a guide to sexual enjoyment without the cares of pregnancy. There is also indirect evidence that the practice of birth control did have a demographic impact on the Muslim population. Like many other parts of the world, the Middle East was hit by devastating epidemics of plague in the fourteenth century, and its population dropped precipitously. Unlike other regions, however, recovery there was slow, and population numbers did not rebound quickly as they did elsewhere. Some historians have argued that the people of the Middle East, armed with information, theological sanction, and a new pessimism about the future, chose to limit their families to the extent that population levels remained permanently depressed. Furthermore, the Qur'anic recommendation that women who are willing and able should nurse each child for a full two years aided in the spacing of children, because nursing, while not a totally effective birth-control method, does help to prevent pregnancy.

Extramarital Relations. Sexual relations outside of marriage or legal concubinage were severely proscribed. *Zina*, or unlawful sexual intercourse, was one of the few acts for which the Qur'an prescribed a specific punishment, stoning or lashing, depending on the marital status of the perpetrators. During the medieval period Muslim jurists,

working with Qur'anic material and the hadiths, tended toward the restriction of the application of *zina* punishments. Although the prohibition of sex outside marriage or concubinage remained in force—as an explicit command of God it could not be otherwise—jurists stressed the equally demanding rules of evidence needed to prove this crime. Indeed, in order to prove a charge of *zina*, the law required four witnesses to the act itself or four separate sworn oaths on the part of the accusing spouse. The accused spouse could avoid punishment by swearing four oaths of innocence. In addition, the person who brought an accusation of *zina* that could not meet these stringent demands for evidence was liable for severe punishment. The apparent outcome of these procedural requirements was to make the prosecution of *zina* a rarity. Recognizing the difficulties of proving and punishing *zina,* some Muslim states modified the law. Early Ottoman legal codes, for example, criminalized sex outside of marriage but prescribed fines and banishment rather than the classic *zina* punishments.

Popular Views. Although Islamic law theoretically held men and women equally culpable in the case of sexual relations outside of marriage, the blame for sexual transgressions was often likely to be laid on women. While male thinkers recognized female sexuality, it could also pose a danger to society. Al-Ghazali, the same writer who exhorted men to be sexual companions for their wives, thought that women should be secluded from all contact with unrelated men because even the sound of their voices might inflame a man's desire. The philosopher Nasir al-Din al-Tusi (1201–1274) advised husbands to keep their wives busy at home because, if a woman saw other men, she would be "emboldened to embark on abominable courses, and even to provoke admirers to quest for her." The idea that women were natural seductresses also appeared in popular literature. Some poets and essayists celebrated sexuality and seduction and railed against the prudishness of the ulama'. The well-known Arabic poet Abu Nuwas (circa 762–813) wrote obscene poems that detailed his sexual intercourse with boys and girls. Much of the erotica featured slaves, both male and female, whose availability for illicit sexual play was a result of their powerlessness. Such activity took place in the world of the elite, who could afford to purchase expensive slaves and had the wealth and power to flaunt social rules, including the ban on homosexuality. Wealthy men made presents of slave girls and boys to favored friends, and the Islamic rule that one could have sexual intercourse only with a concubine one personally owned was often violated, at least according to literary accounts. Whether this kind of sexual license filtered down the majority of the population is not easy to ascertain, but there is little evidence that homosexuality or prostitution was particularly common.

Shahrazad. Perhaps the best-known piece of literature from the medieval period was the collection of tales known as *Alf Laylah wa-Laylah* (The Thousand and One Nights), set in the world of the elite. The earliest essentially complete edition dates to the fourteenth century. The frame for these tales is a story of women's lust and perfidy, and men's fear for their honor should their women betray them. Two brothers, Shahzaman and Shahrayar, each king in his own country, experience similar misfortunes: they discover that their wives are being secretly unfaithful to them. They kill their wives and their lovers, but Shahrayar does not stop there:

> he went to his own palace and ordered his chief vizier . . . and said to him, "Take that wife of mine and put her to death." The Shahrayar went to her himself, bound her, and handed her over to the vizier, who took her out and put her to death. The King Shahrayar grabbed his sword, brandished it, and, entering the palace chambers, killed every one of his slave-girls and replaced them with others. He then swore to marry for one night only and kill the woman the next morning, in order to save himself from the wickedness and cunning of women, saying, "There is not a single chaste woman anywhere on the entire face of the earth."

After considerable slaughter, he is diverted from this terrible course of action by the brave and clever Shahrazad, the daughter of his vizier, who volunteers to marry him and then keeps him spellbound with her storytelling each night so that he postpones and eventually cancels her execution and makes her his permanent wife. Her stories compose the tales, which feature many women of strength and intelligence, but also sound a cautionary note: several women in the tales are unfaithful and conniving wives, and they come to bad ends.

Princess Nura. Other narratives, including epics, had a wide and eager audience in the period. One such twelfth-century epic, the *Sirat Dhat al-Himma* (Epic of Dhat al-Himma), includes an episode featuring a Byzantine warrior-princess, Nura, whose strength and beauty wreaks havoc among her Muslim opponents. She is an effective fighter who takes up arms to defend Byzantine territory, and on the battlefield she is not above using her feminine charms to disarm her opponents. At one point during battle she uncovers her face and even her breasts, and her opponent's eyes pop out of his head. One of the chief heroes of the Muslim army, Abu Muhammad al-Battal, is bewitched by her beauty and spirit, and he falls hopelessly in love with her. His lovesickness has no bounds and destroys his manly virtue: he faints, cries, betrays his comrades, and tries to leave the fighting in order to be with Nura. She has a similar effect on other soldiers—so much so that her power as a seductress threatens to imperil the success of the Muslim army. Nura is finally brought under control by her marriage to al-Battal, but their wedding night is anything but tranquil. He attempts to drug her to ensure her compliance; she is discovered slipping lethal poison into his drink and then refuses to let him touch her; he finally resorts to having his commander in chief (who is also a woman) beat Nura and tie her up so that he can consummate the marriage. In the end Nura comes to love al-Battal, converts to Islam, and takes up arms for the Muslims. The marriage is a narrow victory over female physical and sexual power, which almost destroyed precious community solidarity and, indeed, the Muslims themselves. The popularity of such narratives, which were widely told in public squares and private living rooms, suggests the widespread acceptance of the belief that the power and allure of female sexuality can drive men to distraction and that it must be controlled and brought under male dominion for the well-being of all members of the community. Of course, all the written versions of these popular narratives, which record long-standing oral traditions, were put on paper by male writers. There may have been "female" versions of these tales that have not survived.

Celibacy. The channeling of such powerful sexuality into marriage was the standard expectation of the day. Although men of the wealthy elite might have multiple sex partners—several wives and/or slave concubines—most marriages were probably monogamous, but the ease of divorce made it possible for both men and women to change their marriage partners more than once. Celibacy was limited in the Islamic tradition as a result of the Prophet Muhammad's example and a widely accepted hadith that "there is no monasticism in Islam." Still, some men and women who were inclined toward Sufism, the mystical tradition in Islam, chose to practice asceticism and not to marry. The eighth-century woman Sufi, Rabi'a al-'Adawiyya, refused to marry on the grounds that she belonged completely to God. Other women eschewed marriage because they believed men were a worldly distraction from the worship of God or because they found it difficult to find a husband who could tolerate their lifestyle of prayer and at least partial asceticism. Some male Sufis felt the same way and saw sex and marriage as temptations that would impede them on their spiritual quest. Within Sufi circles there was considerable relaxation of concerns about unregulated male-female association. Female Sufis frequented masjids, studied with their male counterparts, and joined them in mystic sessions. One thirteenth-century Sufi biographer, Farid al-Din 'Attar, explained that adept Sufi women were not really women any more. Indeed, it is possible that such women, who lived with minimal food and sleep, grew so thin that they stopped menstruating and thus lost many of their secondary sex characteristics. Most Sufis, both male and female, did marry and have sexual relations, but the option of celibacy remained available.

Sources:

Lois Beck and Nikki Keddie, eds., *Women in the Muslim World* (Cambridge, Mass.: Harvard University Press, 1978).

Abu Hamid al-Ghazali, *Marriage and Sexuality in Islam: A Translation of al-Ghazali's Book on the Etiquette of Marriage from the Ihya'*, translated by Madelain Farah (Salt Lake City: University of Utah Press, 1984).

Husain Haddawy, trans., *The Arabian Nights*, edited by Muhsin Mahdi (New York & London: Norton, 1990).

Gavin R. G. Hambly, ed., *Women in the Medieval Islamic World: Power, Patronage, and Piety* (New York: St. Martin's Press, 1998).

B. F. Musallam, *Sex and Society in Islam* (Cambridge: Cambridge University Press, 1983).

Guity Nashat and Judith Tucker, *Women in the Middle East and North Africa: Restoring Women to History* (Bloomington: Indiana University Press, 1998).

Leslie Peirce, *The Imperial Harem: Women and Sovereignty in the Ottoman Empire* (New York: Oxford University Press, 1993).

Ruth Roded, ed., *Women in Islam and the Middle East, A Reader* (London: Tauris, 1999).

Margaret Smith, *Rabi'a the Mystic and Her Fellow-Saints in Islam* (Cambridge: Cambridge University Press, 1928).

SOCIAL ROLES AND RESPONSIBILITIES

The Family. Education equipped men and women for the social roles and responsibilities that they assumed in their families and communities. Expectations for their behavior and their contributions to family and community life varied according to age, gender, and class. As with most other facets of life during the medieval period, scholars know most about life in urban areas, and it would be wrong to assume that the social roles and responsibilities of rural people were necessarily the same as those of the urbanized population. The family, the most basic and important social unit, first and foremost shaped social life. Husbands and wives were bound by legal rules and social expectations that defined the husband as provider and the wife as obedient keeper of the household. The power and authority of the husband and father was largely unquestioned. In the ideal Muslim family, the father provided for all members of the household and exercised absolute control over his wife and children, who owed him obedience and deference. His power was modified in principle by certain rights of his wife and children to fair treatment and independent property, but law and social custom seemed to accord the male head of household almost unlimited power. Yet, it is impossible to judge to what extent this ideal family actually existed or if there was a gap between the ideal and the reality of many families in this period. Scholars do know that high mortality rates and the ease of divorce rendered marriage unstable. Widows or divorced women might gain rights of guardianship over their children, and they were likely to remarry at some point in the future. In the elite Mamluk circles of thirteenth–fifteenth-century Egypt, for example, women often made a series of marriages, in part because their husbands tended to die in the frequent conflicts within the ruling group.

Serial Marriages. The few records relating to ordinary people suggest that multiple marriages were not uncommon among them either. The impermanence of marriage made families fluid. Both men and women might have several serial marriages, and children could move from one household to another in the wake of a death or divorce. The laws and customs that assigned the role of exclusive provider and ruler of the household to the father and husband were no doubt often modified by real-life events that might make a woman head of household and responsible for her children.

The Extended Family. Although Islamic law focused on the rights and responsibilities of members of a nuclear family (wife, husband, and children), other family relationships were important in people's lives. In an era before the rise of state welfare systems, the extended family played a central role in the provision of material security. Siblings, aunts, uncles, and cousins all shared a sense of mutual responsibil-

ity. Brothers often played a major role in the lives of their sisters. In one legal proceeding in fourteenth-century Jerusalem, a brother acted as legal executor of his sister's late husband's estate, ensuring that she received the inheritance portion due her. The same brother was also responsible for their late father's property; he was the one handling the financial affairs of the family, including those of his sister. A woman's relationship with her brother was lifelong, and she no doubt found support and shelter in his house if her marriage did not work out. Ties to aunts, uncles, and cousins were highlighted and reinforced by the practice of cousin marriage. Islamic law permitted the marriage of first cousins, and there is some evidence that it was, in fact, a frequent occurrence. The marrying of cousins helped to bind families together, to preserve family property that might be lost if a female took her inheritance outside the family, and to ensure that the bride would have a mother-in-law who would be predisposed to treat her kindly.

Career Paths. Beyond basic issues of mutual support and the sharing of resources, families also molded the career paths of their members. Most occupations tended to be passed along. Whether scholars, merchants, or butchers, many men followed in the footsteps of a father or uncle. Periods of training or apprenticeship were usually served within the family, so there was little social mobility. In the world of the scholar—the profession about which the most information is available—certain families established over time virtual monopolies on the teaching and judicial posts in different cities. The recruitment practices of the ruling elite in Mamluk times, however, represented a dramatic departure from this system of hereditary occupations. Mamluk "households" were composed of male military retinues and their female concubines and servants, all of whom were imported as slaves from outside Mamluk territory. The biological children of the Mamluk rulers tended to leave the ruling group and blend into local society while the newly imported recruits took over as the next generation of the elite. Even in this case, however, people felt the need for fictive kinship. The head of a Mamluk household referred to his retinue as "my sons," and the women of slave origins were treated like daughters for whom suitable marriages to men of the elite class were carefully arranged. The ties of loyalty and dependence among members of a Mamluk household were invariably expressed in the terms of blood and kin so familiar to the society at large.

Public Space. Just as roles within the family were strongly gender defined in the sense that men and women were assigned distinct responsibilities, so too was life outside the family colored by views of what was appropriate for males and females. The issue of female access to public space during the medieval period is one of the most difficult to assess because of some rather contradictory evidence on the practice of female seclusion. At the time of the Prophet Muhammad, only his wives were secluded in accordance with a revelation addressed to them (Qur'an, 33: 32). Other Muslim women appear to have moved about in public with considerable freedom, participating in warfare and court life. In the Umayyad

Muslim women playing chess at a private all-female gathering; thirteenth-century Andalusian miniature
(Museu Institut Amatller d'Art Hispanic, Barcelona)

and Abbasid periods, however, practices of female veiling and seclusion, which had long been part of Middle Eastern urban culture in the pre-Islamic period, reasserted themselves. Abbasid rulers were the first to establish the harem, the separate women's quarters where the women of the household could be completely secluded and denied all contact with unrelated males. The ideal of the woman who never left her house except to be married or buried became a powerful image of "purity" that filtered down from the ruling groups. Veiling spread as a form of portable seclusion, enabling women who had to leave the house for practical reasons to hide their bodies and faces from the eyes of strange men. Such customs became so widespread that the fourteenth-century traveler Ibn Battuta could claim that during his travels in the Muslim world, from Morocco to China, he encountered unveiled women only twice, in the Maldives and among the Tuareg in West Africa. Yet, other sources challenge the idea that public space was the exclusive domain of men, where women were present only veiled and on sufferance. Another fourteenth-century observer, Ibn al-Hajj, a religious scholar in Cairo, lamented the extent to which women could be found mingling with men in the market, at religious celebrations, and in the workplace: "Some of our worthy ancestors [al-salaf] may God be pleased with them said: 'A woman is permitted three exits: one to the house of her husband when she is married to him; one when her parents die; and one when she is carried to her grave.' By God, listen to this *salafi* advice, and observe the kind of chaos and corruption caused by women's frequent exits nowadays." He went on to advise that the shopkeeper

must be careful when a woman comes to buy something, to look at her behavior, for if she was one of those women dressed in delicate clothes, exposing her wrists, or some of her adornments, and speaking in a tender and soft voice, he should leave the selling transaction and give her his back until she leaves the shop peacefully. . . . This is a great affliction nowadays, for one rarely sees the shop of a cloth merchant without the presence of women dressed in delicate clothes which expose their adornment, and behaving as if they were with their husbands, or members of their family.

In his long treatise, *al-Madkhal ila tanmiyat al-a'mal bi tahsin al-niyyat,* Ibn al-Hajj dealt with the many ways women were violating the boundaries of private and public space in his day, describing women who routinely went out to shop and flirted with the shopkeepers or fraternized with the male peddlers who came to their houses. Religious rituals provided yet another venue for unauthorized behavior. Women were avid visitors to cemeteries, where they might camp out for a night or two and participate along with men in the Egyptian rituals of singing and talking with a dead saint or relative. At Sufi celebrations women danced unveiled in the streets of Cairo as they participated with men in spiritual dance, chant, and song. Even on ordinary days of leisure, women, along with men and children, flocked to the banks of the Nile, where they strolled, took boat rides, or swam apparently with little regard for the notions of seclusion and modesty dear to Ibn al-Hajj. Furthermore, according to Ibn al-Hajj, if a husband objected to the immodest behavior of his wife in public space, she was likely to threaten him with the withdrawal of her sexual services.

Men and women seated separately in a masjid; illumination from a medieval Persian manuscript (Bodleian Library, Oxford)

Public Women. That female seclusion was far from absolute is also demonstrated by the kinds of occupations women pursued. The women of Cairo are known to have practiced some two dozen occupations during the thirteenth and fourteenth centuries. In many cases, middle- and lower-class women were engaged in work that met the needs of the more-secluded upper class. Female peddlers specializing in purveying goods to the upper-class harems or female bath attendants, who served as the beauticians of their day, provided services essential to the upper-class lifestyle. Midwives and female doctors, governesses, domestic servants, wet nurses, morticians, professional mourners, and matchmakers found employment through assisting other women with some of the most significant events of life—marriage, childbirth, child rearing, and death. Other female occupations, however, must have brought women into contact with men. Some women who worked as merchants were managers of long-distance trade. Other women labored in entertainment fields as musicians, singers, dancers, or prostitutes. Some highly educated women could acquire a reputation as teachers, and there are records of religious women of a mystical bent who rose to the status

of *shaykha*, or adept, in Sufi orders. Women were not found in all occupations, however. There was a wide range of urban crafts and services—including metalworking, dyeing, butchering, and donkey transport—from which women appear to have been totally excluded. The ability of women to enter some public occupations despite ambivalence about their role in public space was aided by their legal status with regard to property. Unlike women in Europe, who in large part did not acquire full rights to independent property holding until the twentieth century, Muslim women in their legal majority had by law the ability to own and manage property without interference from husbands, fathers, or others. Any inherited or earned property or income belonged to a woman herself, and she could dispose of it as she wished. This legal framework enabled women to buy and sell real estate, invest in trade ventures, or endow *waqf* properties. Many upper-class women thus acquired behind-the-scenes power as they pursued business and philanthropic ventures by employing agents to represent them in public. Women of middle- and lower-class backgrounds, with more modest incomes, could still retain control of their property. Although there is not much information on what poor women did with their assets, they probably gave those women leverage within their families and communities. There is even less information on rural women. Travelers during the period commented on the extent to which rural women were seen doing fieldwork, so they were probably an important part of the labor force on family holdings. There seems to have been some division of farm labor according to gender: men worked with the plough to prepare the soil, and women planted seeds and participated in the harvest. In many places, women had special responsibility for herding domestic animals—such as cows, sheep, goats, or camels—and processing their milk and hair for family consumption and for the market. The demands for labor in rural areas, in light of what appears to have been a chronic undersupply of farm labor in this period, probably ensured that women worked alongside their menfolk in most rural settings.

Spiritual Equality. The division of social roles by gender was also modified by an ideological commitment to the spiritual equality of men and women. The Qur'an was abundantly clear that men and women had the same religious duties and religious rewards. Men and women are addressed in equal terms and called on to be believing, devout, truthful, humble, charitable, and chaste, and to pray and keep the fast. The rewards for such virtue are promised to both men and women (Qur'an 33: 35–36). The social roles of men and women were perhaps the most similar in the areas of religious ritual and spiritual quest. Women, like men, were supposed to pray five times a day whether at home or in the masjid. Most masjids were reserved for men, although some masjids of the period were constructed with special sections designated for women. Women and men alike were required to make the pilgrimage to Makkah if they had the ability and resources to do so. Many women of the Mamluk elite, for example, made the pilgrimage from Cairo at least once in their lifetimes, and their departure for the journey to Makkah was the occasion for much pomp and circumstance. They rode in procession in huge palanquins mounted on the backs of camels, accompanied by lesser princes, eunuchs, servants, slaves, and drummers. Their departures and returns were public spectacles: the women and their entourages, dressed in the finest of silks and brocades, paraded through Cairo, much to the chagrin of the conservative ulama'. In addition to prayer and pilgrimage, both men and women were also expected to keep the Ramadan fast and to give alms. The distinctions in male and female roles were least marked in the realm of spiritual quest. The mystical, or Sufi, path was an important element of religious practice of the time, and women were well ensconced in Sufi orders. Women had a strong precedent for following the Sufi way in the person of Rabi'a al-'Adawiyya, an eighth-century Sufi saint who became among the most revered of all time. In her utter devotion to union with God, Rabi'a transcended the notion of maleness and femaleness and achieved spiritual purity. Her legacy no doubt helped to make Sufi orders receptive

to the idea of female adepts, and, indeed, many women were active in Sufi orders during the medieval period, participating fully in public rituals and even assuming leadership roles.

Women as Rulers. Royal wives could play a significant role in governance of Muslim states and sometimes, though rarely, even attain power in their own right. In two of these cases, when male observers were confronted by women who were playing the male role of ruler, they mused about what made a man a man and a woman a woman, rather than criticizing this reversal of the usual order of things. Their comments reveal much about how people of the time thought about social roles and the question of male and female. In the first case, a Muslim scholar reflected with irony on Radiyya bint Iltutmish, who reigned as Sultan of Delhi for three years in the thirteenth century: "Sultan Radiyya—may she rest in peace—was a great sovereign, and wise, just, and beneficent, the patron of the learned, a dispenser of justice, the cherisher of her subjects, and of warlike skills, and was endowed with all the admirable attributes and qualities required of kings; but, as she did not attain her destiny, in her creation, of being computed among men, of what advantage were all these excellent qualifications unto her?" In the second case, a fourteenth-century Ottoman poet wrote a eulogy of the Ilkhanid princess Sati Beg:

> Although she was a woman, she was wise,
> She was experienced and she had good judgment.
>
> Whatever task she undertook, she accomplished,
> She succeeded at the exercise of sovereignty.
>
> There are many women who are greater than men,
> There are many men who are baser than women.
>
> What is manhood? It is generosity, intelligence, and piety,
> Whoever possesses these three things is surely a man.

Sources:
Leila Ahmed, *Women and Gender in Islam: Historical Roots of a Modern Debate* (New Haven: Yale University Press, 1992).

Maulana Muhammad Ali, trans., *A Manual of Hadith* (Guilford, U.K.: Curzon Press, 1983).

Ibn Battuta, *Travels in Asia and Africa, 1325–1354*, 3 volumes, translated by H. A. R. Gibb (London: Routledge, 1929).

Gavin Hambly, ed., *Women in the Medieval Muslim World* (New York: St. Martin's Press, 1998).

Nikki R. Keddie and Beth Baron, eds., *Women in Middle Eastern History: Shifting Boundaries in Sex and Gender* (New Haven: Yale University Press, 1991).

Guity Nashat and Judith Tucker, *Women in the Middle East and North Africa: Restoring Women to History* (Bloomington: Indiana University Press, 1998).

Leslie Peirce, *The Imperial Harem: Women and Sovereignty in the Ottoman Empire* (New York: Oxford University Press, 1993).

Margaret Smith, *Rabi'a the Mystic and Her Fellow-Saints in Islam* (Cambridge: Cambridge University Press, 1928).

SIGNIFICANT PEOPLE

'A'ISHA BINT ABI BAKR

CIRCA 614 - 678
WIFE OF MUHAMMAD

The Prophet's Wife. 'A'isha bint Abi Bakr was the daughter of Abu Bakr, a trusted Companion of the Prophet. She was married to the Prophet Muhammad when she was nine and became his favorite wife and confidante. She was also the subject of one of Muhammad's divine revelations, which exonerated her of a charge of adultery brought against her when she was fourteen. She never bore children.

Political Role. After Muhammad's death in 632, when 'A'isha was only eighteen, her father became the Prophet's successor as political leader of the Islamic community, where 'A'isha also played a key political role, lending her support to the opponents of 'Ali ibn Abi Talib, the fourth political successor to the Prophet, who was accused of complicity in the murder of his predecessor, 'Uthman (ruled 644–656). She participated in the major military confrontation that decided the succession issue, which was named the Battle of the Camel (656) because she entered the fray borne on the back of a camel in order to inspire the troops. After 'Ali's resounding victory, 'A'isha was returned to Madinah as a virtual prisoner and spent the next two decades transmitting information about the words and deeds of the Prophet Muhammad. She is the original source of many traditions (hadiths) that have continued to guide Muslims over the years.

'A'isha's Legacy. While she has been revered as the beloved wife of the Prophet and an important source of authentic material about the Prophet's life, her political role has been more controversial. She was criticized by later Muslim writers for encouraging discord in the community and for intruding into the male world of politics and warfare. Others, however, have maintained that her political activism can serve as a model for Muslim women and their full participation in religious, social, and political life. She is popular among modern Muslim feminists, who emphasize her success in combining the roles of faithful wife, public person, and Islamic scholar.

Source:
Denise Spellburg, *Politics, Gender, and the Islamic Past: The Legacy of 'A'isha bint Abi Bakr* (New York: Columbia University Press, 1994).

AHMAD IBN 'ABD AL-RAHIM

DIED 1423
SCHOLAR

Traveling Scholar. Ahmad ibn 'Abd al-Rahim, known as Ibn al-'Iraqi, was born in Cairo in 1360 into a prominent intellectual family. His father, also known as Ibn al-'Iraqi, took an early hand in his son's education and, before the boy was three years of age, took him before some of the best-known teachers in Cairo. At age three, Ahmad made his first journey of "learning" with his father, traveling to Damascus and Jerusalem, where he visited the leading scholars and hadith transmitters of the time, hearing their lessons and hadiths firsthand. Although it seems doubtful that he would remember much of anything from these encounters, his father was able to secure *ijazahs* that later gave his son the distinction of having connections to a previous generation of transmitters. Ahmad's education in Cairo focused on law, grammar, and hadiths, and he received fellowships in several different madrasahs. He undertook at least two more study tours as a youth, traveling with his father to Makkah and Madinah to study hadiths and stopping on the return journey in Syria to hear hadiths again from the next generation of transmitters.

Teacher. While still in his twenties, Ahmad assumed his father's teaching posts in several Cairo madrasahs after his father was appointed a judge in Makkah and "inherited" the posts permanently on the death of his father. As Ahmad became known as an important legal scholar and transmitter of hadiths, the number of those who studied with him increased dramatically. In fact, there were few top students from any Islamic school of law who had not studied with him. He also was appointed a judge in an Islamic court. In 1422 he resigned his judgeship and outside teaching posts, retiring to his house where he taught and wrote until he died a year later.

A Typical Scholar. Many elements of Ahmad's life seem typical for a prominent scholar, including the care that was taken with his education under the watchful eye of his father, who then passed on his teaching posts to his son. His scholarly career was further fostered by his connections to and contacts with other prominent intellectuals, who provided him with the certificates as well as substantive learning. Ultimately, however, Ahmad's success as a teacher and scholar was based on his own reputation and his ability to attract students.

Source:
Jonathan Berkey, *The Transmission of Knowledge in Medieval Cairo* (Princeton: Princeton University Press, 1992).

'AISH'A BINT MUHAMMAD IBN 'ABD AL-HADI

FOURTEENTH CENTURY
SCHOLAR

Quest for Knowledge. 'Aish'a bint Muhammad ibn 'Abd al-Hadi was born in Damascus in the early fourteenth century to a family of the intellectual elite. Her education began as early as age four, when she was brought before al-Hajjar, a well-known transmitter of hadiths, from whom she heard two hadith collections. Her education continued under several scholars, most of whom were friends of her father. Focusing on the study of hadiths and the biography of the Prophet Muham-

mad, she acquired *ijazahs* from prominent scholars of Aleppo, Hama, Nablus, and Hebron. Scholars do not know if she traveled to all these cities as part of her knowledge quest or took advantage of their temporary presence in Damascus.

Teacher. Eventually visits to 'Aish'a became a popular part of the learning tours of male scholars, who listed her as their teacher in hadith studies. She also instructed some thirty-five women. Part of her success as a teacher was linked to her longevity (she lived to age eighty-four), which ensured that she alone spoke for the hadith transmitters of her generation. Of particular importance was her early contact with al-Hajjar. She was 4, and he was 103, when she heard his transmission, so in the later part of her life she was the only individual who had had personal contact with him.

Career. 'Aish'a's career was typical for the female scholar. Her family connections, and especially her father's interest in her learning, helped her gain access to higher education. Although she was not formally enrolled in a school, she managed to study with some of the most prominent scholars of the day. Like most female scholars, she focused on the field of hadiths, where the reputed female capacity for memory served her well, and her career reached its high point only when she was an elderly person who could claim direct intellectual connections to other scholars long deceased. Her life illustrates how a woman—despite exclusion from formal educational institutions—might still carve out a scholarly career and gain a position of considerable respect in intellectual circles.

Sources:
Jonathan Berkey, *The Transmission of Knowledge in Medieval Cairo* (Princeton: Princeton University Press, 1992).

Ruth Roded, *Women in Islamic Biographical Collections: From Ibn Sa'd to Who's Who* (Boulder: Lynne Rienner, 1994).

DOCUMENTARY SOURCES

Alf Laylah wa-Laylah (The Thousand and One Nights) —A collection of stories that circulated orally and were collected in essentially final form during the fourteenth century; also translated as *The Arabian Nights,* the stories include many details of palace life and relations between men and women.

Muhammad ibn Ismail al-Bukhari (810–870), *Sahih* (Traditions of the Prophet) — A canonical collection of hadiths, the narratives of the Prophet Muham-mad's life that served as guides and precedents for the religious and social lives of Muslims.

Abu Hamid al-Ghazali (1058–1111), *Nasihat al-muluk* (Council for Kings) — A manual of advice for rulers by a prominent philosopher and theologian, which includes reflections on the proper behavior rulers should enforce; the book includes several passages on men's and women's social roles, including a strong endorsement of female seclusion.

Abu Abd Allah Muhammad Ibn Battuta (1304 – circa 1378), *Rihlah* (Travels) — A travel record of a North African who between 1325 and 1354 journeyed from Morocco in the West as far as China in the East; his journal includes observations of the lifestyles he encountered throughout the Muslim world and beyond.

'Ali ibn Abi Bakr al-Marghinini (died 1196 or 1197), *Hidayah* (Guidance) — An Islamic legal text by a prominent jurist of the Hanafi school, which includes discussion of Islamic rules regarding marriage, divorce, child custody, inheritance, and business arrangements.

Mourning for Layla's husband, Ibn Salam; illumination attributed to Qasim Ali from a 1494 manuscript for *Khamsah* (Five) by Nizami (British Library, London)

RELIGION
AND PHILOSOPHY

by VINCENT J. CORNELL

CONTENTS

CHRONOLOGY

324

OVERVIEW

332

**TOPICS IN RELIGION
AND PHILOSOPHY**

Din and Theology in
Qur'an and Sunnah 335

Free Will and the Rise of
Islamic Sectarianism 343

Sayings of Imam 'Ali. 344

Divine Rights of Khalifahs 350

Origins and Development of
Systematic Theology 354

Heredity and Sin 356

The Rise of Falsafah:
The Philosophical
Tradition 366

Ibn Sina's Poetry 371

The Sunni Critique of
Kalam and Falsafah 381

Ibn Rushd Versus al-Ghazali . . . 387

**SIGNIFICANT
PEOPLE**

Abu Hamid Muhammad
al-Tusi al-Ghazali 393

Muhyi al-Din Ibn
al-'Arabi 393

Muhammad 394

Rabi'ah al-Adawiyyah 395

Jalal al-Din Rumi 396

**DOCUMENTARY
SOURCES**

397

Sidebars and tables are listed in italics.

622
- Muhammad and his followers migrate from Makkah (Mecca) to Madinah (Medina), where he is offered asylum from Makkan persecution and leadership of the city. He establishes the first Islamic polity.

628
- Muhammad dispatches letters to the emperor of Byzantium, the shah of Persia, and the "Muqawqis" of Egypt, inviting them to convert to Islam.

630
- Muhammad gains control of Makkah. He grants amnesty to the population and removes the symbols of idol worship from the Ka'bah, rededicating the Haram (holy sanctuary) to the worship of the One God.

632
- Muhammad leads Muslims on his Farewell Pilgrimage, establishing the hajj (pilgrimage) rites that are still practiced annually.
- Muhammad dies in Madinah. Abu Bakr succeeds him as leader of the Muslim state and becomes the first of the *Khulafa' al-Rashidun*, or Rightly Guided Khalifahs (caliphs).

634
- Abu Bakr dies in Madinah. 'Umar ibn al-Khattab succeeds him as khalifah.

637
- Jerusalem comes under Muslim rule; 'Umar ibn al-Khattab visits the city, guaranteeing the safety of Christian and Jewish holy places.

644
- 'Umar ibn al-Khattab is assassinated by a disgruntled Christian slave. An appointed committee selects 'Uthman ibn Affan as his successor.

650*
- Under the khilafah (caliphate) of 'Uthman, the Qur'an is standardized by a committee headed by the Prophet's secretary, Zayd ibn Thabit, who has checked the text against the recitations of those who had memorized the Qur'an and the sections of the Qur'an copied by the Prophet's scribes.

656
- 'Uthman is murdered by Muslim rebels, and 'Ali ibn Abi Talib succeeds him as khalifah, beginning the first fitna (period of civil strife). 'Ali's followers create the Shi'ite movement. Mu'awiyyah, the governor of Syria, challenges 'Ali's khilafah. The Prophet's wife 'A'isha and the Prophet's Companions Talhah and Zubayr also resist 'Ali.

657
- Arbitration ends the battle of Siffin between 'Ali and Mu'awiyyah. Elements of 'Ali's army secede and create the Kharijite (Secessionist) movement.

* Denotes Circa Date

658
- 'Ali defeats the Kharijites at the Battle of Nahrawan.

661
- 'Ali is murdered by a Kharijite, leaving Mu'awiyyah undisputed leader and the first Umayyad ruler; 'Ali's eldest son, Hasan ibn 'Ali, reaches agreement with Mu'awiyyah and renounces his rights to the khilafah.

661–750
- The Umayyad dynasty rules the khilafah.

670
- Hasan ibn 'Ali, the second Shi'ite Imam, dies in Madinah. (Hasan is the ancestor of the present-day kings of Jordan and Morocco.)

680
- 'Ali's son Husayn ibn 'Ali, the third Shi'ite Imam, and his followers are killed at Karbala' in Iraq during the reign of Khalifah Yazid ibn Mu'awiyyah (ruled 680–683).

683–693
- The Najdite Kharijites, who believe that an individual who repeats a sin is an idolater, revolt against the Umayyad khilafah.

684*
- Ibadite Kharijism is born. Communities of Ibadites, who believe that only those who reject God should be considered idolaters, continue to exist in Oman, Tunisia, and Algeria.

686–687
- Led by Mukhtar al-Thaqafi, the Kaysaniyyah Shi'ites revolt against the Umayyads. Mukhtar proclaims 'Ali's third son, Muhammad ibn al-Hanafiyyah, Imam and Mahdi (Guided One).

687
- The first Muslim scholar to espouse doctrine of the "uncreated Qur'an," 'Abd Allah ibn 'Abbas, cousin of the Prophet Muhammad and commentator on the Qur'an, dies in Madinah.

690*
- Mu'adhah al-Adawiyyah founds a school for female ascetics at Basrah.

700
- Mahdist pretender Muhammad ibn al-Hanafiyyah dies.

* DENOTES CIRCA DATE

717
- 'Ali Zayn al-'Abidin, the fourth Shi'ite Imam, dies in Madinah.

- Descendants of 'Abd Allah ibn 'Abbas (died 687), cousin of the Prophet Muhammad, create the Abbasid movement, which eventually overthrows the Umayyad khilafah.

717-720
- Umayyad khalifah 'Umar ibn 'Abd al-'Aziz, who is known for his piety and evenhandedness, attempts to integrate converts to Islam into Umayyad society.

728
- Hasan al-Basri, theologian and influential traditionist, dies in Basrah.

735
- Muhammad al-Baqir, the fifth Shi'ite Imam, dies in Madinah. Modern scholars consider him to be the founder of Shi'ism as a separate religious sect within Islam.

740
- Zayd ibn 'Ali, son of Imam 'Ali Zayn al-'Abidin, founds the Zaydi Shi'ite movement and is killed in a revolt against the Umayyads.

748
- Wasil ibn 'Ata', a student of Hasan al-Basri, dies. Wasil is the reputed founder of the rationalist theological movement known as the Mu'tazila.

750-1256
- Having finally defeated the Umayyads, the Abbasids rule the khilafah.

754*
- St. John of Damascus, an Arab Christian theologian and an Umayyad official, dies.

754-763*
- Ismail al-Mubarak, first son and designated successor of Shi'ite Imam Ja'far al-Sadiq, dies.

754-775
- During the khilafah of al-Mansur, Greek, Persian, and Syriac works of science and philosophy are translated into Arabic.

757-1034
- The Umayyads rule Islamic Spain (al-Andalus). This period is considered the high point of Muslim civilization in Spain.

***DENOTES CIRCA DATE**

762
- Khalifah al-Mansur founds Baghdad as the Abbasid capital.

765
- After the death of Ja'far al-Sadiq, sixth Shi'ite Imam, creator of Shi'ite jurisprudence, and influential commentator on the Qur'an, the dispute over the succession to the Imamate creates a rift between Imami and Ismaili Shi'ites.

767
- Abu Hanifah, reputed founder of the Hanafi school of jurisprudence, dies in Baghdad.

786-809
- Kalam (Islamic theology) comes into its own as a formal discipline during the reign of Abbasid khalifah Harun al-Rashid.

791
- Idris ibn 'Abd Allah, a descendant of Imam Hasan ibn 'Ali, is proclaimed Imam in Morocco. Worried about the threat he poses to the Abbasids, Harun al-Rashid sends agents who murder Idris.

795
- Malik ibn Anas, founder of the Maliki school of jurisprudence, dies in Madinah.

796*
- Muhammad ibn Ismail, seventh Imam of Ismaili Shi'ism, dies somewhere in eastern Iran. Ismaili Shi'ites consider him to have been the successor to Imam Ja'far al-Sadiq.

799
- Musa al-Kazim, seventh Imam of Imami Shi'ism, is poisoned in Baghdad on orders from Khalifah Harun al-Rashid.

801
- Sufi mystic Rabi'ah al-'Adawiyyah, a well-known woman saint, dies in Basrah.

813-833
- The khilafah of al-Ma'mun is considered a high point of Islamic rationalism.

817*
- Bishr ibn al-Mu'tamir, founder of the Mu'tazilite school of Baghdad, dies.

817
- In Merv, Turkmenistan, Abbasid khalifah al-Ma'mun proclaims 'Ali al-Rida, eighth Imam of Imami Shi'ism, heir to the khilafah.

* Denotes Circa Date

818
- Imam 'Ali al-Rida dies near the city of Tus in eastern Iran.

820
- Muhammad ibn Idris al-Shafi'i, founder of the Shafi'i school of jurisprudence, dies in al-Fustat (Old Cairo).

830
- Al-Ma'mun founds the Bayt al-Hikmah (House of Wisdom) in Baghdad.

833-850
- Mu'tazilism is the official theology of the Abbasid state. Non-Mu'tazilite theologians and hadith scholars are persecuted.

836
- Mu'tazilite theologian Ibrahim al-Nazzam dies. He taught that the Qur'an was created in time, rather than being the eternal, uncreated word of God.

840*
- Abu al-Hudhayl, who founded the Mu'tazilite school of Basrah, dies.

850
- Khalifah al-Mutawwakil ends dominance of the Mu'tazila and revives Sunni Muslim theology.

854
- Sahnun 'Abd al-Salam, the systematizer of Maliki jurisprudence, dies in Tunisia.

855
- Ahmad ibn Hanbal, hadith scholar and a founder of the Hanbali school of jurisprudence, dies in Baghdad.

857
- Sufi theologian al-Harith ibn Asad al-Muhasibi dies in Baghdad. He is known as the founder of Sufi psychology and the originator of the tripartite concept of the soul.

866
- Abu Yusuf Ya'qub al-Kindi, "Philosopher of the Arabs," patron of the translation movement, and the first major Islamic philosopher, dies in Baghdad.

868
- Al-Jahiz, essayist and Mu'tazilite theologian, dies in Baghdad.

* **Denotes Circa Date**

874-962

- During the period of the Short Occultation of Muhammad al-Mahdi, twelfth Imam of the Imami Shi'ites, the Imam communicates with his followers through four Imami scholars. During the Complete Occultation, which begins in 962 and is ongoing, he communicates through inspiration to select followers.

874-999

- The rule of the Samanids in eastern Iran and Central Asia is one of the greatest periods of the flowering of Islamic thought.

909-1171

- During this period the Fatimid dynasty of Ismaili Shi'ites rules North Africa, Egypt, and Syria.

910

- Abu al-Qasim al-Junayd dies in Baghdad. He is known as "Master of the Sufi Way" and the founder of the Sufi doctrine of divine oneness.

915

- Abu 'Ali al-Jubba'i, "First Master" of the Basrah school of the Mu'tazila, dies.

922

- Mansur al-Hallaj, a Sufi mystic and ecstatic, is executed for heresy in Baghdad. Later Sufis revere him as a martyr.

933

- Abu Hashim ibn al-Jubba'i, "Second Master" of the Basrah school of the Mu'tazila, dies.

935

- Abu al-Hasan al-Ash'ari dies. He was founder of the Ash'arite school of Kalam, which subsequently dominates Sunni theology.

944

- Abu Mansur al-Maturidi, founder of the Maturidi school of Kalam, dies in Central Asia.

945-1055

- Buyid emirs dominate the Abbasid khilafah in Iraq and Iran. They are major promoters of Imami Shi'ism and philosophical speculation.

950

- Abu Nasr Muhammad al-Farabi (known in the West as Alfarabius or Abunaser), the "Second Teacher" of Islamic philosophy after Aristotle, dies in Damascus. He combined the doctrines of Plato and Aristotle and excelled in metaphysics, the philosophy of language, and the philosophy of knowledge.

* DENOTES CIRCA DATE

998
- Muhammad ibn Abi Zayd, Maliki jurist and opponent of philosophers and Shi'ites, dies in Qayrawan, Tunisia.

1021
- Abu 'Abd al-Rahman al-Sulami, Sufi biographer, Qur'an commentator, and major figure in the Sunni "usulization" of knowledge movement, dies in the Iranian city of Nishapur. The movement seeks to unify and limit sources of religious knowledge.

1022
- Al-Shaykh al-Mufid, biographer of the Shi'ite Imams, dies in Baghdad.

1024
- Qadi 'Abd al-Jabbar, judge of Rayy (modern Tehran) and Mu'tazilite theologian, dies.

1037
- Ibn Sina (known in the West as Avicenna), the greatest Islamic philosopher of Iran and exponent of "Oriental Wisdom," dies in the city of Hamadan.

1067
- Saljuk wazir Nizam al-Mulk founds the Nizamiyyah madrasah in Baghdad to educate Sunni scholars and to promote Sunni orthodoxy.

1074
- Abu al-Qasim al-Qushayri, an Ash'arite theologian and author of the most important Sufi handbook of orthodox mysticism, dies in Nishapur.

1111
- Abu Hamid al-Ghazali, a Shafi'i jurist, Ash'arite theologian, and Sufi, dies in eastern Iran. Called "The Proof of Islam," he wrote the decisive Sunni critique of Islamic philosophy.

1150-1250*
- Sufi Tariqahs (Orders) are founded as Sufism becomes established at all levels of society.

1166
- 'Abd al-Qadir al-Jilani, the Hanbali scholar for whom the Qadiriyyah Sufi order is named, dies in Baghdad.

1198
- Ibn Rushd (known in the West as Averroës), commentator on Aristotle and the greatest philosopher of Muslim Spain, dies in Córdoba.

* DENOTES CIRCA DATE

1236
- Córdoba falls to Christian forces, marking the beginning of the end of Muslim rule in Spain.

1240
- Spanish Muslim mystic Muhammad (Muhyi al-Din) Ibn al-'Arabi of Murcia, Spain, widely regarded as the greatest Sufi theologian, dies in Damascus.

1254
- In Seville, systematic translation of Arabic works into Latin takes place under the aegis of King Alfonso X of Castile and León.

1273
- Jalal al-Din Rumi, Persian Sufi and poet, dies in Konya, Turkey.

1406
- Ibn Khaldun, Islamic historian, jurist, and father of the discipline of sociology, dies in Cairo.

1492
- Granada, the last Muslim state in Spain, falls to Christian forces.

* **DENOTES CIRCA DATE**

Lustreware bowl with a depiction of a priest swinging a censer, made for a Christian living in Muslim territory during the first half of the twelfth century (Victoria and Albert Museum, London)

OVERVIEW

Islam. The name *Islam* and the concepts associated with its teachings are found in the Qur'an, which Muslims believe to be the Word of God revealed to the Prophet Muhammad during roughly twenty-two years between 610 and Muhammad's death in 632. The Islamic belief system is not named after a leader or the person who established the faith community. Muhammad is understood to be the human vessel for the revelation. His mission was to receive and transmit the message of Islam and also to live as the embodiment of Islam. The name *Islam* designates the goal for the believer—entering "the state of submission to God." Understanding of Islamic teachings presupposes use of terminology from within the faith, beginning with the term *din*, which is generically translated as "religion." The English term may be used to designate any one of several religious traditions, but the Arabic term *din* means religion as such. The meaning of *din* includes concepts defining the relationship between the Creator and each human being and describing the human condition itself, one of inborn inclination toward submission to the authority of God and fulfillment of the obligation to worship (the Five Pillars of Islam) and to do good works. The term for a follower of Islam—*Muslim*—does not refer to adherence to any earthly manifestation such as a human leader, institution, or cult. Just as the word *Islam* refers to a goal, the word *Muslim* refers to an aspiration—to be a person who submits to God in knowledge and practice. Thus, the claim that the prophets and messengers of God are Muslim refers to this quality rather than being a partisan designation. The designation embraces the whole line of prophethood that begins with Adam and includes Noah, Abraham, Moses, Jesus, and Muhammad.

The Qur'an. The primary source of religious knowledge in Islam is the Qur'an, the book revealed to humankind through Muhammad and recorded in memory and in writing before his death. The Qur'an was transmitted and interpreted by the Prophet's example, called the Sunnah, which was in turn transmitted in the form of the hadiths (records of his words and deeds) and in accounts of Muhammad's life. The Qur'anic text describes the nature of God and His relation to creation, both human and natural, and points to the natural world as a sign of God. In addition, the Qur'an includes prescriptions for individual and collective moral behavior, social organization, and worship. The description of God in the Qur'an is embodied in the concept of *tawhid,* a simple expression of monotheism. The sum total of Qur'anic statements about Allah is sufficiently complex to have engendered a theological discourse that has reverberated through the centuries and has interacted with other philosophical and theological systems. Intellectual discourse in the Muslim tradition unfolded in four major directions: the system of Shari'ah (Islamic law), systematic theology and philosophy, the natural sciences, and Islamic mysticism, or Sufism.

Shari'ah. Shari'ah is the path of Islamic practice, integrating the teachings of the Qur'an into individual and community life. Islamic jurisprudence meant acquisition of knowledge from the divine sources (Qur'an and Sunnah) and training in *fiqh,* the analytical process of applying human reason to understanding how this knowledge should be applied. Muslim jurists were the most important ulama' (scholars) in premodern Muslim society. The often-repeated statement that Islam is a complete way of life stems from the nature of Shari'ah as a comprehensive system. All human behavior is understood to fall under the purview of Islamic law on a spectrum ranging from obligatory, approved, neutral, disapproved, or forbidden acts. The jurist's role was to draw on his knowledge to evaluate actions based on interpretation of the context and relationship of the act to the text. The flexibility of Shari'ah stems from the application of the text to principles and to new circumstances that did not arise during the time of the Prophet. Differences of approach and interpretation resulted in the development of schools of Islamic law, called *madhhabs,* which were based on the teaching of a founding jurist and characterized by their methods of reasoning. Four main Sunni madhhabs—the Hanafi, Maliki, Shafi'i, and Hanbali schools—emerged in the eighth and ninth centuries and came to dominate in certain geographic regions. The Shafi'i school became especially influential for its principles of applied reason, called *usul al-fiqh* (literally, roots of jurisprudence).

Sunnites and Shi'ites. Closely related to the development of Shari'ah were the doctrinal differences that arose from recurrent disputes over the legitimacy of political leadership of the Muslim community after the death of the Prophet Muhammad in 632. Those who attained power and their opposition differed in their views on the criteria for selection of leadership and the nature of the office of Muhammad's successor. The best-known division giving rise to sectarianism in Islam was the dispute in 658–661 between 'Ali ibn Abi Talib (circa 596 – 661) and the Umayyad ruler Mu'awiyyah (circa 605 – 680), which gave rise to the Shi'ite branch of Islam and various offshoots from it in the following centuries. Those who acquiesced to Umayyad rule and rejected the belief that 'Ali was the sole legitimate successor to Muhammad later came to be known as Ahl al-Sunnah, or Sunnites. Beliefs about the criteria for leadership of the Muslim *ummah* (community) led to differences in doctrine, theology, and law and influenced the concepts of khilafah (caliphate) and imamate as political and religious institutions.

Free Will versus Predestination. Among the most important theological disputes were opposing claims about free will and predestination that took on political overtones surrounding the issue of the legitimacy of the leadership. Though the Qur'an clearly indicates that human beings are granted free will corresponding to their responsibility and accountability for their actions, interpretations of scripture just as clearly state that Allah's omnipotence encompasses the fate of nations and individuals. These seemingly paradoxical teachings gave rise to different interpretations. Partisans of 'Ali—the literal meaning of Shi'at 'Ali, for example—held that leadership was divinely vested in the house of the Prophet through 'Ali and his first wife, Fatimah, who was Muhammad's daughter, but they relied on a doctrine of individual choice to support the ideal of seeking justice in the face of oppression. Even so, the use of reason in applying the divine message to practice seemed limited among many Shi'ite groups by their belief that true knowledge and religious authority were vested in a series of Imams and their designated representatives. The Umayyad rulers, on the other hand, came to espouse a doctrine of predestination that supported not only the inevitability of the Umayyad rulers, but the rightness of their decrees. At their most extreme, disagreements over the succession resulted in the accusation that opponents had strayed outside the community of Muslims. The Murjiah took a neutral position that allowed faith to coexist with flawed behavior, offering a way out of the impasse created by the opponents and supporters of the Umayyads. This position restored the belief that human beings choose between good and evil as a logical condition for the doctrine of human accountability before God on Judgment Day.

Other Intellectual Traditions. As the geographic horizons of Muslim society widened to include many cultures, Muslims were exposed to a broad heritage of knowledge and the conceptual vocabulary of Islamic discourse expanded as well. Chief among these influences were the intellectual traditions of the Greeks, Persians, and Indians, as well as the interactions of Muslims with adherents and former adherents of other faith traditions, including Christianity, Judaism, and Zoroastrianism. Issues and terminology from outside Islamic sources became part of an eclectic intellectual discourse. An elaborate theology, or *kalam*, developed around the application of these concepts, fostering debates in which Muslims retained confidence in Islamic institutions while exhibiting their openness to eclectic influences. Discussions in the *kalam* tradition concentrated on the attributes of God and the problem of comprehending the nature of God within the limitations of the human mind and the earthly experience. For Muslims, intellectual discourse over the eternity and transcendence of God had implications for the human sphere. Disputes about the universal and eternal nature of the Qur'an were seen to be tied to the legitimacy of Islamic jurisprudence. Issues surrounding free will, human responsibility for good and evil acts, and the status of Muslims who committed sins absorbed the interest of writers and debaters for centuries.

Mu'tazilism. Disputes over Mu'tazilism, a movement that emphasized theological rationalism over the authority of Islamic tradition, arose in the ninth century, becoming the official theology of the Abbasid khilafah in 833–850. This dispute over tradition and reason engendered an inquisition that targeted Muslim scholars. Mu'tazilism was influential for approximately four hundred years, from the second half of the eighth to the twelfth century, during which its proponents and opponents advanced Muslim theological discourse by weighing the conceptual vocabulary and core beliefs of the Islamic sources against ideas from Greek, Christian, and other sources. Ultimately, these debates brought forth systematic Sunni and Shi'i Muslim responses to rationalist thought and arguments over the scope of human action and divine justice. Abu Mansur al-Maturidi (died 944) was influential in beginning efforts to work out a theory of knowledge and perception that placed investigation of the natural sciences in a theological context. While these theological movements were centered on Baghdad and elsewhere in Iraq, the geographic range of the discourse expanded into Central Asia, the eastern Mediterranean, and North Africa. The spread of paper-manufacturing knowledge and the expansion of markets that accompanied increased urbanization resulted in growth of the availability of books, while the rise in Arabic literacy created demand.

The Greek Influence. Greek philosophy, which had been cultivated in the late Persian empire and continued under Persian influence at the Abbasid court, entered Muslim intellectual life with the surge of translation activity that began in Baghdad during the mid eighth century. Subsequent development of a sophisticated body of *Falsafah* (philosophy) by Muslims included al-Kindi (circa 801 – 866), al-Farabi (circa 870 – 950), Ibn Sina (980–1037), and Ibn Rushd (1126–1198). The philosophers strove to explain every phenomenon by logic and rational demonstration and tended to dismiss faith-based arguments. Contrary to some modern commentators on Islam, reconciling religion and philosophy was not a question of whether it was permissible for Muslims to use the human faculty of reason. Many passages in the Qur'an call on the believer to exercise reason as a way to know God and His creation. Clearly, however, the knowledge of God could not be encompassed through reason alone. The critical process of coming to terms with the power of the Greek rationalist model to explain the creation, without contradicting the letter and spirit of the Qur'an and Sunnah, was a challenging enterprise. It was not, however, an either/or proposition between faith and reason. The proof of the value and the complexity of the effort lies in the fact that the major writers in the Falsafah tradition also made major contributions in scientific studies. They were comprehensive thinkers and seekers of knowledge wherever it could be found, writing theoretical and empirical studies in fields that included mathematics, astronomy, medicine, music, chemistry, and politics. Just as the Qur'an is not a scientific work, it is not a detailed philosophical or legal work. Just as the idea of the oneness of God and the invitation to the believers to investigate and appreciate the creation led to human activity in many spheres, the *faylasuf* (philosopher) was stimulated by the Qur'an and carried that impetus forward in the sphere of human speculative thought. The challenge was to remain firmly within the Qur'anic framework and not to write God out of the equation in their enthusiasm for what could be rationally demonstrated. There was no shortage of critics to warn that their ideas were heretical, nor did some thinkers in the Falsafah tradition fail to go outside the bounds of orthodoxy. Among the defenses they put forth were notions that Greek thinkers, who lived before Islam, displayed an affinity to Islam, and that the Greeks were influenced by the Hebrew prophets. Others emphasized the centrality of God to their systems and justified the search for universal truths. By the eleventh century, the movement away from Falsafah was carried by a Sunni revival represented by al-Ghazali (1059–1111) and the dominance of Shafi'i jurisprudence based on the legal model of usul al-fiqh, which hewed closely to the Qur'an and the hadiths. The spread of training in this method through a growing education system of colleges made it a standard part of the curriculum in the education of Muslim elites and prospective officials.

Asceticism. The tendency of asceticism could be traced directly back to Prophet Muhammad and some of his Companions. Ascetic practice developed into Sufism, often called the mystical branch of Islam, an egalitarian movement that included many women. While the historical evidence indicates that early asceticism was sometimes taken to extremes, it did not develop into a monastic tradition, as in Christianity or Buddhism. Such tendencies were moderated by the Prophet's teachings about the middle way, expressed in the supplication for "guidance to the straight path" in the Opening (Fatihah) chapter of the Qur'an, which every Muslim recites in each daily prayer. Extremism in any form is disavowed in Islam as counterproductive, and tendencies toward isolationism are counterbalanced by the exhortation to serve one's fellow humans rather than turning away from them. Beginning with a tradition of ascetic experience, by the ninth century, Sufi writers began to lay out the principles supporting Sufism and systematic methodologies for overcoming the shackles of the self and its attachment to the world. Al-Junayd (died 910) developed a theology of Sunni Sufism and contributed to the institutionalization of Sufism, which sought to replicate the experience of nearness to God in a wider following. Sufi brotherhoods and formal orders developed in the ensuing centuries, playing important roles in the organization of urban and rural life and spreading Islam along the trade routes beyond the periphery of territory under Muslim rule.

TOPICS IN RELIGION AND PHILOSOPHY

DIN AND THEOLOGY IN QUR'AN AND SUNNAH

Interpreting Islam. Muslims and non-Muslims often ask what Islam says about God and religion, but these questions are posed the wrong way. Islam does not say anything. Muslims, believers in Islam, say and write things about God, the prophets, and the requirements of the Islamic religion. The Qur'an, the Holy Scripture of Islam, states, "Verily, the religion [*din*] of God [*Allah*] is Islam" (3: 19). To understand this passage in its full context, it is important to know exactly what Arabic terms such as *din* and *Allah* mean. Defining such religious concepts requires interpretation. Interpreting the religion of Islam is the subject of Islamic dogma. Interpreting the nature of God (*Allah*) is the subject of Islamic theology.

The Concept of *Din* and Religious Practice. Islamic dogma is based on the term *din*. In general, *din* is the Arabic word for "religion." But *din* means more than the Western idea of a "church" or institutional religion. A Semitic language like Hebrew, Arabic is structured in a system of roots—two to five consonants in length—that form words that are related in meaning. The root of the Arabic word *din* is *d-y-n*. This root has four primary meanings: mutual obligation, submission or acknowledgment, judicial authority, and natural inclination or tendency. For example, the word *dana*, which comes from *din*, means "being indebted"; this term conveys an entire group of meanings related to the idea of debt. The word *da'in*, depending on the way in which it is used, can mean either "debtor" or "creditor," words that have opposite meanings but are based on the same concept. To be *da'in* means that one is obliged to follow all of the laws, customs, and ordinances covering indebtedness. Being in debt also implies obligation, which is expressed in Arabic by the term *dayn*, another word that comes from the same root. Indebtedness may also involve formal judgment (*daynunah*) or conviction (*idanah*), terms that relate to one's obligation to pay or otherwise fulfill a debt or a contract. Commercial life, which is based to a large extent on the responsibility to fulfill one's contracts and debts, is centered in a town or a city, both of which are designated in Arabic by the term *madinah*. A city has a judge, ruler, or governor, each of whom may be desig-

nated by the term *dayyan*. In Islamic society, belonging to a community, whether a family, a tribe, or an urban community, is fundamental to the human condition. Similarly, the concept of civilization has always been associated in Islam with towns and cities. Thus, it is not surprising to find that some of the Arabic terms for civilization are also derived from the root *dyn: tamaddana* means "to build or found cities" or "to refine" or "to humanize," while *tamaddun* means "civilization" or "refinement of society." When one considers the four primary meanings of the root *dyn*, one realizes that in Islam, religion (*din*) is natural to the human condition. Religion conveys the idea of obligation or indebtedness, the acknowledgment of indebtedness, and the requirement to repay one's debts.

Responsibility. The logic that underlies the concept of religion in Islam can be summed up in two additional concepts that have important ethical and theological implications: responsibility and reciprocity. In Islam, human beings are indebted to *Allah*, the One God, for creating them, providing for them, and maintaining their existence. The spiritually aware human being believes that human intelligence and creativity are only pale imitations of divine knowledge and creativity. The human being cannot create a race of new beings or maintain an entire universe. According to the Qur'an, every human being acknowledges a debt to God at the core of his or her being. This debt is expressed as a covenant, established between humanity and its Creator even before the human race was placed on earth: "When thy Lord drew forth their descendants from the children of Adam, He made them testify concerning themselves [saying]: 'Am I not your Lord?' They replied, 'Yes, we do so testify'" (7: 172).

The Pious Slave of God. In Islam, the most important debt that the human being owes to God is that of his or her existence. Thus, the Qur'an often portrays the human being as a "slave of God" (*'Abd Allah*). Because he owes his existence to God, the spiritually aware person knows that he is the substance of his own debt and must repay God by giving himself over to the service of his Creator and submitting to God's commands and ordinances. This total submission to God is what is meant by the term *Islam*. The person who submits to God is called a *Muslim* (feminine: *muslimah*). In a saying of the Prophet Muhammad, Islam is described metaphorically as a form of indentured servitude: "The intelligent man is he who indentures himself (*dana nafsahu*) to God and works for that which shall be after death." This saying is echoed in the Qur'an by the statement, "Verily God has purchased from the believers their persons and possessions in return for Paradise. . . . So rejoice in the sale of yourself which you have concluded; for it is the supreme achievement" (9: 111). Today, the idea of being the slave of anyone, even God, is difficult to accept. When the subject of slavery is brought up, people usually associate it with abuse, exploitation, and the denial of the inalienable human right of freedom. However, when the Qur'an was revealed in the seventh century, slavery was a more complex phenomenon, and the metaphor of slavery as a form of salvation was commonly employed. People often sold themselves or members of their families into slavery to pay off debts, and in certain cases a trusted slave might be given a wide degree of individual freedom. Educated slaves often managed the business affairs of their masters and at times traveled hundreds of miles from their homes to conduct transactions. In early Christianity, the Apostles of Jesus were called "slaves of God," not as a term of disrespect but as a token of the high esteem accorded them in the Christian community. Only as a "slave of God" could a believer become a "friend of God" and attain honor in heaven. A similar idea of divine friendship arising from divine slavery also exists in Islam. The Islamic word for worship, *'ibadah*, comes from the same Arabic root as *'Abd*, the word for slave. *'Ubudiyyah*, the term used to describe the state of worship in Islam, literally means "slavery." The pious Muslim was often called *muta'abbid*, "one who makes himself into a slave." *Muta'abbid* is also used in Islam to describe the friend of God, who "shall neither fear nor grieve" (10: 62).

Reciprocity. The responsibility to acknowledge and repay one's debt to God demands reciprocity. In a sense God "owes" the human being a fair return for his worship. "Who is the one who will lend to God a goodly loan, which God will double to his credit and multiply many times?" asks the Qur'an (2: 245). The Qur'an also affirms that the human being's "loan" to God is to be paid not only in worship but also in charitable works: "Verily, we will ease the path to salvation for the person who gives out of fear of God and testifies to the best. But we will ease the path to damnation for the greedy miser who thinks himself self-sufficient and rejects what is best" (92: 5–10). The idea that a merciful God rewards human beings for their acts of mercy was an important doctrine for the Spanish Sufi Ibn al-'Arabi (1165–1240). The Moroccan Sufi Abu al-'Abbas Sabti (died 1205) once said, "Divine grace is stimulated by acts of generosity." For Sabti, each charitable act performed by a person calls forth a response from God that rewards the giver in proportion to the gift. Sabti, the patron saint of the Moroc-

Pilgrims at the Ka'bah in Makkah (photograph by S. M. Amin)

can city of Marrakesh, used this doctrine to encourage the elite classes of the city to provide charity for the poor.

Religious Knowledge and Religious Practice. The relationship between the concept of *din* and religious practice in Islam is summarized in a well-known tradition of the Prophet Muhammad, the Tradition of Jibril (Gabriel), which Muslims take as a semi-official creed. In this account, the angel Jibril comes to the Prophet in the form of a man and says, "Oh Muhammad, tell me about Islam." The Prophet replies, "Islam means to bear witness that there is no god but Allah, that Muhammad is the Messenger of Allah, to maintain the required prayers, to pay the poor-tax, to fast in the month of Ramadan, and to perform the pilgrimage to the House of God at Mecca if you are able to do so." Then Jibril says, "Tell me about faith [*iman*]." The Prophet replies, "*Iman* is to believe in Allah, His angels, His books, His messengers, and the Last Day, and to believe in Allah's determination of affairs, whether good comes of it or bad." "You are correct," Jibril replies. "Now tell me about the perfection of religion [*ihsan*]." The Prophet responds, "*Ihsan* is to worship Allah as if you see Him; for if you do not see Him, surely He sees you." In this tradition, *Islam* represents religious practice; *iman* represents religious knowledge; and *ihsan* represents the union of knowledge and practice. Most scholars of religion think of religious practice as coming after religious knowledge. People follow the rules and commandments of God because they believe in God and know that His rules must be obeyed, but in the Tradition of Jibril these roles are reversed. Instead of faith coming before practice, practice defines and confirms faith. To be a true Muslim, it is not enough to be born a Muslim or to call oneself a Muslim. The believer must also perform the actions that confirm one as a Muslim before God. These actions are summarized in the "Five Pillars of Islam" that appear in the first part of the Tradition of Jibril:

1. To affirm that there is no god but Allah and that Muhammad is the Messenger of Allah (*Shahadah*)
2. To maintain the five required daily prayers (*Salat*)
3. To pay the poor-tax (*Zakat*)
4. To fast during the lunar month of Ramadan (*Sawm Ramadan*)
5. To perform the pilgrimage to Makkah at least once in one's lifetime (*Hajj*).

The key to the Five Pillars of Islam is the *Shahadah*, the "Act of Bearing Witness," which symbolizes the complementarity of faith and practice in Islam. The statement "There is no god but Allah" confirms the believer's acceptance of divine reality. As a formal proclamation of divine oneness, it represents the essence of knowledge (*'ilm*). The statement "Muhammad is the Messenger of Allah" confirms the believer's submission to God, which is the meaning of the word *Islam*. By making this statement, the believer responds to God by acknowledging the Prophet Muhammad, both as the transmitter of the Islamic message and as the quintessential Muslim. The person of knowledge in Islam is both a "knower" and a "doer." The knowledge of the nature of God informs religious practice and is confirmed by it. By maintaining a complementarity between faith and practice, the sincere Muslim follows the example of the Prophet Muhammad, who was exalted (*muhammad*) above all others because he embodied religion both inwardly and outwardly. This dual embodiment is exemplified in the final portion of the Tradition of Jibril, where *ihsan*, the perfection of religion, is defined as "worshipping Allah as if you see Him; for if you do not see Him, surely He sees you."

Sources of Religious Knowledge. The primary source of religious knowledge in Islam is the Qur'an, the "Speech" of God. The Arabic term *Qur'an* is most often translated as "reading" or "recital." It can also be translated as "scripture." Grammatically, *Qur'an* is a verbal noun that carries the connotation of a "continuous reading" or something that is recited and listened to over and over again. For Muslims, the Qur'an is a spiritual touchstone and a literary model. As a spiritual touchstone, it is the revelation sent down by God to the Prophet Muhammad between the years 610 and 632. The Qur'an calls itself *Umm al-Kitab*, "Mother of the Book" or "Sourcebook," a model of divine communication (13: 39). As a form of literature, it is often regarded as the source of the Classical Arabic language. The Qur'an is the earliest known major text to appear in Classical Arabic, and it includes all the rules of Arabic grammar. It is regarded as a literary model not only by Muslims but also by Arab Christians.

Revelation from God. For Muslims, the Qur'an consists of the actual "word" or "speech" of God (9: 6) and is written exactly as it was revealed to the Prophet Muhammad. As a revelation from God, the entire text of the Qur'an is sacred. Its significance for Muslims is similar to that of the *logos* (divine word) in Christianity. In Christianity, the divine word is embodied in the person of Jesus Christ. In Islam, the divine word is not embodied in the Prophet Muhammad. Muhammad was only the bearer of the divine word; as a prophet and a mortal man, he transmitted and interpreted the word of God, but he was not the word of God himself. This divine attribute is reserved for the Qur'an alone.

Reading the Qur'an. The Qur'an is divided into 114 sections (*surah*), each of which includes from 3 to 286 or 287 "signs" or "verses" (*ayah*). An *ayah* is a "statement in the speech of God." The purpose of these divine statements, which may include anything from the written text of the Qur'an to the signs of God in nature, is to awaken the human spirit to the reality of God's existence. To be a person of knowledge in Islam, one must learn two levels of discourse: the Arabic text of the Qur'an and the "text" of the natural world, which is also seen as an *ayah* in the speech of God. The person of knowledge in Islam must learn to "read" the signs of God in the world as a "book." This aspect of knowledge is exemplified in the Qur'an by the prophet Abraham, who understood God to be the cause of heavenly events (6: 75–79), and the prophet Solomon, who was inspired by God to understand the "discourse of the birds" (27: 16). This attitude toward knowledge also inspired the great achievements of Muslim scholars in philosophy, science, and medicine.

Divine Transcendence in the Qur'an. As a theological document, the Qur'an demonstrates the existence and nature of *Allah*, the One God. In doing so, it refers to itself as a "criterion of discernment" (*furqan*). The discernment or certainty that is gained by a Muslim who assimilates the message of the Qur'an is the same as that bestowed by God on His prophets and messengers. A messenger of God (*Rasul Allah*) is a bearer of divine scripture. The prophets Muhammad, Abraham, Moses, David, and Jesus are messengers because they were the bearers of divine books. A prophet of God (*Nabi Allah*) does not bring a revealed book but is chosen by God to remind humanity of Allah's message. In the Qur'an, these messengers include biblical prophets such as Lot and Solomon and nonbiblical ones such as Luqman and the Arabian prophets Salih and Hud. The knowledge brought by prophets and messengers leads the spiritually aware human being to perceive an absolute and all-encompassing reality—Allah—whose nature, unique and exalted, lies beyond the limits of the human imagination: "Say: He is Allah the One; Allah the Perfect beyond compare; He gives not birth, nor is He begotten, and He is, in Himself, not dependent on anything" (112).

Interior of the Dome of the Rock in Jerusalem, completed in 691 and decorated with
the earliest surviving written verses from the Qur'an

This short surah of the Qur'an provides the classic Islamic expression of divine transcendence, the idea that God is beyond all comparison with the physical world.

Divine Immanence in the Qur'an. In the Qur'an the image of a unique and transcendent deity is complemented by a more complex image of a deity who is present, or immanent, in the world because He is the source of existence itself: "He is the First and the Last, the Outward and the Inward; And He is the Knower of every thing" (57: 3). Through an understanding of divine transcendence and divine immanence, the Muslim gains knowledge of *tawhid,* the concept of divine oneness that is the fundamental premise of Islamic theology.

Monotheism. Islam has often been called the most radically monotheistic of world religions. The Qur'an repeat- edly stresses that Allah is one, unique, perfect, and incomparable; He has no spouse, children, or partners and does not form part of a trinity. Despite this radical monotheism, however, the discourse of the Qur'an often fluctuates between transcendence and immanence, abstract and concrete, logical and analogical: although God is not tied to place, He is Lord of the East and the West (55: 17). He is beyond the world; yet, he sends rain and revives the earth (29: 63). He is unlike anything; yet, his "face" will abide forever (55: 27). To aid the understanding of God's nature, the Qur'an uses ninety-nine terms to convey aspects of divine being. These terms are known as the ninety-nine "Excellent Names of Allah" (7: 180). Many of these divine names are incorporated into personal names, such as 'Abd al-Rahman (Slave of the Merciful), 'Abd al-Jabbar (Slave of the Overpowering), or 'Abd al-Aziz (Slave of the Glorious). Most of the divine names in the Qur'an can also be applied to people, thus reminding believers of Allah's immanence in the world. With the exception of the supreme name *Allah* and the name *al-Rahman*, which refers to the divine mercy that creates and maintains the universe, divine names refer to attributes that are shared by both God and humans.

God and Humanity in the Qur'an. The sharing of the "Excellent Names of Allah" with human attributes is an important aspect of the spiritual humanism of the Qur'an. In the Qur'an, the human being is the key to the divine plan and the ultimate beneficiary of God's creation of the world. Significantly, the word *insan*, the term used in the Qur'an to designate the human being, is generic: it includes both men and women. The use of a term for "human being" rather than "man" or "woman" in the Qur'an demonstrates that men and women are spiritually equal. It is not man or woman but humanity in general that occupies an intermediate position between heaven and earth. All human beings are faced with the existential and moral choices that make up the "criterion of discernment" in the Qur'an. Each person, man and woman alike, is responsible for his or her own soul. The most significant duty of every Muslim is to submit his or her personal will to the criterion of truth in the Qur'an. Choosing between fundamental truth and falsehood is what separates Islam from unbelief (*kufr*): a denial of truth that "covers up," falsifies, or rejects God's message as expressed in His revelations.

Covenant. In the Qur'an human accountability is epitomized by a covenant in which humanity takes responsibility for the heavens and the earth before creation. This covenant constitutes another criterion by which faith and actions are judged. Sometimes called "God's covenant" (2: 27), it separates hypocrites and those who assign spiritual or material partners to God from true believers who maintain their trust in the Qur'anic message (33: 73). The person who trusts in Allah and is true to God's trust in him by not breaking the covenant in thought, word, or deed is the trustee or vice-regent (*khalifah*) of God on earth (2: 30–33). A society made up of such individuals constitutes a normative community, one that serves as an example and is a collective witness to the truth (2: 143). The Qur'an calls this normative community *Ummah Muslimah* (2: 128). In Islamic salvation history, the first Ummah Muslimah was the community created by the Prophet Muhammad and his Companions in Madinah between the years 622 and 632.

The Prophet Muhammad. Although Muslims do not believe that the Prophet Muhammad wrote the Qur'an, neither do they believe that he was an ordinary person. A well-known Sufi saying states: "Muhammad was 'merely' a man as a ruby is 'merely' a stone." Muhammad and the Qur'an are inseparable. First, the Prophet Muhammad was the vehicle of the Qur'an's revelation. For Muslims, this "unlettered prophet" (7: 157) was chosen by God to transmit the divine word because he uniquely exemplified the goodness, justice, and spirituality required for a bearer of the divine message. When asked about Muhammad's personality, the Prophet's wife 'A'isha summarized it by saying, "His way of

life was the Qur'an." Second, as the messenger of the divine word, Muhammad was more qualified than anyone else to interpret the meaning of the Qur'an. The Qur'an says to Muhammad: "We have revealed unto you the Remembrance, so that you may explain to humanity that which has been revealed to them" (16: 44). It is reported that in the last year of his life, the Prophet reviewed and edited the text of the Qur'an with the scribes of his community so that the written Qur'an would be an exact copy of the revelation sent down to him. Third, Muhammad was the first political leader in Islam. The Qur'an admonishes Muslims to heed the Prophet's advice and follow his injunctions. Finally, the Prophet Muhammad was a *paradigm*, a human norm of Islam in all of its aspects, ranging from the spiritual to the terrestrial and from the individual to the collective. The Qur'an calls the Prophet a "fine example" (33: 21) and a "sufficiency to all of humanity" (34: 28). He exemplified in a single, integrated personality all three facets of the Islamic concept of *din*: Islam as practice, Islam as knowledge, and Islam as the combination of knowledge and practice.

Prophetic and Divine Traditions. In Arabia before the coming of Islam, the leaders of towns and tribes kept the records of important decisions, local laws, and customary practices in special places, such as temples or sacred precincts. Collectively, these records of a community's traditions were known as its *sunnah*. When referring to the way things were done in a particular locality in Arabia, people would speak of the "Sunnah of Ta'if," or the "Sunnah of Makkah." With the advent of Islam, *sunnah* gradually lost its local connotation, and came to be understood as the "way of the Prophet Muhammad." Sunnah comprises all aspects of the Prophet's life and teachings and is derived from four sources: (1) the Qur'an, which at times refers to incidents in the Prophet's life, hints at the nature of his personality, and corrects his behavior; (2) orally transmitted traditions (*hadiths*), which recount the Prophet's actions and decisions; (3) "battle accounts" (*maghazi*), which describe the battles fought by the Prophet; and (4) later biographical works (*sirah*) that detail the life and career of the Prophet. Sirah biographies often attempt to draw parallels between events in the life of Muhammad and the lives of biblical prophets.

Hadiths. Of the four sources of Sunnah, the most important are the orally transmitted traditions known as hadiths. Literally, *hadith* means "saying" or "event." As a source of Islamic knowledge, hadiths are second only to the Qur'an in significance and authority. In some collections, hadith accounts are paired with accounts of the actions and sayings of the Prophet's Companions and the first generations of Muslim leaders. One can also find collections of so-called holy traditions (*hadith qudsi*): inspirational sayings revealed by God to the Prophet Muhammad, but not part of the Qur'an.

Wisdom and Guidance. As a body of knowledge, Sunnah is a compendium of wisdom and guidance covering every facet of Islamic thought and life. The hadith traditions that make up Sunnah describe how the Prophet ate, slept, treated his neighbors, practiced hygiene, and earned a

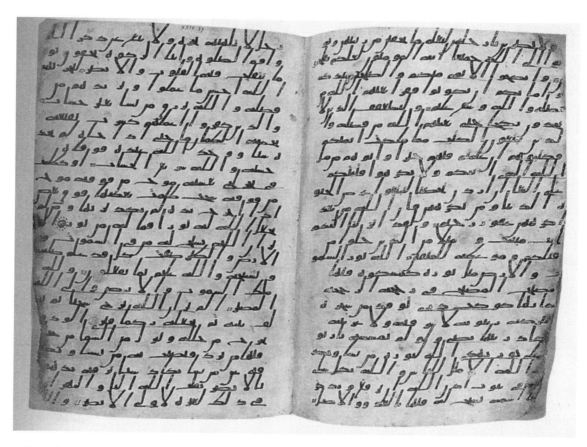

Pages from the earliest surviving manuscript for the Qur'an, transcribed in the eighth century (British Library, London)

livelihood. Other traditions deal with the social, economic, and political regulation of Muslim society. Many traditions deal with the ritual aspects of Muslim life, such as the rules for prayer, fasting, alms giving, pilgrimage, and ablutions. Still others, including the "holy traditions," are more theological in nature and deal with metaphysics, cosmology, and eschatology (accounts of the afterlife).

'Ilm. For most of Islamic history, *'ilm*, the Arabic word for knowledge, primarily meant "knowledge of traditions." The "person of knowledge" (*'alim*) was trained in hadiths before being trained in more-specialized disciplines. Although some traditions were collected and disseminated in written form during the Prophet Muhammad's lifetime, it was only in the ninth century that they were systematically organized into collections. When the Prophet was alive, traditions were disseminated in three ways. The most direct method was dictation. Since Muhammad could not write, he dictated portions of the Qur'an and administrative correspondence to his scribes. At least forty-five such scribes are known by name. The most common form of hadith transmission was verbal teaching. It was the practice of the Prophet to repeat important regulations and interpretations of Qur'anic passages, so that listeners could learn them by heart or write them down. The final form of hadith transmission was practical demonstration. In matters of ritual, such as ablution, prayer, and pilgrimage, the Prophet demonstrated required behaviors to observers, who would then pass on his example to others. Hadiths that were not written

down were discussed in study circles. The Prophet commissioned teachers to organize study circles in regions of Arabia beyond Makkah and Madinah, such as Najran, Yemen, and Hadramawt.

Hadith Dissemination. About 150 years after the Prophet's death, the dissemination of hadiths became more formalized. New forms of dissemination included oral recitation of traditions by a teacher, dictation of traditions from a written collection, and recitation back to a teacher by a student. Although written traditions became more common, the transmission of hadiths retained its original oral character throughout the medieval period. In order to teach hadiths to others, a student had to obtain a written document known as an *ijazah* from his teacher. A sort of diploma, the *ijazah* confirmed the ability of the student to recite traditions accurately from memory. The *ijazah* also confirmed that the student knew the entire chain of transmission of each hadith account, leading back to the Prophet Muhammad. By the end of the eighth century, a formal discipline of hadith criticism had grown up, which judged hadith accounts on the basis of their content and the truthfulness of their transmitters. Evidence of faulty memory or questionable personal behavior weakened the reputation of a hadith transmitter and lessened the authority of the accounts he transmitted. A significant number of women attained notoriety as hadith transmitters. One of the earliest of these was the Prophet's wife 'A'isha, who was also an important political figure.

Shari'ah: The Road to God. One of the most important reasons for the collection of hadiths was the need to find a model for integrating the teachings of the Qur'an into the lives of believers. Besides providing a common standard for religious practices, hadiths gave Muslims rules by which to regulate social and political life, following the example set by the Prophet in Makkah and Madinah. Just as knowledge came to be associated with knowledge of Qur'an and Sunnah, so "understanding" (*fiqh*) came to be associated with the analysis and application of the rules and regulations in the Qur'an and hadiths. The outcome of applying such analysis to the Qur'an and hadiths is Shari'ah: the "path," or road, of Islamic practice that leads the believer to God. *Shari'ah* is the generic term for Islamic law. *Fiqh* is the analytical process by which Shari'ah is understood and applied. Its practitioners were specialists in Islamic jurisprudence, the most important "people of knowledge" in premodern Islamic society.

Divine Law, Human Application. The most important distinction between Shari'ah and fiqh is that the source of Shari'ah is divine, whereas the source of fiqh is human reasoning. That is, the primary source of Shari'ah is the Qur'an, which is believed by Muslims to be the word of God. The divinity of Shari'ah even extends to the rulings that are derived from hadiths because the Prophet Muhammad was divinely inspired. Thus, any rule or regulation from a hadith text that conveys the words or intent of the Prophet Muhammad is nearly as authoritative as a ruling based on the Qur'an. Some medieval jurists even went so far as to say that the text of the Qur'an is authoritative because each verse meets the strongest criteria of source criticism applied to hadiths.

Legal Interpretation. Muslim legal scholars were aware that a text could be interpreted in different ways and that experts trained in the methods of text interpretation were needed by the Muslim community. Early jurists understood that every text—even one that is divine in origin—has a context, and that many questions had to be asked before a ruling of God or the Prophet could be applied in practice. Human behavior was judged on a scale of five values, which set the standard for Islamic morality: (1) *obligatory actions:* the major obligations of Islam, such as prayer, fasting, and pilgrimage; (2) *approved actions:* deeds that are morally positive but are not required by the Qur'an or Sunnah, such as treating the poor with kindness or giving charity beyond the minimum; (3) *neutral actions:* most acts performed by human beings, which are not deemed to fall under religious supervision; (4) *disapproved actions:* deeds that are morally negative but are not specifically forbidden in Qur'an or Sunnah, including many interpersonal issues, such as treating a spouse badly or acting inappropriately in business; (5) *forbidden actions:* behaviors that are banned in the Qur'an and Sunnah, including religious transgressions, such as rejecting the obligations of Islam, or moral transgressions such as wine drinking, gambling, theft, and murder.

Schools of Law in Islam. Before an action could be placed on the scale of five values, questions relating to background and context had to be asked: Which is primary in judging an act, permission or prohibition? If an act is not specifically prohibited in Qur'an or Sunnah, is it allowed? Which obligations should everyone perform, and which obligations may be performed by only a sufficient number of Muslims, who act for the community as a whole? If an act is forbidden, is it forbidden because the act is wrong in and of itself or because it may lead to a moral transgression in the future? Is the application of a legal ruling limited to the context in which it appears, or does it have a wider application? Questions such as these led to the development, by the mid eighth century, of the first "schools" of Islamic law. The Arabic term for a school of law is *madhhab,* which means "traveled path." When applied to Islamic law, the term means "method of reasoning" or "methodology." Each madhhab follows its own method of reasoning and interpretation of legal sources, which include the Qur'an and Sunnah. Many schools of legal interpretation were created between the eighth and the tenth centuries, but in Sunni Islam the number was eventually reduced to four.

The Hanafi School. The oldest Sunni madhhab is the Hanafi, named after the jurist Abu Hanifah (circa 699 – 767). This school originated in the Iraqi city of Kufah and is noted for its skeptical attitude toward traditions. During the lifetime of Abu Hanifah, hadith accounts proliferated throughout the Muslim world. Many of these accounts were political in nature and sought to justify either the rulers of the time or their opponents. Clearly, most such accounts did not represent the true words and opinions of the Prophet Muhammad. For this reason early jurists of the Hanafi madhhab relied more on the text of the Qur'an than on hadith accounts. To be acceptable, a hadith had to pass rigorous tests of authenticity, which included a form of content criticism that compared the text of the hadith with texts in the Qur'an. If the hadith seemed to contradict the meaning of a Qur'anic passage, it was rejected as unsound. This method derives from the Hanafi school's reliance on *ray,* the interpretation of a text based on the rules of logic. This reliance on reasoned opinion led the Hanafi madhhab to associate with rationalist trends in Islamic thought, such as the theological movement known as the Mu'tazila. In addition, relatively few Hanafi scholars were Sufi mystics because the rationalism of their method led to skepticism about Sufi claims of extraordinary spirituality and the miracles of saints. Historically, the Hanafi school was the official madhhab of the Abbasid khilafah (caliphate) and was the dominant school of Islamic law from the eighth through the eleventh centuries. In the later medieval period, it was associated with Turkish regimes, such as those of the Saljuks of Iran and Anatolia. It was also the official madhhab of the Ottoman Empire.

The Maliki School. The second madhhab in chronological terms was the Maliki, named for its founder, Malik ibn Anas (circa 712 – 795). Like the Hanafi, the Maliki school was relatively skeptical of hadiths. But unlike the Hanafis, the Malikis were not content to base their madhhab as heavily on the logical reasoning of jurists. Malik ibn Anas looked instead to the local tradition that had the best chance of preserving a record of the Prophet's words and deeds. He found this tradition in Madinah, the capital of the first Muslim state. Malik's reliance on the traditions of Madinah preserves the earlier, pre-Islamic notion of a local sunnah. It also meant that he had to rely heavily on the Prophet Muhammad's Companions and their successors as sources of information. For this reason, *al-Muwatta* (The Trodden Path), Malik's collection of traditions from Madinah, includes many accounts that are not reported directly from the Prophet but come instead from his Companions. In the ninth century, the traditions of the Maliki madhhab were codified by Sahnun 'Abd al-Salam (died 854), who wrote a multivolume collection of the decisions of Malik and his students, which was called *al-Mudawwanah* (The Compendium). After Sahnun, Maliki jurists relied on logic-based interpretation much like that of the Hanafis, with the exception that the Malikis traced many decisions back to Malik and his students. Other characteristics of the Maliki madhhab included a relatively open attitude toward the incorporation of local custom into Islamic law and the requirement that a believer give evidence of his or her adherence to Islam through public participation in Islamic rituals. Historically, the Maliki madhhab was dominant in North and West Africa, upper Egypt, Islamic Spain, and Sicily. The Maliki attitude toward Sufism was divided. Although some of the strongest opponents of Sufism were Malikis, many of the best-known mystics of North Africa and Islamic Spain belonged to this school of law.

The Shafi'i School. The third and most influential school of Islamic law is the Shafi'i, named after Muhammad ibn Idris al-Shafi'i (767–820). A native of Gaza in Palestine, Shafi'i studied under Malik ibn Anas in Madinah and under students of Abu Hanifah in Iraq. Living at a time when the discipline of hadith criticism had succeeded in eliminating many false accounts, Shafi'i was concerned that both the Hanafi and the Maliki schools of law were in danger of adding unwarranted innovations to the body of Islamic law. In the case of the Malikis, Shafi'i opposed their reliance on the traditions of Madinah and the tendency of Maliki jurists to develop their legal school in isolation from other trends in Islamic thought. He reserved his strongest criticism for *ray*, the method of logical reasoning employed by both Hanafi and Maliki jurists. For Shafi'i, *ray* was little more than opinion mongering: he portrayed the "people of *ray*" as making arbitrary decisions about legal matters with little regard for their compatibility with either the Qur'an or Sunnah.

Usul al-Fiqh. Although this critique of *ray* was unfair, it received a sympathetic hearing. There was clearly a need to unite Islamic legal thought under a common standard. In addition, the association of many Hanafi and Maliki jurists with the ruling classes led Muslims to suspect them of tailoring their opinions for

political or personal reasons. Shafi'i's answer to this problem was the doctrine of *usul al-fiqh*—"roots" or "principles of jurisprudence"—which he laid out in *al-Risalah* (The Treatise). This book, which Shafi'i wrote in Egypt during the latter part of his life, was the first theoretical treatise on Islamic law. Shafi'i's *usul* method relies heavily on tradition; that is, he considered the two most fundamental sources of Islamic jurisprudence to be the Qur'an and Sunnah, as given in accepted hadith collections. Only after the jurist fails to find guidance in the Qur'an or hadiths should he use his own reasoning in judging whether an action conforms to the teachings of Islam. This reasoning process, called *qiyas*, must conform to strict rules of analogy. The jurist starts by finding a Qur'an or hadith text that matches the new case as closely as possible. Then, by deducing the inner logic of the text, he sees whether or not the new case conforms to the same logic. Shafi'i's conception of *qiyas* is similar to what modern judges do when they use the example, or precedent of earlier cases, to guide their decisions. In Islamic law, the decisions resulting from this process are not necessarily binding. The closest equivalent to binding precedent is to be found in Shafi'i's fourth principle of jurisprudence, *ijma'*: the unanimous consensus by legal scholars on a single issue. In practice, however, such unanimous consensus was nearly impossible to obtain. Thus, the *usul* method allowed a wide range of disagreement among scholars in legal matters.

Shafi'i's Influence. Shafi'i's teachings have had a great influence on Islamic legal thought: so much so, in fact, that the Hanafi and Maliki schools were eventually forced to adopt them, and even Shi'ite Islam could not escape being affected by the *usul* method. The Shafi'i madhhab was also a favorite of Sufis. According to the Iranian Sufi Abu Sa'id ibn Abi al-Khayr (967–1049), the Sunnis embraced the Shafi'i method because it exacted a greater rigor in the performance of religious obligations. Geographically, the Shafi'i madhhab was first dominant in Egypt, where it was developed, and was later spread by the juridical and mercantile classes throughout the eastern Muslim lands, from Iran to Indonesia.

The Hanbali School. The fourth Sunni madhhab is the Hanbali, named after the jurist and hadith scholar Ahmad ibn Hanbal (780–855). A student of Shafi'i from Baghdad, Ibn Hanbal created a legal doctrine that was quite similar to that of his teacher, except that it relied even more heavily on hadiths and imposed greater restrictions on the process of juridical reasoning. During his lifetime, Ibn Hanbal became well-known as the compiler of *al-Musnad* (The Authoritative Collection), one of the largest hadith collections in Sunni Islam. Although he was sometimes accused of not being critical enough of hadith accounts, Ibn Hanbal's collection was so comprehensive that he could refer most legal questions to texts included in *al-Musnad*. The Hanbali madhhab has been extremely influential in modern times because it is the official madhhab of Saudi Arabia, and its doctrines form the basis of so-called Islamic fundamentalism. In medieval Islam, however, it was in the minority. It was associated with the most conservative elements among the "people of Hadith" and was geographically restricted to Iraq and parts of Syria and Iran. Its most important claim was that it was popular among the lower classes of Muslim society and promoted an ethic that stressed personal virtue and the denial of wealth and luxury. For this reason, despite the literalistic and antimystical nature of Hanbali teachings, one occasionally finds Sufis who followed Hanbali legal doctrines. Such a Sufi was 'Abd al-Qadir al-Jilani (1077–1166), the great teacher and saint of Baghdad who founded the Qadiriyyah Sufi order.

Sources:

Abdullah Yusuf Ali, trans., *The Holy Quran* (N.p.: Holy Koran Publishing House, 1934).

Muhammad Asad, trans., *The Message of the Qur'an* (Gibraltar: Dar al-Andalus, 1980).

Syed Muhammad Naquib al-Attas, *Prolegomena to the Metaphysics of Islam: An Exposition of the Fundamental Elements of the Worldview of Islam* (Kuala Lumpur, Malaysia: International Institute of Islamic Thought and Civilization, 1995).

Vincent J. Cornell, *Realm of the Saint: Power and Authority in Moroccan Sufism* (Austin: University of Texas Press, 1998).

Mohammad Hashim Kamali, *Principles of Islamic Jurisprudence*, revised edition (Cambridge: Islamic Texts Society, 1991).

Marmaduke Pickthall, trans., *Holy Quran* (Karachi: Dawood Foundation, 1930).

FREE WILL AND THE RISE OF ISLAMIC SECTARIANISM

Free Will and Predestination in the Qur'an. The first major theological controversy in Islam, over free will and predestination, was particularly an issue during the period 661–750, when the Umayyad khalifahs (caliphs) ruled the Muslim empire from their capital at Damascus. The strictly theological portion of the debate revolved around the Arabic term *qadar*, which refers to God's ability to predetermine events, including all human acts. This theological discussion, however, masked an underlying political controversy. Those who believed that God determined everything, leaving little or no room for human initiative, tended to be apologists for the Umayyad regime and resisted calls to reform the Umayyad state or correct abuses of power. Many of the partisans of free will, who were known as "Qadarites" (*al-Qadariyyah*), were opponents of the Umayyads and used this doctrine to justify their right to condemn official misdeeds and rise up against injustice.

Free Will and the Qur'an. At first glance, this controversy seems ill conceived. Many verses in the Qur'an affirm the freedom of human initiative and the moral, ethical, and theological importance of personal choice: "Whatever good befalls you, it is from Allah, and whatever evil befalls you it is from yourself" (4: 79); "Whoever will, let him believe, and whoever will, let him disbelieve" (18: 29); "Whoever goes aright, it is only for the sake of his own soul that he goes aright, and whoever goes wrong, goes wrong to his own detriment. No soul can bear the burden of another"

(17: 15). As the last verse implies, it would make no sense to punish human beings for their actions if they were not free to choose them. The choice between Islam and unbelief, or between good and evil, would have no theological or moral significance if a person could not make such a choice freely. The divine-human covenant would have no meaning if there were no freedom of choice; that is, if a court cannot punish a person for a crime that was not committed by choice, how could God do such a thing?

The Qur'an and Divine Omnipotence. Yet, as often as it affirms personal initiative, the Qur'an limits it by stressing divine omnipotence: "Whatever is in the heavens and the earth is [Allah's]. All things are subservient to Him. He is the Originator of the heavens and the earth. When He decrees a thing, he merely says unto it, 'Be!' And it is" (2: 116–117); "They will not heed unless Allah wills it; He is the source of God-consciousness; He is the source of mercy" (74: 56); "You do not will, unless Allah wills; verily, Allah is the All-Knowing, the All-Wise" (76: 30); "No misfortune occurs on earth or to yourselves that has not been written down in a book before we bring it into being" (57: 22). The contradiction that is revealed in these two sets of verses can be found in Christianity and Judaism as well as Islam. These various verses on free will and divine omnipotence illustrate the paradox of *theodicy*, the problem of divine justice. In a monotheistic religion, where God is one and everything comes from Him, one might ask how injustice can arise in the world; what are the limits of humanity's responsibility, and what pertains to God; and why a just God lets bad things happen to good people.

Free Will and Revolution. In the field of Islamic studies, theology cannot be studied apart from history. Theological disputes often conceal underlying political or social issues. To this day, Islamic activists continue to cast political disputes in theological terms, just as Muslims did during the first century of Islam. The death of the Prophet Muhammad in 632 was followed by a violent era marked by the murders of three of the first four khalifahs, three major revolts by Muslims against a Muslim ruler, and the birth of the Sunni, Shi'ite, and Kharijite sects. At the same time, the territory under Muslim rule expanded as far as Afghanistan in the East and Morocco in the West. Because of these conquests, Islam became transformed from a religion made up largely of Arabs to a universal commonwealth, encompassing many of the countries and peoples of the world of classical antiquity. Although the history of dynasties and conquests in this period is well known, the details of the revolution of ideas that accompanied them remain obscure.

The Abbasids. Part of the problem is that history is written by the victors. The victors in this case were the Abbasids, who overthrew the Umayyads in 750 and moved the capital of the Muslim empire from Damascus to Baghdad. All of the best-known historical and doctrinal sources that deal with the Umayyad period were written after the Abbasid victory, and some of them were written under Abbasid patronage. For this reason, it is difficult to get a clear idea of the religious doctrines that were prevalent in the Umayyad period. Abbasid-era writers and those who followed them portrayed the Umayyads as illegitimate Arab "kings" rather than as legitimate Islamic khalifahs, and many Shi'ite and Kharijite activists were cast as extremists, terrorists, or both. Though the recent publication of Shi'ite and Kharijite works has changed such perceptions, this early period of Muslim history remains insufficiently understood.

Internal Disputes. One of the major problems of this period was Muslims branding other Muslims as unbelievers. During Muhammad's lifetime, the line between believer and unbeliever was clearly drawn. All who acknowledged Muhammad as Prophet, followed the message of the Qur'an, and adhered to a minimum of Islamic practice were believers (*mu'min*); those who rejected Muhammad and the Qur'an and refused to acknowledge the *din* of Islam were unbelievers (*kafir*). In the decades after Muhammad's death, however, Muslims began to accuse each other of unbelief because they "sinned" by not belonging to the correct political factions. In the words of the noted Hanbali jurist Ibn Taymiyyah (1263–1328): "The dispute over what belief and unbelief meant was the first internal dispute to occur among the Muslims. Because of this problem, the Muslim community was divided into sects and factions, which began to differ over the Sacred Book and the Sunnah and began to call one another unbelievers."

The Problem of Succession. The problem of succession to the Prophet Muhammad remains unresolved. For Sunnis and Kharijites, the Prophet never named a successor. For Shi'ites, the Prophet named his cousin and son-in-law 'Ali ibn Abi Talib (circa 596 – 661) to succeed him. According to the Shi'ites, the Prophet's Companions Abu Bakr (circa 570 – 634) and 'Umar ibn al-Khattab (592–644) staged a coup while 'Ali was preparing Muhammad's body for burial; they pressured the Muslims into accepting Abu Bakr as khalifah and agreeing to 'Umar as his successor. In the Sunni and Kharijite versions, Abu Bakr was chosen by acclamation and only later appointed 'Umar as his successor. There is even disagreement about the meaning of the term *khalifah*. Most Sunnis and Kharijites, following Abu Bakr, define the term as "successor to Muhammad." But for the Umayyad khalifahs and their supporters, the term meant "deputy of God." For Shi'ites, *khalifah* means both "deputy of God" and "successor to Muhammad," but in a sense that leadership is an extension of the prophetic mission. Instead of *khalifah*, Shi'ites prefer to use the term *imam* (religious leader) and assert that the true leader of the Muslims is a designated member of the Prophet's family.

'Uthman. All Muslims agree that the issue of succession came to a head under the Khalifah 'Uthman (ruled 644–656). An early convert to Islam and a highly respected companion of Muhammad, 'Uthman married the Prophet's daughters Ruqayyah and Umm Kulthum. Yet, he came from the clan of Banu Umayyah, the chief

clan of the Quraysh tribe of Makkah, and was a nephew of Abu Sufyan (died circa 653), the leader of the pagan opposition to Muhammad. On becoming khalifah, 'Uthman was faced with ruling a rapidly expanding Muslim state. To govern such an empire, he needed administrators who were experienced in the management of large numbers of men and large sums of money. He found many of these administrators within his own clan. Some of these officials were late converts to Islam and cared little about the teachings of their religion. 'Uthman was accused of favoritism for appointing family members to high positions and moral laxity for refusing to punish officials such as the governor of Basrah, who was found drunk in his palace. In 656 a group of rebels surrounded 'Uthman's house in Madinah, and when he refused to accede to their demands, they killed him. After committing this deed, the rebels named 'Ali the new khalifah.

Interior of the Great Masjid of Damascus, founded by the Umayyad khalifah al-Walid I in 705

Kharijism. Before his death, 'Uthman had appointed his cousin Mu'awiyyah (circa 605–680), the son of Abu Sufyan, governor of Syria. After 'Uthman's murder, Mu'awiyyah took up 'Uthman's cause and demanded that the murderers be brought to justice. 'Ali, who had taken no part in the crime, refused to punish those who committed it. Instead, he moved his capital from Madinah to the garrison city of Kufah in Iraq. 'Ali's refusal to punish the killers of 'Uthman outraged those who were not personally loyal to 'Ali. Some joined Mu'awiyyah in Damascus, while others rose against 'Ali. At the end of 656, 'Ali defeated an army led by the Prophet Muhammad's widow 'A'isha and the Prophet's Companions Talhah and Zubayr. The following year, the armies of 'Ali and Mu'awiyyah faced each other at Siffin, on the upper Euphrates River. A long standoff was eventually settled by arbitration in which it was decided that 'Uthman had been killed unjustly. Although no decision was reached on the legitimacy of 'Ali's khilafah, the judgment of the arbitrators weakened 'Ali's position and strengthened Mu'awiyyah's. Angered by the arbitration, a large group of 'Ali's supporters withdrew from his army; they became known as the Kharijites (*al-Khawarij*), the "Secessionists." In July 658 'Ali attacked the Kharijites at Nahrawan in Iraq and killed many of them. In 661 a Kharijite assassin killed 'Ali in revenge for this battle.

The Doctrine of Sin. In the conflict between Mu'awiyyah and 'Ali, there was moral ambiguity on both sides. Dissatisfied with the arbitration at Siffin, the Kharijites proclaimed the slogan "Neither this one nor that one" and rejected the need for a khalifah altogether. The Kharijites, who were religiously pious and idealistic, opposed on ethical grounds the claims of both 'Ali and Mu'awiyyah to the khilafah. Although they agreed with 'Uthman's removal and originally supported 'Ali as khalifah, they felt that 'Ali had erred in accepting arbitration. Following the maxim "No judgment but that of God," the Kharijites believed 'Ali had disobeyed the divine command that had made him the leader of the Muslims. As for Mu'awiyyah, they felt that none of his claims was valid: his Umayyad family background was unsuited for the leadership of Islam, and he upheld the rights of 'Uthman, whom they regarded as corrupt.

Doctrinal Differences. The Kharijites considered political "sins" such as those of 'Uthman, 'Ali, and Mu'awiyyah to be "grave sins," equating them with sins such as adultery, murder, theft, and apostasy. Doctrinal differences among groups of Kharijites revolved around differences in the definition of sin and its punishments. The most extreme Kharijites felt that people who committed grave sins were unbelievers and that military action was required against them. None of these groups survived the Umayyad period. Moderate Kharijites adhered to more carefully thought-out doctrines. The Najdites (683–693) felt that a single instance of a common sin such as theft or adultery would not turn a person into an unbeliever; one who repeats such a sin, however, is an idolater (*mushrik*) and must be punished. The Ibadites (circa 684 – present) held that idolaters were only those who rejected God.

Non-Kharijite Muslims were considered monotheists but not true believers. However, since they lived in the "domain of monotheism," it was permissible for Kharijites to live among them and associate with them.

Kharijite Views on Choice. The Kharijite position on free will and predestination was ambiguous. Although freedom of choice is implied in their decision to oppose 'Ali, predestination is implied in their belief that 'Ali's "sin" was his rejection of the destiny that Allah had determined for him. For the Kharijites, salvation or damnation was collective, rather than individual outcomes of human acts. Kharijite writings are full of references to "the people of the Garden" and "the people of the Fire," implying that salvation depends on which group one belongs to: if one is a Kharijite, he or she is counted among "the people of the Garden"; if one is not a Kharijite, he or she is counted among "the people of the Fire" and will be punished eternally. The extremist followers of Ibn al-Azraq (died 685) believed that any Muslim who did not join their camp was an unbeliever and could be put to death. In their terrorist raids they spared Christians and Jews but put non-Kharijite Muslims to the sword.

Communal Leadership. The earliest Kharijites went beyond rejecting 'Ali and Mu'awiyyah. Seeing the majority of Muslims as sinful and corrupt, they withdrew from Islamic cities such as Kufah and Basrah and sought to create a purer version of Islam in the countryside. They believed that they were following the example of the Prophet Muhammad when he migrated from Makkah to Madinah to escape the pagan Arabs. As justification for this practice, they cited the following verse of the Qur'an: "Whoever migrates for the sake of Allah will find refuge and abundance in the earth; and whoever forsakes his home as a fugitive on behalf of Allah and His Messenger, and death overtakes him, his reward is incumbent on Allah" (4: 100).

Kharijite Leaders. Believing that the Prophet Muhammad's leadership could not be duplicated, the Kharijites refused to appoint a khalifah. Instead, they preferred the temporary leadership of a military commander (*amir*), who would also act as a religious leader (*imam*). Recent scholarship has shown that most of the early Kharijites came from Bedouin or Christian backgrounds. Perhaps echoing an egalitarianism born out of Bedouin or Christian ideals, they rejected the Umayyad claim that the leader of the Muslims should come from the noble tribe of Quraysh and the Shi'ite claim that the leader should come from the noble "house" of Muhammad. Instead, the leader of the Kharijites could come from any family or social class, including slaves. What was most important was that this person be the best of his community in piety, knowledge, and good works. In addition, the choice of leadership was a matter for the entire community to decide. The Kharijite imam was appointed by consensus of the community; if he proved unable to carry out his functions, the community was empowered to remove him.

Kharijism and Democracy. Although Kharijite doctrines may seem egalitarian and democratic, these early Muslim idealists did not adhere to modern conceptions of individual freedom. For the most part, groups, not individuals, came together to form Kharijite communities. The Kharijites strongly rejected the middle-of-the-road opinion that one's status as believer or sinner was a private matter between the individual and God. On the contrary, the person who held such an opinion was likely to be considered a "grave sinner" because ethical neutrality allowed corruption to continue. The advantage of Kharijism was that its doctrines stressed social equality and focused attention on the highest moral and ethical principles of Islam. The disadvantage of this movement was that it perpetuated ancient, tribal notions of group solidarity and dangerously oversimplified complex ethical and theological issues. At its best, it pointed the way toward Islamic ideals; at its worst, it created dissension among Muslims and led to outbreaks of terrorism.

Shi'ism. Because they arose from the same political conflict, early Shi'ism and Kharijism shared much in common. Both groups started out as part of the political opposition to 'Uthman, which later continued as opposition to the Umayyads. After 750, this opposition was extended to the Abbasid khalifahs as well. As a social movement, both groups claimed to represent the lower classes and disaffected elements of Muslim society, including non-Arab converts to Islam, the poor, and the pious who advocated poverty and service as religious virtues. Kharijism first took root in the Arabian peninsula and nearby regions; later, it spread widely among the Berbers of North Africa. The Ibadite form of Kharijism remains today in Oman and parts of Tunisia and Algeria. Shi'ism was initially popular among South Arabian immigrants in Iraq, who had a long tradition of charismatic leadership. Eventually, it spread among converts to Islam in Iraq and Iran. Like Kharijism, Shi'ism also took root among the Berbers of North Africa, who formed the backbone of the Fatimid movement in the tenth century. Doctrinally, the more extreme groups of Shi'ites and Kharijites shared a tendency to call their enemies unbelievers. A group of Shi'ites called "Rejecters" (*al-Rowafid*) in Sunni sources rejected the rule of Abu Bakr, 'Umar, and 'Uthman, claiming that all three khalifahs had usurped the rightful inheritance of 'Ali. These "Rejecters" were the forerunners of present-day Imami and Ismaili Shi'ites.

'Ali and Fatimah. The terms *Shi'ism* and *Shi'ite* come from the Arabic word *shi'ah*, which means "party" or "faction." A Shi'ite is one of the *Shi'at 'Ali* (Party of 'Ali), who believes that 'Ali was the true successor to the Prophet Muhammad. Shi'ites also believe that leadership is vested in the family of the Prophet Muhammad, who are called the "Prophet's Household" (*Ahl al-Bayt*). Among the earliest Shi'ites, the Prophet's household was understood to include all twenty-seven children of 'Ali and even members of the Prophet's clan of Banu Hashim. Since the ninth century, however, the Prophet's household has been restricted to the descendants of Muhammad through his daughter Fatimah (died 633), 'Ali's first wife. 'Ali and Fatimah had two sons, Hasan (624–669) and Husayn (626–680). After

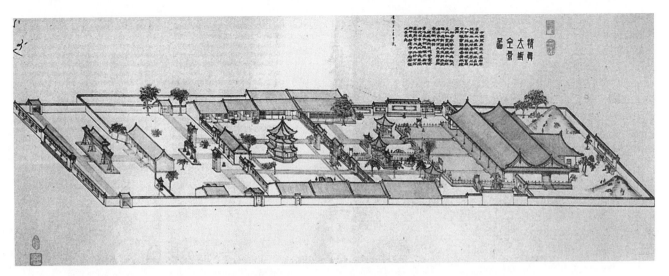

Painting on silk of the courtyard and garden complex at the Great Masjid of Xian, China, founded in the eighth century
(from *Aramco World*, July-August 1985)

Fatimah's death, 'Ali married a woman from the tribe of Banu Hanifah. His son from this marriage, Muhammad ibn al-Hanafiyyah (died 700), was also regarded as an Imam by some early Shi'ites.

Succession. The idea that succession is vested in the household of a charismatic leader is a custom that goes back to pre-Islamic Arabia, but under the Shi'ites it was taken to unprecedented levels. In the creed of al-Shaykh al-Mufid (948–1022), an Imami Shi'ite theologian from Baghdad, 'Ali is called "Commander of the Faithful, first of the Imams of the Believers, who are the rulers of the Muslims and the Deputies of God in religion after the Messenger of God." 'Ali is also "the 'brother' of the Messenger of God, his paternal cousin, the trustee of his affairs, and his son-in-law, who was married to Fatimah the Virtuous, Mistress of the Women of the Universe." In this creed one can find many of the major tenets of Shi'ite doctrine: the idea that 'Ali was the most qualified khalifah, or "Commander of the Faithful"; the designation of his successors, the Shi'ite Imams, as "Imams of the Believers"; the claim that the Imams, and not the Umayyad khalifahs, are "Deputies of God"; and the belief that the Imam is the official spokesman for Islam. The Shi'ites describe Fatimah in terms that are strikingly reminiscent of Christians' characterizations of the Virgin Mary: like Mary, she is called "The Virtuous" (*al-Batul;* literally "The Virgin") and "Mistress of the Women of the Universe," a title that recalls the Qur'anic description of Mary as "chosen over all the women of the worlds" (3: 42).

The Light of Muhammad. A major tenet of Shi'ite theology is the mystical doctrine of the "Light of Muhammad," which teaches that Allah created Muhammad and 'Ali from a single light before the creation of Adam. After the death of the Prophet, the Light of Muhammad was transmitted by the Holy Spirit to the Shi'ite Imams and formed the basis of their religious authority. In some versions, the Light of Muhammad comes to the Imams through 'Ali alone. In an account related by al-Shaykh al-

Mufid, 'Ali was holding the Prophet's head in his lap as he lay dying; when Muhammad breathed his final breath, 'Ali caught the Prophet's breath in his right hand and rubbed it over his face, thus taking the Muhammadan Light upon himself. In other versions of the Muhammadan Light legend, this mystical light was transmitted through Muhammad's blood to his daughter Fatimah, who passed it on through herself to her sons, Hasan and Husayn.

The Imamate. There is considerable dispute over when the Shi'ite doctrine of the Imamate was first formulated. Most Shi'ite scholars ascribe this doctrine to the fifth and sixth Imams, Muhammad al-Baqir (died 735) and Ja'far al-Sadiq (circa 702 – 765). The importance of these two figures is attested by the fact that the majority of Shi'ite traditions are attributed to them. In addition, the political and doctrinal legacy of Ja'far al-Sadiq is key to the differences between Imami and Ismaili Shi'ism, and he lent his name to the Imami school of law, which is called Ja'fari. For both Imami and Ismaili Shi'ites, the Imam is the "Proof of God" to humanity and the "Sign of God" (*Ayat Allah*) on earth. All political order and sovereignty belongs to him. Obedience to the Imam is obligatory for all Muslims. In religious matters, the Imam is the sole authorized interpreter of the Qur'an. Other scholars may interpret the Qur'an only by his permission. To be accorded this status, the Imam must possess five qualities:

His Imamate must be conferred on him by his predecessor.
He must be immune from sin and error.
He must be the best of humankind.
He must have extensive general and religious knowledge.
He must give spiritual guidance on all matters relating to the Qur'an and the Sunnah.

According to Imami Shi'ite sources, Ja'far al-Sadiq considered himself and his descendants to be heirs to the prophets. From his father, Muhammad al-Baqir, Ja'far is said to have inherited the "Scrolls of Comprehensive Knowledge," twelve scrolls that contain secret messages from the Archangel Jibril. Another tradition mentions the "Scripture of

Fatimah," a copy of the Qur'an that originally belonged to Fatimah and included references to the Shi'ite Imams that were deleted from the Qur'an by the khalifah 'Uthman. Ja'far was also said to have possessed the Red Casket (al-Jafr al-Ahmar), which contained the weapons of the Prophet Muhammad, and the White Casket (al-Jafr al-Abyad), which held the original copies of the Torah of Moses, the Gospel of Jesus, and the Psalms of David. (The English word cipher came from this use of the Arabic word jafr.)

Justice and Leadership. The Shi'ite doctrine of the Imamate is built on the twin foundations of justice ('adl) and leadership (imamah). If an Islamic society is to be legitimate, it must be built on the same foundations as the society governed by the Prophet in Madinah. For this reason, the principles of justice and leadership cannot derive their authority from a purely human source. For Shi'ites, justice is equivalent to the divine command in the Qur'an. Leadership belongs to the Imam, who is chosen by God to carry out his mandates. In order to be chosen by God, Imams, like prophets, must be endowed with special attributes. The most important of these attributes is knowledge. Religious knowledge, of which the Qur'an is the epitome, must be transmitted personally, on a one-to-one basis. For Shi'ites, the Imamate is a mirror of prophethood. The authority of the Imam depends on the knowledge of the divine command that is taught to him by his predecessor. This knowledge is perfected by the charismatic "Light of Muhammad," which the Imam inherits from his predecessor. When an Imam designates his successor, he confirms that the knowledge he has passed on is authentically divine in origin.

The Doctrine of Choice. In addition to accepting the Five Pillars of Islam like every other Muslim, Shi'ites must also accept the "Five Pillars of Shi'ism." The first pillar, justice, refers to the social aspect of Shi'ism. In theological terms, justice comes from God, and injustice comes from man. This formulation was a common way of expressing the divine origin of the Qadarite doctrine of free will, but in Shi'ism, as in Kharijism, justice also has a human dimension: besides requiring that the Imams act justly, this pillar encourages ordinary Shi'ites to practice justice as well. This requirement is expressed in the concept of service (khidmah), which is fundamental to both Imami and Ismaili Shi'ism and which has led Shi'ites historically to identify with the exploited, the poor, and the disadvantaged.

Divine Oneness. The second pillar of Shi'ism is divine oneness. Although this doctrine is fundamental to Islam, among Shi'ites it is understood to mean that God is simple and abstract, beyond likeness or number. A Shi'ite tradition ascribed to 'Ali defines this concept:

To say that God is one has four meanings: two of them are false and two are correct. As for the two false meanings, one is that a person should say "God is one" and be thinking of number and counting. This is false because that which has no second cannot enter into the category of number. Do you not see that those who say that God is the third of a trinity fall into this infidelity? Another meaning is to say, "So-and-so is one of his people," namely, a species

of this genus or a member of this species. This meaning is also false when applied to God, because it implies likening something to God, whereas God is above all likeness. As to the two meanings that are correct when applied to God, one is that it should be said that "God is one" in the sense that there is no likeness to him among things. And one is to say that "God is one" in the sense that there is no multiplicity or division conceivable in Him, neither outwardly, nor in the mind, nor in the imagination. God alone possesses such a unity.

The Shi'ite definition of divine oneness shares much in common with that of the Mu'tazila, a theological movement of non-Shi'ite rationalists.

Prophecy and Eschatology. The remaining pillars of Shi'ism are primarily concerned with the Imamate. Prophecy, the third pillar of Shi'ism, describes how the Imamate continues and completes the prophetic mission. The designation of the Imam by his predecessor imitates Moses' designation of Joshua as his successor and John the Baptist's proclamation of the coming of Jesus. Moses also provides the example of a "speaking," or active, prophet who is accompanied by a "silent," or latent, prophet, his brother Aaron. Likewise, each "Speaking Imam" is accompanied by a "Silent Imam," his designated successor. The fourth pillar of Shi'ism, eschatology, links the fate of the believer after death to one's acceptance of the Imam. In Shi'ism, recognition of the Imam is a prerequisite for salvation. Sunni and Kharijite Muslims, who do not recognize the Shi'ite Imam, are "grave sinners" and will not enter paradise.

The Imamate. As a theological doctrine, the fifth pillar of Shi'ism, the Imamate, is Qadarite because it stresses freedom of choice. In Shi'ite theology the choice of the Imamate over other models of Islamic leadership depends on humanity's being endowed with two essential attributes. These are reason ('aql) and choice (ikhtiyar). Since God does not will injustice, He cannot punish a person for committing a sin unless the person is endowed with reason. In Shi'ism, children, the ignorant, and the intellectually challenged are not held accountable for their actions. Reason entails the ability to make a considered choice between alternatives. Free choice, however, is not exactly the same as free will. Shi'ism depends too much on the influence of the divine will to allow humans to completely determine their own affairs. To use a well-known analogy created by the Sufi poet Jalal al-Din Rumi (1207–1273), human destiny is played out on a sort of polo field, where the soul is the horse; reason is the rider; choice is the polo stick; and the game is governed by the law of cause and effect. God predetermines the nature of what the player brings to the match: geographical location, social status, access to education, level of intelligence, and personality are all determined before one begins the match of life. The player makes choices that have moral and practical consequences: such as whether to follow sin or virtue, whether to act selfishly or altruistically, and whether to acknowledge or reject the Imam. By the end of the match, the totality of one's choices has led the player to either salvation or damnation. Looking

Courtyard of the Great Masjid at Kariouan, Tunisia, founded in 670 and completed in 875

back on the course of his life, the player may feel that his destiny was predetermined. But in fact, much of what he calls "destiny" was determined by how he played the game.

Shi'ite Sectarianism. Because Shi'ism developed as a movement of political opposition that drew many of its adherents from non-Arab converts to Islam, much of its early history was affected by the beliefs and aspirations of people who were not yet fully acculturated to Islamic teachings and who still retained elements of their previous Christian, Jewish, or Manichaean belief systems. Shi'ism did not develop as a mature set of doctrines until the end of the ninth century, more than two hundred years after the death of 'Ali. In this period, Shi'ism was associated with a variety of extremist doctrines. During 'Ali's lifetime, a follower named 'Abd Allah ibn Saba', a Jewish convert to Islam, believed that 'Ali was the awaited messiah. Ibn Saba' proclaimed 'Ali's divinity and said that the Imam had not died but was alive in the clouds and would return to fill the earth with justice. Another extremist sect, the Ulyaniyyah (circa 800), claimed that 'Ali was God and Muhammad his messenger. Sometimes called "The Blamers," this group blamed the Prophet Muhammad for concealing 'Ali's true nature out of jealousy.

The Kaysaniyyah. Other Shi'ite sects put forth candidates for leadership who were not descended from 'Ali and Fatimah. The most important of these sects was the Kaysaniyyah, founded by the anti-Umayyad rebel Mukhtar al-Thaqafi (died 687). This movement claimed that after the death of Husayn, the Imamate passed to 'Ali's third son, Muhammad ibn al-Hanafiyyah. Drawing on non-Arab aspirations for equality with Arab Muslims, Mukhtar proclaimed Ibn al-Hanafiyyah the "Guided One" (*Mahdi*), who would deliver newly converted Muslims from oppression. Although this movement was powerful enough to take over the city of Kufah in 686, it fell apart because its Mahdi, Ibn al-Hanafiyyah, refused to support it. Although the Kaysaniyyah movement died out fairly quickly, Kaysaniyyah concepts such as that of the Mahdi remained influential. A later group held that Ibn al-Hanafiyyah had not died but was in a state of concealment on a mountain near Madinah. They believed that the Mahdi would eventually return to restore justice among Muslims. Another group, the Hashimiyyah, claimed that Ibn al-Hanafiyyah had passed on the Imamate to his son Abu Hashim (died 717). After Abu Hashim's death, a group called the Abbasiyyah claimed that the Imamate had passed to the descendants of the

Prophet's cousin 'Abd Allah al-'Abbas (619–686). This group started the revolt against the Umayyads that led to the establishment of the Abbasid khilafah.

Zaydi Shi'ism. After the death of 'Ali, the most important event in the history of Shi'ism was the martyrdom of Husayn at Karbala' in southern Iraq, which took place on 10 October 680 and is commemorated in the Islamic world as Ashura. The last stand of Husayn and his seventy-two companions against five thousand Umayyad troops is one of the most important paradigms of Shi'ism and symbolizes the responsibility of Shi'ites to fight injustice whatever the cost. The memory of this event, which is commemorated in highly emotional festivals that include parades and staged pageants, reminds Shi'ites of the cost of failing to honor their commitment to the Imam and encourages bravery in the face of overwhelming odds.

Zayd ibn 'Ali. One of the few survivors of the massacre at Karbala' was Husayn's son 'Ali Zayn al-'Abidin (died 717), who lived the remainder of his life in Madinah and did not take part in political disputes. His son Zayd ibn 'Ali died in 740 during a short-lived revolt against the Umayyads. Zayd asserted his claim to the Imamate on the grounds that the Imamate belonged to any descendant of 'Ali and Fatimah who was learned and pious and raised his sword in defense of justice. Unlike other Shi'ite groups, the Zaydis, the followers of Zayd ibn 'Ali, did not reject Abu Bakr and 'Umar. Although they felt that 'Ali was better suited for the khilafah, they accepted what they called the "Imamate of the Second-Best" because 'Ali himself had not chosen to oppose Abu Bakr and 'Umar. In their theological doctrines, the Zaydis shared much in common with non-Shi'ite rationalists, such as the Mu'tazila. Zayd ibn 'Ali is said to have been a pupil of one of the founders of the Mu'tazila, Wasil ibn 'Ata' (699–748).

Revolt. After the Abbasids took power, Zaydi Shi'ism provided an opportunity for the descendants of 'Ali and Fatimah's son Hasan to assert their claims to the Imamate. Since the Zaydis recognized no hereditary succession to the Imamate, any descendant of 'Ali and Fatimah could assert his claim to leadership by raising a revolt. The most significant revolt led by a descendant of Hasan was that of Muhammad al-Nafs al-Zakiyyah (died 762), who in 758 staged an abortive rising against the Abbasids in Madinah. After escaping from this defeat, his brother Idris (died 791) proclaimed an Imamate in the western part of North Africa. This Imamate resulted in the creation of the Idrisid state, the first independent Muslim state in Morocco. Over the next 150 years, the Idrisid Imams taught a distinctive brand of Shi'ism based on the excellence of Hasan and his descendants. This doctrine, known in Morocco as Sharifism, was purely political and did not include the theological and eschatological doctrines of the Imamate. Sharifism remains the ideological basis of the Moroccan monarchy. Although the present king of Morocco is not a descendant of Idris, he traces his ancestry to Hasan. At the beginning of the tenth century, a Zaydi Imamate was also established in Yemen, where the sect continues to survive.

DIVINE RIGHTS OF KHALIFAHS

The following statement by the Umayyad khalifah al-Walid II (ruled 743–744) in a letter to his provincial governors illustrates how the Umayyads used the doctrine of predestination to justify their claims for the legitimacy of their rule and the rightness of their decrees. The insistent tone of this letter may be a result of the degree to which the legitimacy of Umayyad rule was being questioned in the years just preceding their overthrow by the Abbasids in 750.

The khalifahs of God followed one another, in charge of that which God had caused them to inherit from His prophets and over which He had delegated them. Nobody can dispute their right without God casting him down, and nobody can separate from their community without God destroying him, nor can anyone hold their government in contempt or question God's decree concerning them without God placing them in the khalifahs' power and giving them mastery over him, thus making him an example and a warning to others. This is how God acts toward anyone who has forsaken the obedience to which He has ordered people to cling, adhere, and devote themselves, and through which it is that heaven and earth came to be supported.

Source: Patricia Crone and Martin Hinds, *God's Caliph: Religious Authority in the First Centuries of Islam* (Cambridge: Cambridge University Press, 1986), pp. 116–126.

Imami Shi'ism. Today, the Imami Shi'ites are the most significant Shi'ite group. They first appeared on the political scene in the ninth century, when Islamic sources began to mention "People of the Imamate" (*Ahl al-Imamah*). Also called "Twelvers" (*Ithna 'Ashariyyah*), Imami Shi'ites believe that the leadership of the Muslim community is vested in twelve Imams. These Imams are 'Ali, Hasan, Husayn, 'Ali Zayn al-'Abidin (died 717), Muhammad al-Baqir (died 735), Ja'far al-Sadiq (circa 702–765), Musa al-Kazim (745–799), 'Ali al-Rida (765–818), Muhammad al-Jawad (died 835), 'Ali al-Hadi (died 868), Hasan al-Askari (died 874), and Muhammad al-Mahdi (circa 824 – ?). Adapting a concept that was first used by the Kaysaniyyah, Imami Shi'ites believe that the twelfth Imam is Mohammad al-Mahdi, the "Guided One" who will return at the end of time to inaugurate a final age of justice on earth. At present, however, the Mahdi is believed to exist in a state of absence or "occultation" (*ghaybah*). During the "Short Occultation," which occurred between 874 and 962, the twelfth Imam is said to have communicated with his followers through four scholars who were leaders of the Imami community. In the "Complete Occultation," which has lasted from 962 until the present, the Imam communicates to selected followers by inspiration.

The Ulama'. Until the return of Muhammad al-Mahdi, the religious scholars (*ulama'*) of the Imami community are to take the Imam's place as his trustees. These scholars retain the right, in the name of the Imam, to interpret matters of dogma, theology, and law. Rather than engage in independent reasoning, Imami Shi'ites follow the decisions of their scholars in all matters pertaining to religion. The scholars of the Imami community follow the decisions of the Imams. Rather than relying on their own reasoning, they are expected to follow the teachings of the Imams whenever possible. This requirement led the Imami Shi'ites to develop their own body of hadiths (*hadith walawi*), which consists of traditions of the Imams. In time, this reliance on tradition led to the development of scholarly institutions that were much like those created by Sunni Muslims.

Ismaili Shi'ism. Ismaili Shi'ism was born out of a conflict among Shi'ites that involved the succession to Ja'far al-Sadiq. The thirty-year Imamate of Ja'far (735–765) marked a watershed in the development of Shi'ite thought. During this period, the doctrine of the Imamate and much of Shi'ite law and theology attained their present form. According to the Ismailis, Ja'far al-Sadiq designated his eldest son, Ismail al-Mubarak (died circa 754), his successor. When Ismail died eleven years before his father, the question of further succession was left unresolved. For Ismailis, the succession after Ja'far should have gone to Ismail's son Muhammad (died circa 796). Ismaili Shi'ites call Muhammad "The Hidden One" (*al-Maktum*), because he and his descendants are believed to have gone into hiding for five generations. Ismailis are also called "Seveners" because they consider Muhammad al-Maktum to be the seventh Imam. Ismaili Shi'ites trace the descent of their Imams through Fatimah alone, because only Fatimah carried the blood of the Prophet Muhammad. For this reason, 'Ali is not counted as the first Imam. Instead, his son Hasan is the first Imam, while 'Ali is called the "Foundation" of the Imamate.

The Fatimids. Ismaili Shi'ism became prominent in Islamic history during the period of the Fatimid khilafah (909–1171), which ruled over much of North Africa and the Middle East from its capital at Cairo in Egypt. The official name of the Fatimid movement was "Mission of the Truth" (*Da'wat al-Haqq*). The Fatimid Imams operated through agents or missionaries, who were sent throughout Muslim lands to propagate Ismaili teachings. The head of the Ismaili mission was the Fatimid khalifah, who was Imam, successor to the Prophet Muhammad, and true repository of knowledge and wisdom. His mouthpiece was the Chief Missionary, who was the most accomplished Ismaili scholar of his time. The Fatimid mission was organized into geographical units called "islands," which were under the command of high-ranking missionaries called "Witnesses." Major Ismaili "islands" included Iraq, Yemen, Sind (now part of Pakistan), and parts of Iran and Central Asia. Regional and local missions were headed by missionaries of lesser rank. The foot soldiers of the Ismaili movement were missionaries known as "Breakers." Their job was to "break down" the resistance of pupils to Ismaili teachings.

Ismaili Doctrines. Fatimid theology was based on the notion of outer (*zahir*) and inner (*batin*) doctrines. The outer aspect of Fatimid doctrine consisted of a distinctive Ismaili school of law. Ismaili law was similar to Sunni schools of law, such as the Hanafi and the Maliki, which stressed *ray,* the logic-based opinion of jurists. In Fatimid Cairo, classes on Ismaili law were held regularly at the al-Azhar masjid (mosque) and were open to all comers, including women and Sunni Muslims. The inner aspect of Ismaili doctrine consisted of the disciplines of theology and philosophy. These were taught in the palace of the Imam in Cairo, and lessons were open only to Ismaili initiates, who were called "Saints."

Inner Truth. According to Ismaili doctrine, the Qur'an includes an inner truth that forms the essential core of divine revelation. This inner truth comes directly from God and can be found in all religions. Part of this truth consists of the doctrines of the Divine Soul and Universal Intellect, concepts that were acquired from the Neoplatonic philosophies of late antiquity. God is identified with the Universal Intellect, which creates and maintains the world through the Divine Soul. Creation emanates from the Divine Soul in a hierarchical manner; descending from man and angelic beings down through the higher animals, lower animals, plants, and minerals. This hierarchical chain of being is replicated by a hierarchy of Islamic knowledge that emanates from God, to the Prophet Muhammad, the Imams, and the Ismaili missionaries, until it reaches ordinary believers. The task of the Ismaili initiate is to use his intellect to ascend in the opposite direction: he must progress up the hierarchy of knowledge and the hierarchy of leadership until he attains the rank most suited to the level of his knowledge and intelligence.

Religious Doctrine as a Tool of State Policy. The Sunni conception of Islamic knowledge assumes that from the time of the Prophet Muhammad there were groups of pious Muslims who devoted themselves exclusively to the study of the Qur'an and hadiths. Known as the "Righteous Ancestors" (*al-Salaf al-Salih*), these men and women included the "Companions of the Prophet Muhammad," the "Followers" of the Companions, and the "Followers of the Followers." These three generations of "Righteous Ancestors" witnessed the revelation of the Qur'an, the death of the Prophet Muhammad, the breakup of the Muslim community into sects, and the establishment of the Umayyad khilafah. The traditions that they disseminated in oral and written form compose the majority of the Sunnah.

Interpreting Traditions. Unfortunately, much of this model is a myth. There is no doubt that such pious people existed and that they studied and taught Qur'an and Sunnah, but recent historical research has demonstrated that these "Righteous Ancestors" were often divided as to how their traditions should be interpreted and how the term *Sunnah* should be understood. Paradoxically, the term "Sunnah of the Messenger of God" appeared first among the Shi'ites and Kharijites and not among the Sunnis.

Minbar, carved in 862, in the Great Masjid at Kairouan

Clearly, the normative model of the Sunnah of the Prophet Muhammad was much less important to Islamic thought in this early period than it was in later generations. Subsequent changes in the concept of the Sunnah had much to do with changes in political ideology after the Abbasids replaced the Umayyads in the mid eighth century.

The Umayyads' Politics of Predestination. For the Umayyad khalifahs (ruled 662–750), "following the Sunnah" meant following their orders. The official title of the Umayyad khalifah was "Deputy of God and Imam of the Muslims." This title indicates that the khalifah claimed authority over matters of both state and religion. The khalifah's authority even extended to power over nature: references to at least three khalifahs in the works of Umayyad-era poets mention their power to bring sustenance to the land. Mu'awiyyah (ruled 661–680), the founder of the Umayyad dynasty, is reported to have said, "The earth belongs to God, and I am the Deputy of God." Opposition to the Umayyads was considered unbelief. After putting

down a political revolt against the Umayyads in 704, the Umayyad governor of Iraq spared the lives of only those rebels who confessed to being unbelievers and reconverted to Islam. In a letter to his provincial governors, the Umayyad khalifah al-Walid II (ruled 743–744) claimed that history has only two eras: the prophetic era and the era of the khilafah. For the Umayyads, the khalifahs, as God's deputies, were appointed by God to administer the legacy of the prophets. They presided over the implementation of the Sunnah, the legal system, the requirements of religion, and rights pertaining to God and humanity. Whoever obeyed the khalifah would flourish, and whoever disobeyed the khalifah would be punished in this world and the next.

Divine Right. The Umayyads believed that they ruled over the Muslims by divine right. Consequently, their theological doctrines denied the concept of free will and stressed God's predetermination of human actions. The Umayyads used the doctrine of predestination to claim that their opponents were unbelievers: since God made the Umayyads

The Great Masjid and minaret at Samarra', built by the Umayyad khalifah al-Mutawakkil in 847–851

khalifahs, it was His will that they should rule over the Muslims; thus, to reject the Umayyad khalifah is to reject God's will, and rejection of God's will is unbelief. The Umayyads did not stop at claiming legitimacy by divine right; they also claimed that since they were deputies of God, each of their decisions was, in effect, a divine decree. This claim put their opponents in a difficult theological situation. To say that the Umayyads' decisions were bad implied either that God's will was imperfect or that God created evil by creating leaders of Islam who disseminated false doctrines. The easiest solution to this dilemma was to say that God creates good, but human beings create evil. Blaming the sins of the Umayyad khalifahs on their own faults and weaknesses prevented the possibility of blaming God for allowing Umayyad injustices to occur. In this way, a theological principle was used to refute a major tenet of Umayyad political doctrine.

Murjiah Neutralists. Although most Sunni Muslims in the Umayyad period supported the Umayyad khalifahs, a significant number of scholars belonged to a group known as the Murjiah. The term *murjiah* comes from two Arabic roots: *arja'a*, meaning "to postpone" or "to defer," and *arja*, meaning "to give hope." In doctrinal discussions, both roots are linked to the Qur'anic verse "And there are others who await Allah's decree, whether He will punish them or forgive them" (9: 106). Politically, the Murjiah were "fence sitters": Muslims who refused to commit clearly to the Umayyads, the Kharijites, or the Shi'ites. In addition, they avoided passing judgment on the ethical merits of 'Uthman and 'Ali, "postponing" the matter for God to decide. Theologically, the Murjiah were religious scholars who separated faith from works. They believed that as long as a person had faith, he or she could "hope" for God's mercy, no matter how many sins he or she had committed. Kharijites and Shi'ites condemned the Murjiah as political obstructionists. By refusing to criticize

'Uthman and by refusing to judge the Umayyad rulers on the basis of their actions alone, they allegedly harmed Islam by acquiescing to the Umayyad regime and doing nothing to eliminate corruption and injustice.

Historical Perspective. Recent scholarship has shown this negative opinion to be unfair. The views held by people who were identified as Murjiah were spread over every facet of Islamic opinion, including those critical of the Umayyad regime. Later Muslim historians often disagreed over who should be included among the Murjiah. Many of the Murjiah were upholders of the Sunnah of the Prophet Muhammad and tried to create a unity among Muslims that would overcome sectarian divisions. A significant number of the Murjiah were noted jurists. Some jurists—such as al-Awza'i (died 773), the most prominent judge of Damascus during the later Umayyad period—were supporters of the Umayyads; others—such as Abu Hanifah, founder of the Hanafi madhhab—were politically neutral; still others—such as Sufyan al-Thawri (715–777), an influential jurist from Kufah who associated with early Sufis—were opponents of the Umayyads.

Murjiite Doctrine. Murjiite political doctrine recognized the khilafahs of both 'Uthman and 'Ali. *Al-Fiqh al-Akbar* (The Great Book of Law), a work attributed to Abu Hanifah, states, "We refer to God the decision about 'Uthman and 'Ali." A later work, called *Wasiyyat Abu Hanifah* (Testament of Abu Hanifah), goes farther and claims that the order of the first four khalifahs matches the order of their excellence; since 'Uthman came before 'Ali, 'Uthman was more suited to be khalifah than 'Ali. Murjiite theological doctrine asserted that faith and works are separate moral issues. *Al-Fiqh al-Akbar* states, "We do not declare anyone an unbeliever through sin, nor do we exclude anyone from faith." Faith is not divisible into parts nor does it decrease or increase. It is an all-or-nothing proposition:

one either has faith or does not have it, and believers are not to be compared to each other because of it. For Abu Hanifah, it is the faith that makes a person a Muslim. There is no halfway house between faith and unbelief. Muslims may differ, however, with respect to acts. The person who neglects to perform required acts such as prayer may be considered a bad Muslim. But as long as one has faith, one is still a Muslim. Muqatil ibn Sulayman (died 767), a noted Murjiite commentator on the Qur'an, summarized this principle by saying, "Where there is faith, sin does no harm."

Hasan al-Basri. A Sunni Muslim who took a middle stance between the Murjiites and their opponents and occupied a middle position on the subjects of free will and predestination was Hasan al-Basri (died 728). The son of a Persian captive who converted to Islam, Hasan settled in Basrah and won a great reputation for his strength of character, piety, learning, and eloquence. At times, he supported the Umayyads and was befriended by the Umayyad governor of Iraq. At other times, he opposed their decisions and was forced to go into hiding. He disagreed with the Kharijites by claiming that the grave sinner could be a believer. But unlike the Murjiites, he felt that the sinner should be held accountable for his actions; accordingly, he called the grave sinner a "hypocrite." He refused to judge between 'Uthman and 'Ali; yet, he rejected the Umayyad doctrine of predestination. A person once said to him of the Umayyads, "These princes shed the blood of Muslims and seize their goods; they do such-and-such and say: 'Our acts occur only according to God's will.'" Hasan replied, "The enemies of God lie." Like the Qadarites, Hasan al-Basri believed that human beings have the ability to choose between good and evil on their own. But he tempered this view with the belief that God determined the outlines of a person's fate and allowed misfortunes to happen to people in order to test them. He used to say, "God created creation and the creatures, and they proceeded as He created them; if a person supposes that by acting on his own he can increase his sustenance, let him by acting on his own increase the span of his life, alter his color, or add to his limbs or his fingers."

Sources:
Patricia Crone and Martin Hinds, *God's Caliph: Religious Authority in the First Centuries of Islam* (Cambridge: Cambridge University Press, 1986).

Farhad Daftary, *The Isma'ilis: Their History and Doctrines* (Cambridge: Cambridge University Press, 1990).

Heinz Halm, *The Fatimids and Their Traditions of Learning* (London: I. B. Tauris and The Institute of Ismaili Studies, 1997).

Marshall G. S. Hodgson, *The Venture of Islam: Conscience and History in a World Civilization*, 3 volumes (Chicago: University of Chicago Press, 1974).

Moojan Momen, *An Introduction to Shi'i Islam* (New Haven & London: Yale University Press, 1985).

Al-Shaykh al-Mufid, *Kitab al-Irshad: The Book of Guidance into the Lives of the Twelve Imams*, translated by I. K. A. Howard (Horsham: Balagha Books / London: Muhammadi Trust, 1981).

W. Montgomery Watt, *The Formative Period of Islamic Thought* (Edinburgh: Edinburgh University Press, 1973).

ORIGINS AND DEVELOPMENT OF SYSTEMATIC THEOLOGY

The Problem of Authenticity. *Kalam,* the Arabic word for "theology," literally means "speech" or "word." It was used in Arabic translations of works by Greek philosophers as a synonym of the Greek word *logos,* which means "word," "reason," or "argument." In the works of Muslim theologians who were influenced by Greek philosophy, *theologoi,* the Greek word for "theologians," was translated as "masters of the divine Kalam" or "practitioners of Kalam in divinity." In this way, *Kalam* came to signify formal or systematic theology. The interchangeability of the terms *logos* and *kalam* reflects one of the major problems of systematic theology in Islam—the reliance of this discipline on methods and terminologies that came from outside the Islamic tradition. For the opponents of Kalam, this problem was proof that systematic theology was an inauthentic discipline, alien in its origins and development from the original sources of Islam.

Kalam as a Formal Discipline. Kalam came into its own as a formal discipline during the reign of the Abbasid khalifah Harun al-Rashid (ruled 786–809). The first century of Abbasid rule (circa 750–850) was a period of great intellectual ferment. The new capital of Baghdad in Iraq, possibly the largest city in the world at that time, attracted visitors from as far away as Byzantium, Africa, and India. A thriving book trade stimulated translations of Greek, Christian, and Indian works. Many scholars of this period came from non-Arab backgrounds. Their parents or grandparents had converted to Islam from Judaism, Christianity, Zoroastrianism, Manichaeism, and other religions of the Middle East and Asia. Christian theologians writing in Arabic, such as Theodore Abu Qurrah (circa 750 – 826) and the Nestorian patriarch Timothy I (died 823), debated Muslims at the Abbasid court and added to Muslims' knowledge of Christian theological arguments. The annotated bibliography of writings in Arabic compiled by Ibn al-Nadim (circa 936–995), a scholar and librarian from Baghdad, mentions eighty Greek authors whose works were translated into Arabic. The multicultural environment of Abbasid Iraq had much to do with the development of Kalam as an intellectual discipline.

Methodology. The hallmark of Kalam was the discussion of theological issues with little or no recourse to tradition as a source of proof texts. When a scriptural passage was used to prove a point, it usually came from the Qur'an, not from hadiths. Instead of a saying of the Prophet, logical arguments—usually taken from Greek philosophical models—were used to prove or disprove assertions. The literary style of Kalam treatises was the dialectical method, also known as the point-counterpoint debate (*munazara* or *jadal*). Kalam treatises were often written as a series of disputations in which an opponent's opinion was signaled by the phrase "if it is said," and the author's opinion was signaled by the phrase "it is said" or "it should be answered." Masjids, private homes, schools, and the audience halls of government officials were the sites of Kalam debates. In the

Courtyard of the Masjid of al-Azhar in Cairo, first constructed in 970–972 and later rebuilt and expanded

intellectual culture of the time, Kalam was a performative discipline: reputations were made and lost in public disputations before highly trained audiences. A frustrating aspect of Kalam texts for the modern reader is that the lively debate that originally gave rise to an argument is not reproduced in the text, and a dry, stylistic formalism takes its place. To regain the flavor of the debate, the medieval reader of a Kalam text would have to reconstruct the original context of the argument, drawing on years of study with Kalam instructors and fellow students.

Christianity and Kalam. During the height of the Abbasid khilafah in the ninth and tenth centuries, Islamic thought was eclectic; that is, it shared many concepts and terminologies with neighboring cultures and intellectual traditions. This eclecticism is evidence of the confidence that Muslims had in their religious and political institutions. For scholars living in the Abbasid era, Islam had created the most powerful empire since ancient Rome; Baghdad was the economic and cultural capital of the world; and the teachings of Allah and the Prophet Muhammad were on the cutting edge of religious history. It was only a matter of time, they believed, before Islam became the universal religion of the world. This optimistic outlook allowed Muslim thinkers to interact freely with representatives of other religions and engage with them in public debates. Texts derived from Christian and Jewish sources were used to amplify arguments that the Qur'an touched on only briefly. Collections of stories and legends

known as *Israiliyat* (Stories of Israel) were used by commentators on the Qur'an to fill in the details of biblical narratives.

Terminology. The writings of Arab Christians provided early Kalam scholars with key theological terms. An example of this influence can be found in the debate over God's attributes. In the eighth century, there arose in Islam the belief that certain of the "names" of Allah in the Qur'an stand for real entities, which have existed in God from eternity. The opponents of this view accused its adherents of borrowing ideas from the Christian concept of the Trinity. To a certain extent, this charge was true. The most common Kalam terms for "divine attribute" are *ma'na* and *sifah*. Kalam scholars who believed in divine attributes conceived of these qualities—such as power, glory, and mercy—as "things" or "entities" that exist co-eternally with God. The Arabic word for "thing" or "entity" is *shay*. Arab Christian theologians, starting with Theodore Abu Qurrah, used *shay* as a translation of the Greek word *pragma*, which also means "thing" or "entity." Christian theologians used the term *pragma* to describe the three parts of the Christian Trinity. The Arab Christian philosopher Yahya ibn 'Adi (died 974), commenting on a work by Abu Qurrah's teacher John of Damascus (circa 675 – circa 754), used the Arabic term *sifah* to describe the attributes of each "person" of the Trinity: existence, essence, and generosity are *sifat* of the Father, life and wisdom are *sifat* of the Son, and knowledge, life, and power are *sifat* of the Holy Spirit. The Muslim use of the term *sifah* for divine attributes dates from the same period. More than a century and a half earlier, the Shi'ite theologian Hisham ibn al-Hakam (died 815) used the related term *ma'na* to describe the essential attributes of God. Like John of Damascus and Abu Qurrah, he believed that divine attributes such as knowledge and power are incorporeal "bodies" or "things" that co-exist with God. The difference was that for Hisham there was no separation of God's attributes into three categories or "persons." These "things" were instead essential attributes of the One God and were paired with the Qur'anic "names" that most closely resembled them.

From the Qadariyyah to the Mu'tazila.

One of the most vehement opponents of the doctrine of divine attributes was Wasil ibn 'Ata' (699–748), a native of Basrah who was a student of Hasan al-Basri. According to Wasil, "he who posits a 'thing' or an 'attribute' as eternal posits two gods." For Wasil, divine unity meant divine simplicity. According to his understanding of the statement "There is no god but Allah," nothing but God is equal to God or is even a part of God, including God's own actions and attributes. Attributes of God cannot be eternal because only God Himself is eternal. Thus, the "names" of God mentioned in the Qur'an are not real entities. They are only metaphors, figures of speech or created "modes" of divine action.

Theological Rationalism.

Wasil ibn 'Ata' is best known as the founder of the Mu'tazila, a movement of theological rationalism that supported the Qadarite doctrine of free choice. Lasting for approximately four hundred years, Mu'tazilism became the official theology of the Abbasid khilafah in the mid ninth century and enjoyed a revival in the guise of Islamic modernism in the twentieth century. Western scholars of Islam have favored the Mu'tazila because their doctrines seemed to foreshadow the rationalistic philosophy of the European Enlightenment. Such scholars forget, however, that the Mu'tazila were not modern liberals. Although they favored reason over tradition, they would not have agreed with the Enlightenment critique of religion, and they followed the decidedly nonliberal policy of persecuting their opponents when they had political power.

Origins of Mu'tazilism.

According to the standard account of the origin of the Mu'tazila, Hasan al-Basri was asked during one of his lessons whether a grave sinner should be counted as a believer or an unbeliever. When Hasan hesitated, his student Wasil replied that the grave sinner was neither a believer nor an unbeliever but occupied an "intermediate position" between the two. Having contradicted his teacher, Wasil withdrew (*i'tazala*) to another part of the masjid, followed by several of Hasan's students. Despite the popularity of this story, historical research has determined that it is no more than a legend. Modern scholars believe that the term *Mu'tazila* was originally political in nature. Like the term *Murjiah*, it connoted "neutrality" or "withdrawal," most probably from the conflicts that raged between the Umayyads and their opponents. During the four centuries of its existence as a major theological movement, Mu'tazilism spread as far as North Africa and Central Asia and left a strong influence on Shi'ite theology, but in its formative years it was confined almost exclusively to Iraq. In the eighth and ninth centuries two Mu'tazilite theological schools formed in Basrah and in the Abbasid capital of Baghdad.

The Basrah School.

The more important of the two schools was the Basrah school. Basrah Mu'tazilism was primarily associated with Abu al-Hudhayl (752 – circa 840), whose most creative period was before the year 800. Abu al-Hudhayl was noted for his debates with Jews, Christians, and Zoroastrians and was eventually asked to settle in Baghdad, near the khalifah and the chief ministers of the Abbasid court. Politically, he was anti-Shi'ite. He believed that the choice of a khalifah was a matter for the Muslim community to decide and that the community would choose the best candidate. On the subject of 'Uthman's khilafah, he argued that 'Uthman was more qualified than 'Ali during the first six years of his rule; as for the remainder of 'Uthman's khilafah, he refused to make a judgment. In doctrinal matters, Abu al-Hudhayl appears to have been the first to formulate the Mu'tazilite Five Principles.

The Baghdad School.

As Basrah Mu'tazilism grew in popularity under Abu al-Hudhayl, another branch of the movement formed in Baghdad under Bishr ibn al-Mu'tamir (died after 817). Bishr was a noted poet as well as a theologian and composed refutations of his theological opponents in verse. Under Bishr, the Baghdad school of

---

HEREDITY AND SIN

A major compiler and systemizer of Mu'tazilite thought, Qadi 'Abd al-Jabbar, *qadi al-qudat* (chief judge) of the city of Rayy in the midst of the period of Shi'ite Buyid rule (949–1055), applied reason to the question of heredity in earthly life and divine judgment and came to the conclusion that children do not inherit their father's disbelief, thus stressing the importance on individual choice and accountability.

Then if it is asked: Is it not the case that in this world, children are virtually the same as their fathers in regard to disbelief? Hence, are they not under virtually the same rule as their fathers in the hereafter regarding divine punishment for disbelief? *Say to him:* If what you said were possible, one could also say that if the father committed adultery, the child should be flogged [for his father's crime], or if the father committed murder, the child should be executed, because he is under the same rule as his father. If that is not valid, then what you have asserted is not valid. The child only has the same judgment as his father in whatever does not relate to punishment. As for divine punishments, may God preserve us from them!

Source: "Qadi 'Abd al-Jabbar's *Kitab al-usul al-khamsah* (Book of the Five Principles)," translated by Richard C. Martin, in *Defenders of Reason in Islam: Mu'tazilism from Medieval School to Modern Symbol,* by Martin and Mark R. Woodward, with Dwi S. Atmaja (Oxford: Oneworld, 1997), pp. 90–115.

The Great Masjid of Isfahan, Iran, commissioned by Saljuk sultan Malik-Shah I (ruled 1073–1092)

the Mu'tazila enjoyed close relations with the Abbasid court. These relations culminated in the proclamation of Mu'tazilism as the official theology of Islam by the khalifahs al-Ma'mun (ruled 813–833), al-Mu'tasim (ruled 833–842), and al-Wathiq (ruled 842–847). Politically, the Baghdad Mu'tazilites held a more favorable view of Shi'ism than did their counterparts in Basrah. Bishr ibn al-Mu'tamir accompanied the khalifah al-Ma'mun to the Central Asian city of Merv in 817 in order to proclaim 'Ali al-Rida, the eighth leader of the Imami Shi'ites, heir to the khilafah.

Free Choice. Both schools of the Mu'tazila supported the Qadarite doctrine of free choice. They believed that it would be unjust for God to punish people for acts for which they were not responsible, and they concluded that if God commands human beings to do something, they must have the ability (*istita'ah*) or independent power (*qudrah*) to do it. Thus, they said that even if God knows that a person will not obey His commands, he cannot be punished until he demonstrates that he has freely chosen to disobey. Children, captives, and the mentally or physically impaired are not held accountable for their actions because they do not have the ability to make a rationally considered choice between moral alternatives. According to Abu al-Hudhayl, the ability to act in a morally correct way is a potential that resides in all human beings. Before acting, each person must decide which of two possibilities will be carried out: he or she will act either as God commands or contrary to God's command. This moment of decision separates the potential act from the actual act. God judges only the actual act, after it has been performed. Expanding on this view, Bishr ibn al-Mu'tamir advocated the doctrine of "secondary effects" (*tawallud*). He asserted that any secondary effect that is generated from a person's act is also that "act," and therefore the person's responsibility. Bishr's doctrine of secondary effects is similar to the modern legal concept of liability, in which a company can be sued for injuries resulting from the fabrication of a faulty product.

Inquisition. Shortly before his death in 833, the khalifah al-Ma'mun instructed the governor of Baghdad to require all state-appointed judges to submit to an examination of their beliefs. This inquisition lasted for seventeen years and resulted in the persecution, imprisonment, and even torture of many Muslim scholars. When the khalifah al-Mutawakkil ended the inquisition in 850, the Baghdad school of the Mu'tazila fell out of favor. During this period, al-Jahiz (circa 776–869), a well-known essayist and theologian of the Baghdad school, wrote *Fadilat al-Mu'tazila* (The Excellence of the Mu'tazila), a treatise defending Mu'tazilism. Later, Ibn al-Rawandi (died 910), a Shi'ite political activist and theological freethinker, wrote *Fadihat al-Mu'tazila* (The Disaster of the Mu'tazila), a refutation of al-Jahiz's work.

The Spread of Mu'tazilism. After the decline of the Baghdad Mu'tazila, the movement continued to be influential in

Basrah, from whence it spread to the rich and heavily populated cities of eastern Iran and Central Asia. The Basrah school reached its zenith under a father and son known as the "Two Masters," Abu 'Ali al-Jubba'i (died 915) and Abu Hashim ibn al-Jubba'i (died 933). These "Two Masters" had an enormous influence on the subsequent development of the Kalam tradition. For the Mu'tazila, the son was more influential than the father. Through his student Abu 'Abd Allah al-Basri (died 977) and al-Basri's student Qadi 'Abd al-Jabbar (died 1024), Abu Hashim's views on Mu'tazilite theology became dominant among the later Mu'tazila. The influence of Abu Hashim's father, Abu 'Ali al-Jubba'i, was also important. Apart from his son, Abu 'Ali's most-prized pupil was Abu al-Hasan al-Ash'ari (died 935). Al-Ash'ari eventually rejected the doctrines of Jubba'i and left to form his own school of theology, that of the Ash'arites, which became the most influential Kalam school of Sunni Islam.

The Five Principles. The most important sources of information on Mu'tazilite theology are the works of al-Ash'ari and Qadi 'Abd al-Jabbar. Originally from Hamadan in Iran, 'Abd al-Jabbar served as chief judge (*qadi al-qudat*) of the city of Rayy, which was located near modern Tehran. Rayy controlled the trade routes from Iran to the Byzantine Empire and was one of the most important cities of the Buyids, a family of Shi'ite military leaders who governed the Abbasid state from 945 to 1055. As patrons of both Imami Shi'ite and Mu'tazilite theologians, the Buyids presided over the period in which Imami Shi'ism became influenced by Mu'tazilite theology and developed the doctrines by which it is known today.

Systematization. Qadi 'Abd al-Jabbar was best known as a compiler and systematizer of Mu'tazilite thought. He built a comprehensive and coherent system of theological thinking on the foundations laid for him by the older generations of Mu'tazila. He considered his greatest merit to be the creation of a systematic approach to theological questions and the elaboration of theological arguments. 'Abd al-Jabbar's most important works are *al-Mughni*, whose full title is translated as "The Comprehensive Book on the Subjects of Divine Unity and Justice," and *Kitab al-usul al-khamsah* (Book of the Five Principles). These works are a synopsis of the teachings of the Basrah school of Mu'tazilism as represented by the followers of Abu Hashim.

Unity. The first and most important principle of Mu'tazilite theology was divine unity (*tawhid*). For 'Abd al-Jabbar, knowledge of divine unity depends first of all on the knowledge that God exists. This sort of knowledge is based on rational thought (*nazar*), which is a responsibility imposed on all human beings. The rational knowledge of God is based on four kinds of evidence: reason, the Qur'an, the Sunnah of the Prophet Muhammad, and the consensus of the Muslims. Of these four kinds of evidence, reason is the most important because the validity of scripture, tradition, and consensus is based on the rational knowledge that God exists, that He is truthful, and that He would not deceive his creatures. One of the

Mihrab (prayer niche) in the Great Masjid of Tlemcen, Tunisia, built in 1082 and restored in 1136

most important Mu'tazilite arguments for the existence of God is the argument from *contingency*. Reason, which is based on experience, tells one that one cannot live forever and that one is limited in one's powers and abilities. Thus, a person is a *contingent* being: one must depend on something outside of oneself for one's creation and support. This noncontingent, necessary being is God, who is unlike human beings in every respect. People die, but God is the Living; God, not people, is the ultimate Creator of all things; God is the Powerful, but people are constantly confronted by their powerlessness.

Negative Theology. The argument from contingency is an example of negative theology, a discourse about the nature of God that is based not on God's positive attributes but on logical oppositions. God is whatever the human being is not. Another approach to negative theology is to describe God in terms of what God is not. According to al-Ash'ari, this approach was also practiced by the Mu'tazila: "The Mu'tazila agree that God is one; there is no thing like Him. . . . He is not a body, not a form, not flesh and blood, not an individual, not a substance or an attribute . . . not begetting nor begotten; magnitudes do not comprehend Him, nor do veils cover Him; the senses do not attain Him; He is not comparable to men and does not resemble creatures in any respect." Because God is exalted above all forms of resemblance, statements of God in the Qur'an such as "What prevents you from prostrating yourself before what I have created with my two hands?" (38: 75) can only be metaphorical. The "hands" of God must stand for something other than real hands, such as God's ability to create and maintain the world. All the other divine names and attributes in the Qur'an are metaphorical as well. They should be understood as partial and approximate descriptions of a divine reality that is ultimately indescribable. The Mu'tazila accused those who believed in the reality of divine attributes of falling into the heresies of *anthropomorphism*, the belief that God has human attributes such as hands or a face, or *corporealism*, the belief that God's attributes are corporeal entities that exist within Him.

Justice. The fundamental principle of Mu'tazilite ethics was divine justice. Justice, as understood by the Mu'tazila, was based on two hypotheses and a corollary: God desires good for human beings; thus, He does not will or create evil; God provides guidance for human beings in the form of divine revelations; thus, He does not want people to go astray; and follows from these hypotheses that God cannot force human beings to commit immoral or unlawful acts. God would be unjust if He punished people for acts that He forced them to perform. In their writings on ethics the Mu'tazila faced a problem that was as old as Socrates: Does God give laws to human beings because the laws themselves are good, or are the laws good because God made them? For most Sunni theologians, God's laws as revealed in the Qur'an and the Sunnah are good and must be obeyed because they come from God. For the Mu'tazila, God's laws are objectively good. That is, reason demonstrates that they are beneficial for humankind, even without the aid of the Qur'an. Following Bishr ibn al-Mu'tamir, Qadi 'Abd al-Jabbar viewed the Shari'ah—the law of Islam—as a grace or blessing (*ni'mah*) bestowed by God on humanity. This grace is like a rope thrown to a drowning man or food given to a starving person. God provides the opportunity for salvation, but it is up to the human being to accept it or reject it.

Explaining Suffering. Another problem discussed by the Mu'tazila had to do with *theodicy:* How should one understand the suffering caused by natural disasters or human actions? 'Abd al-Jabbar argued that bad things happen in the world, but to attribute injustice to God would mean that God willed something that He hated or prohibited something that He wanted. This idea, said 'Abd al-Jabbar, was absurd. Other Mu'tazilites tried to posit reasons for God's appearing to make bad things happen to good people. Bishr ibn al-Mu'tamir argued that, when innocents were killed in acts of war or natural disasters, God was punishing them for hidden sins or preventing them from committing evil in the future. 'Abd al-Jabbar tried to soften Bishr's harsh judgment by arguing that God granted an indemnity to innocent people for their sufferings. As proof, he cited the following saying of the Prophet Muhammad: "The pen [of judgment] is raised in three instances: a man sleeping until he awakens, a child until he reaches puberty, and a madman until he recuperates." Even

animals earned an indemnity for their suffering. Some Mu'tazilites suggested that grazing animals killed for food would be granted everlasting enjoyment in the pastures of Paradise. Beasts of prey posed a greater moral problem because their survival depended on the suffering of other animals. The Baghdad Mu'tazilite Ja'far ibn Harb (died 850) believed that carnivorous beasts were condemned to prey on each other in a "stopping place" (*mawqif*) between heaven and hell. Others said that beasts of prey would go to hell, but only in order to punish human evildoers.

Divine Promise and Threat. The Mu'tazilite principle of promise and threat (*al-wa'd wa al-wa'iz*) was a corollary of the principle of justice. Most simply, it meant that whatever God promises is bound to come to pass. For some Mu'tazilites, this "promise" included a predetermined date for the end of a person's life (*ajal*). Abu al-Hudhayl was so convinced that a person's days were numbered that he said, if a murdered man were somehow spared from being killed, he would die on the same day from another cause. Other Mu'tazilites, seeing that Abu al-Hudhayl's fatalism might contradict the concept of free choice, sought to draw a distinction between a person's sustenance (*rizq*), which was predetermined by God, and the moral course of one's life, which was a matter of personal choice.

Intercession. Among the later Mu'tazila, discussions about the principle of promise and threat were mostly about eschatology. 'Abd al-Jabbar discussed the promise of heaven for the virtuous believer and the threat of hellfire for the grave sinner. In particular, he sought to disprove the Murjiite assertion that the grave sinner may have access to salvation through the intercession of prophets and saints. Although Mu'tazilite theology, which stresses divine transcendence over divine immanence, seems to rule out the possibility of intercession, 'Abd al-Jabbar did not deny that intercession exists, but he limited the scope of intercession by saying that it increases only the degree of virtue that a person already possesses: intercession cannot transform a vice into a virtue. For 'Abd al-Jabbar, the Murjiite statement "Where there is faith, there is no sin" contradicts the logic of the Qur'anic arguments about justice. As a Mu'tazilite, he believed that hadith accounts affirming intercession for the grave sinner should not be allowed to contradict a statement made by God in the Qur'an or the logic based on it.

The Intermediate Position. The "intermediate position" (*al-manzilah bayn al-manzilatayn*) was one of the two principles of Mu'tazilite theology that defined Mu'tazilism for Sunni historians. It is said that this principle caused Wasil ibn 'Ata' to remove himself from the circle of Hasan al-Basri and start a new theological movement. For the Mu'tazila, however, the "intermediate position" was merely another corollary of the principle of justice. Just as the principle of divine justice defined theodicy for the Mu'tazila, the "intermediate position," along with the "promise and threat," defined Mu'tazilite ethics. As with the rest of the Five Principles, Mu'tazilite arguments about the interme-

An Imam delivering a sermon from a minbar in a masjid; illumination by al-Wasiti from a 1237 manuscript for the *Maqamat* (Assemblies) of al-Hariri (Bibliothèque Nationale, Paris)

diate position depended on conclusions that were drawn logically from statements of God in the Qur'an.

Defining the Believer. Qadi 'Abd al-Jabbar opened his discussion of the intermediate position with the question "Why do you say that one who fornicates and commits murder is a grave sinner, and not a believer?" He answered by saying that the term *believer* (*mu'min*) is a noun of praise in the Qur'an. Citing Qur'anic verses to prove his point, he argued that a fornicator or a murderer is not a praiseworthy person and thus does not meet God's definition of a believer. "Then why," he was asked, "Do you say that the grave sinner is not an unbeliever?" Because, replied 'Abd al-Jabbar, if the grave sinner were an unbeliever, the Qur'an would require that he pay the tax levied on unbelievers and the Shari'ah would allow such a person to be enslaved as a prisoner of war. Since neither the Qur'an nor the Sunnah mandates such punishments for the grave sinner, such a person cannot be considered an unbeliever. Finally, Hasan al-Basri's opinion of the grave sinner was raised: "Do you say, then, that he is a hypocrite?" No, said 'Abd al-Jabbar. The hypocrite is a person who hides his unbelief within

himself while outwardly professing Islam. The grave sinner hides nothing; because his sins are there for everyone to see, he cannot be called a hypocrite. In any case, the grave sinner would still face punishment after death, for the Qur'an says: "Oh Lord! Twice you have made us die" (40: 11), and "They will be exposed to hellfire morning and evening" (40: 46).

Commanding Good and Forbidding Evil. The third corollary of the Mu'tazilite principle of justice was the last of the Five Principles: "commanding good and forbidding evil" (*al-amr bi-l-ma'ruf wa al-nahy 'an al-munkar*). Like the previous two principles, it also served as a hallmark of the Mu'tazilite definition of ethics. Although the Mu'tazila shared this principle with Kharijites and Shi'ites, unlike these two groups, they did not apply it to sectarian conflicts. Instead, they made it the foundation principle for a strict ethic of right and wrong. According to 'Abd al-Jabbar, the person who does not prohibit wrongdoing has disobeyed God. The same applies to commanding the good. The only exception would be in the case of one who might be persecuted for carrying out this principle. In such a case, a person would be justified in keeping his opinions to himself. This position is similar to the Shi'ite doctrine of "dissimulation" (taqiyah), which allows a person to hide his true opinions if they might bring danger to himself or his family.

The Doctrine of the Created Qur'an. Apart from the "intermediate position," the best-known doctrine of the Mu'tazila was the concept of the created Qur'an (khalq al-Qur'an). For Sunni theologians, this doctrine set the Mu'tazila apart from the Sunnis as a theological movement. This doctrine also lay at the heart of the Mu'tazilite inquisition of 833–850. In 833 the khalifah al-Ma'mun declared: "He who does not believe that the Qur'an is created has no belief in God's unity." After the inquisition, Sunni theologians transformed this hallmark of Mu'tazilite doctrine into proof of Mu'tazilite heresy. Ironically, the argument over whether the Qur'an is created or uncreated is still one of the least understood theological disputes in Islam.

Creation versus Eternal Existence. For the Mu'tazila, the doctrine of the created Qur'an was derived from the principle of divine unity and was related to their rejection of eternal divine attributes. The Qur'an variously describes itself as an "Arabic Qur'an . . . in the Mother of the Book" (43: 3-4); a "Noble Qur'an, in a Hidden Book" (56: 77-78); and a "Glorious Qur'an on a Preserved Tablet" (85: 21-22). To Mu'tazilite theologians, these passages implied that the Qur'an was created as a model or archetype of divine scripture before the creation of the world. The Qur'an that was revealed to the Prophet Muhammad was a copy of this pre-existent Qur'an and was sent down to confirm Muhammad's role as the Seal of the Prophets. In its most basic form, the Mu'tazilite doctrine of the created Qur'an was similar to the Jewish doctrine of the pre-existent Torah. In Judaism, the Torah, as the source of the Divine Law, is both pre-existent and created; that is, God created His law before He created the world. Less than fifty years after the death of the Prophet Muhammad, 'Abd Allah ibn 'Abbas, a noted hadith scholar and cousin of the Prophet, claimed that God's speech was uncreated and co-eternal with God. According to this doctrine, the Qur'an was also uncreated and eternal because it contained the word of God. Evidence that Ibn Abbas's doctrine of the uncreated Qur'an was widely accepted in the Umayyad period can be found in the "Debate Between a Saracen and a Christian" by the Arab Christian theologian John of Damascus. In this work, the Christian tries to get the Muslim to admit the divinity of Christ by acknowledging that both the Qur'an and Christ are the uncreated word of God.

The Case for Eternal Existence. In the Abbasid period, the best-known proponent of the doctrine of the uncreated Qur'an was Ahmad Ibn Hanbal. Ibn Hanbal, who suffered severe persecution at the hands of the Mu'tazilite inquisition, claimed that "the word of God is His eternal knowledge, and hence it is uncreated." He further claimed that "what is between the covers of the Qur'an is the word of God, and what we read and hear and write is the word of God. It therefore follows that the words and letters of the Qur'an are the word of God. Inasmuch as agreement has established that the word of God is uncreated, it follows that the words of the Qur'an are also uncreated." Ibn Hanbal and his successors realized that the concept of the created Qur'an had a serious theological shortcoming. If the verses of the Qur'an were created at the moment of their revelation, the text of the Qur'an would be fixed in historical time, and thus its relevance would be limited to the period in which it appeared. If the Qur'an were seen historically as a product of seventh-century Arabia, it would follow that its statements and injunctions addressed seventh-century Arabian concerns. Thus, certain Qur'anic injunctions might be suspended if the conditions that gave rise to them changed. An uncreated Qur'an, however, not fixed in historical time and space, would have no such limitations. Such a Qur'an would be truly universal. Being free of the limitations of both culture and history, its injunctions would be valid for all peoples and all historical periods, whether in seventh-century Arabia or in twenty-first-century America.

The Case for Creation. However, the extreme, historicist interpretation of the doctrine of the created Qur'an feared by Ibn Hanbal was held by only a few of the Mu'tazila. One of them was the libertarian Ibrahim al-Nazzam (died 836). For Nazzam, the verses of the Qur'an were created "in the air" at the moment of their revelation. This belief meant not only that the Qur'an was fixed in time and space but also that human beings could copy, and even improve, its literary style. According to Nazzam, the content of the Qur'an, not the style of its verses, proves the truth of Muhammad's prophetic mission. A similarly libertarian view was held by Mu'ammar of Basrah (died 830), who taught that the word of God was a capacity that belonged to the "body" in which it appeared. Thus, the word of God that Moses heard in the burning bush belonged not to God, but to the bush; likewise, the word of God in the Qur'an belonged to the Prophet Muhammad. Since Nazzam denied the uniqueness of the Qur'an and appeared to allow the abrogation of its verses—and since Mu'ammar appeared to deny the divinity of the word of God—it was understandable that Sunni theologians would suspect them of heresy. But most Mu'tazilites were not libertarians such as Nazzam and Mu'ammar. Instead, they more commonly held that God created the Qur'an as a pre-existent, heavenly scripture, and that the text of this created, yet pre-existent, scripture was sent down to Muhammad as a divine revelation. The idea that the Qur'an, although created in time, exists as a heavenly archetype eliminated the danger that the word of God might be suspended or abrogated by later generations of Muslims. Whether created or uncreated, its existence on a heavenly "Preserved Tablet" ensured that it would retain its universal and timeless validity. The "Two Ja'fars" of Baghdad Mu'tazilism, Ja'far ibn Harb and Ja'far ibn Mubashshir (died 851) taught that the Qur'an was created in an "abode," which was another term for the Preserved Tablet.

Quanzhou Masjid in China, built in 1310

This pre-existent Qur'an has exactly the same form as the Qur'an that was revealed to the Prophet Muhammad, including the same letters, sentences, and arrangement of verses. But the true word of God, the real Qur'an that "none but the purified may touch" (56: 79), is the pre-existent Qur'an, which subsists in its "abode" on the Preserved Tablet. The Qur'an that Muslims read and recite is an "imitation" of this pre-existent Qur'an, and whatever is recited or held in the believer's mind is an imitation of the divine word, not the divine word itself.

The Sunni Critique of Mu'tazilism. In the year 850 the khalifah al-Mutawakkil put an end to the Mu'tazilite inquisition by forbidding public disputes about the nature of the Qur'an. His decree led to the decline of the Baghdad school of the Mu'tazila and the rise of Sunni theology, which held that the Qur'an was the uncreated word of God and that the doctrine of the created Qur'an was an innovation (*bid'ah*), a departure from the authentic teachings of the Qur'an and the Prophet Muhammad. One of the side effects of the Mu'tazilite inquisition was that Sunni theologians became acquainted with the doctrines and methods of the Kalam. Some Sunni theologians adopted positions that were not too different from those of the Mu'tazila. One such scholar, Husayn al-Karabisi (died 862), taught that although the Qur'an is uncreated, a person's utterance (*lafz*) of the Qur'an—whether by voice (as in recitation) or by writing its verses with a pen—is created. Karabisi and his followers, who were known as the Lafziyyah, attempted to address an important paradox of the written word that Ibn Hanbal and other Sunni literalists did not take into account. When one reads the works of a long-dead writer such as Ibn Hanbal, one can say metaphorically that Ibn Hanbal "speaks" through his writings. Similarly, one can say that Ibn Hanbal's "speech," as expressed in his writings, is "re-created" whenever his works are read. Thus, one can also say that God "speaks" through the text of the Qur'an, which is "re-created" metaphorically whenever its verses are recited or read. By framing the doctrine of the uncreated Qur'an in terms of what today would be called communication theory, Karabisi hoped to counter the argument of the two Ja'fars that the Qur'an was created in an "abode." For strict literalists such as Ibn Hanbal, however, Karabisi's approach was no improvement on the Mu'tazilite position. To Ibn Hanbal, Karabisi was even worse than a Mu'tazilite, because as a Sunni theologian, he gave legitimacy to Mu'tazilite arguments while denying their conclusions.

Al-Ash'ari versus the Mu'tazila. The most significant Sunni theological response to Mu'tazilism was formulated by Abu al-Hasan al-Ash'ari (died 935). This former Mu'tazilite scholar converted to Sunni Islam in the year 912 and attempted to combine the logical arguments of Kalam with Ibn Hanbal's reliance on tradition. Born in Basrah to a family of religious notables, al-Ash'ari spent the formative years of his life studying Mu'tazilism under his stepfather, Abu 'Ali al-Jubba'i. Al-Ash'ari remained with Jubba'i until the age of forty and shared with his stepbrother Abu Hashim ibn al-Jubba'i the status of favorite pupil. There are several stories about why al-Ash'ari left Jubba'i and the Mu'tazila. Some claim that the break had to do with rivalry over who was to head the Basrah school of the Mu'tazila when Jubba'i retired. When it became clear that Jubba'i preferred his son to his stepson, al-Ash'ari left and formed a rival Kalam school. Other accounts speak of a spiritual conversion. According to them, al-Ash'ari had three dreams of the Prophet Muhammad during the fasting month of Ramadan. In the first dream, the Prophet commanded al-Ash'ari to defend tradition, as contained in the hadiths. When al-Ash'ari began to study hadith accounts about the vision of God, intercession, and visionary dreams of the Prophet, Muhammad appeared to him a second time and asked about his progress. In the third dream, the Prophet commanded al-Ash'ari to defend tradition by using the intellectual tools of Kalam that he had learned from his Mu'tazilite teachers. Another account states that al-Ash'ari went into seclusion for fifteen days and then publicly proclaimed his change of mind from the pulpit of the great masjid of Basrah, saying "I divest myself of all I have believed just as I divest myself of my cloak."

Divine Power. Al-Ash'ari's greatest dispute with the Mu'tazila was over the subject of divine power (*qudrah*). This problem lay at the heart of the differences between the Qadarites, who included the Mu'tazila and the Shi'a, and their opponents, the Sunni predestinarians, who included the Ash'arites and the followers of Ibn Hanbal. For the Qadarites, a just God must share His power with human beings, and thus humans were given the power of free choice. For the Sunnis, however, all power belongs to God. Because God is the Creator of the universe, divine power is unlimited. As the Creator of all things, God has no limit to the extent of His power and ability. If God granted people the power of free choice, then He must have relinquished the power to determine the fate of His creatures. For Sunni theologians such as al-Ash'ari, it was absurd to imagine that God would give up any of His power. Al-Ash'ari states this problem as a question of "whether God has power over that concerning which He has endowed people with power."

The Mu'tazilite View. For the Mu'tazila, God endowed human beings with the power of free choice because of their unique place in the hierarchy of creation. Of all creatures, only humans possess the faculty of reason. Since God endowed people with reason, He could not prevent them from using reason to make their own decisions. It would be unjust and absurd for God to give people reason and then prevent them from using it. For al-Ash'ari, it was absurd to consider anything impossible for God. If God's power were truly infinite, then even theoretical limitations on divine power were unacceptable. In his theological writings, al-Ash'ari tried to reconcile the issues of divine power and freedom of choice by using the concept of *acquisition* (*kasb*).

The Qadarite View of Acquisition. The concept of acquisition originally came from the Qadarites. In its original form, the term was used to describe the moral accountability of human beings. Wasil ibn 'Ata', the "founder" of the Mu'tazila, said that "goodness and evil, nobility and baseness" are the "acquisitions" of human beings. This use of the term *acquisition* in the sense of "earnings" or "consequences" follows the Qur'an, which states, "Every person is a hostage to what he has earned (*bi-ma kasaba*)" (52: 21). For most Qadarites, such verses meant that the consequences of a person's actions are his acquisitions. Later, some of the Mu'tazila, such as the theologians of the Baghdad school, changed the meaning of the term so that it signified the powers granted by God to humanity. In this formulation, God endows human beings with the power to

act and then allows them to "acquire" responsibility for their actions. People create their own actions and bear responsibility for them. But the freedom with which they carry out their actions is a gift from God, who chooses not to exercise His omnipotence so that people may be judged by their deeds. In this way, the "acquisition" of human responsibility is conceived as an aspect of divine justice.

Necessary and Acquired Actions. Al-Ash'ari agreed with the Baghdad Mu'tazila that the "acquisition" of human responsibility is a divine gift, but he denied that human beings have the power to act independently. For al-Ash'ari, God not only grants people the freedom to act, but He also creates their actions. According to al-Ash'ari, the Qur'anic verse "[God is the] Doer of what He wills" (11: 109) means that God is the Creator of everything, including the actions of human beings. Al-Ash'ari distinguished between "necessary" actions and "acquired" actions. Necessary actions are those that occur involuntarily, such as shivering from a fever or trembling from palsy. Acquired actions are those that involve voluntary movements, such as walking in a certain direction, choosing which food to eat, or making moral choices between right and wrong. In all cases, God is both the creator and the agent of human actions; the human being acquires only the capacity to carry them out. Al-Ash'ari stated that this capacity, which is created at the time of the act itself, "includes both the power to act and its contrary." In other words, the human being acquires the capacity to make one of two choices. Like binary switches on a computer chip, these choices are limited to the simplest questions, such as "stop?" or "go?"—or "yes?" or "no?" Even these limited choices are not really the human being's to make. For al-Ash'ari, "acquiring the power to do something" means only the power to do what God has created one to do; the human being cannot produce anything for which he was not created. As the Qur'an states, "God created you and that which you do" (37: 96).

Response. The response of the Mu'tazila and the Islamic philosophers to al-Ash'ari's doctrine of acquisition was that he had merely revived the long-discredited doctrines of the Compulsionists (*Jabriyyah*), who believed that the human being had no freedom of choice whatsoever. To the Mu'tazila, al-Ash'ari's attempt to reconcile divine power and human freedom was "unintelligible." The philosopher Ibn Rushd of Córdoba (1126–1198) also refuted al-Ash'ari's doctrine as illogical: "if both the acquisition and that which is acquired are created by God, then the human being is compelled in his acquisition." If the "acquisition" of an act created by God enables a person neither to own the act nor to create it, the act cannot in any sense be described as a "power" possessed by the human being. It would therefore be unjust for a person to be judged by God for committing a sin that did not, in reality, belong to him. As a way of countering such arguments, the Ash'arite theologian Abu Bakr al-Baqillani (died 1013) revised the doctrine of acquisition so that people could take personal responsibility for their actions. For al-Baqillani, God creates the generic "subject" of each act, whereas the human being acquires its "mode" or "context" (*hal*). For example, if God creates in a person the "subject" of motion, it is up to the person to decide in which "mode"—such as sitting down, standing up, or walking—this motion will occur. In such a way, it can be said that the person owns his acts. The context of an action is most important when moral alternatives are involved: if God wills that a person seek a livelihood (the "subject" of an act), it is up to the individual to choose whether the context or "mode" in which he earns his livelihood will be lawful or unlawful.

The Place of Revelation. Ash'arite theology became dominant in Islam partly because it provided a simple and consistent solution to the problems associated with creation, divine knowledge, and revelation. By basing their arguments on the concepts of divine power and omnipotence, al-Ash'ari and his successors were able to formulate a Qur'an-centered theology more successfully than their opponents. By relying too heavily on Greek philosophical theories that were alien to Islam, the Greek-inspired Muslim philosophers (*falasifah*) risked making the Qur'an irrelevant in their theological formulations. The same was true for the Mu'tazila. Although Mu'tazilite theology was more clearly based on the Qur'an, its emphasis on the independent use of reason in attaining knowledge of God led to the criticism that divine revelation was either unnecessary or was reserved for those who were too simpleminded or uneducated to think for themselves. Although most Ash'arites continued to stress the importance of human reason in the study of religion, revelation was seen as fundamental because it provided the divine guidance necessary for reason to function properly. Ash'arite theologians saw themselves as taking a middle path between revelation and reason. In the words of Abu Hamid al-Ghazali (1059–1111), "Revelation is understood through tradition, but its underlying truth is understood through reason."

Atomism. A centerpiece of Ash'arite Kalam was the theory of atomism. According to this theory, the universe is divided into atoms of matter, qualities, space, and time. Every action or event may be broken down into a series of separate and unconnected moments, which are completely independent of each other. Such moments are joined together solely through the agency of the divine will. No logical continuity or order connects a series of events. For Kalam atomists, the act of hitting a nail with a hammer was not perceived as a single motion. Instead, the act of bringing down the hammer and striking the nail was conceptualized as a series of discrete events, in which the hammer is brought closer and closer to the nail until it finally strikes it. This view of action can be compared to a movie, in which what appears to be a single moving picture is in reality a series of still pictures of different events, which appear continuous because of the speed at which the individual pictures are run through the projector. In Kalam atomic theory, objects, actions, and events exist for only a single instant. They continue to exist by being created again and again by God in a series of creations (*khalq fi kull waqt*) that appear to have continuity but in reality do not. Implicit in

Glass masjid lamp with enameled decorations, made in Syria for Saif al-Din Tuquz-Timur, assessor to Sultan al-Malik al-Nasir, 1340 (British Museum, London)

this theory is the rejection of any idea of "Nature" or even a natural order. Everything is possible for God, who can change reality at any moment. The only impossibilities are logical impossibilities: no natural limitations on divine power are allowed to exist.

Atoms. The two most common Arabic terms for atom were *juz* (part) and *jawhar* (substance or element). Kalam texts often referred to atoms as "unique elements" or "indivisible parts." Modern atomic theory is based on the atomism of the Greek philosopher Democritus (died 370 B.C.E.), who taught that atoms were the primary, indivisible units of matter. These units came in various forms and sizes, and their shapes and combinations determined the properties of bodies (an early form of molecular theory). Democritus also taught that the space between atoms is occupied by a void, an idea that provided the basis for the modern concept of empty space. While the doctrines of Democritus were translated into Arabic by the tenth century, the atomism of the Kalam differed in many respects from the atomism of Democritus. For example, certain Kalam atomists and Indian atomists of the Vaisesika school of Brahmanism shared the theory that atoms, unlike bodies, had no dimension. This theory was not found among the Greek atomists or the Islamic philosophers. However, this fact alone does not prove that Kalam atomism was derived from Indian atomism. While Islamic scholars were aware of some of the philosophical doctrines of Brahmanism, no specific link between Kalam atomism and Indian atomism can be proved conclusively.

Atomism and Theology. It is easy to understand the attraction that atomism held for the Ash'arites. Because their theology stressed the omnipotence and unlimited power of God, a theory of existence that depended entirely on the divine will was irresistible. It is surprising that the atomic theories of the Kalam did not originate with the Ash'arites but were first formulated by the Mu'tazila, whose belief in free choice and human agency seems more suited to a theory of existence that postulates the continuity of actions in time. If a person had the power to make free choices and determine the course of his or her life, his or her plans would depend on the law of cause and effect: if he or she did *x* over a certain period of time, *y* would be the result. As long as he or she continued to perform the same actions, the result of these actions would be the same. But Kalam atomic theory accepts neither continuity nor the law of cause and effect. Instead, the regularity of natural occurrences is explained by means of a "habit" or "custom" ('adah), which God may interrupt at any moment. Among the Ash'arites, a miracle was called a "rupture of habit" (kharq al-'adah), literally, a "ripping" of the fabric of custom. To the average person, a miracle is an "impossible" event because it goes against normal expectations, but from the point of view of Ash'arism, a miracle is completely "normal." Because God creates everything at every moment, all creation is a miracle. What people think of as a "miracle" is simply an example of God changing His customary way of doing things (Sunnat Allah). Sufi mystics adopted the Ash'arite concept of a "rupture of habit" to explain their doctrine of the miracles of saints. From the time of al-Ash'ari to 1500, most Sufis were followers of Ash'arite theology and most Ash'arite theologians accepted Sufism as a legitimate expression of Islam.

The Theology of al-Maturidi. The most successful theological alternative to Ash'arism in Sunni Islam was formulated by Abu Mansur al-Maturidi (died 944). A contemporary of al-Ash'ari, al-Maturidi was born near the city of Samarqand in present-day Uzbekistan and spent most of his life in Central Asia. He developed a theology that was similar to Ash'arism in many respects, but its main points were developed independently and were a response to Mu'tazilite, Shi'ite, and non-Islamic Persian theologies that were widely held in Central Asia. Although there is no direct relationship between schools of theology and schools of law in Sunni Islam, Maturidi theology eventually became associated with the Hanafi legal tradition, whereas Ash'arism became the theological counterpart of the Shafi'i legal tradition. Al-Maturidi's theology became known in the western Islamic lands under the Ottoman Empire, which officially practiced Hanafi jurisprudence.

Al-Maturidi versus al-Ash'ari. The most important difference between the theologies of al-Maturidi and al-Ash'ari lay in their views of human freedom and responsi-

bility. According to al-Maturidi, action is divided between God and the human being. When an action is attributed to God, it is called *creation* (khalq), and when an action is attributed to the human being, it is called *acquisition* (kasb). Actions that belong entirely to God are those that the human mind cannot fully comprehend, such as how God makes things come to be from nonexistence. Actions such as movement or rest and obeying or disobeying divine commands belong to the human being, who "acquires" responsibility for his or her actions from God. Unlike al-Ash'ari, al-Maturidi believed that human beings were fully responsible for their acquired actions. Before the human being acts, God creates in the person both the capacity and the means to carry out an action. Then the human being decides whether or not to perform the action. This decision or intention (niyyah) to act in a certain way earns the person reward or punishment. Since al-Maturidi conceived of the human being as a semi-independent actor who acquires the ability to choose his actions freely, he was better able than al-Ash'ari to account for paradoxes in human behavior, such as when a person who has the capacity for evil acts in a way that is good, or when an otherwise good person inexplicably commits a crime. Al-Ash'ari was less able to resolve such paradoxes because he denied the human being the capacity for making truly independent decisions.

Al-Maturidi's Theory of Knowledge. Another important contribution of al-Maturidi to the development of Islamic thought was his theory of knowledge. Before al-Maturidi, it was rare for a Muslim theologian to begin his treatise with a discussion of knowledge; after al-Maturidi, hardly any theologian could neglect such a discussion. Like the Mu'tazilites and the Ash'arites, Al-Maturidi strongly condemned the unquestioning acceptance of another's teachings (taqlid). This stress on reason was particularly important with respect to conceptions of God because the Qur'an admonishes believers not to follow blindly in the footsteps of their forefathers (43: 23). Al-Maturidi felt that it was the responsibility of every Muslim to use the faculty of reason that God had created in him. As the Hanbali theologian Ibn al-Jawzi (1126–1200) remarked, "How abominable it is that one who is given a candle with which to light his way should extinguish it and walk in darkness!"

Three Kinds of Knowledge. According to al-Maturidi, there are three kinds of knowledge: that derived from the senses, that derived from testimony, and that derived from reason. The knowledge of the senses includes knowledge derived from experience, which today would be called *empirical*. Empirical knowledge tells people what causes pleasure or pain and what preserves or harms them. Someone who denies empirical knowledge, says al-Maturidi, is willful and obstinate because he denies "what he sees with his own eyes." Knowledge derived from testimony includes what today would be called *history*. It is the means of knowing about past events, distant countries, what is useful and harmful, and all that people cannot witness for themselves. A special kind of historical knowledge is the testimony of prophets, which includes scriptural sources such as the Qur'an and Sunnah and is believable "because of the signs the prophets have which demonstrate the truth." The most important form of knowledge is reason. Reason provides the critical faculty by which people assess the empirical and historical forms of knowledge. By means of reason, says al-Maturidi, it is possible to understand the divine wisdom in creation, and from the evidence of the world one can infer the existence of God. Reason is the faculty that mediates between the knowledge of experience and the knowledge of testimony. Without submitting testimony to reason and experience, the human being falls into the trap of blind traditionalism. Without submitting the knowledge of experience to reason and revelation, the human being falls into the trap of materialism (*ilhad*).

Sources:

Abdul-Amir al-A'asam, *Ibn ar-Riwandi's Kitab Fadihat al-Mu'tazilah: Analytical Study of Ibn ar-Riwandi's Method in His Criticism of the Rational Foundation of Polemics in Islam* (Beirut & Paris: Editions Ouedat, 1977).

Dimitri Gutas, *Greek Thought, Arabic Culture: The Graeco-Arabic Translation Movement in Baghdad and Early 'Abbasid Society (2nd–4th/8th–10th centuries)* (London & New York: Routledge, 1998).

Imam al-Haramayn al-Juwayni, *A Guide to Conclusive Proofs for the Principles of Belief: Kitab al-irshad ila qawati' al-adilla fi usul al-i'tiqad*, translated by Paul E. Walker (Reading, U.K.: Garnet, 2000).

Richard C. Martin and Mark R. Woodward, with Dwi S. Atmaja, *Defenders of Reason in Islam: Mu'tazilism from Medieval School to Modern Symbol* (Oxford: Oneworld, 1997).

Abu Mansur Muhammad al-Maturidi al-Samarqandi, *Kitab al-Tawhid*, edited by Fathalla Kholeif (Beirut: Dar El Machreq, 1982).

Abu al-Faraj Ibn al-Nadim, *The Fihrist of al-Nadim: A Tenth-Century Survey of Muslim Culture*, 2 volumes, edited and translated by Bayard Dodge (New York: Columbia University Press, 1970).

Shlomo Pines, *Studies in Islamic Atomism* (Jerusalem: Magnes Press/Hebrew University, 1997).

Harry Austryn Wolfson, *The Philosophy of the Kalam* (Cambridge, Mass. & London: Harvard University Press, 1976).

THE RISE OF FALSAFAH: THE PHILOSOPHICAL TRADITION

The Heritage of Pre-Islamic Philosophy and Science. During the two and a half centuries between 750 and 1000, nearly all the Greek works that were available in the Byzantine Empire and the Middle East were translated into Arabic. The only Greek works that were not translated into Arabic were literary and historical works and books of Christian theology. Muslim theologians avoided books of Christian theology for religious and political reasons, just as Christian theologians avoided books of Islamic theology. Modern scholars do not know why Muslims did not translate Greek literary and historical works. Perhaps they avoided these works because they referred to pagan gods. However, Aristotle's *Rhetoric* and *Poetics,* the two best-known sources of Greek literary theory, had been translated into Arabic by the tenth century. Traces of Aristotle's teachings on these subjects can be found in a variety of Muslim texts, ranging from books of law to the biographies of saints. The issue of Greek influence on Muslim historical writing and literature remains to be investigated. Although Aristotle was the "Greatest Sage" of both Greek

and Islamic philosophy, his name seldom appears in Arabic works on literary stylistics. Nor do the historians of classical antiquity appear in medieval Arabic discussions of pre-Islamic history. Instead, Muslim authors preferred to rely on sources from the Arab and Persian cultural traditions. One Muslim theologian, 'Abd al-Qahir al-Baghdadi (died 1037), even went so far as to claim that the Greeks stole their knowledge from ancient Arab sages.

The Translation Movement. Like the Kalam tradition of theology, the translation movement from Greek into Arabic is historically associated with the Abbasid khilafah. The foundation of the Abbasid capital of Baghdad in Iraq united as never before the cultural worlds of Greece and Persia and served as a bridge for communication with India and China. In addition, the development of paper, which reached the Muslim world from China as early as 751, greatly reduced the price of books and allowed the transmission of knowledge on an unprecedented scale. Paradoxically, the popularity of Persian culture at the Abbasid court also helped to stimulate the process of translating Greek works. The Abbasid khalifah al-Mansur (ruled 754–775), the founder of Baghdad, started the translation movement. He surrounded himself with Persian court officials and saw the Abbasids as continuing the Persian tradition of combining religion and state under an imperial ideology. The Sasanid kings, who ruled Iran from 226 until 642, believed that Greek philosophy and science developed from knowledge that Alexander the Great took from the Persians. Ardashir I (ruled 226–241), the founder of the Sasanid dynasty, ordered all available works of Greek philosophy and science to be translated into Persian, so that Persia could reclaim the intellectual heritage it had supposedly lost. By similarly ordering the translation of Greek works into Arabic, al-Mansur continued the process started by Ardashir five centuries earlier.

Islam and Late Antiquity. In many ways the Umayyad and Abbasid khilafahs shared more in common with the Byzantine and Persian empires of late antiquity than they did with the newly developing kingdoms of western Europe. Like the Byzantine and Persian empires, but unlike the kingdoms of Europe, the Islamic khilafah was a highly centralized state that made use of the contributions from a variety of cultures. The Umayyads relied heavily on Greek-speaking functionaries in their administration, while the Abbasids made use of Persians. Both regimes sought the services of the Arab Christians who lived in Syria and Iraq and Aramaic-speaking Christians and Jews who inhabited Iraq and western Iran. The first group of scholars and court officials translated books from Greek or Syriac into Arabic while the second translated Persian into Aramaic or Aramaic into Arabic. Indian works on astronomy, astrology, mathematics, and medicine passed into Arabic through the mediation of Persian translations.

Alexandria. In the sixth century, just before the coming of Islam, the Egyptian city of Alexandria was the foremost center for the study of Greek philosophy. For centuries, it

"There is no god but God, and Muhammad is the Messenger of God": inscription at the Masjid and Madrasah of Sultan al-Malik al-Mu'ayyad Shaykh (ruled 1412–1421) in Cairo

had played host to a variety of religions, theologies, and philosophies, including Platonism, Neoplatonism, Aristotelianism, Gnosticism, Judaism, and Christianity. After the fall of Alexandria to the Muslims in 642, the philosophical traditions of the city spread eastward to Iraq and Central Asia. Particularly important were the Aristotelian and Neoplatonic traditions, which were introduced to Islam through the influence of works that were studied in Alexandria. The *Isagoge* (Introduction) by the Neoplatonist Porphyry of Tyre (circa 234 – circa 305) to Aristotle's *Categories* was the most important handbook of logic. First translated into Arabic during the reign of al-Mansur, it became the standard introductory work for Muslim philosophers. Another important Neoplatonic work was *Elements of Theology* by Proclus (circa 410? – 485), an introduction to metaphysics, the study of the nature of God and immaterial entities such as mind and spirit. Drawing on the works of Plotinus (205–270), the great Egyptian teacher of Neoplatonic philosophy, as well as earlier varieties of Greek mystical philosophy, Proclus sought to propagate the "true though hidden meaning of Plato" through a discussion of metaphysical concepts such as the One, the Universal Intellect, and the Soul. These concepts later had an impor-

tant influence on Islamic philosophy and mysticism. Another work that included the teachings of Plotinus and Proclus was a work known as *Theology of Aristotle*—which was, in fact, not written by Aristotle. It was actually the last three books of Plotinus's *Enneads* (Nine Books) and parts of Proclus's *Elements of Theology*. First translated into Arabic for use by the Muslim philosopher al-Kindi (circa 801 – 866), it discusses Neoplatonic concepts such as the Universal Intellect and *effusion,* the "out-flowing" of being from the One. Works such as the *Theology of Aristotle* were as much mystical as philosophical and helped to foster the belief in an ancient wisdom tradition that prefigured the teachings of Islam. It was common for Muslim philosophers to think of Plato, Aristotle, Plotinus, and other great figures of Greek philosophy as monotheists who would have become Muslims if they had been exposed to the Qur'anic revelation. According to al-Kindi, the true purpose of Aristotle's metaphysics was to clarify the Islamic concept of divine unity (*tawhid*) and to elucidate the meanings of the ninety-nine "Beautiful Names of God" mentioned in the Qur'an.

Other Centers of Greek Learning. Besides Alexandria, other centers of Greek learning included Antioch, Harran, Edessa, and Qinnasrin in northern Syria, and Nisibis and Gondeshapur in Iraq. Greek works on logic were translated into Syriac and Arabic at Christian monasteries throughout the Middle East. The monastery of Qinnasrin in Syria, which was founded in the mid sixth century, produced several noted scholars, including Jacob of Edessa (died 708), who wrote a treatise on philosophical terms and translated Aristotle's *Categories* into Syriac. Another Qinnasrin scholar, George, Bishop of the Arabs (died 724), produced translations of and commentaries on Aristotle's *Categories, On Interpretation,* and *Prior Analytics.* The scholars of Harran preserved the mystical traditions and astronomical knowledge of Greece and Babylonia. Passing themselves off as Sabians, a sect that is associated with Christianity in the Qur'an, pagan Harranians served the Abbasid court as astrologers and provided an important link between Islam and the mystical traditions of late antiquity, such as Gnosticism and Hermetism. The best-known scholar of Harran was Thabit ibn Qurrah (died 901). Along with his son and grandsons, he made major contributions to the fields of mathematics and astronomy.

Gondeshapur. Named after the Sasanid king Shapur I (ruled 241–271), the city of Gondeshapur in Iraq was the site of an academy, founded by the Sasanids in 555, that served as a center for the revival of "Persian" knowledge appropriated by the Greeks. The directors of this academy were Nestorian Christians who had fled persecution by the Orthodox Christian Church of the Byzantine Empire and sought refuge among the Sasanids. After the Byzantine emperor Justinian I (ruled 527–565) closed down the academy of Athens in 529, the Persians also welcomed pagan Greek scholars. The Greek philosopher Damascius, a student of Proclus, lived in Gondeshapur until his death in 553. By the time the Abbasids founded Baghdad in 762, the city of Gondeshapur had become a major center of science and philosophy that included a medical school, a philosophical academy, and an observatory. The Nestorian Christian family of Bakhtishu, from Gondeshapur, served the Abbasids for more than two centuries as court physicians. Another Nestorian from Gondeshapur, Yuhannah ibn Masawayh (died 857) was director of the Bayt al-Hikmah (House of Wisdom) at the khalifah's palace in Baghdad. His student, the Arab Christian Hunayn ibn Ishaq (died 873), was the greatest translator of Greek works into Arabic. Hunayn's translations include Plato's *Parmenides, The Sophist, Timaeus, The Republic,* and *The Laws.* His son Ishaq ibn Hunayn (died 911) made important translations of nearly all the works of Aristotle.

The Bayt al-Hikmah. Several Arabic sources, starting with the tenth-century *Fihrist* (Index) by Ibn al-Nadim, claim that in the year 830 the Abbasid khalifah al-Ma'mun created a palace archive known as the Bayt al-Hikmah (House of Wisdom). Modern Western scholars took these accounts as evidence that al-Ma'mun had created an official institute and library for translation and research that formed the basis for subsequent translations of Greek scientific and philosophical works. In order to stock the library, al-Ma'mun reportedly sent emissaries to Byzantium to purchase books of ancient learning. He then ordered these books to be translated by a panel of scholars, who were mostly Nestorian Christians from Gondeshapur. In 1998, however, Dimitri Gutas challenged the legend of the Bayt al-Hikmah, arguing that it appears to be inaccurate in two major respects. First, he produced evidence suggesting that it was not a major center for research and translation. Western scholars seem to have projected the modern image of a research institute onto ninth-century Baghdad and given what was actually a private palace library more importance than it was due. Gutas points out that *Bayt al-Hikmah* was the term used by the Sasanids to denote any library. Before Islam, Persian "houses of wisdom" were archives of Sasanid royal tradition, which contained Zoroastrian religious works and accounts of the sayings and deeds of Persian kings. Whatever wisdom they contained was confined to Persia alone. The most detailed accounts in medieval Arabic sources about the Abbasid Bayt al-Hikmah indicate that it too preserved the royal traditions of Persia. If any translation was done in this library, it was from Persian into Arabic, not from Greek into Arabic. Later Muslim scholars, who looked back at al-Ma'mun's khilafah as a time of scientific and philosophical progress, ascribed the translation of nearly every rare or ancient book to this collection. These legendary accounts were then passed on by Western scholars, who sought in the intellectual rationalism of al-Ma'mun's era a precursor to the modern scientific age.

Aristotle and Plato Meet the Qur'an. Gutas's research also suggests a second problem: though there was a translation movement during the reign of al-Ma'mun, the legend gives him too much credit for it. The systematic translation of Greek, Persian, and Indian works into Arabic began with al-Mansur (ruled 745–775) and dates at least as far back as the founding of Baghdad. Yet, even this correction is insufficient because it gives all of the credit for the translation movement to kings. In reality, the translation of the works of classical and late antiquity was part of a widespread cultural movement that affected all the educated classes of Abbasid society. Abbasid khalifahs and princes—even some princesses—ordered many translations of Greek scientific and philosophical works, but most patrons of such translations were not from the Abbasid ruling family. They included courtiers such as Ahmad al-Sarakhsi (died 899), who studied philosophy and was a tutor to princes, and al-Fath ibn Khaqan, the commander of the Abbasid royal guard, who was a personal friend of the khalifah al-Mutawakkil (ruled 847–861). Another general who sponsored scientific translations was "Tahir of the Two Oaths" (died 823). Tahir's grandson Mansur, who was the Abbasid governor of the eastern provinces at the end of the ninth century, was an authority on philosophy, music, astronomy, and mathematics. Musa ibn Shakir, a friend of the khalifah al-Ma'mun, was a former highwayman. His descendants, the Banu Musa, reportedly spent 500 gold dinars per month for full-time translation services by the best scholars and linguists of the age.

Religious Ramifications. As a product of the elite culture of Abbasid society, the translation movement eventually influenced the rest of the educated classes. In this way, Greek, Persian, and Indian works came to play a decisive role in the formation of Arabic literary culture. Besides stimulating the development of science in the Muslim world, foreign methods of inquiry and argumentation also influenced the way in which the religion of Islam was expressed. The Kalam tradition of systematic theology could not have developed without the influence of Greek logic. Throughout the ninth and tenth centuries, it was widely understood in the Muslim world that the truth was not the exclusive property of any single nation or belief system. The philosopher al-Kindi said, "We ought not to be afraid of appreciating the truth and acquiring it wherever it comes from, even if it comes from nations that are distant from us and races that are different from us. The status of no one is diminished by the truth. Instead, the truth ennobles us all." This open-minded attitude toward the knowledge transmitted by non-Muslim peoples extended even to traditionalist scholars such as Ibn Qutaybah (died 889), who had little interest in philosophy. In his book *'Uyun al-Akhbar* (The Sources of Knowledge), he observed that "the ways to God are many and the doors of the good are wide." He also commented:

> Knowledge is the stray camel of the believer; it benefits him regardless from where he takes it. It will not lessen the truth if you hear it from pagans, nor can those who harbor hatred derive any advice from it. Shabby clothes do no injustice to a beautiful woman, nor do shells to pearls, nor does gold's origin from dust. Whoever neglects to take the good from the place where it is found misses an opportunity, and opportunities are as fleeting as the clouds. . . . Ibn 'Abbas (the cousin of the Prophet Muhammad) said: "Take wisdom from whomever you hear it, for the fool may utter a wise saying and a target may be hit by a beginner."

Qayrawan in Tunisia, Ibn Abi Zayd was both politically and ideologically opposed to the Abbasids. Seeing the translation movement as part of a Persian plot to undermine the Arab origins of Islam, he concocted an imaginative story that laid the blame for the influence of Greek philosophy at the feet of the Byzantine emperor. According to this story, the ruler of Byzantium was afraid that if his people studied Greek philosophy, they would abandon Christianity in favor of paganism, so he collected all of the Greek philosophical works in his empire and locked them up in a secret building. When the Persian wazir of the Abbasid khalifah heard about these books, he asked the Byzantine emperor if he could have them. The emperor was delighted to comply with this request. He informed the Orthodox bishops that the works of Greek philosophy, which were a danger to Christianity, could be sent to Baghdad, where they would instead undermine the beliefs of the Muslims. Ibn Abi Zayd ended his story with a warning: "Very few of the people who applied themselves to the study of these books avoided falling into heresy."

Falsafah and Hikmah. *Falsafah*, the Greek-inspired philosophical tradition in Islam, is a complex field of knowledge. To the premodern Muslim, the Arabic term *Falsafah* did not mean "philosophy" in the sense that modern people understand the term. The common modern definition of philosophy as a body of knowledge that governs a person's way of life, was expressed instead by the Arabic term *hikmah* (wisdom). In premodern Islam hikmah comprised several forms of knowledge, including those that now would be considered "philosophical," "scientific," or even "religious." In his *Kitab ihsa' al-'ulum* (The Enumeration of the Sciences), the philosopher al-Farabi (circa 870 – 950) divided formal knowledge into six fields of inquiry: (1) science of language (linguistics, semantics, stylistics, reading, writing, and poetry); (2) logic (formal logic, rhetoric, and poetics); (3) mathematical science (arithmetic and geometry, optics, astronomy, music, and engineering); (4) physical science (properties of bodies, minerals, plants, and animals); (5) metaphysics or "divine science" (beings and their attributes, theoretical proofs, and incorporeal beings); and (6) civic science (ethics, political theory, law, religious practices, and religious dogma). Hikmah could be found in all of these fields, but to be true hikmah, a field of inquiry had to have ancient roots: its authenticity was proven by its validity throughout the ages. Just as Islam was seen as the continuation and culmination of a religious truth that went back to Adam, other forms of knowledge also had to have roots that could be traced back to antiquity. No ancient philosophical system was more widely revered than that of Aristotle. Muslim philosophers and theologians alike called Aristotle "The Sage" (*al-Hakim*) or "The First Teacher" (*al-Mu'allim al-Awwal*). Because Aristotle's treatment of logic set standards that were accepted by almost everybody, his "wisdom" extended beyond *Falsafah* alone. But the typical *faylasuf*, the Muslim philosopher, did not enjoy Aristotle's wide acceptance. To many Muslim theologians and jurists, the faylasuf was primarily loyal to the traditions of

A carved-wood and ivory minbar built in Egypt, circa 1470 (Victoria and Albert Museum, London)

Not every traditionalist scholar was as open to foreign knowledge as Ibn Qutaybah. Islamic philosophy, like the Kalam tradition that developed at the same time, continually suffered from problems of authenticity. Although Muslim philosophers were fond of viewing Plato and Aristotle as near Muslims, other Muslim scholars were aware that many of the teachings of Greek philosophy contradicted the Qur'an and the Sunnah. After the khalifah al-Ma'mun tried to impose Mu'tazilite theology as state orthodoxy in 832, much of the skepticism displayed toward the philosophical portion of the translated sciences turned into hostility. One extreme reaction came from the Maliki jurist Ibn Abi Zayd (died 998). A resident of the city of

ancient Greece and only secondarily loyal to Islam. Hence, the knowledge he taught was not considered authentic and was not accepted by the majority of Muslims.

Criticism of Falsafah. The Ash'arite theologian al-Ghazali, who was one of the most important critics of Islamic philosophy, defined the faylasuf as a "practitioner of formal logic and rational demonstration." The employment of logic and reason, in itself, was not a problem. Most theologians of the Kalam, including al-Ghazali, did the same thing. The main methodological problem for Sunni theologians was that the faylasuf believed that the most accurate knowledge was demonstrative reason and that everything, including miracles and prophecy, could be explained by logic and rational demonstration. Furthermore, the faylasuf's uncritical belief in the traditions of ancient Greece led him to advocate doctrines that either contradicted the Qur'an and Sunnah or led to unwarranted interpretations of scripture. In *Tahafut al-Falasifah* (Incoherence of the Philosophers), his well-known critique of the Falsafah tradition, al-Ghazali mentions no fewer than twenty philosophical doctrines that were major sources of heresy. They included: a metaphysics that defined the existence and nature of God in Aristotelian or Neoplatonic rather than Qur'anic terms; a belief in the everlasting nature of the world, time, and motion; and an Aristotelian model of the soul that denied miracles and denied prophecy as an example of a divine miracle. These "heresies" applied to some of the best-known Islamic philosophers.

Al-Kindi. Known as "The Philosopher of the Arabs," Abu Yusuf Ya'qub al-Kindi (circa 801 – 866) was the first Muslim philosopher to gain a lasting reputation. He was also one of the few who came from a purely Arab background. A descendant of South Arabian kings and the son of a governor of Kufah, al-Kindi was part of the Abbasid elite from birth. Al-Kindi was the upholder of an ecumenical tradition by which Greeks and Arabs were considered people of the same origin who were separated by different languages. He was a major patron and promoter of the Abbasid-era translation movement and fought against the attempt by more-conservative Muslims to limit the adoption of foreign methods and concepts in Islamic thought. After studying Arabic grammar and logic in Basrah, al-Kindi moved to Baghdad, where he enjoyed the patronage of the pro-Mu'tazila khalifahs al-Ma'mun (ruled 813–833), al-Mu'tasim (ruled 833–842), and al-Wathiq (ruled 842–847). As a member of the Abbasid court, he sponsored and supervised the translation of many of the most important Greek philosophical works. During the Sunni revival under al-Mutawakkil (ruled 847–861), he suffered a reversal of fortune that included the confiscation of his personal library. His fortunes were partially restored in his final years, following the death of al-Mutawakkil.

Al-Kindi's Writings. Al-Kindi was one of the most prolific writers and most comprehensive thinkers in all Islamic history. The 260 works attributed to him by the bibliographer Ibn al-Nadim include writings on logic, metaphysics, arithmetic, music, astronomy, geometry, medicine, astrology, theology, psychology, politics, meteorology, topography, prophecy, and alchemy. Fewer than 10 percent of these works have survived. The variety of al-Kindi's writings was so great that some Muslim historians who were familiar only with his scientific works classified him as a scientist or a mathematician, while others who were familiar mainly with his philosophical writings considered him a faylasuf. Although some of his critics accused him of trying to combine heresy and Islam, al-Kindi was the only major figure of the Falsafah tradition to attempt to make philosophy conform in both letter and spirit to the teachings of Islam. His rationalism and use of Qur'anic proof texts have led some historians to label him a Mu'tazilite. Unlike the philosophers criticized by al-Ghazali, he defended the Islamic doctrines of the creation of the world, the resurrection of the body, prophetic revelation, and the eventual destruction of the world by God. However, his metaphysics depended heavily on the teachings of Aristotle, and he saw Greek philosophy as part of a wisdom tradition that led from ancient times to its final culmination in the religion of Islam.

Al-Kindi's Definition of God. For al-Kindi, God is deeply rooted in the Qur'an, but al-Kindi described Him in terms borrowed from Aristotle: Allah is Creator and Completer of all things, and an active Doer; yet, He is also First Cause and Unmoved. While the first three of these attributes resemble the Qur'anic conception of God, the final two evoke Aristotle's definition of God as the "Unmoved First Mover." Al-Kindi was perhaps closest to the Qur'an when he affirmed God's absolute unity: "The True One [*Wahid Haqq*] is pure and simple unity, nothing other than unity, while every other one is multiple." God is absolute unity. Apart from God, every other apparent unity is divisible into parts. There is nothing in the world that cannot be divided into smaller components. Thus, the "unity" of worldly phenomena is an accidental unity, not an essential unity.

Accident and Essence. *Accident* and *essence* were two of the most important concepts inherited by Islamic philosophy from the Greeks. *Accident* is a property that belongs to a subject in a particular context. It can be defined only in relation to its subject and may exist in one or more of the following modes: quality, quantity, relation, time, place, position, condition, action, or reaction. For example, speed is an "accidental" property of a runner. It is accidental because it describes the runner only in certain, identifiable contexts: in relation to the other runners in a race, the place where the race is held, the time of the race, the movements of the runner's body, the condition of the track, or the position of the runner on the track. *Essence* is a property that belongs to a subject in and of itself. It does not depend on the context in which the subject is found, and the subject cannot be conceived without it. For al-Kindi, unity and simplicity are essential attributes of God because The True One cannot be conceived without them: "He is not many but One, without multiplicity. He

As he tried to resolve the contradictions between religion and philosophy, and Eastern and Western thought, Ibn Sina was widely criticized by his fellow Muslims. His poetry includes responses to his critics and attempts to work through religious issues:

I. Reply to His Critics

It is not an easy thing to call me a heretic.
No belief in religion is firmer than my own.

I am unique in this world, so if I am a heretic,
There is not a Muslim to be found anywhere!

II. Commentary on the Qur'anic "Verse of Light" (24: 35)

Accustom the soul to knowledge so that it may progress,
And leave aside all else, for the soul is everything's abode.

The soul is like glass, and knowledge
A lamp, and God's wisdom is the oil.

When you are illuminated you are alive,
But when you are in darkness you live no more.

III. On the Descent of the Soul

Why, then, was she cast down from her high peak
Into this degraded depth? It was God who brought her low,

For a wise purpose that is concealed
Even from the keenest mind and the liveliest wit.

If the tangled net impeded her,
And the narrow cage prevented her wings from soaring

Freely in heaven's high ranges, she was yet
A flash of lightning that brightly glowed

Momentarily over the tents, and then was concealed,
As if its gleam had never been seen below.

Sources: "Commentary on the Qur'anic 'Verse of Light'," translated from the Arabic by Vincent J. Cornell, from *An Introduction to Islamic Cosmological Doctrines*, by Seyyed Hossein Nasr (Albany: State University of New York Press, 1993), p. 16.

"On the Descent of the Soul," translation revised by Cornell, from Nasr, pp. 259–260.

"Reply to His Critics," translated from the Persian by Cornell, from Nasr, p. 183, n. 12.

does not resemble His creation, for multiplicity exists in all creation but absolutely not in Him. He is the Creator and they are the created." Al-Kindi also stressed the essential nature of divine simplicity by defining God negatively: "God is no element, no genus, no species, no individual, no part, no attribute, no accident."

God and Creation. Unlike most other Muslim philosophers, al-Kindi did not believe in the eternity of the world. Instead, he was a firm believer in the Islamic doctrine of creation out of nothing. In *Fi Hudud al-ashya' wa rusumiha* (The Treatise on Definitions) al-Kindi stated, "creation means making something appear from nothing (*lays*)." The

Arabic term *lays*, which al-Kindi used to mean "nothing," is an example of a neologism, a new Arabic term created to express a Greek philosophical concept. *Lays* comes from the Arabic *laysa*, which means "not." Al-Kindi used it in the sense of "non-being" or "not-ness." This concept is contrasted with another Kindian neologism, *ays*, which can be translated as "being" or "is-ness." When describing God's ability to create the world out of nothing, al-Kindi said that God produces "being" (*ays*) from "non-being" (*lays*). His tendency to create neologisms makes al-Kindi's works difficult to read for those who are not masters of the Arabic language.

Al-Kindi versus Aristotle. Despite his belief that the essential teachings of Aristotle agreed with the doctrines of Islam, al-Kindi's conception of God was different from that of his Greek predecessor. Aristotle's Unmoved First Mover is an eternal, motionless, and unchanging principle. This Necessary Pure Being is the source of all form and movement but is not concerned with the details of His creation. His only real activity is the contemplation of Himself. Aristotle's God "loves" and motivates the world because the world is good, but He does not create the world. The most significant action of Aristotle's God is to give form to matter. According to al-Kindi's metaphysics, God, "The True One," is similarly an eternal, necessary, and uncaused being, neither genus nor species, unchanging, indestructible, and perfect. God cannot be characterized as a body because bodies are divisible, and divisibility contradicts the Islamic concept of divine unity. Yet, unlike Aristotle's Unmoved First Mover, al-Kindi's God is an active Generator and Creator, who creates the world out of nothing and in time. According to al-Kindi, humankind knows that the world is created because everything in the world is characterized by accidents: if the world were eternal, it would have to be essential and thus could not contain accidents. Accidents, by definition, are not essential, so a world full of accidents cannot be eternal.

Astrology. Like other masters of Falsafah, al-Kindi believed in the law of cause and effect and denied the atomistic and occasionalistic model of the universe shared by the Ash'arites and most Mu'tazilites, but he betrays his distance from modern conceptions of causality by his belief in astrology. Astrology was widely accepted in premodern Islam. Rulers employed astrologers, and philosophers, theologians, and jurists believed that the stars and planets influenced affairs on earth. The cities of Baghdad and Cairo were founded and laid out on the basis of astrological prognostications. Al-Kindi's belief in astrology stemmed from his acceptance of Ptolemaic astronomy and his interest in the astrological traditions of Harran. Both Harranian astrology and Ptolemaic astronomy described the stars and planets as "intelligences" that resided in spheres beyond the moon. These celestial spheres were interconnected, and the movement of the higher spheres influenced the spheres below them. For al-Kindi, it was clear from empirical observation that the movement of the spheres of the sun and the moon affected life on earth; for example, the passage of the sun in the sky gives rise to the seasons, and the motion of the moon affects the tides. He also believed that the motion of the spheres caused historical changes. These changes produced variations in the character and mores of nations and resulted in the rise and fall of political regimes. Interpreting literally the Qur'anic statement that "the stars and the trees" prostrate themselves before God (55: 6), al-Kindi concluded that "superior entities" such as the planets and the stars must possess life and intelligence. Furthermore, because the planets and the stars reside in the highest spheres, he believed that they are more perfect and intelligent than beings on earth. Not composed of the four terrestrial elements (air, earth, fire, and water) and having no opposites, they exist in an everlasting state of life and motion. According to Ibn al-Nadim, al-Kindi's official position at the court of the Abbasid khalifahs in Baghdad was that of astrologer, not philosopher.

The Doctrine of the Soul. For al-Kindi, the soul (*nafs*) is affiliated with the heavenly spheres because it is not a body but an *incorporeal* substance. In the human being, the union of soul and body is not essential but accidental. The soul is the source of life; it governs the body for a time and then gives it up, leaving an empty husk. Because it is an incorporeal substance and hence superior to matter, the soul defines the body it inhabits: it constitutes the body's identity or personality (*shakhs*). In relation to the body the soul is like form, which gives identity to formless matter. "The soul is a simple entity," wrote al-Kindi, "whose substance is analogous to the Creator's own substance, just as the light of the sun is analogous to the sun." Al-Kindi's model of the soul was typical of the Falsafah tradition, and it aroused the suspicion of conservative Muslims, who felt that it implied an identity between the soul and God. This model was influenced by Aristotle, who taught that the soul illuminated the body, and by Plato, who believed that the body imprisons the soul on earth, drawing it away from its celestial origin. When a person dies, the human or "partial" soul (*al-nafs al-juz'iyah*) leaves the body and returns to its true home, the abode of "intelligibles" (*ma'qulat*), which lies beyond the spheres. In this abode, the human soul joins with the Universal Soul (*al-nafs al-kulliyah*), where it is illuminated by God and shares in all forms of knowledge. Al-Kindi did not specify whether human souls actually "link up" with the Universal Soul, a concept that later philosophers called *ittisal*. He did, however, make it clear that the Universal Soul is not God, for the True One is beyond both soul and intellect.

Reason and Belief. According to al-Kindi, not every human soul joins the Universal Soul in the abode of the intelligibles. Some souls need to be cleansed by residing successively in each of the heavenly spheres until they are purified. These are the souls of people who have fallen victim to the senses. Al-Kindi likened people who are overcome by the appetites to pigs, those who are overcome by the passions to dogs, and those who are ruled by reason to kings. Reason and religious belief come together in the imaginative or representational faculty of the human mind

(*al-musawwirah*). This faculty, which is natural to all human beings, creates images of things that are not seen on earth. Under the wrong conditions, the imaginative faculty may create monsters, but when it is not distracted by the senses, it can create representations of sublime things, such as those described in the Qur'an and other holy scriptures. Prophecy and revelation are the means by which God communicates ideas to the human imagination. By acting on this natural human faculty, God shows the way to salvation and ultimate happiness. For al-Kindi, true happiness lies in the pursuit of philosophical knowledge and the vision of God. The goal of the philosophical path is to come as near to the Creator as possible in the intellect. In general terms, this goal is the same as that of religion: "To know things in their reality is to know divinity, oneness, virtue, the knowledge of all that is useful, and the way to accomplish it. God's messengers have similarly taught us how to recognize the divinity of the One God, to follow the virtues, and to abandon the vices that are opposed to the virtues."

Al-Farabi. Known in the Latin West as Alfarabius or Abunaser, Abu Nasr Muhammad al-Farabi (circa 870 – 950) was the second great Islamic philosopher after al-Kindi, master of logic in the Falsafah tradition and the father of Muslim political philosophy. Because of his originality and importance to Islamic philosophy, he was called the "Second Teacher" (*al-Mu'allim al-Thani*), surpassed only by Aristotle. Born near the city of Farab, in Turkmenistan, al-Farabi was the son of a military officer, and his grandfather, who also held a military post, was a Turkish convert to Islam. According to some biographical sources, al-Farabi "knew every language," which meant that apart from Arabic, he knew Persian and several dialects of Turkish, and perhaps could read Syriac and Greek. To further his education, al-Farabi moved to Bukhara in Uzbekistan, where he studied Persian and music. His *Kitab al-Musiqa al-kabir* (Great Book of Music) was the most influential treatise on music in the Islamic world. His temporary service as a judge led to an interest in logic and the techniques of debate and dialectical reasoning. Unlike al-Kindi, who took his philosophical knowledge mainly from books, al-Farabi represented the living tradition of the school of Alexandria, which he traced from teacher to teacher back to the masters of late antiquity. Surviving fragments of al-Farabi's autobiography reveal that he was first exposed to Alexandrian philosophy in Marv, in Turkmenistan. His teacher was the Nestorian monk Yuhannah ibn Haylan (died 910), who lived at the monastery of Masergasan near Marv. Al-Farabi was devoted to Ibn Haylan as his teacher and his personal mentor and followed him to Baghdad, Harran, and possibly Constantinople. On returning to Baghdad, al-Farabi studied under the Nestorian philosopher Matta ibn Yunus (died 940), who was one of the foremost translators of Aristotle. While in Baghdad, al-Farabi gave many lectures on Aristotle's *Physics* and *On the Soul*. In 942 al-Farabi left Baghdad for Damascus, where he wrote some of his most important works, including his masterpiece of political philosophy,

Mabadi' ara' ahl al-madinah al-fadila (Principles of the Beliefs of the Inhabitants of the Virtuous City). He died in Damascus at the end of the year 950 and is buried in the cemetery outside of the southern gate of that Syrian capital.

"Farabian" Theology. When compared with al-Kindi's, al-Farabi's conception of God is less dependent on the Qur'an and more dependent on Aristotle and Plato. In fact, his philosophy is such an original synthesis of Plato, Aristotle, and the Qur'an that some modern scholars have refused to characterize it as Platonic, Aristotelian, or Islamic but instead have called it uniquely "Farabian." Al-Farabi did not neglect to use Qur'anic terminology or cite Qur'anic verses. He began his works with the traditional formula "In the name of Allah, the Beneficent, the Merciful" and praised God as "Lord of the Worlds" and "God of the east and the west." But he also described God as "Necessarily Existent," "Cause of Causes," and "Eternal, Unchanging." In a religious work titled *Al-Du'a' al-'Azim* ('The Magnificent Invocation), al-Farabi asked God to bestow on him "an emanation from the Active Intellect" and to purify his soul from the "filth of matter" and the "murkiness of nature." After asking to be guided by the "brightness of the Intellect," he ended the invocation with a Qur'anic verse: "God is the Protector of the believers; He brings them forth from darkness into light" (11: 258). To Muslim traditionalists, such interpretations of Qur'anic verses in Greek philosophical terms exemplified the heretical nature of the Falsafah tradition.

Platonic Interpretations. When al-Farabi read the Qur'an, he did so through Platonic glasses. In a work comparing the philosophies of Plato and Aristotle, he argued that Aristotle's ideas are compatible with those of religion and hence compatible with the ideas of Plato. In other words, it is not the Qur'an, but Plato, that defines religion. In al-Farabi's works Platonic and Qur'anic terms and concepts are shuffled together, producing a synthesis that owes more to Neoplatonism than it does to the Prophet Muhammad. God is the First Being and the First Cause. He is without beginning, eternal, and necessarily existent. His absolute unity is a function of His essence: "His being by which He is distinguished from other beings cannot be other than that by which He Himself in essence exists." God has no partner and no opposite. He is total simplicity: indivisible in His substance, He is indescribable, immaterial, and without form. Reproducing Aristotle's definition of God as "thought thinking itself" (Latin: *intellectus intelligens intellectum*), al-Farabi said that God is "a thinking Intellect that thinks up its own essence."

Essence and Existence. One of al-Farabi's most important contributions to the field of metaphysics was his explanation of the difference between *essence* and *existence*. His views on essence and existence were later adopted by Ibn Sina (980–1037), who in turn influenced the Catholic theologian Thomas Aquinas (1225–1274). Al-Farabi claimed that the essence of a thing is both different from and independent of its existence. Thus, whenever a thing

"exists," it owes its existence to something outside itself. In other words, existence is an "accident" of essence. Essence and existence are discussed in several of al-Farabi's works, including *Mabadi' ara' ahl al-madinah al-fadila* and *Kitab al-Huruf* (The Book of Letters). At times, these concepts appear under different Arabic names. The most common Arabic term for essence is *dhat*, but al-Farabi also used the neologism *mahiyyah* (what-is-it-ness) to denote essence as a subject. Existence is most often expressed by *wujud*, but at times al-Farabi uses the neologism *huwiyyah* (he-ness). *Huwiyyah* comes from the Arabic pronoun *huwwa* (he). The Arabic word for "pronoun" is *damir*, meaning a term that stands in place of something whose identity is hidden from view. Thus, according to Arabic grammar, another subject at which al-Farabi excelled, existence is a predicate of essence because it describes an essence that remains beyond definition. God, however, is not a predicate. God is the Originator of existence directly from His essence. He bestows existence on all things, but in Himself, both essence and existence are inseparable parts of His nature. By making God an exception to the normal essence-existence distinction, al-Farabi harmonized the teachings of Greek philosophy and the Qur'an. Although "The Existent" (*al-Wujud*) is not a name of God in the Qur'an, a related term, *al-Wajid*, is one of the ninety-nine names of God. For al-Farabi, *al-Wajid* meant "He Who Brings Things into Existence." This meaning is identical with God the Originator (*al-Badi'*), a concept that appears both in the Qur'an and in the metaphysical writings of Aristotle.

The Doctrine of Emanation. Bringing things into existence is not necessarily the same as creating them. The Qur'anic Creator (*al-Khaliq*) is a self-determined, purposeful deity who both wills things into being and actively brings them into existence. In Qur'anic terminology, "When [God] decrees a thing, He merely says unto it, 'Be!' and it is" (2: 117). Al-Farabi's God does not really create the world. Instead, God allows the world to come forth from Him as an emanation (*sudur*). This outflowing of being from God is involuntary; it is neither willed nor chosen by God and cannot be prevented. Since the world emanates from God as part of the divine nature, it is not completely separate from God. Thus, it must have existed as long as God has existed. For this reason, it is impossible to claim that the world was created in time. This view is the doctrine of the eternity of the world to which Al-Ghazali and other Muslim theologians objected so strenuously. It is difficult to see how al-Farabi could reconcile the doctrines of Greek philosophy and Islam on this important point. Either God wills and creates the world or He does not. Only by saying that the concepts of "willing" and "creating" are metaphors can one claim that the Farabian doctrine of emanation agrees with the Islamic doctrine of creation.

The Stages of Emanation. Al-Farabi tried to overcome this problem by combining a multistage model of emanation taken from the Neoplatonists with a model of the soul taken from Aristotle. Creation is a function of what al-Farabi calls the "Active" or "Agent" Intellect (*al-'Aql* *al-Fa'al*). This Intellect gives form to matter and actualizes the human intellect, which mirrors the Active Intellect in its rational faculties. However, the Active Intellect is not God. Instead, it corresponds to the "Holy Spirit" or "Trustworthy Spirit" mentioned in the Qur'an (26: 193). But in the Qur'an, the "Holy Spirit" and the "Trustworthy Spirit" are agents of revelation, not of creation. Thus, the Active Intellect, in the guise of the Holy Spirit, does not really create the world. Rather, it "illuminates" or reveals the universal forms of things in the world, bringing them out of potentiality into actuality. For al-Farabi, God is The First (*al-Awwal*)—a motionless, perfect being, beyond both form and substance. Substance, form, soul, and matter all emanate from God in an automatic, ten-step process that proceeds downward, like the rungs of a ladder. The closest thing to an initial "Creator" in this process is the First Intellect, which al-Farabi, following Plotinus, calls "The Second." The form and substance of the First Heaven, where the universal forms of things are established, emanate from the First Intellect. The Second Intellect is another emanation of the First Intellect, and shares with the First Heaven the highest rung of the ladder of existence. The Second Intellect is the source of the Third Intellect, which provides the "soul" of the Sphere of the Fixed Stars. This process of emanation then continues down the rungs of the ladder through the spheres of Saturn, Jupiter, Mars, the Sun, Venus, and Mercury, each sphere paired with a particular intellect, until the ladder of existence reaches the lowest rung, the Tenth Intellect, which corresponds to the sphere of the moon. This Tenth Intellect is the Active Intellect, which, besides being known as the Holy Spirit and the Trustworthy Spirit, is also the angel Jibril.

The Active Intellect. In addition to giving form to matter, the Active Intellect fills the world with mind and spirit. Following the ancient adage that "only like can know like," al-Farabi assumed that the Active Intellect and the human intellect are related organically. He called the Active Intellect "a separate form of human being" or the "True Human Being" (*al-Insan 'ala al-Haqiqah*). Humanity attains its full potential when it realizes within itself the intellectual nature of the True Human Being; that is, when the human intellect begins to take on the qualities of the Active Intellect. According to al-Farabi, every human being has a "Potential Intellect," which exists in the person as an inborn capacity to know objects, concepts, and ideas. The forms of these "intelligibles" lie dormant in the human mind until the Active Intellect illuminates them. Once illuminated, they "come to life" and become the concepts and ideas that enable one to live in the world. When reason and logic come to govern the mind, the Potential Intellect becomes the "Actual Intellect." The hallmark of the Actual Intellect is the ability to engage in abstract thinking and theoretical reasoning. When a person's theoretical knowledge allows the mind to transcend the senses and perceive the universal forms of things abstracted from matter, the Actual Intellect becomes the "Acquired Intellect." This

highest form of the human intellect is called the "Acquired" Intellect because it takes on, to a limited extent, the creative capacity of the Active Intellect. In a few rare cases, the Acquired Intellect absorbs so much illumination from the Active Intellect that continuity (*ittisal*) occurs between the two intellects. Al-Farabi calls the person in whom this continuity is established the Prophet, the Imam, or the "Perfect Philosopher."

Religion and Philosophy. The revelation of a holy scripture such as the Qur'an comes about when the Active Intellect communicates knowledge of the intelligibles to the Acquired Intellect of the Prophet. On receiving this knowledge, the Acquired Intellect becomes the "Prophetic Intellect." The Prophetic Intellect translates the knowledge imparted by the Active Intellect into human language, which the Prophet communicates to the general public. The public, however, is not able to discern the true nature of the Prophet's revelation. Instead of seeing how knowledge is passed from the Active Intellect to the Prophetic Intellect through emanation, they conceive of this emanation as a "miraculous" revelation of scripture. Instead of seeing the Active Intellect as the true agent of revelation, they imagine the angel Jibril in bodily form. For al-Farabi, a revealed religion such as Islam is necessary for the guidance of humanity. But as a source of knowledge it is limited, because its message is abridged for "general audiences." Religion teaches the same truths as philosophy, but it teaches these truths through a persuasive method that works on the imagination. As such, it can impart only beliefs. Philosophy, however, teaches through a superior method of rational demonstration that works on the mind. Thus, its teachings go beyond mere beliefs and impart rational certainty to the human intellect.

Political Terminology. Nearly all of al-Farabi's discussions of religion are to be found in his works of political philosophy. Consequently, he tends to define religion in political terms. The term he chooses for "religion" is *millah*, which denotes a religious community, not a set of beliefs. For al-Farabi, "*Millah* and 'religion' (*din*) are nearly synonymous, as are 'law' (*shari'ah*) and 'tradition' (*Sunnah*)." Theology is limited to dogma, and thus is not an intellectual science: "Religion is beliefs and actions, determined and restricted by regulations and prescribed for a community by their First Ruler [the Prophet]." This view of religion deals only with its outward form, not with its inner, spiritual dimension. For al-Farabi, a religion is a community of believers who believe and act according to what has been determined for them by the Prophet, who is also their political leader. The required forms of religious practice and the limits of belief are restricted by laws set down by the Prophet and are guided by his personal example. Although al-Farabi acknowledged that theology is the theoretical aspect of religion, its function is mainly descriptive. It provides a "likeness of the truth" rather than the truth itself. Both religion and philosophy have theoretical and practical aspects, but the "universals," or inner meaning, of the laws and customs of religion are to be found only in philosophy. Thus, for al-Farabi, religion was an inferior version of philosophy.

Ibn Sina. Known in the Latin West as Avicenna, Abu 'Ali al-Husayn Ibn Sina (circa 980 – 1037) was one of the best-known Islamic philosophers among European scholars. Although he is also well known in the Islamic world, his influence on Islamic thought is more limited and has been confined mainly to Shi'ism. His ideas were largely discredited in Sunni Islam, mostly because of attacks leveled against him by the Sunni theologian al-Ghazali and the philosopher Ibn Rushd (1126–1198). Ibn Sina's works on medicine and the natural sciences were more universally accepted than his philosophical writings. They were frequently copied and disseminated in both the Muslim world and in medieval Europe. In Shi'ism, Ibn Sina is best known for the system of thought he called "Oriental Philosophy" or "Eastern Wisdom" (*al-Hikmah al-Mashriqiyah*).

Exposure to Islamic Sects. Ibn Sina was born in the region of Bukhara, Uzbekistan. His father was a district official who followed the Ismaili sect of Shi'ism. Although Ibn Sina was exposed to Ismaili doctrines from an early age, he did not consider himself an Ismaili. Instead, he preferred to maintain his independence from any sect, and his teachers included both Sunnis and Shi'ites. In religion, as well as in philosophy, he adopted what suited him and left the rest. Ibn Sina was a prodigy as a child and a genius as an adult. He had memorized the Qur'an by the age of ten and Aristotle's *Metaphysics* by the age of eighteen. As a teenager, he mastered the disciplines of logic, Islamic law, astronomy, and medicine. At the age of seventeen, he cured the ruler of Bukhara of a major illness. Often, he solved difficult philosophical problems in his sleep. By the age of twenty-one he had written important works on mathematics, the natural sciences, and ethics. During a turbulent career in which his fortunes rose and fell several times, Ibn Sina traveled throughout Iran and Central Asia. He served a variety of rulers as both physician and government official and met several Sufi masters. Many of his best-known works were written during a fifteen-year sojourn in the Iranian city of Isfahan. He died in the Iranian city of Hamadan, where he sought refuge after an Afghan army attacked Isfahan.

Philosophy and "Oriental Wisdom." Ibn Sina's *al-Qanun fi'l-tibb* (Canon of Medicine) was translated into Latin and was the most important book on medicine in Western Europe until the seventeenth century. It is still the authoritative text on traditional Muslim medicine in countries such as Pakistan, where premodern techniques of healing are practiced alongside modern medicine. Ibn Sina's other masterwork was the *Kitab al-Shifa'* (Book of Healing). Although its title suggests that its subject is medicine, it is a work of philosophy that covers logic, physics, mathematics, and metaphysics. The *Kitab al-Shifa'* is a masterpiece of Aristotelian and Platonic thought and shares much in common with the works of al-Farabi. Toward the end of his life, Ibn Sina began to compose works on "Oriental Wisdom." These works—*Hayy ibn*

Yaqzan (Living Son of Awake), *Risalat wa al-Ta'ir* (Epistle of the Bird), *Salaman was Absal* (Salaman and Absal), and *Mantiq al-Mashriqiyin* (The Logic of the Easterners)—mark an important departure from his earlier philosophical writings. Written in symbolic and allegorical form, they describe visionary experiences that demonstrate how the soul may achieve continuity with God. These mystical works, more than his writings on rational philosophy, became influential in the Shi'ite tradition of esoteric theology.

A Perennial Tradition. Like al-Farabi, Ibn Sina tried to reconcile the conflicting claims of religion and philosophy, and like al-Farabi as well, he was often accused of heresy. He resisted these charges and proclaimed himself a sincere Muslim. His ideal was a system of thought that combined the wisdom of the Greeks and the Hebrew prophets, a tradition that was completed with the coming of Islam. This ideal of a philosophical religion hinted at the existence of a perennial wisdom, a universal form of knowledge that was common to Greek philosophy and Islam alike. Shihab al-Din al-Suhrawardi (circa 1155 – 1191), the founder of the Illuminationist (*ishraqi*) school of Islamic mysticism, reacted favorably to this "oriental" aspect of Ibn Sina's thought. In his *Qissat al-Ghurbal Gharbiyyah* (Story of the Western Exile), al-Suhrawardi refered to *Hayy ibn Yaqzan* and claimed that Ibn Sina's Oriental Philosophy was the inspiration for his own philosophy of illumination. Observing that the Arabic words for "illumination" (*ishraq*) and "eastern" (*mashriqi*) come from the same root, al-Suhrawardi argued for a perennial philosophy that was the inner truth of all religions. Some modern scholars have suggested that Ibn Sina's poetic compositions were also attempts to draw inspiration from this tradition of perennial wisdom.

Being and Existence. Ibn Sina's rational philosophy is similar to al-Farabi's. In fact, most of Ibn Sina's philosophical works may be seen as commentaries on al-Farabi's. The Turkish bibliographer Hajji Khalifah (died 1657) claimed that Ibn Sina's *Kitab al-Shifa'* was based on an earlier, lost work by al-Farabi titled *Al-Ta'lim al-thani* (The Second Teaching). Both al-Farabi and Ibn Sina placed great importance on the difference between essence and existence, and both made use of a hierarchical model of existence that has ten levels of manifestation. Whereas al-Farabi stressed the concept of essence as the key to his philosophy, however, Ibn Sina focused on existence and argued for a clearly articulated theory that unites essence and existence as twin aspects of a wider, universal category of Being. For Ibn Sina, God was First Being, a sort of Existence-before-existence that makes all other existence necessary: *Wajib al-Wujud*. This Arabic term is usually translated as "Necessary Being," but its literal meaning is "Necessarily Existent." In this wider category of Being, essence and existence are unified, as in the well-known Chinese symbol of yin and yang. For Ibn Sina as well as al-Farabi, the existence of all things other than God is accidental, and their apparent unity is an illusion. God is the only Necessary Being. Other beings are either necessary in a limited sense, such as the Intelligences

The Firdaws Madrasah in Aleppo, Syria, built in 1236. Its walls are inscribed with quotations from Shihab al-Din al-Suhrawardi's philosophy of Illumination.

or angelic substances that maintain the universe, or they are accidental bodies that come into existence and pass away. God alone is pure Truth and Goodness. The world emanates from God as an object of His Love, and out of love for Him all things return to God. The universe is nothing but the manifestation and effusion of divine Being. The products of the human imagination are true and good according to how much they correspond to Necessary Being and are evil and false according to their rejection of Necessary Being. All things find true happiness in union with Necessary Being, on which they completely depend and without which they would not exist.

Knowledge and Revelation. Ibn Sina also shared with al-Farabi a belief in intellectual revelation. For al-Farabi, a prophet is a man endowed with inborn wisdom who progresses to the knowledge of the universals by developing his rational faculties and by achieving continuity with the Active Intellect. Although the prophet does not need a teacher to guide him, he still must progress through the stages of intellectual development like any other person. For Ibn Sina, however, divine knowledge does not come to the prophet through the development of his rational faculties. Instead, the soul of the prophet is ignited by the sudden effusion of wisdom from the Active Intellect. Like a bolt of lightning, knowledge of the universals comes to the prophet independently of any rational training or development. The philosopher experiences a similar "ignition" of

the soul when he acquires knowledge of the universals. But, unlike the prophet, the philosopher must follow the route laid out for him by al-Farabi: the "lightning" of divine knowledge can strike the philosopher only when his mind has progressed through the normal stages of intellectual development. By making the illumination of the prophet an exception to this rule, Ibn Sina preserved the Islamic sense of miracle and the revelatory nature of divine communication that al-Farabi risked losing with his more rationalistic model of intellectual illumination.

Philosophy and Medicine. Although Ibn Sina was one of the most important Islamic philosophers to combine philosophy and medicine, he was not alone. Philosophy was an important part of medical training. In premodern Islam, the study of nature complemented the study of religion. Unlike today, there was no conception of randomness in nature, and everything that existed was thought to have meaning. Both reason and the senses had important roles to play in understanding God's plan. The world of nature was where the wisdom of God was made manifest. By observing nature, the philosopher could learn God's plan for the world. As a form of traditional wisdom, the study of nature was associated in the Qur'an with the prophet Solomon, who studied the "language of the birds" (27: 16), and with the prophet Luqman "The Sage," who learned hikmah so that he would "be thankful to God" (31: 12).

Motion and Inclination. For Islamic philosophers, the world of nature was a world of motion. God moved all things according to a natural purpose. But motion did not just consist of moving a thing from place to place. For Aristotle, motion meant going from potentiality to actuality. For Ibn Sina, motion was a process of becoming. Motion may be accidental, as when cookies in a cookie jar are moved when the jar is shaken. Motion may be "impulsive," as when an outside force acts on an object and causes it to move. Motion may be natural, as when an object possesses something within itself that impels it toward movement. Ibn Sina also believed that motion could be quantitative: that is, it comprised the processes of growth, shrinkage, expansion, and contraction. Physical motion, such as throwing a ball, was thought to occur in two stages. First, an impulsive (*qasri*) force puts the ball in motion; next an inclination (*mayl*) sees the act through to its completion. Ibn Sina identified three kinds of inclination: psychic or spiritual inclination (*mayl nafsi*), impulsive inclination (*mayl qasri*), and natural inclination (*mayl tabi'i*). The desire of a person to throw the ball is an example of "psychic inclination" (*mayl nafsi*). The force of the arm that throws the ball constitutes "impulsive inclination" (*mayl qasri*). The inner desire of the ball to reach its target is "natural inclination" (*mayl tabi'i*). Ibn Sina equated inclination with love (*'ishq*), which, he believed, pervaded the entire universe. In modern physics, gravity causes an object to drop from a tower to earth. For Ibn Sina, the attraction, or "mutual love" of the object and the earth causes the object to fall. By equating inclination with love, Ibn Sina revived the ancient vision of a living cosmos where all change is caused by the love of things for each other and the love of the universe for God.

Equilibrium. In Ibn Sina's philosophy all things naturally incline toward a state of goodness and perfection. Nature always tries to restore a sense of balance, to establish or re-establish equilibrium. In medieval medicine, illness was often thought to be caused by an excess of some "humor" (blood, phlegm, yellow bile, or black bile) or "quality" (hot, cold, dry, or wet). One of the ways to cure illness was to restore the original balance of humors—usually by applying the opposite humor to that which originally seemed to have caused the disease. Death was not considered evil because it restored an equilibrium that had been upset at a higher level. Evil was not caused by nature but by matter, which was the only thing in the universe that was truly "dead."

Form and Matter. Following the Neoplatonists, Ibn Sina believed that matter had no independent reality of its own. It could exist only when combined with form. Ibn Sina defined form as "the quality of the essence by which a body is what it is." Matter was "that which supports the quality or form." Matter could exist only through the form imparted to it by the Active Intellect, which he also called the "Giver of Form." Without form, matter would have no reality: "Matter is created for form and its purpose is to have form imposed on it, but form is not cre-

ated for matter." Body, which is made up of form and matter, is that which possesses the possibility of being divided. A body is a substance that contains within itself both potentiality and actuality; its potentiality is matter, and its actuality is form. Matter is nothing on its own, but "receives" the form that is imposed on it. As such, it is the furthest thing from Being, which is the source of life and form. Thus, insofar as there is evil in the world, evil can always be traced to "dead" matter.

Time and Space. Composed of form and matter, bodies exist in the world through the mediation of time and space. For Ibn Sina, time and space were not independent realities but were accidental conditions that depended on the existence of bodies. The modern notion of "empty space" had no meaning for him. The space or "place" (*makan*) of a body was the boundary that surrounded it. For example, with regard to the "elements" of fire and air, the "place" of fire is in the heavens and the "place" of air is in fire. Ibn Sina defined the orientation of objects in the universe according to six primary directions: up and down, right and left, and front and back. The *length* of a body was defined as the plane between the two poles, with south as the *up* direction and north as the *down* direction; the *width* of a body was the plane between *right* and *left*; the *thickness* of a body was the depth between *front* and *back*. The model Ibn Sina used to determine the orientation of space was the human body: "If a person lies down, facing the heavens with his right hand toward the east, his head will be toward the south." Because the head, or "up" direction of the human body was associated with the south, premodern Islamic maps appear upside down in comparison with modern maps, in which the "up" direction is north.

Time. For Ibn Sina, time, like space, was also relative. Time depended entirely on change: "If there is no change and no motion there is no time." According to Ibn Sina, time was a continuous quantity that could be divided indefinitely without ever reaching an end point, or "atom of time." Because time is continuous, it must accept division. This division is the "moment." Because time has no end point, however, Ibn Sina's "moments" are not measurable moments but purely theoretical divisions. Because space also extends indefinitely, the point in space is similarly a theoretical entity. Thus, for Ibn Sina, the passing of time in the universe was like the passing of plasma through space: it could only be observed through its motion, or "flow."

A Living Universe. The universe of the Greek and Islamic philosophers was vastly different from the universe a modern person imagines. Their universe was made up of living beings: planets and stars possessed intelligence; the motion of the heavenly spheres affected the lives of humans on earth; and the all-pervading presence of the Active Intellect ensured that the natural order possessed meaning and purpose. God's will and plan could be found everywhere. By contrast, the modern idea of a universe of inanimate matter and energy would have appeared dead to these philosophers. A cosmology of galactic clusters, black holes, dark matter, red giants, white dwarfs, and subatomic particles such as protons, electrons, and quarks—all governed by the impersonal forces of relativity, chaos, and uncertainty—would have seemed sinister and demonic to philosophers whose universe was motivated by a "love" that sought goodness and perfection in order and equilibrium. It is important to remember that the universe of the Greek and Islamic philosophers was not only based on mistakes of empirical observation. Empirical science existed in the premodern world, just as it exists today. Yet, for the Greek and Islamic philosophers, a world without an underlying meaning was a world without God. A science or philosophy that constructed a world without God was atheistic and therefore evil. For Plato and Aristotle, as much as for Ibn Sina, such a world was inconceivable.

Ibn Rushd. Known in the Latin West as Averroës, Abu al-Walid Muhammad ibn Rushd (1126–1198) was the greatest Aristotelian philosopher in the Islamic world. Like Ibn Sina's, however, his writings were more widely accepted in the West than among his own people. He was born in Córdoba, the former capital of Islamic Spain, and was named after his grandfather, who had been a renowned jurist of the Maliki school of Islamic law. When Ibn Rushd was in his twenties, North Africa and Islamic Spain fell under the control of the Almohads (Arabic: *al-Muwahhidun,* "Unitarians"). These religious reformers from the mountains of Morocco and western Algeria sought to harmonize the differences among the schools of Islamic law by creating a new, synthetic legal system that combined the best of all methods. In both law and theology, the Almohads based their doctrines on the apparent meaning of the Qur'an and selected hadith accounts whose authenticity could be clearly verified. While ordinary believers were prohibited from speculating about ambiguous passages in the Qur'an, the scholars of Almohad doctrine (*talabah*) and the non-Almohad "urban scholars" (*talabat al-hadar*) who specialized in the rational sciences were allowed to use dialectical and demonstrative reasoning to examine theological issues. Falsafah was taught at the court of the second Almohad ruler, Abu Ya'qub Yusuf I (ruled 1163–1184). Ibn Rushd's attempt to harmonize Falsafah and the Shari'ah was greatly influenced by the Almohad approach to law and theology.

Physician-Philosopher. Like his predecessor Ibn Sina, Ibn Rushd combined the theoretical study of philosophy with the practical study of medicine. Like Ibn Sina, he wrote a celebrated work on medicine, which he titled *Al-Kulliyyat fi al-Tibb* (The General Book of Medicine). In 1169, shortly after the completion of this work, Abu Ya'qub Yusuf invited Ibn Rushd to Marrakesh, the capital of the Almohad empire, and commissioned him to compose commentaries on the works of Aristotle, a project on which Ibn Rushd spent the next ten years. He also wrote important critiques of the works of Ibn Sina and al-Ghazali. During Ibn Rushd's lifetime his commentaries on Aristotle were translated into Hebrew and were highly regarded by the Jewish philosopher Moses Maimonides (1135–1204). In the thirteenth century, translations of

Ibn Rushd's works from either Hebrew or Arabic influenced such important European philosophers as Thomas Aquinas (1225–1274) and Siger of Brabant (circa 1240 – circa 1284).

Philosopher-Jurist. Unlike other Islamic philosophers, Ibn Rushd spent a considerable part of his career as a practicing jurist. He wrote two treatises on legal interpretation. His best-known legal work, *Bidayat al-mujtahid wanihayat al-muqtasid* (The Jurist's Beginning and the Layman's End), uses Aristotelian logic to resolve differences among the schools of Islamic law. By resolving these differences, he hoped to create a universal approach to Islamic jurisprudence that would fulfill the spirit of Almohad reform. Despite his acceptance of Almohadism, however, the Almohad religious establishment never accepted Ibn Rushd. After his royal patron died, his philosophical beliefs came under increasing attack. In 1194 he was accused of heresy and brought before the current Almohad ruler, Ya'qub al-Mansur. Al-Mansur ordered Ibn Rushd's books to be burned and kept the philosopher and his followers under house arrest in the town of Lucena, near Córdoba. According to Ibn Rushd, the saddest moment of his life came during this period, when he was thrown out of a masjid by the other worshipers because they thought he was not a Muslim.

Making the Case for Falsafah. Apart from his commentaries on Aristotle, most of Ibn Rushd's philosophical writ-

Ibn Rushd (known in the West as Averroës), as depicted in *The Triumph of St. Thomas Aquinas,* a fourteenth-century fresco in the Church of Santa Maria Novella, Florence

ings fall under the category of *apologetics*. These works were composed as critiques of specific philosophical theories or to refute the accusation that Falsafah was a heretical system of thought. Ibn Rushd's best-known apologetic works are *Fasl al-maqal fi ma bayna al-shari'ah wa-al hikmah min al-ittisal* (The Decisive Discourse and Affirmation of the Connection between Shari'ah and Philosophy), a discussion of the relationship between Falsafah and Shari'ah (or more properly, between philosophical knowledge and knowledge derived from revelation), and *Tahafut al-Tahafut* (The Incoherence of the "Incoherence"), his answer to al-Ghazali's critique of the Falsafah tradition.

The Decisive Discourse. Ibn Rushd wrote *The Decisive Discourse* at the end of the period in which he completed his commentaries on Aristotle. Although he lived this portion of his life in safety under the patronage of a powerful monarch, the intellectual climate of the day was antiphilosophical. The literalists (*Hashwiyyah*) among Maliki jurists and partisans of the doctrines of Ahmad ibn Hanbal resisted any speculation about the nature of God or the divine attributes. The Ash'arite theologians, who were favored by the Almohads, held theories of natural philosophy, such as atomism and occasionalism, that were opposed to the Falsafah tradition. As a judge Ibn Rushd found himself in a particularly difficult position because he was expected to maintain an unimpeachable belief in the Qur'an and the Sunnah, while at the same time holding philosophical beliefs that were unpopular. His commentaries on Aristotle aroused the suspicion of fellow jurists, who accused him of using his position to advocate heretical ideas. The legalistic style in which *The Decisive Discourse* is written indicates that Ibn Rushd had such people in mind when he wrote this important work.

Defending Philosophy. Ibn Rushd poses the central problem of *The Decisive Discourse* in legal terms: Can one determine, "from the standpoint of the study of the Shari'ah, whether the study of philosophy and logic is permitted by the Shari'ah, or prohibited, or commanded, or recommended, or obligatory?" The answer that he gives to this question is based on the sources of Islamic jurisprudence as outlined by Shafi'i: the evidence of the Qur'an and the Sunnah, plus the conclusions of syllogistic reasoning (*qiyas*) and scholarly consensus (*ijma'*). Because of the way its arguments are formulated, *The Decisive Discourse* should not be regarded as a work of philosophy but rather as a legal work about philosophy. Ibn Rushd wrote as a legal scholar who shared the philosophers' beliefs. Unlike the legal scholars who were his opponents, he did not view philosophy as a speculative science that is opposed to the certainty of revelation. Instead, he portrayed philosophy as a demonstrative science that leads to true conclusions because its methodology is based on sound premises. According to Ibn Rushd, the Qur'anic statement that human beings should observe the natural world and reflect on the signs of God (59: 2) is proof that God intends scholars to combine natural philosophy and metaphysics so that the data of empirical science and the theories of

demonstrative philosophy support one another. His opponents saw a fallacy in this position that Ibn Rushd overlooked: no science can be both empirical and demonstrative at the same time. The observation of the natural world can provide evidence that helps generate theories, but this evidence can never be sufficient to prove universal concepts. This fallacy is a major reason why what used to be called "natural philosophy" is now called "science" and is a separate discipline from philosophy.

Religion and Philosophy. Ibn Rushd encountered a similar problem when he claimed that religion and philosophy must always agree on every point. His successors in the Christian West avoided having to redefine religion and philosophy by separating knowledge into two domains. Revealed truths were true in the "religious realm," whereas facts about the world were true in the "philosophic realm." In this scheme there was no inherent contradiction between religion and philosophy because each dealt with a separate conceptual world. Ibn Rushd, however, committed a logical fallacy that still causes problems for Muslim intellectuals. He equated the theological concept of *tawhid*, the unity of God, with a totalizing concept of unity that implied the unification of all forms of knowledge. In such a unitary system, religion and philosophy are forced to make the same claims. The Qur'an is expected to express truths about science and history, while philosophy is expected to express truths about God and the universe. Reason and revelation are thus potentially in conflict, and if either can be proved to have made false assertions, the entire edifice of logic that supports them can come tumbling down. The inability of demonstrative reason to deal with all religious matters led to the refutation of both Falsafah and Kalam in premodern Islam. Today, the inability of scripture to deal with all knowledge outside the physical sciences is a major weakness of Islamic fundamentalism, which shares a similar totalizing vision of knowledge.

Agreement through Allegory. Ibn Rushd tried to resolve this contradiction between religion and philosophy through the use of allegory. He claimed that apparent contradictions between the teachings of the Qur'an and the theories of the philosophers could be resolved through "the extension of the meaning of an expression from real to metaphorical significance, without forsaking the standard metaphorical practices of the Arabic language." Some form of allegorical reasoning is allowed in all schools of Islamic law, where it is part of the process of deriving a ruling from an ambiguous case or an unclear passage of scripture. According to Ibn Rushd, the resolution of ambiguity through allegory is part of God's plan for humanity; scripture has both apparent and allegorical meanings in accordance with the different intellectual capacities of human beings. In addition, scripture includes passages that are apparently contradictory in order to provide religious scholars with thought experiments to sharpen their intellects. Since it is clear that unanimity can never been achieved in theoretical matters, it is God's will that the

Qur'an may be interpreted in different ways by jurists, Kalam theologians, or philosophers.

An Apparent Contradiction. As an example of a contradiction that is more apparent than real, Ibn Rushd cited al-Ghazali's claim that the philosophers went against the Qur'an by denying the creation of the world. He replied that if *creation* means that something is brought into existence by something other than itself that precedes it in time, there is no disagreement between the theologians and the philosophers. Both groups agree that entities such as water, air, earth, animals, and plants originated in time. Both agree as well that God is unoriginated and pre-eternal. That is, God is not made from or by anything else and is not preceded in time. The only real disagreement is over the one entity that, according to the philosophers, is not made from anything else and is not preceded in time, but is still brought into existence by an agent: the cosmos. In the view of Falsafah, the cosmos is neither originated nor pre-eternal. According to Ibn Rushd, this view of the cosmos corresponds more closely to the Qur'anic view than does that of the theologians who advocate creation out of nothing. The Qur'an states: "He it is who created the heavens and the earth in six days, and His throne was on the water" (13: 78); "He turned His attention toward the sky, and it was smoke" (13: 11–12); "on the day when the earth shall be changed into other than earth, and the heavens as well" (14: 48). For Ibn Rushd, these verses provide conclusive proof that matter (that is, water and smoke) came before the origination of objects in the universe, thus refuting the doctrine of creation out of nothing. In addition, these verses demonstrate that at the end of time the earth will be changed into a different entity rather than being dissolved into nothingness. Finally, argued Ibn Rushd, nowhere in the Qur'an does it say that God ever existed with absolutely nothing else around Him. Thus, he said, it is the theologians' assertion of creation out of nothing—not the philosophers' theory of the origination of the universe—that is truly heretical, for creation out of nothing cannot be supported by the statements of the Qur'an.

The Limits of Interpretation. Not everyone should engage in allegorical interpretation. According to Ibn Rushd, the rise of Islamic sectarianism and the abuses that it created were owed to allegory being employed by people who were not intellectually prepared for it. There are three classes of people with regard to interpretation: the *rhetorical* class, who are not suited for interpretation at all; this group comprises the majority of believers; the *dialectical* class, who are suited only for the give-and-take of dialectical argument; this group comprises the jurists and the Kalam theologians; and the *demonstrative* class, who, by their nature and training, are exclusively suited for philosophy. Since the primary purpose of revelation is to provide for the needs of the majority, the majority of the verses of the Qur'an should not be subjected to allegorical interpretation, and only the demonstrative class should attempt to interpret verses that are suited to allegorical readings.

The mausoleum complex of Sultan al-Malik al-Ashraf Qa'itbay in Cairo, built in 1472–1474

When allegorical interpretations are taught to those who are not suited to understand them, the result is unbelief, because allegorical interpretation entails rejecting the apparent meaning of a verse in favor of its allegorical meaning. Only the demonstrative class of philosophers has the intellectual tools to engage in this sort of interpretation, and, thus, the philosophers should be the foremost of those who are empowered to interpret Islam. "Philosophy is the milk-sister of religion," wrote Ibn Rushd at the end of *The Decisive Discourse*. Unfortunately, he said, the Kalam theologians, who claim an affinity with philosophy but do not understand its methods and principles, have lost sight of this relationship. Their misunderstanding of the true relationship between philosophy and religion led to the "evil fancies and perverted beliefs that have infiltrated this religion" and caused philosophy to be rejected, thus subverting God's plan for the world and impoverishing Islam intellectually.

Sources:

Osman Bakar, *Classification of Knowledge in Islam: A Study in Islamic Philosophies of Science* (Cambridge: Islamic Texts Society, 1998).

Majid Fakhry, *A History of Islamic Philosophy* (New York & London: Columbia University Press, 1983).

Abu Nasr al-Farabi, *The Political Writings: "Selected Aphorisms" and Other Texts*, translated by Charles E. Butterworth (Ithaca, N.Y. & London: Cornell University Press, 2001).

Dimitri Gutas, *Greek Thought, Arabic Culture: The Greco-Arabic Translation Movement in Baghdad and Early 'Abbasid Society* (London & New York: Routledge, 1998).

Arthur Hyman and James J. Walsh, eds., *Philosophy in the Middle Ages: The Christian, Islamic, and Jewish Traditions* (Indianapolis & Cambridge: Hackett, 1973).

Ibn Rushd, *Averroës: On the Harmony of Religion and Philosophy*, translated by George F. Hourani (London: Luzac, 1976).

Ibn Rushd, *Averroës' Tahafut al-Tahafut (The Incoherence of the Incoherence)*, 2 volumes, translated by Simon van den Bergh (London: Luzac, 1954).

Ibn Rushd, *The Distinguished Jurist's Primer (Bidayat al-Mujtahid)*, 2 volumes, translated by Imran Ahsan Khan Nyazee (Reading, U.K.: Garnet, 1994, 1996).

Muhsin Mahdi, *Alfarabi and the Foundation of Islamic Political Philosophy* (Chicago & London: University of Chicago Press, 2001).

Seyyed Hossein Nasr, *An Introduction to Islamic Cosmological Doctrines* (Albany: State University of New York Press, 1993).

Nasr and Oliver Leaman, eds., *History of Islamic Philosophy* (London & New York: Routledge, 1996).

Ian Richard Netton, *Allah Transcendent: Studies in the Structure and Semiotics of Islamic Philosophy, Theology and Cosmology* (Richmond, U.K.: Curzon Press, 1994).

Emilio Tornero Poveda, *Al-Kindi: La Transformacion de un Pensamiento Religioso en un Pensamiento Racional* (Madrid: Consejo Superior de Investigaciones Cientificas, 1992).

Fazlur Rahman, *Prophecy in Islam: Philosophy and Orthodoxy* (Chicago & London: University of Chicago Press, 1979).

THE SUNNI CRITIQUE OF KALAM AND FALSAFAH

Background to the Sunni Revival. Except for al-Kindi (circa 801 – 866) and Ibn Rushd (1126–1198), most of the important figures of the Falsafah tradition lived at least part of their lives in the fourth Islamic century, the tenth century of the Common Era. Modern historians have called it the "Shi'ite Century" because during this period Shi'ism had political dominance throughout the Islamic world. In the West, the Ismaili Shi'ite Fatimid dynasty ruled over Egypt, Syria, and much of North Africa. The Fatimids conquered Egypt in 969 and moved their court from Tunisia to their new capital of Cairo. Over the next one hundred years, Cairo thrived as the center of a wealthy mercantile empire, which diverted the Indian Ocean trade from Iraq to the Red Sea and opened the markets of western Europe to the goods of India and the Far East. In Iraq and the eastern Muslim lands, the Abbasid khilafah was an empire in name only. Significant regions, such as North Africa, Egypt, Syria, and Central Asia, had broken free of direct Abbasid control, and Abbasid khalifahs were virtual prisoners in their palaces, rendered impotent by Buyid emirs (circa 945–1055), who ruled Iraq and Iran as military dictators. The Buyids, a clan of Shi'ites from the mountains of northwestern Iran, allowed both Imami and Ismaili Shi'ism to flourish under their patronage and sponsored works of Falsafah and Mu'tazilite theology. In the second half of the tenth century, no fewer than three separate khilafahs competed for dominance in the Muslim world: the nearly powerless Abbasids in the East, the wealthy and vigorous Fatimids in the center, and the Umayyads of Muslim Spain (al-Andalus) in the West.

Sunni Challengers. The only Sunni rulers that could challenge the Fatimids militarily were the Umayyads of Spain (ruled 757–1034). But Umayyad Spain was too far from the center of the Muslim world to threaten Fatimid power in Egypt. Furthermore, the Umayyads were unlikely to support the Abbasids because in 750 the Abbasids had overthrown the Umayyad khilafah ruled from Damascus. The only other Sunni state of any consequence was that of the Samanids (ruled 874–999), who ruled over Central Asia and eastern Iran from their capital of Bukhara in Uzbekistan. The Samanids were descendants of pre-Islamic Persian notables whose power was based on the control of the well-known Silk Route, the trade network that funneled the luxury goods of India and China to the markets of the Middle East and Byzantium. Apart from Bukhara, the most important urban centers of the Samanid state were the trading emporia of Nishapur and Rayy. As merchant princes, the Samanids were more interested in profits than in religious dogma. Consequently, they presided over a principality in which members of all Islamic sects could practice their beliefs free of governmental interference. The Samanid state thus was home to a "free market of ideas," where Sunnis, Shi'ites, Mu'tazilites, philosophers, and other thinkers debated each other and competed for the patronage of high officials. It is no coincidence that the regions ruled by the Samanids produced many of the most important religious thinkers of the fourth and fifth Islamic centuries, including al-Farabi, Ibn Sina, al-Ash'ari, al-Maturidi, and Qadi 'Abd al-Jabbar. It is also significant that the twin pillars of the eventual Sunni revival, Ash'arite theology and Shafi'i jurisprudence, developed as major intellectual movements in these regions.

The "Usulization" of Intellectual Life. Although the "free market of ideas" that characterized intellectual life under the Samanids was meant to foster religious tolerance, on the local level it resulted in intense and sometimes violent competition among Islamic sects and schools of law. The Palestinian geographer al-Muqaddasi, who visited eastern Iran and Central Asia in the year 980, observed the high level of sectarian violence and remarked, "An owl cannot drink from the water of this region without becoming a fanatic!" Although the Samanid rulers themselves followed the Hanafi school of law, many of the most influential jurists belonged to the Shafi'i school and sought to put an end to the climate of sectarianism by uniting all Muslims under a single approach to religious knowledge. This approach, first proposed by Muhammad ibn Idris al-Shafi'i (767–820) in *al-Risalah* (The Treatise), the first systematic work on legal methodology in Islam, came to be known as the *usul* (sources, or roots) approach because it was based on the fundamental sources of Islamic knowledge. In the field of jurisprudence, this approach was known as *usul al-fiqh* (sources of jurisprudence); in theology and dogmatics, it was called *usul al-din* (sources of religion).

Sources of Knowledge. As outlined by Shafi'i, the *usul* approach relied first and foremost on the Qur'an and Sunnah as sources of religious and legal knowledge. The truest form of knowledge was thought to come from God, either by means of revelation, as in the Qur'an, or by means of divine inspiration, as in the hadith accounts that made

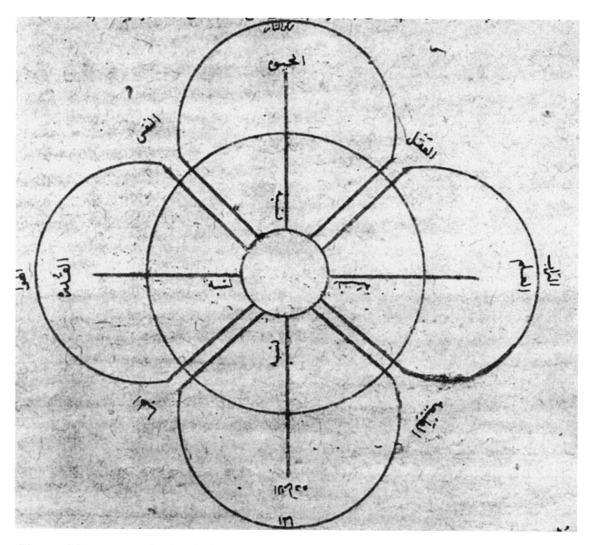

Diagram of the many emanating from the One Being in an early-sixteenth-century manuscript for *al-Futuhat al-Makkiyyah* (The Makkan Revelations, written 1202–1237), by Sufi theologian Ibn al-ʿArabi (British Library, London)

up the Sunnah. Only when the answer to a legal or theological question could not be found in the Qur'an or the Sunnah was a scholar allowed to resort to his own reasoning (*ijtihad*). Even in this case, a scholar's reasoning was to be limited to strict analogy (*qiyas*), which had to be based on a text found in the Qur'an or in approved hadith collections. To further aid his reasoning, a scholar could also turn to the traditions of the Prophet's Companions and the two generations of Muslims who followed them. These "Righteous Ancestors" (*al-Salaf al-Salih*) were the main sources of hadith reports about the Prophet Muhammad and were considered more pious and trustworthy than Muslims of later times.

Rejection of Innovation. Only rarely could a matter of law or religious doctrine depart from these sources of tradition. Although the Hanafi school of law recognized the concept of "positive innovation" (*bid'ah hasanah*), the other legal schools regarded all overt innovation as an abandonment of the path laid out by the Prophet and the Righteous Ancestors. Consequently, schools of thought, such as Falsafah, that depended heavily on pre-Islamic sources of knowledge were branded as heresies by the practitioners of

usul, as were schools of more purely Islamic theology, such as the Mu'tazila, which depended on human reason more than on tradition. Approved schools of theology, such as that of al-Ash'ari, did not entirely abandon their reliance on logic and human reasoning but were careful not to overstep the bounds of tradition and made sure that the scope of divine power did not appear to be limited in any way.

Orthodoxy and Education. By the late eleventh century, the growing popularity of Shafi'i jurisprudence and the *usul* approach to knowledge led to the "usulization" of intellectual life in the eastern Islamic lands. Because the *usul* approach was based on a legal model, training in the "roots of jurisprudence" became fundamental to all forms of higher education. Under the Saljuks, a tribe of Turks who during the eleventh century came to power in Central Asia, Iran, and Iraq as defenders of Sunni Islam, religious schools known as madrasahs were established. These schools featured legal training as part of the core curriculum. Whether the graduates of these schools became jurists, theologians, Sufis, government officials, historians, scientists, or mathematicians, all shared the same *usul*-based education. In many cases, they even studied the same books. The process of "usulization" was designed to combat the intellectual effects of "heresies" such as Falsafah and Shi'ism and to promote a new sense of Sunni orthodoxy. Nizam al-Mulk (circa 1019 – 1092), the Saljuk wazir who founded the Nizamiyyah madrasahs of Nishapur and Baghdad, defined the goal of this endeavor as the promotion of "correct belief" (Persian: *niku i'tiqad*). Within a century after the death of Nizam al-Mulk, the "usulization" of intellectual life had become so widespread in the Muslim world that even an Aristotelian philosopher such as Ibn Rushd had to be trained in the *usul* method.

The Sunni Critique of Falsafah. The "usulization" of Islamic knowledge left little room for competing traditions such as Falsafah. Students of the *usul* method were taught that the only valid sources of knowledge about God and other metaphysical subjects were the Qur'an, the Sunnah, and the traditions of the Righteous Ancestors, so they believed that the pre-Islamic metaphysics of "the divine Plato" and "The Greatest Sage" Aristotle had to be refuted. The person who took on this task, with devastating consequences for Falsafah, was Abu Hamid al-Ghazali. *Tahafut al-Falasifah* (The Incoherence of the Philosophers), al-Ghazali's critique of Falsafah, is widely regarded as one of the best examples of polemical writing in Islam. A masterpiece of faith-based theology, its effectiveness in refuting the main points of the Falsafah worldview earned its author the honorific *Hujjat al-Islam* (The Proof of Islam). Although some modern scholars have characterized *Tahafut al-Falasifah* as an antirationalistic work, this view is not correct. Rather, the book seeks to demonstrate in a systematic manner that the claims of the philosophers are either logically unsupportable or are themselves based on a blind faith in reason that is no more valid than the "simple" faith of those who believe in the miraculous origin of revealed religion.

Al-Ghazali's "Higher Theology." Al-Ghazali's thought is a difficult subject to summarize because he resists categorization. Although he was an Ash'arite theologian, his "higher theology" differed from traditional Ash'arism in several respects. For example, there is ample evidence that he rejected the atomism and occasionalism of classical Ash'arite theology in favor of a determinism in which God chooses to govern the world through the law of cause and effect. This view of causality had much in common with the philosophical teachings of Aristotle and Ibn Rushd, though al-Ghazali gave more room than the philosophers for miracles and other occasions where God "rends the fabric of custom." However, al-Ghazali does not openly espouse this "higher theology" in the majority of his works. Instead, he poses as a traditional Ash'arite scholar in works that are designed for public consumption and conceals his actual doctrines in disparate threads of argumentation that appear in other, more mystical or intellectual writings. These doctrinal contradictions did not go unnoticed by al-Ghazali's critics. The Spanish mystic and philosopher Ibn Sab'in of Ricote (1217–1270) characterized al-Ghazali's writings as "a language without expression, a voice without

speech, a mixture that combines opposites, and a perplexity that tears the heart. At one time he is a Sufi, at another a philosopher. A third time he is an Ash'arite, a fourth a jurist, and a fifth merely confused."

Polemical Strategy. Most modern scholars have been more forgiving than Ibn Sab'in and attribute al-Ghazali's contradictions to political cautiousness. In 1091 the Saljuk wazir Nizam al-Mulk appointed the thirty-three-year-old al-Ghazali to the chair of Shafi'i law at the Nizamiyyah madrasah of Baghdad. It would not have been wise for an officially sponsored scholar of such renown to advocate doctrines openly that disagreed with the views he was supposed to uphold. Rather than attempt to teach his higher theology at that time, he found it both wiser and safer to confine his activities to the refutation of the philosophers, a project that all Ash'arite theologians would approve. Consequently, during his tenure at the Nizamiyyah madrasah al-Ghazali wrote his two-part refutation of the Falsafah tradition. First, he set up the philosophers for his attack by detailing the "essence" of their tradition in *Maqasid al-Falasifah* (The Goals of the Philosophers). Then, he demolished the doctrines of the philosophers by detailing their "incoherencies" in *Tahafut al-Falasifah.*

Tahafut al-Falasifah. The crux of al-Ghazali's argument in *Tahafut al-Falasifah* is that the Islamic philosophers are guilty of the same blind traditionalism for which they blame less sophisticated Muslims. Believing themselves intellectually superior, they are deceived by the exaggerated claims made by the followers of Socrates, Plato, and Aristotle. They assert that

> the ancient masters possessed extraordinary intellectual powers; that the principles they have discovered are unquestionable; that the mathematical, logical, physical, and metaphysical sciences developed by them are the most profound; that their profound intelligence justifies their bold attempts to discover the unseen by demonstrative methods; and that with all the subtlety of their intelligence and the originality of their accomplishments they repudiated the authority of the religious laws, denied the validity of the revealed religions, and believed that such things were only sanctimonious lies and trivialities.

The primary targets of al-Ghazali's attack were the Islamic philosophers al-Farabi and Ibn Sina, whose views on the superiority of philosophy over religion were well known. Al-Farabi and Ibn Sina, said al-Ghazali,

> failed to see that a change from one kind of intellectual bondage to another is only a self-deception, a stupidity. What position in God's world is baser than that of one who thinks that it is honorable to renounce a truth that is accepted on authority, and then relapses into an acceptance of falsehood, which is still a matter of blind faith, unaided by independent inquiry? Such a scandalous attitude is never taken by the unsophisticated masses of men. For they have an instinctive aversion to following the example of misguided genius. Surely, their "simplicity" is nearer to salvation than sterile genius can ever be!

The Value of the Ancients. Despite the strength of his criticism, al-Ghazali had no intention of abandoning the

Sufis dancing in a khanqah; illumination from a 1458–1459 manuscript for *Mathnawi-i ma'nawi* (Spiritual Couplets) by
Jalal al-Din Rumi (Vever Collection, Arthur M. Sackler Gallery, The National Museum of Asian Art,
Smithsonian Institution, Washington, D.C.)

legacy of Plato and Aristotle entirely. There are things in which the ancient philosophers believed that do not come into conflict with revealed religion. Such is the case with the conclusions they drew from empirical science. Al-Ghazali cites the example of a lunar eclipse. When the ancient philosophers maintained that a lunar eclipse occurs because the earth comes between the moon and the sun, this view is correct because it is based on what today would be called the "scientific method." Other problems arose because of the mistranslation of Greek philosophical terms into Arabic. Often, these terms were as much in dispute as the ideas of the philosophers themselves. Apparent contradictions such as these, said al-Ghazali, may be resolved by showing how the terms used by the Greek philosophers actually correspond to the terms used by Muslim theologians. As an example of such a false disagreement, al-Ghazali cited the concepts of *logic* and *dialectic*. Although the Islamic philosophers regarded the "logical" method of Falsafah as superior to the "dialectical" method of Kalam, al-Ghazali demonstrated that the two methods are in fact equivalent.

Theology and the Ancients. For al-Ghazali, the real problem of the Greek philosophers and their Muslim followers lay in their espousal of beliefs that directly contradicted the teachings of the Qur'an, the Sunnah, or Sunni

Kalam. Al-Ghazali cited twenty such disagreements, which can be reduced to five essential theological issues: (1) the philosophers' belief in the eternity of the world; (2) the philosophers' inability to demonstrate that God is a true Creator; (3) the denial of the divine attributes; (4) the denial of God's power to know the particulars of His creation and to determine the destinies of created things; and (5) the denial of bodily resurrection. It is important to keep in mind that in *Tahafut al-Falasifah* al-Ghazali challenged Falsafah from the standpoint of classical Ash'arite theology and not from the standpoint of his own "higher theology." This approach is sufficient to refute certain of the philosophers' arguments but not to refute others. For example, in his attempt to argue against the "atheism" of philosophers who claimed that the world is governed by the laws of cause and effect, Al-Ghazali defended the occasionalistic worldview of classical Ash'arism, which sees God as both the ultimate and the immediate cause of every occurrence. In some of his later works, al-Ghazali abandoned this extreme doctrine of occasionalism as unsupportable. Two generations after al-Ghazali's death, the Spanish philosopher Ibn Rushd seized on this same point to condemn Ash'arism as illogical. This argument appears in Ibn Rushd's refutation of *Tahafut*, which he titled *Tahafut al-Tahafut* (The Incoherence of The Incoherence).

Courtyard of the Zahiriyyah madrasah in Cairo, completed circa 1337, where Ibn Khaldun spent the last years of his life

Ibn Khaldun's Critique of Kalam and Falsafah. 'Abd al-Rahman ibn Khaldun (1332–1406), statesman, jurist, historian, and Sunni rationalist, was born in the North African city of Tunis. The first truly modern thinker in Islam, he traveled in the course of his career to all of the capitals of the Muslim West, as well as to Damascus and Cairo. His career, like that of Ibn Sina, was characterized by reversals of fortune. At various times he was an adviser to princes, a political prisoner, an exile among Bedouins, and a Maliki judge. In 1384 he lost his entire family when the ship that was carrying them from Tunis to Egypt sank just outside the harbor of Alexandria. He wrote his best-known work, his *Muqaddimah* (Introduction) to his history of the world, in 1377, "with words and ideas pouring into my head like cream into a churn." On his death in Egypt, he was buried in the Sufi cemetery of Cairo.

Ibn Khaldun's Rationalism. It is ironic that Ibn Khaldun was buried among the Sufis because his rationalism prevented him from accepting the more mystical aspects of Sufi doctrine. As a late medieval Sunni thinker, he stood somewhere between al-Ghazali and Ibn Rushd. Like al-Ghazali, Ibn Khaldun accepted and promoted the worldview of Sunni Islam, including a modified form of occasionalistic theology that had more in common with al-Maturidi than with al-Ash'ari. But like Ibn Rushd, Ibn Khaldun respected much of the Greek philosophical tradition and was a clear supporter of Aristotle's opinions concerning cause and effect. More empirical and less tied to a specific theological doctrine than al-Ghazali, he was better able to offer a balanced critique of Falsafah, which rejected its shortcomings while retaining the positive influences of the Greek philosophical tradition in the fields of science and logic.

Critique of Falsafah. Ibn Khaldun's critique of Falsafah appears in the last section of the *Muqaddimah,* which is devoted to an enumeration of the sciences and modes of instruction. He began the chapter with a theory of perception that divides the human mind into three types of intellect: the *discerning intellect* helps the human being make sense of the natural world; the *experimental intellect* helps the person function in society through experiences with other people; and the *speculative intellect* allows the person to deal with hypothetical knowledge, which goes beyond the knowledge derived from the senses. These three types of intellect allow the human being to perceive three worlds of consciousness: the sensual world, the intellectual world, and the spiritual-angelic world. The spiritual-angelic world is the domain of the prophets, who have the ability to transform their human natures into angelic natures. Returning to their human natures, the prophets communicate news of the spiritual-angelic world to humanity via revelation and divine inspiration. The knowledge possessed by the prophets is derived from direct observation and spiritual vision. Because the veil of the supernatural has been removed, this knowledge is never subject to error or mistaken assumptions. Although Ibn Khaldun did not cite him as a source, this model of the spiritual-angelic world and the nature of prophecy owes much to Ibn Sina's "Oriental Wisdom."

Social Science. The social scientific side of Ibn Khaldun becomes apparent in his characterization of scientific instruction, including philosophy, as a craft that is produced by urban civilization. Like a modern sociologist, he thought that science is a product of the division of labor in sedentary society and comes about through the leisure time that is made possible by economic surpluses. Science was particularly well developed in Egypt, he claimed, because Egypt had been a settled farming culture for thousands of years. According to Ibn Khaldun, two kinds of science exist in urban civilization: *natural science,* which includes philosophy and depends on the natural workings of human reason, and *traditional science,* which depends on the authority of the religious law. There is no place for intellect in traditional science, except in relating problems of detail to basic principles. The most important traditional science is that of the Shari'ah, which includes the disciplines of *usul al-fiqh* and *usul al-din.* Another traditional science is Sufism, which, in its most positive form, seeks to provide the believer with a momentary experience of the spiritual-angelic realm.

The Search for Causes. Kalam and Falsafah belong to the speculative side of natural science. The problem with the speculative sciences is that those who seek all answers through logic will ultimately be frustrated because the chain of cause and effect must ultimately lead to a Causer of Causes that is beyond the realm of the human intellect. Causes of human actions multiply vertically and horizontally. They include intention and volition, as well as the "accidents" that determine the course of future events. The causes of perception are other perceptions, and "the

cause of all the perceptions taking place in the soul is unknown, since no one is able to know the beginnings or order of matters pertaining to the soul." Therefore, wrote Ibn Khaldun:

> a person who stops at the search for causes is bound to be frustrated. He is rightly said to be an unbeliever. If he ventures to swim in the ocean of speculation and research, seeking each one of the causes that cause them and the influence they exercise, I can guarantee that he will return unsuccessful. This is why the Prophet Muhammad forbade us to study causes. We were only commanded to recognize the absolute oneness of God.

However, this statement does not mean that all intellectual speculation is forbidden. The intellect can indeed serve as a correct measure of things, but it should not be used to weigh such matters as the oneness of God, the spiritual-angelic world, the truth of prophecy, the real character of the divine attributes, or anything else that lies beyond its own level. This attempt would amount to desiring the impossible. According to Ibn Khaldun, using the intellect to understand such matters is like trying to weigh a mountain on a scale that is made for weighing gold.

The Superiority of Kalam. Although they share the defect of putting too much faith in reason, according to Ibn Khaldun, Kalam is superior to Falsafah because it starts with the articles of faith revealed by God to the Prophet Muhammad. Thus, despite its excessive rationalism, it maintains a foothold in the spiritual-angelic world. It starts from divinely revealed principles and works downward. Falsafah, however, starts from the physical world and tries to work upward. It seeks to prove the existence of God and the validity of the Shari'ah by resorting to logic and rational demonstration alone. According to the philosophers, even if no religious law had been revealed, humans would have learned to distinguish between vice and virtue by means of the intellect. In the same way, the intellect would have led them to a complete understanding of God and First Principles. Not only does this view contradict the teachings of Islam, it also contradicts the teachings of Plato. According to Ibn Khaldun, Plato said, "No certainty can be achieved with regard to the divine, and one can state about the divine only what is suitable and proper—that is, conjectures." He came to this conclusion because the immaterial world cannot be proved by demonstrative arguments. It is a condition of demonstrative arguments that their premises be essential, but essential premises founded on the experience of the material world cannot prove the existence of immaterial entities.

The Sufi Alternative. The doctrinal origins of Sufism (*tasawwuf*) are as obscure as the origins of its name. As early as the tenth century a noted Sufi remarked: "Sufism was once a reality without a name. Now it is a name without a reality." Often, Sufism is defined as "Islamic mysticism." But the concept of mysticism is problematical because it refers to individual, inward experiences of spirituality that vary from person to person. For this reason, many scholars assume that mysticism is *ineffable:* that is, it cannot be

In his *Tahafut al-Tahafut* (The Incoherence of the Inco-herence) Ibn Rushd contrasted his views on the nature of causality with those expressed by al-Ghazali in his *Tahafut al-Falasifah* (Incoherence of the Philosophers):

Al-Ghazali says: Our opponent claims that the agent of the burning is the fire exclusively; this is a natural, not a volun-tary agent, and cannot abstain from what is in its nature when it is brought into contact with a receptive substratum. This we deny, saying: The agent of the burning is God, through His creating the black in the cotton and the discon-nection of its parts, and it is God who made the cotton burn and made it ashes either through the intermediation of angels or without intermediation. For fire is a dead body which has no action, and what is the proof that it is the agent? Indeed, the philosophers have no other proof than the observation of the occurrence of the burning, when there is contact with fire. But observation proves only simultane-ity, not causation, and in reality, there is no other cause but God. . . .

I say: To deny the existence of efficient causes which are observed in sensible things is sophistry, and he who defends this doctrine either denies with his tongue what is present in his mind or is carried away by a sophistical doubt which occurs to him concerning this question. For he who denies this can no longer acknowledge that every act must have an agent. The question whether these causes by themselves are sufficient to perform the acts that proceed from them, or need an external cause for the perfection of their act . . . is not self-evident and requires much investigation and research. And if the theologians have doubts about the effi-cient causes that are perceived to cause each other, because there are also effects whose cause is not perceived, this is illogical. . . . The man who reasons like the theologians does not distinguish between what is self-evident and what is unknown, and everything Al-Ghazali says in this passage is sophistical.

Source: Ibn Rushd, *Averroës' Tahafut al-Tahafut (The Incoherence of the Inco-herence)*, 2 volumes, translated by Simon van den Bergh (London: Luzac, 1954).

described or analyzed in any meaningful sense. Yet, if per-sonal experiences were truly incommunicable to others, human beings would have no language, no literature, and no art. The fact that not everyone can understand a painting by the abstract expressionist Vassily Kandinsky does not mean that Kandinsky was a bad artist or that people cannot study his technique after his death. The same is true for Sufism. Despite the fact that a major part of Sufi practice is based on inward experiences, Sufis have written detailed and sys-tematic works on Sufi doctrine. Many of these works rival the finest treatises of Kalam and Falsafah in their contribu-tion to Islamic thought. In addition, many Sufis such as the Persian master Jalal al-Din Rumi (1207–1273) produced poetic works of great beauty that are still revered today.

Derivations of Terms. What is called "Sufism" in English comprises three terms in Arabic: *sufi, tasawwuf,* and *al-sufiyyah.* A *Sufi* is a practitioner of Sufism, *tasawwuf.* The only Arabic word directly related to these terms is *suf* (wool). Literally, therefore, a *sufi* is a "wooly" person, and *tasawwuf* means to practice "wooliness." These definitions do not make any sense. It has long been assumed that the term *sufi,* which was first used in the eighth century, denoted world-denying Islamic spiritualists who wore woolen garments. But wool was not particularly cheap in premodern times. It would often have been more cost-effective to wear clothing made of other materials, such as linen or cotton. So the origins of the term *sufi* remain a matter of conjecture, as they have been for more than 1,200 years. The Arabic term *al-sufiyyah* denotes the formal body of doctrines and practices that speakers of English call "Sufism." No Arabic root exactly corresponds to this term. The closest equivalent is the Greek word *sophia,* which means "wisdom." Sufism has long included an esoteric wis-

dom tradition, much like the *hikmah* tradition of the philos-ophers. Also, the closest counterparts to the Sufis in pre-Islamic times were itinerant Cynic and Neoplatonic philos-ophers, who renounced the world, practiced spiritual exer-cises, performed miracles, and wore white linen garments like those in which some Sufis dressed. But Sufis have been careful to stress the purely Islamic origins of their doctrines and practices, which they trace to the Righteous Ancestors who followed the Prophet Muhammad. Thus, the modern scholar of Sufism is left in a quandary: either one accepts the Sufi version of their origins and admits that Sufism is "a reality without a name," or one accepts the Greek etymol-ogy of the term *al-sufiyyah* and assumes that the Sufis hid the true origins of their beliefs and practices for centuries. Neither alternative is satisfactory.

The Ascetic Tradition. According to Sufi manuals and biographical works, the earliest Sufis were *ascetics,* people who denied worldly luxuries and practiced rigorous aus-terities such as fasting and solitude. Asceticism was com-mon in the first and second centuries of Islam. Several of the Companions of the Prophet Muhammad were noted ascetics. The ascetic movement of the following century included not only early Sufis but also Kharijites, Murji-ites, and even some Shi'ites. There is little doubt that the ascetic movement in Islam was influenced by Christian asceticism. Syria and Egypt, two of the first lands con-quered for Islam, were noted centers of Christian asceti-cism, where "desert fathers" and other holy people were well known for their austerities. Sufi biographical works include accounts of Muslim ascetics "comparing notes" with their Christian counterparts, and some early Sufis were called "monks" (*ruhban*). Muhammad ibn Wasi' (died 738), a student of Hasan al-Basri, was one of these people. As an ascetic, he practiced self-mortification and wore rough wool and chains on his body when he prayed. He was also a noted hadith transmitter and reciter of the Qur'an, and he died as a holy warrior in Central Asia. He is said to have remarked: "I have never looked at anything without seeing God therein."

Women Sufis. Many of the early Sufi ascetics were women. Abu 'Abd al-Rahman al-Sulami (died 1021), a biographer and systematizer of Sufi doctrines who was one of the scholars most responsible for the "usulization" of Islamic mysticism, wrote the earliest book devoted to women's spirituality in Islam. He mentioned eighty Sufi women who lived between the eighth and tenth centuries and who spanned the Muslim world from Egypt to Iran. In his short spiritual portraits of these women, al-Sulami demonstrated that there was a thriving tradition of women's spirituality in early Islam, which included local "schools" of women's asceticism. One of the earliest of these schools existed for more than a century in the Iraqi city of Basrah, and included the great woman saint Rabi'ah al-'Adawiyyah (circa 714 – 801). The practices of this school included the complete reliance on God for worldly support, weeping for the sins of the world, and *wara'*, a form of negative piety that included the denial of anything that might be physically or morally impure. Mu'adhah al-'Adawiyyah (died circa 702–719), the apparent founder of this school of women's asceticism, believed that her body was a temple that could be polluted and made unfit for worship if she ignored her prayers or ate anything that came from an unlawful source. Umm al-Aswad, a student of Mu'adhah who nursed at her breast as a child, remembered her teacher saying "I would not eat anything suspicious lest it cause me to neglect either an obligatory prayer or an additional invocation." Mu'adhah also said to Umm al-Aswad: "Do not spoil the breast-feeding I have given you by eating forbidden food, for when I was nursing you I made every effort to eat only what was lawful. So make every effort after this to eat only what is lawful. Perhaps you will succeed in your service to your Lord and in your acceptance of His will."

Seeking a Middle Way. By the ninth century, Sufis began to understand that "heroic virtues" such as asceticism and *wara'* were not for everybody. In the worst cases, such practices might lead to religious extremism because they went against the Islamic rule to seek the "middle way" in all activities. They could also be harmful to the spiritual life because a Sufi ascetic, believing himself purer and more pious than other Muslims, might develop an egoistic form of self-admiration that could actually lead him away from God. Sufis soon understood that their separation from the rest of Muslim society could lead to an elitism that caused them to deviate from the goals of the spiritual path. For this reason, they began to stress the practices of *muhasabah* and *muraqabah*, the sustained, critical examination of their actions, motives, and spiritual states. This interest in critical self-examination led to the development of the first theories of psychology in Islam.

Al-Muhasibi and Sufi Psychology. The father of Sufi psychology was a native of Baghdad named Harith al-Muhasibi (died 857). His deep understanding of human nature and his theory of the soul gave his writings an importance to Sufism that can be compared only with that of Sigmund Freud in the field of modern psychology. Al-Muhasibi's father was a Muslim heretic who may have held Manichaean or Zoroastrian beliefs. Al-Muhasibi refused to take the large inheritance his father left him because he believed that the money was tainted by his father's unbelief. In Arabic, *muhasibi* means "practitioner of *muhasabah*," rigorous self-examination. Al-Muhasibi earned this name by acting as an exemplar for other Sufis in moral conduct and in his refusal to allow any kind of self-deception, no matter how insignificant. His motto was "Be God's or be nothing." He taught his disciples to follow the dictates of reason and common sense in all matters. He never accepted gifts without providing some service in return. He was contemplative by nature and tried to remain detached from human affairs. He also disliked emotionalism. When one of his disciples cried out after hearing a bird sing during a session of invocation, he remarked: "If a senseless bird sings capriciously, out of its own habit, why should we act as if it were the voice of God?" Al-Muhasibi was a contemporary of Ahmad ibn Hanbal, namesake of the Hanbali school of Islamic law. But rather than approving of Muhasibi for his scrupulous adherence to Islam, Ibn Hanbal condemned him for his rationalism and his use of dialectical reasoning. According to Sufi accounts, Ibn Hanbal incited the lower classes of Baghdad to intimidate al-Muhasibi and prevent people from attending his lessons. Consequently, in the last years of his life, al-Muhasibi was barely able to venture outside of his house. When he died, only a few people attended his funeral because his disciples were afraid that Ibn Hanbal's followers would attack them.

Al-Muhasibi's Theories. Al-Muhasibi's psychological theories are found in *al-Ri'ayah li-huquq Allah wa al-qiyam biha* (How to Observe and Abide by the Rights of God). After al-Muhasibi's death, this book became one of the most important works of the orthodox-mystical tradition in Islam. Al-Ghazali cited it as influential in his conversion from Kalam to Sufism. In *al-Ri'ayah*, al-Muhasibi outlined what he called the "science of hearts." The "heart" is al-Muhasibi's metaphor for the human soul. According to his psychological theory, the soul has two parts: the conscience (*sirr*), which is the spiritual center, and the *nafs*, which can be translated as "psyche," "self," or "ego." The *nafs* is the realm of the "enemy," al-Muhasibi's term for Satan. It is the seat of the appetites, desires, and lust, and it strives against the higher nature of the human being. The "enemy" is also a metaphor for the instincts of the ego. Satan only incites people to do evil; people choose to do evil themselves by following the lust and passions of the *nafs*. Unlike earlier Christian ascetics, al-Muhasibi did not advocate "killing" the ego through self-denial and physical austerities. He understood that the ego is necessary for human existence. It provides the "spirit" and ability to think that allow people to survive in the world and attain the necessities of life. Rather than killing the *nafs,* one must tame it, just as one might tame a wild horse. The instrument that God provides human beings for taming the *nafs* is reason (*'aql*).

Taming the *Nafs*. The process of taming the *nafs* is in three stages. The first is that of the "commanding *nafs*" (*al-nafs al-ammarah*). In this stage the rebellious self commands the person to commit sins. In the vocabulary of modern psychoanalysis, this stage corresponds to the concepts that Freud termed the "id" and the "ego." According to al-Muhasibi, the key to taming the "commanding *nafs*" is self-examination (*muhasabah*). When a person is fully aware of the consequences of his or her actions, he or she is in a position to exercise self-control and turn negative qualities into virtues. This process corresponds to what a modern psychiatrist would call "analysis." Al-Muhasibi's view of psychotherapy shared the Freudian emphasis on sessions of counseling and self-examination. But because it was religious, al-Muhasibi's method also made use of the tools of fear and hope. Fear and hope were his way of ensuring that the process of *muhasabah* did not go on forever. To help inform people of the consequences of their actions in this life and the hereafter, he produced short pamphlets that illustrated in graphic detail the horrors of hell and the delights of heaven. This "carrot and stick" approach was designed to frighten people away from doing evil and to entice them to practice goodness in their daily lives.

The "Self-Blaming" *Nafs*. The second stage of taming the soul is the stage of the "self-blaming *nafs*" (*al-nafs al-lawwamah*). This stage corresponds to the Freudian concept of the "superego." Through the application of self-examination and the stimuli of fear and hope, a person becomes aware of the damage he or she has done to himself or herself and others by allowing the *nafs* to control his or her life without restraint. This person turns inward and engages in a more intense form of self-examination, desirous of rooting out the last vestiges of the "enemy" in the soul. This process corresponds to the various types of "depth-analysis" used in modern psychology. For al-Muhasibi, the main techniques of dealing with the "self-blaming *nafs*" were guided forms of religious meditation and self-examination. Although the stage of the "self-blaming *nafs*" constitutes a certain amount of progress in the development of self-awareness, the process is by no means complete. The *nafs* has gone only from the stage of proclaiming "I am the greatest!" to the stage of proclaiming "I am worthless." The person who occupies this stage is still obsessed with self. He or she may be less of a danger to others but is still in danger of committing inward sins, such as self-hatred and suicide.

The *Nafs* at Peace. For al-Muhasibi, the key to spiritual health was to "get out of one's self" entirely. Only by transcending the ego is it possible to attain the third and final stage of self-awareness, the "*nafs* at peace" (*al-nafs al-mutma'innah*). Although, as a Muslim, al-Muhasibi did not believe in the concept of original sin, he did believe in an

original human weakness: the problem of the "almighty I"—the egoism, selfishness, and self-absorption of the human being on which the literatures of all religions remark. According to al-Muhasibi, the ego exists in human beings from birth. It first manifests itself when a baby learns to differentiate its body from that of its mother, and it continues to develop into the "commanding *nafs*" unless it is checked through self-examination and the application of "the science of hearts." The Spanish Sufi Abu Madyan (circa 1116 – 1198), who followed al-Muhasibi's teachings closely, stated in one of his poems: "I seek the forgiveness of God for saying 'I' and 'with me,' for saying 'belonging to me' and 'mine,' and for my suspicions and my limited understanding." This intense concern with inner sincerity and the blandishments of the ego should not be dismissed as mere Sufi perfectionism. A multitude of human sins can be traced in one way or another to al-Muhasibi's "commanding *nafs*" or "self-blaming *nafs*." Such sins range from corruption, murder, fraud, and unsavory business practices to suicide, drug addiction, and terrorism.

Al-Junayd and Sufi Theology. The first great theologian of Sufism was a Baghdad native named Abu al-Qasim al-Junayd (died 910). Known as the "Peacock of the Scholars," he came from a merchant background, like most of the members of the religious elites of premodern Islam. As an early follower of the Shafi'i school of law and a practitioner of the *usul* method, he was critical of Kalam scholars for wasting their time in arguments over trivialities. Along with his teacher and uncle Sari al-Saqati (died 867), al-Junayd is considered the founder of the "Baghdad school" of Sufism, which set the standard for "Sunni" or "orthodox" Sufism. Although the Sufis of the "Baghdad school" were Sunni Muslims, they included the Shi'ite Imams among the Righteous Ancestors. Ma'ruf al-Karkhi (died 816), the teacher of al-Junayd's teacher, was a close associate of 'Ali al-Rida, the eighth Shi'ite Imam. Because of pressure from the followers of Ibn Hanbal, al-Junayd restricted his study circle to no more than twenty people. He and his followers were accused of being atheists, infidels, and believers in reincarnation. Every one of his associates and disciples was formally accused of infidelity at least once. These charges could not be made to stick, however, because al-Junayd's extensive legal training allowed him to defend the orthodoxy of his opinions successfully. Today he is regarded as the touchstone for all forms of legitimate Sufi doctrine.

Al-Junayd's Letters. Al-Junayd's doctrinal writings consist of letters that have been copied and passed down among Sufis from generation to generation. Although many subjects are discussed in these letters, the most important is al-Junayd's definition of *tawhid,* the Islamic doctrine of the oneness of God. For most Muslims, *tawhid* simply means that God is one, and not many. Al-Junayd, however, has a deeper and more meaningful definition in mind: "*Tawhid* means distinguishing the Eternal from that which is created in time." 'Ali al-Hujwiri (died after 1072), a Sufi from Afghanistan who wrote the first Persian-language treatise on Sufism, said of al-Junayd's definition: "You must

Page from a 1495 manuscript for *Ihya' 'ulum al-din* (The Revival of the Religious Sciences) by Abu Hamid al-Ghazali (Los Angeles County Museum of Art)

not regard the Eternal as a place of phenomena, or phenomena as a place of the Eternal. You must know that God alone is Eternal and that you are phenomena, that nothing of your species is connected with Him, that none of His attributes are commingled with yours, and that there is no homogeneity between the Eternal and the phenomenal."

Levels of *Tawhid*. According to Junayd, there are four levels of *tawhid*. For the majority of believers, *tawhid* is the intellectual assertion that God is one and that God has no companions, opposites, equals, or likenesses. However, despite the fact that the believer acknowledges the oneness of God in his mind, in his worldly hopes and aspirations he still relies on people and external powers other than God. The *tawhid* of the religious scholars, which al-Junayd terms the "Way of Reason and Virtue," builds on the *tawhid* of the ordinary believer and adds the avoidance of all that is forbidden by the Shari'ah. Such a person hopes that by purifying his external actions, God will allay his fears and help him realize his hopes and desires in the world. The first level of *tawhid* for the Sufis builds on the *tawhid* of the religious scholars, but the Sufis exceed the scholars in their understanding because they have ceased to place their hopes, fears, and aspirations in anything other than God. The Sufis know through self-awareness that God is always present with them and that when God calls to one's heart, the heart always responds. The supreme *tawhid* of the Sufi is characterized by the complete effacement or obliteration of the human self in the divine. It is "existence without individuality before God, with no intermediary or third party in between." The knower of God (*'arif*) "is drowned in the flooding seas of God's oneness, completely obliterated both from himself and from God's call to him, as well as from his answer to God. It is a state where the devotee has achieved the true realization of the oneness of God in true proximity to Him. He is lost to all sense and action because God has fulfilled in him what He has willed."

Annihilation. This third level of *tawhid* is the state that the Sufis, following al-Junayd, call "annihilation" or "obliteration" (*fana'*). The most complete form of this mystical annihilation leads to a spiritual vision or manifestation of the divine and the erasure of all sense of individual identity. For mystically minded philosophers such as Ibn Sina, the Sufi concept of annihilation corresponds to what they would call "conjunction" (*ittisal*) with the Active Intellect. Ibn Khaldun would have called this state the vision of the "spiritual-angelic realm." Yet, annihilation in the divine presence is only a temporary state. It is like a state of drunkenness in which a person has lost his wits and no longer has a grasp of "objective" reality. Sometimes Sufis become lost in this state. They wander in town and countryside like holy fools, shocking more-sober believers with their unkempt appearance, cryptic sayings, and sometimes-outrageous behavior. In Sufi parlance, these holy fools are "attracted" (*majdhub*) to God like iron to a magnet or like a moth to a flame. A permanent state of such drunkenness is a sign of ultimate failure on the way. The true master of the "*tawhid* of the elect" is the Sufi who has come back to his senses in a state of spiritual sobriety, whose experience of annihilation has transformed his heart so that the divine presence abides within him (*baqa'*) like an inner light. Whereas a holy fool fails to realize that the qualities of God are not God, the master of the divine presence knows that annihilation does not mean the passing away of man's being in God's being. Rather, it means the passing away of man's will in God's will. Only such a person is able to maintain himself continuously under God's guidance.

Institutional Sufism. The two centuries following the death of al-Junayd were a period of intense activity in Sufi circles. As with Sunni Islam in general, this period was characterized by the adoption of the *usul* approach to knowledge and a move toward *orthopraxy*, standardizing and systematizing the Sufi way on the basis of universally accepted principles. For Sufism, as for the rest of Sunni Islam, eastern Iran and Central Asia were the major centers of this activity. In the lands under Samanid control, Sufism became so popular that it amounted to another *madhhab*, or "school" of Islamic practice. The earliest Sufi manuals, which were all written in this region, tend to speak of Sufism as a separate and distinct intellectual discipline, much like Kalam or Falsafah. Al-Ghazali took this approach in his spiritual autobiography, *al-Munqidh min al-Dalal* (The Deliverer from Error). In this work, al-Ghazali contrasts Sufism with Kalam, Falsafah, and the doctrines of the Ismailis, portraying Sufism as a distinct school of thought that seeks to transcend the limitations of rationalism by combining formal study with guided spiritual disciplines and the "taste" of personal spiritual experiences. In his depiction of Sufism, al-Ghazali was strongly influenced by the doctrines of al-Muhasibi and al-Junayd. His previous reputation as a defender of Sunni Islam against the "heresies" of Falsafah and Shi'ism gave his opinions an aura of credibility that other Sufi writers were unable to match. Although his views on Sufi doctrine were not particularly profound when compared with those of his better-known Sufi predecessors, Al-Ghazali has justifiably earned credit for securing a place for Sufism among the formal disciplines of Sunni Islam. Largely because of the influence of *al-Munqidh* and al-Ghazali's multivolume masterwork, *Ihya' 'ulum al-din* (The Revival of the Religious Sciences), Sufism enjoyed a wide measure of acceptance among Sunni scholars until modern times.

Systematization of Doctrine. Al-Ghazali's generation was the last in which individual masters taught Sufism on a personal basis to small groups of disciples. Starting in the late tenth century, systematizers of Sufi doctrine, such as al-Sulami and his student Abu al-Qasim al-Qushayri (died 1074), began to produce a variety of written works for general Sufi audiences, including Sufi manuals, individual treatises on aspects of Sufi practice, and biographical accounts of famous Sufis. These works were designed to promote a commonality of doctrine and practice by differentiating "proper" Sufism from the more "heretical" varieties of mysticism. One of the most important of these works by al-Sulami dealt with the practice of *futuw-*

wah. The Arabic term *futuwwah* (young manliness) referred to organized groups of young men, headed by an older teacher known as a *shaykh* (old man, or elder), who met together on a regular basis to engage in spiritual exercises and develop a sense of mutual brotherhood. Sometimes, *futuwwah* groups lived together and wore distinctive clothing. As voluntary associations, they ran the gamut from Muslim street gangs to disciplined groups of Sufi adepts. Al-Sulami's *Kitab al-Futuwwah* (Book of Futuwwah) showed how the organizational aspects of *futuwwah* might be incorporated into Sufism.

Institutionalization. Coincident with the occupation of Baghdad by the Saljuk Turks in the mid eleventh century, the *futuwwah* phenomenon spread from eastern Iran and Central Asia to Iraq. There the combination of *futuwwah* organizational principles and Sufi doctrine led to the creation of a new institutionalized form of Sufism. Formerly known as a *ta'ifah* (faction) but now more often called a *tariqah* (way), this new institution comprised a corporately self-defined group of Sufis that adhered, more or less exclusively and over several generations, to the transmitted doctrines of an individual Sufi teacher and his appointed successors. Because an individual Sufi teacher could appoint several successors to disseminate his doctrines in different regions, the new phenomenon of "*tariqah* Sufism" led to the first international Sufi orders. Named after their founding teachers, these orders sometimes had a life span of centuries, and in many cases they spread throughout all regions of the Muslim world. The first international Sufi order to develop was the Qadiriyyah *tariqah*, named after 'Abd al-Qadir al-Jilani (died 1166), a Hanbali preacher and Sufi from Baghdad. Within two generations after his death, 'Abd al-Qadir's successors had founded branches of the Qadiriyyah in Arabia, Yemen, Syria, and Egypt. The Qadiriyyah is still the most widespread Sufi order in the world, with affiliated groups in nearly every Muslim country from Morocco to Malaysia. Other major international Sufi orders include the Rifa'iyyah, named after the Iraqi Sufi Ahmad al-Rifa'i (died 1183) and the Shadhiliyyah, named after the North African Sufi Abu al-Hasan al-Shadhili (died 1258).

Sources:

Ali Hassan Abdel-Kader, *The Life, Personality, and Writings of al-Junayd: A Study of a Third/Ninth Century Mystic* (London: Luzac, 1976).

Tor Andrae, *In the Garden of Myrtles: Studies in Early Islamic Mysticism*, translated by Birgitta Sharpe (Albany: State University of New York Press, 1987).

Vincent J. Cornell, *The Way of Abu Madyan: Doctrinal and Poetic Works of Abu Madyan Shu'ayb ibn al-Husayn al-Ansari (c. 509/1115-16–594/1198)* (Cambridge: Islamic Texts Society, 1996).

Cornell, "The Way of the Axial Intellect: The Islamic Hermetism of Ibn Sab'in," *Journal of the Muhyiddin Ibn 'Arabi Society*, 23 (1997): 41–79.

Carl W. Ernst, *The Shambhala Guide to Sufism: An Essential Introduction to the Philosophy and Practice of the Mystical Tradition of Islam* (Boston & London: Shambhala Publications, 1997).

Richard M. Frank, *Al-Ghazali and the Ash'arite School* (Durham, N.C. & London: Duke University Press, 1994).

Abu Hamid al-Ghazali, *Deliverance from Error: Five Key Texts Including His Spiritual Autobiography, al-Munqidh min al-Dalal*, translated by R. J. McCarthy (Louisville, Ky.: Fons Vitae, 2001).

al-Ghazali, *The Incoherence of the Philosophers*, translated by Michael E. Marmura (Provo: Brigham Young University Press, 1997); also translated by Sabih Ahmad Kamali as *Al-Ghazali's Tahafut al-Falasifah (Incoherence of the Philosophers)* (Lahore: Pakistan Philosophical Congress, 1963).

'Ali ibn 'Uthman al-Hujwiri, *The Kashf al-Mahjub: The Oldest Persian Treatise on Sufism*, translated by Reynold A. Nicholson (London: Luzac, 1976).

Abd al-Rahman Ibn Khaldun, *The Muqaddimah: An Introduction to History*, translated by Franz Rosenthal, edited by N. J. Dawood (Princeton: Princeton University Press, 1967).

Ibn Rushd, *Averroës' Tahafut al-Tahafut (The Incoherence of the Incoherence)*, 2 volumes, translated by Simon van den Bergh (London: Luzac, 1954).

Majid Khadduri, *Al-Imam Muhammad ibn Idris al-Shafi'i's al-Risala fi Usul al-Fiqh: Treatise on the Foundations of Islamic Jurisprudence* (Cambridge: Islamic Texts Society, 1987).

Louis Massignon, *Essay on the Origins of the Technical Language of Islamic Mysticism*, translated by Benjamin Clark (Notre Dame: Notre Dame University Press, 1997).

Annemarie Schimmel, *Mystical Dimensions of Islam* (Chapel Hill: University of North Carolina Press, 1975).

Margaret Smith, *An Early Mystic of Baghdad: A Study of the Life and Teaching of Harith b. Asad al-Muhasibi, A.D. 781–857* (London: Sheldon Press, 1977).

Abu 'Abd al-Rahman al-Sulami, *The Book of Sufi Chivalry: Futuwwah, Lessons to a Son of the Moment*, translated by Sheikh Tosun Bayrak al-Jerrahi al-Halveti (New York: Inner Traditions International, 1983).

Al-Sulami, *Early Sufi Women: Dhikr an-niswa al-muta'abbidat as-sufiyyat*, translated by Rkia Elaroui Cornell (Louisville: Fons Vitae, 1999).

SIGNIFICANT PEOPLE

ABU HAMID MUHAMMAD AL-TUSI AL-GHAZALI

1058-1111

PHILOSOPHER

Early Years. Abu Hamid Muhammad al-Tusi al-Ghazali was born in 1058 in Tus, near the present-day city of Mashhad in eastern Iran. He and his brother, Ahmad, were orphaned at an early age, but their father had directed a friend to help them get an education. Although the meager funds left for this purpose soon ran out, they were fortunate to live in a time when education for young people of humble origins was sponsored by many private foundations and by the Saljuk rulers of Iran. After acquiring a basic education, al-Ghazali studied throughout Iran, completing his studies in Nishapur, the site of a well-known Nizamiyyah religious college, where he studied under the renowned theologian Abu al-Ma'ali al-Juwayni.

Career. In 1085 al-Juwayni introduced al-Ghazali to the Saljuk wazir Nizam al-Mulk, and in 1091 al-Ghazali was appointed chair of Shafi'i law at the Nizamiyyah madrasah in Baghdad. He was well received there, and within a few years he became a prominent lecturer with hundreds of students. During this period he wrote several works, including his refutations of the Ismaili Shi'ites and the philosophers. Although he had attained great success, al-Ghazali was not satisfied, and on the pretense of making the hajj, he left Baghdad, renouncing his career as a jurist and theologian. In his autobiography he stated that he was disillusioned with the corruption among scholars, the dangerous political atmosphere in ruling circles, and the adulation that he feared might corrupt him. During his withdrawal from academic life, he lived in Damascus and Jerusalem. He became a Sufi, and he devoted himself to spiritual exercises, prayer, and meditation and became committed to the mystic way. He composed his greatest work, *Ihya' 'Ulum al-Din* (Revival of the Religious Sciences), during his retreat in Jerusalem. In 1106 the son of Nizam al-Mulk encouraged al-Ghazali to return to academic life. He began teaching once again, this time at the Nizamiyyah in Nishapur. There he wrote an autobiographical work called *al-Munqidh min al-*

Dalal (The Deliverer from Error). Shortly before his death in 1111, he returned to his native city of Tus, where he is said to have established a Sufi hermitage.

Writings. Al-Ghazali wrote several important works on theology in the Kalam tradition, as well as mystical treatises and works on ethics. Many of his writings were intended for general audiences. Certain of his books, such as the Persian-language *Kimiya-i saadeh* (Alchemy of Salvation), are thought to have been written on two levels: the apparent text, a straightforward essay on religious life, is believed to mask a hidden text that reveals mystical secrets. One of al-Ghazali's best-known works is *Tahafut al-Falasifa* (Incoherence of the Philosophers). This work is a Kalam critique of the philosophies of al-Farabi and Ibn Sina, in which al-Ghazali attempted to prove that the philosophers held many views that were both illogical and inconsistent with Sunni Islam. His masterwork, *Ihya' 'Ulum al-Din*, is a veritable encyclopedia of Sunni Islam. Written as a blueprint for attaining purification and progress along the spiritual path, it is also a statement against blind traditionalism and the sterility of religious knowledge wielded for worldly gain and prestige.

Sources:

Richard M. Frank, *Al-Ghazali and the Ash'arite School* (Durham & London: Duke University Press, 1994).

Abu Hamid al-Ghazali, *Deliverance from Error: Five Key Texts, including His Spiritual Autobiography, al-Munqidh min al-Dalal*, translated by R. J. McCarthy (Louisville, Ky.: Fons Vitae, 2001).

al-Ghazali, *The Incoherence of the Philosophers*, translated by Michael E. Marmura (Provo, Utah: Brigham Young University Press, 1997); also translated by Sabih Ahmad Kamali as *Al-Ghazali's Tahafut al-Falasifah (Incoherence of the Philosophers)* (Lahore: Pakistan Philosophical Congress, 1963).

MUHYI AL-DIN IBN AL-'ARABI

1165-1240

SUFI THEOLOGIAN

Career. Born in Murcia, Spain, Ibn al-'Arabi moved at a young age to the large Andalusian metropolis of Seville, where he received his education. At the age of eight, he experienced his first mystical vision, which eventually led him to seek out inspired Sufi shaykhs. After the year 1193, he traveled frequently between Spain and North Africa, until he set out for the East for good in 1202. Traveling via Egypt, he made the hajj pilgrimage to Makkah, where he stayed until 1204. He traveled around the Near East, visiting Syria, Iraq, and Turkey, where he settled at Malatya, circa 1215. Around 1220 he returned to Syria and settled in Damascus, dying there in 1240.

Writings. Ibn al-'Arabi wrote some four hundred works, of which many survive. Most of his works are short treatises, but a few are works of considerable length, especially *al-Futuhat al-Makkiyyah* (The Makkan Revelations). This multivolume masterwork of Sufi theology was begun in 1202 at Makkah, completed in Damascus in 1231, and revised 1233–1237. The *Futuhat* is an enormous encyclopedia of mystical and philosophical knowledge (comprising seventeen thousand pages in a modern critical edition). His controversial *Fusus al-hikam* (The Bezels of Wisdom), which discussed the inner wisdom of each of the Islamic prophets, was written in Damascus in 1232 and 1233. Ibn al-'Arabi also produced a book of mystical love poetry, *Tarjuman al-ashwaq* (The Interpreter of Desires), circa 1201–1213. This work was inspired by a Persian girl who was the daughter of one of his associates during his stay in Makkah.

The Greatest Master. Ibn al-'Arabi's deep Sufi thought has led his followers to describe him as "The Greatest Master." In all his teachings, he was careful to insist on strict practice of Islam according to the Qur'an and the Sunnah of the Prophet Muhammad. He taught that what can be learned through reason or the senses is extremely limited and that those with a special aptitude may journey to new levels of knowledge through another, more intuitive means. The ultimate goal of the Sufi way is the effacement of the self and the immediate knowledge of God, who cannot be defined in worldly language. God can be known only through enlightenment, which is attainable only through the Sufi path. Ibn al-'Arabi had a major impact on Islamic mystical thinking, but he was also quite controversial. Some Sunni doctors of the law accused him of harboring heretical ideas—in particular his claim that *al-Futuhat al-Makkiyyah* had been revealed to him in a dream.

Sources:
Claude Addas, *Quest for the Red Sulphur: The Life of Ibn 'Arabi*, translated by Peter Kingsley (Cambridge, U.K.: Islamic Texts Society, 1993).

Seyyed Hossein Nasr, *Three Muslim Sages: Avicenna, Suhrawardi, Ibn 'Arabi* (Cambridge, Mass.: Harvard University Press, 1964).

MUHAMMAD

CIRCA 570 - 632

THE PROPHET OF ISLAM

The Last Prophet. According to Islamic beliefs, Muhammad ibn 'Abd Allah ibn 'Abd al-Muttalib, also known as Prophet Muhammad, was the last prophet to receive revelation from God. He is so honored that Muslims, when they mention him, always pronounce a blessing.

Childhood. Muhammad was born into the Makkan tribe of Quraysh, as a member of the noble clan of Banu Hashim. The Makkans were custodians of the Ka'bah, a simple house of worship whose construction was attributed to the patriarch Abraham and which later was the source of the sacred status of Makkah in Arabia. The Quraysh were the traditional hosts of the annual pilgrimage to this sacred house. By the time of Muhammad, the Ka'bah had become the focus of idol worship. The Prophet's father, 'Abd Allah, died before Muhammad was born, and his mother, Aminah, died when he was a child. Muhammad was placed in the care of his grandfather 'Abd al-Muttalib, who took great pride in his grandson and kept him by his side. The death of 'Abd al-Muttalib, a prestigious man, a few years later was a blow to the entire clan. Muhammad was then taken into the care of his paternal uncle Abu Talib, a merchant of narrow means but broad generosity. The boy grew up with the favor of his uncle, looked after his family's flocks for a time, and learned the caravan trade by accompanying Abu Talib on his journeys.

Marriage. The wealthy Makkan widow Khadijah contracted Muhammad to manage her caravan business. Though much older and wealthier than Muhammad, she proposed marriage to him in about 595, and he accepted. For the next twenty-five years Muhammad and Khadijah were a devoted couple with four surviving daughters and two sons who died in infancy. Muhammad was recognized in Makkah for his good character and noble bearing. He supervised the reconstruction of the Ka'bah after a flood, averting through diplomacy a feud between clans over the placing of its cornerstone. He rejected the worship of idols.

Revelation of the Qur'an. Muhammad used to withdraw to the hills around Makkah in order to meditate. During one such retreat, in the lunar month of Ramadan in 610, when he was about forty years old, Muhammad experienced the first revelation of the Qur'an. The angel Jibril appeared to him on all four horizons and said: "Read! In the name of thy Lord who creates, creates the human being from a clot of blood. Read! Verily, thy Lord is the Most Bounteous, Who teaches by the pen, teaches the human being what he does not know" (Qur'an 96: 1-5). Worried that he might be insane, Muhammad returned to Khadijah, who took him to her Christian cousin, Waraqah. Waraqah reassured Muhammad of the truthfulness of the message and its divine source. When the revelations resumed, Muhammad was ordered to arise and warn (Qur'an 74: 2) the members of his family and tribe to believe in one God alone and to accept his prophethood. For the next thirteen years, he gathered the followers who became the first Muslims, in the face of increasing persecution by the leadership of Makkah. During this period, the revelation continued, constituting the Makkan surahs, describe the nature of God, the reward and punishment of the afterlife, the obligations of worship, and exhortations to help the weak and honor parents. After the deaths of Khadijah and 'Abu Talib in about 619, a plot by the Makkan clans to murder the Prophet caused him to flee to Yathrib, a city north of Makkah whose leading tribes had invited him and pledged to protect him.

The Hijrah. The migration, or Hijrah, of Muhammad and his followers to Yathrib, renamed Madinat al-Nabi (City of the Prophet), marks the beginning of the Islamic calendar in 622 C.E. An agreement drawn up between the Prophet and the resident tribes granted him leadership of the city and marked his ascendancy to political authority over the nascent Muslim state. He joined the Makkan migrants (Muhajirun) to the Muslims of Madinah (Ansar) in compacts of brotherhood. The revelations he received in Madinah are characterized by attention to arrangements and commands concerning the functioning of society and its internal and external relations. During the years at Madinah, Muhammad married several women, including 'A'isha ahd Hafsa, daughters of two prominent Companions. He also married widows and other women in order to cement alliances. Continuing to revere Khadijah's memory, he was known as a fair and affectionate husband to all his wives. In Madinah, Muhammad faced an all-out military and political assault by Quraysh, which forced him to become a diplomat and military leader. Following several battles and the acceptance of Islam by allied tribes, Muhammad returned to Makkah and accepted the city's surrender in about 630. The Prophet or his deputies led additional campaigns against outside threats in the Arabian peninsula. These campaigns helped to spread Islam across Arabia and brought Islam to the attention of regional powers.

Death. By the time of Muhammad's death in 632, the revelation of the Qur'an had been completed with a farewell pilgrimage to Makkah. Muhammad was buried in Madinah in the house-masjid complex where he died. This site is now called Masjid al-Nabawi. Since his death, Muslims have sought to pattern their lives according to his example, and the Prophet has been the subject of intense study by both Muslim and non-Muslim scholars over the centuries.

Sources:

Martin Lings, *Muhammad: His Life Based on the Earliest Sources* (Rochester, Vt.: Inner Traditions International, 1983).

Marmaduke M. Pickthall, *The Life of the Prophet Muhammad: A Brief History* (Beltsville, Md.: Amana, 1998).

RABI'AH AL-'ADAWIYYAH

CIRCA 714 - 801
SUFI SAINT

A Great Woman Saint. Rabi'ah al-'Adawiyyah, also known as Rabi'ah al-Qaysiyyah, was born in the second decade of the eighth century and died in her native city of Basrah in 801. Along with the well-known female ascetics and hadith transmitters Mu'adhah al-'Adawiyyah and Umm al-Darda', Rabi'ah was one of the three great woman saints of Basrah. Her tomb on the outskirts of Basrah was revered as a place of pilgrimage for centuries. Little objective information is available about Rabi'ah's life. She was a client (*mawlat*) of the Arab tribe of Adiyy ibn Qays, which adopted her and allowed her to use its name. In the Umayyad period, every convert to Islam had to be adopted by a member of an Arab tribe, which served as the convert's patron. Thus, Rabi'ah's relationship of clientage to this Arab tribe indicates that either she, or perhaps her father, was a convert. She may also have been a freed slave, but this information is found only in later sources.

Career. Rabi'ah was a noted ascetic and teacher. Her best-known students were the jurist Sufyan al-Thawri (715–778) and the hadith transmitter Shu'bah ibn al-Hajjaj (died 782). Sufyan relied on Rabi'ah extensively for her knowledge of *fiqh al-'ibadat*, the Islamic rules pertaining to worship. As a follower of the Basrah tradition of women's asceticism started by Mu'adhah al-'Adawiyyah, Rabi'ah practiced a spiritual method that stressed detachment from the world, absorption in the love of God, and inward and outward sincerity. She appears to have shared the Murjiite beliefs of Hasan al-Basri. Some of her statements can be read with more than one meaning. When asked whether she loved the Prophet Muhammad, she replied: "Truly I love him. But love for the Creator has turned me away from love for created things." This comment may mean that nothing came between Rabi'ah and her love for God, but it may also mean that the words of God in the Qur'an are more important than the words of the Prophet in the hadiths. Because Hanbali scholar Jamal al-Din ibn al-Jawzi (died 1201) wrote a book about Rabi'ah, now lost, entitled *Rabi'ah al-Mu'tazila*. This title may indicate that she withdrew from the world or that Ibn al-Jawzi thought she had Mu'tazilite sympathies.

Legendary Reputation. There are as many versions of Rabi'ah's legendary persona as there are accounts attributed to her. These accounts appear in the most-influential collections of Sufi biography. Farid al-Din al-'Attar (died 1220) portrayed her as a second Mary. Abu Nasr al-Sarraj (died 988) highlighted her as a model of Sufi knowledge. Abu Talib al-Makki (died 996) credited her with introducing the concept of divine love into Islamic asceticism. Hanbali scholars such as Ibn al-Jawzi accepted her because of her asceticism and otherworldliness. Abu 'Abd al-Rahman al-Sulami (died 1021) was the first to portray her as the quintessential Sufi woman and female saint. Some biographers, such as Ibn al-Jawzi, portrayed Rabi'ah as an antisocial recluse whose reactions bordered on hysteria. Others, such as al-Sulami, portrayed her as a perceptive and somewhat cynical critic of the world and human weakness. When Sufyan al-Thawri complained to Rabi'ah of his sorrows, she replied: "Do not lie! Say instead, 'How little is my sorrow!' If you were truly sorrowful, life itself would not please you." Accounts about Rabi'ah often confuse her with other Sufi women with similar names or from the same region. Some of her statements on love mysticism may actually have have been made by her servant and student, Maryam of Basrah, who died of a ruptured spleen while listening to a sermon on love. Rabi'ah is often confused with another Sufi woman,

Rabi'ah bint Isma'il, who lived in Damascus and died about fifty years after Rabi'ah al-'Adawiyyah. Rabi'ah bint Isma'il's tomb in Jerusalem is still thought to be that of Rabi'ah al-Adawiyyah, and many of her poems have been attributed to her Basran predecessor.

Source:
Abu 'Abd al-Rahman al-Sulami, *Early Sufi Women: Dhikr an-niswa al-muta'abbidat as-sufiyyat*, translated by Rkia Elaroui Cornell (Louisville, Ky.: Fons Vitae, 1999).

JALAL AL-DIN RUMI

1207-1273

SUFI POET AND THEOLOGIAN

Career. Jalal al-Din Rumi was born in Balkh in northwestern Afghanistan and migrated with his father to present-day Turkey around 1217. In 1229 he settled in Konya, where he made his home for the rest of his life. His father, Baha' al-Din, was a religious scholar and a Sufi who wrote an important Sufi work, *al-Ma'arif* (Ways of Knowledge). After his father's death in 1231, Rumi became a disciple of Burhan al-Din Muhaqqiq, who had been one of his father's associates. By 1241 Rumi had become established as a scholar and Sufi shaykh in his own right. The inspiration for his Sufi poetry about the love of God came about through his meeting with another Sufi, Shams al-Din of Tabriz, whom Rumi regarded as his spiritual mentor. For three years Rumi and Shams were inseparable companions. When Shams fled to Damascus to escape the hostility of Rumi's followers, Rumi sent his son after him to plead for him to return (1246). In the following year, Shams disappeared. (A much later story claimed Shams was secretly murdered.) After Shams disappeared, Rumi continued to teach and lead his disciples and entered into his most fruitful period of literary production.

Writings. Rumi's writings consist mostly of two large poetic works: *Diwan-i Shams-i Tabriz* (The Collected Poems of Shams-i Tabriz), a collection of Persian mystical poems totaling more than forty thousand lines, and *Mathnawi-i ma'nawi* (Spiritual Couplets), a collection of poetic narratives totaling some twenty-six thousand lines. In his teachings and poems Rumi always remained loyal to the normative practices of Islam and never favored deviation from the law. Rumi's sense of loneliness and desolation after the disappearance of Shams led him at the same time to emphasize total, selfless love of God. In his writings the fire of spiritual passion burns away the arrogance of the self, until the self is no more, and the lover becomes identified with and one with the beloved, God. The achievement of this state is facilitated by the practice of *dhikr* (remembrance), which is done in a group and accompanied by music and dance. The latter-day followers of Rumi, the Mawlawis, or so-called Whirling Dervishes, may practice a more stylized form of dance than Rumi's followers did during his lifetime, but there is little doubt that he laid considerable emphasis on dance from the outset. Because of his love poetry, Rumi is popular with modern audiences. His translated works are among the best-selling works of poetry in the English language.

Sources:
Coleman Barks and others, trans., *The Essential Rumi* (San Francisco: Harper, 1995).

Afzal Iqbal, *The Life and Work of Muhammad Jalal-ud-Din Rumi* (Lahore: Institute of Islamic Culture, 1964).

Franklin D. Lewis, *Rumi Past and Present, East and West: The Life, Teaching and Poetry of Jalal al-Din Rumi* (Oxford & Boston: Oneworld, 2000).

Reynold A. Nicholson, trans., *The Mathnawi of Jalalu'ddin Rumi*, 8 volumes, edited by Nicholson (London: Luzac, 1925–1933).

Nicholson, trans., *Rumi, Poet and Mystic, 1207–1273: Selections from His Writings* (New York: S. Weiser, 1974).

DOCUMENTARY SOURCES

Abu Nasr al-Farabi (circa 870 – 950), *Mabadi' ara' ahl al-madinah al-fadila* (Principles of the Beliefs of the Inhabitants of the Virtuous City) — An exposition of the author's philosophical principles and his master-work of political philosophy.

Abu Hamid al-Ghazali (1058–1111), *al-Munqidh min al-Dalal* (The Deliverer from Error) — A spiritual and intellectual autobiography, or confession as it is sometimes called, that grew out of a period of spiritual crisis in which al-Ghazali explored issues of knowledge and certainty, as well as the connection between the soul and the intellect.

Al-Ghazali (1058–1111), *Tahafut al-Falasifah* (The Incoherence of the Philosophers) — A work that criticizes philosophy, with the intent of defending theology against rationalism; Ibn Rushd later wrote a refutation called *Tahafut al-Tahafut* (The Incoherence of the Incoherence).

'Ali ibn 'Uthman al-Hujwiri (died after 1072), *Kashf al-Mahjub* (Unveiling of the Veiled) — The earliest comprehensive treatise on Islamic mysticism, or Sufism, which describes the means to achieve unity with the divine as separating oneself from the attractions of earthly life.

'Abd al-Rahman ibn Khaldun (1332–1406), *Kitab al-'Ibar, Muqaddimah* (The Book of World History, Introduction, 1377) — An important discussion of the philosophy and methodology of history and sociology, which includes a critique of the Falsafah tradition.

Abu al-Faraj Ibn al-Nadim (tenth century), *al-Fihrist* (Index) — A bibliography of Arabic works written during the first four centuries of Islam; based on Ibn al-Nadim's knowledge as a bookseller and on extensive research, including perhaps at the khalifal library in Baghdad; many of the works listed are no longer extant.

Ibn al-Rawandi (died 910), *Fadihat al-Mu'tazila* (The Disaster of the Mu'tazila) — A refutation of al-Jahiz's defense of the Mu'tazila movement, which emphasized the existence of free will rather than predestination, by a Shi'ite political activist and critic of the rational foundation of polemics in Islam.

Abu al-Walid Muhammad ibn Rushd (1126–1198), *Bidayat al-Mujtahid* (The Distinguished Jurist's Primer) — A significant work of classical Muslim jurisprudence that systematically discusses the differences among the schools of Islamic law, as well as the application and practice of the law.

Ibn Rushd (1126–1198), *Fasl al-maqal fima bayna al-shari'ah wa-al-hikmah min al-ittisal* (The Decisive Discourse and Affirmation of the Connection between Shari'ah and Philosophy) — A legal work describing the relationship between philosophical knowledge and knowledge based on revelation, in which Ibn Rushd portrayed philosophy as a demonstrative science based on a sound methodology.

Ibn Rushd (1126–1198), *Tahafut al-Tahafut* (The Incoherence of the Incoherence) — A reply to al-Ghazali's critique of the Falsafah tradition, in which Ibn Rushd argues for the validity of philosophy.

Qadi 'Abd al-Jabbar (died 1024), *Kitab al-usul al-khamsah* (Book of the Five Principles) — A work on the teachings of the Basrah school of Mu'tazilism, which argues that reason is the most important evidence for the existence of God because the validity of the other forms of evidence (the Qur'an, the Sunnah of the Prophet Muhammad, and the consensus of the Muslims) is based on the rational knowledge that God exists, that He is truthful, and that He would not deceive His creatures.

Abu 'Uthman al-Jahiz (circa 776 – 869), *Fadilat al-Mu'tazila* (The Excellence of the Mu'tazila) — A defense of the Mu'tazila religious doctrines that were the official theology of the Abbasid khilafah from 833 until 850.

Abu al-Qasim al-Junayd (died 910), *Kitab al-Fana'* (Book of the Annihilation of the Self) — A discussion of the path to unity with the divine through the struggle to overcome the self, preferring what cultivates awe of Allah rather than engagement in theological disputations about the nature of Allah carried on within the tradition of kalam.

Abu al-Ma'ali al-Juwayni (1028–1085), *Kitab al-irshad ila qawati' al-adilla fi usul al-i'tiqad* (The Guide to the Cogent Proofs of the Principles of Faith) — A detailed account of al-Juwayni's theological principles as an Ash'arite theorist, in which he discusses the omnipotence of God as an argument against rationalism and Mu'tazilite ideas.

Abu Mansur Muhammad al-Maturidi (died 944), *Kitab al-Tawhid* (Book of the Unity of God) — A refutation of Mu'tazilite ideas and affirmation of the omnipotence of God, by one of the foremost Imams of the Sunni *mutakallimun* (practitioner of [the written or oral debate] of kalam).

Shaykh al-Mufid (948–1022), *Kitab al-Irshad* (Book of Guidance into the Lives of the Twelve Imams) — An important statement of Shi'i belief that names the twelve Shi'i Imams and describes their virtues and the circumstances of their deaths up to the disappearance of the last Imam.

Shams al-Din 'Abd Allah Muhammad al-Muqaddasi (circa 945 – circa 990), *Ahsan al-Taqasim fi Ma'rifat al-Aqalim* (The Best Divisions for Knowledge of the Regions, 985) — A geographic work based on the author's twenty-year journey in regions where Muslim religious and political institutions were dominant; the work also documents the intellectual activity of places he visited.

Muhammad ibn Idris al-Shafi'i, *al-Risalat fi al-Fiqh* (Treatise on the Foundations of Islamic Jurisprudence) — The first systematic work on legal methodology in Islam.

Abu 'Abd al-Rahman al-Sulami (died 1021), *Dhikr an-niswa al-muta'abbidat as-sufiyyat* (Early Sufi Women) — The earliest known work in Islam devoted entirely to women's spirituality; written by a Persian Sufi, it portrays eighty Sufi women who lived in central Muslim lands in the eighth and eleventh centuries; the book provides evidence that women served as spiritual masters, respected teachers, and guides, demonstrating their understanding of Sufi doctrine, the Qur'an, and Islamic spirituality.

Al-Sulami (died 1021), *Kitab al-Futuwwah* (Book of Futuwwah) — A work on Sufi chivalry, or the personal qualities of *futuwwah,* and the *malamitiyya,* a Sufi order following "the way of blame," of which the author's father was a member; the work includes a large catalogue of given names.

Al-Walid II (ruled 743–744), Letter to his Provincial Governors — A letter by an Umayyad khalifah advancing the theological notion that God appointed the khalifahs as his deputies to administer the legacy of the prophets; the letter is one of many by various khalifahs to their appointees that document khalifal policies and the political, intellectual, and spiritual ideas that underpinned them.

CHAPTER TEN

SCIENCE, TECHNOLOGY, AND HEALTH

by KARIMA DIANA ALAVI

CONTENTS

CHRONOLOGY
400

OVERVIEW
403

TOPICS IN SCIENCE, TECHNOLOGY, AND HEALTH

The 'Alim and
Muslim Science 405

The Qur'an and the Pursuit
of Knowledge 405

Astronomy 407

The Gregorian Calendar 408

Botany 409

Cartography and
Navigation 411

Chemistry 413

Cultural Exchange 414

Mathematics 415

The Legacy of the Banu Musa . . 417

Mechanics 418

Medicine and Health 419

Al-Tasrif 421

Military Advances 424

Mineralogy and Geology 426

The Muslim
Agricultural Revolution . . 426

Optics and Ophthalmology . . 428

Technology 429

Arab Paper 429

From East to West:
A Crusader-Era Treaty . . . 432

Zoology 432

SIGNIFICANT PEOPLE

Jabir ibn Hayyan 434

Abu Bakr Muhammad
ibn Zakariya al-Razi 435

Nasir al-Din al-Tusi 435

DOCUMENTARY SOURCES
436

Sidebars and tables are listed in italics.

750
- The Abbasid dynasty moves the center of the Muslim khilafah (caliphate) to the east, where they establish the city of Baghdad.

751
- At the Battle of Talas River, the Muslim army defeats the Chinese army and, according to some accounts, acquires the technology of paper manufacture from Chinese captives.

770
- Al-Khawarizmi, who is credited with the invention of al-jabr (algebra), is born in Baghdad. During his lifetime, he also writes about geography and the links between mathematics and time.

786-809
- During his reign Khalifah (Caliph) Harun al-Rashid contributes to the development of high-court culture in Baghdad and establishes a diplomatic relationship with Charlemagne, ruler of the Holy Roman Empire in western Europe.

800*
- Jabir ibn Hayyan (circa 721 – circa 815), the "Father of Chemistry," is credited with many inventions that lay the foundation of modern scientific experimentation. Other Arab alchemists also contribute to the development of the scientific method for controlled and recorded experimentation.

809
- The first public hospital is established in Baghdad and is soon followed by similar institutions of healing and teaching in other Muslim cities. The physicians and pharmacists at these hospitals are licensed by the government.

830
- During his reign Khalifah al-Ma'mun creates the Bayt al-Hikmah (House of Wisdom) in Baghdad and brings some of the greatest scholars in the world to his magnificent round capital city to collect and translate precious ancient manuscripts.

860*
- Astronomer and geographer al-Farghani learns how to identify one's location by calculating latitude and longitude and becomes the first scientist to discover that planets travel on elliptical, rather than circular, paths.

864
- Al-Razi is born in Persia (present-day Iran). The author of 184 books and considered the greatest medieval physician, he is the first to differentiate between smallpox and measles.

* DENOTES CIRCA DATE

936
- Al-Zahrawi is born near Córdoba, in Muslim Spain. Known as the "Father of Modern Surgery," he writes textbooks that describe surgical procedures and the tools needed to conduct them. He is also an expert in oral surgery and dentistry.

- Ibn Sina (known in the West as Avicenna) is born in Persia. His *al-Qanun fi al-tibb* (Canon of Medicine) is thought to be the most widely read medical book in history.

1000*
- Pope Sylvester II becomes a strong proponent of translating Islamic and Arabic texts for use in the Latin world. His use of Arabic, instead of Roman, numerals becomes the subject of a scandal.

1017
- Geographer and geologist al-Biruni is captured as a prisoner of war by Sultan Mahmud of Ghazna, who appoints al-Biruni to the post of royal geographer. His *Tahqiq al-Hind* (Facts about India, circa 1030) is the first text to describe the geography and people of an entire subcontinent.

1085
- The Muslim city of Toledo falls to the Catholic armies of northern Spain. Its library is saved in the battle, and European scholars begin visiting the city to translate the Arabic manuscripts they discover in the library.

1120*
- European scholars flock to the regions of Spain that have fallen to the armies of the Christian Reconquista and start the long process of translating Muslim scientific texts into Latin and Hebrew, creating enormous changes in the curriculum of European universities. Latin translations of al-Khawarizmi's books by British philosopher Adelard of Bath and later by Italian scholar Gerard of Cremona become standard mathematics textbooks in Europe.

1201
- Nasir al-Din Tusi is born in Khorasan. A mathematician, astronomer, philosopher, theologian, and physician, he makes major corrections to the writings of the Greek scholar Ptolemy and expands the field of mathematical astronomy with his own discoveries.

1236
- The Muslim city of Córdoba falls to Christian armies of northern Spain.

1248
- The Muslim city of Seville falls to Spanish Christian forces.

* DENOTES CIRCA DATE

1252-1284	• During his reign Alfonso X (the Wise), ruler of the Spanish Christian kingdoms of Castile and Léon, encourages the translation and dissemination of knowledge from Arabic sources.
1258	• After Baghdad is devastated by Mongol armies, the Muslim cities of Spain become the new centers of Muslim scholarship.
1479	• Isabella of Castile inherits her father's throne, uniting her kingdom with that of her husband, King Ferdinand of Aragon. The united armies of these two Spanish Catholic kingdoms move south to continue the Reconquista.
1492	• Granada, the last Muslim stronghold in Spain, is defeated by the armies of Isabella and Ferdinand, bringing an end to Islamic rule in Andalusia, or southern Spain.

* DENOTES CIRCA DATE

A Muslim cavalryman firing a blunderbuss in an illumination of a battle scene from a 1493–1494 manuscript for the *Shahnameh* (Book of Kings) by Abu'l Qasim Firdawsi (Vever Collection, Arthur M. Sackler Gallery, The National Museum of Islamic Art, Smithsonian Institution, Washington, D.C.)

OVERVIEW

Religion and Science. One of the greatest challenges that humanity has faced is finding a balance between religious faith and science. Learned men and women of the ancient civilizations of China, the Middle East, and Africa all asked if those things that everyone experiences (such as life, death, natural phenomena, and disease) could be explained by religious beliefs or by scientific study and exploration. In the Western tradition ancient Greek philosophers such as Aristotle asked the same question, and people continue to do so today. The so-called Age of Reason or Age of Enlightenment in seventeenth-century Europe laid the foundation for the modern dependence on science to explain the world; but earlier scholars did not see science as separate from religion. Scholars within the Islamic and Judeo-Christian traditions often believed that their attempt to explain the world around them, even through scientific observation and study, was a religious act; a way of understanding what God is trying to reveal to humanity about the nature of life. This sense of the connection between religion and science was the foundation of Muslim science until modern times. For this reason, even though early Muslim scientists often turned first to the teachings of ancient masters—such as the Greeks, Persians, Chinese, and Indians—every subject they studied had to pass the "acid test" of being in harmony with the beliefs of Islam, and any idea that failed was discarded as lacking Truth and being useless to humanity. Any area of scientific study had to serve both God and his creation in order for the scientist to pursue it.

The First Flowering. The ninth-century city of Baghdad was the crowning glory of the Abbasid dynasty, whose leader, al-Mansur, began building the city as its capital in 750. After Khalifah al-Ma'mun (ruled 813–833) founded the Bayt al-Hikmah (House of Wisdom) there in 830, this City of Peace attracted major scholars from all over the world to join the effort to summarize and expand all the knowledge they could gather. Jews, Christians, Buddhists, Zoroastrians, and Muslims were among the people who joined this effort. Their first aim was to gather as much ancient knowledge in one place as they could. Then they translated these texts and made corrections based on their own scientific observations. The same scholars also wrote original works, many of which have survived, either as orig-inal documents or as translations into languages such as Latin, Hebrew, French, Spanish, and English.

Muslim Contributions to Science. With encouragement from the Qur'an and the hadiths (or sayings and examples of the Prophet Muhammad)—as well as hefty financial incentives offered by royal sponsors—Muslim scientists set out to understand and explain their world as thoroughly as they possibly could. In the process, they made tremendous strides in fields such as mathematics, botany, geography, geology, technology, and medicine. Many of their discoveries have been credited to European Renaissance scholars, but in fact many of these later scientists were borrowing—at times almost verbatim—from Muslim texts that had been translated into European languages. Historians have attributed some important discoveries to the wrong people, and textbooks have perpetuated these errors through the centuries. For example, textbooks say that Italian Leonardo da Vinci was the first person to invent machines that would enable man to fly, but Ibn Firnas, a Muslim scientist in Spain, constructed and tested a flying machine seven centuries before Leonardo. Isaac Newton, a seventeenth-century English scholar, is often credited with discovering that white light is formed from a whole rainbow of colored light; yet, Muslim scientist Ibn al-Haytham made this discovery in the eleventh century. In medicine the seventeenth-century Englishman William Harvey is frequently said to have discovered that blood circulates and thought to have been the first to understand how the heart, arteries, and veins function; a Muslim scholar named al-Razi (865–925) accurately described the whole circulatory system, including details of the major and minor arteries and veins, as well as the function of heart valves.

The Spread of Muslim Knowledge. During the twelfth century, Latin translations of Muslim scientific works—as well as ancient texts that had survived only in Arabic translations—began to flood western European universities and became a major part of the curriculum. Ancient and new scientific knowledge fanned the imaginations of many European researchers. Because of the prevailing views on intellectual property at that time, it was normal for writers to use others' work, even verbatim, without attribution. Often scholars assumed that their readers (almost exclusively other scholars) would be aware of the existing body of knowledge in their field and its origins. As a result, many scientific writings failed to acknowledge their debt to Greco-Arab science. Modern historians, however, have begun to acknowledge European scientists' debt to earlier Arabs and Muslims. During the first part of the medieval period, while Europe was still emerging from the so-called Dark Ages, Muslim scholars were not only preserving ancient knowledge but also making many important discoveries in science, medicine, and technology. As Philip Khuri Hitti has pointed out, "For centuries, Arabic was the language of learning, culture and intellectual progress for the whole of the civilized world with the exception of the Far East. From the ninth to the twelfth century there were more philosophical, medical, historical, religious, astronomical and geographical works written in Arabic than in any other human tongue."

Exchanges of Knowledge. The learning of the West and that of Muslim regions often crossed cultural and physical barriers. Some sharing of knowledge took place during the era of the Crusades (1095–1271) or during the pandemic of plague known as the Black Death in the mid fourteenth century. At other times people who were open-minded about cultures other than their own traveled to far-off lands to study and to share their own knowledge. Muslims were specifically encouraged to travel by their religious beliefs, which made it incumbent on all Muslims (male and female) to seek knowledge, even if they had to travel to China to get it. As early as the eighth century, Muslim rule had spread as far as China in the East and Spain in the West. This expansion of the Dar al-Islam (Abode of Islam) facilitated the diffusion of Muslim scholarship across the region. Muslim rulers in southern Spain developed large libraries that attracted some of the best scholars from northern Europe as well as Africa, the Middle East, and Asia.

The Destruction of Muslim Knowledge. Scholars will never know how many Muslim scientific texts have been destroyed by natural phenomena such as mold, dry rot, and worms and the man-made phenomena that accompany war and religious intolerance. Purposeful destruction of enormous libraries took place when the Mongols invaded Baghdad in 1258, when Europeans fought Muslims in the Crusades, and when the Spanish Christians took the Muslim cities of Andalusian Spain during the eleventh through the fifteenth centuries. In 1085 the city of Toledo fell to Christian armies. Córdoba fell in 1236 and Seville in 1248. The final blow to Islamic rule in Europe took place in 1492 when Granada fell to the armies of Isabella and Ferdinand, marking the end of Muslim rule in Spain.

The Transfer of Muslim Scholarship to Europe. Fortunately, not all conquerors destroyed libraries and private book collections. In fact, many Christian Europeans devoted their lives to the study of Arabic and the translation of Arabic texts into languages that could be understood by Westerners, particularly those who were attending the growing universities of Europe. As each Muslim city fell in Spain, European scholars flocked to their libraries and returned home with a wealth of knowledge. Muslims and Europeans alike owe a great debt to the people who were part of this massive transmission of scholarship to western Europe. Some of the people who helped in this process were members of the Christian Church hierarchy, such as Raimundo, who was archbishop of Toledo in 1124–1152 and established a school for translators of Muslim texts in that city, and Pope Sylvester II (reigned 999–1003), who was an excellent scholar of science and mathematics. The great theologian Thomas Aquinas, who quoted the Muslim scholar Ibn Rushd more than two hundred times in his writings, was a major link between Christian and Islamic philosophy.

European Translators. One of the first scholars to travel to Muslim libraries in search of knowledge was the English cleric Adelard of Bath, who during the early twelfth century traveled to Spain and translated important mathematical texts from Arabic into Latin. He was followed by other men such as Robert of Chester, Michael Scot, and Gerard of Cremona, who is perhaps the most important translator of Arabic texts into Latin. Gerard is said to have translated more than eighty works during the twelfth century. These same translations were printed in the fifteenth century and became a foundation on which the Scientific Revolution was built.

Royal Patrons. Some European rulers also participated in the study and transmission of Muslim scholarship to Europe. Roger II of Sicily (ruled 1105–1154) and a later king of that island, Frederick II (ruled 1197–1250), became so captivated with Muslim court culture that they wore long Arab robes, spoke Arabic, and continued the Muslim tradition of inviting scholars of all faiths to their courts. Other European rulers were so dismayed with their behavior that they called these men the "Baptized Sultans of Sicily." The Spanish ruler Alfonso X (the Wise) of Castile and León supported Muslim scholars and sought their help in his studies of astronomy and other sciences.

Book Burning. Other Christian Europeans, however, were eager to burn and destroy Muslim libraries. During the Spanish Inquisition of the late fifteenth and early sixteenth centuries, Muslims were subjected to forced conversions, expulsion, and torture under the direction of church leaders such as Inquisitor General Tomás de Torquemada and Cardinal Francisco Jiménez Cisneros, who during his tenure (1507–1517) ordered the forcible conversion of the Muslims of Granada. As part of their effort to expel or convert Muslims and eradicate their cultural influence from Europe, inquisitors burned thousands of books in city squares as crowds of excited onlookers cheered. Jewish and Christian scholars, as well as Muslims, were devastated by this destruction of ancient and new knowledge.

Survivals. During the twentieth century many libraries around the world began to discover that they had many Arabic manuscripts that had somehow survived through the centuries and awaited wider dissemination as Arabic printed books, as well as their first translation into a Western language. There are still more than 250,000 Arabic texts that no one has studied and translated, but scholars from all over the world are rising to the challenge.

TOPICS IN SCIENCE, TECHNOLOGY, AND HEALTH

THE 'ALIM AND MUSLIM SCIENCE

Faith and Science. Traditional Muslim culture is characterized by the interweaving of faith into every aspect of life, including government, economics, and scientific study. In fact, the first revelation of the Qur'an mentions reading, teaching (or proclaiming), and writing: "Read! In the name of thy Lord and Cherisher, who created man out of a mere clot of congealed blood. Proclaim! And thy Lord is Most Bountiful, He Who taught the use of the Pen, Taught man that which he knew not" (96: 1–5). The hadiths, or sayings and actions of the Prophet Muhammad, also encourage scholarship and scientific study, with words such as

Verily, the men of knowledge are the heirs of the Prophets.

Seek ye knowledge, from the cradle to the grave.

Those who leave home in the quest of knowledge walk the path of God.

Seek ye knowledge, even unto China.

A person who became a scholar in the Islamic tradition is called an *'alim*. Because studying is one of the religious obligations of all Muslims, male and female, the study of God's creation is considered a religious pursuit. As people gain an understanding of the world around them, it is assumed that they will also learn more about the interconnectedness of the physical world and how it is a reflection of the Divine. This sort of scholarship, which combines science and religion, is best exemplified by the Ikhwan al-Safa (Brethren of Purity), a tenth-century fraternity of intellectuals who lived in Basrah (in present-day Iraq) and produced a body of writings that were combined into fifty-two *Risalat* (Epistles). Their teachings summarized the knowledge of their time in virtually every field of scientific study, including zoology, medicine, agricultural technology, astronomy, and mathematics, which was their primary interest. Strongly influenced by the Pythagorean-Hermetic school of ancient Greek thought, they emphasized the metaphysical aspect of arithmetic and geometry, including number symbolism. In their treatise "The Metaphysical Significance of Unity and Multiplicity" the Brethren wrote: "Know, oh Brother (may God assist thee and us by His Spirit) that Pythagoras . . . . used to say 'The knowledge of

numbers, and of their origin from unity (which is before two), is the knowledge of the Unity of God, May He Be Exalted; and the knowledge of the properties of numbers, their classification and order, is the knowledge of the beings created by the Exalted Creator, and of His handiwork.'" The writings of the Brethren of Purity influenced the classification of plants and animals, the study of the properties of minerals, and ideas about the proper relationship between humans and the natural world, which the Brethren felt should always be in a state of harmony and balance.

Scientific Legacies. As Islam spread outward from the Arabian Peninsula, it came into contact with many cultures that also had long traditions of scholarship—including Greece, Persia, India, Africa, and China. As traveling Muslim scholars visited or settled in these regions, their influences were absorbed into Muslim thought. Because of the link between religion and science within Islamic thought, the more widespread Muslim civilization became, the more dedication its leaders showed to supporting the pursuit of knowledge. In fact, rulers competed to attract the

---

THE QUR'AN AND THE PURSUIT OF KNOWLEDGE

The Qur'an instructs Muslims to learn about God's creation in order to further their faith. Scientists drew particular inspiration from passages such as the following, which point to the wonders of the natural world as signs of God's mercy, majesty, and power.

It is He Who makes the stars as beacons for you, that you may guide yourselves with their help, through the dark spaces of land and sea. (6: 97)

And among His Signs, He shows you the lightning, By way both of fear, and of hope, and He sends down rain from the sky and with it gives life to the earth after it is dead: Verily in that are Signs for those who are wise. (30: 24)

Source: Yusif Ali, trans., *The Holy Qur'an* (Brentwood, Md.: Amana, 1989).

"The Author and His Attendants"; illumination from an 1287 Baghdad manuscript for the *Risalat* (Epistles) by the Ikhwan al-Safa (Brethren of Purity), tenth-century mystics and scientists (Suleymaniye Library, Istanbul)

greatest scholars, poets, musicians, and philosophers to their courts. Some members of the educated elite traveled during their careers from Africa to China in pursuit of great teachers, libraries, and rare manuscripts. During their travels they encountered peoples of many faiths and cultures who taught Muslims about science and literature while learning about the Islamic faith. The result was one of the greatest exchanges in history of religious, philosophical, and scientific ideas. As one modern scholar, Munir ud-Din Ahmed, has stated, "It seemed as if all the world from the Caliph down to the humblest of citizens suddenly became students. . . . In quest of knowledge, men traveled over three continents and returned home, like bees laden with honey, to impart the precious stores which they had accumulated to crowds of eager disciples."

The Bayt al-Hikmah. Before the rise of Islam there was already a tradition of gathering together great minds in an effort to consolidate the wisdom of the time with that of earlier cultures. Egypt, Greece, India, and Persia had all hosted great centers of learning. Yet, historians consider the Bayt al-Hikmah (House of Wisdom), established in 830 in Baghdad, the most significant of these centers because it linked together so many different traditions of ancient learning. Founded by the Abbasid dynasty in 750, Baghdad had become an important center of court culture, scholarly exchange, and world trade by the early ninth century, and because of its location at a major crossroads between the Chinese empire and the markets of the Middle East and Europe, it developed into one of the largest and most prosperous cities in the world during the centuries that followed. The city included the palace of the khalifah (caliph), many masjids (mosques), magnificent gardens, enormous libraries, hospitals, and public baths for a population of about one and a half million people. At that time the only city in the world that was larger was Xian, China, with about two million people. Barges from all over the known world made their way up the Tigris and Euphrates Rivers to Baghdad, bringing goods that eventually made their way, either by ship or land, to Africa, India, Central Asia, the Middle East, Spain, and northern Europe. Ships brought luxury goods such as silk, porcelain, spices, ivory, and gold to the great bazaar of Baghdad. From the overland trade routes came furs, jewels, perfumes, and frankincense. The gathering of merchants from the far reaches of several continents brought Baghdad a level of wealth seldom before attained. These riches were not only monetary but cultural as well.

Transfer of Knowledge. In 1258 Mongol invaders from the steppes of Central Asia conquered and laid waste to the city of Baghdad. So complete was their destruction that contemporary writers claimed nothing was left alive when the Mongols rode away from the smoldering ruins of that great city. Though most of the libraries in the city were lost, many scholars were able to flee Baghdad before the onslaught and copies of many of the destroyed books existed in other Muslim libraries. Some settled in Persia, Syria, or North Africa, but a large number of them fled to Muslim Spain, or al-Andalus (Andalusia), which had become a center of scholarship for western Muslim regions. Spain thus became the major conduit through which Muslim learning spread to western Europe. Even before that time, Arabic influences had permeated the Spanish language, and the Arab-Muslim art of refined living—including poetry, music, elegant textiles, and books—had permeated Spanish culture. As a result, the attitude of western Europe toward the Arabs had two contrasting elements: fear of Muslims as non-Christian "infidels" and admiration for the culture and intellect of Arab-Hispanic society, including its magnificent libraries and universities. The elite of Christian Europe sent their sons to Muslim universities in Spain to study the Arabic language as well as Muslim science and philosophy. As early as 854 Bishop Alvar of Córdoba was lamenting the fact that Europe's young male scholars were turning their backs on Latin and focusing on the study of Arabic. Later, Pope Sylvester II (reigned 999–1003) gained respect from some people (and criticism from others) for his important scholarship on Arabic science. By the twelfth century, scholars were flocking to Spain in search of Arabic manuscripts in the libraries of Muslim cities conquered by Christian rulers.

Muslim Influences. Traces of medieval Europeans' admiration for the high level of scholarship in Muslim culture are still apparent today. Degree recipients at college graduation ceremonies wear long black robes, and flat, square "mortarboard" hats. Some modern scholars believe that the robe was worn by scholars at early European universities because they equated the long, dark robe worn by Arab scholars with wisdom. The doctoral hood draped over the robe corresponds to the taylasan (hood) worn by Muslim jurists. Modern scholars have also suggested that the traditional mortarboard hat may represent the writing board used by Muslim students. When their teacher quizzed them, they had to put their boards on their heads so they could not cheat by looking at their notes. In some Muslim regions, young students of the Qur'an still sit at the feet of their teachers and write their lessons on these simple boards.

Sources:

Munir-ud-Din Ahmed, *Muslim Education and the Scholar's Social Status up to the 5th Muslim Era* (Zurich: "Der Islam," 1968).

Philip Khuri Hitti, *History of the Arabs*, tenth edition (New York: St. Martin's Press, 1974).

Seyyed Hossein Nasr, *Science and Civilization in Islam* (Cambridge, Mass.: Harvard University Press, 1968).

Francis Robinson, "Knowledge, Its Transmission, and the Making of Muslim Societies," in *The Cambridge Illustrated History of the Islamic World*, edited by Robinson (Cambridge: Cambridge University Press, 1996), pp. 208–249.

W. Montgomery Watt, *The Influence of Islam on Medieval Europe*. Islamic Surveys 9 (Edinburgh: Edinburgh University Press, 1972).

ASTRONOMY

Stargazers. Islamic religious beliefs and practices provide a particularly strong incentive for Muslims to study astronomy. All three Abrahamic faiths—Judaism, Christianity, and Islam—developed among tribal peoples who traversed the forbidding deserts. It is easy to get lost in desert terrain, and once lost, chances for survival are slim. For this reason pastoral peoples developed a thorough understanding of the stars as their most crucial navigational tool. One group in particular, the Sabaean stargazers, combined Greek tradition with ancient Babylonian learning in mathematics and astronomy. Later, Muslim scientists greatly respected the Sabaeans for their advanced knowledge of the heavenly bodies and studied their works closely. Muslim astronomers also had access to the knowledge of the Persian and Indian scholars who had studied at Jundi-Shapur in Persia. When the Abbasids moved the center of Muslim rule to Baghdad in the eighth century, the city planners turned to Indian astronomical sources to help them position the city in a way that would bring it the most auspicious blessings. The first official astronomer under the Abbasids was Muhammad al-Fazari (died 777). Shortly before his death, he brought Indian scholars to Baghdad to teach science and assist with the translation of manuscripts into Arabic.

Religious Calculations. The stars were important to Muslims for religious as well as practical reasons. The Qur'an calls the stars, the sun, and the moon signs of God's mercy. Because Muslims saw the navigational help offered by the stars as a symbol of the guidance offered by God, they were inspired to reflect upon the movement of the heavenly bodies. According to the Qur'an, God "has made subject to you the night and the day, the sun and the moon and the stars are in subjection by His command. Verily in this are signs for men who are wise" (16: 12). Muslims also used heavenly bodies for calculations that helped them perform their religious duties. They needed accurate computations of times for the five daily prayers and fasting, and they needed to establish the calendar for each lunar year so they could calculate the correct times for religious observances such as the Ramadan fast and the hajj (pilgrimage) to Makkah. For this reason, Muslim scholars analyzed the phases of the moon in great detail, plotted the movements of the planets, and developed elaborate zij (star charts). In addition to their use in determining the dates and times for religious activities, these calculations aided navigation.

The House of Wisdom. After 830, when Khalifah al-Ma'mun built the Bayt al-Hikmah (House of Wisdom) in Baghdad and brought scholars to his city to develop Islamic sciences, Muslim astronomers began to rely less on Indian traditions and turned toward the Greeks as the foundation for their studies. One of the first original calculations made by a team of Muslim astronomers was the height of the meridian of the sun (the point at which it reaches its highest altitude) near Mosul, in present-day Iraq. They measured it as 111,814 meters. Modern scientists have found it to be 110,938 meters—a difference of 876 meters, or about

As people gained a deeper understanding of how mathematics and astronomy could be used to determine time, they were able to create more-accurate calendars. Some of the earliest calendars, such as those employed by the Sumerians and Egyptians, were based on the phases of the moon. In Western Europe a solar calendar, the Julian Calendar, first introduced by the Romans, was in use until the late 1500s. Under this particular system, the year is too long by 11 minutes, 14 seconds, an excess that amounts to almost 1.5 days every two centuries and seven days every one thousand years. As a result, by 1545 the vernal equinox, which marked the first day of Spring (21 March) and was used in determining Easter, had moved ten days from its proper date.

In the sixteenth century Pope Gregory VIII decided to rectify the problem. He assembled church, civic, and scientific leaders to create a calendar that would definitively set the times and dates for church holidays and sacred observances. The Pope challenged those present to find the most accurate charts in the world that described the movement of the stars and planets in such detail that a calendar for all time could be set by their calculations.

Such charts were discovered in the manuscripts of Ulugh Beg, a fifteenth-century Tatar prince. Ulugh Beg ruled Samarkand in present-day Turkestan and he turned that city into a center of Muslim culture. He compiled *zij* (star charts) in an astronomical observatory built next to his mosque and palace in the 1420s; without the aid of a telescope, he mapped more than 1,220 stars.

The new calendar, which was developed from the *Zij,* is called the Gregorian Calendar. It is the one still in use today, but it needed a little "adjustment" when it was introduced because of the inaccuracies of the Julian Calendar. It was first put into use on the day after Thursday, 5 October 1582; that Friday became 15 October, which means that ten days were purposely omitted.

Source: *Grolier Multimedia Encyclopedia,* version 7.0 (New York: Grolier Electronic, 1995).

2,870 feet. Some time between 820 and 833, Muslim scientists also measured one degree of the meridian, which enabled them to calculate the circumference of the earth. Considerable effort also went to the development of observational instruments such as the astrolabe, the quadrant, and the armillary sphere, a model of the heavens with rings representing the paths of stars and planets.

Observatories. Also during the reign of al-Ma'mun, the Muslim tradition of building elaborate astronomical observatories began. There were already observatories in other regions, such as India, and, as their influence and rule spread, the Muslims built impressive facilities in various parts of the Middle East. Shiraz, Iran, had an observatory by the tenth century, Cairo and Ghazna by the eleventh, and the magnificent observatory of Samarqand was built during the rule of Ulugh Beg (1447–1449).

Ptolemaic Foundations. Muslim scholars focused much effort on translating the works of Ptolemy, the second-century Greek master of astronomy, as well as correcting his mistakes and expanding on his foundation of astronomical knowledge. They called this revised and expanded work *Al-Majisti* (The Majesty), and it became one of the primary vehicles through which Ptolemaic astronomy was transmitted to western Europe, where the work became known as the *Almagest.*

Early Muslim Discoveries. Much astronomical research had been done between the time of Ptolemy and the rise of Islam. Using the Indian and Greek sciences as the basis of their studies, Muslims soon began to develop their own astronomical theories. They wrote about the heavenly spheres, planetary motions, the distance and size of planets, and the relationship between mathematics and time—all sophisticated topics of study. By the ninth century several notable scientists were contributing to Muslim astronomy, including al-Khawarizmi and al-Farghani. Best known for his development of algebra, al-Khawarizmi developed astronomical tables (or charts of the stars) that influenced Muslim and European scientists for centuries. Around 820–833, al-Farghani participated in the project of determining one degree of the meridian and then used that information to accurately measure the diameter of the earth. He also calculated the size and distance from the earth of each planet, and he was the first person known to have realized that planets travel on an elliptical, rather than circular, path. His *Kitab fi'l-harakat al-samawiyyah wa jawami 'ilm al-nujum* (Principles of Astronomy) laid the foundation for later Muslim scientific works, and after Gerard of Cremona translated the work into Latin in the twelfth century, it strongly influenced European astronomical sciences. One of al-Farghani's contemporaries was al-Battani, whom some historians consider the greatest of all Muslim astronomers. Known for the accuracy of his observations, he discovered that the apogee of the sun (the point of its greatest distance from the earth) had varied since the time of Ptolemy in the second century. This discovery led to another, the motion of the apsides of the sun (the line connecting its highest and lowest point from a specific spot on the earth). With this information, he determined that the movement of

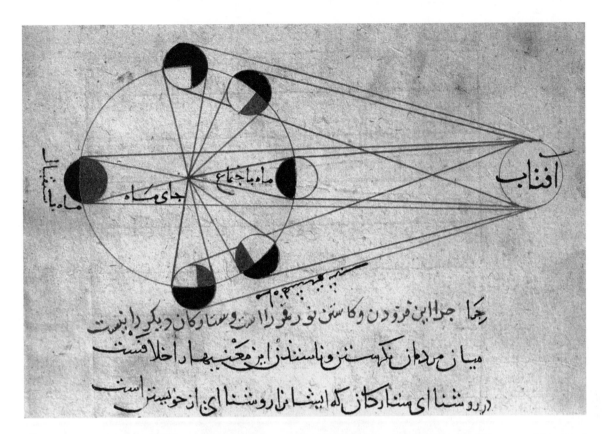

Al-Biruni's explanation of an eclipse of the moon; illumination from a manuscript for *Kitab al-tafhim* (Elements of Astrology),
written in the eleventh century (Majles Library, Tehran)

the sun changes by 54½ inches per year. Al-Battani also offered a scientific explanation for eclipses, which had been viewed as a sign of God's anger. During the eleventh century Muslim astronomers reached a new level of scholarship, particularly with the work of al-Biruni, whose determinations of longitude and latitude brought about major changes in exploration. Another high point was reached in the thirteenth century, when Nasr al-din al-Tusi led a team of scientists at the astronomical observatory in Maraghah, Persia. This team included some of the best scholars of the time, such as al-Shirazi, al-Maghribi, and a Chinese scholar named Fao-mun-ji. Their efforts included a planetary theory that brought previous astronomical discoveries into accord with the religious tenets of Islam.

Muslim Influences in the West. The discoveries and theories of Muslim astronomers astounded and influenced scholars not only in their own region but in Europe as well. For example, modern scholars have pointed out the close similarity of the lunar theory proposed by Copernicus in the sixteenth century to that of Ibn al-Shatir, a fourteenth-century Muslim astronomer, as evidence that Copernicus knew of the earlier astronomer's work. Early Muslim astronomers also influenced the scientific language of the West. Words such as *zenith*, *azimuth*, and *nadir* all have Arabic roots. The bright orange star in the shoulder of the constellation Orion was discovered by an Arab, who called it Bayt al-Jizya (House of Jizya)—which became Betelgeuse in English.

Sources:

Nafis Ahmad, *Muslim Contribution to Geography* (New Delhi: Adam, 1945).

Ahmad Y. al-Hassan and Donald R. Hill, *Islamic Technology: An Illustrated History* (Cambridge: Cambridge University Press / Paris: Unesco, 1987).

John R. Hayes, ed., *The Genius of Arab Civilization: Source of Renaissance,* third edition (New York: New York University Press, 1992).

Seyyed Hossein Nasr, *Islamic Science: An Illustrated Study* (London: World of Islam Festival Publishing, 1976).

BOTANY

Signs. The natural sciences of botany, geology, and zoology have held a central position in the Muslims' world-view, which sees all objects in nature as signs of God's mercy and majesty. The Qur'an encourages Muslims to reflect on the inner, religious meaning of nature and to live in harmony with the natural world: "By the sun and its glorious splendor; By the moon, as it follows the sun; By the day as it shows up the sun's glory; By the night as it conceals it; By the earth and its wide expanse; Truly he succeeds that purifies it, and he fails that corrupts it" (91: 1–10). Early Muslim manuscripts on natural history covered vast numbers of subjects. Some gave detailed descriptions of natural phenomena, while others took a symbolic and mythological outlook, but they all viewed nature as a source of wisdom beyond the merely scientific. One underlying theme of these writings was the idea that the natural world had an inner soul. This "World Soul" was divided into three parts: the Animal Soul, the Vegetative Soul, and the Mineral Soul. With this theory as a guide, Muslim scholars borrowed from Aristotle's work on the natural world, *De Anima*, and then expanded on its

دباعل بريان كنه ويربيشا ننه خورش سازه واستجان بيضه
داگوشت بيوشد و تكين كند درد سر داركه به باسرگ و
روغن گل صاحك و نيزروسن كرده اندنشانكار عدسى و خالها را
ازوشكاف رايرومركه كونيد ياپوست خوبن شنيد و
كرم كنه دعل وطلاسازند و كاه آب بيخته
مرمها و قراح وبا روغنها بلال
نافع بود ازحبت ما مدگى و منافع او
بسبارست
واقدا علم

Illuminations of an iris and a lily in a fifteenth-century manuscript for a Persian translation of *Materia Medica* by Dioscorides (Topkapi Museum, Istanbul)

scientific and philosophical aspects, placing it in an Islamic context.

Practical Uses. Muslims also studied plants for agricultural and medicinal purposes. The great chemist Jabir ibn Hayyan (circa 725 – circa 815) also wrote texts on botany and agriculture, setting an example that later scholars followed. From the ninth century onward, Muslim botany books listed, classified, and described each plant, explaining how it grows, discussing its medicinal uses, and at times indicating its religious importance.

Writings on Plants. The most influential ninth-century botany text is al-Dinawari's *Kitab al-nabat* (Book of Plants). In the tenth century the Ikhwan al-Safa (Brethren of Purity) wrote a book on the numerical symbolism of the various parts of plants, and how they fit into the total cosmic order, and in the eleventh century Ibn Sina (980–1037) dealt extensively with the healing nature of plants as well as the philosophy of botany, in his *Kitab al-shifa'* (Book of Healing). Al-Baghdadi (died 1164) wrote *Kitab al-i'tibar* (The Eastern Key), a treatise on the plants of Egypt. During the twelfth and thirteenth centuries, Muslims in Spain also produced some major works on botany, mainly agricultural and pharmaceutical manuscripts. These works identi-

fied the flora of the western part of the Muslim region and systematized the study of them. By the fourteenth century the Muslims' botanical knowledge was so extensive that their works became nearly "encyclopedic" in nature. Ibn al-Athir's *Tuhfat al-'aja'ib* (The Gift of Wonders) compiled the wisdom of earlier studies and included new discoveries.

Spiritual Meanings. Many Muslim scientists focused on the study of plants to further their spiritual understanding of the world around them. Plants are not only mentioned often in the Qur'an as signs of God's mercy to humankind, but they also figure prominently in Qur'anic descriptions of Paradise. In Islamic art, stylized plants can be found decorating the minaret of a masjid or the ceramic tiles that surround a prayer room. These works of art are meant to remind the viewer of the Qur'anic verses that point to plants as an integral part of God's creation. Persia and Muslim Spain became particularly well known for their elaborate gardens in which plants were chosen for their symbolic meanings to sophisticated viewers. Muslim music and poetry also used flowers and greenery as symbols of Paradise and love.

Sources:
Seyyed Hossein Nasr, *Islamic Science: An Illustrated Study* (London: World of Islam Festival Publishing, 1976).

Nasr, *Science and Civilization in Islam* (Cambridge, Mass.: Harvard University Press, 1968).

Andrew Watson, *Agricultural Innovation in the Early Islamic World* (Cambridge: Cambridge University Press, 1983).

CARTOGRAPHY AND NAVIGATION

Some historians have claimed that Arabs were desert travelers who were afraid to travel by sea. It has been well established, however, that long before the rise of Islam, seafarers from the Arabian Peninsula were shipping Arab wares to far-off lands. When one considers the geography of the region, it becomes obvious that areas that eventually came under Muslim rule were located at the hubs of several hemispheric trade routes that extended from northern Europe to China. Western historians tend to focus on trade across the Mediterranean Sea, but equally important trade routes departed from the Red Sea, the Gulf of Aden, the Arabian Sea, the Euphrates River, and the Indian Ocean.

Islam and Trade. Islam arose primarily in a mercantile, rather than a nomadic or agricultural, milieu, although some of the early adherents to the faith were members of nomadic Bedouin tribes of the region. The Prophet Muhammad was a merchant and managed caravans that traveled along the trade routes between Arabia, Palestine, and Syria. The Qur'an mentions trade and points out how God facilitates trade among Muslims and non-Muslims by providing the winds that carry ships to distant lands. By the end of the eighth century, Arab traders had well-developed sea routes to Baghdad, India, Madagascar, Ceylon, Indonesia, and China. The first Arab vessel arrived at Guangcho, China, around the year 787, and for the next five centuries the Arabs held a virtual monopoly on trade between China and the West. These merchants had continued the ancient tradition of following monsoon winds from Arabia to the Indian Ocean. The Arab-Muslim presence was so strong in Canton that the Chinese emperor appointed a Muslim official to govern the area and lead the Friday prayers at the local mosque, which is the oldest one in China. By tracing the production of Muslim coinage, historians have also documented Muslim mercantile activities northward from the Caspian Sea along the Volga River and into the southern regions of Finland, Norway, and Sweden. The Scandinavian traders set up trading posts that developed into commercial towns such as Kiev in present-day Ukraine. Here Arab merchants purchased European goods such as animal pelts, wax, leather, and Slavic captives (from which the English word *slave* is derived). Other words that have come into English from Muslim traders include *check, tariff, coffer, cipher, risk, traffic* (in the sense of distribution), and *magazine* (in the sense of storage facility).

Orienting Worship. In addition to the need for accurate means of plotting trade routes, there were strong religious foundations for the rapid development of geographic skills among Muslims. No matter where Muslims are in the world, they have to pray facing toward Makkah, and they need a good understanding of geography to do so. Also, all Muslims who have sufficient means are expected to make the pilgrimage to Makkah, and there was the concept within Islam of *Rihla fi talab al-'ilm* (Travel for the Sake of Knowledge), so there was a need for accurate maps.

Scientific Geography. Under the Abbasid dynasty, which moved the political center of Islam to Baghdad in the eighth century, geography began to develop as a science in Muslim culture. Scholars at the Bayt al-Hikmah (House of Wisdom) in Baghdad translated into Arabic the major astronomical text of India, the *Surya-siddhanta*. Muslims quickly mastered Indian and Persian geographic knowledge and then expanded on it, turning, in particular, to the works of the second-century Greek scholar Ptolemy. The Khalifah al-Ma'mun (ruled 813–833) supported the efforts of Muslim geographers to make a map of the world.

Sacred Geography. Early Muslim geography texts combined scientific geography with sacred, or symbolic, geography, making no sharp distinction between the two. In sacred geography, mountains, rivers, islands, and points of the compass were symbols of the celestial world. The earth was divided into seven different climate zones that corresponded with the belief that the celestial region had seven levels. Each climate was also connected to a planet and a zodiac sign.

Practical Geography. The writings of the ninth-century geographer al-Farghani (called Alfraganus in the West) were of practical use to travelers. Like his contemporaries among Chinese scholars, al-Farghani developed ways to determine location through the calculation of longitude and latitude. Christopher Columbus used al-Farghani's measurement of the length of the degree when planning the voyage on which he discovered the New World, and he quoted the Muslim scientist in his marginal notes in a fifteenth-century atlas now at the Biblioteca Colombina in Seville. Unfortunately, Columbus did not realize that the Arab mile in which the measurement was expressed was different from the Italian nautical mile he was using, and thus his calculations were inaccurate. The most important achievements in this field, however, were the work of al-Biruni (973 – circa 1050), who is credited with joining mathematics and geography in his *Tahdid nihayat al-amakin* (The Determination of the Coordinates of Cities). This book is still considered remarkably accurate, even when compared with maps based on satellite photographs and computerized measurements. Perhaps the greatest of all Muslim geographers, al-Biruni is well known for mapping Persia, Central Asia, and India. As the royal geographer to Sultan Mahmud of Ghazna, al-Biruni accompanied the sultan on military expeditions and became an expert on the peoples, cultures, and geography of India. His greatest achievement is probably his *Tahqiq al-Hind* (Facts About India, circa 1030), one of the earliest works of ethnography and regional geography.

Patronage. As Muslim Spain and Sicily lost territory to the Christians, several Christian rulers adopted the Muslim tradition of gathering renowned scholars at their courts and supporting their studies. The best known of

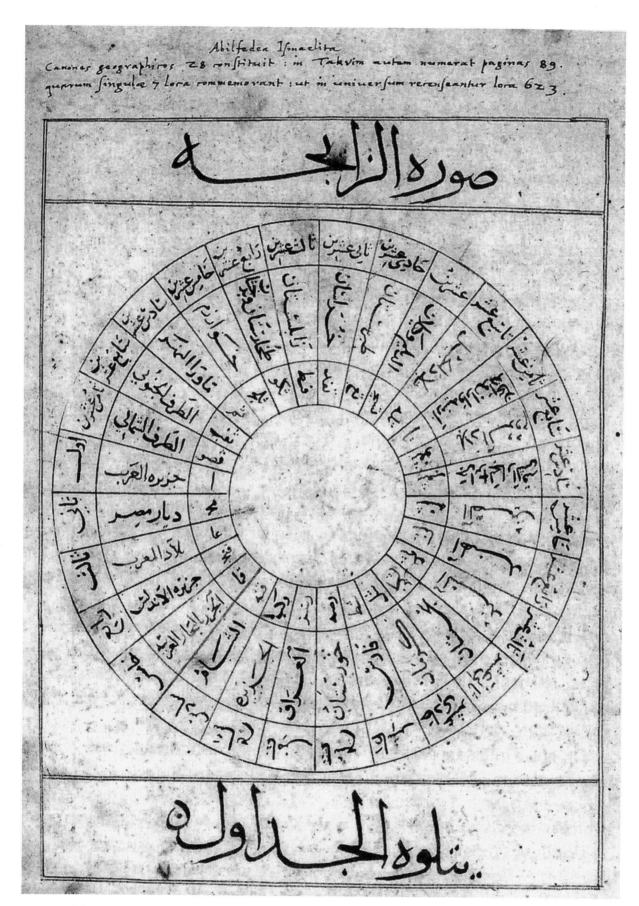

Diagram of the twenty-eight traditional divisions of the world; illumination from a manuscript, circa 1320, for a
work by Abu al-Fida (Vatican Library, Rome)

these Christian scholar-kings was the wealthy and powerful King Roger II of Sicily (ruled 1105–1154), who had studied under Greek and Arabic tutors as a youth. He invited Muslim scholars to join Jews and Christians at his court to work on translating and writing scholarly works. Practicing a lifestyle similar to that of Muslim courts, Roger wore Arab robes and often spoke in Arabic, causing concern among his fellow European monarchs, many of whom were involved in the Crusades against Muslims in the Holy Land. One of the Muslim scholars Roger invited to his court was the geographer al-Idrisi, who—in an effort to create the most scientifically accurate map—gathered together all the known geographic knowledge of their time. To assist al-Idrisi on his project, Roger formed the Academy of Geographers and brought in other scholars to help. This team of geographers began by distinguishing between fables and scientific knowledge—a difficult task at a time when travel to far-off places was arduous and time-consuming. Maps of the period were filled with warnings about dangerous monsters and bizarre creatures said to live in distant lands. The scholars of Roger's academy had to debate whether there really were humans with crocodile tails, females whose eyes could flash lightning, and people with dogs' heads who could rip someone apart. Deciding to create a physical, rather than "cultural," map of the world, al-Idrisi studied the writings of twelve earlier geographers, ten of whom were from the Muslim world. After fifteen years of effort, the final result was *Kitab al-Rujari* (The Book of Roger), the most important gathering of geographic knowledge up to that time. Al-Idrisi also presented King Roger with a three-hundred-pound solid silver disk bearing a map of the entire known world. Shortly after Roger's death, his court was attacked by Byzantine invaders. They melted down the silver disk to make weapons and burned the Latin version of the *Book of Roger*. Al-Idrisi managed to escape with the only remaining copy, written in Arabic, and the work was not translated into Latin again until the seventeenth century, when it caused great excitement in Europe.

Navigational Technology. Heading out to sea was a terrifying experience for ancient and medieval sailors, and history books are filled with stories of ships that became lost and never returned home. Muslim scientists devised several instruments to help mariners determine their location. Of these, the astrolabe is considered the most important. Like the sextant and the quadrant (another Muslim invention), the astrolabe can help the navigator determine his location by measuring the altitude of the stars, sun, moon, and planets, but the astrolabe can also be used to tell time, measure the height of a mountain, and determine latitude and longitude on land. Muslims also made maps of the sea called Portelan charts. Based on *zij* (star charts) made by Muslim astronomers, Portelan charts also included information about coastlines, tidal conditions, wind directions, weather conditions, and a map of the sea divided into squares of longitude and latitude. Muslim navigators also had compasses. It is uncertain when Muslim navigators first used

them at sea, but it is known that Muslim navigators transferred this technology to the West.

Sources:

Nafis Ahmad, *Muslim Contributions to Geography* (New Delhi: Adam, 1945).

Ahmad Y. al-Hassan and Donald R. Hill, *Islamic Technology: An Illustrated History* (Cambridge & New York: Cambridge University Press / Paris: Unesco, 1986).

David A. King, "Some Illustrations in Islamic Scientific Manuscripts and Their Secrets," in *The Book in the Islamic World*, edited by George N. Atiyah (Albany: State University of New York Press, 1995), pp. 149–177.

Seyyed Hossein Nasr, *Islamic Science: An Illustrated Study* (London: World of Islam Festival Publishing, 1976).

Nasr, *Science and Civilization in Islam* (Cambridge, Mass.: Harvard University Press, 1968).

CHEMISTRY

Alchemy. The English word *alchemy* comes from the Arabic word *al-chemi* (the change), which is also the root of the English word *chemistry*. The roots of alchemy can be traced to ancient cultures ranging from China to Egypt, where it developed from a mixture of religion, philosophy, and science. While modern people have often dismissed alchemy as an occult (or magical) pseudoscience, historians of science have come to realize that it was a serious form of scientific research. In fact, alchemists made important contributions to chemistry, medicine, and physics.

Scientific Method. Perhaps their most valuable contribution was what is now known as the scientific method, which was a revolutionary development when the Arab alchemists introduced it in the ninth century. Alchemists learned that by doing certain things to natural substances—such as mixing them, heating them, or distilling them—they could bring about changes in matter. The need to repeat such experiments in exactly the same way led to the development of the scientific method. For the first time Arab scientists began to keep detailed scientific records of the physical properties of such things as alum, sulfur, lime, glass, and metals. Scientists such as Jabir ibn Hayyan (circa 725 – circa 815), known in the West by the Latinized name Geber, and al-Razi (865–925), known in the west as Rhazes, wrote books on chemistry that were widely used by European scholars. These books described what happened when minerals were exposed to heat, air, or other chemical substances. Many of their discoveries had practical applications in areas as diverse as cosmetics (making perfumes by distilling the oils of flowers), pharmacy, ceramics, glass, glazes, textiles, and mining.

Equipment and Operations. Muslim alchemists developed equipment that enabled them to conduct controlled experiments. Some of their inventions, or improvements on earlier equipment, are still in use today, including the crucible, the alembic, and the retort. Their most significant invention was the furnace, which was described in many manuscripts. The anthanor, a special kind of furnace, has segments that represent certain parts of the human body. They made tremendous advancements in chemical operations such as distillation, filtration, calcination, crystallization, and the preparation of chemical compounds. Many of these compounds were used as medicine. For example, to make a medicinal herbal distillation, the alchemist boiled herbs and a small amount of liquid, collected the rising steam in a glass vessel, and sealed it. When the steam returned to a liquid state, the final product was a potent medication.

Metallurgy. Much of modern historians' knowledge about Muslim metallurgy comes from the writings of Muslim alchemists, whose careful observation and recording of process and results led to the development of methods for smelting, oxidation, liquidation, leaching, and amalgamation (combining metals). These alchemists did extensive studies on the characteristics of gold, silver, lead, tin, copper, brass, and steel. The knowledge derived from these experiments was put to use by medieval Muslim craftsmen, who created beautiful works of art, some of which are now in museums. In fact, Muslim decorative art reached one of its peaks in the medieval period with the inlaying of brass or bronze with silver, copper, and gold. Some of these finely wrought objects made by Arab craftsmen were taken to Europe by merchants and Crusaders.

Classification. Considered the founder of Islamic alchemy and the Father of Chemistry, Jabir ibn Hayyan began the long and tedious project of classifying the substances of the natural world. He divided them into three classes based on their main characteristics. He called the first group "The Spirits," because they could be vaporized with fire. His second group was "Metallic Bodies," lustrous or shiny substances that could be hammered into shape and could make a sound. The third group he called "The Bodies," mineral substances that could not be hammered, but are easy to pulverize, or break into fine powder. He also wrote about the "inner spirit" of substances and the important balance between their inner physical qualities.

Elements and Processes. The physician al-Razi linked alchemy, pure science (which led to the modern concept of chemistry), and medicine. His books, particularly *Kitab sirr al-asrar* (The Book of the Secret of Secrets), were studied by later generations of Muslims and Europeans. Al-Razi expanded earlier works that divided metals into seven categories, making progress in the field of geology possible. His well-known classification of all substances as either mineral, vegetable, or animal laid the foundation for the modern classification system used today. Some historians claim that al-Razi was the first scientist to chemically separate and make use of *al-kohl* (alcohol), which could be used as a disinfectant. That advance enabled physicians to perform surgery with a reduced risk of postoperative infection. The tenth-century alchemist Ibn Umayl wrote several influential works, including his *Kitab al-ma' al-waraqi wa'l-ard al-najmiyyah* (Book of the Silvery Water and Starry Earth), which was translated into Latin as the *Tabula Chemica* and influenced the development of chemistry in the West. The continued study of such processes as the fusion of elements, distillation, and crystallization continued over the centuries.

CULTURAL EXCHANGE

The thirst for artistic exchange among the elites of different cultures often brings about an intermingling of technology and art from several regions. One particular example of this kind of exchange is the intricately designed hand warmers Muslim artists made for the European market. The idea of a circular metal heater seems to have originated in China, where small round fire pots with hinged tops were filled with burning embers and hung from the ceiling. Using a similar design, Muslim craftsmen made spherical incense burners, piercing the round body of each burner and decorating it with silver and gold inlaid designs. After merchants exported them to Europe, they discovered that the people in the cold climates of Europe were using the incense burners as hand warmers. Seeing a market for a new item, Muslim artisans inserted a brass pan inside each burner to hold hot coals, and to keep the burning embers from spilling they added a gimbal inside of the spherical. This device enabled people to roll the round hand warmer in any direction while keeping the inner pan holding the hot coals completely level. These hand warmers were so popular that by the 1700s European artisans in Venice were copying the design and competing for the hand-warmer market. Some Muslim artisans moved to Venice, where they taught Islamic metal-working skills to the Italians. Venetian metalworkers who copied Muslim styles called themselves *al-Azzimina*, a term derived from the Arabic word for non-Arabs. Working with Muslim craftsmen, these Venetians made "Islamic style" trays, bowls, buckets, hand warmers, vases, and elaborately designed pitchers called ewers, copies of those Muslims used for ritual cleansing before their five daily prayers.

Source: Esin Atil, W. T. Chase, and Paul Jett, *Islamic Metalwork* (Washington, D.C.: Freer Gallery of Art, Smithsonian Institution, 1985).

Alchemy and Religious Beliefs. The spiritual expression of alchemy is rooted in the belief that if physical matter could be transformed from one substance to another, then the spiritual realm of humans could be altered as well. Alchemists thought that, if they could bring about perfection in the physical world (by attempting to turn base lead into gold, for example), then they could also bring about spiritual rebirth—by turning the crudest element of the individual human soul into something that could connect with the Divine. This symbolic and spiritual side of Muslim alchemy appealed to European Christians because of the doctrine of the death and resurrection of Christ. Alchemy was closely allied to astrology, with each field serving as a complement to the other. Astrology focused on the heavens while alchemy explored how one can move from the lower, or earthly, realm to the higher, heavenly

A still used to make rosewater; illumination from a ninth-century manuscript for *Kitab Kimya' al-'Itr wa al-Tas'idat* (Book of Perfume Chemistry and Distillation) by al-Kindi (Suleymaniye Library, Istanbul)

haps the most interesting of twelfth-century Spanish alchemists was al-Jayyani, who combined alchemy and the art of poetry in his *Shu-dur al-dhahab* (Particles of Gold). A fifteenth-century Spanish scientist, al-Marrakushi, described chemical processes in the form of a dream. Many of these manuscripts were difficult to translate because Muslim alchemists often used language that was deliberately confusing, particularly if they were writing about something bordering on the occult. They did not want anyone except other alchemists to decipher their seemingly strange experiments. It was particularly difficult for "outsiders" to make sense of the writings of Jabir ibn Hayyan, and the English word *gibberish* is derived from his name. Among the Europeans influenced by Arabic alchemical writings were the well-known French alchemist and student of the occult Nicolas Flamel (1330–1418), the philosopher-scientists Roger Bacon (circa 1214/1220 – circa 1292), Albertus Magnus (circa 1200 – 1280), Frances Bacon (1561–1626), and Isaac Newton (1642–1727).

Sources:

Esin Atil, W. T. Chase, and Paul Jett, *Islamic Metalwork* (Washington, D.C.: Freer Gallery of Art, Smithsonian Institution, 1985).

Seyyed Hossein Nasr, *Islamic Science: An Illustrated Study* (London: World of Islam Festival Publishing, 1976).

Nasr, *Science and Civilization in Islam* (Cambridge, Mass.: Harvard University Press, 1968).

Rachel Ward, *Islamic Metalwork* (New York: Thames & Hudson, 1993).

W. Montgomery Watt, *The Influence of Islam on Medieval Europe.* Islamic Surveys 9 (Edinburgh: Edinburgh University Press, 1972).

MATHEMATICS

Numbers. Muslim scholars agreed with the ancient Greek notion that mathematics is the underlying foundation of all knowledge. They knew that studying mathematics gives one skill in logic and reasoning. Furthermore, one of the main foundations of Islam is the concept of *Tawhid* (Oneness) of the whole interconnected world, and Muslims viewed mathematics as a way to make sense of the physical world and its union with the spiritual world. This link between the science of numbers and understanding of the divine reality was so critical to early Muslim scholars that they referred to mathematics as "the tongue which speaks of Unity and Transcendence." Their affinity for mathematics as spiritual symbolism is apparent in Muslim art and architecture, which often includes the number 1, or a single, central design element, to remind the viewer that there is only one God. Hence, the number 1 is often called "The Source" because God is seen as the source of all creation. Similarly, a series of numbers is sometimes interpreted as symbolizing the steps Muslims must take to reach an understanding of Muslim beliefs. In a treatise written by the Ikhwan al-Safa (Brethren of Purity), a tenth-century brotherhood of mystical Muslim scholars, the primary position of mathematics among the sciences was clearly stated: "The science of numbers is the root of the sciences, the element of wisdom, the origin of the divine sciences, the pillar of meaning, the first elixir and the great alchemy." These scholars had their strongest influence on

realm. Alchemy deals with the four qualities identified by ancient philosophers (cold, humid, hot, and dry) and the seven metals commonly used in antiquity. These seven metals in the earthly realm were linked to, and symbolized, the sun, moon, and planets in the heavenly realm:

Saturn: lead
Venus: copper
Jupiter: tin
Mercury: quicksilver
Mars: iron
Moon: silver
Sun: gold

Alchemists considered nature to be the Divine Breath on earth.

Achievements. Working within a unifying religious framework, Muslim alchemists made advances in medicine, geology, philosophy, chemistry, biology, and botany. Many Arabic alchemical texts were among the works translated into Latin in the twelfth century. Because of their close proximity to the rest of western Europe, alchemists working in Andalusia (Muslim Spain) had a more immediate effect on the West than those in the Middle East. Per-

First page of al-Tusi's thirteenth-century commentary on Euclid's *Elements;* from a fifteenth-century Persian manuscript for the work (Millet Library, Istanbul)

Western mathematics in the fields of algebra and trigonometry. In fact, the word *algebra* is a Latinized form of the Arabic term *al-jabr*, which stems from the word for "bone setting" and means restoration, putting together parts, or completion of a whole. Arab mathematicians drew mainly on ancient Greek and Indian mathematics, correcting the mistakes in these earlier sources and expanding on the work of the ancients. The "Arabic" numerals in use today get their name from the fact that Muslim mathematicians used them as symbols of quantities in their mathematical theories. These symbols—which revolutionized the field of mathematics—actually originated in India, where Indian mathematicians saw that the ancient numbering systems, including those devised by the Greeks and Romans, were adequate for expressing quantities but cumbersome and difficult to use in solving even the simplest mathematical equation. Once Indian scholars began to use symbols (such as 5 or 7) to express quantity and came up with the concept of place values (such as "thousandth," "hundredth," or "tenth" place), people were able to perform basic tasks such as adding and subtracting with relative ease (and without using stones, fingers, or an abacus). Finally, the Indians came up with the concept of a circular symbol to represent the concept of *emptiness,* or *nothing*—the origin of the universal mathematical symbol for *zero.* It is essential in writing a number like 608 without a zero, making it impossible to distinguish between 68 and 608, for example. Muslim scholars embraced these new Indian ideas with enthusiasm, applied them in new ways, and disseminated them widely, including to western Europe. The Muslim study of mathematics included the same four subjects as the Latin "Quadrivium," the four parts of the liberal arts: arithmetic, geometry, astronomy, and music, which was considered a mathematical science. But Muslim scholars also included optics in the field of mathematics.

Algebra and Trigonometry. Scholars of the Muslim world developed both geometry and trigonometry as new scientific fields and first defined the sine, cosine, and cotangent mathematical functions. The best-known Muslim mathematician was al-Khawarizmi, whose name is the source of the English word *algorithm*. Working in the ninth century, he also developed tables of trigonometry that contained sine functions and theories of calculus, as well as studying the geometric qualities of cones. Though he spent most of his life in Baghdad, some historians think he may have traveled to India to study there. His work on the astronomical project in which Muslim scientists measured one degree of the meridian led him to write the first extensive Muslim treatise on mathematical geography, using triangulation to measure distances. During the twelfth century his *Kitab al-mukhtasar fi hisab al-jabr wa'l-muqabalah* (The Book of Summary Concerning the Process of Calculating Compulsion and Equation) was translated into Latin by Robert of Chester and led to the wide dissemination of algebra throughout European intellectual circles.

THE LEGACY OF THE BANU MUSA

When Khalifah al-Ma'mun (ruled 813–833) of Baghdad appointed Musa ibn Shakir as his court astronomer, he began a long tradition of scholars who brought renown to his Bayt al Hikmah (House of Wisdom). Musa's three sons, Muhammad, Ahmad, and al-Hasan, known collectively as the Banu Musa, that is, Sons of Musa (Moses), all devoted their lives to the pursuit of knowledge. They focused their efforts on geometry, mechanics, dynamics, astronomy, and music (which medieval scholars considered a theoretical science). After first studying ancient texts, particularly those of the Greeks, the Banu Musa wrote a large number of books based on their own research, mostly in geometry and other areas of mathematics. Muhammad wrote *The Measurement of the Sphere, Trisection of the Angle, and Determination of Two Mean Proportionals to Form a Single Division Between Two Given Quantities,* as well as books on the atom, the movement of celestial bodies, and the origin of the earth. Ahmad wrote about mechanics, and al-Hasan focused much of his work on the geometrical properties of the ellipse. The Banu Musa book that had the greatest influence in the West was *Kitab ma'rifah misahat al-ashkal* (The Book of Knowledge of the Area of Figures), which was translated by Gerard of Cremona in the twelfth century.

The Banu Musa also contributed to Muslim scholarship in another way. While returning home from a trip to Byzantium, where they gone in search of manuscripts to study, Muhammad stopped in the town of Harran, where he met Thabit ibn Qurra, who had a thorough knowledge of math and astronomy and was quite fluent in Syriac, Greek, and Arabic. Muhammad took Thabit to the court of Baghdad, where the khalifah immediately appointed Thabit court astrologer. Because he knew both Greek and Syriac, Thabit was able to work with Nestorian Christians' Syriac translations of Greek texts. After correcting and expanding earlier translations, Thabit also wrote more than seventy scientific works based on his own studies in mathematics, astronomy, astrology, ethics, mechanics, music, medicine, physics, philosophy, and scientific instrumentation. His sons became well-known physicians who also wrote about history, mathematics, and politics.

Source: Paul Lunde, "Science in the Golden Age," *Aramco World,* 33 (May-June 1982): 6–13.

Geometry. Other important ninth-century mathematical texts were written by the Banu Musa (Sons of Moses), three brothers working in Baghdad who wrote several works about geometry. Their *Kitab ma'rifah misahat al-ashkal* (The Book of Knowledge of the Area of Figures) created much interest in geometry among the scholars of Baghdad. After Gerard of Cremona translated the Banu Musa manuscripts into Latin in the twelfth century, these works brought to Europe a wealth of new information on mathematics, physics, and mechanical science.

Numerical Series. Another popular field of studies within mathematics was the area of numerical series. The geographer al-Biruni (973 – circa 1050) wrote several works on this subject, many of which offered mathematical puzzles to be solved. The best known of these is the fictitious story of the man who invented the game of chess. It was said that, when he presented his new invention to his ruler, the ruler absolutely insisted that he accept some sort of favor in return. The man asked for some grain, which would be measured according to the mathematics of the chessboard: there would be one grain for the first square, and then the number of kernels would double with each subsequent square. Thus, the second square would hold two grains, the third square four, the fourth square eight, and so on, up to the sixty-fourth square. The ruler accepted this proposal without doing the math first. Much to his dismay, he discovered that he owed his subject 18,446,774,073,709,551,615 pieces of grain—more than all the grain in the kingdom.

'Umar Khayyam. The development of algebra among the Muslims reached its peak with the studies of the Persian 'Umar Khayyam (1048–1131), better known in the West as a poet than as a mathematical genius. In his best-known mathematical text, *Maqalat fi al-Jabr wa al-Muqabalah,* he classified algebraic equations according to their level of complexity. He was also the first scholar to develop the binomial theorem and determine binomial coefficients, and he did work on the multiplication of ratios and the mathematical theory of parallel lines. Also interested in physics and metaphysics, he did extensive research on how to determine specific gravity. When the Saljuk sultan Malik-Shah (ruled 1072–1092) asked Khayyam to update and make corrections to the Persian calendar, he undertook a massive project involving intense study of mathematics and astronomy and produced a solar calendar called the Jalali calendar, which is still in use today and is more accurate than the Gregorian calendar used in the West. Only about a dozen of Khayyam's works on mathematics have survived. Most of them express his interest in philosophy and its relationship to science. One of the major goals of Muslim sages such as 'Umar Khayyam was to show disciples how to see spiritual signs in the realm of numbers. This philosophy also influenced the study of geometry, a field that the Banu Musa called "one of the gates through which we move to the knowledge of the essence of the soul."

Nasir al Din al-Tusi. Khayyam's work in algebra and geometry was continued by Nasir al-Din al-Tusi (1201–1274), who is credited with much developmental work in geometry and trigonometry and also wrote about medicine, ethics, and religion. Tusi's *Kitab shikl al-qita'* (Book of the Figure of the Sector) is considered the first independent work on trigonometry. He also wrote an extensive commentary on Euclid's *Elements,* an ancient Greek mathematical work on which several Muslim scholars expanded. Tusi also discovered many mistakes in the mathematics of the astronomical models put forth by Ptolemy.

Sources:

John R. Hayes, ed., *The Genius of Arab Civilization: Source of Renaissance,* third edition (New York: New York University Press, 1992).

Seyyed Hossein Nasr, *Islamic Science: An Illustrated Study* (London: World of Islam Festival Publishing, 1976).

Nasr, *Science and Civilization in Islam* (Cambridge, Mass.: Harvard University Press, 1968).

MECHANICS

New Inventions. The Banu Musa (Sons of Moses), whose books on geometry aroused so much interest in the ninth century, also wrote extensively on the relationship between physics and mechanics. Mechanics so fascinated people that this field of study became known in Arabic as *ilm al-hiyal* (knowledge of the ruse, or deception)—expressing the wonder people felt at new inventions that seemed impossible to explain during that time. Many of these mechanical objects were made for the entertainment of the wealthy, including mechanical servants that poured drinks for guests and mechanical musicians that entertained people while they dined.

Water Clocks. Some of the earliest mechanical clocks used water to measure the passage of time. The simplest water clock is thought to be an Egyptian invention dated around 1500 B.C.E. This cone-shaped vessel narrowed toward the base, and a hole at the bottom released one drop of water at a time. The Chinese used water to power their clocks and made elaborate timekeepers to amuse the royal courts. These clocks served as inspiration for the Muslims, and during the reign of Abbasid Khalifah Harun al-Rashid (ruled 786–809), engineers produced an elaborate water clock that the khalifah presented to Charlemagne, the powerful ruler of the Holy Roman Empire in western Europe. Muslim engineers vied with each other to create devices that marked time and performed simple tasks to entertain the elegant courts of Muslim rulers. In the arched gate on one water clock, which looked like the facade of a palace, mechanical musicians played music. Above the roof was a semicircular disc that rotated to show the signs of the zodiac, and at certain intervals a window opened to reveal a figure within the palace. This clock was operated by a hydraulic system hidden behind the facade.

Candle Power. Another clock was powered by the heat released from a large burning candle on a tall brass candlestick in the center of the clock. At the base was a mechanical falcon that released a round ball from his beak every hour. At the top was a figure of a man with a sword. Each

Sources:

Esin Atil, *Art of the Arab World* (Washington, D.C.: Smithsonian Institution, 1975).

Ahmad Y. al-Hassan and Donald R. Hill, *Islamic Technology: An Illustrated History* (Cambridge & New York: Cambridge University Press / Paris: Unesco, 1986).

David A. King, "Some Illustrations in Islamic Scientific Manuscripts and Their Secrets," in *The Book in the Islamic World*, edited by George N. Atiyah (Albany: State University of New York Press, 1995), pp. 149–177.

A mechanical handwashing device; illumination from a 1315 Syrian manuscript for *Kitab fi ma'rifat al-hiyal al-handasiyyah* (Book of Knowledge of Ingenious Mechanical Devices) by al-Jazari (Freer Gallery of Art, The National Museum of Asian Art, Smithsonian Institution, Washington, D.C.)

time the bird dropped a ball, the man swung his sword, striking off the burned wick from the candle.

Mechanical Clocks. Eventually water clocks gave way to mechanical clocks. Some had mechanical servants who poured drinks for their viewer on command and scribes who "wrote" at intervals of one hour. One of the most elaborate timepieces displayed a bearded man seated on an elephant. Every half hour, the man moved his head, looked to one side, caught a ball with one hand, and dropped it into the mouth of a dragon with the other.

Mechanical Innovation. In 1206 an engineer named al-Jazari wrote *Kitab fi ma'rifat al-hiyal al-handasiyyah* (Book of Knowledge of Ingenious Mechanical Devices), which described many ingenious Muslim mechanical inventions. While some may view them as trivial mechanical toys that catered to the tastes of the Muslim leisure class, work on such objects fostered the development of engineering. To create these mechanisms, engineers invented an extremely sophisticated technology of pulleys, weights, air pressure, steam, water pressure, and gears that had useful applications in other areas and influenced the development of the machine technology in use today.

MEDICINE AND HEALTH

Prophetic Foundations. Muslim medicine has an important theological basis. Both the Qur'an and the hadiths make many references to taking care of the body, which is a religious obligation for Muslims. An instrumental aspect of Islamic theology is the divinely ordained balance of life. Muslims are expected to protect that delicate balance, including care of their bodies, so they are able to perform religious duties and be valuable citizens. This concept was clearly put forth by the fifteenth-century Muslim physician Jalal al-Din al-Suyuti in his *Tibb ul-Nabbi* (Medicine of the Prophet):

> It is obligatory upon every Muslim that he draw as close to the Almighty God as he can and that he put forth all his powers in attention to His commands and obedience to Him, and that he make the best use of his means and that he . . . [refrains] from what is forbidden and that he strive for what gives benefit to Mankind by the preservation of good health and the treatment of disease. For good health is essential for the performance of religious obligations and for the worship of God.

Public Health. Along with advances in health care came innovations in public health and hygiene. Medical schools were attached to teaching hospitals in cities such as Baghdad, Cairo, Damascus, and Córdoba. Medical facilities traditionally closed each night, but by the tenth century laws were passed to keep hospitals open twenty-four hours a day. Hospitals were also forbidden to turn away patients who were unable to pay. Eventually charitable foundations called *waqfs* were formed to support public institutions such as hospitals and schools. This money supported free medical care for all citizens. Muslim cities also maintained public baths to facilitate the fulfillment of religious duties related to personal hygiene. Muslims must perform a ritual washing five times per day before saying their obligatory prayers, and Muslim scholars realized early the links among clean water, public hygiene, and health.

Medical Theory. Muslim physicians used Greek, Chinese, and Indian medical theories as the bases from which to develop their own. Like the ancient Greeks, Muslims believed that a balanced body is a healthy body and did their best to maintain a delicate balance between the four humors: blood, phlegm, yellow bile, and black bile. As in Greek medical theory, the humors were linked between the four natures—hot, dry, cold, and humid—and the four elements—earth, water, air, and fire. Muslim scientists are considered the first medical scholars to understand the pathology of contagion, and as a result they created hospi-

Portraits of Andromachos and eight physicians of ancient Greece in a thirteenth-century manuscript for Yahya al-Nahwi's summary of Galen's treatise on antidotes (Österreichische Nationalbibliothek, Vienna)

In his encyclopedic work on surgery, diseases, and their cures, al-Zahrawi devoted much attention to the healing properties of duhn, oil extracted from various natural substances. His list includes:

The Duhn of Bitter Almond: if mixed with wine and applied to the scalp will be useful against open sores and dandruff therein.

The Duhn of Sweet Almond: is soothing to the chest and lung. It also dissolves hard tumors and relaxes spasms everywhere.

The Duhn of Laurel: helps to widen the opening of the veins. It relieves pain of the organs as well as chills, ear aches, and headaches.

The Duhn of Wheat: is hot and helpful in stopping ringworm at the start. Rub the ringworm with course cloth until it is almost going to bleed, then apply the Duhn on it. Repeat the same procedure until it is healed—God the Almighty willing.

The Duhn of Mustard: is hot and mild, and good for a chronic cold. It also helps in joint pain, paralysis, tremors, and trembling. It helps against forgetfulness, strengthens the memory, and warms the nerves.

The Duhn of Wild Mint: is useful in fatigue if applied externally in the sun or in the bath. It will help in facial paralysis and if used in nose drops it drives out a cold. Use it as ear drops to stop ringing of the ears. It will also help cure the sting of a scorpion.

The Duhn of Rose: is moderately cold and astringent. It relieves pain caused by heat and if used internally it helps against inflammation of the stomach. It can also cure hepatitis. If taken with ewe's milk it helps relieve the pain of the bladder and helps sugar diabetes- the disease in which the patient drinks too much water and quickly passes it. In the case of a severe blow to the head resulting in a fracture of the bone wherein the inner skin of the brain appears, pour over the injured head the warm duhn of rose instead of the blood of a dove, for it will help to quiet the pain and the hot swelling therein.

Source: Sami Khalaf Hamarneh and Glenn Sonnedecker, *A Pharmaceutical View of Abulcasis al-Zahrawi in Moorish Spain* (Leiden: Brill, 1963).

tals with separate wards for specific illnesses, so that people with contagious diseases could be kept away from others. Before this innovation in health care, a patient hospitalized for a broken leg might have been placed next to someone with the highly contagious bubonic plague.

Aids to Recovery. As early as the eighth century Muslims were aware of the connection between psychological well-being and physical health. In the tenth century, the renowned Adudi hospital in Baghdad offered soothing music, poetry, and the sound of running water as aids to recovery. Patients were also permitted to work in the herb gardens as a relaxing form of exercise. Eventually Muslim physicians developed a holistic form of treatment that involved a combination of diet management, herbal medication, isolation of communicable diseases, prayers, fresh air, exercise, healing scents, and reduction of stress. When patients were released, they were often given a small sum of money to facilitate their return to the community.

Folk Traditions. Arab-Muslim and Latin-Christian cultures both had a wealth of folk traditions, as well as religious faith, to draw on when confronted with illness. Often treatments combined remedies from several sources in search of anything that might offer relief to the afflicted. Like their European counterparts, Muslim physicians often turned to unscientific treatment methods. For instance, Islam developed in a region that had a strong tradition of believing in the power of the "evil eye." Suyuti mentions it in his *Tibb ul-Nabbi:*

If any one of you is struck by the Evil Eye and asks for water in order to perform an ablution (ritual cleansing before prayer) then his request should be granted. And he who is struck by the Evil Eye will wash his face, his hands, his elbows and knees, and the tips of his feet, and what lies within his breeches. He will collect this water in a cup and pour it over the possessor of the Evil Eye. He will turn the cup upside down behind him on the ground. It is said that this pouring upon him will bury the effects and he will be cured by the permission of Almighty Allah.

Although some Muslims disagreed with the practice, astrology, numerology, protective charms, and amulets were also used in medieval times to ward off disease and the evil eye. These practices were particularly prevalent during the mid fourteenth century, when both the Muslim and Christian worlds were devastated by the rampant spread of bubonic plague, known as the Black Death. People seeking cures often made little distinction among religion, science, and superstition. Muslims often tried to protect themselves by wearing charms and rings that bore Arabic inscriptions, believing these letters had healing powers because the Qur'an was revealed in the Arabic language. Many believed they could protect themselves from illness or injury by wearing either an entire verse from the sacred text, or even a few letters.

The Black Death. The devastating plague that struck the Muslim world and Europe in the mid fourteenth century sparked an important exchange of medical knowledge between the Muslim empire and Latin Christendom. Contemporary comments describing the plague and how people tried to deal with it reveal much about the time and how sometimes, in their effort to avoid the plague, people did things that probably increased their exposure to the highly contagious disease. The Moroccan traveling scholar Ibn Battuta (1304 – circa 1378) described how the people of Damascus tried to deal with the plague:

The people fasted for three successive days, the last of which was a Thursday. At the end of this period the amirs, sharifs, qadis, Doctors of the Law, and all other classes of the people in their several degrees, assembled in the Great Mosque, until it was filled to overflowing with them, and

Hospital built by Ottoman Sultan Bayazid II in Edirne (in present-day Turkey), 1484–1488

spent Thursday night there in prayers and liturgies and supplications. Then, after performing the dawn prayer, they all went out together on foot carrying Qur'ans in their hands; the amirs too, barefooted. The entire population of the city joined in the exodus, male and female, small and large. The Jews went out with their Book of the Law and the Christians with their Gospel, their women and children with them; the whole concourse of them in tears and humble supplications, imploring the favor of God through His Books and His Prophets.

In fourteenth-century Germany and Flanders the Christian flagellants—who went from village to village flogging themselves in an attempt to end the plague by penance for the sins of mankind—probably spread the plague through every village they visited. The many efforts to combat the plague throughout Europe and the Middle East combined common sense (such as quarantining victims) with superstition. Another "protective measure" that was instrumental in spreading the plague was fleeing the disease by leaving a city where the plague had struck and going to a place that was so far disease free. Ibn Battuta always seemed to be just one step ahead of the plague, but others were not so lucky, and their behavior proved deadly to people they encountered in their flight. One of the most effective treatments developed by Muslim physicians was to open and drain the "bubos" (boils) and then soak the area with vinegar and oil of roses. People were also told to keep their homes clean and to avoid the "miasma" (bad air) of crowded places. Finally, they were told to turn to the Qur'an for help.

Medical Exchange During the Crusades. The Crusades (1095–1271) offered an opportunity for an exchange of medical knowledge between European physicians and those of the Middle East. Most of the time the sharing of

medical procedures was a positive experience, but sometimes cultural prejudices prevented European doctors from learning from their more-advanced Middle Eastern counterparts. A journal entry by Usamah ibn Munqidh (1095–1188), a prominent Muslim living in Syria, tells the story of a European Christian doctor and Syrian Arab physician:

One day, the Frankish [French] governor of Munaytra, in the Lebanese mountains, wrote to my uncle the sultan, asking him to send a physician to treat several urgent cases. My uncle selected one of our Christian doctors, a man named Thabit. He was gone for just a few days, and then returned home. We were all very curious to know how he had been able to cure the patients so quickly, and we besieged him with questions. Thabit answered: "They brought before me a knight who had an abscess on his leg and a woman suffering from consumption [excessive fatigue and general poor health]. I made a plaster for the knight, and the swelling opened and improved. For the woman I prescribed a diet to revive her constitution. But a Frankish doctor then arrived and objected, 'This man does not know how to care for them.' And, addressing the knight, he asked him, 'Which do you prefer, to live with one leg or die with two?' When the patient answered that he preferred to live with just one leg, the physician ordered, 'Bring me a strong knight with a well-sharpened battle axe.' The knight and the axe soon arrived. The Frankish doctor placed the man's leg on a chopping block, telling the new arrival, 'Strike a sharp blow to cut cleanly.' Before my very eyes, the man struck an initial blow, but then, since the leg was still attached, he struck a second time. The marrow of the leg spurted out and the wounded man died that very instant. As for the woman, the Frankish doctor examined her and said, 'She has a demon in her head who has fallen in love with her. Cut her hair.' They cut her hair. The woman then began to eat their food again, with its garlic and mustard, which aggravated the consumption. Their doctor affirmed, 'The devil himself must have entered her head.' Then, grasping a razor, he cut an incision in the shape of a cross, exposed the bone of the skull, and rubbed it with salt. The woman expired on the spot. I then asked, 'Have you any further need of me?' They said no, and I returned home, having learned much that I had never known about the medicine of the Franj (French).

Arab Medicine. By the twelfth century, however, many European physicians were enthusiastically studying works by Arab medical authorities such as al-Razi (865–925), known in the West as Rhazes, and Ibn Sina (980–1037), well known to European scholars as Avicenna. When asked to choose the location for a new hospital in Baghdad, al-Razi hung large pieces of raw meat on poles in various sections of the city. After a few days, he determined the site by finding the place where the meat had rotted the least. He concluded that the circulation of the air must be best at that site, which would make it a good place for treating sick people. In his medical texts he put forth new ideas about the need to improve the mental health of patients in order to cure their diseases. He was also one of the earliest physicians to see pediatrics as a separate field of medical research. Until this time, people tended to view children as "small adults" and ignored their different psychological and physical needs. Al-Razi's *Kitab al-Mansuri* (Book of Mansur) describes diseases and treatments in a systematic and scientific way. He kept careful clinical records and instructed his readers on how to diagnose and cure diseases. The philosopher-physician Ibn Sina's enormous *Qanun fi'l-tibb* (Canon of Medicine) listed every disease known at that time and their cures. He also included a pharmacopoeia in which he described medicinal plants and other remedies in detail. In the twelfth century Ibn Sina's *Qanun* was translated into Latin by Gerard of Cremona. Thought to be the most widely read medical text in the world, it served as the primary medical text of European universities until the seventeenth century. In his study of the nervous system, Ibn Sina concluded that muscles move through impulses sent through the nerves and also noted that some organs, such as the liver and the kidney, do not have any nerves inside them but are surrounded by nerves in their outer layer. Ibn Sina's *Kitab al-shifa'* (Book of Healing) is not a medical text: instead it covers a wide variety of scientific fields and focuses on explaining how science and theology together could solve the great mysteries of life.

Surgery and Anatomy. An area in which Muslim physicians excelled was surgery. Ibn Sina's detailed descriptions of the structure of the human eye and how the heart valves let blood enter the heart as the heart contracts are obviously the observations of a physician who performed many surgical procedures. An entire chapter of al-Razi's *Kitab al-Mansuri* is devoted to surgical procedures. In this chapter he was the first physi-

cian to write about spinal cord injuries and how a patient could be paralyzed if the connection between the nerves and the brain was severed. Arab physicians were also the first scholars to describe the four chambers of the heart and how the valves kept the blood flowing in one direction. They were also the first to use inhalation anesthesia by putting a sponge soaked in narcotics over the face of the patient during surgery. They eventually created sedatives that enabled them to perform major surgery, and they invented more than two hundred surgical instruments. Medieval Muslim surgeons used hollow needles and suction to remove cataracts from their patients' eyes—a procedure that was revived in 1846 by a French doctor. Muslim scholars also wrote books on how the eyes, optic nerves, and brain give people sight. (Earlier scientists thought that beings saw by sending rays out of their eyes, rather than by receiving light rays through the eyes and transmitting them to the brain.) After performing surgery, Muslim physicians sewed their patients up with sutures (stitches) made of animal guts or silk. As early as the tenth century, to lower the risk of postsurgical infection, they had created a new antiseptic called *al-kohl* (alcohol) using a distillation process invented by Arab chemists. Once surgery was completed, patients entered a recovery ward, where they received continued medical care while listening to prayers, poetry, and music.

Al-Zahrawi. In his *Kitab al-Tasrif* (Encyclopedia of Surgery and Instruments), Abu al-Qasim al-Zahrawi (known in the West as Albucasis), an eleventh-century surgeon from Andalusia (Muslim Spain), wrote a clear description of the pulmonary circulatory system as well as the "lesser circulation" of smaller vessels. He also described surgical procedures he had invented—including dissecting organs, removing stones from the bladder, and cauterizing wounds—and was the first physician to identify hemophilia as a disease. Skilled at oral surgery and dentistry as well, he explained how to make artificial teeth from animal bones. After the twelfth century, when Gerard of Cremona translated al-Zahrawi's medical text into Latin, the thirty-volume work revolutionized European medicine. In addition to its instructions on how to perform surgery, the text included diagrams of the surgical instruments that al-Zahrawi had invented and detailed descriptions of human anatomy. A large portion of this work was dedicated to the description of how to prepare and use *duhn*, the oil or "essence" of various plant and animal matter—such as roses, balsam, almonds, chick peas, chamomile, eggs, snakes, and flying ants. These remedies were administered for ailments such as inflamed eyes, bladder infections, chest colds, skin rashes, tumors, and asthma. In fact, al-Zahrawi offered a treatment for virtually all known diseases.

Sources:

Michael W. Dols, *The Black Death in the Middle East* (Princeton, N.J.: Princeton University Press, 1977).

Ross E. Dunn, *Adventures of Ibn Battuta, A Muslim Traveler of the Fourteenth Century* (Berkeley: University of California Press, 1986).

Sami Khalaf Hamarneh and Glenn Sonnedecker, *A Pharmaceutical View of Abulcasis al-Zahrawi in Moorish Spain* (Leiden: Brill, 1963).

Amin Maalouf, *The Crusades through Arab Eyes*, translated by Jon Rothschild (New York: Schocken, 1984).

Seyyed Hossein Nasr, *Science and Civilization in Islam* (Cambridge, Mass.: Harvard University Press, 1968).

Jalal al-Din al-Suyuti, *Tibb ul-Nabbi of al-Suyuti, The Medicine of the Prophet*, translated by Cyril Elgood (Cookeville, Tenn., n.d.).

Philip Ziegler, *The Black Death* (New York: John Day, 1969).

MILITARY ADVANCES

Military Challenges. Islam arose during the seventh century, during a period when the Christian Byzantine Empire and the Zoroastrian Sasanid (Persian) Empire were battling for control of the region. As the Muslim empire expanded, they had to face formidable enemies and contend with various nomadic tribes. Later, Muslim territory came under attack from various Turkic and Mongol ethnic groups and Christian Crusaders from western Europe. The outcome of a battle was often decided by who had the strongest and best-trained horses or the latest in military technology. Many Arab military manuscripts describe early Muslims' development of military technology to counter the superior weaponry of the sophisticated and experienced Byzantine and Persian cavalries.

Edged Weapons. The sword was a cavalryman's most important weapon, and one form of metallurgy in which Muslim artisans excelled was the art of making swords, which were not only weapons but works of art. Muslim swords from Muslim lands were coveted by soldiers everywhere, including Europe. The best swords were made of Damascus steel, which was strong, but flexible enough not to break in battle, and hard enough to hold a sharp edge. It was produced by adding carbon to iron and melting it in a hot crucible, a process that originated in India and was perfected in Persia, Damascus, and then in Toledo in Muslim Spain. Fine cutlery is still made at some of these centers. After the iron and carbon became molten steel, other ingredients were added—including pomegranate rinds, salt, and pearl shells—to make patterns in the steel once it was beaten into a sword. Early swords were slightly curved, single-edged weapons and were often decorated with inlaid designs or religious inscriptions. On the best swords, the grip and the scabbard were also highly decorated. The lance was a good weapon for keeping one's enemy at a distance, and it was less expensive than a sword. Typically, a lance was made by attaching an iron spearhead to a long piece of wood or even a thin tree branch. Other equipment for cavalrymen included javelins, knives, maces, and shields.

Bows. Archers were particularly important to the outcome of a battle, and bows were used in ancient Egypt. After they defeated the Persians, who were skilled archers, in the seventh century, the Muslims adopted the bow from their new subjects and soon improved it. Unlike the wooden bows used in the West, the Turkic "composite" bow had a wooden core that was reinforced with animal horn on the side that faced the archer, and it was covered with sinew (animal tendons). The power of this complex weapon came from the fact that it was a "reflex" bow; that is, it was first curved in one direction and then bent the opposite way when it was strung, usually with a silk or gut bowstring. This technique created an extremely taut weapon that could shoot an arrow a long distance, and this bow has been called the most effective weapon developed before the invention of firearms. It had a range of 1,500 feet. When fitted with an arrowhead that had a triangular cross section, an arrow shot from it had the force to penetrate mail armor from almost 500 feet away. While Muslims held archers in high esteem, European knights initially viewed the bow as an infantry weapon of little importance until their defeat by highly skilled Muslim archers changed their minds. Because it was difficult to draw and cumbersome for a man on horseback, the crossbow was not widely used by Muslim armies until the twelfth century, and even then it was primarily used as a siege weapon or in naval warfare. Once it was modified for use on horseback, however, it became the preferred weapon in Muslim Spain. The new version allowed a cavalryman to hold the bow in place with a stirrup and shoot arrows while riding at a fast pace.

Siege Equipment. One of the most effective methods of defeating an enemy in medieval times was the military siege, in which an army surrounded a fortified city and either attacked it and entered its gates or cut off its food and water supplies and waited for the inhabitants to surrender while harassing them by various means. Since ancient times catapults had been used to throw large rocks and various sorts of missiles. The trebuchet catapult, which was developed in China and introduced to Muslim warriors during the seventh century, had a sling attached to one end of a long wooden beam that was mounted on a tall framework. When people holding ropes pulled the other end of the beam downward, the sling end launched a projectile at or over the city walls. Because of their limited power, early trebuchets had to be within 150 feet of their target to be effective. By the twelfth century, however, the powerful counterweight trebuchet had come into use. This weapon replaced people pulling ropes with a heavy lead weight or stones, and the increased weight countering the missiles in the sling made the machine able to lob as much as five hundred pounds from a distance of 1,000 feet. Its place of origin has been disputed, but the bulk of historical evidence points to the Muslim world. For example, when the Chinese were using it in the thirteenth century, they called the counterweight trebuchet the "Muslim Phao" (Muslim throwing machine). By that time it was in widespread use and had proved an extremely effective weapon for both the Christian Crusaders and their Muslim enemies.

Incendiary Weapons. Fire has been used as a military weapon since ancient times, particularly in areas of the Near East where *naft* (petroleum) seeps naturally from the ground. The word *naft* came to denote various kinds of military incendiary materials, even if they were not derived from petroleum. In addition to liquid petroleum,

Incendiary troops wearing fireproof clothing covered with lit firecrackers and carrying flaming devices to throw at enemies (top) and men preparing to fire rockets (bottom); illumination from a fourteenth-century manuscript for a military treatise
(Keir Collection, Richmond, U.K.)

the incendiary materials used in pre-Islamic times included liquid pitch; mixtures of pitch, resin, and sulfur; and mixtures of quicklime and sulfur with materials such as bitumen, resin, or petroleum. The best-known medieval incendiary weapon is the so-called Greek fire, an unknown flammable substance given to the Byzantines in about 673 by an architect who had defected from Arab Syria to Byzantium. This secret weapon helped the Byzantines protect themselves from Muslim attacks for centuries, until Constantinople finally fell to the Ottomans in 1453. The Crusaders called it "Greek fire," but the Byzantines never used that name. After the eighth century, Muslim innovations increased the efficiency of incendiary weapons. Many historians believe that the secret ingredient they added to the flammable substances used earlier was saltpeter (potassium nitrate), while others point to the Muslims' expertise at distillation, which would have enabled them to increase the effectiveness of *naft*. By the time of the Abbasid dynasty in the eighth-thirteenth centuries, Muslim armies included special

troops trained in using weapons of fire. Practicing an early form of psychological warfare, these soldiers and their specially-trained horses wore fireproof uniforms that were covered with burning firecrackers. While approaching their enemies at high speed, the fire warriors lobbed incendiary devices filled with burning *naft*.

Gunpowder. The first use of gunpowder by the Muslims is unknown. Archaeological excavations at Fustat (old Cairo) have uncovered traces of gunpowder in the firepots used to burn the city in 1168. According to many historians, the use of incendiary explosives filled with gunpowder was the deciding factor in the Battle of Mansura (1250), at which the Muslim forces of Turan Shah defeated the Crusaders and captured King Louis IX of France. The exact nature of these weapons is unknown, though some historians believe they were "real artillery." The French chronicler Jean de Joinville, who fought in the battle, described one of these weapons: "It was like a big cask and had a trail the length of a large spear: the noise it made resembled thunder and it appeared like a great fiery dragon flying through the air." Primitive cannon, which used gunpowder to shoot iron balls, were used by Muslim troops in North Africa as early as 1204 and in Spain by 1248. By the middle of the thirteenth century, they were used in the Muslim East.

Sources:

Michael D. Coe and others, *Swords and Hilt Weapons* (New York: Weidenfeld & Nicolson, 1989).

Frances and Joseph Gies, *Cathedral, Forge and Waterwheel: Technology and Invention in the Middle Ages* (New York: HarperCollins, 1994).

Ahmad Y. al-Hassan and Donald R. Hill, *Islamic Technology: An Illustrated History* (Cambridge: Cambridge University Press / Paris: Unesco, 1987).

MINERALOGY AND GEOLOGY

Natural Formations. Because they saw objects in nature as symbols of God's mercy and majesty, Muslims examined soil, rocks, and minerals as one way of seeking an understanding of the relation between the earthly world of humans and the divine world of the angels and God. Muslims studied rock formations to unlock the mysteries of geological changes that had taken place on the surface of the earth: changes of landmasses into seas and seas into landmasses, or massive disruptions such as erupting volcanoes or earthquakes. The writings of the Ikhwan al-Safa (Brethren of Purity), a tenth-century brotherhood of mystical Muslim scholars, described fossils as petrified sea creatures in deserts that had once been covered by seas. (In western geological histories the mystery of the origin of fossils was not solved with confidence until the 1700s.) Muslim scientists also wrote about the ways in which sand and wind can alter rock formations. Describing how sedimentary rocks are formed, they divided them into three major categories. The first is rock such as sandstone, or shale, which is made of rock fragments from one place that are deposited in another, usually by flowing water. The second, such as rock salt, or gypsum, is formed by the combination of minerals and water. The third, which includes limestone, is formed from the remains (such as shells or skeletons) of living organisms. Perhaps the most remarkable geological discovery made by a Muslim scientist was al-Biruni's eleventh-century identification of the Ganges Plain of India as a sedimentary deposit (which he viewed as evidence that it had once been under water). In his *Tahqiq al-Hind* (Facts About India, circa 1030), he wrote about discovering rocks in forms that were completely opposite from what one might expect: "if you see the soil of India with your own eyes and meditate on its nature, if you consider the rounded stones found in the earth however deeply you dig, stones that are huge near the mountains and where the rivers have violent currents, stones that are of smaller size at the greater distance from the mountains and where the streams flow more slowly, stones that appear pulverized in the shape of sand where the streams begin to stagnate near their mouths and near the sea—if you consider all this, you can scarcely help thinking that India was once a sea, which by degrees had been filled up by the alluvium (deposits) of the streams."

Gems. Within Islam the study of mineralogy weaves together many different fields, including alchemy, chemistry, metallurgy, and medicine. Muslim scientists not only described the outward, physical properties of gems, but they also wrote down their thoughts about the "inner" characteristics of these stones. They believed that gemstones had powers that could be used to heal a person or change one's psychological state. For this reason studies of minerals found their way into medical textbooks and works on philosophy or religion, as well as purely scientific writings. Al-Kindi (circa 801 – circa 866) wrote of the earliest Muslim texts on mineralogy. His *Risalah fi anwa' al-jawahir al-thaminah wa ghayriha* (Treatise on Various Types of Stones and Jewels) laid the foundation for later studies in the field. Another of al-Kindi's books discussed the properties of various metals, as well as the art of making swords. Ibn Sina (980–1037) wove mineralogy and metallurgy into the study of medicine, classifying metals and minerals in his *Kitab al-shifa'* (Book of Healing) and expanding on the study in his *Qanun fi'l-tibb* (Canon of Medicine). In the eleventh century al-Biruni wrote his important *Kitab al-jamahir fi ma'rifat al-jawahir* (Book of the Multitude of Knowledge of Precious Stones), which treated mineralogy from the viewpoint of a scientist working in the field. During the late tenth and early eleventh centuries, studies were also done in the Maghrib region of northwest Africa and in Muslim Spain. In the Mahgrib, al-Majriti included a section about minerals in his *Rawdat al-hada'iq wariyad al-haqa'iq* (The Garden of Gardens and Meadow of Truth), which links the science of mineralogy with alchemy, philosophy, and the occult. Ibn al-'Arabi (1165–1240), the great Sufi philosopher of Spain, included a section on the mystical nature of gems in his book on how divine influence will restore the human kingdom through natural creation. After this time, most of the notable Muslim works on mineralogy were written in Persia, India, and Turkey.

Sources:

Seyyed Hossein Nasr, *Islamic Science: An Illustrated Study* (London: World of Islam Festival Publishing, 1976).

Nasr, *Science and Civilization in Islam* (Cambridge, Mass.: Harvard University Press, 1968).

THE MUSLIM AGRICULTURAL REVOLUTION

Agricultural Technology. Some historians have called the diffusion of new crops and agricultural methods to the West through Muslim Spain an agricultural revolution because they had a major impact not only on agricultural production but also on incomes, population levels, urban growth, distribution of labor, industrial output, clothing, cooking, and diet. Moreover, agricultural technologies Muslims took to Spain eventually reached the New World. As many as 40 percent of the Spanish immigrants to South and Central America between 1493 and 1600 were from Andalusia (Muslim Spain), and they took with them their crops and irrigation technology. The most important of these crops were *sukker* (sugar) and *qutn* (cotton), which became two of the most prominent "cash crops" in the world during the late Middle Ages and the Renaissance. (Cotton may have been taken to the Americas from Asia in antiquity, or there may be indigenous varieties because the inhabitants of the Americas were already cultivating and weaving cotton when the first Europeans arrived.) When the resources of the New World were combined with plants and technologies from the Old World, the global economy was vastly expanded. Cash crops are grown for export, not for local consumption, and these crops can be highly profitable to those who grow them, particularly if a cheap labor force is available. As the cultivation of popular new crops spread around the world, the European craving for products such as sugar, coffee, indigo dyes, and cotton also brought an increase in slavery.

Coffee. The first cultivation of coffee has been traced to about 1100 in the area of Arabia along the Red Sea. Though this variety is classified as Coffea Arabica, botanical evidence indicates that it was discovered around 850 on the plateaus of central Ethiopia, several thousand feet above sea level. There are several legends about a shepherd who noticed his goats behaving in a strange manner after eating the red coffee beans. According to one legend, he took some of the beans to his village, where everyone liked the way the berries kept them awake during prayer. Initially, coffee was brewed from green unroasted beans, which created a beverage similar to tea. The great Persian physician Ibn Sina (980–1037) is known to have administered coffee as a medical treatment. By the thirteenth century Arabs were roasting and brewing the beans to make coffee and using it as a beverage as well as for medicinal purposes. Large-scale cultivation of the coffee bean was rare until the fifteenth century, when extensive orchards were planted in Yemen. From there the plant spread throughout the Arabian peninsula and into the Ottoman Empire of Turkey. One of the earliest documented coffee shops is the Kiva Han, which opened in Constantinople in 1475, but there were probably earlier coffee shops on the Arabian peninsula. Coffea Arabica became so popular that laws were passed to forbid anyone from exporting fertile coffee plants to non-Muslim regions. This law, of course, was unenforceable. When coffee became popular in Europe, many fortunes were made by exporting it from ports such as Alexandria, Egypt.

Citrus Fruits. The earliest citrus fruits were rather bitter and considered undesirable for human consumption. The flowering trees that produced these fruits first appeared in Southeast Asia and India, and the modern versions of oranges, lemons, and limes probably evolved naturally by insect cross-pollination in China, which had a wide range of citrus varieties. As early as 4000 B.C.E. the domestic cultivation of lemons, limes, and oranges was occurring at several sites in China, India, and Malaysia. These new hybrid fruits spread westward through trade and were well known in the Mediterranean region before the time of Christ. Sweet oranges were depicted on a mausoleum erected by the Byzantine emperor Constantine I in the fourth century. During the Middle Ages, Arab traders introduced many new varieties of citrus fruits to Europe, where lemons, limes, and oranges were once so rare that they were given to children as Christmas gifts. Eventually Spain became well known for gardens that included citrus trees. Citrus became important during the Age of Exploration (1400–1700), when ship captains learned that these fruits could prevent outbreaks of scurvy, a disease caused by lack of vitamin C.

Cotton. An important Muslim fiber crop, cotton probably originated in India or Egypt, both of which have a long his-

tory of cultivation and weaving of cotton fabrics. During pre-Islamic times it spread to China and—via the Indian Ocean maritime trade—as far as East Africa. Muslims developed a stronger, higher-yielding variety of cotton, which was disseminated by traders, facilitating the economic development of Muslim regions and stimulating a vast industry that produced many kinds of textiles. When this variety of cotton was grafted to the cotton discovered in the New World, the result was a stronger variety with longer fibers. This new cash crop became one of the greatest sources of the income that supported European colonization and economic growth in the Americas.

Dyes. As cotton cultivation spread, the production of dyes also became important. Indigo, a blue dye obtained from the leaves of a plant that originated in India, spread to Muslim lands, where it was cultivated in Persia, Egypt, and Morocco. Indigo-dyed textiles have been found in Roman graves of the second and third centuries. Indigo dye became so valuable that imitations were developed in Europe, leading indigo traders to produce pamphlets explaining how to test fabrics for "true blue," an expression still in use today. Another highly valued dye was the brilliant red hue that came from crushing female cochineal insects found on grasses in Persia and Armenia. Because of its high price, other cheaper and less brilliant reds were later produced from cochineal insects found growing on cacti in Mexico and the Andes Mountains of South America.

Sugarcane. A high-yield staple crop, sugar owes much of its dissemination to Islamic technology. The cultivation of sugarcane was introduced to Persia from India shortly after the Muslim conquest at Nihavand in 642. Sugar cultivation followed the spread of Muslim rule from Persia across North Africa to Muslim Sicily and Spain, and from Spain to the Atlantic islands off the coast of southern Europe, reaching the Canary Islands by the 1500s. It also traveled east, reaching China. According to Marco Polo, Egyptian sugar technicians were brought to China so they could teach the people of Fukien Province how to refine the crop.

Sugar Plantations. The high level of technology needed to irrigate sugarcane and refine the sugar made it difficult for small, independent farmers to produce and process this crop, and throughout the Muslim Mediterranean region sugar production became controlled by large, state-owned farms and factories. The sugarcane was broken and peeled on the farm and then transported to the refinery, which processed it into various forms. Sugar was the earliest cash crop grown in the New World. On his second voyage Columbus took sugarcane to the West Indies, where it thrived, and the Spanish introduced the production of sugarcane to the Caribbean island of Hispaniola in 1517, providing labor by importing slaves from West Africa and thus stimulating the African slave trade.

Sources:

Ahmad Y. al-Hassan and Donald R. Hill, *Islamic Technology: An Illustrated History* (Cambridge: Cambridge University Press / Paris: Unesco, 1987).

Paul Lunde, "Muslims and Muslim Technology in the New World," *Aramco World*, 43 (May–June 1992): 38–41.

Andrew M. Watson, *Agricultural Innovation in the Early Islamic World* (Cambridge: Cambridge University Press, 1983).

OPTICS AND OPHTHALMOLOGY

Vision and Light. Closely related to mathematics and physics, the field of optics attempts to answer questions of what and how people see. By reflecting on what people see, Muslim scientists delved into the realm of philosophy and religion. People in several faith traditions have questioned whether the physical world is actual reality or some sort of unreal entity that veils the reality of God. While Muslims joined other traditions in that debate, they also made enormous strides in discovering how vision works. Optics also looks at the physical properties of light, examining questions about what makes a rainbow or why images look dis- torted when reflected on a convex or concave surface as opposed to a flat one. Mathematics and physics were the tools needed to answer these questions.

The Father of Modern Optics. While earlier Muslim scholars also studied modern optics, they mostly accepted Greek sources—especially Aristotle, Ptolemy, and Euclid—including their claim that vision shoots from the eyes. Aristotle in particular had written that the eyes send out rays of light that illuminate the objects one sees. In the eleventh century, however, the Muslim scholar Ibn al-Haytham (called Alhazen in the West) did research in Egypt and Spain that led him to reach conclusions about

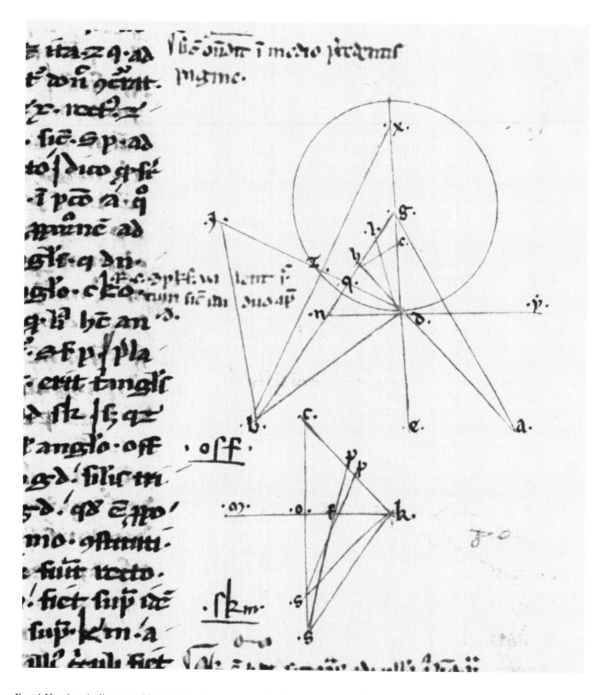

Ibn al-Haytham's diagram of how to find the point of reflection between an object and its image in a spherical mirror, a solution to what is known as "Alhazen's Problem"; illumination from a 1269 manuscript for *Kitab al-Manazir* (Book of Optics), written in the eleventh century (Royal Observatory, Edinburgh)

the nature of light and vision that contradicted the teachings of the Greeks and earned him the title "Father of Modern Optics." Ibn al-Haytham discovered that the eyes receive reflected light from objects, rather than emitting it. He thus established the true scientific basis for vision. The next step was to understand the nature of light and how the eye transforms light into vision. Ibn al-Haytham devoted virtually all his adult life to sophisticated experiments designed to answer some of these questions.

The Nature of Light. Ibn al-Haytham and the Muslim scientists contributed much to the understanding of the nature of refracted light. Ibn al-Haytham wrote about what happened to light when it passed through clear substances such as water, air, and glass. He also did experiments on the dispersion of white light into the colors of the spectrum and was thus able to explain how light traveling through the atmosphere can create a rainbow. These studies led him to other discoveries about the atmosphere. He found that it becomes less dense at higher elevations and thus refracts light in different ways. By discovering that twilight begins when the sun is nineteen degrees below the horizon, he was able to calculate the thickness of the earth's atmosphere. He wrote an entire book describing how various atmospheric conditions create different colors of a sunset. Ibn al-Haytham's works on light and on mirrors and their reflective qualities had a strong influence on Renaissance artists and architects, who were trying to understand the concept of perspective and how to reproduce on canvas the visual effect of three-dimensional space.

The Human Eye. Ibn al-Haytham drew diagrams of how vision enters the eye through light that is reflected or refracted off of physical objects. He was the first scientist to put forth the theory that vision is the result of the workings of the eye, the optic nerve, and the brain. These studies influenced the works of Roger Bacon and Leonardo da Vinci. Another Muslim scholar, al-Zahrawi, had done extensive studies of the eye in the tenth and early eleventh centuries, writing texts on eye surgery and describing how he had removed cataracts by siphoning them out of the eye with a hollow needle. The eleventh-century physician Ibn Sina (Avicenna in Latin) was the first scientist to describe the anatomy of the eye in great detail, identifying parts such as the cornea, iris, retina, layer lens, the inner water, the optic nerve, and the optic chiasma that conducts the optic nerves to the brain.

Sources:
Seyyed Hossein Nasr, *Islamic Science: An Illustrated Study* (London: World of Islam Festival Publishing, 1976).

Nasr, *Science and Civilization in Islam* (Cambridge, Mass.: Harvard University Press, 1968).

TECHNOLOGY

Irrigation. Finding enough water for agriculture, industrial power, and domestic use has always been a problem in the Middle East, where the low rainfall makes the terrain quite different from that of Europe, with its lush forests and abundant rivers. Out of necessity, Arab farmers expanded on many of the technological achievements of

ARAB PAPER

A Greek manuscript, which is now in the Vatican Library, is believed to be the oldest surviving document that was written on Arab paper. It contains several teachings of the early Christian Church Fathers. Dated to around 800 C.E., it was probably written in Damascus, a city controlled by the Muslims at that time. The Syrian Christians played an important part in the efforts of the government to translate and encourage commentary on ancient manuscripts, so many of the official documents of the era were composed by Christian administrators.

Another discovery indicates that an elaborate postal system was transferring documents across vast territories long before the Islamic empire spread across the Middle East and Asia. In 1907 the British-Hungarian explorer Sir Aurel Stein discovered a stash of documents from Soghdia that were abandoned in a watchtower. The tower was somewhere between Dunhuang, site of the famous painted caves of western China, and Loulan, farther to the west. They are thought to be the contents of an abandoned mailbag. One of the letters was wrapped in silk and, according to the address on the envelope, had been on its way to Samarkand, a destiny that lay about 2,000 miles away! Obviously Chinese paper was traveling along the cities of the Silk Route even before the eighth century burst of literary activity in the Islamic city of Baghdad made it such an important commodity.

Source: Jonathan Bloom, "Revolution by the Ream, A History of Paper" *Aramco World*, 50 (May–June 1999): 26–39.

the Greco-Roman world and developed efficient ways of moving water from one place to another. Through the use of an elaborate system of gears and wheels for raising and moving water, Arab farmers greatly expanded the amount of land on which they could plant their crops. Use of these devices in Andalusia (Muslim Spain) resulted in the transfer of this technology to Europe. One of the most efficient early tools for bringing underground water to the surface was the *saqiya*, an animal-driven machine that consists of two gears meeting at right angles, so that one is vertical and one is horizontal. The vertical cogwheel is mounted on an axle just above the water source, such as a well. A series of ceramic pots attached to the cogs of the wheel fill with water as they go into the well and dump the water into an irrigation channel when they come up. The vertical wheel is powered by the horizontal wheel as it is moved by an ox or mule that walks in a circle around the well. This machine, which spread to the Syrians from the Romans, moved eastward first and then westward. The vertical waterwheel, which was used in the Middle East alongside major waterways, was an efficient way of lifting water and

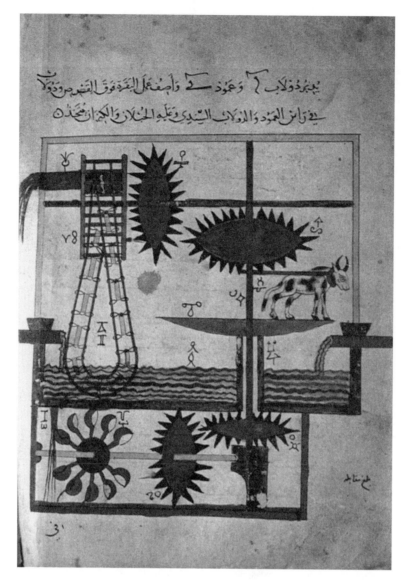

Plan for a water-raising device; illumination from a thirteenth-century manuscript for *Kitab fi ma'rifat al-hiyal al-handasiyyah* (Book of Knowledge of Ingenious Mechanical Devices) by al-Jazari (Suleymaniye Library, Istanbul)

placing it in an aqueduct that irrigated fields. The most original advances in water raising were made by the time al-Jazari wrote his *Fi ma 'rifat al-hiyal al-handasiyyah* (The Book of Knowledge of Ingenious Mechanical Devices) in 1206. By this time the system of gears for pulling water out of the ground had become so elaborate that they provided hours of entertainment to awed spectators. Al-Jazari described one work in particular that was built next to a small lake. Some of its working parts were purposely left visible so that people could watch it operate. At the bottom of the structure was a tank into which water flowed. A "chain-of-pots" attached to a vertical waterwheel raised the water out of the tank, and—much to the amazement of onlookers—a wooden cow on top of the device seemed to be doing all the work. (The secret was that another, more-elaborate mechanism hidden from view contained additional machinery that really did the bulk of the work.) Other machines used even more complex gears and wheels, as well as a crank for turning them. These elaborate meth-

ods of moving water did not reach Europe until the fifteenth century.

Water Power. Besides raising water out of the ground, people with limited water resources also needed to develop efficient ways of using the power of moving water to irrigate land and provide energy for other work. Many writings of Muslim travelers describe the use of large waterwheels along the edges of rivers. As Muslim cities grew in size and population, waterwheels helped irrigate large tracts of farmland. The increase in demand for food necessitated milling (or grinding) large quantities of cereal grains. For this reason there were eventually seventy water mills located near the city of Nishapur in present-day Iran. The most remarkable accomplishment in harnessing water power, however, was in the city of Baghdad. By the tenth century, large mills made of wood and iron rested on boats that were moored along the banks of the Tigris and Euphrates Rivers. Each mill worked day and night, grinding about fifty donkey loads of grain per day. Since each load weighed about one hundred kilograms, their production was at about ten tons per mill each day. Water-powered mills and trip-hammers were also used in the Central Asian city of Samarqand for pounding pulp that would be used for producing paper. This idea traveled to Baghdad and southern Spain. Highly developed techniques for milling grains in Muslim lands could produce all grades of flour, including white flour and semolina. Millstones were made from a coarse sandstone supplied by quarries in Mesopotamia (Iraq) and Persia (Iran). Another important Muslim crop was rice, which they husked using water-powered trip-hammers. This rice-mill technology spread from the Middle East to western Muslim regions and from there to Europe. Water power was also used to refine sugar. Recent excavations in Jordan have revealed thirty-two water-driven sugar mills.

Wind Power. Windmills have their origin in Muslim culture, specifically in Iran. The earliest recorded windmills—which are mentioned by the ninth-century Muslim explorers the Banu Musa brothers in their *Kitab al-Hiyal* (Book on Mechanical Devices)—were horizontal. In his twelfth-century *Kitab Nukhbat al-Dahr* (Cosmography), al-Dimashqi included detailed descriptions of horizontal windmills. They were surrounded on three sides by mud-brick walls that intensified the power of the wind that drove them. Acting as a turbine, the wind caused the mill inside to turn. This invention, which took advantage of the strong winds in many Muslim regions, spread to the Far East and Europe by the twelfth century. (The vertical windmill is believed to have been a European invention.) The power from the horizontal windmill could be used to pull underground water to the surface, to grind grain, or to power hammers that crushed sugar cane. One can still find horizontal windmills in Iran.

Paper. According to a traditional account, when the Muslims defeated the Chinese in 751, they took some prisoners of war who are said to have possessed a skill the Muslims had never seen before: producing sheets of paper by pulverizing fiber and mulberry-wood pulp and molding it into flat sheets. Muslim civilization spread the production of paper to Central Asia, Iraq, Syria, Egypt, North Africa, and Spain. Because paper was cheaper and easier to produce than parchment or papyrus, this diffusion of paper-making skills created a virtual revolution in the dissemination of knowledge in such diverse areas as religion (with increased production of the Qur'an and eventually the Bible), literature, mathematics, commerce, and the arts. The first Muslim city to embrace this new product with enthusiasm was the Central Asian city of Samarqand, which came under Muslim rule in the eighth century. By the ninth century, the advantages of paper over papyrus and parchment had become obvious, and paper became one of the major exports of Samarqand.

The Paper Market. After the establishment of the Bayt al-Hikmah (House of Wisdom) in ninth-century Baghdad, scholars' growing need for paper fueled its production. The rapid expansion of the Muslim empire created a demand for more and more copies of the Qur'an. Baghdad also began to manufacture paper in quantity. By the tenth century, Baghdad had an entire market, the Suq al-Warraqin, devoted to the sale of paper and books. This covered *suq* (bazaar) was lined with more than one hundred booksellers' and papermakers' shops and soon became the center of Baghdad literary life. In this *suq* people produced ink from the soot of oil lamps; books were bound in leather carved with intricate designs; and artisans decorated the edges of manuscripts with geometric designs in colorful pigment and gold. Merchants sold highly prized rice paper and mulberry paper from China, as well as *qutni*, paper made from cotton fibers in Baghdad. Coarse, brown *qutni* filled the needs of those with little money, while smooth, white *qutni* appealed to the wealthy. At first, the best *qutni* came from Samarqand, but the paper manufacturers of that city were eventually unable to compete against heavy competition from the paper factories of Cairo. With the advent of paper technology, special agents traveled to newly developed book markets in cities such as Damascus, Cairo, and Fez. Some of the books sold along this route reached Europe, often through diplomatic exchanges. While at first some people preferred parchment, paper gradually replaced it among the literary elite and in government offices, which produced large numbers of documents.

Glass. During the Middle Ages, Muslim artisans used the techniques of molding, blowing, cutting, and etching to create fine glassware for the wealthy. By the Renaissance period, owning even a few samples of Muslim glassware became a status symbol for the urban bourgeoisie of Europe. In the Muslim regions, glass was used to produce lamps for masjids (mosques) and containers for food and cosmetics. Muslim artisans made glass by fusing two main ingredients: woody ashes called *al-qali* (alkali) and silica, or sand. By adding manganese dioxide, they could make glass colorless. Alchemists learned how to make stained glass by adding other ingredients, such as the various metallic oxides used to create black, sapphire blue, red, yellow, and green glass. Syrian craftsmen created a technique for making enameled glass by painting the finished piece with different colors and then reheating it to melt the color into the glass. Much of the surviving information about early glass-making comes from the writings of al-Razi (865–925). Many beautiful pieces created by Muslim glass artisans are now in museums throughout the world.

Ceramics. Pottery is one of the oldest art forms in the world. Ancient pottery shards have been found in virtually all parts of the globe. Most cultures produced early pots using the same technology. Primitive pots shaped by hand later gave way to those formed on pottery wheels or in molds. One important Muslim innovation was the development of different glazes. When a glazed pot is fired, brilliant colors are permanently baked into the piece. Glazes were used on pots, platters, drinking vessels, and the tiles used to cover the facades of many masjids. Isfahan, Iran, for instance, has several masjids that are well known for their brilliant blue, green, and white tiles—some of which

oring agent because it produced a brilliant turquoise blue. In the ninth century the Muslims rediscovered tin glazing, which had been practiced in ancient Mesopotamia. By adding a tin glaze to a lead-silicate glaze they could create a cream-colored glaze similar to that of Chinese porcelain. One of the most sophisticated glazing methods developed in the Muslim world was lustre, an iridescent, or shiny, glaze that enabled potters to imitate expensive metal pieces. A molded ceramic plate from ninth-century Iraq is an early example of lustre ware. These pieces, which often had floral decorations or depictions of hunting scenes or musicians, appealed to members of Muslim royal courts. By the eleventh century ceramic techniques were spreading from Iran and Syria to the rest of the Muslim world. One of the first techniques to be discovered in Iran and then travel westward was the sgraffito technique, in which a rough, red paste was coated with a thin layer of fine-grained white clay. A design was incised into the white clay and then glazes of various colors were applied to embellish the design. The purpose of the deep incisions into the clay was to keep the colors from running together and mixing. A final clear glaze was applied to the finished piece. By the fourteenth century brilliant blue "turquoise ware" had developed into a refined and elegant product. Many of these pieces were decorated with a black pigment that depicts animals, plants, or birds. For the Muslim elite Persian ceramic artisans developed a style called *haft rang* (seven colors). These pieces were fired twice; once after the application of the underglaze colors (which require a high temperature) and again at a lower temperature to affix pigments that were added after the first firing. These pieces are significant for their innovative use of *mina'i*, enamel created by melting alkaline with other pigments and powdered when cooled. During the late Middle Ages and the Renaissance, Chinese porcelain (a delicate ceramic fired at high temperatures) and colorful glazed ceramics from the Muslim world were much sought after in Europe. The Delft tiles made in Holland that became popular in Europe during the 1700s and 1800s were strongly influenced by Muslim ceramics.

Sources:

Jonathan Bloom, "Revolution by the Ream, A History of Paper," *Aramco World*, 50 (May-June 1999): 26–39.

Ahmad Y. al-Hassan and Donald R. Hill, *Islamic Technology: An Illustrated History* (Cambridge: Cambridge University Press / Paris: Unesco, 1987).

David Talbot Rice, *Islamic Art*, revised edition (London: Thames & Hudson, 1979).

ZOOLOGY

Literature. Animals have a sanctified place in Islamic theology, so early Muslim writings about the animal world combined religion, scientific observation, and morality tales in which humans are reminded that they have a lot to learn from animals. Muslims inherited three pre-Islamic traditions concerning animals from the Arabic, Greco-Alexandrian, and Indo-Persian cultures. The Indo-Persian tradition was quite different from that of the Greeks. While the Greeks had many "morality tales" in which animals were charac-

have Qur'anic verses on them. These tiles were glazed by using a combination of metal oxides and the salts of other metals. Muslim craftsmen closely guarded their knowledge of innovative glazing techniques such as how to create various methods of applying the glaze, and the time and temperature at which to fire ceramics in their kilns (ovens).

Glazes. The two glazes most often used in Muslim ceramics were an alkaline glaze and a lead glaze, refinements on glazes that originated in ancient Egypt and Mesopotamia. Alkaline glazes were made from quartz, soda, potash, and salt. They were clear but tended to become iridescent. Lead glazes contained red lead and were colored with the addition of metallic oxides. These lead glazes created the brilliant colors for which Muslim pottery became so well known. Copper was the most popular col-

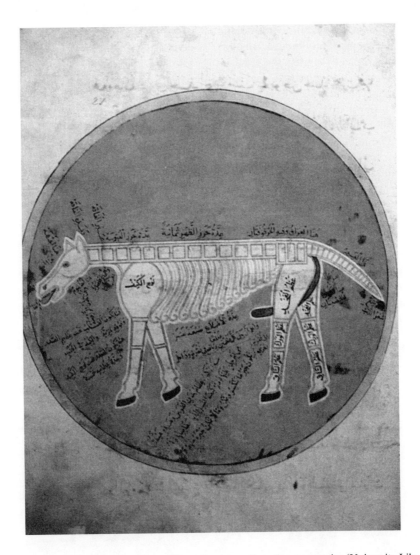

Anatomical chart of a horse; illumination from a fifteenth-century Egyptian manuscript (University Library, Istanbul)

ters, the Greeks wrote predominantly scientific descriptions of animals. In contrast, the Indians and Persians paid attention to the spiritual and moral aspects of the animal world. The best-known Indian animal legends of this era were the Indian tales of Bidpai, which became the Arabic collection *Kalilah wa Dimnah* (Kalilah and Dimnah). The main point of these stories is that people can learn from animals as well as about them. For practical reasons, many of the earliest Muslim zoological manuscripts dealt with horses and camels. In the eighth and ninth centuries these studies created the methodology for dissecting, studying, and describing animals in a scientific manner.

Arabian Horses. The Arabs became particularly adept at breeding the animals on which they depended for survival in the rough terrain of the extensive trade routes on which they traveled from one part of the vast Muslim empire to another. What is now known today as the Arabian Horse came about as the result of extensive care in breeding. Known for their amazing energy, intelligence, and devotion to their owners, these horses were originally bred by Bedouin tribes as war mounts or for long treks. The legendary endurance of these horses is due in part to their large lungs. In the seventh century the Prophet

Muhammad was instrumental in encouraging the breeding of Arabian horses because they were considered crucial to Muslim military efforts against large armies of the Persians and Byzantines. These horses took on a religious significance as well after the Prophet pointed out that they had been created by Allah and that people who treated these beautiful horses kindly would be rewarded in the afterlife. Over the centuries, through their selective breeding, Arabian horses have retained characteristics such as large, wide-set eyes (good for seeing to both sides during battle), small ears (which collect less sand) and large nostrils (for taking in more air and strengthening endurance). Arabian horses are popular all over the world and were ridden by major military figures such as Alexander the Great, Genghis Khan, Napoleon, and George Washington.

Zoological Writings. The most significant early Muslim work on zoology is *Kitab al-hayawan* (Book of Animals) by al-Jahiz (circa 776–869), a scholar from Basrah, in present-day Iraq. In his book al-Jahiz compiled, corrected, and expanded on the zoological knowledge of the Greeks, Persians, and Indians, using Aristotle's works but criticizing them because Aristotle seemed to leave God out of his studies. As a devout Muslim, al-Jahiz felt that one should study zoology primarily to prove the existence of God and to discover the wisdom of his creation. Indeed, al-Jahiz wrote that one should have respect for even the smallest natural phenomenon, because the wonders of creation were as visible in it as in the grandest of creation: "I would have you know that a pebble proves the existence of God just as much as a mountain, and the human body is evidence as strong as the universe that contains our world: for this purpose the small and slight carries as much weight as the great and vast." In the tenth century, philosophers such as the Ikhwan al-Safa (Brethren of Purity) began devoting much attention to zoology. One of their "Epistles" is a commentary on the seemingly "natural" conflict between humans and the animal world—an early reflection on issues that are the basis for battles between conservationists and business interests in the modern world. The Brethren describe a debate between the animals and man that begins with man arguing that, because of his intellect and powers of invention, he has the right to dominate and even destroy the animal kingdom. The animals argue against this contention until they note that there are saints among humans. Recognizing saints as people who demonstrate that humans are capable of fulfilling their divine purpose on earth, the animals agree to serve humans, but only on condition that they remain conscious of their religiously ordained responsibility (mentioned in the Qur'an) to take care of the natural world and live in harmony with it. Humans are then warned that they will pay dearly if they fail in this respect. The foremost of Muslim zoology texts after al-Jahiz's *Kitab al-hayawan*, is Kamal al-Din al-Damiri's fourteenth-century *Hayat al-hayawan al-kubra* (Great Book on the Life of Animals). This enormous work is a systematic study of animals, including information on their religious status according to the Qur'an, how they are to be treated according to Islamic law, traditions concerning their medical benefits to humans, their occult (or magical) properties, and their significance in the interpretation of dreams. Because this text combined religious as well as scientific perspectives on the study of animals, it became quite popular in the Muslim world, even among children. It eventually became a source of folklore as well as an inspiration to artists who painted many of the animals described in the text.

Sources:

Paul Lunde, "The Book of Animals," *Aramco World*, 33 (May–June 1982): 15–19.

Seyyed Hossein Nasr, *Islamic Science: An Illustrated Study* (London: World of Islam Festival Publishing, 1976).

Nasr, *Science and Civilization in Islam* (Cambridge, Mass.: Harvard University Press, 1968).

SIGNIFICANT PEOPLE

JABIR IBN HAYYAN

CIRCA 725 - CIRCA 815
ALCHEMIST

Scientific Method. Jabir ibn Hayyan is considered the father of modern chemistry because his work in alchemy led to the development of the scientific method. His books combine science, religion, astrology, and numerology (the belief in the esoteric symbolism of numbers and how they relate to things such as metals and other natural substances).

Life and Legacy. A member of the Azd tribe of southern Arabia, Jabir spent much of his youth in Kufah, in modern-day Iraq. During the reign of the Khalifah Harun al-Rashid (ruled 786–809), Jabir went to Baghdad, where he found employment at the court of this powerful and scholarly ruler. Though he is also known for his contributions to the studies of botany and agriculture, Jabir is remembered most for his long and widely influential *Kitab al-Chemi* (Book of Chemistry)—the source of the English words *alchemy* and *chemistry*. In it he began the tedious job of classifying natural substances into groups according to their physical qualities, gave detailed descriptions of scientific experiments, and—perhaps most important—set the pattern for the scientific method, by which scholars carefully document each of their experiments. After British scholar Robert of Chester translated this work into Latin in 1144, it had a major impact on the teaching of science in European universities, where Jabir was known as Geber. The influence of this text is still apparent in the Arabic derivations of many scientific terms and names for laboratory.

Source:

Seyyed Hossein Nasr, *Islamic Science: An Illustrated Study* (London: World of Islam Festival Publishing, 1976).

ABU BAKR MUHAMMAD IBN ZAKARIYA AL-RAZI

865-925
HAKIM

Renaissance Man. With the spread of Islam, a group of learned Muslim scholars developed whose renown spread from Baghdad to the universities of Europe. In the Muslim world such a scholar is called a *hakim*—a word that stems from *hikmah* (wisdom). A *hakim* was expected to be a scholar of religion and philosophy, a writer, a teacher, and a scientist. Since the focus of Muslim higher education was on medicine and law, it was assumed that all *hakims* were also competent physicians and judges. Known as Rhazes in the West, al-Razi has been called the unchallenged chief physician of the Muslims and the most brilliant genius of the Middle Ages. He wrote books about philosophy, logic, astronomy, mathematics, physics, medicine, and music.

Life. Al-Razi was born in 864 in Persia, near the present-day city of Tehran. He had a wide range of interests that included mathematics, music, philosophy, chemistry, ethics, and especially medicine. He was also an accomplished musician who specialized in playing the *ud*, which is a forerunner of the guitar. At an early age, al-Razi showed a strong interest in the healing arts. He traveled to the city of Baghdad, then the center of Muslim scholarship and medical studies. While in Baghdad, he wrote his best-known book, *Kitab al-Mansuri* (Book of Mansur), which he dedicated to the ruler who supported many of his scholarly efforts. Al-Razi eventually returned to Persia, where he died in 925. As al-Razi's renown spread, many students traveled far distances to study medicine under him. Like the ancient Greek physician Hippocrates, al-Razi urged the licensing and formal training of all those entering the medical field. He called on doctors to live, eat, and dress in a simple manner in order to serve as role models to their patients.

Writings. Al-Razi is said to have written 184 books, but only a few survive. He studied the writings of ancient Greek physicians, translated them into Arabic, corrected their mistakes, and expanded them with medical knowledge unavailable to the Greeks. His *Kitab al-Mansuri* includes detailed descriptions of human anatomy and of diseases and their cures. This book also links injuries of the spine and brain to the paralysis of various parts of the body. After it was translated into Latin as *Liber medicinalis ad Almansorem* in the twelfth century, it became an extremely influential medical text in European universities. Another important work by al-Razi, which was translated at about the same time, is *al-Hawi* (translated into Latin as *Continens*), a twenty-volume encyclopedia of medical knowledge that circulated in several Latin versions because of its popularity in European medical circles. His *Kitab al-jadari wa'l-hasbah* (Treatise on Smallpox and Measles) also became well known in Europe after it was translated into Latin as *De Pestilentia*.

Source:
Seyyed Hossein Nasr, *Islamic Science: An Illustrated Study* (London: World of Islam Festival Publishing, 1976).

NASIR AL-DIN AL-TUSI

1201-1274
ASTRONOMER

Life. Born in Tus, Khorasan, al-Tusi became astrologer to the Ismaili governor of Persia at a time when the Mongol armies were advancing on the Muslim empire. After the Mongol ruler Hulagu conquered Persia, al-Tusi offered his services to him, hoping to diminish the usual destruction of libraries that accompanied Mongol onslaughts. He was able to gain the confidence of Hulagu, who supported al-Tusi's every scientific effort, including the establishment of the Maraghah observatory, where al-Tusi headed a large team of astronomers and mathematicians.

Writings. At this observatory al-Tusi and his team created the Ilkhanid astronomical star tables, which later had a major influence on European Renaissance studies of astronomy. Al-Tusi also wrote extensively on how the movements of the earth, sun, and moon were related, a study that led him to a scientific explanation for eclipses and a means of determining the times of the solar equinox. One of al-Tusi's students went on to devise a mathematical explanation for the rainbow. Copernicus's 1543 work, *Concerning the Revolution of Heavenly Bodies,* borrowed heavily from the works of al-Tusi and his followers.

Source:
Seyyed Hossein Nasr, *Islamic Science: An Illustrated Study* (London: World of Islam Festival Publishing, 1976).

Documentary Sources

Banu Musa (ninth century), *Kitab ma'rifah misahat al-ashkal* (Book of Knowledge of the Area of Figures) — An early mathematical work that strongly influenced Baghdad scholars who were interested in the new field of geometry and was later influential in Europe.

Abu Rayhan Al-Biruni (973 – circa 1050), *Kitab al-jamahir fi ma'rifat al-jawahir* (Book of the Multitude of Knowledge of Precious Stones) — A work describing the physical properties of stones and gems, which influenced the works of later geologists.

Al-Biruni (973 – circa 1050), *Qanun al-Mas'udi* (The Mas'udic Canon, 1030) — A compendium of scientific knowledge on subjects including trigonometry and astronomy.

Al-Biruni (973 – circa 1050), *Tahdid nihayat al-amakin* (The Determination of the Coordinates of Cities) — Al-Biruni's most important work, which enabled Muslim geographers to pinpoint the exact location of any city on earth by accurately determining the longitude and latitude of the site; extremely accurate even by modern standards, this book was also one of the first works to describe how the earth rotates on its axis.

Al-Biruni (973 – circa 1050), *Tahqiq al-Hind* (Facts About India, circa 1030) — Considered the first book to combine physical geography and sociological analysis of an entire region; this book includes information on such subjects as Indian death and burial rituals as well as Indian languages, dress, and cultural traditions.

Abu l-'Abbas al-Farghani, *Kitab fi'l-harakat al-samawiyyah wa jawami 'ilm al-nujum* (Principles of Astronomy, circa 820–833) — A work that includes statistics on the size of each known planet and its distance from the earth; this work laid the foundation for later Muslim astronomical works and had a major influence in Europe after Gerard of Cremona translated it into Latin during the twelfth century.

Ibn al-Haytham (eleventh century), *Kitab al Manazir* (Book of Optics) — A work by the Father of Optics, who discovered that sight results from rays of light entering the eyes and being "translated" by the brain into vision.

Ibn Rushd (1126–1198), *Kitab al-kulliyyat* (Book of General Principles) — A medical book by the Andalusian physician best known as the greatest medieval commentator on the philosophy of Aristotle; known in the West as Averroes, he also wrote more than seventy-eight texts on scientific subjects such as astronomy, physics, religion, philosophy, and medicine.

Ibn Sina (980–1037), *Qanun fi'l-tibb* (Canon of Medicine) — Possibly the most widely read medical textbook in the world, used by European medical students for more than six centuries; Known in the West as Avicenna, Ibn Sina wrote more than 250 books, including works on medicine, mathematics, chemistry, logic, and philosophy.

Ikhwan al-Safa (Brethren of Purity), *Risalat* (Epistles, tenth century) — a series of fifty-one works by a group of Sufi scholars that form one of the foundations of Muslim scientific study, covering virtually every field from astronomy to zoology; these works include some of the earliest scientific explanations for tides and earthquakes and offer a clear description of sound waves; these works were burned as heretical in 1150, but one complete set survived in Spain.

Jabir ibn Hayyan (circa 725 – circa 815), *Kitab al-Chemi* (Book of Chemistry) — An early work that began the classification of natural substances according to their physical qualities and set the pattern for the modern scientific method.

Abu Uthman al-Jahiz (circa 776–869), *Kitab al-hayawan* (Book of Animals) — One of the earliest zoological studies by a Muslim scholar, which was influenced by Aristotle's writings on animals but adds knowledge gained since Aristotle's time.

al-Jazari, *Fi ma 'rifat al-hiyal al-handasiyyah* (The Book of Knowledge of Ingenious Mechanical Devices, 1206) — A text by a mechanical engineer who described new technological advances such as water clocks, fountains, military machinery, and agricultural devices raising water from the ground; while previous books had described such machinery, al-Jazari also gave directions on how to construct them.

Muhammad ibn Musa al-Khawarizmi, *Kitab al-mukhtasar fi hisab al-jabr wa'l-muqabalah* (The Book of Summary Concerning the Process of Calculating Compulsion and Equation, ninth century) — An important mathematical work by the librarian at the Bayt al-Hikmah (House of Wisdom) in Baghdad, who is one of the best-known mathematicians in history.

Abu Bakr Muhammad ibn Zakariya al-Razi (865–925), *al-Hawi* — A twenty-volume encyclopedia of medical knowledge that was widely influential in the Muslim world and the West.

Al-Razi (865–925), *Kitab al-Mansuri* (Book of Mansur) — An important medical text that includes detailed descriptions of human anatomy and diseases.

Abu al-Qasim al-Zahrawi (circa 936 – circa 1013) *Kitab al-Tasrif* (Encyclopedia of Surgery and Instruments) — A thirty-volume work that includes illustrations of early surgical tools, detailed descriptions of the human circulatory system from the heart to minor blood vessels, and instructions on how to perform surgery, including cataract surgery; it also explains how to deliver a healthy baby and remove a dead fetus from a womb without harming the mother, as well as how to amputate limbs and sew up surgical incisions with silk thread.

Modern Arabic (western)	1	2	3	4	5	6	7	8	9	0
Early Arabic (western)	1	2	₹	ﻉ	9	6	7	8	9	0
Arabic letters used as numerals	ا	ب	ج	د	ه	و	ز	ح	ط	ي
Modern Arabic (eastern)	١	٢	٣	٤	٥	٦	٧	٨	٩	٠
Early Arabic (eastern)	١	٢	٣	٤	٥	٦	٧	٨	٩	٠
Early Devanagari (Indian)	ح	て	ℐ	Ⴑ	ⴹ	Ⴒ	Ⴗ	ყ	۶	
Later Devanagari (tenth-century Sanskrit)	१	२	३	४	५	६	७	८	९	०

The development of Arabic numerals (from *Aramco and Its World: Arabia and the Middle East*, 1980)

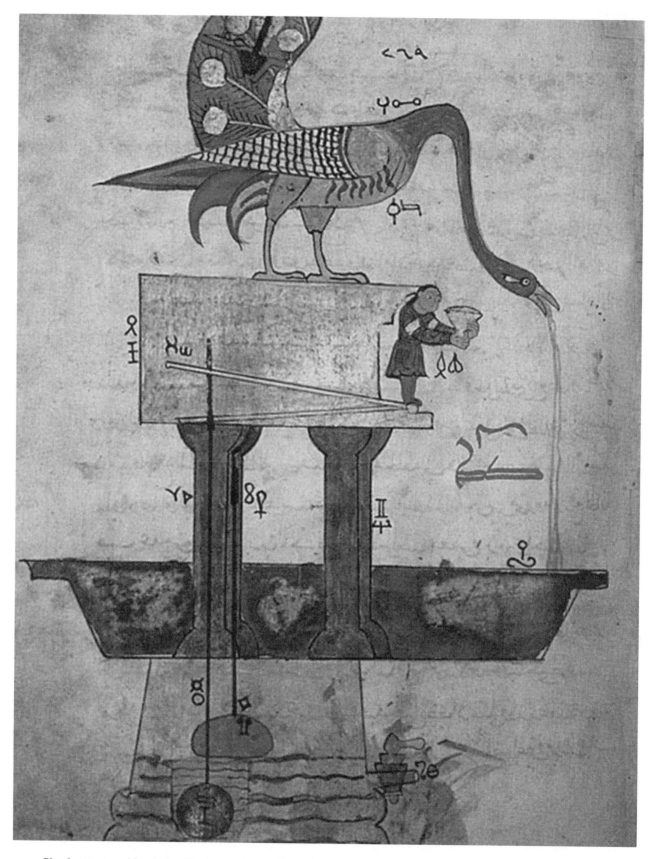

Plan for a water-raising device; illumination from a thirteenth-century manuscript for *Kitab fi ma'rifat al-hiyal al-handasiyyah* (Book of Knowledge of Ingenious Mechanical Devices) by al-Jazari (Suleymaniye Library, Istanbul)

GLOSSARY

Abbasids: A dynasty of **khalifahs** (caliphs) who ruled the **Islamic** empire for more than five hundred years (749–1258) after defeating the **Umayyads** in a revolution; they claimed descent from 'Abbas, uncle of Muhammad.

Adab: A habit or norm of good conduct; the definition of *adab* came to include the sum total of learning and knowledge that makes a person courteous and sophisticated; it is also a synonym for literature and the humanities.

Aghlabids: A dynasty that ruled Tunisia, eastern Algeria, and Sicily from 800 until 909.

Ahl al-dhimmah: Beneficiaries of the indefinitely renewed contract through which the **Muslim** community accords tolerance and protection to members of other revealed religions, originally only Jews and Christians (People of the Book) but later Zoroastrians and members of other faiths Muslims encountered as the territory under their rule expanded.

al-'Aja'lib: Marvels or wonders of God's creation or of antiquity; a genre of geographical literature.

'Alim: *See* **ulama'**.

Almohads: A dynasty of Berber origin (Arabic name: *al-Muwahhidun*) that ruled in North Africa and Spain in 1130–1269; al-Muwahhidun was the name given to reformist promulgators of the **Islamic** doctrine of **tawhid** (divine unity).

Almoravids: A dynasty of Berber origin (Arabic name: *al-Murabitun*) that ruled in North Africa and then Spain (circa 1050–1147). It was replaced by the **Almohads**.

Aman: Safety, or protection; in law, a safe conduct or pledge of security.

Amir: Commander, governor, or prince; a person invested with a command (*amr*), especially a military command.

'Amma (*plural:* 'awamm): The common people.

Ansab: *See* **nasab**.

Ansar: A title meaning "The Helpers"; that is, the people of Madinah who aided Muhammad and the immigrants (**Muhajirun**) after their flight (**Hijrah**) from Makkah.

Asnam (*singular:* sanam): Idols or objects that were worshiped.

A'yan: Notables or elites; in philosophy, this term refers to things that are perceived in the exterior world as opposed to what exists in the mind.

Ayat: Literally, a sign or manifestation; a single verse of the **Qur'an**.

Ayyarun: Rascals, tramps, or vagabonds; also members of the **futuwwah**, or militarized gangs, who terrorized the wealthy in **Muslim** towns.

Badu (*or* badw): Pastoral nomads of Arabian ethnicity and culture; Bedouins.

Basmalah: The saying of the initiatory blessing over any act performed by a **Muslim**; in complete form the blessing is *"Bi ismi Allah al-rahman al-rahim"* (In the Name of God, the Beneficent, the Merciful), and this expression begins nearly every chapter of the **Qur'an**.

Bay'a: An individual or collective oath recognizing the authority of another person, such as a **khalifah**.

Bayt al-mal: A state treasury.

Bimaristan: A hospital.

Burdah poems: A genre of verse in praise of the Prophet Muhammad; the name comes from the term *burdah*, a wrap of striped woolen cloth produced in Yemen and worn by men during the Prophet's time. The term marks the acceptance of poetry as a **Muslim** literary form after a poet who had been attacking the Prophet asked forgiveness and recited a poem praising him; in response Muhammad signaled his approval of poetry by giving his cloak to the poet as a present.

Byzantine Empire: The Eastern Christian successor to the Roman Empire and the chief military rival of **Muslim** states for much of the medieval period. Armies of the **khilafah** made significant territorial gains at the Byzantines' expense. The Byzantine capital, Constantinople, fell to the Ottomans in 1453.

Caravanserai: An imperial establishment at which travelers on major caravan routes could find protection, provisions, and rest; also, a complex of buildings with shops, workshops, warehouses, and lodgings with covered galleries and a courtyard, often protected by a high wall; similar to a **khan.**

Dahr: Time in the absolute sense; infinitely extended time.

Dar al-harb: Foreign territory or those countries in which **Islamic** law is not in force for the protection of **Muslims** and **dhimmis;** also, territories under the threat of war or threatening war.

Dar al-Islam: The land of **Islam;** that is, the whole territory in which the law of Islam prevails with its guarantees to members of the **Muslim** community and non-Muslim (**dhimmis**) under its protection.

Daʻwa: A call or invitation; in the **Qurʼanic** sense, it is the call to the dead to rise from their graves on the Day of Judgment; in the religious sense, it is the invitation addressed to humankind by God and the prophets to believe in the true religion.

Dhikr: Remembering God or reciting and repeating the names of God or praises to God as individuals or groups, especially the religious services of remembrance common to **Sufism,** the mystical branch of **Islam.**

Dhimmi: In **Islamic** law, a beneficiary of the tolerance and protection accorded to non-**Muslims** of recognized faiths, such as Judaism and Christianity. *Dhimma* is the term for the legal status granted to such individuals.

Diwan: A register or office in government bureaucracy; or, a collection of poetry or prose.

Duff: In music, the general term for an instrument in the tambourine family.

Faiʼ: Immovable property acquired by conquest; also, a foundation established in perpetuity for the benefit of successive generations of the community.

Fajr: Dawn or daybreak; the time of the **salat** al-fajr (dawn prayer), the first of the five obligatory prayers in **Islam.**

Falsafah: Greek thought or philosophy.

Fard: Something made obligatory; in **Islamic** law it is a term for a religious obligation, as in *fard ʻayn* (individual obligation) and *fard kefaya* (collective or community obligation).

Fatihah: The opening **surah** (chapter) of the **Qurʼan,** which is recited in each **rakʻa** (unit of prayer).

Fatimids: A **Shiʻi** dynasty that ruled North Africa, Egypt, and Syria, 909–1171.

Fatwa: A judgment or opinion on a point of civil or religious law.

Fiqh: Understanding, knowledge, or intelligence; the technical term in **Islamic** law for jurisprudence and for the laws regulating religious rituals and observances, as well as orders and prohibitions, family law, inheritance law, property and commercial law and procedure, constitutional law, and laws regulating administration of the state and the conduct of war.

Fitna: A revolt, civil disturbance, or war. In the **Qurʼan** this term means "temptation, or trial of faith." The term is also used for the great struggles over the succession to the **khilafah** after the murder of Khalifah ʻUthman in 656.

Five Pillars of Islam: The formal acts of worship that confirm one as a **Muslim** before God: shahadah, salat, zakat, siyam (or sawm Ramadan), and hajj.

Funduq: A North African term for a hostelry, hotel, **caravanserai,** or **khan.**

Futuwwah: Movements and organizations common in urban communities of the eastern **Muslim** regions, or Muslim chivalric orders. As voluntary associations, they ranged from Muslim street gangs to craft brotherhoods to disciplined groups of **Sufi** adepts. The literal meaning of the term *futuwwah* is "young manliness."

Ghazal: An elegy of love.

Ghusl: The general ablution, or washing of the whole body and hair in pure water, which is obligatory before the performance of prayer after the completion of a woman's menses and after men and women have sexual relations; also, the washing of a **Muslim's** corpse.

Hadd: A boundary, frontier, or limit; in **Islamic** law, *hadd* is the technical term for punishments of certain acts forbidden in the **Qurʼan.**

Hadith: A narrative or tradition; an account passed down from the time of the Prophet Muhammad reporting what he said or did, or recording things said or done in his presence to which he gave tacit approval.

Hajj: The **Islamic** pilgrimage to **Makkah** during the month of Dhu al-Hijjah and the performance of rites at the **Kaʻbah** and at other sites in and around Makkah. The hajj is the last of the **Five Pillars** of Islamic personal obligations; every **Muslim** who is physically, mentally, and financially able to do so is expected to go on the hajj once in a lifetime. One who has performed the pilgrimage is called *hajji* (masculine) or *hajjah* (feminine).

Hakim: A sage, physician, or ʻalim of great learning and accomplishment.

Halal: In **Islamic** law and practice, everything that is not forbidden.

Hanafi school: One of the four major **Sunni** schools or tendencies of **Islamic** law, developed by Abu Hanafah (699–767) and others. (*See also* **Hanbali school, Maliki school, Shafiʻi school, Jaʻfari [or Imami] school, Zaydi school,** and **Ismaʻili school.**)

Hanbali school: One of the four major **Sunni** schools or tendencies of **Islamic** law, developed by Ahmad Ibn Hanbal (780–855) and others. (*See also* **Hanafi school, Maliki school, Shafiʻi school, Jaʻfari [or Imami] school, Zaydi school,** and **Ismaʻili school.**)

Hanif: In **Islamic** writings, one who follows the original and true (monotheistic) religion. In the **Qurʼan** the term is used especially in reference to Ibrahim (Abraham); in later

Islamic usage the term is occasionally employed as the equivalent of "Muslim."

Haram (pronounced *harAM*): In Islamic law, a term for everything that is forbidden to Muslims. The term *haram*, when pronounced *HARam*, refers to a sacred area around a shrine; a place where a holy power manifests itself; the sacred territory of Makkah; the two holy places—usually Makkah and Madinah but also, in Mamluk and Ottoman usage, Jerusalem and Hebron.

Hijab: The veil (in modern usage, head covering or scarf) worn by Muslim women; the practice of wearing the veil; or a shorthand term for women's "Islamic dress." *Hijab* is also the term for the curtain behind which khalifahs and other rulers concealed themselves and for an amulet worn for protection; in mysticism, *hijab* represents everything that veils the true end and makes humans insensitive to Divine Reality.

Hijaz: The region in the vicinity of Makkah and Madinah, the area of the Haram (pronounced *HARam*).

Hijrah: The migration in 622 of Muhammad and his Muslim followers from the city of Makkah, where they were persecuted, to the city of Yathrib, renamed Madinat al-Nabi (*see* Madinah), where they were offered sanctuary and Muhammad's authority was recognized; in Islamic law, emigration of Muslims from the dar al-harb to the dar al-Islam.

Hisbah: The duty of every Muslim to "promote good and forbid evil"; the function of the muhtasib, the person in each town who is entrusted with making sure the duty is fulfilled.

'Ibadat: The practice of religious duties; literally, submissive obedience to a master, the ritual acts required by Islamic law; also the branch of Islamic law concerning those rituals and acts of worship, as opposed to mu'amalat, meaning worldly acts and relations between individuals.

'Id al-Adha: The Feast of the Sacrifice, the major annual celebration in Islam, which commemorates the obedience and willingness of Ibrahim (Abraham) to sacrifice his firstborn son, who was redeemed when God sent a ram to be sacrificed in his place; the feast takes place on the tenth day of the lunar month of Dhu al-Hijjah and marks the end of the pilgrimage, or Hajj.

'Id al-Fitr: The Feast of the Fast-Breaking, the minor annual celebration, which is signaled by the appearance of the new moon that begins the tenth lunar month of Shawwal.

'Iddah: In Islamic law, the legal period of abstention from sexual relations imposed on widows, divorced women, or women whose marriages have been annulled; women cannot legally remarry until the end of this period.

'Ilm: Knowledge; the word from which the term *'alim* (*plural:* ulama')—one who has knowledge; that is, a scholar—is derived.

Imam: Leader of the salat (prayer rituals). In the earliest days of Islam, the ruler was imam as the commander in war, the head of the government, and the leader of the communal prayer. Later, as the ruler's representatives, the governors of the provinces became the leaders of prayer, conducting the Friday prayer and sermon; during the Abbasid period (750–1258), the office lost its political function and the term *imam* began to designate the prayer leader at a masjid.

Imamate: Supreme leadership of the Muslim community.

Imami school: *See* Ja'fari (or Imami) school.

In sha' Allah: "If God wills," the formula Muslims recite when speaking of an intended act or describing a future state of affairs.

Injil: In the Qur'an, the revealed word of God received by Jesus.

Iqta': In fiscal administration, granting a member, or members, of the military the tax revenues from a district on behalf of the state.

Islam: The state of seeking peace through submission and total surrender to God; the name given in the Qur'an to revealed religion.

Isma'ili school: One of the four major Shi'i schools or tendencies of Islamic law. (*See also* Hanafi school, Hanbali school, Maliki school, Shafi'i school, Ja'fari [or Imami] school, and Zaydi school.)

Isnad (*singular:* sanad): The chain of transmitters of a hadith, whose authority is established by tracing it back to the Prophet Muhammad; identifying such a chain is an essential part of verifying the authenticity of a hadith.

Iwan: A chamber or hall that is open to the outside at one end, either directly or through a portico; ancient and medieval iwans generally had vaulted roofs. Palaces and other official buildings were often built in this style, as were halls in masjids and madrasahs. The term *iwan* is sometimes also used to refer to the raised part of a floor.

Izar (or mi'zar): A large sheet-like wrap originally worn as a mantle, a long loincloth, or a waist wrap; later, the term was applied to a large, enveloping body wrap for women and a fringed shawl worn by Jewish women in western Muslim lands.

Ja'fari (or Imami) school: One of the four major *Shi'i* schools or tendencies of Islamic law, developed by Ja'far al-Sadiq (circa 702 – 765) and others. (*See also* Hanafi school, Hanbali school, Maliki school, Shafi'i school, Zaydi school, and Isma'ili school.)

Jahiliyyah: The term used to describe the state of affairs in Arabia before the mission of the Prophet, or the pre-Islamic period and the men of that time. Used more broadly to describe any sort of paganism, the word *jahiliyyah* is derived from *jahil*, which means "ignorant" or "pre-Islamic."

Janazah: A funeral.

Jannah: The heavenly Paradise promised as salvation in the afterlife to one who submits to God (a Muslim).

Jinn: A Qur'anic term for creatures composed of vapor and flame who came to play a large role in folklore. The English word *genie* is derived from *jinn*.

Jizya: The poll, or head, tax that **Muslim** states levied on non-Muslims in lieu of military service.

Jund: Armed troops; in the **Umayyad** period, the term was applied especially to Syrian military garrisons where Arab soldiers lived; under **Mamluk** rule, it meant the sultan's service, but not his personal guard.

Ka'bah: The House of God (Bayt Allah) situated in the center of the Great **Masjid** in **Makkah**. The name *Ka'bah* is derived from the roughly cubic shape of the simple stone structure, which the **Qur'an** says was built by the patriarch Ibrahim (Abraham) at God's command. **Muslims** pray in the direction of the Ka'bah and circumambulate it as part of the rites of the **Hajj** and **'Umrah**.

Kaftan: A wide, full-length robe with sleeves and buttons down the front. This garment originated in Persia and became extremely popular throughout Arab regions.

Kalam: Literally, "speech" or "word"; formal or systematic theology.

Khalifah: Caliph (literally, *successor*), a shortened version of *Khalifat Rasul Allah* (Successor of the Messenger of God). (*Khalifat* is the genitive form of *khalifah*.) This title was given to the first four rulers after the death of Muhammad in 632: Abu Bakr, 'Umar, 'Uthman, and 'Ali, and it passed to the **Umayyads**, the **Abbasids**, and other major dynasties such as the **Fatimids**. It was never officially transferred to the **Ottomans**, who took the title of sultan. In political theory, *khalifah* is the title of the leader of the **Muslim** community; in the **Qur'an**, the term *Khalifat Allah* is used to describe the role of mankind as vice-regent of God on earth.

Khan: In Turkish military usage, a commander of ten thousand soldiers. The same word in Persian designates a staging post and lodging place on a main communication route, a warehouse, or a hostelry in an urban center. (*See also* **funduq** and **caravanserai**.) The Persian word is also used to describe a group of specialized markets or an enclosed concourse of shops with two gateways.

Khanqah: A lodging place used by **Sufis**.

Kharaj: A land tax.

Khatt: A style of handwriting, as in calligraphy.

Khilafah: Caliphate; the **Islamic** state under the authority of a **khalifah**.

Khul': In law, a negotiated divorce; a divorce requested by the wife, who may pay compensation in the form of the **mahr** (bride gift) she has received from the husband.

Khutbah: A sermon, or address, especially during the Friday service.

Kiswah: The brocaded, embroidered fabric covering for the Ka'bah—usually black, gold, and silver—which was replaced each year. It was often carried to Makkah on spe-cial camel litters from textile centers such as Cairo, where it was manufactured.

Kunya: An element of a name composed of *abu* (father) or *umm* (mother) plus a name, generally the eldest son's name, but sometimes the name of a younger son or even a daughter. Some people without children are also referred to by a kunya name, such as Abu Abdullah (father of the servant of God), as a token of formality and respect.

Kursi: A seat. Though *kursi* refers to any kind of seat (such as a chair, couch, throne, stool, or bench), in the daily life of medieval **Muslims**, *kursi* referred to a stool, a stand for an object, or the desk for the **Qur'an** and the seat for the reader. In the Qur'an, *kursi* means "throne," as in Ayat al-Kursi (The Throne Verses).

Kuttab: A beginners', or primary, school, often held in a **masjid** for the purpose of teaching memorization of the Qur'an and the basics of religious practice; an **Islamic** traditional school, also known as a *maktab*.

Madhhab: A way of thinking or persuasion; generally the schools of law in **Islam**. (*See also* **Hanafi school, Hanbali school, Maliki school, Shafi'i school, Ja'fari [or Imami] school, Zaydi school,** and **Isma'ili school**.)

Madinah: A word meaning *city* or *civitas*; in particular, the shortened version of Madinat al-Nabi (City of the Prophet), formerly known as Yathrib, where Muhammad founded the **Islamic** polity after migrating there from **Makkah** with his followers in 622.

Madrasah: An institution and place of learning where the **Islamic** sciences are taught; that is, a college for higher studies as opposed to an elementary school; in medieval usage, a college of law in which Islamic, literary, and philosophical sciences were taught; in Persia during the eleventh century, a center for **Sufis**.

Mahr: The bride gift, or dowry; a sum of money or valuable property given by the groom to the bride for her personal use and as her personal property; the mahr is a condition of completing the marriage contract in **Islam**; if the groom has few means it may be a token gift, on the condition that the bride agrees to accept it.

Majlis: A meeting place or a reception hall of an official; also, a session of a consultative body held in such a hall.

Makkah: The birthplace of Muhammad, a city in the western part of the Arabian peninsula, near the Red Sea coast, where the Ka'bah is located.

Maliki school: One of the four major **Sunni** schools, or tendencies of **Islamic** law, developed by Malik Ibn Abas (circa 712 – 795) and others. (*See also* **Hanafi school, Hanbali school, Shafi'i school, Ja'fari [or Imami] school, Zaydi school,** and **Isma'ili school**.)

Mamluk: Literally, "a thing possessed," hence a "slave"; especially used in the sense of military servants who were formally the property of the ruler. The Mamluks were a dynasty of former soldier-slaves who established and ruled a sultanate in Egypt (1250–1517) and Syria (1260–1516).

Manara: A lighthouse, or an elevated place where a light or beacon is established; the means of marking (originally fire) routes for caravans or for the army in war; or especially a minaret, the tower alongside (or atop) a **masjid,** from which the call to prayer is made.

Mandharah: A large room in an Egyptian house, whose central part, a substitute for the courtyard, is paved, adorned with a fountain, and surrounded by two or three **iwans.**

Maqamat (*singular:* **maqamah**): An Arabic literary genre of rhyming prose anecdotes; literally, *maqamat* means "assemblies" or "session," which may refer to the settings where such anecdotes were told. The genre was created by al-Hamadhani (968–1008). A maqamat collection usually features a picaresque hero whose adventures and eloquent speeches are related by a narrator to the author who, in turn, conveys the stories to his readers, whom he hopes to entertain not only with the content of his anecdotes but also with his literary and linguistic prowess.

Maqsurah: A compartment set apart for the ruler near the **mihrab** in a **masjid.**

Mashrabiyyah: In traditional Arab architecture, a turned-wood latticed panel, usually forming a large bay window on the upper stories of a house; the term derives from *mashraba,* a niche where porous earthenware water jars were exposed to breezes that kept their contents cool for drinking. The niche was incorporated into the lattice-work, which let breezes into the house while keeping the interior screened for privacy.

Masjid: A mosque; literally, a place of **sujud,** or kneeling in prayer with the forehead to the ground; the modern Western European words (English: *mosque,* French: *mosquée,* German: *Moschee,* Italian: *moschea*) come from the Spanish word *mezquita,* a corruption of the original Arabic term; in the **Qur'an,** a sanctuary, especially the **Haram** in **Makkah,** but also a place of worship for any religion.

Mathnawi: Literally, "things in pairs"; a term used in Persian, Turkish, and Urdu for a poem written in rhyming couplets.

Mawat: In law, "dead lands," property that is uncultivated or lying fallow and belongs to no one; in **Islamic** law ownership of such land could be established by bringing it into use through improvement, especially irrigation.

Mawla (*plural:* **Mawali**): A person linked to another by proximity; a patron, client, freedman, or a party to a mutual relationship of assistance, as a kinsman, confederate, ally, or friend; in the **Qur'an** and **hadiths,** *mawla* is applied to God with the meaning of tutor, trustee, and lord.

Mawlid: Celebration of the birth of a person, especially the Prophet Muhammad or a saint; or a panegyric poem in honor of the Prophet. In Egypt, Mawlid is a festival related to the spring equinox and the summer solstice.

Mazlima (*plural:* **Mazalim**): An unjust or oppressive action, an antonym of *'adl* (just action); the plural form, *mazalim,* is the structure through which worldly authorities took direct responsibility for dispensing justice and were obliged to make themselves available to hear the grievances and difficulties of the people; mazalim was also the name for such sessions held regularly under some **Abbasid khalifahs,** as well as the name of a tax levied under the **Aghlabids.**

Mihrab: A prayer niche with the general shape of a doorway and located in a **masjid** so that it indicates the **qiblah** (direction of **Makkah**); the imam stands in it to lead prayers.

Minbar: A raised platform, stairway, or pulpit in a **masjid** from which sermons are preached and announcements are made to the **Muslim** community.

Mi'zar. *See* **izar.**

Mu'amalat: In law, acts that define human relations and ensure that the **Muslims'** behavior conforms to **Islamic** moral norms; these acts are interpersonal acts (literally, "bilateral contracts"), as opposed to the **'ibadat.**

Muezzin, or Muadthin: The prayer caller in a **masjid** or gathering of **Muslims,** either as an informal and temporary appointment for a specific prayer or as a formal appointment, an employee in a masjid.

Mufti: A person who gives a **fatwa** (an opinion on a point of law) or is qualified to do so by dint of knowledge and judgment.

Mughal: A title given for a successor of the Mongol rulers.

Muhajirun: The collective name for the Makkan **Muslims** who migrated with Muhammad to Yathrib, or **Madinah,** in the **Hijrah.**

Muhtasib: A town official who is entrusted with the application of **hisbah** through the supervision of moral behavior and especially inspecting the markets.

Muqarnas: Literally, "stalactites"; a form of decoration used in **Islamic** architecture throughout the central and eastern parts of the **Muslim** lands; usually a series of niches within an architectural frame or arch, forming a three-dimensional composition; in the western Muslim lands, it is called *muqarbas.*

Murshid: Literally, "one who gives right guidance"; the spiritual director (also called *baba, pir,* or *shaykh*) who initiates into a **Sufi** order a novice who is following the Sufi path.

Muruwwa: Manliness, honor, the sum of the physical and moral qualities, virtue; also chastity, good nature, and observance of **Qur'anic** laws; good conduct.

Musharaka: In Islamic economic law, "participation financing"; a contractual partnership for the joint exploitation of capital, work, and/or skills of individuals in a credit or investment partnership, with joint participation in profits and losses.

Muslim: A person who is an adherent of **Islam;** literally, one who submits to God; as an adjective, what is relative to Islam, which includes cultural phenomena influenced by or conducted by Muslims.

Musta'min: Under **Islamic** law, a non-Muslim from a land not under **Muslim** rule who is given an **aman** (safe conduct or a pledge of protection for his life and property) during the period of his presence or mission in a Muslim-ruled territory.

Mutawatir: A narrated report of the highest degree of reliability, which was transmitted from its source to many, who then transmitted to many others; in contrast to *ahad*, a narration in a single chain transmitted from the source to one person to another, and so on. Literally, the term *mutawatir* means "uninterrupted," and a mutawatir report has the highest degree of reliability. The transmission of the **Qur'an** is classified as mutawatir.

Muwahhidun: The name given to the adherents of the reformist movement whose principal element of belief was the divine unity, or **tawhid**; the ruling group known in the West as the **Almohads**.

Muwashshah poetry: A genre of poetry that developed in eleventh-century al-Andalus (**Muslim** Spain), characterized by the complex rhyming structures and the addition of a final stanza composed in Arabic and Romance vernacular; one of the seven postclassical genres of Arabic poetry.

Nasab (*singular:* **ansab**): Kinship or ancestral relations; the genealogy of a person or tribe; a list of ancestors in an Arabic name as designated by *ibn* (son of) for a man or by *bint* (daughter of) for a woman.

Nay: In Persian, a reed pipe or flute.

Nikah: Marriage; literally, marital or conjugal relations.

Nisba: The part of a person's name made up of an adjective ending in *i*, formed originally from the name of the individual's tribe or clan, place of birth or residence, sometimes from a **madhhab**, or occasionally from an occupation. In Arabic, but not in Persian, the nisba is always preceded by the definite article *al-*.

Niyyah: An intention, as in the **Muslim**'s required spoken or silent declaration of intent to perform an obligatory or other act; without such an intention, some acts, such as fasting or purification, are null.

Ordu: A royal tent or royal encampment, a term that became widespread in the **sultan**'s service but not the personal guard.

Ottomans: A Turkic dynasty that ruled much of Southwest Asia, North Africa, and southern Europe from 1299 until 1922. The Ottomans claimed descent from 'Uthman, or Osman (1258–1324), the tribal leader who began the Ottomans' territorial expansion into the **Byzantine Empire**.

Qa'ah: In Egyptian houses, the principal room in the private quarters; a rectangular hall with two **iwans** and a square sunken central area called the *durkha*.

Qada': Literally, "decision"; in the **Qur'an**, this word had many meanings, including: doomsday, jurisdiction, revelation of the truth, predestination, determination, or decree; in theology, it means God's eternal decision or decree and the carrying out of a decree at the appointed time; in law, it is the office and the sentence of a judge.

Qadi: A judge; a representative of the **khalifah**'s authority who is invested with the power and responsibility to do justice in person, to apply the **Shari'ah** law in civil and penal cases, and to administer **masjids** and pious endowments. (*See* **waqf**.)

Qasidah: An ode, or classical Arabic poetic form; other **Muslim** poetic forms were later derived from or influenced by the qasidah.

Qiblah: The direction of **Makkah** (or, more exactly, the **Ka'bah**), toward which the **Muslim** worshiper must direct himself for prayer; in Muslim lands, or those where Muslims reside, it is the name of a point on the compass indicating the direction of Makkah.

Qur'an: The holy scripture of **Islam**; in Islamic belief, the revelation given by God through the Angel Jibril (Gabriel) to Prophet Muhammad from 610 until 632; derived from the words *recitation* or *reading*, the word **Qur'an** is the name that the Qur'an itself gives for the book of Islam.

Quraysh: The Makkan tribal group into which Muhammad was born; a powerful tribe in pre-**Islamic** Arabia, the Quraysh were the custodians of the **Ka'bah** and providers for pilgrims to it, as well as prominent merchants and leaders of a federation of tribes in the Arabian peninsula.

Rabab (or ribab): A viol, or any stringed instrument played with a bow; the instrument known as a rebec.

Rajaz meter: The simplest meter in Arabic poetry, and according to tradition, the oldest; it was most often used for short poems and improvisations in pre-**Islamic** and early Islamic times; in poetry, halved (that is, three-foot) lines unbroken by caesuras.

Rak'a (*plural:* **rakat**): Literally, the act of bowing; in **Islamic** prayer, a sequence of recitations and movements performed during prayer; the name of one unit of prayer.

Ramadan: The ninth month of the **Islamic** lunar calendar, during which **Muslims** fast from dawn to sunset.

Rasul: A messenger or apostle, as in "Muhammad, rasul Allah" (Muhammad, messenger of God); specifically, those prophets entrusted with revealed books; in the secular sense, an envoy or ambassador.

Ra'y: Personal opinion; the result of independent exercise of judgment; in **Islamic** law, the decision of legal matters according to one's judgment in a case on which no known traditional ruling has bearing.

Ribat: A building or lodge used by **Muslim Sufi**, or mystical orders; synonyms are **khanqah**, **tekke**, and **zawiyyah**. A ribat is different from a Christian monastery because members of Sufi orders were not cloistered, nor did they practice celibacy or take monastic vows.

Rida': A piece of white seamless cloth wrapped around the upper half of the wearer's body, which, with the **izar**, is the garment men wear during a pilgrimage.

Rihla fi talab al-'ilm: A journey in search of knowledge; especially the travels of scholars to research **hadiths,** but later, any exploration of a known or unknown territory for the purpose of learning about it.

Rub' al-Khali: The Empty Quarter, a region of extremely arid, sandy desert in the southeastern Arabian peninsula.

Ruba'i (*plural:* ruba'iyyat): A Persian verse form, the shortest formulaic poem (often inaccurately called a quatrain), defined by number of lines, rhyme scheme (*a a b a* or *a a a a*), and meter.

Ruh: Literally, breath, or wind; in the **Qur'an,** an angelic messenger or divine spirit, for example: *al-ruh al-qudus* (the Holy Spirit).

Sadaqa: An act, or sum of money, given as voluntary charity, as opposed to obligatory charity (**zakat**).

Sahabah: The Companions of the Prophet, dating from the first conversions (from 610) at **Makkah** and **Madinah** until the death of Anas ibn Malik (circa 700); in early **Islam,** the term was restricted to those people who were close to the Prophet, but later it included those who had met or seen him during his lifetime.

Sahih: Literally, sound or healthy, correct; in the science of **hadith** authentication, a sound tradition is one whose chain of transmitters goes back to the Prophet without interruption; the term *sahih* is also used for a whole collection of such hadiths.

Saj: Rhymed prose, and the basis of an ornate style.

Sajjada: A prayer carpet or rug; or the mystical path of a Sufi master.

Sakk: In classical **Muslim** administration, an inventory or payroll; in finance, a check, or letter of credit; that is, a means of transferring and remitting payments from a distance for commercial purposes. The English word "check" is derived from *sakk.*

Salaam: Safety, salvation; peace and tranquillity; a salutation; the obligatory greeting of peace among **Muslims** is *al-salaamu 'alaikum* (peace be upon you). In communal prayer, it is a litany pronounced from minarets every Friday about half an hour before the beginning of the call to midday prayer, and it is repeated in the **masjid** before the beginning of the sermon. *Salaam* is also the name for benedictions on the Prophet sung from the minaret during the month of Ramadan about half an hour after midnight.

Salaf: The "pious ancients," the forefathers, **Sahabah,** of early **Islam,** whose example was to be emulated.

Salat: The five obligatory daily prayers in **Islam,** the second of the **Five Pillars of Islam.**

Sanam: A graven idol or image of a deity.

Sawm Ramadan: *See* **siyam.**

Sayyid: Originally a chief, or head, of an Arab tribe; in **Islamic** history, a title of honor designating a descendant of the Prophet (also called *Sharif*); origin of the dialect term *sidi,* a Sufi master.

Saz: A Turkish stringed instrument played to accompany religious folk poetry; or, in Persian, a stringed or wind instrument or musical ensemble of such intruments.

Sha'b: In politics, "a people" or "the people," meaning the common people, lower classes, or the masses.

Shafi'i school: One of the four major **Sunni** schools or tendencies of **Islamic** law developed by al-Shafi'i (762–820) and others. (*See also* **Hanafi school, Hanbali school, Maliki school, Ja'fari [or Imami] school, Zaydi school,** and **Isma'ili school.**)

Shah: King; also the piece called the king in chess, giving rise to the term *checkmate* because the game was won by declaring *shah mat* (the king is dead).

Shahadah: The testimony of faith consisting of the words *la ilaha illa Allah wa Muhammadun rasul Allah* (There is no god but God, and Muhammad is the messenger of God); it is the creed of **Islam** and the first of the **Five Pillars;** pronouncing these words is the only condition for entry into the faith community of Islam.

Shari'ah: Literally, "the trodden way to a watering place"; in the **Qur'an** and in **hadiths,** a divinely appointed way or path; a prophetic religion in its totality; **Islamic** law and practice, meaning the rules and regulations governing the lives of **Muslims;** Islamic jurisprudence.

Shatranj: The game of chess, with chess pieces such as *shah* (king), *rukhkh* (rook), and *faras* (horse).

Shaykh: Literally, an elder; a person of authority and prestige; the chief of any group such as a family, tribe, guild, or religious establishment or order; an **'alim** (scholar) of recognized achievement; a person designated as the master in a field of specialization; in **Sufi** mysticism, the spiritual master.

Sherbet: A sweet, cold drink made of iced or chilled fruit juices.

Shi'a (*adjective form:* **Shi'i**): Originally, *Shi'at 'Ali* (the party or partisans of 'Ali) in 'Ali's struggle with Mu'awiyyah for the **khilafah** in 658–661, and later the opposition to the **Umayyads;** the branch or sect of **Islam** that arose from this opposition, as distinct from **Sunni Muslims.**

Shura: The practice of mutual consultation, recommended in the **Qur'an** as a method of decision making.

Shurta: During early **Muslim** history, a special corps, formed in the early centuries of Muslim history, that was linked to the **khalifah** or governor rather than the army and was mainly responsible for maintaining public order; a police force.

Shuubiyya movement: A movement in early **Islam** that opposed the privileged position of Arab **Muslims** over converts of other ethnic origins.

Sinf: A group of men practicing the same craft, trade, or profession, similar to a guild.

Sirah: Literally, path or way; in **Islamic** history and literature, biography, especially the *Sirah Nabawiyya* (biography of Prophet Muhammad).

Siyam (*or* **Sawm Ramadan**): Fasting, the fourth of the **Five Pillars of Islam.**

Siyar: In jurisprudence, the field concerned with the rules governing war and dealings of non-**Muslims,** apostates, and rebels.

Sufi: A member of the mystical branch of **Islam.**

Suhur: The meal eaten before the break of dawn during Ramadan or before any day of fasting for a **Muslim.**

Sujud: The **Islamic** prayer posture in which the worshiper kneels with forehead, palms, and toes touching the ground; *sujud* is often mistranslated as "prostration"; each unit, or rak'a, of prayer ends with sujud. *See also* **masjid.**

Sultan: A holder of power of authority, the title of a ruler.

Sunnah (*plural:* **sunan**): Literally, the way or path; a habit, custom or hereditary norm of conduct; a normative custom practiced by the Prophet Muhammad or a member of the early **Muslim** community. In its plural form, *sunan,* it refers to several important collections of hadiths and legal pronouncements and is the generic name for such works.

Sunni Muslims: Muslims who designate themselves as Ahl al-**Sunnah** (People of the Sunnah).

Surah: A chapter of the **Qur'an.**

Tabl: A large, wooden, double-headed drum suspended from a strap and beaten with two sticks; the basic percussion instrument of the Ottoman ensemble.

Tafsir: An exegesis, or commentary and interpretation, of the **Qur'an.**

Tanbur: A large, long-necked lute.

Tarh: In alchemy, an inert or molten substance.

Tawaf: The circumambulation of the **Ka'bah** as a rite of the pilgrimage (**hajj** or '**umrah**).

Tawhid: The oneness of God, the divine unity.

Tekke: See **khanqah.**

Timar: A "tax farm" from which a portion of the revenues are allotted to the holder of that privilege and a portion are given over to the imperial administration.

Tiraz: Silken fabrics and brocades designed for ceremonial robes or robes of honor; embroidery, especially embroidered bands incorporating calligraphy in the design; embroidered robes worn by a ruler or a member of the court; such robes were bestowed as tokens of royal favor, appreciation, or obligation and were among the standard diplomatic gifts carried on foreign embassies.

'**Ud:** A lute.

Ulama' (*singular:* '**alim**): People possessing knowledge ('**ilm**) of things; the scholarly class in **Muslim** society; in

Islamic law, the technical term for a specialist in religious law.

Umayyads: A dynasty of **khalifahs** (caliphs) who ruled the **Islamic** empire from 661 until 750, when they were defeated by the **Abba.**

Ummah: A community, in particular, of believers in **Islam;** the worldwide **Muslim** community.

'**Umrah:** The lesser pilgrimage, which includes some of the major pilgrimage (**Hajj**) rites, such as walking seven times around the **Ka'bah,** praying two **rak'at** while facing the Ka'bah and the maqam Ibrahim (standing place of Abraham) next to the Ka'bah, and finally traversing seven times the distance between Safa and Marwa, two nearby hills.

'**Ushr:** A tax on agricultural produce.

Wa'd: A promise or covenant.

Wakalah: An urban meeting place for commercial agents or brokers.

Waqf (*plural:* **awqaf**): In law, an endowment of property or its income as a pledge to the service of God; a charitable foundation.

Wazir: A minister of state or head of a bureaucracy.

Wudu': Ritual purification for prayer, performed by washing the hands, mouth, nostrils, face and head, arms, and feet in a prescribed way.

Zajal: A poetic genre of **Muslim** Spain, written only in the Arabic dialect of Spain, usually with the rhyme scheme *aa bbb a ccc a.*

Zakat: Obligatory charity given from personal or family means beyond the money required for one's basic needs, generally 2.5 percent of one's cash savings, with varying percentages of other assets; the third of the **Five Pillars of Islam.**

Zawiyyah: A religious foundation, usually a small building where a shaykh resided, with rooms for students; a center of mysticism and religious instruction; in Abbasid society, a place where an ascetic lived in solitude; by the fourteenth century *zawiyyah* had come to be synonymous with **ribat,** a center for mysticism and religious instruction.

Zaydi school: One of the four major **Shi'i** schools or tendencies of **Islamic** law, developed by Zayd ibn 'Ali (699–740) and his followers. (*See also* **Hanafi school, Hanbali school, Maliki school, Shafi'i school, Ja'fari [or Imami] school,** and **Isma'ili school.**)

Zij: Astronomical tables or charts of the stars and planets, including theoretical writings; the original meaning of the term was "threads used in weaving."

Zina: Fornication or illicit sexual intercourse by married or unmarried persons.

GENERAL REFERENCES

GENERAL

The Alim for Windows, Multimedia Edition, Release 4.5 (Baltimore: ISL Software, 1996).

Encyclopædia Britannica Online <http://www.search.eb.com>

Encyclopedia of Islam, CD-ROM version (Leiden: E. J. Brill, 1999).

John Esposito, ed., *The Oxford History of Islam* (London & New York: Oxford University Press, 1999).

Isma'il R. and Lois L. al-Faruqi, *The Cultural Atlas of Islam* (London: Collier Macmillan, 1986).

John R. Hayes, ed., *The Genius of Arab Civilization: Source of Renaissance* (New York: New York University Press, 1975).

Philip Khuri Hitti, *History of the Arabs,* tenth edition (New York: St. Martin's Press, 1974).

Marshall G. S. Hodgson, *The Venture of Islam: Conscience and History in a World Civilization,* 3 volumes (Chicago: University of Chicago Press, 1974).

Peter M. Holt, *The Age of the Crusades: The Near East from the Eleventh Century to 1517* (London & New York: Longman, 1985).

Albert H. Hourani, *A History of the Arab People* (Cambridge & New York: Cambridge University Press, 1991).

Hugh Kennedy, *The Prophet and the Age of the Caliphates: The Islamic Near East from the Sixth to the Eleventh Century* (London & New York: Longman, 1986).

Tarif Khalidi, *Arabic Historical Thought in the Classical Period* (Cambridge: Cambridge University Press, 1994).

Ira M. Lapidus, *A History of Islamic Societies* (Cambridge & New York: Cambridge University Press, 1988).

Francis Robinson, ed., *The Cambridge Illustrated History of the Islamic World* (Cambridge: Cambridge University Press, 1996).

Edward Said, *Orientalism* (New York: Pantheon, 1978).

GEOGRAPHY

Nafis Ahmad, *Muslim Contribution to Geography* (Lahore: Sh. Muhammad Ashraf, 1972).

S. M. Ziauddin Alavi, *Geography in the Middle Ages* (Delhi: Sterling, 1966).

S. M. Ali, *Arab Geography* (Aligarh: Muslim University, 1960).

Thomas Arnold and Alfred Guillaume, eds., *The Legacy of Islam* (Oxford: Clarendon Press, 1931).

Ainslie Embree, *Alberuni's India* (New York: Norton, 1971).

J. B. Harley and D. Woodward, *History of Cartography* (Chicago: University of Chicago Press, 1987).

Marshall G. S. Hodgson, *The Venture of Islam: Conscience and History in a World Civilization,* 3 volumes (Chicago: University of Chicago Press, 1974).

George H. T. Kimble, *Geography in the Middle Ages* (London: Methuen, 1938).

Geoffrey J. Martin and Preston E. James, *All Possible Worlds: A History of Geographical Ideas,* third edition, enlarged (New York: Wiley, 1993).

Seyyed Hossein Nasr, *Science and Civilization in Islam* (New York: State University of New York Press, 1987).

Ahmad Nazmi, "Some Aspects of the Image of the World in Muslim Tradition, Legends, and Geographical Literature," *Studia Arabistyczne i Islamistyczne,* 6 (1998): 87–102.

Francis Robinson, *Atlas of the Islamic World since 1500* (New York: Facts On File, 1982).

Roelof Roolvink, with Saleh A. el Ali, Hussain Mones, and Mohd Salim, *Historical Atlas of the Muslim Peoples* (Amsterdam: Djambatan, 1957).

Tim Unwin, *The Place of Geography* (Harlow, U.K.: Longman Scientific & Technical / New York: Wiley, 1992).

THE ARTS

A. J. Arberry, *Classical Persian Literature* (New York: Macmillan, 1958).

Julia Ashtiany and others, *Abbasid Belles Lettres* (Cambridge & New York: Cambridge University Press, 1990).

Nurhan Atasoy and others, *The Art of Islam* (Paris: Unesco, 1990).

Esin Atil, W. T. Chase, and Paul Jett, *Islamic Metalwork* (Washington, D.C.: Freer Gallery of Art, Smithsonian Institution, 1985).

Gertrude Bell, *The Teachings of Hafiz* (London: Octagon Press, 1985).

Sheila S. Blair and Jonathan M. Bloom, *The Art and Architecture of Islam 1250–1800* (New Haven: Yale University Press, 1994).

Blair and Bloom, *Islamic Arts* (London: Phaidon, 1997).

Muhammad ibn Ismail al-Bukhari, *The Translation of the Meanings of Sahih Al-Bukhari: Arabic-English*, 9 volumes, edited and translated by Muhammad Muhsin Khan (Beirut: Dar al-Fikr, 1981).

K. A. C. Creswell, *Early Muslim Architecture* (New York: Hacker Art Books, 1979).

Creswell, *A Short Account of Early Muslim Architecture*, revised by James W. Allan (Cairo: American University in Cairo Press, 1989).

Abbas Daneshvari, ed., *Essays in Islamic Art and Architecture: In Honor of Katharina Otto-Dorn* (Malibu, Cal: Undena, 1981).

Isma'il R. and Lois L. al-Faruqi, *The Cultural Atlas of Islam* (London: Collier Macmillan, 1986).

Martin Frishman and Hasan-Uddin Khan, ed., *The Mosque: History, Architectural Development and Regional Diversity* (New York: Thames & Hudson, 1994).

H. A. R. Gibb, *Arabic Literature: An Introduction*, second revised edition (Oxford: Clarendon Press, 1963).

Basil Gray, ed., *The Arts of the Book in Central Asia, 14th-16th Centuries* (Boulder, Colo.: Shambhala, 1980).

Hafiz, *The Green Sea of Heaven: Fifty Ghazals from the Díwán of Háfiz*, translated by Elizabeth T. Gray (Ashland, Ore.: White Cloud, 1995).

Al-Hariri, *The Assemblies*, 2 volumes, translated by Thomas Chenery (London: Williams & Norgate, 1867, 1898).

John R. Hayes, ed., *The Genius of Arab Civilization: Source of Renaissance* (Cambridge, Mass.: MIT Press, 1983).

Michael C. Hillmann, *Unity in the Ghazals of Hafez* (Minneapolis: Bibliotheca Islamica, 1976).

Ibn Khaldun, *The Muqaddimah: An Introduction to History*, 3 volumes, translated by Franz Rosenthal (London: Routledge & Kegan Paul, 1958; corrected edition, 1967); 1 volume, abridged by N. J. Dawood (London: Routledge & Kegan Paul, 1967).

Al-Jahiz, *Nine Essays of al-Jahiz*, translated by William M. Hutchins (New York: Peter Lang, 1989).

Al-Jurjani, *Asrar al-balagha, The Mysteries of Eloquence*, edited by Hellmut Ritter (Istanbul: Government Press, 1954).

Gabriel Mandel Khan, *Arabic Script: Styles, Variants, and Calligraphic Adaptations* (New York: Abbeville Press, 2001).

James Kritzeck, *Anthology of Islamic Literature, from the Rise of Islam to Modern Times* (New York: Holt, Rinehart & Winston, 1964).

Aptullah Kuran, *The Mosque in Early Ottoman Architecture* (Chicago: University of Chicago Press, 1968).

Reuben Levy, *An Introduction to Persian Literature* (New York: Columbia University Press, 1969).

Franklin D. Lewis, *Rumi Past and Present, East and West: The Life, Teaching and Poetry of Jalal al-Din Rumi* (Oxford & Boston: Oneworld, 2000).

Ilse Lichtenstadter, *Introduction to Classical Arabic Literature* (New York: Twayne, 1974).

Al-Mas'udi, *The Meadows of Gold: The Abbasids*, translated and edited by Paul Lunde and Caroline Stone (London: Kegan Paul International, 1989).

George Michell, ed., *Architecture of the Islamic World: Its History and Social Meaning* (New York: Morrow, 1978).

Mustansir Mir and Jarl E. Fossum, eds., *Literary Heritage of Classical Islam* (Princeton: Darwin, 1993).

George Morrison, ed., *History of Persian Literature: From the Beginning of the Islamic Period to the Present Day* (Leiden: Brill, 1981).

Abu al-Husayn Muslim, *Sahih Muslim*, 4 volumes, translated by Abdul Hamid Siddiqi (Lahore: Shaikh Muhammad Ashraf, 1971–1975).

Al-Nadim, *The Fihrist of al-Nadim: A Tenth-Century Survey of Muslim Culture*, 2 volumes, edited and translated by Bayard Dodge (New York: Columbia University Press, 1970).

Seyyed Hossein Nasr, *Islamic Art and Spirituality* (New York: State University of New York Press, 1987).

Charles Pellat, *The Life and Works of Jahiz*, translated by D. M. Hawke (London: Routledge & Kegan Paul, 1969).

Arthur Upham Pope, *An Introduction to Persian Art Since the Seventh Century A.D.* (Westport, Conn.: Greenwood Press, 1977).

Venetia Porter, *Islamic Tiles* (New York: Interlink, 1995).

David Talbot Rice, *Islamic Art*, revised edition (London: Thames & Hudson, 1975).

B. W. Robinson and others, eds., *Islamic Painting and the Arts of the Book* (London: Faber & Faber, 1976).

Rumi, *The Mathnawi of Jalalu'ddin Rumi*, 8 volumes, edited and translated by R. A. Nicholson (London: Luzac, 1925–1933).

Ahmad M. H. Shboul, *Al-Masudi and His World: A Muslim Humanist and His Interest in Non-Muslims* (London: Ithaca Press, 1979).

Henri Stierlin, *Turkey: From the Selcuks to the Ottomans* (Köln, Germany & New York: Taschen, 1998).

Henri and Anne Stierlin, *Splendours of an Islamic World: Mamluk Art in Cairo 1250–1517* (London & New York: Tauris Parke, 1997).

Rachel Ward, *Islamic Metalwork* (New York: Thames & Hudson, 1993).

John Alden Williams, *The Word of Islam* (Austin: University of Texas Press, 1994).

Michael Zwettler, *The Oral Tradition of Classical Arabic Poetry: Its Character and Implications* (Columbus: Ohio State University Press, 1978).

COMMUNICATION, TRANSPORTATION, AND EXPLORATION

Al-Biruni, *Alberuni's India*, translated by Edward C. Sachau, edited by Ainslie T. Embree (New York: Norton, 1971).

Richard W. Bulliet, *The Camel and the Wheel* (Cambridge, Mass.: Harvard University Press, 1975).

Basil Anthony Collins, *Al-Muqaddasi: The Man and His Work, with Selected Passages Translated from the Arabic* (Ann Arbor: Department of Geography, University of Michigan, 1974).

Ross E. Dunn, *Adventures of Ibn Battuta, A Muslim Traveler of the Fourteenth Century* (Berkeley: University of California Press, 1986).

Dale F. Eickelman and James Piscatori, eds. *Muslim Travellers: Pilgrimage, Migration, and the Religious Imagination* (London: Routledge, 1990).

C. M. Fraehn, *Ibn Fozlan's und anderer Araber Berichte über die Russen älterer Zeit: Nachdruck der Ausgabe von 1823* (Habsburg: Helmut Buske, 1976).

Derek Hill and Oleg Grabar, *Islamic Architecture and Its Decoration, A.D. 800–1500; A Photographic Survey* (Chicago: University of Chicago Press, 1964).

Ibn Battuta, *Travels in Asia and Africa, 1325–1354*, 3 volumes, translated by H. A. R. Gibb (London: Routledge, 1929).

Ibn Jubair, *The Travels of Ibn Jubayr*, translated by R. J. C. Broadhurst (London: Cape, 1952).

Owen Lattimore, *The Desert Road to Turkestan* (New York: Kodansha International, 1995).

Guy Le Strange, *The Lands of the Eastern Caliphate: Mesopotamia, Persia, and Central Asia, from the Moslem conquest to the Time of Timur* (Cambridge: Cambridge University Press, 1905).

N. Levtzion, ed., *Corpus of Early Arabic Sources for West African History*, translated by J. F. P. Hopkins (Cambridge & New York: Cambridge University Press, 1981).

Amin Maalouf, *Leo Africanus*, translated by Peter Sluglett (New York: Norton, 1989).

H. T. Norris, *The Berbers in Arabic Literature* (London & New York: Longman, 1982).

G. R. Tibbetts, *A Study of the Arabic Texts Containing Material on South-east Asia* (Leiden: E. J. Brill, 1979).

Kees Versteegh, *The Arabic Language* (New York: Columbia University Press, 1997).

Alan Villiers, *Sons of Sinbad: An Account of Sailing with the Arabs in Their Dhows, in the Red Sea, around the Coasts of Arabia, and to Zanzibar and Tanganyika: Pearling in the Persian Gulf: and The Life of the Shipmasters, the Mariners and Merchants of Kuwait* (New York: Scribners, 1940).

M. Zaki, ed., *Arab Accounts of India during the Fourteenth Century* (Delhi: Idarah-i Adabiyat-i Delli, 1981).

SOCIAL CLASS SYSTEM AND THE ECONOMY

Nabia Abbot, *Two Queens of Baghdad: Mother and Wife of Harun al-Rashid* (Chicago: University of Chicago Press, 1946).

Leila Ahmad, *Women and Gender in Islam: Historical Roots of a Modern Debate* (New Haven: Yale University Press, 1992).

Muhammad M. Ahsan, *Social Life Under the Abbasids, 786–902 A.D.* (London & New York: Longman, 1979).

Julia Ashtiyani and others, eds., *The Cambridge History of Arabic Literature: Abbasid Belles Lettres* (Cambridge & New York: Cambridge University Press, 1983).

Eliyahu Ashtor, *A Social and Economic History of the Near East in the Middle Ages* (Berkeley: University of California Press, 1976).

George N. Atiyeh and others, *The Genius of Arab Civilization: Source of Renaissance*, third edition (New York & London: New York University Press, 1992).

Al-Baladhuri, *The Origins of the Islamic State: Being a Translation from the Arabic, Accompanied with Annotations, Geographic and Historic Notes of the Kitab Fituh al-Buldan of al-Imam Abu-l Abbas Ahmad Ibn-Jabir al-Baladhuri*, 2 volumes, translated by Philip K. Hitti (New York: Columbia University, 1916, 1924);

Daniel G. Bates and Amal Rassam, *Peoples and Cultures of the Middle East*, second edition (Saddle River, N.J.: Prentice Hall, 2001).

Donna Lee Bowen and Evelyn A. Early, eds., *Everyday Life in the Muslim Middle East* (Bloomington: Indiana University Press, 1993).

George W. Braswell Jr., *Islam: Its Prophet, Peoples, Politics, and Power* (Nashville: Broadman & Holman, 1996).

Michael A. Cook, ed., *Studies in the Economic History of the Middle East: From the Rise of Islam to the Present Day* (Oxford: Oxford University Press, 1970).

Fredrick Mathewson Denny, *An Introduction to Islam*, second edition (New York: Macmillan, 1994).

Beha ed-Din, *The Life of Saladin* (London: Committee of the Palestine Exploration Fund, 1897).

Michael Dols, *The Black Death in the Middle East* (Princeton: Princeton University Press, 1977).

Fred McGraw Donner, *The Early Islamic Conquests* (Princeton: Princeton University Press, 1981).

Ross E. Dunn, *Adventures of Ibn Battuta, A Muslim Traveler of the Fourteenth Century* (Berkeley: University of California Press, 1986).

Elizabeth Warnock Fernea, ed., *Children in the Muslim Middle East* (Austin: University of Texas Press, 1995).

Fernea, ed., *Women and the Family in the Middle East: New Voices of Change* (Austin: University of Texas Press, 1985).

Al-Ghazzali, *Deliverance From Error: An Annotated Translation of al-Munqidh min al Dal-al and Other Relevant Works of al-Ghazzali*, translated by Richard Joseph McCarthy (Louisville, Ky.: Fons Vitae, 1999).

Dimitri Gutas, *Greek Thought, Arabic Culture: The Greco-Arabic Translation Movement in Baghdad and Early 'Abbasid Society* (London & New York: Routledge, 1988).

Shirley Guthrie, *Arab Women in the Middle Ages: Private Lives and Public Roles* (London: Saqi Books, 2000).

Suzanne Haneef, *What Everyone Should Know about Islam and Muslims* (Chicago: Kazi, 1979).

G. R. Hawting, *The First Dynasty of Islam: The Umayyad Caliphate A.D. 661–750* (Carbondale: Southern Illinois University Press, 1987).

Tayeb El-Hibri, *Reinterpreting Islamic Historiography: Harun al-Rashid and the Narrative of the 'Abbasid Caliphate* (Cambridge & New York: Cambridge University Press, 1999).

Philip Khuri Hitti, *History of the Arabs*, tenth edition (New York: St. Martin's Press, 1974).

Peter M. Holt, *The Age of the Crusades: The Near East from the Eleventh Century to 1517* (London & New York: Longman, 1985).

Albert H. Hourani, *A History of the Arab People* (Cambridge & New York: Cambridge University Press, 1991).

Hourani and S. M. Stern, eds., *The Islamic City: A Colloquium* (Philadelphia: University of Pennsylvania Press, 1970).

R. Stephen Humphreys, *From Saladin to the Mongols: The Ayyubids of Damascus 1193–1260* (Albany: State University of New York Press, 1977).

Alice C. Hunsberger, *Nasir Khusraw, The Ruby of Badakhshan: A Portrait of the Persian Poet, Traveller and Philosopher* (London & New York: I. B. Tauris, 2000).

Muhammad ibn Ishaq, *The Life of Muhammad*, translated by Alfred Guillaume (London & New York: Oxford University Press, 1955).

Usama ibn Munqidh, *An Arab Syrian Gentleman and Warrior in the Period of the Crusades*, translated by Philip K. Hitti (Princeton: Princeton University Press, 1981).

Ibn al-Nadim, *The Fihrist of al-Nadim: A Tenth-Century Survey of Muslim Culture*, 2 volumes, edited and translated by Bayard Dodge (New York: Columbia University Press, 1970).

Mahmood Ibrahim, *Merchant Capital and Islam* (Austin: University of Texas Press, 1990).

Robert Irwin, *The Middle East in the Middle Ages: The Early Mamluk Sultanate, 1250–1382* (Carbondale: Southern Illinois University Press, 1986).

Al-Jahiz, *Avarice & the Avaricious = Kitab al-Bukhala*, by Abu Uthman Amr ibn Bahr al-Jahiz, translated by Jim Colville (London & New York: Kegan Paul, 1999).

Nikki R. Keddie and Beth Baron, eds., *Women in Middle Eastern History: Shifting Boundaries in Sex and Gender* (New Haven: Yale University Press, 1991).

Hugh Kennedy, *The Prophet and the Age of the Caliphates: The Islamic Near East from the Sixth to the Eleventh Century* (London & New York: Longman, 1986).

Tarif Khalidi, *Arabic Historical Thought in the Classical Period* (Cambridge: Cambridge University Press, 1994).

Ira M. Lapidus, *A History of Islamic Societies* (Cambridge & New York: Cambridge University Press, 1988).

Lapidus, *Muslim Cities in the Later Middle Ages* (Cambridge & New York: Cambridge University Press, 1984).

Amin Maalouf, *The Crusades Through Arab Eyes*, translated by Jon Rothschild (London: al-Saqi, 1983).

George Makdisi, *The Rise of Colleges: Institutions of Higher Learning in Islam and the West* (Edinburgh: Edinburgh University Press, 1981).

Al-Maqrizi, *A History of the Ayyubid Sultans of Egypt*, translated by R. J. C. Broadhurst (Boston: Twayne, 1980).

Louise Marlow, *Hierarchy and Egalitarianism in Islamic Thought* (Cambridge: Cambridge University Press, 1997).

David Morgan, *Medieval Persia: 1040–1797* (London & New York: Longman, 1988).

Carl F. Petry, ed., *The Cambridge History of Egypt*, volume 1: *The Islamic Period, 640–1517* (Cambridge: Cambridge University Press, 1999).

Fazlur Rahman, *Major Themes of the Qur'an* (Minneapolis: Bibliotheca Islamica, 1988).

Geoffrey Regan, *Lionhearts: Saladin, Richard I, and the Era of the Third Crusade* (New York: Walker, 1999).

Patricia Risso, *Merchants and Faith: Muslim Commerce and Culture in the Indian Ocean* (Boulder, Colo.: Westview Press, 1995).

Maxime Rodinson, *Islam and Capitalism* (New York: Pantheon, 1973).

Syedah Fatima Sadeque, ed., *Baybars I of Egypt* (Dacca: Oxford University Press, 1956).

M. A. Shaban, *The 'Abbasid Revolution* (London: Cambridge University Press, 1970).

Shaban, *Islamic History: A New Interpretation, Vol. I, A.D. 600–750 (A. H. 132)* (Cambridge: Cambridge University Press, 1971).

D. A. Spellberg, *Politics, Gender, and the Islamic Past: The Legacy of 'A'isha bint Abi Bakr* (New York: Columbia University Press, 1994).

Al-Tabari, *The Early 'Abbasid Empire*, 2 volumes, translated by John Alden Williams (Cambridge & New York: Cambridge University Press, 1988, 1989).

Al-Tabari, *The History of al-Tabari*, 39 volumes (Albany: State University of New York, 1985–1999).

Peter Thorau, *The Lion of Egypt: Sultan Baybars I and the Near East in the Thirteenth Century*, translated by P. M. Holt (London & New York: Longman, 1992).

Abraham L. Udavitch, *Partnership and Profit in Medieval Islam* (Princeton: Princeton University Press, 1970).

Abdullah al-Udhari, *Classical Poems by Arab Women: A Bilingual Anthology* (London: Saqi Books, 2000).

Andrew M. Watson, *Agricultural Innovation in the Early Islamic World: The Diffusion of Crops and Farming Techniques, 700–1100* (Cambridge: Cambridge University Press, 1983).

W. Montgomery Watt, *The Formative Period of Islamic Thought* (Edinburgh: Edinburgh University Press, 1973).

Watt, *A History of Islamic Spain* (Edinburgh: Edinburgh University Press, 1965).

Watt, *The Majesty That Was Islam: The Islamic World, 611–1100* (London: Sidgwick & Jackson, 1974).

Watt, *Muhammad: Prophet and Statesman* (London: Oxford University Press, 1961).

Julius Wellhausen, *The Arab Kingdom and Its Fall*, translated by Margaret Graham Weir (Calcutta: University of Calcutta, 1927).

John Alden Williams, ed., *Themes of Islamic Civilization* (Berkeley: University of California Press, 1971).

M. J. L. Young, J. D. Latham, and R. B. Serjeant, eds., *The Cambridge History of Arabic Literature: Religion, Learning and Science in the Abbasid Period* (Cambridge & New York: Cambridge University Press, 1990).

POLITICS, LAW, AND THE MILITARY

K. N. Ahmad, *Muslim Law of Divorce* (New Delhi: Kitab Bhavan, 1978).

Mohamed S. El-Awa, *Punishment in Islamic Law* (Indianapolis: American Trust Publications, 1982).

M. Cherif Bassiouni, ed., *The Islamic Criminal Justice System* (London: Oceana Publications, 1982).

Antony Black, *The History of Islamic Political Thought: From the Prophet to the Present* (New York: Routledge, 2001).

Khalid Yahya Blankinship, *The End of the Jihad State: The Reign of Hisham ibn 'Abd al-Malik and the Collapse of the Umayyads* (Albany: State University of New York Press, 1994).

Michael Brett, *Ibn Khaldun and the Medieval Maghrib* (Aldershot, U.K.: Ashgate Variorum, 1999).

Jonathan E. Brockop, *Early Maliki Law: Ibn 'Abd al-Hakam and His Major Compendium of Jurisprudence* (Leiden: Brill, 2000).

Richard W. Bulliet, *Conversion to Islam in the Medieval Period: An Essay in Quantitative History* (Cambridge, Mass: Harvard University Press, 1979).

N. J. Coulson, *A History of Islamic Law* (Edinburgh: Edinburgh University Press, 1964).

Yasin Dutton, *The Origins of Islamic Law: The Qur'an, the Muwatta' and Madinan 'Amal* (Richmond, U.K.: Curzon Press, 1999).

Asaf A. A. Fyzee, *Outlines of Muhammadan Law*, fourth edition (Oxford: Oxford University Press, 1974).

Wael B. Hallaq, *A History of Islamic Legal Theories: An Introduction to Sunni Usul al-Fiqh* (Cambridge: Cambridge University Press, 1997).

Muhammad Hamidullah, *Muslim Conduct of State*, seventh edition (Lahore: Sh. Muhammad Ashraf, 1977).

Ahmad Hasan, *Analogical Reasoning in Islamic Jurisprudence: A Study of the Juridical Principle of Qiyas* (Islamabad: Islamic Research Institute, 1986).

Hasan, *The Early Development of Islamic Jurisprudence* (Islamabad: Islamic Research Institute, 1970).

Muhammad ibn Ahmad Ibn Rushd, *The Distinguished Jurist's Primer: A Translation of Bidayat Al-Mujtahid*, 2 volumes, translated by Imran Ahsan Khan Nyazee (Reading, U.K.: Garnet, 1994, 1996).

Ibn Khaldun, *al-Muqaddimah: An Introduction to History*, translated by Franz Rosenthal, edited and abridged by N. J. Dawood (Princeton: Princeton University Press, 1967).

Ibn Taymiya, *Public Duties in Islam: The Institution of the Hisba*, translated by Muhtar Holland (Leicester: Islamic Foundation, 1982).

Syed Husain M. Jafri, *The Origins and Early Development of Shi'a Islam* (London & New York: Longman, 1979).

'Ala'al-Din 'Ata-Malik Juwayni, *The History of the World-Conqueror*, translated by J. A. Boyle (Manchester: Manchester University Press, 1958).

Walter Emil Kaegi, *Byzantium and the Early Islamic Conquests* (Cambridge: Cambridge University Press, 1992).

Mohammad Hashim Kamali, *Principles of Islamic Jurisprudence*, revised edition (Cambridge: Islamic Texts Society, 1991).

John Kelsay and James Turner Johnson, eds., *Just War and Jihad: Historical and Theoretical Perspectives on War and Peace in Western and Islamic Traditions* (New York: Greenwood Press, 1991).

Majid Khadduri, *War and Peace in the Law of Islam* (Baltimore: Johns Hopkins Press, 1955).

Bruce B. Lawrence, ed., *Ibn Khaldun and Islamic Ideology* (Leiden: Brill, 1984).

Wilferd Madelung, *The Succession to Muhammad: A Study of the Early Caliphate* (Cambridge: Cambridge University Press, 1997).

Malik ibn Anas, *al-Muwatta'*, translated by 'A'isha 'Abdarahman al-Tarjumana and Ya'qub Johnson (Norwich: Diwan Press, 1982); also translated as *Al-Muwatta' of Imam Malik ibn Anas: The First Formulation of Islamic Law*, translated by 'A'isha 'Abdurrahman Bewley (London: Kegan Paul International, 1989).

Chibli Mallat, ed., *Islam and Public Law: Classical and Contemporary Studies* (London: Graham & Trotman, 1993).

Mallat and Jane Connors, eds., *Islamic Family Law* (London: Graham & Trotman, 1989).

Mansour Hasan Mansour, *The Maliki School of Law: Spread and Domination in North and West Africa 8th to 14th Centuries C.E.* (San Francisco: Austin & Winfield, 1995).

Burhan al-Din al-Marghinani, *The Hedaya, or Guide: A Commentary on the Mussulman Laws*, translated by Charles Hamilton (London: Bensley, 1791).

Al-Mawardi, *The Ordinances of Government: Al-Ahkam al-Sultaniyyah*, translated by Wafaa Wahba (Reading, U.K.: Garnet, 1996); also published as *Al-Ahkam As-Sultaniyyah: The Laws of Islamic Governance*, translated by Asadullah Yate (London: Ta-Ha, 1996).

Ahmad Ibn Naqib al-Misri, *The Reliance of the Traveller: The Classic Manual of Islamic Sacred Law 'Umdat al-Salik*, 2 volumes, edited and translated by Nuh Ha Mim Keller (Evanston, Ill.: Sunna Books, 1994).

Moojan Momen, *An Introduction to Shi'i Islam: The History and Doctrines of Twelver Shi'ism* (New Haven: Yale University Press, 1985).

David O. Morgan, *The Mongols* (Oxford: Blackwell, 1986).

Nizam al-Mulk, *The Book of Government or, Rules for Kings: The Siyar al-Muluk or Siyasatnama*, translated by Hubert Darke, revised edition (London: Routledge & Kegan Paul, 1978).

Shibli Nu'mani, *Imam Abu Hanifah: Life and Work: English Translation of Allamah Shibli Nu'mani's "Sirat-i- Nu'man,"* translated by M. Hadi Hussain (Lahore: Institute of Islamic Culture, 1977).

S. A. A. Rizvi, *Nizam al-Mulk Tusi, His Contribution to Statecraft, Political Theory and the Art of Government* (Lahore, 1978).

Francis Robinson, ed., *The Cambridge Illustrated History of the Islamic World* (Cambridge: Cambridge University Press, 1996).

Joseph Schacht, *An Introduction to Islamic Law* (Oxford: Clarendon Press, 1964).

Muhammad ibn Idris al-Shafi'i, *al-Shafi'i's Risala: Treatise on the Foundations of Islamic Jurisprudence*, translated by Majid Khadduri (Baltimore: Johns Hopkins Press, 1961).

Muhammad ibn Hasan al-Shaybani, *The Islamic Law of Nations: Shaybani's Siyar*, translated by Majid Khadduri (Baltimore: Johns Hopkins Press, 1966).

Al-Tabari, *The History of al-Tabari*, 39 volumes (Albany: State University of New York, 1985–1999).

Emil Tyan, *Histoire de l'organisation judiciaire en pays d'Islam*, second edition (Leiden: Brill, 1960).

Tyan, *Sultanate et califat* (Paris: Recueil Sirey, 1956).

LEISURE, RECREATION, AND DAILY LIFE

Muhammad M. Ahsan, *Social Life Under the Abbasids, 786–902 A.D.* (London & New York: Longman, 1979).

Khatib al-Baghdadi, *The Topography of Baghdad in the Early Middle Ages*, translated by Jacob Lassner (Detroit: Wayne State University Press, 1970).

Richard W. Bulliet, *Islam: The View from the Edge* (New York: Columbia University Press, 1994).

Andre Clot, *Harun al-Rashid and the World of the Thousand and One Nights*, translated by John Howe (New York: New Amsterdam Press, 1989).

Susan L. Douglass, *Beyond A Thousand & One Nights: A Sampler of Literature from Muslim Civilization* (Fountain Valley, Cal.: Council on Islamic Education, 2000).

Isma'il R. al-Faruqi and Lois Lamya', *The Cultural Atlas of Islam* (New York: Macmillan / London: Collier Macmillan, 1986).

Ahmad Badi al-Zaman al-Hamadhani, *The Maqamat of Badi al-Zaman al-Hamadhani*, translated by W. J. Prendergast (London: Curzon Press, 1973).

Al-Harari, *The Assemblies of al-Hariri: Fifty Encounters with the Shaykh Abu Zayd of Seruj*, translated by Amina Shah (London: Octagon Press, 1980).

Jennifer Harris, ed., *Textiles, 5000 Years: An International History and Illustrated Survey* (New York: Abrams, 1993).

Ahmad Y. al-Hassan and Donald R. Hill, *Islamic Technology: An Illustrated History* (Cambridge & New York: Cambridge University Press / Paris: Unesco, 1986).

J. R. Hayes, ed., *The Genius of Arab Civilization: Source of Renaissance* (New York: New York University Press, 1975).

Timothy Insoll, *The Archaeology of Islam* (Oxford: Blackwell, 1999).

Al-Jahiz, *The Life and Works of Jahiz*, translated by Charles Pellat, translated from French by D. M. Hawke (Berkeley: University of California Press, 1969).

Denys Johnson-Davies, *Goha* (Cairo: Hoopoe, in cooperation with the British Council, 1993).

Ibn Khallikan, *Biographical Dictionary*, 4 volumes, translated by Bn Mac Guckin de Slane (Paris: Oriental Translation Fund of Great Britain and Ireland, 1843–1871).

Ira M. Lapidus, *Muslim Cities in the Later Middle Ages* (Cambridge & New York: Cambridge University Press, 1984).

Lapidus, ed., *Middle Eastern Cities: A Symposium on Ancient, Islamic, and Contemporary Middle Eastern Urbanism* (Berkeley: University of California Press, 1969).

Martin Lings, *Muhammad: His Life Based on the Earliest Sources,* revised edition (London: Islamic Texts Society, 1991).

Ibn Said al-Maghibri, *The Banners of the Champions: An Anthology of Medieval Arabic Poetry from Andalusia and Beyond,* translated by James Bellamy and Patricia Owen Steiner (Madison, Wis.: Hispanic Seminary of Medieval Studies, 1989).

Rebecca Martin, *Textiles in Daily Life in the Middle Ages* (Cleveland: Cleveland Museum of Art in cooperation with Indiana University Press, 1985).

Al-Masudi, *The Meadows of Gold: The Abbasids,* translated by Paul Lunde and Caroline Stone (London & New York: Kegan Paul, 1989).

Ian Richard Netton, *Seek Knowledge: Thought and Travel in the House of Islam* (Surrey, U.K.: Curzon Press, 1996).

F. E. Peters, *The Hajj: The Muslim Pilgrimage to Mecca and the Holy Places* (Princeton: Princeton University Press, 1994).

Francis Robinson, *Atlas of the Islamic World Since 1500* (New York: Facts on File, 1982).

Robinson, ed., *Cambridge Illustrated History of the Islamic World* (Cambridge: Cambridge University Press, 1996).

Clive Rogers, ed. *Early Islamic Textiles* (Brighton, U.K.: Rogers & Podmore, 1983).

Muhammad Ibn Sa'd, *Kitab al Tabaqat al-Kabir,* translated by S. Moinul Haq and H. K. Ghazanfar (Karachi: Pakistan Historical Society, 1967).

Nezar al-Sayyad, *Cities and Caliphs: On the Genesis of Arab Muslim Urbanism* (New York & London: Greenwood Press, 1991).

'Abd al-Rahman ibn Nasr al-Shayzari, *The Book of the Islamic Market Inspector: Nihayat al-Rutba fi Talab al-Hisba (the Utmost Authority in the Pursuit of Hisba),* translated by R. P. Buckley (Oxford: Oxford University Press on behalf of the University of Manchester, 1999).

Andrew M. Watson, *Agricultural Innovation in the Early Islamic World: The Diffusion of Crops and Farming Techniques, 700–1100* (Cambridge: Cambridge University Press, 1983).

Liu Xinru, "Silks and Religions in Eurasia, c. AD 600–1200," *Journal of World History,* 6 (Spring 1995): 25–48.

FAMILY AND SOCIAL TRENDS

Leila Ahmed, *Women and Gender in Islam: Historical Roots of a Modern Debate* (New Haven: Yale University Press, 1992).

Maulana Muhammad Ali, trans., *A Manual of Hadith* (Guilford, U.K.: Curzon Press, 1983).

Lois Beck and Nikki Keddie, eds., *Women in the Muslim World* (Cambridge, Mass.: Harvard University Press, 1978).

Jonathan Berkey, *The Transmission of Knowledge in Medieval Cairo* (Princeton: Princeton University Press, 1992).

Abu Hamid al-Ghazali, *Ghazali's Book of Council for Kings,* translated by F. R. C. Bagley (London & New York: Oxford University Press, 1964).

Avner Giladi, *Infants, Parents and Wet Nurses: Medieval Islamic Views on Breastfeeding and Their Social Implications* (Leiden: Brill, 1999).

Husain Haddawy, trans., *The Arabian Nights,* edited by Muhsin Mahdi (New York & London: Norton, 1990).

Gavin Hambly, ed., *Women in the Medieval Muslim World* (New York: St. Martin's Press, 1998).

Ibn Battuta, *Travels in Asia and Africa, 1325–1354,* 3 volumes, translated by H. A. R. Gibb (London: Routledge, 1929).

Nikki R. Keddie and Beth Baron, eds., *Women in Middle Eastern History: Shifting Boundaries in Sex and Gender* (New Haven: Yale University Press, 1991).

Muhammad M. Khan, *The Translation of the Meanings of the Sahih al-Bukhari,* 9 volumes (Madinah: Dar al-Fikr, 1981).

B. F. Musallam, *Sex and Society in Islam* (Cambridge: Cambridge University Press, 1983).

Guity Nashat and Judith Tucker, *Women in the Middle East and North Africa: Restoring Women to History* (Bloomington: Indiana University Press, 1998).

Leslie Peirce, *The Imperial Harem: Women and Sovereignty in the Ottoman Empire* (New York: Oxford University Press, 1993).

Ruth Roded, *Women in Islamic Biographical Collections: From Ibn Sa`d to Who's Who* (Boulder, Colo.: Lynne Rienner, 1994).

Roded, ed., *Women in Islam and the Middle East, A Reader* (London: Tauris, 1999).

Margaret Smith, *Rabi'a the Mystic and Her Fellow-Saints in Islam* (Cambridge: Cambridge University Press, 1928).

Denise Spellburg, *Politics, Gender, and the Islamic Past: The Legacy of 'A'isha bint Abi Bakr* (New York: Columbia University Press, 1994).

Barbara Stowasser, *Women in the Qur'an, Traditions, and Interpretations* (New York & Oxford: Oxford University Press, 1984).

RELIGION AND PHILOSOPHY

Abdul-Amir al-A'asam, *Ibn ar-Riwandi's Kitab Fadihat al-Mu'tazilah: Analytical Study of Ibn ar-Riwandi's Method in His Criticism of the Rational Foundation of Polemics in Islam* (Beirut & Paris: Editions Ouedat, 1977).

Ali Hassan Abdel-Kader, *The Life, Personality, and Writings of al-Junayd: A Study of a Third/Ninth Century Mystic* (London: Luzac, 1976).

Abdullah Yusuf Ali, trans., *The Holy Quran* (N.p.: Holy Koran Publishing House, 1934).

Tor Andrae, *In the Garden of Myrtles: Studies in Early Islamic Mysticism*, translated by Birgitta Sharpe (Albany: State University of New York Press, 1987).

Muhammad Asad, trans., *The Message of the Qur'an* (Gibralter: Dar al-Andalus, 1980).

Syed Muhammad Naquib al-Attas, *Prologomena to the Metaphysics of Islam: An Exposition of the Fundamental Elements of the Worldview of Islam* (Kuala Lumpur, Malaysia: International Institute of Islamic Thought and Civilization, 1995).

Osman Bakar, *Classification of Knowledge in Islam: A Study in Islamic Philosophies of Science* (Cambridge: Islamic Texts Society, 1998).

Vincent J. Cornell, *Realm of the Saint: Power and Authority in Moroccan Sufism* (Austin: University of Texas Press, 1998).

Cornell, *The Way of Abu Madyan: Doctrinal and Poetic Works of Abu Madyan Shu'ayb ibn al-Husayn al-Ansari (c. 509/ 1115-16–594/1198)* (Cambridge: Islamic Texts Society, 1996).

Cornell, "The Way of the Axial Intellect: The Islamic Hermetism of Ibn Sab'in," *Journal of the Muhyiddin Ibn 'Arabi Society*, 23 (1997): 41–79.

Patricia Crone and Martin Hinds, *God's Caliph: Religious Authority in the First Centuries of Islam* (Cambridge: Cambridge University Press, 1986).

Farhad Daftary, *The Isma'ilis: Their History and Doctrines* (Cambridge: Cambridge University Press, 1990).

Carl W. Ernst, *The Shambhala Guide to Sufism: An Essential Introduction to the Philosophy and Practice of the Mystical Tradition of Islam* (Boston & London: Shambhala Publications, 1997).

Majid Fakhry, *A History of Islamic Philosophy* (New York & London: Columbia University Press, 1983).

Fakhry, *A Short Introduction to Islamic Philosophy, Theology, and Mysticism* (Oxford: One World, 1998).

Abu Nasr al-Farabi, *The Political Writings: "Selected Aphorisms" and Other Texts*, translated by Charles E. Butterworth (Ithaca & London: Cornell University Press, 2001).

Richard M. Frank, *Al-Ghazali and the Ash'arite School* (Durham & London: Duke University Press, 1994).

Abu Hamid al-Ghazali, *Deliverance from Error: Five Key Texts Including His Spiritual Autobiography, al-Munqidh min al-Dalal*, translated by R. J. McCarthy (Louisville: Fons Vitae, 2001).

al-Ghazali, *The Incoherence of the Philosophers*, translated by Michael E. Marmura (Provo: Brigham Young University Press, 1997); also translated by Sabih Ahmad Kamali as *Al-Ghazali's Tahafut al-Falasifah (Incoherence of the Philosophers)* (Lahore: Pakistan Philosophical Congress, 1963).

Dimitri Gutas, *Greek Thought, Arabic Culture: The Graeco-Arabic Translation Movement in Baghdad and Early 'Abbasid Society (2nd–4th / 8th–10th centuries)* (London & New York: Routledge, 1998).

Heinz Halm, *The Fatimids and Their Traditions of Learning* (London: I. B. Tauris and The Institute of Ismaili Studies, 1997).

Marshall G. S. Hodgson, *The Venture of Islam: Conscience and History in a World Civilization*, 3 volumes (Chicago: University of Chicago Press, 1974).

'Ali ibn 'Uthman al-Hujwiri, *The Kashf al-Mahjub: The Oldest Persian Treatise on Sufism*, translated by Reynold A. Nicholson (London: Luzac, 1976).

Abd al-Rahman Ibn Khaldun, *The Muqaddimah: An Introduction to History*, translated by Franz Rosenthal, edited by N. J. Dawood (Princeton: Princeton University Press, 1967).

Ibn Rushd, *Averroës: On the Harmony of Religion and Philosophy*, translated by George F. Hourani (London: Luzac, 1976).

Ibn Rushd, *Averroës' Tahafut al-Tahafut (The Incoherence of the Incoherence)*, 2 volumes, translated by Simon van den Bergh (London: Luzac, 1954).

Ibn Rushd, *The Distinguished Jurist's Primer (Bidayat al-Mujtahid)*, 2 volumes, translated by Imran Ahsan Khan Nyazee (Reading, U.K.: Garnet, 1994, 1996).

Imam al-Haramayn al-Juwayni, *A Guide to Conclusive Proofs for the Principles of Belief: Kitab al-irshad ila qawati' al-adilla fi usul al-i'tiqad*, translated by Paul E. Walker (Reading, U.K.: Garnet, 2000).

Martin Lings, *Muhammad: His Life Based on the Earliest Sources* (Rochester, Vt.: Inner Traditions International, 1983).

Muhsin Mahdi, *Alfarabi and the Foundation of Islamic Political Philosophy* (Chicago & London: University of Chicago Press, 2001).

Richard C. Martin and Mark R. Woodward, with Dwi S. Atmaja, *Defenders of Reason in Islam: Mu'tazilism from Medieval School to Modern Symbol* (Oxford: Oneworld, 1997).

Louis Massignon, *Essay on the Origins of the Technical Language of Islamic Mysticism*, translated by Benjamin Clark (Notre Dame: Notre Dame University Press, 1997).

Abu Mansur Muhammad al-Maturidi al-Samarqandi, *Kitab al-Tawhid*, edited by Fathalla Kholeif (Beirut: Dar El Machreq, 1982).

Moojan Momen, *An Introduction to Shi'i Islam: The History and Doctrines of Twelver Shi'ism* (New Haven: Yale University Press, 1985).

Shaykh al-Mufid, *Kitab al-Irshad: The Book of Guidance into the Lives of the Twelve Imams*, translated by I. K. A. Howard (Horsham: Balagha Books / London: Muhammadi Trust, 1981).

Abu al-Faraj al-Nadim, *The Fihrist of al-Nadim: A Tenth-Century Survey of Muslim Culture*, 2 volumes, edited and translated by Bayard Dodge (New York: Columbia University Press, 1970).

Seyyed Hossein Nasr, *An Introduction to Islamic Cosmological Doctrines* (Albany: State University of New York Press, 1993).

Nasr and Oliver Leaman, eds., *History of Islamic Philosophy* (London & New York: Routledge, 1996).

Ian Richard Netton, *Allah Transcendent: Studies in the Structure and Semiotics of Islamic Philosophy, Theology and Cosmology* (Richmond, U.K.: Curzon Press, 1994).

Marmaduke M. Pickthall, *The Life of the Prophet Muhammad: A Brief History* (Beltsville, Md.: Amana, 1998).

Pickthall, trans., *Holy Quran* (Karachi: Dawood Foundation, 1930).

Shlomo Pines, *Studies in Islamic Atomism* (Jerusalem: Magnes Press / Hebrew University, 1997).

Emilio Tornero Poveda, *Al-Kindi: La Transformacion de un Pensamiento Religioso en un Pensamiento Racional* (Madrid: Consejo Superior de Investigaciones Cientificas, 1992).

Fazlur Rahman, *Prophecy in Islam: Philosophy and Orthodoxy* (Chicago & London: University of Chicago Press, 1979).

Annemarie Schimmel, *Mystical Dimensions of Islam* (Chapel Hill: University of North Carolina Press, 1975).

Margaret Smith, *An Early Mystic of Baghdad: A Study of the Life and Teaching of Harith b. Asad al-Muhasibi*, A.D. 781–857 (London: Sheldon Press, 1977).

Abu 'Abd al-Rahman al-Sulami, *Early Sufi Women: Dhikr an-niswa al-muta'abbidat as-sufiyyat*, translated by Rkia Elaroui Cornell (Louisville, Ky.: Fons Vitae, 1999).

Al-Sulami, *The Book of Sufi Chivalry: Futuwwah, Lessons to a Son of the Moment*, translated by Sheikh Tosun Bayrak al-Jerrahi al-Halveti (New York: Inner Traditions International, 1983).

W. Montgomery Watt, *The Formative Period of Islamic Thought* (Edinburgh: Edinburgh University Press, 1973).

Harry Austryn Wolfson, *The Philosophy of the Kalam* (Cambridge, Mass. & London: Harvard University Press, 1976).

SCIENCE, TECHNOLOGY, AND MEDICINE

Nafis Ahmad, *Muslim Contribution to Geography* (New Delhi: Adam, 1945).

Munir-ud-Din Ahmed, *Muslim Education and the Scholar's Social Status up to the 5th Muslim Era* (Zurich: "Der Islam," 1968).

Esin Atil, W. T. Chase, and Paul Jett, *Islamic Metalwork* (Washington, D.C.: Freer Gallery of Art, Smithsonian Institution, 1985).

Jonathan Bloom, "Revolution by the Ream, A History of Paper," *Aramco World*, 50 (May–June 1999): 26–39.

Michael D. Coe and others, *Swords and Hilt Weapons* (New York: Weidenfeld & Nicolson, 1989).

Norman Daniel, *The Arabs and Medieval Europe* (London: Longman, 1979).

Michael W. Dols, *The Black Death in the Middle East* (Princeton: Princeton University Press, 1977).

Zvi Dor-Ner, *Columbus and the Age of Discovery* (New York: Morrow, 1991).

Susan L. Douglass and Karima Diane Alavi, *Emergence of Renaissance: Cultural Interactions between Europeans and Muslims* (Fountain Valley, Cal.: Council on Islamic Education, 1999).

Ross E. Dunn, *Adventures of Ibn Battuta, A Muslim Traveler of the Fourteenth Century* (Berkeley: University of California Press, 1986).

Dale Eickelman and James Piscatori, *Muslim Travelers: Pilgrimage, Migration and the Religious Imagination* (Berkeley: University of California Press, 1990).

Frances and Joseph Gies, *Cathedral, Forge and Waterwheel: Technology and Invention in the Middle Ages* (New York: HarperCollins, 1994).

Sami Khalaf Hamarneh and Glenn Sonnedecker, *A Pharmaceutical View of Abulcasis al-Zahrawi in Moorish Spain* (Leiden: Brill, 1963).

Ahmad Y. al-Hassan and Donald R. Hill, *Islamic Technology: An Illustrated History* (Cambridge & New York: Cambridge University Press / Paris: Unesco, 1986).

John R. Hayes, ed., *The Genius of Arab Civilization: Source of Renaissance* (Cambridge, Mass.: MIT Press, 1983).

Philip Khuri Hitti, *History of the Arabs,* tenth edition (New York: St. Martin's Press, 1974).

Jacob Lassner, *The Topography of Baghdad in the Early Middle Ages* (Detroit: Wayne State University Press, 1970).

Paul Lunde, "The Book of Animals," *Aramco World,* 33 (May–June 1982): 15–19.

Lunde, "Muslims and Muslim Technology in the New World," *Aramco World,* 43 (May–June 1992): 38–41.

Lunde, "Science in the Golden Age," *Aramco World,* 33 (May–June 1982): 6–13.

Amin Maalouf, *The Crusades through Arab Eyes,* translated by Jon Rothschild (New York: Schocken, 1984).

George Makdisi, *The Rise of Colleges: Institutions of Learning in Islam and the West* (Edinburgh: Edinburgh University Press, 1981).

Mehdi Nakosteen, *History of Islamic Origins of Western Education, A.D. 800–1350* (Boulder, Colo.: University of Colorado Press, 1964).

Seyyed Hossein Nasr, *Islamic Art and Spirituality* (New York: State University of New York Press, 1987).

Nasr, *Islamic Science: An Illustrated Study* (London: World of Islam Festival Publishing, 1976).

Nasr, *Science and Civilization in Islam* (Cambridge, Mass.: Harvard University Press, 1968).

Venetia Porter, *Islamic Tiles* (New York: Interlink Books, 1995).

Margaret B. Stillwell, *The Awakening Interest in Science during the First Century of Printing, 1450–1550* (New York: Bibliographical Society of America, 1970).

Jalal al-Din al-Suyuti, *Tibb ul-Nabbi of al-Suyuti, The Medicine of the Prophet,* translated by Cyril Elgood (Cookeville, Tenn., n.d.).

Otto von Simson, *The Gothic Cathedral* (New York: Pantheon, 1956).

Rachel Ward, *Islamic Metalwork* (New York: Thames & Hudson, 1993).

Andrew M. Watson, *Agricultural Innovation in the Early Islamic World* (Cambridge: Cambridge University Press, 1983).

W. Montgomery Watt, *The Influence of Islam on Medieval Europe,* Islamic Surveys 9 (Edinburgh: Edinburgh University Press, 1972).

Philip Ziegler, *The Black Death* (New York: John Day, 1969).

CONTRIBUTORS

Karima Diane Alavi is Director of the Dar al-Islam Teacher Institutes on Understanding and Teaching about Islam in Abiquiu, New Mexico. She received her master's degree in Asian Studies and history from Kent State University, studying language, history, and art in Iran on a Bicentennial Scholarship and returning to Iran in 1978 to teach English at the University of Isfahan. She was one of the few nongovernmental Americans who remained in Iran throughout the Islamic Revolution. She has also taught Islamic Studies at the Sidwell Friends School in Washington, D.C. She is co-author of the curriculum unit *Emergence of Renaissance: Cultural Interactions Between Europeans and Muslims* (co-author with Susan L. Douglass, 1999) and has published articles such as "Ramadan: More Than Fasting," *Journal of the Near East* (South Asia Council of Overseas Schools, Spring 1998); "Life in the House of Wisdom," in "Al-Ma'mun, Caliph of Baghdad," *Calliope History Magazine* (2000); and "At Risk of Prejudice: Teaching Tolerance About Muslim Americans," *Social Education* (October 2001).

Khalid Yahya Blankinship is associate professor of religion and chair of the Department of Religion at Temple University in Philadelphia. He holds an M.A. in Islamic history from Cairo University and a Ph.D. in history (1988) from the University of Washington. He is the author of *The End of the Jihad State: The Reign of Hisham ibn 'Abd al-Malik and the Collapse of the Umayyads* (1994) and "Imarah, Khilafah, and Imamah: The Origins of the Succession to the Prophet Muhammad," in *Shi'ite Heritage: Essays on Classical and Modern Tradition*, edited by Lynda Clarke (2001). He translated two of the thirty-eight volumes of *The History of al-Tabari:* volume 25, *The End of Expansion (covering the years 105–20/724–38)* (1989) and volume 11, *The Challenge to the Empires (covering the years 12–13/633–35)* (1993). He is also the author of several articles, including "The Tribal Factor in the 'Abbasid Revolution: An Analysis of the Betrayal of the Imam Ibrahim b. Muhammad," *Journal of the American Oriental Society* (1988) and "Islam and World History: Towards a New Periodization," *American Journal of the Islamic Social Sciences* (1991), which was

translated into Arabic as "al-Islam wa-al-ta'rikh al-'alami," *Islamiyyat al-ma'rifah* (1995).

Richard W. Bulliet is a professor of history at Columbia University and served for twelve years as the Director of the Middle East Institute at Columbia. His books include *The Columbia History of the Twentieth Century* (editor, 1998), *The Earth and Its Peoples: A Global History* (co-author, 1997), *Islam: The View from the Edge* (1993), *Conversion to Islam in the Medieval Period* (1979), *The Camel and the Wheel* (1975), and *The Patricians of Nishapur* (1972).

Vincent J. Cornell is professor of history and Director of the King Fahd Center for Middle East and Islamic Studies at the University of Arkansas. He is a summa cum laude graduate of the University of California, Berkeley, and received his Ph.D. in Islamic Studies from the University of California, Los Angeles, in 1989. He has taught at Northwestern University, the University of Georgia, and Duke University. He has published *The Way of Abu Madyan* (1996) and *Realm of the Saint: Power and Authority in Moroccan Sufism* (1998). His premodern interests cover Islamic thought from Sufism, to philosophy, to Islamic law. He has lived and worked in Morocco for nearly six years and has taught and done research in Egypt, Tunisia, Malaysia, and Indonesia.

Manar Darwish is an instructor in the Modern Languages Department at the College of New Jersey at Ewing. She has taught art history, art appreciation, and Islamic history courses and has lectured extensively on Islamic art as well as Egyptian history and culture past and present.

Susan L. Douglass is Principal Writer and Researcher for the Council on Islamic Education. She holds an M.A. in Arab Studies (history) from Georgetown University. Her publications include *Strategies and Structures for Presenting World History* (1994) and instructional resources such as *Beyond A Thousand and One Nights: Literature from Muslim Civilization* (2000), *The Emergence of Renaissance: Cultural Interactions between Europeans and Muslims* (co-author with Karima Diane Alavi, 1999), *Images of the Orient: European Travelers to Muslim Lands* (1998), and an elementary series on Muslim history and culture (Kendall/Hunt, 1994–1996). She is also author of the report *Teaching About Religion in National and State Social Studies Standards* (2000) as well as many articles, including "Interpreting Islam in American Schools," with Ross E. Dunn, in *Interpreting Islam*, edited by Hastings Donnan (2002).

Mahmood Ibrahim is a professor of Islamic and Middle Eastern history and the Chairman of the Department of History at California Polytechnic University, Pomona. He is the author of *Merchant Capital and Islam* (1991) and *The Oral History of the Intifada* (in Arabic, 1995). He has also written several articles and many book reviews on Islam, Islamic fundamentalism, and the modern Middle East. He has also been chairman of the Department of History, Geography, and Political Science at Birzeit University in the West Bank (1985–1989).

Munir A. Shaikh is completing a Ph.D. in Islamic Studies at the University of California, Los Angeles. His research interests include the history and culture of medieval Islamic Iberia as well as contemporary American Islam and Muslim institutions. He is the author of the Council on Islamic Education teachers' handbook *Teaching About Islam and Muslims in the Public School Classroom* (1995) and has contributed to other council publications on Islam and Muslim history for secondary

educators. He has also served as editor in chief of *Jusur: The UCLA Journal of Middle East Studies*.

Judith E. Tucker is professor of history and Director of Academic Programs in Arab Studies at Georgetown University. She holds a B.A. from Radcliffe College of Harvard University (1969) and an M.A. and Ph.D. in history and Middle East Studies from Harvard (1981). Her publications include *Women in Nineteenth Century Egypt* (1985); *Arab Women: Old Boundaries, New Frontiers* (editor, 1993); *In the House of the Law: Gender and Islamic Law in Ottoman Syria and Palestine* (1998); *Women in the Middle East and North Africa. Restoring Women to History* (co-author with Guity Nashat, 1999); *A Social History of Women and the Family in the Middle East* (editor with Margaret Meriwether, 1999); "Women in the Middle East and North Africa," in *Restoring Women to History*, edited by Cheryl Johnson-Odim and Margaret Strobel (1988); "Gender and Islamic History," in *Themes in Islamic and European Expansion*, edited by Michael Adas (1993; reprinted in pamphlet form, 1994); "Muftis and Matrimony: Islamic Law in Ottoman Syria and Palestine," *Islamic Law and Society* (1994); and "Revisiting Reform: Women and the Ottoman Law of Family Rights," *Arab Studies Journal* (Fall 1996).

INDEX OF PHOTOGRAPHS

Abbasid coins found in a tenth-century grave near Oslo, Norway (from *Aramco World*, November–December 1999) 187

Abu al-Fida's diagram of the twenty-eight traditional divisions of the world; illumination in a circa 1320 manuscript (Vatican Library, Rome) 412

Abu Zyd and al-Harith arriving in a Muslim village; illumination from a manuscript for the *Maqamat* (Assemblies) of al-Hariri (Bibliothèque Nationale, Paris) 174

An Abyssinian court receiving a Muslim embassy; illumination from a 1306–1307 Tabriz manuscript for *Jami' al-tawarikh* (Collected Histories) by Rashid al-Din (Edinburgh University Library) 216

Adoration of the Magi (fifteenth century) by Gentile da Fabriano; detail of a woman wearing tiraz fabrics (Uffizi Gallery, Florence) 261

An Afghan princess and her attendants; illumination from a 1335–1340 manuscript for the *Shahnameh* (Book of Kings) by Firdawsi (Vever Collection, Arthur M. Sackler Gallery, The National Museum of Asian Art, Smithsonian Institution, Washington, D.C.) 313

Pierre d'Ailly, *Imago Mundi*, Christopher Columbus's copy, with notes about al-Farghani's calculation of the circumference of the earth (Biblioteca Colombina, Seville) 77

Alanya, Turkey, covered berths for ships, built by the Saljuks in 1228 181

Album of the Conqueror: illumination from a fifteenth-century manuscript (Topkapi Library, Istanbul) 168

Aleppo, Syria, Firdaws Madrasah 376; plan of the medieval city, from the itinerary of Nasuh al-Matraki, Istanbul, circa 1536 (Istanbul University Library) 186

Alf Laylah wa Laylah (The Thousand and One Nights), the earliest known fragment, written on paper in 879 by legal scholar Ahmad Ibn Mahfouz (Robert C. Williams American Museum of Papermaking, Atlanta) 145

Alhambra palace (thirteenth century), Granada, Spain: fountains in the Court of Lions and a double-arched window with muqarnas (stalactite) decoration and Arabic calligraphy 106

'Ali ibn Abi Talib (reigned 656–661), calligraphy (from Isma'il R. al-Faruqi, and Lois Lamya', *The Cultural Atlas of Islam*, 1986) 203

Qasim Ali, illuminations in a 1494 manuscript for *Khamsah* (Five) by Nizami (British Library, London) 305, 322

Qadi Jalal al-Din 'Ali's tile gravestone, early fourteenth century (British Museum, London) 209

Anatomical chart of a horse; illumination from a fifteenth-century Egyptian manuscript (University Library, Istanbul) 433

Andromachos and eight physicians of ancient Greece, portraits in a thirteenth-century manuscript for Yahya al-Nahwi's summary of Galen's treatise on antidotes

(Österreichische Nationalbibliothek, Vienna) 420

Aq Suray (ruins), a Timurid palace built at Shahr-I Sabz, Uzbekistan, during the early fifteenth century 120

An Arab dhow (illustration by Susan L. Douglass) 152

The Arabic alphabet (from Francis Robinson, *Atlas of the Islamic World Since 1500*, 1982) 143

Arabic calligraphy styles (from Francis Robinson, *Atlas of the Islamic World Since 1500*, 1982) 95

Arabic numerals, development of (from *Aramco and Its World: Arabia and the Middle East*, 1980) 437

The astrolabe, described in a twelfth-century manuscript for al-Biruni's *Kitab al-Tafhim* (Book of Astrology) (Majles Library, Tehran) 75

An astrolabe from Iraq, circa 927–928 (Kuwait National Museum) 74

The Attarine madrasah in medieval Fez, calligraphy and geometric designs in the carved plaster and tilework of the façade 129

"The Author and His Attendants"; illumination from a 1287 Baghdad manuscript for the *Risalat* (Epistles) by the Ikhwan al-Safa (Brethren of Purity), tenth-century mystics and scientists (Suleymaniye Library, Istanbul) 406

Al-Azhar Masjid, Cairo, courtyard 355

Baghdad, artist's reconstructions of the gates to the Abbasids' round city (from Friedrich Sarre and Ernst Herzfeld, *Archäologische Reise im Euphrat- und Tigris-Gebiet*, volume 2, 1920) 165; Mongol sack of (1258), illumination from a fourteenth-century manuscript for *Jami' al-tawarikh* by Rashid al-Din (Bibliothèque Nationale, Paris) 226; plan of the Abbasid city as it was in the years 772–992 (from Guy Le Strange, *Baghdad During the Abbasid Caliphate*, 1924) 177

Banquet dishes, metalwork, with blessings and the owner's name engraved around the borders, circa 1000 (drawing by Ann Searwright) 271

Battle standard thought to have been the ensign of an Almohad general at the Battle of Las Navas de Tolosa in 1212 (Patrimonio Nacional, Madrid) 222

Bayad singing and playing the 'ud; illumination from a thirteenth-century Spanish or Moroccan manuscript for *Bayad wa Riyad* (Vatican Library, Rome) 277

Bayad wa Riyad (Bayad and Riyad): illumination from a thirteenth-century Spanish or Moroccan manuscript (Vatican Library, Rome) 277

Berths for ships at Alanya, Turkey, built by the Saljuks in 1228 181

Bihzad, illuminations in a circa 1400 manuscript for the *Shahnameh* of Firdawsi (Topkapi Museum, Istanbul) 279; in a circa 1494 manuscript for the *Khamsah* of Nizami (British Library, London) 224; in a 1488–1489 manuscript for the *Bustan* (Garden) by al-Sa'di (General Egyptian Book Organization, Cairo) 208; in a 1494–1495 manuscript for the *Khamsah* of Nizami (British Library, London) 266

Bihzad, student of, illumination in a 1485 manuscript for *Layla wa-Majnun* (Layla and Majnun) by Amir Khosrow Dihlavi (Chester Beatty Library, Dublin) 300

Al-Biruni's description of the astrolabe, in a twelfth-century manuscript for his *Kitab al-Tafhim* (Book of Astrology) (Majles Library, Tehran) 75

Al-Biruni's explanation of an eclipse of the moon; illumination from a manuscript for *Kitab al-tafhim* (El-

ements of Astrology), written in the eleventh century (Majles Library, Tehran) 409

A blunderbuss being fired by a Muslim cavalryman, illumination of a battle scene from a 1493–1494 manuscript for the *Shahnameh* by Abu'l Qasim Firdawsi (Vever Collection, Arthur M. Sackler Gallery, The National Museum of Islamic Art, Smithsonian Institution, Washington, D.C.) 402

Bowl and handwarmer (inlaid brass) typical of vessels Muslim craftsmen made for the European market during the fifteenth century (British Museum, London) 103

A bowl (lustreware) with a depiction of a priest swinging a censer, made for a Christian living in Muslim territory during the first half of the twelfth century (Victoria and Albert Museum, London) 331

Brass and silver-inlaid canteen made in Syria by a Muslim craftsman for sale to a Christian visitor to the Holy Land during the thirteenth century (Freer Gallery of Art, The National Museum of Islamic Art, Smithsonian Institution, Washington, D.C.) 292

Brass bowl and handwarmer (inlaid) typical of vessels Muslim craftsmen made for the European market during the fifteenth century (British Museum, London) 103

Brass candlestick inlaid with copper and silver, made in Iran, circa 1220–1250 (Victoria and Albert Museum, London) 268

Brass handwarmer and bowl (inlaid) typical of vessels Muslim craftsmen made for the European market during the fifteenth century (British Museum, London) 103

Brass penbox with silver and copper inlay made in thirteenth-century Iraq (Victoria and Albert Museum, London) 104

Brass (pierced) and silver-inlaid globe made in Syria for Badr al-Din Baysari, circa 1270 (British Museum, London) 244

Brethren of Purity (Ikhwan al-Safa), *Risalat* (Epistles); illumination of "The Author and His Attendants" from a 1287 Baghdad manuscript

(Suleymaniye Library, Istanbul) 406

Bronze astrolabe from Iraq, circa 927–928 (Kuwait National Museum) 74

Bukhara, Samanid dynasty tomb with decorative brickwork, built during the first half of the tenth century 119

Bustan (Garden) by al-Sa'di: illumination by Bihzad in a 1488–1489 manuscript (General Egyptian Book Organization, Cairo) 208

Cairo, Masjid and Madrasah of Sultan al-Malik al-Mu'ayyad Shaykh (ruled 1412–1421), inscription reading "There is no god but God, and Muhammad is the Messenger of God" 367

Cairo, Masjid of al-Azhar, courtyard 355

Cairo, Sultan Hassan madrasah, mihrab (prayer niche) in the Mamluk masjid 117

Cairo, Sultan al-Malik al-Ashraf Qa'itbay mausoleum complex 380

Cairo, Zahiriyyah madrasah, courtyard 385

Calligraphy and geometric designs in the carved plaster and tilework of the façade of the Attarine madrasah in medieval Fez 129

Calligraphy attributed to Khalifah 'Ali ibn Abi Talib, who reigned 656–661 (from Isma'il R. al-Faruqi and Lois Lamya', *The Cultural Atlas of Islam*, 1986) 203

Calligraphy styles (from Francis Robinson, *Atlas of the Islamic World Since 1500*, 1982) 95

Camel train, Mongol, depicted on a ceramic plate made in fourteenth-century Iran (Landesbildstelle Rheinland, Düsseldorf) 148

Candlestick of brass inlaid with copper and silver, made in Iran, circa 1220–1250 (Victoria and Albert Museum, London) 268

Canteen of brass with silver inlays, made in Syria by a Muslim craftsman for sale to a Christian visitor to the Holy Land during the thirteenth century (Freer Gallery of Art, The National Museum of Islamic Art, Smithsonian Institution, Washington, D.C.) 292

A catapult; illumination from a 1306 manuscript for Rashid al-Din's *Jami' al-tawarikh* (Edinburgh University Library) 225

A cavalryman firing a blunderbuss; illumination from a 1493–1494 manuscript for the *Shahnameh* by Abu'l Qasim Firdawsi (Vever Collection, Arthur M. Sackler Gallery, The National Museum of Islamic Art, Smithsonian Institution, Washington, D.C.) 402

Cavalrymen jousting; illumination from *Kitab al-Baytarah* (Book of Veterinary Medicine), a fourteenth-century Egyptian manuscript (Museum of Islamic Art, Cairo) 221

Celebration of a child's birth; illumination by a student of Bihzad from a 1485 manuscript for *Layla wa-Majnun* (Layla and Majnun) by Amir Khosrow Dihlavi (Chester Beatty Library, Dublin) 300

A ceramic dish, lustre-glazed, made in Valencia, Spain, during the early fifteenth century (Victoria and Albert Museum, London) 274

A ceramic plate decorated with a picture of a Mongol camel train, made in fourteenth-century Iran (Landesbildstelle Rheinland, Düsseldorf) 148

Children in a masjid school; illumination by al-Wasiti from a 1237 Baghdad manuscript for the *Maqamat* of al-Hariri (Bibliothèque Nationale, Paris) 304

Christopher Columbus, notes about al-Farghani's calculation of the circumference of the earth; in Columbus's copy of *Imago Mundi,* a fifteenth-century work by Pierre d'Ailly (Biblioteca Colombina, Seville) 77

Coins from the Abbasid era found in a tenth-century grave near Oslo, Norway (from *Aramco World,* November–December 1999) 187

Córdoba, Spain, the Great Masjid, interior 110

Damascus, Syria, the Great Masjid, interior 345

Decorative brickwork on a tomb built in Bukhara for a member of the Samanid dynasty during the first half of the tenth century 119

A dhow (illustration by Susan L. Douglass) 152

Amir Khosrow Dihlavi, *Layla wa-Majnun* (Layla and Majnun): illumination from a 1485 manuscript (Chester Beatty Library, Dublin) 300

Diwan (Collected Poems) by Khwaju Kirmani: illumination from a 1396 Baghdad manuscript (British Library, London) 310

Djenné, Mali, masjid built of plastered mudbrick in as early as the thirteenth century (drawing by Pierre Maas; from *Aramco World,* November–December 199) 116

The Dome of the Rock, Jerusalem 691 107; interior decorated with the earliest surviving written verses from the Qur'an 338

An eclipse of the moon explained in an illumination from a manuscript for al-Biruni's *Kitab al-tafhim* (Elements of Astrology), written in the eleventh century (Majles Library, Tehran) 409

Edirne, Turkey, hospital built by Ottoman Sultan Bayazid II, in 1484–1488 422

Elements by Euclid; first page of al-Tusi's thirteenth-century commentary on the work, from a fifteenth-century Persian manuscript (Millet Library, Istanbul) 416

Euclid's *Elements;* first page of al-Tusi's thirteenth-century commentary on the work, from a fifteenth-century Persian manuscript (Millet Library, Istanbul) 416

Expansion of the Islamic World to 1500 (from Francis Robinson, *Atlas of the Islamic World Since 1500,* 1982) 231

Al-Farghani's calculation of the circumference of the earth, Christopher Columbus's notes about, in his copy of *Imago Mundi,* a fifteenth-century work by Pierre d'Ailly (Biblioteca Colombina, Seville) 77

Farm laborers cultivating medicinal plants; illumination from *Kitab ad-Diryad* (Book of Antidotes), a late twelfth-century Muslim medical manuscript (Bibliothèque Nationale, Paris) 172

Fez, the Attarine madrasah, calligraphy and geometric designs in the carved plaster and tilework of the façade 129

The Firdaws Madrasah in Aleppo, Syria, built in 1236 376

Firdawsi, *Shahnameh* (Book of Kings): illuminations by Bihzad from a circa 1400 manuscript (Topkapi Museum, Istanbul) 279; from a 1493–1494 manuscript (Vever Collection, Arthur M. Sackler Gallery, The National Museum of Islamic Art, Smithsonian Institution, Washington, D.C.) 402; from a 1335–1340 manuscript (Vever Collection, Arthur M. Sackler Gallery, The National Museum of Asian Art, Smithsonian Institution, Washington, D.C.) 313

Funeral procession of Ghazan (ruled 1295–1304), the first Ilkhanid (Mongol) ruler to embrace Islam; illumination from a fourteenth-century manuscript for Rashid al-Din's *Jami' al-tawarikh* (Bibliothèque Nationale, Paris) 227

Al-Futuhat al-Makkiyyah (The Makkan Revelations): diagram from an early-sixteenth-century manuscript (British Library, London) 382

Gentile da Fabriano, *Adoration of the Magi* (fifteenth century); detail of a woman wearing tiraz fabrics (Uffizi Gallery, Florence) 261

Al-Ghazali, *Ihya' 'ulum al-din* (The Revival of the Religious Sciences), page from a 1495 manuscript (Los Angeles County Museum of Art) 390

Ghazan (ruled 1295–1304), funeral procession for the first Ilkhanid (Mongol) ruler to embrace Islam; illumination from a fourteenth-century manuscript for Rashid al-Din's *Jami' al-tawarikh* (Bibliothèque Nationale, Paris) 227

Globe (pierced brass and silver inlaid) made in Syria for Badr al-Din Baysari, circa 1270 (British Museum, London) 244

Gravestone (early fourteenth-century tile) of Qadi Jalal al-Din 'Ali (British Museum, London) 209

The Great Masjid and minaret at Samarra', built by the Umayyad khalifah al-Mutawakkil in 847–851 353

The Great Masjid at Córdoba, Spain, interior 110

The Great Masjid at Damascus, Syria, interior 345

The Great Masjid at Isfahan, Iran, commissioned by Saljuk sultan Malik-Shah I (ruled 1073–1092) 357

The Great Masjid at Kariouan, Tunisia, courtyard 349; minbar 352

The Great Masjid at Tlemcen, Tunisia, mihrab (prayer niche) 358

The Great Masjid at Xian, China, courtyard and garden complex, painting on silk (from *Aramco World*, July-August 1985) 347

Handwarmer and bowl (inlaid brass), typical of vessels Muslim craftsmen made for the European market during the fifteenth century (British Museum, London) 103

Al-Hariri, *Maqamat* (Assemblies): illuminations by al-Wasiti in a 1237 Baghdad manuscript (Bibliothèque Nationale, Paris) 281, 283, 298, 304, 311, 360; from a circa 1256 manuscript (British Library, London) 121; from a circa 1237 manuscript (Bibliothèque Nationale, Paris) 89, 113; from a thirteenth-century manuscript (Bibliothèque Nationale, Paris) 154, 174; from a 1237 manuscript (British Library, London) 258; from an early thirteenth-century Baghdad manuscript (Bibliothèque Nationale, Paris) 179, 184

Horse, anatomical chart; illumination from a fifteenth-century Egyptian manuscript (University Library, Istanbul) 433

Hospital built by Ottoman Sultan Bayazid II in Edirne (in present-day Turkey), 1484–1488 422

A hunter attacking a lion; illumination by Bihzad in a manuscript for the *Shahnameh* of Firdawsi, circa 1400 (Topkapi Museum, Istanbul) 279

Ibn al-'Arabi, *al-Futuhat al-Makkiyyah* (The Makkan Revelations, written 1202–1237): diagram from an early-

sixteenth-century manuscript (British Library, London) 382

Ibn al-Haytham's diagram of how to find the point of reflection between an object and its image in a spherical mirror, a solution to what is known as "Alhazen's Problem"; illumination from a 1269 manuscript for *Kitab al-Manazir* (Book of Optics), written in the eleventh century (Royal Observatory, Edinburgh) 428

Ibn al-Muqatta', *Kalilah wa-Dimmah* (Kalilah and Dimmah, eighth century), page from a manuscript (Bodleian Library, Oxford) 91

Ibn Hawqal's tenth-century map of western Asia and the eastern Mediterranean (Suleymaniye Library, Istanbul) 71

Ibn Rushd (known in the West as Averroës), as depicted in *The Triumph of St. Thomas Aquinas*, a fourteenth-century fresco in the Church of Santa Maria Novella, Florence 378

Al-Idrisi's twelfth-century map of the Mediterranean, northern Africa, and southwestern Asia (Bodleian Library, Oxford) 73

Ihya' 'ulum al-din (The Revival of the Religious Sciences) by al-Ghazali, page from a 1495 manuscript (Los Angeles County Museum of Art) 390

Ikat velvet Turkestani man's coat (chalat) with brocade lining and embroidered cuffs and bindings (Whitworth Art Gallery, University of Manchester) 254

Ikhwan al-Safa (Brethren of Purity), *Risalat* (Epistles): illumination from a 1287 Baghdad manuscript (Suleymaniye Library, Istanbul) 406

Imago Mundi by Pierre d'Ailly, Christopher Columbus's copy with notes about al-Farghani's calculation of the circumference of the earth (Biblioteca Colombina, Seville) 77

An imam delivering a sermon from a minbar in a masjid; illumination by al-Wasiti from a 1237 manuscript for the *Maqamat* of al-Hariri (Bibliothèque Nationale, Paris) 360

Incendiary troops wearing fireproof clothing covered with lit firecrackers and carrying flaming devices to throw at enemies (top) and men preparing to fire rockets (bottom); illumination from a fourteenth-century manuscript for a military treatise (Keir Collection, Richmond, U.K.) 425

An iris and a lily; illuminations from a fifteenth-century manuscript for a Persian translation of *Materia Medica* by Dioscorides (Topkapi Museum, Istanbul) 410

Isfahan, Iran, the Great Masjid, commissioned by Saljuk sultan Malik-Shah I (ruled 1073–1092) 357

Islamic law, chart showing how a Muslim judge arrives at a decision on its validity (from Marshall G. S. Hodgson, *The Venture of Islam*, 1977) 219

The Islamic World, expansion to 1500 (from Francis Robinson, *Atlas of the Islamic World Since 1500*, 1982) 231

Al-Jahiz, *Kitab al-hayawan* (The Book of Animals, ninth century): illumination from a manuscript (Ambrosiana Library, Milan) 93

Jami' al-tawarikh (Collected Histories) by Rashid al-Din: illuminations from a fourteenth-century manuscript (Bibliothèque Nationale, Paris) 226, 227; from a 1306–1307 Tabriz manuscript (Edinburgh University Library) 215, 216, 225

Al-Jazari, *Kitab fi ma 'rifat al-hiyal al-handasiyah* (Book of Knowledge of Ingenious Mechanical Devices): illuminations from a 1315 Syrian manuscript (Freer Gallery of Art, The National Museum of Asian Art, Smithsonian Institution, Washington, D.C.) 419; from a thirteenth-century Iranian manuscript (Topkapi Museum, Istanbul) 212; from a thirteenth-century manuscript (Suleymaniye Library, Istanbul) 430, 438

Jerusalem, the Dome of the Rock, completed 691, 107; interior decorated with the earliest surviving written verses from the Qur'an 338

The Ka'bah in Makkah (photograph by S. M. Amin) 336

Kalilah wa-Dimmah (Kalilah and Dimmah, eighth century) by Ibn al-Muqatta', page from a manuscript (Bodleian Library, Oxford) 91

Kariouan, Tunisia, Great Masjid, courtyard 349; minbar 352

A khalifah in the bath house; illumination by Bihzad in a 1494–1495 manuscript for the *Khamsah* of Nizami (British Library, London) 266

Khamsah (Five) by Nizami: illuminations attributed to Qasim Ali from a 1494 manuscript (British Library, London) 305, 322; by Bihzad from a circa 1494 manuscript (British Library, London) 224; by Bihzad from a 1494–1495 manuscript (British Library, London) 266

Khawarnaq, Iraq, construction of the fort; illumination from a manuscript for Nizami's *Khamsah*, circa 1494, illuminated by Bihzad (British Library, London) 224

Khirbat al-Mafjah, mosaic floor from the bath (Palestine Archaeological Museum) 205

Khwaju Kirmani, *Diwan* (Collected Poems): illumination from a 1396 Baghdad manuscript (British Library, London) 310

Al-Kindi, *Kitab Kimya' al-'Itr wa al-Tas'idat* (Book of Perfume Chemistry and Distillation): illumination (Suleymaniye Library, Istanbul) 415

Kitab ad-Diryad (Book of Antidotes): illumination from a late twelfth-century manuscript (Bibliothèque Nationale, Paris) 172

Kitab al-Baytarah (Book of Veterinary Medicine): illumination from a fourteenth-century Egyptian manuscript (Museum of Islamic Art, Cairo) 221

Kitab al-hayawan (The Book of Animals, ninth century) by al-Jahiz: illumination from a manuscript (Ambrosiana Library, Milan) 93

Kitab al-Manazir (Book of Optics, written eleventh century) by Ibn al-Haytham: illumination from a 1269 manuscript (Royal Observatory, Edinburgh) 428

Kitab al-tafhim (Elements of Astrology) by al-Biruni: illuminations (Majles Library, Tehran) 75, 409

Kitab fi ma 'rifat al-hiyal al-handasiyah (Book of Knowledge of Ingenious Mechanical Devices) by al-Jazari: illuminations from a 1315 Syrian manuscript (Freer Gallery of Art, The National Museum of Asian Art, Smithsonian Institution, Washington, D.C.) 419; from a thirteenth-century Iranian manuscript (Topkapi Museum, Istanbul) 212; from a thirteenth-century manuscript (Suleymaniye Library, Istanbul) 430, 438

Kitab Kimya' al-'Itr wa al-Tas'idat (Book of Perfume Chemistry and Distillation) by al-Kindi: illumination from a ninth-century manuscript (Suleymaniye Library, Istanbul) 415

Konya, Turkey, gates of Sultan Khan, 189

Laborers building the fort at Khawarnaq, on the Euphrates River in present-day Iraq; from a manuscript for Nizami's *Khamsah*, circa 1494, illuminated by Bihzad (British Library, London) 224

Land and sea routes (from Francis Robinson, ed., *The Cambridge Illustrated History of the Islamic World*, 1996) 150

"Layla and Majnun at School"; illumination attributed to Qasim Ali from a 1494 manuscript for *Khamsah* by Nizami (British Library, London) 305

Layla wa-Majnun (Layla and Majnun) by Amir Khosrow Dihlavi: illumination by a student of Bihzad from a 1485 manuscript (Chester Beatty Library, Dublin) 300

A literary group in a Baghdad garden, circa 1237; illumination from a manuscript for the *Maqamat* (Assemblies) of al-Hariri (Bibliothèque Nationale, Paris) 89

Loom, horizontal; illumination from a mid-twelfth-century manuscript (Trinity College, Cambridge) 256

A lustre-glazed ceramic dish made in Valencia, Spain, during the early fifteenth century (Victoria and Albert Museum, London) 274

Lustreware bowl with a depiction of a priest swinging a censer, made for a Christian living in Muslim territory during the first half of the twelfth century (Victoria and Albert Museum, London) 331

Madinah, the Prophet Muhammad's masjid (plan from Isma'il R. al-Faruqi and Lois Lamya', *The Cultural Atlas of Islam*, 1986) 249

Mahmud of Ghazna (998–1030), in eastern Afghanistan, putting on the robe of honor sent to him by the Abbasid khalifah al-Qahir; from a 1306–1307 Tabriz manuscript for *Jami' al-tawarikh* by Rashid al-Din (Edinburgh University Library) 215

Makkah, the Ka'bah (photograph by S. M. Amin) 336

A man hurrying home for the birth of his son; illumination by al-Wasiti from a 1237 Baghdad manuscript for the *Maqamat* (Assemblies) of al-Hariri (Bibliothèque Nationale, Paris) 298

Man's coat (chalat), Turkestani, made of ikat velvet with brocade lining and embroidered cuffs and bindings (Whitworth Art Gallery, University of Manchester) 254

A man's wool tunic with tapestry ornamentation, made in sixth- or seventh-century Egypt (Whitworth Art Gallery, University of Manchester) 251

The many emanating from the One Being; illumination in an early-sixteenth-century manuscript for al-*Futuhat al-Makkiyyah* (The Makkan Revelations, 1202–1237), by Sufi theologian Ibn al-'Arabi (British Library, London) 382

Maqamat (Assemblies) by al-Hariri: illuminations by al-Wasiti in a 1237 Baghdad manuscript (Bibliothèque Nationale, Paris) 281, 283, 298, 304, 311, 360; from a circa 1256 manuscript (British Library, London) 121; from a circa 1237 manuscript (Bibliothèque Nationale, Paris) 89, 113; from a thirteenth-century manuscript (Bibliothèque Nationale, Paris) 154, 174; from a 1237 manuscript (British Library, London) 258; from an early-thirteenth-century Baghdad manuscript (Bibliothèque Nationale, Paris) 179, 184

Masjid lamp, glass with enameled decorations, made in Syria for Saif al-Din Tuquz-Timur, assessor to Sultan al-Malik al-Nasir, 1340 (British Museum, London) 364

A masjid school; illumination by al-Wasiti from a 1237 Baghdad manuscript for the *Maqamat* of al-Hariri (Bibliothèque Nationale, Paris) 304

Materia Medica by Dioscorides: illuminations from a fifteenth-century manuscript for a Persian translation (Topkapi Museum, Istanbul) 410

Mathnawi-i ma'nawi (Spiritual Couplets) by Rumi: illumination from a 1458–1459 manuscript (Vever Collection, Arthur M. Sackler Gallery, The National Museum of Asian Art, Smithsonian Institution, Washington, D.C.) 384

A mechanical beverage dispenser; illumination from a thirteenth-century Iranian manuscript for al-Jazari's *Kitab fi ma 'rifat al-hiyal al-handasiyah* (Book of Knowledge of Ingenious Mechanical Devices) (Topkapi Museum, Istanbul) 212

A mechanical hand-washing device; illumination from a 1315 Syrian manuscript for *Kitab fi ma'rifat al-hiyal al-handasiyyah* by al-Jazari (Freer Gallery of Art, The National Museum of Asian Art, Smithsonian Institution, Washington, D.C.) 419

A medieval horizontal loom; illumination from a mid-twelfth-century manuscript (Trinity College, Cambridge) 256

The Mediterranean, northern Africa, and southwestern Asia; a twelfth-century map by al-Idrisi (Bodleian Library, Oxford) 73

Men and women seated separately in a masjid; illumination from a medieval Persian manuscript (Bodleian Library, Oxford) 317

A merchant and his porter; illumination from an early-thirteenth-century Baghdad manuscript for the *Maqamat* of al-Hariri (Bibliothèque Nationale, Paris) 179

Metalwork banquet dishes with blessings and the owner's name engraved around the borders, circa 1000 (drawing by Ann Searwright) 271

Mihrab (prayer niche) in the Great Masjid of Tlemcen, Tunisia, built in 1082 and restored in 1136 358

Mihrab in the Mamluk masjid at the Sultan Hassan madrasah, built in Cairo in 1356 117

Minbar, carved in 862, in the Great Masjid at Kairouan 352

Minbar made of carved wood and ivory, Egypt, circa 1470 (Victoria and Albert Museum, London) 369

A Mongol camel train depicted on a ceramic plate made in fourteenth-century Iran (Landesbildstelle Rheinland, Düsseldorf) 148

The Mongol sack of Baghdad (1258); illumination from a fourteenth-century manuscript for *Jami' al-tawarikh* by Rashid al-Din (Bibliothèque Nationale, Paris) 226

Mosaic floor from the bath at the Umayyad desert palace of Khirbat al-Mafjah (Palestine Archaeological Museum) 205

Mourning for Layla's husband, Ibn Salam; illumination attributed to Qasim Ali from a 1494 manuscript for *Khamsah* by Nizami (British Library, London) 322

Musicians in a tavern playing a tambourine, short-necked lute, and harp; illumination from a circa 1256 manuscript for al-Hariri's *Maqamat* (British Library, London) 121

A Muslim burial scene; illumination by al-Wasiti from a 1237 manuscript for the *Maqamat* of al-Hariri (Bibliothèque Nationale, Paris) 283

A Muslim embassy to the court of an Abyssinian ruler; illumination from a 1306–1307 Tabriz manuscript for *Jami' al-tawarikh* by Rashid al-Din (Edinburgh University Library) 216

Yahya al-Nahwi's summary of Galen's treatise on antidotes: illumination from a thirteenth-century manuscript for (Österreichische Nationalbibliothek, Vienna) 420

Las Navas de Tolosa, Battle of (1212), banner thought to have been the ensign of an Almohad general (Patrimonio Nacional, Madrid) 222

Nizami, *Khamsah* (Five): illuminations attributed to Qasim Ali from a 1494 manuscript (British Library, London) 305, 322; by Bihzad from a circa 1494 manuscript (British Library, London) 224; by Bihzad from a 1494–1495 manuscript (British Library, London) 266

A nomadic encampment; illumination from a fifteenth-century manuscript for *Album of the Conqueror* (Topkapi Library, Istanbul) 168

An ostrich sitting on its eggs; illumination from a manuscript for *Kitab al-hayawan* (The Book of Animals) by the ninth-century writer al-Jahiz (Ambrosiana Library, Milan) 93

Penbox of brass with silver and copper inlay, made in thirteenth-century Iraq (Victoria and Albert Museum, London) 104

People pouring gold coins over a groom as he leaves his bride's room on the day after their wedding; illumination from a 1396 Baghdad manuscript for the *Diwan* (Collected Poems) of Khwaju Kirmani (British Library, London) 310

Peter of Eboli, writings; illumination from an 1195 Sicilian manuscript (Burgerbibliothek, Bern) 144

Pilgrimage certificate (fragment) issued at Makkah and Madinah in the twelfth century (Museum of Islamic Art, Istanbul) 156

Pilgrims at the Ka'bah in Makkah (photograph by S. M. Amin) 336

Pilgrims on the road to Makkah, accompanied by drummers and trumpeters playing festive music; illumination by al-Wasiti from a 1237 manuscript for the *Maqamat* of al-Hariri (Bibliothèque Nationale, Paris) 281

The Prophet Muhammad's masjid in Madinah (plan from Isma'il R. al-Faruqi and Lois Lamya', *The Cultural Atlas of Islam*, 1986) 249

A qadi (magistrate) hearing a dispute between a husband and wife; illumination by al-Wasiti from a 1237 manuscript for the *Maqamat* of al-Hariri (Bibliothèque Nationale, Paris) 311

A qadi settling a dispute between a young woman and her father; illumination from an early thirteenth-century Baghdad manuscript for the *Maqamat* of al-Hariri (Bibliothèque Nationale, Paris) 184

A qadi's court; illumination by Bihzad in a 1488–1489 manuscript for the *Bustan* (Garden) by al-Sa'di (General Egyptian Book Organization, Cairo) 208

Qa'itbay mausoleum complex, Cairo, built in 1472–1474 380

Qasr Mushatta, ruins of the desert palace built by Umayyad khalifah al-Walid II, circa 743–744 108

Quanzhou Masjid, China, built in 1310 362

Qur'an, pages from copies in Kufic script, eleventh century (Vever Collection, Arthur M. Sackler Gallery, The National Museum of Asian Art, Smithsonian Institution, Washington, D.C.) 100; Kufic script, ninth-century Iraq (British Library, London) 98; Maghribi script from tenth-century Andalusia (from *Aramco World*, September–October 1989) 98; Muhaqqaq script by Yaqut al-Musta'simi of Baghdad, 1282–1283 (Khalili Collection, Isfahan) 100; Muhaqqaq script under Mamluk patronage in Egypt or Syria, 1425 (Bayt al-Qur'an, Bahrain) 101; the earliest surviving manuscript for the Qur'an, transcribed in the eighth century (British Library, London) 340

Rashid al-Din, *Jami' al-tawarikh* (Collected Histories): illuminations from a fourteenth-century manuscript (Bibliothèque Nationale, Paris) 226, 227; from a 1306–1307 Tabriz manuscript (Edinburgh University Library) 215, 216, 225

Risalat (Epistles) by the Ikhwan al-Safa (Brethren of Purity): illumination from a 1287 Baghdad manuscript (Suleymaniye Library, Istanbul) 406

Rumi, *Mathnawi-i ma'nawi* (Spiritual Couplets): illumination from a 1458–1459 manuscript (Vever Collection, Arthur M. Sackler Gallery, The National Museum of Asian Art, Smithsonian Institution, Washington, D.C.) 384

Al-Sa'di, *Bustan* (Garden): illumination by Bihzad in a 1488–1489 manuscript (General Egyptian Book Organization, Cairo) 208

Samanid dynasty tomb with decorative brickwork, built in Bukhara during the first half of the tenth century 119

Samarra', the Great Masjid and minaret, built by the Umayyad khalifah al-Mutawakkil in 847–851 353

Santa Maria Novella, Florence; Ibn Rushd as depicted in *The Triumph of St. Thomas Aquinas*, a fourteenth-century fresco 378

Scholars in a public library at Hulwan, near Baghdad; illumination from a 1237 manuscript for al-Hariri's *Maqamat* (Bibliothèque Nationale, Paris) 113

Sea and land routes (from Francis Robinson, ed., *The Cambridge Illustrated History of the Islamic World*, 1996) 150

Secretaries of the Abassid period; illumination from an 1195 Sicilian Christian manuscript by Peter of Eboli (Burgerbibliothek, Bern) 144

Shahnameh (Book of Kings) by Firdawsi: illuminations by Bihzad from a circa 1400 manuscript (Topkapi Museum, Istanbul) 279; from a 1493–1494 manuscript (Vever Collection, Arthur M. Sackler Gallery, The National Museum of Islamic Art, Smithsonian Institution, Washington, D.C.) 402; from a 1335–1340 manuscript (Vever Collection, Arthur M. Sackler Gallery, The National Museum of Asian Art, Smithsonian Institution, Washington, D.C.) 313

Shahr-I Sabz, Uzbekistan, ruins of Aq Suray, a Timurid palace built during the early fifteenth century 120

A ship sailing in the Persian Gulf to the port of Basrah; illumination from a thirteenth-century manuscript for the *Maqamat* of al-Hariri (Bibliothèque Nationale, Paris) 154

Silk fabric made in fourteenth-century Spain with a geometric pattern similar in style to designs at the Alhambra Palace in Granada (Musée Historique des Tissus, Lyon) 260

A sixth- or seventh-century Egyptian man's wool tunic with tapestry ornamentation (Whitworth Art Gallery, University of Manchester) 251

Soldiers using a catapult; illumination for a 1306 manuscript for Rashid al-Din's *Jami' al-tawarikh* (Edinburgh University Library) 225

A still used to make rosewater; illumination from a ninth-century manuscript for *Kitab Kimya' al-'Itr wa al-Tas'idat* (Book of Perfume Chemistry and Distillation) by al-Kindi (Suleymaniye Library, Istanbul) 415

Sufis dancing in a khanqah; illumination from a 1458–1459 manuscript for *Mathnawi-i ma'nawi* (Spiritual Couplets) by Jalal al-Din Rumi (Vever Collection, Arthur M. Sackler Gallery, The National Museum of Asian Art, Smithsonian Institution, Washington, D.C.) 384

Sultan al-Malik al-Ashraf Qa'itbay mausoleum complex, Cairo, built in 1472–1474 380

Sultan al-Malik al-Mu'ayyad Shaykh Masjid and Madrasah, Cairo; inscription reading "There is no god but God, and Muhammad is the Messenger of God" 367

Sultan Hassan madrasah, Cairo, mihrab (prayer niche) in the Mamluk masjid 117

Sultan Khan, gates to a travelers' inn built by Saljuk ruler 'Ala' al-Din Kayqubad outside Konya, Turkey, during the thirteenth century 189

A suq (bazaar); interior view from an early-thirteenth-century manuscript for the love story of Warqa and Gulsah (Topkapi Museum, Istanbul) 264

Syrian dress and home furnishings during the Mamluk period; illumination from a 1237 manuscript for the *Maqamat* (Assemblies) of al-

Hariri (British Library, London) 258

"There is no god but God, and Muhammad is the Messenger of God": inscription at the Masjid and Madrasah of Sultan al-Malik al-Mu'ayyad Shaykh (ruled 1412–1421) in Cairo 367

The Thousand and One Nights (*Alf Laylah wa Laylah*), the earliest known fragment, written on paper in 879 by legal scholar Ahmad Ibn Mahfouz (Robert C. Williams American Museum of Papermaking, Atlanta) 145

Tile made in Egypt or Syria during the first half of the fifteenth century (British Museum, London) 84

Tiraz brocaded silk (fragment) woven during the twelfth century in Muslim Spain (Musée de Cluny) 252

Tiraz fabrics worn by a woman; in a fifteenth-century *Adoration of the Magi,* by Gentile da Fabriano (Uffizi Gallery, Florence) 261

Tlemcen, Tunisia, mihrab (prayer niche) in the Great Masjid 1136 358

The Triumph of St. Thomas Aquinas (detail: portrait of Ibn Rushd), a fourteenth-century fresco in the Church of Santa Maria Novella, Florence 378

Trumpeters; illumination from a 1468–1469 manuscript for a Persian glossary of rare words (British Library, London) 122

A tunic with tapestry ornamentation, made in sixth- or seventh-century Egypt (Whitworth Art Gallery, University of Manchester) 251

Turkestani man's coat (chalat) of ikat velvet with brocade lining and embroidered cuffs and bindings (Whitworth Art Gallery, University of Manchester) 254

Al-Tusi's thirteenth-century commentary on Euclid's *Elements,* first page from a fifteenth-century Persian manuscript (Millet Library, Istanbul) 416

The twenty-eight traditional divisions of the world; diagram by Abu al-Fida in a circa 1320 manuscript (Vatican Library, Rome) 412

Al-Wasiti, illuminations in a 1237 Baghdad manuscript for the *Maqamat* (Assemblies) of al-Hariri (Bibliothèque Nationale, Paris) 281, 283, 298, 311, 304, 360

Water-raising devices; illuminations from a thirteenth-century manuscript *for Kitab fi ma'rifat al-hiyal al-handasiyyah* (Book of Knowledge of Ingenious Mechanical Devices) by al-Jazari (Suleymaniye Library, Istanbul) 430, 438

Western Asia and the eastern Mediterranean, Ibn Hawqal's tenth-century map (Suleymaniye Library, Istanbul) 71

Women playing chess at a private all-female gathering; thirteenth-century Andalusian miniature (Museu Institut Amatller d'Art Hispanic, Barcelona) 316

The world known to the Muslims, circa 700–1500 (from Nafis Ahmad, *Muslim Contributions to Geography,* 1945) 140

Xian, China, the Great Masjid, courtyard and garden complex, painting on silk (from *Aramco World,* July-August 1985) 347

Zahiriyyah madrasah, Cairo, courtyard 385

INDEX

Page numbers in boldface refer to a topic upon which an essay is based.
Page numbers in italics refer to illustrations, figures, and tables.

A

Abbasid dynasty
architecture, 114, 115
Bayt al-Hikmah, 368
building of Baghdad, 173–174
clothing, 256–257
concubines, 309
conversion, 166–167
development of Kalam, 354–355
law, 219
military campaigns, 223
Mu'tazilism, 333
non-Arab Muslims, 182
non-Muslim influence, 366
poetry, 88–89
political power, 205–206
translation movement, 366, 368–369
'Abd al-Jabbar, Qadi, 356, 358–360
Ibn Abi Zayd, 369
Abode of Islam, 70, 155
Abu al-Hudhayl, 356
Abu Hanifah, **233–234**
Abu Hurayrah, **288**
Academy of Geographers, 413
Adab literature, 97, 99
Adelard of Bath, 404
Adhan, 248–249
Africa
building materials, 263
clothing, 259–260
cooking, 275
spread of Islam, 70, 232
sub-Saharan, 150–151
Agriculture and pastoralism, **168–171, 426–427**
citrus fruits, 427
coffee, 427
cotton, 427
crop transfers, 269–270
crops, 169, 426–427
decline of, 171
dyes, 427
farmers, 167, **168–171,** *172*
irrigation, 429–430
landlords, 170
pastoral communities, 247, 264
sugarcane, 427
taxation, 169, 170–171
technology, 426–427
Ahmad ibn 'Abd al-Rahim, **319–320**
'A'isha bint Abi Bakr, 307–308, **319**

'Aish'a bint Muhammad ibn 'Abd al-Hadi, **320**
'A'ishah bint Ahmad al-Qurtubiyyah, 89–90
Alchemy, 413–415, 434
Alcoholic beverages, 268–269, 271
Aleppo, *186*
Alexandria, 366–367
Alf Laylah wa-Laylah, 123–124, 276, 313–314
Alfraganus. *See* al-Farghani
Algebra. *See* Mathematics
Alhambra Palace, 105–106, *106*
'Ali ibn Abi Talib, 204, **234–235,** 344–345, 346–347
'Alim, **405–407**
See also Scholars
Alive, The Son of Awake, 99, 128
Allegory, 379–380
Alphabet, Arabic, *143*
Analogies, legal, 202, 218–219
Anas Ibn Malik, **290**
Anatolia, 223, 225, 231
Anatomy. *See* Medicine and health
Animals
camels, 147–151
horses, 149–150, 433
literature and, 432–433
transportation, 146–147
zoology, **432–434**
Apologetics, 379
Aq Suray ruins, *120*
Ibn al-'Arabi, Myhyi al-Din, **393–394**
Arabian horses, 433
Arabs
alliance with Berbers, 150
alphabet, *143*
architecture, **114–118**
business and economy, 168
diet, 269
expansion and, 144
language, 126, 132–133, 135, 141–144
merchants, 168
poetry, **86–90**
prose, **90–99**
script, 145–146
transportation economy, 147–148
Architecture, **105–120**
Abbasid, 114, 115
Alhambra Palace, 105–106, *106*
Aq Suray ruins, *120*
Arab and African religious, **114–118**
Ayyubid dynasty, 116
building materials, 117

Cairo, Egypt, 116
construction, 117, 263–264
decorative tomb brickwork, *119*
developments, 117
Dome of the Rock, *107,* 112, *338*
domes, 116, 117, 118–119
domestic and secular, **105–106**
early religious, **107–114**
Egypt, 115–117
houses, 105–106
Indian, 119–120
Iranian, 118–119
Iraqi, 115
later religious, **114–120**
Mausoleum of Qa'itbay, 117
public lodging, 106
Qasr Mushatta ruins, *108*
regional styles, 114
South Asian, 119–120
Syria, 113
tombs, 116
Turco-Iranian and Indian, **118–120**
Umayyad dynasty, 112–114
See also Art; Masjids
Aristotle, 369, 371, 378, 383–384
Arranged marriages, 301
Art
calligraphy, *95, 98,* **99–101,** *106,* 129, *203*
ceramics, 103, 431–432
common motifs, 85–86
decorative art, 101–102
Egypt, 112–113
geometric decoration, 101–102, *129*
glassmaking, 102–103, 431, 432
Greco-Roman influence, 85
hand warmers, 414
illumination, 104–105
kiswah, 104
Mamluk lamps, 102–103
metalworking, 102, *103,* 104
miniatures, 105
Near East influence, 85
overview, **85–86**
Persian influence, 85, 105
private, 130
prohibition of images, **127–130**
public, 129
regional variations, 86
rugs, 104
standards, 85–86
style, 128–129

textiles, 103–104
woodworking, 102
See also Architecture
Artisans, 171–172, 414
Asceticism, 334, 387–388
al-Ash'ari, Abu al-Hasan, 362–365
Ash'arism
  atomism, 364–365
  al-Baqillani, Abu Bakr, 363–364
  divine power, 363
  doctrine of acquisition, 363
  al-Ghazali, 383, 384
  Mu'tazilism *vs.*, 362–365
  See also Falsafah; Kalam; Muhammad;
    Mu'tazilism; Qur'an; Religion and
    philosophy; Sufism; Sunnis
Asia
  architecture, 119–120
  clothing, 260
  cooking, 275
  expansion into, 70
  trade routes, 149
  See also China
Asia Minor, 223, 225
The Assemblies of al-Hamadhani, 110, 115, 285
Astrolabes, *74, 75*
Astrology, 371–372, 414–415
Astronomy, 76, 180–181, **407–409**, 435
Atomism, 364–365
  See also Ash'arism
al-'Attar, Farid al-Din, 125
Averroës. *See* Ibn Rushd, Abu al-Walid
  Muhammad
Avestan language, 124
Avicenna. *See* Ibn Sina, Abu 'Ali al-Husayn
Ayyubid dynasty
  architecture, 116
  decentralization, 188–189

B

Backgammon, 278
Baghdad
  architecture, 114
  Bayt al-Hikmah, 368, 403, 406, 407–408, 417
  city plan, *177*
  commercial activity, 153, 173–174
  Mongol destruction of, *226*, 406–407
Baghdad school of Mu'tazilism, 356–357
Bal'ami, 126
Balkans, 231–232
Bananas, 273
Banu Musa, 417, 418
al-Baqillani, Abu Bakr, 363–364
Barani, Ziya' al-Din, 126
Basrah, 153
Basrah school of Mu'tazilism, 356
Baths, 263, *266*
al-Battani, 408–409
Ibn Battuta, 97, 147, **158**, 263, 421–422
Baybars, al-Zahir, 116–117, **190–191**
Bayhaqi, Abu al-Fazl, 126
Bayt al-Hikmah, 368, 403, 406, 407–408, 417
Berbers
  alliance with Arabs, 150
  conversion, 230–231
  states, 206

Berke, 229
Beverage dispenser, *212*
Beverages, 268–269, 270–271, 427
Bidayat al-mujtahid wanihayat al-muqtasid, 378
Biographical works, 96–97
Birth control, 312–313
al-Biruni, Abu Rayhan, **79**, 157, 409, 411, 418, 426
Bishr ibn al-Mu'tamir, 356–357
Black Death, 421–422
Book burning, 404
Book of Animals, 93, 433–434
Book of Enjoyment and Good Company, 183
Book of Healing, 375
Book of Historical Lessons, 236
Book of Mansur, 423
Book of Roger, 413
Book of Songs, 122
Botany, **409–411**
Bows and arrows, 424
Boys. *See* Gender
Breads, 272
Breast feeding, 297
Buddhism, 231, 232
Building materials, 263–264
Al-Bukhari, Muhammad ibn Ismail, **288–289**
Burial
  burial scene, *283*
  funerals, *227*, 286–287
  gravestone, *209*
  mourning, *322*
Business and economy, **171–176**
  Arab transportation economy, 147–148
  Arabian peninsula, 168
  Baghdad, 173–174
  caravan trade, 147–151
  cities, 171–172
  commerce, 172–173
  commercial law, **211–212**
  economic development, 171–172
  financial instruments, 211–212
  foreign competition, 174–175
  government policy, 173
  interest, 211
  market inspectors, 174, 175
  marketplaces, 172, 262–263, *264*
  merchants, *179*, 191, 285
  paper, 431
  textiles, 255–256
  ulama', 142
  usury, 211
  See also Trade
Byzantines
  art, 128–129
  Greek philosophy and, 369
  military campaigns, 223, 225
  naval dominance, 228

C

Cairo, 116, 155
Calendars
  Gregorian, 408
  Jalali, 418
Calligraphy, *95, 98*, **99–101**, *106, 129, 203*
Camels, 147–151
Candle power, 418–419
Canon of Medicine, 375, 423

Caravan cities, 147–148
Caravanserais, 106
Carpets, 267
Cartography. *See* Maps
Carts, 149
Catapults, *225*, 424
Cavalrymen jousting, *221*
Celibacy, 314
Central Asia
  clothing, 260
  cooking, 275
  trade routes, 149
Ceramics, 103, 431–432
Charity, 178, 302–303, 336
Cheese and curds, 270
Chemistry, **413–415**
Chess, 278
Children
  child-rearing methods, **297–302**
  games, 278
  guardianship, 214, 299
  Islamic instruction, 300–301
  orphans, 301
  See also Family life and social trends
China
  ceramics, 103
  Islamic expansion into, 70
  Mongol invasions, 228
  See also Asia
Christians, 180, 355
  See also Crusades; Non-Muslims
Cities. *See* Urban life
Civil order, 184
Civil War, 235
Class system
  Christians and Jews, 180
  cities, 180, 185
  converts, **182–184**
  corporate society, 189
  cultural division, 189–190
  daily life, 247–248
  education and common folk, 306–307
  expansionism, 180–181
  farmers, 169
  landlords, 170
  Makkah, 177–178
  marriage, 309, 311
  merchants, 171–175
  nomads, 176
  non-Arab Muslims, 182
  notables, 189–190
  overview, **166–167**
  people of the book, 180
  Persians, 182–183
  pre-Islamic society, 176–178
  scholars, 142, 167, 180–181
  shaykhs, 190
  social change and, **176–181**
  Sufis, 187–188
  Turks, 188
  Umayyad dynasty, 166
  women, 176, 178, 306
  See also Family life and social trends
Climate, 78, 146–147, **247–248**
Clocks, 418–419
Clothing and textiles, **250–260**
  Abbasid dynasty, 256–257
  art in textiles, 103–104
  Central Asia, 260

cotton, 427
courtly dress, 257
decline of production, 172
dyes, 427
East Africa, 260
Egypt, 258–259
expansion and, 263
Fatimid dynasty, 257–259
headdresses, 251–252
leather and fur, 256
loom, *256*
man's coat, *254*
Mongol influences, 260
mourning, 252–253, 287
non-Muslims, 254–255
northwestern Africa and Iberian peninsula, 259
production, 255–256
regional styles, 254–255
rugs, 104, 267
silk, 255–256, *260*
textile furnishings, 267
textiles as currency, 253–254
tiraz fabrics, 253, 257–258, *261*
tunics, *251*
Turkish influence, 259
Umayyad dynasty, 253
West Africa, 259–260
Coffee cultivation, 427
Coins, 128, *187*
Colleges. *See* Education
Columbus, Christopher, *77*
Commentaries, 92, 94, 96
Commerce. *See* Business and economy
Commercial law, **211–212**
Communication, **141–146**
   See also Language
Community, 178
Concubines, 309
Consensus, legal, 202
Consolation treatises, 302
Construction. *See* Architecture
Conversion
   Abbasid dynasty, 166–167
   class system, **182–184**
   communication, 141–142
   Mongols, 229–230
   overview, 140
   process, 230–231
Corporate society, 189
Cotton, 427
Courtly love, 88, 90
Courts, *208, 209*
Courtyards, 105, 111, 261
Creation, 371, 373–374, 380
Criminal law, **212–213**
Crops. *See* Agriculture and pastoralism
Crusades, 188–189, 225–226, 239, 422–423
   See also Christians
Custody rights, 214, 299
Customs and practices, 246

D

Daily life
   characteristics, **248–251**
   diversity of, 247–248
      environmental influences, **247–248**
      hygiene and cleanliness, 250
      merchants, 285
      overview, **245–246**
      personal objects, 267–268
      pillars of Islam, 248
      prayer, 248–250
      purification, 249–250
      social class, 247–248
      See also Family life and social trends
al-Damiri, Kamal al-Din, 434
Dar al-Islam, 70, 155
Decentralization, **184–190**
The Decisive Discourse, 379–380
The Deliverer from Error, 391
Democracy, 346
Democritus, 364
Devotional prose, 96
Dhikr, 187
al-Dimashqi, Abu al-Fadl Ja'far Ibn 'Ali, **191**
Din defined, 332, 335
Diversity, ethnic, 144, 146, 183, 190
Divine right, 352–353
Divorce, 213–214, 308
Dome of the Rock, *107,* 112, *338*
Domes, 116, 117, 118–119
Domestic architecture, **105–106**
Durum wheat, 273
Dyes, 427

E

East Africa
   clothing, 260
   cooking, 275
Economy. *See* Business and economy
Education, **302–307**
   charitable foundations, 302–303
   cities, 306–307
   endowments, 181
   higher, 238, 303–304
   importance of knowledge, 302
   Islamic instruction, 300–301
   madrasahs, 302
   Nizamiyyah colleges, 238
   oral transmission, 304–305
   religious sciences, 304
   schools, 302
   teaching, 303, 304–305
   traveling scholars, 305–306
   women, 306
Egypt
   architecture, 115–117
   art, 112–113
   Cairo, 116, 155
   clothing, 258–259
   Islamization, 231
Elements, al-Tusi's commentary on, *416,* 418
Elements of Astrology, 409
Endowments, 116, 181
Epic of Dhat al-Himma, 314
Epigraphic coins, 128
Epistles, 406
Equestrian sports, 278–279
Equilibrium, 377
Eschatology, 348
Ethnic diversity, 144, 146, 183, 190

Europe
   alchemy, 415
   astronomy, 409
   Islamic expansion into, 70–71
   knowledge transfer, 404, 406–407
   regional differences from Chinese and
      Muslim worlds, 139
Expansion
   Arab transportation economy, 147–148
   camel routes, 147–151
   chronology, 223
   class system, 180–181
   cultural interactions, 245
   effect on law, 218
   Egypt, 231
   Europe, 70–71
   language and, 141–145
   military, 221, 223
   overview, 139–140
   political, 144
   religious, 229, **230–232**
   science and, 403–404, 405–407
   second wave, 149
   social consequences, 179–180
   trade and, 70–71
   See also Government and politics
Exploration, **155–157**
Extramarital relations, 313

F

Facts About India, 426
Ibn Fadlan, **158**
Falsafah, **366–381**
   accident and essence, 370–371
   Active Intellect, 373–374
   Alexandria, 366–367
   allegory, 379–380
   Aristotle, 371
   astrology, 371–372
   creation, 371, 373–374
   criticism, 370
   divine knowledge, 376
   doctrine of emanation, 373–374
   doctrine of the soul, 372
   equilibrium, 377
   essence and existence, 373, 375–376
   al-Farabi, Abu Nasr Muhammad, 372–375
   al-Ghazali, Abu Hamid Muhammad al-
      Tusi, 370
   God, 370–371, 373
   Greek influence, 366–367
   as heresy, 370
   hikmah and, 369–370
   Ibn Khaldun's critique of, 385–386
   al-Kindi, Abu Yusuf Ya'qub, 370–372
   limits of interpretation, 380
   motion, 377
   Plato, 373
   religion and philosophy, 374
   Ibn Rushd, Abu al-Walid Muhammad,
      378–380
   Ibn Sina, Abu 'Ali al-Husayn, 375–378
   Sunni critique of, **381–392**
   universal soul, 372

See also Ash'arism; Kalam; Muhammad; Mu'tazilism; Qur'an; Religion and philosophy; Sufism; Sunnis
Family life and social trends, **294–322**
  age of legal majority, 301
  arranged marriages, 301
  birth, 284, *300*
  birth control, 312–313
  breast feeding, 297–298
  careers, 315
  child-rearing methods, **297–302**
  children, 214, 299–301
  concubines, 309
  consolation treatises, 302
  custody rights, 214, 299
  diversity, 296
  divorce, 213–214, 308
  emotional ties, 301–302
  extended, 315
  extramarital relations, 313
  funerals, 286–287
  housing, 105–106
  infants, 297–299
  inheritance, 214–215, 301
  Islamic instruction, 300–301
  kinship ties, 176, 178
  law, **213–215**, 308–309
  lifestyle, 245
  love, 88, 90, 125, 311–312
  marriage, 301, **307–312**, 315
  motherhood, 298–300
  mourning, *322*
  orphans, 301
  overview, **296**
  parental grief, 302
  patrilineage, 299
  privacy, 105
  procreation, 297
  roles and responsibilities, **315–318**
  serial marriages, 315
  sexuality, **312–314**
  wedlock, 213, 284
  See also Class system; Daily life
al-Farabi, Abu Nasr Muhammad, 369, 372–375
al-Farghani, 408, 411
Farmers. See Agriculture and pastoralism
Fatimah, 346–347
Fatimid dynasty
  architecture, 115–116
  clothing, 257–259
  Ismaili Shi'ism, 351
  Sunni challenge, 381
Fatwas, 208–209
Festivals. See Holidays and religious observances
Figural representation, 127–130
Financial instruments, 211–212
Fiqh schools of law, 220–221, 341
Firdaws Madrasah, *376*
Folk traditions and medicine, 421
Folklore, 123–124
Food and diet, **268–276**
  Arab fare, 269
  bananas, 273
  breads, 272
  cheese and curds, 270
  cities, 270
  durum wheat, 273
  fats, 270
  flavorings and spices, 274

fruits, 273, 427
nuts, 273
olive oil, 270
permitted and prohibited foods, 268–269
regional differences, 169, 275
rice, 271, 273
salt, 270
sugar, 273–274
sweeteners, 274
vegetables, 273
Foreign relations law, **215–217**
Free will, 333, **343–354**
Friday prayer, 109–110, 280
Frontiers, 148–149
Fundamentalism, 342–343
Funerals. See Burial
Furnishings, 265, 267

G

Gangs, youth, 185, 187
Gardens, 265
Garrison cities, 166, 180
Gates of Sultan Khan, *189*
Gender
  Islamic instruction, 301
  roles and responsibilities, 296, **315–318**
  spiritual equality, 339
  See also Family life and social trends; Women
The General Book of Medicine, 378
Genghis Khan, 228
Geography, **69–80**
  abode of Islam, 70, 155
  Academy of Geographers, 413
  astronomy and, 76
  al-Biruni, Abu Rayhan, **79**, 157, 411
  The Book of Roger, 413
  boundaries, 70, 78
  climate, 78, 146–147, **247–248**
  Dar al-Islam, 70, 155
  dynasties and boundaries, 78
  early writings, 73
  al-Farghani, 411
  geographic literature, 72, 156
  holistic view of, 69
  al-Idrisi, **79**, 413
  importance to religion, 72–73
  influences on, 72
  information sources, 76
  Kitab al-Rujari, 413
  known world, 157
  al-Muqaddasi, Abu 'Abd Allah Muhammad, 74, **159**
  Muslim influence on European thinking, 69
  natural boundaries, 78
  navigational charts, 76
  overview, 69
  pilgrimages, 283–284
  sacred, 411
  scientific, 411
  study of, 72
  technology, 76
  topography, 78
  travel writing, 73–74, 97, 126, 147, 155–156

world divisions, *412*
  See also Maps
Geology, **426**
Geometric design, 101–102, *129*
Geometry. See Mathematics
Ghadir Khumm, 286
al-Ghazali, Abu Hamid Muhammad al-Tusi, 370, 383–384, 387, 391, **393**
Ghazals, 125
Ghazan, *227*
Ghurids, 223
Girls. See Gender; Women
Glassmaking, 102–103, 431, 432
Gondeshapur, 367–368
Government and politics
  advice books for rulers, 126, 217
  Ali's exposition on just rule, 204
  Berber states, 206
  cities, 180
  concubines, 309
  decentralization, **184–190**
  divine right, 352–353
  factions, 234–235
  functions, 205
  Kharijism, 346
  major ruling groups, 207
  military rule, 205–206
  notables, 189–190
  overview, **201–203**
  peasant revolts, 170–171
  political philosophy, 374–375
  Prophet's lack of political system, 201
  royal celebrations, 284
  rulers' wives, 309
  state manufactured fabric, 253–254, 257–258
  state-sponsored histories, 126
  strength of and spread of Islam, 232
  sultanates, **232–233**
  titles, 203–204
  Turks, 171, 188
  women, 191–192, 318
  See also Expansion; Khalifahs; Individual dynasties; Individual rulers
Grammar, 94, 135
Great Book on the Life of Animals, 434
Greek influence
  Alexandria, 366–367
  art, 85
  atomism, 364–365
  geography, 72
  philosophy, 180–181, 333–334, 383–384
Gregorian calendar, 408

H

Ibn Habal, Ahmad, 220, **235**
Hadiths
  Al-Bukhari, Muhammad ibn Ismail, **288–289**
  collections, 94–96, 202–203
  daily living, 245
  dissemination, 340
  fatherly grief, 302
  Ibn Hanbal, Ahmad, **235**
  ijazah, 340
  motherhood, 299–300

Muslim, Muslim Abu al-Husayn, **291**
penalties for crimes, 212–213
traditions, 339–340
transmission, 340
women, 306
Hafiz, 123, **131**
Hajj. *See* Pilgrimages
Ibn al-Hajj, 302, 316
Halima, 297–298
al-Hamadhani, Ahmad Badi al-Zaman, 99, **289**, 311–312
Hanafi school of law, 210, 341
Ibn Hanbal, Ahmad, **235**, 342–343, 361, 388
Hanbali school of law, 210, 342–343
Hand warmers, 414
Hanifah, Abu, 341
Hanifi school of law, 233–234
al-Haram al-Sharif, 112
Harams, 110–112
Harbor at Tyre, 153
al-Hariri, 99, **131–132**
Harran, scholars of, 367
Harun al-Rashid, **191–192**
Hasan al-Basri, 354
Ibn Hawqal, map by, *71*
Hayat al-hayawan al-kubra, 434
Ibn al-Haytham, 428–429
Hayy ibn Yaqzan, 99, 128
Hayyan, Abu, 303
Hijrah, 178, 395
Hikmah, 369–370
Hinduism, 231
Hisham ibn al-Hakam, 356
History, 96, 126, **133–134**, 276
Holidays and religious observances, **280–287**
births, 284, *300*
cross-cultural influences, 286
Friday prayer, 280
funerals, 286–287
Ghadir Khumm, 286
'Id al-Adha, 281–282
'Id al Fitr, 280–282
Mawlid un-Nabi, 284, 286
Persian festivals, 286
pilgrimages, 282–284
Ramadan, 280
regional, 284, 286
royal celebrations, 284
weddings, 284
Holy sites, 110–112
Homosexuality, 313
Horses, 149–150, 433
Hospital in Edirne, *422*
Hotels, 106
House of Wisdom. *See* Bayt al-Hikmah
Housing, **261–268**
decoration, 264–265
design, 105–106
diversity in materials, 263–264
furnishings, 265, 267
gardens, 265
household items, 267, *268, 271, 274*
reception rooms, 265
yurt, 264
How to Observe and Abide by the Rights of God, 388–389
Hulagu, 228–229
Hunting, 279–280
Hygiene, 250

I

'Id al-Adha, 280–282
'Id al Fitr, 280–282
al-Idrisi, **79**, 413
Ihya' 'ulum al-din, 390
Ijazah, 340
Ilkhan empire, 228–229
Illumination, 104–105
Imaili Shi'ism, 351
Imami Shi'ism, 350–351
The Incoherence of the Philosophers, 383–384
India
architecture, 119–120
Islamization, 232
mathematics, 417
trade routes, 149
Indian Ocean, 153
Inheritance, 214–215, 301
International law, **215–217**
Introduction, 385, 386
Inventions. *See* Technology
Iran
architecture, 118–119
art, 85
cooking, 275
festivals, 286
Islamization, 231
migration from, 144–145
miniatures, 105
Persian language, 124, 143–144, 145, 238
poetry, 123
rugs, 104
social status of Persians, 182–183
Iraq
architecture, 115
cities, 114
cooking, 275
law, 218–220
Ibn al-'Iraqi. *See* Ahmad ibn 'Abd al-Rahim
Irrigation, 429–430
Islam defined, 332
Ismaili law, 351
Iwan-style masjids, 109, 118

J

Jabir ibn Hayyan, 414, **434**
Ja'far al-Sadiq, 347–348
Jahili poetry, 86–88
al-Jahiz, Abu Uthman, 97, **132**, 433–434
Jalali calendar, 418
Jami, 125
Jerusalem, 111–112
Jewelry, 102
Jews, 180
   See also Non-Muslims
Jihad, 215–216
Ibn Jubayr, 142, 153, **159**
Judicial system. *See* Law and judicial system
Juha, 269, **290**
Jum'ah, 280
al-Junayd, Abu al-Qasim, 389, 391
The Jurist's Beginning and the Layman's End, 378
al-Jurjani, Abd al-Qahir, **132–133**
Juzjani, Minhaj-i Siraj, 126

K

Ka'b ibn Zuhayr ibn Abi Salma, 88
Ka'bah, 111, 177, *336*
Kalam, **354–366**
attributes of God, 355–356
Christianity and, 355
critique of, **381–392**
development of, 354–355
Hisham ibn al-Hakam, 356
methodology, 354–355
Wasil ibn 'Ata', 356
See also Ash'arism; Falsafah; Muhammad; Mu'tazilism; Qur'an; Religion and philosophy; Sufism; Sunnis
Kalilah wa Dimnah, 433
al-Karabisi, Husayn, 362
Kaysaniyyah, 349–350
Khadijah, 307
Ibn Khaldun, 'Abd al-Rahman, **235–236**, 312, 385–388
Khalifahs
authority, 167, **203–206**
clothing, 257
divine right, 350, 352–353
end of, 206
sultanates and, 232–233
Umayyad dynasty, 206
See also Government and politics; Individual rulers
Ibn Khallikan, **289**
Khanate of the Golden Horde, 229–230
al-Khansa', **133**
Kharijism, 345–346
Khawarnaq fort, *224*
Khayyam, 'Umar, 418
al-Khazraji, Abu Dulaf, **159**
l-Kindi, Abu Yusuf Ya'qub, 370–372, 426
Kinship ties, 176, 178
Kiswah, 104
Kitab al-aghani, 122
Kitab al-hayawan, 433–434
Kitab al-'ibar, 236
Kitab al-Imta'wa al Mu'anasah, 183
Kitab al-Irshad, 344
Kitab al-Mansuri, 423
Kitab al-Rujari, 413
Kitab al-Shifa', 375
Kitab al-tafhim, 409
Knowledge
Ash'arism, 365–366
non-Muslim sources, 368–369
six fields of inquiry, 369
Kufic script, 101
al-Kulliyyat fi al-Tibb, 378

L

Land transportation, **146–151**
Language
Arabs, 126, 132–133, 135, 141–144
Avestan, 124
ethnic diversity, 144
expansion and, 141–145
grammar, 94, 135
al-Jurjani, Abd al-Qahir, 132–133

Persian and Turkish, 126–127, 143–144, 145
  See also Communication
Law and judicial system, **206–209**
  Abbasid dynasty, 219
  Abu Hanifah, **233–234**
  age of legal majority, 301
  aliens and travelers, 216–217
  analogies, 202, 218–219
  application, 213
  cities, 184–185, 187
  commercial law, **211–212**
  consensus, 202
  courts, *208*, 209, 213
  criminal law, **212–213**
  developments, **217–221**
  effect of expansion on, 218
  family, **213–215**, 308–309
  fiqh school, 220–221, 341
  foreign relations and war, **215–217**
  Ibn Hanbal, Ahmad, 220, **235**
  Hanifi school of law, 233–234
  inheritance, 214–215, 301
  interpretation, 341
  Iraq, 218–220
  Ismaili, 351
  judges, *184*, 206, 207, 218–219
  Ibn Khaldun, 'Abd al-Rahman, **235–236**
  Ibn Khallikan, **289**
  Madinah, 220
  madrasahs, 302, *376*, 382–383
  Malik Ibn Anas, 220, **237–238**
  marriage and divorce, 308–309
  mawali, 218
  methodology, 381–382
  non-Muslims, 216–217
  overview, **201–203**
  payment of tribute, 215–216
  penalties, 212–213
  philosophy and, 378–379
  principles of jurisprudence, 342
  prohibition of images, 127–128
  property rights, 211
  punishment, 212–213
  Qur'an, 217–218
  sacred law, 206, 209, 211
  schools of law, 210, 219–220, 332, 341–343, 382–383
  al-Shafi'i, Muhammad ibn Idris, 220, **238–239**
  Shari'ah, 206, 209, 211, 332–333, 341
  Shi'i schools, 221
  sources, 202, 239
  standards, 202–203
  texts, 208–209
  treaties, 215–216
  Umayyad dynasty, 218
  usulization, 381–383
  writings, 94–96
Layla wa-Majnun, 125
Leather and fur, 256
Leisure and games, **276–280**
  backgammon, 278
  chess, 278, *316*
  children's games, 278
  equestrian sports, 278–279
  hunting, 279–280
  military sports, 278
  recitation, 276

song and dance, 277–278
storytelling, 276–277
Libraries, 368, 404
Light. *See* Optics and opthamology
Light of Muhammad, 347
Literature
  al-'Attar, Farid al-Din, 125
  adab, 97, 99
  animals and, 432–433
  Bal'ami, 126
  Barani, Ziya' al-Din, 126
  Bayhaqi, Abu al-Fazl, 126
  biographical works, 96–97
  book burning, 404
  centers of knowledge, 92
  chain of sources, 92
  commentaries, 92, 94, 96
  courtly, 125–126
  creativity, 92, 93
  devotional prose, 96
  geographic, 72, 156
  hadiths, 94–96
  Hafiz, 123, **131**
  al-Hamadhani, Ahmad Badi al-Zaman, **289**, 311–312
  al-Hariri, 99, **131–132**
  history, 96, 126, 133–134
  al-Jahiz, Abu Uthman, 97, **132**
  Jami, 125
  Juha, 269, **290**
  al-Jurjani, Abd al-Qahir, **132–133**
  Juzjani, Minhaj-i Siraj, 126
  Ibn Khallikan, **289**
  al-Khansa', **133**
  language and rhetoric, 94, 126–127
  legal writings, 94–96
  literary group in Baghdad garden, *89*
  Ma'arri, Abu al-'Ala', 102
  maqamat, 99, 110, *113*, 115, 289
  al-Mas'udi, **133–134**
  al-Mutanabbi, **134**
  Nasr al-Din Khoja, **290–291**
  Nizami of Ganjah, 125
  oral, 123–124
  originality, 92, 93
  Persian poetry, 123
  philosophical prose, 96
  popular, 125–126
  prose, Arabic, **90–99**
  Qur'an commentaries, 92, 94
  Ibn Qutaybah, 97, 368
  rhymed prose, 99
  Rumi, Jalal al-Din, 125, **396**
  Sa'di, 125
  Sana'i, 125
  travel, 73–74, 97, 126, 147, 155–156, 159
  Ibn Tufayl, Abu Bakr Muhammad, 99, 128
  See also Poetry; Individual works
Love, 88, 90, 125, 311–312

M

Ma'arri, Abu al-'Ala', 102
Madinah
  establishment of Islam, 178
  masjids, 110

  Muhammad's migration to, 395
  pilgrimages, 111
  school of law, 220
Madrasahs, 302, *376*, 382–383, *385*
Mahmud of Ghazna, 144, *215*
Makkah
  Ka'bah, 111, 177
  pilgrimages, 72–73, 104, 111, 172
  pre-Islamic, 177–178
  settlement by the Quraysh, 176–177
  social structure, 177–178
Malik ibn Anas, 92, 220, **237–238**, 341–342
Maliki school of law, 210, 237, 341–342
Mamluks
  architecture, 116–117
  Baybars, al-Zahir, **190–191**
  Crusades, 188–189
  lamps, 102–103
  Mongols and, 188–189
  occupations, 315
  rugs, 104
al-Ma'mum, 368
al-Mansur, 366, 367
Maps
  Baghdad, *177*
  expansion of Islam to 1500, *231*
  known world, *140*
  mapmaking, 74, 76, 78, 156, **411–413**
  Mediterranean, northern Africa, *73*
  western Asia and eastern Mediterranean, *71*
  See also Geography
The Maqama of the Spindle (al-Hamadhani), 115
The Maqama of the Yellow One (al-Hamadhani), 110
Maqamat, 99, 110, *113*, 115, 285, 289
Maqamat al-Hamadhani, 110, 115, 285
Maqsurah, 113–114
Maritime zones, 152
Market inspectors, 174, 175
Marketplaces, 172, 262–263, *264*
Marriage, **307–312**
  arranged, 301
  ceremony, *310*
  elite class, 309, 311
  serial, 315
  See also Family life and social trends
Masjids
  activities in, 249
  al-Aqsa, 112
  arcaded, 109
  al-Azhar, 115, *355*
  Cairo, 367
  calligraphy, 99, 101
  cities, 262
  Córdoba, Spain, *110*
  daily prayer, 248–249
  Damascus, 113–114, *345*
  Djenné, Mali, *116*
  domes, 109, 118–119
  Egypt, 115–117
  endowment, 116
  expansion and, 109–110
  Fatimid dynasty, 115–116
  Friday congregations, 109–110
  glass masjid lamp, *364*
  India, 119–120
  Iran, 118
  Iraq, 114

Isfahan, *357*
iwan, 109, 118
Kariouan, *349, 352*
Madinah, 108–109, 111, *249*
maqsurah, 113–114
mausoleums, 117
men and women seated separately, *317*
minarets, 110, 114
origins, 107–109
plans, 109
preservation, 107
prohibition of images, 130
Qala'un, 117
Quanzhou, *362*
al-Salih Tala'i', 115–116
Samarra', *353*
schools, 303, *304*
size, 109–110
Syrian, 110
Tlemcen, *358*
Umayyad dynasty, 112–114
women, 249, 318
Xian, *347*
See also Architecture
al-Mas'udi, **133–134**
Materia Medica, 410
Mathematics, **415–418**
algebra, 417
al-Biruni, Abu Rayhan, 418
geometry, 418
India, 417
Khayyam, 'Umar, 418
numbers, 415, 417, *437*
numerical series, 418
trigonometry, 417
al-Tusi, Nasir al Din, *416*, 418, **435**
See also Science
Matter, 377
al-Maturidi, Abu Mansur, 365–366
Mausoleums, 117, *380*
Mawali. *See* Non-Arab Muslims
Mawlid un-Nabi, 284, 286
Mechanics, **418–419**
Medicine and health, **419–424**
alchemy, 413–414
anatomy, 423
Black Death, 421–422
contagions, 419, 421
Crusades and medical exchange, 422–423
Edirne hospital, *422*
folk traditions, 421
mental health, 421
oil extracts, 421
philosophy, 376, 378
physicians' portraits, *420*
public health, 419
al-Razi, Abu Bakr Muhammad ibn Zakariya, 423
religion, 419
ibn Sina, Abu 'Ali al-Husayn, 423
surgery, 423
al-Zahrawi, Abu al-Qasim, 421, 423
Mediterranean sea, 151–153
Merchants, *179*, 191, 285
Metallurgy, 414
Metalworking, 102, *103, 104*
Migration, 141
Mihrab, *358*
Military and warfare

Abbasid dynasty, 223
Anatolia, 223, 225
Asia Minor, 223, 225
banner, *222*
Byzantines, 223, 225, 228
camels, 147
catapult, *225*
cavalryman firing blunderbuss, *402*
cavalrymen jousting, *221*
Civil War, 235
Crusades, 188–189, 225–226, 239
developments, **221–228**
expansion, 221, 223
Genghis Khan, 228
Ghurids, 223
gunpowder, 425–426
Hulagu, 228–229
incendiary weapons, 424–425
Khawarnaq fort, *224*
law, 216
Mamluks, 188–189, 190–191
maritime power, 152–153
military rule, 205–206
Mongol invasions, *226*, **228–230**
naval forces, 227–228
organization, 226–228
political influence of the Turks, 171
professional soldiers, 226–227
Qur'an, 226
raising troops, 226
Salah al-Din al-Ayyubi, **192**
Saljuks, 223, 225
siege equipment, 424
Spain, 225
sports, 278
sultanates, **232–233**
tax farming, 170–171
technology, 226, 227, **424–426**
Umayyad dynasty, 223
weapons, 102, **424–426**
Mills, 430–431
Minarets, 110, 114
Minbar, *369*
Mineralogy, **426**
Mongols
clothing influence, 260
conversion to Islam, 229–230
destruction of Baghdad, *226*, 406–407
funeral procession of Ghazan, *227*
invasions of Muslim world, **228–230**
Mamluk defense against, 188–189
marriage, 309
Monotheism, *367*
Moses, 299
Mosques. *See* Masjids
Motion, 377
Mu'adhah al-'Adawiyyah, 388
Mu'awiyyah, 345
al-Mufid, al-Shaykh, 344
Muhammad
biographical information, **394–395**
commemoration of the birth of, 284, 286
daily life, 245
horse breeding, 433
house at Madinah, 261
lack of political system, 201
marriages, 307–308
Qur'an and, 339
social reforms, 178

status of women, 178
tomb of, 111
wet nursing, 297–298
See also Ash'arism; Falsafah; Kalam; Mu'tazilism; Qur'an; Religion and philosophy; Sufism; Sunnis
al-Muhasibi, Harith, 388–389
Muhtasibs, 174, 175
ibn Munqidh, Usamah, 422
al-Munqidh min al-Dalal, 391
al-Muqaddasi, Abu 'Abd Allah Muhammad, 74, **159**
Muqaddinamah, 236, 385, 386
Ibn al-Muqaffa', 90–92
Murjiah, 353–354
Music, **120–123**
Bayad singing and playing, *277*
classical, 122
instruments, 122–123
musicians, *121, 122*
religion and, 121
secular, 122
song and dance, 277–278
Sufi music, 122
Muslim, Muslim Abu al-Husayn, **291**
Muslim defined, 332
al-Mutanabbi, **134**
Mu'tazilism
Abbasid dynasty, 333
'Abd al-Jabbar, Qadi, 356, 358–360
belief and non-belief, 360
created Qur'an, 361
development of, 356
divine justice, 359–361
divine promise and threat, 359
divine unity, 358
five principles, 358
free choice, 357, 363
inquisition, 357
intercession, 359
intermediate position, 359–361
al-Karabisi, Husayn, 362
al-Nazzam, Ibrahim, 361
negative theology, 358–359
rationalism, 356
right and wrong, 361
schools of, 356–357
spread of, 357–358
suffering, 359
Sunni response, 361–363
See also Ash'arism; Falsafah; Kalam; Muhammad; Qur'an; Sufism; Sunnis
al-Muwatta', 237
Mysticism. *See* Sufism

N

Nasr al-Din Khoja, **290–291**
Nasta'liq script, 101
Nature, 337
Naval force, 227–228
Navigation, 76, 151–155, **411–413**
al-Nazzam, Ibrahim, 361
Neoplatonic thought, 367
New Persian, 144
Nizam al-Mulk, 126, 217, **238**
Nizami of Ganjah, 125

Nomads, *168*, 176, 264
Non-Arab Muslims, 182, 218, 230–232
Non-Muslims, 216–217, 230, 254–255, 366
North Africa, 275
Notables, 189–190
Nudar, 303
Numbers. *See* Mathematics
Nura, 314

O

Observatories, 408
Observatories, astronomical, 76
Occupations
    family and, 315
    Mamluks, 315
    urban, 185
    women, 317–318
Olive oil, 270
Optics and opthamology, **428–429**
Oral epics, 123–124
Oriental wisdom, 375
Orphans, 301
Ottomans, 225, 231–232

P

Paper, 146, 429, 431
Pastoralism. *See* Agriculture and pastoralism
Patrilineage, 299
Peasant revolts, 170–171
Pedestrian roads, 151
Perception, 386
Perfume still, *415*
Persia. *See* Iran
Personal objects, 267–268
Philosophy. *See* Religion and philosophy
Pilgrimages
    certificate, *156*
    harams, 111
    Madinah, 111
    Makkah, 72–73, 104, 111, 172, *336*
    rituals, 282–284
    social benefits, 283–284
    transportation and, 155–156
Plants, 409–410
Plato, 373, 383–384, 386
Plotinus, 367
Poetry
    Abbasid khilafah, 88–89
    'A'ishah bint Ahmad al-Qurtubiyyah, 89–90
    Arabic, **86–90**
    courtly love, 88, 90
    devotional, 125
    ghazals, 125
    love, 125
    meter, 86, 88
    models, 124
    music and, 122
    oral, 88, 276
    Persian, 123
    "The Poem of Antar," 87
    pre-Islamic, 86–88
    rajaz meter, 86, 88
    Rumi, Jalal al-Din, **396**

Spanish Muslim, 89–90
    Umayyad khilafah, 88
    See also Literature
Political philosophy, 374–375
Political Treatise, 238
Politics. *See* Government and politics
Polygamy, 213
Pork, 268
Port cities, 151–152
Postal system, 429
Pottery, 103
Prayer, 107–108, 248–250, 280
Pre-Islamic society
    class system, 176–178
    marriage, 307
    poetry, 86–88
    storytelling, 276
    trade, 171
The Precise Description of India, 157
Predestination, 333, 352
Privacy, 105
Proclus, 367
Property rights, 211
Prose, Arabic, **90–99**
Psychology, Sufi, 388–389
Ptolemy, 408
Public health, 419
Punishment, 212–213
Purification for prayer, 249

Q

Qadarites, 363
Qanum fi'l-tibb, 375, 423
Qasr Mushatta ruins, *108*
Qur'an
    as basis of Islam, 332
    breast feeding, 298
    charity, 178, 336
    commentaries, 92, 94
    created *vs.* uncreated, 361–362
    creation of the world, 380
    divine immanence, 338
    divine omnipotence, 343
    divine transcendance, 337–338
    as divine word of God, 337
    extramarital relations, 313
    free will and predestination, 343
    God's covenant, 339
    illumination, 104–105
    importance as literature, 90
    influence on communication, 146
    interpretation, 170
    knowledge, pursuit of, 405
    law, 217–218
    marriage, 307
    messengers of God, 337–338
    monotheism, 338–339
    Moses, story of, 299
    Muhammad and, 339
    natural world, 409–410
    nature, 337
    pages from, *340*
    penalties for crimes, 212–213
    permitted and prohibited foods, 268–269
    philosophy and, 334
    prayer, 107–108

    as primary source of religious knowledge, 337–339
    procreation, 297
    prohibition of images, **127–130**
    reading, 337
    revelation through Muhammad, 394–395
    sexuality, 312
    slavery, 178–179
    status of women, 178, 339
    "The Verse of Light," 97
    warfare, 226
    See also Ash'arism; Falsafah; Kalam; Muhammad; Mu'tazilism; Religion and philosophy; Sufism; Sunnis
Quraysh, 176–177
Ibn Qutaybah, 97, 368

R

Rabi'ah al-'Adawiyyah, 318, **395–396**
Ramadan, 280
Rationalism, 356, 385
al-Razi, Abu Bakr Muhammad ibn Zakariya, 414, 423, **435**
Recitation, 276
Reconquista, 188
Religion and philosophy, **323–398**
    alchemy, 414–415
    allegory, 379–380
    apologetics, 379
    Aristotle, 367, 378, 383–384
    ascetic practice, 334, 387–388
    assimilation, 230
    astronomy, 407
    belief and unbelief, 344
    charity, 336
    classes of philosophers, 380
    din defined, 332, 335
    divine oneness, 348
    divine right, 352–353
    equilibrium, 377
    eschatology, 348
    expansion, 229, **230–232**
    Fatimids, 351
    Five Pillars of Islam, 337
    Five Pillars of Shi'ism, 348–349
    form, 377
    free choice, 348–349
    free will, 333, **343–354**
    Friday congregation, 109–110, 280
    fundamentalism, 342–343
    geography, 72–73, 411
    God, 333
    Gondeshapur, 367–368
    government strength and spread of Islam, 232
    Greek influence, 180–181, 333–334, 364–367, 383–384
    Hasan al-Basri, 354
    holidays and religious observances, **280–287**
    holy sites, 110–112
    idol worship, 127
    Imaili Shi'ites, 351
    Imam delivering a sermon, *360*
    Imamate, doctrine of, 347–348
    Imami Shi'ism, 350–351

indebtedness, 335–336
inner truth, 351
Islam defined, 332
Ka'bah, 111
Kaysaniyyah, 349–350
Kharijism, 345–346
al-Kindi's definition of God, 370–371
law and, 378–379
Light of Muhammad, 347
limits of interpretation, 380
literature, 96, 277
al-Maturidi, Abu Mansur, 365–366
medicine, 376, 378, 419
metaphor of slavery, 335–336
missionaries, 230
monotheism, *367*
motion, 377
Murjiah, 353–354
music and, 121
Muslim defined, 332
natural world, 409
neoplatonic, 367
non-Muslims, 231
numbers, symbolism of, 415
overview, **332–334**
pillars of Islam, 248
Plato, 383–384
political philosophy of al-Farabi, 374–375
prayer, 248–250
prohibition of images, **127–130**
purification for prayer, 249–250
Qadarites, 363
rationalism, 385
religious practice, 336–337
religious sciences, 304
religious stories, 277
responsibility and reciprocity, 335–336
Righteous Ancestors, 351
scholars, 350–351
science, 403, 405
Shari'ah, 332
Shi'ism, 333, 346–351
sin, doctrine of, 345–346
sources of knowledge, 337
spiritual equality, 318
succession, 344, 347–354
Sunnah, 201–202, 339, 352
Sunnites, 333
systematic theology, **354–366**
theological disputes, 333
time and space, 377
Umayyad dynasty, 343–344, 351–353
universe, 377–378
usulization, 381–382
"World Soul," 409
Zaydi Shi'ism, 350
zoology, 433–434
See also Ash'arism; Conversion; Falsafah;
    Kalam; Mu'tazilism; Sufism; Systematic
    theology
The Revival of the Religious Sciences, 390
Rhetoric, 94, 126–127
al-Ri'ayah li-huquq Allah wa qiyam biha, 388–389
Rice, 271, 273
Righteous Ancestors, 382
al-Risalah, 342
Risalat, 406
River transport, 153–154
Roads, 151, 283–284

Roger II of Sicily, 411, 413
Roman influence on art, 85
Rugs, 104, 267
Rumi, Jalal al-Din, 125, **396**
Rural housing, 265
Ibn Rushd, Abu al-Walid Muhammad, 363,
    378–380, 384, 387

S

Sabaeans, 407
Sacred law. *See* Shari'ah
Sa'di, 125
Sahara, 150
Sahihs, 96
Salah al-Din al-Ayyubi, 188, **192**
Saljuks
    khalifahs, 206
    Mongol invasions, 228
    Nizam al-Mulk, **238**
    sultanates, 232
Salt, 270
Samanids, 381
Samarra', Iraq, 114
Sana'i, 125
Scholars
    Abu Hanifah, **233–234**
    Ahmad ibn 'Abd al-Rahim, **319–320**
    'Aish'a bint Muhammad ibn 'Abd al-Hadi,
        320
    Banu Musa, 417, 418
    cities, 142
    class system, 167, 180–181
    endowments, 181
    female, 306
    Ibn Hanbal, Ahmad, **235**
    Imami Shi'ites and, 350–351
    Iranian migrant, 144–145
    Ibn al-'Iraqi, **319–320**
    Ibn Khaldun, 'Abd al-Rahman, **235–236**
    Malik Ibn Anas, **237–238**
    patronage, 411, 413
    al-Razi, Abu Bakr Muhammad ibn
        Zakariya, 414, 423, **435**
    travels, 142–143, 155–156, 405–406
Schools, 302
Schools of law, 219–220, 332, 341–343
Science
    alchemy, 413–415, 434
    'alim, **405–407**
    astronomy, 76, 180–181, **407–409**, 435
    Banu Musa, 417, 418
    al-Battani, 408–409
    Bayt al-Hikmah, 368, 403, 406, 407–408,
        417
    al-Biruni, Abu Rayhan, 409, 411, 418, 426
    botany, **409–411**
    calendars, 408, 418
    chemistry, **413–415**
    classification, 414
    Europeans, influence on, 409
    expansion, 403–407
    exploration, **155–157**
    al-Farghani, 408, 411
    geography as, 411
    geology, **426**
    Ibn al-Haytham, 428–429

Jabir ibn Hayyan, 414, **434**
Khayyam, 'Umar, 418
al-Kindi, Abu Yusuf Ya'qub, 426
knowledge sharing, 404–407
mechanics, **418–419**
metallurgy, 414
mineralogy, **426**
motion, 377
observatories, 408
optics and opthamology, **428–429**
overview, **403–404**
patronage, 411, 413
Persian influence on Arab thought, 72
al-Razi, Abu Bakr Muhammad ibn
    Zakariya, 414
religion, 403, 405, 414–415
Sabaeans, 407
scientific method, 413–414
study of, 367–368
Thabit, 417
translation of scientific works, 72
al-Tusi, Nasir al-Din, *416,* 418, **435**
zoology, **432–434**
See also Mathematics
Script, Arabic, 145–146
Sea trade, 152
Secretaries of the Abassid period, *144*
Settlement, 146–147
Sexuality, **312–314**
al-Shafi'i, Muhammad ibn Idris, 220, **238–239,**
    342, 381–382
Shafi'i school, 342
Shahrazad, 313–314
Shajarat al-Durr, **239**
Shari'ah, 206, 209, 211, 332–333, 341
al-Shayzari, 175
Shi'i schools of law, 221
Shi'ism, 333, 346–351
Shipbuilding, 152
Sibawayh, **135**
Silk, 255–256, *260*
Silk Road, 149
Ibn Sina, Abu 'Ali al-Husayn, 304, 371,
    375–378, 423
Sind, 231
Sirat Dhat al-Himma, 314
Siyasat-namah, 238
Slavery, 176, 178–179
Social change, **176–181**
Social class system. *See* Class system
Social reforms, 178
Social roles and responsibilities, **315–318**
Social science, 386
Social trends. *See* Family life and social trends
South Asia, 119–120
Southeast Asian expansion, 70
Spain
    agricultural technology, 426
    cooking, 275
    figural representation, 130
    knowledge transfer, 407
    military campaigns, 225
    poetry, 89–90
Spices, 274
Sports, 278–279
Storytelling, 123–124, 276–277
Sub-Saharan trade, 150–151
Succession, 347–354
Sufism

as alternative to Kalam and Falsafah, 386–388
annihilation, 391
Ibn al-ʿArabi, **393–394**
asceticism, 334, 387–388
Baghdad school, 389, 391
celibacy, 314
cities, 187–188
futuwwah, 392
al-Ghazali, Abu Hamid Muhammad al-Tusi, *390, 391,* **393**
institutional, 391–392
al-Junayd, Abu al-Qasim, 389, 391
"middle way," 388
Muʾadhah al-ʿAdawiyyah, 388
al-Muhasibi, Harith, 388–389
music, 122, *384*
"nafs," 388–389
oneness of God, 389, 391
psychology, 388–389
Rabiʿah al-ʿAdawiyyah, **395–396**
Rumi, Jalal al-Din, **396**
al-Sulami, 391–392
systemization, 391–392
tariqah Sufism, 392
tawhid, 389, 391
Umm al-Aswad, 388
women, 318, 388
See also Ashʿarism; Falsafah; Kalam; Muhammad; Muʿtazilism; Qurʾan; Religion and philosophy; Sunnis
Sugar, 273–274, 427
al-Suhrawardi, Shihab al-Din, 375
al-Sulami, Abu ʿAbd al-Rahman, 388, 391–392
Sultanates, **232–233**
Sunnah, 201–202, 339, 352
Sunnis
challenge to Fatimids power, 381
critique of Kalam and Falsafah, **381–392**
doctrine of the uncreated Qurʾan, 361–363
al-Ghazali, 383–384
Ibn Hanbal, Ahmad, 235
intellect, 386
Ibn Khaldun, ʿAbd al-Rahman, 385–388
rejection of innovation, 382
Righteous Ancestors, 382
al-Shafiʿi, Muhammad ibn Idris, 381–382
social science, 386
Umayyad dynasty, 351–354
usulization, 381–383
See also Ashʿarism; Falsafah; Kalam; Muhammad; Muʿtazilism; Qurʾan; Religion and philosophy; Sufism
Surgery. *See* Medicine and health
al-Suyuti, Jalal al-Din, 419, 421
Swords, 424
Symbolism, numbers and, 415
Syria
architecture, 113
clothing, *258*
Islamization, 231
Masjids, 110
Systematic theology, **354–366**

T

Tahafut al-Falsaifah, 383–384

Tahqiq al-Hind, 157, 426
Tariqah Sufism, 392
Tax farming, 170–171
Taxation, 169, 170–171, 176
Tayyibat, 268
Teachers, 303
Technology, **429–432**
agricultural, 426–427
candle power, 418–419
ceramics, 431–432
clocks, 418–419
furnace, 413
geography and, 76
glassmaking, 431, 432
handwashing device, *419*
inventions, 403
mechanical innovation, 419
military, 226, 227, **424–426**
mills, 430–431
navigational, 413
paper, 429, 431
still, rosewater, *415*
water power, 430–431
water raising machines, 429–430, *438*
wind power, 431
Tents, 264
Textiles. *See* Clothing and textiles
Thabit, 417
The Thousand and One Nights, 123–124, 276, 313–314
Tibb ul-Nabbi, 419, 421
Time, 377
Time measurement. *See* Calendars; Clocks
Tiraz fabrics, 253, 257–258, *261*
Tombs
decorative brickwork, *119*
domed, 118–119
Fatimid, 116
Topography, 78
Trade
central Asian trade routes, 149
expansion and, 70–71, 144–146, 146–149
maritime, 152–153, 411
Mediterranean, 149
pre-Islamic, 171
routes, 148–149, 172–173, 411
Sahara, 150
sea, 152–153
Sub-Saharan, 150–151
See also Business and economy
Trade winds, 152
Translation movement, 366, 368–369
Transportation and travel
Ibn Battuta, 97, 147, **158,** 263
Ibn Fadlan, **158**
frontiers, 148–149
Ibn Jubayr, 142, 153, **159**
maritime zones, 152
overland, **146–151**
pedestrian roads, 151
pilgrimages, 155–156
public lodging, 106
river transport, 153–154
scholarly, 142, 155–156, 405–406
sea and river, **151–155,** 411
shipbuilding, 152
ships' berths, *181*
trade winds, 152

travel writing, 73–74, 97, 126, 147, 155–156, 159
travelers arriving in a Muslim village, *174*
urban life, 151
wheeled vehicles, 146, 149
Travel and transportation
navigational technology, 413
Treaties, 215–216
The Treatise, 342
Tribute, payment of, 215–216
Trigonometry. *See* Mathematics
The Trodden Path, 237
Ibn Tufayl, Abu Bakr Muhammad, 99, 128
Turkish influence
clothing, 259
horses, 149–150
Islamization, 231–232
language, 143–144, 145
marriage, 309
political, 171, 188
al-Tusi, Nasir al-Din, *416, 418,* **435**

U

Ulamaʾ. *See* Scholars
ʿUmar I. *See* ʿUmar ibn al-Khattab
ʿUmar II. *See* ʿUmar ibn ʿAbd al-ʿAziz
ʿUmar ibn ʿAbd al-ʿAziz, **192–193**
ʿUmar ibn al-Khattab, **193**
Umayyad dynasty
architecture, 112–114
class system, 166
clothing, 253
divine right, 352–353
khalifahs, 206
law, 218
military campaigns, 223
Murjiah, 353–354
non-Arab Muslims, 182
non-Muslims, 230, 366
poetry, 88
predestination, 333, 352
religious doctrine, 343–344, 351–353
rulers' wives and concubines, 309
Sunni Muslims, 352–353
taxation, 170
Umm al-Aswad, 388
Ummah, 178
United States, 71
Universal soul, 372
Universe, 377–378
Urban life
architecture, 114
caravan cities, 147–148
civil order, 184–185
class system, 180, 185
daily life, 247
economic development, 171–172
education, 306–307
food distribution, 270
garrison, 166, 180
government, 180
layout, 262, 264
market places, 172, 262–263, *264*
masjids, 262
occupations, 185
sacred centers, 176–177

Sufism, 187–188
transportation, 151
ulama', 142
urbanization, 180
violence, 184–185, 187
youth gangs, 185, 187
See also Individual cities
Usulization, 381–383
Usury, 211
'Uthman, 344–345

V

Vegetables, 273
Vehicles, 146
Veils, 252, 315–316
"The Verse of Light," 97
Violence, 184–185, 187
Vision. *See* Optics and opthamology

W

al-Walid Ibn Abd al-Malik, 112, 113, **135**
al-Walid II, 350
Wasil ibn 'Ata', 356
Water clocks, 418
Water power, 430–431
Water raising machines, 429–430, *438*
Water supply and drainage, 265

Water transportation, **151–155**
Weapons. *See* Military and warfare
Wedlock, 213, 284
West Africa
building materials, 263
clothing, 259–260
Wet nurses, 297
Wheat, durum, 273
Wind power, 431
Wine. *See* Alcoholic beverages
Women
'A'isha bint Abi Bakr, 307–308, **319**
'Aish'a bint Muhammad ibn 'Abd al-Hadi, **320**
'A'ishah bint Ahmad al-Qurtubiyyah, 89–90
clothing, 251, 252
concubines, 309
education, 306
elegy for a scholarly daughter, 303
extramarital relations, 313
fictional, 313–314
Halima, 297–298
housing, 261
Khadijah, 307
masjids, 249
motherhood, 298–300
Mu'adhah al-'Adawiyyah, 388
occupations, 317–318
political influence, 191–192, 318
public spaces, 315–316
Qur'an, 178, 339

Rabi'ah al-'Adawiyyah, 318, **395–396**
right to divorce, 214
rulers, 318
sexuality, 312
Shajarat al-Durr, **239**
spiritual equality, 318
status, 176, 178
Sufism, 318, 388
Umm al-Aswad, 388
veiling and seclusion, 315–316
women playing chess, *316*
Woodworking, 102
Writing, Arabic, 145–146

Y

Yathrib. *See* Madinah
Yemen, 168
Youth gangs, 185, 187
Yurt, 264

Z

Zahiri school of law, 210
al-Zahrawi, Abu al-Qasim, 421, 423
Zayd ibn 'Ali, 350
Zaydi Shi'ism, 350
Zoology, **432–434**